Complete Multilingual Dictionary
of Advertising, Marketing, and Communications

Complete
Multilingual
Dictionary

of

ADVERTISING

MARKETING

and

COMMUNICATIONS

English   French   German

Hans W. Paetzel

 **PASSPORT BOOKS**

Trade Imprint of National Textbook Company
Lincolnwood, Illinois U.S.A.

Foreword

This multilingual dictionary is an impressive initiative. We have witnessed the increasing globalization of marketing and advertising, and this valuable reference will surely serve all communicators well.

Images may be easy and quick to transfer across borders, but so often the effectiveness of advertising and marketing strategy depends on how well an idea translates—and that is where language comes in.

This definitive reference lists more than 8,000 technical and general communications terms in three important languages: English, French, and German. Translations are done with scholarly attention to precision, yet with a communicator's need to interpret ideas and emotions.

I know that my colleagues of the International Advertising Association, the worldwide association of advertising and marketing professionals, will welcome this dictionary as a real contribution to clearer and more effective communication.

Russell J. Melvin
Chairman, International Advertising Association

Avant-propos

Ce dictionnaire multilingue représente une initiative remarquable. Nous avons été les témoins de la globalisation croissante du marketing et de la publicité, et cet ouvrage de référence sera certainement précieux à tous les communicateurs.

Il est peut-être facile et rapide de transmettre les images par delà les frontières, mais l'efficacité des stratégies de publicité et de marketing dépend bien souvent de la façon dont une idée se traduit d'une langue à une autre—et c'est précisément là que le langage entre en jeu.

Cet important ouvrage de référence répertorie plus de 8.000 termes techniques et généraux relatifs à l'industrie de la communication. Ces termes apparaissent dans trois langues importantes: l'anglais, le français et l'allemand. Les traductions ont été réalisées grâce à la précision et à la compétence d'experts. Les traducteurs ont cependant gardé à l'esprit le besoin qu'ont les communicateurs d'exprimer des idées et des émotions.

Je suis sûr que mes collègues de l'IAA, l'association mondiale des professionnels de la publicité et du marketing, seront heureux d'accueillir ce dictionnaire en tant que véritable contribution à une communication plus claire et plus efficace.

Russell J. Melvin
Président, International Advertising Association

Vorwort

Dieses mehrsprachige Wörterbuch stellt eine einmalige Leistung dar. Wir haben in den letzten Jahren miterlebt, wie sich Marketing und Werbung weltweit verbreitet haben. Dieses wertvolle Nachschlagewerk wird bestimmt allen Benutzern als Quelle der kommunikativen Ausdrucksformen bestens dienen.

Bilder lassen sich leicht und schnell über Landesgrenzen senden, aber oft hängt die Wirkung der Werbung und des Marketings von der Übersetzungskraft des Gedankens ab—das ist die Rolle der Sprache.

Dieses ausführliche Nachschlagewerk enthält über 8.000 technische und allgemeine Fachausdrücke und Redewendungen in drei wichtigen Sprachen: Englisch, Französisch und Deutsch. Die Übersetzungen sind wissenschaftlich präzise, werden jedoch unter Berücksichtigung des Emotions- und Sinngehalts eines jeweiligen Stichwortes erläutert.

Ich weiß, daß meine Kollegen in der IAA, der weltweiten Gesellschaft von Werbe- und Marketingfachleuten, dieses Wörterbuch als Beitrag zur klareren und effektiveren Kommunikation begrüßen werden.

Russell J. Melvin
Vorstandsvorsitzender, International Advertising Association

Complete Multilingual Dictionary of Advertising, Marketing, and Communications

German • Deutsch
English • Englisch
French • Französisch

List of Abbreviations/Verzeichnis der Abkürzungen:

	German/Deutsch	English/Englisch	French/Französisch
am	amerikanisch	American	américain
brit	britisch	British	britannique
f	weiblich	feminine	féminin
f/pl	weibliche Mehrzahl	feminine plural	féminin pluriel
m	männlich	masculine	masculin
m/pl	männliche Mehrzahl	masculine plural	masculin pluriel
n	sächlich	neuter	neutre
n/pl	sächliche Mehrzahl	neuter plural	neutre pluriel
pl	Mehrzahl	plural	pluriel
s.	siehe	see	voir
stereotyp.	Stereotypie	stereotyping	stéréotypie
typogr.	Buchdruck	typography	typographie

Die Umlaute ä, ö und ü wurden eingeordnet wie ae, oe und ue.

A

abändern	to modify	modifier
abbestellen	to cancel	annuler
abbestellen, ein Abonnement	to withdraw a subscription	se désabonner à
Abbestellung *f*	cancellation	annulation *f*
Abbildung *f*	illustration, picture	illustration *f*
abblenden	to wipe off	baisser les phares *m/pl*
Abbreviatur *f*	abbreviation	abréviation *f*
abdecken	to block out, to cover, to mask out	caviarder, couvrir, masquer, recouvrir
Abdeckmaske *f*	frisket, mask	cache *f*
Abdeckpapier *n*	golden-rod paper, masking paper	papier-cache *m*
Abdeckrahmen *m*	masking frame	cache *f*, frisquette *f*
Abdeckstreifen *m*	masking tape	bande *f* à masquer
Abdeckung *f*	mask	détourage *m*
Abdruck *m*	impression, imprint	empreinte *f*
Abdruckhöhe *f*	advertisement height	hauteur *f* d'annonce *f*
Abdrucksrecht *n*	copyright, right of reproduction	droit *m* de reproduction *f*
abendfüllender Film *m*	full-length film	long métrage *m*
Abendzeitung *f*	evening newspaper	journal *m* du soir *m*
Abenteuerfilm *m*	adventure film	film *m* d'aventures *f/pl*
Abfahrtsplan *m*	time-table	horaire *m*
Abfall *m*	offcut	déchet *m*, reste *m* de papier *m*
Abfassung *f*	composition	rédaction *f*
abformen	to duplicate	surmouler
abgedroschene Redensart *f*	hackneyed phrase, stock phrase	cliché *m*, phrase *f* rebattue
abgedroschenes Zeug *n*	threadbare story	vieille rengaine *f*
abgegriffen	trite	poncif
abgenutzte Schrift *f*	worn-out type	têtes *f/pl* de clou *m*
abgepackte Waren *f/pl*	packaged goods *pl*	marchandises *f/pl* empaquetées
Abguß *m*	casting	moulage *m*
Abhandlung *f*	treatise	traité *m*
Abhandlung *f*, **kurze**	essay	essai *m*
Abholabonnements *n/pl*	call-at-office subscriptions *pl*	abonnements *m/pl* pour retrait *m* au guichet *m*
Abholwaren *f/pl*	cash-and-carry-wares *pl*	marchandises *f/pl* à transporter par l'acheteur *m*
Abklatsch *m*	copy, poor imitation	copie *f*, pastichage *m*
Abkommen *n*	agreement, settlement	accord *m*, arrangement *m*
abkürzen	to curtail, to cut down, to cut short	abréger, élaguer
Abkürzung *f*	abbreviation	abréviation *f*
Ablage *f*	depot, file, filing system	classement *m*, dépôt *m*
Ablauf *m*	expiration, expiry	expiration *f*
Ablegekorb *m*	filing basket	corbeille *f* de distribution *f*
ablegen	to file	classer, distribuer
ablegen (Satz) *m*	to diss (composition), to kill (composition)	distribuer, mettre en casse *f*
Ablegeregal *n*	galley for dead matter	galée *f* à distribution *f*
Ablegesatz *m*	dead matter	composition *f* à distribuer
Ablegeschiff *n*	galley for dead matter	galée *f* à distribution *f*
Ablehnung *f*	rejection	refus *m*, rejet *m*
Ablehnung *f* **eines Manuskripts** *n*	spike	refus *m* d'un manuscrit *m*
Ablichtung *f*	blue print, photostatic copy	copie *f* héliographique, photocopie *f*

abmachen	to agree, to arrange, to settle	arranger, fixer
Abmachung *f*	agreement, arrangement	accord *m*, arrangement *m*, convention *f*
Abnahmemenge *f*	size of the order	volume *m* publicitaire
abnehmbar	to be published	à épuiser
Abnehmer *m*	buyer, client (for a service), customer	acheteur *m*, client *m*
Abonnement *n*	subscription	abonnement *m*
Abonnement aufgeben, ein	to withdraw a subscription	se désabonner à
Abonnement *n*, kombiniertes	clubbing offer	abonnement *m* combiné
Abonnementserneuerung *f*	renewal of subscription	réabonnement *m*
Abonnementskündigung *f*	subscription stop	résiliation *f* de l'abonnement *m*
Abonnements *n/pl*, bezahlte	paid subscriptions *pl*	abonnements *m/pl* payants
Abonnementspreis *m*	subscription rates *pl*	prix *m* d'abonnement *m*
Abonnementszeitung *f*	firm order newspaper, subscribers' paper	journal *m* d'abonnés *m/pl*
Abonnent *m*	subscriber	abonné *m*, souscripteur *m*
Abonnentenanalyse *f*	subscriber analysis	analyse *f* des abonnés *m/pl*
Abonnentenkartei *f*	list of subscribers *pl*	fichier *m* d'abonnés *m/pl*
Abonnentenschwund *m*	downward trend in subscription	désabonnement *m*
Abonnentenversicherung *f*	assurance of subscribers *pl*	assurance *f* des abonnés *m/pl*
Abonnentenwerber *m*	sheet-writer, subscription canvasser, subscription salesman, subscription solicitor	courtier *m*
Abonnentenzahl *f*	number of subscribers *pl*	nombre *m* des abonnés *m/pl*
abonnieren	to subscribe	s'abonner à
Abpächter *m*	site getter	prospecteur *m* d'emplacements *m/pl*
abquetschen	to batter	écraser
abrechnen	to account, to invoice	boucler un compte *m*, facturer, faire un décompte *m*, solder
Abrechnung *f*	settlement, statement	décompte *m*, liquidation *f*
Abrechnungszeitraum *m*	accounting period	période *f* comptable
Abrede *f*	agreement	stipulation *f*
Abreißkalender *m*	tear-off calendar	calendrier *m* à effeuiller, éphémerides *f/pl*
Abriß *m*	summary	résumé *m*
Abruf *m*, auf	at our convenience, on call	à notre convenance *f*, sur appel *m*
abrufen	to call	appeler
Absatz *m* des Herstellers *m* an den Großhändler *m*	selling of the manufacturer to the wholesale dealer	circuit *m* long
Absatz *m* (im Text *m*)	paragraph	alinéa *m*, paragraphe *m*
Absatz *m*, kein!	run-in!	pas d'alinéa *m* !
Absatz *m*, neuer !	run out!	nouvel alinéa *m* !
Absatz *m* setzen, ohne	to run on	faire suivre sans alinéa *m*
Absatz *m* (Vertrieb *m*)	distribution	distribution *f*
Absatzanalyse *f*	market analysis	analyse *f* du marché *m*
Absatzbemühungen *f/pl*	marketing	commercialisation *f*
Absatzberater *m*	marketing consultant	conseil *m* en marketing *m*
Absatzbereich *m*	sales *pl* area, trading area	débouché *m*, territoire *m* de vente *f*
Absatzchance *f*	sales *pl* prospects *pl*	chance *f* d'écoulement *m*
Absatzflaute *f*	period of dull sales *pl*	mévente *f*
Absatzförderung *f*	sales *pl* promotion	promotion *f* de vente *f*
Absatzforschung *f*	marketing research	étude *f* de marché *m*
Absatzgebiet *n*	outlet, sales *pl* area, trading area	débouché *m*, marché *m*

Absatzinstrument *n*	sales *pl* instrument	instrument *m* de vente *f*
Absatzkanal *m*	channel of distribution	voie *f* de distribution *f*
Absatzkontrolle *f*	marketing control	contrôle *m* de la vente *f*
Absatzkosten *pl*	distribution costs *pl*	frais *m/pl* de distribution *f*
Absatzmarkt *m*, erfolgversprechender	promising market	débouché *m* plein de promesses *f/pl*
Absatzmethoden *f/pl*	distribution methods *pl*, marketing techniques *pl*	méthode *f* de distribution *f*
Absatzplan *m*	distribution plan	plan *m* de vente *f*
absatzpolitische Maßnahmen *f/pl*	merchandizing	mise *f* en valeur *f*, techniques *f/pl* marchandes
Absatzschwankung *f*	market fluctuation	fluctuations *f/pl* des ventes *f/pl*
Absatzsteigerung *f*	sales *pl* promotion	promotion *f* de vente *f*
Absatzstockung *f*	standstill in market	stagnation *f* des ventes *f/pl*
Absatzstrategie *f*	marketing strategy	stratégie *f* de distribution *f*
Absatzvorbereitung *f* durch Vertriebsplannung *f*	merchandizing	techniques *f/pl* marchandes
Absatzweg *m*	channel of distribution, sales *pl* channel	voie *f* de distribution *f*
Absatzzählung *f*	census of distribution	recensement *m* de la distribution *f*
Absatzzeichen *n*	section mark	paragraphe *m*, signe *m* d'alinéa *m*
abschleifen	to bevel	biseauter
abschließende Frage *f*	rider	phrase *f* finale
abschließender Kaufappell *m*	rider	message *m* additionnel à la fin *f* d'un message *m* publicitaire
Abschluß *m*	contract, deal	contrat *m*
Abschluß *m*, kurzfristiger	short term contract	contrat *m* à court terme *m*
Abschluß *m*, provisorischer	provisional booking	ordre *m* provisoire
Abschlußjahr *n*	contract year, legal year	année *f* légale
Abschlußmenge *f*	size of the order	volume *m* publicitaire
Abschlußrabatt *m*	time discount	dégressif *m* sur volume *m* publicitaire
Abschmutzbogen *m*	set-off sheet, tympan-paper	papier *m* anti-macule, papier *m* de décharge *f*
abschneiden	to break up	découper
Abschnitt *m*	paragraph	alinéa *m*, paragraphe *m*
abschreiben	to pilfer	piller
Abschrift *f* anfertigen	to copy	faire un duplicata *m*
absenden	to dispatch	expédier
Absender *m*	sender	expéditeur *m*
absetzen (Druck)	to compose, to set up, to tap, to typeset	composer
absetzen (Verkauf)	to sell	vendre
abspielen, noch einmal	to play back	faire repasser la bande *f*
Absprache *f*	convention	convention *f*
Abstimmung *f*	tuning	syntonisation *f*
Abstimmung *f*, zeitliche	timing	coordination *f* des termes *m/pl*
Abstufung *f*	shading	nuance *f*
Abteilplakat *n*	compartment panel	emplacement *m* dans compartiment *m*
Abteilung *f*	department, division, section	département *m*, rayon *m*, section *f*
Abteilung *f*, fotografische	art department	service *m* photographique
Abteilungstitel *m*	section title	titre *m* de chapitre *m*
Abtretung *f*	cession	cession *f*

Abwandlung f	variation	modification f, variante f
Abwehrwerbung f	counter advertising	contre-publicité f
Abweichung f	deviation	déviation f
abwerben	to entice away	débaucher
abwickeln	to wind up	utiliser
Abwicklung f	implementation, unrolling	déroulement m
Abwicklungskosten pl	handling costs pl	frais m/pl de manutention f
Abzahlungsverkauf m	instalment sale	vente f à tempérament m
Abzeichen n	badge	insigne m, signe m distinctif
Abziehbild n	transfer picture	image f de décalcomanie f
Abziehbogen m	tympan-sheet	papier m de décharge f
abziehen (Druck)	to proof, to pull	tirer
abziehen (Foto)	to make a print	faire une épreuve f
Abzieher m	proofer	tireur m des épreuves f/pl
Abziehplakat n	decalcomania, paint transfer, transparency am	décalcomanie f
Abziehpresse f	proof press	presse f à épreuves f/pl
Abzüge m/pl lesen	to hold copies pl	lire les épreuves f/pl
Abzug m	print, proof, pull	contre-type m, épreuve f
Abzug m auf Kunstdruckpapier n	art pull, glossy print proof am	épreuve f sur papier m couché
Abzug m, erster	first proof	épreuve f en première
Abzug m, sauberer	clean proof	épreuve f corrigée
Abzug m, schmutziger	smutty proof	épreuve f boueuse
Abzugpapier n	flimsy paper	papier m pour copies f/pl
abzunehmen innerhalb eines Jahres n	to be published within one year	à épuiser dans le délai m d'une année f
Accent m aigu	acute accent	accent m aigu
Accent m circonflexe	circumflex	accent m circonflexe
Accent m grave	grave accent	accent grave
Achtelgeviert n	em-space	huitième m de cadratin m
Achtelpetit f (siehe Anhang!)	12-to-pica (see appendix!)	1 point (voir appendice!)
Achtelseite f	eighth of page	huitième de page f
adaptieren	to adapt	adapter
Adaptierung f	adaptation	adaptation f
Administration f	administration	administration f
Administrator m	administrator	administrateur m
Adremaplatte f	addressograph plate	plaque-adresse f
Adressat m	addressee, consignee	destinataire m
Adreßbuch n	address book, directory	annuaire m, indicateur m d'adresses f/pl, livre m d'adresses f/pl
Adresse f	address	adresse f
Adressenaufkleber m	adhesive address label	adresse f adhésive
Adressenkartei — Vermietung f	list-broking	bail m de fichiers m/pl d'adresses f/pl
Adressenkontrolle f	mailing list control	contrôle m des adresses f/pl
Adressenliste f	list of addresses pl, mailing list	liste f d'adresses f/pl
Adressenquelle f	address source	source f d'adresses f/pl
Adressenverkauf m	letter shop	vente f d'adresses f/pl
Adressenverlag m	address broker, supplier of addresses pl	éditeur m d'adresses f/pl, loueurs m/pl d'adresses f/pl
Adressiermaschine f	addressing machine, addressographe	adressographe m
Adressierung f	addressing	adressage m
Änderung f	amendment	amendement m, changement m, modification f

ästhetische Qualität *f*	aesthetic quality	qualité *f* esthétique
ätzen	to bite, to engrave, to etch	creuser, graver, mordre
Ätzer *m*	engraver, etcher	graveur *m*
Ätzmaschine *f*	etching machine	machine *f* à graver
Ätzstufen *f/pl*	powderless etching	gravure *f* sans poudrage *m*
Ätztiefe *f*	bite	morsure *f*
Ätzung *f*	block (brit), engraving, etching	cliché *m*, eau-forte *f*, gravure *f*
Ätzung *f*, kombinierte	combination plate, combined line and half-tone block *brit*	cliché *m* trait *m* -simili combiné
Ätzung *f*, seitenverkehrte	flop, reversed plate	cliché *m* inversé, cliché *m* retourné
Ätzverfahren *n*	engraving process, etching process	procédé *m* de gravure *f*, procédé *m* de morsure *f*
äußerer Papierrand *m*	fore-edge, outside margin	marge *f* extérieure
äußerster Termin *m*	deadline	terme *m* de rigueur *f*
Äußerung *f*	utterance	expression *f*, propos *m*
Affiche *f*	poster	affiche-papier *f*, placard *m*
Affichierung *f*	billposting	affichage *m*
Agate *f* (siehe Anhang!)	Ruby *f* (see appendix!)	Parisienne *f* (voir appendice!)
Agenda *f*	memorandum book, pocket diary	agenda *m*, carnet *m*
Agent *m*	selling agent	agent *m*
Agentur *f*	agency	agence *f*
Agentur *f*, vorgeschobene	house agency	agence *f* fictive
Agenturerfahrung *f*	agency experience	expérience *f* d'agence *f*
Agenturkette *f*	chain of agencies *pl*	chaîne *f* d'agences *f/pl*
Agenturprovision *f*	agency commission, commission fee, media discount	commission *f* d'agence *f*
Agenturvergütung *f*	service fee	honoraires *m/pl*
Agenturvertrag *m*	agency agreement, agency contract	contrat *m* d'agence *f*
Agenturvertreter *m*	agency representative	représentant *m* d'une agence *f* de publicité *f*
aggressive Werbung *f*	competitive copy *am*, disparaging copy, hard approach, knocking copy *brit*	publicité *f* agressive
Agitation *f*	agitation	agitation *f*
Agitator *m*	agitator	agitateur *m*
Agrarpresse *f*	farm press	presse *f* rurale
Akkumulierung *f*	accumulation	effet *m* cumulatif
Akquisiteur *m*	canvasser	démarcheur *m*, solliciteur *m*
Akquisition *f*	canvassing	acqisition *f*
Aktenzeichen *n*	reference number	cote *f*
Aktualität *f*	actuality	actualité *f*
Aktualitätenkino *n*	non-stop cinema	cinéma *m* d'actualités *f/pl*
aktuell	topical	actuel
aktuelle Bedeutung *f*	topicality	actualité *f*
akustische Werbung *f*	acoustic advertising	publicité *f* acoustique
Akzent *m*	accent	accent *m*
Akzidenzarbeit *f*	jobbing work	bibelots *m/pl*
Akzidenzdruck *m*	job printing, jobbing work	bilboquet *m*, travail *m* à la pièce *f*, travail *m* de ville *f*
Akzidenzdrucker *m*	job printer	imprimeur *m* de travaux *m/pl* de ville *f*
Akzidenzdruckerei *f*	jobbing office	imprimerie *f* de travaux *m/pl* de ville *f*
Akzidenzen *f/pl*	jobbing work	travaux *m/pl* de ville *f*
Akzidenzkasten *m*	job case	casseau *m*

Akzidenzsatz *m*	display composition	composition *f* de travaux *m/pl* de ville *f*
Akzidenzschriften *f/pl*	display faces *pl*	caractères *m/pl* de travaux *m/pl* de ville *f*
Akzidenzsetzer *m*	advertographer, job compositor	compositeur *m* de travaux *m/pl* de ville *f*, ouvrier *m* en conscience *f*
Akzidenzsetzerei *f*	jobbing case room, trade compositors *pl*	atelier *m* de composition *f* des travaux *m/pl* de ville *f*
alarmierende Überschrift *f*	scare headline	gros titre *m* à sensation *f*, manchette *f* sensationnelle
alle drei Monate *m/pl*	quarterly	trimestriel
alle Rechte *n/pl* vorbehalten	all rights *pl* reserved	tous droits *m/pl* réservés
alle zwei Monate *m/pl*	bi-monthly	bimestriel
Allegorie *f*	allegory	allégorie *f*
Alleinmeldung *f*, sensationelle	scoop	exclusivité *f*
alleinstehend (Anzeige *f*)	island position, solus position *brit*	position *f* isolée
alleinstehend (Außenwerbung *f*)	solus site	emplacement *m* unique
alleinstehende Anzeige *f*	sole advertisement	annonce *f* isolée
Alleinverkauf *m*	exclusive distribution, sole sale	vente *f* exclusive
Alleinverkaufsrecht *n*	franchise, sole rights *pl* of sale	exclusivité *f*
Alleinvertreter *m*	sole agent	concessionaire *m*
Alleinvertretung *f*	exclusive agency	agence *f* exclusive
Alleinwerbung *f*	individual advertising, isolated advertising	publicité *f* individuelle, publicité *f* isolée
Alleskönner *m*	allround man	homme *m* universel
allgemein ansprechender Film *m*	film of universal appeal	film *m* passe-partout
allgemeine Anschlagstelle *f*	usually used site	emplacement *m* utilisé habituellement
allgemeine Anzeigen *f/pl*	display advertisements *pl*	publicité *f* non classifiée
allgemeine Bedingungen *f/pl*	general conditions *pl*	conditions *f/pl* générales
Allgemeininteresse *n*	public interest	intérêt *m* général
Allonge *f*	fly-leaf	allonge *f*, feuille *f* attachée
Allzweckschrift *f*	all-purpose type face	type *m* à toutes fins *f/pl*
Almanach *m*	almanac, calendar	almanach *m*
Alphabet *n*	alphabet	alphabet *m*
alphabetisch	alphabetic	par ordre *m* alphabétique
alphabetisieren	to place in alphabetical order	mettre en ordre *m* alphabétique
alte Klischees *n/pl*	dead plates *pl*	vieux clichés *m/pl*
alte Zeitungsnummer *f*	back-number	exemplaire *m* périmé
alter Text *m*	dead copy	texte *m* déjà employé
Altersgruppen *f/pl*	age groups *pl*	groupes *m/pl* d'âge *m*
altgotische Schrift *f*	old black type	caractères *m/pl* gothiques
altmodisch	old fashioned, out-of-fashion	démodé
Altpapier *n*	waste paper	vieux papiers *m/pl*
Altzeug *n*	old metal	vieille matière *f*
Aluminiumfolie *f*	aluminium foil	feuille *f* d'aluminium *m*
am Fuß *m* einer Seite *f*	bottom of page, foot of page	bas *m* de page *f*, pied *m* de page *f*
Amateurfilm *m*	amateur film	film *m* d'amateur *m*
ambulanter Zeitungsverkäufer *m*	news-butcher	vendeur *m* ambulant de journaux *m/pl*
amtliche Anzeige *f*	official announcement, statutory announcement	annonce *f* légale
amtliche Bekanntmachung *f*	legal notice, official notice	avis *m* officiel

amtliche Nachrichten *f/pl*	official news	nouvelles *f/pl* authentiques
amtliche Zeitung *f*	gazette	journal *m* officiel
amtliches Organ *n*	official organ	organe *m* officiel
amtliches Plakat *n*	official notice, official poster	affiche *f* officielle, avis *m* officiel
Amtsblatt *n*	official gazette	bulletin *m* officiel
Anaglyphendruck *m*	anaglyphic print	impression *f* d'anaglyphes *f/pl*
Analyse *f*	analysis	analyse *f*
anastatischer Druck *m*	anastatic printing	impression *f* anastatique
anaxiale Satzform *f*	anaxial composition	composition *f* anaxiale
anbieten	to offer	offrir
anbringen (Plakat)	to post	afficher
andeuten	to hint	dire à mots *m/pl* couverts
Andruck *m*	preprint, proof, proofing	épreuve *f*, exemplaire *m* d'essai *m*
Andruck *m*, endgültiger	final pull	épreuve *f* définitive
andrucken	to pull a proof	tirer des épreuves *f/pl*
Andruckpapier *n*	proofing paper	papier *m* pour tirage *m* d'épreuves *f/pl*
Anekdote *f*	anecdote	anecdote *f*
anerkannt	accredited, recognised	accrédité, reconnu
anerkannte Werbeagentur *f*	recognised advertising agency	agence *f* de publicité *f* reconnue
anerkannter Werbungsmittler *m*	recognised advertising agency	agence *f* de publicité *f* reconnue
anerkennen	to recognise	reconnaître
Anerkennung *f*	recognition	reconnaissance *f*
Anerkennungsschreiben *n*	applause mail *am*, testimonial	courrier *m* des auditeurs *m/pl*
Anfänger *m*	cub	débutant *m*
Anfang *m* einer Anzeige *f*	lead-in	entrée *f* d'une annonce *f*
Anfangsbuchstabe *m*	initial letter	initiale *f*
Anfrage *f*	query, question	demande *f*
Anfrage *f*, auf	on request	sur demande *f*
Anfragentest *m*	inquiry test	test *m* de demandes *f/pl*
Anführungsstriche *m/pl*	double quotation marks *pl*, inverted commas *pl/brit*	guillemets *m/pl*
Angabe *f*	declaration, statement	déclaration *f*, indication *f*
angeben	to state	déclarer, indiquer
Angebot *n*	offer	offre *f*
Angebot *n*, freibleibendes	offer without obligation	offre *f* sans engagement *m*
Angebot *n*, verborgenes	buried offer, hidden offer	offre *f* clandestine
Angebot *n*, verstecktes	blind offer, buried offer, hidden offer, subordinate offer	offre *f* clandestine
Angebot *n* zum Selbstkostenpreis *m*	selfliquidation offer	offre *f* au prix *m* coûtant
Angebotsmappe *f*	advertising portfolio, offer case	carton *m* pour des offres *f/pl*
angekündigter Preis *m*	posted price	prix *m* affiché
Angelegenheit *f*	matter	affaire *f*
Angelegenheit *f*, bewußte	matter	affaire *f* en question *f*
angemessener Preis *m*	adequate price	juste prix *m*
Angemessenheit *f*	appropriateness	convenance *f*
angeschlossene Zeitung *f*	member of a group of publishers *pl*	membre *m* d'un cercle *m* d'édition *f*
angeschnittene Anzeige *f*	bleed advertisement	annonce *f* à fond *m* perdu, annonce *f* à franc-bord *m*
angeschnittene Seite *f*	bleed-off page	fond *m* perdu
angestaubt	shop-soiled	défraîchi

angestrahlte Werbefläche *f*	floodlight advertisement	publicité *f* éclairée
angewandte Kunst *f*	applied art	arts *m/pl* industriels
anhängen *typog*	to run on	faire suivre, joindre
Anhänger *m* (Beiwagen *m*)	trailer	remorque *f*
Anhängezettel *m*	tag	étiquette *f* à attacher, étiquette *f* à ficelle *f*
anhäufen	to accumulate	cumuler
Anhäufung *f*	accumulation	accumulation *f*
Anhang *m*	annex, appendix, supplement	appendice *m*, supplément *m*
Anilindruck *m*	aniline printing, flexographic printing	flexographie *f*, impression *f* à l'aniline *f*
Ankleben *n*	placing, posting	affichage *m*, collage *m*
Ankleber *m*	sticker	afficheur *m*
Anknüpfungswerbung *f*	tie-in advertising	publicité *f* d'association *f*
ankündigen	to announce	annoncer
Ankündigung *f*	announcement	annonce *f*, information *f*
Ankündigung *f* im Rundfunk *m*	broadcast announcement	avis *m* radiodiffusé
Ankurbelung *f*	launching	déclenchement *m*
Anlage *f*	appendix, enclosure	annexe *f*
Anlage *typog*	lays *pl*	marge *f*
Anlauf *m*	start	démarrage *m*
Anlaufzeit *f*	start time	période *f* de démarrage *m*
Anlaufzeit *f*, mittlere	average date of posting	date *f* moyenne de pose *f*
Anlegeapparat *m*	feeder, margin stop	margeur *m*, régulateur *m* de marges *f/pl*
anlegen	to dress a form	garnir la forme *f*
anmaßende Werbung *f*	insolent advertising	publicité *f* envahissante
Anmerkung *f*	note	note *f*
Annahmeschluß *m*	closing hour	heure *f* limite de remise *f*
Annahmestelle *f*	newspaper's office	bureau *m* du journal *m*
Annalen *f/pl*	annals *pl*, records *pl*	annales *f/pl*
annehmbar	acceptable	acceptable
Annonce *f*	ad, advertisement	annonce *f*, insertion *f*
Annoncenexpedition *f*	space broker	agence *f* de publicité *f*, expédition *f* d'annonces *f/pl*, intermédiaire *m* publicitaire
annoncieren	to insert, to publish	insérer
annullieren	to cancel	annuler
Annullierung *f*	cancellation	annulation *f*, résiliation *f*
anonym	anonymous	anonyme
anonymer Briefschreiber *m*	poison pen	corbeau *m*
anonymer Produkttest *m*	blind product test	test *m* de produit *m* anonyme
Anonymität *f*	anonymity	anonymat *m*
Anordnung *f*	arrangement	agencement *m*
Anordnung *f*, asymmetrische	informal balance, off-center arrangement	arrangement *m* asymétrique
anpassen	to adapt	adapter
Anpassung *f*	adaptation, adjustment	accommodation *f*
anpreisen	to plug	prôner
Anreißer *m*	tout	bonisseur *m*, racoleur *m*
anreißerische Werbung *f*	puffing publicity	publicité *f* raccrocheuse
Anreiz *m*	appeal, incitement	appel *m*, incitation *f*
Anreizartikel *m*	loss leader	marchandise *f* d'appel *m*
Anreizprämie *f*	incentive	prime *f* d'encouragement *m*
Ansage *f*	announcement	annonce *f*
Ansager *m*	announcer. compère. emcee	compère *m*, speaker *m*

Ansagerin *f*	female announcer	présentatrice *f,* speakerine *f*
Ansatzpunkt *m*	approach, hook	accrochage *m* publicitaire, angle *m* d'approche *f*
Anschläger *m*	bill-sticker	afficheur *m*
Anschlag *m*	sticking up	collage *m*
Anschlag *m,* **faltenfreier**	nonwrinkle posting	affichage *m* sans plis *m/pl*
Anschlag *m* **in Verkehrsmitteln** *n/pl*	car card advertising	affichette *f* d'autobus *m* ou de tramway *m*
Anschlag *m,* **kurzfristiger**	temporary posting	affichage *m* temporaire
Anschlag *m,* **verdeckter**	obstructed site	emplacement *m* masqué
Anschlagbeginn *m*	start of the bill posting	date *f* de départ *m* de l'affichage *m*
Anschlagbogen *m*	bill, placard, poster	affiche *f*-papier *f*
Anschlagdauer *f*	period of display, posting period	conservation *f*
anschlagen	to place bills *pl,* to post bills *pl,* to stick bills *pl*	afficher, coller, poser une affiche *f*
Anschlagen *n* **verboten**	post no bills *pl*	défense *f* d'afficher
Anschlagfläche *f*	street hoarding	palissade *f*
Anschlagfläche *f,* **gemalte**	painted display	panneau *m* peint
Anschlagkontrolle *f*	site inspection	inspection *f* d'emplacements *m/pl*
Anschlagkontrolleur *m*	site inspector	inspecteur *m* d'emplacements *m/pl*
Anschlagkosten *pl*	space charge	dépenses *f/pl* d'affichage *m*
Anschlagort *m*	place of posting	lieu *m* d'affichage *m*
Anschlagpächter *m*	site leaseholder	concessionaire *m* d'affichage *m*
Anschlagsäule *f*	poster pillar	colonne *f* d'affichage *m,* colonne *f* Morris (à Paris)
Anschlagstelle *f*	billboard, site	emplacement *m,* place *f* d'affichage *m*
Anschlagstelle *f,* **allgemeine**	usually used site	emplacement *m* utilisé habituellement
Anschlagstellen *f/pl,* **verdeckt stehende**	sites *pl* hidden from view	masquage *m*
Anschlagtafel *f*	billboard, notice board, poster panel	panneau *m* d'affichage *m*
Anschlagtafelgruppe *f*	hoarding	ensemble *m* de panneaux *m/pl*
Anschlagunternehmen *n*	billposting company, plant operator	entreprise *f* d'affichage *m*
Anschlagwand *f*	poster hoarding	panneau *m* d'affichage *m*
Anschlagwerbung *f*	poster advertising	publicité *f* par affiches *f/pl*
Anschlagzaun *m*	poster hoarding	panneau *m* d'affichage *m*
Anschlußauftrag *m*	follow-on order, follow-up order	commande *f* de suite *f*
Anschlußwerbung *f*	connexion advertising	campagne *f* de suite *f*
Anschnitt *m*	bleed	rogne *f*
Anschrift *f*	address	adresse *f*
Anschwärzung *f*	slander	dénigrement *m*
Ansehen *n*	reputation	notoriété *f,* prestige *m,* réputation *f*
Ansichtsexemplar *f*	sample copy, specimen copy	numéro *m* spécimen *m*
Ansichtskarte *f*	picture postcard	carte *f* postale illustrée
Ansichtsmuster *n*	sample for inspection	échantillon *m* à l'examen *m*
Ansichtssendung *f*	consignment for inspection	envoi *m* à l'examen *m*
Ansichtsskizze *f*	visual	maquette *f*

Ansprache *f*	speech	harangue *f*
Ansprache *f* auf dem Wege *m* über das Kind *n*	kid appeal	appel *m* via l'enfant *m*
Ansprache *f* des Familiengefühls *n*	family appeal	appel *m* au bonheur *m* domestique, appel *m* au sentiment *m* de famille *f*
Ansprache *f* des Menschlichen *n*	human appeal	appel *m* à l'humanité *f*
Ansprache *f* des Snobismus *m*	snob appeal	appel *m* au snobisme *m*
Ansprache *f*, persönliche	personal approach	appel *m* personnel
ansprechende Werbung *f*	appealing advertising	publicité *f* attrayante
Anstalt *f*, lithografische	lithographic plant	atelier *m* de lithographie *f*
Anstalt *f*, öffentlich-rechtliche	body corporate, public institution	établissement *m* de droit *m* public
Ansteckplakette *f*	button	bouton *m*
anstößige Werbung *f*	indecent advertising	publicité *f* indécente
Anstrich *m*	paint	peinture *f*
Anstrich *m* (Buchstabe *m*)	up-stroke	plein *m*
Anteil *m*	quota	contingent *m*
Anthologie *f*	anthology	anthologie *f*
antik (Papier)	antique wove	papier *m* édition *f*
Antiqua *f*	old face type, Roman type	caractère *m* ancien, caractère *m* romain
Antiqua *f*, klassische	classicistic Latin	Didot *m*
antizyklische Werbung *f*	anticyclic advertising	publicité *f* anticyclique
Antwort *f*, telegrafische	reply by wire	réponse *f* télégraphique
Antwortkarte *f*	reply card, return card	carte *f* de retour *m*, carte-réponse *f*
Antwortkupon *m*	reply coupon	coupon-réponse *f*
Antwortschreiben *n*	written reply	lettre *f*-réponse*f*
Anweisung *f* (für Satz *m*)	composition pattern	donnée *f* de composition *f*
Anweisung *f* von Werbekosten *pl*	advertising allocation	allocation *f* publicitaire, lotissement *m* publicitaire
Anweisungen *f/pl*	instructions *pl*	directives *f/pl*
Anzahlung *f*	down payment, part payment	acompte *m*
Anzapfung *f* der Telefonleitungen *f/pl*	wire-tapping	captage *m* des messages *m/pl* télégraphiques
Anzeige *f*	ad, advertisement, announcement	annonce *f*, insertion *f*
Anzeige *f*, alleinstehende	sole advertisement	annonce *f* isolée
Anzeige *f*, amtliche	official announcement	annonce *f* légale
Anzeige *f* im Anschluß *m* an mehrere Textspalten *f/pl*	cut-in advertisement	annonce *f* se joignant à plusieurs colonnes *f/pl* rédactionnelles *f/pl*
Anzeige *f*, angeschnittene	bleed advertisement	annonce *f* à fond *m* perdu, annonce *f* à franc-bord *m*
Anzeige *f* aufgeben	to have an advertisement inserted	faire insérer une annonce *f*
Anzeige *f*, die verschiedene Arten *f/pl* eines Produktes *n* zeigt	umbrella-ad	annonce *f* montrant de diverses sortes *f/pl* d'un produit *m*
Anzeige *f*, doppelseitige	double truck, double-page spread	double page *f* centrale
Anzeige *f*, einzige einer Seite *f*	sole advertisement	seule annonce *f*
Anzeige *f*, feuilletonistische	advertisement in feuilleton style, advertisement in short story style	reportage *m* publicitaire
Anzeige *f*, fingierte	dummy advertisement	annonce *f* fictive
Anzeige *f*, ganzseitige	full page ad, spread	annonce *f* d'une page *f* entière

Anzeige *f*, **gerichtliche**	legal notice	annonce *f* judiciaire
Anzeige *f*, **getarnte**	veiled advertisement	annonce *f* déguisée
Anzeige *f*, **großflächige**	big splurge ad, large space ad	annonce *f* de grandes dimensions *f/pl*
Anzeige *f* **im Rundfunk** *m*	advergram	annonce *f* radiophonique
Anzeige *f* **in einer Teilauflage** *f/pl*	split-run advertisement	annonce *f* à variantes *f/pl*
Anzeige *f*, **luftige**	advertisement with much white space	annonce *f* bien aérée
Anzeige *f*, **maskierte**	advertisement masked out in part	annonce *f* masquée en partie *f*
Anzeige *f*, **mehrfarbige**	colored ad *am*, coloured ad *brit*	annonce *f* multicolore
Anzeige *f* **neben Zeitungskopf** *m*	box on the right of the masthead, ear-pieces *pl*, ears *pl*	manchette *f* à droite du titre *m*
Anzeige *f*, **Neugier erregende**	teaser	annonce *f* piquant la curiosité *f*
Anzeige *f*, **nichtgebrachte**	hold over	reporter
Anzeige *f*, **örtliche**	local advertisement	annonce *f* locale
Anzeige *f*, **redaktionell aufgemachte**	advertorial, editorial advertisement, reader advertisement, reading notice *am*	annonce *f* à apparence *f* rédactionnelle
Anzeige *f*, **seitenbeherrschende**	page dominance	emplacement *m* prédominant dans une page *f*
Anzeige *f*, **seitenteilige**	fractional-page advertisement	publicité *f* au format *m* annonce *f* flamboyante
Anzeige *f*, **sensationell aufgemachte**	flaring advertisement	décroché *m*
Anzeige *f*, **stufenförmige**	disconnected advertisement	annonce *f* téléphonée
Anzeige *f*, **telefonisch aufgegebene**	telephoned advertisement	annonce *f* surchargée
Anzeige *f*, **überladene**	buckeye	annonce *f* encadrée
Anzeige *f*, **umrandete**	boxed advertisement	annonce *f* complémentaire pour bénéficier du dégressif *m*
Anzeige *f* **zur Erreichung** *f* **eines höheren Nachlasses** *m*	rate holder, rate maker	insertion *f* supplémentaire
Anzeige *f*, **zusätzliche**	additional insertion	annoncer
anzeigen	to advertise	publicité *f* non classifiée
Anzeigen *f/pl*, **allgemeine**	display advertisements *pl*	petites annonces *f/pl*
Anzeigen *f/pl*, **kleine**	classified advertisements *pl*, small ads *pl*	annonces *f/pl* personnelles
Anzeigen *f/pl*, **persönliche**	agony column	annonces *f/pl* groupées, petites annonces *f/pl*
Anzeigen *f/pl*, **rubrizierte**	classified advertisements *pl*, composite advertisements *pl*, small ads *pl*	disposition *f*
Anzeigenabruf *m*	release	contrat *m* d'insertion *f*
Anzeigenabschluß *m*	advertising contract	service *m* des annonces *f/pl*,
Anzeigenabteilung *f*	advertising department	service *m* publicité *f* épreuve *f* pour archives *f/pl*
Anzeigenabzug *m* **für Archivzwecke** *m/pl*	file proof	démarcheur *m* en publicité *f*, vendeur *m* d'espace *m*
Anzeigenakquisiteur *m*	advertisement canvasser, advertising solicitor *am*, space salesman	réception *f* d'annonces *f/pl*
Anzeigenannahme *f*	reception of advertisements *pl*	genres *m/pl* d'annonces *f/pl*
Anzeigenarten *f/pl*	kinds *pl* of advertisements *pl*	corrélations *f/pl* entre
Anzeigen-Auflagen-Spirale *f*	interrelations *pl* between advertisements *pl* and circulation	annonces *f/pl* et tirage *m*

Anzeigenauftrag *m*	advertisement order, insertion order, space order	commande *f* d'insertion *f*
Anzeigenausschnitt *m*	clipping, press cutting	coupure *f*
Anzeigenbeachtung *f*	ad-audience	audience *f* d'insertion *f*
Anzeigenbeilage *f*	advertisement supplement	supplément *m* d'annonces *f/pl*
Anzeigenbeleg *m*	voucher copy	justificatif *m* d'annonce *f*
Anzeigenbelegung *f*	space buying	achat *m* d'espace *m*
Anzeigenberechnung *f*	advertisement calculation	calculation *f* d'annonces *f/pl*
Anzeigenblatt *n*	admag, advertisement magazine, advertiser, free sheet, shopper	annoncier *m*, feuille *f* d'annonces *f/pl*, journal *m* publicitaire
Anzeigenbüro *n*	advertisement office	bureau *m* d'annonces *f/pl*
Anzeigendienst *m*	advertising service	service *m* de publicité *f*
Anzeigendirektor *m*	advertisement director	directeur *m* du service *m* de publicité *f*
Anzeigendisposition *f*	placing orders *pl* for space	retenue *f* des emplacements *m/pl*
Anzeigeneinfassung *f*	advertisement border	bordure *f* d'annonce *f*
Anzeigeneinkauf *m*	space buying	achat *m* d'annonces *f/pl*
Anzeigeneinnahmen *f/pl*	ad revenues *pl*	revenus *m/pl* d'annonces *f/pl*
Anzeigenelement *m*, wiederkehrendes	standing detail	détail *m* permanent
Anzeigenerfolgskontrolle *f*	advertisement rating, advertising control	contrôle *m* du rendement *m* publicitaire
Anzeigenerinnerungstest *m*	blind product test	test *m* sans visibilité *f* du produit *m*
Anzeigenerlöse *m/pl*	advertisement proceeds *pl*	montant *m* d'annonces *f/pl*
Anzeigenexpedition *f*	advertising space buyer	intermédiaire *m* publicitaire
Anzeigenfachmann *m*	adman	publicitaire *m*
Anzeigenfestpreis *m*	flat rate	prix *m* fixe
Anzeigenflaute *f*	flatness in advertising business	période *f* creuse pour la publicité *f*
Anzeigenformat *n*	advertisement size	format *m* d'annonce *f*
Anzeigenfriedhof *m*	buried advertisements *pl*	annonces *f/pl* enterrées
Anzeigengeschäft *n*	advertising business	métier *m* publicitaire
Anzeigengestaltung *f*	creative copy and artwork	conception *f* de l'annonce *f*, présentation *f* de l'annonce *f*
Anzeigengröße *f*	advertisement lineage, space size	lignage *m* d'une annonce *f*
Anzeigengrundpreis *m*	basic rate, open rate	tarif *m* de base *f*
Anzeigeninhalt *m*	advertising contents *pl*	contenu *m* publicitaire
Anzeigenkäufer *m*	space buyer	acheteur *m* d'espace *m*
Anzeigenkennzeichnung *f*	keying an advertisement	codification *f* d'une annonce *f*
Anzeigenklischee *n*	advertising block	cliché *m* d'annonce *f*
Anzeigenkollektiv *n*	collective page	page *f* collective
Anzeigenkosten *pl*	advertising charges *pl*	dépenses *f/pl* d'insertion *f*
Anzeigenkunde *m*	advertising customer	client *m* de publicité *f*
Anzeigenleiter *m*	advertisement director, advertising manager	chef *m* de publicité *f*, chef *m* des annonces *f/pl*, directeur *m* du service *m* de publicité *f*
Anzeigenmangel *m*	defection from advertisements *pl*	défection *f* publicitaire
Anzeigenmittler *m*	advertising contractor, space broker	acheteur *m* d'espace *m*, courtier *m* d'annonces *f/pl*, intermédiaire *m* publicitaire
Anzeigenmonopol *n*	advertising monopoly	monopole *m* publicitaire
Anzeigenpächter *m*	advertising operator	concessionaire *m*, régisseur *m*
Anzeigenplantage *f*	cocktail of ads *pl*	juxtaposition *f* désordonnée d'annonces *f/pl*

Anzeigenplatz *m*, **reservierter**	reserved position	emplacement *m* réservé
Anzeigenplazierung *f*	advertisement placing	emplacement *m* d'annonce *f*
Anzeigenpreis *m* **entsprechend**	earned rate	tarif *m* dégressif
der tatsächlich		
abgenommenen Menge *f*		
Anzeigenpreis *m*, **kombinierter**	combination rate	tarif *m* combiné
Anzeigenpreise *m/pl*	adrates *pl*, advertising charges *pl*,	tarifs *m/pl* de publicité *f*
	costs *f* of advertisement	
Anzeigenpreisliste *f*	advertisement rate card, space	tarif *m* d'annonces *f/pl*
	rates *pl*	
Anzeigenpreisliste *f*, **z.Zt.**	temporary rate sheet	tarif *m* d'annonces *f/pl* valide
gültige		actuellement
Anzeigenrabatt *m* **bei**	clubbing offer	rabais *m* commun
Belegung *f* **mehrerer**		
Blätter *n/pl* **eines Verlages** *m*		
Anzeigenraum *m*	advertising space, amount of	espace *m* d'annonces *f/pl*,
	space, lineage	lignage *m*
Anzeigenraum *m* **bestellen**	space buying	acheter d'espace *m*
Anzeigenraum *m* **buchen**	to book space	enregistrer d'espace *m*
Anzeigenregie *f*	advertisement administration	régie *f* d'annonces *f/pl*
Anzeigenring *m*	group of publishers *pl*	cercle *m* d'édition *f*, couplage *m*
		publicitaire
Anzeigensatz *m*	advertising composition	composition *f* des annonces *f/pl*
Anzeigenschluß *m*	closing date, closing down,	date *f* limite de remise *f*,
	closing hour, copy deadline,	délai *m* des annonces *f/pl*
	forms *pl* close	
Anzeigenseite *f*	advertisement page,	feuille *f* d'annonces *f/pl*, page *f*
	advertising sheet	d'annonces *f/pl*
Anzeigenserie *f*	serial advertisements *pl*	série *f* d'annonces *f/pl*
Anzeigensetzer *m*	advertisement compositor	annoncier *m*
Anzeigenspalte *f*	advertisement colums *pl*	colonne *f* d'annonce *f*
Anzeigenspiegel *m*	advertisement make-up,	maquette *f* de la partie *f*
	advertisement type area,	publicitaire
	advertising page plan	
Anzeigensplit *m*	split run	tirage *m* partagé
Anzeigensteuer *f*	advertisement duty	impôt *m* sur la publicité *f*
Anzeigentarif *m*	advertisement rate schedule,	tarif *m* d'annonces *f/pl*, tarif *m*
	advertising charges *pl*,	de publicité *f*, tarif *m*
	advertising rates *pl*, space	d'insertion *f*
	rates *pl*	
Anzeigenteil *m*	advertising section	partie *f* publicitaire
Anzeigenteil *m* **pachten**	to lease the advertisement	affermer la publicité *f*
	business	
Anzeigentest *m*	copy test, folder test, impact-test	test *m* d'annonce *f*
Anzeigentext *m*	copy, text	texte *m* de l'annonce *f*
Anzeigenumbruch *m*	advertisement make-up	mise *f* en pages *f/pl* des
		annonces *f/pl*
Anzeigenumfang *m*	advertisement volume	volume *m* d'annonces *f/pl*
Anzeigenvertreter *m*	advertisement representative,	courtier *m* en publicité *f*,
	advertising sales *pl* executive	représentant *m* publicitaire
Anzeigenverwaltung *f*	advertisement administration,	concessionaire *m*, régie *f* de
	advertising management, sole	publicité *f*, régie *f*
	advertising representative	d'annonces *f/pl*
Anzeigenvolumen *n*	advertising volume	volume *m* publicitaire
Anzeigenvortest *m*	pre-test	test *m* préalable
Anzeigenwerbeleiter *m*	ad sales *pl* promotion manager	chef *m* de la vente *f*
		d'annonces *f/pl*

Anzeigenwerbung f	press advertising	publicité-presse f
Anzeigenzunahme f	advertising growth	accroissement m de publicité f
Anziehungskraft f	appeal, attraction, attractive power	attrait m, force f d'attraction f
Aphorismus m	aphorism	aphorisme m
Apostroph m	apostrophe	apostrophe f
Apparatur f **zur Prüfung** f **der Werbewirkung** f	program analyzer	appareil m pour tester l'effet m publicitaire
Appell m	appeal	appel m
appetitanregende Aufmachung f	appetizing appeal	présentation f appétissante
Aquarell n	wash drawing, water colour	aquarelle f
Aquarellfarben f/pl	aquarelle colours pl	couleurs f/pl aquarelles
aquarellierte Strichzeichnung f	line and wash drawing	dessin m au trait m aquarellé
Aquatinta f	aquatint	aquatinte f
Arabeske f	arabesque	arabesque f
arabische Ziffern f/pl	arabic numerals pl	chiffres m/pl arabes
Arbeiten f/pl, **künstlerische**	art work	ouvrages m/pl artistiques
Arbeitsablauf m	procedure	procédure f
Arbeitsablaufblatt n	job memorandum, work order	note f sur les étapes f/pl de déroulement m
Arbeitsabwicklung f	progress of work	cours m de travail m
Arbeitsanweisung f	briefing	instructions f/pl
Arbeitsaufwand m	expenditure of work	ampleur f du travail m
Arbeitsgang m	process of work, working operation	opération f, phase f de travail m
Arbeitsgebiet n	field of activities pl	ressort m d'activité f
Arbeitsgemeinschaft f	team	communauté f de travail m, coopération f, équipe f
Arbeitsgerät n	tool	outil m
Arbeitsgrundsätze m/pl	rules pl of work	règles f/pl de travail m
Arbeitsgruppe f	working party	groupe m de travail m
Arbeitsplaner m	programmer	préparateur m
Arbeitsprogramm n	programme of work	programme m des travaux m/pl
Arbeitsrückstand m	backlog	arriéré m de travail m
Arbeitssitzung f	research pl plans pl board meeting	séance f de travail m
Arbeitstasche f	job bag	chemise f de travail m
Arbeitstitel m	provisional title	titre m provisoire
Arbeitsvorgang m	operating process	mode m de travail m
Arbeitsweise f	method of operation	manière f de travailler
Archiv n	archives pl, record office	archives f/pl
Archivbild n	stock-shot	plan m d'archives f/pl
Archivexemplar n	copy on file, file-copy, record copy	exemplaire m des archives f/pl, exemplaire m en collection f
Argumentation f	talking points pl	argumentation f
Artdirektor m	art buyer, art director	concepteur m graphique, directeur m artistique, ordonnateur m d'art m
Artikel m	article	article m
Artikel m, **auffallender**	stunt article	article m tapageur
Artikel m, **aufsehenerregender**	blockbuster	papier m du tonnerre m
Artikel m, **der vor dem Ereignis** n **geschrieben wurde**	advance story	avant-papier m
Artikel m, **gezeichneter**	bylined story	article m signé

Artikel *m* gleichzeitig in mehreren Zeitungen *f/pl* veröffentlichen	to syndicate	publier un article *m* simultanément dans plusieurs journaux *m/pl*
Artikel *m* mit viel Zwischenschlag *m*	double-leaded article	article *m* blanchi
Artikel *m*, objektiver	balanced article	article *m* objectif
Artikel *m*, redaktioneller	editorial	éditorial *m*
Artikel *m*, überlaufender	jump story	article *m* à cheval *m*
Artikel *m*, unverdaulicher	pig iron	article *m* lourd et indigeste
Artikel *m*, zurechtgepfuschter	patched-up story	article *m* bâclé
Artikelserie *f*	series *pl* of articles *pl*	série *f* d'articles *m/pl*
Assistent *m*	assistant	adjoint *m*, assistant *m*
Assoziationstest *m*	association test	test *m* d'association *f*
Asymmetrie *f*	asymmetry	asymétrie *f*
asymmetrische Anordnung *f*	informal balance, off-center arrangement	arrangement *m* asymétrique
Atelier *n*	studio, workshop	atelier *m*, studio *m*
Atelierleiter *m*	art director, studio manager	chef *m* de studio *m*, directeur *m* artistique
Atlaspapier *n*	satin paper	papier *m* imprégné et gaufré
Attraktivität *f* der Anzeigenaussage *f*	copy appeal	attrait *m* du message *m* publicitaire
Attrappe *f*	dummy pack	attrape *f*, emballage *m* factice
Audimeter *m*	audimeter	audimètre *m*
audiovisuelle Geräte *n/pl*	audio-visual equipment	appareils *m/pl* audio-visuels
audiovisuelle Werbung *f*	audio-visual advertising	publicité *f* audio-visuelle
auf dem Blei *n* korrigieren	to correct in the metal	corriger sur le plomb *m*
auf den neuesten Stand *m* bringen	to update	mettre à jour *m*
auf einer anderen Seite *f* fortsetzen	to run over	décrocher
auf Leinwand *f* gemaltes Plakat *n*	poster painted on canvas	affiche *f* toile *f* peinte
auf Provisionsbasis *f*	on commission	à la commission *f*
Auf- und Abverschiebung *f* von Bildschirmzeilen *f/pl*	roll up and down, scroll up and down	décalage *m* des lignes *f/pl*
aufbauen	to build-up	élever
aufbauschen	to blow up, to puff up	enfler, faire mousser
Aufbauskizze *f*	layout	maquette *f*
aufbewahren	to hold for release	à conserver
aufblasbare Werbefiguren *f/pl*	inflatable advertising figures *pl*	figures *f/pl* de publicité *f* gonflables
aufblenden	to wipe on	arriver dans un fondu *m*
aufdecken	to disclose	divulguer
Aufdruck *m*	imprint, overprint	repiquage *m*, surimpression *f*
aufeinander abgestimmte Werbung *f*	coordinated advertising	publicité *f* coordonnée
aufeinanderfolgend	successive	successif
auffallende Titelseite *f*	flag	titre *m* flamboyant
auffallender Artikel *m*	stunt article	article *m* tapageur
auffallender Satz *m*	display composition	composition *f* tape-à-l'œil *m*
Aufgabengebiet *n*	assignment, field, scope	fonctions *f/pl*, tâche *f* assignée
aufgeben, ein Inserat *n*	to order an advertisement	remettre une annonce *f*
aufgelegter Raster *m*	sticked screen	trame *f* collée
aufgezeichnete Sendung *f*	pre-recorded broadcast	émission *f* différée
Aufgliederung *f*	breakdown	détail *m*, détaillé *m*, ventilation *f*
Aufhängedekoration *f*	mobile	décoration *f* mobile

Aufhänger *m*	approach, hook, topical peg	accrochage *m* publicitaire, angle *m* d'approche *f*
Aufhellung *f*	clarification	clarification *f*
aufklärende Etikettierung *f*	informative labeling	étiquettage *m* informatif
Aufklärungsschrift *f*	popular pamphlet	brochure *f* de vulgarisation *f*
Aufklärungswerbung *f*	product publicity, reason-why advertising	publicité *f* argumentée, publicité *f* produits *m/pl*
Aufkleben *n*	pasting	collage *m*
Aufkleber *m*	gummed label, sticker slip	étiquette *f* gommée, papillon *m*, timbre *m* adhésif *m*
aufklotzen	to block, to mount	clouer
Auflage *f*	circulation, press run	tirage *m*
Auflage *f*, **beglaubigte**	audited circulation	tirage *m* contrôlé
Auflage *f*, **beschränkte**	limited edition	édition *f* à tirage *m* limité
Auflage *f*, **bezahlte**	paid circulation	tirage *m* payé
Auflage *f*, **durchschnittliche**	average circulation	diffusion *f* moyenne
Auflage *f*, **erhöhte**	run-on	tirage *m* supplémentaire
Auflage *f*, **erweiterte**	enlarged edition	édition *f* augmentée
Auflage *f*, **hohe**	mass-circulation	haut tirage *m*
Auflage *f*, **kleine**	short run	petit tirage *m*
Auflage *f*, **verkaufte**	total net paid circulation	diffusion *f* bouillon *m* déduit
Auflagebeglaubigung *f*	certified statement of circulation	certificat *m* de contrôle *m* du tirage *m*, constat *m* de tirage *m*
Auflageerweiterung *f*	run-on	tirage *m* supplémentaire
Auflagemeldung *f*	publisher's statement	rapport *m* sur les tirages *m/pl*
Auflagenanalyse *f*	circulation analysis	analyse *f* des tirages *m/pl*
Auflagenanstieg *m*	circulation growth	accroissement *m* des tirages *m/pl*
Auflagenbestätigung *f*	certification of circulation	certification *f* des tirages *m/pl*
Auflagendruck *m*	circulation run	tirage *m* (impression *f*)
Auflagenentwicklung *f*	development of circulation	évolution *f* des tirages *m/pl*
Auflagengarantie *f*	circulation guarantee	garantie *f* de la circulation *f*
Auflagenhöhe *f*	circulation base, print run, printing-number	chiffre *m* du tirage *m*
Auflagenkontrolle *f*	circulation control	contrôle *m* des tirages *m/pl*
Auflagenminderung *f*	decrease of circulation	diminution *f* des tirages *m/pl*
Auflagenprüfung *f*	circulation control	contrôle *m* des tirages *m/pl*
Auflagenrückgang *m*	decline in circulation	régression *f* des tirages *m/pl*
Auflagensplit *m* **unter Partnern** *m/pl*	partner split	tirage *m* partagé entre des partenaires *m/pl*
auflagenstarke Presse *f*	press with a large circulation	grande presse *f*, presse *f* à grand tirage *m*
Auflagenstillstand *m*	circulation dullness	stagnation *f* des tirages *m/pl*
Auflagenüberwachungsstelle *f*	Audit Bureau of Circulations *pl*	Office *m* de Justification *f* des Tirages *m/pl*
Auflagenveränderung *f*	change in circulation	changement *m* des tirages *m/pl*
Auflagenverteilung	circulation breakdown	répartition *f* des tirages *m/pl*
Auflageschwankungen *f/pl*	fluctuations *pl* of circulation	fluctuations *f/pl* des tirages *m/pl*
Auflegemaske *f*	overlay	cache *f*, masque *m*
Auflösung *f*	cancellation, dissolution	dissolution *f*, résiliation *f*
aufmachen	to dress, to make up	arranger, présenter
Aufmacher *m*	leader	article *m* de tête *f*
Aufmachung *f*	make up	arrangement *m*, présentation *f*

Aufmachung f, appetitanregende	appetizing appeal	présentation f appétissante
Aufmachung f, ausgewogene	balanced make up	mise f en page f équilibrée
Aufmachung f bringen, in großer	to make a splash	mettre en manchette f
Aufmachung f, überladene	crowded make up	mise f en page f surchargée
Aufmachungsmuster n	dummy	maquette f
Aufmerksamkeit f	attention	attention f
Aufmerksamkeitserreger m	advertising approach, attention getter	accrochage m initial, angle m d'approche f
Aufmerksamkeitsfaktor m	attention factor, interest factor	facteur m d'attention f
Aufmerksamkeitswert m	attention value	valeur f d'attention f
Aufnahme f	acceptance	acceptation f
Aufnahme f (Film)	take	prise f de vue f
Aufnahme f, fotografische	shot, taking of photographs pl	photographie f, prise f de vue f
Aufnahmeapparat m zur Feststellung f der Hörerzahl f	audimeter	audimètre m, audiomètre m
Aufnahmebereitschaft f	consumer acceptance	faveur f du public m
Aufnahmefähigkeit f	receptivity	réceptivité f
Aufnahmefreudigkeit f	consumer acceptance	faveur f du public m
Aufnahmegerät n	tape recorder	appareil m enregistrateur
Aufnahmeleiter m	director	metteur m en scène f
Aufnahmeraum m	studio	atelier m, film m studio m
Aufnahmetechnik f	photographic technique	technique f photographique
aufnehmen (Foto)	to photograph, to shoot	photographier
Aufrasterung f	Ben Day process, screening	tramage m
Aufriß m	layout	maquette f
Aufsatz m	essay	article m
Aufsaugung f	absorption	absorption f
Aufschlag m	extra charge, rate increase	majoration f de tarif m, supplément m
Aufschlagseite f	eye-catching right-hand page	belle page f
Aufschlüsselung f	breakdown, classification	répartition f, ventilation f
aufschweißen	to weld on	thermosouder
aufsehenerregende Nachricht f	sensational piece of news	pétard m
aufsehenerregender Artikel m	blockbuster	papier m du tonnerre m
Aufstecker m	crowner	capsule f de bouteille f
Aufstellplakat n	counter card, show card	affiche f de comptoir m, affiche f mobile, pancarte f
Aufstellung f	list	liste f, relevé m
Auftakt m	opening phase	ouverture f
aufteilen	to split	diviser, partager
Aufteilung f	breakdown	répartition f
Aufteilung f des Werbebudgets n	assignment of advertising expenditure	allocation f du budget m publicitaire
Aufträge m/pl hereinholen	canvassing	prospection f
Auftrag m	commission, order	commande f, commission f, ordre m
Auftrag m auf Widerruf m	open order, until cancelled order	ordre m valable jusqu'à révocation f
Auftrag m buchen	to book an order	noter un ordre m
Auftrag m, freibleibender	order without obligation	ordre m sans engagement m
Auftrag m, laufender	continuous order, standing order	ordre m permanent
Auftrag m, mündlich erteilter	order by word of mouth	commande f verbale
Auftrag m, telegrafisch erteilter	order by wire	commande f télégraphique
Auftrag m vergeben	to place an order	donner un ordre m, passer une commande f

Auftraggeber *m*	client, commissioned by, customer	client *m*, commettant *m*, mandant *m*
Auftraggeber *m* eines Ghostwriters *m*	mummy	commettant *m* d'un nègre *m*
Auftraggeber *m* freier Künstler *m/pl*	art buyer	acheteur *m* d'art *m*
Auftragnehmer *m*	supplier	fournisseur *m*, mandataire *m*
Auftragsablehnung *f*	refusal of an order	refus *m* de commande *f*
Auftragsabteilung *f*	order department	service *m* des commandes *f/pl*
Auftragsabwicklung *f*	filling of a contract, order processing	exécution *f* d'un ordre *m*
Auftragsannahme *f*	acceptance of an order	acceptation *f* d'une commande *f*
Auftragsannullierung *f*	cancellation of an order	annulation *f* d'un ordre *m*
Auftragsausführung *f*	execution of an order	exécution *f* d'une commande *f*
Auftragsbesprechung *f*	briefing conference	conférence *f* d'instruction *f*
Auftragsbestätigung *f*	confirmation of order	confirmation *f* de la commande *f*
Auftragsbestand *m*	stock of orders *pl*	portefeuille *m* de commandes *f/pl*
Auftragsbuch *n*	order-book	carnet *m* de commandes *f/pl*
Auftragseingang *m*	incoming of orders *pl*	entrée *f* de commandes *f/pl*
Auftragserledigung *f*	carrying out of an order, order filling	réalisation *f* de commandes *f/pl*
Auftragserneuerung *f*	repeating of an order	renouvellement *m* d'un ordre *m*
Auftragserteilung *f*	placing of orders *pl*	passation *f* d'un ordre *m*
Auftragserweiterung *f*	enlargement of an order, extension of an order	augmentation *f* de commande *f*, complément *m* de commande *f*
Auftragsformular *n*	order form	bon *m* de commande *f*
auftragsgemäß	as per instructions *pl*	suivant l'ordre *m*
Auftragskartei *f*	card-index of orders *pl*, order register	fichier *m* des commandes *f/pl* en exécution *f*
Auftragskürzung *f*	reduction of an order	réduction *f* d'un mandat *m*
Auftragsnummer *f*	order number	numéro *m* de la commande *f*
Auftragspolster *n*	backlog of orders *pl*	commandes *f/pl* en suspens *m*
Auftragsrückgang *m*	decline of orders *pl*, falling off of orders *pl*	fléchissement *m* dans les rentrées *f/pl* de commande *f*
Auftragsrückstand *m*	back orders *pl*, delay in the execution of orders *pl*	retard *m* dans l'exécution *f* des commandes *f/pl*
Auftragssperre *f*	blockade of orders *pl*	blocage *m* de commandes *f/pl*
Auftragsstreichung *f*	cancelling of an order	suppression *f* d'un mandat *m*
Auftragstasche *f*	docket, job bag	dossier *m* d'une commande *f*
Auftragsüberhänge *m/pl*	surplus of orders *pl*	surplus *m* de commandes *f/pl*
Auftragsüberschreibung *f*	remittance of an order	attribution *f* de la commande *f*
Auftragsumfang *m*	insertion and size	grandeur *f* et arrangement *m*
Aufwand *m*	expenditure	dépenses *f/pl*
Aufwendung *f*	expenditure, expense	dépenses *f/pl*, frais *m/pl*
Aufzeichnung *f* einer Rundfunksendung *f*	air check	enregistrement *m* d'une émission *f* radiophonique
Aufzeichnungsgerät *n*	video recorder	magnétoscope *m*
Aufzeichnungsgerät *n* zur Hörerschaftsforschung *f*	audiometer	audiomètre *m*
aufziehen (Foto)	to mount	monter
Augenzeugenbericht *m*	eyewitness account	récit *m* d'un témoin *m* oculaire
aus erster Hand *f*	from first source	de première main *f*

ausarbeiten	to elaborate	élaborer
ausbedingen	to stipulate	stipuler
Ausbildung *f*	education, training	formation *f*
ausbinden	to tie up	lier
Ausbindeschnur *f*	page cord	ficelle *f*
ausbleichen	to bleach out	décolorer
Ausblenden *n*	fade-out	fondu *m*
Ausblick *m*	vista	perspective *f*
ausblocken	to block out, to turn a letter	bloquer une lettre *f*, caviarder
ausdecken	to mask out	couvrir, masquer
Ausdruck *m*	expression	expression *f*
Ausdruck *m*, bildlicher	metaphor	métaphore *f*
ausdrucken	to work off	achever de tirer, terminer l'impression *f*
Ausdrucksform *f*	form of expression	mode *m* d'expression *f*
Ausdruckskraft *f*	expressive force, force expressiveness	expressivité *f*, force *f* d'expression *f*
Ausdrucksmittel *n*	means *pl* of expression	moyen *m* d'expression *f*
Ausdrucksökonomie *f*	economy of expression	économie *f* d'expression *f*
Ausdrucksweise *f*	diction, phraseology, style	diction *f*, élocution *f*, manière *f* de s'exprimer, phraséologie *f*
Ausdrucksweise *f*, klare	plain style	style *m* sans fioritures *f/pl*
Ausfall *m*	failure rates *pl*, turnout	rebut *m*
ausfallen lassen	to kill	éliminer
Ausfallmuster *n*	quality sample, reference pattern	échantillon *m* de comparaison *f*
Ausfertigung *f*, zweifache	duplicate	double exemplaire *m*
ausfräsen	to cut out, to rout out	fraiser, toupiller
Ausfräsung *f*	routing	fraisage *m*
ausführen	to implement	exécuter
Ausführung *f*	execution, realization	exécution *f*, réalisation *f*
Ausgabe *f*, erste	bulldog edition	première édition *f*
Ausgabe *f*, je	per issue	par édition *f*
Ausgabe *f*, letzte	current number	dernier numéro *m* paru
Ausgabe *f* (Nummer)	copy, edition, issue, number	édition *f*, exemplaire *m*, numéro *m*
Ausgaben *f/pl*, frühere	back copies *pl*	exemplaires *m/pl* précédents
Ausgaben *f/pl* (Unkosten)	costs *pl*, expenses *pl*	dépenses *f/pl*, frais *m/pl*
Ausgabe *f/typog*	output	information *f* traitée
Ausgangszeile *f*	break-line, last line, short line	dernière ligne *f*, fin *f* d'alinéa *m*, ligne *f* courte
ausgedruckter Druckbogen *m*	folded printed sheet	cahier *m*
ausgefallene Idee *f*	gimmick	coup *m*, truc *m*
ausgefräster Druckstock *m*	routed plate	cliché *m* fraisé, cliché *m* toupillé
ausgestanztes Emblem *n*	die cut	découpé, emblème *m*
ausgewogene Aufmachung *f*	balanced make up	mise *f* en page *f* équilibrée
Ausgleich *m*	compensation	compensation *f*
Ausgleich *typog m*	alignment	alignement *m*
ausgleichen (Zeile)	to space evenly	rectifier les approches *f/pl*
ausgleichen (Zurichtung *f*)	to equalize	égaliser
Aushängebogen *m*	advance sheet, specimen sheet	bonne feuille *f*
Aushängeschild *n*	sign	panonceau *m*
aushandeln	to bargain, to negotiate	marchander, négocier
Aushang *m*	display, exhibition	étalage *m*, exposition *f*
Aushangdauer *f*	period of display	conservation *f*, durée *f* d'affichage *m*
Aushangzeit *f*	period of display	période *f* de conservation *f*

aushecken, eine Nachricht f	to fabricate an information	forger une information f
Auskleidepapier n	blanking paper	papier m de fond m
Auskleidung f der Anschlagstellen f/pl	dressing of the sites pl	habillage m des emplacements m/pl
ausklinken	to mortise, to pierce for type	encocher, entailler
Auskunftsperson f	informant	informateur m, informatrice f
Auslage f	display	présentation f, vitrine f
Auslage f, offene	open display	exposition f libre
Auslageapparat m	delivery apparatus roll	rouleau m de sortie f ralentisseur m
Auslandsauftrag m	foreign order	commande f de l'étranger m
Auslandsberichterstatter m	foreign correspondent	correspondant m à l'étranger m
Auslandsmarkt m	foreign market	marché m étranger m
Auslandsnachrichten f/pl	foreign news	nouvelles f/pl de l'étranger m
Auslandspresse f	foreign press	presse f de l'étranger m
Auslandssender m	foreign station	station-radio f de l'étranger m
Auslandsverbreitung f	foreign circulation	diffussion f à l'étranger m
Auslandswerbung f	foreign advertising	publicité f à l'étranger m
Auslassung f	out	bourdon m
Auslassungszeichen n	caret mark	renvoi m de marge f, signe m d'omission f
auslaufen (Farbe)	to run (colour)	couler (couleur)
Auslaufzeit f	stop time	période f transitoire
Ausleger m (Bogenfänger)	sheet-delivery	sortie f des feuilles f/pl
Auslegetisch m	delivery table	banc m de presse f
Auslegung f	interpretation	interprétation f
Auslese f	digest	condensé m
ausleuchten	to illuminate	illuminer
Auslieferer m	distributor, supplier	dépositaire m
Ausmaße n/pl	size	dimensions f/pl
ausmerzen	to expurgate, to sort	expurger, trier
ausplaudern, eine Sache f	to blab out a secret	vendre la mèche f
Ausrede f, fadenscheinige	quibble	argutie f, faux-fuyant m
ausreißen	to pull out	séparer
Ausrüstung f	equipment, finishing	équipement m, façonnage m
Ausrufezeichen n	exclamation mark, exclamation point am	point m d'exclamation f
Aussage f	statement	déclaration f
Aussageform f	form of assertion	forme f d'assertion f
aussagekräftige Überschrift f	action	manchette f verbale
Aussagekraft f	force of expression	puissance f d'expression f
ausschlachten	to pick	désosser
ausschlagbare Seite f	gatefold	pli m en portefeuille m
ausschließen, nach links	to move to the left	justifier à la gauche
ausschließen, nach rechts	to move to the right	justifier à droite
ausschließen (typog)	to align, to justify	aligner, justifier
Ausschließkeil m	space band	espace-bande f
Ausschluß m	exclusion	exclusion f
Ausschluß typog m	blank space, stick space	cadrats m/pl, espace f
Ausschnitt m (Stanze f)	cut out, piercing, trimming	découpe f, encoche f, perforation f
Ausschnitt m (Zeitung f)	clipping, press-cutting	coupure f
Ausschnittdienst m	press-cutting agency	bureau m de coupure f de journaux m/pl
Ausschreibung f	invitation to bid	adjucation f

Ausschuß *m*	committee	comité *f*
Ausschuß (Abfall) *m*	dross, refuse	déchet *m*
Außenaufnahme *f*	outdoor photo	photo *f* en plein air *m*
Außenbericht *m*	outside broadcast	reportage *m* en extérieur
Außendienst *m*	field service, outdoor duty	service *m* extérieur
Außendienstmitarbeiter *m/pl*	field force, field staff	personnel *m* du service *m* extérieur
Außenhandel *m*	foreign commerce	commerce *m* extérieur
Außenschild *n*	outdoor sign	enseigne *f*, panneau *m*
Außenseiter *m*	outsider	non-conformiste *m*, outsider *m*
Außenspalte *f*	outside position	bord *m* extérieur
Außensteg *m*	fore-edge margin, outside margin	marge *f* extérieure
Außenwerbung *f*	outdoor advertising	publicité *f* extérieure
Außenwerbung *f* **an** **Verkehrsmitteln** *n/pl*	parade poster, travelling display	publicité *f* sur l'extérieur *m* de voitures *f/pl*
Außenwerbung *f*, **gemalte**	painted displays *pl*	affiches *f/pl* peintes, panneaux *m/pl* peints
Außenwerbungsunternehmen *n*	outdoor advertising plant	entrepreneur *m* de publicité *f* extérieure
außergewöhnlicher **Werbetext** *m*	creative copy	texte *m* publicitaire extraordinaire
Aussortierung *f*	sorting out	tri *m*
aussparen *typog*	to clear away	laisser en blanc
Aussparung *f*	recess	blanc *m*, évidement *m*, niche *f*
Aussprache *f*, **freie**	open forum	point *m* de vue *f* des lecteurs *m/pl*
Ausstanzstück *n*	cut out, die cut	découpage *m*, silhouette *f* découpée
Ausstattung *f*	make-up	présentation *f*
ausstellen (Rechnung *f*)	to make out	établir
ausstellen (Waren *f/pl*)	to exhibit, to expose	exposer
Aussteller *m*	exhibitor	exposant *m*
Ausstellkarton *m*	showcard	affiche *f* mobile
Ausstellung *f*	exhibition, exposition *am*, show	exposition *f*
Ausstellungsbau *m*	exhibition stand construction	construction *f* des expositions *f/pl*
Ausstellungsfläche *f*	exhibition space	aire *f* de l'exposition *f*
Ausstellungsgelände *n*	exhibition grounds *pl*	terrain *m* de l'exposition *f*
Ausstellungshalle *f*	exhibition hall	hall *m* d'exposition *f*
Ausstellungskatalog *m*	exhibition catalogue	catalogue *m* d'exposition *f*
Ausstellungsmaterial *n*	material for exhibitions *pl*	matériel *m* de vitrine *f*, matériel *m* d'exposition *f*
Ausstellungsplakat *n*	exhibition poster	affiche *f* d'exposition *f*
Ausstellungsraum *m*	show-room	salle *f* d'exposition *f*
Ausstellungsständer *m*	floor-stand	présentoir *m* de sol *m*
Ausstellungsstand *m*	exhibition stand	stand *m* d'exposition *f*
Ausstellungsstück *n*	exhibits *pl*, show-piece	pièce *f* spécimen *m*
Ausstellungswagen *m*	exhibition van	voiture *f* d'exposition *f*
Ausstellungszug *m*	exhibition train	train *m* d'exposition *f*
Ausstrahlung *f*	emission	émission *f*
Ausstrahlungstermin *m*	play date	terme *m* d'émission *f*
ausstreichen	to cross, to delete	biffer, effacer
Austastlücke *f*	field blanking interval	blocage *m* effacement *m*
Austräger *m*	delivery man	porteur *m*
Ausverkauf *m*	clearance sale, selling off	vente *f* de soldes *m/pl*
ausverkaufen	to sell off	liquider, solder
auswählen	to choose, to select	choisir, sélectionner

Auswahl *f*	assessment, choice, selection	choix *m*, sélection *f*
Auswahlsendung *f*	consignment for choice	envoi *m* à choix *m*
auswechselbare Werbefläche *f*	portable panel	panneau *m* transportable
auswechseln	to transpose	transposer
Auswechselung *f*	change	mutation *f*
Ausweitung *f*	diversification	élargissement *m*
Auswertung *f*	evaluation, exploitation	évaluation *f*, exploitation *f*, interprétation *f*
auszählen (Manuskript)	to cast off	calibrer la copie *f*
Auszeichnen *n* eines Textes *m*	to accentuate, to display text matter	mettre un texte *m* en évidence *f*
Auszeichnungsschrift *f*	display type	caractères *m/pl* duplexés
Auszeichnungszeile *f*	display line	ligne *f* duplexée
Auszubildender *m*	probationer, trainee	stagiaire *m*
Auszug *m*	excerpt, extract	extrait *m*, résumé *m*
Autobuswerbung *f*	bus advertising	publicité *f* dans ou sur un autobus *m*
Autochromdruck *m*	autochrome printing	impression *f* en autochromie *f*
autografisches Papier *n*	transfer paper	papier *m* autographique
Autokino *n*	drive-in cinema	cinéma *m* en plein air *m* pour automobilistes *m/pl*
Autolithografie *f*	lithography drawn on plate	autolithographie *f*
Automat *m*	vending machine	distributeur *m* automatique
Automatenbecher *m*	plastic drinking-cup	gobelet *m* pour distributeur *m* automatique
Automaten *m/pl*, Verkauf *m* durch	automatic selling, vending	vente *f* d'articles *m/pl* dans des machines *f/pl* distributrices automatiques
automatische Schreibmaschine *f*	automatic typewriter	machine *f* à écrire automatique
automatische Setzmaschine *f*	teletypesetter	télétypesetter *m*
Autor *m*	author	auteur *m*
Autor *m*, anonymer	ghostwriter	nègre *m*
Autorenkorrektur *f*	author's alteration, author's correction	corrections *f/pl* d'auteur *m*
Autorenrecht *n*	copyright	droit *m* d'auteur *m*
Autorentantieme *f*	royalties *pl*	redevance *f*
Autosalon *m*	motor-show	salon *m* de l'automobile *f*
Autotypie *f*	autotype, half-tone block, half-tone plate *am*, process engraving	autotypie *f*, similigravure *f*
Autotypie *f*, flachgeätzte	shallow half-tone	simili *m* manquant de creux *m*
Autotypie *f*, freistehende	blocked-out half-tone, outline half-tone, silhouette half-tone	autotypie *f* en silhouette *f*, simili *m* détouré
Autotypie *f*, spitzgeätzte	drop-out halftone	autotypie *f* détourée
Autotypie *f*, tiefgeätzte	deep-etched half-tone	simili *m* avec blanc pur
Autotypieätzer *m*	process engraver	similiste *m*
Autotypieätzung *f*	half-tone block	cliché *m* simili
Autotypiepapier *n*	half-tone paper	papier *m* très calandré pour simili *m*
Autotypieraster *m*	halftone screen	trame *f* de simili *m*
Autotypiereproduktion *f*	block – process	photo-typographie *f*
axiale Satzform *f*	axial composition	composition *f* axiale
Azetatfolie *f*	acetate film	feuille *f* d'acétate *m*

B

Bäderanzeige *f*	travel advertisement	publicité *f* balnéaire
Bäderbeilage *f*	health resort supplement	supplément *m* balnéaire
Bahnhofsbuchhandlung *f*	bookstall	bibliothèque *f* de gare *f*
Bahnhofshallenwerbung *f*	station interior site	panneau *m* de gare *f*
Bahnhofsplakat *n*	station poster	affiche *f* dans les gares *f/pl*
Bahnhofswerbung *f*	railway station advertising	publicité *f* dans les gares *f/pl*
Balkenüberschrift *f*	banner-headline	titre *m* en caractères *m/pl* d'affiches *f/pl*
Ballenbrett *n*	baling board	planche *f*
Ballonleinen *n*	balloon linen	toile-ballon *f*
Ballonwerbung *f*	balloon advertising	publicité *f* par ballons *m/pl*
Bandaufnahme *f*	tape recording	enregistrement *m* sur bande *f* magnétique
Bandaufnahmesendung *f*	delayed broadcast	différé *m*
Bandenwerbung *f*	advertising in sport fields *pl*	publicité *f* dans les stades *m/pl*
Bandsäge *f*	band saw	scie *f* à ruban *m*
Bankpostpapier *n*	bond paper	papier *m* coquille *f*
Bankscheck *m*	bank cheque *brit*, check *am*	chèque *m* bancaire, mandat *m* bancaire
Bannerschlepper *m*	airplane banner	bannière *f* tractée par un avion *m*
Barfrankatur *f*	cash endorsement	affranchissement *m* en timbres *m/pl*
Barytpapier *n*	baryta paper	papier *m* baryté
Barzahlung *f*	spot cash	paiement *m* comptant, règlement *m* comptant
Barzahlungsrabatt *m*	cash discount, sales *pl* discount	escompte *m* de caisse *f*
Bastardschrift *f*	bastard face, bastard type	lettres *f/pl* bâtardes
Bauchbinde *f*	band	bande *f* de publicité *f*
baumartiges Entscheidungsschema *n*	decision tree	arbre *m* de décision *f*
bauschiges Papier *n*	bulky paper	papier *m* fort pour l'impression *f*
Bauzaunwerbung *f*	billposting on hoardings *pl*, billposting on plank fences *pl*	affichage *m* sur palissades *f/pl*
Beachtung *f*	attention	attention *f*
Beanstandung *f*	complaint	réclamation *f*
bearbeiten	to adapt, to arrange	adapter, arranger
Bearbeitung *f*	adaptation	adaptation *f*
Bearbeitung *f*, redaktionelle	editorializing	rédaction *f*
bebildert	illustrated	illustré, imagé
Bedarf *m*	need, want	besoin *m*
Bedarf *m*, latenter	hidden demand	besoin *m* latent
Bedarfsdeckung *f*	supply covering all requirements *pl*	satisfaction *f* des besoins *m/pl*
Bedarfsweckung *f*	demand stimulation	stimulation *f* de la demande *f*
Bedeutung *f*, aktuelle	topicality	actualité *f*
Bedeutung *f* des Textes *m* als Anzeigenelement *n*	copy function	importance *f* du texte *m* comme élément *m* publicitaire
Bedingungen *f/pl*	conditions *pl*, requirements *pl*, terms *pl*	conditions *f/pl*
Bedingungen *f/pl*, allgemeine	general conditions *pl*	conditions *f/pl* générales
bedruckt, frisch	wet print	impression *f* fraîche
bedruckte Vorderseite *f*	face	première page *f*

beeinflussen	to influence	influencer
beeinflussen, einseitig	to angle	influencer partialement
Beflockung *f*	covering with fibers *pl*	flocage *m*
befragen	to interview	interviewer
Befragter *m*	interviewee, respondent	interviewé *m*, répondant *m*
Befragung *f*	interview, poll, questioning, survey	enquête *f*, interrogatoire *m*, interview *f*
Befragung *f*, briefliche	mail research, mail survey	enquête *f* postale, recherche *f* par lettre *f*
Befragung *f*, mündliche	oral interview	interrogatoire *m* direct
Begebenheit *f*	happening	événement *m*
beglaubigen	to authenticate	certifier conforme, légaliser
beglaubigte Auflage *f*	audited circulation	tirage *m* contrôlé, ventes *f/pl* réelles certifiées
Beglaubigung *f*	authentication	légalisation *f*
Begleitbrief *m*	covering letter	lettre *f* d'envoi *m*
begleitende Werbung *f*	accessory advertising	publicité *f* de complément *m*
begrenzt	limited	limité
Begriff *m*	notion	notion *f*
begründende Werbung *f*	reason-why advertising	publicité *f* argumentée
Behauptungen *f/pl*	claims *pl*	prétentions *f/pl*
beidseitig satiniert	calendered on both sides *pl*	satiné des deux côtés *m/pl*
Beifilm *m*	fill-up, supplementary film	court-métrage *m*, hors-programme *m*
beifügen	to affix	ajouter
Beigabe *f*	addition	annexe *f*, prime *f*
Beihefter *m*, Beikleber *m*	bound-in, insert, tip-in	encart *m* broché
Beilage *f*	enclosure, insert, inset, supplement	encart *m*, supplément *m*
Beilage *f*, lose	loose insert	encart *m* libre
Beilagenpreis *m*	cost of the insert	prix *m* de l'encart *m*
Beilagenzettel *m*	stuffer	encart *m*, papillon *m*
beilegen	to enclose	ajouter, annexer
Beilegung *f*	inserting	encartage *m*
Beipack *m*	insert	annexe *f*
Beipack *m* von Werbedrucksachen *f/pl*	envelope stuffer	imprimés *m/pl* publicitaires comme annexes *f/pl* d'un packetage *m*
Beiprogramm *n*	adjacency, supplementary film	hors-programme *m*, programme *m* adjacent, programme *m* d'accompagnement *m*
Beitrag *m*, gelegentlicher	casual contribution	contribution *f* fortuite
Beitrag *m*, redaktioneller	contribution	contribution *f*
Bekanntheitsgrad *m*	degree of familiarity, degree of notoriety	dégré *m* de notoriété *f*
Bekanntmachung *f*	announcement, news release	communiqué *m*
Bekanntmachung *f*, amtliche	legal notice, official notice	avis *m* officiel
bekleben	to paste up, to stick on	coller
Beleg *m*	voucher	justificatif *m*
Belegexemplar *n*	advertisers' copy, checking copy, voucher copy	numéro *m* justificatif
Belegkontrolle *f*	voucher audit, watching of order filling	pige *f*
Belegnummer *f*, komplette	complete voucher copy	justificatif *m* complet
Belegseite *f*	tear sheet	épreuve *f* d'une page *f*, page *f* justificative

Belegung f	booking, placing	mise f en place f
Belegungsdaten n/pl	booked dates pl	dates f/pl retenues
Belegungsliste f	marked list	pointage m
Belegversand m	sending of vouchers pl	envoi m de justificatifs m/pl
belehrende Werbung f	educational advertising	publicité f éducative
beleuchten	to light	éclairer
Beleuchtung f	illumination, lighting	éclairage m, illumination f
belichten	to expose	insoler
Belichtung f	exposure, insolation	exposition f, insolation f
Belichtungszeit f	exposure	temps m de pose f
Belletristik f	fiction	belles-lettres f/pl
bemalen	to paint in	peindre
bemalte Flächen f/pl	painted surfaces pl	surfaces f/pl peintes
bemalte Großfläche f	bulletin board, painted bulletin	bulletin m
bemalte Leinwand f	painted cloth	toile f peinte
bemaltes Schild n	painted plate	plaque f peinte
Bemerkung f, witzige	quip	raillerie f
Bemerkungen f/pl	observations pl	observations f/pl
Bemerkungen f/pl, persönliche	personal remarks pl	personnalités f/pl
bemustern	to sample	échantillonner
benachrichtigen	to inform	informer
Benutzer m	user	consommateur m
Beobachtung f	observation	observation f
Berater m	advisor, consultant	conseil m, conseiller m
Berater m für Marktverhalten n	marketing consultant	conseil m en marketing m
Beratung f	consultation, consulting	conseil m, consultation f
Berechnung f	calculation, computation	calcul m, compte m
Berechnungsbeginn m	in charge date of advertising	date f de départ m
Berechnungsgrundlage f	base of calculation	base f de calcul m
Bericht m	report	rapport m
Bericht m, kurzgefaßter	pony report	bref sommaire m des nouvelles f/pl
berichten	to report	rapporter
Berichterstatter m	chronicler, correspondent, reporter	chroniqueur m, correspondant m, rapporteur m
Berichterstatter m, reisender	roving reporter	reporter m itinérant
berichtigen	to correct, to rectify	corriger
Berichtigung f	corrigendum, rectification	rectificatif m, rectification f
Berufsgruppe f	occupational group	catégorie f professionnelle
Berufspresse f	professional press	presse f professionnelle
Berufsverband m	professional organization	organisme m professionnel
Berufszeitschrift f	professional magazine	revue f professionnelle
beschädigte Buchstaben m/pl	battered letters pl, broken letters pl	lettres f/pl écrasées
beschädigtes Plakat n	torn poster	affiche f abîmée, affiche f déchirée, affiche f détériorée
Beschädigung f	damage	détérioration f
Beschaffung f von Informationen f/pl	gathering of information	récolte f des informations f/pl
beschallen	to provide with sound	sonoriser
Beschallung f	providing of sound effects pl	sonorisation f
Beschlagnahme f	confiscation	confiscation f
beschneiden	to crop, to make cuts pl, to prune, to slash, to trim	ébarber, rogner, taillader, tailler
Beschnitt m	cutting, trimming	coupe f, rognage m

Beschnittzugabe *f*	bleed difference, trim	coupure *f*
beschränkte Auflage *f*	limited edition	édition *f* à tirage *m* limité
Beschränkung *f*	limitation, restriction	limitation *f*, restriction *f*
Beschränkungen *f/pl*, gesetzliche	legal restrictions *pl*	restrictions *f/pl* légales
Beschränkungen *f/pl*, zeitliche	time limitations *pl*	restrictions *f/pl* dans le temps *m*
beschreiben	to describe	décrire
Beschreibung *f*	description	description *f*
beschriften	to letter	mettre une inscription *f* sur
Beschriftung *f*	lettering	inscription *f*
Besichtigung *f*	sightseeing	visite *f* des curiosités *f/pl*
Besichtigung *f* vor der Eröffnung *f*	varnishing – day	vernissage *m*
besonders gestalteter aktueller Tatsachenbericht *m*	feature	rapport *m* spécial d'actualité *f*, varia
besprechen	to discuss, to review (a book)	discuter, faire un compte *m* rendu
Besprechung *f*	discussion, meeting	conférence *f*, discussion *f*, entretien *m*
Besprechungsbericht *m*	call report	rapport *m* de conférence *f*
Bestätigung *f*	acknowledgement, confirmation, validation	confirmation *f*
Bestätigungsschreiben *n*	letter of confirmation	lettre *f* de confirmation *f*
bestäuben	to bronze	soupoudrer
Bestandsüberprüfung *f*	shop audit	vérification *f* des stocks *m/pl*
Bestandteil *m*	component, constituent	élément *m*, partie *f* composante
Bestellabschnitt *m*	order coupon	coupon *m* détachable de commande *f*
Bestellbuch *n*	order-book	carnet *m* de commandes *f/pl*
bestellen	to command, to order	commander
Bestellkarte *f*	order form	carte *f* de commande *f*
Bestellschein *m*	order form, subscription form	bon *m* de commande *f*
Bestellung *f*	commission, order	commande *f*, commission *f*, ordre *m*
Bestellung *f*, telefonische	order by telephone	commande *f* téléphonique
Bestimmung *f* des Insertionsorgans *n*	domiciliation	domiciliation *f*
Bestimmung *f* eines Bildausschnitts *m*	cropping	détermination *f* de la coupe *f*
bestossen	to trim	couper
Bestoßhobel *m*	letter-cutter	coupoir *m*
Bestoßmaschine *f*	router	fraiseuse *f*
Bestzahl *f*	optimum number	nombre *m* optimal
Besuchsbericht *m*	call report	rapport *m* de visite *f*
Besuchsziffer *f*	frequency	fréquence *f*
betitelt	entitled, headed	intitulé
Betitelung *f*	entitling	titrage *m*
betonen	to accentuate	accentuer
Betrachtungsweise *f*	slant	manière *f* de considérer
Betrachtungszeit *f*	looking time, stopping power	temps *m* d'observation *f*
Betrag *m*	amount	compte *m*, montant *m*, somme *f*
betreffend	reference, referring to	concernant, relatif à, se référant à
Betriebskosten *pl*	running expenses *pl*	charges *f/pl* d'exploitation *f*, dépenses *pl* courantes
Betriebszeitung *f*	house journal	journal *m* d'entreprise *f*

betrügerische Werbung *f*	deceptive advertising	publicité *f* déceptive, publicité *f* mensongère
Beurteilung *f*	valuation	compte *m* rendu, jugement *m*
Beutel *m*	bag	sac *m*
Bevölkerungsschichten *f/pl*	classes *pl* of population, strata *pl* of population	catégories *f* de population *f*, couches *f/pl* de la population *f*
bevorzugte Plazierung *f*	preferred position, special position	emplacement *m* privilégié
Beweggrund *m*	motive	motif *m*
bewegliche Lichtwerbung *f*	animated electric sign advertising, electric spectaculars *pl/am*	publicité *f* lumineuse animée
bewegliche Werbung *f*	mechanical advertising	publicité *f* mobile
Bewegung *f*	motion, movement	mouvement *m*
Bewerkstelligung *f*	implementation	mise *f* en œuvre *f*
bewerten	to value, to weight	estimer, évaluer
Bewertung *f*	assessment, evaluation	estimation *f*, évaluation *f*
bewilligter Werbeetat *m*	advertising appropriation	budget *m* alloué de publicité *f*
Bewilligung *f*	permit	autorisation *f*, permission *f*
bewußte Angelegenheit *f*	matter	affaire *f* en question *f*
bewußte Wahrnehmung *f*	apperception	apperception *f*
bezahlte Abonnements *n/pl*	paid subscriptions *pl*	abonnements *m/pl* payants
bezahlte Auflage *f*	paid circulation	tirage *m* payé
Bezahlung *f*	payment	paiement *m*, règlement *m*
beziehen (abonnieren)	to subscribe	s'abonner à
Bezieher *m*	subscriber	abonné *m*
Bezieheranalyse *f*	analysis of subscribers *pl*	analyse *f* du cercle *m* des abonnés *m/pl*
Bezieherwerber *f*	subscription agent	agent *m* d'abonnement *m*
Beziehung *f*	relation	relation *f*
Beziehungen *f/pl*, innerbetriebliche	intraflow	relations *f/pl* internes
Beziehungen *f/pl*, zwischenmenschliche	human relations *pl*	relations *f/pl* humaines
Beziehungskauf *m*	direct selling, industrial selling	vente *f* directe
Bezirk *m*	district	district *m*
Bezirksausgabe *f*	local issue, territorial edition	édition *f* départementale, édition *f* locale
Bezirksseite *f*	departmental page	page *f* départementale
Bezirksvertreter *m*	special representative	agent *m* régional
Bezug *m*	subscription	abonnement *m*
Bezugsbedingungen *f/pl*	delivery conditions *pl*	conditions *f/pl* de livraison *f*
Bezugspreis *m*	advertised price, subscription rate	prix *m* d'abonnement *m*
Bezugsquellenverzeichnis *n*	directory of suppliers *pl*, list of suppliers *pl*	liste *f* des fournisseurs *m/pl*, répertoire *m* de fournisseurs *m/pl*
Bibeldruckpapier *n*	bible paper, India paper	papier *m* bible
Bibliografie *f*	bibliography	bibliographie *f*
Bibliothek *f*	library	bibliothèque *f*
Bibliothekar *m*	librarian	bibliothécaire *m*
Bierdeckelwerbung *f*	advertising on beer mats *pl*	publicité *f* sur les soucoupes *f/pl* de la bière *f*
Bild *n*	illustration, picture	illustration *f*, image *f*
Bild *n*, eingeklebtes	tip-in	hors-texte *m*
Bild *n*, ganzseitiges	full-page illustration	hors-texte *m*

Bild- oder Tonspur *f* **eines Films** *m*	track	trace *f* d'un film *m*
Bild *n*, **verlaufendes**	vignette	photo *f* en dégradé
Bildanzeige *f*	illustrated advertisement, pictorial advertisement	annonce *f* illustrée
Bildarchiv *n*	picture library	dépôts *m/pl* illustrations *f/pl*
Bildausschnitt *m*	cutting	coupe *f*
Bildbericht *m*	documentary report	report *m* documentaire
Bildberichterstatter *m*	reporter-cameraman	reporteur *m* d'images *f/pl*
Bilddokumentation *f*	pictorial documentation	documentation *f* par l'image *f*
Bild-Drehbuch *n*	storyboard	storyboard *m*
Bildelement *n*	pictorial element	élément *m* pictural
Bildelement *n*, **ungewöhnliches**	Hathaway touch	élément *m* figuratif extraordinaire
Bilderbeilage *f*	pictorial supplement	supplément *m* illustré
Bilderbrief *m*	illustrated letter	lettre *f* illustrée
Bilderbuch *n*, **unzerreißbares**	rag-book	livre *m* d'images *f/pl* sur toile *f*
Bilderdienst *m*	photographic service	service *m* photographique
Bilderdruckpapier *n*	art paper	papier *m* surglacé
Bilderrätsel *n*	picture puzzle	rébus *m*
Bilderreihe *f*	picture series *pl*	série *f* d'images *m/pl*
Bilderscheck *m*	picture cheque	chèque-image *f*
Bilderschrift *f*	hieroglyphics *pl*	hiéroglyphes *m/pl*
Bilderserie *f*	strip	bande *f* d'illustrations *f/pl*
Bilderstreifen *m*, **humoristischer**	comic strip	bandes *f/pl* dessinées
Bildfläche *f*	surface screen	écran *m*
Bildfolge *f* **im Film**	sequence	séquence *f*
Bildform *f*	shape of the picture	forme *f* picturale
Bildfunk *m*	wireless picture transmission, wirephoto	bélinographie *f*, téléphotographie *f*
Bildgeschichte *f*	picture story	conte *f* illustrée, histoire *f* en images *f/pl*
Bildgestaltung *f*	art work	travail *m* artistique
Bildjournalismus *m*	photojournalism, pictorial journalism	photojournalisme *m*
Bildkassette *f*	video cassette	cassette *f* vidéo
bildliche Darstellung *f*	diagram, schema	schéma *m*
bildlicher Ausdruck *m*	metaphor	métaphore *f*
Bildmarke *f*	symbol	marque *f* symbolique
Bildmaterial *n*	illustrative material	éléments *m/pl* d'illustration *f*
Bildmaterialbeschaffer *m*	art buyer	ravitailleur *m* des éléments *m/pl* d'illustrations *f/pl*
Bildmotiv *n*	publicity motif	motif *m* publicitaire
Bildplakat *n*	pictorial poster	affiche *f* illustrée
Bildplatte *f*	coloured disc	disque *m* en couleurs *f/pl*
Bildredakteur *m*	pictures *pl* editor	rédacteur *m* des illustrations *f/pl*
Bildreporter *m*	camera-man, press photographer	photographe *m* de presse *f*, reporter-photographe *m*
Bildschallplatte *f*	picture record	disque *m* de photographe *m* illustré
Bildschirm *m*	video display screen	écran *m*
Bildschirmdame *f*	female announcer	speakerine *f*
Bildschirmformat *n*	aspect ratio	format *m* de l'écran *m*
Bildschirmgerät *n*	video display terminal, video display unit	écran *m* de visualisation *f*

Bildschirmtext m	viewdata	télétexte m interactif
Bildschnitt m	cut	coupure f
Bildserienwerbung f	band advertising, strip advertising	publicité f avec des bandes f/pl dessinées
Bildstreifen m	film strip	bande f de film m
Bildteil m	pictorial part	partie f picturale
Bildteil m **einer Fernsehsendung** f	video	partie f d'images f/pl d'une émission f télévisée
Bildtelegrafie f	photo-telegraphy	bélinographie f, téléphotographie f
Bildtelegramm n	telephotograph	bélinogramme m, phototélégramme m
Bildüberblendung f, **weiche**	to dissolve am, to fade over, to mix to brit	fondu m enchaîné
Bildübertragung f	photo-telegraphy	transmission f phototélégraphique
Bildungsgrad m	level of education	dégré m de culture f
Bildunterschrift f	caption, legend, outline	légende f
Bildwerbung f	pictorial advertising	publicité f illustrée
Bildwerfer m	epidiascope, slide projector	appareil m de projection f, épidiascope m
bildwirksam	photogenic	photogénique
Bildzeichen n	symbol	marque f figurative
Bildzeitung f	illustrated paper	journal m illustré
Bimetallplatte f	bimetal plate	plaque f bi-métal
Bindemittel n	binder	liant m
Bindestrich m	hyphen	trait m d'union f
Binnenhandel m	domestic commerce, home trade brit	commerce m intérieur
Biografie f	biography	biographie f
biografische Skizze f	profile	portrait m biographique
Blätterwald m	the whole of newspapers pl	ensemble m des journaux m/pl
blank schlagen	to leave blank	laisser en blanc
Blankoformular n	blank	formule f en blanc
Blankoprospekt m	leaflet in blank	dépliant m en blanc
Blankoscheck m	blank cheque	chèque m en blanc
Blatt n (Seite f)	page, sheet	feuille f, page f
Blatt n (Zeitung f)	journal, paper	feuille f, journal m, revue f
Blatt n, **minderwertiges**	trashy paper	journal m médiocre
Blatt n **mit vielen Anzeigen** f/pl	tight paper	journal m avec beaucoup d'annonces f/pl
Blatt n **mit wenigen Anzeigen** f/pl	wide open paper	journal m avec peu d'annonces f/pl
Blatt n, **oft zitiertes**	newspaper of record	journal m sérieux qu'on cite
Blatt n, **pornografisches**	smut sheet	journal m pornographique
Blatt n **wenden**	to turn over the page	tourner la page f
Blatt n, **wissenschaftliches**	scientific paper	feuille f scientifique
Blattbreite f	page width	largeur f de page f
Blattgold n	gold leaf	or m en feuilles f/pl
Blattrand m, **unterer**	tail	marge f de pied m
Blaupause f	blue print, cyanotype, ozalide	cyanotypie f, ozalide m
Blechdruck m	metal-decorating, tin-printing	impression f sur fer-blanc m, impression f sur tôle f
Blechplakat n, **Blechplatte** f	metal sheet	tôle f métallique
Blechschild n	tin plate sign	panneau m métallique
Blei n	lead	plomb m

Blei *n* **korrigieren, auf dem**	to correct in the metal	corriger sur le plomb *m*
Blei *n* **lesen, auf dem**	to read in the metal	lire sur le plomb *m*
bleibe stehen, es *typog*	stet!	à maintenir
Bleifuß *m*, **auf**	mounted on metal	monté sur plomb *m*
Bleisatz *m*	hot metal composition, lead composition	composition *f* au plomb *m*
Bleisatzkorrektur *f*	correction on lead	correction *f* sur plomb *m*
Bleisteg *m*	lead furniture	lingot *m* de plomb *m*
Bleistift *m*	pencil	crayon *m*
Bleistiftskizze *f*	pencil-drawing, rough	crayonné *m*, dessin *m* au crayon *m*
Blende *f*	diaphragm	diaphragme *m*
Blick *m* **hinter die Kulissen** *f/pl*	inside story	regard *m* en coulisses *f/pl*
Blickfang *m*	approach, catch phrase, eye appeal, eye catcher, hook, stopper	accrochage *m*, accroche-œil *m*, amorce *f*, attrape-regard *m*, tape-à-l'œil *m*, tire-l'œil *m*
Blickfangwerbung *f*	eye-catching advertising	publicité *f* attrape-regard *m*
Blickverlauf *m* **auf einer Anzeigenseite** *f*	ad-page traffic	mouvement *m* des yeux *m/pl* sur une page *f* d'annonces *f/pl*
blind schlagen	to leave blank	laisser en blanc
Blindband *m*	dummy	maquette *f*
Blinddruck *m*	blind stamping, embossing	bombage *m*, estampage *m*, gaufrage *m*
Blindenschrift *f*	Braille	braille *m*
blinder Bogen *m*	blank sheet	feinte *f*
Blindgänger *m*	damp squib	affaire *f* ratée
Blindmaterial *n*	blank material, spacing material	blancs *m/pl*
Blindmuster *n*	dummy	maquette *f* d'imprimerie *f*
Blindmuster *n* **von Zeitschriften** *f/pl*	dummy magazine	maquette *f* d'une revue *f*
Blindprägung *f*	blind blocking, blind embossing	gaufrage *m* à sec, impression *f* en blanc
blindpressen	to blind	dorer à froid
Blindpressung *f*	blind tooling	dorure *f* à froid
Blindtest *m*	blind test	test *m* à l'aveugle
Blindzeile *f*	blank line, white line	ligne *f* de blanc
Blinklichtwerbung *f*	flashing sign, flashing-winking of lights *pl*	clignotement *m*
Blitzlicht *n*	flash	éclair *m* au magnésium *m*
Blockade *f*	black, turned letter	blocage *m*, caractère *m* retourné, lettre *f* bloquée
blockbuchen	to buy the whole stock	acheter en bloc *m*
Blockbuchstabe *m*	block capital, block letter	capitale *f* bâton *m*, lettre *m* moulée, majuscule *f* imitée
Blockheftung *f*	block stitching	piqûre *f* au bloc *m*
blockieren	to turn a letter	bloquer une lettre *f*
Blockleimung *f*	spine gluing	encollage *m* des dos *m/pl*
Blocksatz *m*	grouped style	composition *f* en forme *f* de carré *m*
Blockschrift *f*	print script	caractères *m/pl* bâtons *m/pl*, écriture *f* script
Blockzeitung *f*	newspaper with concentration of its readership in a large territory	journal *m* d'une concentration *f* de lecteurs *m/pl* dans un grand territoire *m*
Börsenzeitung *f*	financial paper	journal *m* financier
Bogen *m*	sheet	feuille *f*, page *f*

Bogen *m*, **blinder**	blank sheet	feinte *f*
Bogen *m* (Plakat *n*) (siehe: Plakatformat)	sheet	feuille *f* (voir: format d'affiche)
Bogenanleger *m*	sheet-feeder	margeur *m* de feuilles *f/pl*
Bogenanschlag *m*	bill posting, poster advertising, sheetage	publicité *f* par affiches *f/pl*
Bogengrösse *f*	sheet size	format *m* de feuille *f*
Bogensignatur *f*	sheet signature	signature *f* de feuille *f*
Bogentagpreis *m*	posting price per day and poster	prix *m* d'affichage *m* par jour *m* et affiche *f*
Bon *m*	coupon, credit slip	bon *m*
Bonus *m*	bonus	bonification *f*
Bordüre *f*	border	bordure *f*
Bordzeitung *f*	ship's newspaper	gazette *f* du bord *m*
Borgis *f* (siehe Anhang)	Bourgeois (see appendix)	corps 9 points (voir appendice)
Bote *m*	messenger	courrier *m*, messager *m*
Botschaft *f*	message	message *m*
Boulevardblatt *n*	penny press, yellow paper	feuille *f* boulevardière
Branche *f*	business line	branche *f*
Branchenadreßbuch *n*	trade directory	annuaire *m* commercial
Branchentelefonbuch *n*	yellow pages *pl*	pages *f/pl* jaunes
Brandmalerei *f*	poker-work	pyrogravure *f*
brandneu	brand-new	tout neuf
brandneue Nachrichten *f/pl*	news hot from the press	nouvelles *f/pl* toutes chaudes
Braunpause *f*	sepia tracing	copie *f* sépia *f*
breit	expanded, wide	large
Breite *f*	width	largeur *f*
breite Drucktype *f*	expanded type, extended type	caractère *m* large
breites Sortiment *n*	variety	assortiment *m* large
Breitformat *n*	wide size	format *m* au largeur *f*
Breitwand *f*	wide-screen	écran *m* large
Breitwandfilm *m*	cinemascope	cinémascope *m*
Brennpunkt *m* **des Verkaufs** *m*	focal point, focus of sale, hot spot	centre *m* d'attraction *f*, point *m* central, point *m* chaud
Brett *n*, **schwarzes**	notice board	tableau *m* noir
Brief *m*, **eingeschriebener**	registered letter	lettre *f* recommandée
Brief *m* **mit fehlerhafter Anschrift** *f*	blind letter	lettre *f* dont l'adresse *f* est défectueuse
Brief *f*, **vervielfältigter**	process letter	lettre *f* reproduite
Briefbeilage *f*	letter enclosure	annexe *f*
Briefbogen *m*	lettersheet	feuille *f* à lettres *f/pl*
Briefkopf *m*	letter-heading	en-tête *f* de lettre *f*
briefliche Befragung *f*	mail research, mail survey	enquête *f* postale, recherche *f* par lettre *f*
Briefmarke *f*	postage stamp	timbre-poste *m*
Briefordner *m*	letter-file	classeur *m* de lettres *f/pl*
Briefpapier *n*	note-paper	papier *m* à lettres *f/pl*
Briefschreiber *m*, **anonymer**	poison pen	corbeau *m*
Brieftelegramm *n*	letter telegram	lettre *f* télégraphique
Briefumschlag *m*	envelope	enveloppe *f*
Briefumschlag *m* **mit eingeschlagener Klappe** *f*	penny saver, postage saver	enveloppe *f* énigma
Briefumschlagwerbung *f*	advertising on envelopes *pl*	publicité *f* sur enveloppes *f/pl* commerciales
Brillant *f* (siehe Anhang)	Brilliant (see appendix)	corps 3 points (voir appendice)
Bristolkarton *m*	Bristol board	carton *m* Bristol

Bromsilberdruck *m*	bromide printing	impression *f* au bromure *m* d'argent *m*
Bromsilberpapier *n*	bromide paper	papier *m* au bromure *m* d'argent *m*
Bronzedruck *m*	bronze printing	bronzage *m*, impression *f* de bronze *m*
Bronzefarbe *f*	metallic ink	couleur *f* de bronze *m*
broschieren	to stitch	brocher
broschiertes Buch *n*	paperback	livre *m* broché
Broschüre *f*	booklet, brochure, folder, pamphlet	plaquette *f*, prospectus *m*
Broschur *f*	stitching	brochage *m*
Brotschrift *f*	body type, bread-and-butter-face, ordinary type	caractères *m/pl* courants, caractères *m/pl* de labeur *m*
Bruch (Falz) *m*	fold	pli *m*
Bruchstrich *m*	oblique stroke	barre *f* de fraction *f* oblique
Bruchstück *n*	fragment	fragment *m*
bruchstückhafte Nachrichten *f/pl*	piecemail information	nouvelles *f/pl* fragmentaires
Bruchteil *m*	fraction	fraction *f*
Bruttoauflage *f*	gross circulation	tirage *m* brut
Bruttopreis *m*	gross price	prix *m* brut
Buch *n*	book	livre *m*
Buch *n*, broschiertes	paperback	livre *m* broché
Buch *n*, extra ausgestattetes	enriched book	livre *m* bien présenté
Buch *n*, fest gebundenes	hardcover	livre *m* relié
Buch *n*, geheftetes	sewn book	livre *m* broché
Buch *n*, langlebiges	long seller, steady seller	livre *m* durable
Buch *n*, leichtverkäufliches	quick seller	livre *m* d'écoulement *m* facile
Buch *n*, meistgekauftes	bestseller	livre *m* à succès *m*
Buch *n* mit alphabetischem Register *n*	thumb-indexed book	livre *m* à onglets *m/pl*
Buch *n* (25 Bogen *m/pl* Papier *n*)	quire (25 sheet)	main *f*
Buchbesprechung *f*	book review	critique *f* littéraire
Buchbinder *m*	bookbinder	relieur *m*
Buchbinderarbeit *f*	binding	travail *m* de relieur *m*
Buchbinderei *f*	binding department, bookbindery	atelier *m* de reliure *f*
Buchdeckel *m*	book cover	couverture *f*
Buchdruck *m*	letter press printing	impression *f* typographique, typographie *f*
Buchdrucker *m*	letterpress printer	imprimeur *m*
Buchdruckpapier *n*	book paper	papier *m* d'édition *f*
Bucheinband *m*	binding, cover	reliure *f*
buchen, einen Auftrag *m*	to book an order	noter un ordre *m*
Buchformat *n*	book size	format *m* du livre *m*
Buchgrafik *f*	book graphic	graphique *m* de livre *m*
Buchgrossist *m*	book wholesaler	grossiste *m* en livres *m/pl*
Buchhändler *m*	bookseller	libraire *m*
Buchhaltungsabteilung *f*	accounting department	service *f* comptabilité *f*
Buchhülle *f*	book jacket	chemise *f* de livre *m*
Buchkritik *f*	book review	critique *f* littéraire
Buchmesse *f*	bookfair	salon *m* du livre *m*
Buchplakat *n*	book poster	affiche *f* de livre *m*
Buchrücken *m*	backbone, backstrip, book spine	dos *m* de livre *m*
Buchstabe *m*	character, letter, type	caractère *m*, lettre *f*
Buchstabe *m*, fehlender	dropped-out letter	lettre *f* manquante
Buchstabe *m*, fetter	fat type	caractère *m* gras

Buchstabe *m*, gestürzter	kerned letter	caractère *m* couché, lettre *f* crénée
Buchstabe *m*, hochstehender	superior letter	exposant *m* supérieur
Buchstabe *m*, überhängender	kerned letter	lettre *f* débordante
Buchstaben *m/pl*, beschädigte	battered letters *pl*, broken letters *pl*	lettres *f/pl* écrasées
Buchstaben *m/pl*, gemeine	lower case letters *pl*	lettres *f/pl* bas-de-casse *f*
Buchstaben *m/pl*, hochgerückte	superior letters *pl*	lettres *f/pl* supérieures
Buchstaben *m/pl*, lädierte	battered letters *pl*	lettres *f/pl* écrasées
Buchstaben *m/pl*, schrägliegende	slant letters *pl*	lettres *f/pl* couchées
Buchstaben *m* wenden!	invert letter!	retournez la lettre *f*!
Buchstabenzeichner *m*	letter designer	lettriste *m*
buchstabieren	to spell	épeler
Buchumschlag *m*	book cover, book jacket	chemise *f*
Buchzeichen *n*	bookmark, bookplate	signet *m* de livre *m*
Budget *n*	account, appropriation	budget *m*
Budgetgliederung *f*	assignment of expenditures *pl*	allocation *f* du budget *m*
Budgetkontrolle *f*	budgetary control	contrôle *m* du budget *m*
Budgetsumme *f*	total billings *pl*	facturation *f*
Büchelchen *n*	booklet	livret *m*
Bücherei *f*	library	bibliothèque *f*
Bücherstützen *f/pl*	book-ends *pl*	appui-livres *m/pl*, serre-livres *m/pl*
bündeln	to bunch, to bundle	passer les cahiers *m/pl* en presse *f*
bürgerlich	middle-class	bourgeois *m*
Bürstenabzug *m*	brush proof, flat proof, galley proof, stone proof	épreuve *f* à la brosse *f*, épreuve *f* au taquoir *m*, morasse *f*
Büttenpapier *n*, handgeschöpftes	hand made deckle-edged paper	papier *m* à la forme *f*, papier *m* à la main *f*
Büttenrand *m*	deckle edge	barbe *f*, bord *m* à la cuve *f*
Bulletin *n*	bulletin	bulletin *m*
Bund *m*	federation	fédération *f*
Bundesbahn *f*	federal railways *pl*	chemin *m* de fer *m* fédéral
Bundespost *f*	federal post	poste *f* fédérale
Bundsteg *m*	back margin, gutter-stick, inner margin	blanc *m* du petit fond *m*, marge *f* intérieure
Bund *m/typog*	back	marge *f* intérieure
Buntdruck *m*	colour printing	impression *f* polychrome, polychromie *f*
buntes Papier *n*	colored paper *am*, coloured paper *brit*	papier *m* de couleur *f*, papier *m* peint

C

Campingplatz *m*	camping-ground	camping *m*
CC-Zeitschrift *f*	controlled circulation paper	périodique *m* d'une circulation *f* contrôlée et qualifiée
Cedille *f*	cedilla	cédille *f*
Cellophan *n*	cellophane	cellophane *f*
cellophanieren	to cellosheen, to clarosheen	cellophaner
Charakteristikum *n*	characteristic, feature	caractéristique *f*
chauvinistische Zeitung *f*	flag waver	journal *m* chauvin
Checkliste *f*	check list, guide-sheet	liste *f* aide-mémoire *m*, liste *f* de contrôle *m*

Chef m **des Redaktions-** sekretariats m	slotman	chef m des sécretaires m/pl de rédaction f
Chef m **vom Dienst** m	managing editor	chef m de service m
Chefgrafiker m	art director	artiste m en chef m
Chefredakteur m	editor-in-chief	rédacteur m en chef m
Chefredakteur m, stellvertretender	associate editor	rédacteur m en chef m adjoint
Cheftexter m	copy chief, copy supervisor	chef m de la conception-rédaction f
Chemigraf m	blockmaker, process engraver	clicheur m, graveur m, photograveur m, zincographe m
Chemigrafie f	photo-engraving	photogravure f, zincographie f
chemische Lichteinwirkung f	photochemistry	photochimie f
Chiffre f	box number, key number	numéro-clé f, numéro m de code m
Chiffreanzeige f	box number advertisement, keyed advertisement	annonce f chiffrée
Chiffregebühr f	box fee	taxe f pour annonce f chiffrée
Chiffregeheimnis n	box security	secret m des chiffres m/pl
chinesisches Papier n	India paper, rice-paper	papier m chiné, papier m de Chine f
Chrombad n	chrome bath	bain m de chrome m
Chromoersatzkarton m	chrome imitation board	carton m contrecollé
Chromokarton m	chromo-board	carton m chromo couché
Chromolithografie f	chromo-lithography	chromolithographie f
Chromopapier n	chromo paper	papier m chromo
Chronik f	chronicle	chronique f
Chronist m	chronicler	chroniqueur m
Cicero f (siehe Anhang)	Pica (see appendix)	cicéro f (voir appendice)
Code m	code	code m
Codewort n	code word	mot m de code m
codieren	to code	coder, mettre en code m
codifizieren	to codify	codifier
Collage f	collage, pasting	collage m
Colloqium n	colloquy	colloque m
Colombier m (siehe: Plakatformat)	Colombier (see: poster size)	colombier (voir: format d'affiche)
Comic Strip m	comic strip	bandes f/pl dessinées
Comicserie f	continuity strip	série f de bandes f/pl dessinées
Computer m	computer	calculatrice f, ordinateur m
Computersatz m	computer setting	composition f par ordinateur m
Computersetzanlage f	computer typesetting installation	installation f de composition f programmée
Computerzeichnung f	computer drawing	dessin m d'ordinateur m
Copyright n	copyright	droit m de publication f, droit m d'impression f
Copytest m	copytest	test m du texte m

D

Dachschild n	banner, roof panel, streamer	banderole f, calicot m, panneau m sur le toit m
Dachwerbung f	roof advertisement	publicité f sur les toits m/pl
Dampfradio n	steam radio	bonne vieille radio f papa m
Dankschreiben n	letter of thanks pl	lettre f de remerciement m
Darbietung f	presentation	présentation f

Darbietung f, effektvolle	showmanship	art m de la mise f en scène f
darstellen	to represent	figurer, représenter
Darstellung f	representation	représentation f
Darstellung f, bildliche	diagram, schema	schéma m
Darstellung f des Inneren n	ghost view	présentation f de l'intérieur m
Darstellung f, falsche	misrepresentation	faux rapport m
Darstellung f, gedrängte	digest, pemmican style	présentation f condensée
Darstellung f, grafische	graphic chart, graphical representation	diagramme m, représentation f graphique
Darstellungsform f	form of presentation	présentation f formelle
Datenerfassungsgerät n	data acquisition terminal, data collection terminal	appareil m pour la saisie f des données f/pl
Daten n/pl, technische	mechanical data pl	données f/pl techniques, renseignements m/pl techniques
Datenplan m	date schedule, schedule of insertions pl, time schedule	calendrier m d'insertion f, plan m de termes m/pl
Datenrechner m	computer	ordinateur m
Datenschema n	date schedule, schedule of insertions pl, time schedule	calendrier m d'insertion f, plan m de termes m/pl
Datensender m	data transmission	transeurdonnées f/pl
datieren	to date	dater
Datum n, vorgeschriebenes	prescribed date	date f de rigueur f, date f imposée
Datumstempel m	date-stamp	dateur m
Dauer f	duration, length of time	durée f
Daueranschlag m	permanent posting	affichage m permanent
Daueranschlag m in Verkehrsmitteln n/pl	car card advertising	emplacement m intérieur de voiture f
Daueranzeige f	permanent advertisement	annonce f permanente
Dauerauftrag m	permanent order, standing order	ordre m permanent
Dauerausstellung f	continuous exhibition	exposition f permanente
Dauerkunde m	regular customer	client m fidèle
Dauerplakat n	permanent poster	affiche f permanente
Dauerwerbung f	permanent publicity	publicité f permanente
Dauerwirkung f	lasting effect	effet m durable
Daumenregister n	thumb-index	registre m avec onglets m/pl -guides m/pl, touches f/pl
Debatte f	debate	débat m
dechiffrieren	to decipher, to decode	déchiffrer
Deckadresse f	accommodation address	adresse f d'emprunt m
Deckblatt n	base sheet	feuille f de couverture f
Deckbogen m	top drawsheet	feuille f de couverture f
Deckenhänger m	dangler	rotair m
Deckenschild n	ceiling panel	voussure f
Decker m	mask, overlay	cache f, masque m
Deckfarbe f	opaque ink	encre f opaque
Deckname m	code-word, pseudonym	nom m de guerre f, pseudonyme m
Deckweiß n	zinc white	blanc couvrant
Defektbogen m	waste print	défet m
dehnen	to stretch	étendre
Dekade f	decade	décade f
Dekorateur m	window-dresser	décorateur-étalagiste m
Dekoration f	decoration	décoration f
Dekoration (Film, TV) f	set	décor m
Dekorationspapier n	decorating paper, fancy paper	papier m de décoration f

Dekorationsstück *n*, farbiges	colour display	étalage *m* en couleur *f*
dekorieren	to decorate, window dressing, window trimming	décorer, faire des étalages *m/pl*
Deleaturzeichen *n*	delete mark	déléatur *m*
Delkredere *n*	delcredere	delcredere *m*, ducroire *m*
Dementi *n*	denial	démenti *m*
dementieren	to belie, to deny	démentir
demografische Merkmale *n/pl*	demographic characteristics *pl*	critères *m/pl* démographiques
demografische Struktur *f*	audience composition, demographical structure	structure *f* démographique
Demonstrationsfilm *m*	demonstrational film	film *m* de démonstration *f*
demonstrieren	to demonstrate	démontrer
Demoskopie *f*	Gallup poll, opinion poll, opinion research, public opinion analysis	enquête *f* sur les opinions *f/pl*, sondage *m* de l'opinion *f* publique
Denkschrift *f*	memorandum, record	exposé *m*, mémoire *m*, mémorandum *m*
Depesche *f*	dispatch, telegram	dépêche *f*
Depeschenbüro *n*	dispatch agency	bureau *m* de télégraphe *m*
Depeschensaal *m*	desk	bureau *m* des dépêches *f/pl*
Detailgeschäft *n*	retail enterprise	établissement *m* de détail *m*
detailliertes Layout *n*	comprehensive	maquette *f* détaillée
Detektivroman *m*	detective novel	roman *m* policier
Deutung *f*	interpretation	interprétation *f*
Dia *n*, tönendes	sound slide	diapositif *m* sonore
Diabildwerfer *m*	slide projector	projecteur-diascope *m*
Diagramm *n*	chart, diagram, graph	diagramme *m*, graphique *m*
Dialekt *m*	dialect, idiom	dialecte *m*, idiome *m*
Diamant *f* (siehe Anhang)	diamond (see appendix)	corps 4 points (voir appendice)
Diapositiv *n*	film slide, transparency slide	diapositif *m*
Diapositivwerbung *f*	slide advertising	publicité *f* par diapositif *m*
Dichte *f*	density	densité *f*
dick	fat	gras
Dicke *f*	thickness	chasse *f*, épaisseur *f*
Dienst *m* nach Mitternacht *f*	lobster shift	service *m* après minuit *m*
Dienstleistung *f*	service	prestation *f* de service *m*
Dienstleistung *f*, zusätzliche	accessorial service	service *m* additionnel
Dienstleistungsgewerbe *n*	service rendering trade	secteur *m* économique des services *m/pl*
digitale Informationen *f/pl*	digital information	information *f* numérique
Diktaphon *n*	dictating machine	appareil *m* à dicter
Diktat *n*	dictation	dictée *f*
Diktiergerät *n*	dictating machine	dictaphone *m*
Diplom *n*	diploma	diplôme *m*
Direktabsatz *m*	direct selling	vente *f* directe
Direktabsatz *m* des Herstellers *m* an den Einzelhandel *m*	direct selling of the manufacturer to the retail firms *pl*	circuit *m* court
direkte Kommunikation *f*	face-to-face communication	communication *f* nez *m* à nez *m*
direkter Kaufappell *m*	direct selling emphasis	appel *m* pressant à l'acheteur *m*
Direktion *f*	management	direction *f*
Direktor *m*	director, manager	directeur *m*
Direktübertragung *f*	live broadcast	prise *f* de vue *f* directe
Direktverkauf *m*	house-to-house selling	vente *f* de porte *f* en porte *f*

Direktwerbung f	direct advertising	publicité f directe
Direktwerbung f durch die Post f	direct mail advertising, mailing shot	publicité f directe par la poste f
Discountladen m	discount shop, discounter	magasin m discount m
Diskothek f	record-library	discothèque f
Diskussionsbasis f	basis for discussion	base f d'une discussion f
Diskussionsleiter m	moderator	directeur m d'une discussion f
Diskussionsveranstaltung f	symposium	colloque m
Display n	display	étalage m
disponieren	to dispose, to give instructions pl	arranger, disposer, prévoir
Disposition f	arrangement, release	disposition f
Distributionsweg m	channel of distribution	circuit m de distribution f
Dokumentaraufnahme f	documentary photograph	prise f de vue f documentaire
Dokumentarbericht m	background story, feature	article m documentaire, rapport m documentaire
Dokumentarfilm m	documentary film	film m documentaire
Dokumentation f	documentation	documentation f
Dokumentationsabteilung f	record office	service m de documentation f
Dolmetscher m	interpreter	interprète m
Doppelfalz m	double fold	double pli m
Doppelkrone f (siehe Plakatformat)	double-crown (see poster size)	format double couronne (voir format d'affiche)
Doppelleser m	double reader	double lecteur m
Doppellinie f	double rulings pl	filets m/pl doubles
Doppelnummer f	combined issues pl	numéros m/pl couplés
Doppelpunkt m	colon	deux points m/pl, double point m
Doppelseite f	double page, double spread, opening	pages f/pl en regard m
Doppelseite f-Blattmitte f	center page spread	double page f centrale
doppelseitige Anzeige f	double truck, double-page spread	double page f centrale
Doppelspalte f	double column	double colonne f, sur deux colonnes f/pl
doppelter Preis m	double rate	prix m double
Doppeltondruck m	double-tone printing	impression f double-ton m
Doppeltonfarbe f	double-tone ink	encre f double-ton m
Double n	stuntman	acrobate m-doublure f
Dozent m	lecturer	chargé m de cours m
Draht m, heißer	hot line	téléphone m rouge
Drahtanschrift f	telegraphic address	adresse f télégraphique
drahten	to telegraph, to wire	télégraphier
Drahtfunk m	broadcasting by wire	radiodiffusion f par fil m, télédiffusion f
Drahtheftung f	saddle stitching	couture f dans le dos m, piquage m dans le pli m au fil m de fer m
drahtlose Telegrafie f	wireless telegraphy	télégraphie f sans fil m
Drahtseilbahn f	funicular railway	funiculaire m
Drahtzieher m	machinator, wire-puller	intrigant m, machinateur m
Dramatisierung f	dramatization	dramatisation f
Dreh m	gimmick	truc m
Drehbuch n	scenario, script	scénario m, script m
Drehbuchentwurf m	treatment	brouillon m d'un scénario m
dreidimensional	three-dimensional	à trois dimensions f/pl
3 D(imensional)-Film m	3 D(imensional) film	film m à réfraction f
Dreifarbenätzung f	three-colour etching	trichromie f

Dreifarbendruck *m*	three-colour printing, trichromatic process work	impression *f* en trois couleurs *f/pl*, impression *f* trichrome, trichromie *f*
dreimal monatlich	thrice monthly	trimensuel
dreimal wöchentlich	thrice weekly	tri-hebdo
Dreischneider *m*	three side trimmer	massicot *m* trilatéral à une seule lame *f*
dreispaltig	for a 3-column	sur trois col *f* de largeur *f*
Dreizeilenfall *m*	centred style	style *m* lapidaire
Drittelseite *f*	one-third-page	tiers *m* de page *f*
Druck *m*	impression, printing	impression *f*
Druck *m*, **anastatischer**	anastatic printing	impression *f* anastatique
Druck *m*, **durchgeschlagener**	blotted print	foulage *m*
Druck *m* **einer bestimmten Anzahl** *f* **von Exemplaren** *n/pl*	printing of a certain number of copies *pl*	tirage *m* à la suite *f*
Druck *m*, **fotomechanischer**	photo-typography	photo-typographie *f*
Druck *m* **freigeben, zum**	to release	permettre la publication *f*
Druck *m* **geben, in**	to send to press	mettre sous presse *f*
Druck *m*, **im**	in the press	sous presse *f*
Druck *m*, **kleiner**	small print	petits caractères *m/pl*
Druck *m*, **schlechter**	poor print	impression *f* de piètre qualité *f*
Druck *m*, **unreiner**	slur	impression *f* boueuse
Druck *m*, **unscharfer**	unsharp impression	papillotage *m*
Druck *m*, **verschwommener**	blurred impression	
Druckarbeiten *f/pl*	printing works *pl*	travaux *m/pl* d'impression *f*
Druckart *f*	kind of printing process	mode *m* d'impression *f*
Druckauflage *f*	print figure, print run	tirage *m* impression *f*
Druckauftrag *m*	commission, printing order	commande *f* d'impression *f*
Druckausfall *m*	quality of prints *pl*	qualité *f* de l'impression *f*
Druckbeginn *m*	start of printing	mise en marche *f*
Druckberichtigung *f*	correction of the press	correction *f* de la presse *f*
Druckbogen *m*	printed sheet, proof	feuille *f* imprimée
Druckbogen *m*, **ausgedruckter**	folded printed sheet	cahier *m*
Druckbuchstaben *m/pl*	block letters *pl*	caractères *m/pl* bâtons *m/pl*
Druckdublee *n*	mackling	doublage *m*
Druckeinstellung *f/typog*	adjustment	justification *f*
drucken	to impress, to print	imprimer, tirer
Drucker *m*	printer	imprimeur *m*
Druckerei *f*	printing office, printing plant	imprimerie *f*
Druckerlaubnis *f*	imprimatur, permission to print	permission *f* d'imprimer
Druckerschwärze *f*	printer's ink	encre *f* d'imprimerie *f*, encre *f* grasse
Druckerzeichen *n*	printer's mark	marque *f* d'imprimeur *m*
Druckerzeugnis *n*	printed matter	imprimé *m*
druckfähig	fit for printing, printable	imprimable
Druckfahne *f*	proof, slip	placard *m*
Druckfarbe *f*	printing ink	encre *f* d'impression *f*
Druckfehler *m*	erratum, misprint, printing error, typographical error	coquille *f*, erreur *f* de composition *f*, faute *f* d'impression *f*, faute *f* typographique
Druckfehlerverzeichnis *n*	corrigenda, errata	errata *m*
druckfertig	passed for press, ready for printing	bon à imprimer, bon à (tirer)

druckfertiger Korrektur-bogen m	press revise	dernière épreuve f
druckfertiges Manuskript n	fair copy	belle copie f
druckfeucht	moist from ink	humide d'encre f grasse
Druckfläche f	printing surface	surface f d'impression f
Druckform f	printing form am, printing forme brit	forme f à impression f
Druckformschluß m	closing down	bouclage m
Druckfreigabe f	release	autorisation f de publier, embargo m levé
Druckfundament n	stone	marbre m
Druckgang m	passage, run	passage m
Druckgenehmigung f	imprimatur, permission to print	permission f d'imprimer
Druckgewerbe n	printing trade	industries f/pl graphiques
Druckjahr n	date of impression	date f d'impression f
Druckkosten pl	printing costs pl	frais m/pl d'impression f
Drucklackierung f	varnished overprinting	vernissage m d'impression f
Drucklegung f	going to press, printing	mise à l'impression f, mise sous presse f
Druckmängel m/pl	imperfection in printing	imperfection f d'impression f
Druckmaschine f	letter press, printing press	machine f à imprimer
Druckmaschine f, **Einrichten** n **der**	to make ready	calage m
Druckoberfläche f	face	côté m image m
Druckort m	place of printing	lieu m d'impression f
Druckpapier n	printing paper	papier m à imprimer
Druckplatte f	engraving plate, printing plate	plaque f d'impression f
Druckpresse f	printing press	presse f à imprimer
Druckpresse f **anhalten**	to hold presses pl	arrêter la presse f à imprimer
Druckprinzip n	printing process	principe m d'impression f
Druckprobe f	proof	épreuve f
druckreif	good for printing, o.k. am, ready for press	bon à tirer, prêt à imprimer
druckreif nach Korrektur f	good for printing with corrections pl	bon à tirer après corrections f/pl
Drucksache f	printed matter, printings pl/am	imprimé m
Drucksache f, **großformatige**	broadsheet	imprimé m de grand format m
Drucksachenversand m	sorting	routage m
Drucksachenverteilung f	distribution of printed matter	distribution f d'imprimés m/pl
Drucksatz m	matter	composition f
Druckschrift f (Veröffentlichung f)	publication	imprimé m, publication f
Druckschrift f/typog	block letters pl	caractères m/pl typographiques
Druckstock m	block brit, cut, engraving, plate	cliché m, planche f
Druckstock m, **ausgefräster**	routed plate	cliché m fraisé, cliché m toupillé
Drucktechnik f	printing techniques pl	technique f d'imprimerie f
Drucktuch n	blanket	blanchet m
Drucktype f	character, printing type	caractère m d'imprimerie f
Drucktype f, **breite**	expanded type, extended type	caractère m large
Druckunterlage f	printing material	documents m/pl d'impression f, matériel m d'impression f
Druckverbot n	prohibition to print	défense f d'imprimer
Druckverfahren n	printing method, printing process	mode m d'impression f, procédé m d'impression f
Druckzylinder m	impression cylinder	cylindre m de foulage m, cylindre m d'impression f

Dublette *f*	double, doublet	doublon *m*
Dünndruckpapier *n*	bible paper, India paper, thin paper	papier *m* bible, papier *m* mince, pelure *f* d'oignon *m*
Dunkelkammer *f*	darkroom	chambre *f* noire
Duplex-Autotypie *f*	duplex half-tone block (brit), duplex half-tone cut *am*	autotypie *f*, cliché *m* simili deux tons *m/pl*
Duplexdruck *m*	duplex printing	impression *f* double-ton *m*
Duplikat *n*	duplicate	duplicata *m*
Duplikatätzung *f*	duplicate block	duplicata *m/pl*
durchblättern	to run over	feuilleter
durchbohren	to pierce	transpercer
Durchdringung *f*	penetration	pénétration *f*
durcheinanderbringen	to scramble	brouiller
durcheinandergefallener Satz *m*	pie	copie *f* chamboulée
Durchführungsbestätigung *f*	voucher	justificatif *m*
durchgehender Satz *m*	full measure setting	composition *f* à pleine justification *f*
durchgehender Titel *m*	running head	titre-courant *m*
durchgeschlagener Druck *m*	blotted print	foulage *m*
durchlesen	to run through	parcourir
Durchmesser *m*	diameter	diamètre *m*
Durchsage *f*	announcement	avis *m*
Durchscheinbild *n*	diorama	diorama *m*
durchscheinen	to show through, to transpierce	transparaître, transpercer
durchscheinendes Papier *n*	translucent paper	papier *m* transparent
durchschießen	to interline, to lead out, to space out	blanchir, espacer, interligner
durchschießen (Bogen)	to cut in	intercaler
durchschlagen *typog*	to come through, to strike through, to transpierce	maculer, pénétrer, transpercer, traverser
Durchschlagpapier *n*	copy paper, flimsy paper	papier *m* pour copies *f/pl*
Durchschlagskraft *f*	penetrating power	force *f* de pénétration *f*
Durchschnitt *m*	average	moyenne *f*
Durchschnitt *m*, repräsentativer	cross section	coupe *f* en travers
durchschnittlich	at an average	en moyenne
durchschnittliche Auflage *f*	average circulation	diffusion *f* moyenne, tirage *m* moyen
durchschnittliche Verkaufsauflage *f*	average net paid circulation, average sold circulation	bouillon *m* déduit moyen
Durchschnittskosten *pl*	average costs *pl*	frais *m/pl* moyens
Durchschnittspreis *m*	average price	prix *m* moyen
Durchschuß *m*	leads *pl*, slugs *pl*	interlignage *m*
durchsehen	to revise	reviser, revoir
durchsichtig	transparent	transparent
durchsichtige Verpackung *f* aus Kunststoff *m*	blister pack	emballage *m* plastique transparent
Durchsichtigkeitsgrad *m*	ink density	transparence *f* de la couleur *f*
Durchsichtsbild *n*, farbiges	ektachrome	diorama *m* en couleurs *f/pl*
durchstreichen	to cross out	raturer
durchstrichener Verkaufspreis *m*	crossed out selling price	prix *m* de vente *f* barré

E

Echo *n*	echo, empathy	écho *m*
Ecke *f*, linke	left-hand corner	coin *m* gauche
Ecke *f*, obere	upper corner	coin *m* supérieur

Ecke f, rechte	right-hand corner	coin m droit
Ecke f, untere	lower corner	coin m inférieur
eckige Klammern f/pl	square brackets pl	crochets m/pl
Eckplatz m oberer, der Titelseite f	box on the right of the masthead	manchette f à droite du titre m
Effekt m	effect	effet m
Effekthascherei f	claptrap, sensationalism	recherche f de l'effet m, recherche f de l'épate m
effektiv	effective	effectif
effektvolle Darbietung f	showmanship	art m de la mise f en scène f
Egyptienne f	Egyptian	égyptienne f
Ehrabschneidung f	libel	diffamation f
Ehrenrettung f	white wash	réhabilitation f
ehrliches Spiel n	fair play	franc-jeu m
eidesstattliche Erklärung f	affidavit	affirmation f sur serment m
Eigenanzeige f	one's own advertisement	propre annonce f
Eigenbedarf m	personal requirements pl	besoin m propre
Eigenmarke f	house brand, own brand, private brand	marque f de distributeur m
Eigentum n, geistiges	intellectual property	propriété f intellectuelle
Eigenwerbung f	house advertising	propre publicité f
Eigenwirkung f einer Ware f	self appeal	effet m propre de la marchandise f elle-même
Eilauftrag m	express order, rush job	commande f urgente, ordre m par exprès m
Einband m	binding, cover	couverture f, reliure f
Einblattdruck m	one-side print	feuille f imprimée au recto m seulement
Einblendung f	fade-in	ouverture f en fondu m
einbringen (Zeile)	to take in	gagner
Eindruck m der Händleradresse f	dealer imprint	impression f de l'adresse f du détaillant m
eindrucken	to print on	repiquer sur
Eindrucksstärke f	impact	effet m de choc m
Eindruckwerk n	auxiliary printing unit	élément m d'impression f auxiliaire
eine Nachricht f hochspielen	to play up an information, to puff up an information	donner une publicité f retentissante, gonfler un papier m, remonter une nouvelle f
eine Sache f ausplaudern	to blab out a secret	vendre la mèche f
einen Skandal m ersticken	to stifle a scandal	étouffer un scandale m
einfacher Stil m	plain style	style m simple
Einfall m	flash, gag, idea	boutade f, idée f, saillie f
einfarbig	monochrome, single-coloured	monochrome, unicolore
einfassen	to border, to box in, to frame	border, encadrer, entourer d'un filet m
Einfassung f	border	bordure f, dentelle f, encadrement m
Einflußgebiet n	sphere of influence	sphère f d'influence f
einfügen	to fill-in, to insert	insérer
Einfügung f	insertion	insertion f
einführen	to introduce	introduire, lancer
Einführungsanzeige f	launch ad	annonce f de lancement m, annonce f d'introduction f

Einführungskampagne *f*	announcement campaign, initial campaign, introduction campaign	campagne *f* de lancement *m*, campagne *f* d'information *f*, campagne *f* d'introduction *f*
Einführungsnummer *f*	introductory number	numéro *m* inaugural
Einführungspreis *m*	early bird price	prix *m* de lancement *m*
Einführungsrabatt *m*	discount of introduction	rabais *m* de lancement *m*
Einführungswerbung *f*	introductory advertising	publicité *f* de lancement *m*, publicité *f* d'information *f*, publicité *f* d'introduction *f*
Eingabe *f/typog*	input	information *f* à traiter
eingeblendete Werbung *f*	tie-in advertising	publicité *f* enchaînée
eingedruckte Händleranschrift *f*	dealer imprint	adresse *f* imprimée du commerçant *m*, empreinte *f* de l'adresse *f* du détaillant *m*
eingefangenes Publikum *n*	captive audience	audience *f* captive
eingehen (stereotyp.)	to shrink	rétrécir
eingeklebtes Bild *n*	tip-in	hors-texte *m*
eingerahmter Titel *m*	box head	titre *m* encadré
eingerückter Satz *m*	hanging indent	composition *f* en sommaire *m*
eingeschriebener Brief *m*	registered letter	lettre *f* recommandée
eingetragenes Warenzeichen *n*	registered trade mark	marque *f* déposée
einhängen	to case in	emboîter
einheften	to bind into, to stitch in	brocher dans, coudre dans
Einhefter *m*	bound insert	encart *m* broché
Einheit *f*, **journalistische**	independent newspaper with a complete editorial staff, journalistic unit	journal *m* indépendant avec une rédaction *f* complète, unité *f* journalistique
Einholetasche *f*	shopping basket	sac *m* cabas
Einkauf *m*	buying	achat *m*
einkaufen	to shop	acheter
Einkaufshäufigkeit *f*	purchase rhythm	fréquence *f* d'achat *m*, périodicité *f* d'achat *m*
Einkaufsrhythmus *m*	purchase rhythm	rythme *m* d'achat *m*
Einkaufstasche *f* (aus Papier *n*)	paper bag, shopping-bag	sac *m* en papier *m*, sac *m* publicitaire
Einkaufsverhalten *n*	buying behaviour, shopping habits *pl*	comportement *m* des acheteurs *m/pl*
Einkaufszentrum *n*	shopping area, shopping center	centre *m* commercial, centre *m* d'achat *m*
einklammern	to bracket, to put in parentheses *pl*	mettre en crochets *m/pl*, mettre en parenthèses *f/pl*
Einklebebuch *n*	scrapbook	album-souvenir *m*
einkleben	to paste on	coller
Einkleben *n* **von Beilagen** *f/pl*	tipping-in of insets *pl*	collage *m* d'encarts *m/pl*
Einkommen *n*	income, revenue	revenu *m*
Einkommensklasse *f*	income group	classe *f* de revenus *m/pl*
einkopieren	to copy in, to superimpose	copier dans, pelliculer
einkreisen	to ring	encercler
einkuvertieren	to put in an envelope	mettre sous enveloppe *f*
Einladungskarte *f*	invitation-card	carte *f* d'invitation *f*
einlaufen (stereotyp.)	to shrink	rétrécir, se retirer
Einleitung *f*	introduction, preamble	introduction *f*, préambule *f*
Einleitungsmelodie *f*	signature tune	générique *m*
Einleitungssatz *m*	lead	démarrage *m*
Einlösung *f*	redemption	dégagement *m*, paiement *m*
Einmannschau *f*	one man show	solo *m*
Einnahmen *f/pl*	receipts *pl*, revenue	recettes *f/pl*

einordnen	to classify	classifier
einpassen	to register	repérer
einrahmen	to border, to box in, to frame	encadrer, entourer d'un filet *m*
Einrahmung *f*	border, frame	bordure *f*
Einrichten *n* der Druckmaschine *f*	to make ready	calage *m*
Einrichtung *f*	installation	installation *f*
einrücken (Anzeige)	to insert	insérer
einrücken (einziehen)	to indent	renfoncer, rentrer
Einsatz *m*	implementing	mise *f* en œuvre *f*
einschalten	to insert	insérer
Einschalthäufigkeit *f*	insertion frequency	fréquence *f* d'insertion *f*
Einschaltjahr *n*	contract year	année *f* légale
Einschaltplan *m*	advertising schedule	calendrier *m* d'insertion *f*
Einschaltpreis *m*	insertion rate	prix *m* d'insertion *f*
Einschaltseite *f*	inset, interpolated sheet	page *f* intercalaire
Einschaltung *f*	insertion	insertion *f*
vor **Einschaltung** *f*	before insertion	avant l'insertion *f*
einschieben	to sandwich	intercaler
Einschießbogen *m*	slip sheets *pl*	maculatures *f/pl*
Einschlagpapier *n*	wrapping paper	papier *m* d'emballage *m*
Einschnitt *m*	notch	entaille *f*
einschränken, Raum *m*	to run short	gagner
einschreiben	to inscribe, to register	enregistrer, inscrire
einseitig beeinflussen	to angle	influencer partialement
einseitig gestrichenes Papier *n*	one-side coated paper	satiné d'un côté *m*
einseitig Glanz *m*	machine glazed (M.G.)	frictionné
einspaltig	one column wide, single-column	à une colonne *f*, sur une col *f*
Einsteckheftung *f*	stabbing	piquer travers
einstellen (Erscheinen *n*)	to discontinue publication	cesser de paraître
Einstellung *f*	attitude, behaviour, mental set	attitude *f*, opinion *f*
Einstufung *f* von Anzeigenentwürfen *m/pl*	order of merit-rating	classification *f* de dessins *m/pl* publicitaires
Einteilung *f*	classification	classement *m*
Einteilung *f* nach Typen *f/pl*	typology	typologie *f*
einträgliche Werbung *f*	lucrative advertising	publicité *f* rentable
Eintrag *m*	entry	inscription *f*
eintragen	to enter	inscrire
einwandfreie Werbung *f*	clean advertising	publicité *f* impeccable, publicité *f* irréprochable
Einwegpackung *f*	expendable package, non-returnable package, one way package, spoil package	emballage *m* non repris, emballage *m* perdu
einweichen	to soak	tremper
einwickeln	to roll up, to wrap	envelopper
Einwickelpapier *n*	Kraft paper, wrapping paper	papier *m* bulle *f*, papier *m* d'emballage *m*
Einwirkung *f*	impact	impact *m*
Einzelauftrag *m*	isolated order	commande *f* isolée
Einzelhändler *m*	retailer	détaillant *m*, revendeur *m*
Einzelhändlerunterstützung *f*	merchandizing	techniques *f/pl* marchandes
Einzelhandelspreis *m*	retail price	prix *m* de détail *m*
Einzelhandelsunternehmen *n*	retail firm	établissement *m* de détail *m*
Einzelhandelswerbung *f*	retail advertising	publicité *f* des établissements *m/pl* de détail *m*
Einzelheit *f*	item	item *m*

Einzelnummer f	single copy	numéro m séparé, spécimen m
Einzelpreis m	flat rate, one-time rate, open rate	tarif m de base f, tarif m fixe
Einzelverkauf m (Zeitungen)	news stand sales pl, sale per copy	vente f au kiosque m, vente f au numéro m
Einzelwerbung f	individual advertising	publicité f individuelle
einziehen (Zeile)	to indent	mettre en renfoncement m
einzige Anzeige f **einer Seite** f	sole advertisement	seule annonce f
Einzug m, **ohne**	flush	sans renfoncement m
Einzugsgebiet n	sales pl area, trading area	débouché m, secteur m de vente f
Einzug m/typog m	indent, indention	renfoncement m
Eis n **legen, auf**	to put into cold-storage	mise f au frigo m
Eisbrecher m	lead-in, warm-up	brise-glace m
Eisenbahnplakat n	railroad showing	emplacement m intérieur de chemin m de fer m
Eisenbahnwerbung f	railway advertising	publicité f par chemin m de fer m
elegante Zeitschriften f/pl	glossy monthlies pl	magazines m/pl chics
elektromechanische Reproduktion f	electromechanical reproduction	reproduction f électro-mécanique
Elektronenrechner m	computer	calculateur m électronique
elektronische Fotosetzmaschine f	electronic phototypesetting machine	photocomposeuse f électronique
elektronische Werbung f	electronical advertising	publicité f électronique
Elfenbeinkarton m	ivory board	carton m -ivoire m
Elfenbeinpapier n	ivory paper	papier m d'ivoire m
Elite f, **geistige**	intelligentsia	élite f intellectuelle
Emailleschild n	enamel plate, enamel sign	plaque f emaillée
Emblem n	emblem	emblème m
Emblem n, **ausgestanztes**	die cut	emblème m découpé
Empfänger m	addressee, recipient	destinataire m, récepteur m
Empfänger m (Radio)	radio set	récepteur m
Empfehlung f	recommendation	recommandation f
Empfehlungsanzeige f	business advertisement with regular basic rate	annonce f commerciale à prix m de base f
Empfehlungsschreiben n	testimonial	attestation f
empfindungsloser Stil m	deadpan style	style m pince-sans-rire
empfohlener Preis m	standard price, suggested price	prix m recommandé
Ende n **des Absatzes** m	break line	fin f d'alinéa m
endgültiger Andruck m	final pull	épreuve f définitive
Endlosdruck m	continuous printing	impression f en continu
endloses Papier n	reel paper, web paper	papier m continu
Endlos-Farbanzeige f	continuous advertisement in colour	encart m en couleur f imprimé en continu m
Endlosformular n	continuous form	formulaire m en continu
Endverbraucher m	final consumer, ultimate consumer	consommateur m final
eng setzen	to space closely	composer serré
enge Schrift f	condensed type	écriture f étroite
englische Linie f	plain swelled rule	filet m anglais
englische Schreibschrift f	English script type	écriture f anglaise
Enquête f	investigation	enquête f
Ente f	fake, hoax	bobard m
Entflechtung f	deconcentration	déconcentration f
enthalten in	included in	compris dans
enthüllen	to dig out	révéler

Enthüllung *f*	disclosure	révélation *f*
Entmantelung *f*	stripping	grattage *m*
Entpolitisierung *f*	depolitization	dépolitisation *f*
Entschädigung *f*	compensation, indemnity	dédommagement *m*, indemnité *f*
Entscheidung *f*	decision	décision *f*
Entscheidungsgrundlagen *f/pl*	fundamentals *pl* of decision	bases *f/pl* de la décision *f*
Entscheidungsschema *n*, baumartiges	decision tree	arbre *m* de décision *f*
Entschlüsselung *f*	decoding	décodage *m*
Entstehung *f*	origination	naissance *f*
entwerfen	to design, to draft, to outline	dessiner, élaborer, esquisser
Entwerfer *m*	lay out man	maquettiste *m*
entwickeln	to develop	développer
Entwickler *m*	developer	révélateur *m*
Entwicklung *f*	development, evolution	développement *m*, évolution *f*
Entwicklungstrend *m*, langfristiger	secular trend	évolution *f* à long terme *m*
Entwurf *m*	design, draft, outline, tentative work	croquis *m*, dessin *m*, ébauche *f*, épreuve *f*, maquette *f*, projet *m*
Entwurf *m*, erster unfertiger	scribble	brouillon *m*, griffonnage *m*
Entwurf *m*, fertiger	comprehensive	maquette *f* très poussée
Entwurfsgrafiker *m*	layouter	dessinateur *m*
Entwurfshonorar *n*	fee for design	honoraires *m/pl* de projet *m*
Entwurfsskizze *f* eines Werbefilms *m*	storyboard	présentation *f* d'un scénario *m* sous forme *f* d'une suite *f* de dessins *m/pl*
Erdichtung *f*	fiction	fiction *f*, ouvrage *m* d'imagination *f*
Ereignis *n*	event	événement *m*
Erfahrung *f*	experience	expérience *f*
Erfahrungsschatz *m*, werblicher	advertising record	expérience *f* publicitaire
erfassen	to cover	couvrir
erfaßte Personen-Gesamtzahl *f*	cumulative audience	auditoire *m* cumulatif
Erfassung *f* der Werbestreuung *f*	census of distribution	recensement *m* de la distribution *f*
Erfassungsterminal *n*	data collection	collection *f* des données *f/pl*
Erfolg *m*	success	succès *m*
Erfolg *m*, großer	smash hit	gros succès *m*
Erfolgsbuch *n*	bestseller	livre *m* à succès *m*
Erfolgskontrolle *f*	rating, result checking	contrôle *m* des résultats *m/pl*, contrôle *m* du rendement *m*, contrôle *m* du succès *m*
erfolgversprechender Absatzmarkt *m*	promising market	débouché *m* plein de promesses *f/pl*
erforschen	to investigate	étudier, sonder
Erforschung *f* der Verbrauchermotive *n/pl*	consumer motivation research	études *f/pl* de la motivation *f* des consommateurs *m/pl*
Erfrischungstuch *n*	refreshment towel	mouchoir *m* en papier *m* rafraîchissant
Erfüllungsort *m*	place of fulfilment	lieu *m* d'exécution *f*
erfundenes Wort *n*	coined word	mot *m* forgé
Ergänzungswerbung *f*	accessory advertising, supplementary advertising	publicité *f* auxiliaire, publicité *f* de soutien *m*
Erhaltungswerbung *f*	maintenance advertising	publicité *f* de maintien *m*
Erhebung *f*	survey	enquête *f*

erhöhte Auflage *f*	run-on	tirage *m* supplémentaire
erhöhter Grundpreis *m*	raised standard rate	prix *m* de base *f* augmenté
Erhöhung *f*	increase	augmentation *f*
Erinnerung *f*, spontane	pure recall, spontaneous remembrance	mémoire *f* spontanée, souvenir *m* spontané
Erinnerungsanzeige *f*	reminder advertisement	annonce *f* de rappel *m*
Erinnerungsgrad *m*	degree of recognition	dégré *m* de mémorabilité *f*
Erinnerungshilfe *f*	aided recall	mémoire *f* aidée
Erinnerungskampagne *f*	reminder campaign	campagne *f* mémorative
Erinnerungstest *m*	recall test, recognition test	test *m* de mémorisation *f*, test *m* de souvenir *m* spontané
Erinnerungswerbung *f*	remembrance advertising	publicité *f* de rappel *m*, publicité *f* de souvenir *m*
Erinnerungswert *m*	memory value, remembrance value, reminder value	souvenir *m* laissé, valeur *f* de mémorisation *f*, valeur *f* de rappel *m*
Erkennbarkeit *f*	perceptibility	perceptibilité *f*
Erkennungsmelodie *f*	signature, theme song	mélodie *f* d'identification *f*
Erkennungszeile *f*	galley line	ligne *f* d'identification *f*
erklären	to declare, to state	déclarer
Erklärung *f*	declaration	déclaration *f*
Erklärung *f*, eidesstattliche	affidavit	affirmation *f* sur serment *m*
erkunden	to investigate	étudier, sonder
Erkundigungen *f/pl* einziehen	to inquire	aller aux informations *f/pl*
Erläuterung *f*	explanation	explication *f*
erleuchten	to illuminate	illuminer
ermäßigter Preis *m*	reduced rate, short rate	tarif *m* réajusté
ermässigter Tarif *m*	short rate	tarif *m* réduit
Ermäßigung *f*	reduction	diminution *f*
Ermittler *m*	research worker, researcher	chercheur *m*, spécialiste *m* de la recherche *f*
Erneuerung *f*	renewal	remplacement *m*, renouvellement *m*
Erneuerung *f* des Abonnements *m*	renewal of subscription	réabonnement *m*
Erörterung *f*	discussion	discussion *f*
Erratum *n*	erratum	erratum *m*
erreichen	to reach	toucher
Ersatzanspruch *m*	claim to compensation	droit *m* de compensation *f*
Ersatzanzeige *f*	make-good, replacement ad	gratuité *f* de compensation *f*, ré-insertion *f*
Ersatzbedarf *m*	replacement demand	besoin *m* de remplacement *m*
Ersatzkarton *m*, zweiseitiger	single-leaf cancel	onglet *m*
Ersatzplakat *n*	poster for replacement	affiche *f* de remplacement *m*
Ersatzplakatierung *f*	change of posters *pl*	mutation *f* d'emplacements *m/pl*
Ersatztermin *m*	substitute date	date *f* succédanée
erscheinen	to appear, to come out	paraître, sortir
Erscheinen *n*	appearance	publication *f*, sortie *f*
vor Erscheinen *n*	before issue	avant la parution *f*
Erscheinungsdatum *n*	date of issue, publication date	date *f* de parution *f*, date *f* de publication *f*
Erscheinungsintervall *n*	interval of publication	intervalle *m* de parution *f*
Erscheinungsort *m*	place of publication	lieu *m* de publication *f*

Erscheinungsplan *m*	advertising schedule, insertion schedule	calendrier *m* des parutions *f/pl*, calendrier *m* d'insertion *f*, plan *m* de termes *m/pl*
Erscheinungsrhythmus *m*	rhythm of publication	rythme *m* de parution *f*
Erscheinungstag *m*	day of publishing, publication date	jour *m* de parution *f*
Erscheinungsweise *f*	frequency of publication, publishing intervals *pl*	mode *m* de parution *f*, périodicité *f*
erschienen, soeben	just out, just published	vient de paraître
Erstausgabe *f*	first edition	première édition *f*
Erstdruck *m*	incunabulum	incunable *m*
erste Ausgabe *f*	bulldog edition	première édition *f*
erste endgültige Filmkopie *f*	standard film copy	copie *f* standard
erste Seite	first page, front page	première page *f*
erster Abzug *m*	first proof	épreuve *f* en première
erster Hand *f*, aus	from first source	de première main *f*
erster unfertiger Entwurf *m*	scribble	brouillon *m*, griffonnage *m*
Erstleser *m*	primary reader	premier lecteur *m*
Erstverkaufstag *m*	first selling day	premier jour *m* de vente *f*
Erträge *m/pl*	revenue	revenu *m*
Erwähnung *f*	mention, quotation	citation *f*, mention *f*
erweiterte Auflage *f*	enlarged edition	édition *f* augmentée
erwiesene Tatsache *f*	ascertained fact	fait *m* établi
Erzeugerpreis *m*	producer's price	prix *m* à la production *f*
Erzeugnis *n*	product	produit *m*
Erzeugung *f*	production	production *f*
erzieherische Werbung *f*	educational advertising	publicité *f* éducative
es bleibe stehen *typog*	stet!	à maintenir
Eselsbrücke *f*	crib	guide-âne *m*
Eselsohren *n/pl*, Seite *f* mit	dog-eared page	page *f* cornée
Eselswiese *f*	correspondence column	courrier *m* du cœur *m*
Espartopapier *n*	esparto	alfa *m*
Essay *m*	essay	essai *m*
Etat *m*	account, budget	budget *m*
Etatdirektor *m*	account manager, senior account supervisor	directeur *m* de la section *f* budgetaire
Etatfestsetzung *f*	budget fixation	fixation *f* du budget *m*
Etatkontrolle *f*	budget checking	contrôle *m* budgétaire
Etatkunde *m*	account	client *m*
Etatplan *m*	allocation draft	projet *m* de budget *m*
Etatsanteil *m*	allocation	budget *m* alloué
Etatsumme *f*	billing	chiffre *m* d'affaires *f/pl*
Etatverteilung *f*	budget distribution, media schedule, space schedule, spread-over	répartition *f* de budget *m*
ethische Werbung *f*	ethical advertising	publicité *f* éthique
Etikett *n*	label, sticker	étiquette *f*, timbre *m*
Etikett *n*, „sprechendes"	self-explanatory label	étiquette *f* s'expliquant elle-même
etikettieren	to label, to ticket	étiqueter
Etikettierung *f*, aufklärende	informative labeling	étiquettage *m* informatif
Europäische Wirtschaftsgemeinschaft *f* (EWG)	European Common Market	Marché *m* Commun Européen
eventueller Kunde *m*	prospect	prospect *m*
Exemplar *n*	copy	exemplaire *m*
Exemplare *n/pl*, überzählige	overquire	main *f* de passe *f*

Exemplare *n/pl*, unverkaufte	unsold copies *pl*	bouillon *m*, exemplaires *m/pl* invendus
Exklusivagentur *f*	exclusive agency	agence *f* exclusive
Exklusivbeitrag *m*	exclusive contribution	article *m* exclusif
Exklusivbericht *m*	exclusive report	rapport *m* exclusif
Exklusivität *f*	exclusivity	exclusivité *f*
Exklusivleser *m*	exclusive reader	lecteur *m* exclusif
Experiment *n*	experiment	expérience *f*
Experimentalfilm *m*	experimental film	film *m* expérimental
experimentelles Plakat *n*	experimental poster	affiche *f* expérimentelle
Experten *m/pl* -Zusammenschluß *m*	brain trust	brain-trust *m*
Exponat *n*	show-piece	pièce *f* d'exposition *f*
Exportförderung *f*	export promotion	aide *f* à l'exportation *f*
Exportwerbung *f*	export advertising	publicité *f* d'exportation *f*
Exposé *n*	proposal, statement	exposé *m*, proposition *f*
extra ausgestattetes Buch *n*	enriched book	livre *m* bien présenté
extra fett	extra bold	extra gras
Extrablatt *n*	special edition	édition *f* spéciale
Extrarabatt *m*	additional account	rabais *m* additionnel
Exzerpt *n*	excerpt, extract	citation *f*, extrait *m*

F

Fabel *f* eines Stückes *n*	plot	affabulation *f*
Fabrikant *m*	maker, manufacturer	constructeur *m*, fabricant *m*
Fabrikmarke *f*	manufacturer's brand, producer's brand	marque *f* de fabricant *m*
Facette *f*	bevel	onglet *m*, talus *m*
Fachadreßbuch *n*	trade address book	annuaire *m* pour le commerce *m* et l'industrie *f*
Fachausdruck *m*	technical term, trade expression	terme *m* technique
Fachbuch *n*	handbook, text-book, trade book	livre *m* professionnel, livre *m* technique, ouvrage *m* spécialisé
Fachgeschäft *n*	specialty shop, specialty store	commerce *m* spécialisé
Fachliteratur *f*	specialised literature	littérature *f* spécialisée
Fachmann *m*	expert, specialist	expert *m*, spécialiste *m*
Fachmesse *f*	spezialised fair	foire *f* spécialisée
Fachpresse *f*	technical press, trade press	presse *f* professionnelle, presse *f* technique
fachsimpeln	to talk shop	parler métier *m*
Fachsprache *f*	technical language	langage *m* technique
Fachwerbung *f*	professional advertising	publicité *f* spécialisée
Fachwissen *n*	special knowledge	science *f* spéciale
Fachwort *n*	trade word	terme *m* technique
Fachzeitschrift *f*	professional magazine	revue *f* professionnelle
Fachzeitung	business publication, technical publication, trade journal	journal *m* professionnel, périodique *m* technique
Fadenheftung *f*	book sewing	couture *f* au fil *m* végétal
Fadenknotenheftung *f*	thread sewing	couture *f* au point *m* noué
Fadenkreuz *n*	register mark	croix *f* de repère *m*
fadenscheinige Ausrede	quibble	argutie *f*, faux-fuyant *m*
Fadenzähler *m*	line tester, screen magnifier	compte-fils *m*
Fading *n*	fading	fading *m*, fondu *m*
Fährschiffwerbung *f*	ferry-boat advertising	publicité *f* dans les ferry-boats *m/pl*

fällig	due	échu
Fälligkeit f	date of payment, maturity	échéance f
Fälschung f	fake, falsification	chiqué m, contrefaction f, falsification f
Fahnenabzug m	galley proof, slip	épreuve f à la brosse f, épreuve f en placard m
Fahne f/typog f	proof, slip	épreuve f, placard m
fahrbare Verkaufsstelle f	mobile shop	camionnette f -boutique f
Fahrplan m	time table	horaire m
Fahrplankasten m	box of time-table	boîte f des horaires m/pl des trains m/pl
Fahrscheinwerbung f	ticket advertising	publicité f sur billets m/pl
Fahrstraße f	roadside	route f carossable
Fahrzeugen n/pl, **Werbung** f **in**	vehicular advertising	publicité f sur ou dans véhicules f/pl de transport m
fairer Wettbewerb m	fair competition	concurrence f loyale
Faksimile n	facsimile	fac-similé m
Faksimiledruck m	facsimile reprint	réimpression f fac-similée
Faktensammlung f	fact-gathering	recueillement m de faits m/pl
Faktor m/typog m	overseer of composing room	prote m
Faktotum n	handy man	bricoleur m
Faktura f	invoice	facture f
Fallstudie f	case study	étude f d'un cas m
falsch angesetzte Werbung f	misplaced advertising	publicité f déplacée
falsch ausgesprochenes Wort n	beard	cuir m
falsche Darstellung f	misrepresentation	faux rapport m
falsche Raumaufteilung f	faulty spacing	espacement m faux
Falschmeldung f	fake report, false news	fausse nouvelle f
Falte f	crimp	pli m
falten	to fold	plisser
faltenfreier Anschlag m	nonwrinkle posting	affichage m sans plis m/pl
Falten f/pl **werfen**	to crease	plisser
Faltplan m	folding map	carte f pliable
Faltprospekt m	folder, leaflet	dépliant m
Faltprospekt m, **großer**	broadsheet, broadside	in-plano m
Faltschachtel f	collapsible carton, folding box	boîte f pliante
Falz m	fold, joint	rainure f
falzen	to fold	plier
Falzung f	folding, grooving	pliage m, rainage m
Familienähnlichkeit f	family likeness	similarité f de présentation f
Familienanzeige f	family announcement, personal announcement	avis m, faire-part m
Familienblatt n	family paper, magazine of general interest	feuille f familiale, revue f d'intérêt m général
Familiengefühls n, **Ansprache** f **des**	family appeal	appel m au sentiment m de famille f
Familiennachrichten f/pl	gossip	échos m/pl familiers
Familienpackung f	giant-size pack	empaquetage m gigantesque
Farbätzer m	chromist	chromiste m
Farbätzung f	colour process etching, four-colour block	cliché m de photogravure f, quadrichromie f
Farbandruck m	colour proof, progressive proof	épreuve f en couleurs f/pl, suite f
Farbanzeige f	colour advertisement	publicité f en couleurs f/pl
Farbaufnahme f	colour photograph	photo f en couleurs f/pl, prise f de vue f en couleurs f/pl

Farbauszug *m*	colour selection, colour separation	sélection *f* des couleurs *f/pl*, séparation *f* des couleurs *f/pl*
Farbband *n*	typewriter ribbon	ruban *m* de machine *f*
Farbbanddruckbrief *m*	ink ribbon printed letter	impression *f* au ruban *m* de machine *f*
Farbdia *n*	colour transparency, colour-slide	diapositif *m* couleur, ektachrome *m*
Farbdiaabzug *m*	dye transfer	transfert *m* de couleur *f*
Farbdruck *m*	chromotype, colour printing	chromolithographie *f*, chromotypie *f*, impression *f* en couleurs *f/pl*, impression *f* polychrome, polychromie *f*
Farbe *f*	color *am*, colour *brit*	couleur *f*
Farbe *f*, lichtempfindliche	fugitive colour	couleur *f* sensible à la lumière *f*
Farbeffekt *m*	colour effect	effet *m* de couleurs *f/pl*
Farbenlithografie *f*	colour lithography	chromolithographie *f*, lithographie *f* en couleurs *f/pl*
Farben *f/pl* reiben	to grind colours *pl*	broyer des couleurs *f/pl*
Farbfernsehen *n*	colour television	télévision *f* couleur *f*
Farbfilm *m*	colour film	film *m* en couleurs *f/pl*
Farbfilter *m*	colour filter	filtre *m* coloré
Farbfoto *n*	colour photography	photo *f* en couleurs *f/pl*
Farbfotodruck *m*	colour photo printing	impression *f* de photos *f/pl* en couleur *f*
Farbfotografie *f*	colour photography	photochromie *f*
Farbgebung *f*	colouring, inking, tinting	encrage *m*
Farbharmonie *f*	matching design	harmonie *f* des couleurs *f/pl*
farbig	coloured	coloré
farbige Schaufensterauslage *f*	colour display	étalage *m* de vitrine *f* en couleur *f*
farbiger Steindruck *m*	photochrome	photochromie *f*
farbiges Dekorationsstück *n*	colour display	étalage *m* en couleur *f*
farbiges Durchsichtsbild *n*	ektachrome	diorama *m* en couleurs *f/pl*
Farbintensität *f*	chromatic intensity	intensité *f* de la couleur *f*
Farbkissen *n*	inkpad	tampon *m* encreur
Farbklischee *n*	color engraving *am*, colour block *brit*	cliché *m* en couleurs *f/pl*
Farbkomposition *f*	colour composition	composition *f* chromatique, composition *f* colorée
Farbkontrast *m*	colour contrast	contraste *m* de couleurs *f/pl*
Farbkorrektur *f*	colour correction	correction *f* de couleur *f*
Farbmischung *f*	ink mixing	mélange *m* des encres *f/pl*
Farbmuster *n*	colour sample, swatch	échantillon *m* de couleur *f*
Farbreihenfolge *f*	sequence of colours *pl*	ordre *m* d'impression *f* des couleurs *f/pl*
Farbretusche *f*	colour retouching, dye transfer	retouche *f* des couleurs *f/pl*
Farbsatz *m*	set of colour plates *pl*	gamme *f* de clichés *m/pl* en couleurs *f/pl*
Farbschattierung *f*	shade	nuance *f*
Farbskala *f*	colour chart, colour range, colour scale	gamme *f* des couleurs *f/pl*, guide *m* des couleurs *f/pl*
Farbskizze *f*	coloured sketch	croquis *m* en couleurs *f/pl*
Farbstein *m*	inking stone	pierre *f* à broyer
Farbstift *m*	coloured pencil	crayon *m* de couleur *f*
Farbton *m*	hue, shade, tint	nuance *f*, teinte *f*, ton *m* de couleur *f*

Farbwalze *f*	inking-roller	rouleau *m* encreur
Farbwerk *n*	inking unit	encrage *m*
Farbwert *m*	value of colour	valeur *f* de couleur *f*
Farbwirkung *f*	colour effect	effet *m* chromatique
Farbzuschlag *m*	colour additional charge, colour surcharge	supplément *m* de prix *m* pour la couleur *f*
Faserpapier *n*	granite paper	papier *m* mélangé de fils *m/pl* de soie *f*
Fassadenbeschriftung *f*	advertising on façades *pl*	publicité *f* sur façades *f/pl*
Fassung *f*, gekürzte	cut version	version *f* abrégée
Fassungsvermögen *n*	capacity	capacité *f*
Faxen *f/pl*	baloney *am*, tomfoolery	fadaises *f/pl*
Feature *n*	feature	caractéristique *f*, rapport *m* d'actualité *f*
Feder *f* führen, die	to wield a pen	manier la plume *f*
Federfuchser *m*	pendriver	plumitif *m*
federführend	acting as leader, centrally handling	compétent, dirigeant
Federleichtpapier *n*	featherweight paper	papier *m* bouffant
Federzeichnung *f*	pen and ink drawing	dessin *m* à la plume *f*
Federzeichnung *f*, getönte	wash drawing	dessin *m* au lavis *m*, épure *f* au lavis *m*
Fehldruck *m*	misprint	impression *f* manquée
fehlender Buchstabe *m*	dropped-out letter	lettre *f* manquante
fehlerhaftes Register *n*	out-of-register	fausse marge *f*, registre *m* défectueux
Fehlerquelle *f*	source of error	source *f* d'erreurs *f/pl*
Fehlinformation *f*	faulty information	information *f* incorrecte
Fehlstreuung *f*	waste circulation	bouillon *m*
feierlich verkünden	to herald	proclamer
feine Linie *f*	fine-face rule	filet *m* maigre
feingerastert	with fine screen	à trame *f* fine
Feinkorn *n*	fine grain	grain *m* fin
Feinraster *m*	fine screen	trame *f* fine
Feldarbeit *f*	field-work	travail *m* sur le terrain *m*
Fensterklebeplakat *n*	window sticker, window streamer	adhésive *f*, autocollant *m* de vitrine *f*, vitrophanie *f*
Fensterumschlag *m*	window envelope	enveloppe *f* à fenêtre *f*, enveloppe *f* transparente vitrifiée
Ferienabonnement *n*	holiday subscription	abonnement *m* de vacances *f/pl*
Fernfotografie *f*	telephotography	téléphotographie *f*
Ferngespräch *n*	trunk call	appel *m* interurbain
Fernsatz *m*	teletypesetting	télécomposition *f*
Fernschreibanschluß *m*	telex	telex *m*
Fernschreiber *m*	teleprinter, teletyper, ticker	téléimprimeur *m*, téléscripteur *m*, télétype *m*
Fernschreibnetz *n*	telegraphic network	réseau *m* télégraphique
Fernsehanstalt *f*	television station	station *f* de télévision *f*
Fernsehapparat *m*	television set	récepteur *m* de télévision *f*, téléviseur *m*
Fernsehbeilage *f*	TV supplement	supplément *m* pour T.V.
Fernsehbild *n*	television picture	image *f* télévisée
Fernsehdichte *f*	television density	pénétration *f* de la télévision *f*
Fernsehempfänger *m*	television receiver	récepteur *m* de télévision *f*
Fernsehempfang *m*	television reception	réception *f* de télévision *f*

Fernsehen *n*	telecast, television (TV) , video	petit écran *m*, télévision *f*, vidéo *m*
Fernsehforschung *f*	television audience research	recherches *f/pl* relatives aux téléspectateurs *m/pl*
Fernsehgerät *n*, **tragbares**	walkie-lookie	téléviseur *m* portatif
Fernsehkonserve *f*	canned television item	émission *f* en différé *m*
Fernsehprogramm *n*	television program	programme *m* télévisé
Fernsehreportage *f*	outside broadcast	téléreportage *m*
Fernsehrequisit *n*	prop	portatif *m*
Fernsehschirm *m*	TV-screen	écran *m* de télévision *f*, petit écran *m*
Fernsehsender *m*	television station	station *f* de télévision *f*
Fernsehsendung *f*	telecast, video	émission *f* de télévision *f*
Fernsehspot *m*	announcement, commercial, spot	émission *f* publicitaire, spot *m*
Fernsehstudio *n*	television studio	studio *m* de télévision *f*
Fernsehsüchtiger *m*	television addict	maniaque *m* de la T.V. *f*
Fernsehteilnehmer *m*	television viewer	abonné *m* de la télévision *f*
Fernsehtelefon *n*	videophone	vidéophone *m*
Fernsehübertragung *f*	telecast, television transmission *brit*	émission *f* de télévision *f*, transmission *f* télévisuelle
Fernsehwerbung *f*	commercial television, television advertising	publicité *f* télévisée
Fernsehwerbung *f* **in Plakatform** *f*	billboard commercial	spot *m* en forme *f* d'affiche *f*
Fernsehzuschauer *m*	television viewer	téléspectateur *m*
Fernsehzuschauerbefragung *f* **während der Sendung** *f*	coincidental survey	enquête *f* aux téléspectateurs *m/pl* pendant une émission *f*
Fernsetzmaschine *f*	teletypesetting machine	télécomposeuse *f*
Fernsprechbuch *n*	telephone directory	annuaire *m* des téléphones *m/pl*, indicateur *m* téléphonique
Fernsprechnetz *n*	telephone network	réseau *m* téléphonique
Fernunterricht *m*	correspondence school	cours *m* par correspondance *f*
Fernwirkung *f*	long-range effect	effet *m* à distance *f*
fertige Zeichnung *f*	finished drawing	dessin *m* au propre, dessin *m* définitif
fertiger Entwurf *m*	comprehensive	maquette *f* très poussée
Fertigprodukte *n/pl*	convenience goods *pl*	produits *m/pl* finis
Fertigstellung *f*	completion	finition *f*
Fesselballonwerbung *f*	advertising by captive balloons *pl*	publicité *f* par ballons *m/pl* captifs
fest gebundenes Buch *n*	hardcover	livre *m* relié
Festangebot *n*	firm offer	offre *f* ferme
Festaufträge *m/pl* **auf bestimmte Zeit** *f*	fixed period orders *pl*	ordres *m/pl* à conservation *f* déterminée
Festauftrag *m*	definite order, firm order, standing order	ordre *m* ferme
feste Kosten *pl*	fixed costs *pl*	coûts *m/pl* fixes
festlegen	to fix	établir, fixer
Festlegung *f*	determination	détermination *f*, établissement *m*
Festpreis *m*	firm price, fixed selling price, one-price, standing price	prix *m* fixe, prix *m* imposé
Festschrift *f*	commemorative volume	brochure *f* commémorative
Festspiele *n/pl*	festival	festival *m*
Feststellung *f*	establishment, statement	établissement *m*

fett	bold	gras
fettdichtes Papier *n*	grease-proof paper	papier beurre *f*, papier *m* parcheminé, papier *m* parchemin *m* imitation *f*
Fettdruck *m*	bold-face, bold printtype	caractères *m/pl* gras
fette Linie *f*	fat line	ligne *f* en gras
fette Schrift *f*	bold-face type, full faced type, heavy type	caractère *m* gras, type *m* gras
fette Umrandung *f*	heavy frame, thick frame	bordure *f* de filet *m* mat
fetter Buchstabe *m*	fat type	caractère *m* gras
fetter Satz *m*	bold type	composition *f* grasse
Fettstift *m*	wax crayon	crayon *m* litho
feuerfestes Papier *n*	uninflammable paper	papier *m* incombustible
Feuilleton *n*	feuilleton	feuilleton *m*, page *f* littéraire
Feuilletonist *m*	par writer	courriériste *m*
feuilletonistische Anzeige *f*	advertisement in feuilleton style, advertisement in short story style	reportage *m* publicitaire
Feuilletonredakteur *m*	literary editor	rédacteur *m* du feuilleton *m*
Figur *f* **in einem Warenzeichen** *n*	trade character	personnage *m* dans une marque *f* de fabrique *f*
Fiktion *f*	invention, pretence	fiction *f*
Filialbetrieb *m*	integrated store	succursale *f*
Filialleiter *m*	store manager	directeur *m* de succursale *f*
Film *m*	film *brit*, motion picture, movie *am*	film *m*
Film *m*, **abendfüllender**	full-length film	long métrage *m*
Film *m*, **allgemein ansprechender**	film of universal appeal	film *m* passe-partout
Film *m* **(für Offset** *m***)**	flat, offset transparency	plat *m*, typon *m*
Film *m*, **rückwärts ablaufender**	fast back	film *m* se déroulant en arrière
Filmarchiv *n*	film library, stock-shots *pl*	cinémathèque *f*, filmothèque *f*
Filmatelier *n*	film studio	studio *m*
Filmaufnahme *f*	shooting of a film	prise *f* de vue *f*, tournage *m*
Filmbearbeitung *f*	film adaptation	adaptation *f* cinématographique
Filmbericht *m*	screen record	reportage *m* filmé
Filmbesucher *m*	film-goer	spectateur *m*
Filmbildzentrierung *f*	centring of film image	cadrage *m*
Filmdekoration *f*	set	décoration *f* de film *m*
Filmdia *n*	silent colour film	court métrage *m* muet en couleurs *f/pl*
Filmdrehbuch *n*	film script, shooting script	scénario *m*, script *m*
filmen	to film, to shoot a film	filmer, tourner un film *m*
Filmfachmann *m*	film expert	cinéaste *m*
Filmfestspiele *n/pl*	film festivals *pl*	festivals *m/pl* cinématographiques
Filmformat *n*	film size	format *m* de pellicule *f*
Filmgröße *f*	star	vedette *f*
Filmindustrie *f*	film industry	industrie *f* cinématographique
Filmkamera *f*	film camera	caméra *f*
Filmklub *m*	cine club, film society	ciné-club *m*
Filmkopie *f*	film copy	copie *f* du film *m*
Filmkopie *f*, **erste endgültige**	standard film copy	copie *f* standard
Filmkorrektur *f*	correction on film	correction *f* sur film *m*
Filmlänge *f*	footage	métrage *m*
Filmleinwand *f*	screen	écran *m*

Filmlet *n*	filmlet, minute movie, short film	court-métrage *m*
Filmmanuskript *n*	script	scénario *m*
Filmmanuskriptverfasser *m*	script-writer	scénariste *m*
Filmpapier *n*	film paper	papier-film *m*, papier-pellicule *f*
Filmplakat *n*	film poster	affiche *f* de cinéma *m*
Filmproduzent *m*	film producer	cinéaste *m*, producteur *m* de films *m/pl*
Filmrechte *n/pl*	film rights *pl*	droits *m/pl* d'adaptation *f* cinématographique
Filmregisseur *m*	film director, film producer	metteur *m* en scène *f*, réalisateur *m*
Filmrolle *f*	film reel, film roll	rouleau *m* de pellicule *f*
Filmrundschau *f*	film review	chronique *f* cinématographique
Filmsammlung *f*	film library	filmothèque *f*
Filmsatz *m*	film setting	composition *f* sur film *m*
Filmschauspieler *m*	film actor	acteur *m* de cinéma *m*
Filmschauspielerin *f*	film actress	actresse *f* de cinéma *m*
Filmschlußteil *m*, **werbewirksamer**	pay off	partie *f* finale efficace d'un film *m*
Filmschnitt *m*	cut	coupure *f*
Filmsekretärin *f*	script-girl	secrétaire *f* de plateau *m*
Filmsetzgerät *n*	photocomposer, phototype setter	composeuse *f* photographique, photocompeuse *f*
Filmspule *f*	film reel	bobine *f* cinématographique
Filmstar *m*	leading lady, star	vedette *f* de l'écran *m*
Filmstreifen *m*	film strip	bande *f* d'un film *m*
Filmstreifen *m* **ohne Ton** *m*	picture track	bande *f* sans ton *m*
Filmstudio *n*	film studio	studio *m*
Filmtheater- *n* **Kategorien** *f/pl*	categories *pl* of cinema theatres *pl*	catégories *f/pl* de salles *f/pl*
Filmverleih *m*	film distributors *pl*, film lending institute	location *f* de films *m/pl*, maison *f* de distribution *f* de films *m/pl*
Filmvoranzeige *f*	trailer	film *m* annonce *f*
Filmvorführung *f*	film projection	projection *f* de film *m*
Filmvorschau *f*	trailer	film *m* annonce *f*
Filmvorstellung *f*	cinema performance	séance *f* cinématographique
Filmwagen *m*	film car	voiture *f* équitée pour la projection *f* de films *m/pl*
Filmwerbung *f*	cinema advertising, moving picture advertising, screen advertising	publicité *f* à l'écran *m*, publicité *f* cinématographique, publicité *f* par film *m*
Filmwiedergabe *f*	film reproduction	projection *f* en salle *f*
Filmzeitschrift *f*	film magazine	revue *f* de cinéma *m*
Filter *m*	filter	filtre *m*
Filz *m*	felt	feutre *m*
Filzimitation *f*	imitation felt	feutrine *f*
Filzschreiber *m*	felt pen	crayon-feutre *m*, marqueur *m*
Finanzanzeige *f*	financial advertisement	avis *m* financier
Finanzblatt *n*	financial paper	journal *m* financier
Finanzwerbung *f*	financial advertising	publicité *f* financière
Fingerzeig *m*	tip	avis *m*
fingierte Anzeige *f*	dummy advertisement	annonce *f* fictive
Firma *f*	firm	maison *f*

firmenbetonte Werbung *f*	institutional advertising	publicité *f* institutionnelle
Firmenbild *n*	corporate image	image *f* de la firme *f*
Firmeneindruck *m* auf Briefumschlag *m*	corner card	repiquage *m* d'un nom *m* commercial sur l'enveloppe *f*
Firmenname *m*	trade name	appellation *f*
Firmenschild *n*	name plate, signboard	enseigne *f* commerciale
Firmenschild *n* mitFremdreklame *f*	fascia	bandeau *m* de magasin *m*
Firmenschriftzug *m*	logotype	logotype *m*
Firmensiegel *n*	signet	emblème *m* d'entreprise *f*
Firmensignet *n*		
Firmentafel *f*	name plate	buteau *m*, enseigne *f*, panneau *m* d'entreprise *f*
Firmenwerbung *f*	institutional advertising	publicité *f* de prestige *m* pour une société *f*
Firmenwert *m*	good will	valeur *f* commerciale
Firmenzeichen *n*	trade-mark	marque *f* de firme *f*
Firnis *m*	varnish	vernis *m*
Fisch (typog) *m*	wrong fount, wrong letter	coquille *f*, mastic *m*
Fixativ *n*	fixative	fixatif *m*
Fixierung *f* von Film *m* -Aufbau *m* und -Ablauf *m*	treatment	fixation *f* de composition *f* et de déroulement *m* d'un film *m*
Fixum *n*	fixed salary	salaire *m* fixe
Flachdruck *m*	flat-bed printing, level printing, planography, straight printing	impression *f* à plat, impression *f* planographique
flachgeätzte Autotypie *f*	shallow half-tone	simili *m* manquant de creux *m*
Flachheftung *f*	flat stitching	couture *f* à plat
Fläche *f*	area, surface	surface *f*
Flächengesteller *m*	owner of site	propriétaire *m* d'emplacement *m*
Flächen *f/pl*, bemalte	painted surfaces *pl*	surfaces *f/pl* peintes
Flächenstichprobe *f*	area sampling	échantillonnage *m* par zone *f*
Flaschenkapsel *f*	crowner	capsule *f* de bouteille *f*, surmontoir *m*
Flattermarke *f*	collation mark	indice *m* de collationnement *m*
Flattersatz *m*	unjustified matter	composition *f* en drapeau *m*
Flausen *f/pl*	blah-blah	bla-bla-bla *m*
Flaute *f*	dullness, flatness	accalmie *f*, période *f* creuse
Fleck *m*	blur, speck	macule *f*, tache *f*
Fleckenbildung *f*	spotting	formation *f* de taches *f/pl*
Fleisch *n* eines Buchstabens *m*	beard, bevelled feet *pl*, blank space, burr	blanc *m*, épaulement *m*, espace *m* vierge *f*, talus *m* de pied *m*
flexibles Taschenbuch *n*	paperback	flexible livre *m* de poche *f*
Flexodruck *m*	flexographic printing	impression *f* flexographique
Flickwerk *n*	patchwork	rapiéçage *m*
Flickwort *n*	expletive, padding	cheville *f*
fliegender Händler *m*	hawker, itinerant salesman	colporteur *m*, marchand *m* ambulant, marchand *m* forain
Fliegenkopf *m/typog*	turned letter	blocage *m*, lettre *f* bloquée
Fließsatz *m*	solid matter, undisplay	composition *f* courante, composition *f* en placards *m/pl*, texte *m* plein
Floskel *f*	flourish	fleur *f* de rhétorique *f*
Flüchtigkeit *f*	fugacity	fugacité *f*

Flüsterpropaganda *f*	whispering campaign	chuchoterie *f*, publicité *f* orale
Flugblatt *n*	handbill, leaflet, pamphlet	brochure *f*, feuillet *m*, tract *m*
Flughafenwerbung *f*	airport advertising	publicité *f* dans les aéroports *m/pl*
Fluglinienzeitschrift *f*	inflight magazine	revue *f* pour les passagers *m/pl*
Flugpostbrief *m*	airmail letter	lettre *f* aérienne
Flugpostpapier *n*	airmail paper	papier *m* -pelure *f*
Flugreisewerbung *f*	airline advertising	publicité *f* pour les voyages *m/pl* d'avion *m*
Flugschrift *f*	chap-book, leaflet, pamphlet, tract	brochure *f*, tract *m*
Flugzettel *m*	handbill, throw-away	tract *m*
Flugzeugwerbung *f*	aeroplane advertising	publicité *f* par avion *m*
Fluoreszenzfarbe *f*	fluorescence colour	couleur *f* fluorescente
fluoreszierend	fluorescent	fluorescent
Flutlicht *n*	floodlight	lampe *f* survoltée, lumière *f* d'ambiance *f*, lumière *f* d'arrosage *m*
Förderer *m*	sponsor	parrain *m*
Förderung *f*	promotion	promotion *f*
Folie *f*	foil	feuille *f*, pellicule *f*
Folioformat *n*	in-folio	in-folio
Fondpapier *n*	blanking paper	papier *m* de fond *m*
Form *f*	form	forme *f*
Form *f* **schließen**	to close the form, to lock up a form	boucler une page *f*, serrer une forme *f*
Format *n*	dimensions *pl*, format	dimensions *f/pl*, format *m*
Format *n* **der Anschlagstellen** *f/pl*	metric volume	métrage *m*
Format *n*, **handliches**	handy size	format *m* facile à manier
Format *n*, **mittleres**	medium-size	de moyen format *m*
Format *n*, **ungewöhnliches**	unusual size	format *m* bâtard *m*
Formatänderung *f*	change of measure, change of size, rescale, scaling	changement *m* de format *m*, modification *f* de format *m*
Formatsteg *m*	furniture	garniture *f*
Formblatt *n*	form	formule *f*
Formgeber *m*	industrial designer	dessinateur *m* industriel
Formgebung *f*	industrial design	esthétique *f* industrielle, façonnage *m*, forme *f* industrielle
Formgefühl *n*	feeling for form	sens *m* des formes *f/pl*
Formgestalter *m*	designer, stylist	dessinateur *m* industriel, styliste *m*
Formgestaltung *f*	fashioning, industrial design, shaping, styling	création *f* de la forme *f*, esthétique *f* industrielle
Formstreifen *m* **im Papier** *n*	wire-mark	vergeure *f* du papier *m*
Formular *n*	blank form	formulaire *m*
Formulierung *f*	formulation	formulation *f*, mise *f* en forme *f*
Formulierung *f* **eines Textes** *m*	sub-editing	cuisine *f* d'un texte *m*
forschen	to investigate	faire des recherches *f/pl*
Forscher *m*	investigator, researcher	chercheur *m*
Forschung *f*	research	recherches *f/pl*
Forschungsarbeit *f*	desk research	recherche *f* documentaire
Fortdruck *m*	production run, running-on	impression *f* du tirage *m*, tiré à part *f*
fortdrucken	to run on	rouler
fortlaufender Text *m*	running text	corps *m* du texte *m*

fortschrittlich	advanced, go-ahead, progressive	avant-garde f, progressiste
fortschrittliche Werbung f	progressive advertising	publicité f moderne
fortsetzen, auf einer anderen Seite f	to run over	décrocher
Fortsetzung f	continuation	suite f
Fortsetzung f **folgt**	more to come, to be continued	à suivre, complément de texte m suivra
Fortsetzungsanzeige f	following on	annonce f de continuation f
Fortsetzungsfilm m	serial film	film m à épisodes f/pl
Fortsetzungsroman m	novel in continuations pl, serial story	roman-feuilleton m, roman m à suites f/pl
Forum n	forum	séance f de discussion f
Foto n	photograph	photo(graphie) f
Foto n **in dunklen Tönen** m/pl	low key	photo f en tons m/pl obscurs
Foto n **in hellen Tönen** m/pl	high key	photo f en tons m/pl clairs
Foto n**, unscharfes**	high key	photo f flou
Fotoabzug m	master print, photographic print	épreuve f de photo f
Fotoapparat m	camera	appareil m cinématographique
Fotoarchiv n	art library	archives f/pl photographiques
Fotochrom n	photochrome	photochromie f
Fotodruck m	collotype	phototypie f
fotogen	photogenic	photogénique
Fotograf m	photographer	photographe m
Fotografie f	photograph, photography	photographie f
fotografieren	to photograph	faire de la photo f, photographier
fotografische Abteilung f	art department	service m photographique
fotografische Aufnahme f	shot, taking of photographs pl	photographie f, prise f de vue f
fotografisches Papier n	photo paper	papier m à prise f de vue f
Fotogravur f	photogravure	photogravure f
Fotojournalismus m	photo journalism	photojournalisme m
Fotokolorierung f	colour toning	coloration f photographique
Fotokopie f	blue print, photo print, photostatic copy	copie f héliographique, photocopie f
Fotokopiergerät n	photo copier, photo copying machine, photostat	appareil m à photocopier, presse f à photocopier
Fotolithografie f	photo-lithography	photolithographie f
fotomechanisch	photomechanical	photomécanique
fotomechanischer Druck m	photo-typography	photo-typographie f
Fotomodell n	photographer's model	mannequin m, modèle m d'un photographe m
Fotomodell n **auf der Titelseite** f	cover girl	cover-girl f
Fotomodell n**, männliches**	dressman	mannequin m mâle
Fotomontage f	photo montage, photocomposition, stripping	composition f photographique, montage m photographique, photomontage m
Fotopapier n	film paper	papier-film m, papier-pellicule f, papier m photographique
Fotoplakat n	photo poster	affiche f photographique
Fotoredakteur m	art editor	chef m du service m photographique
Fotoreportage f	photographic report, picture story	reportage m photographique
Fotosatz m	photo(graphic) composition	composition f photographique, phototypie f

Fotosetzerei *f*	phototypesetting room	service *m* photocomposition
Fotosetzmaschine *f*	photocomposing machine, phototype setter	photocompeuse *f*
Fotosetzverfahren *n*	photo lettering	composition *f* photographique
Fotothek *f*	photographic library	photothèque *f*
Fototiefdruck *m*	photogravure, rotogravure *f*	héliogravure *f*, rotogravure *f*
Fotounterlage *f*	photographic record	matériel *m* photographique
Fräsapparat *m*	router	fraiseuse *f*
fräsen	to mill, to rout	fraiser
Frage *f*	query, question	interrogation *f*, question *f*
Fragebogen *m*	question form, questionnaire	questionnaire *m*
Fragezeichen *n*	interrogation point (am) , question mark	point *m* d'interrogation *f*
Fragment *n*	fragment	fragment *m*
Fraktur *f*	black letter, German type, Gothic type	caractères *m/pl* allemands, caractères *m/pl* gothiques, fracture *f*
Franchising *n*	franchising system	attribution *f* d'une licence *f*
Frankiermaschine *f*	franking machine	machine *f* à affranchir
Frankierung *f*	franking	affranchissement *m*
Frauenbeilage *f*	ladies' *pl* supplement	supplément *m* pour les dames *f/pl*
Frauenblatt *n*	women's *pl* magazine	revue *f* féminine
Frauenseite *f*	women's topics *pl*	page *f* de la femme *f*
Frauenzeitschrift *f*	women's *pl* magazine	revue *f* féminine
Freiaushang *m*	free posting	affichage *m* gracieux
freiberuflicher Mitarbeiter *m*	free lance contributor	collaborateur *m* à son compte *m*, collaborateur *m* extérieur, collaborateur *m* libre
freibleibender Auftrag *m*	order without obligation	ordre *m* sans engagement *m*
freibleibendes Angebot *n*	offer without obligation	offre *f* sans engagement *m*
freie Aussprache *f*	open forum	point *m* de vue *f* des lecteurs *m/pl*, tribune *f* libre
freier Grafiker *m*	free lance artist	dessinateur *m* libre
freier Journalist *m*	free lance reporter	journaliste *m* indépendant, pigiste *m*
freier Korrespondent *m*	stringer	correspondant *m* qui n'appartient pas à la rédaction *f*
freier künstlerischer Mitarbeiter *m*	outside artist	collaborateur *m* artistique à son compte *m*
freier Lokalberichterstatter *m*	free lance reporter	stringer *m*
freier Raum *m*	blank space	espace *m* blanc, espace *m* vierge *f*
freier Werbeberater *m*	advertising consultant	conseil *m* en publicité *f* libre
Freiexemplar *n*	complimentary copy, free copy, specimen copy	exemplaire *m* gratuit, spécimen *m*
Freigabe *f*	handout, release	disposition *f*, transmission *f* à la presse *f*
freistehende Autotypie *f*	blocked-out half-tone, outline half-tone, silhouette half-tone	autotypie *f* en silhouette *f*, simili *m* détouré
freistehendes Klischee *n*	cut-out block, outlined cut	cliché *m* détouré, cliché *m* isolé
freistellen	to drop out, to silhouette	détourer, silhouetter
Freistempelung *f*	pre-franked stamp	timbre *m* pré-oblitéré
Freiumschlag *m*	stamped envelope	enveloppe *f* timbrée

Freizeitbereichswerbung *f*	leisure time publicity	publicité *f* du domaine *m* des loisirs *m*/*pl*
Fremdenverkehrsplakat *n*	tourist poster	affiche *f* touristique
Fremdenverkehrswerbung *f*	holiday resorts *pl* advertising, tourism advertising, tourist publicity	publicité *f* de tourisme *m*, publicité *f* de villégiature *f*
Fremdsprachensatz *m*	setting in foreign language	composition *f* en langue *f* étrangère
fremdsprachliche Werbung *f*	advertising in foreign language	publicité *f* en langue *f* étrangère
Fremdwort *n*	foreign word	mot *m* étranger
Frequenz *f*	frequency	fréquence *f*
frisch bedruckt	wet print	impression *f* fraîche
Froschperspektive *f*	worm's eye – view	contre-plongée *f*
frühere Ausgaben *f*/*pl*	back copies *pl*	exemplaires *m*/*pl* précédents
Frühjahrsmesse *f*	spring fair	foire *f* de printemps *m*
Führungsschicht *f*	upper class	les gens *pl* du monde *m*
Füllanzeige *f*	filler, plugger ad, stop gap advertisement	annonce *f* bouche-trou *m*
Füller *m*	cushion, fill-up, filler, quadder	annonce *f* d'opportunité *f*, bouche-trou *m*, remplissage *m*
Füllfederhalter *m*	fountain-pen	stylo *m*
Füllmaterial *n*	clumps *pl*, leads *pl*	blancs *m*/*pl*
Füßchen *n*/*typog*	serif	empattement *m*
full-service-Agentur *f*	agency with full service	agence *f* à service *m* complet
Fundament *n* (Schließplatte *f*)	bed	marbre *m*
Fundgrube *f*	godsend, lucky find	trouvaille *f*
Funkprogramm *n*	radio programme *brit*, radio program *am*	calendrier *m* des émissions *f*/*pl*
Funksprechgerät *n*, **tragbares**	walkie-talkie	mobilophone *m*, poste *m* de radio *f* portatif
Funktionen *f*/*pl* **der Werbung** *f*	advertising functions *pl*	fonctions *f*/*pl* de la publicité *f*
Funkübertragung *f*	radiocommunication	radiocommunication *f*
Funkwerbung *f*	broadcast advertising, radio advertising	publicité *f* radiophonique
Funkwerbung *f*, **integrierte**	straight commercial	émission *f* publicitaire intégrée
Fusionierung *f*	fusion, merger	fusion *f*
Fusionsbestrebungen *f*/*pl*	merger movement	tendances *f*/*pl* de fusion *f*
Fuß *m*	foot, tail	marge *f* de pied *m*
Fuß *m* **einer Seite** *f*, **am**	bottom of page, foot of page	bas *m* de page *f*, pied *m* de page *f*
Fußballplatz *m*	football ground	terrain *m* de football *m*
Fussel *m*	fuzz	peluches *f*/*pl*
fusselnd	fluffy	peluché
Fußlinie *f*	foot rule	filet *m* de pied *m*
Fußnote *f*	footnote	note *f* au bas *m* de la page *f*, note *f* courante, note *f* de pied *m*
Fußsteg *m*	footstick	blanc *m* de pied *m*
Fußzeile *f*	bottom line, foot rule	ligne *f* de pied *m*

G

Galvano *n*	electro *am*, electrotype	galvano *m*, galvanotype *m*
Galvanoplastik *f*	electrotyping	galvanoplastie *f*
Galvanotechnik *f*	galvanotechnics *pl*	technique *f* galvanoplastique

Gangschild n	corridor panel, corridor site	emplacement m couloir m
ganze Seite f	full page	page f entière
ganzseitige Anzeige f	full-page ad, spread	annonce f d'une page f entière
ganzseitiges Bild n	full-page illustration	hors-texte m
Ganzstelle f	solus site	emplacement m isolé
Garantie f	guarantee, warranty	garantie f
Garantiefrist f	guarantee period	période f de garantie f
Garantieprovision f	underwriting commission	commission f de garantie f
garantieren	to guarantee	garantir
garantierte Mindestauflage f	guaranted minimum circulation	tirage m minimum m garanti
Garmond f (siehe Anhang)	long primer (see appendix)	corps m 10 points m/pl (voir appendice)
geballte Werbung f	mass advertising	campagne f de saturation f
Gebiet n	geographical sector	région f, secteur m géographique, territoire m
gebilligter Preis m	approved price	prix m approuvé
Gebrauchsanweisung f	directions pl for use, instruction booklet	mode m d'emploi m
Gebrauchsgrafik f	advertising art, applied art, commercial art	art m publicitaire, graphisme m publicitaire, publicité f artistique
Gebrauchsgrafiker m	commercial artist, designer	dessinateur m en publicité f
Gebrauchsgüter n/pl, **langlebige**	hard goods pl	biens m/pl de consommation f durables
Gebrauchsmuster n	industrial design	modèle m d'utilité f
Gebrauchsmusterschutz m	protection of registered design	protection f des modèles m/pl et dessins m/pl
Gebrauchtwarenmarkt m	second hand market	brocantage m, commerce m d'objets m/pl d'occasion f
Gebühr f	fee	honoraires m/pl
gebundener Preis m	controlled price, fixed selling price	prix m fixe, prix m imposé
Geburtsanzeige f	announcement of birth	faire-part m de naissance f
Gedächtnishilfe f	memory aid, recall aid	moyen m mnémotechnique
Gedächtnisprüfung f	recall test	test m de souvenir m aidé
Gedächtnisstütze f	aided recall	souvenir m aidé
Gedankenaustausch m	exchange of thoughts pl	échange m d'idées f/pl
Gedankenfreiheit f	freedom of thought	liberté f de la pensée f
Gedankengang m	train of thought	suite f des idées f/pl
Gedankenstrich m	dash, em-rule	tiret m
Gedankenübertragung f	telepathy	télépathie f
gedrängte Darstellung f	digest, pemmican style	présentation f condensée
gedruckten Medien m/pl, **Werbung** f **in**	print advertising	publicité f dans des médias m/pl imprimés
gefalzt	folded	plié
gefräst	routed	fraisé
Gefühlsansprache f	human appeal	valeur f affective
gefühlsbetonte Werbung f	emotional advertising	publicité f émotive
Gefühlssphäre f	emotional atmosphere	sphère f d'affectivité f
Gegebenheiten f/pl	data pl	données f/pl
Gegenantwort f	replication	réplique f
Gegendarstellung f	counterstatement	contre-déclaration f
Gegenentwurf m	counter-project	contre-projet m
Gegengeschäft n	barter	affaire f en échange m, contre-affaire f, troc m

gegenkaschiert	laminated on the back	plastifié sur le dos *m*
Gegenstand *m*	subject	sujet *m*
gegenüber der ersten	facing first editorial page	face *f* première de texte *m*
Textseite *f*		
gegenüber der letzten	facing last editorial page	face *f* dernière de texte *m*
Textseite *f*		
gegenüber Inhaltsverzeichnis *n*	facing contents *pl*	face *f* sommaire *m*
gegenüber Leitartikel *m*	facing leader	face *f* éditorial *m*
gegenüber redaktionellem	facing editorial matter	face *f* texte *m* rédactionnel
Teil *m*		
gegenüber Text *m*	against text, facing text, next to	contre texte *m*, face *f* texte *m*
	editorial matter, opposite text	
gegenüberliegende Seite *f*	opposite page	ci-contre
Gegenvorschlag *m*	counter-proposition	contreproposition *f*
gegenwärtig laufende	current advertising	publicité *f* courante
Werbekampagne *f*		
gegenwärtige Ereignisse *n/pl*	current happenings *pl*	événements *m/pl* en cours *m*
geglättetes Papier *n*	calendered paper, glazed paper	papier *m* calandré, papier *m*
		satiné
gegründet	established	fondé
geheftet	stitched	broché
geheftetes Buch *n*	sewn book	livre *m* broché
Geheimbotschaft *f*	cipher message	message *m* chiffré
geheime Verführer *m/pl*	hidden persuaders *pl*	séducteurs *m/pl* clandestins
geheimhalten	to keep secret	tenir secret
Geheimmikrophon *n*	bug	mouchard *m*
Geheimniskrämer *m*	mystery-monger	cachottier *m*
Geheimschrift *f*	cipher	écriture *f* secrète
Geheimsender *m*	clandestine radio transmitter	émetteur *m* clandestin
Gehirntrust *m*	brain trust	brain-trust *m*
Gehirnwäsche *f*	brain washing	lavage *m* de cerveau *f*,
		lavage *m* de crâne *m*
Gehrung *f*	bevel	onglet *m*
Gehweg *m*	footpath	trottoir *m*
Geisterbild *n*	double image, phantom	fantôme *m*, image *f* spectre
Geisterzeitung *f*	bogus publication	journal *m* fantôme, journal *m*
		trompeur
Geistesblitz *m*	brain-wave	saillie *f*
Geisteshaltung *f*	mentality	mentalité *f*
Geistesverwandtschaft *f*	congeniality	affinité *f* intellectuelle
geistige Elite *f*	intelligentsia	élite *f* intellectuelle
geistiges Eigentum *n*	intellectual property	propriété *f* intellectuelle
gekabelte Nachrichten *f/pl*	overhead	nouvelles *f/pl* câblées
gekörntes Papier *n*	grained paper	papier *m* grainé, papier *m*
		granulé
gekoppelter Tarif *m*	coupled rate	tarif *m* couplé
Gekritzel *n*	scrawl	griffonnage *m*
gekünstelt	over-elaborate	tarabiscoté
gekürzte Fassung *f*	cut version	version *f* abrégée
gelbe Seiten *f/pl*	yellow pages *pl*	pages *f/pl* jaunes
Gelegenheitsanzeige *f*	classified advertisement	petite annonce *f*
Gelegenheitsauftrag *m*	casual order	ordre *m* occasionnel
Gelegenheitskauf *m*	bargain	achat *m* occasionnel, occasion *f*
Gelegenheitskunde *m*	casual costumer, chance	client *m* de passage *m*, client *m*
	costumer, stray costumer	occasionnel
Gelegenheitsleser *m*	casual reader, occasional reader	lecteur *m* occasionnel

Gelegenheitspublikation f	occasional publication	publication f occasionnelle
Gelegenheitswerbung f	opportunity advertising	publicité f d'opportunité f
gelegentlicher Beitrag m	casual contribution	contribution f fortuite
gelegentlicher Mitarbeiter m	casual contributor, guest writer, string-correspondent	collaborateur m occasionnel, collaborateur m part-time
geleimtes Papier n	sized paper	papier m collé
gemalte Anschlagfläche f	painted display	panneau m peint
gemalte Außenwerbung f	painted displays pl	affiches f/pl peintes, panneaux m/pl peints
gemalte Großfläche f	bulletin board, painted bulletin	bulletin m
gemaltes Plakat n	painted placard	affiche f peinte
gemasertes Papier n	grained paper	papier m grainé, papier m granulé
Gemeindewerbung f	community advertising	publicité f communale
gemeine Buchstaben m/pl	lower case letters pl	lettres f/pl bas-de-casse f
gemeinnützige Plakatierung f	public service posters pl	affiches f/pl pour le service m public
Gemeinplatz m	commonplace, platitude	banalité f, lieu m commun
gemeinsamer Markt m	common market	marché m commun
Gemeinschaftsarbeit f	cooperative work, team-work	collaboration f, travail m en équipe f
Gemeinschaftswerbung f	collective advertising, cooperative advertising brit, group advertising, joint advertising	publicité f collective, publicité f en commun
gemischter Satz m	mixed matter, mixture	composition f lardée, composition f mêlée
genau nach Vorlage f **setzen**	to follow copy	composer fidèle au modèle m
genehmigte Werbemittel n/pl	appropriation of advertising	budget m publicitaire
genehmigter Preis m	approved price	prix m approuvé
Genehmigung f	consent	consentement m
Genehmigungsgebühr f	license fee	droit m de voirie f
Generalanzeigerpresse f	information press	presse f d'information f
Generaldirektor m	chairman	directeur m en chef f
genormte Größe f	basic size	format m standard m
Gepäckhalter m	luggage-rack	porte-bagages m/pl
geprägt	embossed	gaufré
geprägtes Papier n	embossed paper	papier m gaufré
gepunkteter Rand m	dotted frame, stippled frame	cadre m de pointillés m/pl
gequirlter Satz m	broken matter	pâté m, soleil m
gerade Seite f	even page	page f paire
gerade Zahl f	even number	nombre m pair
Gerät n **für Filme** m/pl **in Kassettenform** f	video-tape recorder	magnétoscope m
Gerät n **zur Aufzeichnung** f **von Fernsehsendungen** f/pl	video recorder	magnétoscope m
Gerät n **zur Messung** f **der Zuschauerbeteiligung** f	tamalyzer	appareil m pour tester la participation f des vidéo-spectateurs m/pl
Gerät n **zur Zuschauerforschung** f	video meter	appareil m pour l'étude f des spectateurs m/pl
Geräte n/pl, **audiovisuelle**	audio-visual equipment	appareils m/pl audio-visuels
Geräuscheffekte m/pl	sound effects pl	bruitage m
gerasteter Rahmen m	backed frame, shaded frame	cadre m de filets m/pl gras-maigre
gerichtliche Anzeige f	legal notice	annonce f judiciaire
Gerichtsstand m	competent court	for m, tribunal m

geringwertiger Werbeartikel *m*	gadget	élément *m* publicitaire de peu de valeur *f*
geripptes Papier *n*	laid paper	papier *m* vergé
Gerücht *n*	rumour	bruit *m*, on dit
Gerüchte *n/pl*, umlaufende	current reports *pl*	bruits *m/pl* qui courent
gesättigter Markt *m*	glutted market	marché *m* encombré
Gesamtabschluß *m*	blanked contract	ensemble *m* des contrats *m/pl*, ensemble *m* des ordres *m/pl*
Gesamtauflage *f*	total circulation, total print run	tirage *m* global, tirage *m* total
Gesamtausgabe *f*	all the issues *pl*	édition *f* complète, toutes les éditions *f/pl*
Gesamtbudget *n*	billing	chiffre *m* d'affaires *f/pl* total
Gesamtgestaltung *f*	total configuration	création *f* d'ensemble
Gesamtherstellung *f*	total production	fabrication *f* totale
Gesamtinhalt *m* einer Anzeige *f*	lineage of an advertisement	lignage *m* d'une annonce *f*
Gesamtpublikum *n*	audience flow	audience *f* totale
Gesamtzahl *f* der Hörer *m/pl*	cumulative audience	audience *f* cumulative
Geschäftsabschlüsse *m/pl*	dealings *pl*	affaires *f/pl* conclues
Geschäftsanzeige *f*	business advertisement with regular basic rate, commercial advertisement	annonce *f* commerciale
Geschäftsaufschwung *m*	boom	hausse *f* rapide
Geschäftsbedingungen *f/pl*	business conditions *pl*, conditions *pl* of trading	conditions *f/pl* commerciales
Geschäftsbuch *n*	ledger	livre *m* de commerce *m*
Geschäftsdrucksachen *f/pl*	commercial stationery	imprimés *m/pl* commerciaux
geschäftsführender Redakteur *m*	managing editor	rédacteur *m* gérant
Geschäftsführer *m*	business manager, director	chef *m* d'entreprise *f*, directeur *m* administratif, gérant *m*, gestionnaire *m*
Geschäftsführung *f*	management	gérance *f*, gestion *f*, manutention *f*
Geschäftsgang *m*	trend of business	marche *f* des affaires *f/pl*
Geschäftsgeheimnis *n*	trade secret	secret *m* commercial
Geschäftsmann *m*	business man	homme *m* d'affaires *f/pl*
Geschäftsstelle *f*	administrative, office	agence *f*, bureau *m*
Geschäftsstunden *f/pl*	store hours *pl*	heures *f/pl* d'ouverture *f*
Geschäftswert *m*	goodwill	valeur *f* commerciale
Geschäftszentrum *n*	business centre	centre *m* commercial
Geschenkabonnement *n*	gift subscription	abonnement *m* cadeau *m*
Geschenkartikel *m*	give-away, novelty	article *m* -cadeau *m*, article *m* prime *f*
Geschenkband *m*	presentation copy	livre-cadeau *m*
Geschenkpackung *f*	gift wrapping	boîte *f* pour cadeaux *m/pl*
Geschenkpackungsdienst *m*	gift parcel services *pl*, parcel distribution service	services *m/pl* de l'empaquetage *m* des présents *m/pl*
Geschichte *f*	story	affaire *f*, conte *f*
Geschichte *f* erfinden, eine	to fake up a story	inventer une histoire *f*
geschlossene Ortschaft *f*	built up area	agglomération *f*
geschlossene Satzform *f*	locked-up form	forme *f* serrée
Geschmack *m*	taste	goût *m*
Geschmacklosigkeit *f*	bad taste	mauvais goût *m*
Geschmackstest *m*	solo test	test *m* monadique
Geschmackswandel *m*	change in taste	changement *m* du goût *m* du consommateur *m*

geschöpftes Papier *n*	hand-made paper	papier *m* de cuve *f*
Geschwätz *n*	balderdash	baratin *m*, bêtises *f/pl*
Geschwätz *n*, leeres	bunkum, hokum	boniments *m/pl*, paroles *f/pl* vides
Geselle *m*	journeyman	compagnon *m*
Gesellschaft *f*	society	société *f*
Gesellschaftschronik *f*	society news	carnet *m* mondain
Gesellschaftsklatsch *m*	social gossip, society item, society news	mondanités *f/pl*, nouvelles *f/pl* à la main *f*, potin *m* mondain
gesetzliche Beschränkungen *f/pl*	legal restrictions *pl*	restrictions *f/pl* légales
Gesichtskreis *m*	mental horizon	horizon *m*
Gesichtspunkt *m*	aspect, point of view	point *m* de vue *f*
Gesichtspunkt *m*, werblicher	advertising angle	angle *m* d'approche *f* publicitaire
Gesinnungslump *m*	opportunist	opportuniste *m*
Gesinnungspresse *f*	opinion press	presse *f* d'opinion *f*
gesperrt *typog*	spaced	espacé
gesperrte Zeit *f* (für Werbesendungen)	block-out	durée *f* du blocage *m*
gespickter Satz *m*	interlarded composition	composition *f* lardée
Gespräch *n*	conversation	conversation *f*
Gespräch *n* am runden Tisch	round-table discussion	réunion *f* paritaire, table *f* ronde
Gesprächspartner *m*	interlocutor	correspondant *m*, interlocuteur *m*
Gesprächspunkte *m/pl*	talking points *pl*	argumentation *f*
Gespür *n*	nose	flair *m*
gestaffelter Preis *m*	differential price, graduated price	prix *m* échelonné, tarif *m* mobile
gestalten	to shape, to visualize	façonner, former, visualiser
Gestalter *m*	creative artist, designer, draughtsman, visualizer	artiste *m* -créateur *m*, dessinateur *m* -concepteur *m*, maquettiste *m*
Gestaltung *f*	creative work, design, visualizing	création *f*, dessin *m*, maquette *f*
Gestaltung *f*, grafische	graphic arrangement	conception *f* graphique
Gestaltungsleiter *m*	art director, creative director	chef *m* du service *m* création *f*, directeur *m* artistique
Gestaltungsmittel *m/pl*	art work	moyens *m/pl* de réalisation *f*
Gestell *n*	trestle	chevalet *m*
gestreiftes Papier *n*	laid paper	papier *m* vergé
gestrichenes Papier *n*	coated paper, glazed paper	papier *m* couché, papier *m* glacé
gestürzter Buchstabe *m*	kerned letter	caractère *m* couché, lettre *f* crénée
gesunder Menschenverstand *m*	common sense	sens *m* commun
getarnte Anzeige *f*	veiled advertisement	annonce *f* déguisée
getarnte Publizistik *f*	camouflage	camouflage *m*
geteilte Provision *f*	split commission	commission *f* partagée
getilgte Stelle *f*	obliterated passage	caviar *m*
getönt	coloured, tinted	teinté
getönte Federzeichnung *f*	wash drawing	dessin *m* au lavis *m*
getöntes Papier *n*	coloured paper	papier *m* de couleur *f*
Getränkewerbung *f*	beverage advertising	publicité *f* des boissons *f/pl*
Geviert *n*	em-quad	cadratin *m*
Gewährsmann *m*	informant	informateur *m*

Gewalt *f*, höhere	absolute necessity, act of providence	force *f* majeure
gewelltes Papier *n*	corrugated paper	papier *m* ondulé
Gewerbe *n*	craft, trade	artisanat *m*, métier *m*
Gewerkschaftszeitung *f*	trade-union paper	revue *f* syndicale
gewichten	to weight	pondérer
Gewinn *m*	gain, profit	bénéfice *m*, profit *m*
Gewinnanteil *m*	quota of profits *pl*	tantième *f*
gewinnbringend	profitable	lucratif, profitable
Gewinnschwelle *f*	break-even point	point *m* mort, seuil *m* de la rentabilité *f*
gewöhnliche Plazierung *f*	run-of-paper position	emplacement *m* ordinaire
Gewohnheit *f*	habit	habitude *f*
gewußt, wie	know how	savoir faire
gezeichnete Schrift *f*	handlettering	repoussage *m*
gezeichneter Artikel *m*	bylined story	article *m* signé
gezielte Werbung *f*	selective advertising	publicité *f* sélective
Giebelwerbung *f*	gable publicity, wall publicity	pignon *m* publicitaire, publicité *f* murale
Gießbach *m*	gutter	rue *f*
Gießer *m*	type founder	fondeur *m* de caractères *m/pl*
Gießerei *f*	foundry	fonderie *f*
Gießform *f*	mould	moule *m*
Gießmaschine *f*	casting machine	machine *f* à fondre
Gießmetall *n*	foundry metal	alliage *m* d'imprimerie *f*
Gießwerk *n*	casting mechanism	fondeuse *f*
Glacépapier *m*	glossy paper	papier *m* glacé
Glätte *f*	smoothness	satiné *m*
Glanz *m*, einseitig	machine glazed (M.G.)	frictionné
Glanzfarbe *f*	glossy colour	couleur *f* de lustre *m*
Glanzfolie *f*	glossy foil	pellicule *f* brillante
Glanzfolienkaschierung *f*	lamination	plastification *f*
Glanzpapier *n*	calendered paper, flint paper, glaced paper	papier *m* calandré, papier *m* lissé, papier *m* satiné
Glanzpunkt *m*	high lights *pl*	événement *m* saillant
Glasschild *n*	glass sign	enseigne *f* en verre *m*
glatter Satz *m*	solid matter, straight matter, undisplay	composition *f* courante
Glaubhaftigkeit *f*	believability	croyabilité *f*
Glaubwürdigkeit *f*	credibility	crédibilité *f*
gleichbleibender Text *m*	same text	texte *m* même
gleichbleibendes Vorstellungsbild *n*	stereotype	cliché *m*
gleicher Markenname *m* für verschiedene Produkte *m/pl*	brand-umbrella	le même nom *m* pour des produits *m/pl* différents
Gleichförmigkeit *f*	uniformity	uniformité *f*
Gleichgewicht *n*	balance	équilibre *m*
Gleichschaltung *f*	bringing into line, equalization	mise *f* au pas *m*
gleichzeitig	concurrent	simultané
gleichzeitige Ton- und Bildband *n* -Vorführung *f*	simultaneous projection of recording tape and image	double-bande *f*
Glossar *n*	glossary	glossaire *m*
Glosse *f*	gloss	glose *f*
Glückwunschdienst *m*	congratulation service	services *m/pl* de la remise *f* de félicitation *f*
Glückwunschkarte *f*	congratulary card, greeting card	carte *f* de vœux *m/pl*
Goldbuchstabe *m*	gilt-letter	lettre *f* d'or *m*

goldener Schnitt *m*	medial section, sectio aurea	sectio *m* aurea
Goldprägung *f*	gold blocking	empreinte *f* dorée
Goldschnitt *m*	gilt edge	tranche *f* d'or *m*
Goodwillwerbung *f*	prestige advertising	publicité *f* de prestige *m*
gotische Schrift *f*	Gothic type, old black type, old English face	caractères *m/pl* gothiques
Grafik *f*	graphics *pl*	graphique *m*
Grafik-Designer *m*	commercial artist, designer	dessinateur *m*
Grafiker *m*	artist	graphiste *m*
Grafiker *m*, freier	freelance artist	dessinateur *m* libre
grafische Darstellung *f*	chart, graphic, graphical representation	diagramme *m*, représentation *f* graphique
grafische Gestaltung *f*	graphic arrangement	conception *f* graphique
granieren	to grain, to stipple	grainer
graniertes Papier *n*	grained paper	papier *m* grainé
gratis	free of charge, gratis	gratuit
Gratisabonnement *n*	free subscription	abonnement *m* gratuit
Gratisangebot *n*	free deal	offre *f* gratuite
Gratisanzeige *f*	free advertisement	insertion *f* gratuite
Gratisblatt *n*	free publication, giveaway	périodique *m* gratuit, publication *f* gratuite
Gratisexemplar *n*	presentation copy, specimen copy	service *m* de presse *f*
Gratiskostprobe *f*	sampling by taste	dégustation *f* gratuite
Gratismuster *n*	free sample	échantillon *m* gratuit
Gratisplakataushang *m*	free posting	affichage *m* gracieux
Gratisprobe *f*	free trial	échantillon *m* gratuit
Gratiszustellung *f*	free delivery	envoi *m* gratuit
grauer Markt	grey market	marché *m* gris
Graupappe *f*	grey paste board	carton *m* gris
Grauskala *f*	grey scale	échelle *f* des gris
Grautöne *m/pl*	grey tints *pl*	teintes *f/pl* grises
gravieren	to engrave	graver
Graviermaschine *f*	engraving machine	machine *f* à graver
Gravierung *f*	engraving	gravure *f*
Gravur *f*	engraved plate	gravure *f*
Greiferkante *f*	gripper edge	bord *m* des pinces *f/pl*
grellfarbiges Plakat *n*	glaring poster, sreaming poster	affiche *f* criarde
Greuelmärchen *n*	atrocity story	atrocités *f/pl* inventées
Griffregister *n*	thumb-index	répertoire *m* encoché
grober Raster *m*	coarse screen	grosse trame *f*
grober Schnitzer *m*	howler	faute *f* énorme
Größe *f*	size	dimensions *f/pl*, format *m*, grandeur *f*
Größe *f* einer Seite *f*	page size	surface *f* de la page *f*
Größe *f*, genormte	basic size	format *m* standard *m*
Größenklasse *f*	category of magnitude	catégorie *f* d'importance *f*
Größenverhältnis *n*	proportionality	rapports *m/pl* de grandeur *f*
Groschenheft *n*	pulp magazine	revue *f* à deux sous *m/pl*, revue *f* de concierge *f*
Groschenroman *m*	dime novel	roman *m* bon marché *m*
Großanzeige *f*	display advertisement	grande annonce *f*
Großaufnahme *f*	close-up, full screen	gros plan *m*, plan *m* serré, vue *f* de premier plan *m*

Großbuchstaben *m/pl*	capital letters *pl*, caps *pl*, large print, upper case letters *pl*	caractères *m/pl* haut de casse *f*, gros caractères *m/pl*, lettres *f/pl* capitales, majuscules *f/pl*
großer Erfolg *m*	smash hit	gros succès *m*
großer Faltprospekt *m*	broadsheet, broadside	in-plano *m*
großes Publikum *n*	public at large	grand public *m*
Großfläche *f*	large hoarding, large panel	grand panneau *m*
Großfläche *f*, **gemalte**	bulletin board, painted bulletin	bulletin *m*
großflächige Anzeige *f*	big splurge ad, large space ad	annonce *f* de grandes dimensions *f/pl*
Großformat *n*	large format, large size	grand format *m*
großformatige Drucksache *f*	broadsheet	imprimé *m* de grand format *m*
großformatige Zeitung *f*	blanket sheet	journal *m* de grand format *m*
großformatiges Plakat *n*	royal poster	affiche *f* de grand format *m*
Großfoto *n*	large-size photo	agrandissement *m* photographique
Großhändler *m*	jobber, wholesale dealer	grossiste *m*, intermédiare *m* revendeur
Großhandel *m*	wholesale trade	commerce *m* de gros
Grosso *n*	newspaper wholesaler	commerce *m* de journaux *m/pl* en gros
Großpackung *f*	economy size, giant-size pack	emballage *m* de grande taille *f*, empaquetage *m* gigantesque
Großprospekt *m*	broadsheet	in-plano *m*
Großsprecherei *f*	bragging	rodomontade *f*
Großstadtpresse *f*	big city press, metropolitan dailies *pl*	presse *f* urbaine, quotidiens *m/pl* métropolitains
Großtuerei *f*	splurging	esbrouffe *f*
Großverbraucher *m*	bulk consumer, heavy user	gros consommateur *m*
großzügige Werbung *f*	large-scale advertising	publicité *f* de grand style *m*
Grotesk *f*	grotesque, sans-serif	antique *f*, bâton *m*
Gründer *m*	founder	fondateur *m*
Gründungsjahr *n*	year of establishment	année *f* de fondation *f*
grüner Tisch *m*	green table	tapis *m* vert
Grund *m* **und Boden** *m*,**öffentlicher**	public property	domaine *m* public
Grundaussage *f*	creative copy	message *m* de base *f*
Grundfarbe *f*	ground colour, primary colour	couleur *f* de base *f*
Grundgestell *n*	mount	socle *m*
Grundidee *f*	fundamental idea	idée *f* de base *f*
Grundkonzeption *f*	basic concept	conception *f* de base *f*
Grundlage *f*	basis	base *f*
Grundlage *f*, **konzeptionelle**	copy platform	conception *f* de base *f*
grundlegendes Material *n*	basic data *pl*	données *f/pl* de base *f*
Grundpreis *m*	basic rate, flat rate, open-time rate *am*, standard rate	prix *m* de base *f*, tarif *m* fixe
Grundpreis *m*, **erhöhter**	raised standard rate	prix *m* de base *f* augmenté
Grundsatz *m*	principle	principe *m*
Grundsatzartikel *m*	summary lead	article *m* d'appel *m*
Grundsatzentscheidung *f*	key decision	décision *f* de principe *m*
Grundschrift *f*	body fount, main type	caractère *m* principal
Grundthema *n*	story	sujet *m*
Grundzüge *m/pl*	groundwork	canevas *m*

Gruppe f von Anschlagstellen f/pl an einem Standort m	hoarding	groupe m de panneaux m/pl d'affichage m sur un emplacement m
Gruppenarbeit f	team-work	collaboration f, travail m en équipe f
Gruppendiskussion f	round-table conference	réunion f paritaire, table f ronde
Guasch f	body colour drawing, gouache	couleur f opaque, gouache f
Guaschfarben f/pl	gouache colours pl	couleurs f/pl pour gouache f
Guaschzeichnung f	gouache drawing	dessin m à la gouache f
gültig	valid	valide
Gültigkeit f	validity	validité f
Güterwagenwerbung f	advertising on goods-trains pl	publicité f sur wagons m/pl de marchandises f/pl
Gütezeichen n	certification mark, quality label, seal of approval	étiquette f de qualité f, label m de qualité f, marque f de garantie f, sigle m
Gummidruck m	offset printing	impression f offset
gummiertes Papier n	gummed paper	papier m gommé
Gummiklischee n	rubber block	cliché m caoutchouc m
Gummistempel m	rubber stamp	cachet m de caoutchouc m
Guß m	fount	fonte f
gut aufgemachte Zeitung f	well made-up newspaper	journal m bien fait
gut aufgezogene Werbung f	well-organized advertising	publicité f bien organisée
gut formulierter Gedanke m	well-phrased opinion	pensée f bien tournée
gut unterrichtet	well-informed	bien informé
gut zum Druck m	good for printing	bon à tirer
Gutachten n	expert opinion	arbitrage m, expertise f
guter Ruf m	good will	bonne réputation f
Gutschein m	coupon, credit slip, gift voucher	bon m à valoir, coupon m de réduction f
Gutscheinverteilung f	couponing	couponnage m
Gutschrift f	credit note	note f de crédit m

H

Haarstrich m	hairline, serif, thin stroke	délié m, empattement m
Hadernpapier n	rag paper	papier m de chiffons m/pl
Händler m	dealer	commerçant m, marchand m, négociant m
Händler m, fliegender	hawker, itinerant salesman	colporteur m, marchand m ambulant, marchand m forain
Händleranschrift f, eingedruckte	dealer imprint	empreinte f de l'adresse f du détaillant m
Händlerbefragung f	dealer survey, retail audit, shop audit, shop-check	enquête f auprès des détaillants m/pl
Händlermarke f	dealer's brand	marque f du distributeur m
Händlerrabatt m	dealer rebate	rabais m pour les commerçants m/pl
Händlerwerbehilfen f/pl	dealer aids pl	aides f/pl publicitaires au détaillant m
Händlerwerbung f	trade advertising	publicité f pour le distributeur m
Hängeplakat n	hanger-card	pendentif m
Hängeschild n	hanging	pendentif m
Häubchen n	tail cap	coiffe f

Häufigkeit f	frequency	fréquence f
Haftetikett n	adhesive label	étiquette f adhésive
Haftung f für Mängel m/pl	liability for insufficiencies pl	responsabilité f pour insuffisances f/pl
Haftung f für Schäden m/pl	liability for damages pl	responsabilité f pour dommages m/pl
halbamtlich	semi-official	officieux, semi-officiel
Halbbelegung f	half showing	affichage m à demi
halbe Seite f	half page	demi-page f
halber Punkt m	hair space	espace m fin
halbfett	half-bold, medium, semi-bold	demi-gras, mi-gras
halbfette Schrift f	medium faced type	caractères m/pl quart-gras
halbfetter Satz m	semi-bold type	caractères m/pl demi-gras
Halbfranzband m	half-binding	demi-reliure f
halbgeleimtes Papier n	soft sized paper	papier m demi-collé
Halbgeviert n	en-quad	demi-cadratin m
halbjährlich	half-yearly, semi-annual, twice yearly	semestriel, tous les six mois m/pl
Halbkarton m	thin board	mi-carton m
Halblederband m	half binding	reliure f en demi-cuir m
halbmonatlich	half-monthly	semi-mensuel
Halbpetit f (Diamant) (siehe Anhang)	Diamond (see appendix)	corps 4 points (voir appendice)
Halbton m	half-tone	demi-teinte, mi-ton
Halbtonzeichnung f	half tone drawing	dessin m mi-ton
halbwöchentlich	half-weekly	semi-hebdomadaire
Haltbarkeit f	solidity	solidité f
Haltestellensäule f	bus stop pillar	poteau m d'arrêt m
Hand f (Hinweiszeichen n)	index mark	main f
Handabzug m	hand proof, hand pull	épreuve f tirée à la main f
Handausschnitt m	handcut	découpage m à la main f
Handbuch n	guide, handbook, manual, vademecum	guide m, manuel m, vade-mecum m
Handdruck m	hand printing	impression f à la main f
Handel m	commerce, trade	commerce m
handeln	to deal	faire commerce m
Handelsadreßbuch n	commercial directory, trade directory	almanach m du commerce m, annuaire m du commerce m, Bottin m
Handelsblatt n	journal of commerce, trade journal	journal m de commerce m
Handelsmarke f	private brand	marque f de distributeur m
Handelsmesse f	trade fair	foire f de commerce m
Handelsregister n-Anzeigen f/pl	advertisements pl of the commercial register	annonces f/pl du registre m du commerce m
Handelsreisender m	travelling salesman	voyageur m de commerce m
Handelsspanne f	trade margin	marge f commerciale
Handelsteil m	commercial section	partie f commerciale
Handelsvertreter m	sales pl representative	représentant m de commerce m
handgemalt	hand painted	peint à la main f
handgeschöpftes Bütten-papier n	hand made deckle-edged paper	papier m à la main f
handgestrickt	homespun	fait à la maison f
Handhabung f	handling	manutention f
Handharmonikafalzung f	concertina folding	pliage m en zig-zag
Handkolorierung f	flexichrome process	procédé m flexichrome

handliches Format *n*	handy size	format *m* facile à manier
Handlung *f*	action	action *f*
Handlung *f*, spannende	thriller	film *m* à sensation *f*, roman *m* à sensation *f*
Handmuster *n*	dummy	maquette *f*
Handpresse *f*	hand-press	presse *f* à bras *m*
Handreichung *f*	helping hand	coup *m* de main *f*
Handsatz *m*	hand composition *am*, hand setting, manual typesetting	composition *f* à la main *f*, composition *f* manuelle
Handsatzschrift *f*	foundry type, hand type	caractères *m/pl* fondeur
Handschrift *f*	handwriting	écriture *f* à la main *f*
Handsetzer *m*	hand composer	compositeur *m* à la main *f*
Handwerksmesse *f*	artisan fair	foire *f* de l'artisanat *m*
Handzettel *m*	dodger *am*, give-away, handbill, throw-away	papillon *m*, prospectus *m*
Harmonikafalzung *f*	concertina folding	plis *m/pl* accordéon *m*
harte Konkurrenz *f*	keen competition	concurrence *f* acharnée
Hartfaserplatte *f*	hardboard	carton *m* compact
hastig hingeworfen	slapdashed	écrit à six-quatre-deux
Hauptabsatzgebiet *m*	main market	marché *m* principal
Hauptausgabe *f*	main edition	feuille *f* principale
Hauptaussage *f*	basic message	message *m* de base *f*
Hauptbestandteil *m* einer Anzeige *f*	body copy, body matter, running text	corps *m* d'une annonce *f*
Hauptblickfang *m*	primary appeal	accroche-œil *m* primaire
Hauptfilm *m* des Programms *m*	feature film	grand film *m* de programme *m*
Hauptgeschäftszeit *f*	rush hour	heure *f* de pointe *f*
Hauptmerkmal *n* (einer Anzeige *f*)	feature	caractéristique *f*, trait *m*
Hauptrolle *f*, Film *m* mit G.G. in der	film featuring G.G.	film *m* avec G.G. en vedette *f*
Hauptsaison *f*	busy season, peak season	saison *f* principale
Hauptschriftleiter *m*	editor-in-chief	rédacteur *m* en chef *m*
Haupttext *m*	body	texte *m* principal
Haupttitel *m*	title page	grand titre *m*
Hauptwerbemittel *n*	basic medium	média *m* de base *f*, média *m* principal
Hauptwerbetext *m*	creative copy	texte *m* principal
Hauptzeile *f*	head line	ligne *f* principale
Hauptzielgruppe *f*	principal consumers *pl*	cible *f* principale
Haus *n* zu Haus *n*, von	door-to door	porte *f* à porte *f*
Hausagentur *f*	house agency, imaginary agency	agence *f* fictive
Hausbesuch *m*	domiciliary visit	visite *f* à domicile *m*
Hausexemplar *n*	publisher's copy	exemplaire-éditeur *m*
Hausfarbe *f*	house colour	couleur *f* privée
Hausfrauenabend *m*	housewives' party	soirée *f* de ménagères *f/pl*
Hausfrauenzeitschriften *f/pl*	housewives' magazines *pl*	magasins *m/pl* pour ménagères *f/pl*
Haushalt *m*	household	foyer *m*
Haushaltsartikel *m*	hard goods *pl*	article *m* de ménage *m*
Haushaltspackung *f*	family size pack	empaquetage *m* de ménage *m*
Haushaltswerbung *f*	house-to-house advertising	publicité *f* de porte *f* en porte *f*
Hausierer *m*	huckster	colporteur *m*
Hauskorrektor *m*	printer's reader	correcteur *m* de l'imprimerie *f*
Hauskorrektur *f*	first proof, reader's proof	épreuve *f* en première, première correction *f*
Hausmarke *f*	house brand, private brand	marque *f* de distributeur *m*

Hausstil *m*	house style	style *m* d'entreprise *f*
Haustelefon *n*	house telephone, interphone	téléphone *m* intérieur
Hauszeitschrift *f*	company publication, house journal, house organ, staff magazine	journal *m* d'entreprise *f*, revue *f* d'entreprise
Hauszustellung *f*	door delivery	porte *f* à porte *f*
Heck *n*	rear	arrière *m*
Heckschild *n*	single back panel	arrière *f* (un seul panneau *m*)
Heckstreifen *m*	rear waistband	bandeau *m* arrière
heften	to fasten, to sew, to stitch	agrafer, brocher
Heftfaden *m*	stitching thread	fil *m* à brocher
Heftgaze *f*	stitching gauze	mousseline *f*
Heftklammer *f*	staple	crochet *m*
Heftpreis *m*	single copy price	prix *m* de vente *f* au numéro *m*
Heftung *f*	stitching	piqûre *f*
Heftung *f*, seitliche	side stabbed	piqûre *f* à plat
Heimatzeitung *f*	local paper	journal *m* local
Heiratsanzeige *f*	marriage advertisement	annonce *f* matrimoniale, faire-part *m* de marriage *m*
heißer Draht *m*	hot line	téléphone *m* rouge
Heißprägung *f*	hot process embossing, thermography	empreinte *f* à chaud
Hektograph *m*	hectograph	polycopiste *m*
Heliogravüre *f*	photogravure	rotogravure *f*
Hellraumprojektor *m*	film projector usuable in daylight-rooms *pl*	projection *f* dans des localités *f* avec lumière *f* de jour *m*
Hellschreiber *m*	teleprinter	téléscripteur *m*, télétype *m*
herabsetzende Werbung *f*	competitive copy *am*, disparaging copy, knocking copy *brit*	publicité *f* agressive, publicité *f* discriminatrice
Herabsetzung *f*	disparagement	dénigrement *m*
Heranrücken *n* bei Großaufnahme *f* (Film)	zooming	rapprochement *m* dans une vue *f* de premier plan *m*
herausgeben	to bring out, to issue, to publish	éditer, publier, sortir
Herausgeber *m*	managing editor, publisher	gérant *m*
Herbstmesse *f*	autumn fair	foire *f* d'automne *m*
hereinholen	to canvass	prospecter
Hering *m* (Tadel *m*)	reprimand, reproof	réprimande *f*
Herkunft *f*	origin	origine *f*
Herkunftszeichen *n*	mark of origin	marque *f* d'origine *f*
Hersteller *m*	producer	producteur *m*
Herstellermarke *f*	trade-mark	marque *f* de fabricant *m*
Herstellervermerk *m*	imprinting	mention *m* du producteur *m*
Herstellerwerbung *f*	producer advertising	publicité *f* des producteurs *m/pl*
Herstellung *f*	production	fabrication *f*, production *f*
Herstellungsfachmann *m*	production expert	expert *m* en fabrication *f*
Herstellungskosten *pl*	manufacturing costs *pl*, production costs *pl*	frais *pl* de fabrication *f*, prix *m* de fabrication *f*
Herstellungsleiter *m*	director of fabrication	chef *m* de fabrication *f*
Herstellungstechnik *f*	technique of production	technique *f* de fabrication *f*
Herstellungsverfahren *n*	manufacturing process	procédé *m* de fabrication *f*
herunterspielen	to play down	minimiser
hervorheben	to accentuate, to emphasize, to feature, to highlight	mettre en évidence *f*, mettre en relief *m*, mettre en vedette *f*, souligner
hervorheben, pomphaft	to blazon	exalter
Hervorhebung *f*	emphasizing	mise *f* en valeur *f*

Herzenserguß *m*	effusion	épanchement *m* de cœur *m*
Hetzartikel *m*	inflammatory article	article *m* incendiaire
Hetzpresse *f*	yellow press	journaille *f*
Heulsuse *f*	sob-sister	journaliste *f* spécialisée en reportages *m/pl* larmoyants
HiFi-Endlosfarbanzeige *f*	HiFi continuous advertisement in colour, wall paper litho	encart *m* en couleur *f* imprimé en continu *m*
Hilfsredakteur *m*	leg man	assistant *m* du rédacteur *m*
Himmelsschrift *f*	sky writing	publicité *f* aérienne
Hin- und Hergerede *n*	palaver	palabre *f*
hintereinander gesendete Werbekurzspots *m/pl* für verschiedene Produkte *n/pl* desselben Werbungtreibenden *m*	piggyback	des spots *m/pl* émis l'un après l'autre pour deux produits *m/pl* différents du même annonceur *m*
hinterer Teil *m* der Ausgabe *f*	back section	cahier *m* de queue *f*
Hintergedanke *m*	mental reservation	arrière-pensée *f*
Hintergrund *m*	background	arrière-plan *m*
Hintergrundbericht *m*	close-up	médaillon *m*
Hintergrundgeräusche *n/pl*	ground noise	bruit *m* de fond *m*
hinterkleben	to back	contre-coller
Hinweisschild *n*	direction sign, road sign	panneau *m* routier, signal *m* de direction *f*
hinzufügen	to add	ajouter
hoch	high	haut
hochätzen	to etch in relief	graver en relief *m*
Hochdruck *m*	relief printing	impression *f* en relief *m*
Hochdruckrollenrotation *f*	web-fed letterpress rotary machine	rotative *f* typographique à bobines *f/pl*
Hochdruckverfahren *n*	surface printing	impression *f* en relief *m*
Hochformat *n*	high size, portrait format, upright format	format *m* en hauteur *f*, format *m* normal, format *m* vertical
hochgerückte Buchstaben *m/pl*	superior letters *pl*	lettres *f/pl* supérieures
Hochglanzabzug *m*	high gloss print	copie *f* sur papier *m* brillant, épreuve *f* glacée
Hochglanzkaschierung *f*	high gloss lamination	pelliculage *m*
Hochkonjunktur *f*	boom	hausse *f* rapide, haute conjoncture *f*, période *f* de vogue *f*
Hochlichtaufnahme *f*	highlight exposure	exposé *m* des grandes lumières *f/pl*
Hochlichtautotypie *f*	dropout half-tone, high-light half-tone	cliché *m* simili avec grandes lumières *f/pl*
Hochsaison *f*	peak season	haute saison *f*
hochsatiniert	super-calendered	surglacé
hochsatiniertes Papier *n*	imitation art paper, supercalendered paper	papier *m* satiné
hochspielen, eine Nachricht *f*	to play up an information, to puff up an information	donner une publicité *f* retentissante, gonfler un papier *m*, remonter une nouvelle *f*
hochstehender Buchstabe *m*	cock-up, superior letter	exposant *m* supérieur
hochtönende Werbung *f*	high-pressure advertising	publicité *f* emphatique
hochwertig	first-rate, of high value	de grande qualité *f*, de haute teneur *f*
Hochzeit *f* (doppelt Gesetztes *n*)	double	doublon *m*

Höchstanschlagzeit *f*	period maximum	période *f* maximum
Höchstformat *n*	maximum size	format *m* maximum
Höchstgewicht *n*	maximum weight	poids *m* maximum
Höchstgröße *f*	maximum lineage	lignage *m* maximum
Höchstpreis *m*	ceiling price	prix *m* maximum
Höchstrabatt *m*	maximum rebate	rabais *m* maximum
Höhe *f*	height, length	hauteur *f*
höher stellen	to move up	placer plus haut
höhere Gewalt *f*	absolute necessity, act of providence	force *f* majeure
Hörbarkeit *f*	audibility	audibilité *f*
Hörbericht *m*	radio report	reportage *m* parlé
Hören *n*, räumliches	stereophony	stéréophonie *f*
Hörer *m*	listener	auditeur *m*
Höreranalyse *f*	audience measurement, listenership research	recherches *f/pl* relatives à l'audience *f*
Hörerforschung *f*	broadcast research	études *f/pl* relatives à l'audience *f*
Hörergesamtzahl *f*	cumulative audience	audience *f* cumulative
Hörerpanel *n*	listening panel	groupe *m* de test *m* des auditeurs *m/pl*, panel *m* des auditeurs *m/pl*
Hörerschaft *f*	audience	auditeurs *m/pl*
Hörerzahl *f*, Aufnahme-apparat *m* zur Feststellung *f* der	audimeter	audimètre *m*
Hörfolge *f*	feature programme	programme *m* de radio *f*
Hörfunk *m*	broadcasting	radiodiffusion *f* sonore
Hörfunkwerbung *f*	radio advertising	publicité *f* radiophonique
Hörspiel *n*	radio drama	pièce *f* radiophonique
hohe Auflage *f*	mass-circulation	haut tirage *m*
Hohlsteg *m*	furniture	lingot *m* évidé
holländisches Papier *n*	hand-made paper	papier *m* de Hollande *f*
holografische Werbung *f*	holographic advertising	publicité *f* holographique
Holzdruck *m*	wood printing	impression *f* sur bois *m*
holzfreies Papier *n*	wood-free paper	papier *m* sans pâte *f* de bois *m*
Holzfuß *m*	wood base, wood mount	pied *m* de bois *m*
holzhaltiges Papier *n*	paper made from wood pulp, wood containing paper	papier *m* avec de bois *m*, papier *m* fait de pâte *f* de bois *m*
Holzpappe *f*	board made from wood pulp	carton *m* de bois *m*
Holzschnitt *m*	wood cut, wood engraving	bois *m* gravé, gravure *f* sur bois *m*
Holzschrift *f*	wooden type	caractères *m/pl* de bois *m*
Holzunterlage *f*	wooden base	socle *m* de bois *m*
Honorar *n*	fee	honoraires *m/pl*
Horizontalwerbung *f*	horizontal co-operative advertising	publicité *f* collective horizontale
Horrorfilm *m*	horror film	film *m* d'épouvante *f*
Hortungskäufe *m/pl*	hoarding purchases *pl*	achats *m/pl* spéculatifs
Hostessendienst *m*	hostess service	personnel *m* pour services *m/pl* d'acceuil *m*
humoristische Zeichnung *f*	cartoon	dessin *m* humoristique
humoristischer Bilderstreifen *m*	comic strip	bandes *f/pl* dessinées
Hurenkind *n* (typog)	bastard type, widow	ligne *f* boiteuse

I

Idee *f*	idea	idée *f*
Idee *f*, ausgefallene	gimmick	coup *m*, truc *m*
Ideenentwurf *m*	thumbnail sketch	croquis *m* minuscule
Ideenfindung *f* durch Gruppendiskussion *f*	brainstorming	orage *m* des cerveaux *m/pl*
Ideengestalter *m*	visualizer	dessinateur *m* -concepteur *m*
Ideengestaltung *f*	visualizing	conception *f*
Ideenskizze *f*	rough	maquette *f*
Identifizierung *f*	identification	identification *f*
illegale Presse *f*	illegal press	presse *f* illégale
Illustration *f*	illustration	illustration *f*
Illustrationsdruck *m*	illustration printing	impression *f* d'illustrations *f/pl*
Illustrationsdruckpapier *n*	supercalendered paper	papier *m* pour illustrations *f/pl*
illustratives Plakat *n*	illustrative poster	affiche *f* illustrative
Illustrator *m*	artist, illustrator	illustrateur *m*
illustrieren	to illustrate	illustrer
Illustrierte *f*	illustrated paper, pictorial, picture paper, review	périodique *m* illustré
im Auftrag *m* und unter dem Namen *m* eines anderen schreibender Autor *m*	ghost writer	nègre *m*
Imitation *f*	imitation	contre-façon *f*
imitiertes Kunstdruckpapier *n*	imitation art paper	papier *m* satiné
Immobilienanzeige *f*	real estate advertisement	annonce *f* immobilière
imprägnieren	to impregnate	imprégner
Impressum *n*	colophon, imprint	notice *f*, repiquage *m*
Imprimatur *n*	o. k. to print, permission to print, ready for press	bon à tirer, permission *f* d'imprimer
Impuls *m*	impulse	impulsion *f*
Impulskauf *m*	impulse buying	achat *m* impulsif, achat *m* spontané
in großen Zügen *m/pl* darstellen	to skeletonize	réduire au strict minimum *m*
inbegriffen	included	inclus, y compris
Inch *n* (Anzeigengrundmaß)	inch (14 agate lines *pl*)	pouce *m* (hauteur 27 mm)
indirekte Werbung *f*	indirect advertising	publicité *f* indirecte
Individualwerbung *f*	individual advertising	publicité *f* individuelle
Industrieausstellung *f*	industrial exhibition	foire *f* industrielle
Industrieblatt *n*	industrial magazine, technical magazine	revue *f* pour industriels *m/pl*
Industriedesigner *m*	industrial designer	dessinateur *m* industriel
Industriefilm *m*	industrial film	film *m* industriel
Industriegüter *n/pl*	industrial goods *pl*	biens *m/pl* industriels
Industriemesse *f*	industries *pl* fair	foire *f* de l'industrie *f*
Industriewerbung *f*	industrial advertising	publicité *f* industrielle
Informant *m*	informant	informateur *m*
Information *f*	information	information *f*
Information *f* aus guter Quelle *f*	inside knowledge	information *f* de bonne source *f*
Information *f* verbreiten	to publicize	faire connaître au public *m*
Information *f*, vertrauliche	off the record information	information *f* confidentielle
Informationen *f/pl*	inquiries *pl*	renseignements *m/pl*
Informationen *f/pl*, digitale	digital information	information *f* numérique
Informationsbericht *m* vor Beginn *f* der Ausarbeitung *f* einer Werbekampagne	start work report	rapport *m* d'information *f* devant le commencement *m* d'une campagne *f* publicitaire

Informationsblatt *n*	newsletter	bulletin *m* d'information *f*
Informationsbroschüre *f*	information brochure	brochure *f* d'information *f*
Informationsdienst *m*	information service	service *m* d'information *f*
Informationsfluß *m*	communication	communication *f*
Informationsfülle *f*	abundance of information	plénitude *f* d'information *f*
Informationsgespräch *n*	exploration	exploration *f*
Informationslücke *f*	information gap	lacune *f* d'information *f*
Informationsmedium *n*	medium of information	moyen *m* d'information *f*
Informationsorgan *n*	newsletter	bulletin *m* d'information *f*
Informationsquelle *f*	source of information	source *f* d'information *f*
Informationswege *m/pl*	channels *pl* of information	chemins *m/pl* de l'information *f*
Informationswert *m*	information value, news value	valeur *f* d'information *f*, valeur *f* indicative
informatives Plakat *n*	informative poster	affiche *f* informative
informieren	to acquaint, to inform	informer
informierende Werbung *f*	informatory advertising, product advertising	publicité *f* informative, publicité *f* instructive
Inhalt *m*	contents *pl*	contenu *m*
Inhalt *m*, redaktioneller	editorial content	contenu *m* rédactionnel
Inhaltsanalyse *f*	content analysis	analyse *f* du contenu *m*
Inhaltsangabe *f*	summary	résumé *m*
inhaltsreich	full of matter	substantiel
Inhaltsverzeichnis *n*	index, table of contents *pl*	index *m*, sommaire *m*, table *f* des matières *f/pl*
Inhaltsverzeichnis *n*, gegenüber	facing contents *pl*	face *f* sommaire *m*
Initiale *f*	initial letter	initiale *f*, lettrine *f*
Initiale *f*, große	cut-in letter	grande lettrine *f*
Initialwerbung *f*	pioneering advertising	publicité *f* de pionnier *m*
Inklusivpreis *m*	price including	prix *m* global
Inkrafttreten *n*	effective date	entrée *f* en vigueur *f*
Inkunabel *f*	incunabulum	incunable *m*
Inland *n*	inland	intéricur *m* du pays *m*
Inlandsauflage *f*	home circulation, national print run	tirage *m* national
Inlandsmarkt *m*	domestic market	marché *m* intérieur
Inlandsnachrichten *f/pl*	home news	nouvelles *f/pl* du pays *m*
Innenaufnahme *f*	indoor photo	photo *f* d'intérieur *m*
Innenausbau *m*	inside decoration	agencement *m*
Innendekoration *f*	interior decoration	décoration *f* à l'intérieur *m*
Innenplakat *n* (in Verkehrsmitteln *n/pl*)	car card advertising, car panel, indoor poster	affiche *f* intérieure, emplacement *m* intérieur de voiture *f*
Innenrand *m*	inner margin	marge *f* intérieure
Innenseite *f*	inner page, inside page	page *f* intérieure
Innenspalte *f*	gutter	petit-fonds *m*
Innentitel *m*	half title	faux titre *m*, titre *m* intérieur
Innenwerbung *f*	indoor advertising	publicité *f* d'intérieur *m*
innerbetriebliche Beziehungen *f/pl*	intraflow	relations *f/pl* internes
inoffiziell	off-stage	non officiellement
Inschrift *f*	inscription	épigraphe *f*, inscription *f*
Inselanzeige *f*	sole advertisement	annonce *f* isolée
Inselplacierung *f*	island position	emplacement *m* isolé
Inserat *n*	ad, advertisement	annonce *f*, insertion *f*
Inserat *n* aufgeben	to order an advertisement	remettre une annonce *f*
Inseratenteil *m*	advertisement columns *pl*	partie *f* publicitaire

Inseratvarianten *f/pl* **in derselben Ausgabe** *f*	split run	tirage *m* partagé
Inserent *m*	advertiser	annonceur *m*
Inserentenverzeichnis *n*	list of advertisers *pl*	répertoire *m* des annonceurs *m/pl*
inserieren	to advertise, to insert	annoncer, insérer
Insertio *f* (siehe Anhang)	Emerald (see appendix)	corps 6 1/2 points (voir appendice)
Insertion *f*, **kostenlose**	free insertion	insertion *f* gratuite
Insertionsauftrag *m*	insertion order, space order	ordre *m* d'annonces *f/pl*, ordre *m* d'insertion *f*
Insertionsjahr *n*	contractual year	année *f* contractuelle
Insertionsmedium *n*	printed medium	média *m* imprimé
Insertionsplan *m*	schedule of insertions *pl*	calendrier *m* d'insertion *f*
Insertionsvertrag *m*	advertising contract	contrat *m* d'insertion *f*
Insettinganzeige *f*	advertisement by insetting, spectacolor advertisement	publicité *f* par insetting
Instandhaltung *f*	maintenance	entretien *m*
Institut *n*	institute	institut *m*
institutionelle Werbung *f*	corporate advertising, good-will advertising, institutional advertising	publicité *f* de notoriété *f*, publicité *f* de prestige *m*, publicité *f* institutionnelle
Instruktionen *f/pl*	briefing	instructions *f/pl*
integrierte Funkwerbung *f*	straight commercial	émission *f* publicitaire intégrée
integriertes Satzsystem *n*	integrated composition system, integrated typesetting system	système *m* intégré des textes *m/pl* composés
Intellektueller *m*	egghead, highbrow	intellectuel *m*
Intensität *f*	intensity	intensité *f*
Intensivierung *f* **des Werbeeffekts** *m*	accumulation	intensification *f* de la publicité *f*
Intensivwerbung *f*	intensive advertising	publicité *f* intensive
interessanter machen	to pep up	corser
Interesse *n*	interest	intérêt *m*
Interessenbereich *m*	interest pattern, sphere of interests *pl*	sphère *f* d'intérêts *m/pl*
Interessengemeinschaft *f*	pool	groupe *m*
Interessent *m*	prospect	prospect *m*
Interessentengruppe *f*	pressure group	groupe *m* de pression *f*
Interessenvertreter *m*	lobbyist	agent *m* qui essaie d'influencer les députés *m/pl*
Intermediavergleich *m*	intermedia comparison	comparaison *f* des médias *m/pl*
interpunktieren	to put in the stops *pl*	ponctuer
Interpunktion *f*	punctuation	ponctuation *f*
Interview *n*	interview	interview *f*
Interview *n* **mit Ungenanntem** *m*	lamp-post interview	interview *f* avec une personne *f* non nommée
Interview *n*, **unvorbereitetes**	candid interview	interview *f* non préparée
Interview *n*, **vorgetäuschtes**	fake interview	interview *m* bidon
Interviewer *m*	field investigator, interviewer, pollster	enquêteur *m*
Interviewerin *f*	interviewer, pollster	enquêtrice *f*
Inventurausverkauf *m*	stock-taking sales *pl*	soldes *m/pl* après inventaire *m*
investieren	to invest	investir
Investitionsgüter *n/pl*	capital goods *pl*	biens *m/pl* de production *f*, biens *m/pl* d'investissement *m*

Investitionsgüterwerbung *f*	industrial advertising	publicité *f* pour des biens *m/pl* d'investissement *m*
Irisdruck *m*	irisdescent printing	impression *f* irisée
irreführen	to mislead	tromper
irreführende Werbung *f*	deceptive advertising, false advertising, misleading advertising	publicité *f* déloyale, publicité *f* fallacieuse, publicité *f* mensongère
Irrtümer *m/pl* und Auslassungen *f/pl* vorbehalten	errors *pl* and omissions *pl* excepted	sauf erreur *f* ou omission *f*

J

jährlich	annually, every year	annuel
Jahrbuch *n*	annual, year-book	annale *f*, annuaire *m*
Jahresabonnement *n*	annual subscription	abonnement *m* annuel
Jahresauftrag *m*	annual order	ordre *m* annuel
Jahresbericht *m*	annual report	rapport *m* annuel, rapport *m* d'exercice *f*
Jahresfrist *f*, innerhalb	within one year	dans le délai *m* d'une année *f*
Jahrgang *m*	volume	année *f*
Japanpapier *n*	India paper, Japan paper	japon *m*, papier *m* japon
Jargon *m*	jargon, slang	argot *m*, jargon *m*
Journalismus *m*	journalism	journalisme *m*
Journalist *m*	journalist, newspaper man	journaliste *m*
Journalist *m*, freier	free lance reporter	journaliste *m* indépendant, pigiste *m*
Journalist *m* mit Zeilen-honorar *n*	space man	journaliste *m* payé à la ligne *f*
Journalist *m*, unabhängiger	free lance journalist	pigiste *m*
Journalistenausweis *m*	press credentials *pl*	carte *f* de presse *f*
Journalistenhonorar *n*	fee for journalists *pl*	honoraires *m/pl* des journalistes *m/pl*, pige *m*
journalistische Einheit *f*	independent newspaper with a complete editorial staff, journalistic unit	journal *m* indépendant avec une rédaction *f* complète, unité *f* journalistique
Jubiläumsschrift *f*	anniversary publication, jubilee publication	publication *f* anniversaire, publication *f* de jubilé *m*
Jugendbeilage *f*	youth supplement	supplément *m* pour la jeunesse *f*
Jugendzeitung *f*	youth paper	journal *m* des jeunes *m/pl*
Jungfer *f/typog*	perfect page	page *f* sans faute *f*
juristische Zeitschrift *f*	law review	revue *f* juridique
justieren	to adjust	justifier
Justierung *f*	justification	justification *f*

K

Kabel *n*	cable	câble *m*
Kabelfernsehen *n*	community antenna television, television via cable	télévision *f* via câble *m*
kabeln	to cable	câbler
Kabelnachricht *f*	news sent by cable	information *f* câblée
Kabeltelegramm *n*	cablegram	câblogramme *m*
Kabeltext *m*	cable-text	câble-texte *m*
Käseblättchen *n*	local rag, trumpery paper	feuille *f* de chou *m*

Kästchen n	box	cassetin m
Käufer m (in f)	buyer, female buyer, purchaser, shopper	acheteur m, acheteuse f
Käufergruppe f	buyer category	catégorie f des acheteurs m/pl
Käufermarkt m	buyer's market	marché m d'acheteurs m/pl
Käuferschicht f	spending group	catégorie f des acheteurs m/pl
Käuferverhalten n	purchase pattern, shopping behaviour	comportement m des acheteurs m/pl, habitudes f/pl des acheteurs m/pl
käufliche Presse f	corrupt press	presse f corrompue
Kalander m	calender	calandre f
kalandriertes Papier n	supercalendered paper	papier m surglacé
Kalender m	almanac, calendar	almanach m, calendrier m
Kalenderjahr n	calendar year	année f civile
Kalibermaß n	calibrator	calibre m
kalibrieren	to calibrate, to cast off, to gauge, to size	calibrer
Kaliko n	calico	calicot m
kalkulieren	to calculate, to estimate	calculer
Kalligrafie f	calligraphy	calligraphie f
Kaltsatz m	cold type composing	composition f sans plomb m à froid
Kamerakran m	camera-crane, dolly	grue f
Kameramann m	camera man	cadreur m, opérateur m
Kamerawagen m	dolly	travelling m
Kampagne f	campaign	campagne f
kampagnegerechtes Denken n	campaign thinking	mentalité f orientée vers la campagne f
Kampfmarke f	fighting brand	marque f de bataille f
Kampforgan n	combat organ	organe m de combat m
Kandelaberwerbung f	lamp post advertising	publicité f sur des mâts m/pl d'éclairage m
Kante f	edge	bord m
Kanzleipapier n	foolscap paper	papier m de chancellerie f
Kapitälchen n	small caps pl	petites caps f/pl
Kapitel n	chapter	chapitre m
Kapitelüberschrift f	section title	titre m de chapitre m
Karbondruck m	carbon coating	carbonnage m
kariertes Papier n	cross hatched paper	papier m quadrillé
Karikatur f	caricature, cartoon	caricature f
Karikaturist m	artist	caricaturiste m
Kartei f	card index, file, filing cabinet	armoire f-classeur m, cartothèque f, fichier m
Karteikarte f	index card	carte f de fichier m, fiche f
Karteikarton m	index card board	carton m pour fichiers m/pl
Kartografie f	cartography, map printing	cartographie f
Karton m	board, cardboard, cartridge	carton m
Kartonagefabrik f	cardboard-box manufactory	fabrique f de cartonnage m
Kartonagen f/pl	boarding	cartonnages m/pl
kartoniert	in paper boards pl	cartonné
Kartonseite f	board page	page f cartonnée
kaschieren	to glue, to laminate, to line	doubler, encoller
Kaschierung f	passe-partout lamination	doublage m
Kassaskonto m	cash discount	escompte m de caisse f
Kassenbon m	shop bill	bon m de caisse f

Kassettenfernsehen *n*	audiovision, commercial	audiovision *f*, télévision *f* à cassettes *f/pl*
Kassetteninsert *n*	av-commercial	av-spot *m*
Kastenfach *n*	box	cassetin *m*
Katalog *m*	catalog *am*, catalogue *brit*	catalogue *m*
Katalog *m* mit losen Seiten *f/pl*	loose-leaf catalogue	catalogue *m* à feuillets *m/pl* mobiles
Katalogpreis *m*	list price	prix *m* au catalogue *m*
Kategorie *f*	bracket, category	catégorie *f*
Kategorisierung *f*	labeling	désignation *f*
Katzenauge *n*	cat's eye, rear reflector, reflector button	catadioptre *m*, cataphote *m*
Kauderwelsch *n*	gibberish, gobbledygook	baragouin *m*, jargon *m* incompréhensible
Kauf *m*	purchase	achat *m*
Kaufabsicht *f*	purchase intention	intention *f* d'achat *m*
Kaufanlaß *m*	buying motive	motif *m* d'achat *m*, raison *f* d'achat *m*
Kaufanreiz *m*	buying incitement, merchandise appeal, stimulus	incitation *f* à l'achat *m*
kaufanreizende Prämie *f*	incentive premium	prime *f* stimulante
Kaufanzeige *f*	direct-action copy	annonce *f* fixée sur l'achat *m*
Kaufappell *m*	sales *pl* appeal, selling emphasis	appel *m* au désir *m* d'achat *m*
Kaufappell *m*, abschließender	rider	message *m* additionnel à la fin *f* d'un message *m* publicitaire
Kaufappell *m*, direkter	direct selling emphasis	appel *m* pressant à l'acheteur *m*
Kaufbeeinflussung *f*	inducement to buy	provocation *f* à l'achat *m*
Kaufbereitschaft *f*	buying intention, consumer acceptance	acceptabilité *f* auprès des consommateurs *m/pl*
Kaufentschluß *m*	buying decision	décision *f* d'acheter
Kaufentschlußanalyse *f*	activation research	analyse *f* de la décision *f* d'acheter
Kaufgewohnheiten *f/pl*	buying habits *pl*	habitudes *f/pl* d'achat *m*
Kaufhaus *n*	department store	bazar *m*, grand magasin *m*
Kaufhemmung *f*	buyer's resistance	résistance *f* de l'acheteur *m*
Kaufinteressent *m*	potential buyer	acheteur *m* potentiel
Kaufkraft *f*	buying power, purchasing power, spending power	capacité *f* d'achat *m*, pouvoir *m* d'achat *m*
Kaufkraftklasse *f*	purchasing power class	catégorie *f* de pouvoir *m* d'achat *m*
Kauflust *f*	buying desire	désir *m* d'achat *m*, envie *f* d'acheter
Kaufmotive *n/pl*	buying motives *pl*, reasons *pl* for buying	motivation *f* d'achat *m*
Kaufort *m*	point of purchase	point *m* d'achat *m*
Kaufpreis *m*	cost price, purchase-money	prix *m* d'achat *m*
Kaufstimmung *f*	buying mood	humeur *f* d'acheter
Kaufunlust *f*	disinclination to buy, sales *pl* resistance	abstention *f* des consommateurs *m/pl*
Kaufvertrag *m*	purchase order	contrat *m* de vente *f*
Kaufwerbung *f*	direct-action advertising	publicité *f* incitant à l'action *f* directe
Kaufzeitung *f*	penny press	feuille *f* boulevardière
Kegel *m*	body size, type body	corps *m* de la lettre *f*
Kennwort *n*	code word	mot *m* d'ordre *m*
Kennzeichen *n*	emblem, sign	emblème *m*, indice *m*

Kennziffer *f*	box number, key number	numéro *m* de code *m*
Kennzifferanzeige *f*	keyed advertisement	annonce *f* à clé *f*, annonce *f* chiffrée
Kennzifferwerbung *f*	keyed advertising	publicité *f* codée, publicité *f* sous chiffre *m*
Kennzifferzeitschrift *f*	ciphered business journal, qualified and controlled circulation paper	périodique *m* d'une circulation *f* contrôlée et qualifiée
Keramiker *m*	potter	céramiste *m*
kerniger Stil *m*	vigorous style	style *m* énergique
Kernspruch *m*	pithy saying	aphorisme *m*
Kernstück *m* einer Anzeige *f*	bold type	pièce *f* de résistance *f* d'une annonce *f*
Kettenladen *m*	chain store	membre *m* d'une chaîne *f* volontaire
Kind *n*, Ansprache *f* auf dem Wege *m* über das	kid appeal	appel *m* via l'enfant *m*
Kino *n*	cinema, movie theater, movies *pl am*	cinéma *m*
Kino *n* mit ununterbrochenem Programm *n*	non-stop cinema	cinéma *m* avec un programme *m* sans arrêt *m*
Kinoanzeige *f*	cinema announcement	annonce *f* d'un cinéma *m*
Kinobesucher *m*	film-goer	spectateur *m*
Kinopublikum *n*	movie audience	public *m* des cinémas *m/pl*
Kinotheaterring *m*	circuit	circuit *m*
Kinowerbung *f*	cinema advertising, film advertising	cinéma *m* publicitaire, publicité *f* dans les cinémas *m/pl*
Kiosk *m*	kiosk *brit*, news stand *am*	kiosque *m*
Kirchenblatt *n*	church paper, religious paper	feuille *f* cléricale
Kitsch *m*	shoddy, sob-stuff, trash	tape-à-l'œil *m*
Klammern *f/pl*, eckige	square brackets *pl*	crochets *m/pl*
Klammern *f/pl*, runde	parentheses *pl*	parenthèses *f/pl*
Klammern *f/pl/typog*	brackets *pl*, fingernails *pl*, toenails *pl*	parenthèses *f/pl*
Klangbrücke *f*	bridge	transition *f* musicale
Klangtreue *f*	high fidelity	haute fidélité *f*
Klappe *f*	flap	rabat *m*
Klappentext *m*	advertising text	texte *m* du rabat *m*
klare Ausdrucksweise *f*	plain style	style *m* sans fioritures *f/pl*
Klarheit *f*	clearness	clarté *f*
Klarsichtpackung *f*	transparent package	emballage *m* transparent
Klartext *m*	fair copy, hard copy	copie-témoin *m*, net d'un texte *m*
Klassifizierung *f*	classification	classification *f*
klassische Antiqua *f*	classicistic Latin	Didot *m*
klassische Medien *n/pl*	basic media *pl*, classic media *pl*	médias *m/pl* classiques
Klatschbase *f*	gossip writer	échotier *m*
Klatschdruck *m*	touch print	faux-trait *m*
Klatschgeschichte *f*	gossip, tittle-tattle	bavardage *m*, chronique *f* scandaleuse
Klatschmaul *n*	scandal-monger	cancanier *m*
Klatschspalte *f*	social gossip	nouvelles *f/pl* à la main *f*
Klatschweib *n*	scandal-monger	cancanière *f*
Klausel *f*	stipulation	stipulation *f*
Klaviatur *f*	keyboard	clavier *m*
Klebearbeit *f*	collage	collage *m*

Klebeband *n*	adhesive tape	bande *f* adhésive, ruban *m* adhésif
Klebeetikett *n*	gummed label	étiquette *f* gommée
Klebefolie *f*	adhesive foil	feuille *f* adhésive
Klebekolonne *f*	team of bill-stickers *pl*	équipe *f* d'afficheurs *m/pl*
Klebemarke *f*	adhesive stamp	vignette *f* collante
Klebeperiode *f*	period of display	conservation *f*
Klebespiegel *m*	make-up	maquette *f*
Klebestreifen *m*	gummed strip	bande *f* gommée
Klebezettel *m*	sticker	papillon *m*
Klebstoff *m*	adhesive, glue	adhésif *m*, colle *f*
Kleinanzeigen *f/pl*	classified advertisements *pl*, small ads *pl*	petites annonces *f/pl*
Kleinanzeigenrubrik *f*	classified column	colonne *f* de petites annonces *f/pl*
Kleinartikelschreiber *m*	paragraphist	courriériste *m*
Kleinbuchstabe *m*	lower case letter, minuscule, small letter	lettre *f* bas de casse *f*, minuscule *f*
in **Kleinbuchstaben** *m/pl* absetzen	to put down	composer en minuscules *f/pl*
Kleinbürgertum *n*	petty-bourgeoisie	petite bourgeoisie *f*
kleine Auflage *f*	short run	petit tirage *m*
kleine Textanzeige *f*	short paragraph	entrefilet *m*
kleiner Druck *m*	small print	petits caractères *m/pl*
Kleinformatzeitung *f*	tabloid	tabloïd *m*
Kleinoffsetmaschine *f*	rotaprint sheet-fed machine	presse *f* rotaprint
Kleinoffsetpresse *f*	small offset press	petite presse *f* offset
Kleinplakat *n* **auf Regalen** *n/pl* **und Theken** *f/pl*	shelf-talker	affichette *f* dans les rayonnages *m/pl*
Kleinprospekt *m*	leaflet	petit prospectus *m*, petite brochure *f*
Kleinstadtzeitung *f*	grass roots *pl* press	presse *f* pour la population *f* rurale
Kleinverkaufspreis *m*	retail price	prix *m* vente *f* au détail *m*
Kleister *m*	paste	colle *f*
Kleisterbesen *m*	brush	brosse *f*
Kleisterpapier *n*	gummed fancy paper	papier *m* marbré
Klischee *n*	block *brit*, cliché, cut, plate	cliché *m*, planche *f* typographique
Klischee *n*, **freistehendes**	cut-out block	cliché *m* détouré, cliché *m* isolé
Klischee *n*, **montiertes**	mounted block	cliché *m* monté
Klischee *n*, **randloses**	bleed	cliché *m* sans marge *f*
Klischee *n*, **rechteckiges**	squared up block	cliché *m* rectangulaire
Klischee *n*, **unmontiertes**	unmounted block	cliché *m* non monté
Klischeeabzug *m*	block pull *brit*, block-maker's proof, engraver's proof *am*	épreuve *f* de cliché *m*, fumée *f*
Klischeeätzer *m*	blockmaker, engraver	photograveur *m*
Klischeeätzmaschine *f*	etching machine	machine *f* à graver
Klischeeanstalt *f*	block maker, cliché manufactory, engraving plant	atelier *m* de photogravure *f*, clichérie *f*
Klischeeanzeige *f*	advertisement with illustration, block advertisement	annonce *f* illustrée
Klischeearchiv *n*	collection of picture blocks *pl*	archives *f/pl* des clichés *m/pl*
Klischeeaufbewahrung *f*	block preservation, block storage	magasinage *m* de cliché *m*
Klischeeausschnitt *m*	piercing	encochage *m* d'un cliché *m*
Klischeefacette *f*	bevelled edge	bord *m* biseauté
Klischeefuß *m*	block base, block mount	pied *m* de cliché *m*

Klischeeherstellung *f*	photo-engraving	photogravure *f*
Klischeekorrektur *f*	hand tooling	retouche *f* à l'outil *m*
Klischeeschrank *m*	block cabinet	armoire *f* pour clichés *m/pl*
Klischees *n/pl*, alte	dead plates *pl*	vieux clichés *m/pl*
Klischeetechnik *f*	block making techniques *pl*	technique *f* de clicher
Klischeeunterlage *f*	underlay	mise *f* de hauteur *f* sous cliché *m*
Klischeeunterschrift *f*	cut-liner	légende *f* de cliché *m*
Klischeur *m*	blockmaker	photograveur *m*
klischieren	to cast, to make blocks *pl*, to stereotype	clicher, faire un cliché *m*
klischierfertig	ready for stereotyping	prêt à être cliché *m*
Klischierung *f*	stereotyping process	clichage *m*
Klopfholz *n*	planer	taquoir *m*
knallige Überschrift *f*	catchline, very striking headline	titre *m* criard
Kniehebelpresse *f*	toggle press	presse *f* à genouillère *f*
Knüller *m*	scoop	reportage *m* sensationnel
Kodierung *f*	coding	codification *f*
Köder *m*	bait, loss leader, lure	appât *m*, leurre *m*
Königsformat *n*	king size	géant *m*
Kohlepapier *n*	carbon paper	papier *m* à calquer, papier *m* carbone *m*
Kohlezeichnung *f*	charcoal-drawing	dessin *m* au fusain *m*
kollationieren	to collate, to compare	collationner
Kollegenrabatt *m*	discount granted to colleagues *pl*	remise *f* à titre *m* de confrère *m*
Kollektion *f*	collection	collection *f*
Kollektivanzeige *f*	composite advertisement, joint insertion	annonce *f* collective
Kollektivseite *f*	collective page	page *f* collective
Kollektivwerbung *f*	collective advertising, group advertising	publicité *f* en commun, publicité *f* groupée
Kollotypie *f*	collotype	phototypie *f*
Kolonel *f* (Mignon) (siehe Anhang)	Minion (see appendix)	corps 7 points (voir appendice)
koloriert	coloured	colorié
Kolorierung *f*	colouring	coloriage *m*
Kolorit *n*	colouring, hue, shade	couleur *f*, teinte *f*
Kolportageroman *m*	penny dreadful, shocker	roman *m* à gros effets *m/pl*, roman *m* à sensation *f*
Kolumne *f*	column	colonne *f*
Kolumnenleiste *f*	running head	titre *m* courant
Kolumnenmaß *n*	page gauge	échelle *f* de page *f*
Kolumnenschnur *f*	page cord, string	ficelle *f* à colonnes *f/pl*
Kolumnentitel *m*	column heading, running head, running title	titre *m* courant, titre *m* de colonne *f*
Kolumnist *m*	syndicated columnist	collaborateur *m* attitré, rubriquard *m*
Kombination *f*	couple	couplage *m*
Kombinationsausgabe *f*	combined edition	éditions *f/pl* couplées
Kombinationsdruck *m*	combined printing	impression *f* combinée
Kombinationspreis *m*	combination rate, combined rate	prix *m* de couplage *m*
Kombinationsrabatt *m*	clubbing offer, combined edition discount	rabais *m* de couplage *m*
kombiniert	combined	combiné
kombinierte Ätzung *f*	combination plate, combined line and half-tone block *brit*	cliché *m* trait *m* -simili combiné

kombinierte Werbeaktion *f*	tie-up advertising	publicité *f* d'association *f*
kombinierte Werbung *f*	co-op advertising	publicité *f* combinée
kombinierter Anzeigenpreis *m*	combination rate	tarif *m* combiné
kombinierter Tarif *m*	combined rate	tarif *m* combiné
kombiniertes Abonnement *n*	clubbing offer	abonnement *m* combiné
Komma *n*	comma	virgule *f*
Kommentar *m*	comment, commentary	commentaire *m*
Kommentator *m*	commentator	commentateur *m*
Kommission *f*	commission	commission *f*, provision *f*
Kommunikation *f*	communication	communication *f*
Kommunikation *f*, direkte	face-to-face communication	communication *f* nez *m* à nez *m*
Kommunikation *f*, visuelle	visual communication	médias *m/pl* visuels
Kommunikationsforschung *f*	communication research	étude *f* de la communication *f*
Kommunikationsmittel *n*	communication medium, means *pl* of communication	moyen *m* de communication *f*, véhicule *m* de communication *f*
Kommunikationsmöglichkeit *f*	possibility of communication	possibilité *f* de la communication *f*
Kommunikationspolitik *f*	communication policy	politique *f* de communication *f*
Kommunikationstheorie *f*	theory of communication	théorie *f* de la communication *f*
Kommuniqué *n*	official statement	communiqué *m*
Komparativwerbung *f*	comparative advertising	publicité *f* discriminatrice
Komplementärfarbe *f*	complementary colour	couleur *f* complémentaire
komplette Belegnummer *f*	complete voucher copy	justificatif *m* complet
kompletter Kundendienst *m*	full service	service *m* complet
kompreß	close-set, solid set	compact, plein, serré
kompreß setzen	to space closely	composer sans interlignes *f/pl*
kompresser Satz *m*	plain matter	composition *f* pleine
kompresser setzen	to close up, to set more solid	diminuner l'espace *m*, resserrer
Konferenz *f*	meeting	conférence *f*
Konferenz *f* am runden Tisch *m*	round-table meeting	réunion *f* de table *f* ronde, réunion *f* paritaire
Konjunkturaufschwung *m*	upward business trend	essor *m*
Konjunkturforschung *f*	business research	étude *f* de la conjoncture *f*
Konjunkturritter *m*	time-server	opportuniste *m*
Konjunkturrückgang *m*	downward business trend	dépression *f*
Konjunkturschwankung *f*	market vacillation	variation *f* de la conjoncture *f*
Konkurrent *m*	competitor, rival	concurrent *m*
Konkurrenz *f*	competition	concurrence *f*
Konkurrenz *f*, harte	keen competition	concurrence *f* acharnée
Konkurrenzangebot *n*	rival supply	offre *f* concurrentielle
Konkurrenzartikel *m*	rival article	article *m* concurrentiel
Konkurrenzausschluß *m*	competition clause, exclusivity stipulation	clause *f* d'exclusivité *f*, clause *f* de non-concurrence *f*
Konkurrenzbeobachtung *f*	watching of competitive advertising	pige *f* de la concurrence *f*
Konkurrenzblatt *n*	rival newspaper	journal *m* concurrent
konkurrenzfähig	competitive	à la hauteur *f* de la concurrence *f*, concurrentiel
Konkurrenzklausel *f*	clause regulating competition	clause *f* de non-concurrence *f*
konkurrenzlos	unrivalled	hors concurrence *f*
Konkurrenzmarken *f/pl*	competing brands *pl*	marques *f/pl* de compétition *f*
Konkurrenzunternehmen *n*	rival business	entreprise *f* concurrente
Konkurrenzwerbung *f*	competitive advertising	publicité *f* concurrente
konkurrieren	to compete	concourir, faire concurrence *f*
Konserve *f*, sendefertige	pre-recorded broadcast	émission *f* en différé *m*

konstruktives Plakat *n*	constructive poster	affiche *f* constructiviste
Konsum *m*	consumption	consommation *f*
Konsumartikel *m*	article of consumption	article *m* de consommation *f*
Konsument *m*	consumer	consommateur *m*
Konsumentenansprache *f*, wiederholte	repeataudience	appel *m* renouvelé aux consommateurs *m/pl*
Konsumentenwerbung *f*	consumer advertising	publicité *f* auprès des consommateurs *m/pl*
Konsumgenossenschaft *f*	co-operative	coopérative *f*
Konsumgüter *f/pl*	consumer goods *pl*, shopping goods *pl*	biens *m/pl* de consommation *f*
Konsumpionier *m*	innovator, taste-maker	pionnier *m* de la consommation *f*
Konsumwerbung *f*	consumer goods *pl* advertising	publicité *f* des biens *m/pl* de consommation *f*
Kontakt *m*	contact	contact *m*
Kontaktdruck *m*	contact print	impression *f* par contact *m*
Kontakter *m*, **Kontaktmann** *m*	account executive, account supervisor, contact man, liaison man	contacteur *m*, homme *m* de relation *f*
Kontaktgruppenleiter *m*	group head	chef *m* de groupe *m*
Kontakthäufigkeit *f*	contact frequency	fréquence *f* de contact *m*
Kontenrahmen *m*	payment plan	plan *m* comptable
Konterdruck *m*	counter-proof, reversed impression	contre-épreuve *f*, noir au blanc
Konterfei *n*	portrait	portrait *m*
kontern	to reverse	faire noir au blanc, inverser, retourner
Konterwerbung *f*	counter-advertising	contre-publicité *f*
kontinuierliche Nachfrage *f*	current demand	demande *f* continue
Kontinuität *f*	continuity	continuité *f*
Konto *n*	account	compte *m*
Kontrast *m*	contrast	contraste *m*
Kontrastfarbe *f*	contrasting colour	couleur *f* d'opposition *f*
Kontrollautsprecher *m*	monitor	haut-parleur *m* de contrôle *m*
Kontrollbildschirm *m*	monitor	écran *m* de contrôle *m*
Kontrolle *f*	check, check-up	contrôle *m*, vérification *f*
Kontrollfahrt *f*	tour of inspection	tour *m* d'inspection *f*
kontrollieren	to check	contrôler
Kontroll-Interview *n*	call-back	interview *m* rappelé
Kontrolliste *f*	check list, guide-sheet	liste *f* aide *f*-mémoire *f*, liste *f* de contrôle *m*
Kontrollziffer *f*	desk number, key	clé *f*
Konturplatte *f*	key plate	planche *f* à contours *m/pl*
Konturzeichnung *f*	definition of contours *pl*	définition *f* des contours *m/pl*, netteté *f* des contours *m/pl*
Konzentrationsprozeß *m*	economic concentration	processus *m* de concentration *f*
Konzept *n*	draft, rough copy	brouillon *m*, minute *f*, projet *m*
Konzeption *f*, **redaktionelle**	editorial conception	conception *f* rédactionnelle
konzeptionelle Grundlage *f*	copy platform	conception *f* de base *f*
Konzeptpapier *n*	scribbling paper	papier *m* commun, papier *m* ordinaire
Konzertplakat *n*	concert poster	affiche *f* de concert *m*
Konzessionierung *f*	licensing	attribution *f* d'une concession *f*
Konzessionsinhaber *m*	franchiser	concessionaire *m*
konzipieren	to draft	dessiner, élaborer
Koordinator *m*	coordinator	coordonnateur *m*

koordinieren	to co-ordinate	coordiner
koordinierte Werbung *f*	coordinated advertising	publicité *f* coordonnée
Koordinierung *f*	co-ordination	coordination *f*
Kopf *m* der Seite *f*	head of page, top of page	tête *f* de page *f*
Kopf *m* der Spalte *f*	top of column	tête *f* de colonne *f*
Kopf *m*, per	per capita	par tête *f*
Kopf *m* (Überschrift *f*)	head, heading, headline	manchette *f*, titre *m*
Kopfblatt *n*	reprint with change of title only	journal *m* se distinguant seulement d'un autre par le titre *m*
Kopfhörer *m*	headphone	casque *f* téléphonique
Kopfleiste *f*	head piece, head rules *pl*, headband	bandeau *m* de tête *f*, chapeau *m*, en-tête *f*
Kopfsteg *m*	head margin, head stick, top margin	marge *f* de tête *f*, marge *f* supérieure
kopfstehend	inverted	renversé
Kopie *f*	copy	copie *f*
Kopierdruck *m*	copying printing	impression *f* aux encres *f/pl* communicatives
kopieren	to copy, to imitate	copier, imiter
Kopiergerät *n*	contact printing machine, photostat	appareil *m* à copier, presse *f* à copier
Kopierpapier *n*	copying paper	papier *m* pour copies *f/pl*
Kopierrahmen *m*	printing-frame	châssis *m*-presse *f*
Kopierraster *m*	copying screen	trame *f* de copie *f*
Koppelanzeige *f*	tie-in advertisement	annonce *f* couplée
Koppelungsverkauf *m*	banded offer, combination sale	promotion *f* jumelée, vente *f* liée
Kornpapier *n*	grained paper	papier *m* grainé
Kornraster *m*	granulated screen	trame *f* à grain *m*
Korpus *f* (Garmond) (siehe Anhang)	Long Primer (see appendix)	corps 10 points (voir appendice)
Korrektor *m*	corrector, press reader	correcteur *m*
Korrektur *f*	correction, page proof	correction *f*
nach Korrektur *f* druckreif	good for printing with corrections *pl*, o. k. with corrections *pl am*	bon à tirer après corrections *f/pl*
Korrektur *f* lesen	proof-reading	correction *f* d'épreuves *f/pl*
Korrektur *f*, letzte	press revise	tierce *f*
Korrekturabzug *m*	proof	épreuve *f*
Korrekturbogen *m*, druckfertiger	press revise	dernière épreuve *f*
Korrekturenzettel *m*	errata slip	papillon *m* des erratas *m/pl*
Korrekturzeichen *f*	correction mark, proofreader's mark	marque *f* du correcteur *m*, signe *m* de correction *f*
Korrespondent *m*	correspondent	correspondant *m*
Korrespondent *m*, freier	stringer	correspondant *m*, qui n'appartient pas à la rédaction *f*
Korrespondenzbüro *n*	press agency	agence *f* de presse *f*
korrigieren	to correct	corriger
kosten	to cost	coûter
Kosten *pl*	costs *pl*, expenses *pl*	coûts *pl*, frais *m/pl*
Kosten *pl*, feste	fixed costs *pl*	coûts *m/pl* fixes
Kostenanschlag *m*	estimate	devis *m*
kostenlos	free of charge	gratuit, sans frais *m/pl*
kostenlose Insertion *f*	free insertion	insertion *f* gratuite

kostenlose redaktionelle Werbung *f*	free puff	gracieuseté *f*
kostenloser Kundendienst *m*	gratuitous service	service *m* bénévole
Kostenüberschreitung *f*	overstepping of estimate	dépassement *m* du devis *m*
Kostenübersicht *f*	guide of cost	sommaire *m* des frais *m/pl*
Kostenverteilung *f*	account distribution, allocation	répartition *f* des charges *f/pl*, répartition *f* des coûts *m/pl*
Kostenvoranschlag *m*	cost estimate, estimating, quotation	devis *m* estimatif, évaluation des frais *m/pl*
kostspielige Werbung *f*	expensive advertising	publicité *f* coûteuse
kraftvoller Stil *m*	style with punch in it	style *m* à l'emporte-pièce *m*
Kratzen *n* der Nadel *f*	scratch	grincement *m* de l'aiguille *f*
Kratzer *m*	scraper, scratch	égratignure *f*, griffe *f*
kreativ	creative	créateur
Kreativagentur *f*	team of creative men *pl*	cellule *f*
Kreativgruppenleiter *m*	creative director	chef *m* d'un groupe *m* créateur
Kreativität *f*	creativity	créativité *f*
Kredit *m*	credit	crédit *m*
Kreidepapier *n*	chalk overlay paper	papier *m* crayonneux
Kreidezeichnung *f*	crayon drawing	dessin *m* de crayon *m*
Kreis *m*	circle	cercle *m*
Kreppapier *n*	crêpe paper, crinkled paper	papier *m* crépon, papier *m* de crêpe *m*
Kreuz *n* (Anmerkungszeichen *n*)	dagger	croix *f*
Kreuzband *n*, unter	by bookpost	sous bande *f*
Kreuzbruchfalzung *f*	French fold, right angle folding	pliage *m* croisé
Kreuzlinienraster *m*	cross-line screen	trame *f* à lignes *f/pl* croisées
Kreuzlinienschraffur *f*	cross hatch	lignes *f/pl* croisées
Kreuzsteg *m*	gutter	blanc *m* transversal
Kreuzworträtselzeitung *f*	crossword paper	journal *m* de mots *m/pl* croisés
Krimi *m*	whodunit	roman *m* policier
Kriminalfilm *m*	action film	film *m* policier
kriminalistischer Stimmungseffekt *m*	Hitchcock appeal	effet *m* policier
Kritik *f* an der Werbung *f*	criticism of advertising	critique *f* de la publicité *f*
Kritikaster *m*	armchair critic, fault-finder	critique *m* en chambre *f*, critiqueur *m*, éplucheur *m*
Kritiker *m*	critic	critique *m*
kubisch	cubic	cubique
Kubus *m*	cube	cube *m*
Kündigungsfrist *f*	period of notice, time for giving notice	délai *m* de dédite *f*
Künstler *m*	artist	artiste *m*
Künstlerarbeit *f*	art work	travail *m* artistique
künstlerische Arbeiten *f/pl*	art work	ouvrages *m/pl* artistiques
künstlerische Werbung *f*	artistic advertising	publicité *f* artistique
künstlerischer Leiter *m*	art director	directeur *m* artistique
künstlerischer Mitarbeiter *m*, freier	outside artist	collaborateur *m* artistique à son compte *m*
Künstlerschriften *f/pl*	fancy types *pl*	caractères *m/pl* fantaisie *f*
künstlich	artificial	artificiel, synthétique
Kürzel *n*	grammalogue	sigle *m*
kürzen	to boil down, to compress, to curtail, to shorten	abréger, couper, raccourcir, rogner
Kürzung *f* der Stellenzahl *f*	reduction of the number of the ordered sites *pl*	réduction *f* du nombre *m* d'affiches *f/pl* commandées

Kugel f	bullet, sphere	boule f, sphère f
Kugelkopf m	golf-ball typing head	tête f imprimante
Kugelschreiber m	ball-point	stylo m à bille f
kultiviert	sophisticated	aux goûts m/pl compliqués
kulturelle Zeitschrift f	cultural magazine, periodical of culture	journal m culturel, périodique m de culture f
Kulturfilm m	documentary film	film m documentaire
Kulturredakteur m	cultural editor	rédacteur m de la rubrique f culturelle
kumulative Wirkung f	cumulative effect	effet m cumulatif
Kunde m	client, contractor, customer	client m
Kunde m, **eventueller, möglicher, voraussichtlicher**	prospect	prospect m
Kundenadressen-Austausch m	list-broking	échange m des adresses f/pl de clients m/pl
Kundenbesuch m	business call, calling on customers pl	visite f des clients m/pl
Kundenbetreuer m	account executive, account supervisor	contacteur m
Kundendienst m	service	service m après-vente f
Kundendienst m, **kostenloser**	gratuitous service	service m bénévole
Kundendienst m, **vollständiger**	full service	service m complet
Kundenfang m	crimping, touting	racolage m
Kundenkartei f	card-index of customers pl	fichier m de clients m/pl
Kundenkreis m	circle of clients pl, range of customers pl	clientèle f
Kunden m/pl **gewinnen**	to acquire customers pl, to attract customers pl, to drum	acquérir des clients m/pl, attirer des clients m/pl
Kundenrabatt m	discount for customers pl	rabais m au client m
Kundentreue f	customer loyalty	fidélité f des clients m/pl
Kundenwerber m	tout	pisteur m
Kundenzeitschrift f	customer magazine, sales pl bulletin, shopping news	journal m pour la clientèle f
Kunst f	art	art m
Kunst f, **angewandte**	applied art	arts m/pl industriels
Kunst f, **schwarze**	black art	magie f noire
Kunstdruck m	art print	impression f artistique
Kunstdruckabzug m	art pull	épreuve f sur papier m couché
Kunstdruckkarton m	art board, coated board	carton m couché
Kunstdruckpapier n	art paper, coated paper, enamelled paper, glossy paper	papier m couché des deux faces f/pl
Kunstdruckpapier n, **Abzug** m **auf**	art pull, glossy print proof am	épreuve f sur papier m couché
Kunstdruckpapier n, **imitiertes**	imitation art paper	papier m satiné
Kunstdruckpapier n, **mattes**	art matt paper brit, art matt am	papier m chromo
Kunstgewerbeschule f	school of applied art	école f des arts m/pl et métiers m/pl
Kunstharz n	synthetic resin	résine f synthétique
Kunstkritiker m	art critic	critique m d'art m
Kunstschule f	art school	école f d'art m
Kunststoffe m/pl	plastics pl, synthetic material	matière f artificielle, matière f synthétique
Kunststoffklischee n	nylonprint, plastic block, plastic cut, plastic stereo	cliché m plastique
Kunststoffolie f	film	film m
Kunststoffverpackung f	plastic packaging	emballage m en matière f synthétique

Kunstwort *n,* **zusammengesetztes**	blend	mot *m* téléscopé
Kupferätzung *f*	copper etching, engraving in copper	gravure *f* sur cuivre *m*
Kupferdruck *m*	copperplate printing	taille-douce *f*
Kupferhaut *f*	electro-shell, galvanic shell	coquille *f* de galvano *m*, pellicule *f* galvanoplastique en cuivre *m*
Kupferstecherkunst *f*	engraving	chalcographie *f*
Kupferstich *m*	chalcography, copperplate engraving	chalcographie *f*, estampe *f* en taille *f* douce, gravure *f*
Kupfertiefdruck *m*	copper gravure, copperplate printing, photogravure, rotogravure	impression *f* en héliogravure *f*, impression *f* en taille-douce *f*, rotogravure *f*
Kupon *m*	coupon	bon *m* à découper, coupon *m*
Kuponrücklauf *m*	response	retour *m* de coupons *m/pl*
Kuponwerbung *f*	coupon advertising	publicité *f* au moyen *m* de coupons *m/pl*
Kuppelwort *n*	hyphenated word	mot *m* à trait *m* d'union *f*
Kurrentschrift *f*	running hand	écriture *f* courante
Kursbuch *n*	railway guide, time-table	indicateur *m*
Kursivschrift *f*	Italic type, script type, sloping letters *pl*	caractère *m* italique, écriture *f* cursive
Kursus *m*	workshop	cours *m*, réunion *f* de travail *m*
Kurzanzeige *f*	short announcement	brève information *f*
Kurzartikel *m*	paragraph	entrefilet *m*
Kurzdepesche *f*	news flash	flash *m*
kurze Abhandlung *f*	essay	essai *m*
kurzer Übergang *m*	flash	transition *f* courte
kurzer Werbefilm *m*	minute movie, quickie	court-métrage *m*
kurzes Pressetelegramm *n*	flash	courte dépêche *f* d'agence *f*
Kurzfilm *m*	filmlet, minute movie, quickie, short film	court-métrage *m*
kurzfristiger Abschluß *m*	short term contract	contrat *m* à court terme *m*
kurzfristiger Anschlag *m*	temporary posting	affichage *m* temporaire
kurzgefaßter Bericht *m*	pony report	bref sommaire *m* des nouvelles *f/pl*
Kurzgeschichte *f*	short story	anecdote *f*, nouvelle *f*
Kurznachrichten *f/pl*	news in brief	faits divers *m/pl*, nouvelles *f/pl* brèves
Kurzschrift *f*	shorthand	sténographie *f*
Kurzszene *f*	blackout	pièce *f* courte
Kurzzeile *f*	broken line, short line, widow	bout *m* de ligne *f*, ligne *f* courte
Kuvert *n*	envelope	enveloppe *f*
Kuvertierung *f*	putting in an envelope	mise sous enveloppes *f/pl*

L

Lack *m*	lacquer, varnish	laque *f*, vernis *m*
lackieren	to lacquer, to varnish	laquer, vernir
Lackierung *f*	varnishing	vernissage *m*
Laden *m*	retail store, shop	magasin *m*
Ladenausstattung *f*	store fittings *pl*	installation *f* de magasin *m*
Ladeneinrichtung *f*	shop fitting	installation *f* de magasin *m*

Ladenhüter *m*	dead article, dormant stock, shelf warmer	fond *m* de tiroir *m*, garde-boutique *f*, rossignol *m*
Ladenschild *n*	on-premise sign, shop sign	enseigne *f* de magasin *m*
Ladenschluß *m*	closing time	fermeture *f* des magasins *m/pl*
Ladentischauslage *f*	counter display, counter display container	étalage *m* de comptoir *m*
Ladenverkaufspreis *m*	shop price	prix *m* de magasin *m*
Ladenwerbung *f*	shop advertising	propagande *f* par stand *m*
lädierte Buchstaben *m/pl*	battered letters *pl*	lettres *f/pl* écrasées
Länge *f*	length	longueur *f*
Lage *f* (Papier *n*)	quire, section, signature	cahier *m*
Lagebericht *m*	background report	rapport *m* sur la situation *f*
Lagerbestand *m*	stock	stock *m*
Lagerverkauf *m*	cash-and-carry	paiement *m* comptant
laminieren	to laminate	laminer
Laminierung *f*	laminating	laminage *m*
Landanschlag *m*	rural areas *pl* posting	affichage *m* rural
Landkarte *f*	map	carte *f*
Landkartenpapier *n*	map paper	papier *m* pour cartes *f/pl* géographiques
Landschaftsaufnahme *f*	landscape photo	prise *f* de vue *f* paysage
Landwirtschaftsbeilage *f*	farmer's supplement	supplément *m* rurale
Landwirtschaftsblatt *n*	agriculture publication, farm publication	feuille *f* rurale, journal *m* agricole
langatmig	long-winded	de longue haleine *f*
Langformat *n*	oblong size	format *m* oblong
langfristig	long-term	à long terme *m*, à longue échéance *f*
langfristig geplante Werbekampagne *f*	pre-planned advertising campaign	campagne *f* à longue échéance *f*
langfristiger Entwicklungs-trend *m*	secular trend	évolution *f* à long terme *m*
langlebige Gebrauchsgüter *n/pl*	hard goods *pl*	biens *m/pl* de consommation *f* durables
langlebiges Buch *n*	long seller, steady seller	livre *m* durable
Langspielplatte *f*	microgroove	microsillon *m*
Langzeitwirkung *f*	longtime-effect	effet *m* continué
lanzieren	to launch	lancer
Lanzierung *f*	launching	lancement *m*
Lasche *f*	flap	gousset *m*
Lasurfarbe *f*	glaze, transparent ink	couleur *f* à vernisser, encre *f* transparente
latenter Bedarf *m*	hidden demand	besoin *m* latent
Laterna *f* magica	living screen	combinaison *f* du cinéma *m* et d'acteurs *m/pl*, lanterne *f* magique
Latrinenparolen *f/pl*	grape-vine	téléphone *m* arabe
Lattenzaun *m*	lattice work	bardage *m*
laufender Auftrag *m*	continuous order, standing order	ordre *m* permanent
Laufkundschaft *f*	irregular customers *pl*	clientèle *f* de passage *m*
Laufrichtung *f*	fiber direction *am*, fibre direction *brit*	sens *m* de fabrication *f*
Laufschrift *f*	illuminated newscaster	écriture *f* courante
Lauftasche *f*	docket	chemise *f* de travail *m*
Laufzeit *f*	propagation time, running time, transit time	rut *m*
Laufzettel *m*	job ticket, slip	fiche *f* de travail *m*

Lautschrift *f*	phonetic transcription	transcription *f* phonétique
Lautsprecheranlage *f*	public address system	ensemble micro-ampli-haut-parleur *m*
Lautsprecherwagen *m*	sound truck	camion *m* publicitaire
Lautsprecherwerbung *f*	loudspeaker advertising	publicité *f* par haut-parleur *m*
Layout *n*	page-plan, rough, tracing	maquette *f*
Layout *n*, detailliertes	comprehensive	maquette *f* détaillée
Lebensdauer *f*	duration of life	durée *f* de vie *f*
Lebensmittelversorgung *f*	catering	approvisionnement *m*
Lebensstandard *m*	economic status, living standard	standard *m* de vie *f*
Leckerbissen *m*, literarischer	tit-bit	miette *f* de la semaine *f*
Lederband *m*	leather binding	reliure *f* peau *f* pleine
Lederpapier *n*	leather paper	papier-cuir *m*
Lederpappe *f*	leather board	carton *m* cuir *m*
Leerdruck *m*	blanks *pl*	blancs *m/pl*
leere Seite *f*	blank page	page *f* blanche, page *f* en blanc, page *f* vierge *f*
leeres Geschwätz *n*	bunkum, hokum	boniments *m/pl*, paroles *f/pl* vides
Leerpackung *f*	dummy	factice *f*
Legende *f*	caption, legend	légende *f*
Lehrfilm *m*	educational film, instructional film	film *m* éducatif
Lehrgang *m*	workshop	cours *m*, réunion *f* de travail *m*
Leibblatt *n*	favourite paper	feuille *f* favorite
Leiche *f* (Auslassung *f*)	missing word, omission, out	bourdon *m*
leicht hingehen über	to slur over	glisser sur
leichte Lektüre *f*	light reading	lecture *f* récréative
leichte Plauderei *f*	chatly article, small talk	article *m* léger, menus *m/pl* propos
leichtverkäufliches Buch *n*	quick seller	livre *m* d'écoulement *m* facile
Leihbuchwerbung *f*	advertising by inserts *pl* in books *pl* of a lending library	publicité *f* par encarts *m/pl* dans les livres *m/pl* en location *f*
Leim *m*	glue, paste	colle *f*
Leimung *f*	sizing	encollage *m*
Leinen *n*	cloth	toile *f*
Leinenpapier *n*	linen-paper	papier *m* entoilé
Leinenstruktur *f* (Papier)	crash finish	structure *f* treillis *m*
Leinwand *f*	canvas, linen, screen	écran *m*, toile *f*
Leinwand *f*, bemalte	painted cloth	toile *f* peinte
Leinwandplakat *n*	linen poster	affiche *f* toile
leise Werbung *f*	soft approach	publicité *f* en douceur *f*
Leistung *f*	performance	accomplissement *m*, prestation *f*, rendement *m*
Leitartikel *m*	editorial, leader, leading article	article *m* de fond *m*, article *m* de tête *f*, éditorial *m*
Leitartikel *m*, gegenüber	facing leader	face *f* éditorial *m*
Leiter *m* der Marktforschung *f*	research director	chef *m* des études *f/pl* de marché *m*
Leiter *m* der Mediaabteilung *f*	media director	chef *m* du service *m* médias *m/pl*
Leiter *m* einer Mediagruppe *f*	media supervisor	chef *m* d'un groupe *m* médias *m/pl*
Leiter *m* einer Unterhaltungssendung *f*	showmaster	directeur *m* d'une émission *f* amusante
Leiter *m*, künstlerischer	art director	directeur *m* artistique

Leiter *m*, **technischer**	technical manager	directeur *m* technique
Leitfaden *m*	guide, handbook, manual	guide *m*, manuel *m*
Leitmotiv *n*	leitmotif	leitmotiv *m*
Leitmotiv *n*, **musikalisches**	jingle	indicatif *m* musical
Leitstudie *f*	pilot study	enquête *f* pilote
Leitungsdraht *m*	wire	fil *m* télégraphique
Lektor *m*	copy editor	lecteur *m* d'une maison *f* d'édition *f*
Lektüre *f*	reading	lecture *f*
Lektüre *f*, **leichte**	light reading	lecture *f* récréative
Leporellofalzung *f*	accordion folding, concertina folding, fanfold form	pli *m* accordéon *m*, pli *m* en zig-zag
Lesart *f*	reading, version	version *f*
Lesbarkeit *f*	legibility	lisibilité *f*
Lesedauer *f*	reading duration	temps *m* de lecture *f*
Lesegeschwindigkeit *f*	reading rate	vitesse *f* de lecture *f*
Lesegewohnheit *f*	reading behaviour, reading habits *pl*	habitudes *f/pl* des lecteurs *m/pl*
Leseintensität *f*	reading intensity	intensité *f* de la lecture *f*
Lesemappe *f*	reading circle case	enveloppe *f* dans les cercles *m/pl* de lecture *f*
Lesen *n*, **maschinelles**	character recognition	lecture *f* mécanique
Leseprobe *f*	specimen	spécimen *m* de texte *m*
Leser *m*	reader	lecteur *m*
Leseranalyse *f*	audience analysis, circulation analysis, reader interest research, readership survey	analyse *f* de l'audience *f*, analyse *f* des lecteurs *m/pl*
Leseratte *f*	book-hunter, paper worm	bouquineur *m*, rat *m* de bibliothèque *f*
Leserblattbindung *f*	connexion of readers *pl* with their paper, reader-magazine-relationship	relations *f/pl* des lecteurs *m/pl* avec leur journal *m*
Leserbriefspalte *f*	letter-bag, letters *pl* column	colonne *f* des lettres *f/pl* à la rédaction *f*, courrier *m* des lecteurs *m/pl*
Leserforum *n*	open forum	point *m* de vue *f* des lecteurs *m/pl*
Leserkreis *m*	circle of readers *pl*, readership	cercle *m* de lecteurs *m/pl*, degré *m* de lecture *f*
Leser *m/pl*, **regelmäßige**	regular readers *pl*	lecteurs *m/pl* réguliers
Leserschaft *f*	audience, readers *pl*, readership	audience *f*, ensemble *m* des lecteurs *m/pl*, lecteurs *m/pl*, masse *f* des lecteurs *m/pl*
Leserschaftsforschung *f*	reader interest research	étude *f* des lecteurs *m/pl*
Leserschaftsumfrage *f*	readership poll	enquête *f* auprès des lecteurs *m/pl*
Leserstamm *m*	stock of regular readers *pl*	noyau *m* de lecteurs *m/pl*
Lesertreue *f*	constancy of readership, reader confidence	fidélité *f* de lecture *f*
Leserverbundenheit *f*	reader's attachment	attachement *m* à la revue *f*
Leserzahl *f*	readership figure	nombre *m* des lecteurs *m/pl*
Leserzuschrift *f*	letter to the editor	lettre *f* à la rédaction *f*
Lesesaal *m*	reading-room	salle *f* de lecture *f*
Lesestoff *m*	reading matter	choses *f/pl* à lire
Lesezeichen *n*	bookmark. reading mark	signet *m*

Lesezirkelwerbung *f*	advertising in circulating magazines *pl*, advertising in reading circles *pl*	publicité *f* dans les cercles *m/pl* de lecture *f*
Letter *f*	letter, type	lettre *f*, type *m*
Letternmetall *n*	type metal	métal *m* à caractères *m/pl*
letzte Ausgabe *f*	current number	dernier numéro *m* paru
letzte Korrektur *f*	final proof, press revise	morasse *f*, tierce *f*
letzte Meldungen *f/pl*	latest intelligence	dernières nouvelles *f/pl*
letzte Modeneuheit *f*	latest fashion	dernier cri *m*
letzte Nachrichten *f/pl*	latest news, stop-press news	informations *f/pl* de dernière heure *f*
letzte Seite *f*	last page	page *f* dernière
letzte Zeile eines Absatzes *m*	break line	dernière ligne *f* d'un paragraphe *m*
letzter Minute *f* einrücken, in	to fudge	insérer en dernière minute *f*
Letztverbraucher *m*	ultimate consumer	consommateur *m* final
Leuchtbuchstabe *m*	illuminated letter	lettre *f* lumineuse
Leuchtdruck *m*	fluorescent ink printing	impression *f* avec encre *f* fluorescente
Leuchtfarbe *f*	luminous ink, luminous paint	encre *f* lumineuse
Leuchtfarbenplakat *n*	day-glo poster	affiche *f* irisée
Leuchtkasten *m*	box sign	caisson *m* lumineux
Leuchtkraft *f*	intensity of light	intensité *f* lumineuse
Leuchtschrift *f*	luminous signs *pl*	annonce *f* lumineuse
Leuchtstoffröhre *f*	fluorescent lamp, luminescent lamp	tube *m* fluorescent
Leuchtwerbung *f*	electric sign advertising, illuminated advertising	publicité *f* lumineuse
Leuchtwerbung *f*, bewegliche	spectacular	publicité *f* lumineuse animée
Lexikon *n*	encyclopaedia, lexicon	encyclopédie *f*, lexique *m*
Lichtbild *n*	photograph	photographie *f*
Lichtbildsammlung *f*	photographic library	photothèque *f*
Lichtdruck *m*	collotype, photogelatine	phototypie *f*
lichte Schrift *f*	light-faced type	caractères *m/pl* éclairés
lichtecht	fast to light	solide à la lumière *f*
Lichteinwirkung *f*, chemische	photochemistry	photochimie *f*
lichtempfindlich	panchromatic	panchromatique
lichtempfindliche Farbe *f*	fugitive colour	couleur *f* sensible à la lumière *f*
lichtempfindliches Papier *n*	sensitized paper	papier *m* sensibilisé
Lichtempfindlichkeit *f*	sensitiveness to light	sensibilité *f* à la lumière *f*
Lichtpausgerät *n*	blue print apparatus	appareil *m* à tirer les bleus *m/pl*
Lichtreflektor *m*	rear reflector	cataphote *m*
Lichtsatz *m*	film setting, photo lettering, photo typesetting, photo(graphic) composition	composition *f* photographique, photocomposition *f*, phototypie *f*
Lichtsatzprogramm *n*	photocomposition programme	programme *m* de photocomposition *f*
Lichtsatzsystem *n*	photocomposing system	système *m* de photocomposition *f*
lichtsetzen	photo lettering	composer photographique
Lichtsetzmaschine *f*	filmsetting machine, phototypesetter, video-setter	composeuse *f* photographique, photocompeuse *f*, phototitreuse *f*
Lichtspielhaus *n*	cinema, movie theater, movies *pl am*, picture house	cinéma *m*
Lichtspieltheaterwerbung *f*	advertising in cinemas *pl*	publicité *f* cinématographique

Lichttonverfahren *n*	photographic sound-recording	prise *f* de son *m* photographique
Lichtwerbung *f*	animation, electric sign advertising	publicité *f* lumineuse
Lichtwerbung *f*, **bewegliche**	animated electric sign advertising	publicité *f* lumineuse animée
Lichtzeichnung *f*	light drawing	dessin *m* phototechnique
Liebesgeschichte *f*	love story	histoire *f* d'amour *m*
Liebhaberei *f*	hobby	passe-temps *m* favori, violon *m* d'Ingres
liederlich zusammengestellte Seite *f*	badly imposed page	feuille *f* bambochée
Lieferant *m*	purveyor, supplier	fournisseur *m*
Lieferbedingungen *f/pl*	terms *pl* of delivery	conditions *f/pl* de livraison *f*
Lieferdatum *n*	delivery date	date *f* de livraison *f*
Lieferfrist *f*	delivery delay	délai *m* de livraison *f*
Lieferpreis *m*	delivery price	prix *m* à la livraison *f*
Lieferschein *m*	delivery note, receipt	décharge *f* de livraison *f*, reçu
Liefertermin *m*	delivery date, term for delivery	date *f* de livraison *f*, délai *m* de livraison *f*
Lieferung *f*	delivery	livraison *f*
Lieferung *f* **frei Haus** *n*	free delivery, house delivery	livraison *f* à domicile *m*
Lieferung *f* (**Heft** *n* **eines Werkes** *n*)	issue	fascicule *m*
Lieferungsangebot *n*	tender	soumission *f*
Lieferzeit *f*	delivery period	délai *m* de livraison *f*
liegengebliebener Satz *m*	crowded out matter	matière *f* restée sur le marbre *m*
Ligatur *f*	double letter, ligature	deux lettres *f/pl* ligaturées, ligature *f*
Lineal *n*	ruler	règle *f*
linear	linear	linéaire
Linenschrägung *f*	slope of line	crênage *m*
Linie *f*	line, rule *typog*	filet *m* (typogr.) , ligne *f*
Linie *f*, **englische**	plain swelled rule	filet *m* anglais
Linie *f*, **feine**	fine-face rule	filet *m* maigre
Linie *f*, **fette**	fat line	ligne *f* en gras
Linie *f* **halten**	to align, to straighten line	parangonner
Linie *f*, **punktierte**	dotted line, dotted rule	filet *m* pointillé, ligne *f* de pointillés *m/pl*
Linie *f*, **stumpffeine**	blunt rule	ligne *f* épointée
Linienblatt *n*	guideline	transparent *m* rayé
Linienmaterial *n*	rules *pl*	filets *m/pl*
Linienrand *m*	line border, ruled frame	bordure *f* en filets *m/pl*, cadre *m* de filets *m/pl*
liniiertes Papier *n*	ruled paper	papier *m* réglé
linke Ecke *f*	left-hand corner	coin *m* gauche
linke Seite *f*	even page, left-hand page	en verso, fausse page *f*, page *f* de gauche
links ausschließen, nach	to move to the left	justifier à la gauche
links oben	top left position	emplacement *m* supérieur à gauche
links unten	bottom left	bas de la page *f* gauche
linkseingestellte Zeitung *f*	leftist paper	journal *m* gauchiste
Linkspresse *f*	leftist press	presse *f* de gauche
linksseitig	reverso	envers
Linoleumdruck *m*	lino printing	impression *f* de linoléum *m*

Linolschnitt *m*	lino-cut	gravure *f* sur lino *m*
Linotypemaschine *f*	linotype machine	machine *f* linotype
Linotypesatz *m*	linotype composition	composition *f* linotype *f*
Linotypesetzer *m*	linotype operator	linotypiste *m*
Linotype-Setzmaschine *f*	linotype	linotype *f*
Liste *f*	catalogue *brit*, list	liste *f*
Liste *f* des verfügbaren Anschlagraums *m*	available sites *pl* list	pointage *m* des emplacements *m/pl* disponibles
Listenpreis *m*	listprice, scale rate	prix *m* au tarif *m*, prix *m* de barême *m*
literarischer Betrug *m*	fabricated account	supercherie *f* littéraire
Literat *m*	man of letters *pl*	homme *m* de lettres *f/pl*
Literatur *f*, rührselige	squish	guimauve *f*
Literatur *f*, schöne	fiction	belles-lettres *f/pl*
Literatur *f*, sentimentale	sob-stuff, squish	bonbon *m* fondant, littérature *f* larmoyante
Literaturbeilage *f*	literary supplement	supplément *m* littéraire
Literaturblatt *n*	notices *pl* of new publications *pl*	bulletin *m* littéraire
Literaturverzeichnis *n*	bibliography	bibliographie *f*
Litfaßsäule *f*	poster pillar	colonne-affiche *f*
Lithograf *m*	lithographer	lithographe *m*
Lithografie *f*	litho, lithography	litho *f*, lithographie *f*
lithografische Anstalt *f*	lithographic plant	atelier *m* de lithographie *f*
Live-Sendung *f*	live broadcast	émission *f* en direct, prise *f* de vue *f* directe
Lizenz *f*	franchise, license	licence *f*
Lizenzausgabe *f*	licensed edition	édition *f* licenciée
Lizenzgebühren *f/pl*	royalties *pl*	droit *m* de license *f*
Lizenzträger *m*	licensee	porteur *m* d'une licence *f*
Lizenzübertragung *f*	franchising	attribution *f* d'une licence *f*
Lobbyismus *m*	lobbying	intrigues *m/pl* de couloirs *m/pl*
Lobrede *f*	eulogy, panegyric	éloge *m*, panégyrique *m*
Lochkarte *f*	punched card	fiche *f* perforée
Lochkartenleser *m*	card reader	lecteur *m* des cartes *f/pl* perforées
Lochstreifen *m*	paper tape, punched tape	bande *f* perforée, ruban *m* perforé
Lockartikel *m*	bait, catch-penny article, loss leader, lure	article *m* d'appel *m*, article *m* de réclame *f*, produit *m* d'appel *m*
lockere Manier *f*	loose	d'une manière *f* dissolue
Löschblattreklame *f*	blotter advertising	publicité *f* sur papier *m* buvard
löschen	to delete	effacer
Löschpapier *n*	blotting-paper	papier *m* buvard
löten	to solder	souder
Logotype *f*	logotype	logotype *m*
Lohnbeutelwerbung *f*	pay envelope advertising	publicité *f* sur les enveloppes *f/pl* de paye *f*
Lohntütenwerbung *f*	pay envelopes advertising	publicité *f* sur enveloppes *f/pl* de paye *m*
Lokalberichterstatter *m*, freier	free lance reporter	stringer *m*
Lokalisierung *f*	localization	localisation *f*
Lokalkolorit *n*	local colour	couleur *f* locale
Lokalnachrichten *f/pl*	local news	chronique *f* locale
Lokalpatriotismus *m*	local patriotism	rivalités *f/pl* de clocher *m*

Lokalredakteur *m*	city editor, local editor	rédacteur *m* local
Lokalseite *f*	regional page	page *f* régionale
Lokaltarif *m*	local rate	tarif *m* local
Lokaltratsch *m*	local item	faits *m/pl* divers locals
Lokalwerbung *f*	local advertising	publicité *f* locale
Lokalzeitung *f*	local paper	feuille *f* locale
Losbriefwerbung *f*	advertising on lottery ticket letters *pl*	publicité *f* sur des billets *m/pl* de loterie *f*
lose Beilage *f*	loose insert	encart *m* libre
Loseblattbuch *n*	loose-leaf book	livre *m* à feuilles *f/pl* mobiles
Losung *f*	watchword	devise *f*
Lotterielos *n*	lottery-ticket	billet *m* de loterie *f*
Lückenbüßer *m*	stopgap advertisement	bouche-trou *m*
Lügendetektor *m*	polygraph	polygraphe *m*
Lügengewebe *n*	web of lies *pl*	tissu *m* de mensonges *m/pl*
lügnerische Werbung *f*	lying advertising	publicité *f* mensongère
Luftaufnahme *f*	aerial photograph	photo *f* aérienne
Luftballonwerbung *f*	dirigible advertising	publicité *f* par dirigeable *m*
Luftbild *n*	aerial photograph	photo *f* aérienne
luftige Anzeige *f*	advertisement with much white space	annonce *f* bien aérée
Luftkursbuch *n*	airline guide	guide *m* aérien
Luftpostausgabe *f*	air edition	édition *f* aéropostale
Luftpostpapier *n*	airmail paper, onionskin	papier *m* -pelure *f*, papier *m* avion *m*
Luftschriftwerbung *f*	sky line advertising, sky typing	publicité *f* aérienne
Luftwerbung *f*	aerial advertising, air advertising, skyline advertising	publicité *f* aérienne
lumbecken	perfect-bind by employing the Lumbeck method, to lumbeck	relier par collage *m*
Lumbeckheftung *f*	Lumbeck binding	brochage *m* Lumbeck
Luxusausgabe *f*	de luxe edition	édition *f* de luxe *m*
Luxusblatt *n*	luxury paper, slick magazine	journal *m* luxueux, périodique *m* de luxe *m*
Luxuswaren *f/pl*	luxury goods *pl*	articles *m/pl* de luxe *m*

M

Mängel *m/pl*	deficiencies *pl*	manques *m/pl*
Mängelrüge *f*	complaint	réclamation *f*
männliches Fotomodell *n*	dressman	mannequin *m* mâle, mannequin *m* masculin
Magazin *n*	magazine, periodical, review	magazine *m*, revue *f*
mager	lean, light, thin	maigre, mince
magere Schrift *f*	lean-faced type	caractères *m/pl* maigres
magerer Satz *m*	thin face	composition *f* maigre
Magnetband *n*	magnetic tape, videotape	bande *f* magnétique vidéo, ruban *m* magnétique
Magnetbandkassette *f*	magnetic tape cassette	cassette *f* à bandes *f/pl* magnétiques
Magnetfilmspule *f*	magnetic film spool	bobine *f* de la bande *f* magnétique
Magnetofon *n*	magnetophone	magnétophone *m*
Magnetschild *n*	magnetic sign	écriteau *m* aimanté
Magnettonband *n*	videotape	bande *f* magnétique vidéo
Mahnbrief *m*	demand-note	lettre *f* de rappel *m*

mahnen	to admonish, to remind	mettre en demeurre *m*, sommer
Mahnung *f*	reminder	mise *f* en demeurre *f*, sommation *f*
Majuskel *f*	cap	capitale *f*, lettre *f* majuscule
Majuskeln *f/pl*	capital letters *pl*	lettres *f/pl* majuscules
Makler *m*	broker	courtier *m*
Makulatur *f*	misprint, spoil, waste paper	maculature *f*, papier *m* de rebut *m*
Makulaturpapier *n*	set-off paper, slip sheets *pl*	papier *m* maculé
Mal- und Mengenstaffel *f*	schedule for discount by frequency and volume	dégressif *m* sur la fréquence *f* et le volume *m*
Malerei *f*	painting	peinture *f*
Mammutplakat *n*	mammoth poster	affiche *f* mammouth
Manager *m*	manager	gestionnaire *m*
Mangelware *f*	shortage goods *pl*	marchandise *f* rare
Manier *f*, lockere	loose	d'une manière *f* dissolue
Manilapapier *n*	manila paper	papier *m* bulle *f*
Manipulation *f* von Nachrichten *f/pl*	news management	manipulation *f* de nouvelles *f/pl*
manipulieren	to manipulate	manipuler
Mann *m* auf der Straße *f*	man-on-street	citoyen *m* moyen, homme *m* de la rue *f*
Mannequin *m*	mannequin	démonstratrice *f*, mannequin *m*
Mannschaft *f*	crew, team	équipe *f*
Manuskript *n*	copy, manuscript, MS	copie *f*, manuscrit *m*, ms
Manuskript *n* beachten	follow copy	à composer tel quel
Manuskript *n*, druckfertiges	fair copy	belle copie *f*
Manuskript *n*, schlechtes	bad copy	cheveu *m*
Manuskript *n* warten, auf	to wait copy	manquer de copie *f*
Manuskriptannahme *f*	acceptance of manuscripts *pl*	acceptation *f* des manuscrits *m/pl*
Manuskriptbearbeitung *f*	copy styling	préparation *f* de la copie *f*
Manuskripthalter *m*	copy-holder	porte-copie *m*
Manuskriptumfang *m*	calibration	calibration *f*
Manuskriptumfangsberechnung *f*	calibrating of a copy	calibrage *m* d'une copie *f*
Maquette *f*	layout	maquette *f*
Marginalien *f/pl*	marginal notes *pl*, side-notes *pl*	notes *f/pl* marginales
Marke *f*	brand, make	marque *f*
Markenartikel *m*	branded goods *pl*, specialty goods *pl*	article *m* de marque *f*, produit *m* de marque *f* déposée
Markenartikelwerbung *f*	brand advertising	publicité *f* de marque *f*
Markenbetreuer *m*	brand manager	spécialiste *m* produit *m*
Markenbevorzugung *f*	brand preference	préférence *f* d'une marque *f*
Markenbild *n*	brand image	image *f* de marque *f*
Markencharakter *m*	product personality	caractère *m* propre d'une marque *f*
Markenerkennung *f*	brand identification	identification *f* d'une marque *f*
Markenindex *m*	brand trend survey	baromètre *m* des marques *f/pl*
Markenname *m*	brand name, trade name	appellation *f*, nom *m* de la marque *f*
Markenschutz *m*	trade mark protection	protection *f* des marques *f/pl*
Markenstil *m*	style of marks *pl*	style *m* de marque *f*
Markentreue *f*	brand loyalty, brand preference, consumer insistence	fidélité *f* à la marque *f*

Markenwechsel *m*	brand switching	changement *m* de marque *f*
Markenwechsler *m*	brand switcher	acheteur *m* passant d'une marque *f* à l'autre
Markenzeichen *n*	device, logotype, trade mark	logotype *m*
Marketing *n*	marketing	commercialisation *f*, marketing *m*
Marketingabteilung *f*	marketing department	bureau *m* marketing
Marketingkonzeption *n*	marketing concept	conception *f* marketing
Marketingmix *n*	marketing mix	marketing *m* mix *m*
Marketingplan *m*	marketing plan	plan *m* de marketing *m*
Marketingpolitik *f*	marketing policy	politique *f* de marketing *m*
Marketingstrategie *f*	marketing strategy	stratégie *f* marketing
Markt *m*	market, outlet	débouché *m*, marché *m*
Markt *m*, **gemeinsamer**	common market	marché *m* commun
Markt *m*, **gesättigter**	glutted market	marché *m* encombré
Markt *m*, **grauer**	gray market	marché *m* gris
Markt *m*, **überschwemmter**	glutted market	marché *m* inondé
Marktanalyse *f*	market analysis	analyse *f* du marché *m*
Marktanalytiker *m*	market analyst	analyste *m* du marché *m*
Marktanteil *m*	market share	part *f* de marché *m*, quote-part *f*
Marktausweitung *f*	market extension	expansion *f* du marché *m*
Marktbeobachtung *f*	market observation	observation *f* du marché *m*
Marktberater *m*	marketing consultant	conseil *m* en marketing *m*
Marktbericht *m*	market report	bulletin *m* financier
Marktfähigmachung *f*	marketing	commercialisation *f*, marketing *m*
Marktforscher *m*	head counter, market researcher	enquêteur *m* commercial
Marktforschung *f*	field investigation, market analysis, market research	étude *f* du marché *m*, recherche *f* du marché *m*
Marktforschungsberater *m*	market research counsellor	conseil *m* en études *f/pl* de marché *m*
Marktforschungsinstitut *n*	market research institute	institut *m* d'études *f/pl* de marché *m*
Marktgeltung *f*	market standard	importance *f* au marché *m*
marktgerecht	marketable	vendable
Marktgestaltung *f*	marketing	commercialisation *f*
Marktlage *f*	level of market demand, market condition, marketing background	situation *f* du marché *m*
Marktlücke *f*	loop-hole in the market, marketing-gap	lacune *f* dans le marché *m*
Marktplan *m*	marketing-mix	marketing *m* mix
Marktplanung *f*	marketing	commercialisation *f*, marketing *m*
Marktsättigung *f*	market saturation	encombrement *m* du marché *m*
Marktschaffung *f*	marketing	commercialisation *f*
marktschreierische Werbung *f*	ballyhoo *am*, noisy advertising, puffing publicity	battage *m* publicitaire, bourrage *m* de crâne *m*, publicité *f* raccrocheuse, publicité *f* tapageuse, tam-tam *m*
Marktsegment *n*	market segment	segment *m* du marché *m*
Marktstrategie *f*	marketing strategy	stratégie *f* de marché *m*
Markttendenz *f*	trend	tendance *f* du marché *m*
Marktüberschwemmung *f*	glut of the market	inondation *f* du marché *m*

Marktuntersuchung *f*	market investigation, market survey	enquête *f* sur le marché *m*
Marktuntersuchung *f*, regionale	area sampling	échantillonnage *m* par zone *f*
Marktuntersuchung *f*, repräsentative	adequate sample	échantillon *m* représentatif
marmoriertes Papier *n*	marbled paper	papier *m* marbré
Maroquin *n*	marocco leather	maroquin *m*
maschinelles Lesen *n*	character recognition	lecture *f* mécanique
Maschinenabzug *m*	press proof	morasse *f*
Maschinenbüttenpapier *n*	mould made paper	papier *m* à la cuve *f* à la machine *f*
maschinenglattes Papier *m*	M. F. (machine finished) paper	papier *m* apprêté machine *f*
Maschinenreinigung *f*	machine washing	lavage *m* de machine *f*
Maschinenrevision *f*	press revise	dernière épreuve *f*, tierce épreuve *f*
Maschinensatz *m*	machine composition, mechanical composition *am*, mechanical typesetting	composition *f* à la machine *f*, composition *f* mécanique
Maschinenschreiber *m*	typist	dactylographe *m*
Maschinensetzer *m*	machine-compositor, operator	claviste *m*, opérateur *m*
Maschinenzeile *f*	slug	ligne-bloc *f*
Maschineschreiben *n*	typewriting	dactylographie *f*
Maserpapier *n*	grained paper	papier *m* grainé
maskierte Anzeige *f*	advertisement masked out in part	annonce *f* masquée en partie *f*
Maßeinheiten *f/pl*, typografische (siehe Anhang)	typographical units *pl* of measurement (see appendix)	mesures *f/pl* typographiques (voir appendice)
Massenabsatz *m*	mass selling	vente *f* massive
Massenartikel *f*	bulk article	article *m* de série *f*
Massenauflage *f*	bulk circulation, mass circulation, mass edition	gros tirage *m*
Massenaufnahme *f*	crowd shot	prise *f* de vue *f* en masse *f*
Massendrucksachen *f/pl*	bulk mail	imprimés *m/pl* expédiés en nombre *m*
Massenkommunikation *f*	mass communication	communication *f* de masse *f*
Massenmedium *n*	mass medium	mass-média *m*
Massenprodukt *n*	mass product	produit *m* de grande consommation *f*
Massensendungen *f/pl*, postalische	bulk posting	envois *m/pl* en nombre *m*
Massensuggestion *f*	mass suggestion	suggestion *f* grégaire
Massenversand *m*	mass mailing	envoi *m* en masse *f*
Massenwahn *m*	mass craziness	folie *f* grégaire
Massewalze *f*	composition roller	rouleau *m* à encrer
Maßnahmen *f/pl*, absatzpolitische	merchandizing	mise *f* en valeur *f*, techniques *f/pl* marchandes
Maßnahmen *f/pl* zur Steigerung *f* des Absatzes *m* beim Einzelhandel *m*	merchandizing	moyens *m/pl* pour aider à la revente *f* par le détaillant *m*
Maßstab *m*	scale, yardstick	échelle *f*, règle *f* graduée
Maßsystem *n*, typografisches (siehe Anhang)	typographic system of measurement (see appendix)	mesures *f/pl* typographiques (voir appendice)
Mastenwerbung *f*	sign mast advertising	mât *m* publicitaire, publicité *f* sur potelets *m/pl*

Mater *f*	flong, mat *am*, matrix	flan *m*, matrice *f*
Material *n*, **grundlegendes**	basic dates *pl*	données *f/pl* de base *f*
matern	to mould	mouler
Materndienst *m*	matrix service	service *m* de matrices *f/pl*
Maternkorrespondenz *f*	mat service, ready print	service *m* matrice
Maternpappe *f*	flong board, matrix board	carton *m* pour flans *m/pl*
Matrize *f*	matrix, mould, stencil	matrice *f*, stencil *m*
Matrizenkarton *m*	mat board	flan *m*
matt satiniert	English finished (E.F.)	satiné mat
Mattdruck *m*	dull-finish printing	impression *f* mate
matte Oberfläche *f*	mat surface	surface *f* mate
mattes Kunstdruckpapier *n*	art matt paper *brit*, art matt *am*	papier *m* chromo, papier *m* couché mat
mattieren	to frost glass	dépolir, mater, matir
mattiertes Papier *n*	dull-finished paper	papier *m* mat
Mattkopie *f*	matt print	épreuve *f* sur papier *m* mat
Mauerbemalung *f*	painting on walls *pl*	peinture *f* murale
Mauerwerbung *f*	wall advertising	publicité *f* murale
mechanische Werbung *f*	mechanical advertising	publicité *f* mécanique
Medaille *f*	medal	médaille *f*
Mediaagentur *f*	independent media services *pl* company	intermédiaire *m* publicitaire
Mediaanalyse *f*	media analysis	analyse *f* des médias *m/pl*
Mediaarten *f/pl*	types *pl* of media	types *m/pl* des médias *m/pl*
Mediaauswahl *f*	media selection	sélection *f* des médias *m/pl*
Mediadisponent *m*	space buyer	acheteur *m* d'espace *m*
Mediaeinsatz *m*	media performance	emploi *m* des médias *m/pl*
Mediäval *f*	old face, old style	caractère *m* mediéval, Elzévir *m*
Mediaforschung *f*	media research	étude *f* des médias *m/pl*
Mediakombination *f*	media mix	combinaison *f* des médias *m/pl*
Medialeiter *m*	media manager	directeur *m* des médias *m/pl*
Medianutzer *m*	media user	usager *m* de médias *m/pl*
Mediaplan *m*	media plan	plan *m* média *m*
Mediaplaner *m*	media planner	media-planneur *m*
Mediaplanung *f*	media planning, scheduling	plan *m* de campagne *f*
Mediaplattform *f*	media platform	plate-forme *f* média *m*
Mediasachbearbeiter *m*	media clerk, media man	acheteur *m* d'espace *m*
Mediaselektion *f*	media selection	choix *m* des médias *m/pl*, sélection *f* des médias *m/pl*
Mediastrategie *f*	media strategy	orchestration *f* des différents supports *m/pl*
Medienabteilung *f*	media department	service *m* médias *m/pl*
Mediengewicht *f*	media weight	poids *m* d'un média *m*
Medienlandschaft *f*	media scenery	paysage *m* des médias *m/pl*
Medien *n/pl* **der Werbung** *f* **im Verkehr** *m*	traffic media	médias *m/pl* de la publicité *f* dans les moyens *m/pl* de transport *m*
Medien *n/pl*, **klassische**	classic media *pl*	médias *m/pl* classiques
Medien *n/pl*, **national verbreitete**	national media *pl*	médias *m/pl* répandus dans tout le pays *m*
Medien *n/pl*, **unterstützende**	supporting media *pl*	médias *m/pl* appuyants
Medienverbund *m*	combination of various means *pl* of communication, combined scheduling	combinaison *f* de divers moyens *m/pl* de communication *f*
Medienverflechtung *f*	cross-channel-ownership	interdépendance *f* des médias *f*
Medienvergleich *m*	media comparison	comparaison *f* des médias *m/pl*

Medium *n*	medium	média *m*, support *m* de publicité *f*
medizinische Zeitschrift *f*	medical journal	publication *f* médicale
Mehrauflage *f*	overs *pl*	excédant *m* de tirage *m*
Mehrdruck *m*	overprint	repiquage *m*, surimpression *f*
mehrere Packungen *f/pl* **eines Produktes** *n*	banded packs *pl*	plusieurs emballages *m/pl* d'un produit *m*
Mehrfachbelichtung *f*	repeated exposures *pl*	exposition *f* multiple
Mehrfachbild *n* **eines Firmen- oder Personennamens** *m*	mutiple image	image *f* multiple d'un nom *m* de maison *f* ou de produit *m*
Mehrfarbendruck *m*	multi-colour printing, process printing	impression *f* en couleurs *f/pl*, impression *f* multicolore
Mehrfarben-Druckpresse *f*	multiple colour press	rotative *f* hélio en couleur *f*
Mehrfarbenklischee *n*	process plate	cliché *m* d'impression *f* couleur *f*
Mehrfarbenzuschlag *m*	surcharge for multi-color	supplément *m* pour polychromie *f*
mehrfarbig	multicoloured, polychromatic	multicolore, polychrome
mehrfarbige Anzeige *f*	colored ad *am*, coloured ad *brit*	annonce *f* multicolore
mehrgleisige Werbung *f*	split run advertising	publicité *f* à plusieurs voies *f/pl*
Mehrpreis *m*	additional price, extra charge	majoration *f* de prix *m*
mehrspaltige Überschrift *f*	spread-head	grand titre *m* sur plusieurs colonnes *f/pl*
mehrsprachig	polyglot	polyglotte
Mehrstückpackung *f*	combipack, multipack, multiple unit item	plusieurs pièces *f/pl* dans un même emballage *m*
mehrteiliges Plakat *n*	poster in several parts *pl*	affiche *f* en plusieurs parties *f/pl*
Mehrthemenumfrage *f*	omnibus survey	enquête *f* omnibus
Mehrwegpackung *f*	dual-use package, re-use package	emballage *m* de remploi *m*, emballage *m* de retour
Mehrwertsteuer *f*	added value tax	taxe *f* sur la valeur *f* ajoutée (T.V.A.)
Mehrzweckhalle *f*	multi-purpose hall	hall *m* à usage *m* multiple
Meinung *f*	opinion	opinion *f*
Meinung *f*, **öffentliche**	public opinion	opinion *f* publique
Meinungsänderung *f*	change of opinion	changement *m* d'avis *m*
Meinungsäußerung *f*	expression of opinion	expression *f* de l'opinion *f*
Meinungsaustausch *m*	interchange of ideas *pl*	échange *m* de vues *f/pl*
Meinungsbildner *m*	opinion leader	faiseur *m* d'opinion *f*
Meinungsblatt *n*	opinion paper	organe *m* d'opinion *f*
Meinungsforscher *m*	pollster, public opinion analyst	enquêteur *m* d'opinion *f*
Meinungsforschung *f*	opinion poll, opinion research, public opinion analysis	enquête *f* sur les opinions *f/pl*, sondage *m* d'opinion *f*
Meinungsfreiheit *f*	freedom of opinion	liberté *f* d'opinion *f*
Meinungsklima *n*	climate of opinion	climat *m* d'opinion *f*
Meinungsmacher *m*	opinion leader	faiseur *m* d'opinion *f*
Meinungspflege *f*	public relations *pl*	relations *f/pl* publiques
Meinungspresse *f*	press of opinion	presse *f* d'opinion *f*
Meinungsseite *f*	editorial page	page *f* d'opinion *f*
Meinungsstreit *m*	controversy, polemics *pl*	polémique *f*
Meinungstest *m*	opinion test	test *m* d'opinion *f*
Meinungstrend *m*	trend of opinion	tendance *f* d'opinion *f*
Meinungsumfrage *f*	opinion poll, opinion survey	enquête *f* sur les opinions *f/pl*
Meinungsunterschied *m*, **feiner**	shade of opinion	nuance *f* d'opinion *f*
Meinungsverschiedenheit *f*	differences *pl* of opinions *pl*	divergence *f* d'opinion *f*
Meisterwerk *n*	master-work	chef *m* d'œuvre *f*

meistgekauftes Buch *n*	bestseller	livre *m* à succès *m*
meistgelesene Zeitung *f*	most read paper	journal *m* le plus lu
Meldung *f*	information, news report	information *f*, nouvelle *f*
Meldungen *f/pl*, **letzte**	latest intelligence	dernières nouvelles *f/pl*
Memorandum *n*	memorandum	aide-mémoire *f*
Mengenrabatt *m*	bulk rate *brit*, frequency discount, quantity discount, space discount, volume discount	dégressif *m* sur volume *m* publicitaire, rabais *m* de quantité *f*, remise *f* de quantité *f*
Menschenverstand *m*, **gesunder**	common sense	sens *m* commun
Menschliche *n*, **Ansprache** *f* **an das**	human appeal	appel *m* à l'humanité *f*
menschliche Note *f*	human touch	rapports *m/pl* humains, ton *m* émouvant
Merchandising *n*	merchandizing	mise *f* en valeur *f*, techniques *f/pl* marchandes
Merkblatt *n*	instruction sheet, leaflet	aide-mémoire *f*
Merkmale *n/pl*	criteria *pl*	critères *m/pl*
Merkmale *n/pl*, **demografische**	demographic characteristics *pl*	critères *m/pl* démographiques
Messe *f*	exhibition, fair, show	exposition *f*, foire *f*
Messeamt *n*	fair authorities *pl*	comité *f* d'organisation *f* de la foire *f*
Messeaussteller *m*	exhibitor	exposant *m*
Messebau *m*	exhibition stand construction	construction *f* de stands *m/pl* de foire *f*
Messegelände *n*	fair site	parc *m* des expositions *f/pl*
Messegestalter *m*	designer for fairs *pl*	expert *m* pour foires *f/pl*
Messekatalog *m*	fair catalogue	catalogue *m* de la foire *f*
Messestand *m*	exhibition stand	stand *m* de foire *f*
Messewerbung *f*	exhibition advertising	publicité *f* de foire *f*
Meßgerät *n* **zur Zuschauerforschung** *f*	video meter	instrument *m* de mesure *f* de l'audience *f*
Metallblock *m*	metal log	bloc *m* de métal *m*
Metalldruckverfahren *n*	woodbury print	impression *f* métallographique
Metallklischee *n*	metal block, metal cut	cliché *m* métal *m*
Metallschild *n*	metal sign	enseigne *f* métallique
metaphorisch	metaphorisch	métaphorique
Meterzahl *f*	metric volume	métrage *m*
Methoden *f/pl*, **wissenschaftliche**	scientific methods *pl*	méthodes *f/pl* scientifiques
Mettageabteilung *f*	make-up section	département *m* de mise *f* en pages *f/pl*
Metteur *m*	clicker, form-man, lay-out man, make-up hand, maker-up	imposeur *m*, metteur *m* en pages *f/pl*
Mignon *f* (Kolonel) (siehe Anhang)	Minion (see appendix)	corps 7 points (voir appendice)
Mikrofilm *m*	microfilm	microfilm *m*
Mikrofon *n*	mike	microphone *m*
Mikrofon *n*, **verstecktes**	bug	micro *m* secret
Mikrofonfieber *n*	mike fever	trac *m* devant le micro *m*
Millimeterabschluß *m*	contract on a line basis	contrat *m* en millimètres *m/pl*
Millimeterpapier *n*	graph paper	papier *m* quadrillé à millimètre *m*
Millimeterpreis *m*	column-millimetre	millimètre-colonne *f*
Millimeterzeile *f*	millimetre line	ligne *f* millimètre *m*
minderwertige Qualität *f*	cheap quality	qualité *f* de peu de valeur *f*
minderwertiges Blatt *n*	trashy paper	journal *m* médiocre

minderwertiges Produkt *n*	inferior product, lemon	produit *m* de mauvaise qualité *f*
Mindestabschluß *m*	minimum contract	commande *f* minimale, contrat *m* minimum
Mindestanschlagdauer *f*	minimum period of display	conservation *f* minimum
Mindestauflage *f*	minimum circulation	tirage *m* minimum *m*
Mindestauflage *f*, **garantierte**	guaranted minimum circulation	tirage *m* minimum garanti
Mindestbreite *f*	minimum width	largeur *f* minimum *m*
Mindestgröße *f*	minimum lineage	lignage *f* minimum *m*
Mindesthöhe *f*	minimum length	hauteur *f* minimum *m*
Mindestpreis *m*	minimum rate	prix *m* minimum
Mindestzahl *f* **von Zuschauern** *m/pl*, **garantierte**	guaranted minimum audience	garantie *f* diffusion *f*
Miniatur *f*	miniature	miniature *f*
Miniaturausgabe *f*	miniature edition	édition *f* minuscule
Miniaturskizze *f*	thumbnail sketch	croquis *m* minuscule
Minimalklischee *n*	minimum cliché	cliché *m* minimum
Minimaltarif *m*	minimum tariff	tarif *m* minimal
Minisketch *m*	black out	pièce de cabaret *m* artistique
Minuskel *f*	small letter	lettre *f* bas de casse *f*, lettre *f* minuscule
Minuszeichen *n*	em-rule	moins *m*
Mißbrauch *m*	misuse	mauvais usage *m*
Mißdeutung *f*	misinterpretation	contresens *m*
Mißerfolg *m*	flop	échec *m*
Mißverhältnis *n*	incongruity	déséquilibre *m*
Mißverständnis *n*	misunderstanding	quiproquo *m*
mit einer Widmung *f* **versehene Ausgabe** *f*	presentation copy	exemplaire *m* dédicacé
Mitarbeiter *m* **eines Skandalblattes** *n*	slandermonger	collaborateur *m* d'un journal *m* à scandale *m*
Mitarbeiter *m*, **freiberuflicher**	free lance contributor	collaborateur *m* à son compte *m*, collaborateur *m* extérieur
Mitarbeiter *m*, **freier künstlerischer**	outside artist	collaborateur *m* artistique à son compte *m*
Mitarbeiter *m*, **gelegentlicher**	casual contributor	collaborateur *m* occasionnel
Mitarbeiter *m*, **ständiger**	permanent contributor	collaborateur *m* permanent
Mitbewerber *m*	rival	concurrent *m*
Mitgliedsabonnement *n*	association subscription	abonnement *m* pour membres *m/pl*
Mittagsblatt *n*	noon paper	journal *m* de midi *m*
Mitte *f* **der Seite** *f*	centre of page	milieu *m* de page *f*
Mitte *f* **gesetzt, auf**	centered	centré
Mitte *f* **stellen, auf**	to place in centre of line	placer au centre *m* de la ligne *f*
mitteilen	to communicate, to impart	communiquer
Mitteilung *f*	statement	communiqué *m*
Mittel *f* (Schriftgrad *m*) (siehe Anhang)	Columbian (see appendix)	corps 14 points (voir appendice)
Mittellänge *f*	x-height	œil *m* de la lettre *f*
Mittelstand *m*	middle-class	bourgeois *m*
Mitteltöne *m/pl*	half-tints *pl*	demi-teintes *f/pl*
mittlere Anlaufzeit *f*	average date of posting	date *f* moyenne de pose *f*
mittleres Format *n*	medium-size	de moyen format *m*
Mittlervergütung *f*	agency commission, media discount	commission *f* d'agence *f*
Mobile *n*	dangler, mobile	mobile *m*, rotair *m*
Modeartikel *m*	fashion article	article *m* de modes *f/pl*

Modebeilage f	fashion supplement	supplément m de mode f
Modeblatt n	fashion magazine	journal m de modes f/pl
Modefotografie f	fashion photography	photographie f de mode f
Modell n	mannequin, model, pattern	mannequin m, modèle m
Modellagentur f	model agency	agence de modèles m/pl
Modeneuheit f, letzte	latest fashion	dernier cri m
modernisieren	to streamline	moderniser
Modernisierung f	modernisation	modernisation f
Modeschau f	fashion parade, style show	defilé m de mode f, exposition f de modes f/pl
Modewerbung f	fashion advertising	publicité f de la mode f
Modewort n	vogue-word	mot m à la mode f, mot m du jour m
Modezeichnung f	fashion design	dessin m de mode f
Modezeitschriften f/pl	fashion magazines pl	magasins m/pl de modes f/pl
modisches Produkt n	fancy article	produit m à la mode f
möglicher Kunde m	prospect	prospect m
Möglichkeit f, nach	according to possibility	selon possibilité f
Mönchsbogen m	friar	moine m
Mogelpackung f	deceptive package	emballage m trompeur
Moiré n	moiré	moiré m
Momentaufnahme f	candid picture, snapshot	instantané m non posé, photographie f instantanée
Monat m	month	mois m
Monate m/pl, alle drei	quarterly	trimestriel
Monate m/pl, alle zwei	bi-monthly	bimestriel
monatlich	monthly	mensuel
Monatsschrift f	monthly paper	revue f mensuelle
Mondpreis m	fancy price, misleading pricing	prix m de fantaisie f
Monitor m	monitor	moniteur m
Monographie f	monograph	monographie f
Monopol n	market monopoly	monopole m
Monopolpreis m	monopoly price	prix m de monopole m
Monopolzeitung f	monopolistic journal	journal m monopolisateur
Monotype-Gießmaschine f	monotype caster	fondeuse f monotype
Monotypesatz m	monotype composition	composition f monotype f
Monotype-Setzmaschine f	monotype keyboard	composeuse f monotypè
Montage f	assembling, mounting, paste up	montage m
Montagetisch m	illuminated line-up table, stripping desk, stripping table	table f de montage m, table f lumineuse
montieren	to mount	monter
montiertes Klischee n	mounted block	cliché m monté
Morgenausgabe f	early morning edition	édition f du matin m, première édition f
Morgenzeitung f	morning newspaper	journal m du matin m
Motiv n	motive	motif m
Motivausschnitt m	cutting out of motive	extrait m du motif m
Motivforscher m	head shrinker, motive analyst	enquêteur m de motivation f
Motivforschung f	motivation research	étude f de motivation f
motivieren	to motivate	motiver
Motivierung f	motivation	motivation f
Motto n	motto	épigraphe f
mündlich erteilter Auftrag m	order by word of mouth	commande f verbale
mündliche Befragung f	oral interview	interview f orale
mündliche Werbung f	advertising by word of mouth	publicité f de bouche f à bouche f, publicité f parlante
Mundart f	dialect, idiom	dialecte m, idiome m

Mundpropaganda *f*	advertising by word of mouth	propagande *f* de bouche *f* à oreille *f*
Mund-zu-Mund-Werbung *f*	word-of-mouth-advertising	publicité *f* parlante, publicité *f* verbale
musikalische Überleitung *f*	bridge, sequel	transition *f* musicale
musikalische Untermalung *f*	background sound effect, underscoring	fond *m* sonore
musikalische Werbung *f*	jingle	refrain *m* radiophonique, ritournelle *f* publicitaire, tintement *m*
musikalisches Leitmotiv *n*	jingle	indicatif *m* musical
Mußestunden *f/pl*, Rubrik *f* für	leisure time	rubrique *f* des loisirs *m/pl*
Muster *n*	pattern, sample	échantillon *m*, patron *m*, spécimen *m*
Musterabzug *m*	film copy	copie *f* pour un film *m*
Musteranforderungskarte *f*	sample request card	carte-demande *f* d'échantillon *m*
Musterbuch *n*	sample book	livre *m* d'échantillons *m/pl*
Musterkollektion *f*	sample collection	collection *f* d'échantillons *m/pl*
Musterlager *n*	sample stock	dépôt *m* d'échantillons *m/pl*
Mustermesse *f*	trade fair	foire *f* d'échantillons *m/pl*
Musterversand *m*	sampling	distribution *f* d'échantillons *m/pl*, envoi *m* d'échantillons *m/pl*
Musterzeichner *m*	designer	dessinateur *m*

N

nach links ausschließen	to move to the left	justifier à la gauche
nach rechts ausschließen	to move to the right	justifier à droite
nachahmen	to imitate	imiter
Nachahmung *f*	counterfeit, imitation, plagiarism	contre-facon *f*, imitation *f*, plagiat *m*
Nachahmung *f* eines Warenzeichens *n*	pirating of a trademark	contrefaction *f* d'une marque *f* de fabrique *f*
nacharbeiten mit der Hand *f*	hand tooling	retoucher à l'outil *m*
Nachbelastung *f*	short-rate	charge *m* réajusté
Nachbesserung *f*	touching-up	retouche *f*
Nachbestellung *f*	repeat order	nouvel ordre *m*
Nachbild *n*	after-image	effet *m* ultérieur
Nachdruck *m* erbeten	please copy	reproduction *f* souhaitée
Nachdruck *m/typog*	reprint	réimpression *f*
nachdrückliche Werbung *f*	vigorous advertising	publicité *f* vigoureuse
Nachfaßbrief *m*	follow-up letter	lettre *f* de retrait *m*, relance *f*
Nachfaßinterview *n*	call-back	interview *m* de rappel *m*
Nachfaßwerbung *f*	follow-up advertising	publicité *f* de relance *f*
Nachforschung *f*	research	recherche *f*
Nachfrage *f*	demand	demande *f*
Nachfrage *f*, kontinuierliche	current demand	demande *f* continue
nachgeahmtes Produkt *n*	imitative product	produit *m* imitatif
Nachkalkulation *f*	cost-effect calculation, final costing	contrôle *m* a posteriori, postcalculation *f*
Nachlaß *m*	discount, rebate, reduction	escompte *m*, rabais *m*, réduction *f*
Nachlaßstaffel *f*	sliding scale discount	échelle *f* mobile
Nachlese *f*	gleanings *pl*	glanes *f/pl*
nachmachen	to copy, to imitate	contre-faire, imiter

Nachnahmesendung *f*	parcel to be paid for on delivery	envoi *m* contre rembousement *m*
Nachprüfung *f*	post-testing	postenquête *f*
Nachrabatt *m*	retroactive discount	rabais *m* rétroactif
Nachrede *f*, **üble**	back-biting	médisance *f*
Nachricht *f*	news	nouvelle *f*
Nachricht *f* **auf der Titelseite** *f*	front-page news	nouvelle *f* sensationnelle
Nachricht *f*, **aufsehenerregende**	sensational piece of news	pétard *m*
Nachricht *f* **aus erster Hand** *f*	inside information	renseignements *m/pl* privés
Nachricht *f* **groß aufmachen**	to feature a piece of news	mettre une nouvelle *f* en manchette *f*
Nachricht *f* **hochspielen, eine**	to play up an information, to puff up an information	gonfler un papier *m*, remonter une nouvelle *f*
Nachricht *f*, **unterdrückte**	blacked out news	nouvelle *f* supprimée, ratage *m*
Nachrichtenamt *n*	information-bureau	bureau *m* d'information *f*
Nachrichtenbeschaffung *f*	collection of information	obtention *f* des informations *f/pl*
Nachrichtenbüro *n*	news agency, press agency	agence *f* d'information *f*
Nachrichtendienst *m*	news service	service *m* des nouvelles *f/pl*
Nachrichtendurchsage *f*	broadcasting of news	diffusion *f* de nouvelles *f/pl*
Nachrichtenkörper *m*	body	texte *m* principal
Nachrichtenkommentator *m*	news analyst, news commentator	commentateur *m* des nouvelles *f/pl*
Nachrichtenmagazin *n*	news magazine	magazine *f* d'information *f*
Nachrichtenmanipulation *f*	news management	manipulation *f* des informations *f/pl*
Nachrichten *f/pl*, **amtliche**	official news	nouvelles *f/pl* authentiques
Nachrichten *f/pl* **beschaffen**	to supply news	fournir des nouvelles *f/pl*
Nachrichten *f/pl*, **brandneue**	news hot from the press	nouvelles *f/pl* toutes chaudes
Nachrichten *f/pl*, **bruchstückhafte**	piecemail information	nouvelles *f/pl* fragmentaires
Nachrichten *f/pl*, **gekabelte**	overhead	nouvelles *f/pl* câblées
Nachrichten *f/pl*, **letzte**	latest news, stop-press news	informations *f/pl* de dernière heure *f*
Nachrichten *f/pl*, **neueste**	latest intelligence, spot-news	dernières nouvelles *f/pl*, nouvelles *f/pl* fraîches
Nachrichten *f/pl*, **schlechte**	black tidings *pl*, ill news	mauvaises nouvelles *f/pl*
Nachrichten *f/pl*, **überholte**	stale news	informations *f/pl* dépassées
Nachrichtenpresse *f*	newspaper press	presse *f* d'information *f*
Nachrichtenquelle *f*	stock of information	source *f* d'information *f*
Nachrichtenredakteur *m*	desk editor, news editor	rédacteur *m* au desk *m*, rédacteur *m* aux informations *f/pl*
Nachrichtensatellit *m*	telecommunication satellite	satellite *m* de télécommunication *f*
Nachrichtensendung *f*	broadcast news, news bulletin, newscast, topical talk	bulletin *m* d'actualités *f/pl*, journal *m* parlé, transmission *f* des informations *f/pl*
Nachrichtensetzer *m*	news compositor	canardier *m*
Nachrichtensperre *f*	ban on news, news blackout	black-out *m*, blocus *m* de nouvelles *f/pl*
Nachrichtensprecher *m*	newscaster, newsreader	présentateur *m* du journal *m* parlé
Nachrichtenstelle *f*	intelligence department	centre *m* de renseignements *m/pl*

Nachrichtenübermittlung *f*	news transmitting, radio communication	radiocommunication *f*, transmission *f* des informations *f/pl*
Nachrichtenübersicht *f*	news summary	sommaire *m* des nouvelles *f/pl*
Nachrichtenverarbeitung *f*	processing of the news	traitement *m* des nouvelles *f/pl*
Nachrichtenzentrale *f*	information centre	centre *m* de renseignements *m/pl*
Nachruf *m*	obituary notice	nécrologe *m*
Nachsaison *f*	post season	arrière-saison *f*
Nachschlagewerk *n*	reference book, work of reference	ouvrage *m* de référence *f*
Nachschlagewerk *n* in Form regelmäßig erscheinender Hefte *n/pl*	part publication	ouvrage *m* de référence *f* sous la forme *f* de livraisons *f/pl* régulières
nachschneiden	to finish	finir
Nachsynchronisierung *f*	post synchronization	post-synchronisation *f*
Nachtausgabe *f*	night edition	édition *f* de nuit *f*
Nachtest *m*	post-test	test *m* après parution *f*, test *m* ultérieur
nachträglich	afterwards, later on	après coup *m*
Nachtredakteur *m*	night editor	rédacteur *m* de nuit *f*
Nachwirkung *f*	after-image	effet *m* ultérieur
Nachwort *n*	epilogue	épilogue *m*
Nachzügler-Werbesendung *f*	hitchhike	publicité *f* retardataire
nackte Tatsache *f*	bald fact	fait *m* pur et simple
Näherungswert *m*	approximation	approximation *f*
Nahaufnahme *f*	close-up	photographie *f* prise de près
Nahrungsmittelanzeige *f*	food ad	annonce *f* pour produits *m/pl* alimentaires
Nahrungsmittel *n/pl*, verbrauchsfertige	convenience foods *pl*	aliments *m/pl* prêts à la consommation *f*
Namensliste *f*	index of names *pl*	table *f* nominale
Namensschildchen *n*	badge	insigne *m*
Namenszeichen *n*	initials *pl*, paraph	paraphe *m*
Namenszug *m*	logotype, name slug	logotype *m*, vignette *f*
Nasenzählen *n*	nose count	évaluation *f* approximative «à vue *f* de nez» *m* du nombre *m* des présents *m/pl*
Naß-in-Naß-Druck *m*	wet-on-wet printing	impression *f* sur humide
Naßklebeverfahren *n*	dry posting	affichage *m* à la brosse *f* sèche
national verbreitete Medien *n/pl*	national media *pl*	médias *m/pl* répandus dans tout le pays *m*
Natronpackpapier *n*	Kraft paper	papier *m* d'emballage *m* à la soude *f*
naturgetreue Wiedergabe *f*	high fidelity	haute fidélité *f*
Naturpapier *n*	uncoated paper	papier *m* non couché
naturwissenschaftlich-technische Utopie *f*	science-fiction	utopie *f* scientifique-technique
Nebenausgabe *f*	sub-edition	édition *f* secondaire
Nebenbedeutung *f*	connotation	signification *f* secondaire
Nebengeräusche *n/pl*	atmospherics *pl*, buzz	bruits *m/pl* parasites, fritures *f/pl*
Nebenkosten *pl*	incidental expenses *pl*	faux frais *m/pl*
Nebenleistung *f*	accessorial service	prestation *f* accessoire
Neckwerbung *f*	teaser advertising	publicité *f* taquine
Negativ *n*	negative	négatif *m*

Negativklischee *n*	block white on black, negative plate, reversed block	cliché *m* négatif, cliché *m* noir au blanc
Negativretusche *f*	negative retouching	retouche *f* sur négatif *m*
Negativschrift *f*	negative type	caractère *m* négatif
Neger *m*, literarischer	ghost writer	nègre *m*
Neon-Leuchtschild *n*	neon sign	enseigne *f* au néon *m*
Neonlichtwerbung *f*	neon tubing	publicité *f* par tube *m* néon
Nettoauflage *f*	net circulation	tirage *m* net
Nettopreis *m*	net price, net rate	prix *m* net
Nettoreichweite *f*	net coverage	couverture *f* nette
Netzätzung *f*	half-tone, screen etching	simili *m*, similigravure *f*
Netzanschlag *m*	full showing	affichage *m* général
neu herausgekommen	just published	vient de paraître
neu schreiben	to rewrite	récrire, remanier
neu umbrechen	to overrun	remanier
neu verfilmen	to remake	refaçonner
Neuauflage *f*	new edition, reprint	nouvelle édition *f*
Neuaufnahme *f*	retake	tourner à nouveau
Neubemalung *f*	repaints *pl*	nouvelle peinture *f*
Neudruck *m*	new edition, reprint	réimpression *f*
neuer Schwung *m*	push	poussée *f*
Neuerung *f*	innovation	innovation *f*
Neues *n* vom Tage *m*	current events *pl*	actualités *f/pl*
neueste Nachrichten *f/pl*	latest intelligence, spot-news	dernières nouvelles *f/pl*, nouvelles *f/pl* fraîches
neuesten Stand *m* bringen, auf den	to update	mettre à jour *m*
Neufassung *f*	new formulation, remaking	nouvelle rédaction *f*, réfection *f*
Neugier erregende Anzeige *f*	teaser	annonce *f* piquant la curiosité *f*
Neuigkeitskrämer *m*	news monger	colporteur *m* de nouvelles *f/pl*
Neuigkeitswert *m*	news value	valeur *f* de nouvelle *f*, valeur *f* d'information *f*
Neujahrskarte *f*	New-Year's greeting card	carte *f* de Nouvel-An *m*
Neuling *m*	beginner, newcomer, tyro	néophyte *m*, nouveau venu
Neusatz *m*	re-setting	recomposition *f*
nicht durchscheinendes Papier *n*	opaque paper	papier *m* opaque
nicht eingezogener Titel *m*	flush head	titre *m* aligné à gauche
nicht erschienen	non-appeared	non-paru
Nichtanzeigenträger *m*	periodical without ads *pl*	périodique *m* sans publicité *f* commerciale
Nichtausführung *f* eines Auftrages *m*	non-performance of an order	non-exécution *f* d'une commande *f*
nichtdruckend	non-printing	en blanc
nichtgebrachte Anzeige *f*	hold over	reporter
Nickelgalvano *n*	nickel electro, nickel-faced stereo	galvano-nickel *m*, stéréo-nickel *m*
niederschreiben	to write down	coucher sur papier *m*
Niederschrift *f*	record, writing down	écrit *m*, procès-verbal *m*
niedrig	low	bas
niedriger Preis *m*	thrift price	prix *m* modique
niedrigst kalkulierter Preis *m*	bargain level	prix *m* minimum
Nimbus *m*	halo effect	auréole *f*
Niveau *n*	level	niveau *m*
Nivellierung *f*	levelling	nivellement *m*
nochmaliges Abspielen *n*	to play back	faire repasser la bande *f*

Nonplusultra *f* (Viertelpetit) (siehe Anhang)	2 points (see appendix)	corps 2 points (voir appendice)
Norm *f*	standard	standard *m*
Normalfilm *m*	standard film	film *m* de format *m* normal
Normalformat *n*	standard size	format *m* normalisé
Normalpackung *f*	standard package	emballage *m* normal
Normalschrift *f*	standard text type	caractères *m/pl* standard
Normaluhrensäule *f*	public clock pillar	colonne *f* des horloges *f/pl* publiques
Normung *f*	standardization	standardisation *f*
Note *f*, **menschliche**	human touch	rapports *m/pl* humains
Note *f*, **weibliche**	female touch	note *f* féminine
Notenkopf *m*	notehead	tête *f* de note *f*
Notenpapier *n*	music paper	papier *m* à musique *f*
Notierung *f*	quotation	citation *f*
Notizblock *m*	scratch-pad	bloc-notes *m/pl*
Notizbuch *n*	memorandum book, note-book	agenda *m*, calepin *m*, carnet *m*
Notzeitung *f*	temporary paper	journal *m* intérimaire
Novelle *f*	short story	nouvelle *f*
Nullnummer *f*	zero edition	édition *f* zéro
numerieren	to number	numéroter
Numeriermaschine *f*	numbering machine	machine *f* à numéroter
Numerierung *f*	numbering, pagination	numérotage *m*, numérotation *f*
Nummer *f* (Ausgabe)	issue	numéro *m*
Nummer *f* **der Seite** *f*	folio	nombre *m* de page *f*
Nummern *f/pl*, **überschüssige**	over copies *pl*	exemplaires *m/pl* de passe *f*
Nummernreglette *f*	galley-slug	réglette *f* numerotée
nuten	to groove	rainer
Nutzen *m*	gain, profit	profit *m*, utilité *f*
Nutzungswert *m*	value in use	valeur *f* d'usage *m*
Nylonklischee *n*	nylon block	cliché *m* nylon

O

obere Ecke *f*	upper corner	coin *m* supérieur
obere Zehntausend *f/pl*	high society	haute société *f*
oberer Eckplatz *m* **der Titelseite** *f*	box on the right of the masthead	manchette *f* à droite du titre *m*
Oberfläche *f*, **matte**	mat surface	surface *f* mate
Oberflächengestaltung *f* **eines Papiers** *n*, **technische**	finish	apprêter le papier *m*
oberflächlich behandeln	to skim	effleurer
Oberlängen *f/pl*	ascenders *pl*	lettres *f/pl* débordantes, longues *f/pl* du haut *m*
Oberleitungsomnibus *m*	trolleybus	trolley-bus *m*
Obertitel *m* **über mehrere Aufsätze** *m/pl* **mit demselben Thema** *n*	binder line	bandeau *m* général
objektiver Artikel *m*	balanced article	article *m* objectif
Objektivität *f*	objectivity	objectivité *f*
obligatorische Werbeträger *m/pl*	obligatory media *pl*	médias *m/pl* obligatoires
öffentlich	public	public
öffentliche Meinung *f*	public opinion	opinion *f* publique
öffentlicher Grund *m* **und Boden** *m*	public property	domaine *m* public
Öffentlichkeit *f*	publicity	publicité *f*

Öffentlichkeitsarbeit *f*	public relations *pl*, publicity	relations *f/pl* extérieures, relations *f/pl* publiques
öffentlich-rechtliche Anstalt *f*	body corporate, public institution	établissement *m* de droit *m* public
Ölbild *n*	oil painting	peinture *f* à l'huile *f*
Ölbogen *m*	tympan	feuille *f* huilée
Öldruck *m*	oleography	chromolithographie *f*, oléographie *f*
Ölfarbe *f*	oil-colour	couleur *f* à l'huile *f*
Ölfarbendruck *m*	oil print	impression *f* aux encres *f/pl*
Ölmalfarbe *f*	oil color (am) , oil colour	couleur *f* à l'huile *f*
Ölpapier *n*	oiled paper	papier *m* huilé
örtliche Anzeige *f*	local advertisement	annonce *f* locale
örtliche Werbung *f*	local campaign	campagne *f* locale
offene Auslage *f*	open display	exposition *f* libre
Offerte *f*	estimate, offer	devis *m*, offre *f*
Offertenblatt *n*	free sheet	feuille *f* d'annonces *f/pl*
Offizin *f*	printing office	imprimerie *f*
offiziös	officious	officieux, semi-officiel
Offsetdruck *m*	offset printing	impression *f* offset, offset lithographie *f*, tirage *m* report *m*
Offsetdrucker *m*	offset printer	imprimeur *m* offset
Offsetfilm *m*	flat	film *m* pour offset *m*
Offsetkopierverfahren *n*	offset printing-down process	procédé *m* de copie *f* offset
Offsetpapier *n*	offset paper	papier *m* pour offset *m*
Offsettiefdruck *m*	offset deep printing	impression *f* offset en creux *m*
oft zitiertes Blatt *n*	newspaper of record	journal *m* sérieux qu'on cite
ohne Zwischenraum *m* setzen	to close up	supprimer l'espace *m*
Ohne-Pause-Kino *n*	non-stop-cinema	cinéma *m* sans arrêt *m*
Ohrenzeuge *m*	ear-witness	témoin *m* auriculaire
Oktavformat *n*	octave	octavo *m*
Omnibuswerbung *f*	bus advertising	publicité *f* dans ou sur un autobus *m*
Opfer *n* der Werbung *f*	admass	victime *m* de la publicité *f*
Oppositionsblatt *n*	opposition paper	feuille *f* d'opposition *f*
Optimalpreis *m*	optimum price	prix *m* optimum
Ordner *m*	file box	classeur *m*
Organ *n*	medium, publication	organe *m*, publication *f*
Organ *n*, amtliches	official organ	organe *m* officiel
Organisation *f*	organization	organisation *f*
Organisationsschema *n*	organization set-up	organigramme *m*
organisieren	to organize	organiser
Orientierung *f*	orientation	orientation *f*
Original *n*	original	document *m*
Originalausgabe *f*	first edition, original edition	édition *f* originale
originalgetreu	true to original	identique à l'original *m*
Originalgröße *f*	as is, same size	tel
Originalklischee *n*	master plate, original block, pattern plate	cliché *m* original
Originalmanuskript *n*	original copy	copie *f* originale
Originalpackung *f*	original package	emballage *m* d'origine *f*
Originalschrift *f*	foundry type	caractères *m/pl* fondeur
Originalsendung *f*	live transmission	émission *f* en direct
Originaltext *m*	original copy, verbatim report	texte *m* original
Originalverpackung *f*	original package, original wrapping	emballage *m* d'origine *f*

Originalzeichnung *f*	key drawing	dessin *m* original
Ornament *m*	ornament	ornement *m*
Ortsanzeigen *f/pl*	local advertising	publicité *f* locale
Ortschaft *f*, geschlossene	built up area	agglomération *f*
Ortsgrößenklasse *f*	town size group	habitat *m*, zone *f* de résidence *f*
Ortsverbindung *f*	local call	communication *f* locale
Ortsverzeichnis *n*	gazetteer	liste *f* de localités *f/pl*
Ortszeitung *f*	!ocal paper	journal *m* local

P

Paarvergleich *m*	duo test, paired comparison	test *m* comparatif
Pachtabgabe *f*	rent	loyer *m*
Pachtblatt *n*	leased paper, tied paper	revue *f* affermée
Pachtorgan *n*	tied paper	organe *m* affermé
Pachtunternehmen *n*	advertising operator, leaseholder	entreprise *f* d'affermage *m*, société *f* d'affermage *m*
Pachtvertrag *m*	contract of lease	bail *m* à ferme *f*, contrat *m* de fermage *m*
Pachtzeitung *f*	tied newspaper	journal affermé *m*
Packpapier *n*	brown paper, wrapping paper	papier *m* d'emballage *m*, papier *m* gris
Packung *f*	pack, package	emballage *m*, paquetage *m*
Packungsbeilage *f*	package insert	encart *m* dans un emballage *m*, papillon *m*
Packungsbild *n* im Film *m*	pack-shot	plan-paquet *m*
Packungstest *m*	packaging test	étude *f* sur un emballage *m*, test *m* d'emballage *m*
Pächter *m*	lessee	concessionaire *m*
Pächter *m* einer Verkaufsfläche *f* im Supermarkt *m*	rack-jobber	fermier *m* d'un rayon *m* spécialisé dans un supermarché *m*
paginieren	to number pages *pl*, to page, to paginate	folioter, marquer les pages *f/pl*, paginer
Paginierung *f*	paging	pagination *f*
Paket *n*	parcel	colis *m*, paquet *m*
Paket *n* (Satzstück *m*)	piece of composition	paquet *m*
Paketangebot *n*	package deal	contrat *m* global
Paketsetzer *m*	piece hand	paquetier *m*
Palette *f*	palette	palette *f*
Pamphlet *m*	lampoon	pamphlet *m*
panchromatische Reproduktion *f*	panchromatic reproduction	reproduction *f* panchromatique
Panikmacher *m*	panic-monger	alarmiste *m*
Panoramaanzeige *f*	panorama advertisement	annonce *f* en double page *f*
Panoramierung *f*	panning	panoramarique *f*
Pantoffelkino *n*	television set	appareil *m* de télévision *f*
Pantograph *m*	pantograph	pantographe *m*
Papier *n*	paper	papier *m*
Papier *n*, autografisches	transfer paper	papier *m* autographique
Papier *n*, bauschiges	bulky paper	papier *m* fort pour l'impression *f*
Papier *n*, buntes	colored paper *am*, coloured paper *brit*	papier *m* de couleur *f*, papier *m* peint
Papier *n*, chinesisches	India paper, rice-paper	papier *m* chiné, papier *m* de Chine *f*
Papier *n*, durchscheinendes	translucent paper	papier *m* transparent

Papier *n*, **einseitig gestrichenes**	one-side coated paper	satiné d'un côté *m*
Papier *n*, **endloses**	reel paper	papier *m* continu
Papier *n*, **federleichtes**	featherweight paper	papier *m* bouffant
Papier *n*, **fettdichtes**	grease-proof paper	papier *m* imperméable à la graisse *f*
Papier *n*, **feuerfestes**	uninflammable paper	papier *m* incombustible
Papier *n*, **fotografisches**	photo paper	papier *m* à prise *f* de vue *f*
Papier *n*, **geglättetes**	calendered paper, glazed paper	papier *m* calandré, papier *m* satiné
Papier *n*, **gekörntes**	grained paper	papier *m* grainé, papier *m* granulé
Papier *n*, **geleimtes**	sized paper	papier *m* collé
Papier *n*, **gemasertes**	grained paper	papier *m* grainé, papier *m* granulé
Papier *n*, **geprägtes**	embossed paper	papier *m* gaufré
Papier *n*, **geripptes**	laid paper	papier *m* vergé
Papier *n*, **geschöpftes**	hand-made paper	papier *m* de cuve *f*
Papier *n*, **gestreiftes**	laid paper	papier *m* vergé
Papier *n*, **gestrichenes**	coated paper, glazed paper	papier *m* couché, papier *m* glacé
Papier *n*, **getöntes**	coloured paper	papier *m* de couleur *f*
Papier *n*, **gewelltes**	corrugated paper	papier *m* ondulé
Papier *n*, **graniertes**	grained paper	papier *m* grainé
Papier *n*, **gummiertes**	gummed paper	papier *m* gommé
Papier *n*, **halbgeleimtes**	soft sized paper	papier *m* demi-collé
Papier *n*, **hochsatiniertes**	imitation art paper, supercalendered paper	papier *m* satiné
Papier *n*, **holländisches**	hand-made paper	papier *m* de Hollande *f*
Papier *n*, **holzfreies**	wood-free paper	papier *m* sans pâte *f* de bois *m*
Papier *n*, **holzhaltiges**	paper made from wood pulp, wood containing paper	papier *m* avec de bois *m*, papier *m* fait de pâte *f* de bois *m*
Papier *n*, **kalandriertes**	supercalendered paper	papier *m* surglacé
Papier *n*, **kariertes**	cross hatched paper	papier *m* quadrillé
Papier *n*, **lichtempfindliches**	sensitized paper	papier *m* sensibilisé
Papier *n*, **liniiertes**	ruled paper	papier *m* réglé
Papier *n*, **marmoriertes**	marbled paper	papier *m* marbré
Papier *n*, **maschinenglattes**	M. F. (machine finished) paper	papier *m* apprêté machine *f*
Papier *n*, **mattes**	matt art paper	papier *m* couché mat
Papier *n*, **mattiertes**	dull-finished paper	papier *m* mat
Papier *n*, **nicht durchscheinendes**	opaque paper	papier *m* opaque
Papier *n*, **parfümiertes**	scented paper	papier *m* parfumé
Papier *n*, **satiniertes**	calendered paper, imitation art paper	papier *m* calandré, papier *m* satiné
Papier *n*, **saugfähiges** (**Saugpost** *f*)	absorbent paper	papier *m* amoureux
Papier *n*, **starkes**	strong paper	papier *m* fort
Papier *n*, **widerstandsfähiges**	paper with some substance	papier *m* de la main *f*
Papier *n*, **zweiseitig gestrichenes**	two-sided coated paper	papier *m* couché de deux pages *f/pl*
Papierabfall *m*	waste paper	chute *f*
Papierabschnitt *m*	offcut	chute *f* de papier *m*
Papierbeutel *m* **mit Werbeaufdruck** *m*	paper bag	sac *m* publicitaire
Papierbogen *m*	sheet	feuille *f*
Papierdicke *f*	paper thickness	épaisseur *m* du papier *m*

Papierfabrik *f*	paper-mill	fabrique *f* de papier *m*, papeterie *f*
Papierfabrikant *m*	papermaker	fabricant *m* de papier *m*
Papierfaser *f*	paper fibre	fibre *f* de papier *m*
Papierformat *n*	paper size, sheet size	format *m* de papier *m*
Papierkante *f*	edge	bord *m* du papier *m*
Papierkorb *m*	waste-paper basket	corbeille *f* à papier *m*
Papierkorrektur *f*	correction on paper	correction *f* sur papier *m*
Papierkrieg *m*	paper-warfare	paperasserie *f*
Papierlage *f*	quire	cahier *m*, main *f*
Papierleimung *f*	paper sizing	encollage *m* du papier *m*
Papiermaché *n*	paper mâché	carton-pâte *m*, papier *m* mâché
Papiermasse *f*	pulp, stuff	pâte *f* de papier *m*
Papiermesser *n*	paper-knife	coupe-papier *m*
Papiernormalformat *n*	standard paper size	format *m* normalisé du papier *m*
Papieroberfläche *f*	surface of paper	surface *f* du papier *m*
Papierrand *m*, äußerer	fore-edge	marge *f* extérieure
Papierrolle *f*	paper roll	bobine *f* de papier *m*
Papierschneidemaschine *f*	paper cutter	massicot *m*
Papiersorte *f*	kind of paper, paper type	sorte *f* de papier *m*
Pappband *m*	stiff paper binding	reliure *f* cartonnée
Pappe *f*	board, millboard, pasteboard	carton *m*
Papprolle *f*	paperboard roll	rouleau *m* de carton *m*
Pappschere *f*	cardboard cutter	cisaille *f* à carton *m*
Paragraph *m*	paragraph	paragraphe *m*
Paragraphzeichen *n*	section mark	paragraphe *m*
parallel zur Straße *f*	parallel position	emplacement *m* parallèle
Parenthesen *f/pl*	parentheses *pl*	parenthèses *f/pl*
parfümiertes Papier *n*	scented paper	papier *m* parfumé
Parlamentsjournalist *m*	lobby journalist	rédacteur *m* parlementaire
Parlamentsstenograf *m*	parliament reporter	sténographe *m* parlementaire
Parodie *f*	parody	parodie *f*
Parole *f*	parole	mot *m* d'ordre *m*
Parteiblatt *n*	party organ	feuille *f* de parti *m*
parteiisch	partial	partial
Partygespräch *n*	small talk	menus *m/pl* propos
Passant *m*	passer-by	passant *m*
Passer *m*	register	repère *m*
Passerdifferenz *f*	colour fringing, register difference	différence *f* de repérage *m*
Passerkreuz *n*	register mark	croix *f* de repère *m*
Paßform *f*	key form	épreuve *f* de repérage *m*
Passus *m*	passage	passage *m*
Pastell *n*	pastel	pastel *m*
Pastellkreiden *f/pl*	pastels *pl*	crayons *m/pl* pastel
Pastellzeichnung *f*	pastel drawing	dessin *m* au pastel *m*
Patenschaftsabonnement *n*	sponsored subscription	abonnement *m* parrainé
Patrize *f*	counter-die, punch	poinçon *m*
Patronatssendung *f*	sponsored broadcast, sponsored programme	émission *f* patronnée, programme *m* patronné
Patronenpapier *n*	cartridge paper	carton *m*
Pauschalfrankatur *f*	post paid	affranchissement *m* forfaitaire
Pauschalhonorar *n*	flat fee	honoraires *m/pl* forfaitaires

Pauschalpreis *m*	blanket rate, flat rate, lump sum price	prix *m* forfaitaire
Pauschalreise *f*	package tour	voyage *m* organisé
Pauschalsumme *f*	lump sum	somme *f* globale
Pausdruck *m*	blue print	minute *f*
pausen	to trace	décalquer
Pausenzeichen *n*	signature tune	indicatif *m*
Pauspapier *n*	blueprinting paper, carbon paper, tracing paper	papier *m* à calquer, papier *m* carbone *m*
Perforation *f*	perforation	perforation *f*
perforieren	to perforate	percer, perforer
Perforierlinie *f*	perforating rule	filet *m* à perforer
Pergament *n*	parchment	parcheminé *m*
Pergamentpapier *n*	thick vellum	papier *m* parchemin *m*
Periodika *n/pl*	periodicals *pl*	périodiques *m/pl*
Periodizität *f*	periodicity	périodicité *f*
perlender Satz *m*	open-spaced setting	composition *f* espacée
Perlonklischee *n*	perlon block	cliché *m* perlon
Perlschrift *f* (siehe Anhang)	pearl (see appendix)	parisienne (voir appendice)
Permastatdruck *m*	permastat, photostat printing on special paper	impression *f* photostat sur papier *m* spécial
Perronfläche *f*	dash sign, platform site	emplacement *m* de quai *m*
persönliche Ansprache *f*	personal approach	appel *m* personnel
persönliche Anzeigen *f/pl*	agony column	annonces *f/pl* personnelles
persönliche Bemerkungen *f/pl*	personal remarks *pl*	personnalités *f/pl*
Personalanzeigen *f/pl*	vacancies *pl*	offres *f/pl* d'emploi *m*
personalisierte Werbung *f*	personalized sales *pl* technique	publicité *f* personnalisée
Personalisierung *f*	personifying	personnalisation *f*
Personenbildnis *n*	portrait	portrait *m*
Personen-Gesamtzahl *f*, erfaßte	cumulative audience	auditoire *m* cumulatif
Personenkreis *m*, willkürlich ausgewählter	chunk	audience *f* choisie arbitrairement
Personenkult *m*	worship of persons *pl*	culte *m* de la personne *f*
Petit *f* (siehe Anhang)	brevier (see appendix)	corps 8 points (voir appendice)
Pfennigartikel *m*	catch-penny article	attrape-sou *m*, camélote *f* de réclame *f*
Pflasterwerbung *f*	pavement advertising	publicité *f* sur trottoir *m*
Pflichtabonnement *n*	obligatory subscription	abonnement *m* obligatoire
Pflichtanzeige *f*	obligatory advertisement	annonce *f* obligatoire
Pflichtblatt *n*	journal in which the law requires public notices *pl* to be inserted	journal *m* d'annonces *f/pl* légales
Pflichteindruck *m*	colophon, imprint	repiquage *m*
Pflichtexemplar *n*	obligatory copy	exemplaire *m* obligatoire
Pfuscharbeit *f*	bingling, scamped work	bousillage *m*
Phantasiemarkenname *m*	coined brand name, fancy name	nom *m* inventé
Phantasieschriften *f/pl*	fancy types *pl*	caractères *m/pl* fantaisie *f*
Phantasiewort *n*	coined word	mot *m* forgé
Pharmawerbung *f*	advertising for drugs *pl*	publicité *f* en faveur *f* des produits *m/pl* pharmaceutiques
Phrasendrescher *m*	phrase-monger	phraseur *m*
Pica *f* (siehe Anhang)	pica (see appendix)	pica (voir appendice)
Pigmentpapier *n*	carbon paper, pigment paper	papier *m* charbon *m*
Piktogramm *n*	pictograph	pictogramme *m*
Pionierleistung *f*	pioneering achievement	œuvre *f* de pionnier *m*
Piratensender *m*	pirate station	émetteur *m* clandestin, station *f* pirate *m*

Plagiat *n*	crib, plagiarism	plagiat *m*
Plagiator *m*	copycat, plagiarist	plagiaire *m*
plagiieren	to plagiarize	plagier
Plakat *n*	bill, placard, poster, sticker *am*	affiche *f*-papier *m*, placard *m*
Plakat *n*, amtliches	official notice, official poster	affiche *f* officielle, avis *m* officiel
Plakat *n* anschlagen	placing of a poster	affichage *m* d'un placard *m*
Plakat *n*, auf Leinwand *f* gemaltes	poster painted on canvas	affiche *f* toile *f* peinte
Plakat *n*, beschädigtes	torn poster	affiche *f* abîmée, affiche *f* déchirée, affiche *f* détériorée
Plakat *n*, experimentelles	experimental poster	affiche *f* expérimentelle
Plakat *n*, gemaltes	painted placard	affiche *f* peinte
Plakat *n*, grellfarbiges	glaring poster, screaming poster	affiche *f* criarde
Plakat *n*, großformatiges	royal poster	affiche *f* de grand format *m*
Plakat *n*, illustratives	illustrative poster	affiche *f* illustrative
Plakat *n*, informatives	informative poster	affiche *f* informative
Plakat *n*, konstruktives	constructive poster	affiche *f* constructiviste
Plakat *n*, mehrteiliges	poster in several parts *pl*	affiche *f* en plusieurs parties *f/pl*
Plakat *n*, politisches	political poster	affiche *f* politique
Plakat *n*, versetzbares	floating piece	placard *m* dont l'emplacement *m* peut varier
Plakatanalyse *f*	poster analysis	analyse *f* d'affichage *m*
Plakatanlieferung *f*	supplying of posters *pl*	fourniture *f* des affiches *f/pl*
Plakatanschläger *m*	bill-poster, bill-sticker, carder (public conveyances *pl*)	afficheur *m*
Plakatanschlag *m*	poster advertising	affichage *m*
Plakatanschlaginstitut *n*	billposting agency, poster contractor, poster plant	entrepreneur *m* d'affichage *m*
Plakatanschlagkampagne *f*	poster campaign	campagne *f* d'affichage *m*, campagne-affiche *f*
Plakatanschlagkontrolle *f*	riding the showing	inspection *f* d'emplacements *m/pl*
Plakatanschlagpreis *m*	space charge	dépenses *f/pl* d'affichage *m*
Plakatanschlagsäule *f*	pillar	colonne *f* d'affichage *m*
Plakatanschlagunternehmen *n*	poster plant	entreprise *f* d'affichage *m*
Plakatanschlagwerbung *f*	billposting, poster advertising, sheetage	publicité *f* par affiches *f/pl*
Plakataushang *m*	display of posters *pl*	présentation *f* de placards *m/pl*
Plakatauswechslung *f*	change of the bill	renouvellement *m* de l'affiche *f*
Plakatbeachtung *f*, Prüfung *f* der	poster audience survey	vérification *f* de l'audience *f* d'affichage *m*
Plakatdruckerei *f*	poster printing plant	imprimerie *f* d'affiches *f/pl*
Plakatentwurf *m*	dummy of a poster, poster design, poster sketch	dessin *m* pour affiche *f*, maquette *f* d'une affiche *f*, projet *m* d'affiche *f*
Plakatersatzreserve *f*	renewals *pl*	supplément *m* d'affiches *f/pl* pour le remplacement *m*
Plakates *n*, Vorleimen *n* eines	preposting	pré-encollage *m*
Plakatfamilie *f*	poster-family	famille *f* d'affiches *f/pl*
Plakatformat *n* (siehe Anhang)	poster size (see appendix)	format *m* d'affiche *f* (voir appendice)
Plakatgestaltung *f*	poster-designing	conception *f* de l'affiche *f*
Plakatgrafiker *m*	poster artist	affichiste *m*
plakatieren	to place bills *pl*, to post bills *pl*, to stick bills *pl*	afficher

Plakatierung *f*	posting	affichage *m*
Plakatierung *f*, gemeinnützige	public service posters *pl*	affiches *f/pl* pour le service *m* public
Plakatierungsauftrag *m*	billposting order	ordre *m* d'affichage *m*
Plakatierungsform *f*	form of bill-posting	forme *f* d'affichage *m*
plakativ	poster-like	placatif
Plakatkleber *m*	bill-sticker	colleur *m* d'affiches *f/pl*
Plakatladen *m*	poster-shop	poste *m* de vente *f* d'affiches *f/pl*
Plakatmaler *m*	poster artist, poster designer	affichiste *m*
Plakatmitte *f*	centre of the poster	centre *m* de l'affiche *f*
Plakatmotiv *n*	subject of the poster	sujet *m* de l'affiche *f*
Plakatmuseum *n*	poster museum	musée *m* de l'affiche *f*
Plakatpachtung *f*	site leasing	régie *f* d'affichage *m*
Plakatpapier *n*	poster paper	papier *m* pour affiches *f/pl*
Plakatsäule *f*	advertising pillar	colonne *f* d'affichage *m*, colonne *f* Morris (à Paris)
Plakatsäulen *f/pl*, Teilbelegung *f* von	partial display on a few pillars *pl*	affichage *m* sur certaines colonnes *f/pl* seulement
Plakatsammlung *f*	poster collection	collection *f* d'affiches *f/pl*
Plakatschrift *f*	poster lettering, poster type	caractères *m/pl* pour affiches *f/pl*
Plakatständer *m*	stand	panneau *m* d'affichage *m*
Plakatträger *m*	sandwich man	homme-sandwich *m*
Plakatwand *f*	poster hoarding	panneau *m* d'affichage *m*
Plakatwerbung *f*	poster advertising	affichage *m*
Plakatzaun *m*	poster hoarding	panneau-réclame *f*
Plakatzeichner *m*	poster artist	affichiste *m*
Plakette *f*	plaquette	plaquette *f*
Plan *m*	plan, schedule	plan *m*, schéma *m*
planmäßig	according to plan	selon plan *m*
Planung *f*	plan, planning	planification *f*, programme *m*
Planungsarbeit *f*	planning activity	élaboration *f* d'un plan *m*
Plappermaul *n*	chatterbox	grand bavard *m*
Plastikeinband *m*	laminated jacket	couverture *f* plastifiée
Plastikerzeugnis *n*	plastic product	produit *m* plastique
Plastikheftung *f*	plastic binding	reliure *f* en matière *f* plastique
Plastikplatte *f*	plastic sheet	plaque *f* de plastique *f*
plastisch	plastic	plastique
plastische Werbemittel *n/pl*	plastic media *pl*	moyens *m/pl* publicitaires synthétiques
Platte *f*	plate, sheet, slab	dalle *f*, plaque *f*
Plattendruck *m*	stereotype	stéréotypage *m*
Plattenspeicher *m*	disc memory, disc storage	mémoire *f* à disques *m/pl*
Plattenspieler *m*	record player, recorder	tourne-disques *m*
Plattform *f*	platform	plate-forme *f*
Plattformanschlag *m*	platform site advertising	emplacement *m* de quai *m*
Platz *m*, immer an demselben	anchored	fixe
Platzmangel *m* haben	to be pressed for space	être à court de place *f*
Platzvorschrift *f*	appointed space, prescribed position	emplacement *m* imposé
Plauderei *f*, leichte	chatly article, small talk	article *m* léger, menus *m/pl* propos
Plaudereien *f/pl* am Kamin *m*	fireside chats *pl*	causeries *f/pl* devant la cheminée *f*
Plazierung *f*	placing, position	emplacement *m*, placement *m*

Plazierung *f*, **bevorzugte**	preferred position, special position	emplacement *m* privilégié
Plazierung *f*, **gewöhnliche**	run-of-paper position	emplacement *m* ordinaire
Plazierung *f* **im Anzeigenteil** *m*	ordinary position	emplacement *m* ordinaire
Plazierung *f* **oben links**	top left position	emplacement *m* supérieur à gauche
Plazierung *f* **oben rechts**	top right position	emplacement *m* supérieur à droit
Plazierung *f*, **vorgeschriebene**	prescribed position, stated position	emplacement *m* de rigueur *f*, emplacement *m* imposé
Plazierungsaufschlag *m*	surcharge for special position	majoration *f* pour emplacement *m* de rigueur *f*
Plazierungsvorschrift *f*	prescribed position	emplacement *m* de rigueur *f*
Pleonasmus *m*	pleonasm	pléonasme *m*
Pointe *f*	gag, point	pointe *f*
Polemik *f*	polemics *pl*	polémique *f*
Politikaster *m*	armchair politician	politicien *m*, tacticien *m*
Politiker *m*	politician	politique *m*
politische Richtung *f*	political adherence	appartenance *f* politique
politische Zeitschrift *f*	political periodical	revue *f* politique
politischer Redakteur *m*	political editor	rédacteur *m* politique
politisches Plakat *n*	political poster	affiche *f* politique
Politisierung *f*	politization	politisation *f*
Politur *f*	burnishing	brunissage *m*, satinage *m*
pomphaft hervorheben	to blazon	exalter
populäre Zeitung *f*	popular newspaper	journal *m* populaire
Popularisierung *f*	popularization	vulgarisation *f*
pornografisches Blatt *n*	smut sheet	journal *m* pornographique
Portepagen *pl*	bearers *pl*	porte-pages *f/pl*
Porto *n*	postage	port *m*
Porzellanschild *n*	porcelain sign	affiche *f* porcelaine
Posse *f*	slapstick comedy	farce *f* bouffonne
Postabonnement *n*	postal subscription	abonnement *m* postal
postalische Massensendungen *f/pl*	bulk posting	envois *m/pl* en nombre *m*
Postausgabe *f*	mail edition	première édition *f* du matin *m*
Postaussendung *f*, **werbliche**	mailing	publipostage *m*
Postkarte *f*	post card	carte *f* postale
Postleitzahl *f*	number of postal district	numéro *m* du secteur *m* postal
Postscheck *m*	postal cheque	chèque *m* postal
Postversand *m*	dispatch by mail	envoi *m* postal
Postwerbung *f*	postal advertising	publicité *f* par poste *f*
Postwurfsendungen *f/pl*	boxholder addressing, bulk posting, mail distribution, mailing piece, post office mailing	distribution *f* postale de messages *m/pl* non adressés, publicité *f* directe par voie *f* postale
Postzeitungsdienst *m*	postal newspaper service	arrangement *m* concernant les abonnements *m/pl* aux journaux *m/pl* et écrits *m/pl* périodiques
potentiell	potential	potentiel
potentieller Verbraucher *m*	potential consumer	consommateur *m* potentiel
Prägedruck *m*	blind stamping, embossing	bombage *m*, estampage *m*, gaufrage *m*
prägen	to emboss, to stamp	empreindre, gaufrer, repousser

Prägeplakat *f*	embossed poster	affiche *f* en relief *m*
Prägepresse *f*	blocking press	presse *f* à empreindre
Prägestempel *m*	stamping die	étampe *f*, poinçon *m*
Prägnanz *f*	precision, terseness	concision *f*
Prägung *f*	embossing	gaufrage *m*, repoussage *m*
Prämie *f*	bonus	prime *f*
Prämie *f* **auf der Verpackung** *f*	on-pack premium	prime *f* attachée à l'emballage *m*
Prämie *f* **bei Verpackungsteileinsendung** *f*	box-top offer *am*	offre *f* réclame *f* (sur emballage *m*)
Prämie *f*, **kaufanreizende**	incentive premium	prime *f* stimulante
Prämie *f*, **selbstfinanzierte**	self-liquidating premium	prime *f* auto-payante
Prämiierung *f*	awarding of a prize	attribution *f* d'une prime *f*
Präsentation *f*	presentation	présentation *f*
Präsentator *m*	introducer, presenter	présentateur *m*
Präventivwerbung *f*	preventive advertising	publicité *f* préventive
PR-Agentur *f*	public relations *pl* agency	agence *f* des relations *f/pl* publiques
praktisches Wissen *n*	know-how	savoir-faire *m*
PR-Anzeige *f*	public relations *pl* report	publi-information *f*, publi-reportage *m*
praxisbezogen	related to practise	relative à la pratique *f*
PR-Bearbeiter *m*	public relations *pl* officer	responsable des relations *pl* avec le public *m*
PR-Berater *m*	public-relations *pl* consultant	conseil *m* en relations *f/pl* publiques
Preis *m*	price, rate	prix *m*, taux *m*
Preis *m* **angeben**	to quote	citer, coter
Preis *m*, **angekündigter**	posted price	prix *m* affiché
Preis *m*, **angemessener**	adequate price	juste prix *m*
Preis *m*, **doppelter**	double rate	prix *m* double
Preis *m*, **empfohlener**	standard price, suggested price	prix *m* recommandé
Preis *m*, **ermäßigter**	reduced rate, short rate	tarif *m* réajusté
Preis *m*, **gebilligter**	approved price	prix *m* approuvé
Preis *m*, **gebundener**	controlled price, fixed selling price	prix *m* fixe, prix *m* imposé
Preis *m*, **genehmigter**	approved price	prix *m* approuvé
Preis *m*, **gestaffelter**	differential price, graduated price	prix *m* échelonné, tarif *m* mobile
Preis *m*, **niedriger**	thrift price	prix *m* modique
Preis *m*, **niedrigst kalkulierter**	bargain level	prix *m* minimum
Preis *m*, **psychologisch richtiger**	psychological price	prix *m* psychologique
Preis *m*, **reduzierter**	short price	prix *m* réduit
Preis *m*, **überhöhter**	excessive charge	prix *m* excessif
Preisabsprache *f*	price-fixing agreement	entente *f* sur les prix *m/pl*
Preisänderung *f*	price alteration, price changes *pl*, price variance	modification *f* du prix *m*
Preisangabe *f*	price quotation	indication *f* du prix *m*
Preisangebot *n*	quotation	offre *f* de prix *m*
Preisangleichung *f*	price adjustment	alignement *m* des prix *m/pl*
Preisanstieg *m*	price advance	montée *f* des prix *m/pl*
Preisaufschlag *m*	extra charge, surcharge	majoration *f* de tarif *m*, majoration *f* de prix *m*, supplément *m* de prix *m*
Preisausschreiben *n*	competition, prize contest	mise *f* au concours *m*
Preisauszeichnung *f*	price marking	affichage *m* des prix *m/pl*
Preisberechnung *f*	calculation of price	calcul *m* des prix *m/pl*

Preisbildung *f*	price making	formation *f* des prix *m/pl*
Preisbindung *f* der zweiten Hand *f*	resale price maintenance	prix *m* imposé
Preisbindungsklausel *f*	tying clause	clause *f* limitative
Preisentwicklung *f*	price development	évolution *f* des prix *m/pl*
Preise *m/pl*, reduzierte	short rates *pl*	rappel *m*
Preiserhöhung *f*	advance in price, mark up, price boost	augmentation *f* de prix *m*
Preisermäßigung *f*	price abatement	rabais *m*, remise *f*
Preisgestaltung *f*	pricing	formation *f* des prix *m/pl*
preisgünstig	budget-priced, economy-priced	à bon marché *m*
Preisherabsetzung *f*	mark down, shrinking of prices *pl*	réduction *f* de prix *m*
Preisheraufsetzung *f*	upward adjustment of prices *pl*	majoration *f* de prix *m/pl*
Preisliste *f*	price list, rate card, rates *pl*, schedule of prices *pl*	liste *f* de prix, prix *m* courant *m*, tarif *m*
Preispolitik *f*	price policy	politique *f* des prix *m/pl*
Preisschild *n*	apron, price marker, price tag, sticker	étiquette *f*, porte-prix *m*
Preisschleuderei *f*	price slashing	avilissement *m* des prix *m/pl*
Preisschutz *m*	price protection	protection *f* des prix *m/pl*
Preisschwelle *f*	price threshold	seuil *m* de prix *m*
Preissteigerung *f*	advance in price, price boost	augmentation *f* de prix *m*
Preistreue *f*	rigid price	prix *m* fixe
Preisunterbietung *f*	dumping, price-cutting	bradage *m*, gâchage *m* de prix *m*
Preisvergleich *m*	price comparison	comparaison *f* des prix *m/pl*
Presse *f*	press	presse *f*
Presse *f*, auflagenstarke	press with a large circulation	grande presse *f*, presse *f* à grand tirage *m*
Presse *f*, illegale	illegal press	presse *f* illégale
Presse *f*, käufliche	corrupt press	presse *f* corrompue
Presseagent *m*	press agent	agent *m* de publicité *f*
Presseagentur *f*	press agency	agence *f* d'information *f*
Presseamt *n*	public relations *pl* office	office *m* de presse *f*
Pressearbeit *f*	presswork	activité *f* du journaliste *m*
Presseattaché *m*	press attaché, press officer	attaché *m* de presse *f*
Presseausweis *m*	press passport	carte *f* de presse *f*
Presseauszüge *m/pl*	press extracts *pl*	extraits *m/pl* de la presse *f*
Pressebeobachtung *f*	watching of the press	surveillance *f* de presse *f*
Pressebericht *m*	press report, write-up *am*	récit *m*, reportage *m*
Pressebilderdienst *m*	picture agency	agence *f* de presse *f* photographique
Pressechef *m*	press chief	chef *m* de presse *f*
Pressedelikt *n*	press offence	délit *m* de presse *f*
Pressedienst *m*	news agency, press service	agence *f* d'information *f*, service *m* de presse *f*
Presseempfang *m*	press reception	réception *f* de la presse *f*
Presseexemplar *n*	press-copy	service *m* de presse *f*
Pressefoto *n*	press photo	photo *f* de presse *f*
Pressefotograf *m*	press photographer	photographe *m* de presse *f*
Pressefreiheit *f*	freedom of the press	liberté *f* de la presse *f*
Pressegesetz *n*	press law	loi *f* sur la presse *f*
Pressehandbuch *n*	press guide	guide *m* de presse *f*
Pressekampagne *f*	crusade, press campaign	campagne *f* de presse *f*
Presseknebelung *f*	gagging of the press, muzzling of the press, stifling of the press	baîllonnement *m* de la presse *f*, muselement *m* de la presse *f*

Pressekommentar m	press commentary	commentaire m de presse f
Pressekonferenz f	press conference	conférence f de presse f
Pressekonzentration f	press concentration	concentration f de la presse f
Presseloge f	press-box	banc m de la presse f
Pressemagnat m	press tycoon	magnat m de la presse f
Pressemedien n/pl	press media	médias m/pl de presse f
Pressemitteilung f	hand out	communiqué m
Pressenachrichten f/pl	press news	nouvelles f/pl de presse f
Pressenotiz f	news release, newspaper notice	entrefilet m
Pressepolemik f	paper war, press controversy	polémique f de presse f
Presserecht n	press law	loi f de presse f
Pressereferent m	press attaché	attaché m de presse f
Presserundschau f	press review	revue f de la presse f
Pressesprecher m	speaker	porte-parole m
Pressestand m	press-box	stand m de la presse f
Pressestelle f	press office, publicity department	office m de presse f
Pressestenograf m	press stenographer	sténo m de presse f
Pressestimmen f/pl	press comments pl	échos m/pl de la presse f
Pressetelegramm n	press telegram	télégramme m de presse f
Pressetelegramm n, kurzes	flash	courte dépêche f d'agence f
Pressetribüne f	press gallery	tribune f de la presse f
Presseverlautbarung f	official statement, press release	communiqué m, déclaration f à la presse f
Presseversand m	prcss release	action f de presse f
Pressevertrieb m	distribution of publications pl, newspaper wholesaling	colportage m, messagerie f
Pressewerbung f	press advertising	publicité-presse f
Pressewesen n	journalism	journalisme m
Pressezeichner m	cartoonist	reporter-dessinateur m
Pressezentrum n	press centre	centre m de la presse f
Pressezitate n/pl	press quotations	citations f/pl de la presse f
Prestigewerbung f	good-will advertising, institutional advertising, prestige advertising	publicité f de notoriété f, publicité f de prestige m, publicité f impériale
Prestigezeitung f	quality paper	journal m de qualité f
Primärwerbung f	primary-demand advertising	publicité f primaire
Privatdruck m	private edition	édition f privée
private Anzeige f	personal advertisement	annonce f privée
privates Werbefernsehen n	independent television	télévision f privée
Privatsender m	private station	station f privée
Privileg-Vertriebsmethode f	franchise circulation	diffusion f privilégiée
PR-Mann m	build-upper	agent m de publicité f
Probe f	specimen	échantillon m, spécimen m
Probeabonnement m	trial subscription	abonnement m d'essai m
Probeabzug m	proof, proofsheet, pull	épreuve f
Probeauftrag m	sample order, trial order	commande f à l'épreuve f, ordre m d'essai m
Probedruck m	dummy volume, specimen volume	épreuve f
Probeexemplar n	complimentary copy	fascicule m spécimen m
Probeheft n, Probenummer f	specimen copy	numéro m d'essai m
Probenverteilung f	sampling	distribution f d'échantillons m/pl
Probepackung f	trial package	emballage m d'essai m
Probeseite f	proof page, specimen page	page f modèle m, page f spécimen m
Probesprechen n	audition	séance f d'essai m

Problemstück n	problem play	pièce f à thèse f
Produkt m	product	produit m
Produkt m, **modisches**	fancy article	produit m à la mode f
Produkt n, **nachgeahmtes**	imitative product	produit m imitatif
Produktanalyse f	product analysis	analyse f du produit m
Produktbeschreibung f	fact sheet	description f d'un produit m
Produkterkennung f	product identification	identification f de produit m
Produktform f	shape of product	forme f de produit m
Produktforschung f	product research	étude f des produits m/pl
Produktgattung f	product category	catégorie f de biens m/pl
Produktgestaltung f	styling	réalisation f d'un produit m
Produktionsablauf m	tempo of production	rythme m de la production f
Produktionsgüter n/pl	industrial goods pl, producer's goods pl	articles m/pl industriels, biens m/pl de production f
Produktionskosten pl	talent costs pl	coûts m/pl de production f
Produktionsleiter m	product manager	directeur m de la production f
Produktionstechnik f	production techniques pl	processus m de production f
Produktmanager m	brand manager, product manager	chef m de produit m, spécialiste m produit m
Produktmarke f	brand of a product	marque f de produit m
Produktname m	name of a product	nom m de produit m
Produkttest m	product testing	contrôle m de produit m, test m de produit m
Produkttest m, **anonymer**	blind product test	test m de produit m anonyme
Produktwerbung f	line advertising, product advertising	publicité f produits m/pl
Produzent m	producer	producteur m
Prognose f	prognosis	pronostic m
Programm n	program am, programme brit	programme m
Programmgestaltung f	programming	programmation f
programmieren	to program	programmer
Programmierer m	programmer	programmateur m
Programmstruktur f	program structure	structure f du programme m
Programmzeitschrift f	television magazine	magazine m de télévision f
Projektionstechnik f	projection technique	technique f de projection f
Projektionswand f	screen	écran m
Projektor m	projector	projecteur m
Propaganda f	propaganda	propagande f
Propagandafilm m	propaganda film	film m à propagande f
Propagandagetöse n	hullabaloo	tintamarre m de propagande f
Propagandist m	builder-upper, propagandist	propagandiste m
propagieren	to propagandize, to propagate	faire de la propagande f, propager
proportional vergrößern	to enlarge proportionally	agrandir à la proportionnelle
proportional verkleinern	to scale down	réduire en proportion f
Prospekt m	booklet, folder, handbill, pamphlet, prospectus	brochure f, dépliant m, prospectus m, tract m
Prospektanzeigen f/pl	Dutch door	annonces f/pl avec des dépliants m/pl cousus sur elles
Prospektverteilung f	distribution of circulars pl	distribution f d'imprimés m/pl
Provinzblatt n	provincial paper	feuille f régionale
Provinzpresse f	provincial press	presse f provinciale
Provision f	commission	commission f
Provision f, **geteilte**	split commission	commission f partagée

Provisionsabgabe *f*	kickback, yielding of commission	cession *f* de ristournes *f/pl*, donner des retours *m/pl* en arrière
Provisionsbasis *n*, auf	on commission	à la commission *f*
provisionspflichtig	commissionable	donnant droit *m* à la commission *f*
Provisionssatz *m*	rate of commission	taux *m* de commission *f*
Provisionsteilung *f*	commission splitting	partage *m* de commission *f*
provisorisch	provisional	provisoire
provisorischer Abschluß *m*	provisional booking	ordre *m* provisoire
Provisorium *n*	makeshift	état *m* provisoire
Prozent *n*	percentage	pour-cent *m*
Prozentsatz *m*	percentage	pourcentage *m*
prüfen	to check, to check up, to examine	contrôler, examiner, vérifier
Prüfer *m*	auditor	contrôleur *m*
Prüfliste *f*	check list	liste *f* de contrôle *m*
Prüfung *f*	examination	examen *m*
Prüfung *f* der gedrehten Szenen *f/pl*	rushes *pl*	épreuve *f* de tournage *m*
Prüfung *f* der Plakatbeachtung *f*	poster audience survey	vérification *f* de l'audience *f* d'affichage *m*
Prüfung *f* des Publikumsverhaltens *n*	concept-test	test *m* d'axe *m*
Prüfungsbericht *m*	audit report	rapport *m* de contrôle *m*
Prüfzeichen *n*	test mark	marque *f* de contrôle *m*
Pseudonym *n*	pen-name, pseudonym	nom *m* de guerre *f*, nom *m* de plume *f*, pseudonyme *m*
psychologisch richtiger Preis *m*	psychological price	prix *m* psychologique
public relations *f/pl*	public relations *pl*	relations *f/pl* publiques
Publikation *f*	publication	publication *f*
Publikationszweck *m*	aim of the publication	but *m* de publication *f*
Publikum *n*	audience	audience *f*, public *m*
Publikum *n*, eingefangenes	captive audience	audience *f* captive
Publikum *n*, großes	public at large	grand public *m*
Publikums *n*, Zusammensetzung *f* des	audience composition, audience profile	composition *f* de l'audience *f*
Publikumsanalyse *f*	audience analysis, audience research	analyse *f* de l'audience *f*
Publikumspropaganda *f*	general publicity	publicité *f* générale
Publikumswerbung *f*	advertising for the general public	publicité *f* auprès le grand public *m*
Publikumszeitschrift *f*	consumer publication	magazine *m*, revue *f*
Publikumszusammensetzung *f*	audience profile	composition *f* du public *m*
publizieren	to publish	publier
Publizist *m*	journalist, publicist	publiciste *m*
Publizistik *f*	journalism	journalisme *m*
Publizistik *f*, getarnte	camouflage	camouflage *m*
Publizität *f*	publicity	publicité *f*
Punkt *m*	dot, full stop, point	point *m*
Punkt *m*, halber	hair space	espace *m* fin
Punkt *m*, typografischer	typographic point	point *m* typographique
Punkte *m/pl*, die die Auslassung *f* eines Wortes *n* anzeigen	leaders *pl*	plusieurs points *m/pl* qui indiquent l'omission *f* d'un mot *m*
punktierte Linie *f*	dotted line, dotted rule	filet *m* pointillé, ligne *f* de pointillés *m/pl*

punktierter Rand *m*	dotted frame, stippled frame	cadre *m* de pointillés *m/pl*
Punktlicht *n*	spotlight	feu *m* de projecteur *m*
Punktlinie *f*	dotted line	ligne *f* de pointillés *m/pl*
Punktraster *m*	dot screen	trame *f* à points *m/pl*
Punktschraffierung *f*	stipple	crachis *m*, grisé *m* fait à la brosse *f*
Punktsystem *n* (siehe Anhang)	point system (see appendix)	mesures *f/pl* typographiques (voir appendice), système *m* en points *m/pl*

Q

Quadrantenwaage *f*	basic weight scales *pl*	pèse-papier *m*
Quadrat *n*	square	carré *m*
Quadrat *n* (Ausschluß *n*)	quad, quadrat	cadrat *m*
Quadratmetergewicht *n*	paper weight by grams *pl* per square meter	grammage *m*, poids *m*
Qualität *f*	quality	qualité *f*
Qualität *f*, **ästhetische**	aesthetic quality	qualité *f* esthétique
Qualität *f*, **minderwertige**	cheap quality	qualité *f* de peu de valeur *f*
Qualitätserzeugnis *n*	quality product	produit *m* de qualité *f*
Qualitätsverbesserung *f* **einer Ware** *f*	up-trading	amélioration *f* de la qualité *f* d'un produit *m*
Qualitätszeitung *f*	high-class paper, prestige paper, quality paper	journal *m* de première qualité *f*, journal *m* de prestige *m*, journal *m* pour l'élite *f*
Quartformat *n*	quarto size	format *m* in-quarto
Quelle *f*	source	source *f*
Quellenangabe *f*	credit	référence *f* de source *f*
Quellenverzeichnis *n*	list of references *pl*	table *f* des sources *f/pl*
Querformat *n*	broadside size, cross size, landscape	format *m* en largeur *f*, format *m* en travers *m*
Querheftung *f*	side stitching	couture *f* à cheval *m*
Querlinie *f*	cross rule	réglure *f*
Querschnitt *m*	cross-cut, cross-section	coupe *f* en travers, coupe *f* transversale
Querulant *m*	grumbler	querelleur *m*
Quote *f*	quota	quota *m*

R

Rabatt *m*	discount, rebate	escompte *m*, rabais *m*, remise *f*
Rabatt *m*, **ohne**	transient rate	sans rabais *m*
Rabattmarke *f*	discount ticket, saving stamp, trading stamp	timbre-primes *f/pl*, timbre *m* de rabais *m*, timbre *m* d'épargne *f*
Rabattmarkenbuch *n*	stamp book	carnet *m* de timbres *m/pl* prime *f*
Rabattnachbelastung *f*	short rate	charge *m* réajusté
Rabattreduzierung *f*	discount reduction	réduction *f* de rabais *m*
Rabattrückbelastung *f*	short rate	débit *m* de rabais *m* rétrograde, rappel *m*
Rabattstaffel *f*	scale of discount, sliding scale	barême *m* dégressif, échelle *f* mobile
Radiernadel *f*	chisel	échoppe *f*, pointe *f*
Radierung *f*	etching	gravure *f* à l'eau-forte *f*

Radioamateur *m*	ham	opérateur *m* amateur *m*
Radioapparat *m*	wireless set	poste *m* de radio *f*, récepteur *m* radio *f*
Radiosendung *f*	broadcast transmission	émission *f* à la radio *f*
Radiostation *f*	broadcasting station	station *f* de radiodiffusion *f*
Radiowerbung *f*	broadcast advertising	publicité *f* radiodiffusée
Radiowerbung *f* **betreiben**	to be on the air	annoncer par radio *f*
Rätselecke *f*	puzzle corner	coin *m* des devinettes *f/pl*
Räuberpistole *f*	penny dreadful	journal *m* pour concierges *f/pl*
räumliches Hören *n*	stereophony	stéréophonie *f*
Rahmen *m*	framework	cadre *m*
Rahmen *m*, **gerasterter**	backed frame, shaded frame	cadre *m* de filets *m/pl* gras-maigre
Rahmenklischee *n*	slip-in block	cliché *m* passe-partout
Rahmenplakat *n*	stock poster	affiche *f* passe-partout
Rahmenprogramm *n*	programme framing the commercials *pl*	programme *m* encadrant les émissions *f/pl* publicitaires
Rakel *f*	blade, squeegee	raclette *f*, racleur *m*
Rakeltiefdruck *m*	photogravure, rotogravure	héliogravure *f*, rotogravure *f*
Rand *m*	edge, margin	bord *m*, marge *f*
Rand *m*, **gepunkteter**	stippled frame	cadre *m* de pointillés *m/pl*
Rand *m* **punktierter**	dotted frame	cadre *m* de pointillés *m/pl*
Rand *m*, **schwarzer**	black border, black frame, thick frame	baguette *f*, bordure *f* de filet *m*
Rand *m*, **unbedruckter**	margin	marge *f*
randangeschnitten	bleed-off	franc bord
Randbemerkung *f*	marginal note	note *f* marginale
randkaschiert	edge-turned passe-partout	bord *m* de coupure *f* doublé
Randlinie *f*	border rule	filet *m* de bordure *f*
randloses Klischee *f*	bleed	cliché *m* sans marge *f*
Randverzierung *f*	cartouche	vignette *f*
Rangordnung *f*	hierarchy, order of precedence	hiérarchie *f*, ordre de préséance *f*
Rangordnungsprüfung *f*	order of merit test	épreuve *f* de l'ordre *m* de préséance *f*
Raster *m*	Ben Day, screen	grisé *m* mécanique, réseau *m*, trame *f*
Raster *m*, **aufgelegter**	sticked screen	trame *f* collée
Raster *m*, **grober**	coarse screen	grosse trame *f*
Rasterfolie *f*	screen foil	pellicule *f* tramée
Rasterlinie *f*	screen line	ligne *f* de la trame *f*
Rasterpapier *n*	printed shading tint	trame *f* imprimée, trame *f* mécanique
Rasterpunkt *m*	halftone dot	point *m* de trame *f*
Rastertiefdruck *m*	screen intaglio	héliogravure *f* tramée
Rastertönungen *f/pl*	half-tone shadings *pl*, tints *pl*	grisés *m/pl*
Rasterweite *f*	screen width	finesse *f* de la trame *f*
Ratengeschäft *n*	tally business	vente *f* à tempérament *m*
Ratenverkauf *m*	hire-purchase	vente *f* à crédit *m*
Ratenzahlung *f*	part payment	paiement *m* par versements *m/pl* fractionnés
Ratespiel *n*	quiz	devinette *f*
Raubdruck *m*	pirated edition	édition *f* frauduleuse
Rauchschriftwerbung *f*	smoke writing	écriture *f* fumigène
Raum *m*	space	espace *m*
Raum *m* **einschränken**	to run short	gagner

Raum *m*, **freier, Raum** *m*, **für redaktionellen Text** *m* **verfügbarer**	newshole	espace *m* disponible pour la rédaction *f*
Raum *m*, **unbedruckter**	blank space	espace *m* blanc, espace *m* non-imprimé, espace *m* vierge *f*
Raumaufteilung *f*, **falsche**	faulty spacing	espacement *m* faux
Raummangel *m*	pressure of space	manque *f* de place *f*
Raumton *m*	stereophony	stéréophonie *f*
Rechenscheibe *f*	calculating disc	disque *m* à calculer
Rechenschieber *m*	slide rule	règle *f* à calculer
Rechercheur *m*	investigator, research man	enquêteur *m*
recherchieren	to investigate	faire des recherches *f/pl*
Rechnung *f*	account, bill, invoice	compte *m*, facture *f*
Rechnung *f* **prüfen**	to check the invoice, to verify the invoice	apurer la facture *f*, vérifier la facture *f*
Rechnungsbetrag *m*	invoice amount	montant *m* de la facture *f*
Rechnungserteilung *f*	invoicing	facturation *f*
Rechnungskontrolleur *m*	checker	pigeur *m*
Rechnungsprüfung *f*	audit	vérification *f* des comptes *m/pl*
Rechnungsstellung *f*	invoicing	établissement *m* de facture *f*
Rechnungswesen *n*	accountancy	comptabilité *f*
rechte Ecke *f*	right-hand corner	coin *m* droit
rechte Seite *f*	odd page, right-hand page	bonne page *f*, page *f* de droite, recto
Rechteck *n*	rightangle	rectangle *m*
rechteckig	rectangular	rectangulaire
rechteckige Vollautotypie *f*	square half-tone	autotypie *f* rectangulaire, simili *m* au carré *m*
rechteckiges Klischee *n*	squared up block	cliché *m* rectangulaire
rechts ausschließen, nach	to move to the right	justifier à droite
rechts oben	top right position	emplacement *m* supérieur à droit
rechts unten	bottom right	bas *m* de la page *f* droite
Rechtsberater *m*	legal adviser	conseiller *m* juridique
Rechtschreibung *f*	spelling	orthographe *f*
rechtseingestellte Zeitung *f*	right-wing paper	journal *m* de droite
Rechtsgutachten *n*	legal opinion	avis *m* juridique
rechtwinklig zum Verkehrsfluß *m*	head on position	barre-route *f*
Redakteur *m*	editor	rédacteur *m*
Redakteur *m* **der Seufzerspalte** *f*	love-lorn editor	titulaire *m* du courrier *m* du cœur *m*
Redakteur *m*, **geschäftsführender**	managing editor	rédacteur *m* gérant
Redakteur *m*, **politischer**	political editor	rédacteur *m* politique
Redakteur *m*, **stellvertretender**	sub-editor	rédacteur *m* adjoint
Redakteur *m*, **verantwortlicher**	responsible editor	rédacteur *m* responsable
Redaktion *f*	editorial board, editorial office, editorial staff	rédaction *f*
redaktionell aufgemachte Anzeige *f*	advertorial, editorial advertisement, reader advertisement, reading notice *am*	annonce *f* à apparence *f* rédactionnelle
redaktionelle Bearbeitung *f*	editorializing	rédaction *f*
redaktionelle Konzeption *f*	editorial conception	conception *f* rédactionnelle
redaktionelle Tendenz *f*	editorial policy	politique *f* rédactionnelle

redaktionelle Unterstützung *f*	editorial assistance, editorial support	assistance *f* rédactionnelle
redaktionelle Werbung *f*	editorial publicity, free puff, write-up *am*	annonce *f* rédactionnelle, publicité *f* rédactionnelle gratuite
redaktionellem Teil *m*, **gegenüber**	facing editorial matter	face *f* texte *m* rédactionnel
redaktioneller Artikel *m*	editorial	article *m* rédactionnel, éditorial *m*
redaktioneller Beitrag *m*	contribution	article *m* écrit pour un journal *m*, cntribution *f*
redaktioneller Inhalt *m*	editorial content	contenu *m* rédactionnel
redaktioneller Teil *m*	editorial matter, editorial section	section *f* rédactionnelle, texte *m* rédactionnel
redaktionelles Umfeld *n*	editorial context	contexte *m* rédactionnel
Redaktionsarbeit *f*, **sitzende**	desk work	travail *m* sédentaire au journal *m*
Redaktionsdirektor *m*	managing editor	rédacteur *m* gérant
Redaktionsgeheimnis *n*	editorial secret	secret *m* de la rédaction *f*
Redaktionsgemeinschaft *f*	joint editorial board	communauté *f* de rédaction *f*, team *m* rédactionnel
Redaktionskonferenz *f*	editorial conference	conférence *f* de rédaction *f*
Redaktionssaal *m*	editorial hall	salle *f* de rédaction *f*
Redaktionsschluß *m*	closing date, closing down, copy deadline, forms *pl* close	bouclage *m*, date *f* limite de remise *f*, remise *f* de copie *f*
Redaktionssekretär *m*	copy reader, sub-editor	sécrétaire *m* de rédaction *f*
Redaktionssekretariat *n*	desk	sécrétariat *m* de rédaction *f*
Redaktionsstab *m*	editorial staff	équipe *f* de rédaction *f*
Redefluß *m*	flow of words *pl*	flux *m* verbal
Redefreiheit *f*	freedom of speech	liberté *f* de parole *f*
Redensart *f*	phrase	locution *f*
Redensart *f*, **abgedroschene**	hackneyed phrase, stock phrase	cliché *m*, phrase *f* rebattue
Redewendung *f*	phrase, turn of a sentence	tournure *f* de phrase *f*
Redewendungen *f/pl*, **Sammlung** *f* **von**	phrase-book	recueil *m* de locutions *f/pl*
redigieren	to edit	rédiger
Redner *m*	speaker	orateur *m*
reduzierter Preis *m*	short price	prix *m* réduit
Reduzierung *f* **des Preises** *m* **gegenüber dem auf Packung** *f* **oder Etikett** *f* **angegebenen**	off-label deal	réduction *f* de prix *m* signalé sur le conditionnement *m* ou l'étiquette *f*
Reflektor *m*	reflector	réflecteur *m*
Regal *n*	rack	étagère *f*, rayon *m*
Regalstreifen *m*	shelf-strip	bande *f* d'étagère *f*, dépassant *m* de rayon *m*
regelmäßige Leser *m/pl*	regular readers *pl*	lecteurs *m/pl* réguliers
Regelung *f*	regulation	réglementation *f*
Regenbogenpresse *f*	light reading weekly	feuille *f* hebdomadaire divertissante
Regionalausgabe *f*	regional issue	édition *f* régionale
regionale Marktuntersuchung *f*	area sampling	échantillonnage *m* par zone *f*
regionale Streuung *f*	regional dispersion	couverture *f* régionale
regionale Tageszeitung *f*	regional daily	quotidien *m* régional
regionale Wahlkampagne *f*	zone campaign	campagne *f* électorale régionale

Regionalpresse *f*	regional press	presse *f* régionale
Register *n*	index, register	index *m*, registre *m*
Register *n*, fehlerhaftes	out-of-register	fausse marge *f*, registre *m* défectueux
Registerblatt *n*	index sheet	feuille *f* de registre *m*
Registratur *f*	filing cabinet, registry	enregistrement *m*
Reglette *f*	clump, lead, line-space, reglet	interligne *f*, réglette *f*
Reichhaltigkeit *f*	abundance	abondance *f*
Reichweite *f*	coverage, penetration, range, reach *am*, turnover	couverture *f*, rayon *m* d'action *f*, taux *m* de pénétration *f*
Reichweite *f* eines Senders *m*	coverage of a station	couverture *f* géographique
Reihenanschlag *m*	series *pl* posting	affichage *m* par massifs *m/pl*
Reihenanschlag *m* auf den Metro-Bahnsteigen *m/pl* für einen einzigen Werbungtreibenden *m*	series *pl* posting on the métro platforms *pl* for one advertiser only	massif quai *m* (métro *m*)
Reihenanschlag *m* in den Gängen *m/pl* für einen einzigen Werbungtreibenden *m* (Untergrundbahn)	series *pl* posting in the passage ways *pl* for one advertiser only (Metro)	massif couloir *m* (métro *m*)
Reihenfolge *f*	order	ordre *m*, suite *f*
Reinabzug *m*	clean proof	épreuve *f* sans fautes *f/pl*
Reindruck *m*	clean print	tirage *m*
Reinlayout *n*	finished layout	dessin *m* définitif, maquette *f* définitive
Reinschrift *f*	fair copy	copie *f* au net *m*
Reinzeichnung *f*	final art work, finished drawing	dessin *m* au net, document *m*, projet *m* définitif
Reisebeilage *f*	travel supplement	supplément *m* touristique
Reiseführer *m*	travel guide	prospectus *m* de voyage *m*
Reisekosten *pl*	travelling-expenses *pl*	frais *m/pl* de déplacement *m*, frais *m/pl* de voyage *m*
Reisender *m*	commercial traveller	voyageur *m* de commerce *m*
reisender Berichterstatter *m*	roving reporter	reporter *m* itinérant
Reispapier *n*	rice-paper	papier *m* de Chine *f*, papier *m* de riz *m*
Reißbrett *n*	drawing board	planche *f* à dessiner
Reißer *m*	thriller	clou *m*, film *m*, pièce *f* à sensation *f*, roman *m*
Reißfeder *f*	drawing pen	tire-ligne *m*
Reißfestigkeit *f*	tensile strength	résistance *f* à la rupture *f*
Reißschiene *f*	drawing rule	règle *f* à dessiner
Reiz *m*	stimulus	stimulation *f*
Reizschwelle *f*	sensation level, threshold of sensation	seuil *m* d'efficacité *f*
Reklamation *f*	complaint	réclamation *f*
Reklame *f* machen	to boom, to boost	faire de la propagande *f*
Reklameartikel *m*	advertising article, door opener	article *m* de réclame *f*
Reklameaufschrift *f*	advertising inscription	inscriptions-réclame *f*
Reklameauswüchse *m/pl*	misdoings *pl* of advertising	excès *m* de la publicité *f*, méfaits *m/pl* de la publicité *f*
Reklamebild *n*	advertising picture	image *f* publicitaire
Reklamechef *m*	build-upper	publicitaire *m*
Reklamedrachen *m*	advertising kite	publicité *f* par cerf-volant *m*

Reklamefläche f	advertising space, hoarding for posters pl	panneau m de publicité f, surface f d'affichage m
Reklamemarke f	advertising seal, poster stamp	timbre m réclame f
Reklamepreis m	cut-rate price	prix m réclame
Reklametrick m	bluff, stunt, trick	ruse f publicitaire
Reklameverkauf m	bargain sale	vente f réclame
Reklamewoche f	propaganda week	semaine f publicitaire
Reliefbuchstabe m	relief letter	lettre f en relief m
Reliefdruck m	die-stamping, embossing, relief-printing	gaufrage m en relief m, impression f gaufrée, impression f thermogravure f
Reliefklischee n	relief etched block	cliché m en relief m
Remittenden f/pl	overrun, remainders pl, returns pl	bouillon m, invendus pl, rendus pl
Rennbahn f	race court	champ m de cours m
Rentabilitätsschwelle f	break-even point	limite f minimum, seuil m de la rentabilité f
Reportage f	feature article, report, reporting, running commentary	reportage m
Reporter m	newshawk, newshound, reporter	reporter m
Reporter m **für besondere Aufgaben** f/pl	assignment-man	reporter m à la tâche f
Repräsentant m	representative	courtier m, représentant m
Repräsentationswerbung f	institutional advertising, prestige advertising	publicité f de prestige m
repräsentative Marktuntersuchung f	adequate sample	échantillon m représentatif
repräsentativer Durchschnitt m	cross section	coupe f en travers
Reproduktion f	copy print, reproduction	contre-type m, reproduction f
Reproduktion f, **elektromechanische**	electromechanical reproduction	reproduction f électro-mécanique
Reproduktion f, **panchromatische**	panchromatic reproduction	reproduction f panchromatique
reproduktionsreif	able to be reproduced	apte à être reproduit
Reproduktionstechnik f	reproduction technique	procédés m/pl photomécaniques
Reproduktionsvorlage f	copy for reproduction	original m à reproduire
Reprolithograf m	reprolithographer	reprolithographe m
reservieren	to reserve	réserver
reservierter Anzeigenplatz m	reserved position	emplacement m réservé
Reservierung f	booking, reservation	réservation f
Resonanz f	echo, empathy	écho m, résonance f
Ressort n	beat, department	ressort m, secteur m
Restauflage f	remainders pl	soldes m/pl
Restbestand m	stock remainder	stock m restant
Retusche f	retouching	maquillage m, retouche f
Retuschefarbe f	retouching ink	encre f de retouche f
Retuscheur m	retoucher	retoucheur m
retuschieren	to artist, to retouch	retoucher
Retuschierung f	retouching	retouchage m
Revolverblatt n	gutter paper, yellow journal	feuille f à scandale m, feuille f de chantage m
Rezensent m	critic	critique m
Rezension f	critique, review	compte m rendu, critique f
Rezensionsexemplar n	review copy, reviewer's copy	exemplaire m de presse f
Rheinländer f (siehe Anhang)	Rheinländer (see appendix)	Rheinländer (voir appendice)

Rhythmus m	rhythm	rythme m
Richtlinien f/pl	guide-lines pl, instructions pl	directives f/pl, normes f/pl
Richtpreis m	basic price	prix m de direction f
Richtschnur f	guidance, rule of conduct	gouverne f, règle f de conduite f
Richtung f, **politische**	political adherence	appartenance f politique
Ries n	ream	rame f
Riesenformat n	blow-up	format m gigantesque
Riesenreklame f	gigantic publicity	réclame f monstre m
rillen	to score	faire des rainures f/pl
Ringbuch n	coil-stitched book	livre m broché par boucles f/pl
Ringhefter m	snap-ring file	dossier m à anneaux m/pl
römische Ziffern f/pl	Roman numerals pl	chiffres m/pl romains
Rohabzug m	first proof, flat proof, foundry proof, rough proof	première épreuve f
Rohdaten n/pl	raw data pl	données f/pl brutes
Rohentwurf m	dummy, layout, rough outline, visual	crayonné m, maquette f, premier jet m
roher Umriß m	rough outline	premier jet m
Rohzeichnung f	scribble	griffonnage m
Rollenbesetzung f	casting	choix m des acteurs m/pl
Rollenbreite f	reel width	laize f
rollende Werbung f	rolling advertising	publicité f roulante
Rollendruckmaschine f	web printing press	machine f à imprimer à bobines f/pl
Rollenoffset n	offset rotary printing	technique-offset m à cylindres m/pl
Rollenoffsetmaschine f	rotary offset press	rotatif m offset m
Rollenpapier n	reel paper	papier m roulé
Rolltreppenschild n	escalator panel, escalator site	emplacement m sur escalier m roulant
Roman m	fiction, novel	roman m
Romanheft f	journal of fiction, penny novellette	journal m de roman m, petit roman m bon marché
Rotaprintverfahren n	multilith, rotaprint process	multilithe m
Rotationsdruck m	rotary printing	impression f sur rotative f
Rotationsfarbdruck m	ROP colour	impression f sur rotative f en couleurs f/pl
Rotationspapier n	newsprint paper	papier m pour impression f rotative
Rotationspresse f	rotary press	machines f/pl rotatives
Rotationstiefdruck m	rotogravure	héliogravure f sur rotative f, hélioroto f, rotogravure f
Rubrik f	special section	rubrique f
Rubrik f **für Mußestunden** f/pl	leisure time	rubrique f des loisirs m/pl
Rubrik f **shopping** n	case shopping	section f shopping m
Rubriktitel m	column title, contents pl heading	titre m de rubrique f
rubrizierte Anzeigen f/pl	classified advertisements pl, composite advertisements pl, small ads pl, smalls pl brit	annonces f/pl groupées, petites annonces f/pl
Rückantwortkarte f	business reply card	carte-réponse f
Rückbelastung f	short rate	rappel m
Rückblende f	flash-back	retour m en arrière, scène f rétrospective
Rückenleimung f	back glueing	encollage m du dos m des livres m/pl
Rückenrand m	back edge	mors m

Rückentitel *m*	spine lettering	titre *m* au dos *m* d'un livre *m*
Rückfrage *f*	call back	demande *f* de précisions *f/pl*
Rückkopplung *f*	feed-back	rétroaction *f*
Rücklieferung *f*	sales *pl* return	livraison *f* renvoyée, retour *m*
Rückporto *n*	return postage	réponse *f* payée
Rückseite *f*	inner form, reverse page	côte *m* de seconde, page *f* verso
Rückseitendruck *m*	backing up	impression *f* verso
Rücksendung *f*	return consignment	renvoi *m* à l'expéditeur *m*
Rückspiel *n*	play back	postsonorisation *f*, rejeu *m*, surjeu *m*
Rückstand *m*, im	in arrears *pl*	en retard *m*
Rückstichbroschur *f*	pamphlet stitching	piqûre à cheval *m*
Rückstichheftung *f*	wire stitching	brochure *f* à cheval *m*
Rücktrittsrecht *n*	cancellation right	droit *m* de résiliation *f*, remise *f* des ordres *m/pl*
Rückvergütung *f*	rebate, refund	rabais *m*, remboursement *m*
rückwärts ablaufender Film *m*	fast back	film *m* se déroulant en arrière
rückwirkend	retro-active	rétroactif
Rückwirkung *f*	feed-back	rétroaction *f*
rührselige Geschichte *f*	sob-story	article *m* sentimental
rührselige Literatur *f*	squish	guimauve *f*
Rührstück *n*	sob-stuff	pièce *f* larmoyante
Ruf *m*	reputation	notoriété *f*, réputation *f*
Ruf *m*, guter	good will	bonne réputation *f*
Ruf *m*, schlechter	bad will	mauvaise réputation *f*
Rufmord *m*	smear campaign	campagne *f* de diffamation *f*
Rumpffläche *f*	side panel	affiche *f* latérale, côté *m*, panneau *m* longitudinal
rund	round	rond
rundbiegen	to bend round	arrondir
runde Klammern *f/pl*	parentheses *pl*	parenthèses *f/pl*
Rundfunk *m*	aircast, broadcasting, radio, wireless	radio *f*
Rundfunk *m* sprechen, im	to be on the air	avoir l'antenne *f*
Rundfunk- und Fernseh-Programmzeitschrift *f*	radio and television program paper	revue-programme *m* de la radio *f* et de la télévision *f*
Rundfunkansage *f*	wireless announcement	annonce *f* radiodiffusée
Rundfunkanstalt *f*	broadcasting station	poste *m* émetteur *m*
Rundfunkanzeige *f*	advergram	annonce *f* radiophonique
Rundfunkbericht *m*	broadcast account	radio-reportage *m*
Rundfunkempfangsgerät *n*	wireless set	poste *m* de radio *f*, récepteur *m*
Rundfunkhörer *m*	listener	auditeur *m*
Rundfunkhörerschaft *f*	broadcast audience, radio audience	audience *f* de la radio *f*
Rundfunknachrichten *f/pl*	broadcast news	journal *m* parlé
Rundfunknetz *n*	web	réseau *m* d'émetteurs *m/pl*
Rundfunksender *m*	wireless transmitter	émetteur *m*
Rundfunksendung *f*	broadcast, radio casting *am*	émission *f* radiophonique, radiodiffusion *f*
Rundfunksendung *f* im Laden *m*	storecasting	publicité *f* radiophonique dans une boutique *f*
Rundfunksprecher *m*	broadcaster, radio announcer, radio communicator *am*	chroniqueur *m*, speaker *m*
Rundfunkstation *f*	broadcasting station	station *f* de radiodiffusion *f*
Rundfunkteilnehmer *m*	radio listener, wireless enthusiast	sans-filiste *m*
Rundfunkübertragung *f*	outside broadcast	transmission *f* radiophonique

Rundfunkwerbung *f*	radio advertising	publicité *f* radiophonique
Rundschreiben *n*	circular letter	lettre *f* circulaire
Rundstereo *n*	curved stereo	stéréo *m* cintré
Rundumbeschriftung *f*	solus bus site	totalité *f* des emplacements *m/pl* extérieurs d'un autobus *m*

S

Sachbearbeiter *m* **der Werbung** *f*	account executive, contact man	chef *m* de publicité *f* d'agence *f*
Sachbearbeiter *m* **für Grafiker-Mitarbeit** *f*	art buyer	acheteur *m* du graphisme *m* publicitaire
Sachbericht *m*	feature	rapport *m* d'actualité *f*
Sachbuchliteratur *f*	nonfiction	littérature *f* spécialisée
Sachgebiet *n*	subject	matière *f*
Sachregister *n*	subject index, table of contents *pl*	index *m* alphabétique, registre *m* par matières *f/pl*, répertoire *m*
Sachverständigengutachten *n*	expert opinion	arbitrage *m*
Sachwörterbuch *n*	encyclopaedia	encyclopédie *f*
Sättigungspunkt *m*	saturation point	point *m* de saturation *f*
säurefest	acid resisting	résistant aux acides *m/pl*
saft- und kraftlos	lanky	efflanqué
Saison *f*, **stille**	slack period	morte-saison *f*
Saison *f*, **tote**	off season	hors saison *f*
Saisonanschlag *m*	seasonal poster advertising	affichage *m* saisonnier
Saisonartikel *m*	seasonal goods *pl*	article *m* saisonnier
Saisonrabatt *m*	period price	prix *m* de saison *f*
Saisonschlußverkauf *m*	seasonal closing-out sale	vente *f* de fin *f* de saison *f*
Saisonschwankung *f*	seasonal fluctuation	fluctuation *f* saisonnière, variation *f* saisonnière
Saisonwerbung *f*	seasonal advertising	publicité *f* saisonnière
Sammelanzeige *f*	composite advertisement	annonce *f* collective
Sammelauftrag *m*	collective order, omnibus order	commande *f* groupée, ordre *m* collectif
Sammelband *m*	collected volume, miscellany	collection *f*, recueil *m* en un volume *m*
Sammelbestellung *f*	centralized buying	commande *f* par groupage *m*
Sammelmappe *f*	collecting portfolio	carton-emboîtage *m*
Sammelplakat *n*	collective advertising poster	affiche *f* collective
Sammlung *f* **von Redewendungen** *f/pl*	phrase-book	recueil *m* de locutions *f/pl*
Sandpapier *n*	sandpaper	papier *n* de verre *f*
Sandwichmann *m*	sandwich board man, sandwich man	homme-affiche *f*, homme-sandwich *m*
Satellitenfernsehen *n*	television by satellites *pl*	mondovision *f*, télévision *f* via satellites *m/pl*
satiniert, beidseitig	calendered on both sides *pl*	satiné des deux côtés *m/pl*
satiniert, matt	English finished (E.F.)	satiné mat
satiniert, scharf	high-glazing	surglacé
satiniertes Papier *n*	calendered paper, imitation art paper	papier *m* calandré, papier *m* satiné
Satire *f*	satire	satire *f*
Sattelheftung *f*	saddle stitching	brochage *m* à cheval *m*
Satz *m* (Sortiment *n*)	set	série *f*
Satz *m/typog*	composition, setting, type matter	composition *f*
Satz *m* **ablegen**	to break up	distribuer
Satz *m*, **auffallender**	display composition	composition *f* tape-à-l'œil *m*

Satz *m*, durcheinandergefallener	pie	copie *f* chamboulée
Satz *m*, durchgehender	full measure setting	composition *f* à pleine justification *f*
Satz *m*, eingerückter	hanging indent	composition *f* en sommaire *m*
Satz *m*, fetter	bold type	composition *f* grasse
Satz *m*, gemischter	mixed matter, mixture	composition *f* lardée, composition *f* mêlée
Satz *m*, gequirlter	broken matter	pâté *m*, soleil *m*
Satz *m*, gespickter	interlarded composition	composition *f* lardée
Satz *m*, glatter	solid matter, straight matter, undisplay	composition *f* courante
Satz *m*, halbfetter	semi-bold type	caractères *m/pl* demi-gras
Satz *m*, kompresser	plain matter	composition *f* pleine
Satz *m*, liegengebliebener	crowded out matter	matière *f* restée sur le marbre *m*
Satz *m*, magerer	thin face	composition *f* maigre
Satz *m*, perlender	open-spaced setting	composition *f* espacée
Satz *m*, spationierter	open-spaced setting	composition *f* espacée
Satz *m* stehen lassen	to hold over, to keep type standing	conserver la composition *f*, garder le plomb *m*
Satz *m* strecken	to white out the matter	chasser la composition *f*
Satzabzug *m*	letter-set proof	épreuve *f* de la composition *f*
Satzanordnung *f*	typographical arrangement	arrangement *m* typographique
Satzanweisungen *f/pl*	rules *pl* of composition	données *f/pl* de composition *f*, instructions *f/pl* pour la composition *f*
Satzarten *f/pl*	kinds *pl* of composition	sortes *f/pl* de composition *f*
Satzberechnung *f*	casting off, character count, estimate of composition	calcul *m* de la composition *f*
Satzbild *n*	typographical aspect	aspect *m* typographique
Satzbreite *f*	measure	justification *f*, largeur *f* de la composition *f*
Satzbreite *f*, verkürzte	run-around	largeur *f* abregée de la composition *f*
Satzerschwernis *f*	difficult matter	surcharge *f*
Satzfehler *m*	compositor's error	erreur *f* de composition *f*, faute *f* de composition *f*
Satzform *f*, anaxiale	anaxial composition	composition *f* anaxiale
Satzform *f*, axiale	axial composition	composition *f* axiale
Satzform *f*, geschlossene	locked-up form	forme *f* serrée
Satzgestaltung *f*	typographical design	disposition *f* typographique
Satzherstellung *f* mit EDV-Anlagen *f/pl*	computer controlled typesetting (CCT)	composition *f* programmée
Satzhöhe *f*	depth of page	hauteur *f* de page *f*
Satzkorrektur *f*	typesetting alteration	correction *f* de la composition *f*
Satzkosten *pl*	cost of composition, expenses *pl* for setting	frais *m/pl* de composition *f*
Satzmaterial *n*	composing material	matériaux *m/pl* de composition *f*
Satzmuster *n*	composition pattern	référence *f* de composition *f*
Satzskizze *f*	type layout	maquette *f* typographique
Satzspiegel *m*	printing space, type area, type page	surface *f* de justification *f*, surface *f* d'impression *f*, surface *f* utile
Satzstück *n*	parcel of type	paquet *m* de composition *f*

Satzsystem *n*, integriertes	integrated composition system, integrated typesetting system	système *m* intégré des textes *m/pl* composés
Satztechnik *f*	typographical technique	technique *f* typographique
Satz *m/typog*	composition, setting, type matter	composition *f*
Satzumfang *m*	volume of composition	volume *m* de la composition *f*
Satzumfang *m* berechnen	to cast-off	calibrer un manuscrit *m*
Satzvorlage *f*	layout, schedule, schema	modèle *m*, schéma *m*
Satzzeichen *n*	punctuation mark	signe *m* de ponctuation *f*
sauberer Abzug *m*	clean proof	épreuve *f* corrigée
saugfähiges Papier *n* (Saugpost *f*)	absorbent paper	papier *m* amoureux
Saure-Gurken-Zeit *f*	dead season, gooseberry season, silly season	mois *m/pl* creux de l'été *m*, morte-saison *f*
Schabekarton *m*	scraper board, scratchboard	carte *f* grattée, carton *m* à racler
Schabemanier *f*	mezzotint technique, scratchboard drawing	manière *f* noire, mezzoteinte, trait *m* anglais
Schablone *f*	cut out, jig, pattern, stencil	découpage *m*, écran *m*, gabarit *m*, pochoir *m*, stencil *m*
Schachbrettform *f*	in sqares *pl*	quinconce *f*
Schadenersatz *m*	compensation for damage, indemnity	dédommagement *m*, dommages-intérêts *m/pl*
Schärfe *f*	sharpness	netteté *f*
schätzen	to rate	évaluer, taxer
Schätzung *f*	estimation	estimation *f*
Schalldichtmachung *f*	sound-proofing	insonorisation *f*
Schallmauer *f*	sound barrier	mur *m* du son *m*
Schallplatte *f*	disc *am*, record (brit)	disque *m*
Schallplatten-Ansager *m*	disc-jockey	animateur *m*, présentateur *m* de disques *m/pl*
Schallplattenform *f*, Zeitschrift *f* in	paper in form of records *pl*	journal *m* sonore
Schallplattenhülle *f*	record cover, record sleeve	pochette *f* de disque *m*
Schallplattenmusik *f*	canned music	musique *f* enregistrée
Schallplattensammlung *f*	record library	discothèque *f*
Schallplattenverzeichnis *n*	catalogue of records *pl*, discography	discographie *f*
Schallplattenwerbung *f*	record advertising	publicité *f* orale
Schalterhalle *f*	ticket-office	halle *f* de guichet *m*
scharf	sharp	net
scharf satiniert	high-glazing	surglacé
Schattendruckanzeige *f*	shadow print advertisement	annonce *f* ombrée, annonce *f* surimprimée
schattiert	shaded	ombré
Schattierung *f*	hard edge, pressure	foulage *m*
Schau *f*	show	exposition *f*, parade *f*
Schaubild *n*	diagram, graph	diagramme *m*, graphique *m*
Schauerfilm *m*	grusical, horror film	film *m* d'épouvante *f*
Schauerroman *m*	shocker, thriller	roman *m* à gros effets *m/pl*, roman *m* sensationnel
Schaufenster *n*	display faces *pl*, display window, shop window, show window	devanture *f*, étalage *m*, vitrine *f*
Schaufensterauslage *f*	window display	étalage *m* de vitrine *f*
Schaufensterauslage *f*, farbige	colour display	étalage *m* de vitrine *f* en couleur *f*

Schaufensterauslagen-Massierung *f*	window display campaign	campagne *f* d'étalages *m/pl*
Schaufensterbeleuchtung *f*	shop window lighting	éclairage *m* des étalages *m/pl*
Schaufensterbeschriftung *f*	window-dressing	inscription *f* des vitrines *f/pl*
Schaufensterbummel *m*	window shopping	lèche-vitrines *m*
Schaufensterdekorateur *m*	window dresser	décorateur *m* de vitrines *f/pl*
Schaufensterdekoration *f*	window display	décoration *f* de vitrine *f*
Schaufenstergestalter *m*	window dresser	décorateur *m* de vitrines *f/pl*, étalagiste *m*
Schaufenstergestaltung *f*	fitting of shop windows *pl*	aménagement *m* de vitrines *f/pl*
Schaufensterkleber *m*	window sticker	autocollant *m* de vitrine *f*
Schaufensterplakat *n*	showcard, windowcard	affiche *f* vitrine *f*, pancarte *f*
Schaufensterständer *m*	bracket	support *m*
Schaufenster-Werbemittel *n/pl*	window display material	matériel *m* d'étalage *m*
Schaufensterwerbung *f*	shop window advertising	publicité *f* en vitrine *f*, publicité *f* par étalage *m*
Schaufensterwettbewerb *m*	shop window competition	concours *m* d'étalages *m/pl*
Schaugeschäft *n*	show business	industrie *f* du spectacle *m*
Schaukasten *m*	showcase	petite vitrine *f* murale, vitrinette *f*
Schaumschläger *m*	windbag	vantard *m*
Schaupackung *f*	display package, dummy pack, mock-up	attrape *f*, boîte *f* factice, emballage *m* factice
Schauseite *f*	recto	belle page *f*
Schausteller *m*	showman	forain *m*
Schaustück *n*	show-piece	pièce *f* d'exposition *f*
Schauwerbegestalter *m*	display man, window dresser	étalagiste *m*
Scheck *m*	cheque	chèque *m*
Scheinwerfer *m*	reflector	catadioptre *m*
Scheinwerferlicht *n*	spotlight	feu *m* de projecteur *m*
scheinwissenschaftliche Werbung *f*	pseudoscientific advertising	publicité *f* pseudo-scientifique
Schema *n*	pattern, schedule	modèle *m*, schéma *m*
Schemabrief *m*	schematic letter	lettre *f* schématique
Schematisierung *f*	schematizing	schématisation *f*
Schere *f*	scissors *pl*	ciseaux *m/pl*
Scherenschnitt *m*	silhouette	silhouette *f*
Schere *f*-und-Kleister *m*-Arbeit *f*	scissors *pl*-and-paste work	méthode *f* colle *f* et ciseaux *m/pl*
scherzhafte Werbung *f*	jesting advertising	publicité *f* humoristique
Schicht *f*, soziale	social and occupational category, social status	catégorie *f* socio-professionnelle, classe *f* sociale
Schicht *f*, untere	lower class	les basses classes *f/pl*
Schiebeblende *f*	wipe	volet *m*
Schiedsgericht *n*	court of arbitration	tribunal *m* arbitral
Schiedsrichter *m*	arbitrator, umpire	arbitre *m*
Schiffsstation *f*	landing-stage	débarcadère *f*
Schild *n*	board, panel, plate, sign	enseigne *f*, panneau *m*, panonceau *m*, plaque *f*
Schild *n*, bemaltes	painted plate	plaque *f* peinte
Schildchen *n*	escutcheon	écusson *m*
Schildermaler *m*	sign writer	peintre *m* en lettres *f/pl*
Schimmel *m/typog*	blank page, blind print	page *f* blanche
Schlager *m*	hit, winner	succès *m*
Schlagersänger *m*	crooner	chanteur *m* de charme *m*

Schlagersendung *f*	hit-parade	palmarès *m*, parade *f* des succès *m/pl*
Schlagkraft *f*	punch	force *f*
Schlagwort *n*	catch word, slogan	mot *m* repère, phrase *f* choc *m*
Schlagzeile *f*	catch line, headline, punch line, shoulder note	ligne *f* principale, ligne *f* repère, manchette *f*, phrase *f* choc *m*, titre *m* en vedette *f*
Schlagzeile *f* **ohne Produktnennung** *f*	blind headline	titre *m* en vedette *f* sans citant le produit *m*
Schlagzeilen *f/pl* **machen**	to crash the headlines *pl*	tenir la manchette *f*
schlechte Nachrichten *f/pl*	black tidings *pl*, ill news	mauvaises nouvelles *f/pl*
schlechter Druck *m*	poor print	impression *f* de piètre qualité *f*
schlechter Ruf *m*	bad will	mauvaise réputation *f*
schlechtes Manuskript *n*	bad copy	cheveu *m*
Schleichwerbung *f*	camouflaged advertising, clandestine advertising, masked advertising, subliminal advertising	publicité *f* camouflée, publicité *f* clandestine, publicité *f* déguisée, publicité *f* occulte, publicité *f* subversive
Schleppfahne *f*	airplane banner	bannière *f* tractée par un avion *m*
Schleuderpreis *m*	cut rate, cut-throat price, give-away price	bradage *m*, gâchage *m* de prix *m*, vil prix *m*
Schleuderverkauf *m*	dumping, underselling	vente *f* à meilleur marché *m*, vente *f* à vil prix *m*
Schlichtungsausschuß *m*	court of arbitration	commission *f* de conciliation *f*
schließen (Form)	to lock up a form, to quoin	boucler, serrer
Schließplatte *f*	imposing stone	marbre *m* de serrage *m*
Schließrahmen *m*	chase	châssis *m*
Schließsteg *m*	furniture	lingot *m*
Schließstege *m/pl*	dead metal	garniture *f/pl* pour protéger un cliché *m* en tirage *m*
Schließzeug *n*	metal quoin	serrage *m*
Schlüssellochbericht *m*	keyhole report	report *m* du trou *m* de serrure *f*
Schlüsselroman *m*	key-novel	roman *m* à clé *f*
Schlüsselwort *n*	code-word, key-word	mot-clé *m*
Schlüsselzahl *f*	key	numéro *m* codique
Schlußabrechnung *f*	final settlement	décompte *m* final
Schlußaussage *f*	base line	ligne *f* de fond *m*
Schlußergebnis *n*	balance	bilan *m*
Schlußpunkt *m*	full stop, period	point *m* final
Schlußstück *n*	tail piece	cul *m* de lampe *f*
Schlußteil *m* **eines Films** *n*, **werbewirksamer**	pay off	partie *f* finale couronnée de succès *m*
Schlußtermin *m*	deadline, forms *pl* close	date *f* limite
Schlußvignette *f*	tail piece	cul *m* de lampe *f*
Schlußwort *n*	concluding word	discours *m* de clôture *f*
Schmähschrift *f*	lampoon	libelle *f*
Schmalschrift *f*	condensed type	caractère *m* étroit
schmieren	to scribble	gribouiller
Schmiergeld *n*	bribe, tip	pot-de-vin *m*
Schmierskizze *f*	layout, rough, sketch	croquis *m*, esquisse *f*, projet *m*
Schmirgelpapier *n*	emery-paper	papier *m* émeri
Schmiß *m*	punch	style *m* énergique
Schmitz *n*	blur	frison *m*
Schmitzleiste *f*	bed bearer	tasseau *m* du marbre *m*
Schmöker *m*	old book	bouquin *m*

Schmuckfarbe f	accompanying colour	couleur f d'accompagnement m
Schmuckfarbenanzeige f	run-of-paper advertisement (ROP)	annonce f avec couleur f d'accompagnement m
Schmuckinitiale f	swash initial	initiale f ornée
Schmuckleiste f	ornamental borders pl	filet m orné
Schmutzbogen m	set-off sheet	feuille f de décharge f
schmutziger Abzug m	smutty proof	épreuve f boueuse
Schmutzliteratur f	pornography	pornographie f
Schmutzpresse f	gutter press	presse f obscène
Schmutztitel m	bastard title, half-title	avant-titre m, faux titre m
Schmutztitelblatt n	halftitle page	page f du faux titre m
Schnappschuß m	snapshot	instantané m
Schneeballsystem n	cumulative returns, snowball system	système m boule f de neige f
Schneidemaschine f	cutting machine	coupoir m
schneiden	to cut	couper
Schnellfotografie f auf Eisenblech n	ferrotype	ferrotypie f
Schnellhefter m	letter-file	classeur-relieur m
Schnellkopie f (Film)	rushes pl	premières épreuves f/pl d'un film m
Schnellpresse f	cylinder machine, flat-bed press	presse f à cylindre m, presse f en blanc
Schnellschuß m	hot shot, priority job, rush job	coup m de feu m, train m urgent
schnellverkäufliches Buch n	quick seller	livre m d'écoulement m facile
Schnitt m	cut, intaglio	coupe f
Schnitt m, goldener	sectio aurea	sectio m aurea
Schnittkante f	butt line	arrête f de coupe f
Schnittmeister m	cutter	cutter m
Schnittmuster n	pattern	patron m
Schnittrand m	bleed	bord m de coupe f
Schnitzer m	fluff	loup m
Schnitzer m, grober	howler	faute f énorme
Schnüffler m	nosy	fouinard m
Schnürlmoiré n	moiré effect	moirage m
Schnulze f	sentimental hit	chanson f sentimentale
Schnulzenzeitung f	sentimental magazine	presse f du cœur m
Schockwirkung f	impact	effet m de choc m
Schön- und Widerdruck m	work and turn	impression f recto-verso
Schöndruck m	first impression, first run, prime, printing one face, sheetwise	côté m de première, impression f au recto m, impression f en blanc, premier folio m
schöne Literatur f	fiction	belles-lettres f/pl
Schönfärberei f	eyewash	optimisme m de commande f
Schönschreiber m	penman	calligraphe m
Schönschrift f	calligraphy	calligraphie f
Schönseite f	felt side	côté m feutre
Schön-und-Widerdruck-Maschine f	perfecting press	machine f à retiration f, presse f à double impression f
schöpferisch	creative	créateur
schrägliegende Buchstaben m/pl	slant letters pl	lettres f/pl couchées
Schrägschrift f	slanting letters pl	lettres f/pl couchées
Schrägstrich m	oblique stroke	barre f de fraction f oblique
Schramme f	scar, scratch	rayure f

Schreckensnachricht *f*	creepy news	nouvelle *f* d'horreur *f*
Schreibarbeiten *f/pl*	written work	travaux *m/pl* d'écritures *f/pl*
Schreibart *f*	style	style *m*
Schreibautomat *m*	automatic typewriter	machine *f* à écrire automatique
Schreibblock *m*	scribbling-pad	bloc-notes *f/pl*
Schreiberei *f*	red tape	paperasse *f*
Schreiberling *f*	grub	écrivassier *m*
Schreibfeder *f*	pen	plume *f*
Schreibfehler *m*	clerical mistake, slip of the pen	erreur *f* matérielle, faute *f* d'orthographe *f*, lapsus *m* calami
Schreibkunst *f*	calligraphy	calligraphie *f*
Schreibmaschine *f*	typewriter	machine *f* à écrire
Schreibmaschine *f*, automatische	automatic typewriter	machine *f* à écrire automatique
Schreibmaschinenpapier *n*	typewriter paper	papier *m* pour machine *f* à écrire
Schreibmaschinenschrift *f*	ribbon-face, type-script	caractères *m/pl* de machine *f*
Schreibpapier *n*	writing-paper	papier *m* à écrire
Schreibschrift *f*	handwriting, script writing, script-type	caractères *m/pl* d'écriture *f*, écriture *f* typographique
Schreibschrift *f*, englische	English script type	écriture *f* anglaise
Schreibtisch *m*	desk	bureau *m*, secrétaire *m*
Schreibunterlage *f*	desk pad	sous-main *m*
Schrift *f*, enge	condensed type	écriture *f* étroite
Schrift *f*, fette	full-faced type	caractères *m/pl* gras
Schrift *f*, gezeichnete	hand lettering	repoussage *m*
Schrift *f*, gotische	Gothic type, old black type	caractères *m/pl* gothiques
Schrift *f*, halbfette	medium-faced type	caractères *m/pl* quart-gras
Schrift *f*, lichte	light-faced type	caractères *m/pl* éclairés
Schrift *f*, magere	lean-faced type	caractères *m/pl* maigres
Schrift *f*, Schwabacher	Schwabacher type	Schwabach *m*
Schriftart *f*	font, fount, kind of type	genre *m* de caractères *m/pl*
Schriftbild *n*	type face	œil *m* de caractère *m*
Schriftenauswahl *f*	choice of type faces *pl*	casse *f*
Schriftenmaler *m*	lettering artist	lettreur *m*
Schriftenzeichner *m*	lettering artist	dessinateur *m* en lettres *f/pl*
Schriftfamilie *f*	family of type	famille *f* de caractères *m/pl*
Schriftfundament *n*	form bed	marbre *m* porte-forme *m*
Schriftgarnitur *f*	series *pl*	série *f* de caractères *m/pl*
Schriftgattung *f*	type family	famille *f* de caractères *m/pl*
Schriftgießer *m*	type caster, type founder	fondeur *m* de caractères *m/pl*, fondeur *m* typographe
Schriftgießerei *f*	letter-foundry, type-foundry	fonderie *f*
Schriftgrad *m*	body type size, point size	force *f* de corps *m*
Schriftgröße *f*	point size, type size	corps *m*
Schriftguß *m*	type casting	fonte *f* de caractères *m/pl*
Schrifthöhe *f*	height-to-paper, type height	hauteur *f* du caractère *m*, hauteur *f* en papier *m*
Schriftkasten *m*	frame, letter-case	casse *f*
Schriftkegel *m*	body of type	corps *m*
Schriftlager *n*	type stock	réserve *f*
Schriftleiter *m*	editor	rédacteur *m*
Schriftleitung *f*	editorial department , editorial staff	rédaction *f*
schriftliche Befragung *f*	mail survey	enquête *f* postale
Schriftlinie *f*	alignment, body line	ligne *f* de lettre *f*

Schriftmaterial *n*	stock of type, type matter	caractères *m/pl* d'impression *f*
Schriftmetall *n*	type metal	métal *m* à caractères *m/pl*
Schriftmuster *n*	type specimen	épreuve *f* de caractères *m/pl*, spécimen *m* de caractères *m/pl*
Schriftmusterbuch *n*	type specimen book	catalogue *m* de caractères *m/pl*
Schriftpinsel *m*	lettering brush	pinceau *m* à lettres *f/pl*
Schriftprobe *f*	type specimen book	catalogue *m* de caractères *m/pl*
Schriftqualität *f*	quality of type	qualité *f* typographique
Schriftrolle *f*	scroll	rouleau *m* d'écriture *f*
Schriftsatz *m/typog*	composition	composition *f*
Schriftschneider *m*	type cutter	graveur *m* de caractères *m/pl*
Schriftsetzer *m*	compositor, lettering man, typographer	compositeur *m*, typographe *m*
Schriftsprache *f*	written language	langue *f* littéraire
Schriftsteller *m*	author, publicist, writer	auteur *m*, écrivain *m*, publiciste *m*
Schriftstellername *m*	pen-name	nom *m* de plume *f*
Schriftstück *n*	document, piece of writing	document *m*, écrit *m*, pièce *f*
Schrifttum *n*	literature	lettres *f/pl*, littérature *f*
Schrifttype *f*	type	caractère *m*
Schriftwahl *f*	choice of type	choix *m* du caractère *m*
Schriftwechsel *m*	correspondence	correspondance *f*
Schriftweite *f*	width of type	approche *f*
Schriftzeichnen *n*	handlettering	repoussage *m*
Schriftzeichner *m*	lettering man	lettreur *m*, lettriste *m*
Schriftzug *m*	flourish, paraph	paraphe *m*, trait *m*
Schrumpfung *f*	shrinkage	retrait *m*
Schubfach *n*	pigeon-hole	tiroir *m*
Schülerzeitung *f*	school journal	journal *m* scolaire
Schund *m*	trash	camelote *f*
Schundblatt *n*	trashy paper	journal *m* médiocre
Schundliteratur *f*	rubbishy literature	littérature *f* de bas étage *m*
Schusterjunge *m/typog*	omitted word in composition	bourdon *m*
Schutzfrist *f*	duration of copyright	durée *f* du droit *m* d'auteur *m*
Schutzgitter *n*	guard	grille *f* de protection *f*
Schutzmarke *f*	trade-mark	marque *f* déposée
Schutzumschlag *m*	dust-cover, jacket	fourre *f* de protection *f*, jaquette *f*, protège-livre *m*
Schwabacher Schrift *f*	Schwabacher type	Schwabach *m*
schwabbeln	to buff	polir au buffle *m*
Schwankung *f*	fluctuation	fluctuation *f*
schwarze Kunst *f*	black art	magie *f* noire
schwarzer Rand *m*	black border, black frame, thick frame	baguette *f*, bordure *f* de filets *m/pl* mat
Schwarzes Brett *n*	advertisement board, notice board	porte-affiches *m*, tableau *m* noir
Schwarzhörer *m*	secret listener	écouteur *m* clandestin
Schwarzsendung *f*	illegal transmitting	émission *f* clandestine
Schwarz-Weiß-Anzeige *f*	advertisement in black and white	annonce *f* en noir
Schwarzweißaufnahme *f*	black and white reproduction	prise *f* de vue *f* noir blanc
Schwarzweißfilm *m*	black and white film	film *m* en noir et blanc
Schweigegeld *n*	hush money	prix *m* du silence *m*
zum Schweigen *n* bringen	to silence	réduire au silence *m*
Schweigen *n* hüllen, sich in	to be wrapped in silence	se renfermer dans le silence *m*
schweißen	to solder	souder

Schweizerdegen m /typog	compositor-pressman	amphibie m, ouvrier m à deux mains f/pl
Schwerarbeit f	hard work	labeur m
Schwerpunkt m	centre of gravity	centre m de gravité f
Schwerpunktwerbung f	zone plan	publicité f concentrée
Schwindelzeitung f	bogus publication	journal m fantôme, journal m trompeur
schwülstiger Stil m	gobbledygook	style m ampoulé
Schwulst m	bombast, pomposity	enflure f
Schwundeffekt m	fading	évanouissement m
Schwung m, **neuer**	push	poussée f
schwungvolle Werbung f	dynamic advertising	publicité f pleine d'élan m
Sechstelseite f	sixth of page	sixième de page f
Sechzehntelseite f	sixteenth of page	seizième de page f
Seeschlange f/fig	mare's nest	bobard m, serpent m de la mer f
Seidendruck m	silk-print	impression f sur soie f
Seidengazedruck m	screen printing	sérigraphie f
Seidenpapier n	tissue paper	papier m de soie f
Seite f	page	page f
Seite f, **am Fuß** m **einer**	bottom of page, foot of page	bas m de page f, pied m de page f
Seite f **angeschnittene**	bleed off page	fond m perdu
Seite f, **ausschlagbare**	gatefold	pli m en portefeuille m
Seite f, **erste**	first page, front page	première page f
Seite f, **gegenüberliegende**	opposite page	ci-contre
Seite f, **gerade**	even page	page f paire
Seite f, **leere**	blank page	page f blanche, page f en blanc, page f vierge f
Seite f, **letzte**	back page, last page	page f dernière
Seite f, **linke**	even page, left-hand page	en verso, fausse page f, page f de gauche
Seite f **mit gerader Nummer** f	even-numbered page	page f paire
Seite f **mit Vorder-** f **und Rückseite** f	page work and turn	page f recto verso
Seite f, **Mitte** f **der**	centre of page	milieu m de page f
Seite f, **rechte**	odd page, right-hand page	bonne page f, page f de droite, recto
Seite f, **ungerade**	odd page, uneven page	page f impaire
seitenbeherrschende Anzeige f	page dominance	emplacement m prédominant dans une page f
Seitenformat n	size of page	format m de la page f, surface f de la page f
Seitengröße f	page size	format m de la page f
Seitenkorrektur f	page proof	correction f en bon à clicher
Seitenmitte f	centre of page	milieu m de page f
Seitennumerierung f	pagination, paging	pagination f
Seitennummer f	page number	folio m, numéro m de la page f
Seiten f/pl, **gelbe**	yellow pages pl	pages f/pl jaunes
Seitenpreis m	page rate	prix m d'une page f entière
Seitenrand m	margin	marge f
seitenrichtig	right reading	à l'endroit m
Seitenscheibenplakat n	side window transfer, window sticker	affichette f sur les vitres f/pl, transparent m sur les glaces f/pl
Seitenteil m	page fraction	fraction f de page f
seitenteilige Anzeige f	fractional page advertisement	publicité f au format m
seitenverkehrt	reversed left to right	à l'envers m, inversé

Seitenziffer *f*	folio, page number	folio *m*, numéro *m* de la page *f*
seitliche Heftung *f*	side stabbed	piqûre *f* à plat
Sekretariat *n* einer Presse-agentur *f*	desk	sécrétariat *m* de rédaction *f* d'une agence *f* de presse *f*
Sekundärerhebung *f*	desk research	étude *f* de la clientèle *f*
Selbstanleger *m*	automatic feeder	margeur *m* automatique
Selbstbedienung *f*	self-service	libre service *m*
Selbstbedienungsladen *m*	supermarket	supermarché *m*
selbstfinanzierte Prämie *f*	self-liquidating premium	prime *f* auto-payante
Selbstklebeschild *n*	self-adhesive label	étiquette *f* autocollante
Selbstkontrolle *f*	self-regulation	autocontrôle *m*
Selbstkosten *pl*	prime cost, selling costs *pl*	prix *m* coûtant, prix *m* de revient
Selbstverlag *m*, im	published by the author	chez l'auteur *m*
selektive Werbung *f*	selective advertising	publicité *f* sélective
Semikolon *n*	semicolon	point virgule *m*
Sendeanstalt *f*	broadcasting station	station *f* d'émission *f*
Sendebereich *m*	listening area	région *f* d'émission *f* radiophonique
sendefertige Konserve *f*	pre-recorded broadcast	émission *f* en différé *m*
Sendefolge *f*	instalment	émission *f* par fragments *m/pl*
Sendegebühren *f/pl*	radio and television rates *pl*	tarif *m* d'antenne *f*
senden (Radio)	to broadcast, to transmit	émettre, radiodiffuser
Sendepause *f*	dead air, station break	silence *m*, temps *m* mort
Sendeplan *m*	guide sheet	programme *m* de la radio *f*
Sender *m*	broadcaster, station	antenne *f*, station-radio *f*
Sendereihe *f*	serial	série *f* d'émission *f*
Sendernetz *n*	network	réseau *m*
Senderpreis *m*	commercial rate cards *pl*	tarif *m* d'antenne *f*
Sendeunterbrechung *f*	break in transmission	incident *m* technique
Sendeunterlagen *f/pl*	broadcasting material	documents *m/pl* d'émission *f*, matériel *m* d'émission *f*
Sendezeichen *n*	call sign	indicatif *m*
Sendezeit *f*	air time, broadcasting time	heures *f/pl* de diffusion *f*, temps *m* d'antenne *f*
Sendezeitvermittler *m*	time buyer	acheteur *m* de temps *m* d'antenne *f*
Sendung *f*	broadcast	émission *f* radiophonique
Sendung *f*, aufgezeichnete	pre-recorded broadcast	émission *f* différée
Sendung *f*, volkstümliche	pop feature	émission *f* à succès *m*
sensationell	sensationel	sensationnel
sensationell aufgemachte Anzeige *f*	flaring advertisement	annonce *f* flamboyante
sensationelle Alleinmeldung *f*	scoop	exclusivité *f*, information *f* sensationnelle et exclusive
sensationelle Werbung *f*	gimmick, stunt advertising	coup *m*, truc *m*
Sensationsmache *f*	sensationalism	sensationnalisme *m*
Sensationsmeldung *f*	scoop	grosse nouvelle *f*, nouvelle *f* à sensation *f*
Sensationspresse *f*	muckraker, stunt press, yellow press	presse *f* à sensation *f*, presse *f* jaune
Sensationsschriftsteller *m*	sensational writer	auteur *m* à effets *m/pl* corsés
senstionelle Überschrift *f*	screamer	titre *m* sensationnel
sentimentale Literatur *f*	sob-stuff, squish	bonbon *m* fondant, littérature *f* larmoyante

Separatdruck *m*	off-print, separate copies *pl*, special impression	édition *f* à part *f*, tirage *m* à part *f*
Sepiazeichnung *f*	sepia-drawing	sépia *f*
Serienartikel *m*	mass produced article	article *m* de série *f*
Serienplakat *n*	series *pl* poster	affiche *f* sérielle
Serienrabatt *m*	frequency discount	rabais *m* de série *f*
Serif *n*	serif	empattement *m*
seriöser Zeitungstext *m*	pig iron	texte *m* sérieux
Sesselbahn *f*	chair-lift	télésiège *m*
setzen *typog*	to compose, to set, to typeset	composer
setzen, genau nach Vorlage *f*	to follow copy	composer fidèle au modèle *m*
setzen, kompresser	to close up, to set more solid	resserrer
Setzer *m*	operator, typesetter	compositeur *m*, typographe *m*
Setzerei *f*	case room, composing room	atelier *m* de composition *f*, services *m/pl* de composition *f*
Setzerkasten *m*	composing-frame	casse *f* de compositeur *m*
Setzersaal *m*	back room, composing room	atelier *m* de composition *f*
Setzfehler *m*	compositor's error, setting mistake	faute *f* de composition *f*
Setzlinie *f*	composing rule, setting-rule	filet *m* à composer, filet *m* de composition *f*
Setzmaschine *f*	composing machine, typesetting machine	composeuse *f* mécanique, machine *f* à composer
Setzmaschine *f*, automatische	teletypesetter	télétypesetter *m*
Setzmaschinenzeile *f*	type bar	ligne *f* bloc
Setzregal *n*	case stand	rang *m*
Setzschiff *n*	make-up galley	galée *f*
Seufzerspalte *f*	agony column	annonces *f/pl* personnelles
sich in Verbindung *f* setzen	to contact	contacter
sich zutragen	to happen	se passer
sicherer Tip *m*	straight tip	tuyau *m* exact
Sichtbarkeit *f*	approach, visibility	visibilité *f*
Sichtbarkeit *f*, weite	long approach site	visibilité *f* étendue
Sichtbehinderung *f*	impediment of visibility	masquage *m*
Sichtfeld *n*	field of vision	champ *m* de vision *f*
Sichtmöglichkeit *f*	opportunity to see	occasion *f* de voir
Sichtvermerk *m*	signature	visa *m*
Sichtweite *f*	length of visibility	longueur *f* de visibilité *f*
Siebdruck *m*	silk screen printing	impression *f* écran *m* de soie *f*, impression *f* sérigraphique, sérigraphie *f*
Siebdruckfarbe *f*	screen printing ink	encre *f* sérigraphie *f*
sieben	to sift	cribler, tamiser
Siegel *n*	seal	sceau *m*
Siegelmarke *f*	paper seal	timbre *m* en relief *m*
Signalwert *m*	signal-value	valeur *f* comme signal *m*
Signatur *f*	signature	signature *f*
Signatur *f* (Buch *n*)	nick	cran *m*
Signet *n*	book mark, colophon	marque *f* graphique, sigle *m*, vignette *f*
Sikkativ *n*	siccative	siccatif *m*
Silbentrennung *f*	hyphenation	coupure *f* syllabique
Silberspritzverfahren *n*	silver spray technique	procédé *m* argenture par pulvérisation *f*
Silhouette *f*	silhouette	silhouette *f*
Simulierung *f*	simulation	simulation *f*

Simultanverarbeitung *f*	multi processing, simultaneous operation	élaboration *f* simultanément, traitement *m* simultané
sistieren	to cancel	annuler
Sistierung *f*	cancellation	annulation *f*
sittenwidrig	immoral	portant atteinte *f* aux bonnes mœurs *f/pl*
Situationsbericht *m*	situation story	article *m* qui fait le point *m*
Sitz *m*	seat	siège *m*
Sitzplatzanzahl *f*	seating capacity	nombre *m* des sièges *m/pl*
Sitzredakteur *m*	prison editor	homme *m* de paille *f* mis en avant en cas *m* de poursuites *f/pl* judiciaires
Sitzung *f*	meeting, session	séance *f,* session *f*
Sitzungsbericht *m*	report of a meeting	reportage *m* de séance *f*
Skandal *m* **ersticken, einen**	to stifle a scandal	étouffer un scandal *m*
Skandalblatt *n*	smut sheet	journal *m* scandaleux
Skandalchronik *f*	scandal cronicle	chronique *f* scandaleuse
Skandalpresse *f*	gutter press	presse *f* à scandale *m,* presse *f* de bas étage *m*
Skelettschrift *f*	skeleton type	caractère *m* squelette *m*
Sketch *m*	blackout	pièce *f* courte
Skizze *f*	dummy, layout, outline, rough, sketch	croquis *m,* ébauche *f,* esquisse *f,* maquette *f*
Skizze *f,* **biografische**	profile	portrait *m* biographique
skizzieren	to outline, to sketch	ébaucher, esquisser
Skonto *m*	discount	escompte *m*
Skribifax *m*	ink-slinger	journaleux *m*
Slang *m*	slang	argot *m*
Slogan *m*	catch word	phrase *f* choc *m*
Snobismus *m,* **Ansprechen von**	snob appeal	appel *m* au snobisme *m*
soeben erschienen	just out, just published	vient de paraître
Sommerloch *n*	hiatus, seasonal summer decline	lacune *f* d'été *m*
Sommerschlußverkauf *m*	summer sales *pl*	vente *f* de soldes *m/pl* d'été *m*
Sonderaktion *f*	special action	action *f* spéciale
Sonderangebot *n*	deal, premium, special offer	offre *f* de faveur *f,* offre *f* spéciale
Sonderausgabe *f*	special edition	édition *f* spéciale
Sonderbeilage *f*	special supplement	supplément *m* spécial
Sonderbericht *m*	feature article	article *m* spécialisé
Sonderberichterstatter *m*	special correspondent	envoyé *m* special
Sonderdruck *m*	off-print, separate copies *pl,* special impression	édition *f* à part *f,* tirage *m* spécial
Sonderexemplar *n*	extra copy	exemplaire *m* supplémentaire
Sonderleistung *f*	extra performance	service *m* spécial, travaux *m/pl* exceptionnels
Sondernummer *f*	special issue, special number	numéro *m* spécial
Sonderplacierung *f*	special position	mise *f* en avant
Sonderpreis *m*	cut price, special rate	prix *m* spécial, prix-réclame *f*
Sonderprovision *f*	special commission	commission *f* exceptionnelle
Sonderrabatt *m*	extra discount, special discount	réduction *f* de faveur *f,* remise *f* spéciale
Sonderseite *f*	special page	page *f* spéciale
Sonderstelle *f*	individual location	emplacement *m* utilisé spécialement
Sonderzuschlag *m*	special additional charge	surtaxe *m* spécial
Sonntagsausgabe *f*	Sunday edition	quotidien *m* du septième jour *m*

Sonntagsbeilage *f*	Sunday supplement	supplément *m* dominical
Sonntagszeitung *f*	Sunday newspaper	journal *m* de dimanche *m*
Sorayapresse *f*	light reading weekly	feuille *f* hebdomadaire divertissante
Sorte *f*	brand, sort	genre *m*, sorte *f*
Sortierung *f*	sorting	routage *m*
Sortiment *n*	assortment, choice	assortiment *m*, choix *m*
Sortiment *n*, breites	variety	assortiment *m* large
soziale Schicht *f*	social and occupational category, social status	catégorie *f* socio-professionnelle, classe *f* sociale
Sozialforschung *f*	social research	recherche *f* sociale
Spätausgabe *f*	evening edition	édition *f* du soir *m*
spätestens	at the latest	au plus tard
Spalte *f*	column	colonne *f*
Spaltenanzahl *f*	number of columns *pl*	nombre *m* des colonnes *f/pl*
Spaltenbreite *f*	column measure, column width	justification *f* de la colonne *f*, largeur *f* de la colonne *f*
Spaltenhöhe *f*	column depth, column length	hauteur *f* de colonne *f*
Spaltenlinie *f*	column line, dividing rule	colombelle *f*, séparation *f* des colonnes *f/pl*
Spaltensatz *m*, voller	full measure	ligne *f* pleine
Spaltensetzer *m*	piece compositor	compositeur *m* aux pièces *f/pl*
Spaltenüberschrift *f*	column heading	titre *m* de paragraphe *m*
Spaltpapier *n*	cheap paper for wrapping and posters *pl*	papier *m* frictionné
Spannband *n*	banner	calicot *m*
spannende Handlung *f*	thriller	film *m* à sensation *f*, roman *m* à sensation *f*
Spannplakat *n*	wall banner	bannière *f* murale
Sparte *f*	branch, subject	section *f*
spationieren	to lead out, to space out	blanchir, espacer, interlettrer
spationierter Satz *m*	open-spaced setting	composition *f* espacée
Spatium *n*	space	espace *f*
Specke *m*	fat	composition *f* courante
Speichelleckerei *f*	toadyism	flagornerie *f*
Speisekarte *f*	menu card	carte *f*, menu *m*
sperren	to lead out, to space out	blanchir, espacer, interlettrer
Sperrfrist *f*	hold for release, waiting period	délai *m* d'attente *f*, période *f* de suspension *f*
Sperrholzplatte *f*	plywood plate	plaque *f* de contreplaqué *m*
Sperrsatz *m*	spaced composition	composition *f* espacée
Sperrung *f*	letter spacing	espacement *m*
Spesenvergütung *f*	expense account	remboursement *m* des frais *m/pl*
Spezialausdruck *m*	technical term	terme *m* technique
Spezialfarbe *f*	extra colour, special colour	couleur *f* spéciale, encre *f* spéciale
Spezialgeschäft *n*	specialty store	magasin *m* specialisé
Spezialpreis *m*	cut price, special rate	prix *m* spécial, prix-réclame *f*
Spezialstelle *f*	individual location	emplacement *m* utilisé spécialement
Spezialwissen *n*, technisches	know-how	savoir faire
Spiel *n*, ehrliches	fair-play	franc-jeu *m*
Spielart *f*	variant	variante *f*
Spielwarenmesse *f*	toy industry fair	foire *f* du jouet *m*

Spieß *m/typog*	rising space, work-up *am*	levage, marque *f* d'une espace *f* haute
Spiralheftung *f*	spiral stitching	couture *f* spirale, reliure *f* spirale
Spitze *f* (redaktionell)	lead story	article *m* de fond *m*
Spitzenleistung *f*	top work	puissance *f* maxima
Spitzenmarke *f*	brand leader	marque *f* de tête *f*
Spitzenverkaufszahlen *f/pl*	peak sales *pl*	pointes *f/pl* de vente *f*
spitzgeätzte Autotypie *f*	drop-out halftone	autotypie *f* détourée
Spitzmarke *f*	heading	mots *m/pl* d'appel *m*
Split-Run-Test *n*	split-run test	split-run *m* test *m*
Sponsor-Sendung *f*	sponsored broadcast, sponsored programme	émission *f* patronnée, programme *m* patronné
spontane Erinnerung *f*	pure recall, spontaneous remembrance	mémoire *f* spontanée, souvenir *m* spontané
Spontankauf *m*	impulse buying	achat *m* impulsif, achat *m* spontané
Sportblatt *n*	sport journal, sporting news	feuille *f* sportive
Sportgelände *n*	playing-field	terrain *m* de sport *m*
Sporthalle *f*	arena	hall *m* de sport *m*
Sportnachrichten *f/pl*	sporting news	nouvelles *f/pl* sportives
Sportplatzwerbung *f*	advertising in sport fields *pl*	publicité *f* dans les stades *m/pl*
Sportredakteur *m*	sports *pl* editor	rédacteur *m* des sports *m/pl*
Sportseite *f*	sporting page, sportsmen's page	nouvelles *f/pl* sportives, page *f* sportive
Sportstadion *n*	sport stadium	champ *m* de cours *m*
Sportteil *m*	sports *pl* page	rubrique *f* sportive
Sportübertragung *f*	broadcasting sports *pl*	transmission *f* radiophonique de sport *m*
Sportzeitschrift *f*	sport magazine	journal *m* sportif
Sprachbarriere *f*	language barrier	barrière *f* de langue *f*
Sprachregelung *f*	regulation of terminology	réglementation *f* de la terminologie *f*
Sprachrohr *n*	mouthpiece, spokesman	porte-parole *m*, porte-voix *m*
Sprachschatz *m*	vocabulary	vocabulaire *m*
Sprachschnitzer *m*	flaw, grammatical blunder	bévue *f*
sprachwissenschaftlich	linguistic	linguistique
Sprechblase *f*	balloon caption, bubble, speech balloon	ballon *m*, bulle *f*, philactère *f*
sprechende Argumente *n/pl*	talking points *pl*	arguments *m/pl* en faveur d'une marchandise *f*
„sprechendes" Etikett *f*	self-explanatory label	étiquette *f* s'expliquant elle-même
Sprechfehler *m*	lapse of the tongue	lapsus *m* linguae
Sprechfunkverbindung *f*	radiotelephony	circuit *m* radio-téléphonique
Sprichwort *n*	proverb	proverbe *m*
Spritzmaske *f*	frisket	frisquette *f*
Spritzpistole *f*	air brush	aérographe *m*, pistolet *m* à peinture *f*
Spritztechnik *f*	air brush technique	aérographie *f*
Spruchband *n*	banner, calico, streamer	banderole *f*, calicot *m*
Stabsarbeit *f*	staffwork	travail *m* d'organisation *f*
Stadion *n*	stadium	stade *m*
Stadtauflage *f*	city zone	tirage *m* urbain
Stadtgespräch *n*	talk of the town	on ne parle que de cela
Stadtplanwerbung *f*	advertising on town maps *pl*	publicité *f* sur des plans *m/pl* de ville *f*

Ständer *m*	bracket, poster site, prop	portatif *m*, présentoir *m*, support *m*
ständig wiederholte Streuung *f*	rotation	publicité *f* répétée
ständige Wiederholung *f*	reiteration	réitération *f*
ständiger Mitarbeiter *m*	permanent contributor	collaborateur *m* permanent, collaborateur *m* régulier
Stahldruck *m*	die stamping	impression *f* sur plaque *f* d'acier *m*
Stahlstich *m*	steel engraving	taille *f* dure
Stahlstichel *m*	burin	échoppe *f*
Stahlstichimitation *f*	thermography	imitation *f* de gravure *f* sur acier *m*
Stammkunde *m*	regular customer, steady customer	client *m* fidèle
Stammkundschaft *f*	goodwill	achalandage *m*, clientèle *f*
Stand *m*	stand	stand *m*
Standardformat *n*	standardized sheet size	format *m* normalisé, format *m* standard *m*
Standardisierung *f*	standardization	standardisation *f*
Standbau *m*	stand construction	construction *f* de stands *m/pl*
Standbogen *m*	correct proof, position pull	feuille *f* d'emplacement *m*, feuille *f* des blancs *m/pl*
Standfoto *n*	action still, cinema still, movie film clip	photo *f* de plateau *m*, photo *f* de scène *f*
Standgestaltung *f*	stand design, stand dressing	aménagement *m* d'un stand *m*, présentation *f* d'un stand *m*
Standort *m*	location	position *f*, stationnement *m*
standortgebunden	bound to the location	lié au lieu *m* d'implantation *f*
Standortnummer *f*	press-mark	numéro *m* de classement *m*
Standortpresse *f*	stationary press	presse *f* stationnaire
Standortverzeichnis *n*	listing, site list	liste *f* d'emplacements *m/pl*
Standpunkt *m*	point of view, standpoint	point *m* de vue *f*
Stanniolpapier *n*	tin foil	papier *m* d'argent *m*, papier *m* d'étain *m*
stanzen	to punch	découper à l'emportepièce *f*, étamper
Stapelware *f*	staple article	article *m* clé *f*, article *m* fondamental
starke Vergrößerung *f*	blow-up	grand agrandissement *m*
starke Werbung *f*	substantial advertising	publicité *f* substantielle
starkes Papier *n*	strong paper	papier *m* fort
Startzeichen *n*	cue, starting signal	indication *f* de rentrée *f*
Stationswerbung *f*	terminal display	publicité *f* dans les terminus *m/pl*
Statistik *f*	statistics *pl*	statistique *f*
Statistiker *m*	statistician	statisticien *m*
Stativ *n*	camera stand, mounting	pied *m* photographique, trépied *m*
Statussymbol *n*	status symbol	marque *f* de standing *m*
Stegreif *m* schreiben, aus dem	to strike off	improviser
Stegreifrede *f*	off-hand speech	discours *m* impromptu
Steg *m/typog*	furniture	lingot *m*
Stehbild *n*	slide	plaque *f*
stehen lassen!	stet!	à maintenir
Stehsatz *m*	live matter, retained composition, standing matter	composition *f* conservée, composition *f* permanente, conserve *f*

Steifleinen *n*	buckram	calicot *m*
Stein *m*	stone	marbre *m*
Steindruck *m*	lithographic print, lithography	lithographie *f*
Steindruck *m*, farbiger	photochrome	photochromie *f*
Steinzeichnung *f*	lithographic design	dessin *m* lithographique
Stelle *f*, getilgte	obliterated passage	caviar *m*
Stellenabbau *m*	removal of a hoarding	démontage *m* d'un panneau *m*
Stellenangebot *n*	situation vacant	offre *f* d'emploi *m*
Stellengesuch *n*	employment wanted	demande *f* d'emploi *m*
Stellenmarkt *m*	labour market	marché *m* du travail *m*
Stellennetz *n*	holding of outdoor advertising sites *pl*, network	circuit *m* indivisible d'emplacements *m/pl*, réseau *m*
Stellennumerierung *f*	numbering of sites *pl*	immatriculation *f* des emplacements *m/pl*
Stellenverzeichnis *n*	site list	liste *f* d'emplacements *m/pl*
Stellenzahl *f*, Kürzung *f* der	reduction of the number of the ordered sites *pl*	réduction *f* du nombre *m* d'affiches *f/pl* commandées
Stellschild *n*	portable panel	panneau *m* transportable
stellvertretender Chefredakteur *m*	associate editor	rédacteur *m* en chef *m* adjoint
stellvertretender Redakteur *m*	sub-editor	rédacteur *m* adjoint
Stempel *m*	stamp	sceau *m*, tampon *m*, timbre *m*
Stempeldruck *m*	seal printing	timbrage *m*
Stempelfabrik *f*	stamp factory	fabrique *f* de tampons *m/pl*
Stempelfarbe *f*	marking ink	encre *f* à tampons *m/pl*
Stempelkissen *n*	stamp pad	coussin *m* à tampons *m/pl*
stempeln	to stamp	tamponner, timbrer
Stenograf *m*	shorthand writer	sténographe *m*
Stereo *n*	electro *am*, electro-type, stereo, stereotype	stéréo *m*
Stereotypeur *m*	plate maker, stereotyper	clicheur *m*, stéréotypeur *m*
Stereotypie *f*	stereotyping	clichage *m*, stéréotypie *f*
Sternchen *n*	asterisk	astérique *m*
Steuer *f*	tax	impôt *m*, taxe *f*
Stichel *m*	steel engraving tool	burin *m*
Stichelei *f*	squib	brocard *m*, raillerie *f*
Stichprobe *f*	sample	échantillon *m*, sondage *m*
stichprobenartige Marktuntersuchung *f*	accidental sampling, haphazard sampling	échantillonnage *m* aléatoire, échantillonnage *m* au hasard *m*
Stichtag *m*	fixed day, key-date	date *f* limite, jour *m* d'échéance *f*
Stichwort *n*	catch word, cue	mot *m* clé *f*, mot *m* souche, mot *m* vedette *f*
Stichwortverzeichnis *n*	classified index	index *m* alphabétique des mots *m/pl* souches
Stil *m*	style	style *m*
Stil *m*, einfacher	plain style	style *m* simple
Stil *m*, empfindungsloser	deadpan style	style *m* pince-sans-rire
Stil *m*, kerniger	vigorous style	style *m* énergique
Stil *m*, kraftvoller	style with punch in it	style *m* à l'emporte-pièce *m*
Stil *m*, schwülstiger	gobbledygook	style *m* ampoulé
Stil *m*, vernachlässigter	slipshod style	style *m* négligé
Stilblüte *f*	bull	bévue *f*
stille Saison *f*	slack period	morte-saison *f*
Stilleben *n*	still life	nature *f* morte

Stilrichtung f	tendency of style	tendance f stylistique
Stimmenfang m	canvassing	sollicitation f de suffrages m/pl
Stimmengeräusch n	buzz	bruit m de voix f
Stimmungsbericht m	background story	report m expressif
Stimmungseffekt m, kriminalistischer	Hitchcock appeal	effet m policier
Stimmungsmache f	belabouring public feeling	bourrage m de crâne m
Stirnwand f	bulkhead	panneau m de fond m
Störsender m	blooper, jamming station	émetteur m brouilleur, poste f de brouillage m
Stoffdruck m	cloth printing, printing on fabrics pl	histotypie f, impression f sur étoffes f/pl
Storchschnabel m	pantograph	pantographe m
stornieren	to cancel	annuler
Stornierung f	cancellation	annulation f
Stoßkraft f	impact	effet m publicitaire
Stoßwerbung f	impact advertising	publicité f par chocs m/pl
Stoßwirkung f	impact	choc m
Straße f, parallel zur	parallel position	emplacement m parallèle
Straße f (Satz m)	channel, river	lézarde f
Straßenbahn f	tramway	tramway m
Straßenbahnanhänger m	tram trailer	remorque f du tramway m
Straßenbahnhaltestelle f	tram stop	point m d'arrêt m
Straßenbahntriebwagen m	bloomer am, traction car brit	voiture f motrice
Straßenbahnwerbung f	street car advertising, tramway advertising	publicité f tram m
Straßenhändler m	street hawker	camelot m
Straßenhandel m	boy sales pl, street sales pl	vente f ambulante
Straßenschild n	road sign, roadside hoarding	panneau m routier
Straßenverkäufer m	street hawker, street vendor	camelot m, crieur m de journaux m/pl
Straßenverkehrsordnung f	highway code	code m de la route f
Straßenwerbung f	roadside advertising	publicité f routière
strecken typog	to drive out	chasser
Streckenplakat n	railroad bulletin, roadside hoarding	enseigne f routière, panneau m d'affichage m le long m d'une voie f ferrée
Streckenwerbung f	roadside advertising	publicité f routière
Streichholzbriefchen n	book of matches pl	pochette f d'allumette f
Streichung f	deletion	rayure f, suppression f
Streifband n	wrapper	bande f de journal m, jeu m de bandes f/pl
Streifen m im Satz m, weißer	river of white	lézarde f, ruelle f
Streifenanzeige f	advertisement panel, band, banner, streamer, strip	bandeau m
Streitschrift f	polemic	écrit m polémique
strenger machen (Farbe)	to strengthen (ink)	charger une couleur f
Streuabteilung f	media department	service m médias m/pl
Streuagentur f	independent media services pl company	intermédiaire m publicitaire
Streuanalyse f	distribution analysis	analyse f de distribution f
Streuarten f/pl	types pl of media	genres m/pl de support m, types m/pl des médias m/pl
Streubereich m	dispersion area	domaine m de la diffusion f
Streubild n	scatter diagram	diagramme m de la diffusion f
Streubreite f	coverage	couverture f

Streudauer *f*	duration of the advertising campaign	durée *f* de la campagne *f* publicitaire
Streudichte *f*	density of diffusion	densité *f* de la diffusion *f*
streuen	to disperse	diffuser, disperser
Streuerfolg *m*	advertising result	résultat *m* de la campagne *f* publicitaire
Streufeld *n*	advertising zone	zone *f* de diffusion *f*
Streukosten *pl*	costs *pl* of circularising, space charge	frais *m/pl* de diffusion *f*
Streumenge *f*	advertising volume	volume *m* de la publicité *f*
Streuort *m*	place of advertising	lieu *m* de publicité *f*
Streupause *f*	hiatus	hiatus *m*
Streuperiode *f*	advertising period	période *f* de diffusion *f*
Streuplan *m*	media schedule, space schedule, spread-over	calendrier *m* d'insertion *f*, plan *m* de diffusion *f*, répartition *f* du budget *m*
Streuplaner *m*	media executive	directeur *m* des médias *m/pl*
Streuplanung *f*	account planning, media planning	plan *m* de campagne *f*, plan *m* des supports *m/pl*
Streuprospekt *m*	throwaway leaflet	prospectus *m* distribué en arrasoir *m*
Streuprüfung *f*	checking	vérification *f*
Streuung *f*	coverage, diffusion, dispersion, spread	couverture *f*, prospection *f*
Streuung *f*, regionale	regional dispersion	couverture *f* régionale
Streuung *f*, ständig wiederholte	rotation	publicité *f* répétée
Streuung *f*, umlaufende	rotation	roulement *m* de publicité *f*
Streuungsfachmann *m*	media man	acheteur *m* d'espace *m*, expert *m* en médias *m/pl*
Streuverlust *m*	waste dispersion	prospection *f* perdue
Streuweg *m*	channel of dispersion	voie *f* de prospection *f*
Streuwirkung *f*	advertising effect	effet *m* publicitaire
Streuzeitpunkt *m*	dispersion period, time of the dispersion of the advertising media	période *f* de la diffusion *f* des moyens *m/pl* publicitaires
Strich *m*	dash, stroke	trait *m*
Strich *m*, unter dem	in the feuilleton	rez-de-chausée *m*
von Strich *m* zu Strich *m*	from rule to rule	de filet *m* à filet *m*
Strichätzung *f*	line block *brit*, line cut *am*, line engraving *am*, line etching, line plate, process block *brit*	cliché *m* au trait *m*, gravure *f* au trait *m*
Strichlinie *f*	hatched rule, shaded rule	filet *m* crémaillère *f*
Strichpunkt *m*	semicolon	point-virgule *m*
Strichzeichnung *f*	line drawing	dessin *m* au trait *m*
Strichzeichnung *f*, aquarellierte	line and wash drawing	dessin *m* au trait *m* aquarellé
Strip *m*, Comic	comic strip	bandes *f/pl* dessinées
Strohmann *m*	man of straw	prête-nom *m*
Strohpappe *f*	straw board	carton *m* de paille *f*
Struktur *f*, demografische	audience composition, demographical structure	structure *f* démographique
Strukturwandel *m*	transformation of structure	transformation *f* de structure *f*
Studio *n*	studio	atelier *m*
Stückdurchschuß *m*	short lead	petite interligne *f*
Stückpreis *m*	unit price	prix *m* unitaire
Stückzahl *f*	number of pieces *pl*	nombre *m* des pièces *f/pl*
stümperhaft	buckeye	moche

Stütze *f*	prop, support	support *m*
Stützpreis *m*	pegged price	prix *m* soutenu
stufenförmige Anzeige *f*	disconnected advertisement	décroché *m*
stufenförmige Überschrift *f*	step head	titre *m* en marche *f* d'escalier *m*
Stufenwerbeplan *m*	cream-plan	publicité *f* en étapes *f/pl*
stummer Verkäufer *m*	counter dispenser, counter display container, dummy salesman	matériel *m* d'étalage *m* de comptoir *m*, vendeur *m* muet
Stummfilm *m*	silent film	film *m* muet
stumpffeine Linie *f*	blunt rule	ligne *f* épointée
Subskriptionspreis *m*	subscription price	prix *m* de souscription *f*
Subvention *f* von Sendungen *f/pl*	sponsorship	patronnage *m*
Subventionierung *f*	subsidizing	subventionnement *m*
Suchanzeigen *f/pl*	want ads *pl*	petites annonces *f/pl*
Suggestivfrage *f*	leading question, suggestive question	question *f* suggestive, question *f* tendancieuse
Suggestivwerbung *f*	suggestive advertising	publicité *f* suggestive
Sujetwechsel *m*	change of design	changement *m* de message *m*
Summe *f*	amount	somme *f*
Superlativwerbung *f*	advertising in superlatives *pl*	publicité *f* au superlatif *m*
Supermarkt *m*	supermarket	libre service *m*, supermarché *m*
Superprovision *f*	supercommission	surcommission *f*, surremise *f*
Symmetrie *f*	symmetry	symétrie *f*
Symposium *n*	symposium	conférence *f*-débat *m*, séminaire *m*
Synchronisation *f*	dubbing, synchronization, voice-over	synchronisation *f*
synchronisieren	to dub	doubler
Szene *f* aus dem täglichen Leben *n*	life story	scène *f* de la vie *f* de tous les jours *m/pl*

T

Tabelle *f*	chart, tabulation	tableau *m*, tabulation *f*
Tabellenkopf *m*	box head	tête *f* de tableau *m*
Tabellensatz *m*	tabular matter, tabulator matter	composition *f* de tableaux *m/pl*, tableautage *m*
tabellieren	to tabulate	mettre en tableau *m*, tabuler
Tabulator *m*	tabulator	tabulateur *m*
Tachistoskop *n*	tachistoscope	tachistoscope *m*
täglich	daily	quotidien
täuschende Werbung *f*	misleading advertising	publicité *f* trompeuse
Täuschung *f*	feint, fraud, shenanigan *am*	mystification *f*
Tagebuch *n*	diary	journal *m* intime
Tagesbericht *m*	daily report	bulletin *m* du jour *m*, rapport *m* journalier
Tagesereignisse *n/pl*	events *pl* today	agenda *m* de la journée *f*
Tagesfragen *f/pl*	topics *pl* of the day	questions *f/pl* d'actualité *f*
Tagesleuchtfarbe *f*	day-glo, daylight fluorescent ink	encre *f* luminescente solaire
Tagesnachrichten *f/pl* im Fernsehen *n*	television news	journal *m* télévisé
Tagesnachrichten *f/pl* im Rundfunk *m*	broadcast news	journal *m* parlé
Tagesnachrichten *f/pl* in der Presse *f*	events *pl* today	agenda *m* de la journée *f*
Tagesneuigkeiten *f/pl*	topical news	événéments *m/pl* du jour *m*

Tagespreis *m*	current price	prix *m* courant
Tagespresse *f*	daily press	presse *f* quotidienne
Tagesschau *f*	television news show	journal *m* télévisé
Tageszeitung *f*	daily newspaper	quotidien *m*
Tageszeitung *f*, **regionale**	regional daily	quotidien *m* régional
Tageszettel *m*	progress report	fiche *f* de travail *m*
Tagschicht *f*	day-side	équipe *f* de jour *m*
Tagung *f*	congress	congrès *m*
Tarif *m*	price list, rate card, rates *pl*	prix *m* courant, tarif *m*
Tarif *m*, **ermäßigter**	short rate	tarif *m* réduit
Tarif *m* **für Verkehrsmittelwerbung** *f*	card rates *pl*	tarif *m* de la publicité *f* moyens *m/pl* de transport *m*
Tarif *m* **für Werbesendungen** *f/pl*	time charge	tarif *m* d'antenne *f*, tarif *m* de la publicité *f* radiophonique
Tarif *m*, **gekoppelter**	coupled rate	tarif *m* couplé
Tarif *m*, **kombinierter**	combined rate	tarif *m* combiné
Tarifabweichung *f*	deviation from rates *pl*	dérogation *f* aux tarifs *m/pl*
Tarifaufbau *m*	rate structure	structure *f* de tarif *m*
Tarifblatt *n*	rate sheet	feuille *f* de tarif *m*
Tarifgemeinschaft *f*	rate association	communauté *f* de tarif *m*
Tarifkartei *f*	rate card index	fichier *m* de tarifs *m/pl*
Tarifkombination *f*	rate combination	couplage *m* de tarif *m*
Tarifstaffel *f*	differential price system	barême *m*
Tarifunterschied *m*	differential	différence *f* de tarif *m*
Tarnung *f*	camouflage	camouflage *m*
Taschenausgabe *f*	pocket edition	édition *f* portative
Taschenbuch *n*	paper book, pocket book	livre *m* de poche *f*
Taschenbuch *n*, **flexibles**	paperback	flexible livre *m* de poche *f*
Taschenformat *n*	pocket size	format *m* de poche *f*
Taschenradio *n*	pocket-radio	récepteur *m* de poche *f*
Tastatur	keyboard	dessus *m* de clavier *m*
Taste *f*	key	touche *f*
Taster *m*	drop fingers *pl*	ardillon *m*
Tatarennachricht *f*	false news	nouvelle *f* à la tatare *m*
Tatsache *f*	fact	fait *m*
Tatsache *f*, **erwiesene**	ascertained fact	fait *m* établi
Tatsache *f*, **nackte**	bald fact	fait *m* pur et simple
Tatsache *f*, **vollendete**	accomplished fact	fait *m* accompli
Tatsachenbericht *m*, **besonders gestalteter aktueller**	feature	rapport *m* spécial d'actualité *f*, varia
Tauschanzeige *f*	barter advertisement, exchange advertisement	annonce *f* d'échange *m*
Tauschexemplar *n*	exchange copy	exemplaire *m* d'échange *m*
Tausenderpreis *m*	cost-per-thousand	prix *m* aux milles lecteurs *m/pl*
Taxiwerbung *f*	taxicab advertising	publicité *f* dans les taxis *m/pl*
technische Daten *m/pl*	mechanical data *pl*	données *f/pl* techniques, renseignements *m/pl* techniques
technische Oberflächengestaltung *f* **eines Papiers** *n*	finish	apprêter le papier *m*
technische Zeitschrift *f*	technical publication	revue *f* technique
technischer Leiter *m*	technical manager	directeur *m* technique
technisches Spezialwissen *n*	know-how	savoir-faire *m*
Teerfarbstoffe *m/pl*	aniline dyes *pl*	couleurs *f/pl* à l'aniline *f*
Teil *m* **der Ausgabe** *f*, **hinterer**	back section	cahier *m* de queue *f*
Teil *m* **der Ausgabe, vorderer**	front section	cahier *m* de tête *f*

Teil *m*, redaktionellem, gegenüber	facing editorial matter	face *f* texte *m* rédactionnel
Teil *m*, redaktioneller	editorial matter, editorial section	section *f* rédactionnelle, texte *m* rédactionnel
Teilauflage *f*	partial circulation	tirage *m* partiel
Teilausgabe *f*	part edition	édition *f* partielle
Teilbelegung *f*	split run advertising	publicité *f* dans un tirage *m* partagé
Teilbelegung *f* von Plakatsäulen *f/pl*	partial display on a few pillars *pl*	affichage *m* sur certaines colonnes *f/pl* seulement
Teilnehmerzahl	audience turnover	nombre *m* des personnes *f/pl* touchées par un support *m*
Teilung *f* der Auflage	splitting	division *f* du tirage *m*
Tektur *f*	overlay, slip	papillon *m*
Telefon *n*	telephone	téléphone *m*
Telefonanruf *m*	telephone call	appel *m* téléphonique, coup *m* de téléphone *m*
Telefonanschluß *m*	telephone connection	communication *f* téléphonique
Telefonat *n*	call	communication *f* téléphonique
Telefonbuch *n*	telephone book *am*, telephone directory	annuaire *m* téléphonique, Bottin *m* téléphonique
Telefongespräch *n*	telephone call	conversation *f* téléphonique
telefonieren	to telephone	téléphoner
Telefoninterview *n*	telephone interview	interview *m* par téléphone *m*
telefonisch	telephonic	téléphonique
telefonisch aufgegebene Anzeige *f*	telephoned advertisement	annonce *f* téléphonée
telefonische Bestellung *f*	order by telephone	commande *f* téléphonique
Telefonist *m*	telephonist	téléphoniste *m*
Telefonkabine *f*	call-box	cabine *f* téléphonique
Telefonleitung *f*	telephone circuit	ligne *f* téléphonique
Telefonnummer *f*	telephone number	numéro *m* de téléphone *m*
Telefonumfrage *f*	telephone survey	enquête *f* par téléphone *m*
Telefonverkaufskunst *f*	phonemanship	technique *f* de la vente *f* par téléphone *m*
Telefonwerbung *f*	bell-sell	vente *f* par téléphone *m*
Telefonzentrale *f*	telephone exchange	centrale *f* téléphonique
Telefoto *n*	telephotography	téléphotographie *f*
telegen	telegenic	télégénique
Telegrafie *f*, drahtlose	wireless telegraphy	télégraphie *f* sans fil *m*
telegrafieren	to telegraph, to wire	télégraphier
telegrafisch	by telegram, telegraphic	télégraphique
telegrafisch erteilter Auftrag *m*	order by wire	commande *f* télégraphique
telegrafische Antwort *f*	reply by wire	réponse *f* télégraphique
Telegrafist *m*	telegraphist	télégraphiste *m*
Telegramm *n*	cable, telegram	télégramme *m*
Telegrammadresse *f*	cable address, telegraphic address	adresse *f* de télégramme *m*, adresse *f* télégraphique
Telegrammschlüssel *m*	code	code *m*
Telegrammstil *m*	telegraphic style	style *m* télégraphique
Teleobjektiv *n*	telephoto lens, telephotography	téléobjectif *m*, téléphotographie *f*
Teletypesetter *m*	teletypesetter	télétypesetter *m*
Telexanschrift *f*	telex address	adresse *f* télex
Tellertiegel *m*	platine	presse *f* à platine *f*
Tempera *f*	gouache	gouache *f*
Temperafarbe *f*	tempera	couleur *f* à détrempe *f*

Tendenz *f*	bias, tendency, trend	tendance *f*
Tendenz *f*, redaktionelle	editorial policy	politique *f* rédactionnelle
Tendenzbetrieb *m*	tendency enterprise	entreprise *f* à tendance *f*
Tendenzblatt *n*	tendentious paper	journal *m* de tendance *f*
tendenzfrei	unbiased	impartial
Tendenzmeldung *f*	tendentious information	information *f* à tendance *f*
Tendenzroman *m*	tendency novel	roman *m* à thèse *f*
Tenor *m*	purport, tenor	teneur *f*
Termin *m*	date, delay	date *f*, délai *m*
Termin *m*, äußerster	deadline	terme *m* de rigueur *f*
Terminabteilung *f*	traffic department	service *m* de surveillance *f* de la production *f*
Terminanzeige *f*	fixed date advertisement	annonce *f* à date *f* fixe
Terminauftrag *m*	wait order	attendre ordre *m* d'insertion *f*
Terminfestlegung *f*	timing	détermination *f* d'un terme *m*
Terminhaftung *f*	term-liability	responsabilité *f* quant au délai *m*
Terminkalender *m*	advertising schedule, deadline schedule	agenda *m*, calendrier *m* de termes *m/pl*, échéancier *m*
Terminkontrolle *f*	progress control, traffic control	contrôle *m* des délais *m/pl*
Terminologie *f*	terminology	terminologie *f*
Terminplan *m*	aging schedule, date plan, time schedule	calendrier *m* d'insertion *f*, plan *m* des délais *m/pl*
Terminüberwacher *m*	accelerator, traffic manager	surveillant *m* de la production *f*
Terminverlegung *f*	postponement of a date	ajournement *m* d'un délai *m*
Terminvorschrift *f*	fixed date	date *f* imposée
Tertia *f* (siehe Anhang)	Emerald (see appendix)	corps 16 points (voir appendice)
Test *m*	test	test *m*
Test *m* einer Rundfunksendung *f*	audition	test *m* d'une émission *f* radiophonique
Testausgabe *f*	pilot edition	édition *f* d'essai *m*
testen	to test	faire un test *m*
Testgebiet *n*	test area	territoire-test *m*
Testgruppe *f*	panel	groupe *m* de test *m*
Testkampagne *f*	launching test, test campaign	test *m* de lancement *m*
Testladen *m*	audit store, test shop	boutique *f* d'essai *m*
Testmarkt *m*	test market	marché *m* d'essai *m*, marché-test *m*
Testort *m*	test-town	lieu *m* d'essai *m*
Text *m*	copy, matter, text	copie *f*, texte *m*
Text *m*, alter	dead copy	texte *m* déjà employé
Text *m*, gegenüber	against text, facing text, next to editorial matter, opposite text	contre texte *m*, face *f* texte *m*
Text *m*, gleichbleibender	same text	texte *m* même
Text *m*, mitten im	in text	dans le texte *m*
Text *m*, neben	next to reading matter	à côté *m* du texte *m*, contre texte *m*
Text *m* (Schriftgrad) (siehe Anhang)	Brevier (see appendix)	corps 20 points (voir appendice)
Text *m*, über und neben	over and next text matter	au-dessus et à côté *m* du texte *m*
Text *m*, überarbeiteter	make-over	copie *f* remaniée
Text *m* umarbeiten	to rewrite a text	remanier un texte *m*
Text *m* umranden	to box in	encadrer, entourer d'un filet *m*
Text *m*, unmittelbar unter	immediately below text	immédiatement après texte *m*
Text *m*, unter	under matter	dessous texte *m*

Text *m*, verbesserter	revised text	texte *m* revu
Text *m*, verstümmelter	mutilated text	texte *m* mutilé
Text *m*, vollständiger	full text	texte *m* intégral
Text *m*, vorbereiteter	canned copy	texte *m* mis en boîte *f*
Text *m*, wechselnder	different text	texte *m* différent
Text *m*, weitschweifiger	padded text	texte *m* délayé
Textabteilung *f*	copy department	service *m* de la rédaction *f*
Textanalyse *f*	copy research	analyse *f* de texte *m*
textanschließend	facing matter, following matter, next to reading matter	à côté *m* du texte *m*, après texte *m*, se joignant au texte *m*, sous le texte *m*
Textanzeige *f*	advertorial, reader advertisement	annonce *f* figurant dans le texte *m* rédactionnel
Textanzeige *f*, kleine	short paragraph	entrefilet *m*
Textblock *m*	bold type, section of copy	pavé *m* de texte *m*
Textbuch *n*	libretto	libretto *m*, livret *m*
Texteinblendung *f* in Film *m*	faded in text	texte *m* enchaîné
texten	to copy-write	rédiger des textes *m/pl*
Textentwurf *m*	draft	projet *m* de texte *m*
Texter *m*	copy-writer, script-writer	rédacteur *m* publicitaire, rédacteur-concepteur *m*
Texterfassung *f*	text generation	saisie *f* des textes *m/pl*
Texterfassungsgerät *n*	text acquisition terminal, text collection terminal	appareil *m* pour la saisie *f* des textes *m/pl*
Textmaterial *n*	feature material	éléments *m/pl* du texte *m*
Textplakat *n*	letterpress poster	affiche-texte *f*
Textprüfung *f*	copy testing	testage *m* des messages *m/pl* publicitaires
Textschrift *f*	text face	caractère *m* du texte *m*
Textseite *f*	text page	page *f* de texte *m*, page *f* rédactionnelle
Textseite *f*, gegenüber der ersten	facing first editorial page	face *f* première de texte *m*
Textseite *f*, gegenüber der letzten	facing last editorial page	face *f* dernière de texte *m*
Textstellen *f/pl*	scraps *pl*	courts passages *m/pl* de texte *m*
Textteilanzeige *f*	textual advertisement	annonce *f*-texte *m*
Textwechsel *m*	change of text	changement *m* de texte *m*
Theaterkritik *f*	dramatic critique	critique *f* théâtrale
Theaterkritiker *m*	dramatic critic	critique *m* théâtral
Theaterplakat *n*	play bill, theater poster	affiche *f* de théâtre *m*, annonce *f* de spectacle *m*
Theaterstück *n*	play	pièce *f* de théâtre *m*
Theaterwelt *f*	entertainment world	monde *m* du théâtre *m*
Thekenaufsteller *m*	counter display, piece	matériel *m* d'étalage *m* de comptoir *m*
Thema *n* einer Anzeige *f*	story, theme	thème *m*
Thermodruck *m*	thermography	typo-relief *m*
Tiefätzung *f*	deep-etching	eau-forte *f* grave, morsure *f* de grand creux *m*
Tiefdruckanstalt *f*	photogravure plant	maison *f* d'héliogravure *f*
Tiefdrucker *m*	photogravure printer	imprimeur *m* en héliogravure *f*
Tiefdruckpapier *n*	gravure paper	papier *m* pour héliogravure *f*

Tiefdruck *m* /*typog*	copperplate printing, intaglio printing, photogravure, rotogravure	gravure *f* en creux *m*/*pl*, impression *f* en creux *m*, impression *f* en héliogravure *f*, rotogravure *f*
Tiefeninterview *n*	depth interview	interview *m* en profondeur *f*
tiefer stellen	to move down	placer plus bas
tiefgeätzte Autotypie *f*	deep-etched half-tone	simili *m* avec blanc pur
tiefstehend	inferior	inférieur
Tiefstpreis *m*	rock-bottom price	prix *m* imbattable, prix *m* minimum
Tiegel *m*	platen machine	presse *f* à platine *f*
Tiegeldruckpresse *f*	platen press	presse *f* à platine *f*
Tilde *f*	tilde	tilde *f*
tilgen	to take out	biffer, rayer
Tip *m*	tip, wrinkle	tuyau *m*
Tip *m*, sicherer	straight tip	tuyau *m* exact
Tippfehler *m*	typist's error	erreur *f* de dactylo *f*, faute *f* de frappe *f*
Tisch *m*, fallen lassen unter den	to ignore, to let drop	écraser un papier *m*, passer sous silence *m*
Tisch *m*, Gespräch am runden	round-table discussion	réunion *f* paritaire, table *f* ronde
Tisch *m*, grüner	green table	tapis *m* vert
Tischkarte *f*	tent card	carte *f* de table *f*
Titel *m*	heading, title	titre *m*
Titel *m* der ersten Seite *f*	flag	titre *m* de première page *f* en gros caractères *m*/*pl*
Titel *m*, eingerahmter	box head	titre *m* encadré
Titel *m*, fetter	fat head	titre *m* en gras
Titel *m*, nicht eingezogener	flush head	titre *m* aligné à gauche
Titel *m* über Blattbreite *f*	streamer	titre *m* sur toute la longueur *f*
Titel *m*, vorspringender	shoulder head	titre *m* en ras de marge *f*
Titeländerung *f*	alteration of title	modification *f* de titre *m*
Titelbild *n*	frontispiece	frontispice *m*, titre-planche *f*
Titelblattmädchen *n*	cover girl	cover-girl *f*
Titelbogen *m*	prelim, title-sheet	feuille *f* de titre *m*, pièce *f* préliminaire
Titelgeschichte *f*	cover story	article *m* annoncé en couverture *f*
Titelkopf *m*	heading	en-tête *f*
Titelleiste *f*	masthead	cartouche *f* de titre *m*
Titelschriften *f*/*pl*	title faces *pl*	caractères *m*/*pl* pour titre *m*
Titelseite *f*	front cover, front page, title page	grand titre *m*, page *f* de titre *m*, première page *f*
Titelseite *f*, auffallende	flag	titre *m* flamboyant
Titelseite *f*, oberer Eckplatz *m* der	box on the right of the masthead	manchette *f* à droite du titre *m*
Tochtergesellschaft *f*	affiliate, affiliated company	société *f* affiliée
Todesanzeige *f*	death announcement, obituary notice	annonce *f* de décès *m*, annonce *f* nécrologique
tönendes Dia *n*	sound slide	diapositif *m* sonore
Tönung *f*	shade, tint	coloris *m*
Ton *m*, widerhallender	resounding	son *m* réverbéré
Tonabnahme *f*	prise pick-up	prise *f* tourne-disque *f*
Tonabnehmer *m*	pickup	pick-up *m*
Tonaufnahmegerät *n*	sound recorder	appareil *m* d'enregistrement *m* de son *m*

Tonausfall *m*	dead mike, off mike	absence *f* du son *m*
Tonband *n*	audio tape	bande *f* magnétique
Tonband *n* **ohne Worte** *n/pl*	tape recording without words *pl*	bande *f* internationale
Tonbandarchiv *n*	record library	phonotèque *f*
Tonbandaufnahme *f*	electrical transcription, tape recording	enregistrement *m* électrique, prise *f* de son *m*
Tonbandgerät *n*	video-tape recorder	appareil *m* enregistreur, magnétoscope *m*
Tonbeschaffenheit *f*	tonality	tonalité *f*
Tonbildschau *f*	film-sound transmission car, sound film strip, sound slide film	film *m* à images *f/pl* fixes, voiture *f* spéciale pour la projection *f* de films *m/pl* sonores
Tondia *n*	slide with sound	diapositif *m* sonore
Tonfilm *m*	sound film, talkie, talking film	film *m* parlant
Tonfilmatelier *n*	sound film studio	studio *m* de prises *f/pl* de vue *f*
Tonfläche *f*	flat tint	à-plat *m*
Toningenieur *m*	monitor man	ingénieur *m* du son *m*
Tonkamera *f*	sound camera	caméra *f* d'enregistrement *m* du son *m*
Tonkonserve *f*	canned music	disque *m* de phono *m*, musique *f* enregistrée
tonlos	cold	sans partie *f* sonore
Tonmedien *n/pl*	sound media *pl*	médias *m/pl* sonnants
Tonmischung *f*	mixing of sounds *pl*	mixage *m*
Tonplatte *f*	background plate, ground-tint plate, tint block	à-plat, planche *f* de fond *m*
Tonspur *f* **eines Films** *m*	sound track	piste *f* sonore, trace *f* de son *m* d'un film *m*
Tonstreifen *m*	sound track	bande *f* internationale
Tonteil *m* **einer Fernseh-sendung** *f*	audio	partie *f* de son *m* d'une émission *f* télévisée
Tonuntermalung *f*	background sound effect	fond *m* sonore
Tonverlauf *m*	vignetting of blocks *pl*	dégradage *m* des bords *m/pl*
Tonwerbung *f*	sound advertising	publicité *f* sonore
Tonwert *m*	tonal value	tonalité *f*
Totalausverkauf *m*	clearing of goods *pl*	liquidation *f* générale
tote Saison *f*	dead season, off season	hors saison *f*, morte-saison *f*
Totschweigen *n*	blackout	silence *m* complet
Träger *m*, **Zustellung** *f* **durch**	delivery by porters *pl*	portage *m*
tränenreiche Phrasen *f/pl*	hokum	phrases *f/pl* lacrymogènes
tragbares Fernsehgerät *n*	walkie-lookie	téléviseur *m* portatif
tragbares Funksprechgerät *n*	walkie-talkie	poste *m* de radio *f* portatif
Tragetasche *f* **aus Papier** *n*	paper bag, paper carrier	pochette *f* à anse *f*
Tragweite *f*	bearing	portée *f*
Transartdruck *m*	3-dimensional reproduction and printing process	impression *f* de planches *f/pl* superposées sur supports *m/pl* transparents
Transistor *m*	transistor	transistor *m*
Transkritdruck *m*	carbon printing	carbonnage *m* à chaud
Transparent *n*	banner, electric sign, streamer	enseigne *f* lumineuse, oriflamme *f*, transparent *m*
Transparentpapier *n*	glassine	papier *m* transparent
Transportband *n*	transport tape	tapis *m* roulant
Trauerrand *m*	heavy frame	bordure *f* de filets *m/pl* mat
treffender formulieren	to strengthen	donner une formulation *f* plus frappante

Treffpunkt *m*	meeting-place	rendez-vous *m*
Trema *n*	diaresis	tréma *m*
Trennkarton *m*	divider card	carton *m* de séparation *f*
Trennlinie *f*	cut-off-rule, dividing rule	couillard *m*, coupure *f*, ligne *f* de division *f*
Trennpunkte *m/pl*	diaeresis	tréma *m*
Trennschärfe *f*	selectivity	sélectivité *f*
Trennungstrich *m*	dash	tiret *m* de séparation *f*
Treppenstufenwerbung *f*	advertising on risers *pl* of staircase, staircase site	emplacement *m* sur contre-marches *f/pl* d'escalier *m*, panneau *m* d'escalier *m*
Treuerabatt *m*	patronage discount	rabais *m* de fidélité *f*, ristourne *f* pour clients *m/pl* habituels
Trick *m*	gimmick	truc *m*
Trickbild *n*	trick picture	trucage *m*
Trickfilm *m*	animated cartoon, stunt film, trick picture	dessin *m* animé, film *m* truqué
Trickfilmzeichner *m*	animator	animateur *m*
Triebwagen *m* (Motorwagen *m*)	tram-car	motrice *f*
Triglotte *f*	trilingual work	ouvrage *m* en trois langues *f/pl*
Trockenkopierverfahren *n*	xerography	xérographie *f*
Trockenmittel *n*	siccative	siccatif *m*
Trocknung *f*	drying	séchage *m*
Trostpreis *m*	consolation price	prime *f* d'encouragement *m*
trügerische Werbung *f*	false advertising	publicité *f* trompeuse
Türken *m/pl* **bauen**	to feign, to make pass false for right, to simulate	faire passer quelque chose *f* de faux pour vrai, feindre, simuler
Türplakat *n*	front-end space	panneau *m* à l'entrée *f*
Türrahmenschild *n*	door panel, poster on door-frames *pl*	panneau *m* de porte *f* d'accès *m*
Tusche *f*	Indian ink	encre *f* de Chine *f*
Tuschzeichnung *f*	wash drawing	épure *f* au lavis *m*
Type *f*	face, letter, type	caractère *m*, lettre *f*
Typenguß-Setzmaschine *f*	monotype	monotype *f*
Typisierung *f*	standardization	standardisation *f*
Typograf *m*	typographer	typographe *m*
Typografie *f*	letterpress, typography	typographie *f*
typografische Maßeinheiten *f/pl* (siehe Anhang)	typographical unit of measurement (see appendix)	mesures *f/pl* typographiques (voir appendice)
typografischer Punkt *m*	typographic point	point *m* typographique
typografisches Bild *m*	typographical aspect	aspect *m* typographique
typografisches Maßsystem *n*	typographic system of measurement (see appendix)	mesures *f/pl* typographiques (voir appendice)
Typometer *m*	type gauge, typometer	typomètre *m*
Typo-Studio *n*	type-design	atelier *m* typographique

U

U-Bahn-Werbung *f*	subway advertising (am), underground railway advertising (brit)	publicité-métro *m*
über und neben Text *m*	over and next text matter	au-dessus et à côté *m* du texte *m*
überarbeiten	to retouch, to revise	remanier, retoucher
überarbeiteter Text *m*	make-over	copie *f* remaniée

Überbelichtung *f*	overexposure, solarization	surexposition *f*
Überblendung *f*	dissolve, shunt	enchaînement *m*, fondu *m*
Überblick *m*	survey	tour *m* d'horizon *m*, vue *f* d'ensemble
Überdruck *m* (Aufdruck)	overprint, surprint	surimpression *f*
Überdruck *m* (Überschuß *m*)	surplus	feuille *f* supernuméraire, main *f* de passe *f*
überdrucken	to overprint	surimprimer
Übereinkunft *f*, **nach**	subject to acceptability	à débattre
übereinstimmen mit	to conform to, to run in with	être conforme à, être d'accord *m* avec
Übereinstimmung *f* **mit Markenbild** *n*	brand identity	identité *f* de marque *f*
überfliegen	to skim	parcourir
Übergang *m* **einer Filmszene** *f* **auf die folgende, schneller**	wipe	fermeture *f* en fondu *m*
Übergang *m*, **kurzer**	flash	transition *f* courte
Übergangszeit *f*	transition period	période *f* transitoire
Übergreifen *n*	run-on-line	enjambement *m*
Übergrößen *f/pl*	display types *pl*	caractères *m/pl* pour titre *m*
überhängender Buchstabe *m*	kerned letter	lettre *f* débordante
Überhangsatz *m*	leftover matter	copies *f/pl* en stock *m*
überhöhter Preis *m*	excessive charge	prix *m* excessif
überholte Nachrichten *f/pl*	stale news	information *f* dépassée
Überkleber *m*	overlay	cache *f*
Überkommerzialisierung *f*	overcommercialization	commercialisation *f* exagérée
überkopieren	overprinting	surimpression *f*
überladene Anzeige *f*	buckeye	annonce *f* surchargée
überladene Aufmachung *f*	crowded make up	mise *f* en page *f* surchargée
überlappen	to overlap	chevaucher, recouvrir
Überlappung *f*	overlapping	double emploi *m*, duplication *f*, imbrication *f*, recouvrement *m*
Überlauf *m*	jump	tourne *f*
Überlauf-Anzeige *f*	overflow indication	indication *f* de dépassement *m*
überlaufender Artikel *m*	jump story	article *m* à cheval *m*
Überleitung *f*, **musikalische**	bridge, sequel	transition *f* musicale
Übermittlung *f*	passing on, transmittal	transmission *f*
überparteilich	neutral, non-partisan	au-dessus des partis *m/pl*, neutre
Überraschungseffekt *m*	surprise effect	effet *m* de surprise *f*
Überraschungswert *m*	surprisal value	valeur *f* de surprise *f*
überregionale Presse *f*	national press	presse *f* nationale
überregionale Werbung *f*	nation-wide advertising	publicité *f* nationale
überregionale Zeitung *f*	national newspaper	grand quotidien *m* national
überregionaler Werbefeldzug *m*	general advertising, national campaign	campagne *f* nationale
überrunden (einen Kollegen *m*)	to race past a colleague	griller un confrère *m*
Übersättigung *f*, **werbliche**	saturation with advertising	saturation *f* publicitaire
Überschneidung *f*	duplication, overlapping	double emploi *m*, duplication *f*, imbrication *f*
überschreiten	to exceed	dépasser
Überschrift *f*	caption, head, heading, headline	en-tête *f*, rubrique *f*, titre *m*
Überschrift *f*, **alarmierende**	scare headline	gros titre *m* à sensation *f*, manchette *f* sensationnelle
Überschrift *f* **in großen Buchstaben** *m/pl* **setzen**	to screamline	mettre un titre *m* en gros caractères *m/pl*

Überschrift *f*, **knallende**	catchline, scare headline, very striking headline	titre *m* criard
Überschrift *f*, **mehrspaltige**	spread-head	grand titre *m* sur plusieurs colonnes *f/pl*
Überschrift *f* **ohne Information** *f*	blind headline	titre *m* sans information *f*
Überschrift *f*, **sensationelle**	screamer	titre *m* sensationnel
Überschrift *f*, **stufenförmige**	step head	titre *m* en marche *f* d'escalier *m*
Überschriftenverfasser *m*	caption writer	titulateur *m*
Überschriftszeilen *f/pl*	banks *pl*	lignes *f/pl* d'une manchette *f*
überschüssige Nummern *f/pl*	over copies *pl*	exemplaires *m/pl* de passe *f*
Überschuß *m*	surplus	surplus *m*
überschwemmter Markt *m*	glutted market	marché *m* inondé
Überseeausgabe *f*	oversea edition	édition *f* pour outre -mer *m*
übersetzen	to translate	traduire
Übersetzer *m*	translator	traducteur *m*
Übersetzung *f*	translation	traduction *f*
Übersetzung *f*, **freie**	loose translation	traduction *f* libre
Übersicht *f*	survey, synopsis	aperçu *m*, résumé *m*
übersichtlich	clearly arranged, standardized	bien disposé, normalisé
Übersichtlichkeit *f*	clarity	bonne vue *f* d'ensemble *m*
Übersichtskarte *f*	general map	carte *f* synoptique
überspielen *n*	rerecording	enregistrement *m* fractionné
überstehender Umschlag *m*	extended covers *pl*, overhang covers *pl*	couverture *f* à rabats *m/pl*, couverture *f* débordante
übertragen	to get across, to relay	relayer, transmettre
Übertragung *f*	transmission	transmission *f*
übertreiben	to exaggerate, to inflate, to speak in superlatives *pl*	exagérer, grossir
Übertreibung *f*	overstatement	exagération *f*
überwachen	to watch-dog	surveiller
Überwacher *m* **des Produktionsablaufs** *m*	dispatcher	surveilleur *m* du déroulement *m* de la production *f*
Überwachung *f*	supervision	contrôle *m*, surveillance *f*
überwältigender Erfolg *m*	smash hit	coup *m* en plein
überzählige Exemplare *n/pl*	overquire	main *f* de passe *f*
überzeugende Werbung *f*	persuasive advertising	publicité *f* persuasive
Überzeugungskraft *f*	persuasive power	force *f* de persuasion *f*
Überzugpapier *n*	lining paper	papier *m* couverture *f*
üble Nachrede *f*	back-biting	médisance *f*
Ukas *m*	ukase	oukase *m*
umarbeiten	to reshape, to rewrite	récrire, remanier
Umarbeitung *f*	adaptation, rescale	adaptation *f*
umbrechen	to break the line, to make up	mettre en pages *f/pl*, sortir de la ligne *f*
Umbruch *m*	imposition, make up	imposition *f*, mise *f* en page *f*
Umbruch-Bildschirm *m*	make-up screen	écran *m* de la mise *f* en pages *f/pl*
Umbruch-Bildschirmgerät *n*	make-up display terminal	écran *m* de visualisation *f* de la mise *f* en pages *f/pl*
Umbruchgerät *n*	make-up terminal	machine *f* de la mise *f* en pages *f/pl*
Umbruchredakteur *m*	make-up editor	maquettiste *m*
Umbruchterminal *n*	graphic terminal, page-proof terminal	terminal *m* de composition *f*
Umbruchtisch *m*	making up table	marbre *m* de mise *f* en pages *f/pl*

Umdruck *m*	transfer	report *m*
Umdruckapparat *m*	offset repro machine	appareil *m* à reporter, reporteur *m*
Umdruckpapier *n*	transfer paper	papier *m* à décalque *f*, papier *m* à report *m*
Umfang *m*	size	nombre *m* des pages *f/pl*
umfangreiche Werbung *f*	substantial advertising	publicité *f* substantielle
Umfangsberechnung *f*	casting off, character count, copy fitting	calibrage *m* d'une copie *f*
Umfeld *n*, redaktionelles	editorial context	contexte *m* rédactionnel
Umfrage *f*	poll, survey	enquête *f*, étude *f*
Umfrageergebnis *n*	survey data	résultat *m* d'enquête *f*
Umgangssprache *f*	colloquial speech	langage *m* courant
Umgegend *f*	environment	environs *m/pl*
Umgestaltung *f*	transfiguration, transformation	transfiguration *f*, transformation *f*
umkehren	to reverse, to turn round	renverser, retourner
Umkehrung *f*	inversion, reversing	inversion *f*
Umkreis *m*	circumference	circonférence *f*
umlaufende Gerüchte *n/pl*	current reports *pl*	bruits *m/pl* qui courent
umlaufende Streuung *f*	rotation	roulement *m* de publicité *f*
Umrahmung *f*	border	encadrement *m*
umrandete Anzeige *f*	boxed advertisement	annonce *f* encadrée
Umrandung *f*	box, frame, panel	contour *m*, encadrement *m*
Umrandung *f*, fette	heavy frame, thick frame	bordure *f* de filets *m/pl* mat
umredigieren	to revise	repatiner
Umriß *m*	shape	contour *m*
Umriß *m*, roher	rough outline	premier jet *m*
Umsatz *m*	turnover	chiffre *m* d'affaires *f/pl*
Umsatzhonorar *n*	royalties *pl*	redevance *f*
Umsatzkurve *f*	sales *pl* curve	courbe *f* de vente *f*
umsatzstarke Stelle *f*	focus	point *m* chaud
Umsatzsteigerung *f*	increase in turnover	augmentation *f* du chiffre *m* d'affaires *f/pl*
Umsatzsteuer *f*	sales *pl* tax, turnover tax	impôt *m* sur le chiffre *m* d'affaires *f/pl*
Umsatzzahlen *f/pl*	sales figures *pl*	chiffres *m/pl* de vente *f*
Umschlag *m*	cover	couverture *f*
Umschlag *m* aus dem gleichen Papier *n* wie die Textseiten *f/pl*	self-cover	couverture *f* de la même qualité *f* que le papier *m* des pages *f/pl* de texte *m*
Umschlag *m* im Format *n* der Textseiten *f/pl*	flush cover	couverture *f* en format des pages *f/pl* de texte *m*
Umschlag *m*, überstehender	extended covers *pl*, overhang covers *pl*	couverture *f* à rabats *m/pl*, couverture *f* débordante
Umschlag *m* (von Waren)	turnover	débit *m* des ventes *f/pl*
Umschlagbild *n*	cover picture	illustration *f* de couverture *f*
umschlagen	to work and turn	basculer
Umschlagkarton *m*	cover cardboard	carton *m* de couverture *f*
Umschlagklappe *f*	flap	rabat *m*
Umschlagpapier *n*	cover paper, cover stock	papier *m* de couverture *f*
Umschlagseite *f*	cover page	page *f* de couverture *f*
1. Umschlagseite *f*	front cover	première de couverture *f*
2. Umschlagseite *f*	inside front cover	deuxième de couverture *f*
3. Umschlagseite *f*	inside back cover	troisième de couverture *f*
4. Umschlagseite *f*	back cover	dernière page *f* de couverture *f*

umschmelzen	to recast	refondre
umschreiben (neu fassen)	rewriting	rédiger à nouveau
Umschreibung f	periphrasis	circonlocution f, périphrase f
umsetzen typog	to reset	recomposer
umstellen typog	to transpose	transposer
umstochen	outline	fileté
umstülpen	to tumble	culbuter
Umwandlung f	change, 'transformation	transformation f
Umwelt f	environment	environnement m
Umworbener m	advertisee	destinataire m
unabhängig	independent	indépendant
unabhängiger Journalist m	free-lance journalist	pigiste m
unbedruckter Rand m	margin	marge f
unbedruckter Raum m	blank space	espace m en blanc, espace m non-imprimé, espace m vierge f
unbeschnitten	untrimmed	non rogné
unbezahlte Werbebotschaft f	plug	message m publicitaire impayé
undurchsichtig	opaque	non transparent, opaque
Undurchsichtigkeit f	opacity	opacité f
„und"-Zeichen n	ampersand	esperluète f, signe m «et» commercial
unehrenhafte Werbung f	dishonest advertising	publicité f déloyale
unentgeltlich	free of charge	sans rémunération f
unerlaubte Werbung f	illicit advertising	publicité f illicite
ungefalzt	non-folded	non plié
ungerade Seite f	odd page, uneven page	page f impaire
ungerade Zahl f	odd number	impair, nombre m impair
Ungeschicklichkeit f	bloop	gaffe f
ungewöhnliche Werbung f	original advertising	publicité f originale
ungewöhnliches Bildelement n	Hathaway touch	élément m d'image f extraordinaire
ungewöhnliches Format n	unusual size	format m bâtard
ungezielte Werbung f	non-selective advertising	publicité f non-sélective
Uniformität f	uniformity	uniformité f
Universaljournalist m	universal journalist	journaliste m universel
Unkosten pl	expenses pl	dépenses f/pl, frais m/pl
Unkostendeckung f	recovery of expenses pl	recouvrement m des frais m/pl
unlauterer Wettbewerb m	unfair competition	concurrence f déloyale
unmittelbar unter Text m	immediately below text	immédiatement après texte m
unmontiertes Klischee n	unmounted block	cliché m non monté
unparteiisch	impartial, non-partisan	impartial
unpolitisch	non-political	sans étiquette f politique
Unregelmäßigkeit f	irregularity	irrégularité f
unreiner Druck f	slur	impression f boueuse
Unschärfe f	lack of sharpness	manque f de netteté f
unscharf	blurred, dull	flou
unscharfer Druck m	unsharp impression	papillotage m
unscharfes Foto n	high key	photo f flou
unterätzen	to undercut	sous-graver
Unterbelichtung f	underexposure	sous-exposition f
Unterbewertung f	understatement	amoindrissement m, sous-estimation f
Unterbietungspreis m	cut rate, give-away price	conditions f/pl spéciales, gâchage m de prix m

Unterbrechung f einer Sendung f	break	interruption f d'une émission f
unterbringen	to place	placer
unterdrückte Nachricht f	blacked out news	nouvelle f supprimée, ratage m
Unterdrückung f einer Information f	burying of an information	faire sauter une information f
untere Ecke f	lower corner	coin m intérieur
untere Schicht f	lower class	les basses classes f/pl
unterer Blattrand m	tail	marge f de pied m
Unterführung f	underground passage	passage m souterrain
Untergrundpresse f	underground press	presse f clandestine
Unterhändler m	intermediary, negotiator	entremetteur m, négociateur m
Unterhalter m	entertainer	amuseur m, diseur m
Unterhaltungen f/pl	entertainments pl	divertissements m/pl, spectacles m/pl, variétés f/pl
Unterhaltungsbeilage f	recreational supplement	supplément m feuilleton
Unterhaltungsfilm m	entertainment film	film m divertissant
Unterhaltungsliteratur f	fiction	littérature f divertissante
Unterhaltungsprogramm n	recreational programme	programme m récréatif
unterkopieren	to underprint	souscopier
Unterlänge f	descender height	jambage m inférieur
Unterlagen f/pl	material	matériel m
unterlegen	to line-up, to underlay	charger, garnir
Untermalung f, musikalische	background sound effect, underscoring	fond m sonore
Unternehmensberater m	management counsellor, management consultant	conseil m en gestion f, conseiller m d'entreprise f
Unternehmensführung f	management	gestion f de l'entreprise f
Unterschlag m	tail	blanc m de pied m
unterschreiben	to approve of, to sign	signer, souscrire à
Unterschrift f	signature	signature f
Unterschriftszeile f	base line	légende f
unterschwellige Werbung f	subliminal advertising	publicité f insidieuse, publicité f subliminale
unterstreichen	to emphasize, to underline	mettre en relief m, souligner
Unterstreichung f	underlining	soulignure f
unterstützende Medien n/pl	supporting media pl	médias m/pl appuyants
unterstützende Werbung f	auxiliary advertising	publicité f auxiliaire
Unterstützung f	support	appui m
Unterstützung f, redaktionelle	editorial assistance, editorial support	assistance f rédactionnelle
Untersuchung f	examination, inquiry, research, survey, test	enquête f, examen m, recherche f
Untersuchung f der Anzeigenwirkung f	folder test	test m de reliure f
Unterteilung f	subdivision	subdivision f
Untertitel m	cut-in, drop head, sub-title, subheading	second titre m, sous-titre m
Untertreibung f	understatement	amoindrissement m, sous-estimation f
untervermieten	to sublet	sous-louer
unverbindlich	without obligation	sans engagement m
unverbindlicher Vorschlag m	speculative work	projet m gratuit
unverblümte Sprache f	cold turkey am, plain speech	déclaration sans ambages f/pl
unverdaulicher Artikel m	pig iron	article m lourd et indigeste
unverkäuflich	not for sale	invendable

unverkaufte Exemplare *n/pl*	unsold copies *pl*	bouillon *m*, exemplaires *m/pl* invendus
unvollständig	half-baked	incomplet
unvorbereitetes Interview *n*	candid interview	interview *f* non préparée
unzerreißbares Bilderbuch *n*	rag-book	livre *m* d'images *f/pl* sur toile *f*
unzulängliche Werbung *f*	inadequate advertising	publicité *f* inadéquate
unzulässige Werbung *f*	forbidden advertising	publicité *f* interdite
Urheber *m*	author	auteur *m*
Urheberrecht *n*	copyright	droit *m* d'auteur *m*
Urheberrechtslizenz *f*	royalty	droits *m/pl* d'auteur *m*
Urkunde *f*	document	document *m*
Urschrift *f*	original manuscript	autographe *m*
urteilsfähiger Leser *m*	discriminating reader	lecteur *m* averti
Urtext *m*	original text	original *m*
Utopie *f*, naturwissenschaftlich-technische	science-fiction	utopie *f* scientifique-technique

V

Vakanz *f*	vacancy	place *f* vacante
Vakatseite *f*	blank page	page *f* en blanc
Variante *f*	variant	alternative *f*, variante *f*
Velinpapier *n*	vellum paper, wove paper	papier *m* du Japon *m*, papier *m* vélin
veräußern	to sell	vendre
Verallgemeinerung *f*	generalization	généralisation *f*
Veralten *n*	obsolescence	obsolescence *f*
veraltet	antiquated, out-of-date	périmé, vieilli
veraltete Ware *f*	stale article	article *m* passé de mode *m*
veraltetes Wort *n*	obsolete word	mot *m* désuet
veranschaulichen	to vizualize	concrétiser, visionner
veranschlagen	to estimate	établir un devis *m*, évaluer
Veranstalter *m*	organizer	organisateur *m*
Veranstaltung *f*	performance	manifestation *f*, réunion *f*
verantwortlicher Redakteur *m*	responsible editor	rédacteur *m* responsable
Verarbeitung *f*	processing, working	façonnage *m*
verballhornen	to bowderize	défigurer, expurger
Verband *m*	association	association *f*
Verbandsblatt *n*	organ of a corporation	feuille *f* corporative, journal *m* d'association *f*
verbessern	to revise	reviser
verbesserte und erweiterte Auflage *f*	revised edition	édition *f* corrigée et augmentée
verbesserter Text *m*	revised text	texte *m* revu
Verbesserung *f*	amendment	amendement *m*
verbindender Text *m*	tie-in	texte *m* de liaison *f*
Verbindung *f* setzen, sich in	to contact	contacter
Verbindungsmann *m*	account executive, contact man, liaison man	contacteur *m*, homme *m* de relation *f*
Verbindungsweg *m*	pipeline	filière *f*
verblassen	to fade	passer
verblüffen	to stun	abasourdir
verborgenes Angebot *n*	buried offer, hidden offer	offre *f* clandestine
Verbrauch *m*	consumption	consommation *f*
Verbraucher *m*	consumer, user	consommateur *m*
Verbraucher *m*, potentieller	potential consumer	consommateur *m* potentiel

Verbraucheranalyse *f*	consumer research	recherche *f* auprès des consommateurs *m/pl*
Verbraucherbefragung *f*	consumer imquiry, consumer survey	enquête *f* auprès des consommateurs *m/pl*
Verbraucherforschung *f*	consumer research	recherche *f* auprès des consommateurs *m/pl*
Verbrauchergenossenschaft *f*	cooperative	coopérative *f* des consommateurs *m/pl*
Verbraucherin *f*	user	consommatrice *f*
Verbraucherinteresse *n*	consumer interest	intérêt *m* des consommateurs *m/pl*
Verbrauchermarkt *m*	consumer market	marché *m* de consommation *f*
Verbrauchermotive *n/pl,* **Erforschung** *f* **der**	consumer motivation research	études *f/pl* de la motivation *f* des consommateurs *m/pl*
Verbrauchernachfrage *f*	consumer demand	demande *f* des consommateurs *m/pl*
verbraucherorientiert	customer-oriented	orienté vers le client *m*
Verbraucherschaft *f*	usership	masse *f* des consommateurs *m/pl*
Verbraucherschicht *f*	class of consumers *pl*	catégorie *f* des consommateurs *m/pl*
Verbraucherschutz *m*	consumer protection	protection *f* des consommateurs *m/pl*
Verbraucherschutzbewegung *f*	consumerism	mouvement *m* pour la protection *f* des consommateurs *m/pl*
Verbrauchertest *m*	consumer test	test *m* de consommation *f*
Verbrauchertestgruppe *f*	consumer panel	groupe *m* d'essai *m* de consommateurs *m/pl,* panel *m* des consommateurs *m/pl*
Verbraucherverhalten *n*	consumer behaviour	comportement *m* des consommateurs *m/pl*
Verbraucherwerbung *f*	consumer advertising	publicité *f* consommateurs *m/pl*
Verbraucherwunsch *m*	consumer desire	désir *m* des consommateurs *m/pl*
Verbraucherzentrale *f*	consumer center	centre *m* de consommateurs *m/pl*
verbrauchsfertige Nahrungsmittel *n/pl*	convenience foods *pl*	aliments *m/pl* prêts à la consommation *f*
Verbrauchsgewohnheiten *f/pl*	consuming habits *pl,* consumption pattern	habitudes *f/pl* de consommation *f*
Verbrauchsgüter *n/pl*	consumer's goods *pl,* nondurable goods *pl*	biens *m/pl* de consommation *f*
verbreiten	to dissiminate	disséminer, propager, répandre
Verbreitung *f*	circulation, coverage, diffusion, dissimination, distribution	circulation *f,* couverture *f,* diffusion *f,* distribution *f,* propagation *f,* rayonnement *m*
Verbreitungsanalyse *f*	circulation analysis	analyse *f* de la diffusion *f*
Verbreitungsdichte *f*	circulation density	densité *f* de la diffusion *f*
Verbreitungsgebiet *n*	circulation area, covered sector	rayon *m* d'action *f,* zone *f* de diffusion *f*
Verbreitungszahlen *f/pl*	circulation figures *pl,* distribution figures *pl*	chiffres *m/pl* de diffusion *f,* chiffres *m/pl* de tirage *m*
Verbundpackung *f*	combipack	plusieurs unités *f/pl* de vente *f* dans un même emballage *m*

Verbundwerbung *f*	association advertising, co-up advertising, tie-up advertising	publicité *f* commune, publicité *f* groupée
Verchromung *f*	chroming	chromage *m*
verdeckt stehende Anschlagstellen *f/pl*	sites *pl* hidden from view	masquage *m*
verdeckter Anschlag *m*	obstructed site	emplacement *m* masqué
verdichten	to boil down	condenser
verdrehen	to slant	gauchir
verdrucken	to misprint	faire de la maculature *f*
Verdünnungsmittel *n*	thinner	diluant *m*
verdunkeln	to black out	occulter
vereinbaren	to agree	stipuler
Vereinbarung *f*	agreement	accord *m*, convention *f*, stipulation *f*
vereinfachen	to simplify	simplifier
Vereinsblatt *n*	journal of a society	feuille *f* corporative
Verfälschung *f*	bias, falsification	falsification *f*
Verfahren *n* **für Breitwandvorführung** *f*	cinemascope	cinémascope *m*
Verfasser *m*	author, writer	auteur *m*
verfilmen	to film, to screen	mettre en images *f/pl*
verfremdet	unfamiliar	dénaturé
Verfremdungseffekt *m*	alienation effect	effet *m* d'éloignement *m*
verfügbar	available	disponible
verfügbarer Anschlagraum *m*	available sites *pl*	emplacements *m/pl* disponibles
Verfügung *f*	disposition	disposition *f*
Verführer *m/pl,* **geheime**	hidden persuaders *pl*	séducteurs *m/pl* clandestins
vergilbt	yellowed	jauni
Vergleich *m* **anonymer Produkte** *n/pl*	blind test	test *m* à l'aveugle
vergleichen	to collate, to compare, to crossprove, to match	collationner, comparer
vergleichen, mit dem Manuskript *n*	to see copy	comparer avec le manuscrit *m*
vergleichende Werbung *f*	comparative advertising	publicité *f* discriminatoire
Vergnügungsanzeige *f*	entertainment advertisement	annonce *f* spectacles *m/pl*
Vergnügungsindustrie *f*	show business	monde *m* des spectacles *m/pl*
Vergoldung *f*	gilding	dorure *f*
vergriffen	exhausted, out-of-print, out-of-stock	épuisé
vergrößern	to enlarge, to increase	agrandir
vergrößern, proportional	to enlarge proportionally	agrandir à la proportionnelle
Vergrößerung *f*	blow-up, enlargement	agrandissement *m*
Vergrößerung *f,* **starke**	blow-up	grand agrandissement *m*
Vergünstigung *f*	sales *pl* allowance	avantage *m*, faveur *f*
Vergütung *f*	bonus, fee	bonification *f,* honoraire *m,* rémunération *f*
Verhalten *n*	attitude, behaviour	attitude *f*
Verhaltensbeobachtung *f*	behaviour research	étude *f* de comportement *m*
Verhaltensgrund *m*	motivation	motivation *f*
Verhaltensprüfung *f*	attitude study, concept-test	étude *f* d'attitude *f,* test *m* d'axe *m*
Verhaltensskala *f*	attitude scale	échelle *f* d'attitudes *f/pl*
Verhaltensweise *f*	habit	coutume *f,* habitude *f,* mode *m* de comportement *m*
Verhandlung *f*	negotiation	négociation *f*
verhobene Zeile *f*	misplaced line	ligne *f* transposée

Verkäufer m	salesman	vendeur m
Verkäufer m, stummer	counter dispenser, counter display container, dummy salesman	matériel m d'étalage m de comptoir m, vendeur m muet
Verkäuferin f	sales pl girl	vendeuse f
Verkäufermarkt m	seller's market	marché m de vendeurs m/pl
Verkäufermerkblatt n	salesfolder, switch over	argumentaire m
verkäuflich	saleable, vendible	vendable
Verkauf m	sale	vente f
Verkauf m durch Automaten m/pl	vending	vente f d'articles m/pl dans des machines f/pl distributrices automatiques
Verkauf m ohne Kredit m und Kundendienst m	cash-and-carry	paiement m comptant
Verkaufen n um jeden Preis m	hard selling	vente f à tout prix m
Verkaufsabteilung f	sales pl department	département m des ventes f/pl, service m commercial
Verkaufsanalyse f	sales pl analysis	analyse f des ventes f/pl
Verkaufsapparat m	sales pl organisation	réseau m de vente f
Verkaufsappell m	sales pl appeal	argumentation f de vente f
Verkaufsargument n	sales pl argument, selling angle, selling point	argument m de vente f
Verkaufsargumentation f	purchase proposition	argumentation f de vente f, propositions f/pl commerciales
Verkaufsauflage f, durchschnittliche	average net paid circulation, average sold circulation	bouillon m déduit moyen
Verkaufsauslage f	sales pl display	étalage m de vente f
Verkaufsautomat m	vending machine	distributeur m automatique
Verkaufsbedingungen f/pl	terms pl of sale	conditions f/pl de vente f
Verkaufsberater m	sales pl consultant	conseil m en matière f de vente f
Verkaufsbezirk m	sales pl territory	région f de vente f
Verkaufsbrennpunkt m	focal point of sales pl	zone f de chalandise f
Verkaufsbüro n	sales pl office	bureau m des ventes f/pl
Verkaufserfolg m	sales pl impact	résultats m/pl des ventes f/pl
Verkaufsfeldzug m	selling campaign	campagne f de vente f
Verkaufsförderung f	sales pl promotion	promotion f de vente f
Verkaufsgespräch n	sales pl talk	boniment m, entretien m de vente f
Verkaufsgondel f	gondola	gondole f
Verkaufshandbuch n	sales pl book, sales pl manual	manuel m de vente f
Verkaufshilfe f	promotion matter	aide f à la vente f
Verkaufskampagne f	sales pl campaign	campagne f de vente f
Verkaufskarton m	cardboard box for dealers pl	carton m vendeur
Verkaufsleiter m	sales pl manager, sales pl promoter	chef m des ventes f/pl, directeur m commercial
Verkaufsleitung f	sales pl management	direction f commerciale
Verkaufsmannschaft f	sales pl force	équipe f de vente f
Verkaufsmethode f	selling method	méthode f de distribution f
Verkaufsorganisation f	sales pl organisation, selling organisation	appareil m commercial, organisation f de vente f
Verkaufsort m	point of sale	point m de vente f
Verkaufsplan m	selling plan	plan m de vente f
Verkaufsplatz m	point of purchase	point m de vente f
Verkaufspolitik f	sales pl policy	politique f de vente f
Verkaufspreis m	selling price	prix m de vente f

Verkaufspreis *m*, **durchstrichener**	crossed out selling price	prix *m* de vente *f* barré
Verkaufspreisermäßigung *f*	deal	réduction *f* du prix *m* de vente *f*
Verkaufspunkt *m*	sales *pl* point	angle *m* d'approche *f* publicitaire
Verkaufsquote *f*	sales *pl* quota	quota *m* de vente *f*
Verkaufsrhythmus *m*	purchase rhythm	fréquence *f* d'achat *m*, rythme *m* d'achat *m*
Verkaufsrichtlinien *f/pl*	principles *pl* of selling	principes *m/pl* de vente *f*
Verkaufsrisiko *n*	sales *pl* risk	risque *m* de vente *f*
Verkaufsschlager *m*	bestseller	article *m* de grosse vente *f*, succès *m* de vente *f*
Verkaufsspitze *f*	sales *pl* peak	maximum *m* des ventes *f/pl*
Verkaufsständer *m*	distribution rack	étagère *f*, rayon *m*
Verkaufsstand *m*	stall	boutique *f* de vente *f*
Verkaufsstelle *f*	sales *pl* office, selling point	poste *m* de vente *f*
Verkaufsstelle *f*, **fahrbare**	mobile shop	camionnette *f* -boutique *f*
Verkaufstechnik *f*	salesmanship	art *m* de vendre
Verkaufstraining *n*	sales *pl* training	entraînement *m* à la vente *f*
Verkaufsunterstützung *f*	trade support	secours *m* de vente *f*
Verkaufswettbewerb *m*	sales *pl* competition	concours *m* de vente *f*
Verkaufswirkung *f*	effect on sales *pl*	efficacité *f* de la vente *f*
Verkaufsziel *n*	sales *pl* objective	but *m* commercial, objectif *m* marketing *m*
Verkaufsziffer *f*	sales *pl* figure	chiffre *m* de vente *f*
verkaufte Auflage *f*	total net paid circulation	diffusion *f* bouillon *m* déduit
Verkehrsfluß *m*, **rechtwinklig zum**	head on position	barre-route *f*
Verkehrsmittel *n*	transport systems *pl*	moyens *m/pl* de transport *m*
Verkehrsmittelwerbung *f*	advertising in transport systems *pl*, transit advertising, transport advertising *brit*, transportation advertising *am*, vehicular advertising	publicité *f* moyens *m/pl* de transport *m*
Verkehrsmittelwerbung *f*, **Tarif** *m* **für**	card rates *pl*	tarif *m* de la publicité *f* moyens *m/pl* de transport *m*
Verkehrsreklamepächter *m*	franchise operator of transport advertising	concessionaire *m* de publicité *f* sur les moyens *m/pl* transports *m/pl*
Verkehrtzeichnung *f*	reverse drawing	dessin *m* renversé
verkleinern	to minimise, to reduce	diminuer, rapetisser, réduire
verkleinern, proportional	to scale down	réduire en proportion *f*
verkleinern, Zwischenraum *m*	to depress space	diminuer l'espace *m* blanc
Verkleinerung *f*	reduction	réduction *f*
verkünden, feierlich	to herald	proclamer
verkürzen	to curtail	élaguer, raccourcir
verkürzte Satzbreite *f*	run-around	largeur *f* abregée de la composition *f*
Verlag *m*	publishing house	maison *f* d'édition *f*
Verlagserscheinung *f*	printing work, publication	publication *f*, titre *m*
Verlagsinhaber *m*	owner-editor	directeur-propriétaire *m*
Verlagskonzentration *f*	concentration of publishing houses *pl*	concentration *f* de maisons *f/pl* d'éditions *f/pl*
Verlagsleiter *m*	business manager	directeur *m* commercial
Verlagsort *m*	town of publication	lieu *m* de publication *f*
Verlagssignet *n*	publisher's colophon, publisher's imprint	marque *f* d'éditeur *m*, signet *m*

Verlagsstück *n*	publisher's copy	exemplaire-éditeur *m*
Verlagsvertreter *m*	publisher's representative	vendeur *m* d'espace *m*
verlaufen (Farben *f/pl*)	to blend, to run (colour)	se fondre
verlaufendes Bild *n*	vignette	photo *f* en dégradé
verlautet, wie	as reported	on indique
verlegen	to publish	éditer
Verleger *m*	publisher	éditeur *m*
Verlegerrabatt *m*	publisher's discount	rabais *m* aux éditeurs *m/pl*
Verleiher *m*	lender	distributeur *m*, prêteur *m*
Verleumder *m*	back-biter	calomniateur *m*, détracteur *m*
Verleumdung *f*	calumny, defamation, libel, slander	calomnie *f*, diffamation *f*
Verleumdungskampagne *f*	smear campaign	campagne *f* de dénigrement *m*
Verlobungsanzeige *f*	announcement of an engagement	faire-part de fiançailles *f/pl*
Verlosungsart *f*	sweepstake	espèce *f* de loterie *f*
Vermietung *f*	leasing, letting	location *f*
Vermischtes *n*	miscellanies *pl*, miscellaneous items *pl*	faits divers *m/pl*, miscellanées *f/pl*
vermitteln	to interpose, to negotiate	entremettre
Vermittler *m*	intermediary, negotiator	entremetteur *m*, négociateur *m*
Vermittlungsprovision *f*	commission fee	commission *f* d'intermédiaire
vernachlässigter Stil *m*	slipshod style	style *m* négligé
verniedlichen	to make light, to soft-pedal	bagatelliser, minimiser
vernünftige Werbung *f*	rational advertising	publicité *f* rationnelle
veröffentlichen	to publish	publier
Veröffentlichung *f*	publication	publication *f*
Veröffentlichung *f*, geeignet zur	publishable	publiable
Veröffentlichungstag *m*	day of publication	date *f* de la publication *f*
verpachten	to farm out, to lease	affermer, donner à bail *m*
Verpachtung *f*	farming out, sub-contracting	affermage *m*, amodiation *f*
verpacken	to pack	emballer
Verpackung *f*	package, packaging, wrapping	conditionnement *m*, emballage *m*
Verpackung *f*, durchsichtige aus Kunststoff *m*	blister pack	emballage *m* plastique transparent
Verpackung *f*, wiederverwendbare	re-use package	emballage *m* à double usage *m*, emballage *m* de remploi *m*
Verpackungsberater *m*	packaging consultant	conseil *m* en matière *f* d'emballage *m*
Verpackungsdatum *n*	date of packing	date *f* de conditionnement *m*
Verpackungsfachmann *m*	cardboard engineer	expert *m* en emballages *m/pl*
Verpackungskosten *pl*	packaging costs *pl*, packing charges *pl*	coût *m* de l'emballage *m*, frais *m/pl* de l'emballage *m*
Verpächter *m*	landlord	bailleur *m*, propriétaire *m*
Verrechnungsscheck *m*	crossed cheque	chèque *m* barré
verreißen	to criticize harshly, to pull to pieces *pl*	critiquer sévèrement, éreinter
Versagung *f*	frustration	frustration *f*
Versalien *f/pl*	capital letters *pl*, caps *pl*, upper case letters *pl*	capitales *f/pl*, majuscules *f/pl*
Versammlung *f*	meeting	assemblée *f*, réunion *f*
Versand *m*	dispatching, forwarding	distribution *f*, envoi *m*, expédition *f*
Versandabteilung *f*	postal department, shipping department	service *m* de routage *m*, service *m* des expéditions *f/pl*

Versandanzeige *f*	advice note	instruction *f* d'expédition *f*
Versandauflage *f*	mail circulation	circulation *f* postale
versandfertig	ready for shipping	prêt à expédier
Versandhandel *m*	mail order trade	vente *f* par correspondance *f*
Versandhaus *n*	mail order house	maison *f* de vente *f* par correspondance *f*, maison *f* d'expédition *f*
Versandhauskatalog *m*	mail-order catalogue	catalogue *m* d'une maison *f* d'expédition *f*
Versandhauswerbung *f*	mail order advertising	publicité *f* de vente *f* par correspondance *f*
Versandkosten *pl*	dispatch-charges *pl*	frais *m/pl* de transport *m*, frais *m/pl* d'expédition *f*
Versandliste *f*	mailing index	liste *f* d'adresses *f/pl*
Versandpapiere *n/pl*	dispatch papers *pl*	documents *m/pl* d'expédition *f*
Versandschachtel *f*	transport case	boîte *f* d'expédition *f*
Versandtasche *f*	American envelope	enveloppe *f* américaine, pochette *f*
Versandtermin *m*	shipping date	date *f* d'envoi *m*
verschieben	to defer, to postpone, to shift	décaler, reporter
Verschiebung *f*	postponement	décalage *m*
Verschiedenes *n*	miscellaneous column	pêle-mêle *m*
verschlüsseln	to code	coder
Verschluß *m*	shutter	volet *m*
Verschlußmarke *f*	sealing label	cachet *m*
Verschmelzung *f* zweier Entwürfe *m/pl*	marriage	fonte *f* de deux dessins *m/pl*
Verschwendung *f*	waste	gaspillage *m*
verschwommener Druck *m*	blurred impression	papillotage *m*
versenden	to dispatch, to forward, to ship	acheminer, envoyer
versetzbare Werbefläche *f*	rotating bulletin	bulletin *m* transférable
versetzbares Plakat *n*	floating piece	placard *m* dont l'emplacement *m* peut varier
Versorgungslücke *f*	gap in supplies *pl*	brèche *f* d'approvisionnement *m*
Verspottung *f*	mocking	persiflage *m*
versprechen, sich	to make a slip of the tongue	se tromper en parlant
Versprecher *m*	fluff	bafouillage *m*, loup *m*
Verständlichkeit *f*	readability	intelligibilité *f*
verstärken	to intensify	renforcer
verstärkte Werbeanstrengungen *f/pl*	advertising efforts *pl*, drive	effort *m* spécial de publicité *f*
verstärkter Werbeeinsatz *m*	sales *pl* drive	effort *m* marqué, effort *m* spécial
verstecktes Angebot *n*	blind offer, buried offer, hidden offer, subordinate offer	offre *f* clandestine
verstecktes Mikrophon *n*	bug	micro *m* secret
Versteigerungen *f/pl*	auctions *pl*	ventes *f/pl* publiques
verstellte Zeile *f*	transposed line	ligne *f* intervertie
verstoßen gegen	to infringe	enfreindre
verstreut	scattered	dispersé
verstümmeln	to garble	tronquer
verstümmelter Text *m*	mutilated text	texte *m* mutilé
verstümmeltes Wort *n*	beard	couac *m*
Versuchsanzeige *f*	preliminary advertisement	annonce *f* préliminaire
Versuchsausgabe *f*	pilot edition	édition *f* d'essai *m*

Versuchsballon *m*	trial balloon	ballon *m* d'essai *m*
Versuchsballon *m* steigen lassen	kite-flying	lancement *m* d'un ballon *m* d'essai *m*
Versuchskampagne *f*	test campaign	campagne *f* d'essai *m*
Versuchswerbung *f*	advertising test	publicité *f* test *m*
verteilen	to distribute	distribuer
Verteiler *m*	distributor	distributeur *m*
Verteilung *f*	distribution	distribution *f*
Vertikalwerbung *f*	vertical co-operative advertising	publicité *f* collective verticale
vertonen	to voice-over	sonoriser
Vertonung *f*	musical setting, scoring	addition *f* du ton *m*, mise *f* en musique *f*, sonorisation *f*
Vertrag *m*	agreement, contract	contrat *m*
Vertragsabschluß *m*	settlement of treaty	conclusion *f* du contrat *m*
Vertragsdauer *f*	contract period	durée *f* du contrat *m*
Vertragspartner *m*	contracting party	contractant *m*
Vertrauenswerbung *f*	public relations *pl*	relations *f/pl* extérieures, relations *f/pl* publiques
vertrauenswürdig	trustworthy	digne de confiance *f*
vertrauliche Information *f*	off the record information	information *f* confidentielle
vertrauliche Winke *m/pl*	inside dopes *pl*	tuyaux *m/pl* confidentiels
vertreiben	to distribute	distribuer, vendre
vertreten	to represent	représenter
Vertreter *m*	agent, representative	agent *m*, représentant *m*
Vertreterbericht *m*	call slip	rapport *m* de visite *f*
Vertreterbezirk *m*	agent's territory	région *f* du représentant *m*
Vertreterhandbuch *n*	sales *pl* manual	manuel *m* pour des représentants *m/pl*
Vertreterprovision *f*	agent commission	commission *f* de l'agent *m*
Vertretung *f*	representation	représentation *f*
Vertrieb *m*	distribution, sale	vente *f*
Vertriebsabteilung *f*	marketing department, sales *pl* department	service *m* de la vente *f*
Vertriebsapparat *m*	sales *pl* organisation	appareil *m* commercial
Vertriebsförderung *f*	sales *pl* promotion	promotion *f* de vente *f*
Vertriebsgefüge *n*	structure of distribution	structure *f* de la distribution *f*
Vertriebskanal *m*	trade channel	débouché *m* commercial
Vertriebskosten *pl*	distribution costs *pl*	coûts *m/pl* de distribution *f*
Vertriebsleiter *m*	circulation manager, distribution manager, sales *pl* promoter	chef *m* de vente *f*
Vertriebsmethode *f*	distribution method	méthode *f* de distribution *f*
Vertriebsstelle *f*	outlet	débouché *m*
Vertriebsunternehmen *n*	distributing enterprise, distribution agency	entreprise *f* de distribution *f*
Vertriebsweg *m*	channel of distribution	canal *m* de distribution *f*, circuit *m* de distribution *f*
verunglimpfen	to defame	diffamer
Verunstaltung *f* der Landschaft *f*	disfigurement of country-side	défiguration *f* du paysage *m*
vervielfältigen	to duplicate, to mimeograph	multicopier, multiplier, polycopier, reproduire
vervielfältigter Brief *m*	process letter	lettre *f* reproduite
Vervielfältigung *f*	duplication, multiplication	multicopie *f*, multiplication *f*, polycopie *f*
Vervielfältigungsapparat *m*	duplicator, hectograph	duplicateur *m*, hectographe *m*, multigraphe *m*
vervollkommnen	to perfect	perfectionner

verwalten	to administer	administrer, gérer
Verwalter *m*	administrator	administrateur *m*
Verwaltung *f*	administration	administration *f*
Verwandlung *f*	metamorphosis	métamorphose *f*
Verweigerung *f*	refusal	refus *m*
Verwendung *f*	utilization	utilisation *f*
Verwertung *f*	utilization	utilisation *f*
verwickeln	to complicate	compliquer
Verwicklung *f*	complication	complication *f*
verwischt	fuzzy	flou
verworrenes Geschwätz *n*	balderdash	amphigourie *f*
Verzeichnis *n*	inventory, list	inventaire *m*, liste *f*
Verzerrung *f*	distortion	distorsion *f*
verzieren	to ornament	orner
Verzierung *f*	decoration	décoration *f*
verzögern, die Ausgabe *f*	to hold an edition	retenir une édition *f*
Verzögerung *f*	time-lag	retard *m*
verzollen	to clear through customs *pl*	payer les droits *m/pl* d'entrée *f*
Videoband *n*	videotape	bande *f* magnétique vidéo
Videotext *m*	ceefax, oracle	antiope *m*
Vielfältigkeit *f*	multiplicity	multiplicité *f*
Vielschreiber *m*	scribbler	écrivailleur *m*, gratte-papier *m*, griffonneur *m*
Viereck *n*	rectangle	quadrangle *m*, rectangle *m*
viereckig	squared-off	carré, quadrangulaire
Vierfarbätzung *f*	four-colour block	cliché *m* de photogravure *f*
Vierfarbendruck *m*	four-colour process	impression *f* en quatre couleurs *f/pl*, impression *f* quadrichrome, quadrichromie *f*
vierspaltig	four columns *pl*	sur quatre colonnes *f/pl*
Viertelcicero *f* (siehe Anhang)	Brillant (see appendix)	corps 3 points (voir appendice)
vierteljährlich	every three months *pl*, quarterly	trimestriel
Vierteljahreszeitschrift *f*	quarterly	revue *f* trimestrielle
Viertelpetit *f* (siehe Anhang)	non plus ultra (see appendix)	corps 2 points (voir appendice)
Viertelseite *f*	quarter page	quart *m* de page *f*
Vignette *f*	mask, ornament, vignette	cache *f*, dégradé *m*, fleuron *m*, vignette *f*
Visitenkarte *f*	card	carte *f* de visite *f*
Visitenkarte *f* eines Verkäufers *m*	salesman's calling card	carte *f* de visite *f*
Visualiser *m*	visualizer	concepteur *m*
visuelle Kommunikation *f*	visual communication	médias *m/pl* visuels
Vitrine *f*	display case	vitrine *f*
Vogelperspektive *f*	bird's eye view	vue *f* à vol *m* d'oiseau *m*
Volksausgabe *f*	cheap reprint	édition *f* populaire
Volkslied *n*	folk-song	chanson *f* populaire, chanson *f* traditionnelle
volkstümliche Sendung *f*	pop feature	émission *f* à succès *m*
Volkstümlichkeit *f*	popularity	popularité *f*
Vollautotypie *f*, rechteckige	square half-tone	simili *m* au carré *m*
Vollbelegung *f*	full showing	affichage *m* général
volle Zeile *f*	full line	ligne *f* pleine
vollendete Tatsache *f*	accomplished fact	fait *m* accompli
voller Spaltensatz *m*	full measure	ligne *f* pleine

Vollklischee *n*	complete block *brit*, complete plate *am*	cliché *m* bloc
Vollkommenheit *f*	perfection	perfection *f*
Vollmacht *f*	fullness of power	plein pouvoir *m*
Vollredaktion *f*	complete editorial staff	rédaction *f* complète
Vollretusche *f*	full retouching	retouche *f* complète
vollständig	complete	complet
vollständiger Text *m*	full text	texte *m* intégral
vollstopfen	to jam-pack	bourrer
Volontär *m*	trainee	élève *m*, stagiaire *m*
Vorabdruck *m`*	advance publication	bonne feuille *f*
Vorankündigung *f*	advance notice	avis *m* préalable
Voranschlag *m*	estimate	devis *m*, évaluation *f*
Vorantreiben *n*	drive	dynamisme *m*
Voranzeige *f*	preliminary announcement	annonce *f* préliminaire, avis *m* préalable
Vorarbeiten *f/pl*	preliminary work	travaux *m/pl* préliminaires, travaux *m/pl* préparatoires
Vorausberechnung *f*	forecast	prévision *f*
Vorausexemplar *n*	advance-copy	exemplaire *m* à l'avance *f*, exemplaire *m* de lancement *m*
voraussichtlicher Kunde *m*	prospect	prospect *m*
Vorauszahlung *f*	advance payment, prepayment	paiement *m* d'avance *m*
Vorbemerkung *f*	prefatory note, preliminary remark	avis *m* au lecteur *m*, chapeau *m*
vorbereiteter Text *m*	canned copy	texte *m* mis en boîte *f*
Vorbesprechung *f*	preliminary discussion	entretien *m* préliminaire
Vorbestellung *f*	advance order	commande *f* préliminaire
Vorbild *n*	prototype	modèle *m*, prototype *m*
vordatierte Zeitung *f*	antedated paper, bulldog edition *am*, early-bird issue *am*, pre-dated paper	journal *m* antidaté, journal *m* prédaté, première édition *f*
vorderer Teil *m* der Ausgabe *f*	front section	cahier *m* de tête *f*
Vorderseite *f*	front page, outer form	côté *m* de première, première page *f*
Vordruck *m* (Formblatt *n*)	blank form	formulaire *m*
Vordruck *m/typog*	preprinting	pré-impression *f*
Voreingenommenheit *f*	bias, prejudice	parti *m* pris, prévention *f*
Vorführdame *f*	mannequin	démonstratrice *f*, mannequin *m*
vorführen	to demonstrate	montrer
Vorführmann *m*	dressman	mannequin *m* masculin
Vorführung *f*	demonstration, projection, show	démonstration *f*, présentation *f*, projection *f*
Vorgehen *n*	procedure	procédé *m*
vorgeschobene Agentur *f*	house agency	agence *f* fictive
vorgeschriebene Plazierung *f*	prescribed position, stated position	emplacement *m* de rigueur *f*, emplacement *m* imposé
vorgeschriebenes Datum *n*	prescribed date	date *f* de rigueur *f*, date *f* imposée
vorgetäuschtes Interview *n*	fake interview	interview *m* bidon
Vorhangwerbung *f*	theatre curtain advertising	rideau *m* réclame *f*
Vorhersage *f*	forecast	prédiction *f*
Vorhut *f*	pioneers *pl*	avant-garde *f*
Vorläufer *m*	forerunner	précurseur *m*
Vorlage *f*	copy, pattern	dessin *m* au propre, modèle *m*
vorleimen, Plakat *n*	preposting	pré-encollage *m*

vorlesen	to read out	lire qch. à qn.
Vorratskasten *m* (Schrift *f*)	fount case	casseau *m*
Vorrede *f*	introduction	avant-propos *m*
vorrichten	to prepare	découronner
Vorsatzblatt *n*	fly bill, fly sheet	feuille *f* volante, page *f* de garde *f*
Vorschau *f*	pre-view, trailer	avant-première *f*, bande *f* de lancement *m*
Vorschlag *m*	proposition	proposition *f*, suggestion *f*
Vorschlag *m*, unverbindlicher	speculative work	projet *m* gratuit
vorschlagen	to propose, to suggest	proposer, suggérer
Vorschrift *f*	prescription	prescription *f*
Vorspann *m*	credit titles *pl*, generic, trailer	film *m* annonce *f*
vorspringender Titel *m*	shoulder head	titre *m* en ras de marge *f*
Vorstellungsbild *n*	image	image *f*
Vorstellungsbild *n*, gleichbleibendes	stereotype	cliché *m*
Vorstudie *f* ·	pilot study	enquête *f* pilote
Vortest *m*	pretest	préenquête *f*, test *m* préalable
Vortragsveranstaltung *f*	lecture	conférence *f*
Voruntersuchung *f*	pilot study, pretesting	enquête *f* pilote, pré-test *m*, préenquête *f*
Vorurteil *n*	bias, prejudice	préjugé *m*
vorverlegen	to put forward	avancer
Vorwerbung *f*	advance publicity	publicité *f* d'amorçage *m*
Vorwort *n*	preface	préface *f*
vorzeigen	to present, to show	montrer, présenter
Vorzensur *f*	preventive censorship	censure *f* préventive
Vorzugsangebot *n*	premium offer	offre *f* de faveur *f*
Vorzugsbedingungen *f/pl*	preferential terms *pl*	conditions *f/pl* exceptionnelles
Vorzugsplazierung *f*	full position *am*, preferred position, special position	emplacement *m* préférentiel, emplacement *m* spécial, placement *m* de faveur *f*
Vorzugspreis *m*	special rate	prix *m* spécial
Vorzugstarif *m*	preferential tariff	tarif *m* de faveur *f*
Vorzurichtung *f*	pre-makeready	pré-mise *f* en train *m*

W

Wachs *n*	wax	cire *f*
Wachspapier *n*	wax paper	papier *m* ciré
Wahl *f*	choice, election	choix *m*, élection *f*
Wahlaufruf *m*	election proclamation	appel *m* aux urnes *f/pl*
Wahlkampagne *f*, regionale	zone campaign	campagne *f* électorale régionale
Wahlplakat *n*	election poster	affiche *f* électorale
Wahlpropaganda *f*	election propaganda	propagande *f* électorale
Wahlspruch *m*	motto	devise *f*
Walzdruck *m*	cylinder print	impression *f* sur rouleaux *m/pl*
Wandanschlag *m*	notices *pl* on wall	avis *m* placardé
Wandbemalung *f*	painted wall	peinture *f* murale
Wanderausstellung *f*	touring exhibition	exposition *f* ambulante, exposition *f* itinérante
Wanderbühne *f*	travelling theatre	théâtre *m* ambulant
Wanderladen *m*	mobile shop	boutique *f* mobile
Wanderlichtspiele *n/pl*	travelling movie theatre	cinéma *m* ambulant

Wanderschriftnachrichten *f/pl*	illuminated newsband, news by electric sign	information *f* lumineuse, journal *m* lumineux
Wandkalender *m*	wall calender	calendrier *m* mural
Wandschild *n*	wall sign	panneau *m* mural
Wandzeitung *f*	wall newspaper	journal *m* mural
Ware *f*	commodity, goods *pl*	denrée *f*, marchandise *f*
Warenanhäufung *f*	mass-display	entassement *m* de produits *m/pl*, exposition *f* en masse *f*, présentation *f* de masse *f*
Warenanpreisung *f*	sales *pl* talk	boniment *m*
Warenautomat *m*	vending machine	distributeur *m* automatique
Warendarbietung *f*	merchandizing	présentation *f* de la marchandise *f*
Warengestalter *m*	merchandizer	styliste *m* de marchandise *f*
Warengestaltung *f*	merchandizing	conditionnement *m* d'une marchandise *f*, contexture *f* d'un produit *m*
Warenhaus *n*	department store	bazar *m*, grand magasin *m*
Waren *f/pl*, **abgepackte**	packaged goods *pl*	marchandises *f/pl* empaquetées
Warenprobe *f*	sample	échantillon *m*
Warenprobenverteilung *f*	free gift advertising, novelty advertising	publicité *f* par l'objet *m*
Warensortiment *n*	assortment of goods *pl*, line	choix *m* de marchandises *f/pl*
Warenzeichen *n*	brand, make, trade mark	marque *f* de fabrique *f*
Warenzeichen *n*, **eingetragenes**	registered trade mark	marque *f* déposée
Warenzeichenrolle *f*	trademark's register	registre *m* de l'office *m* de la propriété *f* industrielle
Warenzeichenschutz *m*	protection of trademarks *pl*	protection *f* des marques *f/pl*
Wartehäuschenwerbung *f*	poster advertising in shelters *pl*	affichage *m* dans les abris-bus *m/pl*
Wartezeit *f*	waiting time	temps *m* d'attente *f*
Waschzettel *m*	dope, hand-out, press-release, publisher's blurb, publisher's note, slip	brouillon *m*, note *f* de critique *f*, papillon *m*, prière *f* d'insérer
Wasserfarben *f/pl*	water colours *pl*	couleurs *f/pl* pour peinture *f* à l'eau *f*
Wasserfarbzeichnung *f*	water-colour drawing	peinture *f* à l'eau *f*
wasserfest	waterproof	imperméable
Wasserzeichen *n*	water mark	filigrane *m*
Wechsel *m*	bill	lettre *f* de change *m*, traite *f*
wechselnder Text *m*	different text	texte *m* différent
Wechselrahmen *m*	interchangeable frame	cadre *m* interchangeable
Wechselstreuung *f*	staggered schedule	couverture *f* alternée
wegfallen lassen	to cut, to kill	couper, éliminer
weglassen	to omit	omettre
wegstechen	to cut out	fraiser
Wegwerfpackung *f*	one-way package	emballage *m* non consigné, emballage *m* perdu
weibliche Note *f*	female touch	note *f* féminine
weiche Bildüberblendung *f*	to dissolve *am*, to fade over, to mix to *brit*	fondu *m* enchaîné
Weihnachtsnummer *f*	Christmas number	édition *f* de Noël *m*
Weißbuch *n*	white paper	livre *m* blanc
weißer Rand *m*, **äußerer**	outside margin	marge *f* extérieure

weißer Streifen *m* im Satz *m*	river of white	lézarde *f*, ruelle *f*
Weisung *f* abwarten vor Veröffentlichung *f*	to withhold until further notice	à ne pas publier jusqu'à nouvel avis *m*
weite Sichtbarkeit *f*	long approach site	visibilité *f* étendue
Weitergabe *f*	forwarding	transmission *f*
weiterleiten	to transmit	transmettre
Weiterverarbeitung *f*	converting	transformation *f*
weiterverkaufen	to resell	revendre
weitschweifiger Text *m*	padded text	texte *m* délayé
Wellenlänge *f*	wave-length	longueur *f* d'onde *f*
Wellenlinie *f*	wavy line, wavy rule	filet *m* tremblé, ligne *f* tremblée
Wellenrand *m*	ondulated frame	cadre *m* ondulé
Wellpappe *f*	corrugated paste-board, grooved paste-board	carton *m* ondulé
Weltanschauung *f*	ideology, philosophy of life	conception *f* du monde *m*, idéologie *f*
Weltblatt *n*	newspaper of a world-wide reputation	feuille *f* de réputation *f* mondiale
Weltformat *n*	international format	format *m* mondial
Weltmarkt *m*	world market	marché *m* mondial
Weltpresse *f*	world press	presse *f* mondiale
wenden an, sich	to check with	consulter
wenden, Blatt *n*	to turn over the page	tourner la page *f*
Werbeabteilung *f*	advertisement department *brit*, advertising department, publicity department	département *m* de publicité *f*, service *m* de publicité *f*
Werbeadreßbuch *n*	advertising directory	annuaire *m* de publicité *f*, indicateur *m* d'adresses *f/pl* publicitaires
Werbeagentur *f*	advertising agency	agence *f* de publicité *f*
Werbeaktion *f*	advertising activity	action *f* publicitaire, opération *f* publicitaire
Werbeaktion *f*, kombinierte	tie-up advertising	publicité *f* d'association *f*
Werbeaktionen *f/pl* mit Kupons *m/pl*	advertising activities *pl* with coupons *pl*	couponnage *m*
Werbealternative *f*	advertising alternative	alternative *f* publicitaire
Werbeanalyse *f*	advertising analysis	étude *f* de préparation *f* et d'orientation *f* d'une campagne *f* publicitaire
Werbeangelegenheit *f*	advertising affair	affaire *f* publicitaire
Werbeankündigung *f* im Rundfunk *m*	commercial	annonce *f* publicitaire
Werbeanlaß *m*	cause for advertising	motif *m* de publicité *f*
Werbeanstrengungen *f/pl*, verstärkte	advertising efforts *pl*, drive	effort *m* spécial de publicité *f*
Werbeanteil *m*	volume of advertising	volume *m* publicitaire
Werbeantwort *f*	reply mail, return	réponse *f*
Werbeappell *m*	advertising appeal	attrait *m* publicitaire
Werbearbeit *f*	publicity work	travail *m* de publicité *f*
Werbeargument *n*	advertising angle, advertising point	argument *m* de publicité *f*
Werbeart *f*	kind of advertising, type of advertising	genre *m* de publicité *f*, type *m* de publicité *f*
Werbeartikel *m*	advertising novelty	cadeau *m* publicitaire, nouveauté *f* publicitaire
Werbeartikel *m*, geringwertiger	gadget	élément *m* publicitaire de peu de valeur *f*

Werbeassistent *m*	advertising assistant	adjoint *m* au chef *m* de publicité *f*, assistant *m* en publicité *f*
Werbeatelier *n*	commercial studio	studio *m* de publicité *f*
Werbeattacke *f*	advertising attack	attaque *f* publicitaire
Werbeaufschrift *f*	advertising label	suscription *f* publicitaire
Werbeaufsteller *m*	counter card, show card	affiche *f* mobile, pancarte *f*
Werbeaufwendungen *f/pl*	advertising expenditures *pl*, advertising investments *pl*	dépenses *f/pl* publicitaires, investissements *m/pl* en publicité *f*
Werbeausgaben *f/pl*	advertising costs *pl*, advertising outlay	dépenses *f/pl* publicitaires
Werbeauslage *f*	display	étalage *m*
Werbeaussage *f*	advertising message	message *m* publicitaire
Werbeauswüchse *m/pl*	advertising extravagances *pl*	débauches *f/pl* de publicité *f*
Werbeballon *m*	advertising balloon	ballon *m* publicitaire
Werbebauten *m/pl*	display kiosks *pl*	constructions *f/pl* publicitaires
Werbebehauptung *f*	claim	allégation *f* de la publicité *f*, assertion *f* publicitaire
Werbebeilage *f*	advertising supplement	supplément *m* publicitaire encartage *m*
Werbeberater *m*	advertising consultant, advertising counsellor, advertising practitioner	conseil *m* en publicité *f*
Werbeberaterhonorar *n*	service fee	honoraires *m/pl* du conseiller *m*
Werbebereich *m*	advertising area	domaine *m* publicitaire
Werbeberufe *m/pl*	advertising professions *pl*	professions *f/pl* de la publicité *f*
Werbebeschränkungen *f/pl*	advertising limitations *pl*, advertising restrictions *pl*	limitations *f/pl* de la publicité *f*, restrictions *f/pl* de la publicité *f*
Werbebestimmungen *f/pl*	advertising regulations *pl*	réglementations *f/pl* publicitaires
Werbebild *n*	commercial photo	photo *f* publicitaire
Werbebild *n*, **das das Innere** *n* **zeigt**	ghost view	illustration *f* montrant l'intérieur *m*
Werbeblatt *n*	advertising handbill	prospectus *m* publicitaire
Werbeblock *m*	block of advertisements *pl*	tranche *f* de publicité *f*
Werbebotschaft *f*	advertising message	message *m* publicitaire
Werbebotschaft *f*, **unbezahlte**	plug	message *m* publicitaire impayé
Werbebox *f*	advertising box	colonne *f* publicitaire carrée
Werbeboykott *m*	boycotting of advertising media *pl*	boycottage *m* de supports *m/pl* publicitaires
Werbebräuche *m/pl*	advertising practices *pl*	usages *m/pl* publicitaires
Werbebrief *m*	advertising letter, sales *pl* letter	lettre *f* de propagande *f*, lettre *f* de vente *f*, lettre *f* publicitaire
Werbebroschüre *f*	advertising brochure	brochure *f* publicitaire
Werbebudget *n*	advertising appropriation	budget *m* publicitaire
Werbebudgets *m*, **Aufteilung** *f* **des**	assignment of advertising expenditure	allocation *f* du budget *m* publicitaire
Werbebüro *n*	advertising office	agence *f* de publicité *f*
Werbecharakter *m*	advertising complexion	caractère *m* publicitaire
Werbechinesisch *n*	advertising argot	argot *m* publicitaire
Werbedame *f*	demonstrator, mannequin	démonstratrice *f*, mannequin *m*
Werbediapositiv *n*	advertising film slide	diapositif *m* publicitaire

Werbediavorführung f	projection of advertising film slides pl	film-fixe m
Werbedienst m	advertising service	service m de publicité f
Werbedirektor m	advertising director	directeur m de publicité f
Werbedosierung f	advertising dosage	dosage m publicitaire
Werbedrucksache f	advertising matter	imprimé m publicitaire
Werbedrucksache f **mit Antwort** f	self-mailer	imprimé m publicitaire avec carte-réponse f
Werbedrucksachen f/pl **als Beipack** m	envelope stuffers pl	imprimés m/pl publicitaires comme annexes f/pl d'un packetage m
Werbedurchführung f	advertising execution	exécution f de la publicité f
Werbedurchsage f	commercial, radio announcement, spot announcement	annonce f à la radio f, bref communiqué m radio f
Werbeeffekt m	advertising effect	effet m publicitaire
Werbeeinblendung f	chain break, spot announcement	bref communiqué m radio f, insertion f publicitaire, réglage m
Werbeeinnahmen f/pl	advertising revenues pl	recettes f/pl publicitaires
Werbeeinsatz m, **verstärkter**	sales pl drive	effort m marqué, effort m spécial
Werbeeinschaltung f	spot	message m publicitaire
Werbeelement n/pl	interest factor	éléments m/pl d'un moyen m
Werbeentwurf m	advertising design	dessin m publicitaire
Werbeerfahrung f	advertising experience	expérience f publicitaire
Werbeerfolg m	advertising result	rendement m publicitaire
Werbeerfolgskontrolle f	advertising control, advertising effectiveness study	contrôle m du rendement m de la publicité f
Werbeetat m	account, advertising budget, budget, media allocation, publicity stock	budget m publicitaire
Werbeetat m, **bewilligter**	advertising appropriation	budget m alloué de publicité f
Werbeetataufzeichnung f	media allocation	budget m publicitaire
Werbeexemplar n	complimentary copy	numéro m de propagande f
Werbefachblatt n	advertising paper	journal m de publicité f
Werbefachmann m	adman, advertising expert, advertising man	expert m en publicité f, publicitaire m, spécialiste m de la publicité f, technicien de publicité f
Werbefachschule f	advertising trade school	école f de publicité f
Werbefachverband m	advertising association	association f de publicité f
Werbefachzeitschrift f	advertising magazine	revue f de publicité f
Werbefahrt f	publicity tour	tournée f de propagande f
Werbefaktoren m/pl	advertising factors pl	éléments m/pl publicitaires
Werbefaltblatt n	booklet	brochure f
Werbefaltblatt n **für Spezialauslage** f	rack folder	dépliant m publicitaire pour étalage m spécial
Werbefeindlichkeit f	antipathy to advertising	publiphobie f
Werbefeldzug m	advertising campaign	campagne f publicitaire
Werbefeldzug m **durch Plakatanschlag** m	poster campaign	campagne f d'affichage m
Werbefeldzug m, **überregionaler**	general advertising, national campaign	campagne f nationale
Werbefernsehen n	television advertising	télévision f commerciale
Werbefernsehen n, **privates**	independent television	télévision f privée

Werbefiguren *f/pl*, aufblasbare	inflatable advertising figures *pl*	figures *f/pl* de publicité *f* gonflables
Werbefilm *m*	advertising film, commercial picture, publicity film	film *m* publicitaire
Werbefilm *m*, kurzer	minute movie, quickie	court-métrage *m*
Werbefilm *m* mit Händler-adresse *f*	open end commercial	film *m* publicitaire avec adresse *f* du détaillant *m*
Werbefilmlänge *f*	length of the advertising film	métrage *m*
Werbefilmproduzent *m*	producer of advertising films *pl*	producteur *m* de films *m/pl* publicitaires
Werbefirma *f*	advertising contractor	entreprise *f* de publicité *f*
Werbefläche *f*	advertising space	panneau *m* de publicité *f*, surface *f* d'affichage *m*
Werbefläche *f*, angestrahlte	floodlight advertisement	publicité *f* éclairée
Werbefläche *f*, auswechselbare	portable panel	panneau *m* transportable
Werbefläche *f* mit Beleuchtung *f*	semi-spectacular	panneau *m* d'affichage *m* avec l'addition *f* d'éclairage *m*
Werbefläche *f*, versetzbare	rotating bulletin	bulletin *m* transférable
Werbeflächengruppe *f*	poster showing	circuit *m* indivisible d'emplacements *m/pl*, réseau *m*
Werbeflächenpächter *m*	advertising franchise operator	concessionaire *m* en publicité *f*, régisseur *m*
Werbeflugblatt *n*	broadsheet	in-plano *m*
Werbeflugzeug *n*	advertising aeroplane	avion *m* publicitaire
Werbefonds *m*	advertising stocks *pl*	fonds *m* de publicité *f*
Werbeformen *f/pl*	forms *pl* of advertising	façons *f/pl* publicitaires
Werbeforschung *f*	advertising research	recherches *f/pl* relatives à la publicité *f*
Werbefoto *n*	commercial photo	photo *f* publicitaire
Werbefunk *m*	commercial broadcasting, commercial radio	émission *f* publicitaire, publicité *f* radiophonique
Werbefunktion *f*	advertising functions *pl*	fonction *f* publicitaire
Werbefunkvertreter *m*	station rep	représentant *m* de radiodiffusion *f* publicitaire
Werbegabe *f*	advertising donation, advertising gift, free gift	cadeau *m* publicitaire
Werbegebühren *f/pl*	advertising rates *pl*	frais *m/pl* de publicité *f*
Werbegelegenheit *f*	advertising facilities *pl*	occasion *f* de faire de la publicité *f*
Werbegeräte *n/pl*	advertising utensils *pl*	accessoires *m/pl* publicitaires
Werbegeschäft *n*	advertising trade	activité *f* publicitaire
Werbegeschenk *n*	advertising gift, free gift, specialty	cadeau *m* publicitaire, prime *f*
Werbegeschenkartikel *m*	novelty	article *m* prime *f*
Werbegesellschaft *f*	advertising company	entreprise *f* publicitaire
Werbegesetz *n*	advertising law	loi *f* publicitaire
Werbegesetzgebung *f*	advertising legislation	législation *f* de la publicité *f*
Werbegesichtswinkel *m*	advertising angle, advertising approach	axe *m* de la publicité *f*
Werbegespräch *n*	advertising talk	discours *m* publicitaire
Werbegestalter *m*	art designer	dessinateur *m*
Werbegestaltung *f*	advertising conception, creative copy and artwork	conception *f* publicitaire

Werbegrafik *f*	advertising art, commercial art	art *m* commercial, créations *f/pl* graphiques
Werbegrafiker *m*	advertising artist, advertising designer	artiste *m* en publicité *f*, dessinateur *m* publicitaire
Werbegroßanlage *f*	spectacular	installation *f* spectaculaire
Werbegrundaussage *f*	basic message	axe *m* de la publicité *f*
Werbegrundsätze *m/pl*	advertising principles *pl*	principes *m/pl* publicitaires
Werbehaushalt *m*	advertising appropriation	budget *m* de publicité *f*
Werbeidee *f*	advertising idea	idée *f* publicitaire
Werbeindustrie *f*	advertising industry	industrie *f* publicitaire
Werbeinhalt *m*	advertising contents *pl*	contenu *m* de la publicité *f*
Werbeinschrift *f*	advertising inscription	inscription *f* publicitaire
Werbeinstruktionsfilm *m*	demonstrational film	film *m* de démonstration *f*
Werbeinstrument *n*	advertising medium	outil *m* de propagande *f*
Werbeintensität *f*	advertising intensity	intensité *f* de la publicité *f*
Werbeintensivierung *f*	advertising accumulation	augmentation *f* de publicité *f*
Werbeinvestitionen *f/pl*	advertising investments *pl*	investissements *m/pl* en publicité *f*
Werbejargon *m*	advertising argot	argot *m* publicitaire
Werbejournal *n*	advertising journal	illustré *m* publicitaire
Werbekampagne *f*	advertising campaign	campagne *f* de publicité *f*
Werbekampagne *f* **für verschiedene Arten** *f/pl* **eines Produkts** *m*	umbrella-campaign	campagne *f* pour des sortes *f/pl* différentes d'un produit *m*
Werbekampagne *f*, **gegenwärtig laufende**	current advertising	publicité *f* courante
Werbekampagne *f*, **langfristig geplante**	pre-planned advertising campaign	campagne *f* à longue échéance *f*
Werbekarawane *f*	caravan advertising	caravane *f* publicitaire
Werbeklub *f*	advertising club	club *m* de publicité *f*
Werbekolonne *f*	group of solicitors *pl*, team of canvassers *pl*	équipe *f* de courtiers *m/pl*
Werbekonstante *f*	advertising constant	constante *f* publicitaire
Werbekontakte *m/pl*	advertising impressions *pl*	contacts *m/pl* publicitaires
Werbekontrolle *f*	advertising control	contrôle *m* de la publicité *f*
Werbekonzeption *f*	advertising conception	conception *f* publicitaire
Werbekosten *pl*	advertising expenses *pl*, costs *pl* of advertising	dépenses *f/pl* publicitaires, frais *m/pl* de publicité *f*
Werbekostenanweisung *f*	allocation	allocation *f*, lotissement *m* publicitaire
Werbekraft *f*	pulling power, selling power	puissance *f* publicitaire
Werbekreation *f*	advertising creation	création *f* publicitaire
Werbekunst *f*	advertising art	art *m* publicitaire
Werbekurzfilm *m*	advertising filmlet	film *m* publicitaire court métrage *m*
Werbekurzspiel *n*	advertising sketch	scène *f* publicitaire
Werbeleistung *f*	advertising performance	rendement *m* publicitaire
Werbeleiter *m*	advertising manager	chef *m* de publicité *f* d'annonceur *m*, directeur *m* publicitaire
Werbeleiter *m* **eines Werbeträgers** *m*	advertisement manager	chef *m* de publicité *f* de support *m* publicitaire
Werbeliteratur *f*	advertising literature	éditions *f/pl* publicitaires, littérature *f* publicitaire
Werbemaßnahmen *f/pl*	advertising measures *pl*	efforts *m/pl* publicitaires, mesures *f/pl* publicitaires
Werbemast *m*	advertising mast	mât *m* publicitaire

Werbematerial *n*	advertising aids *pl*, advertising material	matériel *m* de publicité *f*
Werbemethoden *f/pl*	publicity methods *pl*	mèthodes *f/pl* publicitaires
Werbemethodik *f*	advertising methodology	méthodologie *f* publicitaire
Werbemittel *n*	advertising medium	moyen *m* de publicité *f*
Werbemittel *n/pl*, **aus Kunststoff** *m*	plastic media *pl*	moyens *m/pl* publicitaires synthétiques
Werbemittel *n/pl*, **genehmigte**	appropriation of advertising	budget *m* publicitaire
Werbemittel *n/pl*, **zusätzliche**	collateral media *pl*	médias *m/pl* additionnels
Werbemittelausstattung *f*	advertising medium outfit	équipement *m* d'un moyen *m* publicitaire
Werbemittelerinnerung *f*	advertising media recall	souvenir *m* de moyens *m/pl* publicitaires
Werbemittelgestaltung *f*	creation of ads *pl*	création *f* des moyens *m/pl* de publicité *f*
Werbemittelherstellung *f*	media *pl* production	production *f* des moyens *m/pl* de publicité *f*
Werbemittelkombination *f*	media mix	combinaison *f* des médias *m/pl*
Werbemöglichkeiten *f/pl*	advertising facilities *pl*, advertising horizons *pl*, possibilities *pl* of advertising	possibilités *f/pl* de publicité *f*
Werbemotiv *n*	advertising motif	motif *m* publicitaire
Werbemotto *n*	advertising device, advertising motto	devise *f* publicitaire, slogan *m* publicitaire
Werbemüdigkeit *f*	oversaturation with advertising	saturation *f* publicitaire
Werbemusik *f*	music in advertising	publicité *f* musicale
Werbemuster *n*	advertising sample	échantillon *m* publicitaire
werben	to advertise	faire de la publicité *f*
Werbenachricht *f*	advertising news	échos *m/pl* publicitaires
Werbeneuheit *f*	advertising novelty	nouveauté *f* publicitaire
Werbenummer *f*	complimentary copy, publicity copy	numéro *m* de propagande *f*
Werbeobjekt *n*	advertising object	objet *m* publicitaire
Werbeorientierung *f*	advertising orientation	orientation *f* publicitaire
Werbepächter *m*	advertising operator	concessionaire *m*, exploitant *m* de la publicité *f*, régisseur *m*, société *f* d'affermage *m*
Werbepause *f*	hiatus	lacune *f* dans la publicité *f*
Werbepavillon *m*	advertising pavilion	pavillon *m* de publicité *f*
Werbeperiode *f*	advertising period	période *f* publicitaire
Werbephonetiker *m*	advertising phonetician	phonéticien *m* publicitaire
Werbepionier *m*	pioneer in advertising	pionnier *m* publicitaire
Werbeplakat *n* **in Verkehrsmitteln** *n/pl*	car card advertising	affichette *f* d'autobus *m* ou de tramway *m*
Werbeplan *m*	advertising programme *brit*, advertising program *am*, advertising schedule, campaign plan	plan *m* de campagne *f*, plan *m* de publicité *f*, plan *m* publicitaire
Werbeplanung *f*	account planning, advertising planning	planning *m* publicitaire
Werbeplattform *f*	copy platform, unique selling proposition	axe *f* de la publicité *f*
Werbepolitik *f*	advertising policy	politique *f* publicitaire
Werbeprämie *f*	premium	prime *f*
Werbepraktiker *m*	practitioner in advertising	praticien *m* de la publicité *f*
Werbepraxis *f*	advertising practise	pratique *f* publicitaire
Werbepreis *m*	knock down price	prix *m* de réclame *f*

Werbepreisausschreiben *n*	advertising contest	compétition *f* publicitaire
Werbepression *f*	advertising pressure	pression *f* publicitaire
Werbeproblem *n*	advertising problem	problème *m* publicitaire
Werbeprogramm *n*	advertising program *am*, advertising programme *brit*	programme *m* de la publicité *f*
Werbeprospekt *m*	advertising leaflet	dépliant *m* publicitaire
Werbepsychologie *f*	advertising psychology	psychologie *f* de la publicité *f*
Werbepublikation *f*	advertising publication	édition *f* publicitaire
Werbepylon *m*	advertising pylon	pylône *m* publicitaire
Werber *m*	propagandist	propagandiste *m*
Werberatschlag *m*	advertising guide	guide *m* publicitaire
Werberecht *n*	advertising law	droit *m* publicitaire
Werberegelung *f*	regulation of advertising	réglementation *f* de la publicité *f*
Werbereserve *f*	advertising reserve	réserve *f* pour la publicité *f*
Werberesultat *n*	results *pl* of advertising	résultat *m* de la publicité *f*
Werberisiko *n*	risks *pl* of advertising	risques *m/pl* de publicité *f*
Werberummel *m*	ballyhoo *am*, hoopla, noisy advertising, puffing publicity	battage *m* publicitaire, publicité *f* raccrocheuse, publicité *f* tapageuse, tam-tam *m*
Werberundschreiben *n*	advertising circular	circulaire *m* publicitaire
Werbesache *f* **mit Rückantwort** *f*	self-mailer	imprimé *m* publicitaire avec carte *f*-réponse *f*
Werbesachverständiger *m*	advertising expert	expert *m* en publicité *f*
Werbesäule *f*	advertising pillar	colonne *f* publicitaire
Werbeschild *n*	billboard, sign	enseigne *f* publicitaire, panneau *m* d'affichage *m*, panonceau *m*, plaque *f* publicitaire
Werbeschild *n* **am Verdeck** *m*	awning	store *m*
Werbeschild *n* **mit Vertikalschrift** *f*	vertical sign	enseigne *f* verticale
Werbeschlagwort *n*	slogan	slogan *m*
Werbeschreiben *n*	sales *pl* letter	lettre *f* publicitaire
Werbeschrift *f*	advertising pamphlet	brochure *f* publicitaire
Werbesektor *m*	advertising sector	secteur *m* publicitaire
Werbesendung *f*	commercial	émission *f* publicitaire
Werbesendung *f* **für Nebenprodukte** *n/pl*	hitch-hike	émission *f* publicitaire pour des sous-produits *m/pl*
Werbesendung *f* **für zwei verschiedene Produkte** *m/pl* **eines Werbungtreibenden**	piggyback	émission *f* pour deux produits *m/pl* d'un annonceur *m*
Werbesendung *f* **zur gleichbleibenden Tageszeit** *f* **an 5 aufeinanderfolgenden Tagen** *m/pl*	across the board	émission *f* quotidienne sauf samedi *m* et dimanche *m*
Werbesendungen *f/pl*, **Tarif** *m* **für**	time charge	tarif *m* de la publicité *f* radiophonique
Werbeserie *f* **in ständiger Wiederholung** *f* **mit gleichem Rhythmus** *m*	rotation	succession *f* de publicité *f* par répétition *f* permanente avec un rythme *m* invariable
Werbesilhouette *f*	sky sign	publicité *f* se découpant sur le ciel *m*
Werbesketch *m*	advertising sketch	sketch *m* publicitaire
Werbeslogan *m*	advertising slogan	slogan *m* publicitaire
Werbespezialisten *m/pl*	hot shops *pl*	spécialistes *m/pl* de publicité *f*

Werbespot *m*	broadcast announcement, commercial, spot announcement, quickie	annonce *f* radiodiffusée, court-métrage *m* publicitaire, message *m* publicitaire, spot *m*, spot *m* court
Werbespot *pl* **in unmittelbarer Nachbarschaft** *f* **einer besonderen Sendung** *f*	adjacencies *pl*	spots *m/pl* dans le voisinage *m* immédiat d'une émission *f* spécifique
Werbesprache *f*	advertising language	langue *f* de la publicité *f*
Werbespruch *m*	advertising slogan, catch line, catch phrase	formule *f* publicitaire, phrase *f* d'accrochage *m*
Werbestatistik *f*	advertising statistics *pl*	statistiques *f/pl* de publicité *f*
Werbestelle *f*	official publicity bureau	office *m* de publicité *f*
Werbesteuer *f*	advertising tax	impôt *m* sur la publicité *f*
Werbestil *m*	graphic design	style *m* de publicité *f*
Werbestrategie *f*	advertising strategy	stratégie *f* publicitaire
Werbestreuung *f*	advertising dispersion	prospection *f* publicitaire
Werbestudio *n*	advertising studio	studio *m* publicitaire
Werbesystem *n*	advertising system	système *m* publicitaire
Werbetätigkeit *f*	advertising activity, propaganda	activité *f* publicitaire, propagande *f*
Werbetafel *f*	poster hoarding	panneau-réclame *f*
Werbetaktik *f*	advertising tactics *pl*	tactique *f* publicitaire
Werbetechnik *f*	advertising technique	technique *f* publicitaire
Werbeterminologie *f*	advertising terminology	terminologie *f* publicitaire
Werbetext *m*	advertising text, copy	texte *m* publicitaire
Werbetext *m,* **außergewöhnlicher**	creative copy	texte *m* publicitaire extraordinaire
Werbetextabfassung *f*	advertising copywriting	rédaction *f* d'annonces *f/pl*
Werbetexter *m*	copy-writer	concepteur-rédacteur *m,* rédacteur *m* publicitaire
Werbetextidee *f*	story	histoire *f* du texte *m*
Werbethema *n*	advertising theme	sujet *m* publicitaire
Werbetheorie *f*	theory of advertising	théorie *f* de la publicité *f*
Werbethermometer *n*	advertising thermometer	thermomètre *m* publicitaire
Werbetournee *f*	advertising tour	tournée *f* publicitaire
Werbeträger *m*	advertising medium, advertising vehicle, means *pl* of advertising	organe *m* de publicité *f,* support *m* publicitaire, véhicule *m* de communication *f*
Werbeträgeranalyse *f*	media analysis	analyse *f* des médias *m/pl*
Werbeträgerart *f*	type of medium	genre *m* de support *m*
Werbeträgerbewertung *f*	media evaluation	évaluation *f* des médias *m/pl*
Werbeträgereinsatz *m*	media performance	accomplissement *m* publicitaire
Werbeträgerforschung *f*	media research, media survey	étude *f* des médias *m/pl*
Werbeträgerkombination *f*	media mix	combinaison *f* des médias *m/pl*
Werbeträgerkontakt *m*	media contact, opportunity to see	contact *m* au média *m*
Werbeträger *m/pl,* **obligatorische**	obligatory media *pl*	médias *m/pl* obligatoires
Werbetransaktionen *f/pl*	advertising transactions *pl*	opérations *f/pl* publicitaires
Werbetrick *m*	advertising gimmick	artifice *m* publicitaire
die **Werbetrommel** *f* **rühren**	to boost, to make propaganda, to push	battre la grosse caisse *f*
Werbeturm *m*	advertising pylon, advertising tower	pylône *m* publicitaire, tour *f* publicitaire

Werbeübertreibung f	puff advertising	outrance f publicitaire
Werbeumsätze m/pl	advertising turnover	chiffre m d'affaires f/pl publicitaires
Werbeunkosten pl	advertising expenses pl	frais m/pl de publicité f
Werbeunterlagen f/pl	promotional material	documents m/pl publicitaires
Werbeunternehmen n	advertising contractor, advertising enterprise	entreprise f de publicité f
Werbeunterstützung f	advertising support	support m publicitaire
Werbeusancen f/pl	advertising practices pl	usages m/pl publicitaires
Werbeveranstaltung f	publicity event	manifestation f publicitaire
Werbeverband m	advertising association	association f de publicité f
Werbeverbot n	prohibition to advertise	défense f de faire de la publicité f
Werbeverkauf m	bargain sale	vente f réclame
Werbevers m	advertising verse	vers m publicitaire
Werbeverwaltung f	advertising operator	concessionaire m de publicité f
Werbeverwaltung f **von Kinos** n/pl	operator of advertising films pl	concessionaire m de salle f
Werbevitrine f	advertising showcase	vitrine f publicitaire
Werbevolumen n	advertising volume	volume m de la publicité f
Werbevorbereitung f	advertising preparations pl	préparatifs m/pl publicitaires
Werbevorschlag m	advertising proposal	proposition f publicitaire
Werbevortest m	pre-test	pré-test m
Werbevortrag m	advertising discussion	discours m publicitaire
Werbewaffe f	advertising weapon	arme f publicitaire
Werbewagen m	advertising van	camionette f publicitaire
Werbewert m	advertising value	valeur f publicitaire
Werbewesen n	publicity	publicité f
Werbewettbewerb m	advertising competition, advertising contest	concours m publicitaire
Werbewimpel m	pennant, streamer	banderole f, fanion m, flamme f
werbewirksam	effective in advertising	d'un bon rendement m publicitaire
werbewirksamer Filmschlußteil m	pay off	partie f finale efficace d'un film m
Werbewirksamkeit f	advertising effectiveness, advertising efficiency	efficacité f de la publicité f
Werbewirkung f	advertising effect, impact	effet m publicitaire
Werbewirtschaft f	advertising business	métier m publicitaire
Werbewissenschaft f	advertising science	science f de la publicité f
Werbewoche f	propaganda week	semaine f de propagande f
Werbezeichner m	advertising artist	dessinateur m publicitaire
Werbezeichnung f	advertising drawing	dessin m publicitaire
Werbezeitenblöcke m/pl	periods pl of commercial emissions pl	tranches f/pl horaires
Werbezeiteneinkäufer m	time buyer	acheteur m de temps m d'antenne f
Werbezeiten f/pl **in Rundfunk** m **und Fernsehen** n	availabilities pl in radio and television	temps m d'antenne f disponible
Werbezeitenreservierung f	to clear time	réservation f de temps m d'antenne f
Werbezensur f	advertising censorship	censure f de la publicité f
Werbeziele n/pl	advertising objectives pl	objectifs m/pl publicitaires
Werbezuschuß m	advertising allowance	allocation f publicitaire
Werbezwecke m/pl	advertising purposes pl	fins f/pl de publicité f
werblich	advertising	publicitaire

werbliche Postaussendung *f*	mailing	publipostage *m*
werbliche Übersättigung *f*	saturation with advertising	saturation *f* publicitaire
werblicher Erfahrungsschatz *m*	advertising record	expérience *f* publicitaire
werblicher Gesichtspunkt *m*	advertising angle	angle *m* d'approche *f* publicitaire
Werbung *f*	advertising, publicity	propagande *f*, publicité *f*, réclame *f*
Werbung *f*, aggressive	competitive copy *am*, disparaging copy, hard approach, knocking copy *brit*	publicité *f* agressive
Werbung *f*, akustische	acoustic advertising	publicité *f* acoustique
Werbung *f* am Kaufort *m*	point-of-purchase advertising	publicité *f* au point *m* d'achat *m*
Werbung *f* am Verkaufspunkt *m*	advertising on the point of sale	publicité *f* sur le lieu *m* de vente *f*
Werbung *f*, anmaßende	insolent advertising	publicité *f* envahissante
Werbung *f*, anreißerische	puffing publicity	publicité *f* raccrocheuse
Werbung *f*, ansprechende	appealing advertising	publicité *f* attrayante
Werbung *f*, anstößige	indecent advertising	publicité *f* indécente
Werbung *f*, antizyklische	anticyclic advertising	publicité *f* anticyclique
Werbung *f*, audiovisuelle	audio-visual advertising	publicité *f* audio-visuelle
Werbung *f* auf dem Dach *n*	sky sign	publicité *f* dans le ciel *m*
Werbung *f* auf Packungen *f/pl*	package advertising	publicité *f* sur l'emballage *m*
Werbung *f*, aufeinander abgestimmte	coordinated advertising	publicité *f* coordonnée
Werbung *f*, ausgewählte	selective advertising	publicité *f* sélective
Werbung *f*, begleitende	accessory advertising	publicité *f* de complément *m*
Werbung *f*, begründende	reason-why advertising	publicité *f* argumentée
Werbung *f*, belehrende	educational advertising	publicité *f* éducative
Werbung *f*, betrügerische	deceptive advertising	publicité *f* déceptive, publicité *f* mensongère
Werbung *f*, bewegliche	mechanical advertising	publicité *f* mobile
Werbung *f*, bezahlte	paid advertising	publicite *f* payée
Werbung *f* der Vergnügungsbranche *f*	entertainment advertising	publicité *f* spectacles *m/pl*
Werbung *f* des Einzelhandels *m*	retail advertising	publicité *f* des détaillants *m/pl*
Werbung *f*, einführende	original advertising	publicité *f* de lancement *m*
Werbung *f*, eingeblendete	tie-in advertising	publicité *f* enchaînée
Werbung *f*, einträgliche	lucrative advertising	publicité *f* rentable
Werbung *f*, einwandfreie	clean advertising	publicité *f* impeccable, publicité *f* irréprochable
Werbung *f*, elektronische	electronical advertising	publicité *f* électronique
Werbung *f*, erzieherische	educational advertising	publicité *f* éducative
Werbung *f*, ethische	ethical advertising	publicité *f* éthique
Werbung *f*, falsch angesetzte	misplaced advertising	publicité *f* déplacée
Werbung *f*, firmenbetonte	institutional advertising	publicité *f* institutionnelle
Werbung *f*, fortschrittliche	progressive advertising	publicité *f* moderne
Werbung *f*, fremdsprachliche	advertising in foreign language	publicité *f* en langue *f* étrangère
Werbung *f* für den Freizeitbereich *m*	leisure time publicity	publicité *f* du domaine *m* des loisirs *m/pl*
Werbung *f*, geballte	mass advertising	campagne *f* de saturation *f*
Werbung *f*, gefühlsbetonte	emotional advertising	publicité *f* émotive
Werbung *f*, gemeinsame	co-operative advertising	publicité *f* commune
Werbung *f*, gezielte	selective advertising	publicité *f* sélective
Werbung *f*, großzügige	large-scale advertising	publicité *f* de grand style *m*
Werbung *f*, gut aufgezogene	well-organized advertising	publicité *f* bien organisée

Werbung f, herabsetzende	competitive copy am, disparaging copy, knocking copy brit	publicité f agressive, publicité f discriminatoire
Werbung f, hochtönende	high-pressure advertising	publicité f emphatique
Werbung f, holografische	holographic advertising	publicité f holographique
Werbung f im Verkehr m, Medien m/pl der	traffic media	médias m/pl de la publicité f dans les moyens m/pl de transport m
Werbung f in Fahrzeugen n/pl	vehicular advertising	publicité f sur ou dans véhicules f/pl de transport m
Werbung f in gedruckten Medien n/pl	print advertising	publicité f dans des médias m/pl imprimés
Werbung f, indirekte	indirect advertising	publicité f indirecte
Werbung f, informierende	informatory advertising, product advertising	publicité f informative, publicité f instructive
Werbung f, institutionelle	corporate advertising, good-will advertising, institutional advertising	publicité f de notoriété f, publicité f de prestige m, publicité f institutionnelle
Werbung f, irreführende	deceptive advertising, misleading advertising	publicité f déloyale, publicité f fallacieuse
Werbung f, kindbezogene	kid appeal advertising	publicité f relative à l'enfant m
Werbung f, kombinierte	co-op advertising	publicité f combinée
Werbung f, koordinierte	coordinated advertising	publicité f coordonnée
Werbung f, kostenlose redaktionelle	free puff	gracieuseté f
Werbung f, kostspielige	expensive advertising	publicité f coûteuse
Werbung f, künstlerische	artistic advertising	publicité f artistique
Werbung f, leise	soft approach	publicité f en douceur f
Werbung f, lügnerische	lying advertising	publicité f mensongère
Werbung f, marktschreierische	ballyhoo am, noisy advertising, puffing publicity	battage m publicitaire, bourrage m de crâne m, publicité f raccrocheuse, publicité f tapageuse, tam-tam m
Werbung f, mechanische	mechanical advertising	publicité f mécanique
Werbung f, mehrgleisige	split run advertising	publicité f à plusieurs voies f/pl
Werbung f mit Kennziffern f/pl	keyed advertising	publicité f sous chiffre m
Werbung f, mündliche	advertising by word of mouth	propagande f de bouche f à oreille f, publicité f parlante
Werbung f, musikalische	jingle	refrain m radiophonique, ritournelle f publicitaire, tintement m
Werbung f, nachdrückliche	vigorous advertising	publicité f vigoureuse
Werbung f, örtliche	local campaign	campagne f locale
Werbung f, personalisierte	personalized sales pl technique	publicité f personnalisée
Werbung f, produktbezogene	product advertising	publicité f relative au produit m
Werbung f, redaktionelle	editorial publicity, free puff, write-up am	annonce f rédactionnelle, publicité f rédactionnelle gratuite
Werbung f, rollende	rolling advertising	publicité f roulante
Werbung f, scheinwissenschaftliche	pseudoscientific advertising	publicité f pseudo-scientifique
Werbung f, scherzhafte	jesting advertising	publicité f humoristique
Werbung f, schwungvolle	dynamic advertising	publicité f pleine d'élan m
Werbung f, selektive	selective advertising	publicité f sélective
Werbung f, sensationelle	gimmick, stunt advertising	coup m, truc m
Werbung f, starke	substantial advertising	publicité f substantielle

Werbung *f*, täuschende	misleading advertising	publicité *f* trompeuse
Werbung *f*, trügerische	false advertising	publicité *f* trompeuse
Werbung *f*, überregionale	nation-wide advertising	publicité *f* nationale
Werbung *f*, überzeugende	persuasive advertising	publicité *f* persuasive
Werbung *f*, umfangreiche	substantial advertising	publicité *f* volumineuse
Werbung *f*, unehrenhafte	dishonest advertising	publicité *f* déloyale
Werbung *f*, unerlaubte	illicit advertising	publicité *f* illicite
Werbung *f*, ungewöhnliche	original advertising	publicité *f* originale
Werbung *f*, ungezielte	non-selective advertising	publicité *f* non-sélective
Werbung *f*, unterschwellige	subliminal advertising	publicité *f* insidieuse, publicité *f* subliminale
Werbung *f*, unterstützende	auxiliary advertising	publicité *f* auxiliaire
Werbung *f*, unzulängliche	inadequate advertising	publicité *f* inadéquate
Werbung *f*, unzulässige	forbidden advertising	publicité *f* interdite
Werbung *f*, vergleichende	comparative advertising	publicité *f* discriminatoire
Werbung *f*, vernünftige	rational advertising	publicité *f* rationnelle
Werbung *f*, wirksame	effective advertising	publicité *f* efficace
Werbung *f*, wissenschaftliche	scientific advertising	publicité *f* scientifique
Werbung *f*, zielbewußte	systematic advertising	publicité *f* systématique
Werbung *f*, zudringliche	obtrusive advertising	publicité *f* obsessionnelle
Werbung *f*, zugkräftige	attractive advertising, audience builder	numéro *m* à succès *m*, publicité *f* attractive
Werbung *f*, zulässige	admissible advertising	publicité *f* autorisée
Werbung *f*, zusätzliche	accessory advertising, auxiliary advertising, supplementary advertising	publicité *f* auxiliaire, publicité *f* de complément *m*, publicité *f* de soutien *m*
Werbung *f*, zyklische	cyclic advertising	publicité *f* cyclique
Werbungskosten *pl*	publicity expenses *pl*	frais *m/pl* de publicité *f*
Werbungsmittler *m*	advertising contractor, advertising intermediary, space broker	acheteur *m* d'espace *m*, courtier *m* de publicité *f*, intermédiaire *m* publicitaire
Werbungsmittler *m*, anerkannter	recognised advertising agency	agence *f* de publicité *f* reconnue
Werbungtreibender *m*	advertiser	annonceur *m*, entreprise *f* annonceuse
Werkdruck *m*	book printing	impression *f* pour éditions *f/pl*
Werkdruckpapier *n*	antique weave paper, book paper	papier *m* d'œuvre *f*
Werkfilm *m*	industrial film	film *m* industriel
Werksatz *m*	book work, text matter	composition *f* de labeurs *m/pl*, composition *f* d'œuvre *f*
Werkstatt *f*	workshop	atelier *m*
Werkstoff *m*	raw material	matériaux *m/pl*
Werkzeitschrift *f*	house journal, staff magazine	journal *m* d'entreprise *f*
Wertgutschein *m*	gift coupon	coupon *m* pour primes *f/pl*
wertloser Hinweis *m*	bum steer	faux tuyau *m*
Wertreklame *f*	free gift advertising	objet-réclame *f*
Werturteil *n*	value judgment	jugement *m* de valeur *f*
Wesensmerkmal *n*	characteristic , feature	caractéristique *f*
Wettbewerb *m*	competition, contest	concours *m*
Wettbewerb *m*, fairer	fair competition	concurrence *f* loyale
Wettbewerb *m*, unlauterer	unfair competition	concurrence *f* déloyale
Wettbewerber *m*	competitor	concurrent *m*
Wettbewerbsbedingungen *f/pl*	competitive conditions *pl*	conditions *f/pl* de concours *m*
Wettbewerbsbeschränkung *f*	reduction of competition	restriction *f* à la concurrence *f*

Wettbewerbsklausel *f*	restraining clause	clause *f* restrictive
Wettbewerbsunternehmen *n*	rival business	entreprise *f* compétitive
Wettbewerbsverzerrung *f*	distortion of competition, falsification of competition	distorsion *f* de la concurrence *f*
Wettbewerbszeitung *f*	rival newspaper	journal *m* concurrentiel
Wetterbericht *m*	weather-forecast, weather-report	bulletin *m* du temps *m*, grenouille *f*, météo *f*
Wetterbeständigkeit *f*	weather resistance	résistance *f* aux intempéries *f/pl*
Wetterkarte *f*	weather-chart	carte *f* du temps *m*
Wettervorhersage *f*	weather-forecast	prévisions *f/pl* météorologiques
Wickelfalz *m*	parallel folding	pli *m* en portefeuille *m*
Widerdruck *m*	backing up, perfecting, second printing, verso printing	impression *f* au verso *n*, retiration *f*, seconde forme *f*
Widerhall *m*	impact, response	pouvoir *m* de choc *m*, retentissement *m*
widerhallender Ton *m*	resounding	son *m* réverbéré
Widerruf *m*, **Auftrag** *m* **auf**	open order, until cancelled order	ordre *m* valable jusqu'à révocation *f*
Widerruf *m*, **bis auf**	till forbid, until cancelled order	jusqu'à nouvel ordre *m*
widerstandsfähiges Papier *n*	paper with some substance	papier *m* de la main *f*
Widerstandsfähigkeit *f*	tear ratio	degré *m* de résistance *f*
Widmung *f*	dedication	dédicace *f*
Widmung *f* **versehene Ausgabe** *f*, **mit einer**	presentation copy	exemplaire *m* dédicacé
Wiederabdruck *m*	new impression, reprint	réimpression *f*
Wiederaufführung *f*	reprise	reprise *f*
Wiedererkennungstest *m*	recognition test	étude *f* d'identification *f*
Wiedererlangung *f*	recovery	récupération *f*
Wiedergabe *f*	reproduction	reproduction *f*
Wiedergabe *f* **einer Tonaufnahme** *f*	play back	faire repasser la bande *f*, lecture *f* sonore
Wiedergabe *f*, **naturgetreue**	high fidelity	haute fidélité *f*
Wiedergabegerät *n*	recorder	appareil *m* enregistreur
wiedergeben	to render, to reproduce	rendre
wiederholte Konsumentenansprache *f*	repeataudience	appel *m* renouvelé aux consommateurs *m/pl*
Wiederholung *f*	duplication, repetition	double emploi *m*, répétition *f*
Wiederholung *f* **einer Anzeigenserie** *f*	rotation	répétition *f* d'une série *f* d'annonces *f/pl*
Wiederholung *f*, **ständige**	reiteration	réiteration *f*
Wiederholungsanzeige *f*	repeat ad, rerun, run-it-again	annonce *f* de répétition *f*, annonce *f* répétée plusieurs fois *f*, ré-insertion *f*
Wiederholungsbesuch *m*	call-back	visite *f* répétée
Wiederholungsrabatt *m*	series *pl* discount	jeu *m* de dégressifs *m/pl*
wiederkehrendes Anzeigenelement *n*	standing detail	détail *m* permanent
Wiederverfilmung *f*	remake	refaçon *m* d'un film *m*
Wiederverkäufer *m*	dealer, retailer	revendeur *m*
Wiedervermarktung *f*	repackage	conditionnement *m* nouveau
wiederverwendbare Packung *f*	re-use package	emballage *m* à double usage *m*, emballage *m* de remploi *m*
Wildanschlag *m*	fly posting, sniping	affichage *m* à la sauvette *f*, affichage *m* volant, pose *f* libre

Wildwestfilm *m*	western	western *m*
willkürlich ausgewählter Personenkreis *m*	chunk	audience *f* choisie arbitrairement
Wimpel *m*	pelmet, pennant, streamer	bandeau *m*, fanion *m*, flamme *f*
Wink *m*	hint, tip	conseil *m*, insinuation *f*, tuyau *m*
Winkelblatt *n*	hedge press, local rag	feuille *f* de chou *m*, presse *f* de réputation *f* douteuse
Winkelhaken *m*	composing stick	composteur *m*
Winkelmaß *n*	angle meter, square	équerre *f*
Winke *m/pl*, vertrauliche	inside dopes *pl*	tuyaux *m/pl* confidentiels
Winterschlußverkauf *m*	winter sale	solde *m* de printemps *m*
wird fortgesetzt	to be continued	à suivre
Wirklichkeitsflucht *f*	escapism	évasion *f* de la réalité *f*
wirksame Werbung *f*	effective advertising	publicité *f* efficace
wirksamer Filmschluß *m*	pay-off	partie *f* finale efficace d'un film *m*
Wirksamkeit *f*	effectiveness, efficiency, impressiveness	efficacité *f*
Wirkung *f*	effect	effet *m*
Wirkung *f*, kumulative	cumulative effect	effet *m* cumulatif
Wirkungsbereich *m*	sphere of action	champ *m* d'action *f*, sphère *f* d'action *f*
Wirkungsgrad *m* der Werbung *f*	sales *pl* impact	efficience *f* de publicité *f*
Wirkungskraft *f*	penetration	pénétration *f*
Wirkungskreis *m*	field of activities *pl*	champ *m* d'action *f*
Wirkungskurve *f*	response-function	courbe *f* de l'acceuil *m*
Wirkungstest *m*	efficiency test	test *m* d'efficacité *f*
wirkungsvolles Bildelement *n*	Hathaway touch	élément *m* figuratif impressionnant
Wirtschaft *f*	economy	économie *f*
Wirtschaftlichkeit *f*	profitability	rentabilité *f*
Wirtschaftsblatt *n*	business paper, commercial journal	feuille *f* commerciale, feuille *f* économique
Wirtschaftsforschung *f*	commercial research	recherche *f* économique
Wirtschaftspresse *f*	commercial press	presse *f* économique
Wirtschaftsredakteur *m*	economic editor	rédacteur *m* de la rubrique *f* économique
Wirtschaftswerbung *f*	business advertising	publicité *f* commerciale
Wischblende *f*	wipe	volet *m*
Wissen *n*, praktisches	know-how	savoir-faire *m*
wissenschaftliche Methoden *f/pl*	scientific methods *pl*	méthodes *f/pl* scientifiques
wissenschaftliche Werbung *f*	scientific advertising	publicité *f* scientifique
wissenschaftliches Blatt *m*	scientific paper	feuille *f* scientifique
Witwe *f/typog*	widow	ligne *f* isolée, veuve *f*
Witzblatt *n*	comic journal, funnies *pl*, funny paper, humorous paper	feuille *f* humoristique, satirique *m*
witzige Bemerkung *f*	quip	raillerie *f*
witziger Einfall *m*	gag	saillie *f*
Wochenblatt *n*	weekly	hebdomadaire *m*
Wochenendzeitung *f*	week-end paper	journal *m* du septième jour *m*
Wochenplauderei *f*	weekly talk	causerie *f* hebdomadaire
Wochenschau *f*	news-reel	actualités *f/pl*
Wochenschaugesellschaft *f*	newsreel company	société *f* ayant pour objet *m* les actualités *f/pl*
Wochenzeitschrift *f*	weekly magazine, weekly paper	feuille *f* hebdomadaire, revue *f* hebdomadaire
Wochenzeitung *f*	weekly newspaper	journal *m* hebdomadaire

wöchentlich	weekly	hebdomadaire *m*
Wörterbuch *n*	dictionary	dictionnaire *m*
Wörterbuchverfasser *m*	lexicographer	lexicographe *m*
wörtlich	verbatim	textuellement
Woge *f* der Volksgunst *f*	band wagon	vague *f* de popularité *f*
Wort *n*	word	mot *m*
Wort *n*, erfundenes	coined word	mot *m* forgé
Wort *n*, falsch ausgesprochenes	beard	cuir *m*
Wort *n*, veraltetes	obsolete word	mot *m* désuet
Wort *n*, verstümmeltes	beard	couac *m*
Wortanzeige *f*	classified advertisement, composite advertisement	annonce *f* groupée, petite annonce *f*
Wortaufwand *m*	verbosity	verbosité *f*
Wortbedeutungslehre *f*	semantic	semantique *f*
Wortbildung *f*	word-formation	formation *f* des mots *m/pl*
Wortemacher *m*	idle talker	bavardeur *m*
Wortführer *m*	spokesman	porte-parole *m*
Wortgebühr *f*	charge per word	tarif *m* par mot *m*
Wortgefecht *n*	dispute	dispute *f*
Wortgruppe *f*	group of word	groupe *m* de mot *m*
Wortklauberei *f*	hair-splitting	chicane *f* sur les mots *m/pl*
Wortlaut *m*	wording	énoncé *m*, teneur *f*
Wortmarke *f*	trade name	marque *f* typographique, marque *f* verbale
Wortneubildung *f*	neologism	néologisme *m*
Wortregister *n*	terms *pl* index	nomenclature *f*
Wortschatz *m*	thesaurus, vocabulary	thésaurus *m*, trésor *m* de mots *m/pl*, vocabulaire *m*
Wortschöpfer *m*	wordsmith	créateur *m* de mots *m/pl*
Wortschwall *m*	redundancy, torrent of words *pl*	flot *m* de paroles *f/pl*, verbiage *m*
Wortsinn *m*	meaning of a word	sens *m* littéral
Wortspiel *n*	pun, quibble	calembour *m*, jeu *m* de mots *m/pl*
Wortstellung *f*	word order	ordre *m* des mots *m/pl*
Worttrennung *f*	word division	division *f* des mots *m/pl*
Wortzahl *f*	number of words *pl*	nombre *m* de mots *m/pl*
Wortzwischenraum *m*	word space	espace *f* entre les mots *m/pl*
Wucherpreis *m*	exorbitant price	prix *m* usuraire
Würfelzuckerverpackung *f*	lump-sugar packing	emballage *m* des portions *f/pl* de sucre *m*

X

Xerografie *f*	xerography	xérographie *f*
Xografie *f*	xography	xographie *f*
Xylograf *m*	wood-engraver	xylographe *m*
Xylografie *f*	wood-engraving	sculpture *f* sur bois *m*, xylographie *f*

Z

Zahl *f*	figure, number	chiffre *m*, nombre *m*
Zahl *f*, gerade	even number	nombre *m* pair
Zahl *f*, ungerade	odd number	nombre *m* impair
Zahlung *f*	payment	paiement *m*, versement *m*

Zahlung f bei Auftragserteilung f	payment with order	paiement m à la commande f
Zahlung f bei Erhalt m der Rechnung f	payment on receipt of invoice	paiement m à la réception f de la facture f
Zahlung f bei Erhalt m der Ware f	cash on delivery	paiement m lors de la réception f de la marchandise f
Zahlungsbedingungen f/pl	terms pl of payment	conditions f/pl de paiement m
Zahlungsbeleg m	voucher	justificatif m
Zahlungsfrist f	date of payment, term of payment, time of payment	délai m de paiement m, terme m de paiement m
Zahlungsminderung f	diminution of payment	diminution f de paiement m
Zahlungsverkehr m	clearing system	traffic m de paiement m
Zahlungsverzug m	delay of payment	retard m de paiement m
Zahlungsweise f	mode of payment	mode m de paiement m
Zahlungsziel n	open terms pl	terme m de règlement m
Zaponlack m	Japan enamel, zapon varnish	laque f zapon
Zehntausend f/pl, obere	high society	haute société f, haute volée f
Zeichen n	mark, sign	indice m, marque f, signe m
Zeichenatelier n	drawing studio	atelier m de dessin m
Zeichenblock m	sketching block, sketchblock am	bloc m à dessin m
Zeichenfeder f	drawing pen	plume f à dessiner
Zeichenkarton m	drawing cardboard, illustration board	carton m à dessin m
Zeichenkohle f	drawing charcoal	fusain m
Zeichenpapier n	drawing paper	papier m à dessin m
Zeichensetzung f	punctuation	ponctuation f
Zeichenstift m	drawing pencil	crayon m à dessin m
Zeichentisch m	drawing table	table f à dessin m
Zeichentrickfilm m	animated cartoon, cartoon film	film m en dessin m animé
zeichnen	to design, to draw	dessiner
Zeichner m	artist, designer	dessinateur m
Zeichnung f	drawing	dessin m
Zeichnung f, fertige	finished drawing	dessin m définitif
Zeichnung f, humorisitische	cartoon	dessin m humoristique
Zeichnungsarchiv n	plan-filing cabinet	armoire f à dessins m/pl
Zeile f	line	ligne f
Zeile f, ausschließen	word space	espacer, justifier
Zeile f halten	to align, to straighten lines pl	aligner, parangonner
Zeile f mit dem Namen m des Autors m	by-line	ligne f avec le nom m de l'auteur m
Zeile f, verhobene	misplaced line	ligne f transposée
Zeile f, verstellte	transposed line	ligne f intervertie
Zeile f, volle	full line	ligne f pleine
Zeilen f/pl umbrechen	to overrun lines pl	remanier
Zeilenabstand m	interlinear space, leading	interlignage m
Zeilenbreite f	length, measure, width of column	justification f de la colonne f
Zeileneinzug m	indent	renfoncement m
Zeilenfall m	typographical arrangement	schéma m d'emplacement m de lignes f/pl
Zeilenguß-Setzmaschine f	linotype	linotype f
Zeilenhonorar n	penny-a-line payment, space fee am	rémunération f à la ligne f
Zeilenlänge f	length of line	justification f, longueur f de ligne f
Zeilenmesser m	line measure, type line scale, type-gauge	lignomètre m, typomètre m

Zeilenpreis *m*	cost per line, price per line.	prix *m* d'une ligne *f*
Zeilenschinder *m*	penny-a-liner	bourreur *m* de lignes *f/pl*, tireur *m* à la ligne *f*
Zeilenzahl *f*	lineage, number of lines *pl*	lignage *m*, nombre *f* de lignes *f/pl*
Zeilenzwischenräume *m/pl*	leads *pl*	interlignes *f/pl*
Zeit *f* (für Werbesendungen), gesperrte	block-out	durée *f* du blocage *m*
Zeitabschnitt *m*	period	période *f*
zeitgemäß	up to date	à la page *f*, au niveau *m* des derniers progrès *m/pl*
zeitliche Abstimmung *f*	timing	coordination *f* des termes *m/pl*
zeitliche Beschränkungen *f/pl*	time limitations *pl*	restrictions *f/pl* dans le temps *m*
zeitlicher Unterschied *m*	time-lag	retard *m*
Zeitlupe *f*	slow-motion method	ralentisseur *m*
Zeitplan *m*	aging schedule	calendrier *m* d'insertion *f*
Zeitplanung *f*	timing	calendrier *m* de la gestion *f*, fixation *f* de date *f* et durée *f*
Zeitraffer *m*	rapid-motion method, time-lapse equipment	accélérateur *m*
Zeitschrift *f*	magazine, periodical, review	magazine *m*, périodique *m*, revue *f*
Zeitschrift *f*, illustrierte	picture paper	illustré *m*
Zeitschrift *f* in Schallplattenform *f*	paper in form of records *pl*	journal *m* sonore
Zeitschrift *f*, juristische	law review	revue *f* juridique
Zeitschrift *f*, kulturelle	periodical of culture	périodique *m* de culture *f*
Zeitschrift *f* mit Auszügen *m/pl* aus Büchern *n/pl* und Zeitschriften *f/pl*	digest	condensé *m*
Zeitschrift *f* mit Sammelcharakter *m*	partwork	revue *f* destinée à être recueillie
Zeitschrift *f*, politische	political periodical	revue *f* politique
Zeitschrift *f*, technische	technical publication	revue *f* technique
Zeitschriften *f/pl*, elegante	glossy monthlies *pl*	magazines *m/pl* chics
Zeitschriftengattungen *f/pl*	categories *pl* of magazines *pl*	catégories *f/pl* de périodiques *m/pl*
Zeitschriftenregal *n*	shelf for magazines *pl*	casier *m* à revues *f/pl*
Zeitschriftenständer *m*	magazine rack	casier *m* à revues *f/pl*
Zeitschriftenwerbung *f*	magazine advertising	publicité *f* dans les revues *f/pl*
Zeitung *f*	journal, newspaper, paper	gazette *f*, journal *m*
Zeitung *f*, amtliche	gazette	journal *m* officiel
Zeitung *f*, angeschlossene	member of a group of publishers *pl*	membre *m* d'un cercle *m* d'édition *f*
Zeitung *f*, chauvinistische	flag waver	journal *m* chauvin
Zeitung *f*, führende	leading paper	journal *m* de tout premier rang *m*
Zeitung *f*, großformatige	blanket sheet	journal *m* de grand format *m*
Zeitung *f*, gut aufgemachte	well made-up newspaper	journal *m* bien fait
Zeitung *f*, linkseingestellte	leftist paper	journal *m* gauchiste
Zeitung *f*, meistgelesene	most read paper	journal *m* le plus lu
Zeitung *f* ohne Anzeigen *f/pl*	adless newspaper	journal *m* sans publicité *f*
Zeitung *f*, populäre	popular newspaper	journal *m* populaire
Zeitung *f*, rechtseingestellte	right-wing paper	journal *m* de droite

Zeitung *f*, **überregionale**	national newspaper	grand quotidien *m* national
Zeitung *f*, **vordatierte**	antedated paper, bulldog edition *am*, early-bird issue *am*, pre-dated paper	journal *m* antidaté, journal *m* prédaté, première édition *f*
Zeitung *f*, **weitverbreitete**	widely read newspaper	journal *m* très répandu
Zeitungsabonnement *n*	subscription to a journal	abonnement *m* à un journal *m*
Zeitungsagentur *f*	newspaper agency	agence *f* d'un journal *m*
Zeitungsanzeige *f*	press advertisement	annonce *f* de presse *f*
Zeitungsarchiv *n*	newspaper archives *pl*	archive *f* des journaux *m/pl*, documentation *f* de presse *f*
Zeitungsartikel *m*	newspaper article	article *m* de journal *m*
Zeitungsauflage *f*	circulation of a newspaper	tirage *m* d'un journal *m*
Zeitungsausschnitt *m*	clipping, press-cutting	coupure *f* de presse *f*
Zeitungsausschnittbüro *n*	clipping agency, press-cutting service	argus *m* de la presse *f*, bureau *m* de coupure *f* de journaux *m/pl*
Zeitungsautomat *m*	newspaper slot-machine	distributeur *m* de journaux *m/pl* automatique
Zeitungsbeilage *f*	supplement	supplément *m*
Zeitungsbericht *m*	report	rapport *m*
Zeitungsbestellung *f*	subscription to a journal	souscription *f* à un abonnement *m*
Zeitungsboykott *m*	boycotting of a journal	boycottage *m* d'un journal *m*
Zeitungsdeutsch *n*	journalese	style *m* de journal *m*
Zeitungsdichte *f*	press density	pénétration *f* de la presse *f*
Zeitungsdruckerei *f*	news house	imprimerie *f* d'un journal *m*
Zeitungsdruckpapier *n*	newsprint paper	papier *m* journal *m*
Zeitungsdrucksache *f*	newspaper packet, second-class matter *am*	expédition *f* sous bande *f*
Zeitungsente *f*	hoax, mare's nest	bobard *m*, canard *m*
Zeitungsformat *n*	newspaper size	format *m* journal *m*
Zeitungsfusion *f*	newspaper merger	fusion *f* de journaux *m/pl*
Zeitungsgruppe *f*	press group, string of newspapers *pl*	groupe *m* de presse *f*
Zeitungshändler *m*	newsdealer *am*, newsvendor	vendeur *m* de journaux *m/pl*
Zeitungshalter *m*	newspaper-holder	tringle *f* à journaux *m/pl*
Zeitungsherausgeber *m*	publisher	éditeur *m*
Zeitungsherstellung *f*	newspaper production	confection *f* du journal *m*
Zeitungsjunge *m*	news boy, paper-boy	vendeur *m* de journaux *m/pl*
Zeitungskatalog *m*	press-guide, rate book, standard media rates *pl*	catalogue *m* des journaux *m/pl*
Zeitungskette *f*	press-group	chaîne *f* de journaux *m/pl*
Zeitungskiosk *m*	kiosk *brit*, newsstand *am*	kiosque *m* à journaux *m/pl*
Zeitungskopf *m*	mast head, newspaper heading, top	en-tête *f*, manchette *f*
Zeitungskorrektur *f*	page proof	correction *f* en bon à tirer
Zeitungsleser *m*	newspaper reader	lecteur *m* de journaux *m/pl*
Zeitungslesesaal *m*	news-room	salle *f* des journaux *m/pl*
Zeitungsleute *pl*	newspapermen *pl*	monde *m* de la presse *f*
Zeitungsnotiz *f*	news item, press item, press notice	communiqué *m* de presse *f*, nouvelle *f*
Zeitungsnummer *f*, **alte**	back-number	exemplaire *m* périmé
Zeitungspapier *n*	news stock, newsprint paper	papier *m* journal *m*, papier *m* rugueux
Zeitungsplakat *n*	newspaper poster	affiche *f* de journal *m*
Zeitungsraster *m*	newsprint screen	trame *f* journal *m*
Zeitungsregal *n*	newspaper rack	casier *m* à journaux *m/pl*

Zeitungsroman *m*	serial story	roman-feuilleton *m*
Zeitungsschrank *m*	newspaper shelf	étagère *f* à journaux *m/pl*
Zeitungsschreiber *m*	hack writer	folliculaire *m*
Zeitungsspanner *m*	newspaper-holder	porte-journaux *m*
Zeitungsstand *m*	kiosk *brit*, newsstall, newsstand *am*	aubette *f*, débit *m* de journaux *m/pl*, kiosque *m* à journaux *m/pl*, stand *m*
Zeitungssterben *n*	mortality of journals *pl*	mortalité *f* des journaux *m/pl*
Zeitungstechnik *f*	newspaper technique	technique *f* du journal *m*
Zeitungstext *m*, seriöser	pig iron	texte *m* sérieux
Zeitungstitel *m*	title of a newspaper	titre *m* d'un journal *m*
Zeitungsträger *m*	carrier of newspapers *pl*, delivery man	porteur *m* de journaux *m/pl*
Zeitungstyp *m*	type of newspaper	type-journal *m*
Zeitungsverkäufer *m*	newsdealer *am*, newsvendor	marchand *m* de journaux *m/pl*, vendeur *m* de journaux *m/pl*
Zeitungsverkäufer *m*, ambulanter	news-butcher	vendeur *m* ambulant de journaux *m/pl*
Zeitungsverleger *m*	newspaper owner, newspaper publisher *am*	éditeur *m* d'un journal *m*
Zeitungsversand *m*	mailing, sorting	routage *m*
Zeitungsvertrieb *m*	distribution of a newspaper	distribution *f* d'un journal *m*
Zeitungswerbung *f*	press advertising	publicité *f* par la presse *f*
Zeitungswesen *n*	journalism, press	journalisme *m*, presse *f*
Zeitungswissenschaft *f*	science of journalism	science *f* du journalisme *m*
Zeitverzögerung *f*	time lag	décalage *m*, retardement *m*
Zellglasfenster *n*	cellophane window	fenêtre *f* en pellicule *f* transparente
Zensur *f*	censorship	censure *f*
zentrieren	centering *brit*, centring *am*	cadrage *m*, centrer
Zentrierung *f* des Filmbildes *m*	centring of film image	cadrage *m*
Zerrbild *n*	caricature	portrait-charge *f*
zerstückeln	to dismember	fragmenter
Zettel *m*	slip	fiche *f*
Zeugkiste *f*	hell box	boîte *f* à défets *m/pl*
Zeugnis *n*	certificate	certificat *m*, témoignage *m*
Zickzackfaltung *f*	concertina folding	plis *m/pl* accordéon *m*
zielbewußte Werbung *f*	systematic advertising	publicité *f* systématique
Zielgruppe *f*	intended group, target audience, target group	audience *f* utile, cible *f*
Zielgruppenkombination *f* von Medien *n/pl*	media audience accumulation	combinaison *f* de cibles *f/pl* publicitaires
Zielgruppenzeitschrift *f*	specialised magazine	revue *f* spécialisée
Zielpublizistik *f*	public relations *pl*	relations *f/pl* publiques
Zierbuchstabe *m*	ornamental letter, swash letter	italique *f* de fantaisie *f*, lettre *f* à queue *f*, lettre *f* ornée
Zierleiste *f*	border, tail piece	bordure *f*, fleuron *m*
Zierlinie *f*	ornamental rule	filet *m* orné
Zierrahmen *m*	cartouche	cartouche *f*
Zierrand *m*	fancy frame	cadre *m* fantaisie *f*
Zierschrift *f*	fancy letters *pl*, ornamental type, swash face	caractère *m* de fantaisie *f*, caractères *m/pl* ornés
Ziffer *f*	cipher, figure, numeral	chiffre *m*
Zifferblatt *n*	dial	cadran *m*
Ziffern *f/pl*, arabische	Arabic numerals *pl*	chiffres *m/pl* arabes
Ziffern *f/pl*, römische	Roman numerals *pl*	chiffres *m/pl* romains

Zink *n*	zinc	zinc *m*
Zinkätzung *f*	zinc block, zinc etching	cliché *m* zinc, zincographie *f*
Zinkautotypie *f*	zinc halftone	autotypie *f* zinc
Zinkdruck *m*	zincography	zincographie *f*
Zinkklischee *n*	zinc block, zinc etching	cliché *m* zinc *m*, zincographie *f*
Zinkplatte *f*	zinc plate	plaque *f* de zinc *m*
Zirkular *n*	circular	circulaire *m*
Zirkusplakat *n*	circus-poster	affiche *f* de cirque *m*
Zitat *n*	quotation	citation *f*
Zitatensammlung *f*	commonplace-book	recueil *m* de citations *f/pl*
Zoll *m*	customs *pl*	douane *f*
zollfreies Geschäft *n*	duty free shop	boutique *f* franche
Zollgebühr *f*	duty	droits *m/pl* de douane *f*
zudringliche Werbung *f*	obtrusive advertising	publicité *f* obsessionnelle
Zügen *m/pl* **darstellen, in großen**	to skeletonize	réduire au strict minimum *m*
Zündholzwerbung *f*	matchbox advertising	publicité *f* sur feuillets *m/pl* d'allumettes *f/pl*
zufällig	random	au hasard *m*
Zufallsleser *m*	pass-along reader	lecteur *m* accidental, lecteur *m* aléatoire
Zufallsstichprobe *f*	random sample	échantillon *m* au hasard *m*
Zugabe *f*	free gift	prime *f*
Zugabeartikel *m*	advertising premium, give-away	article *m* prime *f*
Zugabewerbung *f*	gift advertising	publicité *f* avec primes *f/pl*, publicité *f* par primes *f/pl*
Zugabewesen *n*	giftgiving	distribution *f* de primes *f/pl*, ventes *f/pl* avec primes *f/pl*
zugkräftige Werbung *f*	attractive advertising, audience builder	numéro *m* à succès *m*, publicité *f* attractive
Zugkraft *f*	attention value, attraction, pulling power	accrochage *m* publicitaire, attrait *m* publicitaire, force *f* d'attraction *f*
Zugnummer *f*	puller	locomotive *f*
Zuhörer *m*	listener	auditeur *m*
Zuhörergewohnheiten *f/pl*	listening habits *pl*	habitudes *f/pl* d'écoute *f*
Zuhörerschaft *f*	audience	audience *f*, ensemble *m* des auditeurs *m/pl*
Zukunftsroman *m*	science-fiction	littérature *f* d'anticipation *f*
zulässige Werbung *f*	admissible advertising	publicité *f* autorisée
z.Z. gültige Anzeigenpreisliste *f*	temporary rate sheet	tarif *m* d'annonces *f/pl* valide actuellement
zurechtgepfuschter Artikel *m*	patched-up story	article *m* bâclé
zurechtstutzen	to doctor	tripatouiller
zurichten	to back-up, to make ready	mettre en page *f*, mettre en train *m*
Zurichtung *f*	make-ready	mise *f* en train *m*
zurückhaltend	non-committal	qui ne prend pas position *f*
zurückstellen	to withhold	retenir
zurückübersetzen	to retranslate	retraduire
zusätzlich	supplementary	supplémentaire
zusätzliche Anzeige *f*	additional insertion	insertion *f* supplémentaire
zusätzliche Dienstleistung *f*	accessorial service	service *m* additionnel
zusätzliche Werbemittel *n/pl*	collateral media *pl*	médias *m/pl* additionnels
zusätzliche Werbung *f*	accessory advertising, auxiliary advertising, supplementary advertising	publicité *f* auxiliaire, publicité *f* de complément *m*, publicité *f* de soutien *m*
zusammenbrauen	to cook up	concocter

zusammenfassen	to accumulate, to cumulate, to recapitulate, to summarize	cumuler, récapituler, résumer
Zusammenfassung *f*	recapitulation, synopsis	récapitulation *f*, résumé *m*
Zusammenfassung *f* **von Unterlagen** *f/pl*	briefing	résumé *m* d'instructions *f/pl*
zusammenfügen	to collate, to collect	assembler
zusammengesetztes Kunstwort *n*	blend	mot *m* téléscopé
zusammengestoppelte Geschichte *f*	patched-up story	article *m* bâclé
Zusammenhang *m*	association, connexion	connexion *f*, liaison *f*
zusammenhanglos	loose	déconsu
Zusammenkunft *f*	appointment, meeting	entrevue *f*
Zusammenschluß *m*	amalgamation, combination	jumelage *m*, regroupement *m*
zusammenschreiben	to write in one word	écrire en un mot *m*
Zusammensetzung *f* **des Publikums** *n*	audience composition, audience profile	composition *f* de l'audience *f*
Zusammenstellung *f*	compilation	compilation *f*
Zusammenstellung *f* **der Seiten** *f/pl*	page make-up	mise *f* en page *f*
zusammenstreichen	to compress, to contract, to shorten, to slash	taillader, triturer
zusammentragen	to compile	compiler
Zusatz *m*	addition	addition *f*, ajout *m*
Zusatz *m* **am Ende eines Artikels** *m*	shirt-tail	pan *m* de chemise *f*
Zusatzfarbe *f*	supplementary colour	couleur *f* de soutien *m*
Zusatzrabatt *m*	additional discount	rabais *m* additionnel
Zusatzwerbung *f*	accessory advertising	publicité *f* additionnelle
Zuschauer *m*, **Zuschauerin** *f*	viewer	spectateur *m*, spectatrice *f*
Zuschaueranalyse *f*	audience analysis	analyse *f* des spectateurs *m/pl*
Zuschlag *m*	additional charge, extra charge	majoration *f*, surtaxe *f*
Zuschuß *m* (**Überschuß** *m*)	overs *pl*	chaperon *m*, passe *f*
Zustelldienst *m*	delivery service	service *m* de distribution *f*
Zustellgebühr *f*	postage	frais *m/pl* postaux
Zustellung *f*	delivery	livraison *f*
Zustellung *f* **durch Träger** *m/pl*	delivery by porters *pl*	portage *m*
zuteilen	to allocate, to allot	allouer, assigner
Zuteilung *f*	allocation, allotment	allocation *f*, lotissement *m* publicitaire
zutragen, sich	to happen	se passer
zuzüglich	additional	en plus
Zwangsabonnement *n*	compulsory subscription	abonnement *m* forcé
Zweckmeldung *f*	tendentious information	nouvelle *f* lancée
Zweidrittelseite *f*	two-thirds page	page *f* de deux tiers
zweifache Ausfertigung *f*	duplicate	double exemplaire *m*
Zweifarbendruck *m*	two-colour process	bichromie *f*, impression *f* bichrome, impression *f* en deux couleurs *f/pl*
Zweigstelle *f*	branch	succursale *f*
zweimal täglich	twice daily	bi-quotidien
zweimal wöchentlich	twice weekly	bi-hebdo
zweimonatlich	bi-monthly	bimestriel
zweiseitig	double-sided, two-sided	à deux côtés *m/pl*, bilatéral, de deux pages *f/pl*, double
zweiseitig gestrichenes Papier *n*	two-sided coated paper	papier *m* couché de deux pages *f/pl*

zweiseitige gegenüberliegende Anzeige *f*	double truck	double page *f* centrale
zweiseitiger Ersatzkarton *m*	single-leaf cancel	onglet *m*
zweispaltig	half measure, in double columns *pl*	face *f* en deux colonnes *f/pl*, sur deux colonnes *f/pl*
zweisprachig	bilingual	bilingue
Zweitabzug *m*	second proof	seconde épreuve *f*
Zweitkorrektur *f*	second revised proof	deuxième épreuve *f* corrigée, seconde revision *f*
Zweitschrift *f*	copy, duplication	duplicata *m*
zweiwöchentlich	bi-weekly	bi-hebdomadaire
Zwiebelfisch *m/typog*	pi *am*, pie, wrong fount, wrong letter	coquille *f*, mastic *m*, pâté *m*
Zwiegespräch *n*	dialogue	dialogue *m*
Zwischenblätter *n/pl*	interleaves *pl*	macules *f/pl*
Zwischenhändler *m*	middleman	intermédiaire *m*
Zwischenhandel *m*	intermediary trade	commerce *m* d'intermédiaire *m*
zwischenmenschliche Beziehungen *f/pl*	human relations *pl*	relations *f/pl* humaines
Zwischenraum *m*	space	espace *m* blanc
Zwischenraum *m*, setzen ohne	to close up	supprimer l'espace *m*
Zwischenraum *m* verkleinern	to close up, to depress space	diminuer l'espace *m* blanc, serrer
Zwischenschlag *m*	lead	interligne *f*
Zwischentitel *m*	caption, sub-title	intertitre *m*, sous-titre *m*
Zwischenträger *m*	go-between, tell-tale	cafard *m*, entremetteur *m*
zyklische Werbung *f*	cyclic advertising	publicité *f* cyclique
Zylinderflachformmaschine *f*	flat-bed cylinder press	presse *f* cylindrique à marbre *m* plan

Complete Multilingual Dictionary of Advertising, Marketing, and Communications

English
German
French

List of abbreviations:

	English	German	French
am	American	amerikanisch	américain
brit	British	britisch	britannique
f	feminine	weiblich	féminin
f/pl	feminine plural	weibliche Mehrzahl	féminin pluriel
m	masculine	männlich	masculin
m/pl	masculine plural	männliche Mehrzahl	masculin pluriel
n	neuter	sächlich	neutre
n/pl	neuter plural	sächliche Mehrzahl	neutre pluriel
pl	plural	Mehrzahl	pluriel
s.	see	siehe	voir
stereotyp.	stereotyping	Stereotypie	stéréotypie
typogr.	typography	Buchdruck	typographie

A

abbreviation	Abbreviatur *f*, Abkürzung *f*	abréviation *f*
able to be reproduced	reproduktionsreif	apte à être reproduit
absolute necessity	höhere Gewalt *f*	force *f* majeure
absorbent paper	saugfähiges Papier *n* (Saugpost *f*)	papier *m* amoureux
absorption	Aufsaugung *f*	absorption *f*
abundance	Reichhaltigkeit *f*	abondance *f*
abundance of information	Informationsfülle *f*	plénitude *f* d'information
accelerator	Terminüberwacher *m*	surveillant *m* de la production *f*
accent	Akzent *m*	accent *m*
to **accentuate**	Auszeichnen *n* eines Textes *m*, betonen, hervorheben	accentuer, mettre en évidence *f*, mettre en relief *m*, mettre en vedette *f*, souligner
acceptable	annehmbar	acceptable
acceptance	Aufnahme *f*	acceptation *f*
acceptance of an order	Auftragsannahme *f*	acceptation *f* d'une commande *f*
acceptance of manuscripts *pl*	Manuskriptannahme *f*	acceptation *f* des manuscrits *m/pl*
accessorial service	Nebenleistung *f*, zusätzliche Dienstleistung *f*	prestation *f* accessoire, service *m* additionnel
accessory advertising	begleitende Werbung *f*, Ergänzungswerbung *f*, zusätzliche Werbung *f*, Zusatzwerbung *f*	publicité *f* additionnelle, publicité *f* auxiliaire, publicité *f* de complément *m*, publicité *f* de soutien *m*
accommodation address	Deckadresse *f*	adresse *f* d'emprunt *m*
accompanying colour	Schmuckfarbe *f*	couleur *f* d'accompagnement *m*
accomplished fact	vollendete Tatsache *f*	fait *m* accompli
according to plan	planmäßig	selon plan *m*
according to possibility	Möglichkeit *f*, nach	selon possibilité *f*
accordion folding	Leporellofalzung *f*	pli *m* accordéon *m*, pli *m* en zig-zag
account	Budget *n*, Etat *m*, Etatkunde *m*, Konto *n*, Rechnung *f*, Werbeetat *m*	budget *m*, budget *m* publicitaire, client *m*, compte *m*, facture *f*
to **account**	abrechnen	boucler un compte *m*, facturer, faire un décompte *m*, solder
account distribution	Kostenverteilung *f*	répartition *f* des charges *f/pl*, répartition *f* des coûts *m/pl*
account executive	Kontakter *m*, Kontaktmann *m*, Kundenbetreuer *m*, Sachbearbeiter *m* der Werbung *f*, Verbindungsmann *m*	chef *m* de publicité *f* d'agence *f*, contacteur *m*, homme *m* de relation *f*
account manager	Etatdirektor *m*	directeur *m* de la section *f* budgetaire

account planning	Streuplanung f, Werbeplanung f	plan m de campagne f, plan m des supports m/pl, planning m publicitaire
account supervisor	Kontakter m, Kontaktmann m, Kundenbetreuer m	contacteur m, homme m de relation f
accountancy	Rechnungswesen n	comptabilité f
accounting department	Buchhaltungsabteilung f	service f comptabilité f
accounting period	Abrechnungszeitraum m	période f comptable
accredited	anerkannt	accrédité, reconnu
to accumulate	anhäufen, zusammenfassen	cumuler, récapituler, résumer
accumulation	Akkumulierung f, Anhäufung f, Intensivierung f des Werbeeffekts m	accumulation f, effet m cumulatif, intensification f de la publicité f
acetate film	Azetatfolie f	feuille f d'acétate m
acid resisting	säurefest	résistant aux acides m/pl
acknowledgement	Bestätigung f	confirmation f
acoustic advertising	akustische Werbung f	publicité f acoustique
to acquaint	informieren	informer
to acquire customers pl	Kunden m/pl gewinnen	acquérir des clients m/pl, attirer des clients m/pl
across the board	Werbesendung f zur gleichbleibenden Tageszeit f an 5 aufeinanderfolgenden Tagen m/pl	émission f quotidienne sauf samedi m et dimanche m
act of providence	höhere Gewalt f	force f majeure
acting as leader	federführend	compétent, dirigeant
action	aussagekräftige Überschrift f, Handlung f	action f, manchette f verbale
action film	Kriminalfilm m	film m policier
action still	Standfoto n	photo f de plateau m, photo f de scène f
activation research	Kaufentschlußanalyse f	analyse f de la décision f d'acheter
actuality	Aktualität f	actualité f
acute accent	Accent m aigu	accent m aigu
ad	Annonce f, Anzeige f, Inserat n	annonce f, insertion f
ad revenues pl	Anzeigeneinnahmen f/pl	revenus m/pl d'annonces f/pl
ad sales pl promotion manager	Anzeigenwerbeleiter m	chef m de la vente f d'annonces f/pl
to adapt	adaptieren, anpassen, bearbeiten	adapter, arranger
adaptation	Adaptierung f, Anpassung f, Bearbeitung f, Umarbeitung f	accommodation f, adaptation f
ad-audience	Anzeigenbeachtung f	audience f d'insertion f
to add	hinzufügen	ajouter
added value tax	Mehrwertsteuer f	taxe f sur la valeur f ajoutée (T.V.A.)
addition	Beigabe f, Zusatz m	addition f, ajout m, annexe f, prime f
additional	zuzüglich	en plus
additional account	Extrarabatt m	rabais m additionnel
additional charge	Zuschlag m	majoration f, surtaxe f
additional discount	Zusatzrabatt m	rabais m additionnel
additional insertion	zusätzliche Anzeige f	insertion f supplémentaire
additional price	Mehrpreis m	majoration f de prix m
address	Adresse f, Anschrift f	adresse f

address book	Adreßbuch *n*	annuaire *m*, indicateur *m* d'adresses *f/pl*, livre *m* d'adresses *f/pl*
address broker	Adressenverlag *m*	éditeur *m* d'adresses *f/pl*, loueurs *m/pl* d'adresses *f/pl*
address source	Adressenquelle *f*	source *f* d'adresses *f/pl*
addressee	Adressat *m*, Empfänger *m*	destinataire *m*, récepteur *m*
addressing	Adressierung *f*	adressage *m*
addressing machine	Adressiermaschine *f*	adressographe *m*
addressograph plate	Adremaplatte *f*	plaque-adresse *f*
adequate price	angemessener Preis *m*	juste prix *m*
adequate sample	repräsentative Marktuntersuchung *f*	échantillon *m* représentatif
adhesive	Klebstoff *m*	adhésif *m*, colle *f*
adhesive address label	Adressenaufkleber *m*	adresse *f* adhésive
adhesive foil	Klebefolie *f*	feuille *f* adhésive
adhesive label	Haftetikett *n*	étiquette *f* adhésive
adhesive stamp	Klebemarke *f*	vignette *f* collante
adhesive tape	Klebeband *n*	bande *f* adhésive, ruban *m* adhésif
adjacencies *pl*	Werbespot *pl* in unmittelbarer Nachbarschaft *f* einer besonderen Sendung *f*	spots *m/pl* dans le voisinage *m* immédiat d'une émission *f* spécifique
adjacency	Beiprogramm *n*	hors-programme *m*, programme *m* adjacent, programme *m* d'accompagnement *m*
to **adjust**	justieren	justifier
adjustment	Anpassung *f*, Druckeinstellung *f/typog*	accommodation *f*, justification *f*
adless newspaper	Zeitung *f* ohne Anzeigen *f/pl*	journal *m* sans publicité *f*
admag	Anzeigenblatt *n*	annoncier *m*, feuille *f* d'annonces *f/pl*, journal *m* publicitaire
adman	Anzeigenfachmann *m*, Werbefachmann *m*	expert *m* en publicité *f*, publicitaire *m*, spécialiste *m* de la publicité *f*, technicien de publicité *f*
admass	Opfer *n* der Werbung *f*	victime *m* de la publicité *f*
to **administer**	verwalten	administrer, gérer
administration	Administration *f*, Verwaltung *f*	administration *f*
administrative	Geschäftsstelle *f*	agence *f*, bureau *m*
administrator	Administrator *m*, Verwalter *m*	administrateur *m*
admissible advertising	zulässige Werbung *f*	publicité *f* autorisée
to **admonish**	mahnen	mettre en demeurre *m*, sommer
ad-page traffic	Blickverlauf *m* auf einer Anzeigenseite *f*	mouvement *m* des yeux *m/pl* sur une page *f* d'annonces *f/pl*
adrates *pl*	Anzeigenpreise *m/pl*	tarifs *m/pl* de publicité *f*
advance-copy	Vorausexemplar *n*	exemplaire *m* à l'avance *f*, exemplaire *m* de lancement *m*
advance in price	Preiserhöhung *f*, Preissteigerung *f*	augmentation *f* de prix *m*

advance notice	Vorankündigung f	avis m préalable
advance order	Vorbestellung f	commande f préliminaire
advance payment	Vorauszahlung f	paiement m d'avance m
advance publication	Vorabdruck m	bonne feuille f
advance publicity	Vorwerbung f	publicité f d'amorçage m
advance sheet	Aushängebogen m	bonne feuille f
advance story	Artikel m, der vor dem	avant-papier m
	Ereignis n geschrieben wurde	
advanced	fortschrittlich	avant-garde f, progressiste
adventure film	Abenteuerfilm m	film m d'aventures f/pl
advergram	Anzeige f im Rundfunk m,	annonce f radiophonique
	Rundfunkanzeige f	
to advertise	anzeigen, inserieren, werben	annoncer, faire de la publicité f,
		insérer
advertised price	Bezugspreis m	prix m d'abonnement m
advertisee	Umworbener m	destinataire m
advertisement	Annonce f, Anzeige f, Inserat n	annonce f, insertion f
advertisement administration	Anzeigenregie f,	concessionaire m, régie f de
	Anzeigenverwaltung f	publicité f, régie f
		d'annonces f/pl
advertisement board	Schwarzes Brett n	porte-affiches m, tableau m
		noir
advertisement border	Anzeigeneinfassung f	bordure f d'annonce f
advertisement by insetting	Insettinganzeige f	publicité f par insetting
advertisement calculation	Anzeigenberechnung f	calculation f d'annonces f/pl
advertisement canvasser	Anzeigenakquisiteur m	démarcheur m en publicité f,
		vendeur m d'espace m
advertisement columns pl	Inseratenteil m,	partie f publicitaire,
	Anzeigenspalte f	colonne f d'annonce f
advertisement compositor	Anzeigensetzer m	annoncier m
advertisement department brit	Werbeabteilung f	département m de publicité f,
		service m de publicité f
advertisement director	Anzeigendirektor m,	chef m de publicité f, chef m
	Anzeigenleiter m	des annonces f/pl,
		directeur m du service m de
		publicité f
advertisement duty	Anzeigensteuer f	impôt m sur la publicité f
advertisement height	Abdruckhöhe f	hauteur f d'annonce f
advertisement in black and white	Schwarz-Weiß-Anzeige f	annonce f en noir
advertisement in feuilleton style	feuilletonistische Anzeige f	reportage m publicitaire
advertisement in short story		
advertisement lineage	Anzeigengröße f	lignage m d'une annonce f
advertisement magazine	Anzeigenblatt n	annoncier m, feuille f
		d'annonces f/pl, journal m
		publicitaire
advertisement make-up	Anzeigenspiegel m,	maquette f de la partie f
	Anzeigenumbruch m	publicitaire, mise f en
		pages f/pl des annonces f/pl
advertisement manager	Werbeleiter m eines	chef m de publicité f de
	Werbeträgers m	support m publicitaire
advertisement masked out in part	maskierte Anzeige f	annonce f masquée en partie f

advertisement office	Anzeigenbüro *n*	bureau *m* d'annonces *f/pl*
advertisement order	Anzeigenauftrag *m*	commande *f* d'insertion *f*
advertisement page	Anzeigenseite *f*	feuille *f* d'annonces *f/pl*, page *f* d'annonces *f/pl*
advertisement panel	Streifenanzeige *f*	bandeau *m*
advertisement placing	Anzeigenplazierung *f*	emplacement *m* d'annonce *f*
advertisement proceeds *pl*	Anzeigenerlöse *m/pl*	montant *m* d'annonces *f/pl*
advertisement rate card	Anzeigenpreisliste *f*	tarif *m* d'annonces *f/pl*
advertisement rate schedule	Anzeigentarif *m*	tarif *m* d'annonces *f/pl*, tarif *m* de publicité *f*, tarif *m* d'insertion *f*
advertisement rating	Anzeigenerfolgskontrolle *f*	contrôle *m* du rendement *m* publicitaire
advertisement representative	Anzeigenvertreter *m*	courtier *m* en publicité *f*, représentant *m* publicitaire
advertisement size	Anzeigenformat *n*	format *m* d'annonce *f*
advertisement supplement	Anzeigenbeilage *f*	supplément *m* d'annonces *f/pl*
advertisement type area	Anzeigenspiegel *m*	maquette *f* de la partie *f* publicitaire
advertisement volume	Anzeigenumfang *m*	volume *m* d'annonces *f/pl*
advertisement with illustration	Klischeeanzeige *f*	annonce *f* illustrée
advertisement with much white space	luftige Anzeige *f*	annonce *f* bien aérée
advertisements *pl* of the commercial register	Handelsregister *n*-Anzeigen *f/pl*	annonces *f/pl* du registre *m* du commerce *m*
advertiser	Anzeigenblatt *n*, Inserent *m*, Werbungtreibender *m*	annonceur *m*, annoncier *m*, entreprise *f* annonceuse, feuille *f* d'annonces *f/pl*, journal *m* publicitaire
advertisers' copy	Belegexemplar *n*	numéro *m* justificatif
advertising	werblich, Werbung *f*	propagande *f*, publicitaire, publicité *f*, réclame *f*
advertising accumulation	Werbeintensivierung *f*	augmentation *f* de publicité *f*
advertising activities *pl* with coupons *pl*	Werbeaktionen *f/pl* mit Kupons *m/pl*	couponnage *m*
advertising activity	Werbeaktion *f*, Werbetätigkeit *f*	action *f* publicitaire, activité *f* publicitaire, opération *f* publicitaire, propagande *f*
advertising aeroplane	Werbeflugzeug *n*	avion *m* publicitaire
advertising affair	Werbeangelegenheit *f*	affaire *f* publicitaire
advertising agency	Werbeagentur *f*	agence *f* de publicité *f*
advertising aids *pl*	Werbematerial *n*	matériel *m* de publicité *f*
advertising allocation	Anweisung *f* von Werbekosten *pl*	allocation *f* publicitaire, lotissement *m* publicitaire
advertising allowance	Werbezuschuß *m*	allocation *f* publicitaire
advertising alternative	Werbealternative *f*	alternative *f* publicitaire
advertising analysis	Werbeanalyse *f*	étude *f* de préparation *f* et d'orientation *f* d'une campagne *f* publicitaire
advertising angle	werblicher Gesichtspunkt *m*, Werbeargument *n*, Werbegesichtswinkel *m*	angle *m* d'approche *f* publicitaire, argument *m* de publicité *f*, axe *m* de la publicité *f*
advertising appeal	Werbeappell *m*	attrait *m* publicitaire
advertising approach	Aufmerksamkeitserreger *m*, Werbegesichtswinkel *m*	accrochage *m* initial, angle *m* d'approche *f*, axe *m* de la publicité *f*

advertising appropriation	bewilligter Werbeetat *m*, Werbebudget *n*, Werbehaushalt *m*	budget *m* alloué de publicité *f*, budget *m* publicitaire
advertising area	Werbebereich *m*	domaine *m* publicitaire
advertising argot	Werbechinesisch *n*, Werbejargon *m*	argot *m* publicitaire
advertising art	Gebrauchsgrafik *f*, Werbegrafik *f*, Werbekunst *f*	art *m* commercial, art *m* publicitaire, créations *f/pl* graphiques, graphisme *m* publicitaire, publicité *f* artistique
advertising article	Reklameartikel *m*	article *m* de réclame *f*
advertising artist	Werbegrafiker *m*, Werbezeichner *m*	artiste *m* en publicité *f*, dessinateur *m* publicitaire
advertising assistant	Werbeassistent *m*	adjoint *m* au chef *m* de publicité *f*, assistant *m* en publicité *f*
advertising association	Werbefachverband *m*, Werbeverband *m*	association *f* de publicité *f*
advertising attack	Werbeattacke *f*	attaque *f* publicitaire
advertising balloon	Werbeballon *m*	ballon *m* publicitaire
advertising block	Anzeigenklischee *n*	cliché *m* d'annonce *f*
advertising box	Werbebox *f*	colonne *f* publicitaire carrée
advertising brochure	Werbebroschüre *f*	brochure *f* publicitaire
advertising budget	Werbeetat *m*	budget *m* publicitaire
advertising business	Anzeigengeschäft *n*, Werbewirtschaft *f*	métier *m* publicitaire
advertising by captive balloons *pl*	Fesselballonwerbung *f*	publicité *f* par ballons *m/pl* captifs
advertising by inserts *pl* in books *pl* of a lending library	Leihbuchwerbung *f*	publicité *f* par encarts *m/pl* dans les livres *m/pl* en location *f*
advertising by word of mouth	mündliche Werbung *f*, Mundpropaganda *f*	propagande *f* de bouche *f* à oreille *f*, publicité *f* de bouche *f* à bouche *f*, publicité *f* parlante
advertising campaign	Werbefeldzug *m*, Werbekampagne *f*	campagne *f* de publicité *f*, campagne *f* publicitaire
advertising censorship	Werbezensur *f*	censure *f* de la publicité *f*
advertising character	Reklamefigur *f*, Werbefigur *f*	figurine *f* publicitaire, personnage *m* publicitaire, personnage *m*-type *m*
advertising charges *pl*	Anzeigenkosten *pl*, Anzeigenpreise *m/pl*, Anzeigentarif *m*	dépenses *f/pl* d'insertion *f*, tarif *m* d'annonces *f/pl*, tarif *m* de publicité *f*, tarif *m* d'insertion *f*, tarif *m/pl* de publicité *f*
advertising circular	Werberundschreiben *n*	circulaire *m* publicitaire
advertising club	Werbeklub *f*	club *m* de publicité *f*
advertising company	Werbegesellschaft *f*	entreprise *f* publicitaire
advertising competition	Werbewettbewerb *m*	concours *m* publicitaire
advertising complexion	Werbecharakter *m*	caractère *m* publicitaire
advertising composition	Anzeigensatz *m*	composition *f* des annonces *f/pl*
advertising conception	Werbegestaltung *f*, Werbekonzeption *f*	conception *f* publicitaire
advertising constant	Werbekonstante *f*	constante *f* publicitaire

advertising consultant	freier Werbeberater *m*, Werbeberater *m*	conseil *m* en publicité *f*, conseil *m* en publicité *f* libre
advertising contents *pl*	Anzeigeninhalt *m*, Werbeinhalt *m*	contenu *m* publicitaire
advertising contest	Werbepreisausschreiben *n*, Werbewettbewerb *m*	compétition *f* publicitaire, concours *m* publicitaire
advertising contract	Anzeigenabschluß *m*, Insertionsvertrag *m*	contrat *m* d'insertion *f*
advertising contractor	Anzeigenmittler *m*, Werbefirma *f*, Werbeunternehmen *n*, Werbungsmittler *m*	acheteur *m* d'espace *m*, courtier *m* d'annonces *f/pl*, courtier *m* de publicité *f*, entreprise *f* de publicité *f*, intermédiaire *m* publicitaire
advertising control	Anzeigenerfolgskontrolle *f*, Werbeerfolgskontrolle *f*, Werbekontrolle *f*	contrôle *m* de la publicité *f*, contrôle *m* du rendement *m* de la publicité *f*
advertising copywriting	Werbetextabfassung *f*	rédaction *f* d'annonces *f/pl*
advertising costs *pl*	Werbeausgaben *f/pl*	dépenses *f/pl* publicitaires
advertising counsellor	Werbeberater *m*	conseil *m* en publicité *f*
advertising creation	Werbekreation *f*	création *f* publicitaire
advertising customer	Anzeigenkunde *m*	client *m* de publicité *f*
advertising department	Anzeigenabteilung *f*, Werbeabteilung *f*	département *m* de publicité *f*, service *m* de publicité *f*, service *m* des annonces *f/pl*
advertising design	Werbeentwurf *m*	dessin *m* publicitaire
advertising designer	Werbegrafiker *m*	artiste *m* en publicité *f*, dessinateur *m* publicitaire
advertising device	Werbemotto *n*	devise *f* publicitaire, slogan *m* publicitaire
advertising director	Werbedirektor *m*	directeur *m* de publicité *f*
advertising directory	Werbeadreßbuch *n*	annuaire *m* de publicité *f*, indicateur *m* d'adresses *f/pl* publicitaires
advertising discussion	Werbevortrag *m*	discours *m* publicitaire
advertising dispersion	Werbestreuung *f*	prospection *f* publicitaire
advertising donation	Werbegabe *f*	cadeau *m* publicitaire
advertising dosage	Werbedosierung *f*	dosage *m* publicitaire
advertising drawing	Werbezeichnung *f*	dessin *m* publicitaire
advertising effect	Streuwirkung *f*, Werbeeffekt *m*, Werbewirkung *f*	effet *m* publicitaire
advertising effectiveness	Werbewirksamkeit *f*	efficacité *f* de la publicité *f*
advertising effectiveness study	Werbeerfolgskontrolle *f*	contrôle *m* du rendement *m* de la publicité *f*
advertising efficiency	Werbewirksamkeit *f*	efficacité *f* de la publicité *f*
advertising efforts *pl*	verstärkte Werbeanstrengungen *f/pl*	effort *m* spécial de publicité *f*
advertising enterprise	Werbeunternehmen *n*	entreprise *f* de publicité *f*
advertising execution	Werbedurchführung *f*	exécution *f* de la publicité *f*
advertising expenditures *pl*	Werbeaufwendungen *f/pl*	dépenses *f/pl* publicitaires, investissements *m/pl* en publicité *f*
advertising expenses *pl*	Werbekosten *pl*, Werbeunkosten *pl*	dépenses *f/pl* publicitaires, frais *m/pl* de publicité *f*
advertising experience	Werbeerfahrung *f*	expérience *f* publicitaire

advertising expert	Werbefachmann *m*, Werbesachverständiger *m*	expert *m* en publicité *f*, publicitaire *m*, spécialiste *m* de la publicité *f*, technicien de publicité *f*
advertising extravagances *pl*	Werbeauswüchse *m/pl*	débauches *f/pl* de publicité *f*
advertising facilities *pl*	Werbegelegenheit *f*, Werbemöglichkeiten *f/pl*	occasion *f* de faire de la publicité *f*, possibilités *f/pl* de publicité *f*
advertising factors *pl*	Werbefaktoren *m/pl*	éléments *m/pl* publicitaires
advertising figure	Werbefigur *f*	figurine *f* publicitaire, personnage *m* publicitaire, personnage *m*-type *m*
advertising film	Werbefilm *m*	film *m* publicitaire
advertising film slide	Werbediapositiv *n*	diapositif *m* publicitaire
advertising filmlet	Werbekurzfilm *m*	film *m* publicitaire court métrage *m*
advertising for drugs *pl*	Pharmawerbung *f*	publicité *f* en faveur *f* des produits *m/pl* pharmaceutiques
advertising for the general public	Publikumswerbung *f*	publicité *f* auprès le grand public *m*
advertising franchise operator	Werbeflächenpächter *m*	concessionaire *m* en publicité *f*, régisseur *m*
advertising functions *pl*	Funktionen *f/pl* der Werbung *f*	fonctions *f/pl* de la publicité *f*
advertising gift	Werbegabe *f*, Werbegeschenk *n*	cadeau *m* publicitaire, prime *f*
advertising gimmick	Werbetrick *m*	artifice *m* publicitaire
advertising growth	Anzeigenzunahme *f*	accroissement *m* de publicité *f*
advertising guide	Werberatschlag *m*	guide *m* publicitaire
advertising handbill	Werbeblatt *n*	prospectus *m* publicitaire
advertising horizons *pl*	Werbemöglichkeiten *f/pl*	possibilités *f/pl* de publicité *f*
advertising idea	Werbeidee *f*	idée *f* publicitaire
advertising impressions *pl*	Werbekontakte *m/pl*	contacts *m/pl* publicitaires
advertising in cinemas *pl*	Lichtspieltheaterwerbung *f*	publicité *f* cinématographique
advertising in circulating magazines *pl*	Lesezirkelwerbung *f*	publicité *f* dans les cercles *m/pl* de lecture *f*
advertising in foreign language	fremdsprachliche Werbung *f*	publicité *f* en langue *f* étrangère
advertising in reading circles *pl*	Lesezirkelwerbung *f*	publicité *f* dans les cercles *m/pl* de lecture *f*
advertising in sport fields *pl*	Bandenwerbung *f*, Sportplatzwerbung *f*	publicité *f* dans les stades *m/pl*
advertising in superlatives *pl*	Superlativwerbung *f*	publicité *f* au superlatif *m*
advertising in transport systems *pl*	Verkehrsmittelwerbung *f*	publicité *f* moyens *m/pl* de transport *m*
advertising industry	Werbeindustrie *f*	industrie *f* publicitaire
advertising inscription	Reklameaufschrift *f*, Werbeinschrift *f*	inscription *f* publicitaire, inscriptions-réclame *f*
advertising intensity	Werbeintensität *f*	intensité *f* de la publicité *f*
advertising intermediary	Werbungsmittler *m*	acheteur *m* d'espace *m*, courtier *m* de publicité *f*, intermédiaire *m* publicitaire
advertising investments *pl*	Werbeaufwendungen *f/pl*, Werbeinvestitionen *f/pl*	dépenses *f/pl* publicitaires, investissements *m/pl* en publicité *f*
advertising journal	Werbejournal *n*	illustré *m* publicitaire

advertising kite	Reklamedrachen *m*	publicité *f* par cerf-volant *m*
advertising label	Werbeaufschrift *f*	suscription *f* publicitaire
advertising language	Werbesprache *f*	langue *f* de la publicité *f*
advertising law	Werbegesetz *n*, Werberecht *n*	droit *m* publicitaire, loi *f* publicitaire
advertising leaflet	Werbeprospekt *m*	dépliant *m* publicitaire
advertising legislation	Werbegesetzgebung *f*	législation *f* de la publicité *f*
advertising letter	Werbebrief *m*	lettre *f* de propagande *f*, lettre *f* de vente *f*, lettre *f* publicitaire
advertising limitations *pl*	Werbebeschränkungen *f/pl*	limitations *f/pl* de la publicité *f*, restrictions *f/pl* de la publicité *f*
advertising literature	Werbeliteratur *f*	éditions *f/pl* publicitaires, littérature *f* publicitaire
advertising magazine	Werbefachzeitschrift *f*	revue *f* de publicité *f*
advertising man	Werbefachmann *m*	expert *m* en publicité *f*, publicitaire *m*, spécialiste *m* de la publicité *f*, technicien de publicité *f*
advertising management	Anzeigenverwaltung *f*	concessionaire *m*, régie *f* de publicité *f*, régie *f* d'annonces *f/pl*
advertising manager	Anzeigenleiter *m*, Werbeleiter *m*	chef *m* de publicité *f*, chef *m* de publicité *f* d'annonceur *m*, chef *m* des annonces *f/pl*, directeur *m* du service *m* de publicité *f*, directeur *m* publicitaire
advertising mast	Werbemast *m*	mât *m* publicitaire
advertising material	Werbematerial *n*	matériel *m* de publicité *f*
advertising matter	Werbedrucksache *f*	imprimé *m* publicitaire
advertising measures *pl*	Werbemaßnahmen *f/pl*	efforts *m/pl* publicitaires, mesures *f/pl* publicitaires
advertising media recall	Werbemittelerinnerung *f*	souvenir *m* de moyens *m/pl* publicitaires
advertising medium	Werbeinstrument *n*, Werbemittel *n*, Werbeträger *m*	moyen *m* de publicité *f*, organe *m* de publicité *f*, outil *m* de propagande *f*, support *m* publicitaire, véhicule *m* de communication *f*
advertising medium outfit	Werbemittelausstattung *f*	équipement *m* d'un moyen *m* publicitaire
advertising message	Werbeaussage *f*, Werbebotschaft *f*	message *m* publicitaire
advertising methodology	Werbemethodik *f*	méthodologie *f* publicitaire
advertising monopoly	Anzeigenmonopol *n*	monopole *m* publicitaire
advertising motif	Werbemotiv *n*	motif *m* publicitaire
advertising motto	Werbemotto *n*	devise *f* publicitaire, slogan *m* publicitaire
advertising news	Werbenachricht *f*	échos *m/pl* publicitaires
advertising novelty	Werbeartikel *m*, Werbeneuheit *f*	cadeau *m* publicitaire, nouveauté *f* publicitaire
advertising object	Werbeobjekt *n*	objet *m* publicitaire
advertising objectives *pl*	Werbeziele *n/pl*	objectifs *m/pl* publicitaires
advertising office	Werbebüro *n*	agence *f* de publicité *f*

advertising on beer mats *pl*	Bierdeckelwerbung *f*	publicité *f* sur les soucoupes *f/pl* de la bière *f*
advertising on envelopes *pl*	Briefumschlagwerbung *f*	publicité *f* sur enveloppes *f/pl* commerciales
advertising on façades *pl*	Fassadenbeschriftung *f*	publicité *f* sur façades *f/pl*
advertising on goods-trains *pl*	Güterwagenwerbung *f*	publicité *f* sur wagons *m/pl* de marchandises *f/pl*
advertising on lottery ticket letters *pl*	Losbriefwerbung *f*	publicité *f* sur des billets *m/pl* de loterie *f*
advertising on risers *pl* of staircase	Treppenstufenwerbung *f*	emplacement *m* sur contremarches *f/pl* d'escalier *m*, panneau *m* d'escalier *m*
advertising on the point of sale	Werbung *f* am Verkaufspunkt *m*	publicité *f* sur le lieu *m* de vente *f*
advertising on town maps *pl*	Stadtplanwerbung *f*	publicité *f* sur des plans *m/pl* de ville *f*
advertising operator	Anzeigenpächter *m*, Pachtunternehmen *n*, Werbepächter *m*, Werbeverwaltung *f*	concessionaire *m* de publicité *f*, entreprise *f* d'affermage *m*, exploitant *m* de la publicité *f*, régisseur *m*, société *f* d'affermage *m*
advertising orientation	Werbeorientierung *f*	orientation *f* publicitaire
advertising outlay	Werbeausgaben *f/pl*	dépenses *f/pl* publicitaires
advertising page plan	Anzeigenspiegel *m*	maquette *f* de la partie *f* publicitaire
advertising pamphlet	Werbeschrift *f*	brochure *f* publicitaire
advertising paper	Werbefachblatt *n*	journal *m* de publicité *f*
advertising pavilion	Werbepavillon *m*	pavillon *m* de publicité *f*
advertising performance	Werbeleistung *f*	rendement *m* publicitaire
advertising period	Streuperiode *f*, Werbeperiode *f*	période *f* de diffusion *f*, période *f* publicitaire
advertising phonetician	Werbephonetiker *m*	phonéticien *m* publicitaire
advertising picture	Reklamebild *n*	image *f* publicitaire
advertising pillar	Plakatsäule *f*, Werbesäule *f*	colonne *f* d'affichage *m*, colonne *f* Morris (à Paris) , colonne *f* publicitaire
advertising planning	Werbeplanung *f*	planning *m* publicitaire
advertising point	Werbeargument *n*	argument *m* de publicité *f*
advertising policy	Werbepolitik *f*	politique *f* publicitaire
advertising portfolio	Angebotsmappe *f*	carton *m* pour des offres *f/pl*
advertising practices *pl*	Werbebräuche *m/pl*, Werbeusancen *f/pl*	usages *m/pl* publicitaires
advertising practise	Werbepraxis *f*	pratique *f* publicitaire
advertising practitioner	Werbeberater *m*	conseil *m* en publicité *f*
advertising premium	Zugabeartikel *m*	article *m* prime *f*
advertising preparations *pl*	Werbevorbereitung *f*	préparatifs *m/pl* publicitaires
advertising pressure	Werbepression *f*	pression *f* publicitaire
advertising principles *pl*	Werbegrundsätze *m/pl*	principes *m/pl* publicitaires
advertising problem	Werbeproblem *n*	problème *m* publicitaire
advertising professions *pl*	Werbeberufe *m/pl*	professions *f/pl* de la publicité *f*
advertising program *am* advertising programme *brit*	Werbeplan *m*, Werbeprogramm *n*	plan *m* de campagne *f*, plan *m* de publicité *f*, plan *m* publicitaire, programme *m* de la publicité *f*

advertising proposal	Werbevorschlag m	proposition f publicitaire
advertising psychology	Werbepsychologie f	psychologie f de la publicité f
advertising publication	Werbepublikation f	édition f publicitaire
advertising purposes pl	Werbezwecke m/pl	fins f/pl de publicité f
advertising pylon	Werbepylon m, Werbeturm m	pylône m publicitaire, tour f publicitaire
advertising rates pl	Anzeigentarif m, Werbegebühren f/pl	frais m/pl de publicité f, tarif m d'annonces f/pl, tarif m de publicité f, tarif m d'insertion f
advertising record	werblicher Erfahrungsschatz m	expérience f publicitaire
advertising regulations pl	Werbebestimmungen f/pl	réglementations f/pl publicitaires
advertising research	Werbeforschung f	recherches f/pl relatives à la publicité f
advertising reserve	Werbereserve f	réserve f pour la publicité f
advertising restrictions pl	Werbebeschränkungen f/pl	limitations f/pl de la publicité f, restrictions f/pl de la publicité f
advertising result	Streuerfolg m, Werbeerfolg m	rendement m publicitaire, résultat m de la campagne f publicitaire
advertising revenues pl	Werbeeinnahmen f/pl	recettes f/pl publicitaires
advertising sales pl executive	Anzeigenvertreter m	courtier m en publicité f, représentant m publicitaire
advertising sample	Werbemuster n	échantillon m publicitaire
advertising schedule	Einschaltplan m, Erscheinungsplan m, Terminkalender m, Werbeplan m	calendrier m de termes m/pl, calendrier m d'insertion f, calendrier m des parutions f/pl, échéancier m, plan m de campagne f, plan m de publicité f, plan m de termes m/pl, plan m publicitaire
advertising science	Werbewissenschaft f	science f de la publicité f
advertising seal	Reklamemarke f	timbre m réclame f
advertising section	Anzeigenteil m	partie f publicitaire
advertising sector	Werbesektor m	secteur m publicitaire
advertising service	Anzeigendienst m, Werbedienst m	service m de publicité f
advertising sheet	Anzeigenseite f	feuille f d'annonces f/pl, page f d'annonces f/pl
advertising showcase	Werbevitrine f	vitrine f publicitaire
advertising sketch	Werbekurzspiel n, Werbesketch m	scène f publicitaire, sketch m publicitaire
advertising slogan	Werbeslogan m, Werbespruch m	formule f publicitaire, phrase f d'accrochage m, slogan m publicitaire
advertising solicitor am	Anzeigenakquisiteur m	démarcheur m en publicité f, vendeur m d'espace m

advertising space	Anzeigenraum *m*, Reklamefläche *f*, Werbefläche *f*	espace *m* d'annonces *f/pl*, lignage *m*, panneau *m* de publicité *f*, surface *f* d'affichage *m*
advertising space buyer	Anzeigenexpedition *f*	intermédiaire *m* publicitaire
advertising statistics *pl*	Werbestatistik *f*	statistiques *f/pl* de publicité *f*
advertising stocks *pl*	Werbefonds *m*	fonds *m* de publicité *f*
advertising strategy	Werbestrategie *f*	stratégie *f* publicitaire
advertising studio	Werbestudio *n*	studio *m* publicitaire
advertising supplement	Werbebeilage *f*	supplément *m* publicitaire encartage *m*
advertising support	Werbeunterstützung *f*	support *m* publicitaire
advertising system	Werbesystem *n*	système *m* publicitaire
advertising tactics *pl*	Werbetaktik *f*	tactique *f* publicitaire
advertising talk	Werbegespräch *n*	discours *m* publicitaire
advertising tax	Werbesteuer *f*	impôt *m* sur la publicité *f*
advertising technique	Werbetechnik *f*	technique *f* publicitaire
advertising terminology	Werbeterminologie *f*	terminologie *f* publicitaire
advertising test	Versuchswerbung *f*	publicité *f* test *m*
advertising text	Klappentext *m*, Werbetext *m*	texte *m* du rabat *m*, texte *m* publicitaire
advertising theme	Werbethema *n*	sujet *m* publicitaire
advertising thermometer	Werbethermometer *n*	thermomètre *m* publicitaire
advertising tour	Werbetournee *f*	tournée *f* publicitaire
advertising tower	Werbeturm *m*	pylône *m* publicitaire, tour *f* publicitaire
advertising trade	Werbegeschäft *n*	activité *f* publicitaire
advertising trade school	Werbefachschule *f*	école *f* de publicité *f*
advertising transactions *pl*	Werbetransaktionen *f/pl*	opérations *f/pl* publicitaires
advertising turnover	Werbeumsätze *m/pl*	chiffre *m* d'affaires *f/pl* publicitaires
advertising utensils *pl*	Werbegeräte *n/pl*	accessoires *m/pl* publicitaires
advertising value	Werbewert *m*	valeur *f* publicitaire
advertising van	Werbewagen *m*	camionette *f* publicitaire
advertising vehicle	Werbeträger *m*	organe *m* de publicité *f*, support *m* publicitaire, véhicule *m* de communication *f*
advertising verse	Werbevers *m*	vers *m* publicitaire
advertising volume	Anzeigenvolumen *n*, Streumenge *f*, Werbevolumen *n*	volume *m* de la publicité *f*, volume *m* publicitaire
advertising weapon	Werbewaffe *f*	arme *f* publicitaire
advertising zone	Streufeld *n*	zone *f* de diffusion *f*
advertographer	Akzidenzsetzer *m*	compositeur *m* de travaux *m/pl* de ville *f*, ouvrier *m* en conscience *f*
advertorial	redaktionell aufgemachte Anzeige *f*, Textanzeige *f*	annonce *f* à apparence *f* rédactionnelle, annonce *f* figurant dans le texte *m* rédactionnel
advice note	Versandanzeige *f*	instruction *f* d'expédition *f*
advisor	Berater *m*	conseil *m*, conseiller *m*
aerial advertising	Luftwerbung *f*	publicité *f* aérienne
aerial photograph	Luftaufnahme *f*, Luftbild *n*	photo *f* aérienne

aeroplane advertising	Flugzeugwerbung f	publicité f par avion m
aesthetic quality	ästhetische Qualität f	qualité f esthétique
affidavit	eidesstattliche Erklärung f	affirmation f sur serment m
affiliate	Tochtergesellschaft f	société f affiliée
affiliated company		
to affix	beifügen	ajouter
after-image	Nachbild n, Nachwirkung f	effet m ultérieur
afterwards	nachträglich	après coup m
against text	gegenüber Text m	contre texte m, face f texte m
age groups pl	Altersgruppen f/pl	groupes m/pl d'âge m
agency	Agentur f	agence f
agency agreement	Agenturvertrag m	contrat m d'agence f
agency commission	Agenturprovision f,	commission f d'agence f
	Mittlervergütung f	
agency contract	Agenturvertrag m	contrat m d'agence f
agency experience	Agenturerfahrung f	expérience f d'agence f
agency representative	Agenturvertreter m	représentant m d'une agence f
		de publicité f
agency with full service	full-service-Agentur f	agence f à service m complet
agent	Vertreter m	agent m, représentant m
agent commission	Vertreterprovision f	commission f de l'agent m
agent's territory	Vertreterbezirk m	région f du représentant m
aging schedule	Terminplan m, Zeitplan m	calendrier m d'insertion f,
		plan m des délais m/pl
agitation	Agitation f	agitation f
agitator	Agitator m	agitateur m
agony column	persönliche Anzeigen f/pl,	annonces f/pl personnelles
	Seufzerspalte f	
to agree	abmachen, vereinbaren	arranger, fixer, stipuler
agreement	Abkommen n, Abmachung f,	accord m, arrangement m,
	Abrede f, Vereinbarung f,	contrat m, convention f,
	Vertrag m	stipulation f
agriculture publication	Landwirtschaftsblatt n	feuille f rurale, journal m
		agricole
aided recall	Erinnerungshilfe f,	mémoire f aidée, souvenir m
	Gedächtnisstütze f	aidé
aim of the publication	Publikationszweck m	but m de publication f
air advertising	Luftwerbung f	publicité f aérienne
air brush	Spritzpistole f	aérographe m, pistolet m à
		peinture f
air brush technique	Spritztechnik f	aérographie f
air check	Aufzeichnung f einer	enregistrement m d'une
	Rundfunksendung f	émission f radiophonique
air edition	Luftpostausgabe f	édition f aéropostale
air time	Sendezeit f	heures f/pl de diffusion f,
		temps m d'antenne f
aircast	Rundfunk m	radio f
airline advertising	Flugreisewerbung f	publicité f pour les
		voyages m/pl d'avion m
airline guide	Luftkursbuch n	guide m aérien
airmail letter	Flugpostbrief m	lettre f aérienne
airmail paper	Flugpostpapier n,	papier m -pelure f, papier m
	Luftpostpapier n	avion m
airplane banner	Bannerschlepper m,	bannière f tractée par un
	Schleppfahne f	avion m
airport advertising	Flughafenwerbung f	publicité f dans les
		aéroports m/pl
alienation effect	Verfremdungseffekt m	effet m d'éloignement m

to **align**	ausschließen (typog) , Linie *f* halten, Zeile *f* halten	aligner, justifier, parangonner
alignment	Ausgleich *typog m*, Schriftlinie *f*	alignement *m*, ligne *f* de lettre *f*
all rights *pl* **reserved**	alle Rechte *n/pl* vorbehalten	tous droits *m/pl* réservés
all the issues *pl*	Gesamtausgabe *f*	édition *f* complète, toutes les éditions *f/pl*
allegory	Allegorie *f*	allégorie *f*
to **allocate**	zuteilen	allouer, assigner
allocation	Etatsanteil *m*, Kostenverteilung *f*, Werbekostenanweisung *f*, Zuteilung *f*	allocation *f*, budget *m* alloué, lotissement *m* publicitaire, répartition *f* des charges *f/pl*, répartition *f* des coûts *m/pl*
allocation draft	Etatplan *m*	projet *m* de budget *m*
to **allot**	zuteilen	allouer, assigner
allotment	Zuteilung *f*	allocation *f*, lotissement *m* publicitaire
all-purpose type face	Allzweckschrift *f*	type *m* à toutes fins *f/pl*
allround man	Alleskönner *m*	homme *m* universel
almanac	Almanach *m*, Kalender *m*	almanach *m*, calendrier *m*
alphabet	Alphabet *n*	alphabet *m*
alphabetic	alphabetisch	par ordre *m* alphabétique
alteration of title	Titeländerung *f*	modification *f* de titre *m*
aluminium foil	Aluminiumfolie *f*	feuille d'aluminium *m*
amalgamation	Zusammenschluß *m*	jumelage *m*, regroupement *m*
amateur film	Amateurfilm *m*	film *m* d'amateur *m*
amendment	Änderung *f*, Verbesserung *f*	amendement *m*, changement *m*, modification *f*
American envelope	Versandtasche *f*	enveloppe *f* américaine, pochette *f*
amount	Betrag *m*, Summe *f*	compte *m*, montant *m*, somme *f*
amount of space	Anzeigenraum *m*	espace *m* d'annonces *f/pl*, lignage *m*
ampersand	„und"-Zeichen *n*	esperluète *f*, signe *m* «et» commercial
anaglyphic print	Anaglyphendruck *m*	impression *f* d'anaglyphes *f/pl*
analysis	Analyse *f*	analyse *f*
analysis of subscribers *pl*	Bezieheranalyse *f*	analyse *f* du cercle *m* des abonnés *m/pl*
anastatic printing	anastatischer Druck *m*	impression *f* anastatique
anaxial composition	anaxiale Satzform *f*	composition *f* anaxiale
anchored	Platz *m*, immer an demselben	fixe
anecdote	Anekdote *f*	anecdote *f*
to **angle**	einseitig beeinflussen	influencer partialement
angle meter	Winkelmaß *n*	équerre *f*
aniline dyes *pl*	Teerfarbstoffe *m/pl*	couleurs *f/pl* à l'aniline *f*
aniline printing	Anilindruck *m*	flexographie *f*, impression *f* à l'aniline *f*
animated cartoon	Trickfilm *m*, Zeichentrickfilm *m*	dessin *m* animé, film *m* en dessin *m* animé, film *m* truqué
animated electric sign advertising	bewegliche Lichtwerbung *f*	publicité *f* lumineuse animée
animation	Lichtwerbung *f*	publicité *f* lumineuse
animator	Trickfilmzeichner *m*	animateur *m*
annals *pl*	Annalen *f/pl*	annales *f/pl*
annex	Anhang *m*	appendice *m*, supplément *m*

anniversary publication	Jubiläumsschrift *f*	publication *f* anniversaire, publication *f* de jubilé *m*
to announce	ankündigen	annoncer
announcement	Ankündigung *f,* Ansage *f,* Anzeige *f,* Bekanntmachung *f,* Durchsage *f,* Fernsehspot *m*	annonce *f,* avis *m,* communiqué *m,* émission *f* publicitaire, information *f,* insertion *f,* spot *m*
announcement campaign	Einführungskampagne *f*	campagne *f* de lancement *m,* campagne *f* d'information *f,* campagne *f* d'introduction *f*
announcement of an engagement	Verlobungsanzeige *f*	faire-part de fiançailles *f/pl*
announcement of birth	Geburtsanzeige *f*	faire-part *m* de naissance *f*
announcer	Ansager *m*	compère *m,* speaker *m*
annual	Jahrbuch *n*	annale *f,* annuaire *m*
annual order	Jahresauftrag *m*	ordre *m* annuel
annual report	Jahresbericht *m*	rapport *m* annuel, rapport *m* d'exercise *f*
annual subscription	Jahresabonnement *n*	abonnement *m* annuel
annually	jährlich	annuel
anonymity	Anonymität *f*	anonymat *m*
anonymous	anonym	anonyme
antedated paper	vordatierte Zeitung *f*	journal *m* antidaté, journal *m* prédaté, première édition *f*
anthology	Anthologie *f*	anthologie *f*
anticyclic advertising	antizyklische Werbung *f*	publicité *f* anticyclique
antipathy to advertising	Werbefeindlichkeit *f*	publiphobie *f*
antiquated	veraltet	périmé, vieilli
antique weave paper	Werkdruckpapier *n*	papier *m* d'œuvre *f*
antique wove	antik (Papier)	papier *m* édition *f*
aphorism	Aphorismus *m*	aphorisme *m*
apostrophe	Apostroph *m*	apostrophe *f*
appeal	Anreiz *m,* Anziehungskraft *f,* Appell *m*	appel *m,* attrait *m,* force *f* d'attraction *f,* incitation *f*
appealing advertising	ansprechende Werbung *f*	publicité *f* attrayante
to appear	erscheinen	paraître, sortir
appearance	Erscheinen *n*	publication *f,* sortie *f*
appendix	Anhang *m,* Anlage *f*	annexe *f,* appendice *m,* supplément *m*
apperception	bewußte Wahrnehmung *f*	apperception *f*
appetizing appeal	appetitanregende Aufmachung *f*	présentation *f* appétissante
applause mail *am*	Anerkennungsschreiben *n*	courrier *m* des auditeurs *m/pl*
applied art	angewandte Kunst *f,* Gebrauchsgrafik *f*	art *m* publicitaire, arts *m/pl* industriels, graphisme *m* publicitaire, publicité *f* artistique
appointed space	Platzvorschrift *f*	emplacement *m* imposé
appointment	Zusammenkunft *f*	entrevue *f*
approach	Ansatzpunkt *m,* Aufhänger *m,* Blickfang *m,* Sichtbarkeit *f*	accrochage *m* publicitaire, accroche-œil *m,* amorce *f,* angle *m* d'approche *f,* attrape-regard *m,* tape -à-l'œil *m,* tire-l'œil *m,* visibilité *f*
appropriateness	Angemessenheit *f*	convenance *f*
appropriation	Budget *n*	budget *m*
appropriation of advertising	genehmigte Werbemittel *n/pl*	budget *m* publicitaire

to **approve of**	unterschreiben	signer, souscrire à
approved price	gebilligter Preis *m*, genehmigter Preis *m*	prix *m* approuvé
approximation	Näherungswert *m*	approximation *f*
apron	Preisschild *n*	étiquette *f*, porte-prix *m*
aquarelle colours *pl*	Aquarellfarben *f/pl*	couleurs *f/pl* aquarelles
aquatint	Aquatinta *f*	aquatinte *f*
arabesque	Arabeske *f*	arabesque *f*
Arabic numerals *pl*	arabische Ziffern *f/pl*	chiffres *m/pl* arabes
arbitrator	Schiedsrichter *m*	arbitre *m*
archives *pl*	Archiv *n*	archives *f/pl*
area	Fläche *f*	surface *f*
area sampling	Flächenstichprobe *f*, regionale Marktuntersuchung *f*	échantillonnage *m* par zone *f*
arena	Sporthalle *f*	hall *m* de sport *m*
armchair critic	Kritikaster *m*	critique *m* en chambre *f*, critiqueur *m*, éplucheur *m*
armchair politician	Politikaster *m*	politicien *m*, tacticien *m*
to **arrange**	abmachen, bearbeiten	adapter, arranger, fixer
arrangement	Abmachung *f*, Anordnung *f*, Disposition *f*	accord *m*, agencement *m*, arrangement *m*, convention *f*, disposition *f*
art	Kunst *f*	art *m*
art board	Kunstdruckkarton *m*	carton *m* couché
art buyer	Artdirektor *m*, Auftraggeber *m* freier Künstler *m/pl*, Bildmaterialbeschaffer *m*, Sachbearbeiter *m* für Grafiker-Mitarbeit *f*	acheteur *m* d'art *m*, acheteur *m* du graphisme *m* publicitaire, concepteur *m* graphique, directeur *m* artistique, ordonnateur *m* d'art *m*, ravitailleur *m* des éléments *m/pl* d'illustrations *f/pl*
art critic	Kunstkritiker *m*	critique *m* d'art *m*
art department	fotografische Abteilung *f*	service *m* photographique
art designer	Werbegestalter *m*	dessinateur *m*
art director	Artdirektor *m*, Atelierleiter *m*, Chefgrafiker *m*, Gestaltungsleiter *m*, künstlerischer Leiter *m*	artiste *m* en chef *m*, chef *m* de studio *m*, chef *m* du service *m* création *f*, concepteur *m* graphique, directeur *m* artistique, ordonnateur *m* d'art *m*
art editor	Fotoredakteur *m*	chef *m* du service *m* photographique
art library	Fotoarchiv *n*	archives *f/pl* photographiques
art matt *am* **art matt paper** *brit*	mattes Kunstdruckpapier *n*	papier *m* chromo, papier *m* couché mat
art paper	Bilderdruckpapier *n*, Kunstdruckpapier *n*	papier *m* couché des deux faces *f/pl*, papier *m* surglacé
art print	Kunstdruck *m*	impression *f* artistique
art pull	Abzug *m* auf Kunstdruckpapier *n*, Kunstdruckabzug *m*	épreuve *f* sur papier *m* couché
art school	Kunstschule *f*	école *f* d'art *m*

art work	Bildgestaltung f, Gestaltungsmittel m/pl, künstlerische Arbeiten f/pl, Künstlerarbeit f	moyens m/pl de réalisation f, ouvrages m/pl artistiques, travail m artistique
article	Artikel m	article m
article of consumption	Konsumartikel m	article m de consommation f
artificial	künstlich	artificiel, synthétique
artisan fair	Handwerksmesse f	foire f de l'artisanat m
artist	Grafiker m, Illustrator m, Karikaturist m, Künstler m, Zeichner m	artiste m, caricaturiste m, dessinateur m, graphiste m, illustrateur m
to artist	retuschieren	retoucher
artistic advertising	künstlerische Werbung f	publicité f artistique
as is	Originalgröße f	tel
as per instructions pl	auftragsgemäß	suivant l'ordre m
as reported	verlautet, wie	on indique
ascenders pl	Oberlängen f/pl	lettres f/pl débordantes, longues f/pl du haut m
ascertained fact	erwiesene Tatsache f	fait m établi
aspect	Gesichtspunkt m	point m de vue f
aspect ratio	Bildschirmformat n	format m de l'écran m
assembling	Montage f	montage m
assessment	Auswahl f, Bewertung f	choix m, estimation f, évaluation f, sélection f
assignment	Aufgabengebiet n	fonctions f/pl, tâche f assignée
assignment of advertising expenditure	Aufteilung f des Werbebudgets n	allocation f du budget m publicitaire
assignment of expenditures pl	Budgetgliederung f	allocation f du budget m
assignment-man	Reporter m für besondere Aufgaben f/pl	reporter m à la tâche f
assistant	Assistent m	adjoint m, assistant m
associate editor	stellvertretender Chefredakteur m	rédacteur m en chef m adjoint
association	Verband m, Zusammenhang m	association f, connexion f, liaison f
association subscription	Mitgliedsabonnement n	abonnement m pour membres m/pl
association test	Assoziationstest m	test m d'association f
assortment	Sortiment n	assortiment m, choix m
assortment of goods pl	Warensortiment n	choix m de marchandises f/pl
assurance of subscribers pl	Abonnentenversicherung f	assurance f des abonnés m/pl
asterisk	Sternchen n	astérique m
asymmetry	Asymmetrie f	asymétrie f
at an average	durchschnittlich	en moyenne
at the latest	spätestens	au plus tard
atmospherics pl	Nebengeräusche n/pl	bruits m/pl parasites, fritures f/pl
atrocity story	Greuelmärchen n	atrocités f/pl inventées
attention	Aufmerksamkeit f, Beachtung f	attention f
attention factor	Aufmerksamkeitsfaktor m	facteur m d'attention f
attention getter	Aufmerksamkeitserreger m	accrochage m initial, angle m d'approche f
attention value	Aufmerksamkeitswert m, Zugkraft f	accrochage m publicitaire, attrait m publicitaire, force f d'attraction f, valeur f d'attention f

attitude	Einstellung f, Verhalten n	attitude f, opinion f
attitude scale	Verhaltensskala f	échelle f d'attitudes f/pl
attitude study	Verhaltensprüfung f	étude f d'attitude f, test m d'axe m
to **attract customers** pl	Kunden m/pl gewinnen	acquérir des clients m/pl, attirer des clients m/pl
attraction	Anziehungskraft f, Zugkraft f	accrochage m publicitaire, attrait m, attrait m publicitaire, force f d'attraction f
attractive advertising	zugkräftige Werbung f	numéro m à succès m, publicité f attractive
attractive power	Anziehungskraft f	attrait m, force f d'attraction f
auctions pl	Versteigerungen f/pl	ventes f/pl publiques
audibility	Hörbarkeit f	audibilité f
audience	Hörerschaft f, Leserschaft f, Publikum n, Zuhörerschaft f	audience f, auditeurs m/pl, ensemble m des auditeurs m/pl, ensemble m des lecteurs m/pl, masse f des lecteurs m/pl, public m
audience analysis	Leseranalyse f, Publikumsanalyse f, Zuschaueranalyse f	analyse f de l'audience f, analyse f des lecteurs m/pl, analyse f des spectateurs m/pl
audience builder	zugkräftige Werbung f	numéro m à succès m, publicité f attractive
audience composition	demografische Struktur f, Zusammensetzung f des Publikums n	composition f de l'audience f, structure f démographique
audience flow	Gesamtpublikum n	audience f totale
audience measurement	Höreranalyse f	recherches f/pl relatives à l'audience f
audience profile	Publikumszusammensetzung f, Zusammensetzung f des Publikums n	composition f de l'audience f, composition f du public m
audience research	Publikumsanalyse f	analyse f de l'audience f
audience turnover	Teilnehmerzahl	nombre m des personnes f/pl touchées par un support m
audimeter	Audimeter m, Aufnahmeapparat m zur Feststellung f der Hörerzahl f	audimètre m, audiomètre m, audimètre m
audio	Tonteil m einer Fernseh-sendung f	partie f de son m d'une émission f télévisée
audio tape	Tonband n	bande f magnétique
audiometer	Aufzeichnungsgerät n zur Hörerschaftsforschung f	audiomètre m
audiovision	Kassettenfernsehen n	audiovision f, télévision f à cassettes f/pl
audio-visual advertising	audiovisuelle Werbung f	publicité f audio-visuelle
audio-visual equipment	audiovisuelle Geräte n/pl	appareils m/pl audio-visuels
audit	Rechnungsprüfung f	vérification f des comptes m/pl
Audit Bureau of Circulations pl	Auflagenüberwachungsstelle f	Office m de Justification f des Tirages m/pl
audit report	Prüfungsbericht m	rapport m de contrôle m
audit store	Testladen m	boutique f d'essai m

audition	Probesprechen *n*, Test *m* einer Rundfunksendung *f*	séance *f* d'essai *m*, test *m* d'une émission *f* radiophonique
auditor	Prüfer *m*	contrôleur *m*
to authenticate	beglaubigen	certifier conforme, légaliser
authentication	Beglaubigung *f*	légalisation *f*
author	Autor *m*, Schriftsteller *m*, Urheber *m*, Verfasser *m*	auteur *m*, écrivain *m*, publiciste *m*
author's alteration, author's correction	Autorenkorrektur *f*	corrections *f/pl* d'auteur *m*
autochrome printing	Autochromdruck *m*	impression *f* en autochromie *f*
automatic feeder	Selbstanleger *m*	margeur *m* automatique
automatic selling	Verkauf *m* durch Automaten *m/pl*	vente *f* d'articles *m/pl* dans des machines *f/pl* distributrices automatiques
automatic typewriter	automatische Schreibmaschine *f*, Schreibautomat *m*	machine *f* à écrire automatique
autotype	Autotypie *f*	autotypie *f*, similigravure *f*
autumn fair	Herbstmesse *f*	foire *f* d'automne *m*
auxiliary advertising	unterstützende Werbung *f*, zusätzliche Werbung *f*	publicité *f* auxiliaire, publicité *f* de complément *m*, publicité *f* de soutien *m*
auxiliary printing unit	Eindruckwerk *n*	élément *m* d'impression *f* auxiliaire
availabilities *pl* in radio and television	Werbezeiten *f/pl* in Rundfunk *m* und Fernsehen *n*	temps *m* d'antenne *f* disponible
available	verfügbar	disponible
available sites *pl*	verfügbarer Anschlagraum *m*	emplacements *m/pl* disponibles
available sites *pl* list	Liste *f* des verfügbaren Anschlagraums *m*	pointage *m* des emplacements *m/pl* disponibles
av-commercial	Kassetteninsert *n*	av-spot *m*
average	Durchschnitt *m*	moyenne
average circulation	durchschnittliche Auflage *f*	diffusion *f* moyenne, tirage *m* moyen
average costs *pl*	Durchschnittskosten *pl*	frais *m/pl* moyens
average date of posting	mittlere Anlaufzeit *f*	date *f* moyenne de pose *f*
average net paid circulation	durchschnittliche Verkaufsauflage *f*	bouillon *m* déduit moyen
average price	Durchschnittspreis *m*	prix *m* moyen
average sold circulation	durchschnittliche Verkaufsauflage *f*	bouillon *m* déduit moyen
awarding of a prize	Prämiierung *f*	attribution *f* d'une prime *f*
awning	Werbeschild *n* am Verdeck *m*	store *m*
axial composition	axiale Satzform *f*	composition *f* axiale

B

back	Bund *m/typog*	marge *f* intérieure
to back	hinterkleben	contre-coller
back copies *pl*	frühere Ausgaben *f/pl*	exemplaires *m/pl* précédents
back cover	4. Umschlagseite *f*	dernière page *f* de couverture *f*
back edge	Rückenrand *m*	mors *m*

back glueing	Rückenleimung *f*	encollage *m* du dos *m* des livres *m/pl*
back margin	Bundsteg *m*	blanc *m* du petit fond *m*, marge *f* intérieure
back orders *pl*	Auftragsrückstand *m*	retard *m* dans l'exécution *f* des commandes *f/pl*
back page	letzte Seite *f*	page *f* dernière
back room	Setzersaal *m*	atelier *m* de composition *f*
back section	hinterer Teil *m* der Ausgabe *f*	cahier *m* de queue *f*
back-biter	Verleumder *m*	calomniateur *m*, détracteur *m*
back-biting	üble Nachrede *f*	médisance *f*
backbone	Buchrücken *m*	dos *m* de livre *m*
backed frame	gerasteter Rahmen *m*	cadre *m* de filets *m/pl* gras-maigre
background	Hintergrund *m*	arrière-plan *m*
background plate	Tonplatte *f*	à-plat, planche *f* de fond *m*
background report	Lagebericht *m*	rapport *m* sur la situation *f*
background sound effect	musikalische Untermalung *f*, Tonuntermalung *f*	fond *m* sonore
background story	Dokumentarbericht *m*, Stimmungsbericht *m*	article *m* documentaire, rapport *m* documentaire, report *m* expressif
backing up	Rückseitendruck *m*, Widerdruck *m*	impression *f* au verso *n*, retiration *f*, seconde forme *f*
backlog	Arbeitsrückstand *m*	arriéré *m* de travail *m*
backlog of orders *pl*	Auftragspolster *n*	commandes *f/pl* en suspens *m*
back-number	alte Zeitungsnummer *f*	exemplaire *m* périmé
backstrip	Buchrücken *m*	dos *m* de livre *m*
to back-up	zurichten	mettre en page *f*, mettre en train *m*
bad copy	schlechtes Manuskript *n*	cheveu *m*
bad taste	Geschmacklosigkeit *f*	mauvais goût *m*
bad will	schlechter Ruf *m*	mauvaise réputation *f*
badge	Abzeichen *n*, Namensschildchen *n*	insigne *m*, signe *m* distinctif
badly imposed page	liederlich zusammengestellte Seite *f*	feuille *f* bambochée
bag	Beutel *m*	sac *m*
bait	Köder *m*, Lockartikel *m*	appât *m*, article *m* d'appel *m*, article *m* de réclame *f*, leurre *m*, produit *m* d'appel *m*
balance	Gleichgewicht *n*, Schlußergebnis *n*	bilan *m*, équilibre *m*
balanced article	objektiver Artikel *m*	article *m* objectif
balanced make up	ausgewogene Aufmachung *f*	mise *f* en page *f* équilibrée
bald fact	nackte Tatsache *f*	fait *m* pur et simple
balderdash	Geschwätz *n*, verworrenes Geschwätz *n*	amphigourie *f*, baratin *m*, bêtises *f/pl*
baling board	Ballenbrett *n*	planche *f*
balloon advertising	Ballonwerbung *f*	publicité *f* par ballons *m/pl*
balloon caption	Sprechblase *f*	ballon *m*, bulle *f*, philactère *f*
balloon linen	Ballonleinen *n*	toile-ballon *f*
ball-point	Kugelschreiber *m*	stylo *m* à bille *f*

ballyhoo *am*	marktschreierische Werbung *f*, Werberummel *m*	battage *m* publicitaire, bourrage *m* de crâne *m*, publicité *f* raccrocheuse, publicité *f* tapageuse, tam-tam *m*
baloney *am*	Faxen *f/pl*	fadaises *f/pl*
ban on news	Nachrichtensperre *f*	black-out *m*, blocus *m* de nouvelles *f/pl*
band	Bauchbinde *f*, Streifenanzeige *f*	bande *f* de publicité *f*, bandeau *m*
band advertising	Bildserienwerbung *f*	publicité *f* avec des bandes *f/pl* dessinées
band saw	Bandsäge *f*	scie *f* à ruban *m*
band wagon	Woge *f* der Volksgunst *f*	vague *f* de popularité *f*
banded offer	Koppelungsverkauf *m*	promotion *f* jumelée, vente *f* liée
banded packs *pl*	mehrere Packungen *f/pl* eines Produktes *n*	plusieurs emballages *m/pl* d'un produit *m*
bank cheque *brit*	Bankscheck *m*	chèque *m* bancaire, mandat *m* bancaire
banks *pl*	Überschriftszeilen *f/pl*	lignes *f/pl* d'une manchette *f*
banner	Dachschild *n*, Spannband *n*, Spruchband *n*, Streifenanzeige *f*, Transparent *n*	bandeau *m*, banderole *f*, calicot *m*, enseigne *f* lumineuse, oriflamme *f*, panneau *m* sur le toit *m*, transparent *m*
banner-headline	Balkenüberschrift *f*	titre *m* en caractères *m/pl* d'affiches *f/pl*
bargain	Gelegenheitskauf *m*	achat *m* occasionnel, occasion *f*
to bargain	aushandeln	marchander, négocier
bargain level	niedrigst kalkulierter Preis *m*	prix *m* minimum
bargain sale	Reklameverkauf *m*, Werbeverkauf *m*	vente *f* réclame
barter	Gegengeschäft *n*	affaire *f* en échange *m*, contre-affaire *f*, troc *m*
barter advertisement	Tauschanzeige *f*	annonce *f* d'échange *m*
baryta paper	Barytpapier *n*	papier *m* baryté
base line	Schlußaussage *f*, Unterschriftszeile *f*	légende *f*, ligne *f* de fond *m*
base of calculation	Berechnungsgrundlage *f*	base *f* de calcul *m*
base sheet	Deckblatt *n*	feuille *f* de couverture *f*
basic concept	Grundkonzeption *f*	conception *f* de base *f*
basic dates *pl*	grundlegendes Material *n*	données *f/pl* de base *f*
basic media *pl*	klassische Medien *n/pl*	médias *m/pl* classiques
basic medium	Hauptwerbemittel *n*	média *m* de base *f*, média *m* principal
basic message	Hauptaussage *f*, Werbegrundaussage *f*	axe *m* de la publicité *f*, message *m* de base *f*
basic price	Richtpreis *m*	prix *m* de direction *f*
basic rate	Anzeigengrundpreis *m*, Grundpreis *m*	prix *m* de base *f*, tarif *m* de base *f*, tarif *m* fixe
basic size	genormte Größe *f*	format *m* standard *m*
basic weight scales *pl*	Quadrantenwaage *f*	pèse-papier *m*
basis	Grundlage *f*	base *f*
basis for discussion	Diskussionsbasis *f*	base *f* d'une discussion *f*
bastard face	Bastardschrift *f*	lettres *f/pl* bâtardes

bastard title	Schmutztitel *m*	avant-titre *m*, faux titre *m*
bastard type	Bastardschrift *f*	lettres *f/pl* bâtardes
to batter	abquetschen	écraser
battered letters *pl*	beschädigte Buchstaben *m/pl*, lädierte Buchstaben *m/pl*	lettres *f/pl* écrasées
to be continued	Fortsetzung *f* folgt, wird fortgesetzt	à suivre, complément de texte *m* suivra
to be on the air	Radiowerbung *f* betreiben, Rundfunk *m* sprechen, im	annoncer par radio *f*, avoir l'antenne *f*
to be pressed for space	Platzmangel *m* haben	être à court de place *f*
to be published	abnehmbar	à épuiser
to be published within one year	abzunehmen innerhalb eines Jahres *n*	à épuiser dans le délai *m* d'une année *f*
to be wrapped in silence	Schweigen *n* hüllen, sich in	se renfermer dans le silence *m*
beard	falsch ausgesprochenes Wort *n*, Fleisch *n* eines Buchstabens *m*, verstümmeltes Wort *n*	blanc *m*, couac *m*, cuir *m*, épaulement *m*, espace *m* vierge *f*, talus *m* de pied *m*
bearers *pl*	Portepagen *pl*	porte-pages *f/pl*
bearing	Tragweite *f*	portée *f*
beat	Ressort *n*	ressort *m*, secteur *m*
bed	Fundament *n* (Schließplatte *f*)	marbre *m*
bed bearer	Schmitzleiste *f*.	tasseau *m* du marbre *m*
before insertion	vor Einschaltung *f*	avant l'insertion *f*
before issue	vor Erscheinen *n*	avant la parution *f*
beginner	Neuling *m*	néophyte *m*, nouveau venu
behaviour	Einstellung *f*, Verhalten *n*	attitude *f*, opinion *f*
behaviour research	Verhaltensbeobachtung *f*	étude *f* de comportement *m*
belabouring public feeling	Stimmungsmache *f*	bourrage *m* de crâne *m*
to belie	dementieren	démentir
believability	Glaubhaftigkeit *f*	croyabilité *f*
bell-sell	Telefonwerbung *f*	vente *f* par téléphone *m*
Ben Day	Raster *m*	grisé *m* mécanique, réseau *m*, trame *f*
Ben Day process, screening	Aufrasterung *f*	tramage *m*
to bend round	rundbiegen	arrondir
bestseller	Erfolgsbuch *n*, meistgekauftes Buch *n*, Verkaufsschlager *m*	article *m* de grosse vente *f*, livre *m* à succès *m*, succès *m* de vente *f*
bevel	Facette *f*, Gehrung *f*	onglet *m*, talus *m*
to bevel	abschleifen	biseauter
bevelled edge	Klischeefacette *f*	bord *m* biseauté
bevelled feet *pl*	Fleisch *n* eines Buchstabens *m*	blanc *m*, épaulement *m*, espace *m* vierge *f*, talus *m* de pied *m*
beverage advertising	Getränkewerbung *f*	publicité *f* des boissons *f/pl*
bias	Tendenz *f*, Verfälschung *f*, Voreingenommenheit *f*, Vorurteil *n*	falsification *f*, parti *m* pris, préjugé *m*, prévention *f*, tendance *f*
bible paper	Bibeldruckpapier *n*, Dünndruckpapier *n*	papier *m* bible, papier *m* mince, pelure *f* d'oignon *m*
bibliography	Bibliografie *f*, Literaturverzeichnis *n*	bibliographie *f*
big city press	Großstadtpresse *f*	presse *f* urbaine, quotidiens *m/pl* métropolitains

big splurge ad	großflächige Anzeige *f*	annonce *f* de grandes dimensions *f/pl*
bilingual	zweisprachig	bilingue
bill	Anschlagbogen *m*, Plakat *n*, Rechnung *f*, Wechsel *m* (Tratte *f*)	affiche *f*-papier *m*, compte *m*, facture *f*, lettre *f* de change *m*, placard *m*, traite *f*
bill posting	Bogenanschlag *m*	publicité *f* par affiches *f/pl*
billboard	Anschlagstelle *f*, Anschlagtafel *f*, Werbeschild *n*	emplacement *m*, enseigne *f* publicitaire, panneau *m* d'affichage *m*, panonceau *m*, place *f* d'affichage *m*, plaque *f* publicitaire
billboard commercial	Fernsehwerbung *f* in Plakatform *f*	spot *m* en forme *f* d'affiche *f*
billing	Etatsumme *f*, Gesamtbudget *n*	chiffre *m* d'affaires *f/pl* total
bill-poster	Plakatanschläger *m*	afficheur *m*
billposting	Affichierung *f*, Plakatanschlagwerbung *f*	affichage *m*, publicité *f* par affiches *f/pl*
billposting agency	Plakatanschlaginstitut *n*	entrepreneur *m* d'affichage *m*
billposting company	Anschlagunternehmen *n*	entreprise *f* d'affichage *m*
billposting on hoardings *pl*, **billposting on plank fences** *pl*	Bauzaunwerbung *f*	affichage *m* sur palissades *f/pl*
billposting order	Plakatierungsauftrag *m*	ordre *m* d'affichage *m*
bill-sticker	Anschläger *m*, Plakatanschläger *m*, Plakatkleber *m*	afficheur *m*, colleur *m* d'affiches *f/pl*
bimetal plate	Bimetallplatte *f*	plaque *f* bi-métal
bi-monthly	alle zwei Monate *m/pl*, zweimonatlich	bimestriel
to **bind into**	einheften	brocher dans, coudre dans
binder	Bindemittel *n*	liant *m*
binder line	Obertitel *m* über mehrere Aufsätze *m/pl* mit demselben Thema *n*	bandeau *m* général
binding	Buchbinderarbeit *f*, Bucheinband *m*, Einband *m*	couverture *f*, reliure *f*, travail *m* de relieur *m*
binding department	Buchbinderei *f*	atelier *m* de reliure *f*
bingling	Pfuscharbeit *f*	bousillage *m*
biography	Biografie *f*	biographie *f*
bird's eye view	Vogelperspektive *f*	vue *f* à vol *m* d'oiseau *m*
bite	Ätztiefe *f*	morsure *f*
to **bite**	ätzen	creuser, graver, mordre
bi-weekly	zweiwöchentlich	bi-hebdomadaire
to **blab out a secret**	eine Sache *f* ausplaudern	vendre la mèche *f*
black	Blockade *f*	blocage *m*, caractère *m* retourné, lettre *f* bloquée
black and white film	Schwarzweißfilm *m*	film *m* en noir et blanc
black and white reproduction	Schwarzweißaufnahme *f*	prise *f* de vue *f* noir blanc
black art	schwarze Kunst *f*	magie *f* noire
black border	schwarzer Rand *m*	baguette *f*, bordure *f* de filets *m/pl* mat
black frame		
black letter	Fraktur *f*	caractères *m/pl* allemands, caractères *m/pl* gothiques, fracture *f*

black out	Minisketch *m*	pièce de cabaret *m* artistique
blackout	Kurzszene *f*, Sketch *m*, Totschweigen *n*	pièce *f* courte, silence *m* complet
to black out	verdunkeln	occulter
black tidings *pl*	schlechte Nachrichten *f/pl*	mauvaises nouvelles *f/pl*
blacked out news	unterdrückte Nachricht *f*	nouvelle *f* supprimée, ratage *m*
blade	Rakel *f*	raclette *f*, racleur *m*
blah-blah	Flausen *f/pl*	bla-bla-bla *m*
blank	Blankoformular *n*	formule *f* en blanc
blank cheque	Blankoscheck *m*	chèque *m* en blanc
blank form	Formular *n*, Vordruck *m* (Formblatt *n*)	formulaire *m*
blank line	Blindzeile *f*	ligne *f* de blanc
blank material	Blindmaterial *n*	blancs *m/pl*
blank page	leere Seite *f*, Schimmel *m*/*typog*, Vakatseite *f*	page *f* blanche, page *f* en blanc, page *f* vierge *f*
blank sheet	blinder Bogen *m*	feinte *f*
blank space	Ausschluß *typog m*, freier Raum *m*, Fleisch *n* eines Buchstabens *m*, unbedruckter Raum *m*	blanc *m*, cadrats *m/pl*, épaulement *m*, espace *m* en blanc, espace *m* non-imprimé, espace *m* vierge *f*, talus *m* de pied *m*
blanked contract	Gesamtabschluß *m*	ensemble *m* des contrats *m/pl*, ensemble *m* des ordres *m/pl*
blanket	Drucktuch *n*	blanchet *m*
blanket rate	Pauschalpreis *m*	prix *m* forfaitaire
blanket sheet	großformatige Zeitung *f*	journal *m* de grand format *m*
blanking paper	Auskleidepapier *n*, Fondpapier *n*	papier *m* de fond *m*
blanks *pl*	Leerdruck *m*	blancs *m/pl*
to blazon	pomphaft hervorheben	exalter
to bleach out	ausbleichen	décolorer
bleed	Anschnitt *m*, randloses Klischee *f*, Schnittrand *m*	bord *m* de coupe *f*, cliché *m* sans marge *f*, rogne *f*
bleed advertisement	angeschnittene Anzeige *f*	annonce *f* à fond *m* perdu, annonce *f* à franc-bord *m*
bleed difference	Beschnittzugabe *f*	coupure *f*
bleed-off	randangeschnitten	franc bord
bleed-off page	angeschnittene Seite *f*	fond *m* perdu
blend	zusammengesetztes Kunstwort *n*	mot *m* téléscopé
to blend	verlaufen (Farben *f/pl*)	se fondre
to blind	blindpressen	dorer à froid
blind blocking, blind embossing	Blindprägung *f*	gaufrage *m* à sec, impression *f* en blanc
blind headline	Schlagzeile *f* ohne Produktnennung *f*, Überschrift *f* ohne Information *f*	titre *m* en vedette *f* sans citant le produit *m*, titre *m* sans information *f*
blind letter	Brief *m* mit fehlerhafter Anschrift *f*	lettre *f* dont l'adresse *f* est défectueuse
blind offer	verstecktes Angebot *n*	offre *f* clandestine
blind print	Schimmel *m*/*typog*	page *f* blanche

blind product test	anonymer Produkttest *m*, Anzeigenerinnerungstest *m*	test *m* de produit *m* anonyme, test *m* sans visibilité *f* du produit *m*
blind stamping	Blinddruck *m*, Prägedruck *m*	bombage *m*, estampage *m*, gaufrage *m*
blind test	Blindtest *m*, Vergleich *m* anonymer Produkte *n/pl*	test *m* à l'aveugle
blind tooling	Blindpressung *f*	dorure *f* à froid
blister pack	durchsichtige Verpackung *f* aus Kunststoff *m*	emballage *m* plastique transparent
block (brit)	Ätzung *f*, Druckstock *m*, Klischee *n*	cliché *m*, eau-forte *f*, gravure *f*, planche *f* typographique
to **block**	aufklotzen	clouer
block advertisement	Klischeeanzeige *f*	annonce *f* illustrée
block base	Klischeefuß *m*	pied *m* de cliché *m*
block cabinet	Klischeeschrank *m*	armoire *f* pour clichés *m/pl*
block capital, block letter	Blockbuchstabe *m*	capitale *f* bâton *m*, lettre *m* moulée, majuscule *f* imitée
block letters *pl*	Druckbuchstaben *m/pl*, Druckschrift *f/typog*	caractères *m/pl* bâtons *m/pl*, caractères *m/pl* typographiques
block maker	Klischeeanstalt *f*	atelier *m* de photogravure *f*, clichérie *f*
block making techniques *pl*	Klischeetechnik *f*	technique *f* de clicher
block mount	Klischeefuß *m*	pied *m* de cliché *m*
block of advertisements *pl*	Werbeblock *m*	tranche *f* de publicité *f*
to **block out**	abdecken, ausblocken	bloquer une lettre *f*, caviarder, couvrir, masquer, recouvrir
block preservation	Klischeeaufbewahrung *f*	magasinage *m* de cliché *m*
block pull *brit*	Klischeeabzug *m*	épreuve *f* de cliché *m*, fumée *f*
block stitching	Blockheftung *f*	piqûre *f* au bloc *m*
block storage	Klischeeaufbewahrung *f*	magasinage *m* de cliché *m*
block white on black	Negativklischee *n*	cliché *m* négatif, cliché *m* noir au blanc
blockade of orders *pl*	Auftragssperre *f*	blocage *m* de commandes *f/pl*
blockbuster	aufsehenerregender Artikel *m*	papier *m* du tonnerre *m*
blocked-out half-tone	freistehende Autotypie *f*	autotypie *f* en silhouette *f*, simili *m* détouré
blocking press	Prägepresse *f*	presse *f* à empreindre
blockmaker	Chemigraf *m*, Klischeeätzer *m*, Klischeur *m*	clicheur *m*, graveur *m*, photograveur *m*, zincographe *m*
block-maker's proof	Klischeeabzug *m*	épreuve *f* de cliché *m*, fumée *f*
block-out	gesperrte Zeit *f* (für Werbesendungen)	durée *f* du blocage *m*
block-process	Autotypiereproduktion *f*	photo-typographie *f*
bloomer *am*	Straßenbahntriebwagen *m*	voiture *f* motrice
bloop	Ungeschicklichkeit *f*	gaffe *f*
blooper	Störsender *m*	émetteur *m* brouilleur, poste *f* de brouillage *m*
blotted print	durchgeschlagener Druck *m*	foulage *m*
blotter advertising	Löschblattreklame *f*	publicité *f* sur papier *m* buvard
blotting-paper	Löschpapier *n*	papier *m* buvard
to **blow up**	aufbauschen	enfler, faire mousser

blow-up	Riesenformat *n*, starke Vergrößerung *f*	agrandissement *m*, format *m* gigantesque, grand agrandissement *m*
blue print	Ablichtung *f*, Blaupause *f*, Fotokopie *f*, Pausdruck *m*	copie *f* héliographique, cyanotypie *f*, minute *f*, ozalide *m*
blue print apparatus	Lichtpausgerät *n*	appareil *m* à tirer les bleus *m/pl*
blueprinting paper	Pauspapier *n*	papier *m* à calquer, papier *m* carbone *m*
bluff	Reklametrick *m*	ruse *f* publicitaire
blunt rule	stumpffeine Linie *f*	ligne *f* épointée
blur	Fleck *m*, Schmitz *n*	frison *m*, macule *f*, tache *f*
blurred	unscharf	flou
blurred impression	verschwommener Druck *m*	papillotage *m*
board	Karton *m*, Pappe *f*, Schild *n*	carton *m*, enseigne *f*, panneau *m*, panonceau *m*, plaque *f*
board made from wood pulp	Holzpappe *f*	carton *m* de bois *m*
board page	Kartonseite *f*	page *f* cartonnée
boarding	Kartonagen *f/pl*	cartonnages *m/pl*
body	Haupttext *m*, Nachrichtenkörper *m*	texte *m* principal
body colour drawing	Guasch *f*	couleur *f* opaque, gouache *f*
body copy	Hauptbestandteil *m* einer Anzeige *f*	corps *m* d'une annonce *f*
body corporate	öffentlich-rechtliche Anstalt *f*	établissement *m* de droit *m* public
body fount	Grundschrift *f*	caractère *m* principal
body line	Schriftlinie *f*	ligne *f* de lettre *f*
body matter	Hauptbestandteil *m* einer Anzeige *f*	corps *m* d'une annonce *f*
body of type	Schriftkegel *m*	corps *m*
body size	Kegel *m*	corps *m* de la lettre *f*
body type	Brotschrift *f*	caractères *m/pl* courants, caractères *m/pl* de labeur *m*
body type size	Schriftgrad *m*	force *f* de corps *m*
bogus publication	Geisterzeitung *f*, Schwindelzeitung *f*	journal *m* fantôme, journal *m* trompeur
to boil down	kürzen, verdichten	abréger, condenser, couper, raccourcir, rogner
bold	fett	gras
bold type	fetter Satz *m*, Kernstück *m* einer Anzeige *f*, Textblock *m*	composition *f* grasse, pavé *m* de texte *m*, pièce *f* de résistance *f* d'une annonce *f*
bold-face, bold printtype	Fettdruck *m*	caractères *m/pl* gras
bold-face type	fette Schrift *f*	caractère *m* gras, type *m* gras
bombast	Schwulst *m*	enflure *f*
bond paper	Bankpostpapier *n*	papier *m* coquille *f*
bonus	Bonus *m*, Prämie *f*, Vergütung *f*	bonification *f*, honoraire *m*, prime *f*, rémunération *f*
book	Buch *n*	livre *m*
to book an order	Auftrag *m* buchen	noter un ordre *m*
book cover	Buchdeckel *m*, Buchumschlag *m*	chemise *f*, couverture *f*
book graphic	Buchgrafik *f*	graphique *m* de livre *m*
book jacket	Buchhülle *f*, Buchumschlag *m*	chemise *f* de livre *m*

book mark	Signet *n*	marque *f* graphique, sigle *m*, vignette *f*
book of matches *pl*	Streichholzbriefchen *n*	pochette *f* d'allumette *f*
book paper	Buchdruckpapier *n*, Werkdruckpapier *n*	papier *m* d'édition *f*, papier *m* d'œuvre *f*
book poster	Buchplakat *n*	affiche *f* de livre *m*
book printing	Werkdruck *m*	impression *f* pour éditions *f/pl*
book review	Buchbesprechung *f*, Buchkritik *f*	critique *f* littéraire
book sewing	Fadenheftung *f*	couture *f* au fil *m* végétal
book size	Buchformat *n*	format *m* du livre *m*
to book space	Anzeigenraum *m* buchen	enregistrer d'espace *m*
book spine	Buchrücken *m*	dos *m* de livre *m*
book wholesaler	Buchgrossist *m*	grossiste *m* en livres *m/pl*
book work	Werksatz *m*	composition *f* de labeurs *m/pl*, composition *f* d'œuvre *f*
bookbinder	Buchbinder *m*	relieur *m*
bookbindery	Buchbinderei *f*	atelier *m* de reliure *f*
booked dates *pl*	Belegungsdaten *n/pl*	dates *f/pl* retenues
book-ends *pl*	Bücherstützen *f/pl*	appui-livres *m/pl*, serre-livres *m/pl*
bookfair	Buchmesse *f*	salon *m* du livre *m*
book-hunter	Leseratte *f*	bouquineur *m*, rat *m* de bibliothèque *f*
booking	Belegung *f*, Reservicrung *f*	mise *f* en place *f*, réservation *f*
booklet	Broschüre *f*, Büchelchen *n*, Prospekt *m*, Werbefaltblatt *n*	brochure *f*, dépliant *m*, livret *m*, plaquette *f*, prospectus *m*, tract *m*
bookmark, bookplate	Buchzeichen *n*, Lesezeichen *n*	signet *m* de livre *m*
book post, by	unter Kreuzband *n*	sous bande *f*
bookseller	Buchhändler *m*	libraire *m*
bookstall	Bahnhofsbuchhandlung *f*	bibliothèque *f* de gare *f*
boom	Geschäftsaufschwung *m*, Hochkonjunktur *f*	hausse *f* rapide, haute conjoncture *f*, période *f* de vogue *f*
to boom	Reklame *f* machen	faire de la propagande *f*
to boost	die Werbetrommel *f* rühren, Reklame *f* machen	battre la grosse caisse *f*, faire de la propagande *f*
border	Bordüre *f*, Einfassung *f*, Einrahmung *f*, Umrahmung *f*, Zierleiste *f*	bordure *f*, dentelle *f*, encadrement *m*, fleuron *m*
to border	einfassen, einrahmen	border, encadrer, entourer d'un filet *m*
border rule	Randlinie *f*	filet *m* de bordure *f*
bottom left	links unten	bas de la page *f* gauche
bottom line	Fußzeile *f*	ligne *f* de pied *m*
bottom of page	am Fuß *m* einer Seite *f*	bas *m* de page *f*, pied *m* de page *f*
bottom right	rechts unten	bas *m* de la page *f* droite
bound insert	Einhefter *m*	encart *m* broché
bound to the location	standortgebunden	lié au lieu *m* d'implantation *f*
bound-in	Beihefter *m*, Beikleber *m*	encart *m* broché
Bourgeois (see appendix)	Borgis *f* (siehe Anhang)	corps 9 points (voir appendice)
to bowderize	verballhornen	défigurer, expurger
box	Kastenfach *n*, Kästchen *n*, Umrandung *f*	cassetin *m*, contour *m*, encadrement *m*
box fee	Chiffregebühr *f*	taxe *f* pour annonce *f* chiffrée
box head	eingerahmter Titel *m*, Tabellenkopf *m*	tête *f* de tableau *m*, titre *m* encadré

to **box in**	einfassen, einrahmen, Text *m* umranden	border, encadrer, entourer d'un filet *m*
box number	Chiffre *f*, Kennziffer *f*	numéro-clé *f*, numéro *m* de code *m*
box number advertisement	Chiffreanzeige *f*	annonce *f* chiffrée
box of time-table	Fahrplankasten *m*	boîte *f* des horaires *m/pl* des trains *m/pl*
box on the right of the masthead	Anzeige *f* neben Zeitungskopf *m*, oberer Eckplatz *m* der Titelseite *f*	manchette *f* à droite du titre *m*
box security	Chiffregeheimnis *n*	secret *m* des chiffres *m/pl*
box sign	Leuchtkasten *m*	caisson *m* lumineux
boxed advertisement	umrandete Anzeige *f*	annonce *f* encadrée
boxholder addressing	Postwurfsendungen *f/pl*	distribution *f* postale de messages *m/pl* non adressés, publicité *f* directe par voie *f* postale
box-top offer *am*	Prämie *f* bei Verpackungsteileinsendung *f*	offre *f* réclame *f* (sur emballage *m*)
boy sales *pl*	Straßenhandel *m*	vente *f* ambulante
boycotting of a journal	Zeitungsboykott *m*	boycottage *m* d'un journal *m*
boycotting of advertising media *pl*	Werbeboykott *m*	boycottage *m* de supports *m/pl* publicitaires
bracket	Kategorie *f*, Schaufensterständer *m*, Ständer *m*	catégorie *f*, portatif *m*, présentoir *m*, support *m*
to **bracket**	einklammern	mettre en crochets *m/pl*, mettre en parenthèses *f/pl*
brackets *pl*	Klammern *f/pl/typog*	parenthèses *f/pl*
bragging	Großsprecherei *f*	rodomontade *f*
Braille	Blindenschrift *f*	braille *m*
brain trust	Experten *m/pl*-Zusammenschluß *m*, Gehirntrust *m*	brain-trust *m*
brain washing	Gehirnwäsche *f*	lavage *m* de cerveau *f*, lavage *m* de crâne *m*
brainstorming	Ideenfindung *f* durch Gruppendiskussion *f*	orage *m* des cerveaux *m/pl*
brain-wave	Geistesblitz *m*	saillie *f*
branch	Sparte *f*, Zweigstelle *f*	section *f*, succursale *f*
brand	Marke *f*, Sorte *f*, Warenzeichen *n*	genre *m*, marque *f* de fabrique *f*, sorte *f*
brand advertising	Markenartikelwerbung *f*	publicité *f* de marque *f*
brand identification	Markenerkennung *f*	identification *f* d'une marque *f*
brand identity	Übereinstimmung *f* mit Markenbild *n*	identité *f* de marque *f*
brand image	Markenbild *n*	image *f* de marque *f*
brand leader	Spitzenmarke *f*	marque *f* de tête *f*
brand loyalty	Markentreue *f*	fidélité *f* à la marque *f*
brand manager	Markenbetreuer *m*, Produktmanager *m*	chef *m* de produit *m*, spécialiste *m* produit *m*
brand name	Markenname *m*	appellation *f*, nom *m* de la marque *f*
brand of a product	Produktmarke *f*	marque *f* de produit *m*
brand preference	Markenbevorzugung *f*, Markentreue *f*	fidélité *f* à la marque *f*, préférence *f* d'une marque *f*

brand switcher	Markenwechsler *m*	acheteur *m* passant d'une marque *f* à l'autre
brand switching	Markenwechsel *m*	changement *m* de marque *f*
brand trend survey	Markenindex *m*	baromètre *m* des marques *f/pl*
branded goods *pl*	Markenartikel *m*	article *m* de marque *f*, produit *m* de marque *f* déposée
brand-new	brandneu	tout neuf
brand-umbrella	gleicher Markenname *m* für verschiedene Produkte *m/pl*	le même nom *m* pour des produits *m/pl* différents
bread-and-butter-face	Brotschrift *f*	caractères *m/pl* courants, caractères *m/pl* de labeur *m*
break	Unterbrechung *f* einer Sendung *f*	interruption *f* d'une émission *f*
break in transmission	Sendeunterbrechung *f*	incident *m* technique
break line	Ende *n* des Absatzes *m*, letzte Zeile eines Absatzes *m*	dernière ligne *f* d'un paragraphe *m*, fin *f* d'alinéa *m*
to **break the line**	umbrechen	mettre en pages *f/pl*, sortir de la ligne *f*
to **break up**	abschneiden, Satz *m* ablegen	découper, distribuer
breakdown	Aufgliederung *f*, Aufschlüsselung *f*, Aufteilung *f*	détail *m*, détaillé *m*, répartition *f*, ventilation *f*
break-even point	Gewinnschwelle *f*, Rentabilitätsschwelle *f*	limite *f* minimum, point *m* mort, seuil *m* de la rentabilité *f*
break-line	Ausgangszeile *f*	dernière ligne *f*, fin *f* d'alinéa *m*, ligne *f* courte
brevier (see appendix)	Petit *f* (siehe Anhang)	corps 8 points (voir appendice)
bribe	Schmiergeld *n*	pot-de-vin *m*
bridge	Klangbrücke *f*, musikalische Überleitung *f*	transition *f* musicale
briefing	Arbeitsanweisung *f*, Instruktionen *f/pl*, Zusammenfassung *f* von Unterlagen *f/pl*	instructions *f/pl*, résumé *m* d'instructions *f/pl*
briefing conference	Auftragsbesprechung *f*	conférence *f* d'instruction *f*
Brillant (see appendix)	Viertelcicero *f* (siehe Anhang)	corps 3 points (voir appendice)
to **bring out**	herausgeben	éditer, publier, sortir
bringing into line	Gleichschaltung *f*	mise *f* au pas *m*
Bristol board	Bristolkarton *m*	carton *m* Bristol
broadcast	Sendung *f*, Rundfunksendung *f*	émission *f* radiophonique, radiodiffusion *f*
to **broadcast**	senden (Radio)	émettre, radiodiffuser
broadcast account	Rundfunkbericht *m*	radio-reportage *m*
broadcast advertising	Funkwerbung *f*, Radiowerbung *f*	publicité *f* radiodiffusée, publicité *f* radiophonique
broadcast announcement	Ankündigung *f* im Rundfunk *m*, Werbespot *m*	annonce *f* radiodiffusée, avis *m* radiodiffusé, court-métrage *m* publicitaire, message *m* publicitaire, spot *m*
broadcast audience	Rundfunkhörerschaft *f*	audience *f* de la radio *f*

broadcast news	Nachrichtensendung f, Rundfunknachrichten f/pl, Tagesnachrichten f/pl im Rundfunk m	bulletin m d'actualités f/pl, journal m parlé, transmission f des informations f/pl
broadcast research	Hörerforschung f	études f/pl relatives à l'audience f
broadcast transmission	Radiosendung f	émission f à la radio f
broadcaster	Sender m, Rundfunksprecher m	antenne f, chroniqueur m, speaker m, station-radio f
broadcasting	Hörfunk m, Rundfunk m	radio f, radiodiffusion f sonore
broadcasting by wire	Drahtfunk m	radiodiffusion f par fil m, télédiffusion f
broadcasting material	Sendeunterlagen f/pl	documents m/pl d'émission f, matériel m d'émission f
broadcasting of news	Nachrichtendurchsage f	diffusion f de nouvelles f/pl
broadcasting sports pl	Sportübertragung f	transmission f radiophonique de sport m
broadcasting station	Radiostation f, Sendeanstalt f, Rundfunkanstalt f, Rundfunkstation f	poste m émetteur m, station f de radiodiffusion f, station f d'émission f
broadcasting time	Sendezeit f	heures f/pl de diffusion f, temps m d'antenne f
broadsheet, broadside	großer Faltprospekt m, großformatige Drucksache f, Großprospekt m, Werbeflugblatt n	imprimé m de grand format m, in-plano m
broadside size	Querformat n	format m en largeur f, format m en travers m
brochure	Broschüre f	plaquette f, prospectus m
broken letters pl	beschädigte Buchstaben m/pl	lettres f/pl écrasées
broken line	Kurzzeile f	bout m de ligne f, ligne f courte
broken matter	gequirlter Satz m	pâté m, soleil m
broker	Makler m	courtier m
bromide paper	Bromsilberpapier n	papier m au bromure m d'argent m
bromide printing	Bromsilberdruck m	impression f au bromure m d'argent m
to bronze	bestäuben	soupoudrer
bronze printing	Bronzedruck m	bronzage m, impression f de bronze m
brown paper	Packpapier n	papier m d'emballage m, papier m gris
brush	Kleisterbesen m	brosse f
brush proof	Bürstenabzug m	épreuve f à la brosse f, épreuve f au taquoir m, morasse f
bubble	Sprechblase f	ballon m, bulle f, philactère f
buckeye	stümperhaft, überladene Anzeige f	annonce f surchargée, moche
buckram	Steifleinen n	calicot m
budget	Etat m, Werbeetat m	budget m, budget m publicitaire
budget checking	Etatkontrolle f	contrôle m budgétaire
budget distribution	Etatverteilung f	répartition f de budget m
budget fixation	Etatfestsetzung f	fixation f du budget m
budgetary control	Budgetkontrolle f	contrôle m du budget m
budget-priced	preisgünstig	à bon marché m

to **buff**	schwabbeln	polir au buffle *m*
bug	Geheimmikrophon *n*, verstecktes Mikrophon *n*, Wanze *f*	micro *m* secret, mouchard *m*
builder-upper	Propagandist *m*	propagandiste *m*
to **build-up**	aufbauen	élever
build-upper	PR-Mann *m*, Reklamechef *m*	agent *m* de publicité *f*, publicitaire *m*
built up area	geschlossene Ortschaft *f*	agglomération *f*
bulk article	Massenartikel *f*	article *m* de série *f*
bulk circulation	Massenauflage *f*	gros tirage *m*
bulk consumer	Großverbraucher *m*	gros consommateur *m*
bulk mail	Massendrucksachen *f/pl*	imprimés *m/pl* expédiés en nombre *m*
bulk posting	postalische Massensendungen *f/pl*, Postwurfsendungen *f/pl*	distribution *f* postale de messages *m/pl* non adressés, envois *m/pl* en nombre *m*, publicité *f* directe par voie *f* postale
bulk rate *brit*	Mengenrabatt *m*	dégressif *m* sur volume *m* publicitaire, rabais *m* de quantité *f*, remise *f* de quantité *f*
bulkhead	Stirnwand *f*	panneau *m* de fond *m*
bulky paper	bauschiges Papier *n*	papier *m* fort pour l'impression *f*
bull	Stilblüte *f*	bévue *f*
bulldog edition	erste Ausgabe *f*, vordatierte Zeitung *f*	première édition *f* journal *m* antidaté, journal *m* prédaté
bullet	Kugel *f*	boule *f*, sphère *f*
bulletin	Bulletin *n*	bulletin *m*
bulletin board	bemalte Großfläche *f*	bulletin *m*
bum steer	wertloser Hinweis *m*	faux tuyau *m*
to **bunch**, to **bundle**	bündeln	passer les cahiers *m/pl* en presse *f*
bunkum	leeres Geschwätz *n*	boniments *m/pl*, paroles *f/pl* vides
buried advertisements *pl*	Anzeigenfriedhof *m*	annonces *f/pl* enterrées
buried offer	verborgenes Angebot *n*, verstecktes Angebot *n*	offre *f* clandestine
burin	Stahlstichel *m*	échoppe *f*
burnishing	Politur *f*	brunissage *m*, satinage *m*
burr	Fleisch *n* eines Buchstabens *m*	blanc *m*, épaulement *m*, espace *m* vierge *f*, talus *m* de pied *m*
burying of an information	Unterdrückung *f* einer Information *f*	faire sauter une information *f*
bus advertising	Autobuswerbung *f*, Omnibuswerbung *f*	publicité *f* dans ou sur un autobus *m*
bus stop pillar	Haltestellensäule *f*	poteau *m* d'arrêt *m*
business advertisement with regular basic rate	Empfehlungsanzeige *f*, Geschäftsanzeige *f*	annonce *f* commerciale à prix *m* de base *f*
business advertising	Wirtschaftswerbung *f*	publicité *f* commerciale
business call	Kundenbesuch *m*	visite *f* des clients *m/pl*
business centre	Geschäftszentrum *n*	centre *m* commercial

business conditions *pl*	Geschäftsbedingungen *f/pl*	conditions *f/pl* commerciales
business line	Branche *f*	branche *f*
business man	Geschäftsmann *m*	homme *m* d'affaires *f/pl*
business manager	Geschäftsführer *m*, Verlagsleiter *m*	chef *m* d'entreprise *f*, directeur *m* administratif, directeur *m* commercial, gérant *m*, gestionnaire *m*
business paper	Wirtschaftsblatt *n*	feuille *f* commerciale, feuille *f* économique
business publication	Fachzeitung	journal *m* professionnel, périodique *m* technique
business reply card	Rückantwortkarte *f*	carte-réponse *f*
business research	Konjunkturforschung *f*	étude *f* de la conjoncture *f*
busy season	Hauptsaison *f*	saison *f* principale
butt line	Schnittkante *f*	arrête *f* de coupe *f*
button	Ansteckplakette *f*	bouton *m*
to buy the whole stock	blockbuchen	acheter en bloc *m*
buyer	Abnehmer *m*, Käufer *m* (in *f*)	acheteur *m*, acheteuse *f*, client *m*
buyer category	Käufergruppe *f*	catégorie *f* des acheteurs *m/pl*
buyer's market	Käufermarkt *m*	marché *m* d'acheteurs *m/pl*
buyer's resistance	Kaufhemmung *f*	résistance *f* de l'acheteur *m*
buying	Einkauf *m*	achat *m*
buying behaviour	Einkaufsverhalten *n*	comportement *m* des acheteurs *m/pl*
buying decision	Kaufentschluß *m*	décision *f* d'acheter
buying desire	Kauflust *f*	désir *m* d'achat *m*, envie *f* d'acheter
buying habits *pl*	Kaufgewohnheiten *f/pl*	habitudes *f/pl* d'achat *m*
buying incitement	Kaufanreiz *m*	incitation *f* à l'achat *m*
buying intention	Kaufbereitschaft *f*	acceptabilité *f* auprès des consommateurs *m/pl*
buying mood	Kaufstimmung *f*	humeur *f* d'acheter
buying motive	Kaufanlaß *m*	motif *m* d'achat *m*, raison *f* d'achat *m*
buying motives *pl*	Kaufmotive *n/pl*	motivation *f* d'achat *m*
buying power	Kaufkraft *f*	capacité *f* d'achat *m*, pouvoir *m* d'achat *m*
buzz	Nebengeräusche *n/pl*, Stimmengeräusch *n*	bruit *m* de voix *f*, bruits *m/pl* parasites, fritures *f/pl*
by bookpost	unter Kreuzband *n*	sous bande *f*
by telegram	telegrafisch	télégraphique
by-line	Zeile *f* mit dem Namen *m* des Autors *m*	ligne *f* avec le nom *m* de l'auteur *m*
bylined story	gezeichneter Artikel *m*	article *m* signé

C

cable	Kabel *n*, Telegramm *n*	câble *m*, télégramme *m*
to cable	kabeln	câbler
cable address	Telegrammadresse *f*	adresse *f* de télégramme *m*, adresse *f* télégraphique
cablegram	Kabeltelegramm *n*	câblogramme *m*
cable-text	Kabeltext *m*	câble-texte *m*
to calculate	kalkulieren	calculer
calculating disc	Rechenscheibe *f*	disque *m* à calculer
calculation	Berechnung *f*	calcul *m*, compte *m*

calculation of price	Preisberechnung *f*	calcul *m* des prix *m/pl*
calendar	Almanach *m*, Kalender *m*	almanach *m*, calendrier *m*
calendar year	Kalenderjahr *n*	année *f* civile
calender	Kalander *m*	calandre *f*
calendered on both sides *pl*	beidseitig satiniert, satiniert, beidseitig	satiné des deux côtés *m/pl*
calendered paper	geglättetes Papier *n*, Glanzpapier *n*, satiniertes Papier *n*	papier *m* calandré, papier *m* lissé, papier *m* satiné
to **calibrate**	kalibrieren	calibrer
calibrating of a copy	Manuskriptumfangsberechnung *f*	calibrage *m* d'une copie *f*
calibration	Manuskriptumfang *m*	calibration *f*
calibrator	Kalibermaß *n*	calibre *m*
calico	Kaliko *n*, Spruchband *n*	banderole *f*, calicot *m*
call	Telefonat *n*	communication *f* téléphonique
on **call**	Abruf *m*, auf	à notre convenance *f*, sur appel *m*
to **call**	abrufen	appeler
call back	Rückfrage *f*	demande *f* de précisions *f/pl*
call report	Besprechungsbericht *m*, Besuchsbericht *m*	rapport *m* de conférence *f*, rapport *m* de visite *f*
call sign	Sendezeichen *n*	indicatif *m*
call slip	Vertreterbericht *m*	rapport *m* de visite *f*
call-at-office subscriptions *pl*	Abholabonnements *n/pl*	abonnements *m/pl* pour retrait *m* au guichet *m*
call-back	Kontroll-Interview *n*, Nachfaßinterview *n*, Wiederholungsbesuch *m*	interview *m* de rappel *m*, interview *m* rappelé, visite *f* répétée
call-box	Telefonkabine *f*	cabine *f* téléphonique
calligraphy	Kalligrafie *f*, Schönschrift *f*, Schreibkunst *f*	calligraphie *f*
calling on customers *pl*	Kundenbesuch *m*	visite *f* des clients *m/pl*
calumny	Verleumdung *f*	calomnie *f*, diffamation *f*
camera	Fotoapparat *m*	appareil *m* cinématographique
camera stand	Stativ *n*	pied *m* photographique, trépied *m*
camera-crane	Kamerakran *m*	grue *f*
camera-man	Bildreporter *m*, Kameramann *m*	photographe *m* de presse *f*, reporter-photographe *m*, cadreur *m*, opérateur *m*
camouflage	getarnte Publizistik *f*, Tarnung *f*	camouflage *m*
camouflaged advertising	Schleichwerbung *f*	publicité *f* camouflée, publicité *f* clandestine, publicité *f* déguisée, publicité *f* occulte, publicité *f* subversive
campaign	Kampagne *f*	campagne *f*
campaign plan	Werbeplan *m*	plan *m* de campagne *f*, plan *m* de publicité *f*, plan *m* publicitaire
campaign thinking	kampagnegerechtes Denken *n*	mentalité *f* orientée vers la campagne *f*
camping-ground	Campingplatz *m*	camping *m*
to **cancel**	abbestellen, annullieren, sistieren, stornieren	annuler

cancellation	Abbestellung *f*, Annullierung *f*, Auflösung *f*, Sistierung *f*, Stornierung *f*	annulation *f*, dissolution *f*, résiliation *f*
cancellation of an order	Auftragsannullierung *f*	annulation *f* d'un ordre *m*
cancellation right	Rücktrittsrecht *n*	droit *m* de résiliation *f*, remise *f* des ordres *m/pl*
cancelling of an order	Auftragsstreichung *f*	suppression *f* d'un mandat *m*
candid interview	unvorbereitetes Interview *n*	interview *f* non préparée
candid picture	Momentaufnahme *f*	instantané *m* non posé, photographie *f* instantanée
canned copy	vorbereiteter Text *m*	texte *m* mis en boîte *f*
canned music	Schallplattenmusik *f*, Tonkonserve *f*	disque *m* de phono *m*, musique *f* enregistrée
canned television item	Fernsehkonserve *f*	émission *f* en différé *m*
canvas	Leinwand *f*	écran *m*, toile *f*
to canvass	hereinholen	prospecter
canvasser	Akquisiteur *m*	démarcheur *m*, solliciteur *m*
canvassing	Akquisition *f*, Aufträge *m/pl* hereinholen, Stimmenfang *m*	acqisition *f*, prospection *f*, sollicitation *f* de suffrages *m/pl*
cap	Majuskel *f*	capitale *f*, lettre *f* majuscule
capacity	Fassungsvermögen *n*	capacité *f*
capital goods *pl*	Investitionsgüter *n/pl*	biens *m/pl* de production *f*, biens *m/pl* d'investissement *m*
capital letters *pl* caps *pl*	Großbuchstaben *m/pl*, Majuskeln *f/pl*, Versalien *f/pl*	capitales *f/pl*, caractères *m/pl* haut de casse *f*, gros caractères *m/pl*, lettres *f/pl* majuscules, lettres *f/pl* capitales, lettres *f/pl* majuscules
caption	Bildunterschrift *f*, Legende *f*, Überschrift *f*, Zwischentitel *m*	en-tête *f*, intertitre *m*, légende *f*, rubrique *f*, sous-titre *m*, titre *m*
caption writer	Überschriftenverfasser *m*	titulateur *m*
captive audience	eingefangenes Publikum *n*	audience *f* captive
car card advertising, car panel	Daueranschlag *m* in Verkehrsmitteln *n/pl*, Innenplakat *n* (in Verkehrsmitteln *n/pl*) Werbeplakat *n* in Verkehrsmitteln *n/pl*	affiche *f* intérieure, affichette *f* d'autobus *m* ou de tramway *m*, emplacement *m* intérieur de voiture *f*
caravan advertising	Werbekarawane *f*	caravane *f* publicitaire
carbon coating	Karbondruck *m*	carbonnage *m*
carbon paper	Kohlepapier *n*, Pauspapier *n*, Pigmentpapier *n*	papier *m* à calquer, papier *m* carbone *m*, papier *m* charbon *m*
carbon printing	Transkritdruck *m*	carbonnage *m* à chaud
card	Visitenkarte *f*	carte *f* de visite *f*
card index	Kartei *f*	armoire *f*-classeur *m*, cartothèque *f*, fichier *m*
card rates *pl*	Tarif *m* für Verkehrsmittelwerbung *f*	tarif *m* de la publicité *f* moyens *m/pl* de transport *m*

card reader	Lochkartenleser *m*	lecteur *m* des cartes *f/pl* perforées
cardboard	Karton *m*	carton *m*
cardboard box for dealers *pl*	Verkaufskarton *m*	carton *m* vendeur
cardboard cutter	Pappschere *f*	cisaille *f* à carton *m*
cardboard engineer	Verpackungsfachmann *m*	expert *m* en emballages *m/pl*
cardboard-box manufactory	Kartonagefabrik *f*	fabrique *f* de cartonnage *m*
carder (public conveyances *pl*)	Plakatanschläger *m*	afficheur *m*
card-index of customers *pl*	Kundenkartei *f*	fichier *m* de clients *m/pl*
card-index of orders *pl*	Auftragskartei *f*	fichier *m* des commandes *f/pl* en exécution *f*
caret mark	Auslassungszeichen *n*	renvoi *m* de marge *f*, signe *m* d'omission *f*
caricature	Karikatur *f*, Zerrbild *n*	caricature *f*, portrait-charge *f*
carrier of newspapers *pl*	Zeitungsträger *m*	porteur *m* de journaux *m/pl*
carrying out of an order	Auftragserledigung *f*	réalisation *f* de commandes *f/pl*
cartography	Kartografie *f*	cartographie *f*
cartoon	humoristische Zeichnung *f*, Karikatur *f*	caricature *f*, dessin *m* humoristique
cartoon film	Zeichentrickfilm *m*	film *m* en dessin *m* animé
cartoonist	Pressezeichner *m*	reporter-dessinateur *m*
cartouche	Randverzierung *f*, Zierrahmen *m*	cartouche *f*, vignette *f*
cartridge	Karton *m*	carton *m*
cartridge paper	Patronenpapier *n*	carton *m*
to case in	einhängen	emboîter
case room	Setzerei *f*	atelier *m* de composition *f*, services *m/pl* de composition *f*
case shopping	Rubrik *f* shopping *n*	section *f* shopping *m*
case stand	Setzregal *n*	rang *m*
case study	Fallstudie *f*	étude *f* d'un cas *m*
cash discount	Barzahlungsrabatt *m*, Kassaskonto *m*	escompte *m* de caisse *f*
cash endorsement	Barfrankatur *f*	affranchisement *m* en timbres *m/pl*
cash on delivery	Zahlung *f* bei Erhalt *m* der Ware *f*	paiement *m* lors de la réception *f* de la marchandise *f*
cash-and-carry	Lagerverkauf *m*, Verkauf *m* ohne Kredit *m* und Kundendienst *m*	paiement *m* comptant
cash-and-carry-wares *pl*	Abholwaren *f/pl*	marchandises *f/pl* à transporter par l'acheteur *m*
to cast	klischieren	clicher, faire un cliché *m*
to cast off	auszählen (Manuskript), kalibrieren	calibrer, calibrer la copie *f*
casting	Abguß *m*, Rollenbesetzung *f*	choix *m* des acteurs *m/pl*, moulage *m*
casting machine	Gießmaschine *f*	machine *f* à fondre
casting mechanism	Gießwerk *n*	fondeuse *f*
casting off	Satzberechnung *f*, Umfangsberechnung *f*	calcul *m* de la composition *f*, calibrage *m* d'une copie *f*
to cast-off	Satzumfang *m* berechnen	calibrer un manuscrit *m*
casual contribution	gelegentlicher Beitrag *m*	contribution *f* fortuite
casual contributor	gelegentlicher Mitarbeiter *m*	collaborateur *m* occasionnel, collaborateur *m* part-time

casual costumer	Gelegenheitskunde *m*	client *m* de passage *m*, client *m* occasionnel
casual order	Gelegenheitsauftrag *m*	ordre *m* occasionnel
casual reader	Gelegenheitsleser *m*	lecteur *m* occasionnel
catalog *am*	Katalog *m*	catalogue *m*
catalogue *brit*	Liste *f*	liste *f*
catalogue of records *pl*	Schallplattenverzeichnis *n*	discographie *f*
catch line	Schlagzeile *f*, Werbespruch *m*, knallige Überschrift *f*	formule *f* publicitaire, ligne *f* principale, ligne *f* repère, manchette *f*, phrase *f* choc *m*, phrase *f* d'accrochage *m*, titre *m* en vedette *f* titre criard
catch phrase	Blickfang *m*, Werbespruch *m*	accrochage *m*, accroche-œil *m*, amorce *f*, attrape-regard *m*, formule *f* publicitaire, phrase *f* d'accrochage *m*, tape-à-l'œil *m*, tire-l'œil *m*
catch word	Schlagwort *n*, Slogan *m*, Stichwort *n*	mot *m* clé *f*, mot *m* repère, mot *m* souche, mot *m* vedette *f*, phrase *f* choc *m*
catch-penny article	Lockartikel *m*, Pfennigartikel *m*	article *m* d'appel *m*, article *m* de réclame *f*, attrape-sou *m*, camélote *f* de réclame *f*, produit *m* d'appel *m*
categories *pl* of cinema theatres *pl*	Filmtheater- *n* Kategorien *f/pl*	catégories *f/pl* de salles *f/pl*
categories *pl* of magazines *pl*	Zeitschriftengattungen *f/pl*	catégories *f/pl* de périodiques *m/pl*
category	Kategorie *f*	catégorie *f*
category of magnitude	Größenklasse *f*	catégorie *f* d'importance *f*
catering	Lebensmittelversorgung *f*	approvisionnement *m*
cat's eye	Katzenauge *n*	catadioptre *m*, cataphote *m*
cause for advertising	Werbeanlaß *m*	motif *m* de publicité *f*
cedilla	Cedille *f*	cédille *f*
ceefax	Videotext *m*	antiope *m*
ceiling panel	Deckenschild *n*	voussure *f*
ceiling price	Höchstpreis *m*	prix *m* maximum
cellophane	Cellophan *n*	cellophane *f*
cellophane window	Zellglasfenster *n*	fenêtre *f* en pellicule *f* transparente
to cellosheen	cellophanieren	cellophaner
censorship	Zensur *f*	censure *f*
census of distribution	Absatzzählung *f*, Erfassung *f* der Werbestreuung *f*	recensement *m* de la distribution *f*
center page spread	Doppelseite *f*-Blattmitte *f*	double page *f* centrale
centered	Mitte *f* gesetzt, auf	centré
centering *brit*	zentrieren	cadrage *m*, centrer
centralized buying	Sammelbestellung *f*	commande *f* par groupage *m*
centrally handling	federführend	compétent, dirigeant
centre of gravity	Schwerpunkt *m*	centre *m* de gravité *f*
centre of page	Mitte *f* der Seite *f*, Seitenmitte *f*	milieu *m* de page *f*
centre of the poster	Plakatmitte *f*	centre *m* de l'affiche *f*
centred style	Dreizeilenfall *m*	style *m* lapidaire
centring *am*	zentrieren	cadrage *m*, centrer

centring of film image	Filmbildzentrierung f, Zentrierung f des Filmbildes m	cadrage m
certificate	Zeugnis n	certificat m, témoignage m
certification mark	Gütezeichen n	étiquette f de qualité f, label m de qualité f, marque f de garantie f, sigle m
certification of circulation	Auflagenbestätigung f	certification f des tirages m/pl
certified statement of circulation	Auflagebeglaubigung f	certificat m de contrôle m du tirage m, constat m de tirage m
cession	Abtretung f	cession f
chain break	Werbeeinblendung f	bref communiqué m radio f, insertion f publicitaire, réglage m
chain of agencies pl	Agenturkette f	chaîne f d'agences f/pl
chain store	Kettenladen m	membre m d'une chaîne f volontaire
chair-lift	Sesselbahn f	télésiège m
chairman	Generaldirektor m	directeur m en chef m
chalcography	Kupferstich m	chalcographie f, estampe f en taille f douce, gravure f
chalk overlay paper	Kreidepapier n	papier m crayonneux
chance costumer	Gelegenheitskunde m	client m de passage m, client m occasionnel
change	Auswechselung f, Umwandlung f	mutation f, transformation f
change in circulation	Auflagenveränderung f	changement m des tirages m/pl
change in taste	Geschmackswandel m	changement m du goût m du consommateur m
change of design	Sujetwechsel m	changement m de message m
change of measure	Formatänderung f	changement m de format m, modification f de format m
change of opinion	Meinungsänderung f	changement m d'avis m
change of posters pl	Ersatzplakatierung f	mutation f d'emplacements m/pl
change of size	Formatänderung f	changement m de format m, modification f de format m
change of text	Textwechsel m	changement m de texte m
change of the bill	Plakatauswechslung f	renouvellement m de l'affiche f
channel	Straße f (Satz m)	lézarde f
channel of dispersion	Streuweg m	voie f de prospection f
channel of distribution	Absatzkanal m, Absatzweg m, Distributionsweg m, Vertriebsweg m	canal m de distribution f, circuit m de distribution f, voie f de distribution f
channels pl of information	Informationswege m/pl	chemins m/pl de l'information f
chap-book	Flugschrift f	brochure f, tract m
chapter	Kapitel n	chapitre m
character	Buchstabe m, Drucktype f	caractère m d'imprimerie f, lettre f
character count	Satzberechnung f, Umfangsberechnung f	calcul m de la composition f, calibrage m d'une copie f
character recognition	maschinelles Lesen n	lecture f mécanique
characteristic	Charakteristikum n, Wesensmerkmal n	caractéristique f
charcoal-drawing	Kohlezeichnung f	dessin m au fusain m
charge per word	Wortgebühr f	tarif m par mot m

chart   242

chart	Diagramm *n*, grafische Darstellung *f*, Tabelle *f*	diagramme *m*, graphique *m*, représentation *f* graphique, tableau *m*, tabulation *f*
chase	Schließrahmen *m*	châssis *m*
chatly article	leichte Plauderei *f*	article *m* léger, menus *m/pl* propos
chatterbox	Plappermaul *n*	grand bavard *m*
cheap paper for wrapping and posters *pl*	Spaltpapier *n*	papier *m* frictionné
cheap quality	minderwertige Qualität *f*	qualité *f* de peu de valeur *f*
cheap reprint	Volksausgabe *f*	édition *f* populaire
check	Kontrolle *f*	contrôle *m*, vérification *f*
to check	kontrollieren, prüfen	contrôler, examiner, vérifier
check *am*	Bankscheck *m*	chèque *m* bancaire, mandat *m* bancaire
check list	Checkliste *f*, Kontrolliste *f*, Prüfliste *f*	liste *f* aide-mémoire *m*, liste *f* de contrôle *m*
to check the invoice	Rechnung *f* prüfen	apurer la facture *f*, vérifier la facture *f*
to check up	prüfen	contrôler, examiner, vérifier
to check with	· wenden an, sich	consulter
checker	Rechnungskontrolleur *m*	pigeur *m*
checking	Streuprüfung *f*	vérification *f*
checking copy	Belegexemplar *n*	numéro *m* justificatif
check-up	Kontrolle *f*	contrôle *m*, vérification *f*
cheque	Scheck *m*	chèque *m*
chisel	Radiernadel *f*	échoppe *f*, pointe *f*
choice	Auswahl *f*, Sortiment *n*, Wahl *f*	assortiment *m*, choix *m*, élection *f*, sélection *f*
choice of type	Schriftwahl *f*	choix *m* du caractère *m*
choice of type faces *pl*	Schriftenauswahl *f*	casse *f*
to choose	auswählen	choisir, sélectionner
Christmas number	Weihnachtsnummer *f*	édition *f* de Noël *m*
chromatic intensity	Farbintensität *f*	intensité *f* de la couleur *f*
chrome bath	Chrombad *n*	bain *m* de chrome *m*
chrome imitation board	Chromoersatzkarton *m*	carton *m* contrecollé
chroming	Verchromung *f*	chromage *m*
chromist	Farbätzer *m*	chromiste *m*
chromo paper	Chromopapier *n*	papier *m* chromo
chromo-board	Chromokarton *m*	carton *m* chromo couché
chromo-lithography	Chromolithografie *f*	chromolithographie *f*
chromotype	Farbdruck *m*	chromotypie *f*, impression *f* en couleurs *f/pl*, impression *f* polychrome, polychromie *f*
chronicle	Chronik *f*	chronique *f*
chronicler	Berichterstatter *m*, Chronist *m*	chroniqueur *m*, correspondant *m*, rapporteur *m*
chunk	willkürlich ausgewählter Personenkreis *m*	audience *f* choisie arbitrairement
church paper	Kirchenblatt *n*	feuille *f* cléricale
cine club	Filmklub *m*	ciné-club *m*
cinema	Kino *n*, Lichtspielhaus *n*	cinéma *m*

cinema advertising	Filmwerbung *f*, Kinowerbung *f*	cinéma *m* publicitaire, publicité *f* à l'écran *m*, publicité *f* cinématographique, publicité *f* dans les cinémas *m/pl*, publicité *f* par film *m*
cinema announcement	Kinoanzeige *f*	annonce *f* d'un cinéma *m*
cinema performance	Filmvorstellung *f*	séance *f* cinématographique
cinema still	Standfoto *n*	photo *f* de plateau *m*, photo *f* de scène *f*
cinemascope	Breitwandfilm *m*, Verfahren *n* für Breitwandvorführung *f*	cinémascope *m*
cipher	Geheimschrift *f*, Ziffer *f*	chiffre *m*, écriture *f* secrète
cipher message	Geheimbotschaft *f*	message *m* chiffré
ciphered business journal	Kennzifferzeitschrift *f*	périodique *m* d'une circulation *f* contrôlée et qualifiée
circle	Kreis *m*	cercle *m*
circle of clients *pl*	Kundenkreis *m*	clientèle *f*
circle of readers *pl*	Leserkreis *m*	cercle *m* de lecteurs *m/pl*, degré *m* de lecture *f*
circuit	Kinotheaterring *m*	circuit *m*
circular	Zirkular *n*	circulaire *m*
circular letter	Rundschreiben *n*	lettre *f* circulaire
circulation	Auflage *f*, Verbreitung *f*	circulation *f*, couverture *f*, diffusion *f*, distribution *f*, propagation *f*, rayonnement *m*, tirage *m*
circulation analysis	Auflagenanalyse *f*, Leseranalyse *f*, Verbreitungsanalyse *f*	analyse *f* de la diffusion *f*, analyse *f* de l'audience *f*, analyse *f* des lecteurs *m/pl*, analyse *f* des tirages *m/pl*
circulation area	Verbreitungsgebiet *n*	rayon *m* d'action *f*, zone *f* de diffusion *f*
circulation base	Auflagenhöhe *f*	chiffre *m* du tirage *m*
circulation breakdown	Auflagenverteilung	répartition *f* des tirages *m/pl*
circulation control	Auflagenprüfung *f*	contrôle *m* des tirages *m/pl*
circulation density	Verbreitungsdichte *f*	densité *f* de la diffusion *f*
circulation dullness	Auflagenstillstand *m*	stagnation *f* des tirages *m/pl*
circulation figures *pl*	Verbreitungszahlen *f/pl*	chiffres *m/pl* de diffusion *f*, chiffres *m/pl* de tirage *m*
circulation growth	Auflagenanstieg *m*	accroissement *m* des tirages *m/pl*
circulation guarantee	Auflagengarantie *f*	garantie *f* de la circulation *f*
circulation manager	Vertriebsleiter *m*	chef *m* de publicité *f*, chef *m* de vente *f*
circulation of a newspaper	Zeitungsauflage *f*	tirage *m* d'un journal *m*
circulation run	Auflagendruck *m*	tirage *m* (impression *f*)
circumference	Umkreis *m*	circonférence *f*
circumflex	Accent *m* circonflexe	accent *m* circonflexe
circus-poster	Zirkusplakat *n*	affiche *f* de cirque *m*
city editor	Lokalredakteur *m*	rédacteur *m* local
city zone	Stadtauflage *f*	tirage *m* urbain
claim	Werbebehauptung *f*	allégation *f* de la publicité *f*, assertion *f* publicitaire
claim to compensation	Ersatzanspruch *m*	droit *m* de compensation *f*
claims *pl*	Behauptungen *f/pl*	prétentions *f/pl*

clandestine advertising	Schleichwerbung *f*	publicité *f* camouflée, publicité *f* clandestine, publicité *f* déguisée, publicité *f* occulte, publicité *f* subversive
clandestine radio transmitter	Geheimsender *m*	émetteur *m* clandestin
claptrap	Effekthascherei *f*	recherche *f* de l'effet *m*, recherche *f* de l'épate *m*
clarification	Aufhellung *f*	clarification *f*
clarity	Übersichtlichkeit *f*	bonne vue *f* d'ensemble *m*
to clarosheen	cellophanieren	cellophaner
class of consumers *pl*	Verbraucherschicht *f*	catégorie *f* des consommateurs *m/pl*
classes *pl* **of population**	Bevölkerungsschichten *f/pl*	catégories *f* de population *f*, couches *f/pl* de la population *f*
classic media *pl*	klassische Medien *n/pl*	médias *m/pl* classiques
classicistic Latin	klassische Antiqua *f*	Didot *m*
classification	Aufschlüsselung *f*, Einteilung *f*, Klassifizierung *f*	classement *m*, classification *f*, répartition *f*, ventilation *f*
classified advertisements *pl*	Gelegenheitsanzeige *f*, Wortanzeige *f*, Anzeigen *f/pl*, kleine, Kleinanzeigen *f/pl*, rubrizierte Anzeigen *f/pl*	annonces *f/pl* groupées, petites annonces *f/pl*
classified column	Kleinanzeigenrubrik *f*	colonne *f* de petites annonces *f/pl*
classified index	Stichwortverzeichnis *n*	index *m* alphabétique des mots *m/pl* souches
to classify	einordnen	classifier
clause regulating competition	Konkurrenzklausel *f*	clause *f* de non-concurrence *f*
clean advertising	einwandfreie Werbung *f*	publicité *f* impeccable, publicité *f* irréprochable
clean print	Reindruck *m*	tirage *m*
clean proof	Reinabzug *m*, sauberer Abzug *m*	épreuve *f* corrigée, épreuve *f* sans fautes *f/pl*
to clear away	aussparen *typog*	laisser en blanc
to clear through customs *pl*	verzollen	payer les droits *m/pl* d'entrée *f*
to clear time	Werbezeitenreservierung *f*	réservation *f* de temps *m* d'antenne *f*
clearance sale	Ausverkauf *m*	vente *f* de soldes *m/pl*
clearing of goods *pl*	Totalausverkauf *m*	liquidation *f* générale
clearing system	Zahlungsverkehr *m*	traffic *m* de paiement *m*
clearly arranged	übersichtlich	bien disposé, normalisé
clearness	Klarheit *f*	clarté *f*
clerical mistake	Schreibfehler *m*	erreur *f* matérielle, faute *f* d'orthographe *f*, lapsus *m* calami
cliché *m*, **cliché**	Klischee *n*	cliché *m*, planche *f* typographique
cliché manufactory	Klischeeanstalt *f*	atelier *m* de photogravure *f*, clichérie *f*
clicker	Metteur *m*	imposeur *m*, metteur *m* en pages *f/pl*
client	Auftraggeber *m*, Kunde *m*	client *m*, commettant *m*, mandant *m*
client (for a service)	Abnehmer *m*	acheteur *m*, client *m*
climate of opinion	Meinungsklima *n*	climat *m* d'opinion *f*

clipping	Anzeigenausschnitt *m*, Zeitungsausschnitt *m*	coupure *f*, coupure *f* de presse *f*
clipping agency	Zeitungsausschnittbüro *n*	argus *m* de la presse *f*, bureau *m* de coupure *f* de journaux *m/pl*
to close the form	Form *f* schließen	boucler une page *f*, serrer une forme *f*
to close up	kompresser setzen, ohne Zwischenraum *m* setzen, Zwischenraum *m* verkleinern	diminuer l'espace *m* blanc, diminuer l'espace *m*, resserrer, serrer, supprimer l'espace *m*
close-set	kompreß	compact, plein, serré
close-up	Großaufnahme *f*, Hintergrundbericht *m*, Nahaufnahme *f*	gros plan *m*, médaillon *m*, photographie *f* prise de près, plan *m* serré, vue *f* de premier plan *m*
closing date, closing down, closing hour	Anzeigenschluß *m*, Redaktionsschluß *m*, Druckformschluß *m*, Annahmeschluß *m*	remise *f* de copie *f*, heure *f* limite de remise *f*
closing time	Ladenschluß *m*	fermeture *f* des magasins *m/pl*
cloth	Leinen *n*	toile *f*
cloth printing	Stoffdruck *m*	histotypie *f*, impression *f* sur étoffes *f/pl*
clubbing offer	Anzeigenrabatt *m* bei Belegung *f* mehrerer Blätter *n/pl* eines Verlages *m*, kombiniertes Abonnement *n*, Kombinationsrabatt *m*	abonnement *m* combiné, rabais *m* commun, rabais *m* de couplage *m*
clump	Reglette *f*	interligne *f*, réglette *f*
clumps *pl*	Füllmaterial *n*	blancs *m/pl*
coarse screen	grober Raster *m*	grosse trame *f*
coated board	Kunstdruckkarton *m*	carton *m* couché
coated paper	gestrichenes Papier *n*, Kunstdruckpapier *n*	papier *m* couché, papier *m* couché des deux faces *f/pl*, papier *m* glacé
cocktail of ads *pl*	Anzeigenplantage *f*	juxtaposition *f* désordonnée d'annonces *f/pl*
cock-up	hochstehender Buchstabe *m*	exposant *m* supérieur
code	Kode *m*, Telegrammschlüssel *m*	code *m*
to code	kodieren, verschlüsseln	coder, mettre en code *m*
code word	Kodewort *n*, Kennwort *n*, Schlüsselwort *n*	mot *m* de code *m*, mot *m* d'ordre *m*, mot-clé *m*
to codify	kodifizieren	codifier
coding	Kodierung *f*	codification *f*
coil-stitched book	Ringbuch *n*	livre *m* broché par boucles *f/pl*
coincidental survey	Fernsehzuschauerbefragung *f* während der Sendung *f*	enquête *f* aux téléspectateurs *m/pl* pendant une émission *f*
coined brand name	Phantasiemarkenname *m*	nom *m* inventé
coined word	erfundenes Wort *n*, Phantasiewort *n*	mot *m* forgé
cold	tonlos	sans partie *f* sonore

cold turkey *am*	unverblümte Sprache *f*	déclaration sans ambages *f/pl*
cold type composing	Kaltsatz *m*	composition *f* sans plomb *m* à froid
collage	Collage *f*, Klebearbeit *f*	collage *m*
collapsible carton	Faltschachtel *f*	boîte *f* pliante
to collate	kollationieren, vergleichen, zusammenfügen	assembler, collationner, comparer
collateral media *pl*	zusätzliche Werbemittel *n/pl*	médias *m/pl* additionnels
collation mark	Flattermarke *f*	indice *m* de collationnement *m*
to collect	zusammenfügen	assembler
collected volume	Sammelband *m*	collection *f*, recueil *m* en un volume *m*
collecting portfolio	Sammelmappe *f*	carton-emboîtage *m*
collection	Kollektion *f*	collection *f*
collection of information	Nachrichtenbeschaffung *f*	obtention *f* des informations *f/pl*
collection of picture blocks *pl*	Klischeearchiv *n*	archives *f/pl* des clichés *m/pl*
collective advertising	Gemeinschaftswerbung *f*, Kollektivwerbung *f*	publicité *f* collective, publicité *f* en commun, publicité *f* groupée
collective advertising poster	Sammelplakat *n*	affiche *f* collective
collective order	Sammelauftrag *m*	commande *f* groupée, ordre *m* collectif
collective page	Anzeigenkollektiv *n*, Kollektivseite *f*	page *f* collective
colloquial speech	Umgangssprache *f*	langage *m* courant
colloquy	Colloqium *n*	colloque *m*
collotype	Fotodruck *m*, Kollotypie *f*, Lichtdruck *m*	phototypie *f*
Colombier (see: poster size)	Colombier *m* (siehe: Plakatformat)	colombier (voir: format d'affiche)
colon	Doppelpunkt *m*	deux points *m/pl*, double point *m*
colophon	Impressum *n*, Pflichteindruck *m*, Signet *n*	marque *f* graphique, notice *f*, repiquage *m*, sigle *m*, vignette *f*
color *am* [see: colour]	Farbe *f*	couleur *f*
color engraving *am*	Farbklischee *n*	cliché *m* en couleurs *f/pl*
colored ad *am*	mehrfarbige Anzeige *f*	annonce *f* multicolore
colored paper *am*	buntes Papier *n*	papier *m* de couleur *f*, papier *m* peint
colour *brit*	Farbe *f*	couleur *f*
colour additional charge	Farbzuschlag *m*	supplément *m* de prix *m* pour la couleur *f*
colour advertisement	Farbanzeige *f*	publicité *f* en couleurs *f/pl*
colour block *brit*	Farbklischee *n*	cliché *m* en couleurs *f/pl*
colour chart	Farbskala *f*	gamme *f* des couleurs *f/pl*, guide *m* des couleurs *f/pl*
colour composition	Farbkomposition *f*	composition *f* chromatique, composition *f* colorée
colour contrast	Farbkontrast *m*	contraste *m* de couleurs *f/pl*
colour correction	Farbkorrektur *f*	correction *f* de couleur *f*
colour display	farbige Schaufensterauslage *f*, farbiges Dekorationsstück *n*	étalage *m* de vitrine *f* en couleur *f*
colour effect	Farbeffekt *m*, Farbwirkung *f*	effet *m* chromatique, effet *m* de couleurs *f/pl*

colour film	Farbfilm *m*	film *m* en couleurs *f/pl*
colour filter	Farbfilter *m*	filtre *m* coloré
colour fringing	Passerdifferenz *f*	différence *f* de repérage *m*
colour lithography	Farbenlithografie *f*	chromolithographie *f*, lithographie *f* en couleurs *f/pl*
colour photo printing	Farbfotodruck *m*	impression *f* de photos *f/pl* en couleur *f*
colour photography	Farbfoto *n*, Farbfotografie *f*	photo *f* en couleurs *f/pl*, prise *f* de vue *f* en couleurs *f/pl* photochromie *f*
colour printing	Buntdruck *m*, Farbdruck *m*	chromolithographie *f*, chromotypie *f*, impression *f* en couleurs *f/pl*, impression *f* polychrome, polychromie *f*
colour process etching	Farbätzung *f*	cliché *m* de photogravure *f*, quadrichromie *f*
colour proof	Farbandruck *m*	épreuve *f* en couleurs *f/pl*
colour range	Farbskala *f*	gamme *f* des couleurs *f/pl*, guide *m* des couleurs *f/pl*
colour retouching	Farbretusche *f*	retouche *f* des couleurs *f/pl*
colour sample	Farbmuster *n*	échantillon *m* dc couleur *f*
colour scale	Farbskala *f*	gamme *f* des couleurs *f/pl*, guide *m* des couleurs *f/pl*
colour selection, colour separation	Farbauszug *m*	sélection *f* des couleurs *f/pl*, séparation *f* des couleurs *f/pl*
colour surcharge	Farbzuschlag *m*	supplément *m* de prix *m* pour la couleur *f*
colour television	Farbfernsehen *n*	télévision *f* couleur *f*
colour toning	Fotokolorierung *f*	coloration *f* photographique
colour transparency	Farbdia *n*	diapositif *m* couleur, ektachrome *m*
coloured	farbig, getönt, koloriert	coloré, colorié, teinté
coloured ad *brit*	mehrfarbige Anzeige *f*	annonce *f* multicolore
coloured disc	Bildplatte *f*	disque *m* en couleurs *f/pl*
coloured paper	getönfes Papier *n*, buntes Papier *n*	papier *m* de couleur *f*, papier *m* peint
coloured pencil	Farbstift *m*	crayon *m* de couleur *f*
coloured sketch	Farbskizze *f*	croquis *m* en couleurs *f/pl*
colouring	Farbgebung *f*, Kolorierung *f*, Kolorit *n*	coloriage *m*, couleur *f*, encrage *m*, teinte *f*
colour-slide	Farbdia *n*	diapositif *m* couleur, ektachrome *m*
Columbian (see appendix)	Mittel *f* (Schriftgrad *m*) (siehe Anhang)	corps 14 points (voir appendice)
column	Kolumne *f*, Spalte *f*	colonne *f*
column depth	Spaltenhöhe *f*	hauteur *f* de colonne *f*
column heading	Kolumnentitel *m*, Spaltenüberschrift *f*	titre *m* courant, titre *m* de colonne *f*, titre *m* de paragraphe *m*
column length	Spaltenhöhe *f*	hauteur *f* de colonne *f*
column line	Spaltenlinie *f*	colombelle *f*, séparation *f* des colonnes *f/pl*

column measure	Spaltenbreite *f*	justification *f* de la colonne *f*, largeur *f* de la colonne *f*
column title	Rubriktitel *m*	titre *m* de rubrique *f*
column width	Spaltenbreite *f*	justification *f* de la colonne *f*, largeur *f* de la colonne *f*
column-millimetre	Millimeterpreis *m*	millimètre-colonne *f*
combat organ	Kampforgan *n*	organe *m* de combat *m*
combination	Zusammenschluß *m*	jumelage *m*, regroupement *m*
combination of various means *pl* **of communication**	Medienverbund *m*	combinaison *f* de divers moyens *m/pl* de communication *f*
combination plate	kombinierte Ätzung *f*	cliché *m* trait *m* -simili combiné
combination rate	kombinierter Anzeigenpreis *m*, Kombinationspreis *m*	prix *m* de couplage *m*, tarif *m* combiné
combination sale	Koppelungsverkauf *m*	promotion *f* jumelée, vente *f* liée
combined	kombiniert	combiné
combined edition	Kombinationsausgabe *f*	éditions *f/pl* couplées
combined edition discount	Kombinationsrabatt *m*	rabais *m* de couplage *m*
combined issues *pl*	Doppelnummer *f*	numéros *m/pl* couplés
combined line and half-tone block *brit*	kombinierte Ätzung *f*	cliché *m* trait *m* -simili combiné
combined printing	Kombinationsdruck *m*	impression *f* combinée
combined rate	kombinierter Tarif *m*, Kombinationspreis *m*	prix *m* de couplage *m*, tarif *m* combiné
combined scheduling	Medienverbund *m*	combinaison *f* de divers moyens *m/pl* de communication *f*
combipack	Mehrstückpackung *f*, Verbundpackung *f*	plusieurs pièces *f/pl* dans un même emballage *m*, plusieurs unités *f/pl* de vente *f* dans un même emballage *m*
to **come out**	erscheinen	paraître, sortir
to **come through**	durchschlagen *typog*	maculer, pénétrer, transpercer, traverser
comic journal	Witzblatt *n*	feuille *f* humoristique, satirique *m*
comic strip	Comic Strip *m*, humoristischer Bilderstreifen *m*	bandes *f/pl* dessinées
comma	Komma *n*	virgule *f*
to **command**	bestellen	commander
commemorative volume	Festschrift *f*	brochure *f* commémorative
comment, commentary	Kommentar *m*	commentaire *m*
commentator	Kommentator *m*	commentateur *m*
commerce	Handel *m*	commerce *m*

commercial	Fernsehspot *m*, Kassettenfernsehen *n*, Werbeankündigung *f* im Rundfunk *m*, Werbedurchsage *f*, Werbesendung *f*, Werbespot *m*	annonce *f* à la radio *f*, annonce *f* publicitaire, annonce *f* radiodiffusée, audiovision *f*, bref communiqué *m* radio *f*, court-métrage *m* publicitaire, émission *f* publicitaire, message *m* publicitaire, spot *m*, télévision *f* à cassettes *f/pl*
commercial advertisement	Geschäftsanzeige *f*	annonce *f* commerciale
commercial art	Gebrauchsgrafik *f*, Werbegrafik *f*	art *m* commercial, art *m* publicitaire, créations *f/pl* graphiques, graphisme *m* publicitaire, publicité *f* artistique
commercial artist	Gebrauchsgrafiker *m*, Grafik-Designer *m*	dessinateur *m*, dessinateur *m* en publicité *f*
commercial broadcasting	Werbefunk *m*	émission *f* publicitaire, publicité *f* radiophonique
commercial directory	Handelsadreßbuch *n*	almanach *m* du commerce *m*, annuaire *m* du commerce *m*, Bottin *m*
commercial journal	Wirtschaftsblatt *n*	feuille *f* commerciale, feuille *f* économique
commercial photo	Werbebild *n*, Werbefoto *n*	photo *f* publicitaire
commercial picture	Werbefilm *m*	film *m* publicitaire
commercial press	Wirtschaftspresse *f*	presse *f* économique
commercial radio	Werbefunk *m*	émission *f* publicitaire, publicité *f* radiophonique
commercial rate cards *pl*	Senderpreis *m*	tarif *m* d'antenne *f*
commercial research	Wirtschaftsforschung *f*	recherche *f* économique
commercial section	Handelsteil *m*	partie *f* commerciale
commercial stationery	Geschäftsdrucksachen *f/pl*	imprimés *m/pl* commerciaux
commercial studio	Werbeatelier *n*	studio *m* de publicité *f*
commercial television	Fernsehwerbung *f*	publicité *f* télévisée
commercial traveller	Reisender *m*	voyageur *m* de commerce *m*
commission	Auftrag *m*, Bestellung *f*, Druckauftrag *m*, Kommission *f*, Provision *f*	commande *f*, commande *f* d'impression *f*, commission *f*, ordre *m*, provision *f*
commission fee	Agenturprovision *f*, Vermittlungsprovision *f*	commission *f* d'agence *f*, commission *f* d'intermédiaire
commission splitting	Provisionsteilung *f*	partage *m* de commission *f*
commissionable	provisionspflichtig	donnant droit *m* à la commission *f*
commissioned by	Auftraggeber *m*	client *m*, commettant *m*, mandant *m*
committee	Ausschuß *m*	comité *f*
commodity	Ware *f*	denrée *f*, marchandise *f*
common market	gemeinsamer Markt *m*	marché *m* commun
common sense	gesunder Menschenverstand *m*	sens *m* commun
commonplace	Gemeinplatz *m*	banalité *f*, lieu *m* commun
commonplace-book	Zitatensammlung *f*	recueil *m* de citations *f/pl*
to communicate	mitteilen	communiquer
communication	Informationsfluß *m*, Kommunikation *f*	communication *f*

communication medium	Kommunikationsmittel *n*	moyen *m* de communication *f*, véhicule *m* de communication *f*
communication policy	Kommunikationspolitik *f*	politique *f* de communication *f*
communication research	Kommunikationsforschung *f*	étude *f* de la communication *f*
community advertising	Gemeindewerbung *f*	publicité *f* communale
community antenna television	Kabelfernsehen *n*	télévision *f* via câble *m*
company publication	Hauszeitschrift *f*	journal *m* d'entreprise *f*, revue *f* d'entreprise
comparative advertising	Komparativwerbung *f*, vergleichende Werbung *f*	publicité *f* discriminatrice, publicité *f* discriminatoire
to compare	kollationieren, vergleichen	collationner, comparer
compartment panel	Abteilplakat *n*	emplacement *m* dans compartiment *m*
compensation	Ausgleich *m*, Entschädigung *f*	compensation *f*, dédommagement *m*, indemnité *f*
compensation for damage	Schadenersatz *m*	dédommagement *m*, dommages-intérêts *m/pl*
compère	Ansager *m*	compère *m*, speaker *m*
to compete	konkurrieren	concourir, faire concurrence *f*
competent court	Gerichtsstand *m*	for *m*, tribunal *m*
competing brands *pl*	Konkurrenzmarken *f/pl*	marques *f/pl* de compétition *f*
competition	Konkurrenz *f*, Preisausschreiben *n*, Wettbewerb *m*	concours *m*, concurrence *f*, mise *f* au concours *m*
competition clause	Konkurrenzausschluß *m*	clause *f* d'exclusivité *f*, clause *f* de non-concurrence *f*
competitive	konkurrenzfähig	à la hauteur *f* de la concurrence *f*, concurrentiel
competitive advertising	Konkurrenzwerbung *f*	publicité *f* concurrente
competitive conditions *pl*	Wettbewerbsbedingungen *f/pl*	conditions *f/pl* de concours *m*
competitive copy *am*	aggressive Werbung *f*, herabsetzende Werbung *f*	publicité *f* agressive, publicité *f* discriminatrice , publicité *f* discriminatoire
competitor	Konkurrent *m*, Wettbewerber *m*	concurrent *m*
compilation	Zusammenstellung *f*	compilation *f*
to compile	zusammentragen	compiler
complaint	Beanstandung *f*, Mängelrüge *f*, Reklamation *f*	réclamation *f*
complementary colour	Komplementärfarbe *f*	couleur *f* complémentaire
complete	vollständig	complet
complete block *brit*	Vollklischee *n*	cliché *m* bloc
complete editorial staff	Vollredaktion *f*	rédaction *f* complète
complete plate *am*	Vollklischee *n*	cliché *m* bloc
complete voucher copy	komplette Belegnummer *f*	justificatif *m* complet
completion	Fertigstellung *f*	finition *f*
to complicate	verwickeln	compliquer
complication	Verwicklung *f*	complication *f*
complimentary copy	Freiexemplar *n*, Probeexemplar *n*, Werbeexemplar *n*, Werbenummer *f*	exemplaire *m* gratuit, fascicule *m* spécimen *m*, numéro *m* de propagande *f*, spécimen *m*
component	Bestandteil *m*	élément *m*, partie *f* composante
to compose	absetzen (Druck) , setzen *typog*	composer
composing machine	Setzmaschine *f*	composeuse *f* mécanique, machine *f* à composer

composing material	Satzmaterial *n*	matériaux *m* de composition *f*
composing room	Setzerei *f*, Setzersaal *m*	atelier *m* de composition *f*, services *m/pl* de composition *f*
composing rule	Setzlinie *f*	filet *m* à composer, filet *m* de composition *f*
composing stick	Winkelhaken *m*	composteur *m*
composing-frame	Setzerkasten *m*	casse *f* de compositeur *m*
composite advertisement	Kollektivanzeige *f*, Sammelanzeige *f*	annonce *f* collective, annonce *f* groupée
composite advertisements *pl*	rubrizierte Anzeigen *f/pl*	annonces *f/pl* groupées, petites annonces *f/pl*
composition	Abfassung *f*, Satz *m/typog*, Schriftsatz *m/typog*	composition *f*, rédaction *f*
composition pattern	Anweisung *f* (für Satz *m*), Satzmuster *n*	donnée *f* de composition *f*, référence *f* de composition *f*
composition roller	Massewalze *f*	rouleau *m* à encrer
compositor	Schriftsetzer *m*	compositeur *m*, typographe *m*
compositor-pressman	Schweizerdegen *m/typog*	amphibie *m*, ouvrier *m* à deux mains *f/pl*
compositor's error	Satzfehler *m*, Setzfehler *m*	erreur *f* de composition *f*, faute *f* de composition *f*
comprehensive	detailliertes Layout *n*, fertiger Entwurf *m*	maquette *f* détaillée, maquette *f* très poussée
to compress	kürzen, zusammenstreichen	abréger, couper, raccourcir, rogner, taillader, triturer
compulsory subscription	Zwangsabonnement *n*	abonnement *m* forcé
computation	Berechnung *f*	calcul *m*, compte *m*
computer	Computer *m*, Datenrechner *m*, Elektronenrechner *m*	calculateur *m* électronique, calculatrice *f*, ordinateur *m*
computer controlled typesetting (CCT)	Satzherstellung *f* mit EDV-Anlagen *f/pl*	composition *f* programmée
computer drawing	Computerzeichnung *f*	dessin *m* d'ordinateur *m*
computer setting	Computersatz *m*	composition *f* par ordinateur *m*
computer typesetting installation	Computersetzanlage *f*	installation *f* de composition *f* programmée
concentration of publishing houses *pl*	Verlagskonzentration *f*	concentration *f* de maisons *f/pl* d'éditions *f/pl*
concept-test	Prüfung *f* des Publikumsverhaltens *n*, Verhaltensprüfung *f*	étude *f* d'attitude *f*, test *m* d'axe *m*
concert poster	Konzertplakat *n*	affiche *f* de concert *m*
concertina folding	Handharmonikafalzung *f*, Harmonikafalzung *f*, Leporellofalzung *f*, Zickzackfaltung *f*	pli *m* accordéon *m*, pli *m* en zig-zag
concluding word	Schlußwort *n*	discours *m* de clôture *f*
concurrent	gleichzeitig	simultané
condensed type	enge Schrift *f*, Schmalschrift *f*	caractère *m* étroit, écriture *f* étroite
conditions *pl*	Bedingungen *f/pl*	conditions *f/pl*
conditions *pl* of trading	Geschäftsbedingungen *f/pl*	conditions *f/pl* commerciales
confirmation	Bestätigung *f*	confirmation *f*
confirmation of order	Auftragsbestätigung *f*	confirmation *f* de la commande *f*
confiscation	Beschlagnahme *f*	confiscation *f*

to **conform to**	übereinstimmen mit	être conforme à, être d'accord *m* avec
congeniality	Geistesverwandtschaft *f*	affinité *f* intellectuelle
congratulary card	Glückwunschkarte *f*	carte *f* de vœux *m/pl*
congratulation service	Glückwunschdienst *m*	services *m/pl* de la remise *f* de félicitation *f*
congress	Tagung *f*	congrès *m*
connexion	Zusammenhang *m*	connexion *f*, liaison *f*
connexion advertising	Anschlußwerbung *f*	campagne *f* de suite *f*
connexion of readers *pl* **with their paper**	Leserblattbindung *f*	relations *f/pl* des lecteurs *m/pl* avec leur journal *m*
connotation	Nebenbedeutung *f*	signification *f* secondaire
consent	Genehmigung *f*	consentement *m*
consignee	Adressat *m*	destinataire *m*
consignment for choice	Auswahlsendung *f*	envoi *m* à choix *m*
consignment for inspection	Ansichtssendung *f*	envoi *m* à l'examen *m*
consolation price	Trostpreis *m*	prime *f* d'encouragement *m*
constancy of readership	Lesertreue *f*	fidélité *f* de lecture *f*
constituent	Bestandteil *m*	élément *m*, partie *f* composante
constructive poster	konstruktives Plakat *n*	affiche *f* constructiviste
consultant	Berater *m*	conseil *m*, conseiller *m*
consultation, consulting	Beratung *f*	conseil *m*, consultation *f*
consumer	Konsument *m*, Verbraucher *m* (in *f*)	consommateur *m*
consumer acceptance	Aufnahmebereitschaft *f*, Aufnahmefreudigkeit *f*, Kaufbereitschaft *f*	acceptabilité *f* auprès des consommateurs *m/pl*, faveur *f* du public *m*
consumer advertising	Konsumentenwerbung *f*, Verbraucherwerbung *f*	publicité *f* auprès des consommateurs *m/pl*
consumer behaviour	Verbraucherverhalten *n*	comportement *m* des consommateurs *m/pl*
consumer center	Verbraucherzentrale *f*	centre *m* de consommateurs *m/pl*
consumer demand	Verbrauchernachfrage *f*	demande *f* des consommateurs *m/pl*
consumer desire	Verbraucherwunsch *m*	désir *m* des consommateurs *m/pl*
consumer goods *pl*	Konsumgüter *f/pl*	biens *m/pl* de consommation *f*
consumer goods *pl* **advertising**	Konsumwerbung *f*	publicité *f* des biens *m/pl* de consommation *f*
consumer inquiry	Verbraucherbefragung *f*	enquête *f* auprès des consommateurs *m/pl*
consumer insistence	Markentreue *f*	fidélité *f* à la marque *f*
consumer interest	Verbraucherinteresse *n*	intérêt *m* des consommateurs *m/pl*
consumer market	Verbrauchermarkt *m*	marché *m* de consommation *f*
consumer motivation research	Erforschung *f* der Verbrauchermotive *n/pl*	études *f/pl* de la motivation *f* des consommateurs *m/pl*
consumer panel	Verbrauchertestgruppe *f*	groupe *m* d'essai *m* de consommateurs *m/pl*, panel *m* des consommateurs *m/pl*

consumer protection	Verbraucherschutz *m*	protection *f* des consommateurs *m/pl*
consumer publication	Publikumszeitschrift *f*	magazine *m*, revue *f*
consumer research	Verbraucheranalyse *f*, Verbraucherforschung *f*	recherche *f* auprès des consommateurs *m/pl*
consumer survey	Verbraucherbefragung *f*	enquête *f* auprès des consommateurs *m/pl*
consumer test	Verbrauchertest *m*	test *m* de consommation *f*
consumerism	Verbraucherschutzbewegung *f*	mouvement *m* pour la protection *f* des consommateurs *m/pl*
consumer's goods *pl*	Verbrauchsgüter *n/pl*	biens *m/pl* de consommation *f*
consuming habits *pl*	Verbrauchsgewohnheiten *f/pl*	habitudes *f/pl* de consommation *f*
consumption	Konsum *m*, Verbrauch *m*	consommation *f*
consumption pattern	Verbrauchsgewohnheiten *f/pl*	habitudes *f/pl* de consommation *f*
contact	Kontakt *m*	contact *m*
to contact	sich in Verbindung *f* setzen	contacter
contact frequency	Kontakthäufigkeit *f*	fréquence *f* de contact *m*
contact man	Kontakter *m*, Kontaktmann *m*, Sachbearbeiter *m* der Werbung *f*, Verbindungsmann *m*	chef *m* de publicité *f* d'agence *f*, contacteur *m*, homme *m* de relation *f*
contact print	Kontaktdruck *m*	impression *f* par contact *m*
contact printing machine	Kopiergerät *n*	appareil *m* à copier, presse *f* à copier
content analysis	Inhaltsanalyse *f*	analyse *f* du contenu *m*
contents *pl*	Inhalt *m*	contenu *m*
contents *pl* **heading**	Rubriktitel *m*	titre *m* de rubrique *f*
contest	Wettbewerb *m*	concours *m*
continuation	Fortsetzung *f*	suite *f*
continued, to be	Fortsetzung *f* folgt, wird fortgesetzt	à suivre, complément de texte *m* suivra
continuity	Kontinuität *f*	continuité *f*
continuity strip	Comicserie *f*	série *f* de bandes *f/pl* dessinées
continuous advertisement in colour	Endlos-Farbanzeige *f*	encart *m* en couleur *f* imprimé en continu *m*
continuous exhibition	Dauerausstellung *f*	exposition *f* permanente
continuous form	Endlosformular *n*	formulaire *m* en continu
continuous order	laufender Auftrag *m*	ordre *m* permanent
continuous printing	Endlosdruck *m*	impression *f* en continu
contract	Abschluß *m*, Vertrag *m*	contrat *m*
to contract	zusammenstreichen	taillader, triturer
contract of lease	Pachtvertrag *m*	bail *m* à ferme *f*, contrat *m* de fermage *m*
contract on a line basis	Zeilenabschluß *m*	contrat *m* en millimètres *m/pl*
contract period	Vertragsdauer *f*	durée *f* du contrat *m*
contract year	Abschlußjahr *n*, Einschaltjahr *n*	année *f* légale
contracting party	Vertragspartner *m*	contractant *m*
contractor	Kunde *m*	client *m*
contractual year	Insertionsjahr *n*	année *f* contractuelle
contrast	Kontrast *m*	contraste *m*
contrasting colour	Kontrastfarbe *f*	couleur *f* d'opposition *f*
contribution	redaktioneller Beitrag *m*	article *m* écrit pour un journal *m*, cntribution *f*, contribution *f*

controlled circulation paper	CC-Zeitschrift f	périodique m d'une circulation f contrôlée et qualifiée
controlled price	gebundener Preis m	prix m fixe, prix m imposé
controversy	Meinungsstreit m	polémique f
convenience, at our	Abruf m, auf	à notre convenance f, sur appel m
convenience foods pl	verbrauchsfertige Nahrungsmittel n/pl	aliments m/pl prêts à la consommation f
convenience goods pl	Fertigprodukte n/pl	produits m/pl finis
convention	Absprache f	convention f
conversation	Gespräch n	conversation f
converting	Weiterverarbeitung f	transformation f
to cook up	zusammenbrauen	concocter
co-op advertising	kombinierte Werbung f	publicité f combinée
cooperative	Konsumgenossenschaft f, Verbrauchergenossenschaft f	coopérative f des consommateurs m/pl
cooperative advertising	Werbung f, gemeinsame, Gemeinschaftswerbung f	publicité f commune, publicité f collective, publicité f en commun
cooperative work	Gemeinschaftsarbeit f	collaboration f, travail m en équipe f
to co-ordinate	koordinieren	coordiner
coordinated advertising	aufeinander abgestimmte Werbung f, koordinierte Werbung f	publicité f coordonnée
co-ordination	Koordinierung f	coordination f
coordinator	Koordinator m	coordonnateur m
copper etching	Kupferätzung f	gravure f sur cuivre m
copper gravure	Kupfertiefdruck m	impression f en héliogravure f, impression f en taille-douce f, rotogravure f
copperplate engraving	Kupferstich m	chalcographie f, estampe f en taille f douce, gravure f
copperplate printing	Kupferdruck m, Kupfertiefdruck m, Tiefdruck m/typog	gravure f en creux m/pl, impression f en creux m, impression f en héliogravure f, impression f en taille-douce f, impression f héliogravure f
copy	Abklatsch m, Anzeigentext m, Ausgabe f (Nummer), Exemplar n, Kopie f, Manuskript n, Text m, Vorlage f, Werbetext m, Zweitschrift f	copie f, dessin m au propre, duplicata m, édition f, exemplaire m, manuscrit m, modèle m, ms, numéro m, pastichage m, texte m, texte m publicitaire
to copy	Abschrift f anfertigen, kopieren, nachmachen	contre-faire, copier, faire un duplicata m, imiter
copy appeal	Attraktivität f der Anzeigenaussage f	attrait m du message m publicitaire
copy chief	Cheftexter m	chef m de la conception-rédaction f

copy deadline	Anzeigenschluß *m*, Redaktionsschluß *m*	bouclage *m*, date *f* limite de remise *f*, délai *m* des annonces *f*/*pl*, remise *f* de copie *f*
copy department	Textabteilung *f*	service *m* de la rédaction *f*
copy editor	Lektor *m*	lecteur *m* d'une maison *f* d'édition *f*
copy fitting	Umfangsberechnung *f*	calibrage *m* d'une copie *f*
copy for reproduction	Reproduktionsvorlage *f*	original *m* à reproduire
copy function	Bedeutung *f* des Textes *m* als Anzeigenelement *n*	importance *f* du texte *m* comme élément *m* publicitaire
to copy in	einkopieren	copier dans, pelliculer
copy on file	Archivexemplar *n*	exemplaire *m* des archives *f*/*pl*, exemplaire *m* en collection *f*
copy paper	Durchschlagpapier *n*	papier *m* pour copies *f*/*pl*
copy platform	konzeptionelle Grundlage *f*, Werbeplattform *f*	axe *f* de la publicité *f*, conception *f* de base *f*
copy print	Reproduktion *f*	contre-type *m*, reproduction *f*
copy reader	Redaktionssekretär *m*	sécrétaire *m* de rédaction *f*
copy research	Textanalyse *f*	analyse *f* de texte *m*
copy styling	Manuskriptbearbeitung *f*	préparation *f* de la copie *f*
copy supervisor	Cheftexter *m*	chef *m* de la conception-rédaction *f*
copy test	Anzeigentest *m*	test *m* d'annonce *f*
copy testing	Textprüfung *f*	testage *m* des messages *m*/*pl* publicitaires
copycat	Plagiator *m*	plagiaire *m*
copy-holder	Manuskripthalter *m*	porte-copie *m*
copying paper	Kopierpapier *n*	papier *m* pour copies *f*/*pl*
copying printing	Kopierdruck *m*	impression *f* aux encres *f*/*pl* communicatives
copying screen	Kopierraster *m*	trame *f* de copie *f*
copyright	Abdrucksrecht *n*, Autorenrecht *n*, Copyright *n*, Urheberrecht *n*	droit *m* d'auteur *m*, droit *m* de publication *f*, droit *m* de reproduction *f*, droit *m* d'impression *f*
copytest	Copytest *m*	test *m* du texte *m*
to copy-write	texten	rédiger des textes *m*/*pl*
copy-writer	Texter *m*, Werbetexter *m*	concepteur-rédacteur *m*, rédacteur *m* publicitaire
corner card	Firmeneindruck *m* auf Briefumschlag *m*	repiquage *m* d'un nom *m* commercial sur l'enveloppe *f*
corporate advertising	institutionelle Werbung *f*	publicité *f* de notoriété *f*, publicité *f* de prestige *m*, publicité *f* institutionnelle
corporate image	Firmenbild *n*	image *f* de la firme *f*
to correct	berichtigen, korrigieren	corriger
to correct in the metal	auf dem Blei *n* korrigieren	corriger sur le plomb *m*
correct proof	Standbogen *m*	feuille *f* d'emplacement *m*, feuille *f* des blancs *m*/*pl*
correction	Korrektur *f*	correction *f*
correction mark	Korrekturzeichen *f*	marque *f* du correcteur *m*, signe *m* de correction *f*
correction of the press	Druckberichtigung *f*	correction *f* de la presse *f*
correction on film	Filmkorrektur *f*	correction *f* sur film *m*

correction on lead	Bleisatzkorrektur *f*	correction *f* sur plomb *m*
correction on paper	Papierkorrektur *f*	correction *f* sur papier *m*
corrector	Korrektor *m*	correcteur *m*
correspondence	Schriftwechsel *m*	correspondance *f*
correspondence column	Eselswiese *f*	courrier *m* du cœur *m*
correspondence school	Fernunterricht *m*	cours *m* par correspondance *f*
correspondent	Berichterstatter *m*, Korrespondent *m*	chroniqueur *m*, correspondant *m*, rapporteur *m*
corridor panel, corridor site	Gangschild *n*	emplacement *m* couloir *m*
corrigenda	Druckfehlerverzeichnis *n*	errata *m*
corrigendum	Berichtigung *f*	rectificatif *m*, rectification *f*
corrugated paper	gewelltes Papier *n*	papier *m* ondulé
corrugated paste-board	Wellpappe *f*	carton *m* ondulé
corrupt press	käufliche Presse *f*	presse *f* corrompue
to cost	kosten	coûter
cost estimate	Kostenvoranschlag *m*	devis *m* estimatif, évaluation des frais *m/pl*
cost of composition	Satzkosten *pl*	frais *m/pl* de composition *f*
cost of the insert	Beilagenpreis *m*	prix *m* de l'encart *m*
cost per line	Zeilenpreis *m*	prix *m* d'une ligne *f*
cost price	Kaufpreis *m*	prix *m* d'achat *m*
cost-effect calculation	Nachkalkulation *f*	contrôle *m* a posteriori, postcalculation *f*
cost-per-thousand	Tausenderpreis *m*	prix *m* aux milles lecteurs *m/pl*
costs *pl*	Ausgaben *f/pl* (Unkosten), Kosten *pl*	coûts *pl*, dépenses *f/pl*, frais *m/pl*
costs *f* of advertisement	Anzeigenpreise *m/pl*	tarifs *m/pl* de publicité *f*
costs *pl* of advertising	Werbekosten *pl*	dépenses *f/pl* publicitaires, frais *m/pl* de publicité *f*
costs *pl* of circularising	Streukosten *pl*	frais *m/pl* de diffusion *f*
counter advertising	Abwehrwerbung *f*	contre-publicité *f*
counter card	Aufstellplakat *n*, Werbeaufsteller *m*	affiche *f* de comptoir *m*, affiche *f* mobile, pancarte *f*
counter dispenser, counter display, counter display container	stummer Verkäufer *m*, Thekenaufsteller *m*, Ladentischauslage *f*	matériel *m* d'étalage *m* de comptoir *m*, vendeur *m* muet
counter-advertising	Konterwerbung *f*	contre-publicité *f*
counter-die	Patrize *f*	poinçon *m*
counterfeit	Nachahmung *f*	contre-facon *f*, imitation *f*, plagiat *m*
counter-project	Gegenentwurf *m*	contre-projet *m*
counter-proof	Konterdruck *m*	contre-épreuve *f*, noir au blanc
counter-proposition	Gegenvorschlag *m*	contreproposition *f*
counterstatement	Gegendarstellung *f*	contre-déclaration *f*
co-up advertising	Verbundwerbung *f*	publicité *f* commune, publicité *f* groupée
couple	Kombination *f*	couplage *m*
coupled rate	gekoppelter Tarif *m*	tarif *m* couplé
coupon	Bon *m*, Gutschein *m*, Kupon *m*	bon *m*, bon *m* à découper, bon *m* à valoir, coupon *m*, coupon *m* de réduction *f*
coupon advertising	Kuponwerbung	publicité *f* au moyen *m* de coupons *m/pl*
couponing	Gutscheinverteilung *f*	couponnage *m*

court of arbitration	Schiedsgericht *n*, Schlichtungsausschuß *m*	commission *f* de conciliation *f*, tribunal *m* arbitral
cover	Bucheinband *m*, Einband *m*, Umschlag *m*	couverture *f*, reliure *f*
to **cover**	abdecken, erfassen	caviarder, couvrir, masquer, recouvrir
cover cardboard	Umschlagkarton *m*	carton *m* de couverture *f*
cover girl	Fotomodell *n* auf der Titelseite *f*, Titelblattmädchen *n*	cover-girl *f*
cover page	Umschlagseite *f*	page *f* de couverture *f*
cover paper	Umschlagpapier *n*	papier *m* de couverture *f*
cover picture	Umschlagbild *n*	illustration *f* de couverture *f*
cover stock	Umschlagpapier *n*	papier *m* de couverture *f*
cover story	Titelgeschichte *f*	article *m* annoncé en couverture *f*
coverage	Reichweite *f*, Streubreite *f*, Streuung *f*, Verbreitung *f*	circulation *f*, couverture *f*, diffusion *f*, distribution *f*, propagation *f*, prospection *f*, rayon *m* d'action *f*, rayonnement *m*, taux *m* de pénétration *f*
coverage of a station	Reichweite *f* eines Senders *m*	couverture *f* géographique
covered sector	Verbreitungsgebiet *n*	rayon *m* d'action *f*, zone *f* de diffusion *f*
covering letter	Begleitbrief *m*	lettre *f* d'envoi *m*
covering with fibers *pl*	Beflockung *f*	flocage *m*
craft	Gewerbe *n*	artisanat *m*, métier *m*
crash finish	Leinenstruktur *f* (Papier)	structure *f* treillis *m*
to **crash the headlines** *pl*	Schlagzeilen *f/pl* machen	tenir la manchette *f*
crayon drawing	Kreidezeichnung *f*	dessin *m* de crayon *m*
cream-plan	Stufenwerbeplan *m*	publicité *f* en étapes *f/pl*
to **crease**	Falten *f/pl* werfen	plisser
creation of ads *pl*	Werbemittelgestaltung *f*	création *f* des moyens *m/pl* de publicité *f*
creative	kreativ, schöpferisch	créateur
creative artist	Gestalter *m*	artiste *m* -créateur *m*, dessinateur *m* -concepteur *m*, maquettiste *m*
creative copy	außergewöhnlicher Werbetext *m*, Grundaussage *f*, Hauptwerbetext *m*	message *m* de base *f*, texte *m* principal, texte *m* publicitaire extraordinaire
creative copy and artwork	Anzeigengestaltung *f*, Werbegestaltung *f*	conception *f* de l'annonce *f*, conception *f* publicitaire, présentation *f* de l'annonce *f*
creative director	Gestaltungsleiter *m*, Kreativgruppenleiter *m*	chef *m* du service *m* création *f*, chef *m* d'un groupe *m* créateur, directeur *m* artistique
creative work	Gestaltung *f*	création *f*, dessin *m*, maquette *f*
creativity	Kreativität *f*	créativité *f*
credibility	Glaubwürdigkeit *f*	crédibilité *f*
credit	Kredit *m*, Quellenangabe *f*	crédit *m*, référence *f* de source *f*
credit note	Gutschrift *f*	note *f* de crédit *m*
credit slip	Bon *m*, Gutschein *m*	bon *m*, bon *m* à valoir, coupon *m* de réduction *f*

credit titles *pl*	Vorspann *m*	film *m* annonce *f*
creepy news	Schreckensnachricht *f*	nouvelle *f* d'horreur *f*
crêpe paper	Kreppapier *n*	papier *m* crépon, papier *m* de crêpe *m*
crew	Mannschaft *f*	équipe *f*
crib	Eselsbrücke *f*, Plagiat *n*	guide-âne *m*, plagiat *m*
crimp	Falte *f*	pli *m*
crimping	Kundenfang *m*	racolage *m*
crinkled paper	Kreppapier *n*	papier *m* crépon, papier *m* de crêpe *m*
criteria *pl*	Merkmale *n/pl*	critères *m/pl*
critic	Kritiker *m*, Rezensent *m*	critique *m*
criticism of advertising	Kritik *f* an der Werbung *f*	critique *f* de la publicité *f*
to criticize harshly	verreißen	critiquer sévèrement, éreinter
critique	Rezension *f*	compte *m* rendu, critique *f*
crooner	Schlagersänger *m*	chanteur *m* de charme *m*
to crop	beschneiden	ébarber, rogner, taillader, tailler
cropping	Bestimmung *f* eines Bildausschnitts *m*	détermination *f* de la coupe *f*
to cross	ausstreichen	biffer, effacer
cross hatch	Kreuzlinienschraffur *f*	lignes *f/pl* croisées
cross hatched paper	kariertes Papier *n*	papier *m* quadrillé
to cross out	durchstreichen	raturer
cross rule	Querlinie *f*	réglure *f*
cross section	repräsentativer Durchschnitt *m*	coupe *f* en travers
cross size	Querformat *n*	format *m* en largeur *f*, format *m* en travers *m*
cross-channel-ownership	Medienverflechtung *f*	interdépendance *f* des médias *f*
cross-cut	Querschnitt *m*	coupe *f* en travers, coupe *f* transversale
crossed cheque	Verrechnungsscheck *m*	chèque *m* barré
crossed out selling price	durchstrichener Verkaufspreis *m*	prix *m* de vente *f* barré
cross-line screen	Kreuzlinienraster *m*	trame *f* à lignes *f/pl* croisées
to crossprove	vergleichen	collationner, comparer
cross-section	Querschnitt *m*	coupe *f* en travers, coupe *f* transversale
crossword paper	Kreuzworträtselzeitung *f*	journal *m* de mots *m/pl* croisés
crowd shot	Massenaufnahme *f*	prise *f* de vue *f* en masse *f*
crowded make up	überladene Aufmachung *f*	mise *f* en page *f* surchargée
crowded out matter	liegengebliebener Satz *m*	matière *f* restée sur le marbre *m*
crowner	Aufstecker *m*, Flaschenkapsel *f*	capsule *f* de bouteille *f*, surmontoir *m*
crusade	Pressekampagne *f*	campagne *f* de presse *f*
cub	Anfänger *m*	débutant *m*
cube	Kubus *m*	cube *m*
cubic	kubisch	cubique
cue	Startzeichen *n*, Stichwort *n*	indication *f* de rentrée *f*, mot *m* clé *f*, mot *m* souche, mot *m* vedette *f*
cultural editor	Kulturredakteur *m*	rédacteur *m* de la rubrique *f* culturelle
cultural magazine	kulturelle Zeitschrift *f*	journal *m* culturel, périodique *m* de culture *f*
to cumulate	zusammenfassen	cumuler, récapituler, résumer

cumulative audience	erfaßte Personen-Gesamtzahl *f*, Gesamtzahl *f* der Hörer *m/pl*, Hörergesamtzahl *f*	audience *f* cumulative, auditoire *m* cumulatif
cumulative effect	kumulative Wirkung *f*	effet *m* cumulatif
cumulative returns	Schneeballsystem *n*	système *m* boule *f* de neige *f*
current advertising	gegenwärtig laufende Werbekampagne *f*	publicité *f* courante
current demand	kontinuierliche Nachfrage *f*	demande *f* continue
current events *pl*	Neues *n* vom Tage *m*	actualités *f/pl*
current happenings *pl*	gegenwärtige Ereignisse *n/pl*	événements *m/pl* en cours *m*
current number	letzte Ausgabe *f*	dernier numéro *m* paru
current price	Tagespreis *m*	prix *m* courant
current reports *pl*	umlaufende Gerüchte *n/pl*	bruits *m/pl* qui courent
to **curtail**	abkürzen, kürzen, verkürzen	abréger, couper, élaguer, raccourcir, rogner
curved stereo	Rundstereo *n*	stéreo *m* cintré
cushion	Füller *m*	annonce *f* d'opportunité *f*, bouche-trou *m*, remplissage *m*
customer	Abnehmer *m*, Auftraggeber *m*, Kunde *m*	acheteur *m*, client *m*, commettant *m*, mandant *m*
customer loyalty	Kundentreue *f*	fidélité *f* des clients *m/pl*
customer magazine	Kundenzeitschrift *f*	journal *m* pour la clientèle *f*
customer-oriented	verbraucherorientiert	orienté vers le client *m*
customs *pl*	Zoll *m*	douane *f*
cut	Bildschnitt *m*, Druckstock *m*, Filmschnitt *m*, Klischee *n*, Schnitt *m*	cliché *m*, coupe *f*, coupure *f*, planche *f* typographique
to **cut**	schneiden, wegfallen lassen	couper, éliminer
to **cut down**	abkürzen	abréger, élaguer
to **cut in**	durchschießen (Bogen)	intercaler
cut out	Ausschnitt *m* (Stanze *f*), Ausstanzstück *n*, Schablone *f*	découpage *m*, découpe *f*, écran *m*, encoche *f*, gabarit *m*, perforation *f*, pochoir *m*, silhouette *f* découpée, stencil *m*
to **cut out**	ausfräsen, wegstechen	fraiser, toupiller
cut price	Sonderpreis *m*, Spezialpreis *m*	prix *m* spécial, prix-réclame *f*
cut rate	Schleuderpreis *m*, Unterbietungspreis *m*	bradage *m*, conditions *f/pl* spéciales, gâchage *m* de prix *m*, vil prix *m*
to **cut short**	abkürzen	abréger, élaguer
cut version	gekürzte Fassung *f*	version *f* abrégée
cut-in	Untertitel *m*	second titre *m*, sous-titre *m*
cut-in advertisement	Anzeige *f* im Anschluß *m* an mehrere Textspalten *f/pl*	annonce *f* se joignant à plusieurs colonnes *f/pl* rédactionnelles *f/pl*
cut-in letter	Initiale *f*, große	grande lettrine *f*
cut-liner	Klischeeunterschrift *f*	légende *f* de cliché *m*
cut-off-rule	Trennlinie *f*	couillard *m*, coupure *f*, ligne *f* de division *f*
cut-out block	freistehendes Klischee *n*	cliché *m* détouré, cliché *m* isolé
cut-rate price	Reklamepreis *m*	prix *m* réclame
cutter	Schnittmeister *m*	cutter *m*
cut-throat price	Schleuderpreis *m*	bradage *m*, gâchage *m* de prix *m*, vil prix *m*

cutting	Beschnitt *m*, Bildausschnitt *m*	coupe *f*, rognage *m*
cutting machine	Schneidemaschine *f*	coupoir *m*
cutting out of motive	Motivausschnitt *m*	extrait *m* du motif *m*
cyanotype	Blaupause *f*	cyanotypie *f*, ozalide *m*
cyclic advertising	zyklische Werbung *f*	publicité *f* cyclique
cylinder machine	Schnellpresse *f*	presse *f* à cylindre *m*, presse *f* en blanc
cylinder print	Walzdruck *m*	impression *f* sur rouleaux *m/pl*

D

dagger	Kreuz *n* (Anmerkungszeichen *n*)	croix *f*
daily	täglich	quotidien
daily newspaper	Tageszeitung *f*	quotidien *m*
daily press	Tagespresse *f*	presse *f* quotidienne
daily report	Tagesbericht *m*	bulletin *m* du jour *m*, rapport *m* journalier
damage	Beschädigung *f*	détérioration *f*
damp squib	Blindgänger *m*	affaire *f* ratée
dangler	Deckenhänger *m*, Mobile *n*	mobile *m*, rotair *m*
darkroom	Dunkelkammer *f*	chambre *f* noire
dash	Gedankenstrich *m*, Strich *m*, Trennungstrich *m*	tiret *m*, tiret *m* de séparation *f*, trait *m*
dash sign	Perronfläche *f*	emplacement *m* de quai *m*
data *pl*	Gegebenheiten *f/pl*	données *f/pl*
data acquisition terminal	Datenerfassungsgerät *n*	appareil *m* pour la saisie *f* des données *f/pl*
data collection	Erfassungsterminal *n*	collection *f* des données *f/pl*
data collection terminal	Datenerfassungsgerät *n*	appareil *m* pour la saisie *f* des données *f/pl*
data transmission	Datensender *m*	transeurdonnées *f/pl*
date	Termin *m*	date *f*, délai *m*
to date	datieren	dater
date of impression	Druckjahr *n*	date *f* d'impression *f*
date of issue	Erscheinungsdatum *n*	date *f* de parution *f*, date *f* de publication *f*
date of packing	Verpackungsdatum *n*	date *f* de conditionnement *m*
date of payment	Fälligkeit *f*, Zahlungsfrist *f*	délai *m* de paiement *m*, échéance *f*, terme *m* de paiement *m*
date plan, date schedule	Datenplan *m*, Terminplan *m*, Datenschema *n*	calendrier *m* d'insertion *f*, plan *m* de termes *m/pl*, plan *m* des délais *m/pl*
date-stamp	Datumstempel *m*	dateur *m*
day of publication	Veröffentlichungstag *m*	date *f* de la publication *f*
day of publishing	Erscheinungstag *m*	jour *m* de parution *f*
day-glo	Tagesleuchtfarbe *f*	encre *f* luminescente solaire
day-glo poster	Leuchtfarbenplakat *n*	affiche *f* irisée
daylight fluorescent ink	Tagesleuchtfarbe *f*	encre *f* luminescente solaire
day-side	Tagschicht *f*	équipe *f* de jour *m*
de luxe edition	Luxusausgabe *f*	édition *f* de luxe *m*
dead air	Sendepause *f*	silence *m*, temps *m* mort
dead article	Ladenhüter *m*	fond *m* de tiroir *m*, garde-boutique *f*, rossignol *m*

dead copy	alter Text *m*	texte *m* déjà employé
dead matter	Ablegesatz *m*	composition *f* à distribuer
dead metal	Schließstege *m/pl*	garniture *f/pl* pour protéger un cliché *m* en tirage *m*
dead mike	Tonausfall *m*	absence *f* du son *m*
dead plates *pl*	alte Klischees *n/pl*	vieux clichés *m/pl*
dead season	Saure-Gurken-Zeit *f*, tote Saison *f*	hors saison *f*, mois *m/pl* creux de l'été *m*, morte-saison *f*
deadline	äußerster Termin *m*, Schlußtermin *m*	date *f* limite, terme *m* de rigueur *f*
deadline schedule	Terminkalender *m*	agenda *m*, calendrier *m* de termes *m/pl*, échéancier *m*
deadpan style	empfindungsloser Stil *m*	style *m* pince-sans-rire
deal	Abschluß *m*, Sonderangebot *n*, Verkaufspreisermäßigung *f*	contrat *m*, offre *f* de faveur *f*, offre *f* spéciale, réduction *f* du prix *m* de vente *f*
to deal	handeln	faire commerce *m*
dealer	Händler *m*, Wiederverkäufer *m*	commerçant *m*, marchand *m*, négociant *m*, revendeur *m*
dealer aids *pl*	Händlerwerbehilfen *f/pl*	aides *f/pl* publicitaires au détaillant *m*
dealer imprint	eingedruckte Händleranschrift *f*, Eindruck *m* der Händler-adresse *f*	adresse *f* imprimée du commerçant *m*, empreinte *f* de l'adresse *f* du détaillant *m*
dealer rebate	Händlerrabatt *m*	rabais *m* pour les commerçants *m/pl*
dealer survey	Händlerbefragung *f*	enquête *f* auprès des détaillants *m/pl*
dealer's brand	Händlermarke *f*	marque *f* du distributeur *m*
dealings *pl*	Geschäftsabschlüsse *m/pl*	affaires *f/pl* conclues
death announcement	Todesanzeige *f*	annonce *f* de décès *m*, annonce *f* nécrologique
debate	Debatte *f*	débat *m*
decade	Dekade *f*	décade *f*
decalcomania	Abziehplakat *n*	décalcomanie *f*
deceptive advertising	betrügerische Werbung *f*, irreführende Werbung *f*	publicité *f* déceptive, publicité *f* déloyale, publicité *f* fallacieuse, publicité *f* mensongère
deceptive package	Mogelpackung *f*	emballage *m* trompeur
to decipher	dechiffrieren	déchiffrer
decision	Entscheidung *f*	décision *f*
decision tree	baumartiges Entscheidungsschema *n*	arbre *m* de décision *f*
deckle edge	Büttenrand *m*	barbe *f*, bord *m* à la cuve *f*
declaration	Angabe *f*, Erklärung *f*	déclaration *f*, indication *f*
to declare	erklären	déclarer
decline in circulation	Auflagenrückgang *m*	régression *f* des tirages *m/pl*
decline of orders *pl*	Auftragsrückgang *m*	fléchissement *m* dans les rentrées *f/pl* de commande *f*
to decode	dechiffrieren	déchiffrer
decoding	Entschlüsselung *f*	décodage *m*
deconcentration	Entflechtung *f*	déconcentration *f*
to decorate	dekorieren	décorer, faire des étalages *m/pl*
decorating paper	Dekorationspapier *n*	papier *m* de décoration *f*

decoration	Dekoration f, Verzierung f	décoration f
decrease of circulation	Auflagenminderung f	diminution f des tirages m/pl
dedication	Widmung f	dédicace f
deep-etched half-tone	tiefgeätzte Autotypie f	simili m avec blanc pur
deep-etching	Tiefätzung f	eau-forte f grave, morsure f de grand creux m
defamation	Verleumdung f	calomnie f, diffamation f
to defame	verunglimpfen	diffamer
defection from advertisements pl	Anzeigenmangel m	défection f publicitaire
to defer	verschieben	décaler, reporter
deficiencies pl	Mängel m/pl	manques m/pl
definite order	Festauftrag m	ordre m ferme
definition of contours pl	Konturzeichnung f	définition f des contours m/pl, netteté f des contours m/pl
degree of familiarity, degree of notoriety	Bekanntheitsgrad m	dégré m de notoriété f
degree of recognition	Erinnerungsgrad m	dégré m de mémorabilité f
delay	Termin m	date f, délai m
delay in the execution of orders pl	Auftragsrückstand m	retard m dans l'exécution f des commandes f/pl
delay of payment	Zahlungsverzug m	retard m de paiement m
delayed broadcast	Bandaufnahmesendung f	différé m
delcredere	Delkredere n	delcredere m, ducroire m
to delete	ausstreichen, löschen	biffer, effacer
delete mark	Deleaturzeichen n	déléatur m
deletion	Streichung f	rayure f, suppression f
delivery	Lieferung f, Zustellung f	livraison f
delivery apparatus roll	Auslageapparat m	rouleau m de sortie f ralentisseur m
delivery by porters pl	Zustellung f durch Träger m/pl	portage m
delivery conditions pl	Bezugsbedingungen f/pl	conditions f/pl de livraison f
delivery date, delivery delay	Lieferdatum n, Lieferfrist f, Liefertermin m	date f de livraison f, délai m de livraison f
delivery man	Austräger m, Zeitungsträger m	porteur m, porteur m de journaux m/pl
delivery note	Lieferschein m	décharge f de livraison f, reçu
delivery period	Lieferzeit f	délai m de livraison f
delivery price	Lieferpreis m	prix m à la livraison f
delivery service	Zustelldienst m	service m de distribution f
delivery table	Auslegetisch m	banc m de presse f
demand	Nachfrage f	demande f
demand stimulation	Bedarfsweckung f	stimulation f de la demande f
demand-note	Mahnbrief m	lettre f de rappel m
demographic characteristics pl	demografische Merkmale n/pl	critères m/pl démographiques
demographical structure	demografische Struktur f	structure f démographique
to demonstrate	demonstrieren, vorführen	démontrer, montrer
demonstration	Vorführung f	démonstration f, présentation f, projection f
demonstrational film	Demonstrationsfilm m, Werbeinstruktionsfilm m	film m de démonstration f
demonstrator	Werbedame f	démonstratrice f, mannequin m
denial	Dementi n	démenti m
density	Dichte f	densité f
density of diffusion	Streudichte f	densité f de la diffusion f
to deny	dementieren	démentir

department	Abteilung f, Ressort n	département m, rayon m, ressort m, secteur m, section f
department store	Kaufhaus n, Warenhaus n	bazar m, grand magasin m
departmental page	Bezirksseite f	page f départementale
depolitization	Entpolitisierung f	dépolitisation f
depot	Ablage f	classement m, dépôt m
to depress space	Zwischenraum m verkleinern	diminuer l'espace m blanc, serrer
depth interview	Tiefeninterview n	interview m en profondeur f
depth of page	Satzhöhe f	hauteur f de page f
descender height	Unterlänge f	jambage m inférieur
to describe	beschreiben	décrire
description	Beschreibung f	description f
design	Entwurf m, Gestaltung f	création f, croquis m, dessin m, ébauche f, épreuve f, maquette f, projet m
to design	entwerfen, zeichnen	dessiner, élaborer, esquisser
designer	Formgestalter m, Gebrauchsgrafiker m, Gestalter m, Grafik-Designer m, Musterzeichner m, Zeichner m	artiste m -créateur m, dessinateur m, dessinateur m -concepteur m, dessinateur m en publicité f, dessinateur m industriel, maquettiste m, styliste m
designer for fairs pl	Messegestalter m	expert m pour foires f/pl
desk	Depeschensaal m, Schreibtisch m, Redaktionssekretariat n, Sekretariat n einer Presse-agentur f	bureau m, bureau m des dépêches f/pl, secrétaire m, sécrétariat m de rédaction f d'une agence f de presse f
desk editor	Nachrichtenredakteur m	rédacteur m au desk m, rédacteur m aux informations f/pl
desk number	Kontrollziffer f	clé f
desk pad	Schreibunterlage f	sous-main m
desk research	Forschungsarbeit f, Sekundärerhebung f	étude f de la clientèle f, recherche f documentaire
desk work	sitzende Redaktionsarbeit f	travail m sédentaire au journal m
detective novel	Detektivroman m	roman m policier
determination	Festlegung f	détermination f, établissement m
to develop	entwickeln	développer
developer	Entwickler m	révélateur m
development	Entwicklung f	développement m, évolution f
development of circulation	Auflagenentwicklung f	évolution f des tirages m/pl
deviation	Abweichung f	déviation f
deviation from rates pl	Tarifabweichung f	dérogation f aux tarifs m/pl
device	Markenzeichen n	logotype m
diaeresis	Trennpunkte m/pl	tréma m
diagram	bildliche Darstellung f, Diagramm n, Schaubild n	diagramme m, graphique m, schéma m
dial	Zifferblatt n	cadran m
dialect	Dialekt m, Mundart f	dialecte m, idiome m
dialogue	Zwiegespräch n	dialogue m
diameter	Durchmesser m	diamètre m

Diamond (see appendix)	Halbpetit f (Diamant) (siehe Anhang)	corps 4 points (voir appendice)
diaphragm	Blende f	diaphragme m
diary	Tagebuch n	journal m intime
dictating machine	Diktaphon n, Diktiergerät n	appareil m à dicter, dictaphone m
dictation	Diktat n	dictée f
diction	Ausdrucksweise f	diction f, élocution f, manière f de s'exprimer, phraséologie f
dictionary	Wörterbuch n	dictionnaire m
die cut	ausgestanztes Emblem n, Ausstanzstück n	découpage m, découpé, emblème m découpé, silhouette f découpée
die stamping	Stahldruck m	impression f sur plaque f d'acier m
die-stamping	Reliefdruck m	gaufrage m en relief m, impression f gaufrée, impression f thermogravure f
differences pl of opinions pl	Meinungsverschiedenheit f	divergence f d'opinion f
different text	wechselnder Text m	texte m différent
differential	Tarifunterschied m	différence f de tarif m
differential price	gestaffelter Preis m	prix m échelonné, tarif m mobile
differential price system	Tarifstaffel f	barème m
difficult matter	Satzerschwernis f	surcharge f
diffusion	Streuung f, Verbreitung f	circulation f, couverture f, diffusion f, distribution f, propagation f, prospection f, rayonnement m
to dig out	enthüllen	révéler
digest	Auslese f, gedrängte Darstellung f, Zeitschrift f mit Auszügen m/pl aus Büchern n/pl und Zeitschriften f/pl	condensé m, présentation f condensée
digital information	digitale Informationen f/pl	informations f/pl numériques
dime novel	Groschenroman m	roman m bon marché m
dimensions pl	Format n	dimensions f/pl, format m
diminution of payment	Zahlungsminderung f	diminution f de paiement m
diorama	Durchscheinbild n	diorama m
diploma	Diplom n	diplôme m
direct advertising	Direktwerbung f	publicité f directe
direct mail advertising	Direktwerbung f durch die Post f	publicité f directe par la poste f
direct selling	Beziehungskauf m, Direktabsatz m	vente f directe
direct selling emphasis	direkter Kaufappell m	appel m pressant à l'acheteur m
direct selling of the manufacturer to the retail firms pl	Direktabsatz m des Herstellers m an den Einzelhandel m	circuit m court

direct-action advertising	Kaufwerbung *f*	publicité *f* incitant à l'action *f* directe
direct-action copy	Kaufanzeige *f*	annonce *f* fixée sur l'achat *m*
direction sign	Hinweisschild *n*	panneau *m* routier, signal *m* de direction *f*
directions *pl* **for use**	Gebrauchsanweisung *f*	mode *m* d'emploi *m*
director	Aufnahmeleiter *m*, Direktor *m*, Geschäftsführer *m*	chef *m* d'entreprise *f*, directeur *m*, directeur *m* administratif, gérant *m*, gestionnaire *m*, metteur *m* en scène *f*
director of fabrication	Herstellungsleiter *m*	chef *m* de fabrication *f*
directory	Adreßbuch *n*	annuaire *m*, indicateur *m* d'adresses *f/pl*, livre *m* d'adresses *f/pl*
directory of suppliers *pl*	Bezugsquellenverzeichnis *n*	liste *f* des fournisseurs *m/pl*, répertoire *m* de fournisseurs *m/pl*
dirigible advertising	Luftballonwerbung *f*	publicité *f* par dirigeable *m*
disc *am*	Schallplatte *f*	disque *m*
disc memory, disc storage	Plattenspeicher *m*	mémoire *f* à disques *m/pl*
disc-jockey	Schallplatten-Ansager *m*	animateur *m*, présentateur *m* de disques *m/pl*
to **disclose**	aufdecken	divulguer
disclosure	Enthüllung *f*	révélation *f*
discography	Schallplattenverzeichnis *n*	discographie *f*
disconnected advertisement	stufenförmige Anzeige *f*	décroché *m*
to **discontinue publication**	einstellen (Erscheinen *n*)	cesser de paraître
discount	Nachlaß *m*, Rabatt *m*, Skonto *m*	escompte *m*, rabais *m*, réduction *f*, remise *f*
discount for customers *pl*	Kundenrabatt *m*	rabais *m* au client *m*
discount granted to colleagues *pl*	Kollegenrabatt *m*	remise *f* à titre *m* de confrère *m*
discount of introduction	Einführungsrabatt *m*	rabais *m* de lancement *m*
discount reduction	Rabattreduzierung *f*	réduction *f* de rabais *m*
discount shop	Discountladen *m*	magasin *m* discount *m*
discount ticket	Rabattmarke *f*	timbre-primes *f/pl*, timbre *m* de rabais *m*, timbre *m* d'épargne *f*
discounter	Discountladen *m*	magasin *m* discount *m*
discriminating reader	urteilsfähiger Leser *m*	lecteur *m* averti
to **discuss**	besprechen	discuter, faire un compte *m* rendu
discussion	Besprechung *f*, Erörterung *f*	conférence *f*, discussion *f*, entretien *m*
disfigurement of country-side	Verunstaltung *f* der Landschaft *f*	défiguration *f* du paysage *m*
dishonest advertising	unehrenhafte Werbung *f*	publicité *f* déloyale
disinclination to buy	Kaufunlust *f*	abstention *f* des consommateurs *m/pl*
to **dismember**	zerstückeln	fragmenter
disparagement	Herabsetzung *f*	dénigrement *m*
disparaging copy	aggressive Werbung *f*, herabsetzende Werbung *f*	publicité *f* agressive, publicité *f* discriminatrice , publicité *f* discriminatoire
dispatch	Depesche *f*	dépêche *f*
to **dispatch**	absenden, versenden	acheminer, envoyer, expédier
dispatch agency	Depeschenbüro *n*	bureau *m* de télégraphe *m*

dispatch by mail	Postversand *m*	envoi *m* postal
dispatch papers *pl*	Versandpapiere *n/pl*	documents *m/pl* d'expédition *f*
dispatch-charges *pl*	Versandkosten *pl*	frais *m/pl* de transport *m*, frais *m/pl* d'expédition *f*
dispatcher	Überwacher *m* des Produktionsablaufs *m*	surveilleur *m* du déroulement *m* de la production *f*
dispatching	Versand *m*	distribution *f*, envoi *m*, expédition *f*
to disperse	streuen	diffuser, disperser
dispersion	Streuung *f*	couverture *f*, prospection *f*
dispersion area	Streubereich *m*	domaine *m* de la diffusion *f*
dispersion period	Streuzeitpunkt *m*	période *f* de diffusion *f*, période *f* de la diffusion *f* des moyens *m/pl* publicitaires
display	Aushang *m*, Auslage *f*, Display *n*, Werbeauslage *f*	étalage *m*, exposition *f*, présentation *f*, vitrine *f*
display advertisements *pl*	Großanzeigen *f/pl* allgemeine Anzeigen *f/pl*	grandes annonces *f/pl* publicité *f* non classifiée
display case	Vitrine *f*	vitrine *f*
display composition	auffallender Satz *m*, Akzidenzsatz *m*	composition *f* de travaux *m/pl* de ville *f*, composition *f* tape-à-l'œil *m*
display faces *pl*	Akzidenzschriften *f/pl*, Schaufenster *n*	caractères *m/pl* de travaux *m/pl* de ville *f*, devanture *f*, étalage *m*, vitrine *f*
display kiosks *pl*	Werbebauten *m/pl*	constructions *f/pl* publicitaires
display line	Auszeichnungszeile *f*	ligne *f* duplexée
display man	Schauwerbegestalter *m*	étalagiste *m*
display of posters *pl*	Plakataushang *m*	présentation *f* de placards *m/pl*
display package	Schaupackung *f*	attrape *f*, boîte *f* factice, emballage *m* factice
to display text matter	Auszeichnen *n* eines Textes *m*	mettre un texte *m* en évidence *f*
display type	Auszeichnungsschrift *f*	caractères *m/pl* duplexés
display types *pl*	Übergrößen *f/pl*	caractères *m/pl* pour titre *m*
display window	Schaufenster *n*	devanture *f*, étalage *m*, vitrine *f*
to dispose	disponieren	arranger, disposer, prévoir
disposition	Verfügung *f*	disposition *f*
dispute	Wortgefecht *n*	dispute *f*
to diss (composition)	ablegen (Satz) *m*	distribuer (composition), mettre en casse *f*
to dissiminate	verbreiten	disséminer, propager, répandre
dissimination	Verbreitung *f*	circulation *f*, couverture *f*, diffusion *f*, distribution *f*, propagation *f*, rayonnement *m*
dissolution	Auflösung *f*	dissolution *f*, résiliation *f*
dissolve	Überblendung *f*	enchaînement *m*, fondu *m*
to dissolve *am*	weiche Bildüberblendung *f*	fondu *m* enchaîné
distortion	Verzerrung *f*	distorsion *f*
distortion of competition	Wettbewerbsverzerrung *f*	distorsion *f* de la concurrence *f*
to distribute	verteilen, vertreiben	distribuer, vendre
distributing enterprise	Vertriebsunternehmen *n*	entreprise *f* de distribution *f*

distribution	Absatz *m* (Vertrieb *m*) , Verbreitung *f*, Verteilung *f*, Vertrieb *m*	circulation *f*, couverture *f*, diffusion *f*, distribution *f*, propagation *f*, rayonnement *m*, vente *f*
distribution agency	Vertriebsunternehmen *n*	entreprise *f* de distribution *f*
distribution analysis	Streuanalyse *f*	analyse *f* de distribution *f*
distribution costs *pl*	Absatzkosten *pl*, Vertriebskosten *pl*	coûts *m/pl* de distribution *f*, frais *m/pl* de distribution *f*
distribution figures *pl*	Verbreitungszahlen *f/pl*	chiffres *m/pl* de diffusion *f*, chiffres *m/pl* de tirage *m*
distribution manager	Vertriebsleiter *m*	chef *m* de publicité *f*, chef *m* de vente *f*
distribution methods *pl*	Vertriebsmethoden *f/pl*, Absatzmethoden *f/pl*	méthodes *f/pl* de distribution *f*
distribution of a newspaper	Zeitungsvertrieb *m*	distribution *f* d'un journal *m*
distribution of circulars *pl*	Prospektverteilung *f*	distribution *f* d'imprimés *m/pl*
distribution of printed matter	Drucksachenverteilung *f*	distribution *f* d'imprimés *m/pl*
distribution of publications *pl*	Pressevertrieb *m*	colportage *m*, messagerie *f*
distribution plan	Absatzplan *m*	plan *m* de vente *f*
distribution rack	Verkaufsständer *m*	étagère *f*, rayon *m*
distributor	Auslieferer *m*, Verteiler *m*	dépositaire *m*, distributeur *m*
district	Bezirk *m*	district *m*
diversification	Ausweitung *f*	élargissement *m*
divider card	Trennkarton *m*	carton *m* de séparation *f*
dividing rule	Spaltenlinie *f*, Trennlinie *f*	colombelle *f*, couillard *m*, coupure *f*, ligne *f* de division *f*, séparation *f* des colonnes *f/pl*
division	Abteilung *f*	département *m*, rayon *m*, section *f*
docket	Auftragstasche *f*, Lauftasche *f*	chemise *f* de travail *m*, dossier *m* d'une commande *f*
to doctor	zurechtstutzen	tripatouiller
document	Schriftstück *n*, Urkunde *f*	document *m*, écrit *m*, pièce *f*
documentary film	Dokumentarfilm *m*, Kulturfilm *m*	film *m* documentaire
documentary photograph	Dokumentaraufnahme *f*	prise *f* de vue *f* documentaire
documentary report	Bildbericht *m*	report *m* documentaire
documentation	Dokumentation *f*	documentation *f*
dodger *am*	Handzettel *m*	papillon *m*, prospectus *m*
dog-eared page	Eselsohren *n/pl*, Seite *f* mit	page *f* cornée
dolly	Kamerakran *m*, Kamerawagen *m*	grue *f*, travelling *m*
domestic commerce	Binnenhandel *m*	commerce *m* intérieur
domestic market	Inlandsmarkt *m*	marché *m* intérieur
domiciliary visit	Hausbesuch *m*	visite *f* à domicile *m*
domiciliation	Bestimmung *f* des Insertionsorgans *n*	domiciliation *f*
door delivery	Hauszustellung *f*	porte *f* à porte *f*
door opener	Reklameartikel *m*	article *m* de réclame *f*
door panel	Türrahmenschild *n*	panneau *m* de porte *f* d'accès *m*
door-to door	Haus *n* zu Haus *n*, von	porte *f* à porte *f*
dope	Waschzettel *m*	brouillon *m*, note *f* de critique *f*, papillon *m*, prière *f* d'insérer
dormant stock	Ladenhüter *m*	fond *m* de tiroir *m*, garde-boutique *f*, rossignol *m*
dot	Punkt *m*	point *m*
dot screen	Punktraster *m*	trame *f* à points *m/pl*

dotted frame	gepunkteter Rand *m*, punktierter Rand *m*	cadre *m* de pointillés *m/pl*
dotted line, dotted rule	punktierte Linie *f*, Punktlinie *f*	filet *m* pointillé, ligne *f* de pointillés *m/pl*
double	Dublette *f*, Hochzeit *f* (doppelt Gesetztes *n*)	doublon *m*
double column	Doppelspalte *f*	double colonne *f*, sur deux colonnes *f/pl*
double fold	Doppelfalz *m*	double pli *m*
double image	Geisterbild *n*	fantôme *m*, image *f* spectre
double letter	Ligatur *f*	deux lettres *f/pl* ligaturées, ligature *f*
double page	Doppelseite *f*	pages *f/pl* en regard *m*
double quotation marks *pl*	Anführungsstriche *m/pl*	guillemets *m/pl*
double rate	doppelter Preis *m*	prix *m* double
double reader	Doppelleser *m*	double lecteur *m*
double rulings *pl*	Doppellinie *f*	filets *m/pl* doubles
double spread	Doppelseite *f*	pages *f/pl* en regard *m*
double truck	doppelseitige Anzeige *f*, zweiseitige gegenüberliegende Anzeige *f*	double page *f* centrale
double-crown (see poster size)	Doppelkrone *f* (siehe Plakatformat)	format double couronne (voir format d'affiche)
double-leaded article	Artikel *m* mit viel Zwischenschlag *m*	article *m* blanchi
double-page spread	doppelseitige Anzeige *f*	double page *f* centrale
double-sided	zweiseitig	à deux côtés *m/pl*, bilatéral, de deux pages *f/pl*, double
doublet	Dublette *f*	doublon *m*
double-tone ink	Doppeltonfarbe *f*	encre *f* double-ton *m*
double-tone printing	Doppeltondruck *m*	impression *f* double-ton *m*
down payment	Anzahlung *f*	acompte *m*
downward business trend	Konjunkturrückgang *m*	dépression *f*
downward trend in subscription	Abonnentenschwund *m*	désabonnement *m*
draft	Entwurf *m*, Konzept *n*, Textentwurf *m*	brouillon *m*, croquis *m*, dessin *m*, ébauche *f*, épreuve *f*, maquette *f*, minute *f*, projet *m*, projet *m* de texte *m*
to draft	entwerfen, konzipieren	dessiner, élaborer, esquisser
dramatic critic	Theaterkritiker *m*	critique *m* théâtral
dramatic critique	Theaterkritik *f*	critique *f* théâtrale
dramatization	Dramatisierung *f*	dramatisation *f*
draughtsman	Gestalter *m*	artiste *m* -créateur *m*, dessinateur *m* -concepteur *m*, maquettiste *m*
to draw	zeichnen	dessiner
drawing	Zeichnung *f*	dessin *m*
drawing board	Reißbrett *n*	planche *f* à dessiner
drawing cardboard	Zeichenkarton *m*	carton *m* à dessin *m*
drawing charcoal	Zeichenkohle *f*	fusain *m*
drawing paper	Zeichenpapier *n*	papier *m* à dessin *m*
drawing pen	Reißfeder *f*, Zeichenfeder *f*	plume *f* à dessiner, tire-ligne *m*
drawing pencil	Zeichenstift *m*	crayon *m* à dessin *m*
drawing rule	Reißschiene *f*	règle *f* à dessiner

drawing studio	Zeichenatelier *n*	atelier *m* de dessin *m*
drawing table	Zeichentisch *m*	table *f* à dessin *m*
to dress	aufmachen	arranger, présenter
to dress a form	anlegen	garnir la forme *f*
dressing of the sites *pl*	Auskleidung *f* der Anschlagstellen *f/pl*	habillage *m* des emplacements *m/pl*
dressman	männliches Fotomodell *n*, Vorführmann *m*	mannequin *m* mâle, mannequin *m* masculin
drive	verstärkte Werbeabstrengungen *f/pl*, Vorantreiben *n*	dynamisme *m*, effort *m* spécial de publicité *f*
to drive out	strecken *typog*	chasser
drive-in cinema	Autokino *n*	cinéma *m* en plein air *m* pour automobilistes *m/pl*
drop fingers *pl*	Taster *m*	ardillon *m*
drop head	Untertitel *m*	second titre *m*, sous-titre *m*
to drop out	freistellen	détourer, silhouetter
drop-out halftone	spitzgeätzte Autotypie *f*	autotypie *f* détourée
dropout half-tone	Hochlichtautotypie *f*	cliché *m* simili avec grandes lumières *f/pl*
dropped-out letter	fehlender Buchstabe *m*	lettre *f* manquante
dross	Ausschuß (Abfall) *m*	déchet *m*
to drum	Kunden *m/pl* gewinnen	acquérir des clients *m/pl*, attirer des clients *m/pl*
dry posting	Naßklebeverfahren *n*	affichage *m* à la brosse *f* sèche
drying	Trocknung *f*	séchage *m*
dual-use package	Mehrwegpackung *f*	emballage *m* de remploi *m*, emballage *m* de retour
to dub	synchronisieren	doubler
dubbing	Synchronisation *f*	synchronisation *f*
due	fällig	échu
dull	unscharf	flou
dull-finish printing	Mattdruck *m*	impression *f* mate
dull-finished paper	mattiertes Papier *n*	papier *m* mat
dullness	Flaute *f*	accalmie *f*, période *f* creuse
dummy	Aufmachungsmuster *n*, Blindband *m*, Blindmuster *n*, Handmuster *n*, Leerpackung *f*, Skizze *f*, Rohentwurf *m*	crayonné *m*, croquis *m*, ébauche *f*, esquisse *f*, factice *f*, maquette *f*, maquette *f* d'imprimerie *f*, premier jet *m*
dummy advertisement	fingierte Anzeige *f*	annonce *f* fictive
dummy magazine	Blindmuster *n* von Zeitschriften *f/pl*	maquette *f* d'une revue *f*
dummy of a poster	Plakatentwurf *m*	dessin *m* pour affiche *f*, maquette *f* d'une affiche *f*, projet *m* d'affiche *f*
dummy pack	Attrappe *f*, Schaupackung *f*	attrape *f*, boîte *f* factice, emballage *m* factice
dummy salesman	stummer Verkäufer *m*	matériel *m* d'étalage *m* de comptoir *m*, vendeur *m* muet
dummy volume	Probedruck *m*	épreuve *f*
dumping	Preisunterbietung *f*, Schleuderverkauf *m*	bradage *m*, gâchage *m* de prix *m*, vente *f* à meilleur marché *m*, vente *f* à vil prix *m*
duo test	Paarvergleich *m*	test *m* comparatif

duplex half-tone block (brit) , duplex half-tone cut *am*	Duplex-Autotypie *f*	autotypie *f*, cliché *m* simili deux tons *m/pl*
duplex printing	Duplexdruck *m*	impression *f* double-ton *m*
duplicate	Duplikat *n*, zweifache Ausfertigung *f*	double exemplaire *m*, duplicata *m*
to duplicate	abformen, vervielfältigen	multicopier, multiplier, polycopier, reproduire, surmouler
duplicate block	Duplikatätzung *f*	duplicata *m/pl*
duplication	Überschneidung *f*, Vervielfältigung *f*, Wiederholung *f*, Zweitschrift *f*	double emploi *m*, duplicata *m*, duplication *f*, imbrication *f*, multicopie *f*, multiplication *f*, polycopie *f*, répétition *f*
duplicator	Vervielfältigungsapparat *m*	duplicateur *m*, hectographe *m*, multigraphe *m*
duration	Dauer *f*	durée *f*
duration of copyright	Schutzfrist *f*	durée *f* du droit *m* d'auteur *m*
duration of life	Lebensdauer *f*	durée *f* de vie *f*
duration of the advertising campaign	Streudauer *f*	durée *f* de la campagne *f* publicitaire
dust-cover	Schutzumschlag *m*	fourre *f* de protection *f*, jaquette *f*, protège-livre *m*
Dutch door	Prospektanzeigen *f/pl*	annonces *f/pl* avec des dépliants *m/pl* cousus sur elles
duty	Zollgebühr *f*	droits *m/pl* de douane *f*
duty free shop	zollfreies Geschäft *n*	boutique *f* franche
dye transfer	Farbdiaabzug *m*, Farbretusche *f*	retouche *f* des couleurs *f/pl*, transfert *m* de couleur *f*
dynamic advertising	schwungvolle Werbung *f*	publicité *f* pleine d'élan *m*

E

early bird price	Einführungspreis *m*	prix *m* de lancement *m*
early morning edition	Morgenausgabe *f*	édition *f* du matin *m*, première édition *f*
early-bird issue *am*	vordatierte Zeitung *f*	journal *m* antidaté, journal *m* prédaté, première édition *f*
earned rate	Anzeigenpreis *m* entsprechend der tatsächlich abgenommenen Menge *f*	tarif *m* dégressif
ear-pieces *pl*, ears *pl*	Anzeige *f* neben Zeitungskopf *m*	manchette *f* à droite du titre *m*
ear-witness	Ohrenzeuge *m*	témoin *m* auriculaire
echo	Echo *n*, Resonanz *f*	écho *m*, résonance *f*
economic concentration	Konzentrationsprozeß *m*	processus *m* de concentration *f*
economic editor	Wirtschaftsredakteur *m*	rédacteur *m* de la rubrique *f* économique
economic status	Lebensstandard *m*	standard *m* de vie *f*
economy	Wirtschaft *f*	économie *f*
economy of expression	Ausdrucksökonomie *f*	économie *f* d'expression *f*
economy size	Großpackung *f*	emballage *m* de grande taille *f*, empaquetage *m* gigantesque
economy-priced	preisgünstig	à bon marché *m*
edge	Kante *f*, Papierkante *f*, Rand *m*	bord *m*, bord *m* du papier *m*, marge *f*
edge-turned passe-partout	randkaschiert	bord *m* de coupure *f* doublé
to edit	redigieren	rédiger

edition	Ausgabe f (Nummer)	édition f, exemplaire m, numéro m
editor	Schriftleiter m, Redakteur m, Herausgeber m	rédacteur m
editorial	Leitartikel m, redaktioneller Artikel m	article m de fond m, article m de tête f, article m rédactionnel, éditorial m
editorial advertisement	redaktionell aufgemachte Anzeige f	annonce f à apparence f rédactionnelle
editorial assistance	redaktionelle Unterstützung f	assistance f rédactionnelle
editorial board	Redaktion f	rédactionf
editorial conception	redaktionelle Konzeption f	conception f rédactionnelle
editorial conference	Redaktionskonferenz f	conférence f de rédaction f
editorial content	redaktioneller Inhalt m	contenu m rédactionnel
editorial context	redaktionelles Umfeld n	contexte m rédactionnel
editorial department	Schriftleitung f	rédaction f
editorial hall	Redaktionssaal m	salle f de rédaction f
editorial matter	redaktioneller Teil m	section f rédactionnelle, texte m rédactionnel
editorial office	Redaktion f	rédactionf
editorial page	Meinungsseite f	page f d'opinion f
editorial policy	redaktionelle Tendenz f	politique f rédactionnelle
editorial publicity	redaktionelle Werbung f	annonce f rédactionnelle, publicité f rédactionnelle gratuite
editorial secret	Redaktionsgeheimnis n	secret m de la rédaction f
editorial section	redaktioneller Teil m	section f rédactionnelle, texte m rédactionnel
editorial staff	Schriftleitung f, Redaktion f, Redaktionsstab m	équipe f de rédaction f, rédaction f
editorial support	redaktionelle Unterstützung f	assistance f rédactionnelle
editorializing	redaktionelle Bearbeitung f	rédaction f
editor-in-chief	Chefredakteur m, Hauptschriftleiter m	rédacteur m en chef m
education	Ausbildung f	formation f
educational advertising	belehrende Werbung f, erzieherische Werbung f	publicité f éducative
educational film	Lehrfilm m	film m éducatif
effect	Effekt m, Wirkung f	effet m
effect on sales pl	Verkaufswirkung f	efficacité f de la vente f
effective	effektiv	effectif
effective advertising	wirksame Werbung f	publicité f efficace
effective date	Inkrafttreten n	entrée f en vigueur f
effective in advertising	werbewirksam	d'un bon rendement m publicitaire
effectiveness, efficiency	Wirksamkeit f	efficacité f
efficiency test	Wirkungstest m	test m d'efficacité f
effusion	Herzenserguß m	épanchement m de cœur m
egghead	Intellektueller m	intellectuel m
Egyptian	Egyptienne f	égyptienne f
eighth of page	Achtelseite f	huitième de page f
ektachrome	farbiges Durchsichtsbild n	diorama m en couleurs f/pl
to elaborate	ausarbeiten	élaborer
election	Wahl f	choix m, élection f
election poster	Wahlplakat n	affiche f électorale
election proclamation	Wahlaufruf m	appel m aux urnes f/pl
election propaganda	Wahlpropaganda f	propagande f électorale

electric sign	Transparent *n*	enseigne *f* lumineuse, oriflamme *f*, transparent *m*
electric sign advertising	Leuchtwerbung *f*, Lichtwerbung *f*	publicité *f* lumineuse
electric spectaculars *pl/am*	bewegliche Lichtwerbung *f*	publicité *f* lumineuse animée
electrical transcription	Tonbandaufnahme *f*	enregistrement *m* électrique, prise *f* de son *m*
electro *am*	Galvano *n*, Stereo *n*	galvano *m*, galvanotype *m*, stéréo *m*
electromechanical reproduction	elektromechanische Reproduktion *f*	reproduction *f* électro-mécanique
electronic phototypesetting machine	elektronische Fotosetzmaschine *f*	photocomposeuse *f* électronique
electronical advertising	elektronische Werbung *f*	publicité *f* électronique
electro-shell	Kupferhaut *f*	coquille *f* de galvano *m*, pellicule *f* galvanoplastique en cuivre *m*
electrotype	Stereo *n*, Galvano *n*	stéréo *m*, galvano *m*, galvanotype *m*
electrotyping	Galvanoplastik *f*	galvanoplastie *f*
emblem	Emblem *n*, Kennzeichen *n*	emblème *m*, indice *m*
to emboss	prägen	empreindre, gaufrer, repousser
embossed	geprägt	gaufré
embossed paper	geprägtes Papier *n*	papier *m* gaufré
embossed poster	Prägeplakat *f*	affiche *f* en relief *m*
embossing	Blinddruck *m*, Prägedruck *m*, Prägung *f*, Reliefdruck *m*	bombage *m*, estampage *m*, gaufrage *m*, gaufrage *m* en relief *m*, impression *f* gaufrée, impression *f* thermogravure *f*, repoussage *m*
emcee	Ansager *m*	compère *m*, speaker *m*
emery-paper	Schmirgelpapier *n*	papier *m* émeri
emission	Ausstrahlung *f*	émission *f*
emotional advertising	gefühlsbetonte Werbung *f*	publicité *f* émotive
emotional atmosphere	Gefühlssphäre *f*	sphère *f* d'affectivité *f*
empathy	Echo *n*, Resonanz *f*	écho *m*, résonance *f*
to emphasize	hervorheben, unterstreichen	mettre en évidence *f*, mettre en relief *m*, mettre en vedette *f*, souligner
emphasizing	Hervorhebung *f*	mise *f* en valeur *f*
employment wanted	Stellengesuch *n*	demande *f* d'emploi *m*
em-quad	Geviert *n*	cadratin *m*
em-rule	Gedankenstrich *m*, Minuszeichen *n*	moins *m*, tiret *m*
em-space	Achtelgeviert *n*	huitième *m* de cadratin *m*
enamel plate, enamel sign	Emailleschild *n*	plaque *f* emaillée
enamelled paper	Kunstdruckpapier *n*	papier *m* couché des deux faces *f/pl*
to enclose	beilegen	ajouter, annexer
enclosure	Anlage *f*, Beilage *f*	annexe *f*, encart *m*, supplément *m*
encyclopaedia	Lexikon *n*, Sachwörterbuch *n*	encyclopédie *f*, lexique *m*
English finished (E.F.)	matt satiniert	satiné mat
English script type	englische Schreibschrift *f*	écriture *f* anglaise

to **engrave**	ätzen, gravieren	creuser, graver, mordre
engraved plate	Gravur *f*	gravure *f*
engraver	Ätzer *m*, Klischeeätzer *m*	graveur *m*, photograveur *m*
engraver's proof *am*	Klischeeabzug *m*	épreuve *f* de cliché *m*, fumée *f*
engraving	Ätzung *f*, Druckstock *m*, Gravierung *f*, Kupferstecherkunst *f*	chalcographie *f*, cliché *m*, eau-forte *f*, gravure *f*, planche *f*
engraving in copper	Kupferätzung *f*	gravure *f* sur cuivre *m*
engraving machine	Graviermaschine *f*	machine *f* à graver
engraving plant	Klischeeanstalt *f*	atelier *m* de photogravure *f*, clichérie *f*
engraving plate	Druckplatte *f*	plaque *f* d'impression *f*
engraving process	Ätzverfahren *n*	procédé *m* de gravure *f*, procédé *m* de morsure *f*
to **enlarge**	vergrößern	agrandir
to **enlarge proportionally**	proportional vergrößern	agrandir à la proportionnelle *f*
enlarged edition	erweiterte Auflage *f*	édition *f* augmentée
enlargement	Vergrößerung *f*	agrandissement *m*
enlargement of an order	Auftragserweiterung *f*	augmentation *f* de commande *f*, complément *m* de commande *f*
en-quad	Halbgeviert *n*	demi-cadratin *m*
enriched book	extra ausgestattetes Buch *n*	livre *m* bien présenté
to **enter**	eintragen	inscrire
entertainer	Unterhalter *m*	amuseur *m*, diseur *m*
entertainment advertisement	Vergnügungsanzeige *f*	annonce *f* spectacles *m/pl*
entertainment advertising	Werbung *f* der Vergnügungsbranche *f*	publicité *f* spectacles *m/pl*
entertainment film	Unterhaltungsfilm *m*	film *m* divertissant
entertainment world	Theaterwelt *f*	monde *m* du théâtre *m*
entertainments *pl*	Unterhaltungen *f/pl*	divertissements *m/pl*, spectacles *m/pl*, variétés *f/pl*
to **entice away**	abwerben	débaucher
entitled	betitelt	intitulé
entitling	Betitelung *f*	titrage *m*
entry	Eintrag *m*	inscription *f*
envelope	Briefumschlag *m*, Kuvert *n*	enveloppe *f*
envelope stuffer	Beipack *m* von Werbedrucksachen *f/pl*	imprimés *m/pl* publicitaires comme annexes *f/pl* d'un packetage *m*
environment	Umgegend *f*, Umwelt *f*	environnement *m*, environs *m/pl*
epidiascope	Bildwerfer *m*	appareil *m* de projection *f*, épidiascope *m*
epilogue	Nachwort *n*	épilogue *m*
equalization	Gleichschaltung *f*	mise *f* au pas *m*
to **equalize**	ausgleichen (Zurichtung *f*)	égaliser
equipment	Ausrüstung *f*	équipement *m*, façonnage *m*
errata	Druckfehlerverzeichnis *n*	errata *m*
errata slip	Korrekturenzettel *m*	papillon *m* des erratas *m/pl*
erratum	Druckfehler *m*, Erratum *n*	coquille *f*, erratum *m*, erreur *f* de composition *f*, faute *f* d'impression *f*, faute *f* typographique

errors *pl* and omissions *pl* excepted	Irrtümer *m/pl* und Auslassungen *f/pl* vorbehalten	sauf erreur *f* ou omission *f*
escalator panel, escalator site	Rolltreppenschild *n*	emplacement *m* sur escalier *m* roulant
escapism	Wirklichkeitsflucht *f*	évasion *f* de la réalité *f*
escutcheon	Schildchen *n*	écusson *m*
esparto	Espartopapier *n*	alfa *m*
essay	Aufsatz *m*, Essay *m*, kurze Abhandlung *f*	article *m*, essai *m*
established	gegründet	fondé
establishment	Feststellung *f*	établissement *m*
estimate	Kostenanschlag *m*, Offerte *f*, Voranschlag *m*	devis *m*, évaluation *f*, offre *f*
to estimate	kalkulieren, veranschlagen	calculer, établir un devis *m*, évaluer
estimate of composition	Satzberechnung *f*	calcul *m* de la composition *f*
estimating	Kostenvoranschlag *m*	devis *m* estimatif, évaluation des frais *m/pl*
estimation	Schätzung *f*	estimation *f*
to etch	ätzen	creuser, graver, mordre
to etch in relief	hochätzen	graver en relief *m*
etcher	Ätzer *m*	graveur *m*
etching	Ätzung *f*, Radierung *f*	cliché *m*, eau-forte *f*, gravure *f*
etching machine	Ätzmaschine *f*, Klischeeätzmaschine *f*	machine *f* à graver
etching process	Ätzverfahren *n*	procédé *m* de gravure *f*, procédé *m* de morsure *f*
ethical advertising	ethische Werbung *f*	publicité *f* éthique
eulogy	Lobrede *f*	éloge *m*, panégyrique *m*
European Common Market	Europäische Wirtschaftsgemeinschaft *f* (EWG)	Marché *m* Commun Européen
evaluation	Auswertung *f*, Bewertung *f*	estimation *f*, évaluation *f*, exploitation *f*, interprétation *f*
even number	gerade Zahl *f*	nombre *m* pair
even page	gerade Seite *f*, linke Seite *f*	en verso, fausse page *f*, page *f* de gauche, page *f* paire
evening edition	Spätausgabe *f*	édition *f* du soir *m*
evening newspaper	Abendzeitung *f*	journal *m* du soir *m*
even-numbered page	Seite mit gerader Nummer	page *f* paire
event	Ereignis *n*	événement *m*
events *pl* today	Tagesereignisse *n/pl*, Tagesnachrichten *f/pl* in der Presse *f*	agenda *m* de la journée *f*
every three months *pl*	vierteljährlich	trimestriel
every year	jährlich	annuel
evolution	Entwicklung *f*	développement *m*, évolution *f*
to exaggerate	übertreiben	exagérer, grossir
examination	Prüfung *f*, Untersuchung *f*	enquête *f*, examen *m*, recherche *f*
to examine	prüfen	contrôler, examiner, vérifier
to exceed	überschreiten	dépasser
excerpt	Auszug *m*, Exzerpt *n*	citation *f*, extrait *m*, résumé *m*
excessive charge	überhöhter Preis *m*	prix *m* excessif

exchange advertisement	Tauschanzeige f	annonce f d'échange m
exchange copy	Tauschexemplar n	exemplaire m d'échange m
exchange of thoughts pl	Gedankenaustausch m	échange m d'idées f/pl
exclamation mark, exclamation point am	Ausrufezeichen n	point m d'exclamation f
exclusion	Ausschluß m	exclusion f
exclusive agency	Alleinvertretung f, Exklusivagentur f	agence f exclusive
exclusive contribution	Exklusivbeitrag m	article m exclusif
exclusive distribution	Alleinverkauf m	vente f exclusive
exclusive reader	Exklusivleser m	lecteur m exclusif
exclusive report	Exklusivbericht m	rapport m exclusif
exclusivity	Exklusivität f	exclusivité f
exclusivity stipulation	Konkurrenzausschluß m	clause f d'exclusivité f, clause f de non-concurrence f
execution	Ausführung f	exécution f, réalisation f
execution of an order	Auftragsausführung f	exécution f d'une commande f
exhausted	vergriffen	épuisé
to exhibit	ausstellen (Waren f/pl)	exposer
exhibition	Aushang m, Ausstellung f, Messe f	étalage m, exposition f, foire f
exhibition advertising	Messewerbung f	publicité f de foire f
exhibition catalogue	Ausstellungskatalog m	catalogue m d'exposition f
exhibition grounds pl	Ausstellungsgelände n	terrain m de l'exposition f
exhibition hall	Ausstellungshalle f	hall m d'exposition f
exhibition poster	Ausstellungsplakat n	affiche f d'exposition f
exhibition space	Ausstellungsfläche f	aire f de l'exposition f
exhibition stand	Ausstellungsstand m, Messestand m	stand m de foire f, stand m d'exposition f
exhibition stand construction	Ausstellungsbau m, Messebau m	construction f de stands m/pl de foire f, construction f des expositions f/pl
exhibition train	Ausstellungszug m	train m d'exposition f
exhibition van	Ausstellungswagen m	voiture f d'exposition f
exhibitor	Aussteller m, Messeaussteller m	exposant m
exhibits pl	Ausstellungsstück n	pièce f spécimen m
exorbitant price	Wucherpreis m	prix m usuraire
expanded	breit	large
expanded type	breite Drucktype f	caractère m large
expendable package	Einwegpackung f	emballage m non repris, emballage m perdu
expenditure	Aufwand m, Aufwendung f	dépenses f/pl, frais m/pl
expenditure of work	Arbeitsaufwand m	ampleur f du travail m
expense	Aufwendung f	dépenses f/pl, frais m/pl
expense account	Spesenvergütung f	remboursement m des frais m/pl
expenses pl	Ausgaben f/pl (Unkosten), Kosten pl	coûts pl, dépenses f/pl, frais m/pl
expenses pl for setting	Satzkosten pl	frais m/pl de composition f
expensive advertising	kostspielige Werbung f	publicité f coûteuse
experience	Erfahrung f	expérience f
experiment	Experiment n	expérience f
experimental film	Experimentalfilm m	film m expérimental
experimental poster	experimentelles Plakat n	affiche f expérimentelle
expert	Fachmann m	expert m, spécialiste m
expert opinion	Gutachten n, Sachverständigengutachten n	arbitrage m, expertise f

expiration, expiry	Ablauf *m*	expiration *f*
explanation	Erläuterung *f*	explication *f*
expletive	Flickwort *n*	cheville *f*
exploitation	Auswertung *f*	évaluation *f*, exploitation *f*, interprétation *f*
exploration	Informationsgespräch *n*	exploration *f*
export advertising	Exportwerbung *f*	publicité *f* d'exportation *f*
export promotion	Exportförderung *f*	aide *f* à l'exportation *f*
to expose	ausstellen (Waren *f/pl*), belichten	exposer, insoler
exposition *am*	Ausstellung *f*	exposition *f*
exposure	Belichtung *f*, Belichtungszeit *f*	exposition *f*, insolation *f*, temps *m* de pose *f*
express order	Eilauftrag *m*	commande *f* urgente, ordre *m* par exprès *m*
expression	Ausdruck *m*	expression *f*
expression of opinion	Meinungsäußerung *f*	expression *f* de l'opinion *f*
expressive force, expressiveness	Ausdruckskraft *f*	expressivité *f*, force *f* d'expression *f*
to expurgate	ausmerzen	expurger, trier
extended covers *pl*	überstehender Umschlag *m*	couverture *f* à rabats *m/pl*, couverture *f* débordante
extended type	breite Drucktype *f*	caractère *m* large
extension of an order	Auftragserweiterung *f*	augmentation *f* de commande *f*, complément *m* de commande *f*
extra bold	extra fett	extra gras
extra charge	Aufschlag *m*, Mehrpreis *m*, Preisaufschlag *m*, Zuschlag *m*	majoration *f*, majoration *f* de tarif *m*, majoration *f* de prix *m*, supplément *m* de prix *m*, surtaxe *f*
extra colour	Spezialfarbe *f*	couleur *f* spéciale, encre *f* spéciale
extra copy	Sonderexemplar *n*	exemplaire *m* supplémentaire
extra discount	Sonderrabatt *m*	réduction *f* de faveur *f*, remise *f* spéciale
extra performance	Sonderleistung *f*	service *m* spécial, travaux *m/pl* exceptionnels
extract	Auszug *m*, Exzerpt *n*	citation *f*, extrait *m*, résumé *m*
eye appeal, eye catcher	Blickfang *m*	accrochage *m*, accroche-œil *m*, amorce *f*, attrape-regard *m*, tape-à-l'œil *m*, tire-l'œil *m*
eye-catching advertising	Blickfangwerbung *f*	publicité *f* attrape – regard *m*
eye-catching right-hand page	Aufschlagseite *f*	belle page *f*
eyewash	Schönfärberei *f*	optimisme *m* de commande *f*
eyewitness account	Augenzeugenbericht *m*	récit *m* d'un témoin *m* oculaire

F

to fabricate an information	aushecken, eine Nachricht *f*	forger une information *f*
fabricated account	literarischer Betrug *m*	supercherie *f* littéraire

face	bedruckte Vorderseite *f,* Druckoberfläche *f,* Type *f*	caractère *m,* côté *m* image *m,* lettre *f,* première page *f*
face-to-face communication	direkte Kommunikation *f*	communication *f* nez *m* à nez *m*
facing contents *pl*	gegenüber Inhaltsverzeichnis *n*	face *f* sommaire *m*
facing editorial matter	gegenüber redaktionellem Teil *m*	face *f* texte *m* rédactionnel
facing first editorial page	gegenüber der ersten Textseite *f*	face *f* première de texte *m*
facing last editorial page	gegenüber der letzten Textseite *f*	face *f* dernière de texte *m*
facing leader	gegenüber Leitartikel *m*	face *f* éditorial *m*
facing matter	textanschließend	à côté *m* du texte *m,* après texte *m,* se joignant au texte *m,* sous le texte *m*
facing text	gegenüber Text *m*	contre texte *m,* face *f* texte *m*
facsimile	Faksimile *n*	fac-similé *m*
facsimile reprint	Faksimiledruck *m*	réimpression *f* fac-similée
fact	Tatsache *f*	fait *m*
fact sheet	Produktbeschreibung *f*	description *f* d'un produit *m*
fact-gathering	Faktensammlung *f*	recueillement *m* de faits *m/pl*
to fade	verblassen	passer
to fade over	weiche Bildüberblendung *f*	fondu *m* enchaîné
faded in text	Texteinblendung *f* in Film *m*	texte *m* enchaîné
fade-in	Einblendung *f*	ouverture *f* en fondu *m*
fading	Fading *n,* Schwundeffekt *m*	évanouissement *m,* fading *m,* fondu *m*
fade-out	Ausblenden *n*	fondu *m*
failure rates *pl*	Ausfall *m*	rebut *m*
fair	Messe *f*	exposition *f,* foire *f*
fair authorities *pl*	Messeamt *n*	comité *f* d'organisation *f* de la foire *f*
fair catalogue	Messekatalog *m*	catalogue *m* de la foire *f*
fair competition	fairer Wettbewerb *m*	concurrence *f* loyale
fair copy	druckfertiges Manuskript *n,* Klartext *m,* Reinschrift *f*	belle copie *f,* copie *f* au net *m,* copie-témoin *m,* net d'un texte *m*
fair play	ehrliches Spiel *n*	franc-jeu *m*
fair site	Messegelände *n*	parc *m* des expositions *f/pl*
fake	Ente *f,* Fälschung *f*	bobard *m,* chiqué *m,* contrefaction *f,* falsification *f*
fake interview	vorgetäuschtes Interview *n*	interview *m* bidon
fake report	Falschmeldung *f*	fausse nouvelle *f*
to fake up a story	Geschichte *f* erfinden, eine	inventer une histoire *f*
falling off of orders *pl*	Auftragsrückgang *m*	fléchissement *m* dans les rentrées *f/pl* de commande *f*
false advertising	irreführende Werbung *f,* trügerische Werbung *f*	publicité *f* déloyale, publicité *f* fallacieuse, publicité *f* mensongère, publicité *f* trompeuse
false news	Falschmeldung *f,* Tatarennachricht *f*	fausse nouvelle *f,* nouvelle *f* à la tatare *m*
falsification	Fälschung *f,* Verfälschung *f*	chiqué *m,* contrefaction *f,* falsification *f*
falsification of competition	Wettbewerbsverzerrung *f*	distorsion *f* de la concurrence *f*
family announcement	Familienanzeige *f*	avis *m,* faire-part *m*

family appeal	Ansprache f des Familiengefühls n	appel m au bonheur m domestique, appel m au sentiment m de famille f
family likeness	Familienähnlichkeit f	similarité f de présentation f
family of type	Schriftfamilie f	famille f de caractères m/pl
family paper	Familienblatt n	feuille f familiale, revue f d'intérêt m général
family size pack	Haushaltspackung f	empaquetage m de ménage m
fancy article	modisches Produkt n	produit m à la mode f
fancy frame	Zierrand m	cadre m fantaisie f
fancy letters pl	Zierschrift f	caractère m de fantaisie f, caractères m/pl ornés
fancy name	Phantasiemarkenname m	nom m inventé
fancy paper	Dekorationspapier n	papier m de décoration f
fancy price	Mondpreis m	prix m de fantaisie f
fancy types pl	Künstlerschriften f/pl, Phantasieschriften f/pl	caractères m/pl fantaisie f
fanfold form	Leporellofalzung f	pli m accordéon m, pli m en zig-zag
to farm out	verpachten	affermer, donner à bail m
farm press	Agrarpresse f	presse f rurale
farm publication	Landwirtschaftsblatt n	feuille f rurale, journal m agricole
farmer's supplement	Landwirtschaftsbeilage f	supplément m rurale
farming out	Verpachtung f	affermage m, amodiation f
fascia	Firmenschild n mit Fremdreklame f	bandeau m de magasin m
fashion advertising	Modewerbung f	publicité f de la mode f
fashion article	Modeartikel m	article m de modes f/pl
fashion design	Modezeichnung f	dessin m de mode f
fashion magazine	Modeblatt n	journal m de modes f/pl
fashion magazines pl	Modezeitschriften f/pl	magasins m/pl de modes f/pl
fashion parade	Modeschau f	defilé m de mode f, exposition f de modes f/pl
fashion photography	Modefotografie f	photographie f de mode f
fashion supplement	Modebeilage f	supplément m de mode f
fashioning	Formgestaltung f	création f de la forme f, esthétique f industrielle
fast back	rückwärts ablaufender Film m	film m se déroulant en arrière
fast to light	lichtecht	solide à la lumière f
to fasten	heften	agrafer, brocher
fat	dick, Specke m	composition f courante, gras
fat head	Titel m, fetter	titre m en gras
fat line	fette Linie f	ligne f en gras
fat type	fetter Buchstabe m	caractère m gras
fault-finder	Kritikaster m	critique m en chambre f, critiqueur m, éplucheur m
faulty information	Fehlinformation f	information f incorrecte
faulty spacing	falsche Raumaufteilung f	espacement m faux
favourite paper	Leibblatt n	feuille f favorite
featherweight paper	Federleichtpapier n	papier m bouffant

feature	besonders gestalteter aktueller Tatsachenbericht *m*, Charakteristikum *n*, Dokumentarbericht *m*, Feature *n*, Hauptmerkmal *n* (einer Anzeige *f*), Sachbericht *m*	article *m* documentaire, caractéristique *f*, rapport *m* d'actualité *f*, rapport *m* documentaire, rapport *m* spécial d'actualité *f*, trait *m*, varia
to **feature**	hervorheben	mettre en évidence *f*, mettre en relief *m*, mettre en vedette *f*, souligner
to **feature a piece of news**	Nachricht *f* groß aufmachen	mettre une nouvelle *f* en manchette *f*
feature article	Reportage *f*, Sonderbericht *m*	article *m* spécialisé, reportage *m*
feature film	Hauptfilm *m* des Programms *m*	grand film *m* de programme *m*
feature material	Textmaterial *n*	éléments *m/pl* du texte *m*
feature programme	Hörfolge *f*	programme *m* de radio *f*
federal post	Bundespost *f*	poste *f* fédérale
federal railways *pl*	Bundesbahn *f*	chemin *m* de fer *m* fédéral
federation	Bund *m*	fédération *f*
fee	Gebühr *f*, Honorar *n*, Vergütung *f*	bonification *f*, honoraire *m*, rémunération *f*
fee for design	Entwurfshonorar *n*	honoraires *m/pl* de projet *m*
fee for journalists *pl*	Journalistenhonorar *n*	honoraires *m/pl* des journalistes *m/pl*, pige *m*
feed-back	Rückkopplung *f*, Rückwirkung *f*	rétroaction *f*
feeder	Anlegeapparat *m*	margeur *m*, régulateur *m* de marges *f/pl*
feeling for form	Formgefühl *n*	sens *m* des formes *f/pl*
to **feign**	Türken *m/pl* bauen	faire passer quelque chose *f* de faux pour vrai, feindre, simuler
feint	Täuschung *f*	mystification *f*
felt	Filz *m*	feutre *m*
felt pen	Filzschreiber *m*	crayon-feutre *m*, marqueur *m*
felt side	Schönseite *f*	côté *m* feutre
female announcer	Ansagerin *f*, Bildschirmdame *f*	présentatrice *f*, speakerine *f*
female buyer	Käufer *m* (in *f*)	acheteur *m*, acheteuse *f*
female touch	weibliche Note *f*	note *f* féminine
ferrotype	Schnellfotografie *f* auf Eisenblech *n*	ferrotypie *f*
ferry-boat advertising	Fährschiffwerbung *f*	publicité *f* dans les ferry-boats *m/pl*
festival	Festspiele *n/pl*	festival *m*
feuilleton	Feuilleton *n*	feuilleton *m*, page *f* littéraire
fiber direction *am* fibre direction *brit*	Laufrichtung *f*	sens *m* de fabrication *f*
fiction	Belletristik *f*, Erdichtung *f*, Roman *m*, schöne Literatur *f*, Unterhaltungsliteratur *f*	belles-lettres *f/pl*, fiction *f*, littérature *f* divertissante, ouvrage *m* d'imagination *f*, roman *m*
field	Aufgabengebiet *n*	fonctions *f/pl*, tâche *f* assignée
field blanking interval	Austastlücke *f*	blocage *m* effacement *m*

field force	Außendienstmitarbeiter *m*/*pl*	personnel *m* du service *m* extérieur
field investigation	Marktforschung *f*	étude *f* du marché *m*, recherche *f* du marché *m*
field investigator	Interviewer *m*	enquêteur *m*
field of activities *pl*	Arbeitsgebiet *n*, Wirkungskreis *m*	champ *m* d'action *f*, ressort *m* d'activité *f*
field of vision	Sichtfeld *n*	champ *m* de vision *f*
field service	Außendienst *m*	service *m* extérieur
field staff	Außendienstmitarbeiter *m*/*pl*	personnel *m* du service *m* extérieur
field-work	Feldarbeit *f*	travail *m* sur le terrain *m*
fighting brand	Kampfmarke *f*	marque *f* de bataille *f*
figure	Zahl *f*, Ziffer *f*	chiffre *m*, nombre *m*
file	Ablage *f*, Kartei *f*	armoire *f*-classeur *m*, cartothèque *f*, classement *m*, dépôt *m*, fichier *m*
to file	ablegen	classer, distribuer
file box	Ordner *m*	classeur *m*
file proof	Anzeigenabzug *m* für Archivzwecke *m*/*pl*	épreuve *f* pour archives *f*/*pl*
file-copy	Archivexemplar *n*	exemplaire *m* des archives *f*/*pl*, exemplaire *m* en collection *f*
filing basket	Ablegekorb *m*	corbeille *f* de distribution *f*
filing cabinet	Kartei *f*, Registratur *f*	armoire *f*-classeur *m*, cartothèque *f*, enregistrement *m*, fichier *m*
filing system	Ablage *f*	classement *m*, dépôt *m*
filler	Füllanzeige *f*, Füller *m*	annonce *f* bouche-trou *m*, annonce *f* d'opportunité *f*, remplissage *m*
to fill-in	einfügen	insérer
filling of a contract	Auftragsabwicklung *f*	exécution *f* d'un ordre *m*
fill-up	Beifilm *m*, Füller *m*	annonce *f* d'opportunité *f*, bouche-trou *m*, court-métrage *m*, hors-programme *m*, remplissage *m*
film	Kunststoffolie *f*	film *m*
film *brit*	Film *m*	film *m*
to film	filmen, verfilmen	filmer, mettre en images *f*/*pl*, tourner un film *m*
film actor	Filmschauspieler *m*	acteur *m* de cinéma *m*
film actress	Filmschauspielerin *f*	actresse *f* de cinéma *m*
film adaptation	Filmbearbeitung *f*	adaptation *f* cinématographique
film advertising	Kinowerbung *f*	cinéma *m* publicitaire, publicité *f* dans les cinémas *m*/*pl*
film camera	Filmkamera *f*	caméra *f*
film car	Filmwagen *m*	voiture *f* équitée pour la projection *f* de films *m*/*pl*
film copy	Filmkopie *f*, Musterabzug *m*	copie *f* du film *m*, copie *f* pour un film *m*
film director	Filmregisseur *m*	metteur *m* en scène *f*, réalisateur *m*

film distributors *pl*	Filmverleih *m*	location *f* de films *m/pl*, maison *f* de distribution *f* de films *m/pl*
film expert	Filmfachmann *m*	cinéaste *m*
film featuring G.G.	Hauptrolle *f*, Film *m* mit G.G. in der	film *m* avec G.G. en vedette *f*
film festivals *pl*	Filmfestspiele *n/pl*	festivals *m/pl* cinématographiques
film industry	Filmindustrie *f*	industrie *f* cinématographique
film lending institute	Filmverleih *m*	location *f* de films *m/pl*, maison *f* de distribution *f* de films *m/pl*
film library	Filmarchiv *n*, Filmsammlung *f*	cinémathèque *f*, filmothèque *f*
film magazine	Filmzeitschrift *f*	revue *f* de cinéma *m*
film of universal appeal	allgemein ansprechender Film *m*	film *m* passe-partout
film paper	Filmpapier *n*, Fotopapier *n*	papier-film *m*, papier-pellicule *f*, papier *m* photographique
film poster	Filmplakat *n*	affiche *f* de cinéma *m*
film producer	Filmproduzent *m*, Filmregisseur *m*	cinéaste *m*, metteur *m* en scène *f*, producteur *m* de films *m/pl*, réalisateur *m*
film projection	Filmvorführung *f*	projection *f* de film *m*
film projector usuable in daylight-rooms *pl*	Hellraumprojektor *m*	projection *f* dans des localités *f* avec lumière *f* de jour *m*
film reel	Filmrolle *f*, Filmspule *f*	bobine *f* cinématographique, rouleau *m* de pellicule *f*
film reproduction	Filmwiedergabe *f*	projection *f* en salle *f*
film review	Filmrundschau *f*	chronique *f* cinématographique
film rights *pl*	Filmrechte *n/pl*	droits *m/pl* d'adaptation *f* cinématographique
film roll	Filmrolle *f*	rouleau *m* de pellicule *f*
film script	Filmdrehbuch *n*	scénario *m*, script *m*
film setting	Filmsatz *m*, Lichtsatz *m*	composition *f* photographique, composition *f* sur film *m*, photocomposition *f*, phototypie *f*
film size	Filmformat *n*	format *m* de pellicule *f*
film slide	Diapositiv *n*	diapositif *m*
film society	Filmklub *m*	ciné-club *m*
film strip	Bildstreifen *m*, Filmstreifen *m*	bande *f* de film *m*
film studio	Filmatelier *n*, Filmstudio *n*	studio *m*
film-goer	Filmbesucher *m*, Kinobesucher *m*	spectateur *m*
filmlet	Filmlet *n*, Kurzfilm *m*	court-métrage *m*
filmsetting machine	Lichtsetzmaschine *f*	composeuse *f* photographique, photocompeuse *f*, phototitreuse *f*
film-sound transmission car	Tonbildschau *f*	film *m* à images *f/pl* fixes, voiture *f* spéciale pour la projection *f* de films *m/pl* sonores
filter	Filter *m*	filtre *m*
final art work	Reinzeichnung *f*	dessin *m* au net, document *m*, projet *m* définitif
final consumer	Endverbraucher *m*	consommateur *m* final

final costing	Nachkalkulation *f*	contrôle *m* a posteriori, postcalculation *f*
final proof	letzte Korrektur *f*	morasse *f*, tierce *f*
final pull	endgültiger Andruck *m*	épreuve *f* définitive
final settlement	Schlußabrechnung *f*	décompte *m* final
financial advertisement	Finanzanzeige *f*	avis *m* financier
financial advertising	Finanzwerbung *f*	publicité *f* financière
financial paper	Börsenzeitung *f*, Finanzblatt *n*	journal *m* financier
fine grain	Feinkorn *n*	grain *m* fin
fine screen	Feinraster *m*	trame *f* fine
fine-face rule	feine Linie *f*	filet *m* maigre
fingernails *pl*	Klammern *f/pl/typog*	parenthèses *f/pl*
finish	technische Oberflächengestaltung *f* eines Papiers *n*	apprêter le papier *m*
to **finish**	nachschneiden	finir
finished drawing	fertige Zeichnung *f*, Reinzeichnung *f*	dessin *m* au net, dessin *m* au propre, dessin *m* définitif, document *m*, projet *m* définitif
finished layout	Reinlayout *n*	dessin *m* définitif, maquette *f* définitive
finishing	Ausrüstung *f*	équipement *m*, façonnage *m*
fireside chats *pl*	Plaudereien *f/pl* am Kamin *m*	causeries *f/pl* devant la cheminée *f*
firm	Firma *f*	maison *f*
firm offer	Festangebot *n*	offre *f* ferme
firm order	Festauftrag *m*	ordre *m* ferme
firm order newspaper	Abonnementszeitung *f*	journal *m* d'abonnés *m/pl*
firm price	Festpreis *m*	prix *m* fixe, prix *m* imposé
first edition	Erstausgabe *f*, Originalausgabe *f*	édition *f* originale, première édition *f*
first impression	Schöndruck *m*	côté *m* de première, impression *f* au recto *m*, impression *f* en blanc, premier folio *m*
first page	erste Seite	première page *f*
first proof	erster Abzug *m*, Hauskorrektur *f*, Rohabzug *m*	épreuve *f* en première, première correction *f*, première épreuve *f*
first run	Schöndruck *m*	côté *m* de première, impression *f* au recto *m*, impression *f* en blanc, premier folio *m*
first selling day	Erstverkaufstag *m*	premier jour *m* de vente *f*
first-rate	hochwertig	de grande qualité *f*, de haute teneur *f*
fit for printing	druckfähig	imprimable
fitting of shop windows *pl*	Schaufenstergestaltung *f*	aménagement *m* de vitrines *f/pl*
to **fix**	festlegen	établir, fixer
fixative	Fixativ *n*	fixatif *m*
fixed costs *pl*	feste Kosten *pl*	coûts *m/pl* fixes
fixed date	Terminvorschrift *f*	date *f* imposée
fixed date advertisement	Terminanzeige *f*	annonce *f* à date *f* fixe
fixed day	Stichtag *m*	date *f* limite, jour *m* d'échéance *f*

fixed period orders *pl*	Festaufträge *m/pl* auf bestimmte Zeit *f*	ordres *m/pl* à conservation *f* déterminée
fixed salary	Fixum *n*	salaire *m* fixe
fixed selling price	Festpreis *m*, gebundener Preis *m*	prix *m* fixe, prix *m* imposé
flag	auffallende Titelseite *f*, Titel *m* der ersten Seite *f*	titre *m* de première page *f* en gros caractères *m/pl*, titre *m* flamboyant
flag waver	chauvinistische Zeitung *f*	journal *m* chauvin
flap	Klappe *f*, Lasche *f*, Umschlagklappe *f*	gousset *m*, rabat *m*
flaring advertisement	sensationell aufgemachte Anzeige *f*	annonce *f* flamboyante
flash	Blitzlicht *n*, Einfall *m*, kurzer Übergang *m*, kurzes Pressetelegramm *n*	boutade *f*, courte dépêche *f* d'agence *f*, éclair *m* au magnésium *m*, idée *f*, saillie *f*, transition *f* courte
flash-back	Rückblende *f*	retour *m* en arrière, scène *f* rétrospective
flashing sign, flashing-winking of lights *pl*	Blinklichtwerbung *f*	clignotement *m*
flat	Film *m* (für Offset *m*) , Offsetfilm *m*	film *m* pour offset *m*, plat *m*, typon *m*
flat fee	Pauschalhonorar *n*	honoraires *m/pl* forfaitaires
flat proof	Bürstenabzug *m*, Rohabzug *m*	épreuve *f* à la brosse *f*, épreuve *f* au taquoir *m*, morasse *f*, première épreuve *f*
flat rate	Anzeigenfestpreis *m*, Einzelpreis *m*, Grundpreis *m*	prix *m* de base *f*, prix *m* fixe, prix *m* forfaitaire, tarif *m* de base *f*, tarif *m* fixe
flat stitching	Flachheftung *f*	couture *f* à plat
flat tint	Tonfläche *f*	à-plat *m*
flat-bed cylinder press	Zylinderflachformmaschine *f*	presse *f* cylindrique à marbre *m* plan
flat-bed press	Schnellpresse *f*	presse *f* à cylindre *m*, presse *f* en blanc
flat-bed printing	Flachdruck *m*	impression *f* à plat, impression *f* planographique
flatness	Flaute *f*	accalmie *f*, période *f* creuse
flatness in advertising business	Anzeigenflaute *f*	période *f* creuse pour la publicité *f*
flaw	Sprachschnitzer *m*	bévue *f*
flexichrome process	Handkolorierung *f*	procédé *m* flexichrome
flexographic printing	Anilindruck *m*, Flexodruck *m*	flexographie *f*, impression *f* à l'aniline *f*, impression *f* flexographique
flimsy paper	Abzugpapier *n*, Durchschlagpapier *n*	papier *m* pour copies *f/pl*
flint paper	Glanzpapier *n*	papier *m* calandré, papier *m* lissé, papier *m* satiné
floating piece	versetzbares Plakat *n*	placard *m* dont l'emplacement *m* peut varier
flong	Mater *f*	flan *m*, matrice *f*
flong board	Maternpappe *f*	carton *m* pour flans *m/pl*
floodlight	Flutlicht *n*	lampe *f* survoltée, lumière *f* d'ambiance *f*, lumière *f* d'arrosage *m*

floodlight advertisement	angestrahlte Werbefläche *f*	publicité *f* éclairée
floor-stand	Ausstellungsständer *m*	présentoir *m* de sol *m*
flop	Mißerfolg *m*	échec *m*
flourish	Floskel *f,* Schriftzug *m*	fleur *f* de rhétorique *f,* paraphe *m,* trait *m*
flow of words *pl*	Redefluß *m*	flux *m* verbal
fluctuation	Schwankung *f*	fluctuation *f*
fluctuations *pl* of circulation	Auflageschwankungen *f/pl*	fluctuations *f/pl* des tirages *m/pl*
fluff	Schnitzer *m,* Versprecher *m*	bafouillage *m,* loup *m*
fluffy	fusselnd	peluché
fluorescence colour	Fluoreszenzfarbe *f*	couleur *f* fluorescente
fluorescent	fluoreszierend	fluorescent
fluorescent ink printing	Leuchtdruck *m*	impression *f* avec encre *f* fluorescente
fluorescent lamp	Leuchtstoffröhre *f*	tube *m* fluorescent
flush	Einzug *m,* ohne	sans renfoncement *m*
flush cover	Umschlag *m* im Format *n* der Textseiten *f/pl*	couverture *f* en format des pages *f/pl* de texte *m*
flush head	nicht eingezogener Titel *m*	titre *m* aligné à gauche
fly bill	Vorsatzblatt *n*	feuille *f* volante, page *f* de garde *f*
fly posting	Wildanschlag *m*	affichage *m* à la sauvette *f,* affichage *m* volant, pose *f* libre
fly sheet	Vorsatzblatt *n*	feuille *f* volante, page *f* de garde *f*
fly-leaf	Allonge *f*	allonge *f,* feuille *f* attachée
focal point	Brennpunkt *m* des Verkaufs *m*	centre *m* d'attraction *f,* point *m* central, point *m* chaud
focal point of sales *pl*	Verkaufsbrennpunkt *m*	zone *f* de chalandise *f*
focus	umsatzstarke Stelle *f*	point *m* chaud
focus of sale	Brennpunkt *m* des Verkaufs *m*	centre *m* d'attraction *f,* point *m* central, point *m* chaud
foil	Folie *f*	feuille *f,* pellicule *f*
fold	Bruch (Falz) *m*	pli *m,* rainure *f*
to fold	falten, falzen	plier, plisser
folded	gefalzt	plié
folded printed sheet	ausgedruckter Druckbogen *m*	cahier *m*
folder	Broschüre *f,* Faltprospekt *m,* Prospekt *m*	brochure *f,* dépliant *m,* plaquette *f,* prospectus *m,* tract *m*
folder test	Anzeigentest *m,* Untersuchung *f* der Anzeigenwirkung *f*	test *m* d'annonce *f,* test *m* de reliure *f*
folding	Falzung *f*	pliage *m,* rainage *m*
folding box	Faltschachtel *f*	boîte *f* pliante
folding map	Faltplan *m*	carte *f* pliable
folio	Nummer *f* der Seite *f,* Seitenziffer *f*	folio *m,* nombre *m* de page *f,* numéro *m* de la page *f*
folk-song	Volkslied *n*	chanson *f* populaire, chanson *f* traditionnelle
follow copy	Manuskript *n* beachten	à composer tel quel
to follow copy	genau nach Vorlage *f* setzen	composer fidèle au modèle *m*
following matter	textanschließend	à côté *m* du texte *m,* après texte *m,* se joignant au texte *m,* sous le texte *m*

following on	Fortsetzungsanzeige *f*	annonce *f* de continuation *f*
follow-on order	Anschlußauftrag *m*	commande *f* de suite *f*
follow-up advertising	Nachfaßwerbung *f*	publicité *f* de relance *f*
follow-up letter	Nachfaßbrief *m*	lettre *f* de retrait *m*, relance *f*
follow-up order	Anschlußauftrag *m*	commande *f* de suite *f*
font	Schriftart *f*	genre *m* de caractères *m/pl*
food ad	Nahrungsmittelanzeige *f*	annonce *f* pour produits *m/pl* alimentaires
foolscap paper	Kanzleipapier *n*	papier *m* de chancellerie *f*
foot	Fuß *m*	marge *f* de pied *m*
foot of page	am Fuß *m* einer Seite *f*	bas *m* de page *f*, pied *m* de page *f*
foot rule	Fußlinie *f*, Fußzeile *f*	filet *m* de pied *m*, ligne *f* de pied *m*
footage	Filmlänge *f*	métrage *m*
football ground	Fußballplatz *m*	terrain *m* de football *m*
footnote	Fußnote *f*	note *f* au bas *m* de la page *f*, note *f* courante, note *f* de pied *m*
footpath	Gehweg *m*	trottoir *m*
footstick	Fußsteg *m*	blanc *m* de pied *m*
for a 3-column	dreispaltig	sur trois col *f* de largeur *f*
forbidden advertising	unzulässige Werbung *f*	publicité *f* interdite
force expressiveness	Ausdruckskraft *f*	expressivité *f*, force *f* d'expression *f*
force of expression	Aussagekraft *f*	puissance *f* d'expression *f*
forecast	Vorausberechnung *f*, Vorhersage *f*	prédiction *f*, prévision *f*
fore-edge	äußerer Papierrand *m*	marge *f* extérieure
fore-edge margin	Außensteg *m*	marge *f* extérieure
foreign advertising	Auslandswerbung *f*	publicité *f* à l'étranger *m*
foreign circulation	Auslandsverbreitung *f*	diffussion *f* à l'étranger *m*
foreign commerce	Außenhandel *m*	commerce *m* extérieur
foreign correspondent	Auslandsberichterstatter *m*	correspondant *m* à l'étranger *m*
foreign market	Auslandsmarkt *m*	marché *m* étranger *m*
foreign news	Auslandsnachrichten *f/pl*	nouvelles *f/pl* de l'étranger *m*
foreign order	Auslandsauftrag *m*	commande *f* de l'étranger *m*
foreign press	Auslandspresse *f*	presse *f* de l'étranger *m*
foreign station	Auslandssender *m*	station-radio *f* de l'étranger *m*
foreign word	Fremdwort *n*	mot *m* étranger
forerunner	Vorläufer *m*	précurseur *m*
form	Form *f*, Formblatt *n*	forme *f*, formule *f*
form bed	Schriftfundament *n*	marbre *m* porte-forme *m*
form of assertion	Aussageform *f*	forme *f* d'assertion *f*
form of bill-posting	Plakatierungsform *f*	forme *f* d'affichage *m*
form of expression	Ausdrucksform *f*	mode *m* d'expression *f*
form of presentation	Darstellungsform *f*	présentation *f* formelle
format	Format *n*	dimensions *f/pl*, format *m*
form-man	Metteur *m*	imposeur *m*, metteur *m* en pages *f/pl*
forms *pl* close	Anzeigenschluß *m*, Schlußtermin *m*, Redaktionsschluß *m*	bouclage *m*, date *f* limite, date *f* limite de remise *f*, délai *m* des annonces *f/pl*, remise *f* de copie *f*
forms *pl* of advertising	Werbeformen *f/pl*	façons *f/pl* publicitaires
formulation	Formulierung *f*	formulation *f*, mise *f* en forme *f*

forum	Forum *n*	séance *f* de discussion *f*
to **forward**	versenden	acheminer, envoyer
forwarding	Versand *m*, Weitergabe *f*	distribution *f*, envoi *m*, expédition *f*, transmission *f*
founder	Gründer *m*	fondateur *m*
foundry	Gießerei *f*	fonderie *f*
foundry metal	Gießmetall *n*	alliage *m* d'imprimerie *f*
foundry proof	Rohabzug *m*	première épreuve *f*
foundry type	Handsatzschrift *f*, Originalschrift *f*	caractères *m/pl* fondeur
fount	Guß *m*, Schriftart *f*	fonte *f*, genre *m* de caractères *m/pl*
fount case	Vorratskasten *m* (Schrift *f*)	casseau *m*
fountain-pen	Füllfederhalter *m*	stylo *m*
four columns *pl*	vierspaltig	sur quatre colonnes *f/pl*
four-colour block	Vierfarbätzung *f*	cliché *m* de photogravure *f*, quadrichromie *f*
four-colour process	Vierfarbendruck *m*	impression *f* en quatre couleurs *f/pl*, impression *f* quadrichrome, quadrichromie *f*
fraction	Bruchteil *m*	fraction *f*
fractional-page advertisement	seitenteilige Anzeige *f*	publicité *f* au format *m*
fragment	Bruchstück *n*, Fragment *n*	fragment *m*
frame	Einrahmung *f*, Schriftkasten *m*, Umrandung *f*	bordure *f*, casse *f*, contour *m*, encadrement *m*
to **frame**	einfassen, einrahmen	border, encadrer, entourer d'un filet *m*
framework	Rahmen *m*	cadre *m*
franchise	Alleinverkaufsrecht *n*, Lizenz *f*	exclusivité *f*, licence *f*
franchise circulation	Privileg-Vertriebsmethode *f*	diffusion *f* privilégiée
franchise operator of transport advertising	Verkehrsreklamepächter *m*	concessionaire *m* de publicité *f* sur les moyens *m/pl* transports *m/pl*
franchiser	Konzessionsinhaber *m*	concessionaire *m*
franchising	Lizenzübertragung *f*	attribution *f* d'une licence *f*
franchising system	Franchising *n*	attribution *f* d'une licence *f*
franking	Frankierung *f*	affranchissement *m*
franking machine	Frankiermaschine *f*	machine *f* à affranchir
fraud	Täuschung *f*	mystification *f*
free advertisement	Gratisanzeige *f*	insertion *f* gratuite
free copy	Freiexemplar *n*	exemplaire *m* gratuit, spécimen *m*
free deal	Gratisangebot *n*	offre *f* gratuite
free delivery	Gratiszustellung *f*, Lieferung *f* frei Haus *n*	envoi *m* gratuit, livraison *f* à domicile *m*
free gift	Werbegabe *f*, Werbegeschenk *n*, Zugabe *f*	cadeau *m* publicitaire, prime *f*
free gift advertising	Warenprobenverteilung *f*, Wertreklame *f*	objet-réclame *f*, publicité *f* par l'objet *m*
free insertion	kostenlose Insertion *f*	insertion *f* gratuite
free lance artist	freier Grafiker *m*	dessinateur *m* libre
free lance contributor	freiberuflicher Mitarbeiter *m*	collaborateur *m* à son compte *m*, collaborateur *m* extérieur, collaborateur *m* libre, collaborateur *m* extérieur

free lance journalist	freier Journalist *m*, freier	pigiste *m*,
free lance reporter	Lokalberichterstatter *m*	journaliste *m* indépendant,
		stringer *m*
free of charge	gratis, kostenlos, unentgeltlich	gratuit, sans frais *m/pl*, sans
		rémunération *f*
free posting	Freiaushang *m*,	affichage *m* gracieux
	Gratisplakataushang *m*	
free publication	Gratisblatt *n*	périodique *m* gratuit,
		publication *f* gratuite
free puff	kostenlose redaktionelle	annonce *f* rédactionnelle,
	Werbung *f*	gracieuseté *f*, publicité *f*
		rédactionnelle gratuite
free sample	Gratismuster *n*	échantillon *m* gratuit
free sheet	Anzeigenblatt *n*, Offertenblatt *n*	annoncier *m*, feuille *f*
		d'annonces *f/pl*, journal *m*
		publicitaire
free subscription	Gratisabonnement *n*	abonnement *m* gratuit
free trial	Gratisprobe *f*	échantillon *m* gratuit
freedom of opinion	Meinungsfreiheit *f*	liberté *f* d'opinion *f*
freedom of speech	Redefreiheit *f*	liberté *f* de parole *f*
freedom of the press	Pressefreiheit *f*	liberté *f* de la presse *f*
freedom of thought	Gedankenfreiheit *f*	liberté *f* de la pensée *f*
freelance artist	freier Grafiker	dessinateur *m* libre
free-lance journalist	unabhängiger Journalist *m*	pigiste *m*
French fold	Kreuzbruchfalzung *f*	pliage *m* croisé
frequency	Besuchsziffer *f*, Frequenz *f*,	fréquence *f*
	Häufigkeit *f*	
frequency discount	Mengenrabatt *m*, Serienrabatt *m*	dégressif *m* sur volume *m*
		publicitaire, rabais *m* de
		quantité *f*, rabais *m* de
		série *f*, remise *f* de quantité *f*
frequency of publication	Erscheinungsweise *f*	mode *m* de parution *f*,
		périodicité *f*
friar	Mönchsbogen *m*	moine *m*
frisket	Abdeckmaske *f*, Spritzmaske *f*	cache *f*, frisquette *f*
from first source	aus erster Hand *f*	de première main *f*
from rule to rule	von Strich *m* zu Strich *m*	de filet *m* à filet *m*
front cover, front page	erste Seite, Titelseite *f*,	côté *m* de première, grand
	Vorderseite *f*, 1.	titre *m*, page *f* de titre *m*,
	Umschlagseite *f*	première de couverture *f*,
		première page *f*
front page	Titelseite *f*	grand titre *m*, page *f* de titre *m*,
		première page *f*
front section	vorderer Teil *m* der Ausgabe *f*	cahier *m* de tête *f*
front-end space	Türplakat *n*	panneau *m* à l'entrée *f*
frontispiece	Titelbild *n*	frontispice *m*, titre-planche *f*
front-page news	Nachricht *f* auf der Titelseite *f*	nouvelle *f* sensationnelle
to frost glass	mattieren	dépolir, mater, matir
frustration	Versagung *f*	frustration *f*
to fudge	letzter Minute *f* einrücken, in	insérer en dernière minute *f*
fugacity	Flüchtigkeit *f*	fugacité *f*
fugitive colour	lichtempfindliche Farbe *f*	couleur *f* sensible à la lumière *f*
full faced type	fette Schrift *f*	caractère *m* gras, type *m* gras
full line	volle Zeile *f*	ligne *f* pleine
full measure	voller Spaltensatz *m*	ligne *f* pleine

full measure setting	durchgehender Satz *m*	composition *f* à pleine justification *f*
full of matter	inhaltsreich	substantiel
full page	ganze Seite *f*	page *f* entière
full page ad	ganzseitige Anzeige	annonce *f* d'une page *f* entière
full position *am*	Vorzugsplazierung *f*	emplacement *m* préférentiel, emplacement *m* spécial, placement *m* de faveur *f*
full retouching	Vollretusche *f*	retouche *f* complète
full screen	Großaufnahme *f*	gros plan *m*, plan *m* serré, vue *f* de premier plan *m*
full service	kompletter Kundendienst *m*	service *m* complet
full showing	Netzanschlag *m*, Vollbelegung *f*	affichage *m* général
full stop	Punkt *m*, Schlußpunkt *m*	point *m*, point *m* final
full text	vollständiger Text *m*	texte *m* intégral
full-faced type	Schrift *f*, fette	caractères *m/pl* gras
full-length film	abendfüllender Film *m*	long métrage *m*
fullness of power	Vollmacht *f*	plein pouvoir *m*
full-page ad	ganzseitige Anzeige *f*	annonce *f* d'une page *f* entière
full-page illustration	ganzseitiges Bild *n*	hors-texte *m*
fundamental idea	Grundidee *f*	idée *f* de base *f*
fundamentals *pl* of decision	Entscheidungsgrundlagen *f/pl*	bases *f/pl* de la décision *f*
funicular railway	Drahtseilbahn *f*	funiculaire *m*
funnies *pl*, funny paper	Witzblatt *n*	feuille *f* humoristique, satirique *m*
furniture	Formatsteg *m*, Hohlsteg *m*, Schließsteg *m*, Steg *m*/*typog*	garniture *f*, lingot *m*, lingot *m* évidé
fusion	Fusionierung *f*	fusion *f*
fuzz	Fussel *m*	peluches *f/pl*
fuzzy	verwischt	flou

G

gable publicity	Giebelwerbung *f*	pignon *m* publicitaire, publicité *f* murale
gadget	geringwertiger Werbeartikel *m*	élément *m* publicitaire de peu de valeur *f*
gag	Einfall *m*, Pointe *f*, witziger Einfall *m*	boutade *f*, idée *f*, pointe *f*, saillie *f*
gagging of the press	Presseknebelung *f*	bâillonnement *m* de la presse *f*, muselement *m* de la presse *f*
gain	Gewinn *m*, Nutzen *m*	bénéfice *m*, profit *m*, utilité *f*
galley for dead matter	Ablegeregal *n*, Ablegeschiff *n*	galée *f* à distribution *f*
galley line	Erkennungszeile *f*	ligne *f* d'identification *f*
galley proof	Bürstenabzug *m*, Fahnenabzug *m*	épreuve *f* à la brosse *f*, épreuve *f* au taquoir *m*, épreuve *f* en placard *m*, morasse *f*
galley-slug	Nummernreglette *f*	réglette *f* numerotée
Gallup poll	Demoskopie *f*	enquête *f* sur les opinions *f/pl*, sondage *m* de l'opinion *f* publique
galvanic shell	Kupferhaut *f*	coquille *f* de galvano *m*, pellicule *f* galvanoplastique en cuivre *m*
galvanotechnics *pl*	Galvanotechnik *f*	technique *f* galvanoplastique

gap in supplies *pl*	Versorgungslücke *f*	brêche *f* d'approvisionnement *m*
to garble	verstümmeln	tronquer
gatefold	ausschlagbare Seite *f*	pli *m* en portefeuille *m*
gathering of information	Beschaffung *f* von Informationen *f/pl*	récolte *f* des informations *f/pl*
to gauge	kalibrieren	calibrer
gazette	amtliche Zeitung *f*	journal *m* officiel
gazetteer	Ortsverzeichnis *n*	liste *f* de localités *f/pl*
general advertising	überregionaler Werbefeldzug *m*	campagne *f* nationale
general conditions *pl*	allgemeine Bedingungen *f/pl*	conditions *f/pl* générales
general map	Übersichtskarte *f*	carte *f* synoptique
general publicity	Publikumspropaganda *f*	publicité *f* générale
generalization	Verallgemeinerung *f*	généralisation *f*
generic	Vorspann *m*	film *m* annonce *f*
geographical sector	Gebiet *n*	région *f*, secteur *m* géographique, territoire *m*
German type	Fraktur *f*	caractères *m/pl* allemands, caractères *m/pl* gothiques, fracture *f*
to get across	übertragen	relayer, transmettre
ghost view	Werbebild *n*, das das Innere *n* zeigt	illustration *f* montrant l'intérieur *m*
ghost writer	im Auftrag *m* und unter dem Namen *m* eines anderen schreibender Autor *m*	nègre *m*
giant-size pack	Familienpackung *f*, Großpackung *f*	emballage *m* de grande taille *f*, empaquetage *m* gigantesque
gibberish	Kauderwelsch *n*	baragouin *m*, jargon *m* incompréhensible
gift advertising	Zugabewerbung *f*	publicité *f* avec primes *f/pl*
gift coupon	Wertgutschein *m*	coupon *m* pour primes *f/pl*
gift parcel services *pl*	Geschenkpackungsdienst *m*	services *m/pl* de l'empaquetage *m* des présents *m/pl*
gift subscription	Geschenkabonnement *n*	abonnement *m* cadeau *m*
gift voucher	Gutschein *m*	bon *m* à valoir, coupon *m* de réduction *f*
gift wrapping	Geschenkpackung *f*	boîte *f* pour cadeaux *m/pl*
giftgiving	Zugabewesen *n*	distribution *f* de primes *f/pl*, ventes *f/pl* avec primes *f/pl*
gigantic publicity	Riesenreklame *f*	réclame *f* monstre *m*
gilding	Vergoldung *f*	dorure *f*
gilt edge	Goldschnitt *m*	tranche *f* d'or *m*
gilt-letter	Goldbuchstabe *m*	lettre *f* d'or *m*
gimmick	ausgefallene Idee *f*, Dreh *m*, sensationelle Werbung *f*, Trick *m*	coup *m*, truc *m*
to give instructions *pl*	disponieren	arranger, disposer, prévoir
give-away	Geschenkartikel *m*, Handzettel *m*, Zugabeartikel *m*	article *m* -cadeau *m*, article *m* prime *f*, papillon *m*, prospectus *m*
giveaway	Gratisblatt *n*	périodique *m* gratuit, publication *f* gratuite

give-away price	Schleuderpreis *m*, Unterbietungspreis *m*	bradage *m*, conditions *f/pl* spéciales, gâchage *m* de prix *m*, vil prix *m*
glaced paper	Glanzpapier *n*	papier *m* calandré, papier *m* lissé, papier *m* satiné
glaring poster	grellfarbiges Plakat *n*	affiche *f* criarde
glass sign	Glasschild *n*	enseigne *f* en verre *m*
glassine	Transparentpapier *n*	papier *m* transparent
glaze	Lasurfarbe *f*	couleur *f* à vernisser, encre *f* transparente
glazed paper	geglättetes Papier *n*, gestrichenes Papier *n*	papier *m* calandré, papier *m* couché, papier *m* glacé, papier *m* satiné
gleanings *pl*	Nachlese *f*	glanes *f/pl*
gloss	Glosse *f*	glose *f*
glossary	Glossar *n*	glossaire *m*
glossy colour	Glanzfarbe *f*	couleur *f* de lustre *m*
glossy foil	Glanzfolie *f*	pellicule *f* brillante
glossy monthlies *pl*	elegante Zeitschriften *f/pl*	magazines *m/pl* chics
glossy paper	Glacépapier *m*, Kunstdruckpapier *n*	papier *m* couché des deux faces *f/pl*, papier *m* glacé
glossy print proof *am*	Abzug *m* auf Kunstdruckpapier *n*	épreuve *f* sur papier *m* couché
glue	Klebstoff *m*, Leim *m*	adhésif *m*, colle *f*
to glue	kaschieren	doubler, encoller
glut of the market	Marktüberschwemmung *f*	inondation *f* du marché *m*
glutted market	gesättigter Markt *m*, überschwemmter Markt *m*	marché *m* encombré, marché *m* inondé
go-ahead	fortschrittlich	avant-garde *f*, progressiste
gobbledygook	Kauderwelsch *n*, schwülstiger Stil *m*	baragouin *m*, jargon *m* incompréhensible, style *m* ampoulé
go-between	Zwischenträger *m*	cafard *m*, entremetteur *m*
godsend	Fundgrube *f*	trouvaille *f*
going to press	Drucklegung *f*	mise à l'impression *f*, mise sous presse *f*
gold blocking	Goldprägung *f*	empreinte *f* dorée
gold leaf	Blattgold *n*	or *m* en feuilles *f/pl*
golden-rod paper	Abdeckpapier *n*	papier-cache *m*
golf-ball typing head	Kugelkopf *m*	tête *f* imprimante
gondola	Verkaufsgondel *f*	gondole *f*
good for printing	druckreif, gut zum Druck *m*	prêt à imprimer
good for printing with corrections *pl*	druckreif nach Korrektur *f*	bon à tirer après corrections *f/pl*
good will	Firmenwert *m*, guter Ruf *m*	bonne réputation *f*, valeur *f* commerciale
goods *pl*	Ware *f*	denrée *f*, marchandise *f*
goodwill	Geschäftswert *m*, Stammkundschaft *f*	achalandage *m*, clientèle *f*, valeur *f* commerciale
good-will advertising	institutionelle Werbung *f*, Prestigewerbung *f*	publicité *f* de notoriété *f*, publicité *f* de prestige *m*, publicité *f* impériale, publicité *f* institutionnelle
gooseberry season	Saure-Gurken-Zeit *f*	mois *m/pl* creux de l'été *m*, morte-saison *f*

gossip	Familiennachrichten f/pl, Klatschgeschichte f	bavardage m, chronique f scandaleuse, échos m/pl familiers
gossip writer	Klatschbase f	échotier m
Gothic type	Fraktur f, gotische Schrift f	caractères m/pl allemands, caractères m/pl gothiques, fracture f
gouache	Guasch f, Tempera f	couleur f opaque, gouache f
gouache colours pl	Guaschfarben f/pl	couleurs f/pl pour gouache f
gouache drawing	Guaschzeichnung f	dessin m à la gouache f
graduated price	gestaffelter Preis m	prix m échelonné, tarif m mobile
to grain	granieren	grainer
grained paper	gekörntes Papier n, gemasertes Papier n, graniertes Papier n, Kornpapier n, Maserpapier n	papier m grainé, papier m granulé
grammalogue	Kürzel n	sigle m
grammatical blunder	Sprachschnitzer m	bévue f
granite paper	Faserpapier n	papier m mélangé de fils m/pl de soie f
granulated screen	Kornraster m	trame f à grain m
grape-vine	Latrinenparolen f/pl	téléphone m arabe
graph	Diagramm n, Schaubild n	diagramme m, graphique m
graph paper	Millimeterpapier n	papier m quadrillé à millimètre m
graphic	grafische Darstellung f	diagramme m, représentation f graphique
graphic arrangement	grafische Gestaltung f	conception f graphique
graphic chart		diagramme m, représentation f graphique
graphic design	Werbestil m	style m de publicité f
graphic terminal	Umbruchterminal n	terminal m de composition f
graphical representation	grafische Darstellung f	diagramme m, représentation f graphique
graphics pl	Grafik f	graphique m
grass roots pl press	Kleinstadtzeitung f	presse f pour la population f rurale
gratis	gratis	gratuit
gratuitous service	kostenloser Kundendienst m	service m bénévole
grave accent	Accent m grave	accent grave
gravure paper	Tiefdruckpapier n	papier m pour héliogravure f
grease-proof paper	fettdichtes Papier n	papier beurre f, papier m imperméable à la graisse f, papier m parcheminé, papier m parchemin m imitation f
green table	grüner Tisch m	tapis m vert
greeting card	Glückwunschkarte f	carte f de vœux m/pl
grey market	grauer Markt	marché m gris
grey paste board	Graupappe f	carton m gris
grey scale	Grauskala f	échelle f des gris
grey tints pl	Grautöne m/pl	teintes f/pl grises
to grind colours pl	Farben f/pl reiben	broyer des couleurs f/pl
gripper edge	Greiferkante f	bord m des pinces f/pl
to groove	nuten	rainer
grooved paste-board	Wellpappe f	carton m ondulé

grooving	Falzung *f*	pliage *m*, rainage *m*
gross circulation	Bruttoauflage *f*	tirage *m* brut
gross price	Bruttopreis *m*	prix *m* brut
grotesque	Grotesk *f*	antique *f*, bâton *m*
ground colour	Grundfarbe *f*	couleur *f* de base *f*
ground noise	Hintergrundgeräusche *n/pl*	bruit *m* de fond *m*
ground-tint plate	Tonplatte *f*	à-plat, planche *f* de fond *m*
groundwork	Grundzüge *m/pl*	canevas *m*
group advertising	Gemeinschaftswerbung *f*, Kollektivwerbung *f*	publicité *f* collective, publicité *f* en commun, publicité *f* groupée
group head	Kontaktgruppenleiter *m*	chef *m* de groupe *m*
group of publishers *pl*	Anzeigenring *m*	cercle *m* d'édition *f*, couplage *m* publicitaire
group of solicitors *pl*	Werbekolonne *f*	équipe *f* de courtiers *m/pl*
group of word	Wortgruppe *f*	groupe *m* de mot *m*
grouped style	Blocksatz *m*	composition *f* en forme *f* de carré *m*
grub	Schreiberling *f*	écrivassier *m*
grumbler	Querulant *m*	querelleur *m*
grusical	Schauerfilm *m*	film *m* d'épouvante *f*
guaranted minimum circulation	garantierte Mindestauflage *f*	tirage *m* minimum garanti
guarantee	Garantie *f*	garantie *f*
to guarantee	garantieren	garantir
guarantee period	Garantiefrist *f*	période *f* de garantie *f*
guard	Schutzgitter *n*	grille *f* de protection *f*
guest writer	gelegentlicher Mitarbeiter *m*	collaborateur *m* occasionnel, collaborateur *m* part-time
guidance	Richtschnur *f*	gouverne *f*, règle *f* de conduite *f*
guide	Handbuch *n*, Leitfaden *m*	guide *m*, manuel *m*, vade-mecum *m*
guide of cost	Kostenübersicht *f*	sommaire *m* des frais *m/pl*
guide sheet	Sendeplan *m*	programme *m* de la radio *f*
guideline	Linienblatt *n*	transparent *m* rayé
guide-lines *pl*	Richtlinien *f/pl*	directives *f/pl*, normes *f/pl*
guide-sheet	Kontrolliste *f*, Checkliste *f*	liste *f* aide *f* -mémoire *f*, liste *f* de contrôle *m*
gummed fancy paper	Kleisterpapier *n*	papier *m* marbré
gummed label	Aufkleber *m*, Klebeetikett *n*	étiquette *f* gommée, papillon *m*, timbre *m* adhésif *m*
gummed paper	gummiertes Papier *n*	papier *m* gommé
gummed strip	Klebestreifen *m*	bande *f* gommée
gutter	Gießbach *m*, Innenspalte *f*, Kreuzsteg *m*	blanc *m* transversal, petit-fonds *m*, rue *f*
gutter paper	Revolverblatt *n*	feuille *f* à scandale *m*, feuille *f* de chantage *m*
gutter press	Schmutzpresse *f*, Skandalpresse *f*	presse *f* à scandale *m*, presse *f* de bas étage *m*, presse *f* obscène

gutter-stick	Bundsteg *m*	blanc *m* du petit fond *m*, marge *f* intérieure

H

habit	Gewohnheit *f,* Verhaltensweise *f*	coutume *f,* habitude *f,* mode *m* de comportement *m*
hack writer	Zeitungsschreiber *m*	folliculaire *m*
hackneyed phrase	abgedroschene Redensart *f*	cliché *m,* phrase *f* rebattue
hair space	halber Punkt *m*	espace *m* fin
hairline	Haarstrich *m*	délié *m,* empattement *m*
hair-splitting	Wortklauberei *f*	chicane *f* sur les mots *m/pl*
half binding	Halblederband *m*	reliure *f* en demi-cuir *m*
half measure	zweispaltig	face *f* en deux colonnes *f/pl,* sur deux colonnes *f/pl*
half page	halbe Seite *f*	demi-page *f*
half showing	Halbbelegung *f*	affichage *m* à demi
half title	Innentitel *m*	faux titre *m,* titre *m* intérieure
half tone drawing	Halbtonzeichnung *f*	dessin *m* mi-ton
half-baked	unvollständig	incomplet
half-binding	Halbfranzband *m*	demi-reliure *f*
half-bold	halbfett	demi gras, mi gras
half-monthly	halbmonatlich	semi-mensuel
half-tints *pl*	Mitteltöne *m/pl*	demi-teintes *f/pl*
half-title	Schmutztitel *m*	avant-titre *m,* faux titre *m*
halftitle page	Schmutztitelblatt *n*	page *f* du faux titre *m*
half-tone	Halbton *m,* Netzätzung *f*	demi-teinte, mi-ton, simili *m,* similigravure *f*
half-tone block	Autotypieätzung *f*	autotypie *f,* cliché *m* simili, similigravure *f*
halftone dot	Rasterpunkt *m*	point *m* de trame *f*
half-tone paper	Autotypiepapier *n*	papier *m* très calandré pour simili *m*
half-tone plate *am*	Autotypie *f*	autotypie *f,* similigravure *f*
halftone screen	Autotypieraster *m*	trame *f* de simili *m*
half-tone shadings *pl*	Rastertönungen *f/pl*	grisés *m/pl*
half-weekly	halbwöchentlich	semi-hebdomadaire
half-yearly	halbjährlich	semestriel, tous les six mois *m/pl*
halo effect	Nimbus *m*	auréole *f*
ham	Radioamateur *m*	opérateur *m* amateur *m*
hand composer	Handsetzer *m*	compositeur *m* à la main *f*
hand composition *am*	Handsatz *m*	composition *f* à la main *f,* composition *f* manuelle
hand made deckle-edged paper	handgeschöpftes Büttenpapier *n*	papier *m* à la forme *f,* papier *m* à la main *f,* papier *m* à la main *f*
hand out	Pressemitteilung *f*	communiqué *m*
hand painted	handgemalt	peint à la main *f*
hand printing	Handdruck *m*	impression *f* à la main *f*
hand proof, hand pull	Handabzug *m*	épreuve *f* tirée à la main *f*
hand setting	Handsatz *m*	composition *f* à la main *f,* composition *f* manuelle
hand tooling	Klischeekorrektur *f,* nacharbeiten mit der Hand *f*	retouche *f* à l'outil *m*
hand type	Handsatzschrift *f*	caractères *m/pl* fondeur

handbill	Flugblatt *n*, Flugzettel *m*, Handzettel *m*, Prospekt *m*	brochure *f*, dépliant *m*, feuillet *m*, papillon *m*, prospectus *m*, tract *m*
handbook	Fachbuch *n*, Handbuch *n*, Leitfaden *m*	guide *m*, livre *m* professionnel, livre *m* technique, manuel *m*, ouvrage *m* spécialisé, vade-mecum *m*
handcut	Handausschnitt *m*	découpage *m* à la main *f*
handlettering	gezeichnete Schrift *f*, Schriftzeichnen *n*	repoussage *m*
handling	Handhabung *f*	manutention *f*
handling costs *pl*	Abwicklungskosten *pl*	frais *m/pl* de manutention *f*
hand-made paper	geschöpftes Papier *n*, holländisches Papier *n*	papier *m* de cuve *f*, papier *m* de Hollande *f*
hand-out	Waschzettel *m*	brouillon *m*, note *f* de critique *f*, papillon *m*, prière *f* d'insérer
handout	Freigabe *f*	disposition *f*, transmission *f* à la presse *f*
hand-press	Handpresse *f*	presse *f* à bras *m*
handwriting	Handschrift *f*, Schreibschrift *f*	caractères *m/pl* d'écriture *f*, écriture *f* à la main *f*, écriture *f* typographique
handy man	Faktotum *n*	bricoleur *m*
handy size	handliches Format *n*	format *m* facile à manier
hanger-card	Hängeplakat *n*	pendentif *m*
hanging	Hängeschild *n*	pendentif *m*
hanging indent	eingerückter Satz *m*	composition *f* en sommaire *m*
to happen	sich zutragen	se passer
happening	Begebenheit *f*	événement *m*
hard approach	aggressive Werbung *f*	publicité *f* agressive
hard copy	Klartext *m*	copie-témoin *m*, net d'un texte *m*
hard edge	Schattierung *f*	foulage *m*
hard goods *pl*	Haushaltsartikel *m*, langlebige Gebrauchsgüter *n/pl*	article *m* de ménage *m*, biens *m/pl* de consommation *f* durables
hard selling	Verkaufen *n* um jeden Preis *m*	vente *f* à tout prix *m*
hard work	Schwerarbeit *f*	labeur *m*
hardboard	Hartfaserplatte *f*	carton *m* compact
hardcover	fest gebundenes Buch *n*	livre *m* relié
hatched rule	Strichlinie *f*	filet *m* crémaillère *f*
Hathaway touch	ungewöhnliches Bildelement *n*, wirkungsvolles Bildelement *n*	élément *m* d'image *f* extraordinaire, élément *m* figuratif extraordinaire, élément *m* figuratif impressionnant
to have an advertisement inserted	Anzeige *f* aufgeben	faire insérer une annonce *f*
hawker	fliegender Händler *m*	colporteur *m*, marchand *m* ambulant, marchand *m* forain

head	Kopf *m* (Überschrift *f*)	en-tête *f*, manchette *f*, rubrique *f*, titre *m*
head counter	Marktforscher *m*	enquêteur *m* commercial
head line	Hauptzeile *f*	ligne *f* principale
head margin	Kopfsteg *m*	marge *f* de tête *f*, marge *f* supérieure
head of page	Kopf *m* der Seite *f*	tête *f* de page *f*
head on position	rechtwinklig zum Verkehrsfluß *m*	barre-route *f*
head piece, head rules *pl*	Kopfleiste *f*	bandeau *m* de tête *f*, chapeau *m*, en-tête *f*
head shrinker	Motivforscher *m*	enquêteur *m* de motivation *f*
head stick	Kopfsteg *m*	marge *f* de tête *f*, marge *f* supérieure
headband	Kopfleiste *f*	bandeau *m* de tête *f*, chapeau *m*, en-tête *f*
headed	betitelt	intitulé
heading, headline	Kopf *m* (Überschrift *f*), Spitzmarke *f*, Titel *m*, Titelkopf *m*, Schlagzeile *f*	en-tête *f*, manchette *f*, mots *m/pl* d'appel *m*, titre *m*, ligne *f* principale, ligne *f* repère, phrase *f*-choc *m*, rubrique *f*, titre *m* en vedette *f*
headphone	Kopfhörer *m*	casque *f* téléphonique
health resort supplement	Bäderbeilage *f*	supplément *m* balnéaire
heavy frame	fette Umrandung *f*, Trauerrand *m*	bordure *f* de filet *m* mat
heavy type	fette Schrift *f*	caractère *m* gras, type *m* gras
heavy user	Großverbraucher *m*	gros consommateur *m*
hectograph	Hektograph *m*, Vervielfältigungsapparat *m*	duplicateur *m*, hectographe *m*, multigraphe *m*, polycopiste *m*
hedge press	Winkelblatt *n*	feuille *f* de chou *m*, presse *f* de réputation *f* douteuse
height	Höhe *f*	hauteur *f*
height-to-paper	Schrifthöhe *f*	hauteur *f* du caractère *m*, hauteur *f* en papier *m*
hell box	Zeugkiste *f*	boîte *f* à défets *m/pl*
helping hand	Handreichung *f*	coup *m* de main *f*
to herald	feierlich verkünden	proclamer
hiatus	Sommerloch *n*, Streupause *f*, Werbepause *f*	hiatus *m*, lacune *f* dans la publicité *f*, lacune *f* d'été *m*
hidden demand	latenter Bedarf *m*	besoin *m* latent
hidden offer	verborgenes Angebot *n*, verstecktes Angebot *n*	offre *f* clandestine
hidden persuaders *pl*	geheime Verführer *m/pl*	séducteurs *m/pl* clandestins
hierarchy	Rangordnung *f*	hiérarchie *f*, ordre de préséance *f*
hieroglyphics *pl*	Bilderschrift *f*	hiéroglyphes *m/pl*
HiFi continuous advertisement in colour	HiFi-Endlosfarbanzeige *f*	encart *m* en couleur *f* imprimé en continu *m*
high	hoch	haut
high fidelity	Klangtreue *f*, naturgetreue Wiedergabe *f*	haute fidélité *f*
high gloss lamination	Hochglanzkaschierung *f*	pelliculage *m*
high gloss print	Hochglanzabzug *m*	copie *f* sur papier *m* brillant, épreuve *f* glacée

high key	Foto *n* in hellen Tönen *m/pl*, unscharfes Foto *n*	photo *f* en tons *m/pl* clairs, photo *f* flou
high lights *pl*	Glanzpunkt *m*	événement *m* saillant
high size	Hochformat *n*	format *m* en hauteur *f*, format *m* normal, format *m* vertical
high society	obere Zehntausend *f/pl*	haute société *f*, haute volée *f*
of high value	hochwertig	de grande qualité *f*, de haute teneur *f*
highbrow	Intellektueller *m*	intellectuel *m*
high-class paper	Qualitätszeitung *f*	journal *m* de première qualité *f*, journal *m* de prestige *m*, journal *m* pour l'élite *f*
high-glazing	scharf satiniert	surglacé
to highlight	hervorheben	mettre en évidence *f*, mettre en relief *m*, mettre en vedette *f*, souligner
highlight exposure	Hochlichtaufnahme *f*	exposé *m* des grandes lumières *f/pl*
high-light half-tone	Hochlichtautotypie *f*	cliché *m* simili avec grandes lumières *f/pl*
high-pressure advertising	hochtönende Werbung *f*	publicité *f* emphatique
highway code	Straßenverkehrsordnung *f*	code *m* de la route *f*
hint	Wink *m*	conseil *m*, insinuation *f*, tuyau *m*
to hint	andeuten	dire à mots *m/pl* couverts
hire-purchase	Ratenverkauf *m*	vente *f* à crédit *m*
hit	Schlager *m*	succès *m*
Hitchcock appeal	kriminalistischer Stimmungseffekt *m*	effet *m* policier
hitch-hike	Werbesendung *f* für Nebenprodukte *n/pl*	émission *f* publicitaire pour des sous-produits *m/pl*
hitchhike	Nachzügler-Werbesendung *f*	publicité *f* retardataire
hit-parade	Schlagersendung *f*	palmarès *m*, parade *f* des succès *m/pl*
hoarding	Gruppe *f* von Anschlagstellen *f/pl* an einem Standort *m*	groupe *m* de panneaux *m/pl* d'affichage *m* sur un emplacement *m*
hoarding for posters *pl*	Reklamefläche *f*	panneau *m* de publicité *f*, surface *f* d'affichage *m*
hoarding purchases *pl*	Hortungskäufe *m/pl*	achàts *m/pl* spéculatifs
hoax	Ente *f*, Zeitungsente *f*	bobard *m*, canard *m*
hobby	Liebhaberei *f*	passe-temps *m* favori, violon *m* d'Ingres
hokum	leeres Geschwätz *n*, tränenreiche Phrasen *f/pl*	boniments *m/pl*, paroles *f/pl* vides, phrases *f/pl* lacrymogènes
to hold an edition	verzögern, die Ausgabe *f*	retenir une édition *f*
to hold copies *pl*	Abzüge *m/pl* lesen	lire les épreuves *f/pl*
hold for release	Sperrfrist *f*	délai *m* d'attente *f*, période *f* de suspension *f*
to hold for release	aufbewahren	à conserver
hold over	nichtgebrachte Anzeige *f*	reporter
to hold over	Satz *m* stehen lassen	conserver la composition *f*, garder le plomb *m*
to hold presses *pl*	Druckpresse *f* anhalten	arrêter la presse *f* à imprimer
holding of outdoor advertising sites *pl*	Stellennetz *n*	circuit *m* indivisible d'emplacements *m/pl*, réseau *m*

holiday resorts *pl* **advertising**	Fremdenverkehrswerbung *f*	publicité *f* de tourisme *m*, publicité *f* de villégiature *f*
holiday subscription	Ferienabonnement *n*	abonnement *m* de vacances *f/pl*
holographic advertising	holografische Werbung *f*	publicité *f* holographique
home circulation	Inlandsauflage *f*	tirage *m* national
home news	Inlandsnachrichten *f/pl*	nouvelles *f/pl* du pays *m*
home trade *brit*	Binnenhandel *m*	commerce *m* intérieur
homespun	handgestrickt	fait à la maison *f*
hook	Ansatzpunkt *m*, Aufhänger *m*, Blickfang *m*	accrochage *m* publicitaire, accroche-œil *m*, amorce *f*, angle *m* d'approche *f*, attrape-regard *m*, tape-à-l'œil *m*, tire-l'œil *m*
hoopla	Werberummel *m*	battage *m* publicitaire, publicité *f* raccrocheuse, publicité *f* tapageuse, tam-tam *m*
horizontal co-operative advertising	Horizontalwerbung *f*	publicité *f* collective horizontale
horror film	Horrorfilm *m*, Schauerfilm *m*	film *m* d'épouvante *f*
hostess service	Hostessendienst *m*	personnel *m* pour services *m/pl* d'acceuil *m*
hot line	heißer Draht *m*	téléphone *m* rouge
hot metal composition	Bleisatz *m*	composition *f* au plomb *m*
hot process embossing	Heißprägung *f*	empreinte *f* à chaud
hot shops *pl*	Werbespezialisten *m/pl*	spécialistes *m/pl* de publicité *f*
hot shot	Schnellschuß *m*	coup *m* de feu *m*, train *m* urgent
hot spot	Brennpunkt *m* des Verkaufs *m*	centre *m* d'attraction *f*, point *m* central, point *m* chaud
house advertising	Eigenwerbung *f*	propre publicité *f*
house agency	Hausagentur *f*, vorgeschobene Agentur *f*	agence *f* fictive
house brand	Eigenmarke *f*, Hausmarke *f*	marque *f* de distributeur *m*
house colour	Hausfarbe *f*	couleur *f* privée
house delivery	Lieferung *f* frei Haus *n*	livraison *f* à domicile *m*
house journal, house organ	Betriebszeitung *f*, Hauszeitschrift *f*, Werkzeitschrift *f*	journal *m* d'entreprise *f*, revue *f* d'entreprise
house style	Hausstil *m*	style *m* d'entreprise *f*
house telephone	Haustelefon *n*	téléphone *m* intérieur
household	Haushalt *m*	foyer *m*
house-to-house advertising	Haushaltswerbung *f*	publicité *f* de porte *f* en porte *f*
house-to-house selling	Direktverkauf *m*	vente *f* de porte *f* en porte *f*
housewives' magazines *pl*	Hausfrauenzeitschriften *f/pl*	magasins *m/pl* pour ménagères *f/pl*
housewives' party	Hausfrauenabend *m*	soirée *f* de ménagères *f/pl*
howler	grober Schnitzer *m*	faute *f* énorme
hucksterer	Hausierer *m*	colporteur *m*
hue	Farbton *m*, Kolorit *n*	couleur *f*, nuance *f*, teinte *f*, ton *m* de couleur *f*
hullabaloo	Propagandagetöse *n*	tintamarre *m* de propagande *f*
human appeal	Ansprache *f* des Menschlichen *n*, Gefühlsansprache *f*	appel *m* à l'humanité *f*, valeur *f* affective
human relations *pl*	zwischenmenschliche Beziehungen *f/pl*	relations *f/pl* humaines

human touch	menschliche Note *f*	rapports *m/pl* humains, ton *m* émouvant
humorous paper	Witzblatt *n*	feuille *f* humoristique, satirique *m*
hush money	Schweigegeld *n*	prix *m* du silence *m*
hyphen	Bindestrich *m*	trait *m* d'union *f*
hyphenated word	Kuppelwort *n*	mot *m* à trait *m* d'union *f*
hyphenation	Silbentrennung *f*	coupure *f* syllabique

I

idea	Einfall *m*, Idee *f*	boutade *f*, idée *f*, saillie *f*
identification	Identifizierung *f*	identification *f*
ideology	Weltanschauung *f*	conception *f* du monde *m*, idéologie *f*
idiom	Dialekt *m*, Mundart *f*	dialecte *m*, idiome *m*
idle talker	Wortemacher *m*	bavardeur *m*
to ignore	Tisch *m*, fallen lassen unter den	écraser un papier *m*, passer sous silence *m*
ill news	schlechte Nachrichten *f/pl*	mauvaises nouvelles *f/pl*
illegal press	illegale Presse *f*	presse *f* illégale
illegal transmitting	Schwarzsendung *f*	émission *f* clandestine
illicit advertising	unerlaubte Werbung *f*	publicité *f* illicite
to illuminate	ausleuchten, erleuchten	illuminer
illuminated advertising	Leuchtwerbung *f*	publicité *f* lumineuse
illuminated letter	Leuchtbuchstabe *m*	lettre *f* lumineuse
illuminated line-up table	Montagetisch *m*	table *f* de montage *m*, table *f* lumineuse
illuminated newsband	Wanderschriftnachrichten *f/pl*	information *f* lumineuse, journal *m* lumineux
illuminated newscaster	Laufschrift *f*	écriture *f* courante
illumination	Beleuchtung *f*	éclairage *m*, illumination *f*
to illustrate	illustrieren	illustrer
illustrated	bebildert	illustré, imagé
illustrated advertisement	Bildanzeige *f*	annonce *f* illustrée
illustrated letter	Bilderbrief *m*	lettre *f* illustrée
illustrated paper	Bildzeitung *f*, Illustrierte *f*	journal *m* illustré, périodique *m* illustré
illustration	Abbildung *f*, Bild *n*, Illustration *f*	illustration *f*, image *f*
illustration board	Zeichenkarton *m*	carton *m* à dessin *m*
illustration printing	Illustrationsdruck *m*	impression *f* d'illustrations *f/pl*
illustrative material	Bildmaterial *n*	éléments *m/pl* d'illustration *f*
illustrative poster	illustratives Plakat *n*	affiche *f* illustrative
illustrator	Illustrator *m*	illustrateur *m*
image	Vorstellungsbild *n*	image *f*
imaginary agency	Hausagentur *f*	agence *f* fictive
to imitate	kopieren, nachahmen, nachmachen	contre-faire, copier, imiter
imitation	Imitation *f*, Nachahmung *f*	contre-façon *f*, imitation *f*, plagiat *m*
imitation art paper	hochsatiniertes Papier *n*, imitiertes Kunstdruckpapier *n*, satiniertes Papier *n*	papier *m* calandré, papier *m* satiné
imitation felt	Filzimitation *f*	feutrine *f*
imitative product	nachgeahmtes Produkt *n*	produit *m* imitatif
immediately below text	unmittelbar unter Text *m*	immédiatement après texte *m*

immoral	sittenwidrig	portant atteinte f aux bonnes mœrs f/pl
impact	Eindrucksstärke f, Einwirkung f, Schockwirkung f, Stoßkraft f, Stoßwirkung f, Werbewirkung f, Widerhall m	choc m, effet m de choc m, effet m publicitaire, impact m, pouvoir m de choc m, retentissement m
impact advertising	Stoßwerbung f	publicité f par chocs m/pl
impact-test	Anzeigentest m	test m d'annonce f
to impart	mitteilen	communiquer
impartial	unparteiisch	impartial
impediment of visibility	Sichtbehinderung f	masquage m
imperfection in printing	Druckmängel m/pl	imperfection f d'impression f
to implement	ausführen	exécuter
implementation	Abwicklung f, Bewerkstelligung f	déroulement m, mise f en œuvre f
implementing	Einsatz m	mise f en œuvre f
imposing stone	Schließplatte f	marbre m de serrage m
imposition	Umbruch m	imposition f, mise f en page f
to impregnate	imprägnieren	imprégner
to impress	drucken	imprimer, tirer
impression	Abdruck m, Druck m	empreinte f, impression f
impression cylinder	Druckzylinder m	cylindre m de foulage m, cylindre m d'impression f
impressiveness	Wirksamkeit f	efficacité f
imprimatur	Druckerlaubnis f, Druckgenehmigung f	permission f d'imprimer
imprint	Abdruck m, Aufdruck m, Impressum n, Pflichteindruck m	empreinte f, notice f, repiquage m, surimpression f
imprinting	Herstellervermerk m	mention m du producteur m
impulse	Impuls m	impulsion f
impulse buying	Impulskauf m, Spontankauf m	achat m impulsif, achat m spontané
in arrears pl	Rückstand m, im	en retard m
in charge date of advertising	Berechnungsbeginn m	date f de départ m
in double columns pl	zweispaltig	face f en deux colonnes f/pl, sur deux colonnes f/pl
in paper boards pl	kartoniert	cartonné
in sqares pl	Schachbrettform f	quinconce f
in text	Text m, mitten im	dans le texte m
in the feuilleton	Strich m, unter dem	rez-de-chausée m
in the press	Druck m, im	sous presse f
inadequate advertising	unzulängliche Werbung f	publicité f inadéquate
incentive	Anreizprämie f	prime f d'encouragement m
incentive premium	kaufanreizende Prämie f	prime f stimulante
inch (14 agate lines pl)	Inch n (Anzeigengrundmaß)	pouce m (hauteur 27 mm)
incidental expenses pl	Nebenkosten pl	faux frais m/pl
incitement	Anreiz m	appel m, incitation f
included	inbegriffen	inclus, y compris
included in	enthalten in	compris dans
income	Einkommen n	revenu m
income group	Einkommensklasse f	classe f de revenus m/pl
incoming of orders pl	Auftragseingang m	entrée f de commandes f/pl
incongruity	Mißverhältnis n	déséquilibre m
increase	Erhöhung f	augmentation f
to increase	vergrößern	agrandir

increase in turnover	Umsatzsteigerung *f*	augmentation *f* du chiffre *m* d'affaires *f/pl*
incunabulum	Erstdruck *m*, Inkunabel *f*	incunable *m*
indecent advertising	anstößige Werbung *f*	publicité *f* indécente
indemnity	Entschädigung *f*, Schadenersatz *m*	dédommagement *m*, dommages-intérêts *m/pl*, indemnité *f*
indent	Einzug *m/typog m*, Zeileneinzug *m*	renfoncement *m*
to indent	einrücken (einziehen), einziehen (Zeile)	mettre en renfoncement *m*, renfoncer, rentrer
indention	Einzug *m/typog m*	renfoncement *m*
independent	unabhängig	indépendant
independent media services *pl* **company**	Mediaagentur *f*, Streuagentur *f*	intermédiaire *m* publicitaire
independent newspaper with a complete editorial staff	journalistische Einheit *f*	journal *m* indépendant avec une rédaction *f* complète, unité *f* journalistique
independent television	privates Werbefernsehen *n*	télévision *f* privée
index	Inhaltsverzeichnis *n*, Register *n*	index *m*, registre *m*, sommaire *m*, table *f* des matières *f/pl*
index card	Karteikarte *f*	carte *f* de fichier *m*, fiche *f*
index card board	Karteikarton *m*	carton *m* pour fichiers *m/pl*
index mark	Hand *f* (Hinweiszeichen *n*)	main *f*
index of names *pl*	Namensliste *f*	table *f* nominale
index sheet	Registerblatt *n*	feuille *f* de registre *m*
India paper	Bibeldruckpapier *n*, chinesisches Papier *n*, Dünndruckpapier *n*, Japanpapier *n*	papier *m* bible, papier *m* chiné, papier *m* de Chine *f*, papier *m* japon, papier *m* mince, pelure *f* d'oignon *m*
Indian ink	Tusche *f*	encre *f* de Chine *f*
indirect advertising	indirekte Werbung *f*	publicité *f* indirecte
individual advertising	Alleinwerbung *f*, Einzelwerbung *f*, Individualwerbung *f*	publicité *f* individuelle, publicité *f* isolée
individual location	Sonderstelle *f*, Spezialstelle *f*	emplacement *m* utilisé spécialement
indoor advertising	Innenwerbung *f*	publicité *f* d'intérieur *m*
indoor photo	Innenaufnahme *f*	photo *f* d'intérieur *m*
indoor poster	Innenplakat *n* (in Verkehrsmitteln *n/pl*)	affiche *f* intérieure, emplacement *m* intérieur de voiture *f*
inducement to buy	Kaufbeeinflussung *f*	provocation *f* à l'achat *m*
industrial advertising	Industriewerbung *f*, Investitionsgüterwerbung *f*	publicité *f* industrielle, publicité *f* pour des biens *m/pl* d'investissement *m*
industrial design	Formgebung *f*, Formgestaltung *f*, Gebrauchsmuster *n*	création *f* de la forme *f*, esthétique *f* industrielle, façonnage *m*, forme *f* industrielle, modèle *m* d'utilité *f*

industrial designer	Formgeber *m*,	dessinateur *m* industriel
	Industriedesigner *m*	
industrial exhibition	Industrieausstellung *f*	foire *f* industrielle
industrial film	Industriefilm *m*, Werkfilm *m*	film *m* industriel
industrial goods *pl*	Industriegüter *n/pl*,	articles *m/pl* industriels,
	Produktionsgüter *n/pl*	biens *m/pl* de production *f*,
		biens *m/pl* industriels
industrial magazine	Industrieblatt *n*	revue *f* pour industriels *m/pl*
industrial selling	Beziehungskauf *m*	vente *f* directe
industries *pl* **fair**	Industriemesse *f*	foire *f* de l'industrie *f*
inferior	tiefstehend	inférieur
inferior product	minderwertiges Produkt *n*	produit *m* de mauvaise qualité *f*
inflammatory article	Hetzartikel *m*	article *m* incendiaire
inflatable advertising figures *pl*	aufblasbare Werbefiguren *f/pl*	figures *f/pl* de publicité *f*
		gonflables
to **inflate**	übertreiben	exagérer, grossir
inflight magazine	Fluglinienzeitschrift *f*	revue *f* pour les passagers *m/pl*
to **influence**	beeinflussen	influencer
in-folio	Folioformat *n*	in-folio
to **inform**	benachrichtigen, informieren	informer
informal balance	asymmetrische Anordnung *f*	arrangement *m* asymétrique
informant	Auskunftsperson *f*,	informateur *m*, informatrice *f*
	Gewährsmann *m*, Informant *m*	
information	Information *f*, Meldung *f*	information *f*, nouvelle *f*
information brochure	Informationsbroschüre *f*	brochure *f* d'information *f*
information centre	Nachrichtenzentrale *f*	centre *m* de
		renseignements *m/pl*
information gap	Informationslücke *f*	lacune *f* d'information *f*
information press	Generalanzeigerpresse *f*	presse *f* d'information *f*
information service	Informationsdienst *m*	service *m* d'information *f*
information value	Informationswert *m*	valeur *f* d'information *f*, valeur *f*
		indicative
information-bureau	Nachrichtenamt *n*	bureau *m* d'information *f*
informative labeling	aufklärende Etikettierung *f*	étiquettage *m* informatif
informative poster	informatives Plakat *n*	affiche *f* informative
informatory advertising	informierende Werbung *f*	publicité *f* informative,
		publicité *f* instructive
to **infringe**	verstoßen gegen	enfreindre
initial campaign	Einführungskampagne *f*	campagne *f* de lancement *m*,
		campagne *f* d'information *f*,
		campagne *f* d'introduction *f*
initial letter	Anfangsbuchstabe *m*, Initiale *f*	initiale *f*, lettrine *f*
initials *pl*	Namenszeichen *n*	paraphe *m*
ink density	Durchsichtigkeitsgrad *m*	transparence *f* de la couleur *f*
ink mixing	Farbmischung *f*	mélange *m* des encres *f/pl*
ink ribbon printed letter	Farbbanddruckbrief *m*	impression *f* au ruban *m* de
		machine *f*
inking	Farbgebung *f*	encrage *m*
inking stone	Farbstein *m*	pierre *f* à broyer
inking unit	Farbwerk *n*	encrage *m*
inking-roller	Farbwalze *f*	rouleau *m* encreur
inkpad	Farbkissen *n*	tampon *m* encreur
ink-slinger	Skribifax *m*	journaleux *m*
inland	Inland *n*	intérieur *m* du pays *m*
inner form	Rückseite *f*	côté *m* de seconde, page *f*
		paire, page *f* verso

inner margin	Bundsteg *m*, Innenrand *m*	blanc *m* du petit fond *m*, marge *f* intérieure
inner page	Innenseite *f*	page *f* intérieure
innovation	Neuerung *f*	innovation *f*
innovator	Konsumpionier *m*	pionnier *m* de la consommation *f*
input	Eingabe *f/typog*	information *f* à traiter
to inquire	Erkundigungen *f/pl* einziehen	aller aux informations *f/pl*
inquiries *pl*	Informationen *f/pl*	renseignements *m/pl*
inquiry	Untersuchung *f*	enquête *f*, examen *m*, recherche *f*
inquiry test	Anfragentest *m*	test *m* de demandes *f/pl*
to inscribe	einschreiben	enregistrer, inscrire
inscription	Inschrift *f*	épigraphe *f*, inscription *f*
insert	Beihefter *m*, Beikleber *m*, Beilage *f*, Beipack *m*	annexe *f*, encart *m*, encart *m* broché, supplément *m*
to insert	annoncieren, einfügen, einrücken (Anzeige) , einschalten, inserieren	annoncer, insérer
inserting	Beilegung *f*	encartage *m*
insertion	Einfügung *f*, Einschaltung *f*	insertion *f*
insertion and size	Auftragsumfang *m*	grandeur *f* et arrangement *m*
insertion frequency	Einschalthäufigkeit *f*	fréquence *f* d'insertion *f*
insertion order	Anzeigenauftrag *m*, Insertionsauftrag *m*	commande *f* d'insertion *f*, ordre *m* d'annonces *f/pl*, ordre *m* d'insertion *f*
insertion rate	Einschaltpreis *m*	prix *m* d'insertion *f*
insertion schedule	Erscheinungsplan *m*	calendrier *m* des parutions *f/pl*, calendrier *m* d'insertion *f*, plan *m* de termes *m/pl*
inset	Beilage *f*, Einschaltseite *f*	encart *m*, page *f* intercalaire, supplément *m*
inside back cover	3. Umschlagseite *f*	troisième de couverture *f*
inside decoration	Innenausbau *m*	agencement *m*
inside dopes *pl*	vertrauliche Winke *m/pl*	tuyaux *m/pl* confidentiels
inside front cover	2. Umschlagseite *f*	deuxième de couverture *f*
inside information	Nachricht *f* aus erster Hand *f*	renseignements *m/pl* privés
inside knowledge	Information *f* aus guter Quelle *f*	information *f* de bonne source *f*
inside page	Innenseite *f*	page *f* intérieure
inside story	Blick *m* hinter die Kulissen *f/pl*	regard *m* en coulisses *f/pl*
insolation	Belichtung *f*	exposition *f*, insolation *f*
insolent advertising	anmaßende Werbung *f*	publicité *f* envahissante
installation	Einrichtung *f*	installation *f*
instalment	Sendefolge *f*	émission *f* par fragments *m/pl*
instalment sale	Abzahlungsverkauf *m*	vente *f* à tempérament *m*
institute	Institut *n*	institut *m*
institutional advertising	firmenbetonte Werbung *f*, Firmenwerbung *f*, institutionelle Werbung *f*, Prestigewerbung *f*, Repräsentationswerbung *f*	publicité *f* de notoriété *f*, publicité *f* de prestige *m*, publicité *f* impériale, publicité *f* institutionnelle
instruction booklet	Gebrauchsanweisung *f*	mode *m* d'emploi *m*
instruction sheet	Merkblatt *n*	aide-mémoire *m*
instructional film	Lehrfilm *m*	film *m* éducatif
instructions *pl*	Anweisungen *f/pl*, Richtlinien *f/pl*	directives *f/pl*, normes *f/pl*
intaglio	Schnitt *m*	coupe *f*

intaglio printing	Tiefdruck *m*/*typog*	gravure *f* en creux *m*/*pl*, impression *f* en creux *m*, impression *f* en héliogravure *f*, rotogravure *f*
intmultraintegrated composition system	integriertes Satzsystem *n*	système *m* intégré des textes *m*/*pl* composés
integrated store	Filialbetrieb *m*	succursale *f*
integrated typesetting system	integriertes Satzsystem *n*	système *m* intégré des textes *m*/*pl* composés
intellectual property	geistiges Eigentum *n*	propriété *f* intellectuelle
intelligence department	Nachrichtenstelle *f*	centre *m* de renseignements *m*/*pl*
intelligentsia	geistige Elite *f*	élite *f* intellectuelle
intended group	Zielgruppe *f*	audience *f* utile, cible *m*
to intensify	verstärken	renforcer
intensity	Intensität *f*	intensité *f*
intensity of light	Leuchtkraft *f*	intensité *f* lumineuse
intensive advertising	Intensivwerbung *f*	publicité *f* intensive
interchange of ideas *pl*	Meinungsaustausch *m*	échange *m* de vues *f*/*pl*
interchangeable frame	Wechselrahmen *m*	cadre *m* interchangeable
interest	Interesse *n*	intérêt *m*
interest factor	Aufmerksamkeitsfaktor *m*, Werbeelement *n*/*pl*	éléments *m*/*pl* d'un moyen *m*, facteur *m* d'attention *f*
interest pattern	Interessenbereich *m*	sphère *f* d'intérêts *m*/*pl*
interior decoration	Innendekoration *f*	décoration *f* à l'intérieur *m*
interlarded composition	gespickter Satz *m*	composition *f* lardée
interleaves *pl*	Zwischenblätter *n*/*pl*	macules *f*/*pl*
to interline	durchschießen	blanchir, espacer, interligner
interlinear space	Zeilenabstand *m*	interlignage *m*
interlocutor	Gesprächspartner *m*	correspondant *m*, interlocuteur *m*
intermedia comparison	Intermediavergleich *m*	comparaison *f* des médias *m*/*pl*
intermediary	Unterhändler *m*, Vermittler *m*	entremetteur *m*, négociateur *m*
intermediary trade	Zwischenhandel *m*	commerce *m* d'intermédiaire *m*
international format	Weltformat *n*	format *m* mondial
interphone	Haustelefon *n*	téléphone *m* intérieur
interpolated sheet	Einschaltseite *f*	page *f* intercalaire
to interpose	vermitteln	entremettre
interpretation	Auslegung *f*, Deutung *f*	interprétation *f*
interpreter	Dolmetscher *m*	interprète *m*
interrelations *pl* between advertisements *pl* and circulation	Anzeigen-Auflagen-Spirale *f*	corrélations *f*/*pl* entre annonces *f*/*pl* et tirage *m*
interrogation point (am)	Fragezeichen *n*	point *m* d'interrogation *f*
interval of publication	Erscheinungsintervall *n*	intervalle *m* de parution *f*
interview	Befragung *f*, Interview *n*	enquête *f*, interrogatoire *m*, interview *f*
to interview	befragen	interviewer
interviewee	Befragter *m*	interviewé *m*, répondant *m*
interviewer	Interviewer *m*, Interviewerin *f*	enquêteur *m*, enquêtrice *f*
intraflow	innerbetriebliche Beziehungen *f*/*pl*	relations *f*/*pl* internes
to introduce	einführen	introduire, lancer
introducer	Präsentator *m*	présentateur *m*
introduction	Einleitung *f*, Vorrede *f*	avant-propos *m*, introduction *f*, préambule *f*

introduction campaign	Einführungskampagne *f*	campagne *f* de lancement *m*, campagne *f* d'information *f*, campagne *f* d'introduction *f*
introductory advertising	Einführungswerbung *f*	publicité *f* de lancement *m*, publicité *f* d'information *f*, publicité *f* d'introduction *f*
introductory number	Einführungsnummer *f*	numéro *m* inaugural
invention	Fiktion *f*	fiction *f*
inventory	Verzeichnis *n*	inventaire *m*, liste *f*
inversion	Umkehrung *f*	inversion *f*
invert letter!	Buchstaben *m* wenden!	retournez la lettre *f*!
inverted	kopfstehend	renversé
inverted commas *pl/brit*	Anführungsstriche *m/pl*	guillemets *m/pl*
to **invest**	investieren	investir
to **investigate**	erforschen, erkunden, forschen, recherchieren	étudier, faire des recherches *f/pl*, sonder
investigation	Enquête *f*	enquête *f*
investigator	Forscher *m*, Rechercheur *m*	chercheur *m*, enquêteur *m*
invitation to bid	Ausschreibung *f*	adjucation *f*
invitation-card	Einladungskarte *f*	carte *f* d'invitation *f*
invoice	Faktura *f*, Rechnung *f*	compte *m*, facture *f*
to **invoice**	abrechnen	boucler un compte *m*, facturer, faire un décompte *m*, solder
invoice amount	Rechnungsbetrag *m*	montant *m* de la facture *f*
invoicing	Rechnungserteilung *f*, Rechnungsstellung *f*	établissement *m* de facture *f*, facturation *f*
irisdescent printing	Irisdruck *m*	impression *f* irisée
irregular customers *pl*	Laufkundschaft *f*	clientèle *f* de passage *m*
irregularity	Unregelmäßigkeit *f*	irrégularité *f*
island position	alleinstehend (Anzeige *f*), Inselplacierung *f*	emplacement *m* isolé, position *f* isolée
isolated advertising	Alleinwerbung *f*	publicité *f* individuelle, publicité *f* isolée
isolated order	Einzelauftrag *m*	commande *f* isolée
issue	Ausgabe *f* (Nummer), Lieferung *f* (Heft *n* eines Werkes *n*), Nummer *f* (Ausgabe)	édition *f*, exemplaire *m*, fascicule *m*, numéro *m*
to **issue**	herausgeben	éditer, publier, sortir
Italic type	Kursivschrift *f*	caractère *m* italique, écriture *f* cursive
item	Einzelheit *f*	item *m*
itinerant salesman	fliegender Händler *m*	colporteur *m*, marchand *m* ambulant, marchand *m* forain
ivory board	Elfenbeinkarton *m*	carton *m* -ivoire *m*
ivory paper	Elfenbeinpapier *n*	papier *m* d'ivoire *m*

J

jacket	Schutzumschlag *m*	fourre *f* de protection *f*, jaquette *f*, protège-livre *m*
jamming station	Störsender *m*	émetteur *m* brouilleur, poste *f* de brouillage *m*
to **jam-pack**	vollstopfen	bourrer
Japan enamel	Zaponlack *m*	laque *f* zapon
Japan paper	Japanpapier *n*	japon *m*, papier *m* japon

jargon	Jargon *m*	argot *m*, jargon *m*
jesting advertising	scherzhafte Werbung *f*	publicité *f* humoristique
jig	Schablone *f*	découpage *m*, écran *m*, gabarit *m*, pochoir *m*, stencil *m*
jingle	musikalische Werbung *f*, musikalisches Leitmotiv *n*	indicatif *m* musical, refrain *m* radiophonique, ritournelle *f* publicitaire, tintement *m*
job bag	Arbeitstasche *f*, Auftragstasche *f*	chemise *f* de travail *m*, dossier *m* d'une commande *f*
job case	Akzidenzkasten *m*	casseau *m*
job compositor	Akzidenzsetzer *m*	compositeur *m* de travaux *m/pl* de ville *f*, ouvrier *m* en conscience *f*
job memorandum	Arbeitsablaufblatt *n*	note *f* sur les étapes *f/pl* de déroulement *m*
job printer	Akzidenzdrucker *m*	imprimeur *m* de travaux *m/pl* de ville *f*
job printing	Akzidenzdruck *m*	bilboquet *m*, travail *m* à la pièce *f*, travail *m* de ville *f*
job ticket	Laufzettel *m*	fiche *f* de travail *m*
jobber	Großhändler *m*	grossiste *m*, intermédiare *m* revendeur
jobbing case room	Akzidenzsetzerei *f*	atelier *m* de composition *f* des travaux *m/pl* de ville *f*
jobbing office	Akzidenzdruckerei *f*	imprimerie *f* de travaux *m/pl* de ville *f*
jobbing work	Akzidenzarbeit *f*, Akzidenzdruck *m*, Akzidenzen *f/pl*	bibelots *m/pl*, bilboquet *m*, travail *m* à la pièce *f*, travail *m* de ville *f*
joint	Falz *m*	rainure *f*
joint advertising	Gemeinschaftswerbung *f*	publicité *f* collective, publicité *f* en commun
joint editorial board	Redaktionsgemeinschaft *f*	communauté *f* de rédaction *f*, team *m* rédactionnel
joint insertion	Kollektivanzeige *f*	annonce *f* collective
journal	Blatt *n* (Zeitung *f*) , Zeitung *f*	feuille *f*, gazette *f*, journal *m*, revue *f*
journal in which the law requires public notices *pl* **to be inserted**	Pflichtblatt *n*	journal *m* d'annonces *f/pl* légales
journal of a society	Vereinsblatt *n*	feuille *f* corporative
journal of commerce	Handelsblatt *n*	journal *m* de commerce *m*
journal of fiction	Romanheft *f*	journal *m* de roman *m*, petit roman *m* bon marché
journalese	Zeitungsdeutsch *n*	style *m* de journal *m*
journalism	Journalismus *m*, Pressewesen *n*, Publizistik *f*, Zeitungswesen *n*	journalisme *m*, presse *f*
journalist	Journalist *m*, Publizist *m*	journaliste *m*, publiciste *m*
journalistic unit	journalistische Einheit *f*	journal *m* indépendant avec une rédaction *f* complète, unité *f* journalistique
journeyman	Geselle *m*	compagnon *m*
jubilee publication	Jubiläumsschrift *f*	publication *f* anniversaire, publication *f* de jubilé *m*
jump	Überlauf *m*	tourne *f*

jump story	überlaufender Artikel *m*	article *m* à cheval *m*
just out, just published	soeben erschienen, neu herausgekommen	vient de paraître
justification	Justierung *f*	justification *f*
to justify	ausschließen (typog)	aligner, justifier

K

keen competition	harte Konkurrenz *f*	concurrence *f* acharnée
to keep secret	geheimhalten	tenir secret
to keep type standing	Satz *m* stehen lassen	conserver la composition *f*, garder le plomb *m*
kerned letter	gestürzter Buchstabe *m*, überhängender Buchstabe *m*	caractère *m* couché, lettre *f* crénée, lettre *f* débordante
key	Kontrollziffer *f*, Schlüsselzahl *f*, Taste *f*	clé *f*, numéro *m* codique, touche *f*
key decision	Grundsatzentscheidung *f*	décision *f* de principe *m*
key drawing	Originalzeichnung *f*	dessin *m* original
key form	Paßform *f*	épreuve *f* de repérage *m*
key number	Chiffre *f*, Kennziffer *f*	numéro-clé *f*, numéro *m* de code *m*
key plate	Konturplatte *f*	planche *f* à contours *m/pl*
keyboard	Klaviatur *f*, Tastatur	clavier *m*, dessus *m* de clavier *m*
key-date	Stichtag *m*	date *f* limite, jour *m* d'échéance *f*
keyed advertisement	Chiffreanzeige *f*, Kennzifferanzeige *f*	annonce *f* à clé *f*, annonce *f* chiffrée
keyed advertising	Kennzifferwerbung *f*, Werbung *f* mit Kennziffern *f/pl*	publicité *f* codée, publicité *f* sous chiffre *m*
keyhole report	Schlüssellochbericht *m*	report *m* du trou *m* de serrure *f*
keying an advertisement	Anzeigenkennzeichnung *f*	codification *f* d'une annonce *f*
key-novel	Schlüsselroman *m*	roman *m* à clé *f*
key-word	Schlüsselwort *n*	mot-clé *m*
kickback	Provisionsabgabe *f*	cession *f* de ristournes *f/pl*, donner des retours *m/pl* en arrière
kid appeal	Ansprache *f* auf dem Wege *m* über das Kind *n*	appel *m* via l'enfant *m*
kid appeal advertising	Werbung *f*, kindbezogene	publicité *f* relative à l'enfant *m*
to kill	ausfallen lassen, wegfallen lassen	couper, éliminer
to kill (composition)	ablegen (Satz) *m*	distribuer, mettre en casse *f*
kind of advertising	Werbeart *f*	genre *m* de publicité *f*, type *m* de publicité *f*
kind of paper	Papiersorte *f*	sorte *f* de papier *m*
kind of printing process	Druckart *f*	mode *m* d'impression *f*
kind of type	Schriftart *f*	genre *m* de caractères *m/pl*
kinds *pl* of advertisements *pl*	Anzeigenarten *f/pl*	genres *m/pl* d'annonces *f/pl*
kinds *pl* of composition	Satzarten *f/pl*	sortes *f/pl* de composition *f*
king size	Königsformat *n*	géant *m*
kiosk *brit*	Kiosk *m*, Zeitungskiosk *m*, Zeitungsstand *m*	aubette *f*, débit *m* de journaux *m/pl*, kiosque *m*, kiosque *m* à journaux *m/pl*, stand *m*
kite-flying	Versuchsballon *m* steigen lassen	lancement *m* d'un ballon *m* d'essai *m*
knock down price	Werbepreis *m*	prix *m* de réclame *f*

knocking copy *brit*	aggressive Werbung *f*, herabsetzende Werbung *f*	publicité *f* agressive, publicité *f* discriminatrice , publicité *f* discriminatoire
know how	gewußt, wie	savoir faire
know-how	praktisches Wissen *n*, technisches Spezialwissen *n*	savoir-faire *m*
Kraft paper	Einwickelpapier *n*, Natronpackpapier *n*	papier *m* bulle *f*, papier *m* d'emballage *m*, papier *m* d'emballage *m* à la soude *f*

L

label	Etikett *n*	étiquette *f*, timbre *m*
to label	etikettieren	étiqueter
labeling	Kategorisierung *f*	désignation *f*
labour market	Stellenmarkt *m*	marché *m* du travail *m*
lack of sharpness	Unschärfe *f*	manque *f* de netteté *f*
lacquer	Lack *m*	laque *f*, vernis *m*
to lacquer	lackieren	laquer, vernir
ladies' *pl* supplement	Frauenbeilage *f*	supplément *m* pour les dames *f/pl*
laid paper	geripptes Papier *n*, gestreiftes Papier *n*	papier *m* vergé
to laminate	kaschieren, laminieren	doubler, encoller, laminer
laminated jacket	Plastikeinband *m*	couverture *f* plastifiée
laminated on the back	gegenkaschiert	plastifié sur le dos *m*
laminating	Laminierung *f*	laminage *m*
lamination	Glanzfolienkaschierung *f*	plastification *f*
lamp post advertising	Kandelaberwerbung *f*	publicité *f* sur des mâts *m/pl* d'éclairage *m*
lampoon	Pamphlet *m*, Schmähschrift *f*	libelle *f*, pamphlet *m*
lamp-post interview	Interview *n* mit Ungenanntem *m*	interview *f* avec une personne *f* non nommée
landing-stage	Schiffsstation *f*	débarcadère *f*
landlord	Verpächter *m*	bailleur *m*, propriétaire *m*
landscape	Querformat *n*	format *m* en largeur *f*, format *m* en travers *m*
landscape photo	Landschaftsaufnahme *f*	prise *f* de vue *f* paysage
language barrier	Sprachbarriere *f*	barrière *f* de langue *f*
lanky	saft- und kraftlos	efflanqué
lapse of the tongue	Sprechfehler *m*	lapsus *m* linguae
large format	Großformat *n*	grand format *m*
large hoarding, large panel	Großfläche *f*	grand panneau *m*
large print	Großbuchstaben *m/pl*	caractères *m/pl* haut de casse *f*, gros caractères *m/pl*, lettres *f/pl* capitales, majuscules *f/pl*
large size	Großformat *n*	grand format *m*
large space ad	großflächige Anzeige *f*	annonce *f* de grandes dimensions *f/pl*
large-scale advertising	großzügige Werbung *f*	publicité *f* de grand style *m*
large-size photo	Großfoto *n*	agrandissement *m* photographique
last line	Ausgangszeile *f*	dernière ligne *f*, fin *f* d'alinéa *m*, ligne *f* courte
last page	letzte Seite *f*	page *f* dernière
lasting effect	Dauerwirkung *f*	effet *m* durable

later on	nachträglich	après coup *m*
latest, at the	spätestens	au plus tard
latest fashion	letzte Modeneuheit *f*	dernier cri *m*
latest intelligence	letzte Meldungen *f/pl*, neueste Nachrichten *f/pl*	dernières nouvelles *f/pl*, nouvelles *f/pl* fraîches
latest news	letzte Nachrichten *f/pl*	information *f* de dernière heure *f*
lattice work	Lattenzaun *m*	bardage *m*
to launch	lanzieren	lancer
launch ad	Einführungsanzeige *f*	annonce *f* de lancement *m*, annonce *f* d'introduction *f*
launching	Ankurbelung *f*, Lanzierung *f*	déclenchement *m*, lancement *m*
launching test	Testkampagne *f*	test *m* de lancement *m*
law review	juristische Zeitschrift *f*	revue *f* juridique
lay out man	Entwerfer *m*	maquettiste *m*
layout	Aufbauskizze *f*, Aufriß *m*, Maquette *f*, Satzvorlage *f*, Schmierskizze *f*, Skizze *f*, Rohentwurf *m*	crayonné *m*, croquis *m*, ébauche *f*, esquisse *f*, maquette *f*, modèle *m*, premier jet *m*, projet *m*, schéma *m*
lay-out man	Metteur *m*	imposeur *m*, metteur *m* en pages *f/pl*
layouter	Entwurfsgrafiker *m*	dessinateur *m*
lays *pl*	Anlage *typog*	marge *f*
lead	Blei *n*, Einleitungssatz *m*, Reglette *f*, Zwischenschlag *m*	démarrage *m*, interligne *f*, plomb *m*, réglette *f*
lead composition	Bleisatz *m*	composition *f* au plomb *m*
lead furniture	Bleisteg *m*	lingot *m* de plomb *m*
to lead out	durchschießen, spationieren, sperren	blanchir, espacer, interlettrer
lead story	Spitze *f* (redaktionell)	article *m* de fond *m*
leader	Aufmacher *m*, Leitartikel *m*	article *m* de fond *m*, article *m* de tête *f*, éditorial *m*
leaders *pl*	Punkte *m/pl*, die die Auslassung *f* eines Wortes *n* anzeigen	plusieurs points *m/pl* qui indiquent l'omission *f* d'un mot *m*
lead-in	Anfang *m* einer Anzeige *f*, Eisbrecher *m*	brise-glace *m*, entrée *f* d'une annonce *f*
leading	Zeilenabstand *m*	interlignage *m*
leading article	Leitartikel *m*	article *m* de fond *m*, article *m* de tête *f*, éditorial *m*
leading lady	Filmstar *m*	vedette *f* de l'écran *m*
leading paper	Zeitung *f*, führende	journal *m* de tout premier rang *m*
leading question	Suggestivfrage *f*	question *f* suggestive, question *f* tendancieuse
leads *pl*	Durchschuß *m*, Füllmaterial *n*, Zeilenzwischenräume *m/pl*	blancs *m/pl*, interlignage *m*, interlignes *f/pl*
leaflet	Faltprospekt *m*, Flugblatt *n*, Flugschrift *f*, Kleinprospekt *m*, Merkblatt *n*	aide-mémoire *m*, brochure *f*, dépliant *m*, feuillet *m*, petit prospectus *m*, petite brochure *f*, tract *m*
leaflet in blank	Blankoprospekt *m*	dépliant *m* en blanc
lean	mager	maigre, mince
lean-faced type	magere Schrift *f*	caractères *m/pl* maigres
to lease	verpachten	affermer, donner à bail *m*

to **lease the advertisement business**	Anzeigenteil *m* pachten	affermer la publicité *f*
leased paper	Pachtblatt *n*	revue *f* affermée
leaseholder	Pachtunternehmen *n*	entreprise *f* d'affermage *m*, société *f* d'affermage *m*
leasing	Vermietung *f*	location *f*
leather binding	Lederband *m*	reliure *f* peau *f* pleine
leather board	Lederpappe *f*	carton *m* cuir *m*
leather paper	Lederpapier *n*	papier-cuir *m*
to **leave blank**	blank schlagen, blind schlagen	laisser en blanc
lecture	Vortragsveranstaltung *f*	conférence *f*
lecturer	Dozent *m*	chargé *m* de cours *m*
ledger	Geschäftsbuch *n*	livre *m* de commerce *m*
left-hand corner	linke Ecke *f*	coin *m* gauche
left-hand page	linke Seite *f*	en verso, fausse page *f*, page *f* de gauche
leftist paper	linkseingestellte Zeitung *f*	journal *m* gauchiste
leftist press	Linkspresse *f*	presse *f* de gauche
leftover matter	Überhangsatz *m*	copies *f/pl* en stock *m*
leg man	Hilfsredakteur *m*	assistant *m* du rédacteur *m*
legal adviser	Rechtsberater *m*	conseiller *m* juridique
legal notice	amtliche Bekanntmachung *f*, gerichtliche Anzeige *f*	annonce *f* judiciaire, avis *m* officiel
legal opinion	Rechtsgutachten *n*	avis *m* juridique
legal restrictions *pl*	gesetzliche Beschränkungen *f/pl*	restrictions *f/pl* légales
legal year	Abschlußjahr *n*	année *f* légale
legend	Bildunterschrift *f*, Legende *f*	légende *f*
legibility	Lesbarkeit *f*	lisibilité *f*
leisure time	Rubrik *f* für Mußestunden *f/pl*	rubrique *f* des loisirs *m/pl*
leisure time publicity	Werbung *f* für den Freizeitbereich *m*	publicité *f* du domaine *m* des loisirs *m/pl*
leitmotif	Leitmotiv *n*	leitmotiv *m*
lemon	minderwertiges Produkt *n*	produit *m* de mauvaise qualité *f*
lender	Verleiher *m*	distributeur *m*, prêteur *m*
length	Höhe *f*, Länge *f*, Zeilenbreite *f*	hauteur *f*, justification *f* de la colonne *f*, longueur *f*
length of line	Zeilenlänge *f*	justification *f*, longueur *f* de ligne *f*
length of the advertising film	Werbefilmlänge *f*	métrage *m*
length of time	Dauer *f*	durée *f*
length of visibility	Sichtweite *f*	longueur *f* de visibilité *f*
lessee	Pächter *m*	concessionaire *m*
to **let drop**	Tisch *m*, fallen lassen unter den	écraser un papier *m*, passer sous silence *m*
letter	Buchstabe *m*, Letter *f*, Type *f*	caractère *m*, lettre *f*, type *m*
to **letter**	beschriften	mettre une inscription *f* sur
letter designer	Buchstabenzeichner *m*	lettriste *m*
letter enclosure	Briefbeilage *f*	annexe *f*
letter of confirmation	Bestätigungsschreiben *n*	lettre *f* de confirmation *f*
letter of thanks *pl*	Dankschreiben *n*	lettre *f* de remerciement *m*
letter press	Druckmaschine *f*	machine *f* à imprimer
letter press printing	Buchdruck *m*	impression *f* typographique, typographie *f*
letter shop	Adressenverkauf *m*	vente *f* d'adresses *f/pl*
letter spacing	Sperrung *f*	espacement *m*
letter telegram	Brieftelegramm *n*	lettre *f* télégraphique

letter to the editor	Leserzuschrift f	lettre f à la rédaction f
letter-bag	Leserbriefspalte f	colonne f des lettres f/pl à la rédaction f, courrier m des lecteurs m/pl
letter-case	Schriftkasten m	casse f
letter-cutter	Bestoßhobel m	coupoir m
letter-file	Briefordner m, Schnellhefter m	classeur m de lettres f/pl, classeur-relieur m
letter-foundry	Schriftgießerei f	fonderie f
letter-heading	Briefkopf m	en-tête f de lettre f
lettering	Beschriftung f	inscription f
lettering artist	Schriftenmaler m, Schriftenzeichner m	dessinateur m en lettres f/pl, lettreur m
lettering brush	Schriftpinsel m	pinceau m à lettres f/pl
lettering man	Schriftsetzer m, Schriftzeichner m	compositeur m, lettreur m, lettriste m, typographe m
letterpress	Typografie f	typographie f
letterpress poster	Textplakat n	affiche-texte f
letterpress printer	Buchdrucker m	imprimeur m
letters pl column	Leserbriefspalte f	colonne f des lettres f/pl à la rédaction f, courrier m des lecteurs m/pl
letter-set proof	Satzabzug m	épreuve f de la composition f
lettersheet	Briefbogen m	feuille f à lettres f/pl
letting	Vermietung f	location f
level	Niveau n	niveau m
level of education	Bildungsgrad m	dégré m de culture f
level of market demand	Marktlage f	situation f du marché m
level printing	Flachdruck m	impression f à plat, impression f planographique
levelling	Nivellierung f	nivellement m
lexicographer	Wörterbuchverfasser m	lexicographe m
lexicon	Lexikon n	encyclopédie f, lexique m
liability for damages pl	Haftung f für Schäden m/pl	responsabilité f pour dommages m/pl
liability for insufficiencies pl	Haftung f für Mängel m/pl	responsabilité f pour insuffisances f/pl
liaison man	Kontakter m, Kontaktmann m, Verbindungsmann m	contacteur m, homme m de relation f
libel	Ehrabschneidung f, Verleumdung f	calomnie f, diffamation f
librarian	Bibliothekar m	bibliothécaire m
library	Bibliothek f, Bücherei f	bibliothèque f
libretto	Textbuch n	libretto m, livret m
license	Lizenz f	licence f
license fee	Genehmigungsgebühr f	droit m de voirie f
licensed edition	Lizenzausgabe f	édition f licenciée
licensee	Lizenzträger m	porteur m d'une licence f
licensing	Konzessionierung f	attribution f d'une concession f
life story	Szene f aus dem täglichen Leben n	scène f de la vie f de tous les jours m/pl
ligature	Ligatur f	deux lettres f/pl ligaturées, ligature f
light	mager	maigre, mince
to light	beleuchten	éclairer
light drawing	Lichtzeichnung f	dessin m phototechnique
light reading	leichte Lektüre f	lecture f récréative

light reading weekly	Regenbogenpresse *f*, Sorayapresse *f*	feuille *f* hebdomadaire divertissante
light-faced type	lichte Schrift *f*	caractères *m/pl* éclairés
lighting	Beleuchtung *f*	éclairage *m*, illumination *f*
limitation	Beschränkung *f*	limitation *f*, restriction *f*
limited	begrenzt	limité
limited edition	beschränkte Auflage *f*	édition *f* à tirage *m* limité
line	Linie *f*, Warensortiment *n*, Zeile *f*	choix *m* de marchandises *f/pl*, filet *m* (typogr.) , ligne *f*
to **line**	kaschieren	doubler, encoller
line advertising	Produktwerbung *f*	publicité *f* produits *m/pl*
line and wash drawing	aquarellierte Strichzeichnung *f*	dessin *m* au trait *m* aquarellé
line block *brit*	Strichätzung *f*	cliché *m* au trait *m*, gravure *f* au trait *m*
line border	Linienrand *m*	bordure *f* en filets *m/pl*, cadre *m* de filets *m/pl*
line cut *am*	Strichätzung *f*	cliché *m* au trait *m*, gravure *f* au trait *m*
line drawing	Strichzeichnung *f*	dessin *m* au trait *m*
line engraving *am*, **line etching**	Strichätzung *f*	cliché *m* au trait *m*, gravure *f* au trait *m*
line measure	Zeilenmesser *m*	lignomètre *m*, typomètre *m*
line plate	Strichätzung *f*	cliché *m* au trait *m*, gravure *f* au trait *m*
line tester	Fadenzähler *m*	compte-fils *m*
lineage	Anzeigenraum *m*, Zeilenzahl *f*	espace *m* d'annonces *f/pl*, lignage *m*, nombre *f* de lignes *f/pl*
lineage of an advertisement	Gesamtinhalt *m* einer Anzeige *f*	lignage *m* d'une annonce *f*
linear	linear	linéaire
linen	Leinwand *f*	écran *m*, toile *f*
linen poster	Leinwandplakat *n*	affiche *f* toile
linen-paper	Leinenpapier *n*	papier *m* entoilé
line-space	Reglette *f*	interligne *f*, réglette *f*
to **line-up**	unterlegen	charger, garnir
linguistic	sprachwissenschaftlich	linguistique
lining paper	Überzugpapier *n*	papier *m* couverture *f*
lino printing	Linoleumdruck *m*	impression *f* de linoléum *m*
lino-cut	Linolschnitt *m*	gravure *f* sur lino *m*
linotype	Zeilenguß-Setzmaschine *f*	linotype *f*
linotype composition	Linotypesatz *m*	composition *f* linotype *f*
linotype machine	Linotypemaschine *f*	machine *f* linotype
linotype operator	Linotypesetzer *m*	linotypiste *m*
list	Aufstellung *f*, Liste *f*, Verzeichnis *n*	inventaire *m*, liste *f*, relevé *m*
list of addresses *pl*	Adressenliste *f*	liste *f* d'adresses *f/pl*
list of advertisers *pl*	Inserentenverzeichnis *n*	répertoire *m* des annonceurs *m/pl*
list of references *pl*	Quellenverzeichnis *n*	table *f* des sources *f/pl*
list of subscribers *pl*	Abonnentenkartei *f*	fichier *m* des abonnés *m/pl*
list of suppliers *pl*	Bezugsquellenverzeichnis *n*	liste *f* des fournisseurs *m/pl*, répertoire *m* de fournisseurs *m/pl*
list price	Katalogpreis *m*	prix *m* au catalogue *m*

list-broking	Adressenkartei — Vermietung *f*, Kundenadressen-Austausch *m*	bail *m* de fichiers *m/pl* d'adresses *f/pl*, échange *m* des adresses *f/pl* de clients *m/pl*
listener	Hörer *m*, Rundfunkhörer *m*, Zuhörer *m*	auditeur *m*
listenership research	Höreranalyse *f*	recherches *f/pl* relatives à l'audience *f*
listening area	Sendebereich *m*	région *f* d'émission *f* radiophonique
listening habits *pl*	Zuhörergewohnheiten *f/pl*	habitudes *f/pl* d'écoute *f*
listening panel	Hörerpanel *n*	groupe *m* de test *m* des auditeurs *m/pl*, panel *m* des auditeurs *m/pl*
listing	Standortverzeichnis *n*	liste *f* d'emplacements *m/pl*
listprice	Listenpreis *m*	prix *m* au tarif *m*, prix *m* de barème *m*
literary editor	Feuilletonredakteur *m*	rédacteur *m* du feuilleton *m*
literary supplement	Literaturbeilage *f*	supplément *m* littéraire
literature	Schrifttum *n*	lettres *f/pl*, littérature *f*
litho	Lithografie *f*	litho *f*, lithographie *f*
lithographer	Lithograf *m*	lithographe *m*
lithographic design	Steinzeichnung *f*	dessin *m* lithographique
lithographic plant	lithografische Anstalt *f*	atelier *m* de lithographie *f*
lithographic print	Steindruck *m*	lithographie *f*
lithography	Lithografie *f*, Steindruck *m*	litho *f*, lithographie *f*
lithography drawn on plate	Autolithografie *f*	autolithographie *f*
live broadcast	Direktübertragung *f*, Live-Sendung *f*	émission *f* en direct, prise *f* de vue *f* directe
live matter	Stehsatz *m*	composition *f* conservée, composition *f* permanente, conserve *f*
live transmission	Originalsendung *f*	émission *f* en direct
living screen	Laterna *f* magica	combinaison *f* du cinéma *m* et d'acteurs *m/pl*, lanterne *f* magique
living standard	Lebensstandard *m*	standard *m* de vie *f*
lobby journalist	Parlamentsjournalist *m*	rédacteur *m* parlementaire
lobbying	Lobbyismus *m*	intrigues *m/pl* de couloirs *m/pl*
lobbyist	Interessenvertreter *m*	agent *m* qui essaie d'influencer les députés *m/pl*
lobster shift	Dienst *m* nach Mitternacht *f*	service *m* après minuit *m*
local advertisement	örtliche Anzeige *f*	annonce *f* locale
local advertising	Lokalwerbung *f*, Ortsanzeigen *f/pl*	publicité *f* locale
local call	Ortsverbindung *f*	communication *f* locale
local campaign	örtliche Werbung *f*	campagne *f* locale
local colour	Lokalkolorit *n*	couleur *f* locale
local editor	Lokalredakteur *m*	rédacteur *m* local
local issue	Bezirksausgabe *f*	édition *f* départementale, édition *f* locale
local item	Lokaltratsch *m*	faits *m/pl* divers locals
local news	Lokalnachrichten *f/pl*	chronique *f* locale
local paper	Heimatzeitung *f*, Lokalzeitung *f*, Ortszeitung *f*	feuille *f* locale, journal *m* local
local patriotism	Lokalpatriotismus *m*	rivalités *f/pl* de clocher *m*

local rag	Käseblättchen n, Winkelblatt n	feuille f de chou m, presse f de réputation f douteuse
local rate	Lokaltarif m	tarif m local
localization	Lokalisierung f	localisation f
location	Standort m	position f, stationnement m
to lock up a form	Form f schließen	boucler une page f, serrer une forme f
locked-up form	geschlossene Satzform f	forme f serrée
logotype	Firmenschriftzug m, Logotype f, Markenzeichen n, Namenszug m	logotype m, vignette f
long approach site	weite Sichtbarkeit f	visibilité f étendue
long primer (see appendix)	Garmond f (siehe Anhang)	corps m 10 points m/pl (voir appendice)
long seller	langlebiges Buch n	livre m durable
long-range effect	Fernwirkung f	effet m à distance f
long-term	langfristig	à long terme m, à longue échéance f
longtime-effect	Langzeitwirkung f	effet m continué
long-winded	langatmig	de longue haleine f
looking time	Betrachtungszeit f	temps m d'observation f
loop-hole in the market	Marktlücke f	lacune f dans le marché m
loose	lockere Manier f, zusammenhanglos	déconsu, d'une manière f dissolue
loose insert	lose Beilage f	encart m libre
loose translation	Übersetzung f, freie	traduction f libre
loose-leaf book	Loseblattbuch n	livre m à feuilles f/pl mobiles
loose-leaf catalogue	Katalog m mit losen Seiten f/pl	catalogue m à feuillets m/pl mobiles
loss leader	Anreizartikel m, Köder m, Lockartikel m	appât m, article m d'appel m, article m de réclame f, leurre m, marchandise f d'appel m, produit m d'appel m
lottery-ticket	Lotterielos n	billet m de loterie f
loudspeaker advertising	Lautsprecherwerbung f	publicité f par haut-parleur m
love story	Liebesgeschichte f	histoire f d'amour m
love-lorn editor	Redakteur m der Seufzerspalte f	titulaire m du courrier m du cœur m
low	niedrig	bas
low key	Foto n in dunklen Tönen m/pl	photo f en tons m/pl obscurs
lower case letters pl	Kleinbuchstaben m, gemeine Buchstaben m/pl	minuscules f/pl, lettres f/pl bas-de-casse f
lower class	untere Schicht f	les basses classes f/pl
lower corner	untere Ecke f	coin m inférieur, coin m intérieur
lucky find	Fundgrube f	trouvaille f
lucrative advertising	einträgliche Werbung f	publicité f rentable
luggage-rack	Gepäckhalter m	porte-bagages m/pl
to lumbeck	lumbecken	relier par collage m
Lumbeck binding	Lumbeckheftung f	brochage m Lumbeck
luminescent lamp	Leuchtstoffröhre f	tube m fluorescent
luminous ink, luminous paint	Leuchtfarbe f	encre f lumineuse
luminous signs pl	Leuchtschrift f	annonce f lumineuse

lump sum	Pauschalsumme *f*	somme *f* globale
lump sum price	Pauschalpreis *m*	prix *m* forfaitaire
lump-sugar packing	Würfelzuckerverpackung *f*	emballage *m* des portions *f/pl* de sucre *m*
lure	Köder *m*, Lockartikel *m*	appât *m*, article *m* d'appel *m*, article *m* de réclame *f*, leurre *m*, produit *m* d'appel *m*
luxury goods *pl*	Luxuswaren *f/pl*	articles *m/pl* de luxe *m*
luxury paper	Luxusblatt *n*	journal *m* luxueux, périodique *m* de luxe *m*
lying advertising	lügnerische Werbung *f*	publicité *f* mensongère

M

M. F. (machine finished) paper	maschinenglattes Papier *m*	papier *m* apprêté machine *f*
machinator	Drahtzieher *m*	intrigant *m*, machinateur *m*
machine composition	Maschinensatz *m*	composition *f* à la machine *f*, composition *f* mécanique
machine glazed (M.G.)	einseitig Glanz *m*	frictionné
machine washing	Maschinenreinigung *f*	lavage *m* de machine *f*
machine-compositor	Maschinensetzer *m*	claviste *m*, opérateur *m*
mackling	Druckdublee *n*	doublage *m*
magazine	Magazin *n*, Zeitschrift *f*	magazine *m*, périodique *m*, revue *f*
magazine advertising	Zeitschriftenwerbung *f*	publicité *f* dans les revues *f/pl*
magazine of general interest	Familienblatt *n*	feuille *f* familiale, revue *f* d'intérêt *m* général
magazine rack	Zeitschriftenständer *m*	casier *m* à revues *f/pl*
magnetic film spool	Magnetfilmspule *f*	bobine *f* de la bande *f* magnétique
magnetic sign	Magnetschild *n*	écriteau *m* aimanté
magnetic tape	Magnetband *n*	bande *f* magnétique vidéo, ruban *m* magnétique
magnetic tape cassette	Magnetbandkassette *f*	cassette *f* à bandes *f/pl* magnétiques
magnetophone	Magnetofon *n*	magnétophone *m*
mail circulation	Versandauflage *f*	circulation *f* postale
mail distribution	Postwurfsendungen *f/pl*	distribution *f* postale de messages *m/pl* non adressés, publicité *f* directe par voie *f* postale
mail edition	Postausgabe *f*	première édition *f* du matin *m*
mail order advertising	Versandhauswerbung *f*	publicité *f* de vente *f* par correspondance *f*
mail order house	Versandhaus *n*	maison *f* de vente *f* par correspondance *f*, maison *f* d'expédition *f*
mail order trade	Versandhandel *m*	vente *f* par correspondance *f*
mail research, mail survey	briefliche Befragung *f*, schriftliche Befragung *f*	enquête *f* postale, recherche *f* par lettre *f*
mailing	werbliche Postaussendung *f*, Zeitungsversand *m*	publipostage *m*, routage *m*
mailing index	Versandliste *f*	liste *f* d'adresses *f/pl*
mailing list	Adressenliste *f*	liste *f* d'adresses *f/pl*
mailing list control	Adressenkontrolle *f*	contrôle *m* des adresses *f/pl*

mailing piece	Postwurfsendungen *f/pl*	distribution *f* postale de messages *m/pl* non adressés, publicité *f* directe par voie *f* postale
mailing shot	Direktwerbung *f* durch die Post *f*	publicité *f* directe par la poste *f*
mail-order catalogue	Versandhauskatalog *m*	catalogue *m* d'une maison *f* d'expédition *f*
main edition	Hauptausgabe *f*	feuille *f* principale
main market	Hauptabsatzgebiet *m*	marché *m* principal
main type	Grundschrift *f*	caractère *m* principal
maintenance	Instandhaltung *f*	entretien *m*
maintenance advertising	Erhaltungswerbung *f*	publicité *f* de maintien *m*
make	Marke *f*, Warenzeichen *n*	marque *f*, marque *f* de fabrique *f*
to **make a print**	abziehen (Foto)	faire une épreuve *f*
to **make a slip of the tongue**	versprechen, sich	se tromper en parlant
to **make a splash**	Aufmachung *f* bringen, in großer	mettre en manchette *f*
to **make blocks** *pl*	klischieren	clicher, faire un cliché *m*
to **make cuts** *pl*	beschneiden	ébarber, rogner, taillader, tailler
to **make light**	verniedlichen	bagatelliser, minimiser
to **make out**	ausstellen (Rechnung *f*)	établir
to **make pass false for right**	Türken *m/pl* bauen	faire passer quelque chose *f* de faux pour vrai, feindre, simuler
to **make propaganda**	die Werbetrommel *f* rühren	battre la grosse caisse *f*
to **make ready**	Einrichten *n* der Druckmaschine *f*, zurichten	calage *m*, mettre en page *f*, mettre en train *m*
make up	Aufmachung *f*, Umbruch *m*	arrangement *m*, imposition *f*, mise *f* en page *f*, présentation *f*
to **make up**	aufmachen, umbrechen	arranger, mettre en pages *f/pl*, présenter, sortir de la ligne *f*
make-good	Ersatzanzeige *f*	gratuité *f* de compensation *f*, ré-insertion *f*
make-over	überarbeiteter Text *m*	copie *f* remaniée
maker	Fabrikant *m*	constructeur *m*, fabricant *m*
make-ready	Zurichtung *f*	mise *f* en train *m*
maker-up	Metteur *m*	imposeur *m*, metteur *m* en pages *f/pl*
makeshift	Provisorium *n*	état *m* provisoire
make-up	Ausstattung *f*, Klebespiegel *m*	maquette *f*, présentation *f*
make-up display terminal	Umbruch-Bildschirmgerät *n*	écran *m* de visualisation *f* de la mise *f* en pages *f/pl*
make-up editor	Umbruchredakteur *m*	maquettiste *m*
make-up galley	Setzschiff *n*	galée *f*
make-up hand	Metteur *m*	imposeur *m*, metteur *m* en pages *f/pl*
make-up screen	Umbruch-Bildschirm *m*	écran *m* de la mise *f* en pages *f/pl*
make-up section	Mettageabteilung *f*	département *m* de mise *f* en pages *f/pl*
make-up terminal	Umbruchgerät *n*	machine *f* de la mise *f* en pages *f/pl*
making up table	Umbruchtisch *m*	marbre *m* de mise *f* en pages *f/pl*

mammoth poster	Mammutplakat *n*	affiche *f* mammouth
man of letters *pl*	Literat *m*	homme *m* de lettres *f/pl*
man of straw	Strohmann *m*	prête-nom *m*
management	Direktion *f*, Geschäftsführung *f*, Unternehmensführung *f*	direction *f*, gérance *f*, gestion *f*, gestion *f* de l'entreprise *f*, manutention *f*
management counsellor, management consultant	Unternehmensberater *m*	conseil *m* en gestion *f*, conseiller *m* d'entreprise *f*
manager	Direktor *m*, Manager *m*	directeur *m*, gestionnaire *m*
managing editor	Chef *m* vom Dienst *m*, geschäftsführender Redakteur *m*, Herausgeber *m*, Redaktionsdirektor *m*	chef *m* de service *m*, gérant *m*, rédacteur *m* gérant
manila paper	Manilapapier *n*	papier *m* bulle *f*
to manipulate	manipulieren	manipuler
mannequin	Mannequin *m*, Modell *n*, Vorführdame *f*, Werbedame *f*	démonstratrice *f*, mannequin *m*, modèle *m*
man-on-street	Mann *m* auf der Straße *f*	citoyen *m* moyen, homme *m* de la rue *f*
manual	Handbuch *n*, Leitfaden *m*	guide *m*, manuel *m*, vade-mecum *m*
manual typesetting	Handsatz *m*	composition *f* à la main *f*, composition *f* manuelle
manufacturer	Fabrikant *m*	constructeur *m*, fabricant *m*
manufacturer's brand	Fabrikmarke *f*	marque *f* de fabricant *m*
manufacturing costs *pl*	Herstellungskosten *pl*	frais *pl* de fabrication *f*, prix *m* de fabrication *f*
manufacturing process	Herstellungsverfahren *n*	procédé *m* de fabrication *f*
manuscript	Manuskript *n*	copie *f*, manuscrit *m*, ms
map	Landkarte *f*	carte *f*
map paper	Landkartenpapier *n*	papier *m* pour cartes *f/pl* géographiques
map printing	Kartografie *f*	cartographie *f*
marbled paper	marmoriertes Papier *n*	papier *m* marbré
mare's nest	Seeschlange *f/fig*, Zeitungsente *f*	bobard *m*, canard *m*, serpent *m* de la mer *f*
margin	unbedruckter Rand *m*	bord *m*, marge *f*
margin stop	Anlegeapparat *m*	margeur *m*, régulateur *m* de marges *f/pl*
marginal note	Randbemerkung *f*, Marginalie *f*	note *f* marginale
mark	Zeichen *n*	indice *m*, marque *f*, signe *m*
mark down	Preisherabsetzung *f*	réduction *f* de prix *m*
mark of origin	Herkunftszeichen *n*	marque *f* d'origine *f*
mark up	Preiserhöhung *f*	augmentation *f* de prix *m*
marked list	Belegungsliste *f*	pointage *m*
market	Markt *m*	débouché *m*, marché *m*
market analysis	Absatzanalyse *f*, Marktanalyse *f*, Marktforschung *f*	analyse *f* du marché *m*, étude *f* du marché *m*, recherche *f* du marché *m*
market analyst	Marktanalytiker *m*	analyste *m* du marché *m*
market condition	Marktlage *f*	situation *f* du marché *m*
market extension	Marktausweitung *f*	expansion *f* du marché *m*
market fluctuation	Absatzschwankung *f*	fluctuations *f/pl* des ventes *f/pl*
market investigation	Marktuntersuchung *f*	enquête *f* sur le marché *m*
market monopoly	Monopol *n*	monopole *m*

market observation	Marktbeobachtung f	observation f du marché m
market report	Marktbericht m	bulletin m financier
market research	Marktforschung f	étude f du marché m, recherche f du marché m
market research counsellor	Marktforschungsberater m	conseil m en études f/pl de marché m
market research institute	Marktforschungsinstitut n	institut m d'études f/pl de marché m
market researcher	Marktforscher m	enquêteur m commercial
market saturation	Marktsättigung f	encombrement m du marché m
market segment	Marktsegment n	segment m du marché m
market share	Marktanteil m	part f de marché m, quote-part f
market standard	Marktgeltung f	importance f au marché m
market survey	Marktuntersuchung f	enquête f sur le marché m
market vacillation	Konjunkturschwankung f	variation f de la conjoncture f
marketable	marktgerecht	vendable
marketing	Absatzbemühungen f/pl, Marketing n, Marktfähigmachung f, Marktgestaltung f, Marktplanung f, Marktschaffung f	commercialisation f, marketing m
marketing background	Marktlage f	situation f du marché m
marketing concept	Marketingkonzeption n	conception f marketing
marketing consultant	Absatzberater m, Berater m für Marktverhalten n, Marktberater m	conseil m en marketing m
marketing control	Absatzkontrolle f	contrôle m de la vente f
marketing department	Marketingabteilung f, Vertriebsabteilung f	bureau m marketing, service m de la vente f
marketing mix	Marketingmix n	marketing m mix m
marketing plan	Marketingplan m	plan m de marketing m
marketing policy	Marketingpolitik f	politique f de marketing m
marketing research	Absatzforschung f	étude f de marché m
marketing strategy	Absatzstrategie f, Marketingstrategie f, Marktstrategie f	stratégie f de distribution f, stratégie f de marché m, stratégie f marketing
marketing techniques pl	Absatzmethoden f/pl	méthode f de distribution f
marketing-gap	Marktlücke f	lacune f dans le marché m
marketing-mix	Marktplan m	marketing m mix
marking ink	Stempelfarbe f	encre f à tampons m/pl
marocco leather	Maroquin n	maroquin m
marriage	Verschmelzung f zweier Entwürfe m/pl	fonte f de deux dessins m/pl
marriage advertisement	Heiratsanzeige f	annonce f matrimoniale, faire-part m de marriage m
mask	Abdeckmaske f, Abdeckung f, Decker m, Vignette f	cache f, dégradé m, détourage m, fleuron m, masque m, vignette f
to mask out	abdecken, ausdecken	caviarder, couvrir, masquer, recouvrir
masked advertising	Schleichwerbung f	publicité f camouflée, publicité f clandestine, publicité f déguisée, publicité f occulte, publicité f subversive
masking frame	Abdeckrahmen m	cache f, frisquette f

masking paper	Abdeckpapier *n*	papier-cache *m*
masking tape	Abdeckstreifen *m*	bande *f* à masquer
mass advertising	geballte Werbung *f*	campagne *f* de saturation *f*
mass circulation	Massenauflage *f*	gros tirage *m*
mass communication	Massenkommunikation *f*	communication *f* de masse *f*
mass craziness	Massenwahn *m*	folie *f* grégaire
mass edition	Massenauflage *f*	gros tirage *m*
mass mailing	Massenversand *m*	envoi *m* en masse *f*
mass medium	Massenmedium *n*	mass-média *m*
mass produced article	Serienartikel *m*	article *m* de série *f*
mass product	Massenprodukt *n*	produit *m* de grande consommation *f*
mass selling	Massenabsatz *m*	vente *f* massive
mass suggestion	Massensuggestion *f*	suggestion *f* grégaire
mass-circulation	hohe Auflage *f*	haut tirage *m*
mass-display	Warenanhäufung *f*	entassement *m* de produits *m*/*pl*, exposition *f* en masse *f*, présentation *f* de masse *f*
mast head	Zeitungskopf *m*	en-tête *f*, manchette *f*
master plate	Originalklischee *n*	cliché *m* original
master print	Fotoabzug *m*	épreuve *f* de photo *f*
master-work	Meisterwerk *n*	chef *m* d'œuvre *f*
masthead	Titelleiste *f*	cartouche *f* de titre *m*
mat *am*	Mater *f*	flan *m*, matrice *f*
mat board	Matrizenkarton *m*	flan *m*
mat service	Maternkorrespondenz *f*	service *m* matrice
mat surface	matte Oberfläche *f*	surface *f* mate
to match	vergleichen	collationner, comparer
matchbox advertising	Zündholzwerbung *f*	publicité *f* sur feuillets *m*/*pl* d'allumettes *f*/*pl*
matching design	Farbharmonie *f*	harmonie *f* des couleurs *f*/*pl*
material	Unterlagen *f*/*pl*	matériel *m*
material for exhibitions *pl*	Ausstellungsmaterial *n*	matériel *m* de vitrine *f*, matériel *m* d'exposition *f*
matrix	Mater *f*, Matrize *f*	flan *m*, matrice *f*, stencil *m*
matrix board	Maternpappe *f*	carton *m* pour flans *m*/*pl*
matrix service	Materndienst *m*	service *m* de matrices *f*/*pl*
matt art paper	Papier *n*, mattes	papier *m* couché mat
matt print	Mattkopie *f*	épreuve *f* sur papier *m* mat
matter	bewußte Angelegenheit *f*, Drucksatz *m*, Text *m*	affaire *f*, affaire *f* en question *f*, composition *f*, copie *f*, texte *m*
maturity	Fälligkeit *f*	échéance *f*
maximum lineage	Höchstgröße *f*	lignage *m* maximum
maximum rebate	Höchstrabatt *m*	rabais *m* maximum
maximum size	Höchstformat *n*	format *m* maximum
maximum weight	Höchstgewicht *n*	poids *m* maximum
meaning of a word	Wortsinn *m*	sens *m* littéral
means *pl* of advertising	Werbeträger *m*	organe *m* de publicité *f*, support *m* publicitaire, véhicule *m* de communication *f*
means *pl* of communication	Kommunikationsmittel *n*	moyen *m* de communication *f*, véhicule *m* de communication *f*
means *pl* of expression	Ausdrucksmittel *n*	moyen *m* d'expression *f*

measure	Satzbreite *f*, Zeilenbreite *f*	justification *f*, justification *f* de la colonne *f*, largeur *f* de la composition *f*
mechanical advertising	bewegliche Werbung *f*, mechanische Werbung *f*	publicité *f* mécanique, publicité *f* mobile
mechanical composition *am*	Maschinensatz *m*	composition *f* à la machine *f*, composition *f* mécanique
mechanical data *pl*	technische Daten *m/pl*	données *f/pl* techniques, renseignements *m/pl* techniques
mechanical typesetting	Maschinensatz *m*	composition *f* à la machine *f*, composition *f* mécanique
medal	Medaille *f*	médaille *f*
media allocation	Werbeetat *m*, Werbeetataufzeichnung *f*	budget *m* publicitaire
media analysis	Mediaanalyse *f*, Werbeträgeranalyse *f*	analyse *f* des médias *m/pl*
media audience accumulation	Zielgruppenkombination *f* von Medien *n/pl*	combinaison *f* de cibles *f/pl* publicitaires
media clerk	Mediasachbearbeiter *m*	acheteur *m* d'espace *m*
media comparison	Medienvergleich *m*	comparaison *f* des médias *m/pl*
media contact	Werbeträgerkontakt *m*	contact *m* au média *m*
media department	Medienabteilung *f*, Streuabteilung *f*	service *m* médias *m/pl*
media director	Leiter *m* der Mediaabteilung *f*	chef *m* du service *m* médias *m/pl*
media discount	Agenturprovision *f*, Mittlervergütung *f*	commission *f* d'agence *f*
media evaluation	Werbeträgerbewertung *f*	évaluation *f* des médias *m/pl*
media executive	Streuplaner *m*	directeur *m* des médias *m/pl*
media man	Mediasachbearbeiter *m*, Streuungsfachmann *m*	acheteur *m* d'espace *m*, expert *m* en médias *m/pl*
media manager	Medialeiter *m*	directeur *m* des médias *m/pl*
media mix	Mediakombination *f*, Werbemittelkombination *f*, Werbeträgerkombination *f*	combinaison *f* des médias *m/pl*
media performance	Mediaeinsatz *m*, Werbeträgereinsatz *m*	accomplissement *m* publicitaire, emploi *m* des médias *m/pl*
media plan	Mediaplan *m*	plan *m* média *m*
media planner	Mediaplaner *m*	media-planneur *m*
media planning	Mediaplanung *f*, Streuplanung *f*	plan *m* de campagne *f*, plan *m* des supports *m/pl*
media platform	Mediaplattform *f*	plate-forme *f* média *m*
media *pl* **production**	Werbemittelherstellung *f*	production *f* des moyens *m/pl* de publicité *f*
media research	Mediaforschung *f*, Werbeträgerforschung *f*	étude *f* des médias *m/pl*
media scenery	Medienlandschaft *f*	paysage *m* des médias *m/pl*
media schedule	Etatverteilung *f*, Streuplan *m*	calendrier *m* d'insertion *f*, plan *m* de diffusion *f*, répartition *f* de budget *m*
media selection	Mediaauswahl *f*, Mediaselektion *f*	choix *m* des médias *m/pl*, sélection *f* des médias *m/pl*
media strategy	Mediastrategie *f*	orchestration *f* des différents supports *m/pl*

media supervisor	Leiter *m* einer Mediagruppe *f*	chef *m* d'un groupe *m* médias *m/pl*
media survey	Werbeträgerforschung *f*	étude *f* des médias *m/pl*
media user	Medianutzer *m*	usager *m* de médias *m/pl*
media weight	Mediengewicht *f*	poids *m* d'un média *m*
medial section	goldener Schnitt *m*	sectio *m* aurea
medical journal	medizinische Zeitschrift *f*	publication *f* médicale
medium	halbfett, Medium *n*, Organ *n*	demi-gras, média *m*, mi-gras, organe *m*, publication *f*, support *m* de publicité *f*
medium faced type	halbfette Schrift *f*	caractères *m/pl* quart-gras
medium of information	Informationsmedium *n*	moyen *m* d'information *f*
medium-faced type	Schrift *f*, halbfette	caractères *m/pl* quart-gras
medium-size	mittleres Format *n*	de moyen format *m*
meeting	Besprechung *f*, Konferenz *f*, Sitzung *f*, Versammlung *f*, Zusammenkunft *f*	assemblée *f*, conférence *f*, discussion *f*, entretien *m*, entrevue *f*, réunion *f*, séance *f*, session *f*
meeting-place	Treffpunkt *m*	rendez-vous *m*
member of a group of publishers *pl*	angeschlossene Zeitung *f*	membre *m* d'un cercle *m* d'édition *f*
memorandum	Denkschrift *f*, Memorandum *n*	aide-mémoire *m*, exposé *m*, mémoire *m*, mémorandum *m*
memorandum book	Agenda *f*, Notizbuch *n*	agenda *m*, calepin *m*, carnet *m*
memory aid	Gedächtnishilfe *f*	moyen *m* mnémotechnique
memory value	Erinnerungswert *m*	souvenir *m* laissé, valeur *f* de mémorisation *f*, valeur *f* de rappel *m*
mental horizon	Gesichtskreis *m*	horizon *m*
mental reservation	Hintergedanke *m*	arrière-pensée *f*
mental set	Einstellung *f*	attitude *f*, opinion *f*
mentality	Geisteshaltung *f*	mentalité *f*
mention	Erwähnung *f*	citation *f*, mention *f*
menu card	Speisekarte *f*	carte *f*, menu *m*
merchandise appeal	Kaufanreiz *m*	incitation *f* à l'achat *m*
merchandizer	Warengestalter *m*	styliste *m* de marchandise *f*
merchandizing	absatzpolitische Maßnahmen *f/pl*, Absatzvorbereitung *f* durch Vertriebsplannung *f*, Einzelhändlerunterstützung *f*, Maßnahmen *f/pl* zur Steigerung *f* des Absatzes *m* beim Einzelhandel *m*, Warendarbietung *f*, Warengestaltung *f*	conditionnement *m* d'une marchandise *f*, contexture *f* d'un produit *m*, mise *f* en valeur *f*, moyens *m/pl* pour aider à la revente *f* par le détaillant *m*, présentation *f* de la marchandise *f*, techniques *f/pl* marchandes
merger	Fusionierung *f*	fusion *f*
merger movement	Fusionsbestrebungen *f/pl*	tendances *f/pl* de fusion *f*
message	Botschaft *f*	message *m*
messenger	Bote *m*	courrier *m*, messager *m*
metal block, metal cut	Metallklischee *n*	cliché *m* métal *m*
metal log	Metallblock *m*	bloc *m* de métal *m*
metal quoin	Schließzeug *n*	serrage *m*
metal sheet	Blechplatte *f*	tôle *f* métallique
metal sign	Metallschild *n*	enseigne *f* métallique

metal-decorating	Blechdruck *m*	impression *f* sur fer-blanc *m*, impression *f* sur tôle *f*
metallic ink	Bronzefarbe *f*	couleur *f* de bronze *m*
metamorphosis	Verwandlung *f*	métamorphose *f*
metaphor	bildlicher Ausdruck *m*	métaphore *f*
metaphorisch	metaphorisch	métaphorique
method of operation	Arbeitsweise *f*	manière *f* de travailler
metric volume	Format *n* der Anschlagstellen *f/pl*, Meterzahl *f*	métrage *m*
metropolitan dailies *pl*	Großstadtpresse *f*	presse *f* urbaine, quotidiens *m/pl* métropolitains
mezzotint technique	Schabemanier *f*	manière *f* noire, mezzoteinte, trait *m* anglais
microfilm	Mikrofilm *m*	microfilm *m*
microgroove	Langspielplatte *f*	microsillon *m*
middle-class	bürgerlich, Mittelstand *m*	bourgeois *m*
middleman	Zwischenhändler *m*	intermédiaire *m*
mike	Mikrofon *n*	microphone *m*
mike fever	Mikrofonfieber *n*	trac *m* devant le micro *m*
to **mill**	fräsen	fraiser
millboard	Pappe *f*	carton *m*
millimetre line	Millimeterzeile *f*	ligne *f* millimètre *m*
to **mimeograph**	vervielfältigen	multicopier, multiplier, polycopier, reproduire
miniature	Miniatur *f*	miniature *f*
miniature edition	Miniaturausgabe *f*	édition *f* minuscule
to **minimise**	verkleinern	diminuer, rapetisser, réduire
minimum circulation	Mindestauflage *f*	tirage *m* minimum *m*
minimum cliché	Minimalklischee *n*	cliché *m* minimum
minimum contract	Mindestabschluß *m*	commande *f* minimale, contrat *m* minimum
minimum length	Mindesthöhe *f*	hauteur *f* minimum *m*
minimum lineage	Mindestgröße *f*	lignage *f* minimum *m*
minimum period of display	Mindestanschlagdauer *f*	conservation *f* minimum
minimum rate	Mindestpreis *m*	prix *m* minimum
minimum tariff	Minimaltarif *m*	tarif *m* minimal
minimum width	Mindestbreite *f*	largeur *f* minimum *m*
Minion (see appendix)	Kolonel *f* (Mignon) (siehe Anhang)	corps 7 points (voir appendice)
minuscule	Kleinbuchstabe *m*	lettre *f* bas de casse *f*, minuscule *f*
minute movie	Filmlet *n*, kurzer Werbefilm *m*, Kurzfilm *m*	court-métrage *m*
miscellaneous column	Verschiedenes *n*	pêle-mêle *m*
miscellaneous items *pl* **miscellanies** *pl*	Vermischtes *n*	faits divers *m/pl*, miscellanées *f/pl*
miscellany	Sammelband *m*	collection *f*, recueil *m* en un volume *m*
misdoings *pl* **of advertising**	Reklameauswüchse *m/pl*	excès *m* de la publicité *f*, méfaits *m/pl* de la publicité *f*
misinterpretation	Mißdeutung *f*	contresens *m*
to **mislead**	irreführen	tromper

misleading advertising	irreführende Werbung f, täuschende Werbung f	publicité f déloyale, publicité f fallacieuse, publicité f mensongère, publicité f trompeuse
misleading pricing	Mondpreis m	prix m de fantaisie f
misplaced advertising	falsch angesetzte Werbung f	publicité f déplacée
misplaced line	verhobene Zeile f	ligne f transposée
misprint	Druckfehler m, Fehldruck m, Makulatur f	coquille f, erreur f de composition f, faute f d'impression f, faute f typographique, impression f manquée, maculature f, papier m de rebut m
to misprint	verdrucken	faire de la maculature f
misrepresentation	falsche Darstellung f	faux rapport m
missing word	Leiche f (Auslassung f)	bourdon m
misunderstanding	Mißverständnis n	quiproquo m
misuse	Mißbrauch m	mauvais usage m
to mix to brit	weiche Bildüberblendung f	fondu m enchaîné
mixed matter	gemischter Satz m	composition f lardée, composition f mêlée
mixing of sounds pl	Tonmischung f	mixage m
mixture	gemischter Satz m	composition f lardée, composition f mêlée
mobile	Aufhängedekoration f, Mobile n	décoration f mobile, mobile m, rotair m
mobile shop	fahrbare Verkaufsstelle f, Wanderladen m	boutique f mobile, camionnette f -boutique f
mocking	Verspottung f	persiflage m
mock-up	Schaupackung f	attrape f, boîte f factice, emballage m factice
mode of payment	Zahlungsweise f	mode m de paiement m
model	Modell n	mannequin m, modèle m
model agency	Modellagentur f	agence de modèles m/pl
moderator	Diskussionsleiter m	directeur m d'une discussion f
modernisation	Modernisierung f	modernisation f
to modify	abändern	modifier
moiré	Moiré n	moiré m
moiré effect	Schnürlmoiré n	moirage m
moist from ink	druckfeucht	humide d'encre f grasse
monitor	Kontrollautsprecher m, Kontrollbildschirm m, Monitor m	écran m de contrôle m, haut-parleur m de contrôle m, moniteur m
monitor man	Toningenieur m	ingénieur m du son m
monochrome	einfarbig	monochrome, unicolore
monograph	Monographie f	monographie f
monopolistic journal	Monopolzeitung f	journal m monopolisateur
monopoly price	Monopolpreis m	prix m de monopole m
monotype	Typenguß-Setzmaschine f	monotype f
monotype caster	Monotype-Gießmaschine f	fondeuse f monotype
monotype composition	Monotypesatz m	composition f monotype f
monotype keyboard	Monotype-Setzmaschine f	composeuse f monotype
month	Monat m	mois m
monthly	monatlich	mensuel
monthly paper	Monatsschrift f	revue f mensuelle
more to come	Fortsetzung f folgt	à suivre, complément de texte m suivra

morning newspaper	Morgenzeitung *f*	journal *m* du matin *m*
mortality of journals *pl*	Zeitungssterben *n*	mortalité *f* des journaux *m/pl*
to mortise	ausklinken	encocher, entailler
most read paper	meistgelesene Zeitung *f*	journal *m* le plus lu
motion	Bewegung *f*	mouvement *m*
motion picture	Film *m*	film *m*
to motivate	motivieren	motiver
motivation	Motivierung *f*, Verhaltensgrund *m*	motivation *f*
motivation research	Motivforschung *f*	étude *f* de motivation *f*
motive	Beweggrund *m*, Motiv *n*	motif *m*
motive analyst	Motivforscher *m*	enquêteur *m* de motivation *f*
motor-show	Autosalon *m*	salon *m* de l'automobile *f*
motto	Motto *n*, Wahlspruch *m*	devise *f*, épigraphe *f*
mould	Gießform *f*, Matrize *f*	matrice *f*, moule *m*, stencil *m*
to mould	matern	mouler
mould made paper	Maschinenbüttenpapier *n*	papier *m* à la cuve *f* à la machine *f*
mount	Grundgestell *n*	socle *m*
to mount	aufklotzen, aufziehen (Foto), montieren	clouer, monter
mounted block	montiertes Klischee *n*	cliché *m* monté
mounted on metal	Bleifuß *m*, auf	monté sur plomb *m*
mounting	Montage *f*, Stativ *n*	montage *m*, pied *m* photographique, trépied *m*
mouthpiece	Sprachrohr *n*	porte-parole *m*, porte-voix *m*
to move down	tiefer stellen	placer plus bas
to move to the left	nach links ausschließen	justifier à la gauche
to move to the right	nach rechts ausschließen	justifier à droite
to move up	höher stellen	placer plus haut
movement	Bewegung *f*	mouvement *m*
movie	Film *m*	film *m*
movie audience	Kinopublikum *n*	public *m* des cinémas *m/pl*
movie film clip	Standfoto *n*	photo *f* de plateau *m*, photo *f* de scène *f*
movie theater	Kino *n*, Lichtspielhaus *n*	cinéma *m*
movies	Kino *n*, Lichtspielhaus *n*	cinéma *m*
moving picture advertising	Filmwerbung *f*	publicité *f* à l'écran *m*, publicité *f* cinématographique, publicité *f* par film *m*
MS	Manuskript *n*	copie *f*, manuscrit *m*, ms
muckraker	Sensationspresse *f*	presse *f* à sensation *f*, presse *f* jaune
multi processing	Simultanverarbeitung *f*	élaboration *f* simultanément, traitement *m* simultané
multi-colour printing	Mehrfarbendruck *m*	impression *f* en couleurs *f/pl*, impression *f* multicolore
multicoloured	mehrfarbig	multicolore, polychrome
multilith	Rotaprintverfahren *n*	multilithe *m*
multipack, multiple unit item	Mehrstückpackung *f*	plusieurs pièces *f/pl* dans un même emballage *m*
multiple colour press	Mehrfarben-Druckpresse *f*	rotative *f* hélio en couleur *f*
multiplication	Vervielfältigung *f*	multicopie *f*, multiplication *f*, polycopie *f*
multiplicity	Vielfältigkeit *f*	multiplicité *f*

multi-purpose hall	Mehrzweckhalle *f*	hall *m* à usage *m* multiple
mummy	Auftraggeber *m* eines Ghostwriters *m*	commettant *m* d'un nègre *m*
music in advertising	Werbemusik *f*	publicité *f* musicale
music paper	Notenpapier *n*	papier *m* à musique *f*
musical setting	Vertonung *f*	addition *f* du ton *m*, mise *f* en musique *f*, sonorisation *f*
mutilated text	verstümmelter Text *m*	texte *m* mutilé
mutiple image	Mehrfachbild *n* eines Firmen- oder Personennamens *m*	image *f* multiple d'un nom *m* de maison *f* ou de produit *m*
muzzling of the press	Presseknebelung *f*	baîllonnement *m* de la presse *f*, muselement *m* de la presse *f*
mystery-monger	Geheimniskrämer *m*	cachottier *m*

N

name of a product	Produktname *m*	nom *m* de produit *m*
name plate	Firmenschild *n*, Firmentafel *f*	buteau *m*, enseigne *f*, enseigne *f* commerciale, panneau *m* d'entreprise *f*
name slug	Namenszug *m*	logotype *m*, vignette *f*
national campaign	überregionaler Werbefeldzug *m*	campagne *f* nationale
national media *pl*	national verbreitete Medien *n/pl*	médias *m/pl* répandus dans tout le pays *m*
national newspaper	überregionale Zeitung *f*	grand quotidien *m* national
national press	überregionale Presse *f*	presse *f* nationale
national print run	Inlandsauflage *f*	tirage *m* national
nation-wide advertising	überregionale Werbung *f*	publicité *f* nationale
need	Bedarf *m*	besoin *m*
negative	Negativ *n*	négatif *m*
negative plate	Negativklischee *n*	cliché *m* négatif, cliché *m* noir au blanc
negative retouching	Negativretusche *f*	retouche *f* sur négatif *m*
negative type	Negativschrift *f*	caractère *m* négatif
to negotiate	aushandeln, vermitteln	entremettre, marchander, négocier
negotiation	Verhandlung *f*	négociation *f*
negotiator	Unterhändler *m*, Vermittler *m*	entremetteur *m*, négociateur *m*
neologism	Wortneubildung *f*	néologisme *m*
neon sign	Neon-Leuchtschild *n*	enseigne *f* au néon *m*
neon tubing	Neonlichtwerbung *f*	publicité *f* par tube *m* néon
net circulation	Nettoauflage *f*	tirage *m* net
net coverage	Nettoreichweite *f*	couverture *f* nette
net price, net rate	Nettopreis *m*	prix *m* net
network	Sendernetz *n*, Stellennetz *n*	circuit *m* indivisible d'emplacements *m/pl*, réseau *m*
neutral	überparteilich	au-dessus des partis *m/pl*, neutre
new edition	Neuauflage *f*, Neudruck *m*	nouvelle édition *f*, réimpression *f*
new formulation	Neufassung *f*	nouvelle rédaction *f*, réfection *f*
new impression	Wiederabdruck *m*	réimpression *f*
newcomer	Neuling *m*	néophyte *m*, nouveau venu

news	Nachricht *f*	nouvelle *f*
news agency	Nachrichtenbüro *n*, Pressedienst *m*	agence *f* d'information *f*, service *m* de presse *f*
news analyst	Nachrichtenkommentator *m*	commentateur *m* des nouvelles *f/pl*
news blackout	Nachrichtensperre *f*	black-out *m*, blocus *m* de nouvelles *f/pl*
news boy	Zeitungsjunge *m*	vendeur *m* de journaux *m/pl*
news bulletin	Nachrichtensendung *f*	bulletin *m* d'actualités *f/pl*, journal *m* parlé, transmission *f* des informations *f/pl*
news by electric sign	Wanderschriftnachrichten *f/pl*	information *f* lumineuse, journal *m* lumineux
news commentator	Nachrichtenkommentator *m*	commentateur *m* des nouvelles *f/pl*
news compositor	Nachrichtensetzer *m*	canardier *m*
news editor	Nachrichtenredakteur *m*	rédacteur *m* au desk *m*, rédacteur *m* aux informations *f/pl*
news flash	Kurzdepesche *f*	flash *m*
news hot from the press	brandneue Nachrichten *f/pl*	nouvelles *f/pl* toutes chaudes
news house	Zeitungsdruckerei *f*	imprimerie *f* d'un journal *m*
news in brief	Kurznachrichten *f/pl*	faits divers *m/pl*, nouvelles *f/pl* brèves
news item	Zeitungsnotiz *f*	communiqué *m* de presse *f*, nouvelle *f*
news magazine	Nachrichtenmagazin *n*	magazine *f* d'information *f*
news management	Manipulation *f* von Nachrichten *f/pl*, Nachrichtenmanipulation *f*	manipulation *f* de nouvelles *f/pl*, manipulation *f* des informations *f/pl*
news monger	Neuigkeitskrämer *m*	colporteur *m* de nouvelles *f/pl*
news release	Bekanntmachung *f*, Pressenotiz *f*	communiqué *m*, entrefilet *m*
news report	Meldung *f*	information *f*, nouvelle *f*
news sent by cable	Kabelnachricht *f*	information *f* câblée
news service	Nachrichtendienst *m*	service *m* des nouvelles *f/pl*
news stand *am*	Kiosk *m*	kiosque *m*
news stand sales *pl*	Einzelverkauf *m* (Zeitungen)	vente *f* au kiosque *m*, vente *f* au numéro *m*
news stock	Zeitungspapier *n*	papier *m* journal *m*, papier *m* rugueux
news summary	Nachrichtenübersicht *f*	sommaire *m* des nouvelles *f/pl*
news transmitting	Nachrichtenübermittlung *f*	radiocommunication *f*, transmission *f* des informations *f/pl*
news value	Informationswert *m*, Neuigkeitswert *m*	valeur *f* de nouvelle *f*, valeur *f* d'information *f*, valeur *f* indicative
news-butcher	ambulanter Zeitungsverkäufer *m*	vendeur *m* ambulant de journaux *m/pl*
newscast	Nachrichtensendung *f*	bulletin *m* d'actualités *f/pl*, journal *m* parlé, transmission *f* des informations *f/pl*
newscaster	Nachrichtensprecher *m*	présentateur *m* du journal *m* parlé

newsdealer *am*	Zeitungshändler *m*, Zeitungsverkäufer *m*	marchand *m* de journaux *m/pl*, vendeur *m* de journaux *m/pl*
newshawk	Reporter *m*	reporter *m*
newshole	Raum *m*, für redaktionellen Text *m* verfügbarer	espace *m* disponible pour la rédaction *f*
newshound	Reporter *m*	reporter *m*
newsletter	Informationsblatt *n*, Informationsorgan *n*	bulletin *m* d'information *f*
newspaper	Zeitung *f*	gazette *f*, journal *m*
newspaper agency	Zeitungsagentur *f*	agence *f* d'un journal *m*
newspaper archives *pl*	Zeitungsarchiv *n*	archive *f* des journaux *m/pl*, documentation *f* de presse *f*
newspaper article	Zeitungsartikel *m*	article *m* de journal *m*
newspaper heading	Zeitungskopf *m*	en-tête *f*, manchette *f*
newspaper man	Journalist *m*	journaliste *m*
newspaper merger	Zeitungsfusion *f*	fusion *f* de journaux *m/pl*
newspaper notice	Pressenotiz *f*	entrefilet *m*
newspaper of a world-wide reputation	Weltblatt *n*	feuille *f* de réputation *f* mondiale
newspaper of record	oft zitiertes Blatt *n*	journal *m* sérieux qu'on cite
newspaper owner	Zeitungsverleger *m*	éditeur *m* d'un journal *m*
newspaper packet	Zeitungsdrucksache *f*	expédition *f* sous bande *f*
newspaper poster	Zeitungsplakat *n*	affiche *f* de journal *m*
newspaper press	Nachrichtenpresse *f*	presse *f* d'information *f*
newspaper production	Zeitungsherstellung *f*	confection *f* du journal *m*
newspaper publisher *am*	Zeitungsverleger *m*	éditeur *m* d'un journal *m*
newspaper rack	Zeitungsregal *n*	casier *m* à journaux *m/pl*
newspaper reader	Zeitungsleser *m*	lecteur *m* de journaux *m/pl*
newspaper shelf	Zeitungsschrank *m*	étagère *f* à journaux *m/pl*
newspaper size	Zeitungsformat *n*	format *m* journal *m*
newspaper slot-machine	Zeitungsautomat *m*	distributeur *m* de journaux *m/pl* automatique
newspaper technique	Zeitungstechnik *f*	technique *f* du journal *m*
newspaper wholesaler	Grosso *n*	commerce *m* de journaux *m/pl* en gros
newspaper wholesaling	Pressevertrieb *m*	colportage *m*, messagerie *f*
newspaper with concentration of its readership in a large territory	Blockzeitung *f*	journal *m* d'une concentration *f* de lecteurs *m/pl* dans un grand territoire *m*
newspaper-holder	Zeitungshalter *m*, Zeitungsspanner *m*	porte-journaux *m*, tringle *f* à journaux *m/pl*
newspapermen *pl*	Zeitungsleute *pl*	monde *m* de la presse *f*
newspaper's office	Annahmestelle *f*	bureau *m* du journal *m*
newsprint paper	Rotationspapier *n*, Zeitungsdruckpapier *n*, Zeitungspapier *n*	papier *m* journal *m*, papier *m* pour impression *f* rotative, papier *m* rugueux
newsprint screen	Zeitungsraster *m*	trame *f* journal *m*
newsreader	Nachrichtensprecher *m*	présentateur *m* du journal *m* parlé
news-reel	Wochenschau *f*	actualités *f/pl*
newsreel company	Wochenschaugesellschaft *f*	société *f* ayant pour objet *m* les actualités *f/pl*
news-room	Zeitungslesesaal *m*	salle *f* des journaux *m/pl*
newsstall	Zeitungsstand *m*	aubette *f*, débit *m* de journaux *m/pl*, kiosque *m* à journaux *m/pl*, stand *m*

newsstand *am*	Zeitungskiosk *m*, Zeitungsstand *m*	aubette *f*, débit *m* de journaux *m/pl*, kiosque *m* à journaux *m/pl*, stand *m*
newsvendor	Zeitungshändler *m*, Zeitungsverkäufer *m*	marchand *m* de journaux *m/pl*, vendeur *m* de journaux *m/pl*
New-Year's greeting card	Neujahrskarte *f*	carte *f* de Nouvel-An *m*
next to editorial matter	gegenüber Text *m*	contre texte *m*, face *f* texte *m*
next to reading matter	textanschließend, Text *m*, neben	à côté *m* du texte *m*, après texte *m*, contre texte *m*, se joignant au texte *m*, sous le texte *m*
nick	Signatur *f* (Buch *n*)	cran *m*
nickel electro, nickel-faced stereo	Nickelgalvano *n*	galvano-nickel *m*, stéréonickel *m*
night edition	Nachtausgabe *f*	édition *f* de nuit *f*
night editor	Nachtredakteur *m*	rédacteur *m* de nuit *f*
noisy advertising	marktschreierische Werbung *f*, Werberummel *m*	battage *m* publicitaire, bourrage *m* de crâne *m*, publicité *f* raccrocheuse, publicité *f* tapageuse, tam-tam *m*
non plus ultra (see appendix)	Viertelpetit *f* (siehe Anhang)	corps 2 points (voir appendice)
non-appeared	nicht erschienen	non-paru
non-committal	zurückhaltend	qui ne prend pas position *f*
nondurable goods *pl*	Verbrauchsgüter *n/pl*	biens *m/pl* de consommation *f*
nonfiction	Sachbuchliteratur *f*	littérature *f* spécialisée
non-folded	ungefalzt	non plié
non-partisan	unparteiisch, überparteilich	au-dessus des partis *m/pl*, impartial, neutre
non-performance of an order	Nichtausführung *f* eines Auftrages *m*	non-exécution *f* d'une commande *f*
non-political	unpolitisch	sans étiquette *f* politique
non-printing	nichtdruckend	en blanc
non-returnable package	Einwegpackung *f*	emballage *m* non repris, emballage *m* perdu
non-selective advertising	ungezielte Werbung *f*	publicité *f* non-sélective
non-stop cinema	Aktualitätenkino *n*, Kino *n* mit ununterbrochenem Programm *n*, Ohne-Pause-Kino *n*	cinéma *m* avec un programme *m* sans arrêt *m*, cinéma *m* d'actualités *f/pl*, cinéma *m* sans arrêt *m*
nonwrinkle posting	faltenfreier Anschlag *m*	affichage *m* sans plis *m/pl*
noon paper	Mittagsblatt *n*	journal *m* de midi *m*
nose	Gespür *n*	flair *m*
nose count	Nasenzählen *n*	évaluation *f* approximative «à vue *f* de nez» *m* du nombre *m* des présents *m/pl*
nosy	Schnüffler *m*	fouinard *m*
not for sale	unverkäuflich	invendable
notch	Einschnitt *m*	entaille *f*
note	Anmerkung *f*	note *f*
note-book	Notizbuch *n*	agenda *m*, calepin *m*, carnet *m*
notehead	Notenkopf *m*	tête *f* de note *f*
note-paper	Briefpapier *n*	papier *m* à lettres *f/pl*
notice board	Anschlagtafel *f*, Schwarzes Brett *n*	panneau *m* d'affichage *m*, porte-affiches *m*, tableau *m* noir
notices *pl* of new publications *pl*	Literaturblatt *n*	bulletin *m* littéraire

notices *pl* on wall	Wandanschlag *m*	avis *m* placardé
notion	Begriff *m*	notion *f*
novel	Roman *m*	roman *m*
novel in continuations *pl*	Fortsetzungsroman *m*	roman-feuilleton *m*, roman *m* à suites *f/pl*
novelty	Geschenkartikel *m*, Werbegeschenkartikel *m*	article *m* -cadeau *m*, article *m* prime *f*
novelty advertising	Warenprobenverteilung *f*	publicité *f* par l'objet *m*
number	Ausgabe *f* (Nummer), Zahl *f*	chiffre *m*, édition *f*, exemplaire *m*, nombre *m*, numéro *m*
to number	numerieren	numéroter
number of columns *pl*	Spaltenanzahl *f*	nombre *m* des colonnes *f/pl*
number of lines *pl*	Zeilenzahl *f*	lignage *m*, nombre *f* de lignes *f/pl*
number of pieces *pl*	Stückzahl *f*	nombre *m* des pièces *f/pl*
number of postal district	Postleitzahl *f*	numéro *m* du secteur *m* postal
number of subscribers *pl*	Abonnentenzahl *f*	nombre *m* des abonnés *m/pl*
number of words *pl*	Wortzahl *f*	nombre *m* de mots *m/pl*
to number pages *pl*	paginieren	folioter, marquer les pages *f/pl*, paginer
numbering	Numerierung *f*	numérotage *m*, numérotation *f*
numbering machine	Numeriermaschine *f*	machine *f* à numéroter
numbering of sites *pl*	Stellennumerierung *f*	immatriculation *f* des emplacements *m/pl*
numeral	Ziffer *f*	chiffre *m*
nylon block	Nylonklischee *n*	cliché *m* nylon
nylonprint	Kunststoffklischee *n*	cliché *m* plastique

O

o. k. to print	Imprimatur *n*	bon à tirer, permission *f* d'imprimer
o. k. with corrections *pl am*	nach Korrektur *f* druckreif	bon à tirer après corrections *f/pl*
obituary notice	Nachruf *m*, Todesanzeige *f*	annonce *f* de décès *m*, annonce *f* nécrologique, nécrologe *m*
objectivity	Objektivität *f*	objectivité *f*
obligatory advertisement	Pflichtanzeige *f*	annonce *f* obligatoire
obligatory copy	Pflichtexemplar *n*	exemplaire *m* obligatoire
obligatory media *pl*	obligatorische Werbeträger *m/pl*	médias *m/pl* obligatoires
obligatory subscription	Pflichtabonnement *n*	abonnement *m* obligatoire
oblique stroke	Bruchstrich *m*, Schrägstrich *m*	barre *f* de fraction *f* oblique
obliterated passage	getilgte Stelle *f*	caviar *m*
oblong size	Langformat *n*	format *m* oblong
observation	Beobachtung *f*	observation *f*
observations *pl*	Bemerkungen *f/pl*	observations *f/pl*
obsolescence	Veralten *n*	obsolescence *f*
obsolete word	veraltetes Wort *n*	mot *m* désuet
obstructed site	verdeckter Anschlag *m*	emplacement *m* masqué
obtrusive advertising	zudringliche Werbung *f*	publicité *f* obsessionnelle
occasional publication	Gelegenheitspublikation *f*	publication *f* occasionnelle
occasional reader	Gelegenheitsleser *m*	lecteur *m* occasionnel
occupational group	Berufsgruppe *f*	catégorie *f* professionnelle
octave	Oktavformat *n*	octavo *m*
odd number	ungerade Zahl *f*	nombre *m* impair

odd page	rechte Seite *f*, ungerade Seite *f*	bonne page *f*, page *f* de droite, page *f* impaire, recto
off mike	Tonausfall *m*	absence *f* du son *m*
off season	tote Saison *f*	hors saison *f*, morte-saison *f*
off the record information	vertrauliche Information *f*	information *f* confidentielle
off-center arrangement	asymmetrische Anordnung *f*	arrangement *m* asymétrique
offcut	Abfall *m*, Papierabschnitt *m*	chute *f* de papier *m*, déchet *m*, reste *m* de papier *m*
offer	Angebot *n*, Offerte *f*	devis *m*, offre *f*
to **offer**	anbieten	offrir
offer case	Angebotsmappe *f*	carton *m* pour des offres *f/pl*
offer without obligation	freibleibendes Angebot *n*	offre *f* sans engagement *m*
off-hand speech	Stegreifrede *f*	discours *m* impromptu
office	Geschäftsstelle *f*	agence *f*, bureau *m*
official announcement	amtliche Anzeige *f*	annonce *f* légale
official gazette	Amtsblatt *n*	bulletin *m* officiel
official news	amtliche Nachrichten *f/pl*	nouvelles *f/pl* authentiques
official notice	amtliche Bekanntmachung *f*, amtliches Plakat *n*	affiche *f* officielle, avis *m* officiel
official organ	amtliches Organ *n*	organe *m* officiel
official poster	amtliches Plakat *n*	affiche *f* officielle, avis *m* officiel
official publicity bureau	Werbestelle *f*	office *m* de publicité *f*
official statement	Kommuniqué *n*, Presseverlautbarung *f*	communiqué *m*, déclaration *f* à la presse *f*
officious	offiziös	officieux, semi-officiel
off-label deal	Reduzierung *f* des Preises *m* gegenüber dem auf Packung *f* oder Etikett *f* angegebenen	réduction *f* de prix *m* signalé sur le conditionnement *m* ou l'étiquette *f*
off-print	Separatdruck *m*, Sonderdruck *m*	édition *f* à part *f*, tirage *m* à part *f*, tirage *m* spécial
offset deep printing	Offsettiefdruck *m*	impression *f* offset en creux *m*
offset paper	Offsetpapier *n*	papier *m* pour offset *m*
offset printer	Offsetdrucker *m*	imprimeur *m* offset
offset printing	Gummidruck *m*, Offsetdruck *m*	impression *f* offset, offset lithographie *f*, tirage *m* report *m*
offset printing-down process	Offsetkopierverfahren *n*	procédé *m* de copie *f* offset
offset repro machine	Umdruckapparat *m*	appareil *m* à reporter, reporteur *m*
offset rotary printing	Rollenoffset *n*	technique-offset *m* à cylindres *m/pl*
offset transparency	Film *m* (für Offset *m*)	plat *m*, typon *m*
off-stage	inoffiziell	non officiellement
oil color (am)	Ölmalfarbe *f*	couleur *f* à l'huile *f*
oil colour	Ölmalfarbe *f*	couleur *f* à l'huile *f*
oil painting	Ölbild *n*	peinture *f* à l'huile *f*
oil print	Ölfarbendruck *m*	impression *f* aux encres *f/pl*
oil-colour	Ölfarbe *f*, Ölmalfarbe *f*	couleur *f* à l'huile *f*
oiled paper	Ölpapier *n*	papier *m* huilé
o.k. am	druckreif	bon à tirer, prêt à imprimer
old black type	altgotische Schrift *f*	caractères *m/pl* gothiques
old book	Schmöker *m*	bouquin *m*
old English face	gotische Schrift *f*	caractères *m/pl* gothiques

old face	Mediäval f	caractère m mediéval, Elzévir m
old face type	Antiqua f	caractère m ancien, caractère m romain
old fashioned	altmodisch	démodé
old metal	Altzeug n	vieille matière f
old style	Mediäval f	caractère m mediéval, Elzévir m
oleography	Öldruck m	chromolithographie f, oléographie f
omission	Leiche f (Auslassung f)	bourdon m
to omit	weglassen	omettre
omitted word in composition	Schusterjunge m /typog	bourdon m
omnibus order	Sammelauftrag m	commande f groupée, ordre m collectif
omnibus survey	Mehrthemenumfrage f	enquête f omnibus
on commission	auf Provisionsbasis f	à la commission f
on the air, to be	Radiowerbung f betreiben, Rundfunk m sprechen, im	annoncer par radio f, avoir l'antenne f
ondulated frame	Wellenrand m	cadre m ondulé
one column wide	einspaltig	à une colonne f, sur une col f
one man show	Einmannschau f	solo m
one way package	Einwegpackung f	emballage m non repris, emballage m perdu
one-price	Festpreis m	prix m fixe, prix m imposé
one's own advertisement	Eigenanzeige f	propre annonce f
one-side coated paper	einseitig gestrichenes Papier n	satiné d'un côté m
one-side print	Einblattdruck m	feuille f imprimée au recto m seulement
one-third-page	Drittelseite f	tiers m de page f
one-time rate	Einzelpreis m	tarif m de base f, tarif m fixe
one-way package	Wegwerfpackung f	emballage m non consigné, emballage m perdu
onionskin	Luftpostpapier n	papier m -pelure f, papier m avion m
on-pack premium	Prämie f auf der Verpackung f	prime f attachée à l'emballage m
on-premise sign	Ladenschild n	enseigne f de magasin m
opacity	Undurchsichtigkeit f	opacité f
opaque	undurchsichtig	non transparent, opaque
opaque ink	Deckfarbe f	encre f opaque
opaque paper	nicht durchscheinendes Papier n	papier m opaque
open display	offene Auslage f	exposition f libre
open end commercial	Werbefilm m mit Händleradresse f	film m publicitaire avec adresse f du détaillant m
open forum	freie Aussprache f, Leserforum n	point m de vue f des lecteurs m /pl, tribune f libre
open order	Auftrag m auf Widerruf m	ordre m valable jusqu'à révocation f
open rate	Anzeigengrundpreis m, Einzelpreis m	tarif m de base f, tarif m fixe
open terms pl	Zahlungsziel n	terme m de règlement m
opening	Doppelseite f	pages f /pl en regard m
opening phase	Auftakt m	ouverture f
open-spaced setting	perlender Satz m, spationierter Satz m	composition f espacée
open-time rate am	Grundpreis m	prix m de base f, tarif m fixe
operating process	Arbeitsvorgang m	mode m de travail m
operator	Maschinensetzer m, Setzer m	claviste m, compositeur m, opérateur m, typographe m

operator of advertising films *pl*	Werbeverwaltung *f* von Kinos *n/pl*	concessionaire *m* de salle *f*
opinion	Meinung *f*	opinion *f*
opinion leader	Meinungsbildner *m*, Meinungsmacher *m*	faiseur *m* d'opinion *f*
opinion paper	Meinungsblatt *n*	organe *m* d'opinion *f*
opinion poll	Demoskopie *f*, Meinungsforschung *f*, Meinungsumfrage *f*	enquête *f* sur les opinions *f/pl*, sondage *m* de l'opinion *f* publique, sondage *m* d'opinion *f*
opinion press	Gesinnungspresse *f*	presse *f* d'opinion *f*
opinion research	Demoskopie *f*, Meinungsforschung *f*	enquête *f* sur les opinions *f/pl*, sondage *m* de l'opinion *f* publique, sondage *m* d'opinion *f*
opinion survey	Meinungsumfrage *f*	enquête *f* sur les opinions *f/pl*
opinion test	Meinungstest *m*	test *m* d'opinion *f*
opportunist	Gesinnungslump *m*	opportuniste *m*
opportunity advertising	Gelegenheitswerbung *f*	publicité *f* d'opportunité *f*
opportunity to see	Sichtmöglichkeit *f*, Werbeträgerkontakt *m*	contact *m* au média *m*, occasion *f* de voir
opposite page	gegenüberliegende Seite *f*	ci contre
opposite text	gegenüber Text *m*	contre texte *m*, face *f* texte *m*
opposition paper	Oppositionsblatt *n*	feuille *f* d'opposition *f*
optimum number	Bestzahl *f*	nombre *m* optimal
optimum price	Optimalpreis *m*	prix *m* optimum
oracle	Videotext *m*	antiope *m*
oral interview	mündliche Befragung *f*	interrogatoire *m* direct, interview *f* orale
order	Auftrag *m*, Bestellung *f*, Reihenfolge *f*	commande *f*, commission *f*, ordre *m*, suite *f*
to order	bestellen	commander
to order an advertisement	Inserat *n* aufgeben	remettre une annonce *f*
order by telephone	telefonische Bestellung *f*	commande *f* téléphonique
order by wire	telegrafisch erteilter Auftrag *m*	commande *f* télégraphique
order by word of mouth	mündlich erteilter Auftrag *m*	commande *f* verbale
order coupon	Bestellabschnitt *m*	coupon *m* détachable de commande *f*
order department	Auftragsabteilung *f*	service *m* des commandes *f/pl*
order filling	Auftragserledigung *f*	réalisation *f* de commandes *f/pl*
order form	Auftragsformular *n*, Bestellkarte *f*, Bestellschein *m*	bon *m* de commande *f*, carte *f* de commande *f*
order number	Auftragsnummer *f*	numéro *m* de la commande *f*
order of merit test	Rangordnungsprüfung *f*	épreuve *f* de l'ordre *m* de préséance *f*
order of merit-rating	Einstufung *f* von Anzeigenentwürfen *m/pl*	classification *f* de dessins *m/pl* publicitaires
order of precedence	Rangordnung *f*	hiérarchie *f*, ordre de préséance *f*
order processing	Auftragsabwicklung *f*	exécution *f* d'un ordre *m*
order register	Auftragskartei *f*	fichier *m* des commandes *f/pl* en exécution *f*
order without obligation	freibleibender Auftrag *m*	ordre *m* sans engagement *m*
order-book	Auftragsbuch *n*, Bestellbuch *n*	carnet *m* de commandes *f/pl*
ordinary position	Plazierung *f* im Anzeigenteil *m*	emplacement *m* ordinaire

ordinary type	Brotschrift *f*	caractères *m/pl* courants, caractères *m/pl* de labeur *m*
organ of a corporation	Verbandsblatt *n*	feuille *f* corporative, journal *m* d'association *f*
organization	Organisation *f*	organisation *f*
organization set-up	Organisationsschema *n*	organigramme *m*
to organize	organisieren	organiser
organizer	Veranstalter *m*	organisateur *m*
orientation	Orientierung *f*	orientation *f*
origin	Herkunft *f*	origine *f*
original	Original *n*	document *m*
original block	Originalklischee *n*	cliché *m* original
original copy	Originalmanuskript *n*, Originaltext *m*	copie *f* originale, texte *m* original
original edition	Originalausgabe *f*	édition *f* originale
original manuscript	Urschrift *f*	autographe *m*
original package	Originalpackung *f*, Originalverpackung *f*	emballage *m* d'origine *f*
original text	Urtext *m*	original *m*
original wrapping	Originalverpackung *f*	emballage *m* d'origine *f*
origination	Entstehung *f*	naissance *f*
ornament	Ornament *m*, Vignette *f*	cache *f*, dégradé *m*, fleuron *m*, ornement *m*, vignette *f*
to ornament	verzieren	orner
ornamental borders *pl*	Schmuckleiste *f*	filet *m* orné
ornamental letter	Zierbuchstabe *m*	italique *f* de fantaisie *f*, lettre *f* à queue *f*, lettre *f* ornée
ornamental rule	Zierlinie *f*	filet *m* orné
ornamental type	Zierschrift *f*	caractère *m* de fantaisie *f*, caractères *m/pl* ornés
out	Auslassung *f*, Leiche *f*	bourdon *m*
outdoor advertising	Außenwerbung *f*	publicité *f* extérieure
outdoor advertising plant	Außenwerbungsunternehmen *n*	entrepreneur *m* de publicité *f* extérieure
outdoor duty	Außendienst *m*	service *m* extérieur
outdoor photo	Außenaufnahme *f*	photo *f* en plein air *m*
outdoor sign	Außenschild *n*	enseigne *f*, panneau *m*
outer form	Vorderseite *f*	côté *m* de première, première page *f*
outlet	Absatzgebiet *n*, Markt *m*, Vertriebsstelle *f*	débouché *m*, marché *m*
outline	Bildunterschrift *f*, Entwurf *m*, Skizze *f*, umstochen	croquis *m*, dessin *m*, ébauche *f*, épreuve *f*, esquisse *f*, fileté, légende *f*, maquette *f*, projet *m*
to outline	entwerfen, skizzieren	dessiner, ébaucher, élaborer, esquisser
outline half-tone	freistehende Autotypie *f*	autotypie *f* en silhouette *f*, simili *m* détouré
outlined cut	freistehendes Klischee *n*	cliché *m* détouré, cliché *m* isolé
out-of-date	veraltet	périmé, vieilli
out-of-fashion	altmodisch	démodé

out-of-print	vergriffen	épuisé
out-of-register	fehlerhaftes Register *n*	fausse marge *f*, registre *m* défectueux
out-of-stock	vergriffen	épuisé
output	Ausgabe *f/typog*	information *f* traitée
outside artist	freier künstlerischer Mitarbeiter *m*	collaborateur *m* artistique à son compte *m*
outside broadcast	Außenbericht *m*, Fernsehreportage *f*, Rundfunkübertragung *f*	reportage *m* en extérieur, téléreportage *m*, transmission *f* radiophonique
outside margin	äußerer Papierrand *m*, Außensteg *m*	marge *f* extérieure
outside position	Außenspalte *f*	bord *m* extérieur
outsider	Außenseiter *m*	non-conformiste *m*, outsider *m*
over and next text matter	über und neben Text *m*	au-dessus et à côté *m* du texte *m*
over copies *pl*	überschüssige Nummern *f/pl*	exemplaires *m/pl* de passe *f*
overcommercialization	Überkommerzialisierung *f*	commercialisation *f* exagérée
over-elaborate	gekünstelt	tarabiscoté
overexposure	Überbelichtung *f*	surexposition *f*
overflow indication	Überlauf-Anzeige *f*	indication *f* de dépassement *m*
overhang covers *pl*	überstehender Umschlag *m*	couverture *f* à rabats *m/pl*, couverture *f* débordante
overhead	gekabelte Nachrichten *f/pl*	nouvelles *f/pl* câblées
to **overlap**	überlappen	chevaucher, recouvrir
overlapping	Überlappung *f*, Überschneidung *f*	double emploi *m*, duplication *f*, imbrication *f*, recouvrement *m*
overlay	Auflegemaske *f*, Decker *m*, Tektur *f*, Überkleber *m*	cache *f*, masque *m*, papillon *m*
overprint	Aufdruck *m*, Mehrdruck *m*, Überdruck *m* (Aufdruck)	repiquage *m*, surimpression *f*
to **overprint**	überdrucken	surimprimer
overprinting	überkopieren	surimpression *f*
overquire	überzählige Exemplare *n/pl*	main *f* de passe *f*
overrun	Remittenden *f/pl*	bouillon *m*, invendus *pl*, rendus *pl*
to **overrun**	neu umbrechen	remanier
to **overrun lines** *pl*	Zeilen *f/pl* umbrechen	remanier
overs *pl*	Mehrauflage *f*, Zuschuß *m* (Überschuß *m*)	chaperon *m*, excédant *m* de tirage *m*, passe *f*
oversaturation with advertising	Werbemüdigkeit *f*	saturation *f* publicitaire
oversea edition	Überseeausgabe *f*	édition *f* pour outre -mer *m*
overseer of composing room	Faktor *m/typog m*	prote *m*
overstatement	Übertreibung *f*	exagération *f*
overstepping of estimate	Kostenüberschreitung *f*	dépassement *m* du devis *m*
own brand	Eigenmarke *f*	marque *f* de distributeur *m*
owner of site	Flächengesteller *m*	propriétaire *m* d'emplacement *m*
owner-editor	Verlagsinhaber *m*	directeur-propriétaire *m*
ozalide	Blaupause *f*	cyanotypie *f*, ozalide *m*

P

pack	Packung *f*	emballage *m*, paquetage *m*
to **pack**	verpacken	emballer

package	Packung f, Verpackung f	conditionnement m, emballage m, paquetage m
package advertising	Werbung f auf Packungen f/pl	publicité f sur l'emballage m
package deal	Paketangebot n	contrat m global
package insert	Packungsbeilage f	encart m dans un emballage m, papillon m
package tour	Pauschalreise f	voyage m organisé
packaged goods pl	abgepackte Waren f/pl	marchandises f/pl empaquetées
packaging	Verpackung f	conditionnement m, emballage m
packaging consultant	Verpackungsberater m	conseil m en matière f d'emballage m
packaging costs pl	Verpackungskosten pl	coût m de l'emballage m, frais m/pl de l'emballage m
packaging test	Packungstest m	étude f sur un emballage m, test m d'emballage m
packing charges pl	Verpackungskosten pl	coût m de l'emballage m, frais m/pl de l'emballage m
pack-shot	Packungsbild n im Film m	plan-paquet m
padded text	weitschweifiger Text m	texte m délayé
padding	Flickwort n	cheville f
page	Blatt n, Seite f	feuille f, page f
to page	paginieren	folioter, marquer les pages f/pl, paginer
page cord	Ausbindeschnur f, Kolumnenschnur f	ficelle f, ficelle f à colonnes f/pl
page dominance	seitenbeherrschende Anzeige f	emplacement m prédominant dans une page f
page fraction	Seitenteil m	fraction f de page f
page gauge	Kolumnenmaß n	échelle f de page f
page make-up	Zusammenstellung f der Seiten f/pl	mise f en page f
page number	Seitennummer f, Seitenziffer f	folio m, numéro m de la page f
page proof	Seitenkorrektur f, Zeitungskorrektur f	correction f, correction f en bon à clicher, correction f en bon à tirer
page rate	Seitenpreis m	prix m d'une page f entière
page size	Größe f einer Seite f, Seitengröße f	format m de la page f, surface f de la page f
page width	Blattbreite f	largeur f de page f
page work and turn	Seite f mit Vorder- f und Rückseite f	page f recto verso
page-plan	Layout n	maquette f
page-proof terminal	Umbruchterminal n	terminal m de composition f
to paginate	paginieren	folioter, marquer les pages f/pl, paginer
pagination, paging	Numerierung f, Paginierung f, Seitennumerierung f	numérotage m, numérotation f, pagination f
paid advertising	Werbung f, bezahlte	publicité f payée
paid circulation	bezahlte Auflage f	tirage m payé
paid subscriptions pl	bezahlte Abonnements n/pl	abonnements m/pl payants
paint	Anstrich m	peinture f
to paint in	bemalen	peindre
paint transfer	Abziehplakat n	décalcomanie f
painted bulletin	bemalte Großfläche f	bulletin m

painted cloth	bemalte Leinwand *f*	toile *f* peinte
painted display	gemalte Anschlagfläche *f*	panneau *m* peint
painted displays *pl*	gemalte Außenwerbung *f*	affiches *f/pl* peintes, panneaux *m/pl* peints
painted placard	gemaltes Plakat *n*	affiche *f* peinte
painted plate	bemaltes Schild *n*	plaque *f* peinte
painted surfaces *pl*	bemalte Flächen *f/pl*	surfaces *f/pl* peintes
painted wall	Wandbemalung *f*	peinture *f* murale
painting	Malerei *f*	peinture *f*
painting on walls *pl*	Mauerbemalung *f*	peinture *f* murale
paired comparison	Paarvergleich *m*	test *m* comparatif
palaver	Hin- und Hergerede *n*	palabre *f*
palette	Palette *f*	palette *f*
pamphlet	Broschüre *f*, Flugblatt *n*, Flugschrift *f*, Prospekt *m*	brochure *f*, dépliant *m*, feuillet *m*, plaquette *f*, prospectus *m*, tract *m*
pamphlet stitching	Rückstichbroschur *f*	piqûre à cheval *m*
panchromatic	lichtempfindlich	panchromatique
panchromatic reproduction	panchromatische Reproduktion *f*	reproduction *f* panchromatique
panegyric	Lobrede *f*	éloge *m*, panégyrique *m*
panel	Schild *n*, Testgruppe *f*, Umrandung *f*	contour *m*, encadrement *m*, enseigne *f*, groupe *m* de test *m*, panneau *m*, panonceau *m*, plaque *f*
panic-monger	Panikmacher *m*	alarmiste *m*
panning	Panoramierung *f*	panoramarique *f*
panorama advertisement	Panoramaanzeige *f*	annonce *f* en double page *f*
pantograph	Pantograph *m*, Storchschnabel *m*	pantographe *m*
paper	Blatt *n*, Papier *n*, Zeitung *f*	feuille *f*, gazette *f*, journal *m*, papier *m*, revue *f*
paper bag	Einkaufstasche *f* (aus Papier *n*), Tragetasche *f* aus Papier *n*	pochette *f* à anse *f*, sac *m* en papier *m*
paper book	Taschenbuch *n*	livre *m* de poche *f*
paper carrier	Tragetasche *f* aus Papier *n*	pochette *f* à anse *f*
paper cutter	Papierschneidemaschine *f*	massicot *m*
paper fibre	Papierfaser *f*	fibre *f* de papier *m*
paper in form of records *pl*	Zeitschrift *f* in Schallplattenform *f*	journal *m* sonore
paper mâché	Papiermaché *n*	carton-pâte *m*, papier *m* mâché
paper made from wood pulp	holzhaltiges Papier *n*	papier *m* avec de bois *m*, papier *m* fait de pâte *f* de bois *m*
paper roll	Papierrolle *f*	bobine *f* de papier *m*
paper seal	Siegelmarke *f*	timbre *m* en relief *m*
paper size	Papierformat *n*	format *m* de papier *m*
paper sizing	Papierleimung *f*	encollage *m* du papier *m*
paper tape	Lochstreifen *m*	bande *f* perforée, ruban *m* perforé
paper thickness	Papierdicke *f*	épaisseur *m* du papier *m*
paper type	Papiersorte *f*	sorte *f* de papier *m*
paper war	Pressepolemik *f*	polémique *f* de presse *f*
paper weight by grams *pl* per square meter	Quadratmetergewicht *n* des Papiers *n*	grammage *m*, poids *m*
paper with some substance	widerstandsfähiges Papier *n*	papier *m* de la main *f*
paper worm	Leseratte *f*	bouquineur *m*, rat *m* de bibliothèque *f*

paperback	broschiertes Buch *n*, flexibles Taschenbuch *n*	flexible livre *m* de poche *f*, livre *m* broché
paperboard roll	Papprolle *f*	rouleau *m* de carton *m*
paper-boy	Zeitungsjunge *m*	vendeur *m* de journaux *m*/*pl*
paper-knife	Papiermesser *n*	coupe-papier *m*
papermaker	Papierfabrikant *m*	fabricant *m* de papier *m*
paper-mill	Papierfabrik *f*	fabrique *f* de papier *m*, papeterie *f*
paper-warfare	Papierkrieg *m*	paperasserie *f*
par writer	Feuilletonist *m*	courriériste *m*
parade poster	Außenwerbung *f* an Verkehrsmitteln *n*/*pl*	publicité *f* sur l'extérieur *m* de voitures *f*/*pl*
paragraph	Absatz *m* (im Text *m*), Abschnitt *m*, Kurzartikel *m*, Paragraph *m*	alinéa *m*, entrefilet *m*, paragraphe *m*
paragraphist	Kleinartikelschreiber *m*	courriériste *m*
parallel folding	Wickelfalz *m*	pli *m* en portefeuille *m*
parallel position	parallel zur Straße *f*	emplacement *m* parallèle
paraph	Namenszeichen *n*, Schriftzug *m*	paraphe *m*, trait *m*
parcel	Paket *n*	colis *m*, paquet *m*
parcel distribution service	Geschenkpackungsdienst *m*	services *m*/*pl* de l'empaquetage *m* des présents *m*/*pl*
parcel of type	Satzstück *n*	paquet *m* de composition *f*
parcel to be paid for on delivery	Nachnahmesendung *f*	envoi *m* contre remboursement *m*
parchment	Pergament *n*	parcheminé *m*
parentheses *pl*	Parenthesen *f*/*pl*, runde Klammern *f*/*pl*	parenthèses *f*/*pl*
parliament reporter	Parlamentsstenograf *m*	sténographe *m* parlementaire
parody	Parodie *f*	parodie *f*
parole	Parole *f*	mot *m* d'ordre *m*
part edition	Teilausgabe *f*	édition *f* partielle
part payment	Anzahlung *f*, Ratenzahlung *f*	acompte *m*, paiement *m* par versements *m*/*pl* fractionnés
part publication	Nachschlagewerk *n* in Form regelmäßig erscheinender Hefte *n*/*pl*	ouvrage *m* de référence *f* sous la forme *f* de livraisons *f*/*pl* régulières
partial	parteiisch	partial
partial circulation	Teilauflage *f*	tirage *m* partiel
partial display on a few pillars *pl*	Teilbelegung *f* von Plakatsäulen *f*/*pl*	affichage *m* sur certaines colonnes *f*/*pl* seulement
partner split	Auflagensplit *m* unter Partnern *m*/*pl*	tirage *m* partagé entre des partenaires *m*/*pl*
partwork	Zeitschrift *f* mit Sammelcharakter *m*	revue *f* destinée à être recueillie
party organ	Parteiblatt *n*	feuille *f* de parti *m*
passage	Druckgang *m*, Passus *m*	passage *m*
pass-along reader	Zufallsleser *m*	lecteur *m* accidental, lecteur *m* (tirer)
passed for press	druckfertig	
passe-partout lamination	Kaschierung *f*	doublage *m*
passer-by	Passant *m*	passant *m*
passing on	Übermittlung *f*	transmission *f*
paste	Kleister *m*, Leim *m*	colle *f*
to paste on	einkleben	coller
paste up	Montage *f*	montage *m*

to **paste up**	bekleben	coller
pasteboard	Pappe *f*	carton *m*
pastel	Pastell *n*	pastel *m*
pastel drawing	Pastellzeichnung *f*	dessin *m* au pastel *m*
pastels *pl*	Pastellkreiden *f/pl*	crayons *m/pl* pastel
pasting	Aufkleben *n*, Collage *f*	collage *m*
patched-up story	zurechtgepfuschter Artikel *m*, zusammengestoppelte Geschichte *f*	article *m* bâclé
patchwork	Flickwerk *n*	rapiéçage *m*
patronage discount	Treuerabatt *m*	rabais *m* de fidélité *f*, ristourne *f* pour clients *m/pl* habituels
pattern	Modell *n*, Muster *n*, Schablone *f*, Schema *n*, Schnittmuster *n*, Vorlàge *f*	découpage *m*, dessin *m* au propre, échantillon *m*, écran *m*, gabarit *m*, mannequin *m*, modèle *m*, patron *m*, pochoir *m*, schéma *m*, spécimen *m*, stencil *m*
pattern plate	Originalklischee *n*	cliché *m* original
pavement advertising	Pflasterwerbung *f*	publicité *f* sur trottoir *m*
pay envelope advertising	Lohnbeutelwerbung *f*, Lohntütenwerbung *f*	publicité *f* sur les enveloppes *f/pl* de paye *f*
pay off	werbewirksamer Filmschlußteil *m*	partie *f* finale couronnée de succès *m*, partie *f* finale efficace d'un film *m*
payment	Bezahlung *f*, Zahlung *f*	paiement *m*, règlement *m*, versement *m*
payment on receipt of invoice	Zahlung *f* bei Erhalt *m* der Rechnung *f*	paiement *m* à la réception *f* de la facture *f*
payment plan	Kontenrahmen *m*	plan *m* comptable
payment with order	Zahlung *f* bei Auftragserteilung *f*	paiement *m* à la commande *f*
peak sales *pl*	Spitzenverkaufszahlen *f/pl*	pointes *f/pl* de vente *f*
peak season	Hauptsaison *f*, Hochsaison *f*	haute saison *f*, saison *f* principale
pearl (see appendix)	Perlschrift *f* (siehe Anhang)	parisienne (voir appendice)
pegged price	Stützpreis *m*	prix *m* soutenu
pelmet	Wimpel *m*	bandeau *m*, fanion *m*, flamme *f*
pemmican style	gedrängte Darstellung *f*	présentation *f* condensée
pen	Schreibfeder *f*	plume *f*
pen and ink drawing	Federzeichnung *f*	dessin *m* à la plume *f*
pencil	Bleistift *m*	crayon *m*
pencil-drawing	Bleistiftskizze *f*	crayonné *m*, dessin *m* au crayon *m*
pendriver	Federfuchser *m*	plumitif *m*
penetrating power	Durchschlagskraft *f*	force *f* de pénétration *f*
penetration	Durchdringung *f*, Reichweite *f*, Wirkungskraft *f*	couverture *f*, pénétration *f*, rayon *m* d'action *f*, taux *m* de pénétration *f*
penman	Schönschreiber *m*	calligraphe *m*
pen-name	Pseudonym *n*, Schriftstellername *m*	nom *m* de guerre *f*, nom *m* de plume *f*, pseudonyme *m*

pennant	Werbewimpel *m*, Wimpel *m*	bandeau *m*, banderole *f*, fanion *m*, flamme *f*
penny dreadful	Kolportageroman *m*, Räuberpistole *f*	journal *m* pour concierges *f/pl*, roman *m* à gros effets *m/pl*, roman *m* à sensation *f*
penny novellette	Romanheft *f*	journal *m* de roman *m*, petit roman *m* bon marché
penny press	Boulevardblatt *n*, Kaufzeitung *f*	feuille *f* boulevardière
penny saver	Briefumschlag *m* mit eingeschlagener Klappe *f*	enveloppe *f* énigma
penny-a-line payment	Zeilenhonorar *n*	rémunération *f* à la ligne *f*
penny-a-liner	Zeilenschinder *m*	bourreur *m* de lignes *f/pl*, tireur *m* à la ligne *f*
to pep up	interessanter machen	corser
per capita	Kopf *m*, per	par tête *f*
per issue	Ausgabe *f*, je	par édition *f*
percentage	Prozent *n*, Prozentsatz *m*	pour-cent *m*, pourcentage *m*
perceptibility	Erkennbarkeit *f*	perceptibilité *f*
to perfect	vervollkommnen	perfectionner
perfect page	Jungfer *f/typog*	page *f* sans faute *f*
perfect-bind by employing the Lumbeck method	lumbecken	relier par collage *m*
perfecting	Widerdruck *m*	impression *f* au verso *n*, retiration *f*, seconde forme *f*
perfecting press	Schön-und-Widerdruck-Maschine *f*	machine *f* à retiration *f*, presse *f* à double impression *f*
perfection	Vollkommenheit *f*	perfection *f*
to perforate	perforieren	percer, perforer
perforating rule	Perforierlinie *f*	filet *m* à perforer
perforation	Perforation *f*	perforation *f*
performance	Leistung *f*, Veranstaltung *f*	accomplissement *m*, manifestation (durée *f* de ...), prestation *f*, rendement *m*, réunion *f*
period	Schlußpunkt *m*, Zeitabschnitt *m*	période *f*, point *m* final
period maximum	Höchstanschlagzeit *f*	période *f* maximum
period of display	Anschlagdauer *f*, Aushangdauer *f*, Aushangzeit *f*, Klebeperiode *f*	conservation *f*, durée *f* d'affichage *m*, période *f* de conservation *f*
period of dull sales *pl*	Absatzflaute *f*	mévente *f*
period of notice	Kündigungsfrist *f*	délai *m* de dédite *f*
period price	Saisonrabatt *m*	prix *m* de saison *f*
periodical	Magazin *n*, Zeitschrift *f*	magazine *m*, périodiqie *m*, revue *f*
periodical of culture	kulturelle Zeitschrift *f*	journal *m* culturel, périodique *m* de culture *f*
periodical without ads *pl*	Nichtanzeigenträger *m*	périodique *m* sans publicité *f* commerciale
periodicals *pl*	Periodika *n/pl*	périodiques *m/pl*
periodicity	Periodizität *f*	périodicité *f*
periods *pl* of commercial emissions *pl*	Werbezeitenblöcke *m/pl*	tranches *f/pl* horaires
periphrasis	Umschreibung *f*	circonlocution *f*, périphrase *f*
perlon block	Perlonklischee *n*	cliché *m* perlon
permanent advertisement	Daueranzeige *f*	annonce *f* permanente
permanent contributor	ständiger Mitarbeiter *m*	collaborateur *m* permanent, collaborateur *m* régulier

permanent order	Dauerauftrag *m*	ordre *m* permanent
permanent poster	Dauerplakat *n*	affiche *f* permanente
permanent posting	Daueranschlag *m*	affichage *m* permanent
permanent publicity	Dauerwerbung *f*	publicité *f* permanente
permastat	Permastatdruck *m*	impression *f* photostat sur papier *m* spécial
permission to print	Druckerlaubnis *f*, Druckgenehmigung *f*, Imprimatur *n*	bon à tirer, permission *f* d'imprimer
permit	Bewilligung *f*	autorisation *f*, permission *f*
personal advertisement	private Anzeige *f*	annonce *f* privée
personal announcement	Familienanzeige *f*	avis *m*, faire-part *m*
personal approach	persönliche Ansprache *f*	appel *m* personnel
personal remarks *pl*	persönliche Bemerkungen *f/pl*	personnalités *f/pl*
personal requirements *pl*	Eigenbedarf *m*	besoin *m* propre
personalized sales *pl* technique	personalisierte Werbung *f*	publicité *f* personnalisée
personifying	Personalisierung *f*	personnalisation *f*
persuasive advertising	überzeugende Werbung *f*	publicité *f* persuasive
persuasive power	Überzeugungskraft *f*	force *f* de persuasion *f*
petty-bourgeoisie	Kleinbürgertum *n*	petite bourgeoisie *f*
phantom	Geisterbild *n*	fantôme *m*, image *f* spectre
philosophy of life	Weltanschauung *f*	conception *f* du monde *m*, idéologie *f*
phonemanship	Telefonverkaufskunst *f*	technique *f* de la vente *f* par téléphone *m*
phonetic transcription	Lautschrift *f*	transcription *f* phonétique
photo(graphic) composition	Fotosatz *m*, Lichtsatz *m*	composition *f* photographique, photocomposition *f*, phototypie *f*
photo copier, photo copying machine	Fotokopiergerät *n*	appareil *m* à photocopier, presse *f* à photocopier
photo journalism	Fotojournalismus *m*	photojournalisme *m*
photo lettering	Fotosetzverfahren *n*, lichtsetzen, Lichtsatz *m*	composer photographique, composition *f* photographique, photocomposition *f*, phototypie *f*
photo montage	Fotomontage *f*	composition *f* photographique, montage *m* photographique, photomontage *m*
photo paper	fotografisches Papier *n*	papier *m* à prise *f* de vue *f*
photo poster	Fotoplakat *n*	affiche *f* photographique
photo print	Fotokopie *f*	copie *f* héliographique, photocopie *f*
photo typesetting	Lichtsatz *m*	composition *f* photographique, photocomposition *f*, phototypie *f*
photochemistry	chemische Lichteinwirkung *f*	photochimie *f*
photochrome	farbiger Steindruck *m*, Fotochrom *n*	photochromie *f*
photocomposer, photocomposing machine	Filmsetzgerät *n*, Fotosetzmaschine *f*	composeuse *f* photographique, photocompeuse *f*
photocomposing system	Lichtsatzsystem *n*	système *m* de photocomposition *f*
photocomposition	Fotomontage *f*	composition *f* photographique, montage *m* photographique, photomontage *m*

photocomposition programme	Lichtsatzprogramm *n*	programme *m* de photocomposition *f*
photo-engraving	Chemigrafie *f*, Klischeeherstellung *f*	photogravure *f*, zincographie *f*
photogenic	bildwirksam, fotogen	photogénique
photograph	Foto *n*, Fotografie *f*, Lichtbild *n*	photo(graphie) *f*
to photograph	aufnehmen (Foto), fotografieren	faire de la photo *f*, photographier
photographer	Fotograf *m*	photographe *m*
photographer's model	Fotomodell *n*	mannequin *m*, modèle *m* d'un photographe *m*
photographic library	Fotothek *f*, Lichtbildsammlung *f*	photothèque *f*
photographic print	Fotoabzug *m*	épreuve *f* de photo *f*
photographic record	Fotounterlage *f*	matériel *m* photographique
photographic report	Fotoreportage *f*	reportage *m* photographique
photographic service	Bilderdienst *m*	service *m* photographique
photographic sound-recording	Lichttonverfahren *n*	prise *f* de son *m* photographique
photographic technique	Aufnahmetechnik *f*	technique *f* photographique
photography	Fotografie *f*	photographie *f*
photogravure	Fotogravur *f*, Fototiefdruck *m*, Heliogravüre *f*, Kupfertiefdruck *m*, Rakeltiefdruck *m*, Tiefdruck *m*/*typog*	gravure *f* en creux *m*/*pl*, héliogravure *f*, impression *f* en creux *m*, impression *f* en héliogravure *f*, impression *f* en taille-douce *f*, photogravure *f*, rotogravure *f*
photogravure plant	Tiefdruckanstalt *f*	maison *f* d'héliogravure *f*
photogravure printer	Tiefdrucker *m*	imprimeur *m* en héliogravure *f*
photojournalism	Bildjournalismus *m*	photojournalisme *m*
photo-lithography	Fotolithografie *f*	photolithographie *f*
photomechanical	fotomechanisch	photomécanique
photostat	Fotokopiergerät *n*, Kopiergerät *n*	appareil *m* à copier, appareil *m* à photocopier, presse *f* à copier, presse *f* à photocopier
photostat printing on special paper	Permastatdruck *m*	impression *f* photostat sur papier *m* spécial
photostatic copy	Ablichtung *f*, Fotokopie *f*	copie *f* héliographique, photocopie *f*
photo-telegraphy	Bildtelegrafie *f*, Bildübertragung *f*	bélinographie *f*, téléphotographie *f*, transmission *f* phototélégraphique
phototype setter, phototypesetter	Filmsetzgerät *n*, Fotosetzmaschine *f*, Lichtsetzmaschine *f*	composeuse *f* photographique, photocompeuse *f*, phototitreuse *f*
phototypesetting room	Fotosetzerei *f*	service *m* photocomposition
photo-typography	fotomechanischer Druck *m*	photo-typographie *f*
phrase	Redensart *f*, Redewendung *f*	locution *f*, tournure *f* de phrase *f*

phrase-book	Sammlung *f* von Redewendungen *f/pl*	recueil *m* de locutions *f/pl*
phrase-monger	Phrasendrescher *m*	phraseur *m*
phraseology	Ausdrucksweise *f*	diction *f*, élocution *f*, manière *f* de s'exprimer, phraséologie *f*
pi *am*	Zwiebelfisch *m/typog*	coquille *f*, mastic *m*, pâté *m*
pica (see appendix)	Pica *f* (siehe Anhang)	pica (voir appendice)
to pick	ausschlachten	désosser
pickup	Tonabnehmer *m*	pick-up *m*
pictograph	Piktogramm *n*	pictogramme *m*
pictorial	Illustrierte *f*	périodique *m* illustré
pictorial advertisement	Bildanzeige *f*	annonce *f* illustrée
pictorial advertising	Bildwerbung *f*	publicité *f* illustrée
pictorial documentation	Bilddokumentation *f*	documentation *f* par l'image *f*
pictorial element	Bildelement *n*	élément *m* pictural
pictorial journalism	Bildjournalismus *m*	photojournalisme *m*
pictorial part	Bildteil *m*	partie *f* picturale
pictorial poster	Bildplakat *n*	affiche *f* illustrée
pictorial supplement	Bilderbeilage *f*	supplément *m* illustré
picture	Abbildung *f*, Bild *n*	illustration *f*, image *f*
picture agency	Pressebilderdienst *m*	agence *f* de presse *f* photographique
picture cheque	Bilderscheck *m*	chèque-image *f*
picture house	Lichtspielhaus *n*	cinéma *m*
picture library	Bildarchiv *n*	dépôts *m/pl* illustrations *f/pl*
picture paper	Illustrierte *f*	illustré *m*, périodique *m* illustré
picture postcard	Ansichtskarte *f*	carte *f* postale illustrée
picture puzzle	Bilderrätsel *n*	rébus *m*
picture record	Bildschallplatte *f*	disque *m* de photographe *m* illustré
picture series *pl*	Bilderreihe *f*	série *f* d'images *m/pl*
picture story	Bildgeschichte *f*, Fotoreportage *f*	conte *f* illustrée, histoire *f* en images *f/pl*, reportage *m* photographique
picture track	Filmstreifen *m* ohne Ton *m*	bande *f* sans ton *m*
pictures *pl* **editor**	Bildredakteur *m*	rédacteur *m* des illustrations *f/pl*
pie	durcheinandergefallener Satz *m*, Zwiebelfisch *m/typog*	copie *f* chamboulée, coquille *f*, mastic *m*, pâté *m*
piece	Thekenaufsteller *m*	matériel *m* d'étalage *m* de comptoir *m*
piece compositor	Spaltensetzer *m*	compositeur *m* aux pièces *f/pl*
piece hand	Paketsetzer *m*	paquetier *m*
piece of composition	Paket *n* (Satzstück *m*)	paquet *m*
piece of writing	Schriftstück *n*	document *m*, écrit *m*, pièce *f*
piecemail information	bruchstückhafte Nachrichten *f/pl*	nouvelles *f/pl* fragmentaires
to pierce	durchbohren	transpercer
to pierce for type	ausklinken	encocher, entailler
piercing	Ausschnitt *m* (Stanze *f*), Klischeeausschnitt *m*	découpe *f*, encochage *m* d'un cliché *m*, encoche *f*, perforation *f*
pig iron	seriöser Zeitungstext *m*, unverdaulicher Artikel *m*	article *m* lourd et indigeste, texte *m* sérieux
pigeon-hole	Schubfach *n*	tiroir *m*

piggyback	hintereinander gesendete Werbekurzspots *m/pl* für verschiedene Produkte *n/pl* desselben Werbungtreibenden *m*	des spots *m/pl* émis l'un après l'autre pour deux produits *m/pl* différents du même annonceur *m*
pigment paper	Pigmentpapier *n*	papier *m* charbon *m*
to pilfer	abschreiben	piller
pillar	Plakatanschlagsäule *f*	colonne *f* d'affichage *m*
pilot edition	Testausgabe *f*, Versuchsausgabe *f*	édition *f* d'essai *m*
pilot study	Leitstudie *f*, Vorstudie *f*, Voruntersuchung *f*	enquête *f* pilote, pré-test *m*, préenquête *f*
pioneer in advertising	Werbepionier *m*	pionnier *m* publicitaire
pioneering achievement	Pionierleistung *f*	œuvre *f* de pionnier *m*
pioneering advertising	Initialwerbung *f*	publicité *f* de pionnier *m*
pioneers *pl*	Vorhut *f*	avant-garde *f*
pipeline	Verbindungsweg *m*	filière *f*
pirate station	Piratensender *m*	émetteur *m* clandestin, station *f* pirate *m*
pirated edition	Raubdruck *m*	édition *f* frauduleuse
pirating of a trademark	Nachahmung *f* eines Warenzeichens *n*	contrefaction *f* d'une marque *f* de fabrique *f*
pithy saying	Kernspruch *m*	aphorisme *m*
placard	Anschlagbogen *m*, Plakat *n*	affiche *f*-papier *m*, placard *m*
to place	unterbringen	placer
to place an order	Auftrag *m* vergeben	donner un ordre *m*, passer une commande *f*
to place bills *pl*	anschlagen, plakatieren	afficher, coller, poser une affiche *f*
to place in alphabetical order	alphabetisieren	mettre en ordre *m* alphabétique
to place in centre of line	Mitte *f* stellen, auf	placer au centre *m* de la ligne *f*
place of advertising	Streuort *m*	lieu *m* de publicité *f*
place of fulfilment	Erfüllungsort *m*	lieu *m* d'exécution *f*
place of posting	Anschlagort *m*	lieu *m* d'affichage *m*
place of printing	Druckort *m*	lieu *m* d'impression *f*
place of publication	Erscheinungsort *m*	lieu *m* de publication *f*
placing	Ankleben *n*, Belegung *f*, Plazierung *f*	affichage *m*, collage *m*, emplacement *m*, mise *f* en place *f*, placement *m*
placing of a poster	Plakat *n* anschlagen	affichage *m* d'un placard *m*
placing of orders *pl*	Auftragserteilung *f*	passation *f* d'un ordre *m*
placing orders *pl* for space	Anzeigendisposition *f*	retenue *f* des emplacements *m/pl*
plagiarism	Nachahmung *f*, Plagiat *n*	contre-facon *f*, imitation *f*, plagiat *m*
plagiarist	Plagiator *m*	plagiaire *m*
to plagiarize	plagiieren	plagier
plain matter	kompresser Satz *m*	composition *f* pleine
plain speech	unverblümte Sprache *f*	déclaration sans ambages *f/pl*
plain style	einfacher Stil *m*, klare Ausdrucksweise *f*	style *m* sans fioritures *f/pl*, style *m* simple
plain swelled rule	englische Linie *f*	filet *m* anglais
plan	Plan *m*, Planung *f*	plan *m*, planification *f*, programme *m*, schéma *m*

planer	Klopfholz n	taquoir m
plan-filing cabinet	Zeichnungsarchiv n	armoire f à dessins m/pl
planning	Planung f	planification f, programme m
planning activity	Planungsarbeit f	élaboration f d'un plan m
planography	Flachdruck m	impression f à plat, impression f planographique
plant operator	Anschlagunternehmen n	entreprise f d'affichage m
plaquette	Plakette f	plaquette f
plastic	plastisch	plastique
plastic binding	Plastikheftung f	reliure f en matière f plastique
plastic block, plastic cut	Kunststoffklischee n	cliché m plastique
plastic drinking-cup	Automatenbecher m	gobelet m pour distributeur m automatique
plastic media pl	plastische Werbemittel n/pl	moyens m/pl publicitaires synthétiques
plastic packaging	Kunststoffverpackung f	emballage m en matière f synthétique
plastic product	Plastikerzeugnis n	produit m plastique
plastic sheet	Plastikplatte f	plaque f de plastique f
plastic stereo	Kunststoffklischee n	cliché m plastique
plastics pl	Kunststoffe m/pl	matière f artificielle, matière f synthétique
plate	Druckstock m, Klischee n, Platte f, Schild n	cliché m, dalle f, enseigne f, panneau m, panonceau m, planche f, planche f typographique, plaque f
plate maker	Stereotypèur m	clicheur m, stéréotypeur m
platen machine	Tiegel m	presse f à platine f
platen press	Tiegeldruckpresse f	presse f à platine f
platform	Plattform f	plate-forme f
platform site	Perronfläche f	emplacement m de quai m
platform site advertising	Plattformanschlag m	emplacement m de quai m
platine	Tellertiegel m	presse f à platine f
platitude	Gemeinplatz m	banalité f, lieu m commun
play	Theaterstück n	pièce f de théâtre m
play back	Rückspiel n, Wiedergabe f einer Tonaufnahme f	faire repasser la bande f, lecture f sonore, postsonorisation f, rejeu m, surjeu m
to play back	nochmaliges Abspielen n	faire repasser la bande f
play bill	Theaterplakat n	affiche f de théâtre m, annonce f de spectacle m
play date	Ausstrahlungstermin m	terme m d'émission f
to play down	herunterspielen	minimiser
to play up an information	eine Nachricht f hochspielen	donner une publicité f retentissante, gonfler un papier m, remonter une nouvelle f
playing-field	Sportgelände n	terrain m de sport m
please copy	Nachdruck m erbeten	reproduction f souhaitée
pleonasm	Pleonasmus m	pléonasme m
plot	Fabel f eines Stückes n	affabulation f
plug	unbezahlte Werbebotschaft f	message m publicitaire impayé
to plug	anpreisen	prôner
plugger ad	Füllanzeige f	annonce f bouche f -trou m
plywood plate	Sperrholzplatte f	plaque f de contreplaqué m
pocket book	Taschenbuch n	livre m de poche f

pocket diary	Agenda *f*	agenda *m*, carnet *m*
pocket edition	Taschenausgabe *f*	édition *f* portative
pocket size	Taschenformat *n*	format *m* de poche *f*
pocket-radio	Taschenradio *n*	récepteur *m* de poche *f*
point	Pointe *f*, Punkt *m*	point *m*, pointe *f*
point of purchase	Kaufort *m*, Verkaufsplatz *m*	point *m* d'achat *m*, point *m* de vente *f*
point of sale	Verkaufsort *m*	point *m* de vente *f*
point of view	Gesichtspunkt *m*, Standpunkt *m*	point *m* de vue *f*
point size	Schriftgrad *m*, Schriftgröße *f*	corps *m*, force *f* de corps *m*
point system (see appendix)	Punktsystem *n* (siehe Anhang)	mesures *f/pl* typographiques (voir appendice), système *m* en points *m/pl*
point-of-purchase advertising	Werbung *f* am Kaufort *m*	publicité *f* au point *m* d'achat *m*
poison pen	anonymer Briefschreiber *m*	corbeau *m*
poker-work	Brandmalerei *f*	pyrogravure *f*
polemic	Streitschrift *f*	écrit *m* polémique
polemics *pl*	Meinungsstreit *m*, Polemik *f*	polémique *f*
political adherence	politische Richtung *f*	appartenance *f* politique
political editor	politischer Redakteur *m*	rédacteur *m* politique
political periodical	politische Zeitschrift *f*	revue *f* politique
political poster	politisches Plakat *n*	affiche *f* politique
politician	Politiker *m*	politique *m*
politization	Politisierung *f*	politisation *f*
poll	Befragung *f*, Umfrage *f*	enquête *f*, étude *f*, interrogatoire *m*, interview *f*
pollster	Interviewer *m*, Interviewerin *f*, Meinungsforscher *m*	enquêteur *m*, enquêteur *m* d'opinion *f*, enquêtrice *f*
polychromatic	mehrfarbig	multicolore, polychrome
polyglot	mehrsprachig	polyglotte
polygraph	Lügendetektor *m*	polygraphe *m*
pomposity	Schwulst *m*	enflure *f*
pony report	kurzgefaßter Bericht *m*	bref sommaire *m* des nouvelles *f/pl*
pool	Interessengemeinschaft *f*	groupe *m*
poor imitation	Abklatsch *m*	copie *f*, pastichage *m*
poor print	schlechter Druck *m*	impression *f* de piètre qualité *f*
pop feature	volkstümliche Sendung *f*	émission *f* à succès *m*
popular newspaper	populäre Zeitung *f*	journal *m* populaire
popular pamphlet	Aufklärungsschrift *f*	brochure *f* de vulgarisation *f*
popularity	Volkstümlichkeit *f*	popularité *f*
popularization	Popularisierung *f*	vulgarisation *f*
porcelain sign	Porzellanschild *n*	affiche *f* porcelaine
pornography	Schmutzliteratur *f*	pornographie *f*
portable panel	auswechselbare Werbefläche *f*, Stellschild *n*	panneau *m* transportable
portrait	Konterfei *n*, Personenbildnis *n*	portrait *m*
portrait format	Hochformat *n*	format *m* en hauteur *f*, format *m* normal, format *m* vertical
position	Plazierung *f*	emplacement *m*, placement *m*
position pull	Standbogen *m*	feuille *f* d'emplacement *m*, feuille *f* des blancs *m/pl*
possibilities *pl* **of advertising**	Werbemöglichkeiten *f/pl*	possibilités *f/pl* de publicité *f*
possibility of communication	Kommunikationsmöglichkeit *f*	possibilité *f* de la communication *f*
to **post**	anbringen (Plakat)	afficher

to **post bills** *pl*	anschlagen, plakatieren	afficher, coller, poser une affiche *f*
post card	Postkarte *f*	carte *f* postale
post no bills *pl*	Anschlagen *n* verboten	défense *f* d'afficher
post office mailing	Postwurfsendungen *f/pl*	distribution *f* postale de messages *m/pl* non adressés, publicité *f* directe par voie *f* postale
post paid	Pauschalfrankatur *f*	affranchissement *m* forfaitaire
post season	Nachsaison *f*	arrière-saison *f*
post synchronization	Nachsynchronisierung *f*	post-synchronisation *f*
postage	Porto *n*, Zustellgebühr *f*	frais *m/pl* postaux, port *m*
postage saver	Briefumschlag *m* mit eingeschlagener Klappe *f*	enveloppe *f* énigma
postage stamp	Briefmarke *f*	timbre-poste *m*
postal advertising	Postwerbung *f*	publicité *f* par poste *f*
postal cheque	Postscheck *m*	chèque *m* postal
postal department	Versandabteilung *f*	service *m* de routage *m*, service *m* des expéditions *f/pl*
postal newspaper service	Postzeitungsdienst *m*	arrangement *m* concernant les abonnements *m/pl* aux journaux *m/pl* et écrits *m/pl* périodiques
postal subscription	Postabonnement *n*	abonnement *m* postal
posted price	angekündigter Preis *m*	prix *m* affiché
poster	Affiche *f*, Anschlagbogen *m*, Plakat *n*	affiche *f*-papier *m*, placard *m*
poster advertising	Bogenanschlag *m*, Plakatanschlagwerbung *f*	affichage *m*, publicité *f* par affiches *f/pl*
poster advertising in shelters *pl*	Wartehäuschenwerbung *f*	affichage *m* dans les abris-bus *m/pl*
poster analysis	Plakatanalyse *f*	analyse *f* d'affichage *m*
poster artist	Plakatgrafiker *m*, Plakatmaler *m*, Plakatzeichner *m*	affichiste *m*
poster audience survey	Prüfung *f* der Plakatbeachtung *f*	vérification *f* de l'audience *f* d'affichage *m*
poster campaign	Plakatanschlagkampagne *f*, Werbefeldzug *m* durch Plakatanschlag *m*	campagne *f* d'affichage *m*
poster collection	Plakatsammlung *f*	collection *f* d'affiches *f/pl*
poster contractor	Plakatanschlaginstitut *n*	entrepreneur *m* d'affichage *m*
poster design	Plakatentwurf *m*	dessin *m* pour affiche *f*, maquette *f* d'une affiche *f*, projet *m* d'affiche *f*
poster designer	Plakatmaler *m*	affichiste *m*
poster for replacement	Ersatzplakat *n*	affiche *f* de remplacement *m*
poster hoarding	Anschlagwand *f*, Anschlagzaun *m*, Plakatwand *f*, Plakatzaun *m*, Werbetafel *f*	panneau *m* d'affichage *m*, panneau-réclame *f*
poster in several parts *pl*	mehrteiliges Plakat *n*	affiche *f* en plusieurs parties *f/pl*
poster lettering	Plakatschrift *f*	caractères *m/pl* pour affiches *f/pl*
poster museum	Plakatmuseum *n*	musée *m* de l'affiche *f*

poster on door-frames *pl*	Türrahmenschild *n*	panneau *m* de porte *f* d'accès *m*
poster painted on canvas	auf Leinwand *f* gemaltes Plakat *n*	affiche *f* toile *f* peinte
poster panel	Anschlagtafel *f*	panneau *m* d'affichage *m*
poster paper	Plakatpapier *n*	papier *m* pour affiches *f/pl*
poster pillar	Anschlagsäule *f*, Litfaßsäule *f*	colonne *f* d'affichage *m*, colonne *f* Morris (à Paris) , colonne-affiche *f*
poster plant	Plakatanschlaginstitut *n*, Plakatanschlagunternehmen *n*	entrepreneur *m* d'affichage *m*, entreprise *f* d'affichage *m*
poster printing plant	Plakatdruckerei *f*	imprimerie *f* d'affiches *f/pl*
poster showing	Werbeflächengruppe *f*	circuit *m* indivisible d'emplacements *m/pl*, réseau *m*
poster site	Ständer *m*	portatif *m*, présentoir *m*, support *m*
poster size (see appendix)	Plakatformat *n* (siehe Anhang)	format *m* d'affiche *f* (voir appendice)
poster sketch	Plakatentwurf *m*	dessin *m* pour affiche *f*, maquette *f* d'une affiche *f*, projet *m* d'affiche *f*
poster stamp	Reklamemarke *f*	timbre *m* réclame *f*
poster type	Plakatschrift *f*	caractères *m/pl* pour affiches *f/pl*
poster-designing	Plakatgestaltung *f*	conception *f* de l'affiche *f*
poster-family	Plakatfamilie *f*	famille *f* d'affiches *f/pl*
poster-like	plakativ	placatif
poster-shop	Plakatladen *m*	poste *m* de vente *f* d'affiches *f/pl*
posting	Ankleben *n*, Plakatierung *f*	affichage *m*, collage *m*
posting period	Anschlagdauer *f*	conservation *f*
posting price per day and poster	Bogentagpreis *m*	prix *m* d'affichage *m* par jour *m* et affiche *f*
to **postpone**	verschieben	décaler, reporter
postponement	Verschiebung *f*	décalage *m*
postponement of a date	Terminverlegung *f*	ajournement *m* d'un délai *m*
post-test	Nachtest *m*	test *m* après parution *f*, test *m* ultérieur
post-testing	Nachprüfung *f*	postenquête *f*
potential	potentiell	potentiel
potential buyer	Kaufinteressent *m*	acheteur *m* potentiel
potential consumer	potentieller Verbraucher *m*	consommateur *m* potentiel
potter	Keramiker *m*	céramiste *m*
powderless etching	Ätzstufen *f/pl*	gravure *f* sans poudrage *m*
practitioner in advertising	Werbepraktiker *m*	praticien *m* de la publicité *f*
preamble	Einleitung *f*	introduction *f*, préambule *f*
precision	Prägnanz *f*	concision *f*
pre-dated paper	vordatierte Zeitung *f*	journal *m* antidaté, journal *m* prédaté, première édition *f*
preface	Vorwort *n*	préface *f*
prefatory note	Vorbemerkung *f*	avis *m* au lecteur *m*, chapeau *m*
preferential tariff	Vorzugstarif *m*	tarif *m* de faveur *f*
preferential terms *pl*	Vorzugsbedingungen *f/pl*	conditions *f/pl* exceptionnelles
preferred position	bevorzugte Plazierung *f*, Vorzugsplazierung *f*	emplacement *m* préférentiel, emplacement *m* privilégié, emplacement *m* spécial, placement *m* de faveur *f*

pre-franked stamp	Freistempelung *f*	timbre *m* pré-oblitéré
prejudice	Voreingenommenheit *f*, Vorurteil *n*	parti *m* pris, préjugé *m*, prévention *f*
prelim	Titelbogen *m*	feuille *f* de titre *m*, pièce *f* préliminaire
preliminary advertisement	Versuchsanzeige *f*	annonce *f* préliminaire
preliminary announcement	Voranzeige *f*	annonce *f* préliminaire, avis *m* préalable
preliminary discussion	Vorbesprechung *f*	entretien *m* préliminaire
preliminary remark	Vorbemerkung *f*	avis *m* au lecteur *m*, chapeau *m*
preliminary work	Vorarbeiten *f/pl*	travaux *m/pl* préliminaires, travaux *m/pl* préparatoires
pre-makeready	Vorzurichtung *f*	pré-mise *f* en train *m*
premium	Sonderangebot *n*, Werbeprämie *f*	offre *f* de faveur *f*, offre *f* spéciale, prime *f*
premium offer	Vorzugsangebot *n*	offre *f* de faveur *f*
to **prepare**	vorrichten	découronner
prepayment	Vorauszahlung *f*	paiement *m* d'avance *m*
pre-planned advertising campaign	langfristig geplante Werbekampagne *f*,	campagne *f* à longue échéance *f*
preposting	Vorleimen *n* eines Plakates *n*	pré-encollage *m*
preprint	Andruck *m*	épreuve *f*, exemplaire *m* d'essai *m*
preprinting	Vordruck *m/typog*	pré-impression *f*
pre-recorded broadcast	aufgezeichnete Sendung *f*, sendefertige Konserve *f*	émission *f* en différé *m*
prescribed date	vorgeschriebenes Datum *n*	date *f* de rigueur *f*, date *f* imposée
prescribed position	Platzvorschrift *f*, Plazierungsvorschrift *f*, vorgeschriebene Plazierung *f*	emplacement *m* imposé, emplacement *m* de rigueur *f*
prescription	Vorschrift *f*	prescription *f*
to **present**	vorzeigen	montrer, présenter
presentation	Darbietung *f*, Präsentation *f*	présentation *f*
presentation copy	Geschenkband *m*, Gratisexemplar *n*, mit Widmung *f* versehene Ausgabe *f*	exemplaire *m* dédicacé, livre-cadeau *m*, service *m* de presse *f*
presenter	Präsentator *m*	présentateur *m*
press	Presse *f*, Zeitungswesen *n*	journalisme *m*, presse *f*
press advertisement	Zeitungsanzeige *f*	annonce *f* de presse *f*
press advertising	Anzeigenwerbung *f*, Pressewerbung *f*, Zeitungswerbung *f*	publicité-presse *f*, publicité *f* par la presse *f*
press agency	Korrespondenzbüro *n*, Nachrichtenbüro *n*, Presseagentur *f*	agence *f* de presse *f*, agence *f* d'information *f*
press agent	Presseagent *m*	agent *m* de publicité *f*
press attaché	Presseattaché *m*, Pressereferent *m*	attaché *m* de presse *f*
press campaign	Pressekampagne *f*	campagne *f* de presse *f*
press centre	Pressezentrum *n*	centre *m* de la presse *f*
press chief	Pressechef *m*	chef *m* de presse *f*

press commentary	Pressekommentar *m*	commentaire *m* de presse *f*
press comments *pl*	Pressestimmen *f/pl*	échos *m/pl* de la presse *f*
press concentration	Pressekonzentration *f*	concentration *f* de la presse *f*
press conference	Pressekonferenz *f*	conférence *f* de presse *f*
press controversy	Pressepolemik *f*	polémique *f* de presse *f*
press credentials *pl*	Journalistenausweis *m*	carte *f* de presse *f*
press cutting	Anzeigenausschnitt *m*	coupure *f*
press density	Zeitungsdichte *f*	pénétration *f* de la presse *f*
press extracts *pl*	Presseauszüge *m/pl*	extraits *m/pl* de la presse *f*
press gallery	Pressetribüne *f*	tribune *f* de la presse *f*
press group	Zeitungsgruppe *f*	groupe *m* de presse *f*
press guide	Pressehandbuch *n*	guide *m* de presse *f*
press item	Zeitungsnotiz *f*	communiqué *m* de presse *f*, nouvelle *f*
press law	Pressegesetz *n*, Presserecht *n*	loi *f* de presse *f*, loi *f* sur la presse *f*
press media	Pressemedien *n/pl*	médias *m/pl* de presse *f*
press news	Pressenachrichten *f/pl*	nouvelles *f/pl* de presse *f*
press notice	Zeitungsnotiz *f*	communiqué *m* de presse *f*, nouvelle *f*
press of opinion	Meinungspresse *f*	presse *f* d'opinion *f*
press offence	Pressedelikt *n*	délit *m* de presse *f*
press office	Pressestelle *f*	office *m* de presse *f*
press officer	Presseattaché *m*	attaché *m* de presse *f*
press passport	Presseausweis *m*	carte *f* de presse *f*
press photo	Pressefoto *n*	photo *f* de presse *f*
press photographer	Bildreporter *m*, Pressefotograf *m*	photographe *m* de presse *f*, reporter-photographe *m*
press proof	Maschinenabzug *m*	morasse *f*
press quotations	Pressezitate *n/pl*	citations *f/pl* de la presse *f*
press reader	Korrektor *m*	correcteur *m*
press reception	Presseempfang *m*	réception *f* de la presse *f*
press release	Presseverlautbarung *f*, Presseversand *m*	action *f* de presse *f*, communiqué *m*, déclaration *f* à la presse *f*
press report	Pressebericht *m*	récit *m*, reportage *m*
press review	Presserundschau *f*	revue *f* de la presse *f*
press revise	druckfertiger Korrektur- bogen *m*, letzte Korrektur *f*, Maschinenrevision *f*	dernière épreuve *f*, morasse *f*, tierce *f*, tierce épreuve *f*
press run	Auflage *f*	tirage *m*
press service	Pressedienst *m*	agence *f* d'information *f*, service *m* de presse *f*
press stenographer	Pressestenograf *m*	sténo *m* de presse *f*
press telegram	Pressetelegramm *n*	télégramme *m* de presse *f*
press tycoon	Pressemagnat *m*	magnat *m* de la presse *f*
press with a large circulation	auflagenstarke Presse *f*	grande presse *f*, presse *f* à grand tirage *m*
press-box	Presseloge *f*, Pressestand *m*	banc *m* de la presse *f*, stand *m* de la presse *f*
press-copy	Presseexemplar *n*	service *m* de presse *f*
press-cutting	Zeitungsausschnitt *m*	coupure *f* de presse *f*
press-cutting agency, press-cutting service	Ausschnittdienst *m*, Zeitungsausschnittbüro *n*	argus *m* de la presse *f*, bureau *m* de coupure *f* de journaux *m/pl*, coupure *f*
pressed for space, to be	Platzmangel *m* haben	être à court de place *f*

press-group	Zeitungskette f	chaîne f de journaux m/pl
press-guide	Zeitungskatalog m	catalogue m des journaux m/pl
press-mark	Standortnummer f	numéro m de classement m
press-release	Waschzettel m	brouillon m, note f de critique f, papillon m, prière f d'insérer
pressure	Schattierung f	foulage m
pressure group	Interessentengruppe f	groupe m de pression f
pressure of space	Raummangel m	manque f de place f
presswork	Pressearbeit f	activité f du journaliste m
prestige advertising	Goodwillwerbung f, Prestigewerbung f, Repräsentationswerbung f	publicité f de notoriété f, publicité f de prestige m, publicité f impériale
prestige paper	Qualitätzeitung f	journal m de première qualité f, journal m de prestige m, journal m pour l'élite f
pretence	Fiktion f	fiction f
pre-test	Anzeigenvortest m, Werbevortest m	pré-test m, test m préalable
pretest	Vortest m	préenquête f, test m préalable
pretesting	Voruntersuchung f	enquête f pilote, pré-test m, préenquête f
preventive advertising	Präventivwerbung f	publicité f préventive
preventive censorship	Vorzensur f	censure f préventive
pre-view	Vorschau f	avant-première f, bande f de lancement m
price	Preis m	prix m, taux m
price abatement	Preisermäßigung f	rabais m, remise f
price adjustment	Preisangleichung f	alignement m des prix m/pl
price advance	Preisanstieg m	montée f des prix m/pl
price alteration	Preisänderung f	modification f du prix m
price boost	Preiserhöhung f, Preissteigerung f	augmentation f de prix m
price changes pl	Preisänderung f	modification f du prix m
price comparison	Preisvergleich m	comparaison f des prix m/pl
price development	Preisentwicklung f	évolution f des prix m/pl
price including	Inklusivpreis m	prix m global
price list	Preisliste f, Tarif m	liste f de prix, prix m courant m, tarif m
price making	Preisbildung f	formation f des prix m/pl
price marker	Preisschild n	étiquette f, porte-prix m
price marking	Preisauszeichnung f	affichage m des prix m/pl
price per line	Zeilenpreis m	prix m d'une ligne f
price policy	Preispolitik f	politique f des prix m/pl
price protection	Preisschutz m	protection f des prix m/pl
price quotation	Preisangabe f	indication f du prix m
price slashing	Preisschleuderei f	avilissement m des prix m/pl
price tag	Preisschild n	étiquette f, porte-prix m
price threshold	Preisschwelle f	seuil m de prix m
price variance	Preisänderung f	modification f du prix m
price-cutting	Preisunterbietung f	bradage m, gâchage m de prix m
price-fixing agreement	Preisabsprache f	entente f sur les prix m/pl
pricing	Preisgestaltung f	formation f des prix m/pl
primary appeal	Hauptblickfang m	accroche-œil m primaire
primary colour	Grundfarbe f	couleur f de base f
primary reader	Erstleser m	premier lecteur m

primary-demand advertising	Primärwerbung f	publicité f primaire
prime	Schöndruck m	côté m de première, impression f au recto m, impression f en blanc, premier folio m
prime cost	Selbstkosten pl	prix m coûtant, prix m de revient
principal consumers pl	Hauptzielgruppe f	cible f principale
principle	Grundsatz m	principe m
principles pl of selling	Verkaufsrichtlinien f/pl	principes m/pl de vente f
print	Abzug m	contre-type m, épreuve f
to print	drucken	imprimer, tirer
print advertising	Werbung f in gedruckten Medien n/pl	publicité f dans des médias m/pl imprimés
print figure	Druckauflage f	tirage m impression f
to print on	eindrucken	repiquer sur
print run	Auflagenhöhe f, Druckauflage f	chiffre m du tirage m, tirage m impression f
print script	Blockschrift f	caractères m/pl bâtons m/pl, écriture f script
printable	druckfähig	imprimable
printed matter	Druckerzeugnis n, Drucksache f	imprimé m
printed medium	Insertionsmedium n	média m imprimé
printed shading tint	Rasterpapier n	trame f imprimée, trame f mécanique
printed sheet	Druckbogen m	feuille f imprimée
printer	Drucker m	imprimeur m
printer's ink	Druckerschwärze f	encre f d'imprimerie f, encre f grasse
printer's mark	Druckerzeichen n	marque f d'imprimeur m
printer's reader	Hauskorrektor m	correcteur m de l'imprimerie f
printing	Druck m, Drucklegung f	impression f, mise à l'impression f, mise sous presse f
printing costs pl	Druckkosten pl	frais m/pl d'impression f
printing error	Druckfehler m	coquille f, erreur f de composition f, faute f d'impression f, faute f typographique
printing form am, printing forme brit	Druckform f	forme f à impression f
printing ink	Druckfarbe f	encre f d'impression f
printing material	Druckunterlage f	documents m/pl d'impression f, matériel m d'impression f
printing method	Druckverfahren n	mode m d'impression f, procédé m d'impression f
printing of a certain number of copies pl	Druck m einer bestimmten Anzahl f von Exemplaren n/pl	tirage m à la suite f
printing office	Druckerei f, Offizin f	imprimerie f
printing on fabrics pl	Stoffdruck m	histotypie f, impression f sur étoffes f/pl
printing one face	Schöndruck m	côté m de première, impression f au recto m, impression f en blanc, premier folio m
printing order	Druckauftrag m	commande f d'impression f

printing paper	Druckpapier *n*	papier *m* à imprimer
printing plant	Druckerei *f*	imprimerie *f*
printing plate	Druckplatte *f*	plaque *f* d'impression *f*
printing press	Druckmaschine *f*, Druckpresse *f*	machine *f* à imprimer, presse *f* à imprimer
printing process	Druckprinzip *n*, Druckverfahren *n*	mode *m* d'impression *f*, principe *m* d'impression *f*, procédé *m* d'impression *f*
printing space	Satzspiegel *m*	surface *f* de justification *f*, surface *f* d'impression *f*, surface *f* utile
printing surface	Druckfläche *f*	surface *f* d'impression *f*
printing techniques *pl*	Drucktechnik *f*	technique *f* d'imprimerie *f*
printing trade	Druckgewerbe *n*	industries *f/pl* graphiques
printing type	Drucktype *f*	caractère *m* d'imprimerie *f*
printing work	Verlagserscheinung *f*	publication *f*, titre *m*
printing works *pl*	Druckarbeiten *f/pl*	travaux *m/pl* d'impression *f*
printing-frame	Kopierrahmen *m*	châssis *m*-presse *f*
printing-number	Auflagenhöhe *f*	chiffre *m* du tirage *m*
printings *pl/am*	Drucksache *f*	imprimé *m*
priority job	Schnellschuß *m*	coup *m* de feu *m*, train *m* urgent
prise pick-up	Tonabnahme *f*	prise *f* tourne-disque *f*
prison editor	Sitzredakteur *m*	homme *m* de paille *f* mis en avant en cas *m* de poursuites *f/pl* judiciaires
private brand	Eigenmarke *f*, Handelsmarke *f*, Hausmarke *f*	marque *f* de distributeur *m*
private edition	Privatdruck *m*	édition *f* privée
private station	Privatsender *m*	station *f* privée
prize contest	Preisausschreiben *n*	mise *f* au concours *m*
probationer	Auszubildender *m*	stagiaire *m*
problem play	Problemstück *n*	pièce *f* à thèse *f*
procedure	Arbeitsablauf *m*, Vorgehen *n*	procédé *m*, procédure *f*
process block *brit*	Strichätzung *f*	cliché *m* au trait *m*, gravure *f* au trait *m*
process engraver	Autotypieätzer *m*, Chemigraf *m*	clicheur *m*, graveur *m*, photograveur *m*, similiste *m*, zincographe *m*
process engraving	Autotypie *f*	autotypie *f*, similigravure *f*
process letter	vervielfältigter Brief *m*	lettre *f* reproduite
process of work	Arbeitsgang *m*	opération *f*, phase *f* de travail *m*
process plate	Mehrfarbenklischee *n*	cliché *m* d'impression *f* couleur *f*
process printing	Mehrfarbendruck *m*	impression *f* en couleurs *f/pl*, impression *f* multicolore
processing	Verarbeitung *f*	façonnage *m*
processing of the news	Nachrichtenverarbeitung *f*	traitement *m* des nouvelles *f/pl*
producer	Hersteller *m*, Produzent *m*	producteur *m*
producer advertising	Herstellerwerbung *f*	publicité *f* des producteurs *m/pl*
producer of advertising films *pl*	Werbefilmproduzent *m*	producteur *m* de films *m/pl* publicitaires
producer's brand	Fabrikmarke *f*	marque *f* de fabricant *m*
producer's goods *pl*	Produktionsgüter *n/pl*	articles *m/pl* industriels, biens *m/pl* de production *f*
producer's price	Erzeugerpreis *m*	prix *m* à la production *f*

product	Erzeugnis *n*, Produkt *m*	produit *m*
product advertising	informierende Werbung *f*, Produktwerbung *f*, Werbung *f*, produktbezogene	publicité *f* informative, publicité *f* instructive, publicité *f* produits *m/pl*, publicité *f* relative au produit *m*
product analysis	Produktanalyse *f*	analyse *f* du produit *m*
product category	Produktgattung *f*	catégorie *f* de biens *m/pl*
product identification	Produkterkennung *f*	identification *f* de produit *m*
product manager	Produktionsleiter *m*, Produktmanager *m*	chef *m* de produit *m*, directeur *m* de la production *f*, spécialiste *m* produit *m*
product personality	Markencharakter *m*	caractère *m* propre d'une marque *f*
product publicity	Aufklärungswerbung *f*	publicité *f* argumentée, publicité *f* produits *m/pl*
product research	Produktforschung *f*	étude *f* des produits *m/pl*
product testing	Produkttest *m*	contrôle *m* de produit *m*, test *m* de produit *m*
production	Erzeugung *f*, Herstellung *f*	fabrication *f*, production *f*
production costs *pl*	Herstellungskosten *pl*	frais *pl* de fabrication *f*, prix *m* · de fabrication *f*
production expert	Herstellungsfachmann *m*	expert *m* en fabrication *f*
production run	Fortdruck *m*	impression *f* du tirage *m*, tiré à part *f*
production techniques *pl*	Produktionstechnik *f*	processus *m* de production *f*
professional advertising	Fachwerbung *f*	publicité *f* spécialisée
professional magazine	Berufszeitschrift *f*, Fachzeitschrift *f*	revue *f* professionnelle
professional organization	Berufsverband *m*	organisme *m* professionnel
professional press	Berufspresse *f*	presse *f* professionnelle
profile	biografische Skizze *f*	portrait *m* biographique
profit	Gewinn *m*, Nutzen *m*	bénéfice *m*, profit *m*, utilité *f*
profitability	Wirtschaftlichkeit *f*	rentabilité *f*
profitable	gewinnbringend	lucratif, profitable
prognosis	Prognose *f*	pronostic *m*
to program	programmieren	programmer
program *am*	Programm *n*	programme *m*
program analyzer	Apparatur *f* zur Prüfung *f* der Werbewirkung *f*	appareil *m* pour tester l'effet *m* publicitaire
program structure	Programmstruktur *f*	structure *f* du programme *m*
programme *brit*	Programm *n*	programme *m*
programme framing the commercials *pl*	Rahmenprogramm *n*	programme *m* encadrant les émissions *f/pl* publicitaires
programme of work	Arbeitsprogramm *n*	programme *m* des travaux *m/pl*
programmer	Arbeitsplaner *m*	préparateur *m*
programming	Programmgestaltung *f*	programmation *f*
progress control	Terminkontrolle *f*	contrôle *m* des délais *m/pl*
progress of work	Arbeitsabwicklung *f*	cours *m* de travail *m*
progress report	Tageszettel *m*	fiche *f* de travail *m*
progressive	fortschrittlich	avant-garde *f*, progressiste
progressive advertising	fortschrittliche Werbung *f*	publicité *f* moderne
progressive proof	Farbandruck *m*	épreuve *f* en couleurs *f/pl*, suite *f*

prohibition to advertise	Werbeverbot n	défense f de faire de la publicité f
prohibition to print	Druckverbot n	défense f d'imprimer
projection	Vorführung f	démonstration f, présentation f, projection f
projection of advertising film slides pl	Werbediavorführung f	film-fixe m
projection technique	Projektionstechnik f	technique f de projection f
projector	Projektor m	projecteur m
promising market	erfolgversprechender Absatzmarkt m	débouché m plein de promesses f/pl
promotion	Förderung f	promotion f
promotion matter	Verkaufshilfe f	aide f à la vente f
promotional material	Werbeunterlagen f/pl	documents m/pl publicitaires
proof	Abzug m, Andruck m, Druckbogen m, Druckfahne f, Druckprobe f, Fahne f/typog f, Korrekturabzug m, Probeabzug m	contre-type m, épreuve f, exemplaire m d'essai m, feuille f imprimée, placard m
to proof	abziehen (Druck)	tirer
proof page	Probeseite f	page f modèle m, page f spécimen m
proof press	Abziehpresse f	presse f à épreuves f/pl
proofer	Abzieher m	tireur m des épreuves f/pl
proofing	Andruck m	épreuve f, exemplaire m d'essai m
proofing paper	Andruckpapier n	papier m pour tirage m d'épreuves f/pl
proofreader's mark	Korrekturzeichen f	marque f du correcteur m, signe m de correction f
proof-reading	Korrektur f lesen	correction f d'épreuves f/pl
proofsheet	Probeabzug m	épreuve f
prop	Fernsehrequisit n, Ständer m, Stütze f	portatif m, présentoir m, support m
propaganda	Propaganda f, Werbetätigkeit f	activité f publicitaire, propagande f
propaganda film	Propagandafilm m	film m à propagande f
propaganda week	Reklamewoche f, Werbewoche f	semaine f de propagande f, semaine f publicitaire
propagandist	Propagandist m, Werber m	propagandiste m
to propagandize, to propagate	propagieren	faire de la propagande f, propager
propagation time	Laufzeit f	rut m
proportionality	Größenverhältnis n	rapports m/pl de grandeur f
proposal	Exposé n	exposé m, proposition f
to propose	vorschlagen	proposer, suggérer
proposition	Vorschlag m	proposition f, suggestion f
prospect	eventueller Kunde m, Interessent m, möglicher Kunde m, voraussichtlicher Kunde m	prospect m
prospectus	Prospekt m	brochure f, dépliant m, prospectus m, tract m
protection of registered design	Gebrauchsmusterschutz m	protection f des modèles m/pl et dessins m/pl
protection of trademarks pl	Warenzeichenschutz m	protection f des marques f/pl
prototype	Vorbild n	modèle m, prototype m

proverb	Sprichwort *n*	proverbe *m*
to **provide with sound**	beschallen	sonoriser
providing of sound effects *pl*	Beschallung *f*	sonorisation *f*
provincial paper	Provinzblatt *n*	feuille *f* régionale
provincial press	Provinzpresse *f*	presse *f* provinciale
provisional	provisorisch	provisoire
provisional booking	provisorischer Abschluß *m*	ordre *m* provisoire
provisional title	Arbeitstitel *m*	titre *m* provisoire
to **prune**	beschneiden	ébarber, rogner, taillader, tailler
pseudonym	Deckname *m*, Pseudonym *n*	nom *m* de guerre *f*, nom *m* de plume *f*, pseudonyme *m*
pseudoscientific advertising	scheinwissenschaftliche Werbung *f*	publicité *f* pseudo-scientifique
psychological price	psychologisch richtiger Preis *m*	prix *m* psychologique
public	öffentlich	public
public address system	Lautsprecheranlage *f*	ensemble micro-ampli-haut-parleur *m*
public at large	großes Publikum *n*	grand public *m*
public clock pillar	Normaluhrensäule *f*	colonne *f* des horloges *f/pl* publiques
public institution	öffentlich-rechtliche Anstalt *f*	établissement *m* de droit *m* public
public interest	Allgemeininteresse *n*	intérêt *m* général
public opinion	öffentliche Meinung *f*	opinion *f* publique
public opinion analysis	Demoskopie *f*, Meinungsforschung *f*	enquête *f* sur les opinions *f/pl*, sondage *m* de l'opinion *f* publique, sondage *m* d'opinion *f*
public opinion analyst	Meinungsforscher *m*	enquêteur *m* d'opinion *f*
public property	öffentlicher Grund *m* und Boden *m*	domaine *m* public
public relations *pl*	Meinungspflege *f*, Öffentlichkeitsarbeit *f*, public relations *f/pl*, Vertrauenswerbung *f*, Zielpublizistik *f*	relations *f/pl* extérieures, relations *f/pl* publiques
public relations *pl* **agency**	PR-Agentur *f*	agence *f* des relations *f/pl* publiques
public relations *pl* **office**	Presseamt *n*	office *m* de presse *f*
public relations *pl* **officer**	PR-Bearbeiter *m*	responsable des relations *pl* avec le public *m*
public relations *pl* **report**	PR-Anzeige *f*	publi-information *f*, publi-reportage *m*
public service posters *pl*	gemeinnützige Plakatierung *f*	affiches *f/pl* pour le service *m* public
publication	Druckschrift *f* (Veröffentlichung *f*), Organ *n*, Publikation *f*, Verlagserscheinung *f*	imprimé *m*, organe *m*, publication *f*, titre *m*
publication date	Erscheinungsdatum *n*, Erscheinungstag *m*	date *f* de parution *f*, date *f* de publication *f*, jour *m* de parution *f*
publicist	Publizist *m*, Schriftsteller *m*	auteur *m*, écrivain *m*, publiciste *m*

publicity	Öffentlichkeit *f,* Öffentlichkeitsarbeit *f,* Publizität *f,* Werbewesen *n,* Werbung *f*	propagande *f,* publicité *f,* réclame *f,* relations *f/pl* publiques
publicity copy	Werbenummer *f*	numéro *m* de propagande *f*
publicity department	Pressestelle *f,* Werbeabteilung *f*	département *m* de publicité *f,* office *m* de presse *f,* service *m* de publicité *f*
publicity event	Werbeveranstaltung *f*	manifestation *f* publicitaire
publicity expenses *pl*	Werbungskosten *pl*	frais *m/pl* de publicité *f*
publicity film	Werbefilm *m*	film *m* publicitaire
publicity methods *pl*	Werbemethoden *f/pl*	méthodes *f/pl* publicitaires
publicity motif	Bildmotiv *n*	motif *m* publicitaire
publicity stock	Werbeetat *m*	budget *m* publicitaire
publicity tour	Werbefahrt *f*	tournée *f* de propagande *f*
publicity work	Werbearbeit *f*	travail *m* de publicité *f*
to **publicize**	Information *f* verbreiten	faire connaître au public *m*
public-relations *pl* **consultant**	PR-Berater *m*	conseil *m* en relations *f/pl* publiques
to **publish**	annoncieren, herausgeben, publizieren, verlegen, veröffentlichen	éditer, insérer, publier, sortir
publishable	Veröffentlichung *f,* geeignet zur	publiable
published, to be	abnehmbar	à épuiser
published by the author	Selbstverlag *m,* im	chez l'auteur *m*
published within one year, to be	abzunehmen innerhalb eines Jahres *n*	à épuiser dans le délai *m* d'une année *f*
publisher	Herausgeber *m,* Verleger *m,* Zeitungsherausgeber *m*	gérant *m*
publisher's blurb	Waschzettel *m*	brouillon *m,* note *f* de critique *f,* papillon *m,* prière *f* d'insérer
publisher's colophon	Verlagssignet *n*	marque *f* d'éditeur *m,* signet *m*
publisher's copy	Hausexemplar *n,* Verlagsstück *n*	exemplaire-éditeur *m*
publisher's discount	Verlegerrabatt *m*	rabais *m* aux éditeurs *m/pl*
publisher's imprint	Verlagssignet *n*	marque *f* d'éditeur *m,* signet *m*
publisher's note	Waschzettel *m*	brouillon *m,* note *f* de critique *f,* papillon *m,* prière *f* d'insérer
publisher's representative	Verlagsvertreter *m*	vendeur *m* d'espace *m*
publisher's statement	Auflagemeldung *f*	rapport *m* sur les tirages *m/pl*
publishing company	Verlag *m*	maison *f* d'édition *f*
publishing house		
publishing intervals *pl*	Erscheinungsweise *f*	mode *m* de parution *f,* périodicité *f*
puff advertising	Werbeübertreibung *f*	outrance *f* publicitaire
to **puff up**	aufbauschen	enfler, faire mousser
to **puff up an information**	eine Nachricht *f* hochspielen	donner une publicité *f* retentissante, gonfler un papier *m,* remonter une nouvelle *f*
puffing publicity	anreißerische Werbung *f,* marktschreierische Werbung *f,* Werberummel *m*	battage *m* publicitaire, bourrage *m* de crâne *m,* publicité *f* raccrocheuse, publicité *f* tapageuse, tam-tam *m*
pull	Abzug *m,* Probeabzug *m*	contre-type *m,* épreuve *f*
to **pull**	abziehen (Druck)	tirer
to **pull a proof**	andrucken	tirer des épreuves *f/pl*
to **pull out**	ausreißen	séparer
to **pull to pieces** *pl*	verreißen	critiquer sévèrement, éreinter

puller	Zugnummer *f*	locomotive *f*
pulling power	Werbekraft *f*, Zugkraft *f*	accrochage *m* publicitaire, attrait *m* publicitaire, force *f* d'attraction *f*, puissance *f* publicitaire
pulp	Papiermasse *f*	pâte *f* de papier *m*
pulp magazine	Groschenheft *n*	revue *f* à deux sous *m/pl*, revue *f* de concierge *f*
pun	Wortspiel *n*	calembour *m*, jeu *m* de mots *m/pl*
punch	Patrize *f*, Schlagkraft *f*, Schmiß *m*	force *f*, poinçon *m*, style *m* énergique
to **punch**	stanzen	découper à l'emportepièce *f*, étamper
punch line	Schlagzeile *f*	ligne *f* principale, ligne *f* repère, manchette *f*, phrase *f* -choc *m*, titre *m* en vedette *f*
punched card	Lochkarte *f*	fiche *f* perforée
punched tape	Lochstreifen *m*	bande *f* perforée, ruban *m* perforé
punctuation	Interpunktion *f*, Zeichensetzung *f*	ponctuation *f*
punctuation mark	Satzzeichen *n*	signe *m* de ponctuation *f*
purchase	Kauf *m*	achat *m*
purchase intention	Kaufabsicht *f*	intention *f* d'achat *m*
purchase order	Kaufvertrag *m*	contrat *m* de vente *f*
purchase pattern	Käuferverhalten *n*	comportement *m* des acheteurs *m/pl*, habitudes *f/pl* des acheteurs *m/pl*
purchase proposition	Verkaufsargumentation *f*	argumentation *f* de vente *f*, propositions *f/pl* commerciales
purchase rhythm	Einkaufshäufigkeit *f*, Einkaufsrhythmus *m*, Verkaufsrhythmus *m*	fréquence *f* d'achat *m*, périodicité *f* d'achat *m*, rythme *m* d'achat *m*
purchase-money	Kaufpreis *m*	prix *m* d'achat *m*
purchaser	Käufer *m* (in *f*)	acheteur *m*, acheteuse *f*
purchasing power	Kaufkraft *f*	capacité *f* d'achat *m*, pouvoir *m* d'achat *m*
purchasing power class	Kaufkraftklasse *f*	catégorie *f* de pouvoir *m* d'achat *m*
pure recall	spontane Erinnerung *f*	mémoire *f* spontanée, souvenir *m* spontané
purport	Tenor *m*	teneur *f*
purveyor	Lieferant *m*	fournisseur *m*
push	neuer Schwung *m*	poussée *f*
to **push**	die Werbetrommel *f* rühren	battre la grosse caisse *f*
to **put down**	in Kleinbuchstaben *m/pl* absetzen	composer en minuscules *f/pl*
to **put forward**	vorverlegen	avancer
to **put in an envelope**	einkuvertieren	mettre sous enveloppe *f*
to **put in parentheses** *pl*	einklammern	mettre en crochets *m/pl*, mettre en parenthèses *f/pl*
to **put in the stops** *pl*	interpunktieren	ponctuer
to **put into cold-storage**	Eis *n* legen, auf	mise *f* au frigo *m*
putting in an envelope	Kuvertierung *f*	mise sous enveloppes *f/pl*
puzzle corner	Rätselecke *f*	coin *m* des devinettes *f/pl*

Q

quad	Quadrat *n*	cadrat *m*
quadder	Füller *m*	annonce *f* d'opportunité *f*, bouche-trou *m*, remplissage *m*
quadrat	Quadrat *n*	cadrat *m*
qualified and controlled circulation paper	Kennzifferzeitschrift *f*	périodique *m* d'une circulation *f* contrôlée et qualifiée
quality	Qualität *f*	qualité *f*
quality label	Gütezeichen *n*	étiquette *f* de qualité *f*, label *m* de qualité *f*, marque *f* de garantie *f*, sigle *m*
quality of prints *pl*	Druckausfall *m*	qualité *f* de l'impression *f*
quality of type	Schriftqualität *f*	qualité *f* typographique
quality paper	Prestigezeitung *f*, Qualitätszeitung *f*	journal *m* de première qualité *f*, journal *m* de prestige *m*, journal *m* de qualité *f*, journal *m* pour l'élite *f*
quality product	Qualitätserzeugnis *n*	produit *m* de qualité *f*
quality sample	Ausfallmuster *n*	échantillon *m* de comparaison *f*
quantity discount	Mengenrabatt *m*	dégressif *m* sur volume *m* publicitaire, rabais *m* de quantité *f*, remise *f* de quantité *f*
quarter page	Viertelseite *f*	quart *m* de page *f*
quarterly	alle drei Monate *m/pl*, vierteljährlich, Vierteljahreszeitschrift *f*	revue *f* trimestrielle, trimestriel
quarto size	Quartformat *n*	format *m* in-quarto
query, question	Anfrage *f*, Frage *f*	demande *f*, interrogation *f*, question *f*
question form	Fragebogen *m*	questionnaire *m*
question mark	Fragezeichen *n*	point *m* d'interrogation *f*
questioning	Befragung *f*	enquête *f*, interrogatoire *m*, interview *f*
questionnaire	Fragebogen *m*	questionnaire *m*
quibble	fadenscheinige Ausrede, Wortspiel *n*	argutie *f*, calembour *m*, faux-fuyant *m*, jeu *m* de mots *m/pl*
quick seller	leichtverkäufliches Buch *n*, schnellverkäufliches Buch *n*	livre *m* d'écoulement *m* facile
quickie	kurzer Werbefilm *m*, Werbespot *m*, Kurzfilm *m*	court-métrage *m*, spot *m* court
quip	witzige Bemerkung *f*	raillerie *f*
quire	Lage *f* (Papier *n*), Papierlage *f*	cahier *m*, main *f*
quire (25 sheet)	Buch *n* (25 Bogen *m/pl* Papier *n*)	main *f*
quiz	Ratespiel *n*	devinette *f*
to quoin	Form *f* schließen	boucler, serrer
quota	Anteil *m*, Quote *f*	contingent *m*, quota *m*
quota of profits *pl*	Gewinnanteil *m*	tantième *f*
quotation	Erwähnung *f*, Kostenvoranschlag *m*, Notierung *f*, Preisangebot *n*, Zitat *n*	citation *f*, devis *m* estimatif, évaluation des frais *m/pl*, mention *f*, offre *f* de prix *m*

to **quote**	Preis *m* angeben	citer, coter

R

race court	Rennbahn *f*	champ *m* de cours *m*
to **race past a colleague**	überrunden (einen Kollegen *m*)	griller un confrère *m*
rack	Regal *n*	étagère *f*, rayon *m*
rack folder	Werbefaltblatt *n* für Spezialauslage *f*	dépliant *m* publicitaire pour étalage *m* spécial
rack-jobber	Pächter *m* einer Verkaufsfläche *f* im Supermarkt *m*	fermier *m* d'un rayon *m* spécialisé dans un supermarché *m*
radio	Rundfunk *m*	radio *f*
radio advertising	Funkwerbung *f*, Hörfunkwerbung *f*, Rundfunkwerbung *f*	publicité *f* radiophonique
radio and television program paper	Rundfunk- und Fernseh- Programmzeitschrift *f*	revue-programme *m* de la radio *f* et de la télévision *f*
radio and television rates *pl*	Sendegebühren *f/pl*	tarif *m* d'antenne *f*
radio announcement	Werbedurchsage *f*	annonce *f* à la radio *f*, bref communiqué *m* radio *f*
radio announcer	Rundfunksprecher *m*	chroniqueur *m*, speaker *m*
radio audience	Rundfunkhörerschaft *f*	audience *f* de la radio *f*
radio casting *am*	Rundfunksendung *f*	émission *f* radiophonique, radiodiffusion *f*
radio communication	Nachrichtenübermittlung *f*	radiocommunication *f*, transmission *f* des informations *f/pl*
radio communicator *am*	Rundfunksprecher *m*	chroniqueur *m*, speaker *m*
radio drama	Hörspiel *n*	pièce *f* radiophonique
radio listener	Rundfunkteilnehmer *m*	sans-filiste *m*
radio program *am* **radio programme** *brit*	Funkprogramm *n*	calendrier *m* des émissions *f/pl*
radio report	Hörbericht *m*	reportage *m* parlé
radio set	Empfänger *m* (Radio)	récepteur *m*
radiocommunication	Funkübertragung *f*	radiocommunication *f*
radiotelephony	Sprechfunkverbindung *f*	circuit *m* radio-téléphonique
rag paper	Hadernpapier *n*	papier *m* de chiffons *m/pl*
rag-book	unzerreißbares Bilderbuch *n*	livre *m* d'images *f/pl* sur toile *f*
railroad bulletin	Streckenplakat *n*	enseigne *f* routière, panneau *m* d'affichage *m* le long *m* d'une voie *f* ferrée
railroad showing	Eisenbahnplakat *n*	emplacement *m* intérieur de chemin *m* de fer *m*
railway advertising	Eisenbahnwerbung *f*	publicité *f* par chemin *m* de fer *m*
railway guide	Kursbuch *n*	indicateur *m*
railway station advertising	Bahnhofswerbung *f*	publicité *f* dans les gares *f/pl*
raised standard rate	erhöhter Grundpreis *m*	prix *m* de base *f* augmenté
random	zufällig	au hasard *m*
random sample	Zufallsstichprobe *f*	échantillon *m* au hasard *m*
range	Reichweite *f*	couverture *f*, rayon *m* d'action *f*, taux *m* de pénétration *f*
range of customers *pl*	Kundenkreis *m*	clientèle *f*
rapid-motion method	Zeitraffer *m*	accélérateur *m*
rate	Preis *m*	prix *m*, taux *m*
to **rate**	schätzen	évaluer, taxer

rate association	Tarifgemeinschaft f	communauté f de tarif m
rate book	Zeitungskatalog m	catalogue m des journaux m/pl
rate card	Preisliste f, Tarif m	liste f de prix, prix m courant, tarif m
rate card index	Tarifkartei f	fichier m de tarifs m/pl
rate combination	Tarifkombination f	couplage m de tarif m
rate holder	Anzeige f zur Erreichung f eines höheren Nachlasses m	annonce f complémentaire pour bénéficier du dégressif m
rate increase	Aufschlag m	majoration f de tarif m, supplément m
rate maker	Anzeige f zur Erreichung f eines höheren Nachlasses m	annonce f complémentaire pour bénéficier du dégressif m
rate of commission	Provisionssatz m	taux m de commission f
rate sheet	Tarifblatt n	feuille f de tarif m
rate structure	Tarifaufbau m	structure f de tarif m
rates pl	Preisliste f, Tarif m	liste f de prix, prix m courant m, prix m courant, tarif m
rating	Erfolgskontrolle f	contrôle m des résultats m/pl, contrôle m du rendement m, contrôle m du succès m
rational advertising	vernünftige Werbung f	publicité f rationnelle
raw data pl	Rohdaten n/pl	données f/pl brutes
raw material	Werkstoff m	matériaux m/pl
to **reach**	erreichen	toucher
reach am	Reichweite f	couverture f, rayon m d'action f, taux m de pénétration f
to **read in the metal**	Blei n lesen, auf dem	lire sur le plomb m
to **read out**	vorlesen	lire qch. à qn.
readability	Verständlichkeit f	intelligibilité f
reader	Leser m	lecteur m
reader advertisement	redaktionell aufgemachte Anzeige f, Textanzeige f	annonce f à apparence f rédactionnelle, annonce f figurant dans le texte m rédactionnel
reader confidence	Lesertreue f	fidélité f de lecture f
reader interest research	Leseranalyse f, Leserschaftsforschung f	analyse f de l'audience f, analyse f des lecteurs m/pl, étude f des lecteurs m/pl
reader-magazine-relationship	Leserblattbindung f	relations f/pl des lecteurs m/pl avec leur journal m
readers pl	Leserschaft f	audience f, ensemble m des lecteurs m/pl, masse f des lecteurs m/pl
reader's attachment	Leserverbundenheit f	attachement m à la revue f
reader's proof	Hauskorrektur f	épreuve f en première, première correction f
readership	Leserkreis m, Leserschaft f	audience f, cercle m de lecteurs m/pl, degré m de lecture f, ensemble m des lecteurs m/pl, masse f des lecteurs m/pl
readership figure	Leserzahl f	nombre m des lecteurs m/pl

readership poll	Leserschaftsumfrage f	enquête f auprès des lecteurs m/pl
readership survey	Leseranalyse f	analyse f de l'audience f, analyse f des lecteurs m/pl
reading	Lektüre f, Lesart f	lecture f, version f
reading behaviour	Lesegewohnheit f	habitudes f/pl des lecteurs m/pl
reading circle case	Lesemappe f	enveloppe f dans les cercles m/pl de lecture f
reading duration	Lesedauer f	temps m de lecture f
reading habits pl	Lesegewohnheit f	habitudes f/pl des lecteurs m/pl
reading intensity	Leseintensität f	intensité f de la lecture f
reading mark	Lesezeichen n	signet m
reading matter	Lesestoff m	choses f/pl à lire
reading notice am	redaktionell aufgemachte Anzeige f	annonce f à apparence f rédactionnelle
reading rate	Lesegeschwindigkeit f	vitesse f de lecture f
reading-room	Lesesaal m	salle f de lecture f
ready for press	druckfertig, druckreif, Imprimatur n	bon à imprimer, bon à tirer, permission f d'imprimer, prêt à imprimer
ready for printing, ready for shipping	versandfertig	prêt à expédier
ready for stereotyping	klischierfertig	prêt à être cliché m
ready print	Maternkorrespondenz f	service m matrice
real estate advertisement	Immobilienanzeige f	annonce f immobilière
realization	Ausführung f	exécution f, réalisation f
ream	Ries n	rame f
rear	Heck n	arrière m
rear reflector	Katzenauge n, Lichtreflektor m	catadioptre m, cataphote m
rear waistband	Heckstreifen m	bandeau m arrière
reasons pl for buying	Kaufmotive n/pl	motivation f d'achat m
reason-why advertising	Aufklärungswerbung f, begründende Werbung f	publicité f argumentée, publicité f produits m/pl
rebate	Nachlaß m, Rabatt m, Rückvergütung f	escompte m, rabais m, réduction f, remboursement m, remise f
recall aid	Gedächtnishilfe f	moyen m mnémotechnique
recall test	Erinnerungstest m, Gedächtnisprüfung f	test m de mémorisation f, test m de souvenir m aidé, test m de souvenir m spontané
to recapitulate	zusammenfassen	cumuler, récapituler, résumer
recapitulation	Zusammenfassung f	récapitulation f, résumé m
to recast	umschmelzen	refondre
receipt	Lieferschein m	décharge f de livraison f, reçu m
receipts pl	Einnahmen f/pl	recettes f/pl
reception of advertisements pl	Anzeigenannahme f	réception f d'annonces f/pl
receptivity	Aufnahmefähigkeit f	réceptivité f
recess	Aussparung f	blanc m, évidement m, niche f
recipient	Empfänger m	destinataire m, récepteur m
to recognise	anerkennen	reconnaître
recognised	anerkannt	accrédité, reconnu

recognised advertising agency	anerkannte Werbeagentur *f*, anerkannter Werbungsmittler *m*	agence *f* de publicité *f* reconnue
recognition	Anerkennung *f*	reconnaissance *f*
recognition test	Erinnerungstest *m*, Wiedererkennungstest *m*	étude *f* d'identification *f*, test *m* de mémorisation *f*, test *m* de souvenir *m* spontané
recommendation	Empfehlung *f*	recommandation *f*
record	Denkschrift *f*, Niederschrift *f*	écrit *m*, exposé *m*, mémoire *m*, mémorandum *m*, procès-verbal *m*
record advertising	Schallplattenwerbung *f*	publicité *f* orale
record *brit*	Schallplatte *f*	disque *m*
record copy	Archivexemplar *n*	exemplaire *m* des archives *f/pl*, exemplaire *m* en collection *f*
record cover	Schallplattenhülle *f*	pochette *f* de disque *m*
record library	Schallplattensammlung *f*, Tonbandarchiv *n*	discothèque *f*, phonotèque *f*
record office	Archiv *n*, Dokumentationsabteilung *f*	archives *f/pl*, service *m* de documentation *f*
record player	Plattenspieler *m*	tourne-disques *m*
record sleeve	Schallplattenhülle *f*	pochette *f* de disque *m*
recorder	Plattenspieler *m*, Wiedergabegerät *n*	appareil *m* enregistreur, tourne-disques *m*
record-library	Diskothek *f*	discothèque *f*
records *pl*	Annalen *f/pl*	annales *f/pl*
recovery	Wiedererlangung *f*	récupération *f*
recovery of expenses *pl*	Unkostendeckung *f*	recouvrement *m* des frais *m/pl*
recreational programme	Unterhaltungsprogramm *n*	programme *m* récréatif
recreational supplement	Unterhaltungsbeilage *f*	supplément *m* feuilleton
rectangle	Viereck *n*	quadrangle *m*, rectangle *m*
rectangular	rechteckig	rectangulaire
rectification	Berichtigung *f*	rectificatif *m*, rectification *f*
to **rectify**	berichtigen	corriger
recto	Schauseite *f*	belle page *f*
red tape	Schreiberei *f*	paperasse *f*
redemption	Einlösung *f*	dégagement *m*, paiement *m*
to **reduce**	verkleinern	diminuer, rapetisser, réduire
reduced rate	ermäßigter Preis *m*	tarif *m* réajusté
reduction	Ermäßigung *f*, Nachlaß *m*, Verkleinerung *f*	diminution *f*, escompte *m*, rabais *m*, réduction *f*
reduction of an order	Auftragskürzung *f*	réduction *f* d'un mandat *m*
reduction of competition	Wettbewerbsbeschränkung *f*	restriction *f* à la concurrence *f*
reduction of the number of the ordered sites *pl*	Kürzung *f* der Stellenzahl *f*	réduction *f* du nombre *m* d'affiches *f/pl* commandées
redundancy	Wortschwall *m*	flot *m* de paroles *f/pl*, verbiage *m*
reel paper	endloses Papier *n*, Rollenpapier *n*	papier *m* continu, papier *m* roulé
reel width	Rollenbreite *f*	laize *f*
reference	betreffend	concernant, relatif à, se référant à
reference book	Nachschlagewerk *n*	ouvrage *m* de référence *f*
reference number	Aktenzeichen *n*	cote *f*
reference pattern	Ausfallmuster *n*	échantillon *m* de comparaison *f*
referring to	betreffend	concernant, relatif à, se référant à

reflector	Scheinwerfer m, Reflektor m	catadioptre m, réflecteur m
reflector button	Katzenauge n	catadioptre m, cataphote m
refreshment towel	Erfrischungstuch n	mouchoir m en papier m rafraîchissant
refund	Rückvergütung f	rabais m, remboursement m
refusal	Verweigerung f	refus m
refusal of an order	Auftragsablehnung f	refus m de commande f
refuse	Ausschuß (Abfall) m	déchet m
regional daily	regionale Tageszeitung f	quotidien m régional
regional dispersion	regionale Streuung f	couverture f régionale
regional issue	Regionalausgabe f	édition f régionale
regional page	Lokalseite f	page f régionale
regional press	Regionalpresse f	presse f régionale
register	Passer m, Register n	index m, registre m, repère m
to register	einpassen, einschreiben	enregistrer, inscrire, repérer
register difference	Passerdifferenz f	différence f de repérage m
register mark	Fadenkreuz n, Passerkreuz n	croix f de repère m
registered letter	eingeschriebener Brief m	lettre f recommandée
registered trade mark	eingetragenes Warenzeichen n	marque f déposée
registry	Registratur f	enregistrement m
reglet	Reglette f	interligne f, réglette f
regular customer	Dauerkunde m, Stammkunde m	client m fidèle
regular readers pl	regelmäßige Leser m/pl	lecteurs m/pl réguliers
regulation	Regelung f	réglementation f
regulation of advertising	Werberegelung f	réglementation f de la publicité f
regulation of terminology	Sprachregelung f	réglementation f de la terminologie f
reiteration	ständige Wiederholung f	réitération f
rejection	Ablehnung f	refus m, rejet m
related to practise	praxisbezogen	relative à la pratique f
relation	Beziehung f	relation f
to relay	übertragen	relayer, transmettre
release	Anzeigenabruf m, Disposition f, Druckfreigabe f, Freigabe f	autorisation f de publier, disposition f, embargo m levé, transmission f à la presse f
to release	Druck m freigeben, zum	permettre la publication f
relief etched block	Reliefklischee n	cliché m en relief m
relief letter	Reliefbuchstabe m	lettre f en relief m
relief printing	Hochdruck m, Reliefdruck m	impression f en relief m gaufrage m en relief m, impression f gaufrée, impression f thermogravure f
religious paper	Kirchenblatt n	feuille f cléricale
remainders pl	Remittenden f/pl, Restauflage f	bouillon m, invendus pl, rendus pl, soldes m/pl
remake	Wiederverfilmung f	refaçon m d'un film m
to remake	neu verfilmen	refaçonner
remaking	Neufassung f	nouvelle rédaction f, réfection f
remembrance advertising	Erinnerungswerbung f	publicité f de rappel m, publicité f de souvenir m
remembrance value	Erinnerungswert m	souvenir m laissé, valeur f de mémorisation f, valeur f de rappel m

to **remind**	mahnen	mettre en demeurre *m*, sommer
reminder	Mahnung *f*	mise *f* en demeurre *f*, sommation *f*
reminder advertisement	Erinnerungsanzeige *f*	annonce *f* de rappel *m*
reminder campaign	Erinnerungskampagne *f*	campagne *f* mémorative
reminder value	Erinnerungswert *m*	souvenir *m* laissé, valeur *f* de mémorisation *f*, valeur *f* de rappel *m*
remittance of an order	Auftragsüberschreibung *f*	attribution *f* de la commande *f*
removal of a hoarding	Stellenabbau *m*	démontage *m* d'un panneau *m*
to **render**	wiedergeben	rendre
renewal	Erneuerung *f*	remplacement *m*, renouvellement *m*
renewal of subscription	Abonnementserneuerung *f*	réabonnement *m*
renewals *pl*	Plakatersatzreserve *f*	supplément *m* d'affiches *f/pl* pour le remplacement *m*
rent	Pachtabgabe *f*	loyer *m*
repackage	Wiedervermarktung *f*	conditionnement *m* nouveau
repaints *pl*	Neubemalung *f*	nouvelle peinture *f*
repeat ad	Wiederholungsanzeige *f*	annonce *f* de répétition *f*, annonce *f* répétée plusieurs fois *f*, ré-insertion *f*
repeat order	Nachbestellung *f*	nouvel ordre *m*
repeataudience	wiederholte Konsumentenansprache *f*	appel *m* renouvelé aux consommateurs *m/pl*
repeated exposures *pl*	Mehrfachbelichtung *f*	exposition *f* multiple
repeating of an order	Auftragserneuerung *f*	renouvellement *m* d'un ordre *m*
repetition	Wiederholung *f*	double emploi *m*, répétition *f*
replacement ad	Ersatzanzeige *f*	gratuité *f* de compensation *f*, ré-insertion *f*
replacement demand	Ersatzbedarf *m*	besoin *m* de remplacement *m*
replication	Gegenantwort *f*	réplique *f*
reply by wire	telegrafische Antwort *f*	réponse *f* télégraphique
reply card	Antwortkarte *f*	carte *f* de retour *m*, carte-réponse *f*
reply coupon	Antwortkupon *m*	coupon-réponse *f*
reply mail	Werbeantwort *f*	réponse *f*
report	Bericht *m*, Reportage *f*, Zeitungsbericht *m*	rapport *m*, reportage *m*
to **report**	berichten	rapporter
report of a meeting	Sitzungsbericht *m*	reportage *m* de séance *f*
reporter	Berichterstatter *m*, Reporter *m*	chroniqueur *m*, correspondant *m*, rapporteur *m*, reporter *m*
reporter-cameraman	Bildberichterstatter *m*	reporteur *m* d'images *f/pl*
reporting	Reportage *f*	reportage *m*
to **represent**	darstellen, vertreten	figurer, représenter
representation	Darstellung *f*, Vertretung *f*	représentation *f*
representative	Repräsentant *m*, Vertreter *m*	agent *m*, courtier *m*, représentant *m*
reprimand	Hering *m* (Tadel *m*)	réprimande *f*
reprint	Nachdruck *m/typog*, Neuauflage *f*, Neudruck *m*, Wiederabdruck *m*	nouvelle édition *f*, réimpression *f*

reprint with change of title only	Kopfblatt *n*	journal *m* se distinguant seulement d'un autre par le titre *m*
reprise	Wiederaufführung *f*	reprise *f*
to reproduce	wiedergeben	rendre
reproduction	Reproduktion *f*, Wiedergabe *f*	contre-type *m*, reproduction *f*
reproduction technique	Reproduktionstechnik *f*	procédés *m*/*pl* photomécaniques
reprolithographer	Reprolithograf *m*	reprolithographe *m*
reproof	Hering *m* (Tadel *m*)	réprimande *f*
reputation	Ansehen *n*, Ruf *m*	notoriété *f*, prestige *m*, réputation *f*
on request	Anfrage *f*, auf	sur demande *f*
requirements *pl*	Bedingungen *f*/*pl*	conditions *f*/*pl*
rerecording	überspielen *n*	enregistrement *m* fractionné
rerun	Wiederholungsanzeige *f*	annonce *f* de répétition *f*, annonce *f* répétée plusieurs fois *f*, ré-insertion *f*
resale price maintenance	Preisbindung *f* der zweiten Hand *f*	prix *m* imposé
rescale	Formatänderung *f*, Umarbeitung *f*	adaptation *f*, changement *m* de format *m*, modification *f* de format *m*
research	Forschung *f*, Nachforschung *f*, Untersuchung *f*	enquête *f*, examen *m*, recherche *f*
research director	Leiter *m* der Marktforschung *f*	chef *m* des études *f*/*pl* de marché *m*
research man	Rechercheur *m*	enquêteur *m*
research *pl* plans *pl* board meeting	Arbeitssitzung *f*	séance *f* de travail *m*
research worker, researcher	Ermittler *m*, Forscher *m*	chercheur *m*, spécialiste *m* de la recherche *f*
to resell	weiterverkaufen	revendre
reservation	Reservierung *f*	réservation *f*
to reserve	reservieren	réserver
reserved position	reservierter Anzeigenplatz *m*	emplacement *m* réservé
to reset	umsetzen *typog*	recomposer
re-setting	Neusatz *m*	recomposition *f*
to reshape	umarbeiten	récrire, remanier
resounding	widerhallender Ton *m*	son *m* réverbéré
respondent	Befragter *m*	interviewé *m*, répondant *m*
response	Kuponrücklauf *m*, Widerhall *m*	pouvoir *m* de choc *m*, retentissement *m*, retour *m* de coupons *m*/*pl*
response-function	Wirkungskurve *f*	courbe *f* de l'acceuil *m*
responsible editor	verantwortlicher Redakteur *m*	rédacteur *m* responsable
restraining clause	Wettbewerbsklausel *f*	clause *f* restrictive
restriction	Beschränkung *f*	limitation *f*, restriction *f*
result checking	Erfolgskontrolle *f*	contrôle *m* des résultats *m*/*pl*, contrôle *m* du rendement *m*, contrôle *m* du succès *m*
results *pl* of advertising	Werberesultat *n*	résultat *m* de la publicité *f*

retail advertising	Einzelhandelswerbung *f*	publicité *f* des détaillants *m*/*pl*, publicité *f* des établissements *m*/*pl* de détail *m*
retail audit	Händlerbefragung *f*	enquête *f* auprès des détaillants *m*/*pl*
retail enterprise	Detailgeschäft *n*	établissement *m* de détail *m*
retail firm	Einzelhandelsunternehmen *n*	
retail price	Einzelhandelspreis *m*, Kleinverkaufspreis *m*	prix *m* de détail *m*, prix *m* vente *f* au détail *m*
retail store	Laden *m*	magasin *m*
retailer	Einzelhändler *m*, Wiederverkäufer *m*	détaillant *m*, revendeur *m*
retained composition	Stehsatz *m*	composition *f* conservée, composition *f* permanente, conserve *f*
retake	Neuaufnahme *f*	tourner à nouveau
to retouch	retuschieren, überarbeiten	remanier, retoucher
retoucher	Retuscheur *m*	retoucheur *m*
retouching	Retusche *f*, Retuschierung *f*	maquillage *m*, retouchage *m*, retouche *f*
retouching ink	Retuschefarbe *f*	encre *f* de retouche *f*
to retranslate	zurückübersetzen	retraduire
retro-active	rückwirkend	rétroactif
retroactive discount	Nachrabatt *m*	rabais *m* rétroactif
return	Werbeantwort *f*	réponse *f*
return card	Antwortkarte *f*	carte *f* de retour *m*, carte-réponse *f*
return consignment	Rücksendung *f*	renvoi *m* à l'expéditeur *m*
return postage	Rückporto *n*	réponse *f* payée
returns *pl*	Remittenden *f*/*pl*	bouillon *m*, invendus *pl*, rendus *pl*
re-use package	Mehrwegpackung *f*, wiederverwendbare Packung *f*	emballage *m* à double usage *m*, emballage *m* de remploi *m*, emballage *m* de retour, emballage *m* de remploi *m*
revenue	Einkommen *n*, Einnahmen *f*/*pl*, Erträge *m*/*pl*	recettes *f*/*pl*, revenu *m*
to reverse	kontern, umkehren	faire noir au blanc, inverser, renverser, retourner
reverse drawing	Verkehrtzeichnung *f*	dessin *m* renversé
reverse page	Rückseite *f*	côté *m* de seconde, page *f* paire, page *f* verso
reversed block	Negativklischee *n*	cliché *m* négatif, cliché *m* noir au blanc
reversed impression	Konterdruck *m*	contre-épreuve *f*, noir au blanc
reversed left to right	seitenverkehrt	à l'envers *m*, inversé
reversing	Umkehrung *f*	inversion *f*
reverso	linksseitig	envers
review	Illustrierte *f*, Magazin *n*, Rezension *f*, Zeitschrift *f*	compte *m* rendu, critique *f*, magazine *m*, périodique *m*, périodique *m* illustré, revue *f*
to review (a book)	besprechen	discuter, faire un compte *m* rendu

review copy, reviewer's copy	Rezensionsexemplar *n*	exemplaire *m* de presse *f*
to **revise**	durchsehen, umredigieren, überarbeiten, verbessern	remanier, repatiner, retoucher, reviser, revoir, reviser
revised edition	verbesserte und erweiterte Auflage *f*	édition *f* corrigée et augmentée
revised text	verbesserter Text *m*	texte *m* revu
to **rewrite**	neu schreiben, umarbeiten	récrire, remanier
to **rewrite a text**	Text *m* umarbeiten	remanier un texte *m*
rewriting	umschreiben (neu fassen)	rédiger à nouveau
Rheinländer (see appendix)	Rheinländer *f* (siehe Anhang)	Rheinländer (voir appendice)
rhythm	Rhythmus *m*	rythme *m*
rhythm of publication	Erscheinungsrhythmus *m*	rythme *m* de parution *f*
ribbon-face	Schreibmaschinenschrift *f*	caractères *m/pl* de machine *f*
rice-paper	chinesisches Papier *n*, Reispapier *n*	papier *m* chiné, papier *m* de Chine *f*, papier *m* de riz *m*
rider	abschließende Frage *f*, abschließender Kaufappell *m*	message *m* additionnel à la fin *f* d'un message *m* publicitaire, phrase *f* finale
riding the showing	Plakatanschlagkontrolle *f*	inspection *f* d'emplacements *m/pl*
right angle folding	Kreuzbruchfalzung *f*	pliage *m* croisé
right of reproduction	Abdrucksrecht *n*	droit *m* de reproduction *f*
right reading	seitenrichtig	à l'endroit *m*
rightangle	Rechteck *n*	rectangle *m*
right-hand corner	rechte Ecke *f*	coin *m* droit
right-hand page	rechte Seite *f*	bonne page *f*, page *f* de droite, recto
right-wing paper	rechtseingestellte Zeitung *f*	journal *m* de droite
rigid price	Preistreue *f*	prix *m* fixe
to **ring**	einkreisen	encercler
rising space	Spieß *m/typog*	levage, marque *f* d'une espace *f* haute
risks *pl* **of advertising**	Werberisiko *n*	risques *m/pl* de publicité *f*
rival	Konkurrent *m*, Mitbewerber *m*	concurrent *m*
rival article	Konkurrenzartikel *m*	article *m* concurrentiel
rival business	Konkurrenzunternehmen *n*, Wettbewerbsunternehmen *n*	entreprise *f* compétitive, entreprise *f* concurrente
rival newspaper	Konkurrenzblatt *n*, Wettbewerbszeitung *f*	journal *m* concurrent, journal *m* concurrentiel
rival supply	Konkurrenzangebot *n*	offre *f* concurrentielle
river	Straße *f* (Satz *m*)	lézarde *f*
river of white	weißer Streifen *m* im Satz *m*	lézarde *f*, ruelle *f*
road sign	Hinweisschild *n*, Straßenschild *n*	panneau *m* routier, signal *m* de direction *f*
roadside	Fahrstraße *f*	route *f* carossable
roadside advertising	Straßenwerbung *f*, Streckenwerbung *f*	publicité *f* routière
roadside hoarding	Straßenschild *n*, Streckenplakat *n*	enseigne *f* routière, panneau *m* d'affichage *m* le long *m* d'une voie *f* ferrée, panneau *m* routier
rock-bottom price	Tiefstpreis *m*	prix *m* imbattable, prix *m* minimum
to **roll up**	einwickeln	envelopper
roll up and down	Auf- und Abverschiebung *f* von Bildschirmzeilen *f/pl*	décalage *m* des lignes *f/pl*
rolling advertising	rollende Werbung *f*	publicité *f* roulante

Roman numerals *pl*	römische Ziffern *f/pl*	chiffres *m/pl* romains
Roman type	Antiqua *f*	caractère *m* ancien, caractère *m* romain
roof advertisement	Dachwerbung *f*	publicité *f* sur les toits *m/pl*
roof panel	Dachschild *n*	banderole *f*, calicot *m*, panneau *m* sur le toit *m*
ROP colour	Rotationsfarbdruck *m*	impression *f* sur rotative *f* en couleurs *f/pl*
rotaprint process	Rotaprintverfahren *n*	multilithe *m*
rotaprint sheet-fed machine	Kleinoffsetmaschine *f*	presse *f* rotaprint
rotary offset press	Rollenoffsetmaschine *f*	rotatif *m* offset *m*
rotary press	Rotationspresse *f*	machines *f/pl* rotatives
rotary printing	Rotationsdruck *m*	impression *f* sur rotative *f*
rotating bulletin	versetzbare Werbefläche *f*	bulletin *m* transférable
rotation	ständig wiederholte Streuung *f*, umlaufende Streuung *f*, Werbeserie *f* in ständiger Wiederholung *f* mit gleichem Rhythmus *m*, Wiederholung *f* einer Anzeigenserie *f*	publicité *f* répétée, répétition *f* d'une série *f* d'annonces *f/pl*, roulement *m* de publicité *f*, succession *f* de publicité *f* par répétition *f* permanente avec un rythme *m* invariable
rotogravure	Fototiefdruck *m*, Kupfertiefdruck *m*, Rakeltiefdruck *m*, Rotationstiefdruck *m*, Tiefdruck *m/typog*	gravure *f* en creux *m/pl*, héliogravure *f*, héliogravure *f* sur rotative *f*, hélioroto *f*, impression *f* en creux *m*, impression *f* en héliogravure *f*, impression *f* en taille-douce *f*, rotogravure *f*
rough	Bleistiftskizze *f*, Ideenskizze *f*, Layout *n*, Schmierskizze *f*, Skizze *f*	crayonné *m*, croquis *m*, dessin *m* au crayon *m*, ébauche *f*, esquisse *f*, maquette *f*, projet *m*
rough copy	Konzept *n*	brouillon *m*, minute *f*, projet *m*
rough outline	roher Umriß *m*, Rohentwurf *m*	crayonné *m*, maquette *f*, premier jet *m*
rough proof	Rohabzug *m*	première épreuve *f*
round	rund	rond
round-table conference, **round-table meeting,**	Gespräch *n* am runden Tisch, Gruppendiskussion *f*, Konferenz *f* am runden Tisch *m*	réunion *f* paritaire, table *f* ronde
to rout	fräsen	fraiser
to rout out	ausfräsen	fraiser, toupiller
routed	gefräst	fraisé
routed plate	ausgefräster Druckstock *m*	cliché *m* fraisé, cliché *m* toupillé
router	Bestoßmaschine *f*, Fräsapparat *m*	fraiseuse *f*
routing	Ausfräsung *f*	fraisage *m*
roving reporter	reisender Berichterstatter *m*	reporter *m* itinérant
royal poster	großformatiges Plakat *n*	affiche *f* de grand format *m*
royalties *pl*	Autorentantieme *f*, Lizenzgebühren *f/pl*, Umsatzhonorar *n*	droit *m* de license *f*, redevance *f*
royalty	Urheberrechtslizenz *f*	droits *m/pl* d'auteur *m*
rubber block	Gummiklischee *n*	cliché *m* caoutchouc *m*
rubber stamp	Gummistempel *m*	cachet *m* de caoutchouc *m*
rubbishy literature	Schundliteratur *f*	littérature *f* de bas étage *m*

Ruby *f* (see appendix!)	Agate *f* (siehe Anhang!)	Parisienne *f* (voir appendice!)
rule *typog*	Linie *f*	filet *m* (typogr.) , ligne *f*
rule of conduct	Richtschnur *f*	gouverne *f*, règle *f* de conduite *f*
ruled frame	Linienrand *m*	bordure *f* en filets *m/pl*, cadre *m* de filets *m/pl*
ruled paper	liniiertes Papier *n*	papier *m* réglé
ruler	Lineal *n*	règle *f*
rules *pl*	Linienmaterial *n*	filets *m/pl*
rules *pl* **of composition**	Satzanweisungen *f/pl*	données *f/pl* de composition *f*, instructions *f/pl* pour la composition *f*
rules *pl* **of work**	Arbeitsgrundsätze *m/pl*	règles *f/pl* de travail *m*
rumour	Gerücht *n*	bruit *m*, on dit
run	Druckgang *m*	passage *m*
to run (colour)	auslaufen (Farbe) , verlaufen (Farben *f/pl*)	couler (couleur) , se fondre
to run in with	übereinstimmen mit	être conforme à, être d'accord *m* avec
to run on	anhängen *typog*, ohne Absatz *m* setzen, fortdrucken	faire suivre, faire suivre sans alinéa *m*, joindre, rouler
run out!	Absatz *m*, neuer !	nouvel alinéa *m* !
to run over	auf einer anderen Seite *f* fortsetzen, durchblättern	décrocher, feuilleter
to run short	Raum *m* einschränken	gagner
to run through	durchlesen	parcourir
run-around	verkürzte Satzbreite *f*	largeur *f* abregée de la composition *f*
run-in!	Absatz *m*, kein!	pas d'alinéa *m* !
run-it-again	Wiederholungsanzeige *f*	annonce *f* de répétition *f*, annonce *f* répétée plusieurs fois *f*, ré-insertion *f*
running commentary	Reportage *f*	reportage *m*
running expenses *pl*	Betriebskosten *pl*	charges *f/pl* d'exploitation *f*, dépenses *pl* courantes
running hand	Kurrentschrift *f*	écriture *f* courante
running head	durchgehender Titel *m*, Kolumnenleiste *f*, Kolumnentitel *m*	titre *m* courant, titre-courant *m*, titre *m* de colonne *f*
running text	fortlaufender Text *m*, Hauptbestandteil *m* einer Anzeige *f*	corps *m* du texte *m*, corps *m* d'une annonce *f*
running time	Laufzeit *f*	rut *m*
running title	Kolumnentitel *m*	titre *m* courant, titre *m* de colonne *f*
running-on	Fortdruck *m*	impression *f* du tirage *m*, tiré à part *f*
run-of-paper advertisement (ROP)	Schmuckfarbenanzeige *f*	annonce *f* avec couleur *f* d'accompagnement *m*
run-of-paper position	gewöhnliche Plazierung *f*	emplacement *m* ordinaire
run-on	Auflageerweiterung *f*, erhöhte Auflage *f*	tirage *m* supplémentaire
run-on-line	Übergreifen *n*	enjambement *m*
rural areas *pl* **posting**	Landanschlag *m*	affichage *m* rural
rush hour	Hauptgeschäftszeit *f*	heure *f* de pointe *f*

rush job	Eilauftrag *m*, Schnellschuß *m*	commande *f* urgente, coup *m* de feu *m*, ordre *m* par exprès *m*, train *m* urgent
rushes *pl*	Prüfung *f* der gedrehten Szenen *f/pl*, Schnellkopie *f* (Film)	épreuve *f* de tournage *m*, premières épreuves *f/pl* d'un film *m*

S

saddle stitching	Drahtheftung *f*, Sattelheftung *f*	brochage *m* à cheval *m*, couture *f* dans le dos *m*, piquage *m* dans le pli *m* au fil *m* de fer *m*
sale	Verkauf *m*, Vertrieb *m*	vente *f*
sale per copy	Einzelverkauf *m* (Zeitungen)	vente *f* au kiosque *m*, vente *f* au numéro *m*
saleable	verkäuflich	vendable
sales figures *pl*	Umsatzzahlen *f/pl*	chiffres *m/pl* de vente *f*
sales *pl* **allowance**	Vergünstigung *f*	avantage *m*, faveur *f*
sales *pl* **analysis**	Verkaufsanalyse *f*	analyse *f* des ventes *f/pl*
sales *pl* **appeal**	Kaufappell *m*, Verkaufsappell *m*	appel *m* au désir *m* d'achat *m*, argumentation *f* de vente *f*
sales *pl* **area**	Absatzbereich *m*, Absatzgebiet *n*, Einzugsgebiet *n*	débouché *m*, marché *m*, secteur *m* de vente *f*, territoire *m* de vente *f*
sales *pl* **argument**	Verkaufsargument *n*	argument *m* de vente *f*
sales *pl* **book**	Verkaufshandbuch *n*	manuel *m* de vente *f*
sales *pl* **bulletin**	Kundenzeitschrift *f*	journal *m* pour la clientèle *f*
sales *pl* **campaign**	Verkaufskampagne *f*	campagne *f* de vente *f*
sales *pl* **channel**	Absatzweg *m*	voie *f* de distribution *f*
sales *pl* **competition**	Verkaufswettbewerb *m*	concours *m* de vente *f*
sales *pl* **consultant**	Verkaufsberater *m*	conseil *m* en matière *f* de vente *f*
sales *pl* **curve**	Umsatzkurve *f*	courbe *f* de vente *f*
sales *pl* **department**	Verkaufsabteilung *f*, Vertriebsabteilung *f*	département *m* des ventes *f/pl*, service *m* commercial, service *m* de la vente *f*
sales *pl* **discount**	Barzahlungsrabatt *m*	escompte *m* de caisse *f*
sales *pl* **display**	Verkaufsauslage *f*	étalage *m* de vente *f*
sales *pl* **drive**	verstärkter Werbeeinsatz *m*	effort *m* marqué, effort *m* spécial
sales *pl* **figure**	Verkaufsziffer *f*	chiffre *m* de vente *f*
sales *pl* **force**	Verkaufsmannschaft *f*	équipe *f* de vente *f*
sales *pl* **girl**	Verkäuferin *f*	vendeuse *f*
sales *pl* **impact**	Verkaufserfolg *m*, Wirkungsgrad *m* der Werbung *f*	efficience *f* de publicité *f*, résultats *m/pl* des ventes *f/pl*
sales *pl* **instrument**	Absatzinstrument *n*	instrument *m* de vente *f*
sales *pl* **letter**	Werbebrief *m*, Werbeschreiben *n*	lettre *f* de propagande *f*, lettre *f* de vente *f*, lettre *f* publicitaire
sales *pl* **management**	Verkaufsleitung *f*	direction *f* commerciale
sales *pl* **manager**	Verkaufsleiter *m*	chef *m* des ventes *f/pl*, directeur *m* commercial
sales *pl* **manual**	Verkaufshandbuch *n*, Vertreterhandbuch *n*	manuel *m* de vente *f*, manuel *m* pour des représentants *m/pl*

sales pl objective	Verkaufsziel n	but m commercial, objectif m marketing m
sales pl office	Verkaufsbüro n, Verkaufsstelle f	bureau m des ventes f/pl, poste m de vente f
sales pl organisation	Verkaufsapparat m, Verkaufsorganisation f, Vertriebsapparat m	appareil m commercial, organisation f de vente f, réseau m de vente f
sales pl peak	Verkaufsspitze f	maximum m des ventes f/pl
sales pl point	Verkaufspunkt m	angle m d'approche f publicitaire
sales pl policy	Verkaufspolitik f	politique f de vente f
sales pl promoter	Verkaufsleiter m, Vertriebsleiter m	chef m de publicité f, chef m de vente f, chef m des ventes f/pl, directeur m commercial
sales pl promotion	Absatzförderung f, Absatzsteigerung f, Verkaufsförderung f, Vertriebsförderung f	promotion f de vente f
sales pl prospects pl	Absatzchance f	chance f d'écoulement m
sales pl quota	Verkaufsquote f	quota m de vente f
sales pl representative	Handelsvertreter m	représentant m de commerce m
sales pl resistance	Kaufunlust f	abstention f des consommateurs m/pl
sales pl return	Rücklieferung f	livraison f renvoyée, retour m
sales pl risk	Verkaufsrisiko n	risque m de vente f
sales pl talk	Verkaufsgespräch n, Warenanpreisung f	boniment m, entretien m de vente f
sales pl tax	Umsatzsteuer f	impôt m sur le chiffre m d'affaires f/pl
sales pl territory	Verkaufsbezirk m	région f de vente f
sales pl training	Verkaufstraining n	entraînement m à la vente f
salesfolder	Verkäufermerkblatt n	argumentaire m
salesman	Verkäufer m	vendeur m
salesman's calling card	Visitenkarte f eines Verkäufers m	carte f de visite f
salesmanship	Verkaufstechnik f	art m de vendre
same size	Originalgröße f	tel
same text	gleichbleibender Text m	texte m même
sample	Muster n, Stichprobe f, Warenprobe f	échantillon m, patron m, sondage m, spécimen m
to sample	bemustern	échantillonner
sample book	Musterbuch n	livre m d'échantillons m/pl
sample collection	Musterkollektion f	collection f d'échantillons m/pl
sample copy	Ansichtsexemplar f	numéro m spécimen m
sample for inspection	Ansichtsmuster n	échantillon m à l'examen m
sample order	Probeauftrag m	commande f à l'épreuve f, ordre m d'essai m
sample request card	Musteranforderungskarte f	carte-demande f d'échantillon m
sample stock	Musterlager n	dépôt m d'échantillons m/pl
sampling	Musterversand m, Probenverteilung f	distribution f d'échantillons m/pl, envoi m d'échantillons m/pl
sampling by taste	Gratiskostprobe f	dégustation f gratuite
sandpaper	Sandpapier n	papier n de verre f

to sandwich	einschieben	intercaler
sandwich board man, sandwich man	Sandwichmann *m*, Plakatträger *m*	homme-affiche *f*, homme-sandwich *m*
sans-serif	Grotesk *f*	antique *f*, bâton *m*
satin paper	Atlaspapier *n*	papier *m* imprégné et gaufré
satire	Satire *f*	satire *f*
saturation point	Sättigungspunkt *m*	point *m* de saturation *f*
saturation with advertising	werbliche Übersättigung *f*	saturation *f* publicitaire
saving stamp	Rabattmarke *f*	timbre-primes *f/pl*, timbre *m* de rabais *m*, timbre *m* d'épargne *f*
scale	Maßstab *m*	échelle *f*, règle *f* graduée
to scale down	proportional verkleinern	réduire en proportion *f*
scale of discount	Rabattstaffel *f*	barème *m* dégressif, échelle *f* mobile
scale rate	Listenpreis *m*	prix *m* au tarif *m*, prix *m* de barème *m*
scaling	Formatänderung *f*	changement *m* de format *m*, modification *f* de format *m*
scamped work	Pfuscharbeit *f*	bousillage *m*
scandal cronicle	Skandalchronik *f*	chronique *f* scandaleuse
scandal-monger	Klatschmaul *n*, Klatschweib *n*	cancanier *m*, cancanière *f*
scar	Schramme *f*	rayure *f*
scare headline	alarmierende Überschrift *f*, knallige Überschrift *f*	gros titre *m* à sensation *f*, manchette *f* sensationnelle, titre *m* criard
scatter diagram	Streubild *n*	diagramme *m* de la diffusion *f*
scattered	verstreut	dispersé
scenario	Drehbuch *n*	scénario *m*, script *m*
scented paper	parfümiertes Papier *n*	papier *m* parfumé
schedule	Plan *m*, Satzvorlage *f*, Schema *n*	modèle *m*, plan *m*, schéma *m*
schedule for discount by frequency and volume	Mal- und Mengenstaffel *f*	dégressif *m* sur la fréquence *f* et le volume *m*
schedule of insertions *pl*	Datenplan *m*, Datenschema *n*, Insertionsplan *m*	calendrier *m* d'insertion *f*, calendrier *m* d'insertion *f*, plan *m* de termes *m/pl*
schedule of prices *pl*	Preisliste *f*	liste *f* de prix, prix *m* courant *m*, tarif *m*
scheduling	Mediaplanung *f*	plan *m* de campagne *f*
schema	bildliche Darstellung *f*, Satzvorlage *f*	modèle *m*, schéma *m*
schematic letter	Schemabrief *m*	lettre *f* schématique
schematizing	Schematisierung *f*	schématisation *f*
school journal	Schülerzeitung *f*	journal *m* scolaire
school of applied art	Kunstgewerbeschule *f*	école *f* des arts *m/pl* et métiers *m/pl*
Schwabacher type	Schwabacher Schrift *f*	Schwabach *m*
science of journalism	Zeitungswissenschaft *f*	science *f* du journalisme *m*
science-fiction	naturwissenschaftlich-technische Utopie *f*, Zukunftsroman *m*	littérature *f* d'anticipation *f*, utopie *f* scientifique-technique
scientific advertising	wissenschaftliche Werbung *f*	publicité *f* scientifique
scientific methods *pl*	wissenschaftliche Methoden *f/pl*	méthodes *f/pl* scientifiques
scientific paper	wissenschaftliches Blatt *m*	feuille *f* scientifique

scissors *pl*	Schere *f*	ciseaux *m/pl*
scissors *pl*-and-paste work	Schere *f*-und-Kleister *m*-Arbeit *f*	méthode *f* colle *f* et ciseaux *m/pl*
scoop	Knüller *m*, Sensationsmeldung *f*, sensationelle Alleinmeldung *f*	exclusivité *f*, grosse nouvelle *f*, information *f* sensationnelle et exclusive, nouvelle *f* à sensation *f*, reportage *m* sensationnel
scope	Aufgabengebiet *n*	fonctions *f/pl*, tâche *f* assignée
to score	rillen	faire des rainures *f/pl*
scoring	Vertonung *f*	addition *f* du ton *m*, mise *f* en musique *f*, sonorisation *f*
to scramble	durcheinanderbringen	brouiller
scrapbook	Einklebebuch *n*	album-souvenir *m*
scraper	Kratzer *m*	égratignure *f*, griffe *f*
scraper board	Schabekarton *m*	carte *f* grattée, carton *m* à racler
scraps *pl*	Textstellen *f/pl*	courts passages *m/pl* de texte *m*
scratch	Kratzen *n* der Nadel *f*, Kratzer *m*, Schramme *f*	égratignure *f*, griffe *f*, grincement *m* de l'aiguille *f*, rayure *f*
scratchboard	Schabekarton *m*	carte *f* grattée, carton *m* à racler
scratchboard drawing	Schabemanier *f*	manière *f* noire, mezzoteinte, trait *m* anglais
scratch-pad	Notizblock *m*	bloc-notes *m/pl*
scrawl	Gekritzel *n*	griffonnage *m*
screamer	senstionelle Überschrift *f*	titre *m* sensationnel
screaming poster		affiche *f* criarde
to screamline	Überschrift *f* in großen Buchstaben *m/pl* setzen	mettre un titre *m* en gros caractères *m/pl*
screen	Filmleinwand *f*, Leinwand *f*, Projektionswand *f*, Raster *m*	écran *m*, grisé *m* mécanique, réseau *m*, toile *f*, trame *f*
to screen	verfilmen	mettre en images *f/pl*
screen advertising	Filmwerbung *f*	publicité *f* à l'écran *m*, publicité *f* cinématographique, publicité *f* par film *m*
screen etching	Netzätzung *f*	simili *m*, similigravure *f*
screen foil	Rasterfolie *f*	pellicule *f* tramée
screen intaglio	Rastertiefdruck *m*	héliogravure *f* tramée
screen line	Rasterlinie *f*	ligne *f* de la trame *f*
screen magnifier	Fadenzähler *m*	compte-fils *m*
screen printing	Seidengazedruck *m*	sérigraphie *f*
screen printing ink	Siebdruckfarbe *f*	encre *f* sérigraphie *f*
screen record	Filmbericht *m*	reportage *m* filmé
screen width	Rasterweite *f*	finesse *f* de la trame *f*
scribble	erster unfertiger Entwurf *m*, Rohzeichnung *f*	brouillon *m*, griffonnage *m*
to scribble	schmieren	gribouiller
scribbler	Vielschreiber *m*	écrivailleur *m*, gratte-papier *m*, griffonneur *m*
scribbling paper	Konzeptpapier *n*	papier *m* commun, papier *m* ordinaire
scribbling-pad	Schreibblock *m*	bloc-notes *f/pl*
script	Drehbuch *n*, Filmmanuskript *n*	scénario *m*, script *m*

script type	Kursivschrift *f*	caractère *m* italique, écriture *f* cursive
script writing	Schreibschrift *f*	caractères *m/pl* d'écriture *f*, écriture *f* typographique
script-girl	Filmsekretärin *f*	secrétaire *f* de plateau *m*
script-type	Schreibschrift *f*	caractères *m/pl* d'écriture *f*, écriture *f* typographique
script-writer	Filmmanuskriptverfasser *m*, Texter *m*	rédacteur *m* publicitaire, rédacteur-concepteur *m*, scénariste *m*
scroll	Schriftrolle *f*	rouleau *m* d'écriture *f*
scroll up and down	Auf- und Abverschiebung *f* von Bildschirmzeilen *f/pl*	décalage *m* des lignes *f/pl*
seal	Siegel *n*	sceau *m*
seal of approval	Gütezeichen *n*	étiquette *f* de qualité *f*, label *m* de qualité *f*, marque *f* de garantie *f*, sigle *m*
seal printing	Stempeldruck *m*	timbrage *m*
sealing label	Verschlußmarke *f*	cachet *m*
seasonal advertising	Saisonwerbung *f*	publicité *f* saisonnière
seasonal closing-out sale	Saisonschlußverkauf *m*	vente *f* de fin *f* de saison *f*
seasonal fluctuation	Saisonschwankung *f*	fluctuation *f* saisonnière, variation *f* saisonnière
seasonal goods *pl*	Saisonartikel *m*	article *m* saisonnier
seasonal poster advertising	Saisonanschlag *m*	affichage *m* saisonnier
seasonal summer decline	Sommerloch *n*	lacune *f* d'été *m*
seat	Sitz *m*	siège *m*
seating capacity	Sitzplatzanzahl *f*	nombre *m* des sièges *m/pl*
second hand market	Gebrauchtwarenmarkt *m*	brocantage *m*, commerce *m* d'objets *m/pl* d'occasion *f*
second printing	Widerdruck *m*	impression *f* au verso *n*, retiration *f*, seconde forme *f*
second proof	Zweitabzug *m*	seconde épreuve *f*
second revised proof	Zweitkorrektur *f*	deuxième épreuve *f* corrigée, seconde revision *f*
second-class matter *am*	Zeitungsdrucksache *f*	expédition *f* sous bande *f*
secret listener	Schwarzhörer *m*	écouteur *m* clandestin
sectio aurea	goldener Schnitt *m*	sectio *m* aurea
section	Abteilung *f*, Lage *f* (Papier *n*)	cahier *m*, département *m*, rayon *m*, section *f*
section mark	Absatzzeichen *n*, Paragraphzeichen *n*	paragraphe *m*, signe *m* d'alinéa *m*
section of copy	Textblock *m*	pavé *m* de texte *m*
section title	Abteilungstitel *m*, Kapitelüberschrift *f*	titre *m* de chapitre *m*
secular trend	langfristiger Entwicklungstrend *m*	évolution *f* à long terme *m*
to **see copy**	vergleichen, mit dem Manuskript *n*	comparer avec le manuscrit *m*
to **select**	auswählen	choisir, sélectionner
selection	Auswahl *f*	choix *m*, sélection *f*
selective advertising	gezielte Werbung *f*, selektive Werbung *f*, ausgewählte Werbung *f*	publicité *f* sélective
selectivity	Trennschärfe *f*	sélectivité *f*

self appeal	Eigenwirkung f einer Ware f	effet m propre de la marchandise f elle-même
self-adhesive label	Selbstklebeschild n	étiquette f autocollante
self-cover	Umschlag m aus dem gleichen Papier n wie die Textseiten f/pl	couverture f de la même qualité f que le papier m des pages f/pl de texte m
self-explanatory label	„sprechendes" Etikett f	étiquette f s'expliquant elle-même
self-liquidating premium	selbstfinanzierte Prämie f	prime f auto-payante
selfliquidation offer	Angebot n zum Selbstkostenpreis m	offre f au prix m coûtant
self-mailer	Werbedrucksache f mit Antwort f	imprimé m publicitaire avec carte-réponse f
self-regulation	Selbstkontrolle f	autocontrôle m
self-service	Selbstbedienung f	libre service m
to sell	absetzen (Verkauf), veräußern	vendre
to sell off	ausverkaufen	liquider, solder
seller's market	Verkäufermarkt m	marché m de vendeurs m/pl
selling agent	Agent m	agent m
selling angle	Verkaufsargument n	argument m de vente f
selling campaign	Verkaufsfeldzug m	campagne f de vente f
selling costs pl	Selbstkosten pl	prix m coûtant, prix m de revient
selling emphasis	Kaufappell m	appel m au désir m d'achat m
selling method	Verkaufsmethode f	méthode f de distribution f
selling of the manufacturer to the wholesale dealer	Absatz m des Herstellers m an den Großhändler m	circuit m long
selling off	Ausverkauf m	vente f de soldes m/pl
selling organisation	Verkaufsorganisation f	appareil m commercial, organisation f de vente f
selling plan	Verkaufsplan m	plan m de vente f
selling point	Verkaufsargument n, Verkaufsstelle f	argument m de vente f, poste m de vente f
selling power	Werbekraft f	puissance f publicitaire
selling price	Verkaufspreis m	prix m de vente f
semantic	Wortbedeutungslehre f	semantique f
semi-annual	halbjährlich	semestriel, tous les six mois m/pl
semi-bold	halbfett	demi-gras, mi-gras
semi-bold type	halbfetter Satz m	caractères m/pl demi-gras
semicolon	Semikolon n, Strichpunkt m	point-virgule m
semi-official	halbamtlich	officieux, semi-officiel
semi-spectacular	Werbefläche f mit Beleuchtung f	panneau m d'affichage m avec l'addition f d'éclairage m
to send to press	Druck m geben, in	mettre sous presse f
sender	Absender m	expéditeur m
sending of vouchers pl	Belegversand m	envoi m de justificatifs m/pl
senior account supervisor	Etatdirektor m	directeur m de la section f budgetaire
sensation level	Reizschwelle f	seuil m d'efficacité f
sensational piece of news	aufsehenerregende Nachricht f	pétard m
sensational writer	Sensationsschriftsteller m	auteur m à effets m/pl corsés
sensationalism	Effekthascherei f, Sensationsmache f	recherche f de l'effet m, recherche f de l'épate m, sensationnalisme m
sensationel	sensationell	sensationnel

sensitiveness to light	Lichtempfindlichkeit *f*	sensibilité *f* à la lumière *f*
sensitized paper	lichtempfindliches Papier *n*	papier *m* sensibilisé
sentimental hit	Schnulze *f*	chanson *f* sentimentale
sentimental magazine	Schnulzenzeitung *f*	presse *f* du cœur *m*
separate copies *pl*	Separatdruck *m*, Sonderdruck *m*	édition *f* à part *f*, tirage *m* à part *f*, tirage *m* spécial
sepia tracing	Braunpause *f*	copie *f* sépia *f*
sepia-drawing	Sepiazeichnung *f*	sépia *f*
sequel	musikalische Überleitung *f*	transition *f* musicale
sequence	Bildfolge *f* im Film	séquence *f*
sequence of colours *pl*	Farbreihenfolge *f*	ordre *m* d'impression *f* des couleurs *f/pl*
serial	Sendereihe *f*	série *f* d'émission *f*
serial advertisements *pl*	Anzeigenserie *f*	série *f* d'annonces *f/pl*
serial film	Fortsetzungsfilm *m*	film *m* à épisodes *f/pl*
serial story	Fortsetzungsroman *m*, Zeitungsroman *m*	roman-feuilleton *m*, roman *m* à suites *f/pl*
series *pl*	Schriftgarnitur *f*	série *f* de caractères *m/pl*
series *pl* discount	Wiederholungsrabatt *m*	jeu *m* de dégressifs *m/pl*
series *pl* of articles *pl*	Artikelserie *f*	série *f* d'articles *m/pl*
series *pl* poster	Serienplakat *n*	affiche *f* sérielle
series *pl* posting	Reihenanschlag *m*	affichage *m* par massifs *m/pl*
series *pl* posting in the passage ways *pl* for one advertiser only (Metro)	Reihenanschlag *m* in den Gängen *m/pl* für einen einzigen Werbungtreibenden *m* (Untergrundbahn)	massif couloir *m* (métro *m*)
series *pl* posting on the métro platforms *pl* for one advertiser only	Reihenanschlag *m* auf den Metro-Bahnsteigen *m/pl* für einen einzigen Werbungtreibenden *m*	massif quai *m* (métro *m*)
serif	Füßchen *n/typog*, Haarstrich *m*, Serif *n*	délié *m*, empattement *m*
service	Dienstleistung *f*, Kundendienst *m*	prestation *f* de service *m*, service *m* après-vente *f*
service fee	Agenturvergütung *f*, Werbeberaterhonorar *n*	honoraires *m/pl*, honoraires *m/pl* du conseiller *m*
service rendering trade	Dienstleistungsgewerbe *n*	secteur *m* économique des services *m/pl*
session	Sitzung *f*	séance *f*, session *f*
set	Dekoration (Film, TV) *f*, Filmdekoration *f*, Satz *m* (Sortiment *n*)	décor *m*, décoration *f* de film *m*, série *f*
to set	setzen *typog*	composer
to set more solid	kompresser setzen	diminuner l'espace *m*, resserrer
set of colour plates *pl*	Farbsatz *m*	gamme *f* de clichés *m/pl* en couleurs *f/pl*
to set up	absetzen (Druck)	composer
set-off paper	Makulaturpapier *n*	papier *m* maculé
set-off sheet	Abschmutzbogen *m*, Schmutzbogen *m*	feuille *f* de décharge *f*, papier *m* anti-macule, papier *m* de décharge *f*
setting	Satz *m/typog*	composition *f*
setting in foreign language	Fremdsprachensatz *m*	composition *f* en langue *f* étrangère
setting mistake	Setzfehler *m*	faute *f* de composition *f*

setting-rule	Setzlinie f	filet m à composer, filet m de composition f
to settle	abmachen	arranger, fixer
settlement	Abkommen n, Abrechnung f	accord m, arrangement m, décompte m, liquidation f
settlement of treaty	Vertragsabschluß m	conclusion f du contrat m
to sew	heften	agrafer, brocher
sewn book	geheftetes Buch n	livre m broché
shade	Farbschattierung f, Farbton m, Kolorit n, Tönung f	coloris m, couleur f, nuance f, teinte f, ton m de couleur f
shade of opinion	Meinungsunterschied m, feiner	nuance f d'opinion f
shaded	schattiert	ombré
shaded frame	gerasteter Rahmen m	cadre m de filets m/pl gras-maigre
shaded rule	Strichlinie f	filet m crémaillère f
shading	Abstufung f	nuance f
shadow print advertisement	Schattendruckanzeige f	annonce f ombrée, annonce f surimprimée
shallow half-tone	flachgeätzte Autotypie f	simili m manquant de creux m
shape	Umriß m	contour m
to shape	gestalten	façonner, former, visualiser
shape of product	Produktform f	forme f de produit m
shape of the picture	Bildform f	forme f picturale
shaping	Formgestaltung f	création f de la forme f, esthétique f industrielle
sharp	scharf	net
sharpness	Schärfe f	netteté f
sheet	Blatt n (Seite f), Bogen m, Papierbogen m, Platte f	dalle f, feuille f, page f, plaque f
sheet signature	Bogensignatur f	signature f de feuille f
sheet size	Bogengröße f, Papierformat n	format m de feuille f, format m de papier m
sheetage	Bogenanschlag m, Plakatanschlagwerbung f	publicité f par affiches f/pl
sheet-delivery	Ausleger m (Bogenfänger)	sortie f des feuilles f/pl
sheet-feeder	Bogenanleger m	margeur m de feuilles f/pl
sheetwise	Schöndruck m	côté m de première, impression f au recto m, impression f en blanc, premier folio m
sheet-writer	Abonnentenwerber m	courtier m
shelf for magazines pl	Zeitschriftenregal n	casier m à revues f/pl
shelf warmer	Ladenhüter m	fond m de tiroir m, garde-boutique f, rossignol m
shelf-strip	Regalstreifen m	bande f d'étagère f, dépassant m de rayon m
shelf-talker	Kleinplakat n auf Regalen n/pl und Theken f/pl	affichette f dans les rayonnages m/pl
shenanigan am	Täuschung f	mystification f
to shift	verschieben	décaler, reporter
to ship	versenden	acheminer, envoyer
shipping date	Versandtermin m	date f d'envoi m
shipping department	Versandabteilung f	service m de routage m, service m des expéditions f/pl

ship's newspaper	Bordzeitung *f*	gazette *f* du bord *m*
shirt-tail	Zusatz *m* am Ende eines Artikels *m*	pan *m* de chemise *f*
shocker	Kolportageroman *m*, Schauerroman *m*	roman *m* à gros effets *m/pl*, roman *m* à sensation *f*, roman *m* sensationnel
shoddy	Kitsch *m*	tape-à-l'œil *m*
to shoot	aufnehmen (Foto)	photographier
to shoot a film	filmen	filmer, tourner un film *m*
shooting of a film	Filmaufnahme *f*	prise *f* de vue *f*, tournage *m*
shooting script	Filmdrehbuch *n*	scénario *m*, script *m*
shop	Laden *m*	magasin *m*
to shop	einkaufen	acheter
shop advertising	Ladenwerbung *f*	propagande *f* par stand *m*
shop audit	Bestandsüberprüfung *f*, Händlerbefragung *f*	enquête *f* auprès des détaillants *m/pl*, vérification *f* des stocks *m/pl*
shop bill	Kassenbon *m*	bon *m* de caisse *f*
shop fitting	Ladeneinrichtung *f*	installation *f* de magasin *m*
shop price	Ladenverkaufspreis *m*	prix *m* de magasin *m*
shop sign	Ladenschild *n*	enseigne *f* de magasin *m*
shop window	Schaufenster *n*	devanture *f*, étalage *m*, vitrine *f*
shop window advertising	Schaufensterwerbung *f*	publicité *f* en vitrine *f*, publicité *f* par étalage *m*
shop window competition	Schaufensterwettbewerb *m*	concours *m* d'étalages *m/pl*
shop window lighting	Schaufensterbeleuchtung *f*	éclairage *m* des étalages *m/pl*
shop-check	Händlerbefragung *f*	enquête *f* auprès des détaillants *m/pl*
shopper	Anzeigenblatt *n*, Käufer *m* (in *f*)	acheteur *m*, acheteuse *f*
shopping area	Einkaufszentrum *n*	centre *m* commercial, centre *m* d'achat *m*
shopping basket	Einholetasche *f*	sac *m* cabas
shopping behaviour	Käuferverhalten *n*	comportement *m* des acheteurs *m/pl*, habitudes *f/pl* des acheteurs *m/pl*
shopping center	Einkaufszentrum *n*	centre *m* commercial, centre *m* d'achat *m*
shopping goods *pl*	Konsumgüter *f/pl*	biens *m/pl* de consommation *f*
shopping habits *pl*	Einkaufsverhalten *n*	comportement *m* des acheteurs *m/pl*
shopping news	Kundenzeitschrift *f*	journal *m* pour la clientèle *f*
shopping-bag	Papierbeutel *m* mit Werbeaufdruck	sac *m* publicitaire
shop-soiled	angestaubt	défraîchi
short announcement	Kurzanzeige *f*	brève information *f*
short film	Filmlet *n*, Kurzfilm *m*	court-métrage *m*
short lead	Stückdurchschuß *m*	petite interligne *f*
short line	Ausgangszeile *f*, Kurzzeile *f*	bout *m* de ligne *f*, dernière ligne *f*, fin *f* d'alinéa *m*, ligne *f* courte
short paragraph	kleine Textanzeige *f*	entrefilet *m*
short price	reduzierter Preis *m*	prix *m* réduit

short rate	ermäßigter Tarif *m*, ermäßigter Preis *m*, Rabattnachbelastung *f*, Rabattrückbelastung *f*	charge *m* réajusté, débit *m* de rabais *m* rétrograde, rappel *m*, tarif *m* réajusté, tarif *m* réduit
short rates *pl*	reduzierte Preise *m/pl*	rappel *m*
short run	kleine Auflage *f*	petit tirage *m*
short story	Kurzgeschichte *f*, Novelle *f*	anecdote *f*, nouvelle *f*
short term contract	kurzfristiger Abschluß *m*	contrat *m* à court terme *m*
shortage goods *pl*	Mangelware *f*	marchandise *f* rare
to shorten	kürzen, zusammenstreichen	abréger, couper, raccourcir, rogner, taillader, triturer
shorthand	Kurzschrift *f*	sténographie *f*
shorthand writer	Stenograf *m*	sténographe *m*
shot	fotografische Aufnahme *f*	photographie *f*, prise *f* de vue *f*
shoulder head	vorspringender Titel *m*	titre *m* en ras de marge *f*
shoulder note	Schlagzeile *f*	ligne *f* principale, ligne *f* repère, manchette *f*, phrase *f* -choc *m*, titre *m* en vedette *f*
show	Ausstellung *f*, Messe *f*, Schau *f*, Vorführung *f*	démonstration *f*, exposition *f*, foire *f*, parade *f*, présentation *f*, projection *f*
to show	vorzeigen	montrer, présenter
show business	Schaugeschäft *n*, Vergnügungsindustrie *f*	industrie *f* du spectacle *m*, monde *m* des spectacles *m/pl*
show card	Aufstellplakat *n*, Werbeaufsteller *m*	affiche *f* de comptoir *m*, affiche *f* mobile, pancarte *f*
to show through	durchscheinen	transparaître, transpercer
show window	Schaufenster *n*	devanture *f*, étalage *m*, vitrine *f*
showcard	Ausstellkarton *m*, Schaufensterplakat *n*	affiche *f* mobile, affiche *f* vitrine *f*, pancarte *f*
showcase	Schaukasten *m*	petite vitrine *f* murale, vitrinette *f*
showman	Schausteller *m*	forain *m*
showmanship	effektvolle Darbietung *f*	art *m* de la mise *f* en scène *f*
showmaster	Leiter *m* einer Unterhaltungssendung *f*	directeur *m* d'une émission *f* amusante
show-piece	Ausstellungsstück *n*, Exponat *n*, Schaustück *n*	pièce *f* d'exposition *f*, pièce *f* spécimen *m*
show-room	Ausstellungsraum *m*	salle *f* d'exposition *f*
to shrink	eingehen (stereotyp.), einlaufen (stereotyp.)	rétrécir, se retirer
shrinkage	Schrumpfung *f*	retrait *m*
shrinking of prices *pl*	Preisherabsetzung *f*	réduction *f* de prix *m*
shunt	Überblendung *f*	enchaînement *m*, fondu *m*
shutter	Verschluß *m*	volet *m*
siccative	Sikkativ *n*, Trockenmittel *n*	siccatif *m*
side panel	Rumpffläche *f*	affiche *f* latérale, côté *m*, panneau *m* longitudinal
side stabbed	seitliche Heftung *f*	piqûre *f* à plat
side stitching	Querheftung *f*	couture *f* à cheval *m*
side window transfer	Seitenscheibenplakat *n*	affichette *f* sur les vitres *f/pl*, transparent *m* sur les glaces *f/pl*
side-notes *pl*	Marginalien *f/pl*	notes *f/pl* marginales

to **sift**	sieben	cribler, tamiser
sightseeing	Besichtigung *f*	visite *f* des curiosités *f/pl*
sign	Aushängeschild *n*, Kennzeichen *n*, Schild *n*, Werbeschild *n*, Zeichen *n*	emblème *m*, enseigne *f*, enseigne *f* publicitaire, indice *m*, marque *f*, panneau *m*, panneau *m* d'affichage *m*, panonceau *m*, plaque *f*, plaque *f* publicitaire, signe *m*
to **sign**	unterschreiben	signer, souscrire à
sign mast advertising	Mastenwerbung *f*	mât *m* publicitaire, publicité *f* sur potelets *m/pl*
sign writer	Schildermaler *m*	peintre *m* en lettres *f/pl*
signal-value	Signalwert *m*	valeur *f* comme signal *m*
signature	Erkennungsmelodie *f*, Lage *f* (Papier *n*), Sichtvermerk *m*, Signatur *f*, Unterschrift *f*	cahier *m*, mélodie *f* d'identification *f*, signature *f*, visa *m*
signature tune	Einleitungsmelodie *f*, Pausenzeichen *n*	générique *m*, indicatif *m*
signboard	Firmenschild *n*	enseigne *f* commerciale
signet	Firmensiegel *n*	emblème *m* d'entreprise *f*
to **silence**	zum Schweigen *n* bringen	réduire au silence *m*
silent colour film	Filmdia *n*	court métrage *m* muet en couleurs *f/pl*
silent film	Stummfilm *m*	film *m* muet
silhouette	Scherenschnitt *m*, Silhouette *f*	silhouette *f*
to **silhouette**	freistellen	détourer, silhouetter
silhouette half-tone	freistehende Autotypie *f*	autotypie *f* en silhouette *f*, simili *m* détouré
silk screen printing	Siebdruck *m*	impression *f* écran *m* de soie *f*, impression *f* sérigraphique, sérigraphie *f*
silk-print	Seidendruck *m*	impression *f* sur soie *f*
silly season	Saure-Gurken-Zeit *f*	mois *m/pl* creux de l'été *m*, morte-saison *f*
silver spray technique	Silberspritzverfahren *n*	procédé *m* argenture par pulvérisation *f*
to **simplify**	vereinfachen	simplifier
to **simulate**	Türken *m/pl* bauen	faire passer quelque chose *f* de faux pour vrai, feindre, simuler
simulation	Simulierung *f*	simulation *f*
simultaneous operation	Simultanverarbeitung *f*	élaboration *f* simultanément, traitement *m* simultané
simultaneous projection of recording tape and image	gleichzeitige Ton- und Bildband *n* -Vorführung *f*	double-bande *f*
single back panel	Heckschild *n*	arrière *f* (un seul panneau *m*)
single copy	Einzelnummer *f*	numéro *m* séparé, spécimen *m*
single copy price	Heftpreis *m*	prix *m* de vente *f* au numéro *m*
single-coloured	einfarbig	monochrome, unicolore
single-column	einspaltig	à une colonne *f*, sur une col *f*
single-leaf cancel	zweiseitiger Ersatzkarton *m*	onglet *m*
site	Anschlagstelle *f*	emplacement *m*, place *f* d'affichage *m*
site getter	Abpächter *m*	prospecteur *m* d'emplacements *m/pl*

site inspection	Anschlagkontrolle f	inspection f d'emplacements m/pl
site inspector	Anschlagkontrolleur m	inspecteur m d'emplacements m/pl
site leaseholder	Anschlagpächter m	concessionaire m d'affichage m
site leasing	Plakatpachtung f	régie f d'affichage m
site list	Standortverzeichnis n, Stellenverzeichnis n	liste f d'emplacements m/pl
sites pl hidden from view	verdeckt stehende Anschlagstellen f/pl	masquage m
situation story	Situationsbericht m	article m qui fait le point m
situation vacant	Stellenangebot n	offre f d'emploi m
sixteenth of page	Sechzehntelseite f	seizième de page f
sixth of page	Sechstelseite f	sixième de page f
size	Ausmaße n/pl, Größe f, Umfang m	dimensions f/pl, format m, grandeur f, nombre m des pages f/pl
to size	kalibrieren	calibrer
size of page	Seitenformat n	format m de la page f, surface f de la page f
size of the order	Abnahmemenge f, Abschlußmenge f	volume m publicitaire
sized paper	geleimtes Papier n	papier m collé
sizing	Leimung f	encollage m
skeleton type	Skelettschrift f	caractère m squelette m
to skeletonize	in großen Zügen m/pl darstellen	réduire au strict minimum m
sketch	Schmierskizze f, Skizze f	croquis m, ébauche f, esquisse f, maquette f, projet m
to sketch	skizzieren	ébaucher, esquisser
sketchblock am, sketching block	Zeichenblock m	bloc m à dessin m
to skim	oberflächlich behandeln, überfliegen	effleurer, parcourir
sky line advertising	Luftschriftwerbung f	publicité f aérienne
sky sign	Werbesilhouette f, Werbung f auf dem Dach n	publicité f dans le ciel m, publicité f se découpant sur le ciel m
sky typing	Luftschriftwerbung f	publicité f aérienne
sky writing	Himmelsschrift f	
skyline advertising	Luftwerbung f	
slab	Platte f	dalle f, plaque f
slack period	stille Saison f	morte-saison f
slander	Anschwärzung f, Verleumdung f	calomnie f, dénigrement m, diffamation f
slandermonger	Mitarbeiter m eines Skandalblattes n	collaborateur m d'un journal m à scandale m
slang	Jargon m, Slang m	argot m, jargon m
slant	Betrachtungsweise f	manière f de considérer
to slant	verdrehen	gauchir
slant letters pl	schrägliegende Buchstaben m/pl	lettres f/pl couchées
slapdashed	hastig hingeworfen	écrit à six-quatre-deux
slapstick comedy	Posse f	farce f bouffonne
to slash	beschneiden, zusammenstreichen	ébarber, rogner, taillader, tailler, triturer
slick magazine	Luxusblatt n	journal m luxueux, périodique m de luxe m

slide	Stehbild *n*	plaque *f*
slide advertising	Diapositivwerbung *f*	publicité *f* par diapositif *m*
slide projector	Bildwerfer *m*, Diabildwerfer *m*	appareil *m* de projection *f*, épidiascope *m*, projecteur-diascope *m*
slide rule	Rechenschieber *m*	règle *f* à calculer
slide with sound	Tondia *n*	diapositif *m* sonore
sliding scale, sliding scale discount	Nachlaßstaffel *f*, Rabattstaffel *f*	barême *m* dégressif, échelle *f* mobile
slip	Druckfahne *f*, Fahnenabzug *m*, Fahne *f*/*typog f*, Laufzettel *m*, Tektur *f*, Waschzettel *m*, Zettel *m*	brouillon *m*, épreuve *f*, épreuve *f* à la brosse *f*, épreuve *f* en placard *m*, fiche *f*, fiche *f* de travail *m*, note *f* de critique *f*, papillon *m*, placard *m*, prière *f* d'insérer
slip of the pen	Schreibfehler *m*	erreur *f* matérielle, faute *f* d'orthographe *f*, lapsus *m* calami *m*
slip sheets *pl*	Einschießbogen *m*, Makulaturpapier *n*	maculatures *f*/*pl*, papier *m* maculé
slip-in block	Rahmenklischee *n*	cliché *m* passe-partout
slipshod style	vernachlässigter Stil *m*	style *m* négligé
slogan	Schlagwort *n*, Werbeschlagwort *n*	mot *m* repère, phrase *f* choc *m*, slogan *m*
slope of line	Linenschrägung *f*	crênage *m*
sloping letters *pl*	Kursivschrift *f*	caractère *m* italique, écriture *f* cursive
slotman	Chef *m* des Redaktions-sekretariats *m*	chef *m* des sécretaires *m*/*pl* de rédaction *f*
slow-motion method	Zeitlupe *f*	ralentisseur *m*
slug	Maschinenzeile *f*	ligne-bloc *f*
slugs *pl*	Durchschuß *m*	interlignage *m*
slur	unreiner Druck *f*	impression *f* boueuse
to slur over	leicht hingehen über	glisser sur
small ads *pl*	kleine Anzeigen *f*/*pl*, rubrizierte Anzeigen *f*/*pl*	annonces *f*/*pl* groupées, petites annonces *f*/*pl*
small caps *pl*	Kapitälchen *n*	petites caps *f*/*pl*
small letter	Kleinbuchstabe *m*, Minuskel *f*	lettre *f* bas de casse *f*, lettre *f* minuscule, minuscule *f*
small offset press	Kleinoffsetpresse *f*	petite presse *f* offset
small print	kleiner Druck *m*	petits caractères *m*/*pl*
small talk	leichte Plauderei *f*, Partygespräch *n*	article *m* léger, menus *m*/*pl* propos
smalls *pl brit*	rubrizierte Anzeigen *f*/*pl*	annonces *f*/*pl* groupées, petites annonces *f*/*pl*
smash hit	großer Erfolg *m*, überwältigender Erfolg *m*	coup *m* en plein, gros succès *m*
smear campaign	Rufmord *m*, Verleumdungskampagne *f*	campagne *f* de dénigrement *m*, campagne *f* de diffamation *f*
smoke writing	Rauchschriftwerbung *f*	écriture *f* fumigène
smoothness	Glätte *f*	satiné *m*
smut sheet	pornografisches Blatt *n*, Skandalblatt *n*	journal *m* pornographique, journal *m* scandaleux
smutty proof	schmutziger Abzug *m*	épreuve *f* boueuse
snap-ring file	Ringhefter *m*	dossier *m* à anneaux *m*/*pl*

snapshot	Momentaufnahme *f*, Schnappschuß *m*	instantané *m*, instantané *m* non posé, photographie *f* instantanée
sniping	Wildanschlag *m*	affichage *m* à la sauvette *f*, affichage *m* volant, pose *f* libre
snob appeal	Ansprache *f* des Snobismus *m*	appel *m* au snobisme *m*
snowball system	Schneeballsystem *n*	système *m* boule *f* de neige *f*
to soak	einweichen	tremper
sob-sister	Heulsuse *f*	journaliste *f* spécialisée en reportages *m/pl* larmoyants
sob-story	rührselige Geschichte *f*	article *m* sentimental
sob-stuff	Kitsch *m*, Rührstück *n*, sentimentale Literatur *f*	bonbon *m* fondant, littérature *f* larmoyante, pièce *f* larmoyante, tape-à-l'œil *m*
social and occupational category	soziale Schicht *f*	catégorie *f* socio-professionnelle, classe *f* sociale
social gossip	Gesellschaftsklatsch *m*, Klatschspalte *f*	mondanités *f/pl*, nouvelles *f/pl* à la main *f*, potin *m* mondain
social research	Sozialforschung *f*	recherche *f* sociale
social status	soziale Schicht *f*	catégorie *f* socio-professionnelle, classe *f* sociale
society	Gesellschaft *f*	société *f*
society item, society news	Gesellschaftsklatsch *m*, Gesellschaftschronik *f*	mondanités *f/pl*, nouvelles *f/pl* à la main *f*, potin *m* mondain, carnet *m* mondain
soft approach	leise Werbung *f*	publicité *f* en douceur *f*
soft sized paper	halbgeleimtes Papier *n*	papier *m* demi-collé
to soft-pedal	verniedlichen	bagatelliser, minimiser
solarization	Überbelichtung *f*	surexposition *f*
to solder	löten, schweißen	souder
sole advertisement	alleinstehende Anzeige *f*, einzige Anzeige *f* einer Seite *f*, Inselanzeige *f*	annonce *f* isolée, seule annonce *f*
sole advertising representative	Anzeigenverwaltung *f*	concessionaire *m*, régie *f* de publicité *f*, régie *f* d'annonces *f/pl*
sole agent	Alleinvertreter *m*	concessionaire *m*
sole rights *pl* of sale	Alleinverkaufsrecht *n*	exclusivité *f*
sole sale	Alleinverkauf *m*	vente *f* exclusive
solid matter	Fließsatz *m*, glatter Satz *m*	composition *f* courante, composition *f* en placards *m/pl*, texte *m* plein
solid set	kompreß	compact, plein, serré
solidity	Haltbarkeit *f*	solidité *f*
solo test	Geschmackstest *m*	test *m* monadique
solus bus site	Rundumbeschriftung *f*	totalité *f* des emplacements *m/pl* extérieurs d'un autobus *m*
solus position *brit*	alleinstehend (Anzeige *f*)	position *f* isolée
solus site	alleinstehend (Außenwerbung *f*), Ganzstelle *f*	emplacement *m* isolé, emplacement *m* unique

sophisticated	kultiviert	aux goûts *m/pl* compliqués
sort	Sorte *f*	genre *m*, sorte *f*
to **sort**	ausmerzen	expurger, trier
sorting	Drucksachenversand *m*, Sortierung *f*, Zeitungsversand *m*	routage *m*
sorting out	Aussortierung *f*	tri *m*
sound advertising	Tonwerbung *f*	publicité *f* sonore
sound barrier	Schallmauer *f*	mur *m* du son *m*
sound camera	Tonkamera *f*	caméra *f* d'enregistrement *m* du son *m*
sound effects *pl*	Geräuscheffekte *m/pl*	bruitage *m*
sound film	Tonfilm *m*	film *m* parlant
sound film strip	Tonbildschau *f*	film *m* à images *f/pl* fixes, voiture *f* spéciale pour la projection *f* de films *m/pl* sonores
sound film studio	Tonfilmatelier *n*	studio *m* de prises *f/pl* de vue *f*
sound media *pl*	Tonmedien *n/pl*	médias *m/pl* sonnants
sound recorder	Tonaufnahmegerät *n*	appareil *m* d'enregistrement *m* de son *m*
sound slide	tönendes Dia *n*	diapositif *m* sonore
sound slide film	Tonbildschau *f*	film *m* à images *f/pl* fixes, voiture *f* spéciale pour la projection *f* de films *m/pl* sonores
sound track	Tonspur *f* eines Films *m*, Tonstreifen *m*	bande *f* internationale, piste *f* sonore, trace *f* de son *m* d'un film *m*
sound truck	Lautsprecherwagen *m*	camion *m* publicitaire
sound-proofing	Schalldichtmachung *f*	insonorisation *f*
source	Quelle *f*	source *f*
source of error	Fehlerquelle *f*	source *f* d'erreurs *f/pl*
source of information	Informationsquelle *f*	source *f* d'information *f*
space	Raum *m*, Spatium *n*, Ausschluß *typog m*	espace *m*, espace *m* blanc, espace *f*
space band	Ausschließkeil *m*	espace-bande *f*
space broker	Annoncenexpedition *f*, Anzeigenmittler *m*, Werbungsmittler *m*	acheteur *m* d'espace *m*, agence *f* de publicité *f*, courtier *m* d'annonces *f/pl*, courtier *m* de publicité *f*, expédition *f* d'annonces *f/pl*, intermédiaire *m* publicitaire
space buyer	Anzeigenkäufer *m*, Mediadisponent *m*	acheteur *m* d'espace *m*
space buying	Anzeigenbelegung *f*, Anzeigeneinkauf *m*, Anzeigenraum *m* bestellen	achat *m* d'annonces *f/pl*, achat *m* d'espace *m*, acheter d'espace *m*
space charge	Anschlagkosten *pl*, Plakatanschlagpreis *m*, Streukosten *pl*	dépenses *f/pl* d'affichage *m*, frais *m/pl* de diffusion *f*
to **space closely**	eng setzen, kompreß setzen	composer sans interlignes *f/pl*, composer serré

space discount	Mengenrabatt *m*	dégressif *m* sur volume *m* publicitaire, rabais *m* de quantité *f,* remise *f* de quantité *f*
to space evenly	ausgleichen (Zeile)	rectifier les approches *f/pl*
space fee *am*	Zeilenhonorar *n*	rémunération *f* à la ligne *f*
space man	Journalist *m* mit Zeilen- honorar *n*	journaliste *m* payé à la ligne *f*
space order	Anzeigenauftrag *m,* Insertionsauftrag *m*	commande *f* d'insertion *f,* ordre *m* d'annonces *f/pl,* ordre *m* d'insertion *f*
to space out	durchschießen, spationieren, sperren	blanchir, espacer, interlettrer, interligner
space rates *pl*	Anzeigenpreisliste *f,* Anzeigentarif *m*	tarif *m* d'annonces *f/pl,* tarif *m* de publicité *f,* tarif *m* d'insertion *f*
space salesman	Anzeigenakquisiteur *m*	démarcheur *m* en publicité *f,* vendeur *m* d'espace *m*
space schedule	Etatverteilung *f,* Streuplan *m*	calendrier *m* d'insertion *f,* plan *m* de diffusion *f,* répartition *f* de budget *m*
space size	Anzeigengröße *f*	lignage *m* d'une annonce *f*
spaced	gesperrt *typog*	espacé
spaced composition	Sperrsatz *m*	composition *f* espacée
spacing material	Blindmaterial *n*	blancs *m/pl*
to speak in superlatives *pl*	übertreiben	exagérer, grossir
speaker	Pressesprecher *m,* Redner *m*	orateur *m,* porte-parole *m*
special action	Sonderaktion *f*	action *f* spéciale
special additional charge	Sonderzuschlag *m*	surtaxe *m* spécial
special colour	Spezialfarbe *f*	couleur *f* spéciale, encre *f* spéciale
special commission	Sonderprovision *f*	commission *f* exceptionnelle
special correspondent	Sonderberichterstatter *m*	envoyé *m* special
special discount	Sonderrabatt *m*	réduction *f* de faveur *f,* remise *f* spéciale
special edition	Extrablatt *n,* Sonderausgabe *f*	édition *f* spéciale
special impression	Separatdruck *m,* Sonderdruck *m*	édition *f* à part *f,* tirage *m* à part *f,* tirage *m* spécial
special issue	Sondernummer *f*	numéro *m* spécial
special knowledge	Fachwissen *n*	science *f* spéciale
special number	Sondernummer *f*	numéro *m* spécial
special offer	Sonderangebot *n*	offre *f* de faveur *f,* offre *f* spéciale
special page	Sonderseite *f*	page *f* spéciale
special position	bevorzugte Plazierung *f,* Sonderplacierung *f,* Vorzugsplazierung *f*	emplacement *m* préférentiel, emplacement *m* privilégié, emplacement *m* spécial, mise *f* en avant, placement *m* de faveur *f*
special rate	Sonderpreis *m,* Spezialpreis *m,* Vorzugspreis *m*	prix *m* spécial, prix-réclame *f*
special representative	Bezirksvertreter *m*	agent *m* régional
special section	Rubrik *f*	rubrique *f*
special supplement	Sonderbeilage *f*	supplément *m* spécial
specialised literature	Fachliteratur *f*	littérature *f* spécialisée
specialised magazine	Zielgruppenzeitschrift *f*	revue *f* spécialisée

specialist	Fachmann *m*	expert *m*, spécialiste *m*
specialty	Werbegeschenk *n*	cadeau *m* publicitaire, prime *f*
specialty goods *pl*	Markenartikel *m*	article *m* de marque *f*, produit *m* de marque *f* déposée
specialty shop, specialty store	Fachgeschäft *n*, Spezialgeschäft *n*	commerce *m* spécialisé, magasin *m* specialisé
specimen	Leseprobe *f*, Probe *f*	échantillon *m*, spécimen *m*, spécimen *m* de texte *m*
specimen copy	Ansichtsexemplar *f*, Freiexemplar *n*, Gratisexemplar *n*, Probenummer *f*	exemplaire *m* gratuit, numéro *m* d'essai *m*, numéro *m* spécimen *m*, service *m* de presse *f*, spécimen *m*
specimen page	Probeseite *f*	page *f* modèle *m*, page *f* spécimen *m*
specimen sheet	Aushängebogen *m*	bonne feuille *f*
specimen volume	Probedruck *m*	épreuve *f*
speck	Fleck *m*	macule *f*, tache *f*
spectacolor advertisement	Insettinganzeige *f*	publicité *f* par insetting
spectacular	Leuchtwerbung *f*, bewegliche, Werbegroßanlage *f*	installation *f* spectaculaire, publicité *f* lumineuse animée
speculative work	unverbindlicher Vorschlag *m*	projet *m* gratuit
speech	Ansprache *f*	harangue *f*
speech balloon	Sprechblase *f*	ballon *m*, bulle *f*, philactère *f*
to spell	buchstabieren	épeler
spelling	Rechtschreibung *f*	orthographe *f*
spending group	Käuferschicht *f*	catégorie *f* des acheteurs *m/pl*
spending power	Kaufkraft *f*	capacité *f* d'achat *m*, pouvoir *m* d'achat *m*
spezialised fair	Fachmesse *f*	foire *f* spécialisée
sphere	Kugel *f*	boule *f*, sphère *f*
sphere of action	Wirkungsbereich *m*	champ *m* d'action *f*, sphère *f* d'action *f*
sphere of influence	Einflußgebiet *n*	sphère *f* d'influence *f*
sphere of interests *pl*	Interessenbereich *m*	sphère *f* d'intérêts *m/pl*
spike	Ablehnung *f* eines Manuskripts *n*	refus *m* d'un manuscrit *m*
spine gluing	Blockleimung *f*	encollage *m* des dos *m/pl*
spine lettering	Rückentitel *m*	titre *m* au dos *m* d'un livre *m*
spiral stitching	Spiralheftung *f*	couture *f* spirale, reliure *f* spirale
to split	aufteilen	diviser, partager
split commission	geteilte Provision *f*	commission *f* partagée
split run	Anzeigensplit *m*, Inseratvarianten *f/pl* in derselben Ausgabe *f*	tirage *m* partagé
split run advertising	mehrgleisige Werbung *f*, Teilbelegung *f*	publicité *f* à plusieurs voies *f/pl*, publicité *f* dans un tirage *m* partagé
split-run advertisement	Anzeige *f* in einer Teilauflage *f/pl*	annonce *f* à variantes *f/pl*
split-run test	Split-Run-Test *n*	split-run *m* test *m*
splitting	Teilung *f* der Auflage	division *f* du tirage *m*
splurging	Großtuerei *f*	esbrouffe *f*
spoil	Makulatur *f*	maculature *f*, papier *m* de rebut *m*

spoil package	Einwegpackung f	emballage m non repris, emballage m perdu
spokesman	Sprachrohr n, Wortführer m	porte-parole m, porte-voix m
sponsor	Förderer m	parrain m
sponsored broadcast, sponsored programme	Patronatssendung f, Sponsor-Sendung f	émission f patronnée, programme m patronné
sponsored subscription	Patenschaftsabonnement n	abonnement m parrainé
sponsorship	Subvention f von Sendungen f/pl	patronnage m
spontaneous remembrance	spontane Erinnerung f	mémoire f spontanée, souvenir m spontané
sport journal	Sportblatt n	feuille f sportive
sport magazine	Sportzeitschrift f	journal m sportif
sport stadium	Sportstadion n	champ m de cours m
sporting news	Sportblatt n, Sportnachrichten f/pl	feuille f sportive, nouvelles f/pl sportives
sporting page	Sportseite f	nouvelles f/pl sportives, page f sportive
sports pl editor	Sportredakteur m	rédacteur m des sports m/pl
sports pl page	Sportteil m	rubrique f sportive
sportsmen's page	Sportseite f	nouvelles f/pl sportives, page f sportive
spot	Fernsehspot m, Werbeeinschaltung f	émission f publicitaire, message m publicitaire, spot m
spot announcement	Werbedurchsage f, Werbeeinblendung f, Werbespot m	annonce f à la radio f, annonce f radiodiffusée, bref communiqué m radio f, court-métrage m publicitaire, insertion f publicitaire, message m publicitaire, réglage m, spot m
spot cash	Barzahlung f	paiement m comptant, règlement m comptant
spotlight	Punktlicht n, Scheinwerferlicht n	feu m de projecteur m
spot-news	neueste Nachrichten f/pl	dernières nouvelles f/pl, nouvelles f/pl fraîches
spotting	Fleckenbildung f	formation f de taches f/pl
spread	ganzseitige Anzeige f, Streuung f	annonce f d'une page f entière, couverture f, prospection f
spread-head	mehrspaltige Überschrift f	grand titre m sur plusieurs colonnes f/pl
spread-over	Etatverteilung f, Streuplan m	calendrier m d'insertion f, plan m de diffusion f, répartition f de budget m
spring fair	Frühjahrsmesse f	foire f de printemps m
square	Quadrat n, Winkelmaß n	carré m, équerre f
square brackets pl	eckige Klammern f/pl	crochets m/pl
square half-tone	rechteckige Vollautotypie f	autotypie f rectangulaire, simili m au carré m
squared up block	rechteckiges Klischee n	cliché m rectangulaire
squared-off	viereckig	carré, quadrangulaire
squeegee	Rakel f	raclette f, racleur m
squib	Stichelei f	brocard m, raillerie f

squish	rührselige Literatur *f*, sentimentale Literatur *f*	bonbon *m* fondant, guimauve *f*, littérature *f* larmoyante
sreaming poster	grellfarbiges Plakat *n*	affiche *f* criarde
stabbing	Einsteckheftung *f*	piquer travers
stadium	Stadion *n*	stade *m*
staff magazine	Hauszeitschrift *f*, Werkzeitschrift *f*	journal *m* d'entreprise *f*, revue *f* d'entreprise
staffwork	Stabsarbeit *f*	travail *m* d'organisation *f*
staggered schedule	Wechselstreuung *f*	couverture *f* alternée
staircase site	Treppenstufenwerbung *f*	emplacement *m* sur contre-marches *f/pl* d'escalier *m*, panneau *m* d'escalier *m*
stale article	veraltete Ware *f*	article *m* passé de mode *m*
stale news	überholte Nachrichten *f/pl*	information *f* dépassée
stall	Verkaufsstand *m*	boutique *f* de vente *f*
stamp	Stempel *m*	sceau *m*, tampon *m*, timbre *m*
to stamp	prägen, stempeln	empreindre, gaufrer, repousser, tamponner, timbrer
stamp book	Rabattmarkenbuch *n*	carnet *m* de timbres *m/pl* prime *f*
stamp factory	Stempelfabrik *f*	fabrique *f* de tampons *m/pl*
stamp pad	Stempelkissen *n*	coussin *m* à tampons *m/pl*
stamped envelope	Freiumschlag *m*	enveloppe *f* timbrée
stamping die	Prägestempel *m*	étampe *f*, poinçon *m*
stand	Plakatständer *m*, Stand *m*	panneau *m* d'affichage *m*, stand *m*
stand construction	Standbau *m*	construction *f* de stands *m/pl*
stand design, stand dressing	Standgestaltung *f*	aménagement *m* d'un stand *m*, présentation *f* d'un stand *m*
standard	Norm *f*	standard *m*
standard film	Normalfilm *m*	film *m* de format *m* normal
standard film copy	erste endgültige Filmkopie *f*	copie *f* standard
standard media rates *pl*	Zeitungskatalog *m*	catalogue *m* des journaux *m/pl*
standard package	Normalpackung *f*	emballage *m* normal
standard paper size	Papiernormalformat *n*	format *m* normalisé du papier *m*
standard price	empfohlener Preis *m*	prix *m* recommandé
standard rate	Grundpreis *m*	prix *m* de base *f*, tarif *m* fixe
standard size	Normalformat *n*	format *m* normalisé
standard text type	Normalschrift *f*	caractères *m/pl* standard
standardization	Normung *f*, Standardisierung *f*, Typisierung *f*	standardisation *f*
standardized	übersichtlich	bien disposé, normalisé
standardized sheet size	Standardformat *n*	format *m* normalisé, format *m* standard *m*
standing detail	wiederkehrendes Anzeigenelement *n*	détail *m* permanent
standing matter	Stehsatz *m*	composition *f* conservée, composition *f* permanente, conserve *f*
standing order	Dauerauftrag *m*, Festauftrag *m*, laufender Auftrag *m*	ordre *m* ferme, ordre *m* permanent
standing price	Festpreis *m*	prix *m* fixe, prix *m* imposé
standpoint	Standpunkt *m*	point *m* de vue *f*
standstill in market	Absatzstockung *f*	stagnation *f* des ventes *f/pl*
staple	Heftklammer *f*	crochet *m*

staple article	Stapelware *f*	article *m* clé *f*, article *m* fondamental
star	Filmgröße *f*, Filmstar *m*	vedette *f*, vedette *f* de l'écran *m*
start	Anlauf *m*	démarrage *m*
start of printing	Druckbeginn *m*	mise en marche *f*
start of the bill posting	Anschlagbeginn *m*	date *f* de départ *m* de l'affichage *m*
start time	Anlaufzeit *f*	période *f* de démarrage *m*
start work report	Informationsbericht *m* vor Beginn *f* der Ausarbeitung *f* einer Werbekampagne	rapport *m* d'information *f* devant le commencement *m* d'une campagne *f* publicitaire
starting signal	Startzeichen *n*	indication *f* de rentrée *f*
to state	angeben, erklären	déclarer, indiquer
stated position	vorgeschriebene Plazierung *f*	emplacement *m* de rigueur *f*, emplacement *m* imposé
statement	Abrechnung *f*, Angabe *f*, Aussage *f*, Exposé *n*, Feststellung *f*, Mitteilung *f*	communiqué *m*, déclaration *f*, décompte *m*, établissement *m*, exposé *m*, indication *f*, liquidation *f*, proposition *f*
station	Sender *m*	antenne *f*, station-radio *f*
station break	Sendepause *f*	silence *m*, temps *m* mort
station interior site	Bahnhofshallenwerbung *f*	panneau *m* de gare *f*
station poster	Bahnhofsplakat *n*	affiche *f* dans les gares *f/pl*
station rep	Werbefunkvertreter *m*	représentant *m* de radiodiffusion *f* publicitaire
stationary press	Standortpresse *f*	presse *f* stationnaire
statistician	Statistiker *m*	statisticien *m*
statistics *pl*	Statistik *f*	statistique *f*
status symbol	Statussymbol *n*	marque *f* de standing *m*
statutory announcement	amtliche Anzeige *f*	annonce *f* légale
steady customer	Stammkunde *m*	client *m* fidèle
steady seller	langlebiges Buch *n*	livre *m* durable
steam radio	Dampfradio *n*	bonne vieille radio *f* papa *m*
steel engraving	Stahlstich *m*	taille *f* dure
steel engraving tool	Stichel *m*	burin *m*
stencil	Matrize *f*, Schablone *f*	découpage *m*, écran *m*, gabarit *m*, matrice *f*, pochoir *m*, stencil *m*
step head	stufenförmige Überschrift *f*	titre *m* en marche *f* d'escalier *m*
stereo	Stereo *n*	stéréo *m*
stereophony	räumliches Hören *n*, Raumton *m*	stéréophonie *f*
stereotype	gleichbleibendes Vorstellungsbild *n*, Plattendruck *m*, Stereo *n*	cliché *m*, stéréo *m*, stéréotypage *m*
to stereotype	klischieren	clicher, faire un cliché *m*
stereotyper	Stereotypeur *m*	clicheur *m*, stéréotypeur *m*
stereotyping	Stereotypie *f*	clichage *m*, stéréotypie *f*
stereotyping process	Klischierung *f*,	clichage *m*
stet!	stehen lassen!	à maintenir
to stick bills *pl*	anschlagen, plakatieren	afficher, coller, poser une affiche *f*

to **stick on**	bekleben	coller
stick space	Ausschluß *typog m*	cadrats *m/pl*, espace *f*
sticked screen	aufgelegter Raster *m*	trame *f* collée
sticker	Ankleber *m*, Etikett *n*, Klebezettel *m*, Preisschild *n*	afficheur *m*, étiquette *f*, papillon *m*, porte-prix *m*, timbre *m*
sticker *am*	Plakat *n*	affiche *f*-papier *m*, placard *m*
sticker slip	Aufkleber *m*	étiquette *f* gommée, papillon *m*, timbre *m* adhésif *m*
sticking up	Anschlag *m*	collage *m*
stiff paper binding	Pappband *m*	reliure *f* cartonnée
to **stifle a scandal**	einen Skandal *m* ersticken	étouffer un scandal *m*
stifling of the press	Presseknebelung *f*	bâillonnement *m* de la presse *f*, muselement *m* de la presse *f*
still life	Stilleben *n*	nature *f* morte
stimulus	Kaufanreiz *m*, Reiz *m*	incitation *f* à l'achat *m*, stimulation *f*
stipple	Punktschraffierung *f*	crachis *m*, grisé *m* fait à la brosse *f*
to **stipple**	granieren	grainer
stippled frame	gepunkteter Rand *m*, punktierter Rand *m*	cadre *m* de pointillés *m/pl*
to **stipulate**	ausbedingen	stipuler
stipulation	Klausel *f*	stipulation *f*
to **stitch**	broschieren, heften	agrafer, brocher
to **stitch in**	einheften	brocher dans, coudre dans
stitched	geheftet	broché
stitching	Broschur *f*, Heftung *f*	brochage *m*, piqûre *f*
stitching gauze	Heftgaze *f*	mousseline *f*
stitching thread	Heftfaden *m*	fil *m* à brocher
stock	Lagerbestand *m*	stock *m*
stock of information	Nachrichtenquelle *f*	source *f* d'information *f*
stock of orders *pl*	Auftragsbestand *m*	portefeuille *m* de commandes *f/pl*
stock of regular readers *pl*	Leserstamm *m*	noyau *m* de lecteurs *m/pl*
stock of type	Schriftmaterial *n*	caractères *m/pl* d'impression *f*
stock phrase	abgedroschene Redensart *f*	cliché *m*, phrase *f* rebattue
stock poster	Rahmenplakat *n*	affiche *f* passe-partout
stock remainder	Restbestand *m*	stock *m* restant
stock-shot	Archivbild *n*	plan *m* d'archives *f/pl*
stock-shots *pl*	Filmarchiv *n*	cinémathèque *f*, filmothèque *f*
stock-taking sales *pl*	Inventurausverkauf *m*	soldes *m/pl* après inventaire *m*
stone	Druckfundament *n*, Stein *m*	marbre *m*
stone proof	Bürstenabzug *m*	épreuve *f* à la brosse *f*, épreuve *f* au taquoir *m*, morasse *f*
stop gap advertisement	Füllanzeige *f*, Lückenbüßer *m*	annonce *f* bouche-trou *m*
stop time	Auslaufzeit *f*	période *f* transitoire
stopper	Blickfang *m*	accrochage *m*, accroche-œil *m*, amorce *f*, attrape-regard *m*, tape-à-l'œil *m*, tire-l'œil *m*
stopping power	Betrachtungszeit *f*	temps *m* d'observation *f*
stop-press news	letzte Nachrichten *f/pl*	information *f* de dernière heure *f*
store fittings *pl*	Ladenausstattung *f*	installation *f* de magasin *m*
store hours *pl*	Geschäftsstunden *f/pl*	heures *f/pl* d'ouverture *f*

store manager	Filialleiter *m*	directeur *m* de succursale *f*
storecasting	Rundfunksendung *f* im Laden *m*	publicité *f* radiophonique dans une boutique *f*
story	Geschichte *f,* Grundthema *n,* Thema *n* einer Anzeige *f,* Werbetextidee *f*	affaire *f,* conte *f,* histoire *f* du texte *m,* sujet *m,* thème *m*
storyboard	Bild-Drehbuch *n,* Entwurfsskizze *f* eines Werbefilms *m*	présentation *f* d'un scénario *m* sous forme *f* d'une suite *f* de dessins *m/pl,* storyboard *m*
straight commercial	integrierte Funkwerbung *f*	émission *f* publicitaire intégrée
straight matter	glatter Satz *m*	composition *f* courante
straight printing	Flachdruck *m*	impression *f* à plat, impression *f* planographique
straight tip	sicherer Tip *m*	tuyau *m* exact
to straighten line	Linie *f* halten, Zeile *f* halten	aligner
strata *pl* of population	Bevölkerungsschichten *f/pl*	catégories *f* de population *f,* couches *f/pl* de la population *f*
straw board	Strohpappe *f*	carton *m* de paille *f*
stray costumer	Gelegenheitskunde *m*	client *m* de passage *m,* client *m* occasionnel
streamer	Dachschild *n,* Spruchband *n,* Streifenanzeige *f,* Titel *m* über Blattbreite *f,* Transparent *n,* Werbewimpel *m,* Wimpel *m*	bandeau *m,* banderole *f,* calicot *m,* enseigne *f* lumineuse, fanion *m,* flamme *f,* oriflamme *f,* panneau *m* sur le toit *m,* titre *m* sur toute la longueur *f,* transparent *m*
to streamline	modernisieren	moderniser
street car advertising	Straßenbahnwerbung *f*	publicité *f* tram *m*
street hawker	Straßenhändler *m,* Straßenverkäufer *m*	camelot *m,* crieur *m* de journaux *m/pl*
street hoarding	Anschlagfläche *f*	palissade *f*
street sales *pl*	Straßenhandel *m*	vente *f* ambulante
street vendor	Straßenverkäufer *m*	camelot *m,* crieur *m* de journaux *m/pl*
to strengthen	treffender formulieren	donner une formulation *f* plus frappante
to strengthen (ink)	strenger machen (Farbe)	charger une couleur *f*
to stretch	dehnen	étendre
to strike off	Stegreif *m* schreiben, aus dem	improviser
to strike through	durchschlagen *typog*	maculer, pénétrer, transpercer, traverser
string	Kolumnenschnur *f*	ficelle *f* à colonnes *f/pl*
string of newspapers *pl*	Zeitungsgruppe *f*	groupe *m* de presse *f*
string-correspondent	gelegentlicher Mitarbeiter *m*	collaborateur *m* occasionnel, collaborateur *m* part-time
stringer	freier Korrespondent *m*	correspondant *m* qui n'appartient pas à la rédaction *f*
strip	Bilderserie *f,* Streifenanzeige *f*	bande *f* d'illustrations *f/pl,* bandeau *m*
strip advertising	Bildserienwerbung *f*	publicité *f* avec des bandes *f/pl* dessinées

stripping	Entmantelung *f*, Fotomontage *f*	composition *f* photographique, grattage *m*, montage *m* photographique, photomontage *m*
stripping desk, stripping table	Montagetisch *m*	table *f* de montage *m*, table *f* lumineuse
stroke	Strich *m*	trait *m*
strong paper	starkes Papier *n*	papier *m* fort
structure of distribution	Vertriebsgefüge *n*	structure *f* de la distribution *f*
studio	Atelier *n*, Aufnahmeraum *m*, Studio *n*	atelier *m*, film *m* studio *m*, studio *m*
studio manager	Atelierleiter *m*	chef *m* de studio *m*, directeur *m* artistique
stuff	Papiermasse *f*	pâte *f* de papier *m*
stuffer	Beilagenzettel *m*	encart *m*, papillon *m*
to **stun**	verblüffen	abasourdir
stunt	Reklametrick *m*	ruse *f* publicitaire
stunt advertising	sensationelle Werbung *f*	coup *m*, truc *m*
stunt article	auffallender Artikel *m*	article *m* tapageur
stunt film	Trickfilm *m*	dessin *m* animé, film *m* truqué
stunt press	Sensationspresse *f*	presse *f* à sensation *f*, presse *f* jaune
stuntman	Double *n*	acrobate *m*-doublure *f*
style	Ausdrucksweise *f*, Schreibart *f*, Stil *m*	diction *f*, élocution *f*, manière *f* de s'exprimer, phraséologie *f*, style *m*
style of marks *pl*	Markenstil *m*	style *m* de marque *f*
style show	Modeschau *f*	defilé *m* de mode *f*, exposition *f* de modes *f/pl*
style with punch in it	kraftvoller Stil *m*	style *m* à l'emporte-pièce *m*
styling	Formgestaltung *f*, Produktgestaltung *f*	création *f* de la forme *f*, esthétique *f* industrielle, réalisation *f* d'un produit *m*
stylist	Formgestalter *m*	dessinateur *m* industriel, styliste *m*
sub-contracting	Verpachtung *f*	affermage *m*, amodiation *f*
subdivision	Unterteilung *f*	subdivision *f*
sub-editing	Formulierung *f* eines Textes *m*	cuisine *f* d'un texte *m*
sub-edition	Nebenausgabe *f*	édition *f* secondaire
sub-editor	Redaktionssekretär *m*, stellvertretender Redakteur *m*	rédacteur *m* adjoint, sécrétaire *m* de rédaction *f*
subheading	Untertitel *m*	second titre *m*, sous-titre *m*
subject	Gegenstand *m*, Sachgebiet *n*, Sparte *f*	matière *f*, section *f*, sujet *m*
subject index	Sachregister *n*	index *m* alphabétique, registre *m* par matières *f/pl*, répertoire *m*
subject of the poster	Plakatmotiv *n*	sujet *m* de l'affiche *f*
subject to acceptability	Übereinkunft *f*, nach	à débattre
to **sublet**	untervermieten	sous-louer
subliminal advertising	Schleichwerbung *f*, unterschwellige Werbung *f*	publicité *f* camouflée, publicité *f* clandestine, publicité *f* déguisée, publicité *f* insidieuse, publicité *f* occulte, publicité *f* subliminale, publicité *f* subversive
subordinate offer	verstecktes Angebot *n*	offre *f* clandestine

to **subscribe**	abonnieren, beziehen	s'abonner à
subscriber	Abonnent *m*, Bezieher *m*	abonné *m*, souscripteur *m*
subscriber analysis	Abonnentenanalyse *f*	analyse *f* des abonnés *m/pl*
subscribers' paper	Abonnementszeitung *f*	journal *m* d'abonnés *m/pl*
subscription	Abonnement *n*, Bezug *m*	abonnement *m*
subscription agent	Bezieherwerber *f*	agent *m* d'abonnement *m*
subscription canvasser	Abonnentenwerber *m*	courtier *m*
subscription form	Bestellschein *m*	bon *m* de commande *f*
subscription price	Subskriptionspreis *m*	prix *m* de souscription *f*
subscription rate	Bezugspreis *m*, Abonnementspreis *m*	prix *m* d'abonnement *m*
subscription salesman, **subscription solicitor**	Abonnentenwerber *m*	courtier *m*
subscription stop	Abonnementskündigung *f*	résiliation *f* de l'abonnement *m*
subscription to a journal	Zeitungsabonnement *n*, Zeitungsbestellung *f*	abonnement *m* à un journal *m*, souscription *f* à un abonnement *m*
subsidizing	Subventionierung *f*	subventionnement *m*
substantial advertising	starke Werbung *f*, umfangreiche Werbung *f*	publicité *f* substantielle, publicité *f* volumineuse
substitute date	Ersatztermin *m*	date *f* succédanée
sub-title	Untertitel *m*, Zwischentitel *m*	intertitre *m*, second titre *m*, sous-titre *m*
subway advertising *am*	U-Bahn-Werbung *f*	publicité-métro *m*
success	Erfolg *m*	succès *m*
successive	aufeinanderfolgend	successif
to **suggest**	vorschlagen	proposer, suggérer
suggested price	empfohlener Preis *m*	prix *m* recommandé
suggestive advertising	Suggestivwerbung *f*	publicité *f* suggestive
suggestive question	Suggestivfrage *f*	question *f* suggestive, question *f* tendancieuse
to **summarize**	zusammenfassen	cumuler, récapituler, résumer
summary	Abriß *m*, Inhaltsangabe *f*	résumé *m*
summary lead	Grundsatzartikel *m*	article *m* d'appel *m*
summer sales *pl*	Sommerschlußverkauf *m*	vente *f* de soldes *m/pl* d'été *m*
Sunday edition	Sonntagsausgabe *f*	quotidien *m* du septième jour *m*
Sunday newspaper	Sonntagszeitung *f*	journal *m* de dimanche *m*
Sunday supplement	Sonntagsbeilage *f*	supplément *m* dominical
super-calendered	hochsatiniert	surglacé
supercalendered paper	hochsatiniertes Papier *n*, Illustrationsdruckpapier *n*, kalandriertes Papier *n*	papier *m* pour illustrations *f/pl*, papier *m* satiné, papier *m* surglacé
supercommission	Superprovision *f*	surcommission *f*, surremise *f*
to **superimpose**	einkopieren	copier dans, pelliculer
superior letter	hochstehender Buchstabe *m*	exposant *m* supérieur
superior letters *pl*	hochgerückte Buchstaben *m/pl*	lettres *f/pl* supérieures
supermarket	Selbstbedienungsladen *m*, Supermarkt *m*	libre service *m*, supermarché *m*
supervision	Überwachung *f*	contrôle *m*, surveillance *f*
supplement	Anhang *m*, Beilage *f*, Zeitungsbeilage *f*	appendice *m*, encart *m*, supplément *m*
supplementary	zusätzlich	supplémentaire
supplementary advertising	Ergänzungswerbung *f*, zusätzliche Werbung *f*	publicité *f* auxiliaire, publicité *f* de complément *m*, publicité *f* de soutien *m*

supplementary colour	Zusatzfarbe f	couleur f de soutien m
supplementary film	Beifilm m, Beiprogramm n	court-métrage m, hors-programme m, programme m adjacent, programme m d'accompagnement m
supplier	Auftragnehmer m, Auslieferer m, Lieferant m	dépositaire m, fournisseur m, mandataire m
supplier of addresses pl	Adressenverlag m	éditeur m d'adresses f/pl, loueurs m/pl d'adresses f/pl
supply covering all requirements pl	Bedarfsdeckung f	satisfaction f des besoins m/pl
to supply news	Nachrichten f/pl beschaffen	fournir des nouvelles f/pl
supplying of posters pl	Plakatanlieferung f	fourniture f des affiches f/pl
support	Stütze f, Unterstützung f	appui m, support m
supporting media pl	unterstützende Medien n/pl	médias m/pl appuyants
surcharge	Preisaufschlag m	majoration f de tarif m, majoration f de prix m, supplément m de prix m
surcharge for multi-color	Mehrfarbenzuschlag m	supplément m pour polychromie f
surcharge for special position	Plazierungsaufschlag m	majoration f pour emplacement m de rigueur f
surface	Fläche f	surface f
surface of paper	Papieroberfläche f	surface f du papier m
surface printing	Hochdruckverfahren n	impression f en relief m
surface screen	Bildfläche f	écran m
surplus	Überdruck m, Überschuß m	feuille f supernuméraire, main f de passe f, surplus m
surplus of orders pl	Auftragsüberhänge m/pl	surplus m de commandes f/pl
surprint	Überdruck m (Aufdruck)	surimpression f
surprisal value	Überraschungswert m	valeur f de surprise f
surprise effect	Überraschungseffekt m	effet m de surprise f
survey	Befragung f, Erhebung f, Umfrage f, Untersuchung f, Überblick m, Übersicht f	aperçu m, enquête f, étude f, examen m, interrogatoire m, interview f, recherche f, résumé m, tour m d'horizon m, vue f d'ensemble
survey data	Umfrageergebnis n	résultat m d'enquête f
swash face	Zierschrift f	caractère m de fantaisie f, caractères m/pl ornés
swash initial	Schmuckinitiale f	initiale f ornée
swash letter	Zierbuchstabe m	italique f de fantaisie f, lettre f à queue f, lettre f ornée
swatch	Farbmuster n	échantillon m de couleur f
sweepstake	Verlosungsart f	espèce f de loterie f
switch over	Verkäufermerkblatt n	argumentaire m
symbol	Bildmarke f, Bildzeichen n	marque f figurative, marque f symbolique
symmetry	Symmetrie f	symétrie f
symposium	Diskussionsveranstaltung f, Symposium n	colloque m, conférence f-débat m, séminaire m
synchronization	Synchronisation f	synchronisation f

to **syndicate**	Artikel *m* gleichzeitig in mehreren Zeitungen *f/pl* veröffentlichen	publier un article *m* simultanément dans plusieurs journaux *m/pl*
syndicated columnist	Kolumnist *m*	collaborateur *m* attitré, rubriquard *m*
synopsis	Übersicht *f,* Zusammenfassung *f*	aperçu *m,* récapitulation *f,* résumé *m*
synthetic material	Kunststoffe *m/pl*	matière *f* artificielle, matière *f* synthétique
synthetic resin	Kunstharz *n*	résine *f* synthétique
systematic advertising	zielbewußte Werbung *f*	publicité *f* systématique

T

table of contents *pl*	Inhaltsverzeichnis *n,* Sachregister *n*	index *m,* index *m* alphabétique, registre *m* par matières *f/pl,* répertoire *m,* sommaire *m,* table *f* des matières *f/pl*
tabloid	Kleinformatzeitung *f*	tabloïd *m*
tabular matter	Tabellensatz *m*	composition *f* de tableaux *m/pl,* tableautage *m*
to **tabulate**	tabellieren	mettre en tableau *m,* tabuler
tabulation	Tabelle *f*	tableau *m,* tabulation *f*
tabulator	Tabulator *m*	tabulateur *m*
tabulator matter	Tabellensatz *m*	composition *f* de tableaux *m/pl,* tableautage *m*
tachistoscope	Tachistoskop *n*	tachistoscope *m*
tag	Anhängezettel *m*	étiquette *f* à attacher, étiquette *f* à ficelle *f*
tail	Fuß *m,* unterer Blattrand *m,* Unterschlag *m*	blanc *m* de pied *m,* marge *f* de pied *m*
tail cap	Häubchen *n*	coiffe *f*
tail piece	Schlußstück *n,* Schlußvignette *f,* Zierleiste *f*	bordure *f,* cul *m* de lampe *f,* fleuron *m*
take	Aufnahme *f* (Film)	prise *f* de vue *f*
to **take in**	einbringen (Zeile)	gagner
to **take out**	tilgen	biffer, rayer
taking of photographs *pl*	fotografische Aufnahme *f*	photographie *f,* prise *f* de vue *f*
talent costs *pl*	Produktionskosten *pl*	coûts *m/pl* de production *f*
talk of the town	Stadtgespräch *n*	on ne parle que de cela
to **talk shop**	fachsimpeln	parler métier *m*
talkie, talking film	Tonfilm *m*	film *m* parlant
talking points *pl*	Argumentation *f,* Gesprächspunkte *m/pl,* sprechende Argumente *n/pl*	argumentation *f,* arguments *m/pl* en faveur d'une marchandise *f*
tally business	Ratengeschäft *n*	vente *f* à tempérament *m*
tamalyzer	Gerät *n* zur Messung *f* der Zuschauerbeteiligung *f*	appareil *m* pour tester la participation *f* des vidéo-spectateurs *m/pl*
to **tap**	absetzen (Druck)	composer
tape recorder	Aufnahmegerät *n*	appareil *m* enregistreur
tape recording	Bandaufnahme *f,* Tonbandaufnahme *f*	enregistrement *m* électrique, enregistrement *m* sur bande *f* magnétique, prise *f* de son *m*
tape recording without words *pl*	Tonband *n* ohne Worte *n/pl*	bande *f* internationale
target audience, target group	Zielgruppe *f*	audience *f* utile, cible *f*

taste	Geschmack *m*	goût *m*
taste-maker	Konsumpionier *m*	pionnier *m* de la consommation *f*
tax	Steuer *f*	impôt *m*, taxe *f*
taxicab advertising	Taxiwerbung *f*	publicité *f* dans les taxis *m/pl*
team	Arbeitsgemeinschaft *f,* Mannschaft *f*	communauté *f* de travail *m,* coopération *f,* équipe *f*
team of bill-stickers *pl*	Klebekolonne *f*	équipe *f* d'afficheurs *m/pl*
team of canvassers *pl*	Werbekolonne *f*	équipe *f* de courtiers *m/pl*
team of creative men *pl*	Kreativagentur *f*	cellule *f*
team-work	Gemeinschaftsarbeit *f,* Gruppenarbeit *f*	collaboration *f,* travail *m* en équipe *f*
tear ratio	Widerstandsfähigkeit *f*	degré *m* de résistance *f*
tear sheet	Belegseite *f*	épreuve *f* d'une page *f,* page *f* justificative
tear-off calendar	Abreißkalender *m*	calendrier *m* à effeuiller, éphémerides *f/pl*
teaser	Neugier erregende Anzeige *f*	annonce *f* piquant la curiosité *f*
teaser advertising	Neckwerbung *f*	publicité *f* taquine
technical language	Fachsprache *f*	langage *m* technique
technical magazine	Industrieblatt *n*	revue *f* pour industriels *m/pl*
technical manager	technischer Leiter *m*	directeur *m* technique
technical press	Fachpresse *f*	presse *f* professionnelle, presse *f* technique
technical publication	Fachzeitung, technische Zeitschrift *f*	journal *m* professionnel, périodique *m* technique, revue *f* technique
technical term	Fachausdruck *m,* Spezialausdruck *m*	terme *m* technique
technique of production	Herstellungstechnik *f*	technique *f* de fabrication *f*
telecast	Fernsehen *n,* Fernsehsendung *f,* Fernsehübertragung *f*	émission *f* de télévision *f,* petit écran *m,* télévision *f,* transmission *f* télévisuelle, vidéo *m*
telecommunication satellite	Nachrichtensatellit *m*	satellite *m* de télécommunication *f*
telegenic	telegen	télégénique
telegram	Depesche *f,* Telegramm *n*	dépêche *f,* télégramme *m*
telegram, by	telegraphisch	télégraphique
to telegraph	drahten, telegrafieren	télégraphier
telegraphic	telegrafisch	télégraphique
telegraphic address	Drahtanschrift *f,* Telegrammadresse *f*	adresse *f* de télégramme *m,* adresse *f* télégraphique
telegraphic network	Fernschreibnetz *n*	réseau *m* télégraphique
telegraphic style	Telegrammstil *m*	style *m* télégraphique
telegraphist	Telegrafist *m*	télégraphiste *m*
telepathy	Gedankenübertragung *f*	télépathie *f*
telephone	Telefon *n*	téléphone *m*
to telephone	telefonieren	téléphoner
telephone book *am*	Telefonbuch *n*	annuaire *m* téléphonique, Bottin *m* téléphonique
telephone call	Telefonanruf *m,* Telefongespräch *n*	appel *m* téléphonique, coup *m* de téléphone *m,* conversation *f* téléphonique
telephone circuit	Telefonleitung *f*	ligne *f* téléphonique
telephone connection	Telefonanschluß *m*	communication *f* téléphonique

telephone directory	Fernsprechbuch *n*, Telefonbuch *n*	annuaire *m* des téléphones *m/pl*, annuaire *m* téléphonique, Bottin *m* téléphonique, indicateur *m* téléphonique
telephone exchange	Telefonzentrale *f*	centrale *f* téléphonique
telephone interview	Telefoninterview *n*	interview *m* par téléphone *m*
telephone network	Fernsprechnetz *n*	réseau *m* téléphonique
telephone number	Telefonnummer *f*	numéro *m* de téléphone *m*
telephone survey	Telefonumfrage *f*	enquête *f* par téléphone *m*
telephoned advertisement	telefonisch aufgegebene Anzeige *f*	annonce *f* téléphonée
telephonic	telefonisch	téléphonique
telephonist	Telefonist *m*	téléphoniste *m*
telephoto lens	Teleobjektiv *n*	téléobjectif *m*, téléphotographie *f*
telephotograph	Bildtelegramm *n*	bélinogramme *m*, phototélégramme *m*
telephotography	Fernfotografie *f*, Telefoto *n*, Teleobjektiv *n*	téléobjectif *m*, téléphotographie *f*
teleprinter	Fernschreiber *m*, Hellschreiber *m*	téléimprimeur *m*, téléscripteur *m*, télétype *m*
teletyper	Fernschreiber *m*	téléimprimeur *m*, téléscripteur *m*, télétype *m*
teletypesetter	automatische Setzmaschine *f*, Teletypesetter *m*	télétypesetter *m*
teletypesetting	Fernsatz *m*	télécomposition *f*
teletypesetting machine	Fernsetzmaschine *f*	télécomposeuse *f*
television (TV)	Fernsehen *n*	petit écran *m*, télévision *f*, vidéo *m*
television addict	Fernsehsüchtiger *m*	maniaque *m* de la T.V. *f*
television advertising	Fernsehwerbung *f*, Werbefernsehen *n*	publicité *f* télévisée, télévision *f* commerciale
television audience research	Fernsehforschung *f*	recherches *f/pl* relatives aux téléspectateurs *m/pl*
television by satellites *pl*	Satellitenfernsehen *n*	mondovision *f*, télévision *f* via satellites *m/pl*
television density	Fernsehdichte *f*	pénétration *f* de la télévision *f*
television magazine	Programmzeitschrift *f*	magazine *m* de télévision *f*
television news, television news show	Tagesnachrichten *f/pl* im Fernsehen *n*, Tagesschau *f*	journal *m* télévisé
television picture	Fernsehbild *n*	image *f* télévisée
television program	Fernsehprogramm *n*	programme *m* télévisé
television receiver	Fernsehempfänger *m*	récepteur *m* de télévision *f*
television reception	Fernsehempfang *m*	réception *f* de télévision *f*
television set	Fernsehapparat *m*, Pantoffelkino *n*	appareil *m* de télévision *f*, récepteur *m* de télévision *f*, téléviseur *m*
television station	Fernsehanstalt *f*, Fernsehsender *m*	station *f* de télévision *f*
television studio	Fernsehstudio *n*	studio *m* de télévision *f*
television transmission *brit*	Fernsehübertragung *f*	émission *f* de télévision *f*, transmission *f* télévisuelle
television via cable	Kabelfernsehen *n*	télévision *f* via câble *m*

television viewer	Fernsehteilnehmer *m*, Fernsehzuschauer *m*	abonné *m* de la télévision *f*, téléspectateur *m*
telex	Fernschreibanschluß *m*	telex *m*
telex address	Telexanschrift *f*	adresse *f* télex
tell-tale	Zwischenträger *m*	cafard *m*, entremetteur *m*
tempera	Temperafarbe *f*	couleur *f* à détrempe *f*
tempo of production	Produktionsablauf *m*	rythme *m* de la production *f*
temporary paper	Notzeitung *f*	journal *m* intérimaire
temporary posting	kurzfristiger Anschlag *m*	affichage *m* temporaire
temporary rate sheet	z.Zt. gültige Anzeigenpreisliste *f*	tarif *m* d'annonces *f/pl* valide actuellement
tendency	Tendenz *f*	tendance *f*
tendency enterprise	Tendenzbetrieb *m*	entreprise *f* à tendance *f*
tendency novel	Tendenzroman *m*	roman *m* à thèse *f*
tendency of style	Stilrichtung *f*	tendance *f* stylistique
tendentious information	Tendenzmeldung *f*, Zweckmeldung *f*	information *f* à tendance *f*, nouvelle *f* lancée
tendentious paper	Tendenzblatt *n*	journal *m* de tendance *f*
tender	Lieferungsangebot *n*	soumission *f*
tenor	Tenor *m*	teneur *f*
tensile strength	Reißfestigkeit *f*	résistance *f* à la rupture *f*
tent card	Tischkarte *f*	carte *f* de table *f*
tentative work	Entwurf *m*	croquis *m*, dessin *m*, ébauche *f*, épreuve *f*, maquette *f*, projet *m*
term for delivery	Liefertermin *m*	date *f* de livraison *f*, délai *m* de livraison *f*
term of payment	Zahlungsfrist *f*	délai *m* de paiement *m*, terme *m* de paiement *m*
terminal display	Stationswerbung *f*	publicité *f* dans les terminus *m/pl*
terminology	Terminologie *f*	terminologie *f*
term-liability	Terminhaftung *f*	responsabilité *f* quant au délai *m*
terms *pl*	Bedingungen *f/pl*	conditions *f/pl*
terms *pl* **index**	Wortregister *n*	nomenclature *f*
terms *pl* **of delivery**	Lieferbedingungen *f/pl*	conditions *f/pl* de livraison *f*
terms *pl* **of payment**	Zahlungsbedingungen *f/pl*	conditions *f/pl* de paiement *m*
terms *pl* **of sale**	Verkaufsbedingungen *f/pl*	conditions *f/pl* de vente *f*
territorial edition	Bezirksausgabe *f*	édition *f* départementale, édition *f* locale
terseness	Prägnanz *f*	concision *f*
test	Test *m*, Untersuchung *f*	enquête *f*, examen *m*, recherche *f*, test *m*
to test	testen	faire un test *m*
test area	Testgebiet *n*	territoire-test *m*
test campaign	Testkampagne *f*, Versuchskampagne *f*	campagne *f* d'essai *m*, test *m* de lancement *m*
test mark	Prüfzeichen *n*	marque *f* de contrôle *m*
test market	Testmarkt *m*	marché *m* d'essai *m*, marché-test *m*
test shop	Testladen *m*	boutique *f* d'essai *m*
testimonial	Anerkennungsschreiben *n*, Empfehlungsschreiben *n*	attestation *f*, courrier *m* des auditeurs *m/pl*
test-town	Testort *m*	lieu *m* d'essai *m*
text	Anzeigentext *m*, Text *m*	copie *f*, texte *m*, texte *m* de l'annonce *f*

text acquisition terminal, text collection terminal	Texterfassungsgerät n	appareil m pour la saisie f des textes m/pl
text face	Textschrift f	caractère m du texte m
text generation	Texterfassung f	saisie f des textes m/pl
text matter	Werksatz m	composition f de labeurs m/pl, composition f d'œuvre f
text page	Textseite f	page f de texte m, page f rédactionnelle
text-book	Fachbuch n	livre m professionnel, livre m technique, ouvrage m spécialisé
textual advertisement	Textteilanzeige f	annonce f-texte m
theater poster	Theaterplakat n	affiche f de théâtre m, annonce f de spectacle m
theatre curtain advertising	Vorhangwerbung f	rideau m réclame f
theme	Thema n einer Anzeige f	thème m
theme song	Erkennungsmelodie f	mélodie f d'identification f
theory of advertising	Werbetheorie f	théorie f de la publicité f
theory of communication	Kommunikationstheorie f	théorie f de la communication f
thermography	Heißprägung f, Stahlstichimitation f, Thermodruck m	empreinte f à chaud, imitation f de gravure f sur acier m, typo-relief m
thesaurus	Wortschatz m	thésaurus m, trésor m de mots m/pl, vocabulaire m
thick frame	fette Umrandung f, schwarzer Rand m	baguette f, bordure f de filet m mat
thick vellum	Pergamentpapier n	papier m parchemin m
thickness	Dicke f	chasse f, épaisseur f
thin	mager	maigre, mince
thin board	Halbkarton m	mi-carton m
thin face	magerer Satz m	composition f maigre
thin paper	Dünndruckpapier n	papier m bible, papier m mince, pelure f d'oignon m
thin stroke	Haarstrich m	délié m, empattement m
thinner	Verdünnungsmittel n	diluant m
thread sewing	Fadenknotenheftung f	couture f au point m noué
threadbare story	abgedroschenes Zeug n	vieille rengaine f
3 D(imensional) film	3 D(imensional)–Film m	film m à réfraction f
3-dimensional reproduction and printing process	Transartdruck m	impression f de planches f/pl superposées sur supports m/pl transparents
three side trimmer	Dreischneider m	massicot m trilatéral à une seule lame f
three-colour etching	Dreifarbenätzung f	trichromie f
three-colour printing	Dreifarbendruck m	impression f en trois couleurs f/pl, impression f trichrome, trichromie f
three-dimensional	dreidimensional	à trois dimensions f/pl
threshold of sensation	Reizschwelle f	seuil m d'efficacité f
thrice monthly	dreimal monatlich	trimensuel
thrice weekly	dreimal wöchentlich	tri-hebdo
thrift price	niedriger Preis m	prix m modique
thriller	Schauerroman m, Reißer m, spannende Handlung f	clou m, film m, film m à sensation f, pièce f à sensation f, roman m à gros effets m/pl, roman m à sensation f, roman m sensationnel

throw-away	Flugzettel *m*, Handzettel *m*	papillon *m*, prospectus *m*, tract *m*
throwaway leaflet	Streuprospekt *m*	prospectus *m* distribué en arrasoir *m*
thumb-index	Daumenregister *n*, Griffregister *n*	registre *m* avec onglets *m/pl* -guides *m/pl*, répertoire *m* encoché, touches *f/pl*
thumb-indexed book	Buch *n* mit alphabetischem Register *n*	livre *m* à onglets *m/pl*
thumbnail sketch	Ideenentwurf *m*, Miniaturskizze *f*	croquis *m* minuscule
ticker	Fernschreiber *m*	téléimprimeur *m*, téléscripteur *m*, télétype *m*
to **ticket**	etikettieren	étiqueter
ticket advertising	Fahrscheinwerbung *f*	publicité *f* sur billets *m/pl*
ticket-office	Schalterhalle *f*	halle *f* de guichet *m*
to **tie up**	ausbinden	lier
tied newspaper	Pachtzeitung *f*	journal affermé *m*
tied paper	Pachtblatt *n*, Pachtorgan *n*	organe *m* affermé, revue *f* affermée
tie-in	verbindender Text *m*	texte *m* de liaison *f*
tie-in advertisement	Koppelanzeige *f*	annonce *f* couplée
tie-in advertising	Anknüpfungswerbung *f*, eingeblendete Werbung *f*	publicité *f* d'association *f*, publicité *f* enchaînée
tie-up advertising	kombinierte Werbeaktion *f*, Verbundwerbung *f*	publicité *f* commune, publicité *f* d'association *f*, publicité *f* groupée
tight paper	Blatt *n* mit vielen Anzeigen *f/pl*	journal *m* avec beaucoup d'annonces *f/pl*
tilde	Tilde *f*	tilde *f*
till forbid	bis auf Widerruf *m*	jusqu'à nouvel ordre *m*
time buyer	Sendezeitvermittler *m*, Werbezeiteneinkäufer *m*	acheteur *m* de temps *m* d'antenne *f*
time charge	Tarif *m* für Werbesendungen *f/pl*	tarif *m* d'antenne *f*, tarif *m* de la publicité *f* radiophonique
time discount	Abschlußrabatt *m*	dégressif *m* sur volume *m* publicitaire
time for giving notice	Kündigungsfrist *f*	délai *m* de dédite *f*
time lag	Zeitverzögerung *f*	décalage *m*, retardement *m*
time limitations *pl*	zeitliche Beschränkungen *f/pl*	restrictions *f/pl* dans le temps *m*
time of payment	Zahlungsfrist *f*	délai *m* de paiement *m*, terme *m* de paiement *m*
time of the dispersion of the advertising media	Streuzeitpunkt *m*	période *f* de diffusion *f*, période *f* de la diffusion *f* des moyens *m/pl* publicitaires
time schedule	Datenplan *m*, Datenschema *n*, Terminplan *m*	calendrier *m* d'insertion *f*, calendrier *m* d'insertion *f*, plan *m* de termes *m/pl*, plan *m* des délais *m/pl*
time table	Fahrplan *m*	horaire *m*
time-lag	Verzögerung *f*, zeitlicher Unterschied *m*	retard *m*
time-lapse equipment	Zeitraffer *m*	accélérateur *m*
time-server	Konjunkturritter *m*	opportuniste *m*
time-table	Abfahrtsplan *m*, Kursbuch *n*	horaire *m*, indicateur *m*

timing	Terminfestlegung *f*, zeitliche Abstimmung *f*, Zeitplanung *f*	calendrier *m* de la gestion *f*, coordination *f* des termes *m*/*pl*, détermination *f* d'un terme *m*, fixation *f* de date *f* et durée *f*
tin foil	Stanniolpapier *n*	papier *m* d'argent *m*, papier *m* d'étain *m*
tin plate sign	Blechschild *n*	panneau *m* métallique
tin-printing	Blechdruck *m*	impression *f* sur fer-blanc *m*, impression *f* sur tôle *f*
tint	Farbton *m*, Tönung *f*	coloris *m*, nuance *f*, teinte *f*, ton *m* de couleur *f*
tint block	Tonplatte *f*	à-plat, planche *f* de fond *m*
tinted	getönt	teinté
tinting	Farbgebung *f*	encrage *m*
tints *pl*	Rastertönungen *f*/*pl*	grisés *m*/*pl*
tip	Fingerzeig *m*, Schmiergeld *n*, Tip *m*, Wink *m*	avis *m*, conseil *m*, insinuation *f*, pot-de-vin *m*, tuyau *m*
tip-in	Beihefter *m*, Beikleber *m*, eingeklebtes Bild *n*	encart *m* broché, hors-texte *m*
tipping-in of insets *pl*	Einkleben *n* von Beilagen *f*/*pl*	collage *m* d'encarts *m*/*pl*
tissue paper	Seidenpapier *n*	papier *m* de soie *f*
tit-bit	Leckerbissen *m*, literarischer	miette *f* de la semaine *f*
title	Titel *m*	titre *m*
title faces *pl*	Titelschriften *f*/*pl*	caractères *m*/*pl* pour titre *m*
title of a newspaper	Zeitungstitel *m*	titre *m* d'un journal *m*
title page	Haupttitel *m*, Titelseite *f*	grand titre *m*, page *f* de titre *m*, première page *f*
title-sheet	Titelbogen *m*	feuille *f* de titre *m*, pièce *f* préliminaire
tittle-tattle	Klatschgeschichte *f*	bavardage *m*, chronique *f* scandaleuse
toadyism	Speichelleckerei *f*	flagornerie *f*
toenails *pl*	Klammern *f*/*pl*/*typog*	parenthèses *f*/*pl*
toggle press	Kniehebelpresse *f*	presse *f* à genouillère *f*
tomfoolery	Faxen *f*/*pl*	fadaises *f*/*pl*
tonal value	Tonwert *m*	tonalité *f*
tonality	Tonbeschaffenheit *f*	
tool	Arbeitsgerät *n*	outil *m*
top	Zeitungskopf *m*	en-tête *f*, manchette *f*
top drawsheet	Deckbogen *m*	feuille *f* de couverture *f*
top left position	Plazierung *f* oben links	emplacement *m* supérieur à gauche
top margin	Kopfsteg *m*	marge *f* de tête *f*, marge *f* supérieure
top of column	Kopf *m* der Spalte *f*	tête *f* de colonne *f*
top of page	Kopf *m* der Seite *f*	tête *f* de page *f*
top right position	Plazierung *f* oben rechts	emplacement *m* supérieur à droite
top work	Spitzenleistung *f*	puissance *f* maxima
topical	aktuell	actuel
topical news	Tagesneuigkeiten *f*/*pl*	événements *m*/*pl* du jour *m*
topical peg	Aufhänger *m*	accrochage *m* publicitaire, angle *m* d'approche *f*

topical talk	Nachrichtensendung *f*	bulletin *m* d'actualités *f/pl*, journal *m* parlé, transmission *f* des informations *f/pl*
topicality	aktuelle Bedeutung *f*	actualité *f*
topics *pl* **of the day**	Tagesfragen *f/pl*	questions *f/pl* d'actualité *f*
torn poster	beschädigtes Plakat *n*	affiche *f* abîmée, affiche *f* déchirée, affiche *f* détériorée
torrent of words *pl*	Wortschwall *m*	flot *m* de paroles *f/pl*, verbiage *m*
total billings *pl*	Budgetsumme *f*	facturation *f*
total circulation	Gesamtauflage *f*	tirage *m* global, tirage *m* total
total configuration	Gesamtgestaltung *f*	création *f* d'ensemble
total net paid circulation	verkaufte Auflage *f*	diffusion *f* bouillon *m* déduit
total print run	Gesamtauflage *f*	tirage *m* global, tirage *m* total
total production	Gesamtherstellung *f*	fabrication *f* totale
touch print	Klatschdruck *m*	faux-trait *m*
touching-up	Nachbesserung *f*	retouche *f*
tour of inspection	Kontrollfahrt *f*	tour *m* d'inspection *f*
touring exhibition	Wanderausstellung *f*	exposition *f* ambulante, exposition *f* itinérante
tourism advertising	Fremdenverkehrswerbung *f*	publicité *f* de tourisme *m*, publicité *f* de villégiature *f*
tourist poster	Fremdenverkehrsplakat *n*	affiche *f* touristique
tourist publicity	Fremdenverkehrswerbung *f*	publicité *f* de tourisme *m*, publicité *f* de villégiature *f*
tout	Anreißer *m*, Kundenwerber *m*	bonisseur *m*, pisteur *m*, racoleur *m*
touting	Kundenfang *m*	racolage *m*
town of publication	Verlagsort *m*	lieu *m* de publication *f*
town size group	Ortsgrößenklasse *f*	habitat *m*, zone *f* de résidence *f*
toy industry fair	Spielwarenmesse *f*	foire *f* du jouet *m*
to **trace**	pausen	décalquer
tracing	Layout *n*	maquette *f*
tracing paper	Pauspapier *n*	papier *m* à calquer, papier *m* carbone *m*
track	Bild- oder Tonspur *f* eines Films *m*	trace *f* d'un film *m*
tract	Flugschrift *f*	brochure *f*, tract *m*
traction car *brit*	Straßenbahntriebwagen *m*	voiture *f* motrice
trade	Gewerbe *n*, Handel *m*	artisanat *m*, commerce *m*, métier *m*
trade address book	Fachadreßbuch *n*	annuaire *m* pour le commerce *m* et l'industrie *f*
trade advertising	Händlerwerbung *f*	publicité *f* pour le distributeur *m*
trade book	Fachbuch *n*	livre *m* professionnel, livre *m* technique, ouvrage *m* spécialisé
trade channel	Vertriebskanal *m*	débouché *m* commercial
trade character	Figur *f* in einem Warenzeichen *n*	personnage *m* dans une marque *f* de fabrique *f*
trade compositors *pl*	Akzidenzsetzerei *f*	atelier *m* de composition *f* des travaux *m/pl* de ville *f*

trade directory	Branchenadreßbuch *n*, Handelsadreßbuch *n*	almanach *m* du commerce *m*, annuaire *m* commercial, annuaire *m* du commerce *m*, Bottin *m*
trade expression	Fachausdruck *m*	terme *m* technique
trade fair	Handelsmesse *f*, Mustermesse *f*	foire *f* de commerce *m*, foire *f* d'échantillons *m/pl*
trade journal	Fachzeitung, Handelsblatt *n*	journal *m* de commerce *m*, journal *m* professionnel, périodique *m* technique
trade margin	Handelsspanne *f*	marge *f* commerciale
trade mark	Markenzeichen *n*, Warenzeichen *n*	logotype *m*, marque *f* de fabrique *f*
trade mark protection	Markenschutz *m*	protection *f* des marques *f/pl*
trade name	Firmenname *m*, Markenname *m*, Wortmarke *f*	appellation *f*, marque *f* typographique, marque *f* verbale, nom *m* de la marque *f*
trade press	Fachpresse *f*	presse *f* professionnelle, presse *f* technique
trade secret	Geschäftsgeheimnis *n*	secret *m* commercial
trade support	Verkaufsunterstützung *f*	secours *m* de vente *f*
trade word	Fachwort *n*	terme *m* technique
trade-mark	Firmenzeichen *n*, Herstellermarke *f*, Schutzmarke *f*	marque *f* de fabricant *m*, marque *f* de firme *f*, marque *f* déposée
trademark's register	Warenzeichenrolle *f*	registre *m* de l'office *m* de la propriété *f* industrielle
trade-union paper	Gewerkschaftszeitung *f*	revue *f* syndicale
trading area	Absatzbereich *m*, Absatzgebiet *n*, Einzugsgebiet *n*	débouché *m*, marché *m*, secteur *m* de vente *f*, territoire *m* de vente *f*
trading stamp	Rabattmarke *f*	timbre-primes *f/pl*, timbre *m* de rabais *m*, timbre *m* d'épargne *f*
traffic control	Terminkontrolle *f*	contrôle *m* des délais *m/pl*
traffic department	Terminabteilung *f*	service *m* de surveillance *f* de la production *f*
traffic manager	Terminüberwacher *m*	surveillant *m* de la production *f*
traffic media	Medien *n/pl* der Werbung *f* im Verkehr *m*	médias *m/pl* de la publicité *f* dans les moyens *m/pl* de transport *m*
trailer	Anhänger *m* (Beiwagen *m*) , Filmvoranzeige *f*, Filmvorschau *f*, Vorschau *f*, Vorspann *m*	avant-première *f*, bande *f* de lancement *m*, film *m* annonce *f*, remorque *f*
train of thought	Gedankengang *m*	suite *f* des idées *f/pl*
trainee	Auszubildender *m*, Volontär *m*	élève *m*, stagiaire *m*
training	Ausbildung *f*	formation *f*
tram stop	Straßenbahnhaltestelle *f*	point *m* d'arrêt *m*
tram trailer	Straßenbahnanhänger *m*	remorque *f* du tramway *m*
tram-car	Triebwagen *m* (Motorwagen *m*)	motrice *f*
tramway	Straßenbahn *f*	tramway *m*
tramway advertising	Straßenbahnwerbung *f*	publicité *f* tram *m*
transfer	Umdruck *m*	report *m*
transfer paper	autografisches Papier *n*, Umdruckpapier *n*	papier *m* à décalque *f*, papier *m* à report *m*, papier *m* autographique

transfer picture	Abziehbild *n*	image *f* de décalcomanie *f*
transfiguration, transformation	Umgestaltung *f*, Umwandlung *f*	transfiguration *f*, transformation *f*
transformation of structure	Strukturwandel *m*	transformation *f* de structure *f*
transient rate	Rabatt *m*, ohne	sans rabais *m*
transistor	Transistor *m*	transistor *m*
transit advertising	Verkehrsmittelwerbung *f*	publicité *f* moyens *m/pl* de transport *m*
transit time	Laufzeit *f*	rut *m*
transition period	Übergangszeit *f*	période *f* transitoire
to translate	übersetzen	traduire
translation	Übersetzung *f*	traduction *f*
translator	Übersetzer *m*	traducteur *m*
translucent paper	durchscheinendes Papier *n*	papier *m* transparent
transmission	Übertragung *f*	transmission *f*
to transmit	senden (Radio), weiterleiten	émettre, radiodiffuser, transmettre
transmittal	Übermittlung *f*	transmission *f*
transparency *am*	Abziehplakat *n*	décalcomanie *f*
transparency slide	Diapositiv *n*	diapositif *m*
transparent	durchsichtig	transparent
transparent ink	Lasurfarbe *f*	couleur *f* à vernisser, encre *f* transparente
transparent package	Klarsichtpackung *f*	emballage *m* transparent
to transpierce	durchscheinen, durchschlagen *typog*	maculer, pénétrer, transparaître, transpercer, traverser
transport advertising *brit*	Verkehrsmittelwerbung *f*	publicité *f* moyens *m/pl* de transport *m*
transport case	Versandschachtel *f*	boîte *f* d'expédition *f*
transport systems *pl*	Verkehrsmittel *n*	moyens *m/pl* de transport *m*
transport tape	Transportband *n*	tapis *m* roulant
transportation advertising *am*	Verkehrsmittelwerbung *f*	publicité *f* moyens *m/pl* de transport *m*
to transpose	auswechseln, umstellen *typog*	transposer
transposed line	verstellte Zeile *f*	ligne *f* intervertie
trash	Kitsch *m*, Schund *m*	camelote *f*, tape-à-l'œil *m*
trashy paper	minderwertiges Blatt *n*, Schundblatt *n*	journal *m* médiocre
travel advertisement	Bäderanzeige *f*	publicité *f* balnéaire
travel guide	Reiseführer *m*	prospectus *m* de voyage *m*
travel supplement	Reisebeilage *f*	supplément *m* touristique
travelling display	Außenwerbung *f* an Verkehrsmitteln *n/pl*	publicité *f* sur l'extérieur *m* de voitures *f/pl*
travelling movie theatre	Wanderlichtspiele *n/pl*	cinéma *m* ambulant
travelling salesman	Handelsreisender *m*	voyageur *m* de commerce *m*
travelling theatre	Wanderbühne *f*	théâtre *m* ambulant
travelling-expenses *pl*	Reisekosten *pl*	frais *m/pl* de déplacement *m*, frais *m/pl* de voyage *m*
treatise	Abhandlung *f*	traité *m*
treatment	Drehbuchentwurf *m*, Fixierung *f* von Film *m* -Aufbau *m* und -Ablauf *m*	brouillon *m* d'un scénario *m*, fixation *f* de composition *f* et de déroulement *m* d'un film *m*
trend	Markttendenz *f*, Tendenz *f*	tendance *f*, tendance *f* du marché *m*
trend of business	Geschäftsgang *m*	marche *f* des affaires *f/pl*

trend of opinion	Meinungstrend *m*	tendance *f* d'opinion *f*
trestle	Gestell *n*	chevalet *m*
trial balloon	Versuchsballon *m*	ballon *m* d'essai *m*
trial order	Probeauftrag *m*	commande *f* à l'épreuve *f*, ordre *m* d'essai *m*
trial package	Probepackung *f*	emballage *m* d'essai *m*
trial subscription	Probeabonnement *m*	abonnement *m* d'essai *m*
trichromatic process work	Dreifarbendruck *m*	impression *f* en trois couleurs *f/pl*, impression *f* trichrome, trichromie *f*
trick	Reklametrick *m*	ruse *f* publicitaire
trick picture	Trickbild *n*, Trickfilm *m*	dessin *m* animé, film *m* truqué, trucage *m*
trilingual work	Triglotte *f*	ouvrage *m* en trois langues *f/pl*
to trim	beschneiden, bestossen	couper, ébarber, rogner, taillader, tailler
trim	Beschnittzugabe *f*	coupure *f*
trimming	Ausschnitt *m* (Stanze *f*), Beschnitt *m*	coupe *f*, découpe *f*, encoche *f*, perforation *f*, rognage *m*
trite	abgegriffen	poncif
trolleybus	Oberleitungsomnibus *m*	trolley-bus *m*
true to original	originalgetreu	identique à l'original *m*
trumpery paper	Käseblättchen *n*	feuille *f* de chou *m*
trunk call	Ferngespräch *n*	appel *m* interurbain
trustworthy	vertrauenswürdig	digne de confiance *f*
to tumble	umstülpen	culbuter
tuning	Abstimmung *f*	syntonisation *f*
to turn a letter	ausblocken, blockieren	bloquer une lettre *f*, caviarder
turn of a sentence	Redewendung *f*	tournure *f* de phrase *f*
to turn over the page	Blatt *n* wenden	tourner la page *f*
to turn round	umkehren	renverser, retourner
turned letter	Blockade *f*, Fliegenkopf *m/typog*	blocage *m*, caractère *m* retourné, lettre *f* bloquée
turnout	Ausfall *m*	rebut *m*
turnover	Reichweite *f*, Umsatz *m*, Umschlag *m* (von Waren)	chiffre *m* d'affaires *f/pl*, couverture *f*, débit *m* des ventes *f/pl*, rayon *m* d'action *f*, taux *m* de pénétration *f*
turnover tax	Umsatzsteuer *f*	impôt *m* sur le chiffre *m* d'affaires *f/pl*
TV supplement	Fernsehbeilage *f*	supplément *m* pour T.V.
TV-screen	Fernsehschirm *m*	écran *m* de télévision *f*, petit écran *m*
12-to-pica (see appendix!)	Achtelpetit *f* (siehe Anhang!)	1 point (voir appendice!)
twice daily	zweimal täglich	bi-quotidien
twice monthly	halbmonatlich	bimensuel
twice weekly	zweimal wöchentlich	bi-hebdo
twice yearly	halbjährlich	semestriel, tous les six mois *m/pl*
2 points (see appendix)	Nonplusultra *f* (Viertelpetit) (siehe Anhang)	corps 2 points (voir appendice)
two-colour process	Zweifarbendruck *m*	bichromie *f*, impression *f* bichrome, impression *f* en deux couleurs *f/pl*
two-sided	zweiseitig	à deux côtés *m/pl*, bilatéral, de deux pages *f/pl*, double

two-sided coated paper	zweiseitig gestrichenes Papier *n*	papier *m* couché de deux pages *f/pl*
two-thirds page	Zweidrittelseite *f*	page *f* de deux tiers
tying clause	Preisbindungsklausel *f*	clause *f* limitative
tympan	Ölbogen *m*	feuille *f* huilée
tympan-paper	Abschmutzbogen *m*	papier *m* anti-macule, papier *m* de décharge *f*
tympan-sheet	Abziehbogen *m*	papier *m* de décharge *f*
type	Buchstabe *m*, Letter *f*, Schrifttype *f*, Type *f*	caractère *m*, lettre *f*, type *m*
type area	Satzspiegel *m*	surface *f* de justification *f*, surface *f* d'impression *f*, surface *f* utile
type bar	Setzmaschinenzeile *f*	ligne *f* bloc
type body	Kegel *m*	corps *m* de la lettre *f*
type caster	Schriftgießer *m*	fondeur *m* de caractères *m/pl*, fondeur *m* typographe
type casting	Schriftguß *m*	fonte *f* de caractères *m/pl*
type cutter	Schriftschneider *m*	graveur *m* de caractères *m/pl*
type face	Schriftbild *n*	œil *m* de caractère *m*
type family	Schriftgattung *f*	famille *f* de caractères *m/pl*
type founder	Gießer *m*, Schriftgießer *m*	fondeur *m* de caractères *m/pl*, fondeur *m* typographe
type gauge	Typometer *m*	typomètre *m*
type height	Schrifthöhe *f*	hauteur *f* du caractère *m*, hauteur *f* en papier *m*
type layout	Satzskizze *f*	maquette *f* typographique
type line scale	Zeilenmesser *m*	lignomètre *m*, typomètre *m*
type matter	Satz *m/typog*, Schriftmaterial *n*	caractères *m/pl* d'impression *f*, composition *f*
type metal	Letternmetall *n*, Schriftmetall *n*	métal *m* à caractères *m/pl*
type of advertising	Werbeart *f*	genre *m* de publicité *f*, type *m* de publicité *f*
type of medium	Werbeträgerart *f*	genre *m* de support *m*
type of newspaper	Zeitungstyp *m*	type-journal *m*
type page	Satzspiegel *m*	surface *f* de justification *f*, surface *f* d'impression *f*, surface *f* utile
type size	Schriftgröße *f*	corps *m*
type specimen	Schriftmuster *n*	épreuve *f* de caractères *m/pl*, spécimen *m* de caractères *m/pl*
type specimen book	Schriftmusterbuch *n*, Schriftprobe *f*	catalogue *m* de caractères *m/pl*
type stock	Schriftlager *n*	réserve *f*
type-design	Typo-Studio *n*	atelier *m* typographique
type-foundry	Schriftgießerei *f*	fonderie *f*
type-gauge	Zeilenmesser *m*	lignomètre *m*, typomètre *m*
types *pl* of media	Mediaarten *f/pl*, Streuarten *f/pl*	genres *m/pl* de support *m*, types *m/pl* des médias *m/pl*
type-script	Schreibmaschinenschrift *f*	caractères *m/pl* de machine *f*
to typeset	absetzen (Druck), setzen *typog*	composer
typesetter	Setzer *m*	compositeur *m*, typographe *m*
typesetting alteration	Satzkorrektur *f*	correction *f* de la composition *f*
typesetting machine	Setzmaschine *f*	composeuse *f* mécanique, machine *f* à composer
typewriter	Schreibmaschine *f*	machine *f* à écrire

typewriter paper	Schreibmaschinenpapier *n*	papier *m* pour machine *f* à écrire
typewriting	Maschineschreiben *n*	dactylographie *f*
typist	Maschinenschreiber *m*	dactylographe *m*
typist's error	Tippfehler *m*	erreur *f* de dactylo *f*, faute *f* de frappe *f*
typographer	Schriftsetzer *m*, Typograf *m*	compositeur *m*, typographe *m*
typographic point	typografischer Punkt *m*	point *m* typographique
typographic system of measurement (see appendix)	Maßsystem *n*, typografisches (siehe Anhang), typografisches Maßsystem *n*	mesures *f/pl* typographiques (voir appendice)
typographical arrangement	Satzanordnung *f*, Zeilenfall *m*	arrangement *m* typographique, schéma *m* d'emplacement *m* de lignes *f/pl*
typographical aspect	Satzbild *n*, typografisches Bild *m*	aspect *m* typographique
typographical design	Satzgestaltung *f*	disposition *f* typographique
typographical error	Druckfehler *m*	coquille *f*, erreur *f* de composition *f*, faute *f* d'impression *f*, faute *f* typographique
typographical technique	Satztechnik *f*	technique *f* typographique
typographical units *pl* of measurement (see appendix)	typografische Maßeinheiten *f/pl* (siehe Anhang)	mesures *f/pl* typographiques (voir appendice)
typography	Typografie *f*	typographie *f*
typology	Einteilung *f* nach Typen *f/pl*	typologie *f*
typometer	Typometer *m*	typomètre *m*
typrewriter ribbon	Farbband *n*	ruban *m* de machine *f*
tyro	Neuling *m*	néophyte *m*, nouveau venu

U

ukase	Ukas *m*	oukase *m*
ultimate consumer	Endverbraucher *m*, Letztverbraucher *m*	consommateur *m* final
umbrella-ad	Anzeige *f*, die verschiedene Arten *f/pl* eines Produktes *n* zeigt	annonce *f* montrant de diverses sortes *f/pl* d'un produit *m*
umbrella-campaign	Werbekampagne *f* für verschiedene Arten *f/pl* eines Produkts *m*	campagne *f* pour des sortes *f/pl* différentes d'un produit *m*
umpire	Schiedsrichter *m*	arbitre *m*
unbiased	tendenzfrei	impartial
uncoated paper	Naturpapier *n*	papier *m* non couché
under matter	Text *m*, unter	dessous texte *m*
to undercut	unterätzen	sous-graver
underexposure	Unterbelichtung *f*	sous-exposition *f*
underground passage	Unterführung *f*	passage *m* souterrain
underground press	Untergrundpresse *f*	presse *f* clandestine
underground railway advertising *brit*	U-Bahn-Werbung *f*	publicité-métro *m*
to underlay	unterlegen	charger, garnir
underlay	Klischeeunterlage *f*	mise *f* de hauteur *f* sous cliché
to underline	unterstreichen	mettre en relief *m*, souligner
underlining	Unterstreichung *f*	soulignure *f*
to underprint	unterkopieren	souscopier
underscoring	musikalische Untermalung *f*	fond *m* sonore

underselling	Schleuderverkauf *m*	vente *f* à meilleur marché *m*, vente *f* à vil prix *m*
understatement	Unterbewertung *f*, Untertreibung *f*	amoindrissement *m*, sous-estimation *f*
underwriting commission	Garantieprovision *f*	commission *f* de garantie *f*
undisplay	Fließsatz *m*, glatter Satz *m*	composition *f* en placards *m/pl*, texte *m* plein
uneven page	ungerade Seite *f*	page *f* impaire
unfair competition	unlauterer Wettbewerb *m*	concurrence *f* déloyale
unfamiliar	verfremdet	dénaturé
uniformity	Gleichförmigkeit *f*, Uniformität *f*	uniformité *f*
uninflammable paper	feuerfestes Papier *n*	papier *m* incombustible
unique selling proposition	Werbeplattform *f*	axe *f* de la publicité *f*
unit price	Stückpreis *m*	prix *m* unitaire
universal journalist	Universaljournalist *m*	journaliste *m* universel
unjustified matter	Flattersatz *m*	composition *f* en drapeau *m*
unmounted block	unmontiertes Klischee *n*	cliché *m* non monté
unrivalled	konkurrenzlos	hors concurrence *f*
unrolling	Abwicklung *f*	déroulement *m*
unsharp impression	unscharfer Druck *m*	papillotage *m*
unsold copies *pl*	unverkaufte Exemplare *n/pl*	bouillon *m*, exemplaires *m/pl* invendus
until cancelled order	Auftrag *m* auf Widerruf *m*	jusqu'à nouvel ordre *m*, ordre *m* valable jusqu'à révocation *f*
untrimmed	unbeschnitten	non rogné
unusual size	ungewöhnliches Format *n*	format *m* bâtard *m*
up to date	zeitgemäß	à la page *f*, au niveau *m* des derniers progrès *m/pl*
to update	auf den neuesten Stand *m* bringen	mettre à jour *m*
upper case letters *pl*	Großbuchstaben *m/pl*, Versalien *f/pl*	capitales *f/pl*, caractères *m/pl* haut de casse *f*, gros caractères *m/pl*, lettres *f/pl* capitales, majuscules *f/pl*
upper class	Führungsschicht *f*	les gens *pl* du monde *m*
upper corner	obere Ecke *f*	coin *m* supérieur
upright format	Hochformat *n*	format *m* en hauteur *f*, format *m* normal, format *m* vertical
up-stroke	Anstrich *m* (Buchstabe *m*)	plein *m*
up-trading	Qualitätsverbesserung *f* einer Ware *f*	amélioration *f* de la qualité *f* d'un produit *m*
upward adjustment of prices *pl*	Preisheraufsetzung *f*	majoration *f* de prix *m/pl*
upward business trend	Konjunkturaufschwung *m*	essor *m*
user	Benutzer *m*, Verbraucher *m*, Verbraucherin *f*	consommateur *m*, consommatrice *f*
usership	Verbraucherschaft *f*	masse *f* des consommateurs *m/pl*
usually used site	allgemeine Anschlagstelle *f*	emplacement *m* utilisé habituellement
utilization	Verwendung *f*, Verwertung *f*	utilisation *f*
utterance	Äußerung *f*	expression *f*, propos *m*

V

| vacancies *pl* | Personalanzeigen *f/pl* | offres *f/pl* d'emploi *m* |

vacancy	Vakanz *f*	place *f* vacante
vademecum	Handbuch *n*	guide *m*, manuel *m*, vade-mecum *m*
valid	gültig	valide
validation	Bestätigung *f*	confirmation *f*
validity	Gültigkeit *f*	validité *f*
valuation	Beurteilung *f*	compte *m* rendu, jugement *m*
to value	bewerten	estimer, évaluer
value in use	Nutzungswert *m*	valeur *f* d'usage *m*
value judgment	Werturteil *n*	jugement *m* de valeur *f*
value of colour	Farbwert *m*	valeur *f* de couleur *f*
variant	Spielart *f*, Variante *f*	alternative *f*, variante *f*
variation	Abwandlung *f*	modification *f*, variante *f*
variety	breites Sortiment *n*	assortiment *m* large
to varnish	lackieren	laquer, vernir
varnish	Firnis *m*, Lack *m*	laque *f*, vernis *m*
varnished overprinting	Drucklackierung *f*	vernissage *m* d'impression *f*
varnishing	Lackierung *f*	vernissage *m*
varnishing – day	Besichtigung *f* vor der Eröffnung *f*	vernissage *m*
vehicular advertising	Verkehrsmittelwerbung *f*, Werbung *f* in Fahrzeugen *n/pl*	publicité *f* moyens *m/pl* de transport *m*, publicité *f* sur ou dans véhicules *f/pl* de transport *m*
veiled advertisement	getarnte Anzeige *f*	annonce *f* déguisée
vellum paper	Velinpapier *n*	papier *m* du Japon *m*, papier *m* vélin
vendible	verkäuflich	vendable
vending	Verkauf *m* durch Automaten *m/pl*	vente *f* d'articles *m/pl* dans des machines *f/pl* distributrices automatiques
vending machine	Automat *m*, Verkaufsautomat *m*, Warenautomat *m*	distributeur *m* automatique
verbatim	wörtlich	textuellement
verbatim report	Originaltext *m*	texte *m* original
verbosity	Wortaufwand *m*	verbosité *f*
to verify the invoice	Rechnung *f* prüfen	apurer la facture *f*, vérifier la facture *f*
version	Lesart *f*	version *f*
verso printing	Widerdruck *m*	impression *f* au verso *n*, retiration *f*, seconde forme *f*
vertical co-operative advertising	Vertikalwerbung *f*	publicité *f* collective verticale
vertical sign	Werbeschild *n* mit Vertikalschrift *f*	enseigne *f* verticale
very striking headline	knallende Überschrift *f*	titre *m* criard
video	Bildteil *m* einer Fernsehsendung *f*, Fernsehen *n*, Fernsehsendung *f*	émission *f* de télévision *f*, partie *f* d'images *f/pl* d'une émission *f* télévisée, petit écran *m*, télévision *f*, vidéo *m*
video cassette	Bildkassette *f*	cassette *f* vidéo
video display screen	Bildschirm *m*	écran *m*
video display terminal, video display unit	Bildschirmgerät *n*	écran *m* de visualisation *f*
videometer	Meßgerät *n* zur Zuschauerforschung *f*	instrument *m* de mesure *f* de l'audience *f*

video recorder	Gerät *n* zur Aufzeichnung *f* von Fernsehsendungen *f/pl*	magnétoscope *m*
videophone	Fernsehtelefon *n*	vidéophone *m*
video-setter	Lichtsetzmaschine *f*	composeuse *f* photographique, photocompeuse *f,* phototitreuse *f*
videotape	Magnetband *n,* Magnettonband *n,* Videoband *n*	bande *f* magnétique vidéo, ruban *m* magnétique
video-tape recorder	Gerät *n* für Filme *m/pl* in Kassettenform *f,* Tonbandgerät *n*	appareil *m* enregistreur, magnétoscope *m*
viewdata	Bildschirmtext *m*	télétexte *m* interactif
viewer	Zuschauer *m,* Zuschauerin *f*	spectateur *m,* spectatrice *f*
vignette	verlaufendes Bild *n,* Vignette *f*	cache *f,* dégradé *m,* fleuron *m,* photo *f* en dégradé, vignette *f*
vignetting of blocks *pl*	Tonverlauf *m*	dégradage *m* des bords *m/pl*
vigorous advertising	nachdrückliche Werbung *f*	publicité *f* vigoureuse
vigorous style	kerniger Stil *m*	style *m* énergique
visibility	Sichtbarkeit *f*	visibilité *f*
vista	Ausblick *m*	perspective *f*
visual	Ansichtsskizze *f,* Rohentwurf *m*	crayonné *m,* maquette *f,* premier jet *m*
visual communication	visuelle Kommunikation *f*	médias *m/pl* visuels
to **visualize**	gestalten	façonner, former, visualiser
visualizer	Gestalter *m,* Ideengestalter *m,* Visualiser *m*	artiste *m* -créateur *m,* concepteur *m,* dessinateur *m* -concepteur *m,* maquettiste *m*
visualizing	Gestaltung *f,* Ideengestaltung *f*	conception *f,* création *f,* dessin *m,* maquette *f*
to **vizualize**	veranschaulichen	concrétiser, visionner
vocabulary	Sprachschatz *m,* Wortschatz *m*	thésaurus *m,* trésor *m* de mots *m/pl,* vocabulaire *m*
vogue-word	Modewort *n*	mot *m* à la mode *f,* mot *m* du jour *m*
to **voice-over**	vertonen	sonoriser
voice-over	Synchronisation *f*	synchronisation *f*
volume	Jahrgang *m*	année *f*
volume discount	Mengenrabatt *m*	dégressif *m* sur volume *m* publicitaire, rabais *m* de quantité *f,* remise *f* de quantité *f*
volume of advertising	Werbeanteil *m*	volume *m* publicitaire
volume of composition	Satzumfang *m*	volume *m* de la composition *f*
voucher	Beleg *m,* Durchführungsbestätigung *f,* Zahlungsbeleg *m*	justificatif *m*
voucher audit	Belegkontrolle *f*	pige *f*
voucher copy	Anzeigenbeleg *m,* Belegexemplar *n*	justificatif *m* d'annonce *f,* numéro *m* justificatif

W

to **wait copy**	Manuskript *n* warten, auf	manquer de copie *f*
wait order	Terminauftrag *m*	attendre ordre *m* d'insertion *f*
waiting period	Sperrfrist *f*	délai *m* d'attente *f*, période *f* de suspension *f*
waiting time	Wartezeit *f*	temps *m* d'attente *f*
walkie-lookie	tragbares Fernsehgerät *n*	téléviseur *m* portatif
walkie-talkie	tragbares Funksprechgerät *n*	mobilophone *m*, poste *m* de radio *f* portatif
wall advertising	Mauerwerbung *f*	publicité *f* murale
wall banner	Spannplakat *n*	bannière *f* murale
wall calender	Wandkalender *m*	calendrier *m* mural
wall newspaper	Wandzeitung *f*	journal *m* mural
wall paper litho	HiFi-Endlosfarbanzeige *f*	encart *m* en couleur *f* imprimé en continu *m*
wall publicity	Giebelwerbung *f*	pignon *m* publicitaire, publicité *f* murale
wall sign	Wandschild *n*	panneau *m* mural
want	Bedarf *m*	besoin *m*
want ads *pl*	Suchanzeigen *f/pl*	petites annonces *f/pl*
warm-up	Eisbrecher *m*	brise-glace *m*
warranty	Garantie *f*	garantie *f*
wash drawing	Aquarell *n*, getönte Federzeichnung *f*, Tuschzeichnung *f*	aquarelle *f*, dessin *m* au lavis *m*, épure *f* au lavis *m*
waste	Verschwendung *f*	gaspillage *m*
waste circulation	Fehlstreuung *f*	bouillon *m*
waste dispersion	Streuverlust *m*	prospection *f* perdue
waste paper	Altpapier *n*, Makulatur *f*, Papierabfall *m*	chute *f*, maculature *f*, papier *m* de rebut *m*, vieux papiers *m/pl*
waste print	Defektbogen *m*	défet *m*
waste-paper basket	Papierkorb *m*	corbeille *f* à papier *m*
to **watch-dog**	überwachen	surveiller
watching of competitive advertising	Konkurrenzbeobachtung *f*	pige *f* de la concurrence *f*
watching of order filling	Belegkontrolle *f*	pige *f*
watching of the press	Pressebeobachtung *f*	surveillance *f* de presse *f*
watchword	Losung *f*	devise *f*
water colour	Aquarell *n*	aquarelle *f*
water colours *pl*	Wasserfarben *f/pl*	couleurs *f/pl* pour peinture *f* à l'eau *f*
water mark	Wasserzeichen *n*	filigrane *m*
water-colour drawing	Wasserfarbzeichnung *f*	peinture *f* à l'eau *f*
waterproof	wasserfest	imperméable
wave-length	Wellenlänge *f*	longueur *f* d'onde *f*
wavy line	Wellenlinie *f*	filet *m* tremblé, ligne *f* tremblée
wavy rule	Wellenlinie *f*	filet *m* tremblé, ligne *f* tremblée
wax	Wachs *n*	cire *f*
wax crayon	Fettstift *m*	crayon *m* litho
wax paper	Wachspapier *n*	papier *m* ciré
weather resistance	Wetterbeständigkeit *f*	résistance *f* aux intempéries *f/pl*
weather-chart	Wetterkarte *f*	carte *f* du temps *m*

weather-forecast	Wetterbericht *m*, Wettervorhersage *f*	bulletin *m* du temps *m*, grenouille *f*, météo *f*, prévisions *f/pl* météorologiques
weather-report	Wetterbericht *m*	bulletin *m* du temps *m*, grenouille *f*, météo *f*
web	Rundfunknetz *n*	réseau *m* d'émetteurs *m/pl*
web of lies *pl*	Lügengewebe *n*	tissu *m* de mensonges *m/pl*
web paper	endloses Papier *n*	papier *m* continu
web printing press	Rollendruckmaschine *f*	machine *f* à imprimer à bobines *f/pl*
web-fed letterpress rotary machine	Hochdruckrollenrotation *f*	rotative *f* typographique à bobines *f/pl*
week-end paper	Wochenendzeitung *f*	journal *m* du septième jour *m*
weekly	wöchentlich, Wochenblatt *n*	hebdomadaire *m*
weekly magazine	Wochenzeitschrift *f*	feuille *f* hebdomadaire, revue *f* hebdomadaire
weekly newspaper	Wochenzeitung *f*	journal *m* hebdomadaire
weekly paper	Wochenzeitschrift *f*	feuille *f* hebdomadaire, revue *f* hebdomadaire
weekly talk	Wochenplauderei *f*	causerie *f* hebdomadaire
to weight	bewerten, gewichten	estimer, évaluer, pondérer
to weld on	aufschweißen	thermosouder
well made-up newspaper	gut aufgemachte Zeitung *f*	journal *m* bien fait
well-informed	gut unterrichtet	bien informé
well-organized advertising	gut aufgezogene Werbung *f*	publicité *f* bien organisée
well-phrased opinion	gut formulierter Gedanke *m*	pensée *f* bien tournée
western	Wildwestfilm *m*	western *m*
wet print	frisch bedruckt	impression *f* fraîche
wet-on-wet printing	Naß-in-Naß-Druck *m*	impression *f* sur humide
whispering campaign	Flüsterpropaganda *f*	chuchoterie *f*, publicité *f* orale
white line	Blindzeile *f*	ligne *f* de blanc
to white out the matter	Satz *m* strecken	chasser la composition *f*
white paper	Weißbuch *n*	livre *m* blanc
white wash	Ehrenrettung *f*	réhabilitation *f*
whodunit	Krimi *m*	roman *m* policier
the whole of newspapers *pl*	Blätterwald *m*	ensemble *m* des journaux *m/pl*
wholesale dealer	Großhändler *m*	grossiste *m*, intermédiare *m* revendeur
wholesale trade	Großhandel *m*	commerce *m* de gros
wide	breit	large
wide open paper	Blatt *n* mit wenigen Anzeigen *f/pl*	journal *m* avec peu d'annonces *f/pl*
wide size	Breitformat *n*	format *m* au largeur *f*
widely read newspaper	Zeitung *f*, weitverbreitete	journal *m* très répandu
wide-screen	Breitwand *f*	écran *m* large
widow	Hurenkind *n* (typog) , Kurzzeile *f*, Witwe *f/typog*	bout *m* de ligne *f*, ligne *f* boiteuse, ligne *f* courte, ligne *f* isolée, veuve *f*
width	Breite *f*	largeur *f*
width of column	Zeilenbreite *f*	justification *f* de la colonne *f*
width of type	Schriftweite *f*	approche *f*
to wield a pen	Feder *f* führen, die	manier la plume *f*
to wind up	abwickeln	utiliser
windbag	Schaumschläger *m*	vantard *m*
window display	Schaufensterauslage *f*, Schaufensterdekoration *f*	décoration *f* de vitrine *f*, étalage *m* de vitrine *f*

window display campaign	Schaufensterauslagen-Massierung f	campagne f d'étalages m/pl
window display material	Schaufenster-Werbemittel n/pl	matériel m d'étalage m
window dresser	Schaufensterdekorateur m, Schaufenstergestalter m, Schauwerbegestalter m	décorateur m de vitrines f/pl, étalagiste m
window dressing	dekorieren	décorer, faire des étalages m/pl
window envelope	Fensterumschlag m	enveloppe f à fenêtre f, enveloppe f transparente vitrifiée
window shopping	Schaufensterbummel m	lèche-vitrines m
window sticker, window streamer	Fensterklebeplakat n, Schaufensterkleber m, Seitenscheibenplakat n	adhésive f, affichette f sur les vitres f/pl, autocollant m de vitrine f, transparent m sur les glaces f/pl, vitrophanie f
window trimming	dekorieren	décorer, faire des étalages m/pl
windowcard	Schaufensterplakat n	affiche f vitrine f, pancarte f
window-dresser	Dekorateur m	décorateur-étalagiste m
window-dressing	Schaufensterbeschriftung f	inscription f des vitrines f/pl
winner	Schlager m	succès m
winter sale	Winterschlußverkauf m	solde m de printemps m
wipe	Schiebeblende f, Übergang m einer Filmszene f auf die folgende, schneller, Wischblende f	fermeture f en fondu m, volet m
to wipe off	abblenden	baisser les phares m/pl
to wipe on	aufblenden	arriver dans un fondu m
to wire	drahten, telegrafieren	télégraphier
wire	Leitungsdraht m	fil m télégraphique
wire stitching	Rückstichheftung f	brochure f à cheval m
wireless	Rundfunk m	radio f
wireless announcement	Rundfunkansage f	annonce f radiodiffusée
wireless enthusiast	Rundfunkteilnehmer m	sans-filiste m
wireless picture transmission	Bildfunk m	bélinographie f, téléphotographie f
wireless set	Radioapparat m, Rundfunkempfangsgerät n	poste m de radio f, récepteur m, récepteur m radio f
wireless telegraphy	drahtlose Telegrafie f	télégraphie f sans fil m
wireless transmitter	Rundfunksender m	émetteur m
wire-mark	Formstreifen m im Papier n	vergeure f du papier m
wirephoto	Bildfunk m	bélinographie f, téléphotographie f
wire-puller	Drahtzieher m	intrigant m, machinateur m
wire-tapping	Anzapfung f der Telefonleitungen f/pl	captage m des messages m/pl télégraphiques
with fine screen	feingerastert	à trame f fine
to withdraw a subscription	ein Abonnement n abbestellen	se désabonner à
to withhold	zurückstellen	retenir
to withhold until further notice	Weisung f abwarten vor Veröffentlichung f	à ne pas publier jusqu'à nouvel avis m
within one year	Jahresfrist f, innerhalb	dans le délai m d'une année f
without obligation	unverbindlich	sans engagement m
women's pl magazine	Frauenblatt n, Frauenzeitschrift f	revue f féminine
women's topics pl	Frauenseite f	page f de la femme f
wood base	Holzfuß m	pied m de bois m

wood containing paper	holzhaltiges Papier *n*	papier *m* avec de bois *m*, papier *m* fait de pâte *f* de bois *m*
wood cut, wood engraving	Holzschnitt *m*	bois *m* gravé, gravure *f* sur bois *m*
wood mount	Holzfuß *m*	pied *m* de bois *m*
wood printing	Holzdruck *m*	impression *f* sur bois *m*
woodbury print	Metalldruckverfahren *n*	impression *f* métallographique
wooden base	Holzunterlage *f*	socle *m* de bois *m*
wooden type	Holzschrift *f*	caractères *m/pl* de bois *m*
wood-engraver	Xylograf *m*	xylographe *m*
wood-engraving	Xylografie *f*	sculpture *f* sur bois *m*, xylographie *f*
wood-free paper	holzfreies Papier *n*	papier *m* sans pâte *f* de bois *m*
word	Wort *n*	mot *m*
word division	Worttrennung *f*	division *f* des mots *m/pl*
word order	Wortstellung *f*	ordre *m* des mots *m/pl*
word space	Wortzwischenraum *m*, Zeile *f*, ausschließen	espace *f* entre les mots *m/pl*, espacer, justifier
word-formation	Wortbildung *f*	formation *f* des mots *m/pl*
wording	Wortlaut *m*	énoncé *m*, teneur *f*
word-of-mouth-advertising	Mund-zu-Mund-Werbung *f*	publicité *f* parlante, publicité *f* verbale
wordsmith	Wortschöpfer *m*	créateur *m* de mots *m/pl*
to **work and turn**	umschlagen	basculer
work and turn	Schön- und Widerdruck *m*	impression *f* recto-verso
work of reference	Nachschlagewerk *n*	ouvrage *m* de référence *f*
to **work off**	ausdrucken	achever de tirer, terminer l'impression *f*
work order	Arbeitsablaufblatt *n*	note *f* sur les étapes *f/pl* de déroulement *m*
working	Verarbeitung *f*	façonnage *m*
working operation	Arbeitsgang *m*	opération *f*, phase *f* de travail *m*
working party	Arbeitsgruppe *f*	groupe *m* de travail *m*
workshop	Atelier *n*, Kursus *m*, Lehrgang *m*, Werkstatt *f*	atelier *m*, cours *m*, réunion *f* de travail *m*, studio *m*
work-up *am*	Spieß *m/typog*	levage, marque *f* d'une espace *f* haute
world market	Weltmarkt *m*	marché *m* mondial
world press	Weltpresse *f*	presse *f* mondiale
worm's eye – view	Froschperspektive *f*	contre-plongée *f*
worn-out type	abgenutzte Schrift *f*	têtes *f/pl* de clou *m*
worship of persons *pl*	Personenkult *m*	culte *m* de la personne *f*
wove paper	Velinpapier *n*	papier *m* du Japon *m*, papier *m* vélin
to **wrap**	einwickeln	envelopper
wrapped in silence, to be	Schweigen *n* hüllen, sich in	se renfermer dans le silence *m*
wrapper	Streifband *n*	bande *f* de journal *m*, jeu *m* de bandes *f/pl*
wrapping	Verpackung *f*	conditionnement *m*, emballage *m*
wrapping paper	Einschlagpapier *n*, Einwickelpapier *n*, Packpapier *n*	papier *m* bulle *f*, papier *m* d'emballage *m*, papier *m* gris
wrinkle	Tip *m*	tuyau *m*
to **write down**	niederschreiben	coucher sur papier *m*
to **write in one word**	zusammenschreiben	écrire en un mot *m*

writer	Schriftsteller *m*, Verfasser *m*	auteur *m*, écrivain *m*, publiciste *m*
write-up *am*	Pressebericht *m*, redaktionelle Werbung *f*	annonce *f* rédactionnelle, publicité *f* rédactionnelle gratuite, récit *m*, reportage *m*
writing down	Niederschrift *f*	écrit *m*, procès-verbal *m*
writing-paper	Schreibpapier *n*	papier *m* à écrire
written language	Schriftsprache *f*	langue *f* littéraire
written reply	Antwortschreiben *n*	lettre *f*-réponse *f*
written work	Schreibarbeiten *f/pl*	travaux *m/pl* d'écritures *f/pl*
wrong fount, wrong letter	Fisch (typog) *m*, Zwiebelfisch *m/typog*	coquille *f*, mastic *m*, pâté *m*

X

xerography	Trockenkopierverfahren *n*, Xerografie *f*	xérographie *f*
x-height	Mittellänge *f*	œil *m* de la lettre *f*
xography	Xografie *f*	xographie *f*

Y

yardstick	Maßstab *m*	échelle *f*, règle *f* graduée
year of establishment	Gründungsjahr *n*	année *f* de fondation *f*
year-book	Jahrbuch *n*	annale *f*, annuaire *m*
yellow journal	Revolverblatt *n*	feuille *f* à scandale *m*, feuille *f* de chantage *m*
yellow pages *pl*	Branchentelefonbuch *n*, gelbe Seiten *f/pl*	pages *f/pl* jaunes
yellow paper	Boulevardblatt *n*	feuille *f* boulevardière
yellow press	Hetzpresse *f*, Sensationspresse *f*	journaille *f*, presse *f* à sensation *f*, presse *f* jaune
yellowed	vergilbt	jauni
yielding of commission	Provisionsabgabe *f*	cession *f* de ristournes *f/pl*, donner des retours *m/pl* en arrière
youth paper	Jugendzeitung *f*	journal *m* des jeunes *m/pl*
youth supplement	Jugendbeilage *f*	supplément *m* pour la jeunesse *f*

Z

zapon varnish	Zaponlack *m*	laque *f* zapon
zero edition	Nullnummer *f*	édition *f* zéro
zinc	Zink *n*	zinc *m*
zinc block, zinc etching	Zinkätzung *f*, Zinkklischee *n*	cliché *m* zinc *m*, zincographie *f*
zinc halftone	Zinkautotypie *f*	autotypie *f* zinc
zinc plate	Zinkplatte *f*	plaque *f* de zinc *m*
zinc white	Deckweiß *n*	blanc couvrant
zincography	Zinkdruck *m*	zincographie *f*
zone campaign	regionale Wahlkampagne *f*	campagne *f* électorale régionale

zone plan   Schwerpunktwerbung *f*   publicité *f* concentrée
zooming   Heranrücken *n* bei   rapprochement *m* dans une
                          Großaufnahme *f* (Film)   vue *f* de premier plan *m*

Complete Multilingual Dictionary of Advertising, Marketing, and Communications

French • Français
German • Allemand
English • Anglais

List of Abbreviations/Liste des abréviations:

	French/Français	German/Allemand	English/Anglais
am	américain	amerikanisch	American
brit	britannique	britisch	British
f	féminin	weiblich	feminine
f/pl	féminin pluriel	weibliche Mehrzahl	feminine plural
m	masculin	männlich	masculine
m/pl	masculin pluriel	männliche Mehrzahl	masculine plural
n	neutre	sächlich	neuter
n/pl	neutre pluriel	sächliche Mehrzahl	neuter plural
pl	pluriel	Mehrzahl	plural
s.	voir	siehe	see
stereotyp.	stéréotypie	Stereotypie	stereotyping
typogr.	typographie	Buchdruck	typography

A

à la commission f	auf Provisionsbasis f	on commission
à notre convenance f	auf Abruf m	at our convinience, on call
abondance f	Reichhaltigkeit f	abundance
abonné m	Abonnent m, Bezieher m	subscriber
abonné m de la télévision f	Fernsehteilnehmer m	television viewer
abonnement m	Abonnement n, Bezug m	subscription
abonnement m à un journal m	Zeitungsabonnement n	subscription to a journal
abonnement m annuel	Jahresabonnement n	annual subscription
abonnement m cadeau m	Geschenkabonnement n	gift subscription
abonnement m combiné	kombiniertes Abonnement n	clubbing offer
abonnement m de vacances f/pl	Ferienabonnement n	holiday subscription
abonnement m d'essai m	Probeabonnement m	trial subscription
abonnement m forcé	Zwangsabonnement n	compulsory subscription
abonnement m gratuit	Gratisabonnement n	free subscription
abonnement m obligatoire	Pflichtabonnement n	obligatory subscription
abonnement m parrainé	Patenschaftsabonnement n	sponsored subscription
abonnement m postal	Postabonnement n	postal subscription
abonnement m pour membres m/pl	Mitgliedsabonnement n	association subscription
abonnements m/pl payants	bezahlte Abonnements n/pl	paid subscriptions pl
abonnements m/pl pour retrait m au guichet m	Abholabonnements n/pl	call-at-office subscriptions pl
abréger	abkürzen, kürzen	to boil down, to compress, to curtail, to cut down, to cut short, to shorten
abréviation f	Abbreviatur f, Abkürzung f	abbreviation
absence f du son m	Tonausfall m	dead mike, off mike
absorption f	Aufsaugung f	absorption
abstention f des consommateurs m/pl	Kaufunlust f	disinclination to buy, sales pl resistance
accalmie f	Flaute f	dullness, flatness
accélérateur m	Zeitraffer m	rapid-motion method, time-lapse equipment
accent m	Akzent m	accent
accent m aigu	Accent m aigu	acute accent
accent m circonflexe	Accent m circonflexe	circumflex
accent grave	Accent m grave	grave accent
accentuer	betonen	to accentuate
acceptabilité f auprès des consommateurs m/pl	Kaufbereitschaft f	buying intention, consumer acceptance
acceptable	annehmbar	acceptable
acceptation f	Aufnahme f	acceptance
acceptation f des manuscrits m/pl	Manuskriptannahme f	acceptance of manuscripts pl
acceptation f d'une commande f	Auftragsannahme f	acceptance of an order
accessoires m/pl publicitaires	Werbegeräte n/pl	advertising utensils pl
accommodation f	Anpassung f	adaptation, adjustment
accomplissement m	Leistung f	performance
accomplissement m publicitaire	Werbeträgereinsatz m	media performance

accord *m*	Abkommen *n*, Abmachung *f*, Vereinbarung *f*	agreement, arrangement, settlement
accrédité	anerkannt	accredited, recognised
accrochage *m*	Blickfang *m*	approach, catch phrase, eye appeal, eye catcher, hook, stopper
accrochage *m* initial	Aufmerksamkeitserreger *m*	advertising approach, attention getter
accrochage *m* publicitaire	Ansatzpunkt *m*, Aufhänger *m*, Zugkraft *f*	approach, attention value, attraction, hook, pulling power, topical peg
accroche-œil *m*	Blickfang *m*	approach, catch phrase, eye appeal, eye catcher, hook, stopper
accroche-œil *m* primaire	Hauptblickfang *m*	primary appeal
accroissement *m* de publicité *f*	Anzeigenzunahme *f*	advertising growth
accroissement *m* des tirages *m/pl*	Auflagenanstieg *m*	circulation growth
accumulation *f*	Anhäufung *f*	accumulation
achalandage *m*	Stammkundschaft *f*	goodwill
achat *m*	Einkauf *m*, Kauf *m*	buying, purchase
achat *m* d'annonces *f/pl*	Anzeigeneinkauf *m*	space buying
achat *m* d'espace *m*	Anzeigenbelegung *f*	space buying
achat *m* impulsif	Impulskauf *m*, Spontankauf *m*	impulse buying
achat *m* occasionnel	Gelegenheitskauf *m*	bargain
achat *m* spontané	Impulskauf *m*, Spontankauf *m*	impulse buying
achats *m/pl* spéculatifs	Hortungskäufe *m/pl*	hoarding purchases *pl*
acheminer	versenden	to dispatch, to forward, to ship
acheter	einkaufen	to shop
acheter d'espace *m*	Anzeigenraum *m* bestellen	space buying
acheter en bloc *m*	blockbuchen	to buy the whole stock
acheteur *m*, acheteuse *f*	Abnehmer *m*, Käufer *m* (in *f*)	buyer, client (for a service), customer, female buyer, purchaser, shopper
acheteur *m* d'art *m*	Auftraggeber *m* freier Künstler *m/pl*	art buyer
acheteur *m* de temps *m* d'antenne *f*	Sendezeitvermittler *m*, Werbezeiteneinkäufer *m*	time buyer
acheteur *m* d'espace *m*	Anzeigeneinkäufer *m*, Anzeigenmittler *m*, Mediadisponent *m*, Mediasachbearbeiter *m*, Streuungsfachmann *m*, Werbungsmittler *m*	advertising contractor, advertising intermediary, media clerk, media man, space broker, space buyer
acheteur *m* du graphisme *m* publicitaire	Sachbearbeiter *m* für Grafiker-Mitarbeit *f*	art buyer
acheteur *m* passant d'une marque *f* à l'autre	Markenwechsler *m*	brand switcher
acheteur *m* potentiel	Kaufinteressent *m*	potential buyer
achever de tirer	ausdrucken	to work off
acompte *m*	Anzahlung *f*	down payment, part payment
acqisition *f*	Akquisition *f*	canvassing
acquérir des clients *m/pl*	Kunden *m/pl* gewinnen	to acquire customers *pl*, to attract customers *pl*, to drum

acrobate *m*-**doublure** *f*	Double *n*	stuntman
acteur *m* **de cinéma** *m*	Filmschauspieler *m*	film actor
action *f*	Handlung *f*	action
action *f* **de presse** *f*	Presseversand *m*	press release
action *f* **publicitaire**	Werbeaktion *f*	advertising activity
action *f* **spéciale**	Sonderaktion *f*	special action
activité *f* **du journaliste** *m*	Pressearbeit *f*	presswork
activité *f* **publicitaire**	Werbegeschäft *n*, Werbetätigkeit *f*	advertising activity, advertising trade, propaganda
actresse *f* **de cinéma** *m*	Filmschauspielerin *f*	film actress
actualité *f*	aktuelle Bedeutung *f*, Aktualität *f*	actuality, topicality
actualités *f/pl*	Neues *n* vom Tage *m*, Wochenschau *f*	current events *pl*, news-reel
actuel	aktuell	topical
adaptation *f*	Adaptierung *f*, Bearbeitung *f*, Umarbeitung *f*	adaptation, rescale
adaptation *f* **cinématographique**	Filmbearbeitung *f*	film adaptation
adapter	adaptieren, anpassen, bearbeiten	to adapt, to arrange
addition *f*	Zusatz *m*	addition
addition *f* **du ton** *m*	Vertonung *f*	musical setting, scoring
adhésif *m*	Klebstoff *m*	adhesive, glue
adhésive *f*	Fensterklebeplakat *n*	window sticker, window streamer
adjoint *m*	Assistent *m*	assistant
adjoint *m* **au chef** *m* **de publicité** *f*	Werbeassistent *m*	advertising assistant
adjucation *f*	Ausschreibung *f*	invitation to bid
administrateur *m*	Administrator *m*, Verwalter *m*	administrator
administration *f*	Administration *f*, Verwaltung *f*	administration
administrer	verwalten	to administer
adressage *m*	Adressierung *f*	addressing
adresse *f*	Adresse *f*, Anschrift *f*	address
adresse *f* **adhésive**	Adressenaufkleber *m*	adhesive address label
adresse *f* **de télégramme** *m*	Telegrammadresse *f*	cable address, telegraphic address
adresse *f* **d'emprunt** *m*	Deckadresse *f*	accommodation address
adresse *f* **imprimée du commerçant** *m*	eingedruckte Händleranschrift *f*	dealer imprint
adresse *f* **télégraphique**	Drahtanschrift *f*, Telegrammadresse *f*	cable address, telegraphic address
adresse *f* **télex**	Telexanschrift *f*	telex address
adressographe *m*	Adressiermaschine *f*	addressing machine, addressographe
aérographe *m*	Spritzpistole *f*	airbrush
aérographie *f*	Spritztechnik *f*	air brush technique
affabulation *f*	Fabel *f* eines Stückes *n*	plot
affaire *f*	Angelegenheit *f*, Geschichte *f*	matter, story
affaire *f* **en échange** *m*	Gegengeschäft *n*	barter
affaire *f* **en question** *f*	bewußte Angelegenheit *f*	matter
affaire *f* **publicitaire**	Werbeangelegenheit *f*	advertising affair
affaire *f* **ratée**	Blindgänger *m*	damp squib
affaires *f/pl* **conclues**	Geschäftsabschlüsse *m/pl*	dealings *pl*
affermage *m*	Verpachtung *f*	farming out, sub-contracting
affermer	verpachten	to farm out, to lease
affermer la publicité *f*	Anzeigenteil *m* pachten	to lease the advertisement business

affichage *m*	Affichierung *f*, Ankleben *n*, Plakatierung *f*, Plakatwerbung *f*	billposting, placing, poster advertising, posting
affichage *m* à demi	Halbbelegung *f*	half showing
affichage *m* à la brosse *f* sèche	Naßklebeverfahren *n*	dry posting
affichage *m* à la sauvette *f*	Wildanschlag *m*	fly posting, sniping
affichage *m* dans les abris-bus *m/pl*	Wartehäuschenwerbung *f*	poster advertising in shelters *pl*
affichage *m* des prix *m/pl*	Preisauszeichnung *f*	price marking
affichage *m* d'un placard *m*	Plakat *n* anschlagen	placing of a poster
affichage *m* général	Netzanschlag *m*, Vollbelegung *f*	full showing
affichage *m* gracieux	Freiaushang *m*, Gratisplakataushang *m*	free posting
affichage *m* par massifs *m/pl*	Reihenanschlag *m*	series *pl* posting
affichage *m* permanent	Daueranschlag *m*	permanent posting
affichage *m* rural	Landanschlag *m*	rural areas *pl* posting
affichage *m* saisonnier	Saisonanschlag *m*	seasonal poster advertising
affichage *m* sans plis *m/pl*	faltenfreier Anschlag *m*	nonwrinkle posting
affichage *m* sur certaines colonnes *f/pl* seulement	Teilbelegung *f* von Plakatsäulen *f/pl*	partial display on a few pillars *pl*
affichage *m* sur palissades *f/pl*	Bauzaunwerbung *f*	billposting on hoardings *pl*, billposting on plank fences *pl*
affichage *m* temporaire	kurzfristiger Anschlag *m*	temporary posting
affichage *m* volant	Wildanschlag *m*	fly posting, sniping
affiche *f* abîmée	beschädigtes Plakat *n*	torn poster
affiche *f* collective	Sammelplakat *n*	collective advertising poster
affiche *f* constructiviste	konstruktives Plakat *n*	constructive poster
affiche *f* criarde	grellfarbiges Plakat *n*	glaring poster, screaming poster
affiche *f* dans les gares *f/pl*	Bahnhofsplakat *n*	station poster
affiche *f* de cinéma *m*	Filmplakat *n*	film poster
affiche *f* de cirque *m*	Zirkusplakat *n*	circus-poster
affiche *f* de comptoir *m*	Aufstellplakat *n*	counter card, show card
affiche *f* de concert *m*	Konzertplakat *n*	concert poster
affiche *f* de grand format *m*	großformatiges Plakat *n*	royal poster
affiche *f* de journal *m*	Zeitungsplakat *n*	newspaper poster
affiche *f* de livre *m*	Buchplakat *n*	book poster
affiche *f* de remplacement *m*	Ersatzplakat *n*	poster for replacement
affiche *f* de théâtre *m*	Theaterplakat *n*	play bill, theater poster
affiche *f* déchirée, affiche *f* détériorée	beschädigtes Plakat *n*	torn poster
affiche *f* d'exposition *f*	Ausstellungsplakat *n*	exhibition poster
affiche *f* électorale	Wahlplakat *n*	election poster
affiche *f* en plusieurs parties *f/pl*	mehrteiliges Plakat *n*	poster in several parts *pl*
affiche *f* en relief *m*	Prägeplakat *f*	embossed poster
affiche *f* expérimentelle	experimentelles Plakat *n*	experimental poster
affiche *f* illustrative	illustratives Plakat *n*	illustrative poster
affiche *f* illustrée	Bildplakat *n*	pictorial poster
affiche *f* informative	informatives Plakat *n*	informative poster
affiche *f* intérieure	Innenplakat *n* (in Verkehrsmitteln *n/pl*)	car card advertising, car panel, indoor poster
affiche *f* irisée	Leuchtfarbenplakat *n*	day-glo poster
affiche *f* latérale	Rumpffläche *f*	side panel
affiche *f* mammouth	Mammutplakat *n*	mammoth poster

affiche *f* mobile	Aufstellplakat *n*, Ausstellkarton *m*, Werbeaufsteller *m*	counter card, show card
affiche *f* officielle	amtliches Plakat *n*	official notice, official poster
affiche *f* passe-partout	Rahmenplakat *n*	stock poster
affiche *f* peinte	gemaltes Plakat *n*	painted placard
affiche *f* permanente	Dauerplakat *n*	permanent poster
affiche *f* photographique	Fotoplakat *n*	photo poster
affiche *f* politique	politisches Plakat *n*	political poster
affiche *f* porcelaine	Porzellanschild *n*	porcelain sign
affiche *f* sérielle	Serienplakat *n*	series *pl* poster
affiche *f* toile	Leinwandplakat *n*	linen poster
affiche *f* toile *f* peinte	auf Leinwand *f* gemaltes Plakat *n*	poster painted on canvas
affiche *f* touristique	Fremdenverkehrsplakat *n*	tourist poster
affiche *f* vitrine *f*	Schaufensterplakat *n*	showcard, windowcard
affiche-papier *m*	Affiche *f*, Anschlagbogen *m*, Plakat *n*	bill, placard, poster, sticker *am*
afficher	anbringen (Plakat), anschlagen, plakatieren	to place bills *pl*, to post, to post bills *pl*, to stick bills *pl*
affiches *f/pl* peintes	gemalte Außenwerbung *f*	painted displays *pl*
affiches *f/pl* pour le service *m* public	gemeinnützige Plakatierung *f*	public service posters *pl*
affiche-texte *f*	Textplakat *n*	letterpress poster
affichette *f* dans les rayonnages *m/pl*	Kleinplakat *n* auf Regalen *n/pl* und Theken *f/pl*	shelf-talker
affichette *f* d'autobus *m* ou de tramway *m*	Anschlag *m* in Verkehrsmitteln *n/pl*, Werbeplakat *n* in Verkehrsmitteln *n/pl*	car card advertising
affichette *f* sur les vitres *f/pl*	Seitenscheibenplakat *n*	side window transfer, window sticker
afficheur *m*	Ankleber *m*, Anschläger *m*, Plakatanschläger *m*	bill-poster, bill-sticker, carder (public conveyances *pl*), sticker
affichiste *m*	Plakatgrafiker *m*, Plakatmaler *m*, Plakatzeichner *m*	poster artist, poster designer
affinité *f* intellectuelle	Geistesverwandtschaft *f*	congeniality
affirmation *f* sur serment *m*	eidesstattliche Erklärung *f*	affidavit
affranchisement *m* en timbres *m/pl*	Barfrankatur *f*	cash endorsement
affranchissement *m*	Frankierung *f*	franking
affranchissement *m* forfaitaire	Pauschalfrankatur *f*	post paid
agence *f*	Agentur *f*, Geschäftsstelle *f*	administrative, agency, office
agence *f* à service *m* complet	full-service-Agentur *f*	agency with full service
agence de modèles *m/pl*	Modellagentur *f*	model agency
agence *f* de presse *f*	Korrespondenzbüro *n*	press agency
agence *f* de presse *f* photographique	Pressebilderdienst *m*	picture agency
agence *f* de publicité *f*	Annoncenexpedition *f*, Werbeagentur *f*, Werbebüro *n*	advertising agency, advertising office, space broker
agence *f* de publicité *f* reconnue	anerkannte Werbeagentur *f*, anerkannter Werbungsmittler *m*	recognised advertising agency
agence *f* des relations *f/pl* publiques	PR-Agentur *f*	public relations *pl* agency

agence f d'information f	Nachrichtenbüro n, Presseagentur f, Pressedienst m	news agency, press agency, press service
agence f d'un journal m	Zeitungsagentur f	newspaper agency
agence f exclusive	Alleinvertretung f, Exklusivagentur f	exclusive agency
agence f fictive	Hausagentur f, vorgeschobene Agentur f	house agency, imaginary agency
agencement m	Anordnung f, Innenausbau m	arrangement, inside decoration
agenda m	Agenda f, Notizbuch n, Terminkalender m	advertising schedule, deadline schedule, memorandum book, note-book, pocket diary
agenda m de la journée f	Tagesereignisse n/pl, Tagesnachrichten f/pl in der Presse f	events pl today
agent m	Agent m, Vertreter m	agent, representative, selling agent
agent m d'abonnement m	Bezieherwerber f	subscription agent
agent m de publicité f	Presseagent m, PR-Mann m	build-upper, press agent
agent m qui essaie d'influencer les députés m/pl	Interessenvertreter m	lobbyist
agent m régional	Bezirksvertreter m	special representative
agglomération f	geschlossene Ortschaft f	built up area
agitateur m	Agitator m	agitator
agitation f	Agitation f	agitation
agrafer	heften	to fasten, to sew, to stitch
agrandir	vergrößern	to enlarge, to increase
agrandir à la proportionnelle	proportional vergrößern	to enlarge proportionally
agrandissement m	Vergrößerung f	blow-up, enlargement
agrandissement m photographique	Großfoto n	large-size photo
aide f à la vente f	Verkaufshilfe f	promotion matter
aide f à l'exportation f	Exportförderung f	export promotion
aide-mémoire m	Memorandum n, Merkblatt n	instruction sheet, leaflet, memorandum
aides f/pl publicitaires au détaillant m	Händlerwerbehilfen f/pl	dealer aids pl
aire f de l'exposition f	Ausstellungsfläche f	exhibition space
ajournement m d'un délai m	Terminverlegung f	postponement of a date
ajout m	Zusatz m	addition
ajouter	beifügen, beilegen, hinzufügen	to add, to affix, to enclose
alarmiste m	Panikmacher m	panic-monger
album-souvenir m	Einklebebuch n	scrapbook
alfa m	Espartopapier n	esparto
alignement m	Ausgleich typog m	alignment
alignement m des prix m/pl	Preisangleichung f	price adjustment
aligner	ausschließen (typog) , Zeile f halten	to align, to justify, to straighten line
aliments m/pl prêts à la consommation f	verbrauchsfertige Nahrungsmittel n/pl	convenience foods pl
alinéa m	Absatz m (im Text m) , Abschnitt m	paragraph
allégation f de la publicité f	Werbebehauptung f	claim
allégorie f	Allegorie f	allegory
aller aux informations f/pl	Erkundigungen f/pl einziehen	to inquire
alliage m d'imprimerie f	Gießmetall n	foundry metal

allocation *f*	Werbekostenanweisung *f*, Zuteilung *f*	allocation, allotment
allocation *f* du budget *m*	Budgetgliederung *f*	assignment of expenditures *pl*
allocation *f* du budget *m* publicitaire	Aufteilung *f* des Werbe- budgets *n*	assignment of advertising expenditure
allocation *f* publicitaire	Anweisung *f* von Werbekosten *pl*, Werbezuschuß *m*	advertising allocation, advertising allowance
allonge *f*	Allonge *f*	fly-leaf
allouer	zuteilen	to allocate, to allot
almanach *m*	Almanach *m*, Kalender *m*	almanac, calendar
almanach *m* du commerce *m*	Handelsadreßbuch *n*	commercial directory, trade directory
alphabet *m*	Alphabet *n*	alphabet
alternative *f*	Variante *f*	variant
alternative *f* publicitaire	Werbealternative *f*	advertising alternative
amélioration *f* de la qualité *f* d'un produit *m*	Qualitätsverbesserung *f* einer Ware *f*	up-trading
aménagement *m* de vitrines *f/pl*	Schaufenstergestaltung *f*	fitting of shop windows *pl*
aménagement *m* d'un stand *m*	Standgestaltung *f*	stand design, stand dressing
amendement *m*	Änderung *f*, Verbesserung *f*	amendment
amodiation *f*	Verpachtung *f*	farming out, sub-contracting
amoindrissement *m*	Unterbewertung *f*, Untertreibung *f*	understatement
amorce *f*	Blickfang *m*	approach, catch phrase, eye appeal, eye catcher, hook, stopper
amphibie *m*	Schweizerdegen *m/typog*	compositor-pressman
amphigourie *f*	verworrenes Geschwätz *n*	balderdash
ampleur *f* du travail *m*	Arbeitsaufwand *m*	expenditure of work
amuseur *m*	Unterhalter *m*	entertainer
analyse *f*	Analyse *f*	analysis
analyse *f* d'affichage *m*	Plakatanalyse *f*	poster analysis
analyse *f* de distribution *f*	Streuanalyse *f*	distribution analysis
analyse *f* de la décision *f* d'acheter	Kaufentschlußanalyse *f*	activation research
analyse *f* de la diffusion *f*	Verbreitungsanalyse *f*	circulation analysis
analyse *f* de l'audience *f*	Leseranalyse *f*, Publikumsanalyse *f*	audience analysis, audience research, circulation analysis, reader interest research, readership survey
analyse *f* de texte *m*	Textanalyse *f*	copy research
analyse *f* des abonnés *m/pl*	Abonnentenanalyse *f*	subscriber analysis
analyse *f* des lecteurs *m/pl*	Leseranalyse *f*	audience analysis, circulation analysis, reader interest research, readership survey
analyse *f* des médias *m/pl*	Mediaanalyse *f*, Werbeträgeranalyse *f*	media analysis
analyse *f* des spectateurs *m/pl*	Zuschaueranalyse *f*	audience analysis
analyse *f* des tirages *m/pl*	Auflagenanalyse *f*	circulation analysis
analyse *f* des ventes *f/pl*	Verkaufsanalyse *f*	sales *pl* analysis
analyse *f* du cercle *m* des abonnés *m/pl*	Bezieheranalyse *f*	analysis of subscribers *pl*
analyse *f* du contenu *m*	Inhaltsanalyse *f*	content analysis
analyse *f* du marché *m*	Absatzanalyse *f*, Marktanalyse *f*	market analysis
analyse *f* du produit *m*	Produktanalyse *f*	product analysis

analyste *m* du marché *m*	Marktanalytiker *m*	market analyst
anecdote *f*	Anekdote *f*, Kurzgeschichte *f*	anecdote, short story
angle *m* d'approche *f*	Ansatzpunkt *m*, Aufhänger *m*, Aufmerksamkeitserreger *m*	advertising approach, attention getter, hook, topical peg
angle *m* d'approche *f* publicitaire	Verkaufspunkt *m*, werblicher Gesichtspunkt *m*	advertising angle, sales *pl* point
animateur *m*	Schallplatten-Ansager *m*, Trickfilmzeichner *m*	animator, disc-jockey
annale *f*	Jahrbuch *n*	annual, year-book
annales *f/pl*	Annalen *f/pl*	annals *pl*, records *pl*
année *f*	Jahrgang *m*	volume
année *f* civile	Kalenderjahr *n*	calendar year
année *f* contractuelle	Insertionsjahr *n*	contractual year
année *f* de fondation *f*	Gründungsjahr *n*	year of establishment
année *f* légale	Abschlußjahr *n*, Einschaltjahr *n*	contract year, legal year
annexe *f*	Anlage *f*, Beigabe *f*, Beipack *m*, Briefbeilage *f*	addition, appendix, enclosure, insert, letter enclosure
annexer	beilegen	to enclose
annonce *f*	Ankündigung *f*, Annonce *f*, Ansage *f*, Anzeige *f*, Inserat *n*	ad, advertisement, announcement
annonce *f* à apparence *f* rédactionnelle	redaktionell aufgemachte Anzeige *f*	advertorial, editorial advertisement, reader advertisement, reading notice *am*
annonce *f* à clé *f*	Kennzifferanzeige *f*	keyed advertisement
annonce *f* à date *f* fixe	Terminanzeige *f*	fixed date advertisement
annonce *f* à fond *m* perdu, annonce *f* à franc-bord *m*	angeschnittene Anzeige *f*	bleed advertisement
annonce *f* à la radio *f*	Werbedurchsage *f*	commercial, radio announcement, spot announcement
annonce *f* à variantes *f/pl*	Anzeige *f* in einer Teilauflage *f/pl*	split-run advertisement
annonce *f* avec couleur *f* d'accompagnement *m*	Schmuckfarbenanzeige *f*	run-of-paper advertisement (ROP)
annonce *f* bien aérée	luftige Anzeige *f*	advertisement with much white space
annonce *f* bouche *f* -trou *m*	Füllanzeige *f*	filler, plugger ad, stop gap advertisement
annonce *f* chiffrée	Chiffreanzeige *f*, Kennzifferanzeige *f*	box number advertisement, keyed advertisement
annonce *f* collective	Kollektivanzeige *f*, Sammelanzeige *f*	composite advertisement, joint insertion
annonce *f* commerciale	Geschäftsanzeige *f*	business advertisement with regular basic rate, commercial advertisement
annonce *f* commerciale à prix *m* de base *f*	Empfehlungsanzeige *f*	business advertisement with regular basic rate
annonce *f* complémentaire pour bénéficier du dégressif *m*	Anzeige *f* zur Erreichung *f* eines höheren Nachlasses *m*	rate holder, rate maker
annonce *f* couplée	Koppelanzeige *f*	tie-in advertisement
annonce *f* de continuation *f*	Fortsetzungsanzeige *f*	following on
annonce *f* de décès *m*	Todesanzeige *f*	death announcement, obituary notice
annonce *f* de grandes dimensions *f/pl*	großflächige Anzeige *f*	big splurge ad, large space ad

annonce f de lancement m	Einführungsanzeige f	launch ad
annonce f de presse f	Zeitungsanzeige f	press advertisement
annonce f de rappel m	Erinnerungsanzeige f	reminder advertisement
annonce f de répétition f	Wiederholungsanzeige f	repeat ad, rerun, run-it-again
annonce f de spectacle m	Theaterplakat n	play bill, theater poster
annonce f d'échange m	Tauschanzeige f	barter advertisement, exchange advertisement
annonce f déguisée	getarnte Anzeige f	veiled advertisement
annonce f d'introduction f	Einführungsanzeige f	launch ad
annonce f d'opportunité f	Füller m	cushion, fill-up, filler, quadder
annonce f d'un cinéma m	Kinoanzeige f	cinema announcement
annonce f d'une page f entière	ganzseitige Anzeige f	full page ad, spread
annonce f en double page f	Panoramaanzeige f	panorama advertisement
annonce f en noir	Schwarz-Weiß-Anzeige f	advertisement in black and white
annonce f encadrée	umrandete Anzeige f	boxed advertisement
annonce f fictive	fingierte Anzeige f	dummy advertisement
annonce f figurant dans le texte m rédactionnel	Textanzeige f	advertorial, reader advertisement
annonce f fixée sur l'achat m	Kaufanzeige f	direct-action copy
annonce f flamboyante	sensationell aufgemachte Anzeige f	flaring advertisement
annonce f groupée	Wortanzeige f	classified advertisement, composite advertisement
annonce f illustrée	Bildanzeige f, Klischeeanzeige f	advertisement with illustration, block advertisement, illustrated advertisement, pictorial advertisement
annonce f immobilière	Immobilienanzeige f	real estate advertisement
annonce f isolée	alleinstehende Anzeige f, Inselanzeige f	sole advertisement
annonce f judiciaire	gerichtliche Anzeige f	legal notice
annonce f légale	amtliche Anzeige f	official announcement, statutory announcement
annonce f locale	örtliche Anzeige f	local advertisement
annonce f lumineuse	Leuchtschrift f	luminous signs pl
annonce f masquée en partie f	maskierte Anzeige f	advertisement masked out in part
annonce f matrimoniale	Heiratsanzeige f	marriage advertisement
annonce f montrant de diverses sortes f/pl d'un produit m	Anzeige f, die verschiedene Arten f/pl eines Produktes n zeigt	umbrella-ad
annonce f multicolore	mehrfarbige Anzeige f	colored ad am, coloured ad brit
annonce f nécrologique	Todesanzeige f	death announcement, obituary notice
annonce f obligatoire	Pflichtanzeige f	obligatory advertisement
annonce f ombrée	Schattendruckanzeige f	shadow print advertisement
annonce f permanente	Daueranzeige f	permanent advertisement
annonce f piquant la curiosité f	Neugier erregende Anzeige f	teaser
annonce f pour produits m/pl alimentaires	Nahrungsmittelanzeige f	food ad
annonce f préliminaire	Versuchsanzeige f, Voranzeige f	preliminary advertisement, preliminary announcement
annonce f privée	private Anzeige f	personal advertisement
annonce f publicitaire	Werbeankündigung f im Rundfunk m	commercial

annonce *f* **radiodiffusée**	Rundfunkansage *f*, Werbespot *m*	broadcast announcement, commercial, spot announcement, wireless announcement
annonce *f* **radiophonique**	Anzeige *f* im Rundfunk *m*, Rundfunkanzeige *f*	advergram
annonce *f* **rédactionnelle**	redaktionelle Werbung *f*	editorial publicity, free puff, write-up *am*
annonce *f* **répétée plusieurs fois** *f*	Wiederholungsanzeige *f*	repeat ad, rerun, run-it-again
annonce *f* **se joignant à plusieurs colonnes** *f/pl* **rédactionnelles** *f/pl*	Anzeige *f* im Anschluß *m* an mehrere Textspalten *f/pl*	cut-in advertisement
annonce *f* **spectacles** *m/pl*	Vergnügungsanzeige *f*	entertainment advertisement
annonce *f* **surchargée**	überladene Anzeige *f*	buckeye
annonce *f* **surimprimée**	Schattendruckanzeige *f*	shadow print advertisement
annonce *f* **téléphonée**	telefonisch aufgegebene Anzeige *f*	telephoned advertisement
annoncer	ankündigen, anzeigen, inserieren	to advertise, to announce, to insert
annoncer par radio *f*	Radiowerbung *f* betreiben	to be on the air
annonces *f/pl* **avec des dépliants** *m/pl* **cousus sur elles**	Prospektanzeigen *f/pl*	Dutch door
annonces *f/pl* **du registre** *m* **du commerce** *m*	Handelsregister *n*-Anzeigen *f/pl*	advertisements *pl* of the commercial register
annonces *f/pl* **enterrées**	Anzeigenfriedhof *m*	buried advertisements *pl*
annonces *f/pl* **groupées**	rubrizierte Anzeigen *f/pl*	classified advertisements *pl*, composite advertisements *pl*, small ads *pl*, smalls *pl brit*
annonces *f/pl* **personnelles**	persönliche Anzeigen *f/pl*, Seufzerspalte *f*	agony column
annonce *f*-**texte** *m*	Textteilanzeige *f*	textual advertisement
annonceur *m*	Inserent *m*, Werbungtreibender *m*	advertiser
annoncier *m*	Anzeigenblatt *n*, Anzeigensetzer *m*	admag, advertisement compositor, advertisement magazine, advertiser, free sheet
annuaire *m*	Adreßbuch *n*, Jahrbuch *n*	address book, annual, directory, year-book
annuaire *m* **commercial**	Branchenadreßbuch *n*	trade directory
annuaire *m* **de publicité** *f*	Werbeadreßbuch *n*	advertising directory
annuaire *m* **des téléphones** *m/pl*	Fernsprechbuch *n*	telephone directory
annuaire *m* **du commerce** *m*	Handelsadreßbuch *n*	commercial directory, trade directory
annuaire *m* **pour le commerce** *m* **et l'industrie** *f*	Fachadreßbuch *n*	trade address book
annuaire *m* **téléphonique**	Telefonbuch *n*	telephone book *am*, telephone directory
annuel	jährlich	annually, every year
annulation *f*	Abbestellung *f*, Annullierung *f*, Sistierung *f*, Stornierung *f*	cancellation
annulation *f* **d'un ordre** *m*	Auftragsannullierung *f*	cancellation of an order
annuler	abbestellen, annullieren, sistieren, stornieren	to cancel
anonymat *m*	Anonymität *f*	anonymity

anonyme	anonym	anonymous
antenne *f*	Sender *m*	broadcaster, station
anthologie *f*	Anthologie *f*	anthology
antiope *m*	Videotext *m*	ceefax, oracle
antique *f*	Grotesk *f*	grotesque, sans-serif
aperçu *m*	Übersicht *f*	survey, synopsis
aphorisme *m*	Aphorismus *m*, Kernspruch *m*	aphorism, pithy saying
à-plat *m*	Tonfläche *f*, Tonplatte *f*	background plate, flat tint, ground-tint plate, tint block
apostrophe *f*	Apostroph *m*	apostrophe
appareil *m* à copier	Kopiergerät *n*	contact printing machine, photostat
appareil *m* à dicter	Diktaphon *n*	dictating machine
appareil *m* à photocopier	Fotokopiergerät *n*	photo copier, photo copying machine, photostat
appareil *m* à reporter	Umdruckapparat *m*	offset repro machine
appareil *m* à tirer les bleus *m/pl*	Lichtpausgerät *n*	blue print apparatus
appareil *m* cinématographique	Fotoapparat *m*	camera
appareil *m* commercial	Verkaufsorganisation *f*, Vertriebsapparat *m*	sales *pl* organisation, selling organisation
appareil *m* de projection *f*	Bildwerfer *m*	epidiascope, slide projector
appareil *m* de télévision *f*	Pantoffelkino *n*	television set
appareil *m* d'enregistrement *m* de son *m*	Tonaufnahmegerät *n*	sound recorder
appareil *m* enregistrateur	Aufnahmegerät *n*	tape recorder
appareil *m* enregistreur	Tonbandgerät *n*, Wiedergabegerät *n*	recorder, video-tape recorder
appareil *m* pour la saisie *f* des données *f/pl*	Datenerfassungsgerät *n*	data acquisition terminal, data collection terminal
appareil *m* pour la saisie *f* des textes *m/pl*	Texterfassungsgerät *n*	text acquisition terminal, text collection terminal
appareil *m* pour tester la participation *f* des vidéo-spectateurs *m/pl*	Gerät *n* zur Messung *f* der Zuschauerbeteiligung *f*	tamalyzer
appareil *m* pour tester l'effet *m* publicitaire	Apparatur *f* zur Prüfung *f* der Werbewirkung *f*	program analyzer
appareils *m/pl* audio-visuels	audiovisuelle Geräte *n/pl*	audio-visual equipment
appartenance *f* politique	politische Richtung *f*	political adherence
appât *m*	Köder *m*	bait, loss leader, lure
appel *m*	Anreiz *m*, Appell *m*	appeal, incitement
appel *m* à l'humanité *f*	Ansprache *f* des Menschlichen *n*	human appeal
appel *m* au bonheur *m* domestique	Ansprache *f* des Familiengefühls *n*	family appeal
appel *m* au désir *m* d'achat *m*	Kaufappell *m*	sales *pl* appeal, selling emphasis
appel *m* au sentiment *m* de famille *f*	Ansprache *f* des Familiengefühls *n*	family appeal
appel *m* au snobisme *m*	Ansprache *f* des Snobismus *m*	snob appeal
appel *m* aux urnes *f/pl*	Wahlaufruf *m*	election proclamation
appel *m* interurbain	Ferngespräch *n*	trunk call
appel *m* personnel	persönliche Ansprache *f*	personal approach
appel *m* pressant à l'acheteur *m*	direkter Kaufappell *m*	direct selling emphasis
appel *m* renouvelé aux consommateurs *m/pl*	wiederholte Konsumentenansprache *f*	repeataudience
appel *m* téléphonique	Telefonanruf *m*	telephone call

appel *m* via l'enfant *m*	Ansprache *f* auf dem Wege *m* über das Kind *n*	kid appeal
appeler	abrufen	to call
appellation *f*	Firmenname *m*, Markenname *m*	brand name, trade name
appendice *m*	Anhang *m*	annex, appendix, supplement
apperception *f*	bewußte Wahrnehmung *f*	apperception
apprêter le papier *m*	technische Oberflächengestaltung *f* eines Papiers *n*	finish
approche *f*	Schriftweite *f*	width of type
approvisionnement *m*	Lebensmittelversorgung *f*	catering
approximation *f*	Näherungswert *m*	approximation
appui *m*	Unterstützung *f*	support
appui-livres *m/pl*	Bücherstützen *f/pl*	book-ends *pl*
après coup *m*	nachträglich	afterwards, later on
après texte *m*	textanschließend	facing matter, following matter, next to reading matter
apte à être reproduit	reproduktionsreif	able to be reproduced
apurer la facture *f*	Rechnung *f* prüfen	to check the invoice, to verify the invoice
aquarelle *f*	Aquarell *n*	wash drawing, water colour
aquatinte *f*	Aquatinta *f*	aquatint
arabesque *f*	Arabeske *f*	arabesque
arbitrage *m*	Gutachten *n*, Sachverständigengutachten *n*	expert opinion
arbitre *m*	Schiedsrichter *m*	arbitrator, umpire
arbre *m* de décision *f*	baumartiges Entscheidungsschema *n*	decision tree
archive *f* des journaux *m/pl*	Zeitungsarchiv *n*	newspaper archives *pl*
archives *f/pl*	Archiv *n*	archives *pl*, record office
archives *f/pl* des clichés *m/pl*	Klischeearchiv *n*	collection of picture blocks *pl*
archives *f/pl* photographiques	Fotoarchiv *n*	art library
ardillon *m*	Taster *m*	drop fingers *pl*
argot *m*	Jargon *m*, Slang *m*	jargon, slang
argot *m* publicitaire	Werbechinesisch *n*, Werbejargon *m*	advertising argot
argument *m* de publicité *f*	Werbeargument *n*	advertising angle, advertising point
argument *m* de vente *f*	Verkaufsargument *n*	sales *pl* argument, selling angle, selling point
argumentaire *m*	Verkäufermerkblatt *n*	salesfolder, switch over
argumentation *f*	Argumentation *f*, Gesprächspunkte *m/pl*	talking points *pl*
argumentation *f* de vente *f*	Verkaufsappell *m*, Verkaufsargumentation *f*	purchase proposition, sales *pl* appeal
arguments *m/pl* en faveur d'une marchandise *f*	sprechende Argumente *n/pl*	talking points *pl*
argus *m* de la presse *f*	Zeitungsausschnittbüro *n*	clipping agency, press-cutting service
argutie *f*	fadenscheinige Ausrede	quibble
arme *f* publicitaire	Werbewaffe *f*	advertising weapon
armoire *f* à dessins *m/pl*	Zeichnungsarchiv *n*	plan-filing cabinet
armoire *f* pour clichés *m/pl*	Klischeeschrank *m*	block cabinet
armoire *f*-classeur *m*	Kartei *f*	card index, file, filing cabinet

arrangement *m*	Abkommen *n*, Abmachung *f*, Aufmachung *f*	agreement, arrangement, make up, settlement
arrangement *m* asymétrique	asymmetrische Anordnung *f*	informal balance, off-center arrangement
arrangement *m* concernant les abonnements *m/pl* aux journaux *m/pl* et écrits *m/pl* périodiques	Postzeitungsdienst *m*	postal newspaper service
arrangement *m* typographique	Satzanordnung *f*	typographical arrangement
arranger	abmachen, aufmachen, bearbeiten, disponieren	to adapt, to agree, to arrange, to dispose, to dress, to give instructions *pl*, to make up, to settle
arrête *f* de coupe *f*	Schnittkante *f*	butt line
arrêter la presse *f* à imprimer	Druckpresse *f* anhalten	to hold presses *pl*
arrière *m*	Heck *n*	rear
arriéré *m* de travail *m*	Arbeitsrückstand *m*	backlog
arrière *f* (un seul panneau *m*)	Heckschild *n*	single back panel
arrière-pensée *f*	Hintergedanke *m*	mental reservation
arrière-plan *m*	Hintergrund *m*	background
arrière-saison *f*	Nachsaison *f*	post season
arriver dans un fondu *m*	aufblenden	to wipe on
arrondir	rundbiegen	to bend round
art *m*	Kunst *f*	art
art *m* commercial	Werbegrafik *f*	advertising art, commercial art
art *m* de la mise *f* en scène *f*	effektvolle Darbietung *f*	showmanship
art *m* de vendre	Verkaufstechnik *f*	salesmanship
art *m* publicitaire	Gebrauchsgrafik *f*, Werbekunst *f*	advertising art, applied art, commercial art
article *m*	Artikel *m*, Aufsatz *m*	article, essay
article *m* à cheval *m*	überlaufender Artikel *m*	jump story
article *m* annoncé en couverture *f*	Titelgeschichte *f*	cover story
article *m* bâclé	zurechtgepfuschter Artikel *m*, zusammengestoppelte Geschichte *f*	patched-up story
article *m* blanchi	Artikel *m* mit viel Zwischenschlag *m*	double-leaded article
article *m* -cadeau *m*	Geschenkartikel *m*	give-away, novelty
article *m* clé *f*	Stapelware *f*	staple article
article *m* concurrentiel	Konkurrenzartikel *m*	rival article
article *m* d'appel *m*	Lockartikel *m*, Grundsatzartikel *m*	bait, catch-penny article, loss leader, lure, summary lead
article *m* de consommation *f*	Konsumartikel *m*	article of consumption
article *m* de fond *m*	Leitartikel *m*, Spitze *f* (redaktionell)	editorial, lead story, leader, leading article
article *m* de grosse vente *f*	Verkaufsschlager *m*	bestseller
article *m* de journal *m*	Zeitungsartikel *m*	newspaper article
article *m* de marque *f*	Markenartikel *m*	branded goods *pl*, specialty goods *pl*
article *m* de ménage *m*	Haushaltsartikel *m*	hard goods *pl*
article *m* de modes *f/pl*	Modeartikel *m*	fashion article
article *m* de réclame *f*	Lockartikel *m*, Reklameartikel *m*	advertising article, bait, catch-penny article, door opener, loss leader, lure
article *m* de série *f*	Massenartikel *f*, Serienartikel *m*	bulk article, mass produced article

article *m* de tête *f*	Aufmacher *m*, Leitartikel *m*	editorial, leader, leading article
article *m* documentaire	Dokumentarbericht *m*	background story, feature
article *m* écrit pour un journal *m*	redaktioneller Beitrag *m*	contribution
article *m* exclusif	Exklusivbeitrag *m*	exclusive contribution
article *m* fondamental	Stapelware *f*	staple article
article *m* incendiaire	Hetzartikel *m*	inflammatory article
article *m* léger	leichte Plauderei *f*	chatly article, small talk
article *m* lourd et indigeste	unverdaulicher Artikel *m*	pig iron
article *m* objectif	objektiver Artikel *m*	balanced article
article *m* passé de mode *m*	veraltete Ware *f*	stale article
article *m* prime *f*	Geschenkartikel *m*, Werbegeschenkartikel *m*, Zugabeartikel *m*	advertising premium, give-away
article *m* qui fait le point *m*	Situationsbericht *m*	situation story
article *m* rédactionnel	redaktioneller Artikel *m*	editorial
article *m* saisonnier	Saisonartikel *m*	seasonal goods *pl*
article *m* sentimental	rührselige Geschichte *f*	sob-story
article *m* signé	gezeichneter Artikel *m*	bylined story
article *m* spécialisé	Sonderbericht *m*	feature article
article *m* tapageur	auffallender Artikel *m*	stunt article
articles *m/pl* de luxe *m*	Luxuswaren *f/pl*	luxury goods *pl*
articles *m/pl* industriels	Produktionsgüter *n/pl*	industrial goods *pl*, producer's goods *pl*
artifice *m* publicitaire	Werbetrick *m*	advertising gimmick
artificiel	künstlich	artificial
artisanat *m*	Gewerbe *n*	craft, trade
artiste *m*	Künstler *m*	artist
artiste *m* -créateur *m*	Gestalter *m*	creative artist, designer, draughtsman, visualizer
artiste *m* en chef *m*	Chefgrafiker *m*	art director
artiste *m* en publicité *f*	Werbegrafiker *m*	advertising artist, advertising designer
arts *m/pl* industriels	angewandte Kunst *f*	applied art
aspect *m* typographique	Satzbild *n*, typografisches Bild *m*	typographical aspect
assemblée *f*	Versammlung *f*	meeting
assembler	zusammenfügen	to collate, to collect
assertion *f* publicitaire	Werbebehauptung *f*	claim
assigner	zuteilen	to allocate, to allot
assistance *f* rédactionnelle	redaktionelle Unterstützung *f*	editorial assistance, editorial support
assistant *m*	Assistent *m*	assistant
assistant *m* du rédacteur *m*	Hilfsredakteur *m*	leg man
assistant *m* en publicité *f*	Werbeassistent *m*	advertising assistant
association *f*	Verband *m*	association
association *f* de publicité *f*	Werbefachverband *m*, Werbeverband *m*	advertising association
assortiment *m*	Sortiment *n*	assortment, choice
assortiment *m* large	breites Sortiment *n*	variety
assurance *f* des abonnés *m/pl*	Abonnentenversicherung *f*	assurance of subscribers *pl*
astérique *f*	Sternchen *n*	asterisk
asymétrie *f*	Asymmetrie *f*	asymmetry
atelier *m*	Atelier *n*, Aufnahmeraum *m*, Studio *n*, Werkstatt *f*	studio, workshop
atelier *m* de composition *f*	Setzerei *f*, Setzersaal *m*	back room, case room, composing room

atelier *m* de composition *f* des travaux *m/pl* de ville *f*	Akzidenzsetzerei *f*	jobbing case room, trade compositors *pl*
atelier *m* de dessin *m*	Zeichenatelier *n*	drawing studio
atelier *m* de lithographie *f*	lithografische Anstalt *f*	lithographic plant
atelier *m* de photogravure *f*	Klischeeanstalt *f*	block maker, cliché manufactory, engraving plant
atelier *m* de reliure *f*	Buchbinderei *f*	binding department, bookbindery
atelier *m* typographique	Typo-Studio *n*	type-design
atrocités *f/pl* inventées	Greuelmärchen *n*	atrocity story
attaché *m* de presse *f*	Presseattaché *m*, Pressereferent *m*	press attaché, press officer
attachement *m* à la revue *f*	Leserverbundenheit *f*	reader's attachment
attaque *f* publicitaire	Werbeattacke *f*	advertising attack
attendre ordre *m* d'insertion *f*	Terminauftrag *m*	wait order
attention *f*	Aufmerksamkeit *f*, Beachtung *f*	attention
attestation *f*	Empfehlungsschreiben *n*	testimonial
attirer des clients *m/pl*	Kunden *m/pl* gewinnen	to acquire customers *pl*, to attract customers *pl*, to drum
attitude *f*	Einstellung *f*, Verhalten *n*	attitude, behaviour, mental set
attrait *m*	Anziehungskraft *f*	appeal, attraction, attractive power
attrait *m* du message *m* publicitaire	Attraktivität *f* der Anzeigenaussage *f*	copy appeal
attrait *m* publicitaire	Werbeappell *m*, Zugkraft *f*	advertising appeal, attention value, attraction, pulling power
attrape *f*	Attrappe *f*, Schaupackung *f*	display package, dummy pack, mock-up
attrape-regard *m*	Blickfang *m*	approach, catch phrase, eye appeal, eye catcher, hook, stopper
attrape-sou *m*	Pfennigartikel *m*	catch-penny article
attribution *f* de la commande *f*	Auftragsüberschreibung *f*	remittance of an order
attribution *f* d'une concession *f*	Konzessionierung *f*	licensing
attribution *f* d'une licence *f*	Franchising *n*, Lizenzübertragung *f*	franchising system
attribution *f* d'une prime *f*	Prämiierung *f*	awarding of a prize
au hasard *m*	zufällig	random
au niveau *m* des derniers progrès *m/pl*	zeitgemäß	up to date
au plus tard	spätestens	at the latest
aubette *f*	Zeitungsstand *m*	kiosk *brit*, newsstall, newsstand *am*
au-dessus des partis *m/pl*	überparteilich	neutral, non-partisan
au-dessus et à côté *m* du texte *m*	über und neben Text *m*	over and next text matter
audibilité *f*	Hörbarkeit *f*	audibility
audience *f*	Leserschaft *f*, Publikum *n*, Zuhörerschaft *f*	audience, readers *pl*, readership
audience *f* captive	eingefangenes Publikum *n*	captive audience
audience *f* choisie arbitrairement	willkürlich ausgewählter Personenkreis *m*	chunk
audience *f* cumulative	Gesamtzahl *f* der Hörer *m/pl*	cumulative audience

audience f de la radio f	Rundfunkhörerschaft f	broadcast audience, radio audience
audience f d'insertion f	Anzeigenbeachtung f	ad-audience
audience f totale	Gesamtpublikum n	audience flow
audience f utile	Zielgruppe f	intended group, target audience, target group
audimètre m, audiomètre m	Audimeter m, Aufnahmeapparat m zur Feststellung f der Hörerzahl f	audimeter, audiometer
audiovision f	Kassettenfernsehen n	audiovision, commercial
auditeur m	Hörer m, Rundfunkhörer m, Zuhörer m	listener
auditeurs m/pl	Hörerschaft f	audience
auditoire m cumulatif	erfaßte Personen-Gesamtzahl f	cumulative audience
augmentation f	Erhöhung f	increase
augmentation f de commande f	Auftragserweiterung f	enlargement of an order, extension of an order
augmentation f de prix m	Preiserhöhung f, Preissteigerung f	advance in price, mark up, price boost
augmentation f de publicité f	Werbeintensivierung f	advertising accumulation
augmentation f du chiffre m d'affaires f/pl	Umsatzsteigerung f	increase in turnover
auréole f	Nimbus m	halo effect
auteur m	Autor m, Schriftsteller m, Urheber m, Verfasser m	author, publicist, writer
auteur m à effets m/pl corsés	Sensationsschriftsteller m	sensational writer
autocollant m de vitrine f	Fensterklebeplakat n, Schaufensterkleber m	window sticker, window streamer
autocontrôle m	Selbstkontrolle f	self-regulation
autographe m	Urschrift f	original manuscript
autolithographie f	Autolithografie f	lithography drawn on plate
autorisation f	Bewilligung f	permit
autorisation f de publier	Druckfreigabe f	release
autotypie f	Autotypie f, Duplex-Autotypie f	autotype, duplex half-tone block (brit), duplex half-tone cut am, half-tone block, half-tone plate am, process engraving
autotypie f détourée	spitzgeätzte Autotypie f	drop-out halftone
autotypie f en silhouette f	freistehende Autotypie f	blocked-out half-tone, outline half-tone, silhouette half-tone
autotypie f rectangulaire	rechteckige Vollautotypie i	square half-tone
autotypie f zinc	Zinkautotypie f	zinc halftone
aux goûts m/pl compliqués	kultiviert	sophisticated
avancer	vorverlegen	to put forward
avant la parution f	vor Erscheinen n	before issue
avant l'insertion f	vor Einschaltung f	before insertion
avantage m	Vergünstigung f	sales pl allowance
avant-garde f	fortschrittlich, Vorhut f	advanced, go-ahead, pioneers pl, progressive
avant-papier m	Artikel m, der vor dem Ereignis n geschrieben wurde	advance story
avant-première f	Vorschau f	pre-view, trailer
avant-propos m	Vorrede f	introduction

avant-titre *m*	Schmutztitel *m*	bastard title, half-title
avilissement *m* **des prix** *m/pl*	Preisschleuderei *f*	price slashing
avion *m* **publicitaire**	Werbeflugzeug *n*	advertising aeroplane
avis *m*	Durchsage *f*, Familienanzeige *f*, Fingerzeig *m*	announcement, family announcement, personal announcement, tip
avis *m* **au lecteur** *m*	Vorbemerkung *f*	prefatory note, preliminary remark
avis *m* **financier**	Finanzanzeige *f*	financial advertisement
avis *m* **juridique**	Rechtsgutachten *n*	legal opinion
avis *m* **officiel**	amtliche Bekanntmachung *f*, amtliches Plakat *n*	legal notice, official notice, official poster
avis *m* **placardé**	Wandanschlag *m*	notices *pl* on wall
avis *m* **préalable**	Vorankündigung *f*, Voranzeige *f*	advance notice, preliminary announcement
avis *m* **radiodiffusé**	Ankündigung *f* im Rundfunk *m*	broadcast announcement
avoir l'antenne *f*	im Rundfunk *m* sprechen,	to be on the air
av-spot *m*	Kasetteninsert *n*	av-commercial
axe *m* **de la publicité** *f*	Werbegesichtswinkel *m*, Werbegrundaussage *f*, Werbeplattform *f*	advertising angle, advertising approach, basic message, copy platform, unique selling proposition

B

bafouillage *m*	Versprecher *m*	fluff
bagatelliser	verniedlichen	to make light, to soft-pedal
baguette *f*	schwarzer Rand *m*	black border, black frame, thick frame
bail *m* **à ferme** *f*	Pachtvertrag *m*	contract of lease
bail *m* **de fichiers** *m/pl* **d'adresses** *f/pl*	Adressenkartei — Vermietung *f*	list-broking
bailleur *m*	Verpächter *m*	landlord
baîllonnement *m* **de la presse** *f*	Presseknebelung *f*	gagging of the press, muzzling of the press, stifling of the press
bain *m* **de chrome** *m*	Chrombad *n*	chrome bath
baisser les phares *m/pl*	abblenden	to wipe off
ballon *m*	Sprechblase *f*	balloon caption, bubble, speech balloon
ballon *m* **d'essai** *m*	Versuchsballon *m*	trial balloon
ballon *m* **publicitaire**	Werbeballon *m*	advertising balloon
banalité *f*	Gemeinplatz *m*	commonplace, platitude
banc *m* **de la presse** *f*	Presseloge *f*	press-box
banc *m* **de presse** *f*	Auslegetisch *m*	delivery table
bande *f* **à masquer**	Abdeckstreifen *m*	masking tape
bande *f* **adhésive**	Klebeband *n*	adhesive tape
bande *f* **de film** *m*	Bildstreifen *m*	film strip
bande *f* **de journal** *m*	Streifband *n*	wrapper
bande *f* **de lancement** *m*	Vorschau *f*	pre-view, trailer
bande *f* **de publicité** *f*	Bauchbinde *f*	band
bande *f* **d'étagère** *f*	Regalstreifen *m*	shelf-strip
bande *f* **d'illustrations** *f/pl*	Bilderserie *f*	strip
bande *f* **d'un film** *m*	Filmstreifen *m*	film strip
bande *f* **gommée**	Klebestreifen *m*	gummed strip

bande *f* internationale	Tonband *n* ohne Worte *n*/*pl*, Tonstreifen *m*	sound track, tape recording without words *pl*
bande *f* magnétique	Tonband *n*	audio tape
bande *f* magnétique vidéo	Magnetband *n*, Magnettonband *n*, Videoband *n*	magnetic tape, videotape
bande *f* perforée	Lochstreifen *m*	paper tape, punched tape
bande *f* sans ton *m*	Filmstreifen *m* ohne Ton *m*	picture track
bandeau *m*	Streifenanzeige *f*, Wimpel *m*	advertisement panel, band, banner, pelmet, pennant, streamer, strip
bandeau *m* arrière	Heckstreifen *m*	rear waistband
bandeau *m* de magasin *m*	Firmenschild *n* mit Fremdreklame *f*	fascia
bandeau *m* de tête *f*	Kopfleiste *f*	head piece, head rules *pl*, headband
bandeau *m* général	Obertitel *m* über mehrere Aufsätze *m*/*pl* mit demselben Thema *n*	binder line
banderole *f*	Dachschild *n*, Spruchband *n*, Werbewimpel *m*	banner, calico, pennant, roof panel, streamer
bandes *f*/*pl* dessinées	Comic Strip *m*, humoristischer Bilderstreifen *m*	comic strip
bannière *f* murale	Spannplakat *n*	wall banner
bannière *f* tractée par avion *m*	Bannerschlepper *m*, Schleppfahne *f*	airplane banner
baragouin *m*	Kauderwelsch *n*	gibberish, gobbledygook
baratin *m*	Geschwätz *n*	balderdash
barbe *f*	Büttenrand *m*	deckle edge
bardage *m*	Lattenzaun *m*	lattice work
barème *m*	Tarifstaffel *f*	differential price system
barème *m* dégressif	Rabattstaffel *f*	scale of discount, sliding scale
baromètre *m* des marques *f*/*pl*	Markenindex *m*	brand trend survey
barre *f* de fraction *f* oblique	Bruchstrich *m*, Schrägstrich *m*	oblique stroke
barre-route *f*	rechtwinklig zum Verkehrsfluß *m*	head on position
barrière *f* de langue *f*	Sprachbarriere *f*	language barrier
bas	niedrig	low
bas *m* de la page *f* droite	rechts unten	bottom right
bas de la page *f* gauche	links unten	bottom left
bas *m* de page *f*	am Fuß *m* einer Seite *f*	bottom of page, foot of page
basculer	umschlagen	to work and turn
base *f*	Grundlage *f*	basis
base *f* de calcul *m*	Berechnungsgrundlage *f*	base of calculation
base *f* d'une discussion *f*	Diskussionsbasis *f*	basis for discussion
bases *f*/*pl* de la décision *f*	Entscheidungsgrundlagen *f*/*pl*	fundamentals *pl* of decision
les basses classes *f*/*pl*	untere Schicht *f*	lower class
bâton *m*	Grotesk *f*	grotesque, sans-serif
battage *m* publicitaire	marktschreierische Werbung *f*, Werberummel *m*	ballyhoo *am*, hoopla, noisy advertising, puffing publicity
battre la grosse caisse *f*	die Werbetrommel *f* rühren	to boost, to make propaganda, to push
bavardage *m*	Klatschgeschichte *f*	gossip, tittle-tattle
bavardeur *m*	Wortemacher *m*	idle talker
bazar *m*	Kaufhaus *n*, Warenhaus *n*	department store
bélinogramme *m*	Bildtelegramm *n*	telephotograph

bélinographie *f*	Bildfunk *m*, Bildtelegrafie *f*	photo-telegraphy, wireless picture transmission, wirephoto
belle copie *f*	druckfertiges Manuskript *n*	fair copy
belle page *f*	Aufschlagseite *f*, Schauseite *f*	eye-catching right-hand page, recto
belles-lettres *f/pl*	Belletristik *f*, schöne Literatur *f*	fiction
bénéfice *m*	Gewinn *m*	gain, profit
besoin *m*	Bedarf *m*	need, want
besoin *m* de remplacement *m*	Ersatzbedarf *m*	replacement demand
besoin *m* latent	latenter Bedarf *m*	hidden demand
besoin *m* propre	Eigenbedarf *m*	personal requirements *pl*
bêtises *f/pl*	Geschwätz *n*	balderdash
bévue *f*	Sprachschnitzer *m*, Stilblüte *f*	bull, flaw, grammatical blunder
bibelots *m/pl*	Akzidenzarbeit *f*	jobbing work
bibliographie *f*	Bibliografie *f*, Literaturverzeichnis *n*	bibliography
bibliothécaire *m*	Bibliothekar *m*	librarian
bibliothèque *f*	Bibliothek *f*, Bücherei *f*	library
bibliothèque *f* de gare *f*	Bahnhofsbuchhandlung *f*	bookstall
bichromie *f*	Zweifarbendruck *m*	two-colour process
bien disposé	übersichtlich	clearly arranged, standardized
bien informé	gut unterrichtet	well-informed
biens *m/pl* de consommation *f*	Konsumgüter *f/pl*, Verbrauchsgüter *n/pl*	consumer goods *pl*, nondurable goods *pl*, shopping goods *pl*
biens *m/pl* de consommation *f* durables	langlebige Gebrauchsgüter *n/pl*	hard goods *pl*
biens *m/pl* de production *f*	Investitionsgüter *n/pl*, Produktionsgüter *n/pl*	capital goods *pl*, industrial goods *pl*, producer's goods *pl*
biens *m/pl* d'investissement *m*		
biens *m/pl* industriels	Industriegüter *n/pl*	industrial goods *pl*
biffer	ausstreichen, tilgen	to cross, to delete, to take out
bi-hebdo	zweimal wöchentlich	twice weekly
bi-hebdomadaire	zweiwöchentlich	bi-weekly
bilan *m*	Schlußergebnis *n*	balance
bilatéral	zweiseitig	double-sided, two-sided
bilboquet *m*	Akzidenzdruck *m*	job printing, jobbing work
bilingue	zweisprachig	bilingual
billet *m* de loterie *f*	Lotterielos *n*	lottery-ticket
bimensuel	halbmonatlich	twice monthly
bimestriel	alle zwei Monate *m/pl*, zweimonatlich	bi-monthly
biographie *f*	Biografie *f*	biography
bi-quotidien	zweimal täglich	twice daily
biseauter	abschleifen	to bevel
bla-bla-bla *m*	Flausen *f/pl*	blah-blah
black-out *m*	Nachrichtensperre *f*	ban on news, news blackout
blanc *m*	Aussparung *f*, Fleisch *n* eines Buchstabens *m*	beard, bevelled feet *pl*, blank space, burr, recess
blanc couvrant	Deckweiß *n*	zinc white
blanc *m* de pied *m*	Fußsteg *m*, Unterschlag *m*	footstick, tail
blanc *m* du petit fond *m*	Bundsteg *m*	back margin, gutter-stick, inner margin
blanc *m* transversal	Kreuzsteg *m*	gutter
blanchet *m*	Drucktuch *n*	blanket

blanchir	durchschießen, spationieren, sperren	to interline, to lead out, to space out
blancs *m/pl*	Blindmaterial *n*, Füllmaterial *n*, Leerdruck *m*	blank material, blanks *pl*, clumps *pl*, leads *pl*, spacing material
bloc *m* à dessin *m*	Zeichenblock *m*	sketching block, sketchblock *am*
bloc *m* de métal *m*	Metallblock *m*	metal log
blocage *m*	Blockade *f*, Fliegenkopf *m/typog*	black, turned letter
blocage *m* de commandes *f/pl*	Auftragssperre *f*	blockade of orders *pl*
blocage *m* effacement *m*	Austastlücke *f*	field blanking interval
bloc-notes *m/pl*	Notizblock *m*, Schreibblock *m*	scratch-pad, scribbling-pad
blocus *m* de nouvelles *f/pl*	Nachrichtensperre *f*	ban on news, news blackout
bloquer une lettre *f*	ausblocken, blockieren	to block out, to turn a letter
bobard *m*	Ente *f*, Seeschlange *f/fig*, Zeitungsente *f*	fake, hoax, mare's nest
bobine *f* cinématographique	Filmspule *f*	film reel
bobine *f* de la bande *f* magnétique	Magnetfilmspule *f*	magnetic film spool
bobine *f* de papier *m*	Papierrolle *f*	paper roll
bois *m* gravé	Holzschnitt *m*	wood cut, wood engraving
boîte *f* à défets *m/pl*	Zeugkiste *f*	hell box
boîte *f* d'expédition *f*	Versandschachtel *f*	transport case
bombage *m*	Blinddruck *m*, Prägedruck *m*	blind stamping, embossing
bon *m*	Bon *m*	coupon, credit slip
bon *m* à découper	Kupon *m*	coupon
bon à imprimer, bon à tirer	druckfertig, druckreif, gut zum Druck *m*, Imprimatur *n*	passed for press, ready for printing, good for printing *brit.*, o. k. to print, o.k. *am*, permission to print, ready for press
bon à tirer après corrections *f/pl*	druckreif nach Korrektur *f*	good for printing with corrections *pl*, o. k. with corrections *pl am*
bon *m* à valoir	Gutschein *m*	coupon, credit slip, gift voucher
bon *m* de caisse *f*	Kassenbon *m*	shop bill
bon *m* de commande *f*	Auftragsformular *n*, Bestellschein *m*	order form, subscription form
à bon marché *m*	preisgünstig	budget-priced, economy-priced
bonbon *m* fondant	sentimentale Literatur *f*	sob-stuff, squish
bonification *f*	Bonus *m*, Vergütung *f*	bonus, fee
boniment *m*	Verkaufsgespräch *n*, Warenanpreisung *f*	sales *pl* talk
boniments *m/pl*	leeres Geschwätz *n*	bunkum, hokum
bonisseur *m*	Anreißer *m*	tout
bonne feuille *f*	Aushängebogen *m*, Vorabdruck *m*	advance publication, advance sheet, specimen sheet
bonne page *f*	rechte Seite *f*	odd page, right-hand page
bonne réputation *f*	guter Ruf *m*	good will
bonne vieille radio *f* papa *m*	Dampfradio *n*	steam radio
bonne vue *f* d'ensemble *m*	Übersichtlichkeit *f*	clarity
bord *m*	Kante *f*, Rand *m*	edge, margin
bord *m* à la cuve *f*	Büttenrand *m*	deckle edge
bord *m* biseauté	Klischeefacette *f*	bevelled edge

bord *m* **de coupe** *f*	Schnittrand *m*	bleed
bord *m* **de coupure** *f* **doublé**	randkaschiert	edge-turned passe-partout
bord *m* **des pinces** *f/pl*	Greiferkante *f*	gripper edge
bord *m* **du papier** *m*	Papierkante *f*	edge
bord *m* **extérieur**	Außenspalte *f*	outside position
border	einfassen	to border, to box in, to frame
bordure *f*	Bordüre *f*, Einfassung *f*, Einrahmung *f*, Zierleiste *f*	border, frame, tail piece
bordure *f* **d'annonce** *f*	Anzeigeneinfassung *f*	advertisement border
bordure *f* **de filet** *m* **mat**	fette Umrandung *f* schwarzer Rand *m*, Trauerrand *m*	black border, black frame, heavy frame, thick frame
bordure *f* **en filets** *m/pl*	Linienrand *m*	line border, ruled frame
boîte *f* **des horaires** *m/pl* **des trains** *m/pl*	Fahrplankasten *m*	box of time-table
boîte *f* **factice**	Schaupackung *f*	display package, dummy pack, mock-up
boîte *f* **pliante**	Faltschachtel *f*	collapsible carton, folding box
boîte *f* **pour cadeaux** *m/pl*	Geschenkpackung *f*	gift wrapping
Bottin *m*	Handelsadreßbuch *n*	commercial directory, trade directory
Bottin *m* **téléphonique**	Telefonbuch *n*	telephone book *am*, telephone directory
bouche-trou *m*	Füller *m*, Lückenbüßer *m*	cushion, fill-up, filler, quadder, stop gap advertisement
bouclage *m*	Druckformschluß *m*, Redaktionsschluß *m*	closing date, closing down, closing down, copy deadline, forms *pl* close
boucler	Form *f* schließen	to lock up a form, to quoin
boucler un compte *m*	abrechnen	to account, to invoice
boucler une page *f*	Form *f* schließen	to close the form, to lock up a form
bouillon *m*	Fehlstreuung *f*, Remittenden *f/pl*, unverkaufte Exemplare *n/pl*	overrun, remainders *pl*, returns *pl*, unsold copies *pl*, waste circulation
bouillon *m* **déduit moyen**	durchschnittliche Verkaufsauflage *f*	average net paid circulation, average sold circulation
boule *f*	Kugel *f*	bullet, sphere
bouquin *m*	Schmöker *m*	old book
bouquineur *m*	Leseratte *f*	book-hunter, paper worm
bourdon *m*	Auslassung *f*, Leiche *f* Schusterjunge *m/typog*	missing word, omission, omitted word in composition, out
bourgeois *m*	bürgerlich, Mittelstand *m*	middle-class
bourrage *m* **de crâne** *m*	marktschreierische Werbung *f*, Stimmungsmache *f*	ballyhoo *am*, belabouring public feeling, noisy advertising, puffing publicity
bourrer	vollstopfen	to jam-pack
bourreur *m* **de lignes** *f/pl*	Zeilenschinder *m*	penny-a-liner
bousillage *m*	Pfuscharbeit *f*	bingling, scamped work
bout *m* **de ligne** *f*	Kurzzeile *f*	broken line, short line, widow
boutade *f*	Einfall *m*	flash, gag, idea
boutique *f* **de vente** *f*	Verkaufsstand *m*	stall
boutique *f* **d'essai** *m*	Testladen *m*	audit store, test shop
boutique *f* **franche**	zollfreies Geschäft *n*	duty free shop

boutique *f* **mobile**	Wanderladen *m*	mobile shop
bouton *m*	Ansteckplakette *f*	button
boycottage *m* **de supports** *m/pl* **publicitaires**	Werbeboykott *m*	boycotting of advertising media *pl*
boycottage *m* **d'un journal** *m*	Zeitungsboykott *m*	boycotting of a journal
bradage *m*	Preisunterbietung *f*, Schleuderpreis *m*	cut rate, cut-throat price, dumping, give-away price, price-cutting
braille *m*	Blindenschrift *f*	Braille
brain-trust *m*	Experten *m/pl* -Zusammenschluß *m*, Gehirntrust *m*	brain trust
branche *f*	Branche *f*	business line
brêche *f* **d'approvisionnement** *m*	Versorgungslücke *f*	gap in supplies *pl*
bref communiqué *m* **radio** *f*	Werbedurchsage *f*, Werbeeinblendung *f*	chain break, commercial, radio announcement, spot announcement
bref sommaire *m* **des nouvelles** *f/pl*	kurzgefaßter Bericht *m*	pony report
brève information *f*	Kurzanzeige *f*	short announcement
bricoleur *m*	Faktotum *n*	handy man
brise-glace *m*	Eisbrecher *m*	lead-in, warm-up
brocantage *m*	Gebrauchtwarenmarkt *m*	second hand market
brocard *m*	Stichelei *f*	squib
brochage *m*	Broschur *f*	stitching
brochage *m* **à cheval** *m*	Sattelheftung *f*	saddle stitching
brochage *m* **Lumbeck**	Lumbeckheftung *f*	Lumbeck binding
broché	geheftet	stitched
brocher	broschieren, heften	to fasten, to sew, to stitch
brocher dans	einheften	to bind into, to stitch in
brochure *f*	Flugblatt *n*, Flugschrift *f*, Prospekt *m*, Werbefaltblatt *n*	booklet, chap-book, folder, handbill, leaflet, pamphlet, prospectus, tract
brochure *f* **à cheval** *m*	Rückstichheftung *f*	wire stitching
brochure *f* **commémorative**	Festschrift *f*	commemorative volume
brochure *f* **de vulgarisation** *f*	Aufklärungsschrift *f*	popular pamphlet
brochure *f* **d'information** *f*	Informationsbroschüre *f*	information brochure
brochure *f* **publicitaire**	Werbebroschüre *f*, Werbeschrift *f*	advertising brochure, advertising pamphlet
bronzage *m*	Bronzedruck *m*	bronze printing
brosse *f*	Kleisterbesen *m*	brush
brouiller	durcheinanderbringen	to scramble
brouillon *m*	erster unfertiger Entwurf *m*, Konzept *n*, Waschzettel *m*	dope, draft, hand-out, press-release, publisher's blurb, publisher's note, rough copy, scribble, slip
brouillon *m* **d'un scénario** *m*	Drehbuchentwurf *m*	treatment
broyer des couleurs *f/pl*	Farben *f/pl* reiben	to grind colours *pl*
bruit *m*	Gerücht *n*	rumour
bruit *m* **de fond** *m*	Hintergrundgeräusche *n/pl*	ground noise
bruit *m* **de voix** *f*	Stimmengeräusch *n*	buzz
bruitage *m*	Geräuscheffekte *m/pl*	sound effects *pl*
bruits *m/pl* **parasites**	Nebengeräusche *n/pl*	atmospherics *pl*, buzz
bruits *m/pl* **qui courent**	umlaufende Gerüchte *n/pl*	current reports *pl*
brunissage *m*	Politur *f*	burnishing
budget *m*	Budget *n*, Etat *m*	account, appropriation, budget
budget *m* **alloué**	Etatsanteil *m*	allocation

budget *m* alloué de publicité *f*	bewilligter Werbeetat *m*	advertising appropriation
budget *m* de publicité *f*	Werbehaushalt *m*	advertising appropriation
budget *m* publicitaire	genehmigte Werbemittel *n/pl*, Werbebudget *n*, Werbeetat *m*, Werbeetataufzeichnung *f*	account, advertising budget, appropriation of advertising, media allocation, publicity stock
bulle *f*	Sprechblase *f*	balloon caption, bubble, speech balloon
bulletin *m*	bemalte Großfläche *f*, Bulletin *n*	bulletin, bulletin board, painted bulletin
bulletin *m* d'actualités *f/pl*	Nachrichtensendung *f*	broadcast news, news bulletin, newscast, topical talk
bulletin *m* d'information *f*	Informationsblatt *n*, Informationsorgan *n*	newsletter
bulletin *m* du jour *m*	Tagesbericht *m*	daily report
bulletin *m* du temps *m*	Wetterbericht *m*	weather-forecast, weather-report
bulletin *m* financier	Marktbericht *m*	market report
bulletin *m* littéraire	Literaturblatt *n*	notices *pl* of new publications *pl*
bulletin *m* officiel	Amtsblatt *n*	official gazette
bulletin *m* transférable	versetzbare Werbefläche *f*	rotating bulletin
bureau *m*	Geschäftsstelle *f*, Schreibtisch *m*	administrative, desk, office,
bureau *m* d'annonces *f/pl*	Anzeigenbüro *n*	advertisement office
bureau *m* de coupure *f* de journaux *m/pl*	Ausschnittdienst *m*, Zeitungsausschnittbüro *n*	clipping agency, press-cutting service, press-cutting agency
bureau *m* de télégraphe *m*	Depeschenbüro *n*	dispatch agency
bureau *m* des dépêches *f/pl*	Depeschensaal *m*	desk
bureau *m* des ventes *f/pl*	Verkaufsbüro *n*	sales *pl* office
bureau *m* d'information *f*	Nachrichtenamt *n*	information-bureau
bureau *m* du journal *m*	Annahmestelle *f*	newspaper's office
bureau *m* marketing	Marketingabteilung *f*	marketing department
burin *m*	Stichel *m*	steel engraving tool
but *m* commercial	Verkaufsziel *n*	sales *pl* objective
but *m* de publication *f*	Publikationszweck *m*	aim of the publication
buteau *m*	Firmentafel *f*	name plate

C

cabine *f* téléphonique	Telefonkabine *f*	call-box
câble *m*	Kabel *n*	cable
câbler	kabeln	to cable
câble-texte *m*	Kabeltext *m*	cable-text
câblogramme *m*	Kabeltelegramm *n*	cablegram
cache *f*	Abdeckmaske *f*, Abdeckrahmen *m*, Auflegemaske *f*, Decker *m*, Überkleber *m*, Vignette *f*	frisket, mask, masking frame, ornament, overlay, vignette
cachet *m*	Verschlußmarke *f*	sealing label
cachet *m* de caoutchouc *m*	Gummistempel *m*	rubber stamp
cachottier *m*	Geheimniskrämer *m*	mystery-monger
cadeau *m* publicitaire	Werbeartikel *m*, Werbegabe *f*, Werbegeschenk *n*	advertising donation, advertising gift, advertising novelty, free gift, specialty

cadrage *m*	Filmbildzentrierung *f*, zentrieren,	centering *brit*, centring *am*, centring of film image
cadran *m*	Zifferblatt *n*	dial
cadrat *m*	Quadrat *n*	quad, quadrat
cadratin *m*	Geviert *n*	em-quad
cadrats *m/pl*	Ausschluß *typog m*	blank space, stick space
cadre *m*	Rahmen *m*	framework
cadre *m* de filets *m/pl*	Linienrand *m*	line border, ruled frame
cadre *m* de filets *m/pl* gras-maigre	gerasteter Rahmen *m*	backed frame, shaded frame
cadre *m* de pointillés *m/pl*	gepunkteter Rand *m*, punktierter Rand *m*	dotted frame, stippled frame
cadre *m* fantaisie *f*	Zierrand *m*	fancy frame
cadre *m* interchangeable	Wechselrahmen *m*	interchangeable frame
cadre *m* ondulé	Wellenrand *m*	ondulated frame
cadreur *m*	Kameramann *m*	camera man
cafard *m*	Zwischenträger *m*	go-between, tell-tale
cahier *m*	ausgedruckter Druckbogen *m*, Lage *f* (Papier *n*), Papierlage *f*	folded printed sheet, quire, section, signature
cahier *m* de queue *f*	hinterer Teil *m* der Ausgabe *f*	back section
cahier *m* de tête *f*	vorderer Teil *m* der Ausgabe *f*	front section
caisson *m* lumineux	Leuchtkasten *m*	box sign
calage *m*	Einrichten *n* der Druckmaschine *f*	to make ready
calandre *f*	Kalander *m*	calender
calcul *m*	Berechnung *f*	calculation, computation
calcul *m* de la composition *f*	Satzberechnung *f*	casting off, character count, estimate of composition
calcul *m* des prix *m/pl*	Preisberechnung *f*	calculation of price
calculateur *m* électronique	Elektronenrechner *m*	computer
calculation *f* d'annonces *f/pl*	Anzeigenberechnung *f*	advertisement calculation
calculatrice *f*	Computer *m*	computer
calculer	kalkulieren	to calculate, to estimate
calembour *m*	Wortspiel *n*	pun, quibble
calendrier *m*	Kalender *m*	almanac, calendar
calendrier *m* à effeuiller	Abreißkalender *m*	tear-off calendar
calendrier *m* de la gestion *f*	Zeitplanung *f*	timing
calendrier *m* de termes *m/pl*	Terminkalender *m*	advertising schedule, deadline schedule
calendrier *m* des émissions *f/pl*	Funkprogramm *n*	radio programme *brit*, radio program *am*
calendrier *m* des parutions *f/pl*	Datenschema *n*, Erscheinungsplan *m*, Insertionsplan *m*, Streuplan *m*, Terminplan *m*, Zeitplan *m*	advertising schedule, aging schedule, date plan, insertion schedule, media schedule, space schedule, spread-over
calendrier *m* d'insertion *f*	Datenplan *m*	date schedule, schedule of insertions *pl*, time schedule
calendrier *m* mural	Wandkalender *m*	wall calender
calepin *m*	Notizbuch *n*	memorandum book, note-book
calibrage *m* d'une copie *f*	Manuskriptumfangsberechnung *f*	calibrating of a copy, casting off, character count, copy fitting
calibration *f*	Manuskriptumfang *m*	calibration
calibre *m*	Kalibermaß *n*	calibrator

calibrer	kalibrieren	to calibrate, to cast off, to gauge, to size
calibrer la copie *f*	auszählen (Manuskript)	to cast off
calibrer un manuscrit *m*	Satzumfang *m* berechnen	to cast-off
calicot *m*	Dachschild *n*, Kaliko *n*, Spannband *n*, Spruchband *n*, Steifleinen *n*	banner, buckram, calico, roof panel, streamer
calligraphe *m*	Schönschreiber *m*	penman
calligraphie *f*	Kalligrafie *f*, Schönschrift *f*, Schreibkunst *f*	calligraphy
calomniateur *m*	Verleumder *m*	back-biter
calomnie *f*	Verleumdung *f*	calumny, defamation, libel, slander
camelot *m*	Straßenhändler *m*, Straßenverkäufer *m*	street hawker, street vendor
camelote *f*	Schund *m*	trash
camélote *f* **de réclame** *f*	Pfennigartikel *m*	catch-penny article
caméra *f*	Filmkamera *f*	film camera
caméra *f* **d'enregistrement** *m* **du son** *m*	Tonkamera *f*	sound camera
camion *m* **publicitaire**	Lautsprecherwagen *m*	sound truck
camionette *f* **d'exposition** *f*	Ausstellungswagen *m*	exhibition van
camionette *f* **publicitaire**	Werbewagen *m*	advertising van
camionnette *f* **-boutique** *f*	fahrbare Verkaufsstelle *f*	mobile shop
camouflage *m*	getarnte Publizistik *f*, Tarnung *f*	camouflage
campagne *f*	Kampagne *f*	campaign
campagne *f* **à longue échéance** *f*	langfristig geplante Werbekampagne *f*	pre-planned advertising campaign
campagne *f* **d'affichage** *m*	Plakatanschlagkampagne *f*, Werbefeldzug *m* durch Plakatanschlag *m*	poster campaign
campagne *f* **de dénigrement** *m*	Verleumdungskampagne *f*	smear campaign
campagne *f* **de diffamation** *f*	Rufmord *m*	smear campaign
campagne *f* **de lancement** *m*	Einführungskampagne *f*	announcement campaign, initial campaign, introduction campaign
campagne *f* **de presse** *f*	Pressekampagne *f*	crusade, press campaign
campagne *f* **de publicité** *f*	Werbekampagne *f*	advertising campaign
campagne *f* **de saturation** *f*	geballte Werbung *f*	mass advertising
campagne *f* **de suite** *f*	Anschlußwerbung *f*	connexion advertising
campagne *f* **de vente** *f*	Verkaufsfeldzug *m*, Verkaufskampagne *f*	sales *pl* campaign, selling campaign
campagne *f* **d'essai** *m*	Versuchskampagne *f*	test campaign
campagne *f* **d'étalages** *m/pl*	Schaufensterauslagen-Massierung *f*	window display campaign
campagne *f* **d'information** *f*, **campagne** *f* **d'introduction** *f*	Einführungskampagne *f*	announcement campaign, initial campaign, introduction campaign
campagne *f* **électorale régionale**	regionale Wahlkampagne *f*	zone campaign
campagne *f* **locale**	örtliche Werbung *f*	local campaign
campagne *f* **mémorative**	Erinnerungskampagne *f*	reminder campaign
campagne *f* **nationale**	überregionaler Werbefeldzug *m*	general advertising, national campaign

campagne f pour des sortes f/pl différentes d'un produit m	Werbekampagne f für verschiedene Arten f/pl eines Produkts m	umbrella-campaign
campagne f publicitaire	Werbefeldzug m	advertising campaign
campagne-affiche f	Plakatanschlagkampagne f	poster campaign
camping m	Campingplatz m	camping-ground
canal m de distribution f	Vertriebsweg m	channel of distribution
canard m	Zeitungsente f	hoax, mare's nest
canardier m	Nachrichtensetzer m	news compositor
cancanier m	Klatschmaul n	scandal-monger
cancanière f	Klatschweib n	scandal-monger
canevas m	Grundzüge m/pl	groundwork
capacité f	Fassungsvermögen n	capacity
capacité f d'achat m	Kaufkraft f	buying power, purchasing power, spending power
capitale f	Majuskel f	cap
capitale f bâton m	Blockbuchstabe m	block capital, block letter
capitales f/pl	Versalien f/pl	capital letters pl, caps pl, upper case letters pl
capsule f de bouteille f	Aufstecker m, Flaschenkapsel f	crowner
captage m des messages m/pl télégraphiques	Anzapfung f der Telefonleitungen f/pl	wire-tapping
caractère m	Buchstabe m, Schrifttype f, Type f	character, face, letter, type
caractère m ancien	Antiqua f	old face type, Roman type
caractère m couché	gestürzter Buchstabe m	kerned letter
caractère m de fantaisie f	Zierschrift f	fancy letters pl, ornamental type, swash face
caractère m d'imprimerie f	Drucktype f	character, printing type
caractère m du texte m	Textschrift f	text face
caractère m étroit	Schmalschrift f	condensed type
caractère m gras	fette Schrift f, fetter Buchstabe m	bold-face type, fat type, full faced type, heavy type
caractère m italique	Kursivschrift f	Italic type, script type, sloping letters pl
caractère m large	breite Drucktype f	expanded type, extended type
caractère m mediéval	Mediäval f	old face, old style
caractère m négatif	Negativschrift f	negative type
caractère m principal	Grundschrift f	body fount, main type
caractère m propre d'une marque f	Markencharakter m	product personality
caractère m publicitaire	Werbecharakter m	advertising complexion
caractère m retourné	Blockade f	black, turned letter
caractère m romain	Antiqua f	old face type, Roman type
caractère m squelette m	Skelettschrift f	skeleton type
caractères m/pl allemands	Fraktur f	black letter, German type, Gothic type
caractères m/pl bâtons m/pl	Blockschrift f, Druckbuchstaben m/pl	block letters pl, print script
caractères m/pl courants	Brotschrift f	body type, bread-and-butter-face, ordinary type
caractères m/pl de bois m	Holzschrift f	wooden type
caractères m/pl de labeur m	Brotschrift f	body type, bread-and-butter-face, ordinary type
caractères m/pl de machine f	Schreibmaschinenschrift f	ribbon-face, type-script
caractères m/pl de travaux m/pl de ville f	Akzidenzschriften f/pl	display faces pl

caractères *m/pl* d'écriture *f*	Schreibschrift *f*	handwriting, script writing, script-type
caractères *m/pl* demi-gras	halbfetter Satz *m*	semi-bold type
caractères *m/pl* d'impression *f*	Schriftmaterial *n*	stock of type, type matter
caractères *m/pl* duplexés	Auszeichnungsschrift *f*	display type
caractères *m/pl* éclairés	lichte Schrift *f*	light-faced type
caractères *m/pl* fantaisie *f*	Künstlerschriften *f/pl*, Phantasieschriften *f/pl*	fancy types *pl*
caractères *m/pl* fondeur	Handsatzschrift *f*, Originalschrift *f*	foundry type, hand type
caractères *m/pl* gothiques	altgotische Schrift *f*, Fraktur *f*	black letter, German type, Gothic type, old black type, old English face
caractères *m/pl* gras	Fettdruck *m*, fette Schrift *f*	bold face, bold printtype, full-faced type
caractères *m/pl* haut de casse *f*	Großbuchstaben *m/pl*	capital letters *pl*, caps *pl*, large print, upper case letters *pl*
caractères *m/pl* maigres	magere Schrift *f*	lean-faced type
caractères *m/pl* ornés	Zierschrift *f*	fancy letters *pl*, ornamental type, swash face
caractères *m/pl* pour affiches *f/pl*	Plakatschrift *f*	poster lettering, poster type
caractères *m/pl* pour titre *m*	Titelschriften *f/pl*, Übergrößen *f/pl*	display types *pl*, title faces *pl*
caractères *m/pl* quart-gras	halbfette Schrift *f*, Schrift *f*, halbfette	medium faced type
caractères *m/pl* standard	Normalschrift *f*	standard text type
caractères *m/pl* typographiques	Druckschrift *f/typog*	block letters *pl*
caractéristique *f*	Charakteristikum *n*, Hauptmerkmal *n* (einer Anzeige *f*), Wesensmerkmal *n*	characteristic, feature
caravane *f* publicitaire	Werbekarawane *f*	caravan advertising
carbonnage *m*	Karbondruck *m*	carbon coating
carbonnage *m* à chaud	Transkritdruck *m*	carbon printing
caricature *f*	Karikatur *f*	caricature, cartoon
caricaturiste *m*	Karikaturist *m*	artist
carnet *m*	Agenda *f*, Notizbuch *n*	memorandum book, note-book, pocket diary
carnet *m* de commandes *f/pl*	Auftragsbuch *n*, Bestellbuch *n*	order-book
carnet *m* de timbres *m/pl* prime *f*	Rabattmarkenbuch *n*	stamp book
carnet *m* mondain	Gesellschaftschronik *f*	society news
carré *m*, carré	Quadrat *n*, viereckig	square, squared-off
carte *f*	Landkarte *f*, Speisekarte *f*	map, menu card
carte *f* de commande *f*	Bestellkarte *f*	order form
carte *f* de fichier *m*	Karteikarte *f*	index card
carte *f* de Nouvel-An *m*	Neujahrskarte *f*	New-Year's greeting card
carte *f* de presse *f*	Journalistenausweis *m*, Presseausweis *m*	press credentials *pl*, press passport
carte *f* de retour *m*	Antwortkarte *f*	reply card, return card
carte *f* de table *f*	Tischkarte *f*	tent card
carte *f* de visite *f*	Visitenkarte *f*, Visitenkarte *f* eines Verkäufers *m*	salesman's calling card, card
carte *f* de vœux *m/pl*	Glückwunschkarte *f*	congratulary card, greeting card
carte *f* d'invitation *f*	Einladungskarte *f*	invitation-card
carte *f* du temps *m*	Wetterkarte *f*	weather-chart

carte f grattée	Schabekarton m	scraper board, scratchboard
carte f pliable	Faltplan m	folding map
carte f postale	Postkarte f	post card
carte f postale illustrée	Ansichtskarte f	picture postcard
carte f synoptique	Übersichtskarte f	general map
carte-demande f d'échantillon m	Musteranforderungskarte f	sample request card
carte-réponse f	Antwortkarte f, Rückantwortkarte f	business reply card, reply card, return card
cartographie f	Kartografie f	cartography, map printing
carton m	Karton m, Pappe f, Patronenpapier n	board, cardboard, cartridge, cartridge paper, millboard, pasteboard
carton m à dessin m	Zeichenkarton m	drawing cardboard, illustration board
carton m à racler	Schabekarton m	scraper board, scratchboard
carton m Bristol	Bristolkarton m	Bristol board
carton m chromo couché	Chromokarton m	chromo-board
carton m compact	Hartfaserplatte f	hardboard
carton m contrecollé	Chromoersatzkarton m	chrome imitation board
carton m couché	Kunstdruckkarton m	art board, coated board
carton m cuir m	Lederpappe f	leather board
carton m de bois m	Holzpappe f	board made from wood pulp
carton m de couverture f	Umschlagkarton m	cover cardboard
carton m de paille f	Strohpappe f	straw board
carton m de séparation f	Trennkarton m	divider card
carton m gris	Graupappe f	grey paste board
carton m -ivoire m	Elfenbeinkarton m	ivory board
carton m ondulé	Wellpappe f	corrugated paste-board, grooved paste-board
carton m pour des offres f/pl	Angebotsmappe f	advertising portfolio, offer case
carton m pour fichiers m/pl	Karteikarton m	index card board
carton m pour flans m/pl	Maternpappe f	flong board, matrix board
carton m vendeur	Verkaufskarton m	cardboard box for dealers pl
carton-emboîtage m	Sammelmappe f	collecting portfolio
cartonnages m/pl	Kartonagen f/pl	boarding
cartonné	kartoniert	in paper boards pl
carton-pâte m	Papiermaché n	paper mâché
cartothèque f	Kartei f	card index, file, filing cabinet
cartouche f	Zierrahmen m	cartouche
cartouche f de titre m	Titelleiste f	masthead
casier m à journaux m/pl	Zeitungsregal n	newspaper rack
casier m à revues f/pl	Zeitschriftenregal n, Zeitschriftenständer m	magazine rack, shelf for magazines pl
casque f téléphonique	Kopfhörer m	headphone
casse f	Schriftenauswahl f, Schriftkasten m	choice of type faces pl, frame, letter-case
casse f de compositeur m	Setzerkasten m	composing-frame
casseau m	Akzidenzkasten m, Vorratskasten m (Schrift f)	fount case, job case
cassetin m	Kastenfach n, Kästchen n	box
cassette f à bandes f/pl magnétiques	Magnetbandkassette f	magnetic tape cassette
cassette f vidéo	Bildkassette f	video cassette
catadioptre m	Katzenauge n, Scheinwerfer m	cat's eye, rear reflector, reflector, reflector button
catalogue m	Katalog m	catalog am, catalogue brit

catalogue *m* à feuillets *m/pl* mobiles	Katalog *m* mit losen Seiten *f/pl*	loose-leaf catalogue
catalogue *m* de la foire *f*	Messekatalog *m*	fair catalogue
catalogue *m* des journaux *m/pl*	Zeitungskatalog *m*	press-guide, rate book, standard media rates *pl*
catalogue *m* d'exposition *f*	Ausstellungskatalog *m*	exhibition catalogue
catalogue *m* d'une maison *f* d'expédition *f*	Versandhauskatalog *m*	mail-order catalogue
cataphote *m*	Katzenauge *n*, Lichtreflektor *m*	cat's eye, rear reflector, reflector button
catégorie *f*	Kategorie *f*	bracket, category
catégorie *f* de biens *m/pl*	Produktgattung *f*	product category
catégorie *f* de pouvoir *m* d'achat *m*	Kaufkraftklasse *f*	purchasing power class
catégorie *f* des acheteurs *m/pl*	Käuferschicht *f*	buyer category, spending group
catégorie *f* des consommateurs *m/pl*	Verbraucherschicht *f*	class of consumers *pl*
catégorie *f* d'importance *f*	Größenklasse *f*	category of magnitude
catégorie *f* professionnelle	Berufsgruppe *f*	occupational group
catégorie *f* socio-professionnelle	soziale Schicht *f*	social and occupational category, social status
catégories *f* de population *f*	Bevölkerungsschichten *f/pl*	classes *pl* of population, strata *pl* of population
catégories *f/pl* de périodiques *m/pl*	Zeitschriftengattungen *f/pl*	categories *pl* of magazines *pl*
catégories *f/pl* de salles *f/pl*	Filmtheater- *n* Kategorien *f/pl*	categories *pl* of cinema theatres *pl*
causerie *f* hebdomadaire	Wochenplauderei *f*	weekly talk
causeries *f/pl* devant la cheminée *f*	Plaudereien *f/pl* am Kamin *m*	fireside chats *pl*
caviar *m*	getilgte Stelle *f*	obliterated passage
caviarder	abdecken, ausblocken	to block out, to cover, to mask out, to turn a letter
cédille *f*	Cedille *f*	cedilla
cellophane *f*	Cellophan *n*	cellophane
cellophaner	cellophanieren	to cellosheen, to clarosheen
cellule *f*	Kreativagentur *f*	team of creative men *pl*
censure *f*	Zensur *f*	censorship
censure *f* de la publicité *f*	Werbezensur *f*	advertising censorship
censure *f* préventive	Vorzensur *f*	preventive censorship
centrale *f* téléphonique	Telefonzentrale *f*	telephone exchange
centré	auf Mitte *f* gesetzt	centered
centre *m* commercial centre *m* d'achat *m*	Einkaufszentrum *n*, Geschäftszentrum *n*	business centre, shopping area, shopping center
centre *m* d'attraction *f*	Brennpunkt *m* des Verkaufs *m*	focal point, focus of sale, hot spot
centre *m* de consommateurs *m/pl*	Verbraucherzentrale *f*	consumer center
centre *m* de gravité *f*	Schwerpunkt *m*	centre of gravity
centre *m* de la presse *f*	Pressezentrum *n*	press centre
centre *m* de l'affiche *f*	Plakatmitte *f*	centre of the poster
centre *m* de renseignements *m/pl*	Nachrichtenstelle *f*, Nachrichtenzentrale *f*	information centre, intelligence department
centrer	zentrieren	centering *brit*, centring *am*

céramiste *m*	Keramiker *m*	potter
cercle *m*	Kreis *m*	circle
cercle *m* de lecteurs *m/pl*	Leserkreis *m*	circle of readers *pl*, readership
cercle *m* d'édition *f*	Anzeigenring *m*	group of publishers *pl*
certificat *m*	Zeugnis *n*	certificate
certificat *m* de contrôle *m* du tirage *m*	Auflagebeglaubigung *f*	certified statement of circulation
certification *f* des tirages *m/pl*	Auflagenbestätigung *f*	certification of circulation
certifier conforme	beglaubigen	to authenticate
cesser de paraître	einstellen (Erscheinen *n*)	to discontinue publication
cession *f*	Abtretung *f*	cession
cession *f* de ristournes *f/pl*	Provisionsabgabe *f*	kickback, yielding of commission
chaîne *f* de journaux *m/pl*	Zeitungskette *f*	press-group
chalcographie *f*	Kupferstecherkunst *f*, Kupferstich *m*	chalcography, copper plate engraving, engraving
chambre *f* noire	Dunkelkammer *f*	darkroom
champ *m* d'action *f*	Wirkungsbereich *m*, Wirkungskreis *m*	field of activities *pl*, sphere of action
champ *m* de cours *m*	Rennbahn *f*, Sportstadion *n*	race court, sport stadium
champ *m* de vision *f*	Sichtfeld *n*	field of vision
chance *f* d'écoulement *m*	Absatzchance *f*	sales *pl* prospects *pl*
chaîne *f* d'agences *f/pl*	Agenturkette *f*	chain of agencies *pl*
changement *m*	Änderung *f*	amendment
changement *m* d'avis *m*	Meinungsänderung *f*	change of opinion
changement *m* de format *m*	Formatänderung *f*	change of measure, change of size, rescale, scaling
changement *m* de marque *f*	Markenwechsel *m*	brand switching
changement *m* de message *m*	Sujetwechsel *m*	change of design
changement *m* de texte *m*	Textwechsel *m*	change of text
changement *m* des tirages *m/pl*	Auflagenveränderung *f*	change in circulation
changement *m* du goût *m* du consommateur *m*	Geschmackswandel *m*	change in taste
chanson *f* populaire	Volkslied *n*	folk-song
chanson *f* sentimentale	Schnulze *f*	sentimental hit
chanson *f* traditionnelle	Volkslied *n*	folk-song
chanteur *m* de charme *m*	Schlagersänger *m*	crooner
chapeau *m*	Kopfleiste *f*, Vorbemerkung *f*	head piece, head rules *pl*, headband, prefatory note, preliminary remark
chaperon *m*	Zuschuß *m* (Überschuß *m*)	overs *pl*
chapitre *m*	Kapitel *n*	chapter
chargé *m* de cours *m*	Dozent *m*	lecturer
charge *m* réajusté	Nachbelastung *f*, Rabattnachbelastung *f*	short rate
charger	unterlegen	to line-up, to underlay
charger une couleur *f*	strenger machen (Farbe)	to strengthen (ink)
charges *f/pl* d'exploitation *f*	Betriebskosten *pl*	running expenses *pl*
chasse *f*	Dicke *f*	thickness
chasser	strecken *typog*	to drive out
chasser la composition *f*	Satz *m* strecken	to white out the matter
châssis *m*	Schließrahmen *m*	chase
châssis *m*-presse *f*	Kopierrahmen *m*	printing-frame
chef *m* de fabrication *f*	Herstellungsleiter *m*	director of fabrication
chef *m* de groupe *m*	Kontaktgruppenleiter *m*	group head

chef *m* de la conception-rédaction *f*	Cheftexter *m*	copy chief, copy supervisor
chef *m* de la vente *f* d'annonces *f/pl*	Anzeigenwerbeleiter *m*	ad sales *pl* promotion manager
chef *m* de presse *f*	Pressechef *m*	press chief
chef *m* de produit *m*	Produktmanager *m*	brand manager, product manager
chef *m* de publicité *f*	Anzeigenleiter *m*	advertisement director, advertising manager
chef *m* de publicité *f* d'agence *f*	Sachbearbeiter *m* der Werbung *f*	account executive, contact man
chef *m* de publicité *f* d'annonceur *m*	Werbeleiter *m*	advertising manager
chef *m* de publicité *f* de support *m* publicitaire	Werbeleiter *m* eines Werbeträgers *m*	advertisement manager
chef *m* de service *m*	Chef *m* vom Dienst *m*	managing editor
chef *m* de studio *m*	Atelierleiter *m*	art director, studio manager
chef *m* de vente *f*	Vertriebsleiter *m*	circulation manager, distribution manager, sales *pl* promoter
chef *m* d'entreprise *f*	Geschäftsführer *m*	business manager, director
chef *m* des annonces *f/pl*	Anzeigenleiter *m*	advertisement director, advertising manager
chef *m* des études *f/pl* de marché *m*	Leiter *m* der Marktforschung *f*	research director
chef *m* des sécretaires *m/pl* de rédaction *f*	Chef *m* des Redaktionssekretariats *m*	slotman
chef *m* des ventes *f/pl*	Verkaufsleiter *m*	sales *pl* manager, sales *pl* promoter
chef *m* d'œuvre *f*	Meisterwerk *n*	master-work
chef *m* du service *m* création *f*	Gestaltungsleiter *m*	art director, creative director
chef *m* du service *m* médias *m/pl*	Leiter *m* der Mediaabteilung *f*	media director
chef *m* du service *m* photographique	Fotoredakteur *m*	art editor
chef *m* d'un groupe *m* créateur	Kreativgruppenleiter *m*	creative director
chef *m* d'un groupe *m* médias *m/pl*	Leiter *m* einer Mediagruppe *f*	media supervisor
chemin *m* de fer *m* fédéral	Bundesbahn *f*	federal railways *pl*
chemins *m/pl* de l'information *f*	Informationswege *m/pl*	channels *pl* of information
chemise *f*	Buchumschlag *m*	book cover, book jacket
chemise *f* de livre *m*	Buchhülle *f*	book jacket
chemise *f* de travail *m*	Arbeitstasche *f*, Lauftasche *f*	docket, job bag
chèque *m*	Scheck *m*	cheque
chèque *m* bancaire	Bankscheck *m*	bank cheque *brit*, check *am*
chèque *m* barré	Verrechnungsscheck *m*	crossed cheque
chèque *m* en blanc	Blankoscheck *m*	blank cheque
chèque-image *f*	Bilderscheck *m*	picture cheque
chèque *m* postal	Postscheck *m*	postal cheque
chercheur *m*	Ermittler *m*, Forscher *m*	investigator, research worker, researcher, researcher
chevalet *m*	Gestell *n*	trestle
chevaucher	überlappen	to overlap
cheveu *m*	schlechtes Manuskript *n*	bad copy
cheville *f*	Flickwort *n*	expletive, padding

chez l'auteur *m*	Selbstverlag *m*, im	published by the author
chicane *f* sur les mots *m/pl*	Wortklauberei *f*	hair-splitting
chiffre *m*	Zahl *f*, Ziffer *f*	cipher, figure, number, numeral
chiffre *m* d'affaires *f/pl*	Etatsumme *f*, Umsatz *m*	billing, turnover
chiffre *m* d'affaires *f/pl* publicitaires	Werbeumsätze *m/pl*	advertising turnover
chiffre *m* d'affaires *f/pl* total	Gesamtbudget *n*	billing
chiffre *m* de vente *f*	Verkaufsziffer *f*	sales *pl* figure
chiffre *m* du tirage *m*	Auflagenhöhe *f*	circulation base, print run, printing-number
chiffres *m/pl* arabes	arabische Ziffern *f/pl*	arabic numerals *pl*, Arabic numerals *pl*
chiffres *m/pl* de diffusion *f*, chiffres *m/pl* de tirage *m*	Verbreitungszahlen *f/pl*	circulation figures *pl*, distribution figures *pl*
chiffres *m/pl* de vente *f*	Umsatzzahlen *f/pl*	sales figures *pl*
chiffres *m/pl* romains	römische Ziffern *f/pl*	Roman numerals *pl*
chiqué *m*	Fälschung *f*	fake, falsification
choc *m*	Stoßwirkung *f*	impact
choisir	auswählen	to choose, to select
choix *m*	Auswahl *f*, Sortiment *n*, Wahl *f*	assessment, assortment, choice, election, selection
choix *m* de marchandises *f/pl*	Warensortiment *n*	assortment of goods *pl*, line
choix *m* des acteurs *m/pl*	Rollenbesetzung *f*	casting
choix *m* des médias *m/pl*	Mediaselektion *f*	media selection
choix *m* du caractère *m*	Schriftwahl *f*	choice of type
choses *f/pl* à lire	Lesestoff *m*	reading matter
chromage *m*	Verchromung *f*	chroming
chromiste *m*	Farbätzer *m*	chromist
chromolithographie *f*, chromotypie *f*	Chromolithografie *f*, Farbdruck *m*, Farbenlithografie *f*, Öldruck *m*	chromo-lithography, chromotype, colour lithography, colour printing, oleography
chronique *f*	Chronik *f*	chronicle
chronique *f* cinématographique	Filmrundschau *f*	film review
chronique *f* locale	Lokalnachrichten *f/pl*	local news
chronique *f* scandaleuse	Klatschgeschichte *f*, Skandalchronik *f*	gossip, scandal cronicle, tittle-tattle
chroniqueur *m*	Berichterstatter *m*, Chronist *m*, Rundfunksprecher *m*	broadcaster, chronicler, correspondent, radio announcer, radio communicator *am*, reporter
chuchoterie *f*	Flüsterpropaganda *f*	whispering campaign
chute *f*	Papierabfall *m*	waste paper
chute *f* de papier *m*	Papierabschnitt *m*	offcut
cible *f*	Zielgruppe *f*	intended group, target audience, target group
cible *f* principale	Hauptzielgruppe *f*	principal consumers *pl*
cicéro *f* (voir appendice)	Cicero *f* (siehe Anhang)	Pica (see appendix)
ci-contre	gegenüberliegende Seite *f*	opposite page
cinéaste *m*	Filmfachmann *m*, Filmproduzent *m*	film expert, film producer
ciné-club *m*	Filmklub *m*	cine club, film society
cinéma *m*	Kino *n*, Lichtspielhaus *n*	cinema, movie theater, movies *pl am*, picture house
cinéma *m* ambulant	Wanderlichtspiele *n/pl*	travelling movie theatre
cinéma *m* avec un programme *m* sans arrêt *m*	Kino *n* mit ununterbrochenem Programm *n*	non-stop cinema

cinéma *m* d'actualités *f/pl*	Aktualitätenkino *n*	non-stop cinema
cinéma *m* en plein air *m* pour automobilistes *m/pl*	Autokino *n*	drive-in cinema
cinéma *m* publicitaire	Kinowerbung *f*	cinema advertising, film advertising
cinéma *m* sans arrêt *m*	Ohne-Pause-Kino *n*	non-stop-cinema
cinémascope *m*	Breitwandfilm *m*, Verfahren *n* für Breitwandvorführung *f*	cinemascope
cinémathèque *f*	Filmarchiv *n*	film library, stock-shots *pl*
circonférence *f*	Umkreis *m*	circumference
circonlocution *f*	Umschreibung *f*	periphrasis
circuit *m*	Kinotheaterring *m*	circuit
circuit *m* court	Direktabsatz *m* des Herstellers *m* an den Einzelhandel *m*	direct selling of the manufacturer to the retail firms *pl*
circuit *m* de distribution *f*	Distributionsweg *m*, Vertriebsweg *m*	channel of distribution
circuit *m* indivisible d'emplacements *m/pl*	Stellennetz *n*, Werbeflächengruppe *f*	holding of outdoor advertising sites *pl*, network, poster showing
circuit *m* long	Absatz *m* des Herstellers *m* an den Großhändler *m*	selling of the manufacturer to the wholesale dealer
circuit *m* radio-téléphonique	Sprechfunkverbindung *f*	radiotelephony
circulaire *m*	Zirkular *n*	circular
circulaire *m* publicitaire	Werberundschreiben *n*	advertising circular
circulation *f*	Verbreitung *f*	circulation, coverage, diffusion, dissimination, distribution
circulation *f* postale	Versandauflage *f*	mail circulation
cire *f*	Wachs *n*	wax
cisaille *f* à carton *m*	Pappschere *f*	cardboard cutter
ciseaux *m/pl*	Schere *f*	scissors *pl*
citation *f*	Erwähnung *f*, Exzerpt *n*, Notierung *f*, Zitat *n*	excerpt, extract, mention, quotation
citations *f/pl* de la presse *f*	Pressezitate *n/pl*	press quotations
citer	Preis *m* angeben	to quote
citoyen *m* moyen	Mann *m* auf der Straße *f*	man-on-street
clarification *f*	Aufhellung *f*	clarification
clarté *f*	Klarheit *f*	clearness
classe *f* de revenus *m/pl*	Einkommensklasse *f*	income group
classe *f* sociale	soziale Schicht *f*	social and occupational category, social status
classement *m*	Ablage *f*, Einteilung *f*	classification, depot, file, filing system
classer	ablegen	to file
classeur *m*	Ordner *m*	file box
classeur *m* de lettres *f/pl*	Briefordner *m*	letter-file
classeur-relieur *m*	Schnellhefter *m*	
classification *f*	Klassifizierung *f*	classification
classification *f* de dessins *m/pl* publicitaires	Einstufung *f* von Anzeigenentwürfen *m/pl*	order of merit-rating
classifier	einordnen	to classify
clause *f* de non-concurrence *f*, clause *f* d'exclusivité *f*	Konkurrenzausschluß *m*, Konkurrenzklausel *f*	clause regulating competition, competition clause, exclusivity stipulation
clause *f* limitative	Preisbindungsklausel *f*	tying clause

clause *f* restrictive	Wettbewerbsklausel *f*	restraining clause
clavier *m*	Klaviatur *f*	keyboard
claviste *m*	Maschinensetzer *m*	machine-compositor, operator
clé *f*	Kontrollziffer *f*	desk number, key
clichage *m*	Klischierung *f*, Stereotypie *f*	stereotyping, stereotyping process
cliché *m*	abgedroschene Redensart *f*, Ätzung *f*, Druckstock *m*, gleichbleibendes Vorstellungsbild *n*, Klischee *n*	block (brit) , cliché, cut, engraving, etching, hackneyed phrase, plate, stereotype, stock phrase
cliché *m* au trait *m*	Strichätzung *f*	line block *brit*, line cut *am*, line engraving *am*, line etching, line plate, process block *brit*
cliché *m* bloc	Vollklischee *n*	complete block *brit*, complete plate *am*
cliché *m* caoutchouc *m*	Gummiklischee *n*	rubber block
cliché *m* d'annonce *f*	Anzeigenklischee *n*	advertising block
cliché *m* de photogravure *f*	Farbätzung *f*	colour process etching
cliché *m* détouré	freistehendes Klischee *n*	cut-out block, outlined cut
cliché *m* d'impression *f* couleur *f*	Mehrfarbenklischee *n*	process plate
cliché *m* en couleurs *f/pl*	Farbklischee *n*	color engraving *am*, colour block *brit*
cliché *m* en relief *m*	Reliefklischee *n*	relief etched block
cliché *m* fraisé	ausgefräster Druckstock *m*	routed plate
cliché *m* inversé	Umkehrätzung	reversed plate
cliché *m* isolé	freistehendes Klischee *n*	cut-out block, outlined cut
cliché *m* métal *m*	Metallklischee *n*	metal block, metal cut
cliché *m* minimum	Minimalklischee *n*	minimum cliché
cliché *m* monté	montiertes Klischee *n*	mounted block
cliché *m* négatif, cliché *m* noir au blanc	Negativklischee *n*	block white on black, negative plate, reversed block
cliché *m* non monté	unmontiertes Klischee *n*	unmounted block
cliché *m* nylon	Nylonklischee *n*	nylon block
cliché *m* original	Originalklischee *n*	master plate, original block, pattern plate
cliché *m* passe-partout	Rahmenklischee *n*	slip-in block
cliché *m* perlon	Perlonklischee *n*	perlon block
cliché *m* plastique	Kunststoffklischee *n*	nylonprint, plastic block, plastic cut, plastic stereo
cliché *m* rectangulaire	rechteckiges Klischee *n*	squared up block
cliché *m* sans marge *f*	randloses Klischee *f*	bleed
cliché *m* simili	Autotypieätzung *f*	half-tone block
cliché *m* simili avec grandes lumières *f/pl*	Hochlichtautotypie *f*	dropout half-tone, high-light half-tone
cliché *m* simili deux tons *m/pl*	Duplex-Autotypie *f*	duplex half-tone block *brit*, duplex half-tone cut *am*
cliché *m* toupillé	ausgefräster Druckstock *m*	routed plate
cliché *m* trait *m* -simili combiné	kombinierte Ätzung *f*	combination plate, combined line and half-tone block *brit*
cliché *m* zinc, cliché *m* zinc *m*	Zinkätzung *f*, Zinkklischee *n*	zinc block, zinc etching, zinc block, zinc etching
clicher	klischieren	to cast, to make blocks *pl*, to stereotype

clichérie f	Klischeeanstalt f	block maker, cliché manufactory, engraving plant
clicheur m	Chemigraf m, Stereotypeur m	blockmaker, plate maker, process engraver, stereotyper
client m	Abnehmer m, Auftraggeber m, Etatkunde m, Kunde m	account, buyer, client, commissioned by, contractor, customer
client m de passage m	Gelegenheitskunde m	casual costumer, chance costumer, stray costumer
client m de publicité f	Anzeigenkunde m	advertising customer
client m fidèle	Dauerkunde m, Stammkunde m	regular customer, steady customer
client m occasionnel	Gelegenheitskunde m	casual costumer, chance costumer, stray costumer
clientèle f	Kundenkreis m, Stammkundschaft f	circle of clients pl, goodwill, range of customers pl
clientèle f de passage m	Laufkundschaft f	irregular customers pl
clignotement m	Blinklichtwerbung f	flashing sign, flashing-winking of lights pl
climat m d'opinion f	Meinungsklima n	climate of opinion
clou m	Reißer m	thriller
clouer	aufklotzen	to block, to mount
club m de publicité f	Werbeklub f	advertising club
cntribution f	redaktioneller Beitrag m	contribution
code m	Kode m, Telegrammschlüssel m	code
code m de la route f	Straßenverkehrsordnung f	highway code
coder	kodieren, verschlüsseln	to code
codification f	Kodierung f	coding
codification f d'une annonce f	Anzeigenkennzeichnung f	keying an advertisement
codifier	kodifizieren	to codify
coiffe f	Häubchen n	tail cap
coin m des devinettes f/pl	Rätselecke f	puzzle corner
coin m droit	rechte Ecke f	right-hand corner
coin m gauche	linke Ecke f	left-hand corner
coin m inférieur, coin m intérieur	untere Ecke f	lower corner
coin m supérieur	obere Ecke f	upper corner
colis m	Paket n	parcel
collaborateur m à son compte m	freiberuflicher Mitarbeiter m	free lance contributor
collaborateur m artistique à son compte m	freier künstlerischer Mitarbeiter m	outside artist
collaborateur m attitré	Kolumnist m	syndicated columnist
collaborateur m d'un journal m à scandale m	Mitarbeiter m eines Skandalblattes n	slandermonger
collaborateur m extérieur, collaborateur m libre	freiberuflicher Mitarbeiter m	free lance contributor
collaborateur m occasionnel, collaborateur m part-time	gelegentlicher Mitarbeiter m	casual contributor, guest writer, string-correspondent
collaborateur m permanent, collaborateur m régulier	ständiger Mitarbeiter m	permanent contributor
collaboration f	Gemeinschaftsarbeit f, Gruppenarbeit f	cooperative work, team-work

collage *m*	Ankleben *n*, Anschlag *m*, Aufkleben *n*, Collage *f*, Klebearbeit *f*	collage, pasting, placing, posting, sticking up
collage *m* d'encarts *m/pl*	Einkleben *n* von Beilagen *f/pl*	tipping-in of insets *pl*
collationner	kollationieren, vergleichen	to collate, to compare, to crossprove, to match
colle *f*	Klebstoff *m*, Kleister *m*, Leim *m*	adhesive, glue, paste
collection *f*	Kollektion *f*, Sammelband *m*	collected volume, collection, miscellany
collection *f* d'affiches *f/pl*	Plakatsammlung *f*	poster collection
collection *f* d'échantillons *m/pl*	Musterkollektion *f*	sample collection
collection *f* des données *f/pl*	Erfassungsterminal *n*	data collection
coller	anschlagen, bekleben, einkleben	to paste on, to paste up, to place bills *pl*, to post bills *pl*, to stick bills *pl*, to stick on
colleur *m* d'affiches *f/pl*	Plakatkleber *m*	bill-sticker
colloque *m*	Colloqium *n*, Diskussionsveranstaltung *f*	colloquy, symposium
colombelle *f*	Spaltenlinie *f*	column line, dividing rule
colombier (voir: format d'affiche)	Colombier *m* (siehe: Plakatformat)	Colombier (see: poster size)
à une colonne *f*	einspaltig	one column wide, single-column
colonne *f*	Kolumne *f*, Spalte *f*	column
colonne *f* d'affichage *m*	Anschlagsäule *f*, Plakatsäule *f*	advertising pillar, poster pillar
colonne *f* d'annonce *f*	Anzeigenspalte *f*	advertisement colums *pl*
colonne *f* de petites annonces *f/pl*	Kleinanzeigenrubrik *f*	classified column
colonne *f* des horloges *f/pl* publiques	Normaluhrensäule *f*	public clock pillar
colonne *f* des lettres *f/pl* à la rédaction *f*	Leserbriefspalte *f*	letter-bag, letters *pl* column
colonne *f* Morris (à Paris)	Anschlagsäule *f*, Plakatsäule *f*	advertising pillar, poster pillar
colonne *f* publicitaire	Werbesäule *f*	
colonne *f* publicitaire carrée	Werbebox *f*	advertising box
colonne-affiche *f*	Litfaßsäule *f*	poster pillar
coloration *f* photographique	Fotokolorierung *f*	colour toning
coloré	farbig	coloured
coloriage *m*	Kolorierung *f*	colouring
colorié	koloriert	coloured
coloris *m*	Tönung *f*	shade, tint
colportage *m*	Pressevertrieb *m*	distribution of publications *pl*, newspaper wholesaling
colporteur *m*	fliegender Händler *m*, Hausierer *m*	hawker, hucksterer, itinerant salesman
colporteur *m* de nouvelles *f/pl*	Neuigkeitskrämer *m*	news monger
combinaison *f* de cibles *f/pl* publicitaires	Zielgruppenkombination *f* von Medien *n/pl*	media audience accumulation
combinaison *f* de divers moyens *m/pl* de communication *f*	Medienverbund *m*	combination of various means *pl* of communication, combined scheduling
combinaison *f* des médias *m/pl*	Mediakombination *f*, Werbemittelkombination *f*, Werbeträgerkombination *f*	media mix

combinaison f du cinéma m et d'acteurs m/pl	Laterna f magica	living screen
combiné	kombiniert	combined
comité f	Ausschuß m	committee
comité f d'organisation f de la foire f	Messeamt n	fair authorities pl
commande f	Auftrag m, Bestellung f	commission, order
commande f à l'épreuve f	Probeauftrag m	sample order, trial order
commande f de l'étranger m	Auslandsauftrag m	foreign order
commande f de suite f	Anschlußauftrag m	follow-on order, follow-up order
commande f d'impression f	Druckauftrag m	commission, printing order
commande f d'insertion f	Anzeigenauftrag m	advertisement order, insertion order, space order
commande f groupée	Sammelauftrag m	collective order, omnibus order
commande f isolée	Einzelauftrag m	isolated order
commande f minimale	Mindestabschluß m	minimum contract
commande f par groupage m	Sammelbestellung f	centralized buying
commande f préliminaire	Vorbestellung f	advance order
commande f télégraphique	telegrafisch erteilter Auftrag m	order by wire
commande f téléphonique	telefonische Bestellung f	order by telephone
commande f urgente	Eilauftrag m	express order, rush job
commande f verbale	mündlich erteilter Auftrag m	order by word of mouth
commander	bestellen	to command, to order
commandes f/pl en suspens m	Auftragspolster n	backlog of orders pl
commentaire m	Kommentar m	comment, commentary
commentaire m de presse f	Pressekommentar m	press commentary
commentateur m	Kommentator m	commentator
commentateur m des nouvelles f/pl	Nachrichtenkommentator m	news analyst, news commentator
commerçant m	Händler m	dealer
commerce m	Handel m	commerce, trade
commerce m de gros	Großhandel m	wholesale trade
commerce m de journaux m/pl en gros	Grosso n	newspaper wholesaler
commerce m d'intermédiaire m	Zwischenhandel m	intermediary trade
commerce m d'objets m/pl d'occasion f	Gebrauchtwarenmarkt m	second hand market
commerce m extérieur	Außenhandel m	foreign commerce
commerce m intérieur	Binnenhandel m	domestic commerce, home trade brit
commerce m spécialisé	Fachgeschäft n	specialty shop, specialty store
commercialisation f	Absatzbemühungen f/pl, Marketing n, Marktfähigmachung f, Marktgestaltung f, Marktplanung f, Marktschaffung f	marketing
commercialisation f exagérée	Überkommerzialisierung f	overcommercialization
commettant m	Auftraggeber m	client, commissioned by, customer
commettant m d'un nègre m	Auftraggeber m eines Ghostwriters m	mummy
commission f	Auftrag m, Bestellung f, Kommission f, Provision f	commission, order

commission *f* d'agence *f*	Agenturprovision *f*, Mittlervergütung *f*	agency commission, commission fee, media discount
commission *f* de conciliation *f*	Schlichtungsausschuß *m*	court of arbitration
commission *f* de garantie *f*	Garantieprovision *f*	underwriting commission
commission *f* de l'agent *m*	Vertreterprovision *f*	agent commission
commission *f* d'intermédiaire	Vermittlungsprovision *f*	commission fee
commission *f* exceptionnelle	Sonderprovision *f*	special commission
commission *f* partagée	geteilte Provision *f*	split commission
communauté *f* de rédaction *f*	Redaktionsgemeinschaft *f*	joint editorial board
communauté *f* de tarif *m*	Tarifgemeinschaft *f*	rate association
communauté *f* de travail *m*	Arbeitsgemeinschaft *f*	team
communication *f*	Informationsfluß *m*, Kommunikation *f*	communication
communication *f* de masse *f*	Massenkommunikation *f*	mass communication
communication *f* locale	Ortsverbindung *f*	local call
communication *f* nez *m* à nez *m*	direkte Kommunikation *f*	face-to-face communication
communication *f* téléphonique	Telefonanschluß *m*, Telefonat *n*	call, telephone connection
communiqué *m*	Bekanntmachung *f*, Kommuniqué *n*, Mitteilung *f*, Pressemitteilung *f*, Presseverlautbarung *f*	announcement, hand out, news release, official statement, press release, statement
communiqué *m* de presse *f*	Zeitungsnotiz *f*	news item, press item, press notice
communiquer	mitteilen	to communicate, to impart
compact	kompreß	close-set, solid set
compagnon *m*	Geselle *m*	journeyman
comparaison *f* des médias *m/pl*	Intermediavergleich *m*, Medienvergleich *m*	intermedia comparison, media comparison
comparaison *f* des prix *m/pl*	Preisvergleich *m*	price comparison
comparer	vergleichen	to collate, to compare, to crossprove, to match
comparer avec le manuscrit *m*	mit dem Manuskript *n* vergleichen	to see copy
compensation *f*	Ausgleich *m*	compensation
compère *m*	Ansager *m*	announcer, compère, emcee
compétent	federführend	acting as leader, centrally handling
compétition *f* publicitaire	Werbepreisausschreiben *n*	advertising contest
compilation *f*	Zusammenstellung *f*	compilation
compiler	zusammentragen	to compile
complément *m* de commande *f*	Auftragserweiterung *f*	enlargement of an order, extension of an order
complément de texte *m* suivra	Fortsetzung *f* folgt	more to come, to be continued
complet	vollständig	complete
complication *f*	Verwicklung *f*	complication
compliquer	verwickeln	to complicate
comportement *m* des acheteurs *m/pl*	Einkaufsverhalten *n*	buying behaviour, shopping habits *pl*
comportement *m* des consommateurs *m/pl*	Verbraucherverhalten *n*	consumer behaviour
composer	absetzen (Druck), setzen *typog*	to compose, to set, to set up, to tap, to typeset
composer en minuscules *f/pl*	in Kleinbuchstaben *m/pl* absetzen	to put down
composer fidèle au modèle *m*	genau nach Vorlage *f* setzen	to follow copy

composer photographique	lichtsetzen	photo lettering
composer sans interlignes f/pl	kompreß setzen	to space closely
composer serré	eng setzen	to space closely
à composer tel quel	Manuskript n beachten	follow copy
composeuse f mécanique	Setzmaschine f	composing machine, typesetting machine
composeuse f monotype	Monotype-Setzmaschine f	monotype keyboard
composeuse f photographique	Filmsetzgerät n, Lichtsetzmaschine f	filmsetting machine, photocomposer, phototype setter, video-setter
compositeur m	Schriftsetzer m, Setzer m	compositor, lettering man, operator, typesetter, typographer
compositeur m à la main f	Handsetzer m	hand composer
compositeur m aux pièces f/pl	Spaltensetzer m	piece compositor
compositeur m de travaux m/pl de ville f	Akzidenzsetzer m	advertographer, job compositor
composition f	Drucksatz m, Satz m/typog, Schriftsatz m/typog	composition, matter, setting, type matter
composition f à distribuer	Ablegesatz m	dead matter
composition f à la machine f	Maschinensatz m	machine composition, mechanical composition am, mechanical typesetting
composition f à la main f	Handsatz m	hand composition am, hand setting, manual typesetting
composition f à pleine justification f	durchgehender Satz m	full measure setting
composition f anaxiale	anaxiale Satzform f	anaxial composition
composition f au plomb m	Bleisatz m	hot metal composition, lead composition
composition f axiale	axiale Satzform f	axial composition
composition f chromatique, composition f colorée	Farbkomposition f	colour composition
composition f conservée	Stehsatz m	live matter, retained composition, standing matter
composition f courante	Fließsatz m, glatter Satz m	fat, solid matter, straight matter, undisplay am
composition f de labeurs m/pl	Werksatz m	book work, text matter
composition f de l'audience f	Zusammensetzung f des Publikums n	audience composition, audience profile
composition f de tableaux m/pl	Tabellensatz m	tabular matter, tabulator matter
composition f de travaux m/pl de ville f	Akzidenzsatz m	display composition
composition f des annonces f/pl	Anzeigensatz m	advertising composition
composition f du public m	Publikumszusammensetzung f	audience profile
composition f d'œuvre f	Werksatz m	book work, text matter
composition f en drapeau m	Flattersatz m	unjustified matter
composition f en forme f de carré m	Blocksatz m	grouped style
composition f en langue f étrangère	Fremdsprachensatz m	setting in foreign language
composition f en placards m/pl	Fließsatz m	solid matter, undisplay
composition f en sommaire m	eingerückter Satz m	hanging indent
composition f espacée	perlender Satz m, Sperrsatz m, spationierter Satz m	open-spaced setting, spaced composition

composition f grasse	fetter Satz m	bold type
composition f lardée	gemischter Satz m, gespickter Satz m	interlarded composition, mixed matter, mixture
composition f linotype f	Linotypesatz m	linotype composition
composition f maigre	magerer Satz m	thin face
composition f manuelle	Handsatz m	hand composition am, hand setting, manual typesetting
composition f mécanique	Maschinensatz m	machine composition, mechanical composition am, mechanical typesetting
composition f mêlée	gemischter Satz m	mixed matter, mixture
composition f monotype f	Monotypesatz m	monotype composition
composition f par ordinateur m	Computersatz m	computer setting
composition f permanente	Stehsatz m	live matter, retained composition, standing matter
composition f photographique	Fotomontage f, Fotosatz m, Fotosetzverfahren n, Lichtsatz m	film setting, photo lettering, photo montage, photo typesetting, photocomposition, photo(graphic) composition, stripping
composition f pleine	kompresser Satz m	plain matter
composition f programmée	Satzherstellung f mit EDV-Anlagen f/pl	computer controlled typesetting (CCT)
composition f sans plomb m à froid	Kaltsatz m	cold type composing
composition f sur film m	Filmsatz m	film setting
composition f tape-à-l'œil m	auffallender Satz m	display composition
composteur m	Winkelhaken m	composing stick
compris dans	enthalten in	included in
comptabilité f	Rechnungswesen n	accountancy
compte m	Berechnung f, Betrag m, Konto n, Rechnung f	account, amount, bill, calculation, computation, invoice
compte m rendu	Beurteilung f, Rezension f	critique, review, valuation
compte-fils m	Fadenzähler m	line tester, screen magnifier
concentration f de la presse f	Pressekonzentration f	press concentration
concentration f de maisons f/pl d'éditions f/pl	Verlagskonzentration f	concentration of publishing houses pl
concepteur m	Visualiser m	visualizer
concepteur m graphique	Artdirektor m	art buyer, art director
concepteur-rédacteur m	Werbetexter m	copy-writer
conception f	Ideengestaltung f	visualizing
conception f de base f	Grundkonzeption f, konzeptionelle Grundlage f	basic concept, copy platform
conception f de l'affiche f	Plakatgestaltung f	poster-designing
conception f de l'annonce f	Anzeigengestaltung f	creative copy and artwork
conception f du monde m	Weltanschauung f	ideology, philosophy of life
conception f graphique	grafische Gestaltung f	graphic arrangement
conception f marketing	Marketingkonzeption n	marketing concept
conception f publicitaire	Werbegestaltung f, Werbekonzeption f	advertising conception, creative copy and artwork
conception f rédactionnelle	redaktionelle Konzeption f	editorial conception
concernant	betreffend	reference, referring to

concessionaire *m*	Alleinvertreter *m*, Anzeigenpächter *m*, Anzeigenverwaltung *f*, Konzessionsinhaber *m*, Pächter *m*, Werbepächter *m*	advertisement administration, advertising management, advertising operator, franchiser, lessee, sole advertising representative, sole agent
concessionaire *m* d'affichage *m*	Anschlagpächter *m*	site leaseholder
concessionaire *m* de publicité *f*	Werbeverwaltung *f*	advertising operator
concessionaire *m* de publicité *f* sur les moyens *m/pl* transports *m/pl*	Verkehrsreklamepächter *m*	franchise operator of transport advertising
concessionaire *m* de salle *f*	Werbeverwaltung *f* von Kinos *n/pl*	operator of advertising films *pl*
concessionaire *m* en publicité *f*	Werbeflächenpächter *m*	advertising franchise operator
concision *f*	Prägnanz *f*	precision, terseness
conclusion *f* du contrat *m*	Vertragsabschluß *m*	settlement of treaty
concocter	zusammenbrauen	to cook up
concourir	konkurrieren	to compete
concours *m*	Wettbewerb *m*	competition, contest
concours *m* de vente *f*	Verkaufswettbewerb *m*	sales *pl* competition
concours *m* d'étalages *m/pl*	Schaufensterwettbewerb *m*	shop window competition
concours *m* publicitaire	Werbewettbewerb *m*	advertising competition, advertising contest
concrétiser	veranschaulichen	to vizualize
concurrence *f*	Konkurrenz *f*	competition
concurrence *f* acharnée	harte Konkurrenz *f*	keen competition
concurrence *f* déloyale	unlauterer Wettbewerb *m*	unfair competition
concurrence *f* loyale	fairer Wettbewerb *m*	fair competition
concurrent *m*	Konkurrent *m*, Mitbewerber *m*, Wettbewerber *m*	competitor, rival
concurrentiel	konkurrenzfähig	competitive
condensé *m*	Auslese *f*, Zeitschrift *f* mit Auszügen *m/pl* aus Büchern *n/pl* und Zeitschriften *f/pl*	digest
condenser	verdichten	to boil down
conditionnement *m*	Verpackung *f*	package, packaging, wrapping
conditionnement *m* d'une marchandise *f*	Warengestaltung *f*	merchandizing
conditionnement *m* nouveau	Wiedervermarktung *f*	repackage
conditions *f/pl*	Bedingungen *f/pl*	conditions *pl*, requirements *pl*, terms *pl*
conditions *f/pl* commerciales	Geschäftsbedingungen *f/pl*	business conditions *pl*, conditions *pl* of trading
conditions *f/pl* de concours *m*	Wettbewerbsbedingungen *f/pl*	competitive conditions *pl*
conditions *f/pl* de livraison *f*	Bezugsbedingungen *f/pl*, Lieferbedingungen *f/pl*	delivery conditions *pl*, terms *pl* of delivery
conditions *f/pl* de paiement *m*	Zahlungsbedingungen *f/pl*	terms *pl* of payment
conditions *f/pl* de vente *f*	Verkaufsbedingungen *f/pl*	terms *pl* of sale
conditions *f/pl* exceptionnelles	Vorzugsbedingungen *f/pl*	preferential terms *pl*
conditions *f/pl* générales	allgemeine Bedingungen *f/pl*	general conditions *pl*
conditions *f/pl* spéciales	Unterbietungspreis *m*	cut rate, give-away price
confection *f* du journal *m*	Zeitungsherstellung *f*	newspaper production
conférence *f*	Besprechung *f*, Konferenz *f*, Vortragsveranstaltung *f*	discussion, lecture, meeting
conférence *f* de presse *f*	Pressekonferenz *f*	press conference
conférence *f* de rédaction *f*	Redaktionskonferenz *f*	editorial conference

conférence *f* d'instruction *f*	Auftragsbesprechung *f*	briefing conference
conférence *f*-débat *m*	Symposium *n*	symposium
confirmation *f*	Bestätigung *f*	acknowledgement, confirmation, validation
confirmation *f* de la commande *f*	Auftragsbestätigung *f*	confirmation of order
confiscation *f*	Beschlagnahme *f*	confiscation
congrès *m*	Tagung *f*	congress
connexion *f*	Zusammenhang *m*	association, connexion
conseil *m*	Berater *m*, Beratung *f*, Wink *m*	advisor, consultant, consultation, **consulting, hint, tip**
conseil *m* en études *f/pl* de marché *m*	Marktforschungsberater *m*	market research counsellor
conseil *m* en gestion *f*	Unternehmensberater *m*	management counsellor, management consultant
conseil *m* en marketing *m*	Absatzberater *m*, Berater *m* für Marktverhalten *n*, Marktberater *m*	marketing consultant
conseil *m* en matière *f* de vente *f*	Verkaufsberater *m*	sales *pl* consultant
conseil *m* en matière *f* d'emballage *m*	Verpackungsberater *m*	packaging consultant
conseil *m* en publicité *f*	Werbeberater *m*	advertising consultant, advertising counsellor, advertising practitioner
conseil *m* en publicité *f* libre	freier Werbeberater *m*	advertising consultant
conseil *m* en relations *f/pl* publiques	PR-Berater *m*	public-relations *pl* consultant
conseiller *m*	Berater *m*	advisor, consultant
conseiller *m* d'entreprise *f*	Unternehmensberater *m*	management counsellor, management consultant
conseiller *m* juridique	Rechtsberater *m*	legal adviser
consentement *m*	Genehmigung *f*	consent
conservation *f*	Anschlagdauer *f*, Aushangdauer *f*, Klebeperiode *f*	period of display, posting period
conservation *f* minimum	Mindestanschlagdauer *f*	minimum period of display
conserve *f*	Stehsatz *m*	live matter, retained composition, standing matter
à conserver	aufbewahren	to hold for release
conserver la composition *f*	Satz *m* stehen lassen	to hold over, to keep type standing
consommateur *m*	Benutzer *m*, Konsument *m*, Verbraucher *m*	consumer, user
consommateur *m* final	Endverbraucher *m*, Letztverbraucher *m*	final consumer, ultimate consumer
consommateur *m* potentiel	potentieller Verbraucher *m*	potential consumer
consommation *f*	Konsum *m*, Verbrauch *m*	consumption
consommatrice *f*	Verbraucherin *f*	user
constante *f* publicitaire	Werbekonstante *f*	advertising constant
constat *m* de tirage *m*	Auflagebeglaubigung *f*	certified statement of circulation
constructeur *m*	Fabrikant *m*	maker, manufacturer
construction *f* de stands *m/pl*	Standbau *m*	stand construction
construction *f* de stands *m/pl* de foire *f*	Messebau *m*	exhibition stand construction

construction *f* des expositions *f/pl*	Ausstellungsbau *m*	exhibition stand construction
constructions *f/pl* publicitaires	Werbebauten *m/pl*	display kiosks *pl*
consultation *f*	Beratung *f*	consultation, consulting
consulter	wenden an, sich	to check with
contact *m*	Kontakt *m*	contact
contact *m* au média *m*	Werbeträgerkontakt *m*	media contact, opportunity to see
contacter	sich in Verbindung *f* setzen	to contact
contacteur *m*	Kontakter *m*, Kontaktmann *m*, Kundenbetreuer *m*, Verbindungsmann *m*	account executive, account supervisor, contact man, liaison man
contacts *m/pl* publicitaires	Werbekontakte *m/pl*	advertising impressions *pl*
conte *f*	Geschichte *f*	story
conte *f* illustrée	Bildgeschichte *f*	picture story
contenu *m*	Inhalt *m*	contents *pl*
contenu *m* de la publicité *f*	Werbeinhalt *m*	advertising contents *pl*
contenu *m* publicitaire	Anzeigeninhalt *m*	advertising contents *pl*
contenu *m* rédactionnel	redaktioneller Inhalt *m*	editorial content
contexte *m* rédactionnel	redaktionelles Umfeld *n*	editorial context
contexture *f* d'un produit *m*	Warengestaltung *f*	merchandizing
contingent *m*	Anteil *m*	quota
continuité *f*	Kontinuität *f*	continuity
contour *m*	Umrandung *f*, Umriß *m*	box, frame, panel, shape
contractant *m*	Vertragspartner *m*	contracting party
contraste *m*	Kontrast *m*	contrast
contraste *m* de couleurs *f/pl*	Farbkontrast *m*	colour contrast
contrat *m*	Abschluß *m*, Vertrag *m*	agreement, contract, deal
contrat *m* à court terme *m*	kurzfristiger Abschluß *m*	short term contract
contrat *m* d'agence *f*	Agenturvertrag *m*	agency agreement, agency contract
contrat *m* de fermage *m*	Pachtvertrag *m*	contract of lease
contrat *m* de vente *f*	Kaufvertrag *m*	purchase order
contrat *m* d'insertion *f*	Anzeigenabschluß *m*, Insertionsvertrag *m*	advertising contract
contrat *m* en millimètres *m/pl*	Millimeterabschluß *m*	contract on a mm basis
contrat *m* global	Paketangebot *n*	package deal
contrat *m* minimum	Mindestabschluß *m*	minimum contract
contre texte *m*	gegenüber Text *m*, Text *m*, neben	against text, facing text, next to editorial matter, next to reading matter, opposite text
contre-affaire *f*	Gegengeschäft *n*	barter
contre-coller	hinterkleben	to back
contre-déclaration *f*	Gegendarstellung *f*	counterstatement
contre-épreuve *f*	Konterdruck *m*	counter-proof, reversed impression
contre-façon *f*	Imitation *f*, Nachahmung *f*	counterfeit, imitation, plagiarism
contrefaction *f*	Fälschung *f*	fake, falsification
contrefaction *f* d'une marque *f* de fabrique *f*	Nachahmung *f* eines Warenzeichens *n*	pirating of a trademark
contre-faire	nachmachen	to copy, to imitate
contre-plongée *f*	Froschperspektive *f*	worm's eye – view
contre-projet *m*	Gegenentwurf *m*	counter-project

contreproposition *f*	Gegenvorschlag *m*	counter-proposition
contre-publicité *f*	Abwehrwerbung *f*, Konterwerbung *f*	counter advertising
contresens *m*	Mißdeutung *f*	misinterpretation
contre-type *m*	Abzug *m*, Reproduktion *f*	copy print, proof, pull, reproduction
contribution *f*	Beitrag	contribution
contribution *f* fortuite	gelegentlicher Beitrag *m*	casual contribution
contrôle *m*	Kontrolle *f*, Überwachung *f*	check, check-up, supervision
contrôle *m* a posteriori	Nachkalkulation *f*	cost-effect calculation, final costing
contrôle *m* budgétaire	Etatkontrolle *f*	budget checking
contrôle *m* de la publicité *f*	Werbekontrolle *f*	advertising control
contrôle *m* de la vente *f*	Absatzkontrolle *f*	marketing control
contrôle *m* de produit *m*	Produkttest *m*	product testing
contrôle *m* des adresses *f/pl*	Adressenkontrolle *f*	mailing list control
contrôle *m* des délais *m/pl*	Terminkontrolle *f*	progress control, traffic control
contrôle *m* des résultats *m/pl*	Erfolgskontrolle *f*	rating, result checking
contrôle *m* des tirages *m/pl*	Auflagenprüfung *f*	circulation control
contrôle *m* du budget *m*	Budgetkontrolle *f*	budgetary control
contrôle *m* du rendement *m*	Erfolgskontrolle *f*	rating, result checking
contrôle·*m* du rendement *m* de la publicité *f*	Werbeerfolgskontrolle *f*	advertising control, advertising effectiveness study
contrôle *m* du rendement *m* publicitaire	Anzeigenerfolgskontrolle *f*	advertisement rating, advertising control
contrôle *m* du succès *m*	Erfolgskontrolle *f*	rating, result checking
contrôler	kontrollieren, prüfen	to check, to check up, to examine
contrôleur *m*	Prüfer *m*	auditor
convenance *f*	Angemessenheit *f*	appropriateness
convenance *f*, à notre	auf Abruf *m*	at our convenience, on call
convention *f*	Abmachung *f*, Absprache *f*, Vereinbarung *f*	agreement, arrangement, convention
conversation *f*	Gespräch *n*	conversation
conversation *f* téléphonique	Telefongespräch *n*	telephonecall
coopération *f*	Arbeitsgemeinschaft *f*	team
coopérative *f*	Konsumgenossenschaft *f*	co-operative
coopérative *f* des consommateurs *m/pl*	Verbrauchergenossenschaft *f*	cooperative
coordination *f*	Koordinierung *f*	co-ordination
coordination *f* des termes *m/pl*	zeitliche Abstimmung *f*	timing
coordiner	koordinieren	to co-ordinate
coordonnateur *m*	Koordinator *m*	coordinator
copie *f*	Abklatsch *m*, Kopie *f*, Manuskript *n*, Text *m*	copy, manuscript, matter, MS, poor imitation, text
copie *f* au net *m*	Reinschrift *f*	fair copy
copie *f* chamboulée	durcheinandergefallener Satz *m*	pie
copie *f* du film *m*	Filmkopie *f*	film copy
copie *f* héliographique	Ablichtung *f*, Fotokopie *f*	photo print
copie *f* originale	Originalmanuskript *n*	original copy
copie *f* pour un film *m*	Musterabzug *m*	film copy
copie *f* remaniée	überarbeiteter Text *m*	make-over
copie *f* sépia *f*	Braunpause *f*	sepia tracing
copie *f* standard	erste endgültige Filmkopie *f*	standard film copy

copie *f* sur papier *m* brillant	Hochglanzabzug *m*	high gloss print
copier	kopieren	to copy, to imitate
copier dans	einkopieren	to copy in, to superimpose
copies *f/pl* en stock *m*	Überhangsatz *m*	leftover matter
copie-témoin *m*	Klartext *m*	fair copy, hard copy
coquille *f*	Druckfehler *m*, Fisch (typog) *m*, Zwiebelfisch *m/typog*	erratum, misprint, pi *am*, pie, printing error, typographical error, wrong fount, wrong letter
coquille *f* de galvano *m*	Kupferhaut *f*	electro-shell, galvanic shell
corbeau *m*	anonymer Briefschreiber *m*	poison pen
corbeille *f* à papier *m*	Papierkorb *m*	waste-paper basket
corbeille *f* de distribution *f*	Ablegekorb *m*	filing basket
corps x points *m/pl* (voir appendice)	siehe Anhang!	see appendix!
correcteur *m*	Korrektor *m*	corrector, press reader
correcteur *m* de l'imprimerie *f*	Hauskorrektor *m*	printer's reader
correction *f*	Korrektur *f*	correction, page proof
correction *f* de couleur *f*	Farbkorrektur *f*	colour correction
correction *f* de la composition *f*	Satzkorrektur *f*	typesetting alteration
correction *f* de la presse *f*	Druckberichtigung *f*	correction of the press
correction *f* d'épreuves *f/pl*	Korrektur *f* lesen	proof-reading
correction *f* en bon à clicher	Seitenkorrektur *f*	page proof
correction *f* en bon à tirer	Zeitungskorrektur *f*	page proof
correction *f* sur film *m*	Filmkorrektur *f*	correction on film
correction *f* sur papier *m*	Papierkorrektur *f*	correction on paper
correction *f* sur plomb *m*	Bleisatzkorrektur *f*	correction on lead
corrections *f/pl* d'auteur *m*	Autorenkorrektur *f*	author's alteration, author's correction
corrélations *f/pl* entre annonces *f/pl* et tirage *m*	Anzeigen-Auflagen-Spirale *f*	interrelations *pl* between advertisements *pl* and circulation
correspondance *f*	Schriftwechsel *m*	correspondence
correspondant *m*	Berichterstatter *m*, Gesprächspartner *m*, Korrespondent *m*	chronicler, correspondent, interlocutor, reporter
correspondant *m* à l'étranger *m*	Auslandsberichterstatter *m*	foreign correspondent
correspondant *m* qui n'appartient pas à la rédaction *f*	freier Korrespondent *m*	stringer
corriger	berichtigen, korrigieren	to correct, to rectify
corriger sur le plomb *m*	auf dem Blei *n* korrigieren	to correct in the metal
corser	interessanter machen	to pep up
cote *f*, côté *m*	Aktenzeichen *n*, Rumpffläche *f*	reference number, side panel
côté *m* de première	Schöndruck *m*, Vorderseite *f*	first impression, first run, front page, outer form, prime, printing one face, sheetwise
côté *m* de seconde	Rückseite *f*	even-numbered page, inner form, reverse page
à côté *m* du texte *m*	textanschließend, Text *m*, neben	facing matter, following matter, next to reading matter
côté *m* feutre	Schönseite *f*	felt side
côté *m* image *m*	Druckoberfläche *f*	face
coter	Preis *m* angeben	to quote
couac *m*	verstümmeltes Wort *n*	beard

coucher sur papier *m*	niederschreiben	to write down
couches *f/pl* de la population *f*	Bevölkerungsschichten *f/pl*	classes *pl* of population, strata *pl* of population
coudre dans	einheften	to bind into, to stitch in
couillard *m*	Trennlinie *f*	cut-off-rule, dividing rule
couler (couleur)	auslaufen (Farbe)	to run (colour)
couleur *f*	Farbe *f*, Kolorit *n*	color *am*, colour *brit*, colouring, hue, shade
couleur *f* à détrempe *f*	Temperafarbe *f*	tempera
couleur *f* à l'huile *f*	Ölfarbe *f*, Ölmalfarbe *f*	oil color (am), oil colour (brit)
couleur *f* à vernisser	Lasurfarbe *f*	glaze, transparent ink
couleur *f* complémentaire	Komplementärfarbe *f*	complementary colour
couleur *f* d'accompagnement *m*	Schmuckfarbe *f*	accompanying colour
couleur *f* de base *f*	Grundfarbe *f*	ground colour, primary colour
couleur *f* de bronze *m*	Bronzefarbe *f*	metallic ink
couleur *f* de lustre *m*	Glanzfarbe *f*	glossy colour
couleur *f* de soutien *m*	Zusatzfarbe *f*	supplementary colour
couleur *f* d'opposition *f*	Kontrastfarbe *f*	contrasting colour
couleur *f* fluorescente	Fluoreszenzfarbe *f*	fluorescence colour
couleur *f* locale	Lokalkolorit *n*	local colour
couleur *f* opaque	Guasch *f*	body colour drawing, gouache
couleur *f* privée	Hausfarbe *f*	house colour
couleur *f* sensible à la lumière *f*	lichtempfindliche Farbe *f*	fugitive color *am*, fugitive colour *brit*
couleur *f* spéciale	Spezialfarbe *f*	extra colour, special colour
couleurs *f/pl* à l'aniline *f*	Teerfarbstoffe *m/pl*	aniline dyes *pl*
couleurs *f/pl* aquarelles	Aquarellfarben *f/pl*	aquarelle colours *pl*
couleurs *f/pl* pour gouache *f*	Guaschfarben *f/pl*	gouache colours *pl*
couleurs *f/pl* pour peinture *f* à l'eau *f*	Wasserfarben *f/pl*	water colours *pl*
coup *m*	ausgefallene Idee *f*, sensationelle Werbung *f*	gimmick, stunt advertising
coup *m* de feu *m*	Schnellschuß *m*	hot shot, priority job, rush job
coup *m* de main *f*	Handreichung *f*	helping hand
coup *m* de téléphone *m*	Telefonanruf *m*	telephone call
coup *m* en plein	überwältigender Erfolg *m*	smash hit
coupe *f*	Beschnitt *m*, Bildausschnitt *m*, Schnitt *m*	cut, cutting, intaglio, trimming
coupe *f* en travers	repräsentativer Querschnitt *m*, repräsentativer Durchschnitt *m*	cross section, cross-cut
coupe *f* transversale	Querschnitt *m*	cross-cut, cross-section
coupe-papier *m*	Papiermesser *n*	paper-knife
couper	bestossen, kürzen, schneiden, wegfallen lassen	to boil down, to compress, to curtail, to cut, to kill , to shorten, to trim
couplage *m*	Kombination *f*	couple
couplage *m* de tarif *m*	Tarifkombination *f*	rate combination
couplage *m* publicitaire	Anzeigenring *m*	group of publishers *pl*
coupoir *m*	Bestoßhobel *m*, Schneidemaschine *f*	cutting machine, letter-cutter
coupon *m*	Kupon *m*	coupon
coupon *m* de réduction *f*	Gutschein *m*	coupon, credit slip, gift voucher
coupon *m* détachable de commande *f*	Bestellabschnitt *m*	order coupon
coupon *m* pour primes *f/pl*	Wertgutschein *m*	gift coupon

couponnage *m*	Gutscheinverteilung *f*, Werbeaktionen *f/pl* mit Kupons *m/pl*	advertising activities *pl* with coupons *pl*, couponing
coupon-réponse *f*	Antwortkupon *m*	reply coupon
coupure *f*	Anzeigenausschnitt *m*, Beschnittzugabe *f*, Bildschnitt *m*, Filmschnitt *m*, Trennlinie *f*	bleed difference, clipping, cut, cut-off-rule, dividing rule, press cutting, trim
coupure *f* **de presse** *f*	Zeitungsausschnitt *m*	clipping, press-cutting
coupure *f* **syllabique**	Silbentrennung *f*	hyphenation
courbe *f* **de l'acceuil** *m*	Wirkungskurve *f*	response-function
courbe *f* **de vente** *f*	Umsatzkurve *f*	sales *pl* curve
courrier *m*	Bote *m*	messenger
courrier *m* **des auditeurs** *m/pl*	Anerkennungsschreiben *n*	applause mail *am*, testimonial
courrier *m* **des lecteurs** *m/pl*	Leserbriefspalte *f*	letter-bag, letters *pl* column
courrier *m* **du cœur** *m*	Eselswiese *f*	correspondence column
courriériste *m*	Feuilletonist *m*, Kleinartikelschreiber *m*	par writer, paragraphist
cours *m*	Kursus *m*, Lehrgang *m*	workshop
cours *m* **de travail** *m*	Arbeitsabwicklung *f*	progress of work
cours *m* **par correspondance** *f*	Fernunterricht *m*	correspondence school
court métrage *m* **muet en couleurs** *f/pl*	Filmdia *n*	silent colour film
courte dépêche *f* **d'agence** *f*	kurzes Pressetelegramm *n*	flash
courtier *m*	Abonnentenwerber *m*, Makler *m*, Repräsentant *m*	broker, representative, sheet-writer, subscription canvasser, subscription salesman, subscription solicitor
courtier *m* **d'annonces** *f/pl*	Anzeigenmittler *m*	advertising contractor, space broker
courtier *m* **de publicité** *f*	Werbungsmittler *m*	advertising contractor, advertising intermediary, space broker
courtier *m* **en publicité** *f*	Anzeigenvertreter *m*	advertisement representative, advertising sales *pl* executive
court-métrage *m*	Beifilm *m*, kurzer Werbefilm *m*	fill-up, filmlet, minute movie, quickie, short film, supplementary film
court-métrage *m* **publicitaire**	Werbespot *m*	broadcast announcement, commercial, spot announcement
courts passages *m/pl* **de texte** *m*	Textstellen *f/pl*	scraps *pl*
coussin *m* **à tampons** *m/pl*	Stempelkissen *n*	stamp pad
coût *m* **de l'emballage** *m*	Verpackungskosten *pl*	packaging costs *pl*, packing charges *pl*
coûter	kosten	to cost
coûts *pl*	Kosten *pl*	costs *pl*, expenses *pl*
coûts *m/pl* **de distribution** *f*	Vertriebskosten *pl*	distribution costs *pl*
coûts *m/pl* **de production** *f*	Produktionskosten *pl*	talent costs *pl*
coûts *m/pl* **fixes**	feste Kosten *pl*	fixed costs *pl*
coutume *f*	Verhaltensweise *f*	habit
couture *f* **à cheval** *m*	Querheftung *f*	side stitching
couture *f* **à plat**	Flachheftung *f*	flat stitching
couture *f* **au fil** *m* **végétal**	Fadenheftung *f*	book sewing
couture *f* **au point** *m* **noué**	Fadenknotenheftung *f*	thread sewing

couture f dans le dos m	Drahtheftung f	saddle stitching
couture f spirale	Spiralheftung f	spiral stitching
couverture f	Buchdeckel m, Einband m, Reichweite f, Streubreite f, Streuung f, Umschlag m, Verbreitung f	binding, book cover, circulation, cover, coverage, diffusion, dispersion, dissimination, distribution, penetration, range, reach am, spread, turnover
couverture f à rabats m/pl	überstehender Umschlag m	extended covers pl, overhang covers pl
couverture f alternée	Wechselstreuung f	staggered schedule
couverture f de la même qualité f que le papier m des pages f/pl de texte m	Umschlag m aus dem gleichen Papier n wie die Textseiten f/pl	self-cover
couverture f débordante	überstehender Umschlag m	extended covers pl, overhang covers pl
couverture f en format des pages f/pl de texte m	Umschlag m im Format n der Textseiten f/pl	flush cover
couverture f géographique	Reichweite f eines Senders m	coverage of a station
couverture f nette	Nettoreichweite f	net coverage
couverture f plastifiée	Plastikeinband m	laminated jacket
couverture f régionale	regionale Streuung f	regional dispersion
couvrir	abdecken, ausdecken, erfassen	to block out, to cover, to mask out
cover-girl f	Fotomodell n auf der Titelseite f, Titelblattmädchen n	cover girl
crachis m	Punktschraffierung f	stipple
cran m	Signatur f (Buch n)	nick
crayon m	Bleistift m	pencil
crayon m à dessin m	Zeichenstift m	drawing pencil
crayon m de couleur f	Farbstift m	coloured pencil
crayon-feutre m	Filzschreiber m	felt pen
crayon m litho	Fettstift m	wax crayon
crayonné m	Bleistiftskizze f, Rohentwurf m	dummy, layout, pencil-drawing, rough, rough outline, visual
crayons m/pl pastel	Pastellkreiden f/pl	pastels pl
créateur	kreativ, schöpferisch	creative
créateur m de mots m/pl	Wortschöpfer m	wordsmith
création f	Gestaltung f	creative work, design, visualizing
création f de la forme f	Formgestaltung f	fashioning, industrial design, shaping, styling
création f d'ensemble	Gesamtgestaltung f	total configuration
création f des moyens m/pl de publicité f	Werbemittelgestaltung f	creation of ads pl
création f publicitaire	Werbekreation f	advertising creation
créations f/pl graphiques	Werbegrafik f	advertising art, commercial art
créativité f	Kreativität f	creativity
crédibilité f	Glaubwürdigkeit f	credibility
crédit m	Kredit m	credit
crênage m	Linenschrägung f	slope of line
creuser	ätzen	to bite, to engrave, to etch
cribler	sieben	to sift
crieur m de journaux m/pl	Straßenverkäufer m	street hawker, street vendor
critères m/pl	Merkmale n/pl	criteria pl
critères m/pl démographiques	demografische Merkmale n/pl	demographic characteristics pl

critique *m*, critique *f*	Kritiker *m*, Rezensent *m*, Rezension *f*	critic, critique, review
critique *m* d'art *m*	Kunstkritiker *m*	art critic
critique *f* de la publicité *f*	Kritik *f* an der Werbung *f*	criticism of advertising
critique *m* en chambre *f*	Kritikaster *m*	armchair critic, fault-finder
critique *f* littéraire	Buchbesprechung *f*, Buchkritik *f*	book review
critique *m* théâtral	Theaterkritiker *m*	dramatic critic
critique *f* théâtrale	Theaterkritik *f*	dramatic critique
critiquer sévèrement	verreißen	to criticize harshly, to pull to pieces *pl*
critiqueur *m*	Kritikaster *m*	armchair critic, fault-finder
crochets *m/pl*	eckige Klammern *f/pl*	square brackets *pl*
croix *f*	Kreuz *n* (Anmerkungszeichen *n*)	dagger
croix *f* de repère *m*	Fadenkreuz *n*, Passerkreuz *n*	register mark
croquis *m*	Entwurf *m*, Schmierskizze *f*, Skizze *f*	design, draft, dummy, layout, outline, rough, sketch, tentative work
croquis *m* en couleurs *f/pl*	Farbskizze *f*	coloured sketch
croquis *m* minuscule	Ideenentwurf *m*, Miniaturskizze *f*	thumbnail sketch
croyabilité *f*	Glaubhaftigkeit *f*	believability
cube *m*	Kubus *m*	cube
cubique	kubisch	cubic
cuir *m*	falsch ausgesprochenes Wort *n*	beard
cuisine *f* d'un texte *m*	Formulierung *f* eines Textes *m*	sub-editing
cul *m* de lampe *f*	Schlußstück *n*, Schlußvignette *f*	tail piece
culbuter	umstülpen	to tumble
culte *m* de la personne *f*	Personenkult *m*	worship of persons *pl*
cumuler	anhäufen, zusammenfassen	to accumulate, to cumulate, to recapitulate, to summarize
cutter *m*	Schnittmeister *m*	cutter
cyanotypie *f*	Blaupause *f*	blue print, cyanotype, ozalide
cylindre *m* de foulage *m*, cylindre *m* d'impression *f*	Druckzylinder *m*	impression cylinder

D

dactylographe *m*	Maschinenschreiber *m*	typist
dactylographie *f*	Maschineschreiben *n*	typewriting
dalle *f*	Platte *f*	plate, sheet, slab
dans le délai *m* d'une année *f*	innerhalb Jahresfrist *f*	within one year
dans le texte *m*	mitten im Text *m*	in text
date *f*	Termin *m*	date, delay
date *f* de conditionnement *m*	Verpackungsdatum *n*	date of packing
date *f* de départ *m*	Berechnungsbeginn *m*	in charge date of advertising
date *f* de départ *m* de l'affichage *m*	Anschlagbeginn *m*	start of the bill posting
date *f* de la publication *f*	Veröffentlichungstag *m*	day of publication
date *f* de livraison *f*	Lieferdatum *n*, Liefertermin *m*	delivery date, term for delivery
date *f* de parution *f*, date *f* de publication *f*	Erscheinungsdatum *n*	date of issue, publication date
date *f* de rigueur *f*	vorgeschriebenes Datum *n*	prescribed date
date *f* d'envoi *m*	Versandtermin *m*	shipping date
date *f* d'impression *f*	Druckjahr *n*	date of impression
date *f* imposée	Terminvorschrift *f*, vorgeschriebenes Datum *n*	fixed date, prescribed date

date *f* limite	Schlußtermin *m*, Stichtag *m*	deadline, fixed day, forms *pl* close, key-date
date *f* limite de remise *f*	Anzeigenschluß *m*, Redaktionsschluß *m*	closing date, closing down, closing hour, closing date, closing down, copy deadline, forms *pl* close
date *f* moyenne de pose *f*	mittlere Anlaufzeit *f*	average date of posting
date *f* succédanée	Ersatztermin *m*	substitute date
dater	datieren	to date
dates *f/pl* retenues	Belegungsdaten *n/pl*	booked dates *pl*
dateur *m*	Datumstempel *m*	date-stamp
débarcadère *f*	Schiffsstation *f*	landing-stage
débat *m*	Debatte *f*	debate
à débattre	Übereinkunft *f*, nach	subject to acceptability
débaucher	abwerben	to entice away
débauches *f/pl* de publicité *f*	Werbeauswüchse *m/pl*	advertising extravagances *pl*
débit *m* de journaux *m/pl*	Zeitungsstand *m*	kiosk *brit*, newsstall, newsstand *am*
débit *m* de rabais *m* rétrograde	Rabattrückbelastung *f*	short rate
débit *m* des ventes *f/pl*	Umschlag *m* (von Waren)	turnover
débouché *m*	Absatzbereich *m*, Absatzgebiet *n*, Einzugsgebiet *n*, Markt *m*, Vertriebsstelle *f*	market, outlet, sales *pl* area, trading area
débouché *m* commercial	Vertriebskanal *m*	trade channel
débouché *m* plein de promesses *f/pl*	erfolgversprechender Absatzmarkt *m*	promising market
débutant *m*	Anfänger *m*	cub
décade *f*	Dekade *f*	decade
décalage *m*	Verschiebung *f*, Zeitverzögerung *f*	postponement, time lag
décalage *m* des lignes *f/pl*	Auf- und Abverschiebung *f* von Bildschirmzeilen *f/pl*	roll up and down, scroll up and down
décalcomanie *f*	Abziehplakat *n*	decalcomania, paint transfer, transparency *am*
décaler	verschieben	to defer, to postpone, to shift
décalquer	pausen	to trace
décharge *f* de livraison *f*	Lieferschein *m*	delivery note, receipt
déchet *m*	Abfall *m*, Ausschuß *m*	dross, offcut, refuse
déchiffrer	dechiffrieren	to decipher, to decode
décision *f*	Entscheidung *f*	decision
décision *f* d'acheter	Kaufentschluß *m*	buying decision
décision *f* de principe *m*	Grundsatzentscheidung *f*	key decision
déclaration *f*	Angabe *f*, Aussage *f*, Erklärung *f*	declaration, statement
déclaration *f* à la presse *f*	Presseverlautbarung *f*	official statement, press release
déclaration sans ambages *f/pl*	unverblümte Sprache *f*	cold turkey *am*, plain speech
déclarer	angeben, erklären	to declare, to state
déclenchement *m*	Ankurbelung *f*	launching
décodage *m*	Entschlüsselung *f*	decoding
décolorer	ausbleichen	to bleach out
décompte *m*	Abrechnung *f*	settlement, statement
décompte *m* final	Schlußabrechnung *f*	final settlement
déconcentration *f*	Entflechtung *f*	deconcentration
déconsu	zusammenhanglos	loose
décor *m*	Dekoration (Film, TV) *f*	set
décorateur *m* de vitrines *f/pl*	Schaufensterdekorateur *m*, Schaufenstergestalter *m*	window dresser
décorateur-étalagiste *m*	Dekorateur *m*	window-dresser

décoration f	Dekoration f, Verzierung f	decoration
décoration f à l'intérieur m	Innendekoration f	interior decoration
décoration f de film m	Filmdekoration f	set
décoration f de vitrine f	Schaufensterdekoration f	window display
décoration f mobile	Aufhängedekoration f	mobile
décorer	dekorieren	to decorate, window dressing, window trimming
découpage m	Ausstanzstück n, Schablone f	cut out, die cut, jig, pattern, stencil
découpage m à la main f	Handausschnitt m	handcut
découpé, découpe f	ausgestanztes Emblem n, Ausschnitt m (Stanze f)	cut out, die cut, piercing, trimming
découper	abschneiden	to break up
découper à l'emportepièce f	stanzen	to punch
découronner	vorrichten	to prepare
décrire	beschreiben	to describe
décroché m	stufenförmige Anzeige f	disconnected advertisement
décrocher	auf einer anderen Seite f fortsetzen	to run over
dédicace f	Widmung f	dedication
dédommagement m	Entschädigung f, Schadenersatz m	compensation, compensation for damage, indemnity
défection f publicitaire	Anzeigenmangel m	defection from advertisements pl
défense f d'afficher	Anschlagen n verboten	post no bills pl
défense f de faire de la publicité f	Werbeverbot n	prohibition to advertise
défense f d'imprimer	Druckverbot n	prohibition to print
défet m	Defektbogen m	waste print
défiguration f du paysage m	Verunstaltung f der Landschaft f	disfigurement of country-side
défigurer	verballhornen	to bowderize
defilé m de mode f	Modeschau f	fashion parade, style show
définition f des contours m/pl	Konturzeichnung f	definition of contours pl
défraîchi	angestaubt	shop-soiled
dégagement m	Einlösung f	redemption
dégradage m des bords m/pl	Tonverlauf m	vignetting of blocks pl
dégradé m	Vignette f	mask, ornament, vignette
dégré m de culture f	Bildungsgrad m	level of education
degré m de lecture f	Leserkreis m	circle of readers pl, readership
dégré m de mémorabilité f	Erinnerungsgrad m	degree of recognition
dégré m de notoriété f	Bekanntheitsgrad m	degree of familiarity, degree of notoriety
degré m de résistance f	Widerstandsfähigkeit f	tear ratio
dégressif m sur la fréquence f et le volume m	Mal- und Mengenstaffel f	schedule for discount by frequency and volume
dégressif m sur volume m publicitaire	Abschlußrabatt m, Mengenrabatt m	bulk rate brit, frequency discount, quantity discount, space discount, time discount, volume discount
dégustation f gratuite	Gratiskostprobe f	sampling by taste
délai m	Termin m	date, delay
délai m d'attente f	Sperrfrist f	hold for release, waiting period
délai m de dédite f	Kündigungsfrist f	period of notice, time for giving notice

délai *m* de livraison *f*	Lieferfrist *f*, Liefertermin *m*, Lieferzeit *f*	delivery delay, delivery date, delivery period, term for delivery
délai *m* de paiement *m*	Zahlungsfrist *f*	date of payment, term of payment, time of payment
délai *m* des annonces *f/pl*	Anzeigenschluß *m*	closing date, closing down, closing hour, copy deadline, forms *pl* close
delcredere *m*	Delkredere *n*	delcredere
déléatur *m*	Deleaturzeichen *n*	delete mark
délié *m*	Haarstrich *m*	hairline, serif, thin stroke
délit *m* de presse *f*	Pressedelikt *n*	press offence
demande *f*	Anfrage *f*, Nachfrage *f*	demand, query, question
demande *f* continue	kontinuierliche Nachfrage *f*	current demand
demande *f* de précisions *f/pl*	Rückfrage *f*	call back
demande *f* d'emploi *m*	Stellengesuch *n*	employment wanted
demande *f* des consommateurs *m/pl*	Verbrauchernachfrage *f*	consumer demand
démarcheur *m*	Akquisiteur *m*	canvasser
démarcheur *m* en publicité *f*	Anzeigenakquisiteur *m*	advertisement canvasser, advertising solicitor *am*, space salesman
démarrage *m*	Anlauf *m*, Einleitungssatz *m*	lead, start
démenti *m*	Dementi *n*	denial
démentir	dementieren	to belie, to deny
demi-cadratin *m*	Halbgeviert *n*	en-quad
demi-gras	halbfett	half-bold, medium, semi-bold
demi-page *f*	halbe Seite *f*	half page
demi-reliure *f*	Halbfranzband *m*	half-binding
demi-teinte	Halbton *m*	half-tone
demi-teintes *f/pl*	Mitteltöne *m/pl*	half-tints *pl*
démodé	altmodisch	old fashioned, out-of-fashion
démonstration *f*	Vorführung *f*	demonstration, projection, show
démonstratrice *f*	Mannequin *m*, Vorführdame *f*, Werbedame *f*	demonstrator, mannequin
démontage *m* d'un panneau *m*	Stellenabbau *m*	removal of a hoarding
démontrer	demonstrieren	to demonstrate
dénaturé	verfremdet	unfamiliar
dénigrement *m*	Anschwärzung *f*, Herabsetzung *f*	disparagement, slander
denrée *f*	Ware *f*	commodity, goods *pl*
densité *f*	Dichte *f*	density
densité *f* de la diffusion *f*	Streudichte *f*, Verbreitungsdichte *f*	circulation density, density of diffusion
dentelle *f*	Einfassung *f*	border
département *m*	Abteilung *f*	department, division, section
département *m* de mise *f* en pages *f/pl*	Mettageabteilung *f*	make-up section
département *m* de publicité *f*	Werbeabteilung *f*	advertisement department *brit*, advertising department, publicity department
département *m* des ventes *f/pl*	Verkaufsabteilung *f*	sales *pl* department
dépassant *m* de rayon *m*	Regalstreifen *m*	shelf-strip
dépassement *m* du devis *m*	Kostenüberschreitung *f*	overstepping of estimate
dépasser	überschreiten	to exceed
dépêche *f*	Depesche *f*	dispatch, telegram

dépenses *f/pl*	Aufwand *m*, Aufwendung *f*, Ausgaben *f/pl* (Unkosten)	expenditure, expense costs *pl*, expenses *pl*
dépenses *f/pl* d'affichage *m*	Anschlagkosten *pl*, Plakatanschlagpreis *m*	space charge
dépenses *f/pl* d'insertion *f*	Anzeigenkosten *pl*	advertising charges *pl*
dépenses *f/pl* publicitaires	Werbeaufwendungen *f/pl*, Werbeausgaben *f/pl*, Werbekosten *pl*	advertising costs *pl*, advertising expenditures *pl*, advertising expenses *pl*, advertising investments *pl*, advertising outlay, costs *pl* of advertising
dépenses *pl* courantes	Betriebskosten *pl*	running expenses *pl*
dépliant *m*	Faltprospekt *m*, Prospekt *m*	booklet, folder, handbill, leaflet, pamphlet, prospectus
dépliant *m* en blanc	Blankoprospekt *m*	leaflet in blank
dépliant *m* publicitaire	Werbeprospekt *m*	advertising leaflet
dépliant *m* publicitaire pour étalage *m* spécial	Werbefaltblatt *n* für Spezialauslage *f*	rack folder
dépolir	mattieren	to frost glass
dépolitisation *f*	Entpolitisierung *f*	depolitization
dépositaire *m*	Auslieferer *m*	distributor, supplier
dépôt *m*	Ablage *f*	depot, file, filing system
dépôt *m* d'échantillons *m/pl*	Musterlager *n*	sample stock
dépôts *m/pl* illustrations *f/pl*	Bildarchiv *n*	picture library
dépression *f*	Konjunkturrückgang *m*	downward business trend
dernier cri *m*	letzte Modeneuheit *f*	latest fashion
dernier numéro *m* paru	letzte Ausgabe *f*	current number
dernière épreuve *f*	druckfertiger Korrektur- bogen *m*, Maschinenrevision *f*	press revise
dernière ligne *f*	Ausgangszeile *f*	break-line, last line, short line
dernière ligne *f* d'un paragraphe *m*	letzte Zeile eines Absatzes *m*	break line
dernière page *f* de couverture *f*	4. Umschlagseite *f*	back cover
dernières nouvelles *f/pl*	letzte Meldungen *f/pl*, neueste Nachrichten *f/pl*	latest intelligence, spot-news
dérogation *f* aux tarifs *m/pl*	Tarifabweichung *f*	deviation from rates *pl*
déroulement *m*	Abwicklung *f*	implementation, unrolling
des spots *m/pl* émis l'un après l'autre pour deux produits *m/pl* différents du même annonceur *m*	hintereinander gesendete Werbekurzspots *m/pl* für verschiedene Produkte *n/pl* desselben Werbungtreibenden *m*	piggyback
désabonnement *m*	Abonnentenschwund *m*	downward trend in subscription
description *f*	Beschreibung *f*	description
description *f* d'un produit *m*	Produktbeschreibung *f*	fact sheet
déséquilibre *m*	Mißverhältnis *n*	incongruity
désignation *f*	Kategorisierung *f*	labeling
désir *m* d'achat *m*	Kauflust *f*	buying desire
désir *m* des consommateurs *m/pl*	Verbraucherwunsch *m*	consumer desire
désosser	ausschlachten	to pick
dessin *m*	Entwurf *m*, Gestaltung *f*, Zeichnung *f*	creative work, design, draft, drawing, outline, tentative work, visualizing

dessin *m* à la gouache *f*	Guaschzeichnung *f*	gouache drawing
dessin *m* à la plume *f*	Federzeichnung *f*	pen and ink drawing
dessin *m* animé	Trickfilm *m*	animated cartoon, stunt film, trick picture
dessin *m* au crayon *m*	Bleistiftskizze *f*	pencil-drawing, rough
dessin *m* au fusain *m*	Kohlezeichnung *f*	charcoal-drawing
dessin *m* au lavis *m*	getönte Federzeichnung *f*	wash drawing
dessin *m* au net	Reinzeichnung *f*	final art work, finished drawing
dessin *m* au pastel *m*	Pastellzeichnung *f*	pastel drawing
dessin *m* au propre	fertige Zeichnung *f*, Vorlage *f*	copy, finished drawing, pattern
dessin *m* au trait *m*	Strichzeichnung *f*	line drawing
dessin *m* au trait *m* aquarellé	aquarellierte Strichzeichnung *f*	line and wash drawing
dessin *m* de crayon *m*	Kreidezeichnung *f*	crayon drawing
dessin *m* de mode *f*	Modezeichnung *f*	fashion design
dessin *m* définitif	fertige Zeichnung *f*, Reinlayout *n*	finished drawing, finished layout
dessin *m* d'ordinateur *m*	Computerzeichnung *f*	computer drawing
dessin *m* humoristique	humoristische Zeichnung *f*	cartoon
dessin *m* lithographique	Steinzeichnung *f*	lithographic design
dessin *m* mi-ton	Halbtonzeichnung *f*	half tone drawing
dessin *m* original	Originalzeichnung *f*	key drawing
dessin *m* phototechnique	Lichtzeichnung *f*	light drawing
dessin *m* pour affiche *f*	Plakatentwurf *m*	dummy of a poster, poster design, poster sketch
dessin *m* publicitaire	Werbeentwurf *m*, Werbezeichnung *f*	advertising design, advertising drawing
dessin *m* renversé	Verkehrtzeichnung *f*	reverse drawing
dessinateur *m*	Entwurfsgrafiker *m*, Grafik-Designer *m*, Musterzeichner *m*, Werbegestalter *m*, Zeichner *m*	art designer, artist, commercial artist, designer, layouter
dessinateur-concepteur *m*	Gestalter *m*	creative artist, designer, draughtsman, visualizer
dessinateur *m* en lettres *f/pl*	Schriftenzeichner *m*	lettering artist
dessinateur *m* en publicité *f*	Gebrauchsgrafiker *m*	commercial artist, designer
dessinateur *m* industriel	Formgeber *m*, Formgestalter *m*, Industriedesigner *m*	designer, industrial designer, stylist
dessinateur *m* libre	freier Grafiker *m*	free lance artist
dessinateur *m* publicitaire	Werbegrafiker *m*, Werbezeichner *m*	advertising artist, advertising designer
dessiner	entwerfen, konzipieren, zeichnen	to design, to draft, to draw, to outline
dessous texte *m*	unter Text *m*	under matter
dessus *m* de clavier *m*	Tastatur	keyboard
destinataire *m*	Adressat *m*, Empfänger *m*, Umworbener *m*	addressee, advertisee, consignee, recipient
détail *m*	Aufgliederung *f*	breakdown
détail *m* permanent	wiederkehrendes Anzeigenelement *n*	standing detail
détaillant *m*	Einzelhändler *m*	retailer
détaillé *m*	Aufgliederung *f*	breakdown
détérioration *f*	Beschädigung *f*	damage
détermination *f*	Festlegung *f*	determination
détermination *f* de la coupe *f*	Bestimmung *f* eines Bildausschnitts *m*	cropping
détermination *f* d'un terme *m*	Terminfestlegung *f*	timing
détourage *m*	Abdeckung *f*	mask

détourer	freistellen	to drop out, to silhouette
détracteur *m*	Verleumder *m*	back-biter
à **deux côtés** *m/pl*	zweiseitig	double-sided, two-sided
deux lettres *f/pl* **ligaturées**	Ligatur *f*	double letter, ligature
de **deux pages** *f/pl*	zweiseitig	double-sided, two-sided
deux points *m/pl*	Doppelpunkt *m*	colon
deuxième de couverture *f*	2. Umschlagseite *f*	inside front cover
deuxième épreuve *f* corrigée	Zweitkorrektur *f*	second revised proof
devanture *f*	Schaufenster *n*	display faces *pl*, display window, shop window, show window
développement *m*	Entwicklung *f*	development, evolution
développer	entwickeln	to develop
déviation *f*	Abweichung *f*	deviation
devinette *f*	Ratespiel *n*	quiz
devis *m*	Kostenanschlag *m*, Offerte *f*, Voranschlag *m*	estimate, offer
devis *m* estimatif	Kostenvoranschlag *m*	cost estimate, estimating, quotation
devise *f*	Losung *f*, Wahlspruch *m*	motto, watchword
devise *f* publicitaire	Werbemotto *n*	advertising device, advertising motto
diagramme *m*	Diagramm *n*, grafische Darstellung *f*, Schaubild *n*	chart, diagram, graph, graphic, graphic chart, graphical representation
diagramme *m* de la diffusion *f*	Streubild *n*	scatter diagram
dialecte *m*	Dialekt *m*, Mundart *f*	dialect, idiom
dialogue *m*	Zwiegespräch *n*	dialogue
diamètre *m*	Durchmesser *m*	diameter
diaphragme *m*	Blende *f*	diaphragm
diapositif *m*	Diapositiv *n*	film slide, transparency slide
diapositif *m* couleur	Farbdia *n*	colour transparency, colour-slide
diapositif *m* publicitaire	Werbediapositiv *n*	advertising film slide
diapositif *m* sonore	tönendes Dia *n*, Tondia *n*	slide with sound, sound slide
dictaphone *m*	Diktiergerät *n*	dictating machine
dictée *f*	Diktat *n*	dictation
diction *f*	Ausdrucksweise *f*	diction, phraseology, style
dictionnaire *m*	Wörterbuch *n*	dictionary
Didot *m*	klassische Antiqua *f*	classicistic Latin
diffamation *f*	Ehrabschneidung *f*, Verleumdung *f*	calumny, defamation, libel, slander
diffamer	verunglimpfen	to defame
différé *m*	Bandaufnahmesendung *f*	delayed broadcast
différence *f* de repérage *m*	Passerdifferenz *f*	colour fringing, register difference
différence *f* de tarif *m*	Tarifunterschied *m*	differential
diffuser	streuen	to disperse
diffusion *f*	Verbreitung *f*	circulation, coverage, diffusion, dissimination, distribution
diffusion *f* bouillon *m* déduit	verkaufte Auflage *f*	total net paid circulation
diffusion *f* de nouvelles *f/pl*	Nachrichtendurchsage *f*	broadcasting of news
diffusion *f* moyenne	durchschnittliche Auflage *f*	average circulation
diffusion *f* privilégiée	Privileg-Vertriebsmethode *f*	franchise circulation
diffussion *f* à l'étranger *m*	Auslandsverbreitung *f*	foreign circulation
digne de confiance *f*	vertrauenswürdig	trustworthy
diluant *m*	Verdünnungsmittel *n*	thinner

dimensions *f/pl*	Ausmaße *n/pl*, Format *n*, Größe *f*	dimensions *pl*, format *brit*, size *am*
diminuer	verkleinern	to minimise, to reduce
diminuer l'espace *m* blanc	Zwischenraum *m* verkleinern	to close up, to depress space
diminuner l'espace *m*	kompresser setzen	to close up, to set more solid
diminution *f*	Ermäßigung *f*	reduction
diminution *f* de paiement *m*	Zahlungsminderung *f*	diminution of payment
diminution *f* des tirages *m/pl*	Auflagenminderung *f*	decrease of circulation
diorama *m*	Durchscheinbild *n*	diorama
diorama *m* en couleurs *f/pl*	farbiges Durchsichtsbild *n*	ektachrome
diplôme *m*	Diplom *n*	diploma
dire à mots *m/pl* couverts	andeuten	to hint
directeur *m*	Direktor *m*	director, manager
directeur *m* administratif	Geschäftsführer *m*	business manager, director
directeur *m* artistique	Artdirektor *m*, Atelierleiter *m*, Gestaltungsleiter *m*, künstlerischer Leiter *m*	art buyer, art director, creative director, studio manager
directeur *m* commercial	Verkaufsleiter *m*, Verlagsleiter *m*	business manager, sales *pl* manager, sales *pl* promoter
directeur *m* de la production *f*	Produktionsleiter *m*	product manager
directeur *m* de la section *f* budgetaire	Etatdirektor *m*	account manager, senior account supervisor
directeur *m* de publicité *f*	Werbedirektor *m*	advertising director
directeur *m* de succursale *f*	Filialleiter *m*	store manager
directeur *m* des médias *m/pl*	Medialeiter *m*, Streuplaner *m*	media executive, media manager
directeur *m* du service *m* de publicité *f*	Anzeigendirektor *m*, Anzeigenleiter *m*	advertisement director, advertising manager
directeur *m* d'une discussion *f*	Diskussionsleiter *m*	moderator
directeur *m* d'une émission *f* amusante	Leiter *m* einer Unterhaltungssendung *f*	showmaster
directeur *m* en chef *m*	Generaldirektor *m*	chairman
directeur *m* publicitaire	Werbeleiter *m*	advertising manager
directeur *m* technique	technischer Leiter *m*	technical manager
directeur-propriétaire *m*	Verlagsinhaber *m*	owner-editor
direction *f*	Direktion *f*	management
direction *f* commerciale	Verkaufsleitung *f*	sales *pl* management
directives *f/pl*	Anweisungen *f/pl*, Richtlinien *f/pl*	guide-lines *pl*, instructions *pl*
dirigeant	federführend	acting as leader, centrally handling
discographie *f*	Schallplattenverzeichnis *n*	catalogue of records *pl*, discography
discothèque *f*	Diskothek *f*, Schallplattensammlung *f*	record library
discours *m* de clôture *f*	Schlußwort *n*	concluding word
discours *m* impromptu	Stegreifrede *f*	off-hand speech
discours *m* publicitaire	Werbegespräch *n*, Werbevortrag *m*	advertising discussion, advertising talk
discussion *f*	Besprechung *f*, Erörterung *f*	discussion, meeting
discuter	besprechen	to discuss, to review (a book)
diseur *m*	Unterhalter *m*	entertainer
dispersé	verstreut	scattered
disperser	streuen	to disperse
disponible	verfügbar	available
disposer	disponieren	to dispose, to give instructions *pl*
disposition *f*	Anzeigenabruf *m*, Disposition *f*, Freigabe *f*, Verfügung *f*	arrangement, disposition, handout, release

disposition *f* **typographique**	Satzgestaltung *f*	typographical design
dispute *f*	Wortgefecht *n*	dispute
disque *m*	Schallplatte *f*	disc *am*, record *brit*
disque *m* **à calculer**	Rechenscheibe *f*	calculating disc
disque *m* **de phono** *m*	Tonkonserve *f*	canned music
disque *m* **de photographe** *m* **illustré**	Bildschallplatte *f*	picture record
disque *m* **en couleurs** *f/pl*	Bildplatte *f*	coloured disc
disséminer	verbreiten	to dissiminate
dissolution *f*	Auflösung *f*	cancellation, dissolution
distorsion *f*	Verzerrung *f*	distortion
distorsion *f* **de la concurrence** *f*	Wettbewerbsverzerrung *f*	distortion of competition, falsification of competition
distribuer	Satz *m* ablegen, verteilen, vertreiben	to break up, to diss, to distribute, to file, to kill (composition)
distributeur *m*	Verleiher *m*, Verteiler *m*	distributor, lender
distributeur *m* **automatique**	Automat *m*, Verkaufsautomat *m*, Warenautomat *m*	vending machine
distributeur *m* **de journaux** *m/pl* **automatique**	Zeitungsautomat *m*	newspaper slot-machine
distribution *f*	Absatz *m* (Vertrieb *m*), Verbreitung *f*, Versand *m*, Verteilung *f*	circulation, coverage, diffusion, dispatching, dissimination, distribution, forwarding
distribution *f* **de primes** *f/pl*	Zugabewesen *n*	giftgiving
distribution *f* **d'échantillons** *m/pl*	Musterversand *m*, Probenverteilung *f*	sampling
distribution *f* **d'imprimés** *m/pl*	Drucksachenverteilung *f*, Prospektverteilung *f*	distribution of circulars *pl*, distribution of printed matter
distribution *f* **d'un journal** *m*	Zeitungsvertrieb *m*	distribution of a newspaper
distribution *f* **postale de messages** *m/pl* **non adressés**	Postwurfsendungen *f/pl*	boxholder addressing, bulk posting, mail distribution, mailing piece, post office mailing
district *m*	Bezirk *m*	district
divergence *f* **d'opinion** *f*	Meinungsverschiedenheit *f*	differences *pl* of opinions *pl*
divertissements *m/pl*	Unterhaltungen *f/pl*	entertainments *pl*
diviser	aufteilen	to split
division *f* **des mots** *m/pl*	Worttrennung *f*	word division
division *f* **du tirage** *m*	Teilung *f* der Auflage	splitting
divulguer	aufdecken	to disclose
document *m*	Original *n*, Schriftstück *n*, Reinzeichnung *f*, Urkunde *f*	document, final art work, finished drawing, original, piece of writing
documentation *f*	Dokumentation *f*	documentation
documentation *f* **de presse** *f*	Zeitungsarchiv *n*	newspaper archives *pl*
documentation *f* **par l'image** *f*	Bilddokumentation *f*	pictorial documentation
documents *m/pl* **d'émission** *f*	Sendeunterlagen *f/pl*	broadcasting material
documents *m/pl* **d'expédition** *f*	Versandpapiere *n/pl*	dispatch papers *pl*
documents *m/pl* **d'impression** *f*	Druckunterlage *f*	printing material
documents *m/pl* **publicitaires**	Werbeunterlagen *f/pl*	promotional material
domaine *m* **de la diffusion** *f*	Streubereich *m*	dispersion area
domaine *m* **public**	öffentlicher Grund *m* und Boden *m*	public property
domaine *m* **publicitaire**	Werbebereich *m*	advertising area

domiciliation f	Bestimmung f des Insertionsorgans n	domiciliation
dommages-intérêts m/pl	Schadenersatz m	compensation for damage, indemnity
donnant droit m à la commission f	provisionspflichtig	commissionable
donnée f de composition f	Anweisung f (für Satz m)	composition pattern
données f/pl	Gegebenheiten f/pl	data pl
données f/pl brutes	Rohdaten n/pl	raw data pl
données f/pl de base f	grundlegendes Material n	basic dates pl
données f/pl de composition f	Satzanweisungen f/pl	rules pl of composition
données f/pl techniques	technische Daten m/pl	mechanical data pl
donner à bail m	verpachten	to farm out, to lease
donner des retours m/pl en arrière	Provisionsabgabe f	kickback, yielding of commission
donner un ordre m	Auftrag m vergeben	to place an order
donner une formulation f plus frappante	treffender formulieren	to strengthen
donner une publicité f retentissante	eine Nachricht f hochspielen	to play up an information, to puff up an information
dorer à froid	blindpressen	to blind
dorure f	Vergoldung f	gilding
dorure f à froid	Blindpressung f	blind tooling
dos m de livre m	Buchrücken m	backbone, backstrip, book spine
dosage m publicitaire	Werbedosierung f	advertising dosage
dossier m à anneaux m/pl	Ringhefter m	snap-ring file
dossier m d'une commande f	Auftragstasche f	docket, job bag
douane f	Zoll m	customs pl
doublage m	Druckdublee n, Kaschierung f	mackling, passe-partout lamination
double point m, double	Doppelpunkt m, zweiseitig	colon, double-sided, two-sided
double colonne f	Doppelspalte f	double column
double emploi m	Überlappung f, Überschneidung f, Wiederholung f	duplication, overlapping, repetition
double exemplaire m	zweifache Ausfertigung f	duplicate
double lecteur m	Doppelleser m	double reader
double page f centrale	doppelseitige Anzeige f, Doppelseite f-Blattmitte f, zweiseitige gegenüberliegende Anzeige f	center page spread, double truck, double-page spread
double pli m	Doppelfalz m	double fold
double-bande f	gleichzeitige Ton- und Bildband n -Vorführung f	simultaneous projection of recording tape and image
doubler	kaschieren, synchronisieren	to dub, to glue, to laminate, to line
doublon m	Dublette f, Hochzeit f (doppelt Gesetztes n)	double, doublet
dramatisation f	Dramatisierung f	dramatization
droit m d'auteur m	Autorenrecht n, Urheberrecht n	copyright
droit m de compensation f	Ersatzanspruch m	claim to compensation
droit m de license f	Lizenzgebühren f/pl	royalties pl
droit m de publication f	Copyright n	copyright
droit m de reproduction f	Abdrucksrecht n	copyright, right of reproduction
droit m de résiliation f	Rücktrittsrecht n	cancellation right
droit m de voirie f	Genehmigungsgebühr f	license fee

droit *m* d'impression *f*	Copyright *n*	copyright
droit *m* publicitaire	Werberecht *n*	advertising law
droits *m/pl* d'adaptation *f* cinématographique	Filmrechte *n/pl*	film rights *pl*
droits *m/pl* d'auteur *m*	Urheberrechtslizenz *f*	royalty
droits *m/pl* de douane *f*	Zollgebühr *f*	duty
ducroire *m*	Delkredere *n*	delcredere
d'un bon rendement *m* publicitaire	werbewirksam	effective in advertising
d'une manière *f* dissolue	lockere Manier *f*	loose
duplicata *m*	Duplikat *n*, Zweitschrift *f*	copy, duplicate, duplication
duplicata *m/pl*	Duplikatätzung *f*	duplicate block
duplicateur *m*	Vervielfältigungsapparat *m*	duplicator, hectograph
duplication *f*	Überlappung *f*, Überschneidung *f*	duplication, overlapping
durée *f*	Dauer *f*	duration, length of time
durée *f* d'affichage *m*	Aushangdauer *f*	period of display
durée *f* de la campagne *f* publicitaire	Streudauer *f*	duration of the advertising campaign
durée *f* de vie *f*	Lebensdauer *f*	duration of life
durée *f* du blocage *m*	gesperrte Zeit *f* (für Werbesendungen)	block-out
durée *f* du contrat *m*	Vertragsdauer *f*	contract period
durée *f* du droit *m* d'auteur *m*	Schutzfrist *f*	duration of copyright
dynamisme *m*	Vorantreiben *n*	drive

E

eau-forte *f*	Ätzung *f*	block (brit) , engraving, etching
eau-forte *f* grave	Tiefätzung *f*	deep-etching
ébarber	beschneiden	to crop, to make cuts *pl*, to prune, to slash, to trim
ébauche *f*	Entwurf *m*, Skizze *f*	design, draft, dummy, layout, outline, rough, sketch, tentative work
ébaucher	skizzieren	to outline, to sketch
échange *m* de vues *f/pl*	Meinungsaustausch *m*	interchange of ideas *pl*
échange *m* des adresses *f/pl* de clients *m/pl*	Kundenadressen-Austausch *m*	list-broking
échange *m* d'idées *f/pl*	Gedankenaustausch *m*	exchange of thoughts *pl*
échantillon *m*	Muster *n*, Probe *f*, Stichprobe *f*, Warenprobe *f*	pattern, sample, specimen
échantillon *m* à l'examen *m*	Ansichtsmuster *n*	sample for inspection
échantillon *m* au hasard *m*	Zufallsstichprobe *f*	random sample
échantillon *m* de comparaison *f*	Ausfallmuster *n*	quality sample, reference pattern
échantillon *m* de couleur *f*	Farbmuster *n*	colour sample, swatch
échantillon *m* gratuit	Gratismuster *n*, Gratisprobe *f*	free sample, free trial
échantillon *m* publicitaire	Werbemuster *n*	advertising sample
échantillon *m* représentatif	repräsentative Marktuntersuchung *f*	adequate sample
échantillonnage *m* par zone *f*	Flächenstichprobe *f*, regionale Marktuntersuchung *f*	area sampling
échantillonner	bemustern	to sample

échéance *f*	Fälligkeit *f*	date of payment, maturity
échéancier *m*	Terminkalender *m*	advertising schedule, deadline schedule
échec *m*	Mißerfolg *m*	flop
échelle *f*	Maßstab *m*	scale, yardstick
échelle *f* d'attitudes *f/pl*	Verhaltensskala *f*	attitude scale
échelle *f* de page *f*	Kolumnenmaß *n*	page gauge
échelle *f* des gris	Grauskala *f*	grey scale
échelle *f* mobile	Nachlaßstaffel *f*, Rabattstaffel *f*	scale of discount, sliding scale discount, sliding scale
écho *m*	Echo *n*, Resonanz *f*	echo, empathy
échoppe *f*	Radiernadel *f*, Stahlstichel *m*	burin, chisel
échos *m/pl* de la presse *f*	Pressestimmen *f/pl*	press comments *pl*
échos *m/pl* familiers	Familiennachrichten *f/pl*	gossip
échos *m/pl* publicitaires	Werbenachricht *f*	advertising news
échotier *m*	Klatschbase *f*	gossip writer
échu	fällig	due
éclair *m* au magnésium *m*	Blitzlicht *n*	flash
éclairage *m*	Beleuchtung *f*	illumination, lighting
éclairage *m* des étalages *m/pl*	Schaufensterbeleuchtung *f*	shop window lighting
éclairer	beleuchten	to light
école *f* d'art *m*	Kunstschule *f*	art school
école *f* de publicité *f*	Werbefachschule *f*	advertising trade school
école *f* des arts *m/pl* et métiers *m/pl*	Kunstgewerbeschule *f*	school of applied art
économie *f*	Wirtschaft *f*	economy
économie *f* d'expression *f*	Ausdrucksökonomie *f*	economy of expression
écouteur *m* clandestin	Schwarzhörer *m*	secret listener
écran *m*	Bildfläche *f*, Bildschirm *m*, Filmleinwand *f*, Leinwand *f*, Projektionswand *f*, Schablone *f*	canvas, cut out, jig, linen, pattern, screen, stencil, surface screen, video display screen
écran *m* de contrôle *m*	Kontrollbildschirm *m*	monitor
écran *m* de la mise *f* en pages *f/pl*	Umbruch-Bildschirm *m*	make-up screen
écran *m* de télévision *f*	Fernsehschirm *m*	TV-screen
écran *m* de visualisation *f*	Bildschirmgerät *n*	video display terminal, video display unit
écran *m* de visualisation *f* de la mise *f* en pages *f/pl*	Umbruch-Bildschirmgerät *n*	make-up display terminal
écran *m* large	Breitwand *f*	wide-screen
écraser	abquetschen	to batter
écraser un papier *m*	unter den Tisch *m* fallen lassen	to ignore, to let drop
écrire en un mot *m*	zusammenschreiben	to write in one word
écrit *m*	Niederschrift *f*, Schriftstück *n*	document, piece of writing, record, writing down
écrit à six-quatre-deux	hastig hingeworfen	slapdashed
écrit *m* polémique	Streitschrift *f*	polemic
écriteau *m* aimanté	Magnetschild *n*	magnetic sign
écriture *f* à la main *f*	Handschrift *f*	handwriting
écriture *f* anglaise	englische Schreibschrift *f*	English script type
écriture *f* courante	Kurrentschrift *f*, Laufschrift *f*	illuminated newscaster, running hand
écriture *f* cursive	Kursivschrift *f*	Italic type, script type, sloping letters *pl*
écriture *f* étroite	enge Schrift *f*	condensed type
écriture *f* fumigène	Rauchschriftwerbung *f*	smoke writing

écriture *f* **script**	Blockschrift *f*	print script
écriture *f* **secrète**	Geheimschrift *f*	cipher
écriture *f* **typographique**	Schreibschrift *f*	handwriting, script writing, script-type
écrivailleur *m*	Vielschreiber *m*	scribbler
écrivain *m*	Schriftsteller *m*	author, publicist, writer
écrivassier *m*	Schreiberling *f*	grub
écusson *m*	Schildchen *n*	escutcheon
éditer	herausgeben, verlegen	to bring out, to issue, to publish
éditeur *m*	Verleger *m*, Zeitungsherausgeber *m*	managing editor, publisher
éditeur *m* **d'adresses** *f/pl*	Adressenverlag *m*	address broker, supplier of addresses *pl*
éditeur *m* **d'un journal** *m*	Zeitungsverleger *m*	newspaper owner, newspaper publisher *am*
édition *f*	Ausgabe *f* (Nummer)	copy, edition, issue, number
édition *f* **à part** *f*	Separatdruck *m*, Sonderdruck *m*	off-print, separate copies *pl*, special impression
édition *f* **à tirage** *m* **limité**	beschränkte Auflage *f*	limited edition
édition *f* **aéropostale**	Luftpostausgabe *f*	air edition
édition *f* **augmentée**	erweiterte Auflage *f*	enlarged edition
édition *f* **complète**	Gesamtausgabe *f*	all the issues *pl*
édition *f* **corrigée et augmentée**	verbesserte und erweiterte Auflage *f*	revised edition
édition *f* **de luxe** *m*	Luxusausgabe *f*	de luxe edition
édition *f* **de Noël** *m*	Weihnachtsnummer *f*	Christmas number
édition *f* **de nuit** *f*	Nachtausgabe *f*	night edition
édition *f* **départementale**	Bezirksausgabe *f*	local issue, territorial edition
édition *f* **d'essai** *m*	Testausgabe *f*, Versuchsausgabe *f*	pilot edition
édition *f* **du matin** *m*	Morgenausgabe *f*	early morning edition
édition *f* **du soir** *m*	Spätausgabe *f*	evening edition
édition *f* **frauduleuse**	Raubdruck *m*	pirated edition
édition *f* **licenciée**	Lizenzausgabe *f*	licensed edition
édition *f* **locale**	Bezirksausgabe *f*	local issue, territorial edition
édition *f* **minuscule**	Miniaturausgabe *f*	miniature edition
édition *f* **originale**	Originalausgabe *f*	first edition, original edition
édition *f* **partielle**	Teilausgabe *f*	part edition
édition *f* **populaire**	Volksausgabe *f*	cheap reprint
édition *f* **portative**	Taschenausgabe *f*	pocket edition
édition *f* **pour outre -mer** *m*	Überseeausgabe *f*	oversea edition
édition *f* **privée**	Privatdruck *m*	private edition
édition *f* **publicitaire**	Werbepublikation *f*	advertising publication
édition *f* **régionale**	Regionalausgabe *f*	regional issue
édition *f* **secondaire**	Nebenausgabe *f*	sub-edition
édition *f* **spéciale**	Extrablatt *n*, Sonderausgabe *f*	special edition
édition *f* **zéro**	Nullnummer *f*	zero edition
éditions *f/pl* **couplées**	Kombinationsausgabe *f*	combined edition
éditions *f/pl* **publicitaires**	Werbeliteratur *f*	advertising literature
éditorial *m*	Leitartikel *m*, redaktioneller Artikel *m*	editorial, leader, leading article
effacer	ausstreichen, löschen	to cross, to delete
effectif	effektiv	effective
effet *m*	Effekt *m*, Wirkung *f*	effect
effet *m* **à distance** *f*	Fernwirkung *f*	long-range effect
effet *m* **chromatique**	Farbwirkung *f*	colour effect
effet *m* **continué**	Langzeitwirkung *f*	longtime-effect

effet *m* cumulatif	Akkumulierung *f*, kumulative Wirkung *f*	accumulation, cumulative effect
effet *m* de choc *m*	Eindrucksstärke *f*, Schockwirkung *f*	impact
effet *m* de couleurs *f/pl*	Farbeffekt *m*	colour effect
effet *m* de surprise *f*	Überraschungseffekt *m*	surprise effect
effet *m* d'éloignement *m*	Verfremdungseffekt *m*	alienation effect
effet *m* durable	Dauerwirkung *f*	lasting effect
effet *m* policier	kriminalistischer Stimmungseffekt *m*	Hitchcock appeal
effet *m* propre de la marchandise *f* elle-même	Eigenwirkung *f* einer Ware *f*	self appeal
effet *m* publicitaire	Stoßkraft *f*, Streuwirkung *f*, Werbeeffekt *m*, Werbewirkung *f*	advertising effect, impact
effet *m* ultérieur	Nachbild *n*, Nachwirkung *f*	after-image
efficacité *f*	Wirksamkeit *f*	effectiveness, efficiency, impressiveness
efficacité *f* de la publicité *f*	Werbewirksamkeit *f*	advertising effectiveness, advertising efficiency
efficacité *f* de la vente *f*	Verkaufswirkung *f*	effect on sales *pl*
efficience *f* de publicité *f*	Wirkungsgrad *m* der Werbung *f*	sales *pl* impact
efflanqué	saft- und kraftlos	lanky
effleurer	oberflächlich behandeln	to skim
effort *m* marqué, effort *m* spécial	verstärkter Werbeeinsatz *m*	sales *pl* drive
effort *m* spécial de publicité *f*	verstärkte Werbeanstrengungen *f/pl*	advertising efforts *pl*, drive
efforts *m/pl* publicitaires	Werbemaßnahmen *f/pl*	advertising measures *pl*
égaliser	ausgleichen (Zurichtung *f*)	to equalize
égratignure *f*	Kratzer *m*	scraper, scratch
égyptienne *f*	Egyptienne *f*	Egyptian
ektachrome *m*	Farbdia *n*	colour transparency, colour-slide
élaboration *f* d'un plan *m*	Planungsarbeit *f*	planning activity
élaboration *f* simultanément	Simultanverarbeitung *f*	multi processing, simultaneous operation
élaborer	ausarbeiten, entwerfen, konzipieren	to design, to draft, to elaborate, to outline
élaguer	abkürzen, verkürzen	to curtail, to cut down, to cut short
élargissement *m*	Ausweitung *f*	diversification
élection *f*	Wahl *f*	choice, election
élément *m*	Bestandteil *m*	component, constituent
élément *m* d'image *f* extraordinaire	ungewöhnliches Bildelement *n*	Hathaway touch
élément *m* d'impression *f* auxiliaire	Eindruckwerk *n*	auxiliary printing unit
élément *m* figuratif extraordinaire	ungewöhnliches Bildelement *n*	Hathaway touch
élément *m* figuratif impressionnant	wirkungsvolles Bildelement *n*	Hathaway touch
élément *m* pictural	Bildelement *n*	pictorial element
élément *m* publicitaire de peu de valeur *f*	geringwertiger Werbeartikel *m*	gadget
éléments *m/pl* d'illustration *f*	Bildmaterial *n*	illustrative material
éléments *m/pl* du texte *m*	Textmaterial *n*	feature material

éléments *m/pl* d'un moyen *m*	Werbeelement *n/pl*	interest factor
éléments *m/pl* publicitaires	Werbefaktoren *m/pl*	advertising factors *pl*
élève *m*	Volontär *m*	trainee
élever	aufbauen	to build-up
éliminer	ausfallen lassen, wegfallen lassen	to cut, to kill
élite *f* intellectuelle	geistige Elite *f*	intelligentsia
élocution *f*	Ausdrucksweise *f*	diction, phraseology, style
éloge *m*	Lobrede *f*	eulogy, panegyric
Elzévir *m*	Mediäval *f*	old face, old style
emballage *m*	Packung *f*, Verpackung *f*	pack, package, packaging, wrapping
emballage *m* à double usage *m*	wiederverwendbare Packung *f*	re-use package
emballage *m* de grande taille *f*	Großpackung *f*	economy size, giant-size pack
emballage *m* de remploi *m*, emballage *m* de retour	Mehrwegpackung *f*, wiederverwendbare Packung *f*	dual-use package, re-use package
emballage *m* des portions *f/pl* de sucre *m*	Würfelzuckerverpackung *f*	lump-sugar packing
emballage *m* d'essai *m*	Probepackung *f*	trial package
emballage *m* d'origine *f*	Originalpackung *f*, Originalverpackung *f*	original package, original wrapping
emballage *m* en matière *f* synthétique	Kunststoffverpackung *f*	plastic packaging
emballage *m* factice	Attrappe *f*, Schaupackung *f*	display package, dummy pack, mock-up
emballage *m* non consigné	Wegwerfpackung *f*	one-way package
emballage *m* non repris	Einwegpackung *f*	expendable package, non-returnable package, one way package, spoil package
emballage *m* normal	Normalpackung *f*	standard package
emballage *m* perdu	Einwegpackung *f*, Wegwerfpackung *f*	expendable package, non-returnable package, one way package, spoil package
emballage *m* plastique transparent	durchsichtige Verpackung *f* aus Kunststoff *m*	blister pack
emballage *m* transparent	Klarsichtpackung *f*	transparent package
emballage *m* trompeur	Mogelpackung *f*	deceptive package
emballer	verpacken	to pack
embargo *m* levé	Druckfreigabe *f*	release
emblème *m*, emblème *m* découpé	ausgestanztes Emblem *n*, Kennzeichen *n*	die cut, emblem, sign
emblème *m* d'entreprise *f*	Firmensiegel *n*	signet
emboîter	einhängen	to case in
émetteur *m*	Rundfunksender *m*	wireless transmitter
émetteur *m* brouilleur	Störsender *m*	blooper, jamming station
émetteur *m* clandestin	Geheimsender *m*, Piratensender *m*	clandestine radio transmitter, pirate station
émettre	senden (Radio)	to broadcast, to transmit
émission *f*	Ausstrahlung *f*	emission
émission *f* à la radio *f*	Radiosendung *f*	broadcast transmission
émission *f* à succès *m*	volkstümliche Sendung *f*	pop feature
émission *f* clandestine	Schwarzsendung *f*	illegal transmitting
émission *f* de télévision *f*	Fernsehsendung *f*, Fernsehübertragung *f*	telecast *am*, television transmission *brit*, video
émission *f* différée	aufgezeichnete Sendung *f*	pre-recorded broadcast

émission f en différé m	Fernsehkonserve f, sendefertige Konserve f	canned television item, pre-recorded broadcast
émission f en direct	Live-Sendung f, Originalsendung f	live broadcast, live transmission
émission f par fragments m/pl	Sendefolge f	instalment
émission f patronnée	Patronatssendung f, Sponsor-Sendung f	sponsored broadcast, sponsored programme
émission f pour deux produits m/pl d'un annonceur m	Werbesendung f für zwei verschiedene Produkte m/pl eines Werbungtreibenden	piggyback
émission f publicitaire	Fernsehspot m, Werbefunk m, Werbesendung f	announcement, commercial, commercial broadcasting, commercial radio, spot
émission f publicitaire intégrée	integrierte Funkwerbung f	straight commercial
émission f publicitaire pour des sous-produits m/pl	Werbesendung f für Nebenprodukte n/pl	hitch-hike
émission f quotidienne sauf samedi m et dimanche m	Werbesendung f zur gleichbleibenden Tageszeit f an 5 aufeinanderfolgenden Tagen m/pl	across the board
émission f radiophonique	Sendung f, Rundfunksendung f	broadcast, radio casting am
empaquetage m de ménage m	Haushaltspackung f	family size pack
empaquetage m gigantesque	Familienpackung f, Großpackung f	economy size, giant-size pack
empattement m	Füßchen n/typog, Haarstrich m, Serif n	hairline, serif, thin stroke
emplacement m	Anschlagstelle f, Plazierung f	billboard, placing, position, site
emplacement m couloir m	Gangschild n	corridor panel, corridor site
emplacement m d'annonce f	Anzeigenplazierung f	advertisement placing
emplacement m dans compartiment m	Abteilplakat n	compartment panel
emplacement m de quai m	Perronfläche f,. Plattformanschlag m	dash sign, platform site, platform site advertising
emplacement m de rigueur f, emplacement m imposé	Platzvorschrift f, Plazierungsvorschrift f, vorgeschriebene Plazierung f	appointed space, prescribed position, stated position
emplacement m intérieur de chemin m de fer m	Eisenbahnplakat n	railroad showing
emplacement m intérieur de voiture f	Daueranschlag m in Verkehrsmitteln n/pl, Innenplakat n (in Verkehrsmitteln n/pl)	car card advertising, car panel, indoor poster
emplacement m isolé	Ganzstelle f, Inselplacierung f	island position, solus site
emplacement m masqué	verdeckter Anschlag m	obstructed site
emplacement m ordinaire	gewöhnliche Plazierung f, Plazierung f im Anzeigenteil m	ordinary position, run-of-paper position
emplacement m parallèle	parallel zur Straße f	parallel position
emplacement m prédominant dans une page f	seitenbeherrschende Anzeige f	page dominance
emplacement m préférentiel	Vorzugsplazierung f	full position am, preferred position, special position
emplacement m privilégié	bevorzugte Plazierung f	preferred position, special position

emplacement *m* réservé	reservierter Anzeigenplatz *m*	reserved position
emplacement *m* spécial	Vorzugsplazierung *f*	full position *am*, preferred position, special position
emplacement *m* supérieur à droit	rechts oben	top right position
emplacement *m* supérieur à gauche	Plazierung *f* oben links	top left position
emplacement *m* sur contre-marches *f/pl* d'escalier *m*	Treppenstufenwerbung *f*	advertising on risers *pl* of staircase, staircase site
emplacement *m* sur escalier *m* roulant	Rolltreppenschild *n*	escalator panel, escalator site
emplacement *m* unique	alleinstehend (Außenwerbung *f*)	solus site
emplacement *m* utilisé habituellement	allgemeine Anschlagstelle *f*	usually used site
emplacement *m* utilisé spécialement	Sonderstelle *f*, Spezialstelle *f*	individual location
emplacements *m/pl* disponibles	verfügbarer Anschlagraum *m*	available sites *pl*
emploi *m* des médias *m/pl*	Mediaeinsatz *m*	media performance
empreindre	prägen	to emboss, to stamp
empreinte *f*	Abdruck *m*	impression, imprint
empreinte *f* à chaud	Heißprägung *f*	hot process embossing, thermography
empreinte *f* de l'adresse *f* du détaillant *m*	eingedruckte Händleranschrift *f*	dealer imprint
empreinte *f* dorée	Goldprägung *f*	gold blocking
en blanc	nichtdruckend	non-printing
en moyenne	durchschnittlich	at an average
en plus	zuzüglich	additional
en retard *m*	Rückstand *m*, im	in arrears *pl*
en verso	linke Seite *f*	even page, left-hand page
encadrement *m*	Einfassung *f*, Umrahmung *f*, Umrandung *f*	border, box, frame, panel
encadrer	Text *m* einfassen, einrahmen, umranden	to border, to box in, to frame
encart *m*	Beilage *f*, Beilagenzettel *m*	enclosure, insert, inset, stuffer, supplement
encart *m* broché	Beihefter *m*, Beikleber *m*, Einhefter *m*	bound insert, bound-in, insert, tip-in
encart *m* dans un emballage *m*	Packungsbeilage *f*	package insert
encart *m* en couleur *f* imprimé en continu *m*	HiFi-Endlosfarbanzeige *f*	continuous advertisement in colour, HiFi continuous advertisement in colour, wall paper litho
encart *m* libre	lose Beilage *f*	loose insert
encartage *m*	Beilegung *f*	inserting
encercler	einkreisen	to ring
enchaînement *m*	Überblendung *f*	dissolve, shunt
encochage *m* d'un cliché *m*	Klischeeausschnitt *m*	piercing
encoche *f*	Ausschnitt *m* (Stanze *f*)	cut out, piercing, trimming
encocher	ausklinken	to mortise, to pierce for type
encollage *m*	Leimung *f*	sizing
encollage *m* des dos *m/pl*	Blockleimung *f*	spine gluing
encollage *m* du dos *m* des livres *m/pl*	Rückenleimung *f*	back glueing
encollage *m* du papier *m*	Papierleimung *f*	paper sizing
encoller	kaschieren	to glue, to laminate, to line
encombrement *m* du marché *m*	Marktsättigung *f*	market saturation

encrage *m*	Farbgebung *f*, Farbwerk *n*	colouring, inking, inking unit, tinting
encre *f* à tampons *m/pl*	Stempelfarbe *f*	marking ink
encre *f* de Chine *f*	Tusche *f*	Indian ink
encre *f* de retouche *f*	Retuschefarbe *f*	retouching ink
encre *f* d'impression *f*	Druckfarbe *f*	printing ink
encre *f* d'imprimerie *f*	Druckerschwärze *f*	printer's ink
encre *f* double-ton *m*	Doppeltonfarbe *f*	double-tone ink
encre *f* grasse	Druckerschwärze *f*	printer's ink
encre *f* luminescente solaire	Tagesleuchtfarbe *f*	day-glo, daylight fluorescent ink
encre *f* lumineuse	Leuchtfarbe *f*	luminous ink, luminous paint
encre *f* opaque	Deckfarbe *f*	opaque ink
encre *f* sérigraphie *f*	Siebdruckfarbe *f*	screen printing ink
encre *f* spéciale	Spezialfarbe *f*	extra colour, special colour
encre *f* transparente	Lasurfarbe *f*	glaze, transparent ink
encyclopédie *f*	Lexikon *n*, Sachwörterbuch *n*	encyclopaedia, lexicon
enfler	aufbauschen	to blow up, to puff up
enflure *f*	Schwulst *m*	bombast, pomposity
enfreindre	verstoßen gegen	to infringe
enjambement *m*	Übergreifen *n*	run-on-line
énoncé *m*	Wortlaut *m*	wording
enquête *f*	Befragung *f*, Enquête *f*, Erhebung *f*, Umfrage *f*, Untersuchung *f*	examination, inquiry, interview, investigation, poll, questioning, research, survey, test
enquête *f* auprès des consommateurs *m/pl*	Verbraucherbefragung *f*	consumer imquiry, consumer survey
enquête *f* auprès des détaillants *m/pl*	Händlerbefragung *f*	dealer survey, retail audit, shop audit, shop-check
enquête *f* auprès des lecteurs *m/pl*	Leserschaftsumfrage *f*	readership poll
enquête *f* aux téléspectateurs *m/pl* pendant une émission *f*	Fernsehzuschauerbefragung *f* während der Sendung *f*	coincidental survey
enquête *f* omnibus	Mehrthemenumfrage *f*	omnibus survey
enquête *f* par téléphone *m*	Telefonumfrage *f*	telephone survey
enquête *f* pilote	Leitstudie *f*, Vorstudie *f*, Voruntersuchung *f*	pilot study, pretesting
enquête *f* postale	briefliche Befragung *f*, schriftliche Befragung *f*	mail research, mail survey, mail research, mail survey
enquête *f* sur le marché *m*	Marktuntersuchung *f*	market investigation, market survey
enquête *f* sur les opinions *f/pl*	Demoskopie *f*, Meinungsforschung *f*, Meinungsumfrage *f*	Gallup poll, opinion poll, opinion research, opinion survey, public opinion analysis
enquêteur *m*	Interviewer *m*, Rechercheur *m*	field investigator, interviewer, investigator, pollster, research man
enquêteur *m* commercial	Marktforscher *m*	head counter, market researcher
enquêteur *m* de motivation *f*	Motivforscher *m*	head shrinker, motive analyst
enquêteur *m* d'opinion *f*	Meinungsforscher *m*	pollster, public opinion analyst
enquêtrice *f*	Interviewerin *f*	interviewer, pollster
enregistrement *m*	Registratur *f*	filing cabinet, registry

enregistrement *m* d'une émission *f* radiophonique	Aufzeichnung *f* einer Rundfunksendung *f*	air check
enregistrement *m* électrique	Tonbandaufnahme *f*	electrical transcription, tape recording
enregistrement *m* fractionné	überspielen *n*	rerecording
enregistrement *m* sur bande *f* magnétique	Bandaufnahme *f*	tape recording
enregistrer	einschreiben	to inscribe, to register
enregistrer d'espace *m*	Anzeigenraum *m* buchen	to book space
enseigne *f*	Außenschild *n*, Firmentafel *f*, Schild *n*	board, name plate, outdoor sign, panel, plate, sign
enseigne *f* au néon *m*	Neon-Leuchtschild *n*	neon sign
enseigne *f* commerciale	Firmenschild *n*	name plate, signboard
enseigne *f* de magasin *m*	Ladenschild *n*	on-premise sign, shop sign
enseigne *f* en verre *m*	Glasschild *n*	glass sign
enseigne *f* lumineuse	Transparent *n*	banner, electric sign, streamer
enseigne *f* métallique	Metallschild *n*	metal sign
enseigne *f* publicitaire	Werbeschild *n*	billboard, sign
enseigne *f* routière	Streckenplakat *n*	railroad bulletin, roadside hoarding
enseigne *f* verticale	Werbeschild *n* mit Vertikalschrift *f*	vertical sign
ensemble *m* de panneaux *m/pl*	Anschlagtafelgruppe *f*	hoarding
ensemble *m* des auditeurs *m/pl*	Zuhörerschaft *f*	audience
ensemble *m* des contrats *m/pl*	Gesamtabschluß *m*	blanked contract
ensemble *m* des journaux *m/pl*	Blätterwald *m*	the whole of newspapers *pl*
ensemble *m* des lecteurs *m/pl*	Leserschaft *f*	audience, readers *pl*, readership
ensemble *m* des ordres *m/pl*	Gesamtabschluß *m*	blanked contract
ensemble micro-ampli-haut-parleur *m*	Lautsprecheranlage *f*	public address system
entaille *f*	Einschnitt *m*	notch
entailler	ausklinken	to mortise, to pierce for type
entassement *m* de produits *m/pl*	Warenanhäufung *f*	mass-display
entente *f* sur les prix *m/pl*	Preisabsprache *f*	price-fixing agreement
en-tête *f*	Kopfleiste *f*, Titelkopf *m*, Überschrift *f*, Zeitungskopf *m*	caption, head piece, head rules *pl*, headband, heading, headline, mast head, newspaper heading, top
en-tête *f* de lettre *f*	Briefkopf *m*	letter-heading
entourer d'un filet *m*	Text *m* einfassen, einrahmen, umranden	to border, to box in, to frame
entraînement *m* à la vente *f*	Verkaufstraining *n*	sales *pl* training
entrée *f* de commandes *f/pl*	Auftragseingang *m*	incoming of orders *pl*
entrée *f* d'une annonce *f*	Anfang *m* einer Anzeige *f*	lead-in
entrée *f* en vigueur *f*	Inkrafttreten *n*	effective date
entrefilet *m*	kleine Textanzeige *f*, Kurzartikel *m*, Pressenotiz *f*	news release, newspaper notice, paragraph, short paragraph
entremetteur *m*	Unterhändler *m*, Vermittler *m*, Zwischenträger *m*	go-between, negotiator, tell-tale
entremettre	vermitteln	to interpose, to negotiate
entrepreneur *m* d'affichage *m*	Plakatanschlaginstitut *n*	billposting agency, poster contractor, poster plant
entrepreneur *m* de publicité *f* extérieure	Außenwerbungsunternehmen *n*	outdoor advertising plant

entreprise f à tendance f	Tendenzbetrieb m	tendency enterprise
entreprise f annonceuse	Werbungtreibender m	advertiser
entreprise f compétitive	Wettbewerbsunternehmen n	rival business
entreprise f concurrente	Konkurrenzunternehmen n	rival business
entreprise f d'affermage m	Pachtunternehmen n	advertising operator, leaseholder
entreprise f d'affichage m	Anschlagunternehmen n, Plakatanschlagunternehmen n	billposting company, plant operator, poster plant
entreprise f de distribution f	Vertriebsunternehmen n	distributing enterprise, distribution agency
entreprise f de publicité f	Werbefirma f, Werbeunternehmen n	advertising contractor, advertising enterprise
entreprise f publicitaire	Werbegesellschaft f	advertising company
entretien m	Besprechung f, Instandhaltung f	discussion, maintenance, meeting
entretien m de vente f	Verkaufsgespräch n	sales pl talk
entretien m préliminaire	Vorbesprechung f	preliminary discussion
entrevue f	Zusammenkunft f	appointment, meeting
enveloppe f	Briefumschlag m, Kuvert n	envelope
enveloppe f à fenêtre f	Fensterumschlag m	window envelope
enveloppe f américaine	Versandtasche f	American envelope
enveloppe f dans les cercles m/pl de lecture f	Lesemappe f	reading circle case
enveloppe f énigma	Briefumschlag m mit eingeschlagener Klappe f	penny saver, postage saver
enveloppe f timbrée	Freiumschlag m	stamped envelope
enveloppe f transparente vitrifiée	Fensterumschlag m	window envelope
envelopper	einwickeln	to roll up, to wrap
envers	linksseitig	reverso
envie f d'acheter	Kauflust f	buying desire
environnement m	Umwelt f	environment
environs m/pl	Umgegend f	environment
envoi m	Versand m	dispatching, forwarding
envoi m à choix m	Auswahlsendung f	consignment for choice
envoi m à l'examen m	Ansichtssendung f	consignment for inspection
envoi m contre remboursement m	Nachnahmesendung f	parcel to be paid for on delivery
envoi m de justificatifs m/pl	Belegversand m	sending of vouchers pl
envoi m d'échantillons m/pl	Musterversand m	sampling
envoi m en masse f	Massenversand m	mass mailing
envoi m gratuit	Gratiszustellung f	free delivery
envoi m postal	Postversand m	dispatch by mail
envois m/pl en nombre m	postalische Massensendungen f/pl	bulk posting
envoyé m special	Sonderberichterstatter m	special correspondent
envoyer	versenden	to dispatch, to forward, to ship
épaisseur f	Dicke f	thickness
épaisseur m du papier m	Papierdicke f	paper thickness
épanchement m de cœur m	Herzenserguß m	effusion
épaulement m	Fleisch n eines Buchstabens m	beard, bevelled feet pl, blank space, burr
épeler	buchstabieren	to spell
éphémerides f/pl	Abreißkalender m	tear-off calendar
épidiascope m	Bildwerfer m	epidiascope, slide projector
épigraphe f	Inschrift f, Motto n	inscription, motto
épilogue m	Nachwort n	epilogue

éplucheur *m*	Kritikaster *m*	armchair critic, fault-finder
épreuve *f*	Abzug *m*, Andruck *m*, Druckprobe *f*, Entwurf *m*, Fahne *f*/*typog f*, Korrekturabzug *m*, Probeabzug *m*, Probedruck *m*	design, draft, dummy volume, outline, preprint, print, proof, proofing, proofsheet, pull, slip, specimen volume, tentative work
épreuve *f* à la brosse *f*	Bürstenabzug *m*, Fahnenabzug *m*	brush proof, flat proof, galley proof, slip, stone proof
épreuve *f* au taquoir *m*	Bürstenabzug *m*	brush proof, flat proof, galley proof, stone proof
épreuve *f* boueuse	schmutziger Abzug *m*	smutty proof
épreuve *f* corrigée	sauberer Abzug *m*	clean proof
épreuve *f* de caractères *m*/*pl*	Schriftmuster *n*	type specimen
épreuve *f* de cliché *m*	Klischeeabzug *m*	block pull *brit*, block-maker's proof, engraver's proof *am*
épreuve *f* de la composition *f*	Satzabzug *m*	letter-set proof
épreuve *f* de l'ordre *m* de préséance *f*	Rangordnungsprüfung *f*	order of merit test
épreuve *f* de photo *f*	Fotoabzug *m*	master print, photographic print
épreuve *f* de repérage *m*	Paßform *f*	key form
épreuve *f* de tournage *m*	Prüfung *f* der gedrehten Szenen *f*/*pl*	rushes *pl*
épreuve *f* définitive	endgültiger Andruck *m*	final pull
épreuve *f* d'une page *f*	Belegseite *f*	tear sheet
épreuve *f* en couleurs *f*/*pl*	Farbandruck *m*	colour proof, progressive proof
épreuve *f* en placard *m*	Fahnenabzug *m*	galley proof, slip
épreuve *f* en première	erster Abzug *m*, Hauskorrektur *f*	first proof, reader's proof
épreuve *f* glacée	Hochglanzabzug *m*	high gloss print
épreuve *f* pour archives *f*/*pl*	Anzeigenabzug *m* für Archivzwecke *m*/*pl*	file proof
épreuve *f* sans fautes *f*/*pl*	Reinabzug *m*	clean proof
épreuve *f* sur papier *m* couché	Abzug *m* auf Kunstdruckpapier *n*, Kunstdruckabzug *m*	art pull *brit*, glossy print proof *am*
épreuve *f* sur papier *m* mat	Mattkopie *f*	matt print
épreuve *f* tirée à la main *f*	Handabzug *m*	hand proof, hand pull
épuisé	vergriffen	exhausted, out-of-print, out-of-stock
à épuiser	abnehmbar	to be published
à épuiser dans le délai *m* d'une année *f*	abzunehmen innerhalb eines Jahres *n*	to be published within one year
épure *f* au lavis *m*	getönte Federzeichnung *f*, Tuschzeichnung *f*	wash drawing
équerre *f*	Winkelmaß *n*	angle meter, square
équilibre *m*	Gleichgewicht *n*	balance
équipe *f*	Arbeitsgemeinschaft *f*, Mannschaft *f*	crew, team
équipe *f* d'afficheurs *m*/*pl*	Klebekolonne *f*	team of bill-stickers *pl*
équipe *f* de courtiers *m*/*pl*	Werbekolonne *f*	group of solicitors *pl*, team of canvassers *pl*
équipe *f* de jour *m*	Tagschicht *f*	day-side
équipe *f* de rédaction *f*	Redaktionsstab *m*	editorial staff
équipe *f* de vente *f*	Verkaufsmannschaft *f*	sales *pl* force
équipement *m*	Ausrüstung *f*	equipment, finishing
équipement *m* d'un moyen *m* publicitaire	Werbemittelausstattung *f*	advertising medium outfit

éreinter	verreißen	to criticize harshly, to pull to pieces pl
errata m	Druckfehlerverzeichnis n	corrigenda, errata
erratum m	Erratum n	erratum
erreur f de composition f	Druckfehler m, Satzfehler m	compositor's error, erratum, misprint, printing error, typographical error
erreur f de dactylo f	Tippfehler m	typist's error
erreur f matérielle	Schreibfehler m	clerical mistake, slip of the pen
esbrouffe f	Großtuerei f	splurging
escompte m	Nachlaß m, Rabatt m, Skonto m	discount, rebate, reduction
escompte m de caisse f	Barzahlungsrabatt m, Kassaskonto m	cash discount, sales pl discount
espacé	gesperrt typog	spaced
espace f	Ausschluß typog/m, spatium n	blanc space, space, stick space
espace m	Raum n	space
espace m blanc	freier Raum m, Zwischenraum m	blank space, space
espace m d'annonces f/pl	Anzeigenraum m	advertising space, amount of space, lineage
espace m disponible pour la rédaction f	Raum m, für redaktionellen Text m verfügbarer	newshole
espace m en blanc	unbedruckter Raum m	blank space
espace f entre les mots m/pl	Wortzwischenraum m	word space
espace m fin	halber Punkt m	hair space
espace m non-imprimé	unbedruckter Raum m	blank space
espace m vierge f	freier Raum m, Fleisch n eines Buchstabens m, unbedruckter Raum m	beard, bevelled feet pl, blank space, burr
espace-bande f	Ausschließkeil m	space band
espacement m	Sperrung f	letter spacing
espacement m faux	falsche Raumaufteilung f	faulty spacing
espacer	durchschießen, spationieren, sperren, ausschließen	to interline, to lead out, to space out, word space
espèce f de loterie f	Verlosungsart f	sweepstake
esperluète f	„und"-Zeichen n	ampersand
esquisse f	Schmierskizze f, Skizze f	dummy, layout, outline, rough, sketch
esquisser	entwerfen, skizzieren	to design, to draft, to outline, to sketch
essai m	Essay m, kurze Abhandlung f	essay
essor m	Konjunkturaufschwung m	upward business trend
estampage m	Blinddruck m, Prägedruck m	blind stamping, embossing
estampe f en taille f douce	Kupferstich m	chalcography, copper plate engraving
esthétique f industrielle	Formgebung f, Formgestaltung f	fashioning, industrial design, shaping, styling
estimation f	Bewertung f, Schätzung f	assessment, estimation, evaluation
estimer	bewerten	to value, to weight
établir	ausstellen (Rechnung f), festlegen	to fix, to make out
établir un devis m	veranschlagen	to estimate
établissement m	Festlegung f, Feststellung f	determination, establishment, statement
établissement m de détail m	Detailgeschäft n, Einzelhandelsunternehmen n	retail enterprise, retail firm
établissement m de droit m public	öffentlich-rechtliche Anstalt f	body corporate, public institution

établissement *m* de facture *f*	Rechnungsstellung *f*	invoicing
étagère *f*	Regal *n*, Verkaufsständer *m*	distribution rack, rack
étagère *f* à journaux *m/pl*	Zeitungsschrank *m*	newspaper shelf
étalage *m*	Aushang *m*, Display *n*, Schaufenster *n*, Werbeauslage *f*	display, display faces *pl*, display window, exhibition, shop window, show window
étalage *m* de comptoir *m*	Ladentischauslage *f*	counter display, counter display container
étalage *m* de vente *f*	Verkaufsauslage *f*	sales *pl* display
étalage *m* de vitrine *f*	Schaufensterauslage *f*	window display
étalage *m* de vitrine *f* en couleur *f*	farbige Schaufenster-auslage *f*	colour display
étalage *m* en couleur *f*	farbiges Dekorationsstück *n*	colour display
étalagiste *m*	Schaufenstergestalter *m*, Schauwerbegestalter *m*	display man, window dresser
étampe *f*	Prägestempel *m*	stamping die
étamper	stanzen	to punch
état *m* provisoire	Provisorium *n*	makeshift
étendre	dehnen	to stretch
étiqueter	etikettieren	to label, to ticket
étiquettage *m* informatif	aufklärende Etikettierung *f*	informative labeling
étiquette *f*	Etikett *n*, Preisschild *n*	apron, label, price marker, price tag, sticker
étiquette *f* à attacher, étiquette *f* à ficelle *f*	Anhängezettel *m*	tag
étiquette *f* adhésive	Haftetikett *n*	adhesive label
étiquette *f* autocollante	Selbstklebeschild *n*	self-adhesive label
étiquette *f* de qualité *f*	Gütezeichen *n*	certification mark, quality label, seal of approval
étiquette *f* gommée	Aufkleber *m*, Klebeetikett *n*	gummed label, sticker slip
étiquette *f* s'expliquant elle-même	„sprechendes" Etikett *f*	self-explanatory label
étouffer un scandal *m*	einen Skandal *m* ersticken	to stifle a scandal
être à court de place *f*	Platzmangel *m* haben	to be pressed for space
être conforme à, être d'accord *m* avec	übereinstimmen mit	to conform to, to run in with
étude *f*	Umfrage *f*	poll, survey
étude *f* d'attitude *f*	Verhaltensprüfung *f*	attitude study, concept-test
étude *f* de comportement *m*	Verhaltensbeobachtung *f*	behaviour research
étude *f* de la clientèle *f*	Sekundärerhebung *f*	desk research
étude *f* de la communication *f*	Kommunikationsforschung *f*	communication research
étude *f* de la conjoncture *f*	Konjunkturforschung *f*	business research
étude *f* de marché *m*	Absatzforschung *f*	marketing research
étude *f* de motivation *f*	Motivforschung *f*	motivation research
étude *f* de préparation *f* et d'orientation *f* d'une campagne *f* publicitaire	Werbeanalyse *f*	advertising analysis
étude *f* des lecteurs *m/pl*	Leserschaftsforschung *f*	reader interest research
étude *f* des médias *m/pl*	Mediaforschung *f*, Werbeträgerforschung *f*	media research, media survey
étude *f* des produits *m/pl*	Produktforschung *f*	product research
étude *f* d'identification *f*	Wiedererkennungstest *m*	recognition test
étude *f* du marché *m*	Marktforschung *f*	field investigation, market analysis, market research
étude *f* d'un cas *m*	Fallstudie *f*	case study
étude *f* sur un emballage *m*	Packungstest *m*	packaging test

études f/pl de la motivation f des consommateurs m/pl	Erforschung f der Verbrauchermotive n/pl	consumer motivation research
études f/pl relatives à l'audience f	Hörerforschung f	broadcast research
étudier	erforschen, erkunden	to investigate
évaluation f	Auswertung f, Bewertung f, Voranschlag m	assessment, estimate, evaluation, exploitation
évaluation f approximative «à vue f de nez» m du nombre m des présents m/pl	Nasenzählen n	nose count
évaluation des frais m/pl	Kostenvoranschlag m	cost estimate, estimating, quotation
évaluation f des médias m/pl	Werbeträgerbewertung f	media evaluation
évaluer	bewerten, schätzen, veranschlagen	to estimate, to rate, to value, to weight
évanouissement m	Schwundeffekt m	fading
évasion f de la réalité f	Wirklichkeitsflucht f	escapism
événement m	Begebenheit f, Ereignis n	event, happening
événement m saillant	Glanzpunkt m	high lights pl
événéments m/pl du jour m	Tagesneuigkeiten f/pl	topical news
événements m/pl en cours m	gegenwärtige Ereignisse n/pl	current happenings pl
évidement m	Aussparung f	recess
évolution f	Entwicklung f	development, evolution
évolution f à long terme m	langfristiger Entwicklungs-trend m	secular trend
évolution f des prix m/pl	Preisentwicklung f	price development
évolution f des tirages m/pl	Auflagenentwicklung f	development of circulation
exagération f	Übertreibung f	overstatement
exagérer	übertreiben	to exaggerate, to inflate, to speak in superlatives pl
exalter	pomphaft hervorheben	to blazon
examen m	Prüfung f, Untersuchung f	examination, inquiry, research, survey, test
examiner	prüfen	to check, to check up, to examine
excédant m de tirage m	Mehrauflage f	overs pl
excès m de la publicité f	Reklameauswüchse m/pl	misdoings pl of advertising
exclusion f	Ausschluß m	exclusion
exclusivité f	Alleinverkaufsrecht n, Exklusivität f, sensationelle Alleinmeldung f	exclusivity, franchise, scoop, sole rights pl of sale
exécuter	ausführen	to implement
exécution f	Ausführung f	execution, realization
exécution f de la publicité f	Werbedurchführung f	advertising execution
exécution f d'un ordre m	Auftragsabwicklung f	filling of a contract, order processing
exécution f d'une commande f	Auftragsausführung f	execution of an order
exemplaire m	Ausgabe f (Nummer), Exemplar n	copy, edition, issue, number
exemplaire m à l'avance f, exemplaire m de lancement m	Vorausexemplar n	advance-copy
exemplaire m de presse f	Rezensionsexemplar n	review copy, reviewer's copy
exemplaire m d'échange m	Tauschexemplar n	exchange copy
exemplaire m dédicacé	mit einer Widmung f versehene Ausgabe f	presentation copy

exemplaire *m* des archives *f/pl*	Archivexemplar *n*	copy on file, file-copy, record copy
exemplaire *m* d'essai *m*	Andruck *m*	preprint, proof, proofing
exemplaire *m* en collection *f*	Archivexemplar *n*	copy on file, file-copy, record copy
exemplaire *m* gratuit	Freiexemplar *n*	complimentary copy, free copy, specimen copy
exemplaire *m* obligatoire	Pflichtexemplar *n*	obligatory copy
exemplaire *m* périmé	alte Zeitungsnummer *f*	back-number
exemplaire *m* supplémentaire	Sonderexemplar *n*	extra copy
exemplaire-éditeur *m*	Hausexemplar *n*, Verlagsstück *n*	publisher's copy
exemplaires *m/pl* de passe *f*	überschüssige Nummern *f/pl*	over copies *pl*
exemplaires *m/pl* invendus	unverkaufte Exemplare *n/pl*	unsold copies *pl*
exemplaires *m/pl* précédents	frühere Ausgaben *f/pl*	back copies *pl*
expansion *f* du marché *m*	Marktausweitung *f*	market extension
expédier	absenden	to dispatch
expéditeur *m*	Absender *m*	sender
expédition *f*	Versand *m*	dispatching, forwarding
expédition *f* d'annonces *f/pl*	Annoncenexpedition *f*	space broker
expédition *f* sous bande *f*	Zeitungsdrucksache *f*	newspaper packet, second-class matter *am*
expérience *f*	Erfahrung *f*, Experiment *n*	experience, experiment
expérience *f* d'agence *f*	Agenturerfahrung *f*	agency experience
expérience *f* publicitaire	werblicher Erfahrungsschatz *m*, Werbeerfahrung *f*	advertising experience, advertising record
expert *m*	Fachmann *m*	expert, specialist
expert *m* en emballages *m/pl*	Verpackungsfachmann *m*	cardboard engineer
expert *m* en fabrication *f*	Herstellungsfachmann *m*	production expert
expert *m* en médias *m/pl*	Streuungsfachmann *m*	media man
expert *m* en publicité *f*	Werbefachmann *m*, Werbesachverständiger *m*	adman, advertising expert, advertising man
expert *m* pour foires *f/pl*	Messegestalter *m*	designer for fairs *pl*
expertise *f*	Gutachten *n*	expert opinion
expiration *f*	Ablauf *m*	expiration, expiry
explication *f*	Erläuterung *f*	explanation
exploitant *m* de la publicité *f*	Werbepächter *m*	advertising operator
exploitation *f*	Auswertung *f*	evaluation, exploitation
exploration *f*	Informationsgespräch *n*	exploration
exposant *m*	Aussteller *m*, Messeaussteller *m*	exhibitor
exposant *m* supérieur	hochstehender Buchstabe *m*	cock-up, superior letter
exposé *m*	Denkschrift *f*, Exposé *n*	memorandum, proposal, record, statement
exposé *m* des grandes lumières *f/pl*	Hochlichtaufnahme *f*	highlight exposure
exposer	ausstellen (Waren *f/pl*)	to exhibit, to expose
exposition *f*	Aushang *m*, Ausstellung *f*, Belichtung *f*, Messe *f*, Schau *f*	display, exhibition, exposition *am*, exposure, fair, insolation, show
exposition *f* ambulante	Wanderausstellung *f*	touring exhibition
exposition *f* de modes *f/pl*	Modeschau *f*	fashion parade, style show
exposition *f* en masse *f*	Warenanhäufung *f*	mass-display
exposition *f* itinérante	Wanderausstellung *f*	touring exhibition
exposition *f* libre	offene Auslage *f*	open display
exposition *f* multiple	Mehrfachbelichtung *f*	repeated exposures *pl*
exposition *f* permanente	Dauerausstellung *f*	continuous exhibition
expression *f*	Ausdruck *m*, Äußerung *f*	expression, utterance
expression *f* de l'opinion *f*	Meinungsäußerung *f*	expression of opinion

expressivité *f*	Ausdruckskraft *f*	expressive force, force expressiveness
expurger	ausmerzen	to expurgate, to sort
extra gras	extra fett	extra bold
extrait *m*	Auszug *m*, Exzerpt *n*	excerpt, extract
extrait *m* du motif *m*	Motivausschnitt *m*	cutting out of motive
extraits *m/pl* de la presse *f*	Presseauszüge *m/pl*	press extracts *pl*

F

fabricant *m*	Fabrikant *m*	maker, manufacturer
fabricant *m* de papier *m*	Papierfabrikant *m*	papermaker
fabrication *f*	Herstellung *f*	production
fabrication *f* totale	Gesamtherstellung *f*	total production
fabrique *f* de cartonnage *m*	Kartonagefabrik *f*	cardboard-box manufactory
fabrique *f* de papier *m*	Papierfabrik *f*	paper-mill
fabrique *f* de tampons *m/pl*	Stempelfabrik *f*	stamp factory
face *f* dernière de texte *m*	gegenüber der letzten Textseite *f*	facing last editorial page
face *f* éditorial *m*	gegenüber Leitartikel *m*	facing leader
face *f* en deux colonnes *f/pl*	zweispaltig	half measure, in double columns *pl*
face *f* première de texte *m*	gegenüber der ersten Textseite *f*	facing first editorial page
face *f* sommaire *m*	gegenüber Inhaltsverzeichnis *n*	facing contents *pl*
face *f* texte *m*	gegenüber Text *m*	against text, facing text, next to editorial matter, opposite text
face *f* texte *m* rédactionnel	gegenüber redaktionellem Teil *m*	facing editorial matter
façonnage *m*	Formgebung *f*, Verarbeitung *f*	equipment, finishing, industrial design, processing, working
façonner	gestalten	to shape, to visualize
façons *f/pl* publicitaires	Werbeformen *f/pl*	forms *pl* of advertising
fac-similé *m*	Faksimile *n*	facsimile
facteur *m* d'attention *f*	Aufmerksamkeitsfaktor *m*	attention factor, interest factor
factice *f*	Leerpackung *f*	dummy
facturation *f*	Budgetsumme *f*, Rechnungserteilung *f*	invoicing, total billings *pl*
facture *f*	Faktura *f*, Rechnung *f*	account, bill, invoice
facturer	abrechnen	to account, to invoice
fadaises *f/pl*	Faxen *f/pl*	baloney *am*, tomfoolery
fading *m*	Fading *n*	fading
faire commerce *m*	handeln	to deal
faire concurrence *f*	konkurrieren	to compete
faire connaître au public *m*	Information *f* verbreiten	to publicize
faire de la maculature *f*	verdrucken	to misprint
faire de la photo *f*	fotografieren	to photograph
faire de la propagande *f*	propagieren, Reklame *f* machen	to boom, to boost, to propagandize, to propagate
faire de la publicité *f*	werben	to advertise
faire des étalages *m/pl*	dekorieren	to decorate, window dressing, window trimming
faire des rainures *f/pl*	rillen	to score
faire des recherches *f/pl*	forschen, recherchieren	to investigate
faire insérer une annonce *f*	Anzeige *f* aufgeben	to have an advertisement inserted

faire mousser	aufbauschen	to blow up, to puff up
faire noir au blanc	kontern	to reverse
faire passer quelque chose f de faux pour vrai	Türken m/pl bauen	to feign, to make pass false for right, to simulate
faire repasser la bande f	nochmaliges Abspielen n, Wiedergabe f einer Tonaufnahme f	to play back
faire sauter une information f	Unterdrückung f einer Information f	burying of an information
faire suivre	anhängen typog	to run on
faire suivre sans alinéa m	ohne Absatz m setzen	to run on
faire un cliché m	klischieren	to cast, to make blocks pl, to stereotype
faire un compte m rendu	besprechen	to discuss, to review (a book)
faire un décompte m	abrechnen	to account, to invoice
faire un duplicata m	Abschrift f anfertigen	to copy
faire un test m	testen	to test
faire une épreuve f	abziehen (Foto)	to make a print
faire-part m	Familienanzeige f	family announcement, personal announcement
faire-part de fiançailles f/pl	Verlobungsanzeige f	announcement of an engagement
faire-part m de marriage m	Heiratsanzeige f	marriage advertisement
faire-part m de naissance f	Geburtsanzeige f	announcement of birth
faiseur m d'opinion f	Meinungsbildner m, Meinungsmacher m	opinion leader
fait m	Tatsache f	fact
fait à la maison f	handgestrickt	homespun
fait m accompli	vollendete Tatsache f	accomplished fact
fait m établi	erwiesene Tatsache f	ascertained fact
fait m pur et simple	nackte Tatsache f	bald fact
faits divers m/pl	Kurznachrichten f/pl, Vermischtes n	miscellanies pl, miscellaneous items pl, news in brief
faits m/pl divers locals	Lokaltratsch m	local item
falsification f	Fälschung f, Verfälschung f	bias, fake, falsification
famille f d'affiches f/pl	Plakatfamilie f	poster-family
famille f de caractères m/pl	Schriftfamilie f, Schriftgattung f	family of type, type family
fanion m	Werbewimpel m, Wimpel m	pelmet, pennant, streamer
fantôme m	Geisterbild n	double image, phantom
farce f bouffonne	Posse f	slapstick comedy
fascicule m	Lieferung f (Heft n eines Werkes n)	issue
fascicule m spécimen m	Probeexemplar n	complimentary copy
fausse marge f	fehlerhaftes Register n	out-of-register
fausse nouvelle f	Falschmeldung f	fake report, false news
fausse page f	linke Seite f	even page, left-hand page
faute f de composition f	Satzfehler m, Setzfehler m	compositor's error, setting mistake
faute f de frappe f	Tippfehler m	typist's error
faute f d'impression f	Druckfehler m	erratum, misprint, printing error, typographical error
faute f d'orthographe f	Schreibfehler m	clerical mistake, slip of the pen
faute f énorme	grober Schnitzer m	howler
faute f typographique	Druckfehler m	erratum, misprint, printing error, typographical error
faux frais m/pl	Nebenkosten pl	incidental expenses pl
faux rapport m	falsche Darstellung f	misrepresentation

faux titre *m*	Innentitel *m*, Schmutztitel *m*	bastard title, half title
faux tuyau *m*	wertloser Hinweis *m*	bum steer
faux-fuyant *m*	fadenscheinige Ausrede	quibble
faux-trait *m*	Klatschdruck *m*	touch print
faveur *f*	Vergünstigung *f*	sales *pl* allowance
faveur *f* du public *m*	Aufnahmebereitschaft *f*, Aufnahmefreudigkeit *f*	consumer acceptance
fédération *f*	Bund *m*	federation
feindre	Türken *m/pl* bauen	to feign, to make pass false for right, to simulate
feinte *f*	blinder Bogen *m*	blank sheet
fenêtre *f* en pellicule *f* transparente	Zellglasfenster *n*	cellophane window
fermeture *f* des magasins *m/pl*	Ladenschluß *m*	closing time
fermeture *f* en fondu *m*	schneller Übergang *m* einer Filmszene *f* auf die folgende	wipe
fermier *m* d'un rayon *m* spécialisé dans un supermarché *m*	Pächter *m* einer Verkaufsfläche *f* im Supermarkt *m*	rack-jobber
ferrotypie *f*	Schnellfotografie *f* auf Eisenblech *n*	ferrotype
festival *m*	Festspiele *n/pl*	festival
festivals *m/pl* cinématographiques	Filmfestspiele *n/pl*	film festivals *pl*
feu *m* de projecteur *m*	Punktlicht *n*, Scheinwerferlicht *n*	spotlight
feuille *f*	Blatt *n* (Seite *f*), Blatt *n* (Zeitung *f*), Bogen *m*, Folie *f*, Papierbogen *m*	foil, journal, page, paper, sheet
feuille *f* à lettres *f/pl*	Briefbogen *m*	lettersheet
feuille *f* à scandale *m*	Revolverblatt *n*	gutter paper, yellow journal
feuille *f* adhésive	Klebefolie *f*	adhesive foil
feuille *f* attachée	Allonge *f*	fly-leaf
feuille *f* bambochée	liederlich zusammengestellte Seite *f*	badly imposed page
feuille *f* boulevardière	Boulevardblatt *n*, Kaufzeitung *f*	penny press, yellow paper
feuille *f* cléricale	Kirchenblatt *n*	church paper, religious paper
feuille *f* commerciale	Wirtschaftsblatt *n*	business paper, commercial journal
feuille *f* corporative	Verbandsblatt *n*, Vereinsblatt *n*	journal of a society, organ of a corporation
feuille *f* d'acétate *m*	Azetatfolie *f*	acetate film
feuille *f* d'aluminium *m*	Aluminiumfolie *f*	aluminium foil
feuille *f* d'annonces *f/pl*	Anzeigenblatt *n*, Anzeigenseite *f*, Offertenblatt *n*	admag, advertisement magazine, advertisement page, advertiser, advertising sheet, free sheet, shopper
feuille *f* de chantage *m*	Revolverblatt *n*	gutter paper, yellow journal
feuille *f* de chou *m*	Käseblättchen *n*, Winkelblatt *n*	hedge press, local rag, trumpery paper
feuille *f* de couverture *f*	Deckblatt *n*, Deckbogen *m*	base sheet, top drawsheet
feuille *f* de décharge *f*	Schmutzbogen *m*	set-off sheet
feuille *f* de parti *m*	Parteiblatt *n*	party organ
feuille *f* de registre *m*	Registerblatt *n*	index sheet
feuille *f* de réputation *f* mondiale	Weltblatt *n*	newspaper of a world-wide reputation
feuille *f* de tarif *m*	Tarifblatt *n*	rate sheet
feuille *f* de titre *m*	Titelbogen *m*	prelim, title-sheet

feuille *f* **d'emplacement** *m*, **feuille** *f* **des blancs** *m/pl*	Standbogen *m*	correct proof, position pull
feuille *f* **d'opposition** *f*	Oppositionsblatt *n*	opposition paper
feuille *f* **économique**	Wirtschaftsblatt *n*	business paper, commercial journal
feuille *f* **familiale**	Familienblatt *n*	family paper, magazine of general interest
feuille *f* **favorite**	Leibblatt *n*	favourite paper
feuille *f* **hebdomadaire**	Wochenzeitschrift *f*	weekly magazine, weekly paper
feuille *f* **hebdomadaire divertissante**	Regenbogenpresse *f*, Sorayapresse *f*	light reading weekly
feuille *f* **huilée**	Ölbogen *m*	tympan
feuille *f* **humoristique**	Witzblatt *n*	comic journal, funnies *pl*, funny paper, humorous paper
feuille *f* **imprimée**	Druckbogen *m*	printed sheet, proof
feuille *f* **imprimée au recto** *m* **seulement**	Einblattdruck *m*	one-side print
feuille *f* **locale**	Lokalzeitung *f*	local paper
feuille *f* **principale**	Hauptausgabe *f*	main edition
feuille *f* **régionale**	Provinzblatt *n*	provincial paper
feuille *f* **rurale**	Landwirtschaftsblatt *n*	agriculture publication, farm publication
feuille *f* **scientifique**	wissenschaftliches Blatt *m*	scientific paper
feuille *f* **sportive**	Sportblatt *n*	sport journal, sporting news
feuille *f* **supernuméraire**	Überdruck *m* (Überschuß *m*)	surplus
feuille *f* (voir: format d'affiche)	Bogen *m* (Plakat *n*) (siehe: Plakatformat)	sheet
feuille *f* **volante**	Vorsatzblatt *n*	fly bill, fly sheet
feuillet *m*	Flugblatt *n*	handbill, leaflet, pamphlet
feuilleter	durchblättern	to run over
feuilleton *m*	Feuilleton *n*	feuilleton
feutre *m*	Filz *m*	felt
feutrine *f*	Filzimitation *f*	imitation felt
fibre *f* **de papier** *m*	Papierfaser *f*	paper fibre
ficelle *f*	Ausbindeschnur *f*	page cord
ficelle *f* **à colonnes** *f/pl*	Kolumnenschnur *f*	page cord, string
fiche *f*	Karteikarte *f*, Zettel *m*	index card, slip
fiche *f* **de travail** *m*	Laufzettel *m*, Tageszettel *m*	job ticket, progress report, slip
fiche *f* **perforée**	Lochkarte *f*	punched card
fichier *m*	Kartei *f*	card index, file, filing cabinet
fichier *m* **d'abonnés** *m/pl*	Abonnentenkartei *f*	list of subscribers *pl*
fichier *m* **de clients** *m/pl*	Kundenkartei *f*	card-index of customers *pl*
fichier *m* **de tarifs** *m/pl*	Tarifkartei *f*	rate card index
fichier *m* **des commandes** *f/pl* **en exécution** *f*	Auftragskartei *f*	card-index of orders *pl*, order register
fiction *f*	Erdichtung *f*, Fiktion *f*	fiction, invention, pretence
fidélité *f* **à la marque** *f*	Markentreue *f*	brand loyalty, brand preference, consumer insistence
fidélité *f* **de lecture** *f*	Lesertreue *f*	constancy of readership, reader confidence
fidélité *f* **des clients** *m/pl*	Kundentreue *f*	customer loyalty
figurer	darstellen	to represent
figures *f/pl* **de publicité** *f* **gonflables**	aufblasbare Werbefiguren *f/pl*	inflatable advertising figures *pl*

fil *m* à brocher	Heftfaden *m*	stitching thread
fil *m* télégraphique	Leitungsdraht *m*	wire
filet *m* à composer	Setzlinie *f*	composing rule, setting-rule
de **filet** *m* **à filet** *m*	von Strich *m* zu Strich *m*	from rule to rule
filet *m* à perforer	Perforierlinie *f*	perforating rule
filet *m* anglais	englische Linie *f*	plain swelled rule
filet *m* crémaillère *f*	Strichlinie *f*	hatched rule, shaded rule
filet *m* de bordure *f*	Randlinie *f*	border rule
filet *m* de composition *f*	Setzlinie *f*	composing rule, setting-rule
filet *m* de pied *m*	Fußlinie *f*	foot rule
filet *m* maigre	feine Linie *f*	fine-face rule
filet *m* orné	Schmuckleiste *f*, Zierlinie *f*	ornamental borders *pl*, ornamental rule
filet *m* pointillé	punktierte Linie *f*	dotted line, dotted rule
filet *m* tremblé	Wellenlinie *f*	wavy line, wavy rule
filet *m* (typogr.)	Linie *f*	line, rule *typog*
fileté	umstochen	outline
filets *m/pl*	Linienmaterial *n*	rules *pl*
filets *m/pl* doubles	Doppellinie *f*	double rulings *pl*
filière *f*	Verbindungsweg *m*	pipeline
filigrane *m*	Wasserzeichen *n*	water mark
film *m*	Film *m*, Kunststofffolie *f*, Reißer *m*	film *brit*, motion picture, movie *am*, thriller
film *m* à épisodes *f/pl*	Fortsetzungsfilm *m*	serial film
film *m* à images *f/pl* fixes	Tonbildschau *f*	film-sound transmission car, sound film strip, sound slide film
film *m* à propagande *f*	Propagandafilm *m*	propaganda film
film *m* à réfraction *f*	3 D(imensional) -Film *m*	3 D(imensional) film
film *m* à sensation *f*	spannende Handlung *f*	thriller
film *m* annonce *f*	Filmvoranzeige *f*, Filmvorschau *f*, Vorspann *m*	credit titles *pl*, generic, trailer
film *m* avec G.G. en vedette *f*	Film *m* mit G.G. in der Hauptrolle *f*	film featuring G.G.
film *m* d'amateur *m*	Amateurfilm *m*	amateur film
film *m* d'aventures *f/pl*	Abenteuerfilm *m*	adventure film
film *m* de démonstration *f*	Demonstrationsfilm *m*, Werbeinstruktionsfilm *m*	demonstrational film
film *m* de format *m* normal	Normalfilm *m*	standard film
film *m* d'épouvante *f*	Horrorfilm *m*, Schauerfilm *m*	grusical, horror film
film *m* divertissant	Unterhaltungsfilm *m*	entertainment film
film *m* documentaire	Dokumentarfilm *m*, Kulturfilm *m*	documentary film
film *m* éducatif	Lehrfilm *m*	educational film, instructional film
film *m* en couleurs *f/pl*	Farbfilm *m*	colour film
film *m* en dessin *m* animé	Zeichentrickfilm *m*	animated cartoon, cartoon film
film *m* en noir et blanc	Schwarzweißfilm *m*	black and white film
film *m* expérimental	Experimentalfilm *m*	experimental film
film *m* industriel	Industriefilm *m*, Werkfilm *m*	industrial film
film *m* muet	Stummfilm *m*	silent film
film *m* parlant	Tonfilm *m*	sound film, talkie, talking film
film *m* passe-partout	allgemein ansprechender Film *m*	film of universal appeal

film *m* policier	Kriminalfilm *m*	action film
film *m* pour offset *m*	Offsetfilm *m*	flat
film *m* publicitaire	Werbefilm *m*	advertising film, commercial picture, publicity film
film *m* publicitaire avec adresse *f* du détaillant *m*	Werbefilm *m* mit Händleradresse *f*	open end commercial
film *m* publicitaire court métrage *m*	Werbekurzfilm *m*	advertising filmlet
film *m* se déroulant en arrière	rückwärts ablaufender Film *m*	fast back
film *m* studio *m*	Aufnahmeraum *m*	studio
film *m* truqué	Trickfilm *m*	animated cartoon, stunt film, trick picture
filmer	filmen	to film, to shoot a film
film-fixe *m*	Werbediavorführung *f*	projection of advertising film slides *pl*
filmothèque *f*	Filmarchiv *n*, Filmsammlung *f*	film library, stock-shots *pl*
filtre *m*	Filter *m*	filter
filtre *m* coloré	Farbfilter *m*	colour filter
fin *f* d'alinéa *m*	Ausgangszeile *f*, Ende *n* des Absatzes *m*	break line, last line, short line
finesse *f* de la trame *f*	Rasterweite *f*	screen width
finir	nachschneiden	to finish
finition *f*	Fertigstellung *f*	completion
fins *f/pl* de publicité *f*	Werbezwecke *m/pl*	advertising purposes *pl*
fixatif *m*	Fixativ *n*	fixative
fixation *f* de composition *f* et de déroulement *m* d'un film *m*	Fixierung *f* von Film *m* -Aufbau *m* und -Ablauf *m*	treatment
fixation *f* de date *f* et durée *f*	Zeitplanung *f*	timing
fixation *f* du budget *m*	Etatfestsetzung *f*	budget fixation
fixe	immer an demselben Platz *m*	anchored
fixer	abmachen, festlegen	to agree, to arrange, to fix, to settle
flagornerie *f*	Speichelleckerei *f*	toadyism
flair *m*	Gespür *n*	nose
flamme *f*	Werbewimpel *m*, Wimpel *m*	pelmet, pennant, streamer
flan *m*	Mater *f*, Matrizenkarton *m*	flong, mat *am*, mat board, matrix
flash *m*	Kurzdepesche *f*	news flash
fléchissement *m* dans les rentrées *f/pl* de commande *f*	Auftragsrückgang *m*	decline of orders *pl*, falling off of orders *pl*
fleur *f* de rhétorique *f*	Floskel *f*	flourish
fleuron *m*	Vignette *f*, Zierleiste *f*	border, mask, ornament, tail piece, vignette
flexible livre *m* de poche *f*	flexibles Taschenbuch *n*	paperback
flexographie *f*	Anilindruck *m*	aniline printing, flexographic printing
flocage *m*	Beflockung *f*	covering with fibers *pl*
flot *m* de paroles *f/pl*	Wortschwall *m*	redundancy, torrent of words *pl*
flou	unscharf, verwischt	blurred, dull, fuzzy
fluctuation *f*	Schwankung *f*	fluctuation
fluctuation *f* saisonnière	Saisonschwankung *f*	seasonal fluctuation
fluctuations *f/pl* des tirages *m/pl*	Auflageschwankungen *f/pl*	fluctuations *pl* of circulation
fluctuations *f/pl* des ventes *f/pl*	Absatzschwankung *f*	market fluctuation
fluorescent	fluoreszierend	fluorescent
flux *m* verbal	Redefluß *m*	flow of words *pl*

foire f	Messe f	exhibition, fair, show
foire f d'automne m	Herbstmesse f	autumn fair
foire f de commerce m	Handelsmesse f	trade fair
foire f de l'artisanat m	Handwerksmesse f	artisan fair
foire f de l'industrie f	Industriemesse f	industries pl fair
foire f de printemps m	Frühjahrsmesse f	spring fair
foire f d'échantillons m/pl	Mustermesse f	trade fair
foire f du jouet m	Spielwarenmesse f	toy industry fair
foire f industrielle	Industrieausstellung f	industrial exhibition
foire f spécialisée	Fachmesse f	spezialised fair
folie f grégaire	Massenwahn m	mass craziness
folio m	Seitennummer f, Seitenziffer f	folio, page number
folioter	paginieren	to number pages pl, to page, to paginate
folliculaire m	Zeitungsschreiber m	hack writer
fonction f publicitaire	Werbefunktion f	advertising functions pl
fonctions f/pl	Aufgabengebiet n	assignment, field, scope
fonctions f/pl de la publicité f	Funktionen f/pl der Werbung f	advertising functions pl
fond m de tiroir m	Ladenhüter m	dead article, dormant stock, shelf warmer
fond m perdu	angeschnittene Seite f	bleed-off page
fond m sonore	musikalische Untermalung f, Tonuntermalung f	background sound effect, underscoring
fondateur m	Gründer m	founder
fondé	gegründet	established
fonderie f	Gießerei f, Schriftgießerei f	foundry, letter-foundry, type-foundry
fondeur m de caractères m/pl	Gießer m, Schriftgießer m	type caster, type founder
fondeur m typographe	Schriftgießer m	type caster, type founder
fondeuse f	Gießwerk n	casting mechanism
fondeuse f monotype	Monotype-Gießmaschine f	monotype caster
fonds m de publicité f	Werbefonds m	advertising stocks pl
fondu m	Ausblenden n, Fading n, Überblendung f	dissolve, fade-out, fading, shunt
fondu m enchaîné	weiche Bildüberblendung f	to dissolve am, to fade over, to mix to brit
fonte f	Guß m	fount
fonte f de caractères m/pl	Schriftguß m	type casting
fonte f de deux dessins m/pl	Verschmelzung f zweier Entwürfe m/pl	marriage
for m	Gerichtsstand m	competent court
forain m	Schausteller m	showman
force f	Schlagkraft f	punch
force f d'attraction f	Anziehungskraft f, Zugkraft f	appeal, attention value, attraction, attractive power, pulling power
force f de corps m	Schriftgrad m	body type size, point size
force f de pénétration f	Durchschlagskraft f	penetrating power
force f de persuasion f	Überzeugungskraft f	persuasive power
force f d'expression f	Ausdruckskraft f	expressive force, force expressiveness
force f majeure	höhere Gewalt f	absolute necessity, act of providence
forger une information f	eine Nachricht f aushecken	to fabricate an information
format m	Format n, Größe f	dimension pl, format brit, size am

format m **bâtard** m	ungewöhnliches Format n	unusual size
format m **d'affiche** f (voir appendice)	Plakatformat n (siehe Anhang)	poster size (see appendix)
format m **d'annonce** f	Anzeigenformat n	advertisement size
format m **de feuille** f	Bogengrösse f	sheet size
format m **de la page** f	Seitenformat n, Seitengröße f	page size, size of page
format m **de l'écran** m	Bildschirmformat n	aspect ratio
format m **de papier** m	Papierformat n	paper size, sheet size
format m **de pellicule** f	Filmformat n	film size
format m **de poche** f	Taschenformat n	pocket size
format double couronne (voir format d'affiche)	Doppelkrone f (siehe Plakatformat)	double-crown (see poster size)
format m **du livre** m	Buchformat n	book size
format m **en hauteur** f	Hochformat n	high size, portrait format, upright format
format m **en largeur** f, **format** m **en travers** m	Breitformat n, Querformat n	broadside size, cross size, landscape, wide size
format m **facile à manier**	handliches Format n	handy size
format m **gigantesque**	Riesenformat n	blow-up
format m **in-quarto**	Quartformat n	quarto size
format m **journal** m	Zeitungsformat n	newspaper size
format m **maximum**	Höchstformat n	maximum size
format m **mondial**	Weltformat n	international format
format m **normal**	Hochformat n	high size, portrait format, upright format
format m **normalisé**	Normalformat n, Standardformat n	standard size, standardized sheet size
format m **normalisé du papier** m	Papiernormalformat n	standard paper size
format m **oblong**	Langformat n	oblong size
format m **standard** m	genormte Größe f, Standardformat n	basic size, standardized sheet size
format m **vertical**	Hochformat n	high size, portrait format, upright format
formation f	Ausbildung f	education, training
formation f **de taches** f/pl	Fleckenbildung f	spotting
formation f **des mots** m/pl	Wortbildung f	word-formation
formation f **des prix** m/pl	Preisbildung f, Preisgestaltung f	price making, pricing
forme f	Form f	form
forme f **à impression** f	Druckform f	printing form am, printing forme brit
forme f **d'affichage** m	Plakatierungsform f	form of bill-posting
forme f **d'assertion** f	Aussageform f	form of assertion
forme f **de produit** m	Produktform f	shape of product
forme f **industrielle**	Formgebung f	industrial design
forme f **picturale**	Bildform f	shape of the picture
forme f **serrée**	geschlossene Satzform f	locked-up form
former	gestalten	to shape, to visualize
formulaire m	Formular n, Vordruck m (Formblatt n)	blank form
formulaire m **en continu**	Endlosformular n	continuous form
formulation f	Formulierung f	formulation
formule f	Formblatt n	form
formule f **en blanc**	Blankoformular n	blank
formule f **publicitaire**	Werbespruch m	advertising slogan, catch line, catch phrase
fouinard m	Schnüffler m	nosy

foulage *m*	durchgeschlagener Druck *m*, Schattierung *f*	blotted print, hard edge, pressure
fournir des nouvelles *f/pl*	Nachrichten *f/pl* beschaffen	to supply news
fournisseur *m*	Auftragnehmer *m*, Lieferant *m*	purveyor, supplier
fourniture *f* **des affiches** *f/pl*	Plakatanlieferung *f*	supplying of posters *pl*
fourre *f* **de protection** *f*	Schutzumschlag *m*	dust-cover, jacket
foyer *m*	Haushalt *m*	household
fraction *f*	Bruchteil *m*	fraction
fraction *f* **de page** *f*	Seitenteil *m*	page fraction
fracture *f*	Fraktur *f*	black letter, German type, Gothic type
fragment *m*	Bruchstück *n*, Fragment *n*	fragment
fragmenter	zerstückeln	to dismember
frais *m/pl*	Aufwendung *f*, Ausgaben *f/pl* (Unkosten) , Kosten *pl*	costs *pl*, expenditure, expense, expenses *pl*
frais *m/pl* **de composition** *f*	Satzkosten *pl*	cost of composition, expenses *pl* for setting
frais *m/pl* **de déplacement** *m*	Reisekosten *pl*	travelling-expenses *pl*
frais *m/pl* **de diffusion** *f*	Streukosten *pl*	costs *pl* of circularising, space charge
frais *m/pl* **de distribution** *f*	Absatzkosten *pl*	distribution costs *pl*
frais *pl* **de fabrication** *f*	Herstellungskosten *pl*	manufacturing costs *pl*, production costs *pl*
frais *m/pl* **de l'emballage** *m*	Verpackungskosten *pl*	packaging costs *pl*, packing charges *pl*
frais *m/pl* **de manutention** *f*	Abwicklungskosten *pl*	handling costs *pl*
frais *m/pl* **de publicité** *f*	Werbegebühren *f/pl*, Werbekosten *pl*, Werbeunkosten *pl*	advertising expenses *pl*, advertising rates *pl*, costs *pl* of advertising, publicity expenses *pl*
frais *m/pl* **de transport** *m*	Versandkosten *pl*	dispatch-charges *pl*
frais *m/pl* **de voyage** *m*	Reisekosten *pl*	travelling-expenses *pl*
frais *m/pl* **d'expédition** *f*	Versandkosten *pl*	dispatch-charges *pl*
frais *m/pl* **d'impression** *f*	Druckkosten *pl*	printing costs *pl*
frais *m/pl* **moyens**	Durchschnittskosten *pl*	average costs *pl*
frais *m/pl* **postaux**	Zustellgebühr *f*	postage
fraisage *m*	Ausfräsung *f*	routing
fraisé	gefräst	routed
fraiser	ausfräsen, fräsen, wegstechen	to cut out, to mill, to rout, to rout out
fraiseuse *f*	Bestoßmaschine *f*, Fräsapparat *m*	router
franc bord	randangeschnitten	bleed-off
franc-jeu *m*	ehrliches Spiel *n*	fair play
fréquence *f*	Besuchsziffer *f*, Frequenz *f*, Häufigkeit *f*	frequency
fréquence *f* **d'achat** *m*	Einkaufshäufigkeit *f*, Verkaufsrhythmus *m*	purchase rhythm
fréquence *f* **de contact** *m*	Kontakthäufigkeit *f*	contact frequency
fréquence *f* **d'insertion** *f*	Einschalthäufigkeit *f*	insertion frequency
frictionné	einseitig Glanz *m*	machine glazed (M.G.)
frison *m*	Schmitz *n*	blur
frisquette *f*	Abdeckrahmen *m*, Spritzmaske *f*	frisket, masking frame
fritures *f/pl*	Nebengeräusche *n/pl*	atmospherics *pl*, buzz
frontispice *m*	Titelbild *n*	frontispiece
frustration *f*	Versagung *f*	frustration
fugacité *f*	Flüchtigkeit *f*	fugacity

fumée *f*	Klischeeabzug *m*	block pull *brit*, block-maker's proof, engraver's proof *am*
funiculaire *m*	Drahtseilbahn *f*	funicular railway
fusain *m*	Zeichenkohle *f*	drawing charcoal
fusion *f*	Fusionierung *f*	fusion, merger
fusion *f* **de journaux** *m/pl*	Zeitungsfusion *f*	newspaper merger

G

gabarit *m*	Schablone *f*	cut out, jig, pattern, stencil
gâchage *m* **de prix** *m*	Preisunterbietung *f*, Schleuderpreis *m*, Unterbietungspreis *m*	cut rate, cut-throat price, dumping, give-away price, price-cutting
gaffe *f*	Ungeschicklichkeit *f*	bloop
gagner	einbringen (Zeile), Raum *m* einschränken	to run short, to take in
galée *f*	Setzschiff *n*	make-up galley
galée *f* **à distribution** *f*	Ablegeregal *n*, Ablegeschiff *n*	galley for dead matter
galvano *m*	Galvano *m*	electro *am*, electrotype
galvano-nickel *m*	Nickelgalvano *n*	nickel electro, nickel-faced stereo
galvanoplastie *f*	Galvanoplastik *f*	electrotyping
galvanotype *m*	Galvano *n*	electro *am*, electrotype
gamme *f* **de clichés** *m/pl* **en couleurs** *f/pl*	Farbsatz *m*	set of colour plates *pl*
gamme *f* **des couleurs** *f/pl*	Farbskala *f*	colour chart, colour range, colour scale
garantie *f*	Garantie *f*	guarantee, warranty
garantie *f* **de la circulation** *f*	Auflagengarantie *f*	circulation guarantee
garantir	garantieren	to guarantee
garde-boutique *f*	Ladenhüter *m*	dead article, dormant stock, shelf warmer
garder le plomb *m*	Satz *m* stehen lassen	to hold over, to keep type standing
garnir	unterlegen	to line-up, to underlay
garnir la forme *f*	anlegen	to dress a form
garniture *f*	Formatsteg *m*	furniture
garniture *f/pl* **pour protéger un cliché** *m* **en tirage** *m*	Schließstege *m/pl*	dead metal
gaspillage *m*	Verschwendung *f*	waste
gauchir	verdrehen	to slant
gaufrage *m*	Blinddruck *m*, Prägedruck *m*, Prägung *f*	blind stamping, embossing
gaufrage *m* **à sec**	Blindprägung *f*	blind blocking, blind embossing
gaufrage *m* **en relief** *m*	Reliefdruck *m*	die-stamping, embossing, relief-printing
gaufré	geprägt	embossed
gaufrer	prägen	to emboss, to stamp
gazette *f*	Zeitung *f*	journal, newspaper, paper
gazette *f* **du bord** *m*	Bordzeitung *f*	ship's newspaper
géant *m*	Königsformat *n*	king size
généralisation *f*	Verallgemeinerung *f*	generalization

générique *m*	Einleitungsmelodie *f*	signature tune
genre *m*	Sorte *f*	brand, sort
genre *m* de caractères *m/pl*	Schriftart *f*	font, fount, kind of type
genre *m* de publicité *f*	Werbeart *f*	kind of advertising, type of advertising
genre *m* de support *m*	Werbeträgerart *f*	type of medium
genres *m/pl* d'annonces *f/pl*	Anzeigenarten *f/pl*	kinds *pl* of advertisements *pl*
genres *m/pl* de support *m*	Streuarten *f/pl*	types *pl* of media
les gens *pl* du monde *m*	Führungsschicht *f*	upper class
gérance *f*	Geschäftsführung *f*	management
gérant *m*	Geschäftsführer *m*, Herausgeber *m*	business manager, director
gérer	verwalten	to administer
gestion *f*	Geschäftsführung *f*	management
gestion *f* de l'entreprise *f*	Unternehmensführung *f*	management
gestionnaire *m*	Geschäftsführer *m*, Manager *m*	business manager, director, manager
glanes *f/pl*	Nachlese *f*	gleanings *pl*
glisser sur	leicht hingehen über	to slur over
glose *f*	Glosse *f*	gloss
glossaire *m*	Glossar *n*	glossary
gobelet *m* pour distributeur *m* automatique	Automatenbecher *m*	plastic drinking-cup
gondole *f*	Verkaufsgondel *f*	gondola
gonfler un papier *m*	eine Nachricht *f* hochspielen	to play up an information, to puff up an information
gouache *f*	Guasch *f*, Tempera *f*	body colour drawing, gouache
gousset *m*	Lasche *f*	flap
goût *m*	Geschmack *m*	taste
gouverne *f*	Richtschnur *f*	guidance, rule of conduct
gracieuseté *f*	kostenlose redaktionelle Werbung *f*	free puff
grain *m* fin	Feinkorn *n*	fine grain
grainer	granieren	to grain, to stipple
grammage *m*	Quadratmetergewicht *n* des Papiers *n*	paper weight by grams *pl* per square meter
grand agrandissement *m*	starke Vergrößerung *f*	blow-up
grand bavard *m*	Plappermaul *n*	chatterbox
grand film *m* de programme *m*	Hauptfilm *m* des Programms *m*	feature film
grand format *m*	Großformat *n*	large format, large size
grand magasin *m*	Kaufhaus *n*, Warenhaus *n*	department store
grand panneau *m*	Großfläche *f*	large hoarding, large panel
grand public *m*	großes Publikum *n*	public at large
grand quotidien *m* national	überregionale Zeitung *f*	national newspaper
grand titre *m*	Haupttitel *m*, Titelseite *f*	front cover, front page, title page
grand titre *m* sur plusieurs colonnes *f/pl*	mehrspaltige Überschrift *f*	spread-head
grande annonce *f*	Großanzeige *f*	display advertisement
grande lettrine *f*	große Initiale *f*	cut-in letter
grande presse *f*	auflagenstarke Presse *f*	press with a large circulation
de grande qualité *f*	hochwertig	first-rate, of high value
grandeur *f*	Größe *f*	size
grandeur *f* et arrangement *m*	Auftragsumfang *m*	insertion and size
graphique *m*	Diagramm *n*, Grafik *f*, Schaubild *n*	chart, diagram, graphics *pl*
graphique *m* de livre *m*	Buchgrafik *f*	book graphic

graphisme m **publicitaire**	Gebrauchsgrafik f	advertising art, applied art, commercial art
graphiste m	Grafiker m	artist
gras	dick, fett	bold, fat
grattage m	Entmantelung f	stripping
gratte-papier m	Vielschreiber m	scribbler
gratuit	gratis, kostenlos	free of charge, gratis
gratuité f **de compensation** f	Ersatzanzeige f	make-good, replacement ad
graver	ätzen, gravieren	to bite, to engrave, to etch
graver en relief m	hochätzen	to etch in relief
graveur m	Ätzer m, Chemigraf m	blockmaker, engraver, etcher, process engraver
graveur m **de caractères** m/pl	Schriftschneider m	type cutter
gravure f	Ätzung f, Gravierung f, Gravur f, Kupferstich m	block brit, chalcography, copperplate engraving, engraved plate, engraving am, etching
gravure f **à l'eau-forte** f	Radierung f	etching
gravure f **au trait** m	Strichätzung f	line block brit, line cut am, line engraving am, line etching, line plate, process block brit
gravure f **en creux** m/pl	Tiefdruck m/typog	copperplate printing, intaglio printing, photogravure, rotogravure
gravure f **sans poudrage** m	Ätzstufen f/pl	powderless etching
gravure f **sur bois** m	Holzschnitt m	wood cut, wood engraving
gravure f **sur cuivre** m	Kupferätzung f	copper etching, engraving in copper
gravure f **sur lino** m	Linolschnitt m	lino-cut
grenouille f	Wetterbericht m	weather-forecast, weather-report
gribouiller	schmieren	to scribble
griffe f	Kratzer m	scraper, scratch
griffonnage m	erster unfertiger Entwurf m, Gekritzel n, Rohzeichnung f	scrawl, scribble
griffonneur m	Vielschreiber m	scribbler
grille f **de protection** f	Schutzgitter n	guard
griller un confrère m	überrunden (einen Kollegen m)	to race past a colleague
grincement m **de l'aiguille** f	Kratzen n der Nadel f	scratch
grisé m **fait à la brosse** f	Punktschraffierung f	stipple
grisé m **mécanique**	Raster m	Ben Day, screen
grisés m/pl	Rastertönungen f/pl	half-tone shadings pl, tints pl
gros caractères m/pl	Großbuchstaben m/pl	capital letters pl, caps pl, large print, upper case letters pl
gros consommateur m	Großverbraucher m	bulk consumer, heavy user
gros plan m	Großaufnahme f	close-up, full screen
gros succès m	großer Erfolg m	smash hit
gros tirage m	Massenauflage f	bulk circulation, mass circulation, mass edition
gros titre m **à sensation** f	alarmierende Überschrift f	scare headline
grosse nouvelle f	Sensationsmeldung f	scoop
grosse trame f	grober Raster m	coarse screen
grossir	übertreiben	to exaggerate, to inflate, to speak in superlatives pl
grossiste m	Großhändler m	jobber, wholesale dealer
grossiste m **en livres** m/pl	Buchgrossist m	book wholesaler
groupe m	Interessengemeinschaft f	pool

groupe *m* de mot *m*	Wortgruppe *f*	group of word
groupe *m* de panneaux *m/pl* d'affichage *m* sur un emplacement *m*	Gruppe *f* von Anschlagstellen *f/pl* an einem Standort *m*	hoarding
groupe *m* de presse *f*	Zeitungsgruppe *f*	press group, string of newspapers *pl*
groupe *m* de pression *f*	Interessentengruppe *f*	pressure group
groupe *m* de test *m*	Testgruppe *f*	panel
groupe *m* de test *m* des auditeurs *m/pl*	Hörerpanel *n*	listening panel
groupe *m* de travail *m*	Arbeitsgruppe *f*	working party
groupe *m* d'essai *m* de consommateurs *m/pl*	Verbrauchertestgruppe *f*	consumer panel
groupes *m/pl* d'âge *m*	Altersgruppen *f/pl*	age groups *pl*
grue *f*	Kamerakran *m*	camera-crane, dolly
guide *m*	Handbuch *n*, Leitfaden *m*	guide, handbook, manual, vademecum
guide *m* aérien	Luftkursbuch *n*	airline guide
guide-âne *m*	Eselsbrücke *f*	crib
guide *m* de presse *f*	Pressehandbuch *n*	press guide
guide *m* des couleurs *f/pl*	Farbskala *f*	colour chart, colour range, colour scale
guide *m* publicitaire	Werberatschlag *m*	advertising guide
guillemets *m/pl*	Anführungsstriche *m/pl*	double quotation marks *pl*, inverted commas *pl/brit*
guimauve *f*	rührselige Literatur *f*	squish

H

habillage *m* des emplacements *m/pl*	Auskleidung *f* der Anschlagstellen *f/pl*	dressing of the sites *pl*
habitat *m*	Ortsgrößenklasse *f*	town size group
habitude *f*	Gewohnheit *f*, Verhaltensweise *f*	habit
habitudes *f/pl* d'achat *m*	Kaufgewohnheiten *f/pl*	buying habits *pl*
habitudes *f/pl* de consommation *f*	Verbrauchsgewohnheiten *f/pl*	consuming habits *pl*, consumption pattern
habitudes *f/pl* d'écoute *f*	Zuhörergewohnheiten *f/pl*	listening habits *pl*
habitudes *f/pl* des acheteurs *m/pl*	Käuferverhalten *n*	purchase pattern, shopping behaviour
habitudes *f/pl* des lecteurs *m/pl*	Lesegewohnheit *f*	reading behaviour, reading habits *pl*
hall *m* à usage *m* multiple	Mehrzweckhalle *f*	multi-purpose hall
hall *m* de sport *m*	Sporthalle *f*	arena
hall *m* d'exposition *f*	Ausstellungshalle *f*	exhibition hall
halle *f* de guichet *m*	Schalterhalle *f*	ticket-office
harangue *f*	Ansprache *f*	speech
harmonie *f* des couleurs *f/pl*	Farbharmonie *f*	matching design
hausse *f* rapide	Geschäftsaufschwung *m*, Hochkonjunktur *f*	boom
haut	hoch	high
haut tirage *m*	hohe Auflage *f*	mass-circulation
haute conjoncture *f*	Hochkonjunktur *f*	boom
haute fidélité *f*	Klangtreue *f*, naturgetreue Wiedergabe *f*	high fidelity
haute saison *f*	Hochsaison *f*	peak season
haute société *f*, haute volée *f*	obere Zehntausend *f/pl*	high society

de **haute teneur** *f*	hochwertig	first-rate, of high value
hauteur *f*	Höhe *f*	height, length
hauteur *f* **d'annonce** *f*	Abdruckhöhe *f*	advertisement height
hauteur *f* **de colonne** *f*	Spaltenhöhe *f*	column depth, column length
à la **hauteur** *f* **de la concurrence** *f*	konkurrenzfähig	competitive
hauteur *f* **de page** *f*	Satzhöhe *f*	depth of page
hauteur *f* **du caractère** *m,* **hauteur** *f* **en papier** *m*	Schrifthöhe *f*	height-to-paper, type height
hauteur *f* **minimum** *m*	Mindesthöhe *f*	minimum length
haut-parleur *m* **de contrôle** *m*	Kontrollautsprecher *m*	monitor
hebdomadaire *m*	wöchentlich, Wochenblatt *n*	weekly
hectographe *m*	Vervielfältigungsapparat *m*	duplicator, hectograph
héliogravure *f*	Fototiefdruck *m,* Rakeltiefdruck *m*	photogravure, rotogravure *f,* rotogravure
héliogravure *f* **sur rotative** *f*	Rotationstiefdruck *m*	rotogravure
héliogravure *f* **tramée**	Rastertiefdruck *m*	screen intaglio
hélioroto *f*	Rotationstiefdruck *m*	rotogravure
heure *f* **de pointe** *f*	Hauptgeschäftszeit *f*	rush hour
heure *f* **limite de remise** *f*	Annahmeschluß *m*	closing hour
heures *f/pl* **de diffusion** *f*	Sendezeit *f*	air time, broadcasting time
heures *f/pl* **d'ouverture** *f*	Geschäftsstunden *f/pl*	store hours *pl*
hiatus *m*	Streupause *f*	hiatus
hiérarchie *f*	Rangordnung *f*	hierarchy, order of precedence
hiéroglyphes *m/pl*	Bilderschrift *f*	hieroglyphics *pl*
histoire *f* **d'amour** *m*	Liebesgeschichte *f*	love story
histoire *f* **du texte** *m*	Werbetextidee *f*	story
histoire *f* **en images** *f/pl*	Bildgeschichte *f*	picture story
histotypie *f*	Stoffdruck *m*	cloth printing, printing on fabrics *pl*
homme *m* **d'affaires** *f/pl*	Geschäftsmann *m*	business man
homme *m* **de la rue** *f*	Mann *m* auf der Straße *f*	man-on-street
homme *m* **de lettres** *f/pl*	Literat *m*	man of letters *pl*
homme *m* **de paille** *f* **mis en avant en cas** *m* **de poursuites** *f/pl* **judiciaires**	Sitzredakteur *m*	prison editor
homme *m* **de relation** *f*	Kontakter *m,* Kontaktmann *m,* Verbindungsmann *m*	account executive, account supervisor, contact man, liaison man
homme *m* **universel**	Alleskönner *m*	allround man
homme-affiche *m,* **homme-sandwich** *m*	Sandwichmann *m,* Plakatträger *m*	sandwich board man, sandwich man
honoraire *m*	Vergütung *f*	bonus, fee
honoraires *m/pl*	Agenturvergütung *f,* Gebühr *f,* Honorar *n*	fee, service fee
honoraires *m/pl* **de projet** *m*	Entwurfshonorar *n*	fee for design
honoraires *m/pl* **des journalistes** *m/pl*	Journalistenhonorar *n*	fee for journalists *pl*
honoraires *m/pl* **du conseiller** *m*	Werbeberaterhonorar *n*	service fee
honoraires *m/pl* **forfaitaires**	Pauschalhonorar *n*	flat fee
horaire *m*	Abfahrtsplan *m,* Fahrplan *m*	time table
horizon *m*	Gesichtskreis *m*	mental horizon
hors concurrence *f*	konkurrenzlos	unrivalled
hors saison *f*	tote Saison *f*	dead season, off season

hors-programme *m*	Beifilm *m*, Beiprogramm *n*	adjacency, fill-up, supplementary film
hors-texte *m*	eingeklebtes Bild *n*, ganzseitiges Bild *n*	full-page illustration, tip-in
huitième *m* de cadratin *m*	Achtelgeviert *n*	em-space
huitième de page *f*	Achtelseite *f*	eighth of page
humeur *f* d'acheter	Kaufstimmung *f*	buying mood
humide d'encre *f* grasse	druckfeucht	moist from ink

I

idée *f*	Einfall *m*, Idee *f*	flash, gag, idea
idée *f* de base *f*	Grundidee *f*	fundamental idea
idée *f* publicitaire	Werbeidee *f*	advertising idea
identification *f*	Identifizierung *f*	identification
identification *f* de produit *m*	Produkterkennung *f*	product identification
identification *f* d'une marque *f*	Markenerkennung *f*	brand identification
identique à l'original *m*	originalgetreu	true to original
identité *f* de marque *f*	Übereinstimmung *f* mit Markenbild *n*	brand identity
idéologie *f*	Weltanschauung *f*	ideology, philosophy of life
idiome *m*	Dialekt *m*, Mundart *f*	dialect, idiom
œil *m* de caractère *m*	Schriftbild *n*	type face
œil *m* de la lettre *f*	Mittellänge *f*	x-height
illumination *f*	Beleuchtung *f*	illumination, lighting
illuminer	ausleuchten, erleuchten	to illuminate
illustrateur *m*	Illustrator *m*	artist, illustrator
illustration *f*	Abbildung *f*, Bild *n*, Illustration *f*	illustration, picture
illustration *f* de couverture *f*	Umschlagbild *n*	cover picture
illustration *f* montrant l'intérieur *m*	Werbebild *n*, das das Innere *n* zeigt	ghost view
illustré	bebildert	illustrated
illustré *m*	illustrierte Zeitschrift *f*	picture paper
illustré *m* publicitaire	Werbejournal *n*	advertising journal
illustrer	illustrieren	to illustrate
imagé, image *f*	bebildert, Bild *n*, Vorstellungsbild *n*	illustrated, illustration, image, picture
image *f* de décalcomanie *f*	Abziehbild *n*	transfer picture
image *f* de la firme *f*	Firmenbild *n*	corporate image
image *f* de marque *f*	Markenbild *n*	brand image
image *f* multiple d'un nom *m* de maison *f* ou de produit *m*	Mehrfachbild *n* eines Firmen- oder Personennamens *m*	mutiple image
image *f* publicitaire	Reklamebild *n*	advertising picture
image *f* spectre	Geisterbild *n*	double image, phantom
image *f* télévisée	Fernsehbild *n*	television picture
imbrication *f*	Überlappung *f*, Überschneidung *f*	duplication, overlapping
imitation *f*	Nachahmung *f*	counterfeit, imitation, plagiarism
imitation *f* de gravure *f* sur acier *m*	Stahlstichimitation *f*	thermography
imiter	kopieren, nachahmen, nachmachen	to copy, to imitate
immatriculation *f* des emplacements *m/pl*	Stellennumerierung *f*	numbering of sites *pl*
immédiatement après texte *m*	unmittelbar unter Text *m*	immediately below text
impact *m*	Einwirkung *f*	impact
impair	ungerade Zahl *f*	odd number

impartial	tendenzfrei, unparteiisch	impartial, non-partisan, unbiased
imperfection *f* **d'impression** *f*	Druckmängel *m/pl*	imperfection in printing
imperméable	wasserfest	waterproof
importance *f* **au marché** *m*	Marktgeltung *f*	market standard
importance *f* **du texte** *m* **comme élément** *m* **publicitaire**	Bedeutung *f* des Textes *m* als Anzeigenelement *n*	copy function
imposeur *m*	Metteur *m*	clicker, form-man, lay-out man, make-up hand, maker-up
imposition *f*	Umbruch *m*	imposition, make up
impôt *m*	Steuer *f*	tax
impôt *m* **sur la publicité** *f*	Anzeigensteuer *f*, Werbesteuer *f*	advertisement duty, advertising tax
impôt *m* **sur le chiffre** *m* **d'affaires** *f/pl*	Umsatzsteuer *f*	sales *pl* tax, turnover tax
imprégner	imprägnieren	to impregnate
impression *f*	Druck *m*	impression, printing
impression *f* **à la main** *f*	Handdruck *m*	hand printing
impression *f* **à l'aniline** *f*	Anilindruck *m*	aniline printing, flexographic printing
impression *f* **à plat**	Flachdruck *m*	flat-bed printing, level printing, planography, straight printing
impression *f* **anastatique**	anastatischer Druck *m*	anastatic printing
impression *f* **artistique**	Kunstdruck *m*	art print
impression *f* **au bromure** *m* **d'argent** *m*	Bromsilberdruck *m*	bromide printing
impression *f* **au recto** *m*	Schöndruck *m*	first impression, first run, prime, printing one face, sheetwise
impression *f* **au ruban** *m* **de machine** *f*	Farbbanddruckbrief *m*	ink ribbon printed letter
impression *f* **au verso** *n*	Widerdruck *m*	backing up, perfecting, second printing, verso printing
impression *f* **aux encres** *f/pl*	Ölfarbendruck *m*	oil print
impression *f* **aux encres** *f/pl* **communicatives**	Kopierdruck *m*	copying printing
impression *f* **avec encre** *f* **fluorescente**	Leuchtdruck *m*	fluorescent ink printing
impression *f* **bichrome**	Zweifarbendruck *m*	two-colour process
impression *f* **boueuse**	unreiner Druck *f*	slur
impression *f* **combinée**	Kombinationsdruck *m*	combined printing
impression *f* **d'anaglyphes** *f/pl*	Anaglyphendruck *m*	anaglyphic print
impression *f* **de bronze** *m*	Bronzedruck *m*	bronze printing
impression *f* **de l'adresse** *f* **du détaillant** *m*	Eindruck *m* der Händleradresse *f*	dealer imprint
impression *f* **de linoléum** *m*	Linoleumdruck *m*	lino printing
impression *f* **de photos** *f/pl* **en couleur** *f*	Farbfotodruck *m*	colour photo printing
impression *f* **de piètre qualité** *f*	schlechter Druck *m*	poor print
impression *f* **de planches** *f/pl* **superposées sur supports** *m/pl* **transparents**	Transartdruck *m*	3-dimensional reproduction and printing process
impression *f* **d'illustrations** *f/pl*	Illustrationsdruck *m*	illustration printing
impression *f* **double-ton** *m*	Doppeltondruck *m*, Duplexdruck *m*	double-tone printing, duplex printing
impression *f* **du tirage** *m*	Fortdruck *m*	production run, running-on

impression *f* écran *m* de soie *f*	Siebdruck *m*	silk screen printing
impression *f* en autochromie *f*	Autochromdruck *m*	autochrome printing
impression *f* en blanc	Blindprägung *f,* Schöndruck *m*	blind blocking, blind embossing, first impression, first run, prime, printing one face, sheetwise
impression *f* en continu	Endlosdruck *m*	continuous printing
impression *f* en couleurs *f/pl*	Farbdruck *m,* Mehrfarbendruck *m*	chromotype, colour printing, multi-colour printing, process printing
impression *f* en creux *m*	Tiefdruck *m/typog*	copperplate printing, intaglio printing, photogravure, rotogravure
impression *f* en deux couleurs *f/pl*	Zweifarbendruck *m*	two-colour process
impression *f* en héliogravure *f*	Kupfertiefdruck *m,* Tiefdruck *m/typog*	copper gravure, copperplate printing, intaglio printing, photogravure, rotogravure
impression *f* en quatre couleurs *f/pl*	Vierfarbendruck *m*	four-colour process
impression *f* en relief *m*	Hochdruck *m,* Hochdruckverfahren *n*	relief printing, surface printing
impression *f* en taille-douce *f*	Kupfertiefdruck *m*	copper gravure, copperplate printing, photogravure, rotogravure
impression *f* en trois couleurs *f/pl*	Dreifarbendruck *m*	three-colour printing, trichromatic process work
impression *f* flexographique	Flexodruck *m*	flexographic printing
impression *f* fraîche	frisch bedruckt	wet print
impression *f* gaufrée	Reliefdruck *m*	die-stamping, embossing, relief-printing
impression *f* héliogravure *f*	Tiefdruck *m typog*	copperplate printing
impression *f* irisée	Irisdruck *m*	irisdescent printing
impression *f* manquée	Fehldruck *m*	misprint
impression *f* mate	Mattdruck *m*	dull-finish printing
impression *f* métallographique	Metalldruckverfahren *n*	woodbury print
impression *f* multicolore	Mehrfarbendruck *m*	multi-colour printing, process printing
impression *f* offset	Gummidruck *m,* Offsetdruck *m*	offset printing
impression *f* offset en creux *m*	Offsettiefdruck *m*	offset deep printing
impression *f* par contact *m*	Kontaktdruck *m*	contact print
impression *f* photostat sur papier *m* spécial	Permastatdruck *m*	permastat, photostat printing on special paper
impression *f* planographique	Flachdruck *m*	flat-bed printing, level printing, planography, straight printing
impression *f* polychrome	Buntdruck *m,* Farbdruck *m*	chromotype, colour printing
impression *f* pour éditions *f/pl*	Werkdruck *m*	book printing
impression *f* quadrichrome	Vierfarbendruck *m*	four-colour process
impression *f* recto-verso	Schön- und Widerdruck *m*	work and turn
impression *f* sérigraphique	Siebdruck *m*	silk screen printing
impression *f* sur bois *m*	Holzdruck *m*	wood printing
impression *f* sur étoffes *f/pl*	Stoffdruck *m*	cloth printing, printing on fabrics *pl*
impression *f* sur fer-blanc *m*	Blechdruck *m*	metal-decorating, tin-printing
impression *f* sur humide	Naß-in-Naß-Druck *m*	wet-on-wet printing

impression *f* **sur plaque** *f* **d'acier** *m*	Stahldruck *m*	die stamping
impression *f* **sur rotative** *f*	Rotationsdruck *m*	rotary printing
impression *f* **sur rotative** *f* **en couleurs** *f/pl*	Rotationsfarbdruck *m*	ROP colour
impression *f* **sur rouleaux** *m/pl*	Walzdruck *m*	cylinder print
impression *f* **sur soie** *f*	Seidendruck *m*	silk-print
impression *f* **sur tôle** *f*	Blechdruck *m*	metal-decorating, tin-printing
impression *f* **thermogravure** *f*	Reliefdruck *m*	die-stamping, embossing, relief-printing
impression *f* **trichrome**	Dreifarbendruck *m*	three-colour printing, trichromatic process work
impression *f* **typographique**	Buchdruck *m*	letter press printing
impression *f* **verso**	Rückseitendruck *m*	backing up
imprimable	druckfähig	fit for printing, printable
imprimé *m*	Druckerzeugnis *n*, Drucksache *f*, Druckschrift *f* (Veröffentlichung *f*)	printed matter, printings *pl/am*, publication
imprimé *m* **de grand format** *m*	großformatige Drucksache *f*	broadsheet
imprimé *m* **publicitaire**	Werbedrucksache *f*	advertising matter
imprimé *m* **publicitaire avec carte-réponse** *f*	Werbedrucksache *f* mit Antwort *f*	self-mailer
imprimer	drucken	to impress, to print
imprimerie *f*	Druckerei *f*, Offizin *f*	printing office, printing plant
imprimerie *f* **d'affiches** *f/pl*	Plakatdruckerei *f*	poster printing plant
imprimerie *f* **de travaux** *m/pl* **de ville** *f*	Akzidenzdruckerei *f*	jobbing office
imprimerie *f* **d'un journal** *m*	Zeitungsdruckerei *f*	news house
imprimés *m/pl* **commerciaux**	Geschäftsdrucksachen *f/pl*	commercial stationery
imprimés *m/pl* **expédiés en nombre** *m*	Massendrucksachen *f/pl*	bulk mail
imprimés *m/pl* **publicitaires comme annexes** *f/pl* **d'un packetage** *m*	Beipack *m* von Werbedrucksachen *f/pl*	envelope stuffers *pl*
imprimeur *m*	Buchdrucker *m*, Drucker *m*	letterpress printer, printer
imprimeur *m* **de travaux** *m/pl* **de ville** *f*	Akzidenzdrucker *m*	job printer
imprimeur *m* **en héliogravure** *f*	Tiefdrucker *m*	photogravure printer
imprimeur *m* **offset**	Offsetdrucker *m*	offset printer
improviser	aus dem Stegreif *m* schreiben	to strike off
impulsion *f*	Impuls *m*	impulse
incident *m* **technique**	Sendeunterbrechung *f*	break in transmission
incitation *f*	Anreiz *m*	appeal, incitement
incitation *f* **à l'achat** *m*	Kaufanreiz *m*	buying incitement, merchandise appeal, stimulus
inclus	inbegriffen	included
incomplet	unvollständig	half-baked
incunable *m*	Erstdruck *m*, Inkunabel *f*	incunabulum
indemnité *f*	Entschädigung *f*	compensation, indemnity
indépendant	unabhängig	independent
index *m*	Inhaltsverzeichnis *n*, Register *n*	index, register, table of contents *pl*

index *m* alphabétique	Sachregister *n*	subject index, table of contents *pl*
index *m* alphabétique des mots *m/pl* souches	Stichwortverzeichnis *n*	classified index
indicateur *m*	Kursbuch *n*	railway guide, time-table
indicateur *m* d'adresses *f/pl*	Adreßbuch *n*	address book, directory
indicateur *m* d'adresses *f/pl* publicitaires	Werbeadreßbuch *n*	advertising directory
indicateur *m* téléphonique	Fernsprechbuch *n*	telephone directory
indicatif *m*	Pausenzeichen *n*, Sendezeichen *n*	call sign, signature tune
indicatif *m* musical	musikalisches Leitmotiv *n*	jingle
indication *f*	Angabe *f*	declaration, statement
indication *f* de dépassement *m*	Überlauf-Anzeige *f*	overflow indication
indication *f* de rentrée *f*	Startzeichen *n*	cue, starting signal
indication *f* du prix *m*	Preisangabe *f*	price quotation
indice *m*	Kennzeichen *n*, Zeichen *n*	emblem, mark, sign
indice *m* de collationnement *m*	Flattermarke *f*	collation mark
indiquer	angeben	to state
industrie *f* cinématographique	Filmindustrie *f*	film industry
industrie *f* du spectacle *m*	Schaugeschäft *n*	show business
industrie *f* publicitaire	Werbeindustrie *f*	advertising industry
industries *f/pl* graphiques	Druckgewerbe *n*	printing trade
inférieur	tiefstehend	inferior
influencer	beeinflussen	to influence
influencer partialement	einseitig beeinflussen	to angle
in-folio	Folioformat *n*	in-folio
informateur *m*	Auskunftsperson *f*, Gewährsmann *m*, Informant *m*	informant
information *f*	Ankündigung *f*, Information *f*, Meldung *f*	announcement, information, news report
information *f* à tendance *f*	Tendenzmeldung *f*	tendentious information
information *f* à traiter	Eingabe *f/typog*	input
information *f* câblée	Kabelnachricht *f*	news sent by cable
information *f* confidentielle	vertrauliche Information *f*	off the record information
information *f* de bonne source *f*	Information *f* aus guter Quelle *f*	inside knowledge
information *f* incorrecte	Fehlinformation *f*	faulty information
information *f* sensationnelle et exclusive	sensationelle Alleinmeldung *f*	scoop
information *f* traitée	Ausgabe *f/typog*	output
information *f* de dernière heure *f*	letzte Nachrichten *f/pl*	latest news, stop-press news
information *f* dépassée	überholte Nachrichten *f/pl*	stale news
information *f* lumineuse	Wanderschriftnachrichten *f/pl*	illuminated newsband, news by electric sign
information *f* numérique	digitale Informationen *f/pl*	digital information
informatrice *f*	Auskunftsperson *f*	informant
informer	benachrichtigen, informieren	to acquaint, to inform
ingénieur *m* du son *m*	Toningenieur *m*	monitor man
initiale *f*	Anfangsbuchstabe *m*, Initiale *f*	initial letter
initiale *f* ornée	Schmuckinitiale *f*	swash initial
innovation *f*	Neuerung *f*	innovation
inondation *f* du marché *m*	Marktüberschwemmung *f*	glut of the market
in-plano *m*	großer Faltprospekt *m*, Großprospekt *m*, Werbeflugblatt *n*	broadsheet, broadside, broadsheet
inscription *f*	Beschriftung *f*, Eintrag *m*, Inschrift *f*	entry, inscription, lettering

inscription f des vitrines f/pl	Schaufensterbeschriftung f	window-dressing
inscription f publicitaire	Werbeinschrift f	advertising inscription
inscriptions-réclame f	Reklameaufschrift f	advertising inscription
inscrire	einschreiben, eintragen	to enter, to inscribe, to register
insérer	annoncieren, einfügen, einrücken (Anzeige), einschalten, inserieren	to advertise, to fill-in, to insert, to publish
insérer en dernière minute f	in letzter Minute f einrücken	to fudge
insertion f	Annonce f, Anzeige f, Einfügung f, Einschaltung f, Inserat n	ad, advertisement, announcement, insertion
insertion f gratuite	Gratisanzeige f, kostenlose Insertion f	free advertisement, free insertion
insertion f publicitaire	Werbeeinblendung f	chain break, spot announcement
insertion f supplémentaire	zusätzliche Anzeige f	additional insertion
insigne m	Abzeichen n, Namensschildchen n	badge
insinuation f	Wink m	hint, tip
insolation f	Belichtung f	exposure, insolation
insoler	belichten	to expose
insonorisation f	Schalldichtmachung f	sound-proofing
inspecteur m d'emplacements m/pl	Anschlagkontrolleur m	site inspector
inspection f d'emplacements m/pl	Anschlagkontrolle f, Plakatanschlagkontrolle f	riding the showing, site inspection
installation f	Einrichtung f	installation
installation f de composition f programmée	Computersetzanlage f	computer typesetting installation
installation f de magasin m	Ladenausstattung f, Ladeneinrichtung f	shop fitting, store fittings pl
installation f spectaculaire	Werbegroßanlage f	spectacular
instantané m	Schnappschuß m	snapshot
instantané m non posé	Momentaufnahme f	candid picture, snapshot
institut m	Institut n	institute
institut m d'études f/pl de marché m	Marktforschungsinstitut n	market research institute
instruction f d'expédition f	Versandanzeige f	advice note
instructions f/pl	Arbeitsanweisung f, Instruktionen f/pl	briefing
instructions f/pl pour la composition f	Satzanweisungen f/pl	rules pl of composition
instrument m de mesure f de l'audience f	Meßgerät n zur Zuschauerforschung f	videometer
instrument m de vente f	Absatzinstrument n	sales pl instrument
intellectuel m	Intellektueller m	egghead, highbrow
intelligibilité f	Verständlichkeit f	readability
intensification f de la publicité f	Intensivierung f des Werbeeffekts m	accumulation
intensité f	Intensität f	intensity
intensité f de la couleur f	Farbintensität f	chromatic intensity
intensité f de la lecture f	Leseintensität f	reading intensity
intensité f de la publicité f	Werbeintensität f	advertising intensity
intensité f lumineuse	Leuchtkraft f	intensity of light
intention f d'achat m	Kaufabsicht f	purchase intention
intercaler	durchschießen (Bogen), einschieben	to cut in, to sandwich

interdépendance *f* des médias *f*	Medienverflechtung *f*	cross-channel-ownership
intérêt *m*	Interesse *n*	interest
intérêt *m* des consommateurs *m/pl*	Verbraucherinteresse *n*	consumer interest
intérêt *m* général	Allgemeininteresse *n*	public interest
intérieur *m* du pays *m*	Inland *n*	inland
interlettrer	spationieren, sperren	to lead out, to space out
interlignage *m*	Durchschuß *m*, Zeilenabstand *m*	interlinear space, leading, leads *pl*, slugs *pl*
interligne *f*	Reglette *f*, Zwischenschlag *m*	clump, lead, line-space, reglet
interligner	durchschießen	to interline, to lead out, to space out
interlignes *f/pl*	Zeilenzwischenräume *m/pl*	leads *pl*
interlocuteur *m*	Gesprächspartner *m*	interlocutor
intermédiaire *m*	Zwischenhändler *m*	middleman
intermédiaire *m* publicitaire	Annoncenexpedition *f*, Anzeigenexpedition *f*, Anzeigenmittler *m*, Mediaagentur *f*, Streuagentur *f*, Werbungsmittler *m*	advertising contractor, advertising intermediary, advertising space buyer, independent media services *pl* company, space broker
intermédiare *m* revendeur	Großhändler *m*	jobber, wholesale dealer
interprétation *f*	Auslegung *f*, Auswertung *f*, Deutung *f*	evaluation, exploitation, interpretation
interprète *m*	Dolmetscher *m*	interpreter
interrogation *f*	Frage *f*	query, question
interrogatoire *m*	Befragung *f*	interview, poll, questioning, survey
interrogatoire *m* direct		oral interview
interruption *f* d'une émission *f*	Unterbrechung *f* einer Sendung *f*	break
intertitre *m*	Zwischentitel *m*	caption, sub-title
intervalle *m* de parution *f*	Erscheinungsintervall *n*	interval of publication
interview *f*	Befragung *f*, Interview *n*	interview, poll, questioning, survey
interview *f* avec une personne *f* non nommée	Interview *n* mit Ungenanntem *m*	lamp-post interview
interview *m* bidon	vorgetäuschtes Interview *n*	fake interview
interview *m* de rappel *m*	Nachfaßinterview *n*	call-back
interview *m* en profondeur *f*	Tiefeninterview *n*	depth interview
interview *f* non préparée	unvorbereitetes Interview *n*	candid interview
interview *f* orale	mündliche Befragung *f*	oral interview
interview *m* par téléphone *m*	Telefoninterview *n*	telephone interview
interview *m* rappelé	Kontroll-Interview *n*	call-back
interviewé *m*	Befragter *m*	interviewee, respondent
interviewer	befragen	to interview
intitulé	betitelt	entitled, headed
intrigant *m*	Drahtzieher *m*	machinator, wire-puller
intrigues *m/pl* de couloirs *m/pl*	Lobbyismus *m*	lobbying
introduction *f*	Einleitung *f*	introduction, preamble
introduire	einführen	to introduce
invendable	unverkäuflich	not for sale
invendus *pl*	Remittenden *f/pl*	overrun, remainders *pl*, returns *pl*
inventaire *m*	Verzeichnis *n*	inventory, list
inventer une histoire *f*	Geschichte *f* erfinden, eine	to fake up a story
inversé	seitenverkehrt	reversed left to right
inverser	kontern	to reverse

inversion *f*	Umkehrung *f*	inversion, reversing
investir	investieren	to invest
investissements *m/pl* en publicité *f*	Werbeaufwendungen *f/pl*, Werbeinvestitionen *f/pl*	advertising expenditures *pl*, advertising investments *pl*
irrégularité *f*	Unregelmäßigkeit *f*	irregularity
italique *f* de fantaisie *f*	Zierbuchstabe *m*	ornamental letter, swash letter
item *m*	Einzelheit *f*	item

J

jambage *m* inférieur	Unterlänge *f*	descender height
japon *m*	Japanpapier *n*	India paper, Japan paper
jaquette *f*	Schutzumschlag *m*	dust-cover, jacket
jargon *m*	Jargon *m*	jargon, slang
jargon *m* incompréhensible	Kauderwelsch *n*	gibberish, gobbledygook
jauni	vergilbt	yellowed
jeu *m* de bandes *f/pl*	Streifband *n*	wrapper
jeu *m* de dégressifs *m/pl*	Wiederholungsrabatt *m*	series *pl* discount
jeu *m* de mots *m/pl*	Wortspiel *n*	pun, quibble
joindre	anhängen *typog*	to run on
jour *m* de parution *f*	Erscheinungstag *m*	day of publishing, publication date
jour *m* d'échéance *f*	Stichtag *m*	fixed day, key-date
journaille *f*	Hetzpresse *f*	yellow press
journal *m*	Blatt *n* (Zeitung *f*), Zeitung *f*	journal, newspaper, paper
journal affermé *m*	Pachtzeitung *f*	tied newspaper
journal *m* agricole	Landwirtschaftsblatt *n*	agriculture publication, farm publication
journal *m* antidaté	vordatierte Zeitung *f*	antedated paper, bulldog edition *am*, early-bird issue *am*, pre-dated paper
journal *m* avec beaucoup d'annonces *f/pl*	Blatt *n* mit vielen Anzeigen *f/pl*	tight paper
journal *m* avec peu d'annonces *f/pl*	Blatt *n* mit wenigen Anzeigen *f/pl*	wide open paper
journal *m* bien fait	gut aufgemachte Zeitung *f*	well made-up newspaper
journal *m* chauvin	chauvinistische Zeitung *f*	flag waver
journal *m* concurrent	Konkurrenzblatt *n*	rival newspaper
journal *m* concurrentiel	Wettbewerbzeitung *f*	rival newspaper
journal *m* culturel	kulturelle Zeitschrift *f*	cultural magazine, periodical of culture
journal *m* d'abonnés *m/pl*	Abonnementszeitung *f*	firm order newspaper, subscribers' paper
journal *m* d'annonces *f/pl* légales	Pflichtblatt *n*	journal in which the law requires public notices *pl* to be inserted
journal *m* d'association *f*	Verbandsblatt *n*	organ of a corporation
journal *m* de commerce *m*	Handelsblatt *n*	journal of commerce, trade journal
journal *m* de dimanche *m*	Sonntagszeitung *f*	Sunday newspaper
journal *m* de droite	rechtseingestellte Zeitung *f*	right-wing paper
journal *m* de grand format *m*	großformatige Zeitung *f*	blanket sheet
journal *m* de midi *m*	Mittagsblatt *n*	noon paper
journal *m* de modes *f/pl*	Modeblatt *n*	fashion magazine
journal *m* de mots *m/pl* croisés	Kreuzworträtselzeitung *f*	crossword paper
journal *m* de première qualité *f*, journal *m* de prestige *m*	Qualitätszeitung *f*	high-class paper, prestige paper, quality paper

journal *m* de publicité *f*	Werbefachblatt *n*	advertising paper
journal *m* de qualité *f*	Prestigezeitung *f*	quality paper
journal *m* de roman *m*	Romanheft *f*	journal of fiction, penny novellette
journal *m* de tendance *f*	Tendenzblatt *n*	tendentious paper
journal *m* de tout premier rang *m*	Zeitung *f*, führende	leading paper
journal *m* d'entreprise *f*	Betriebszeitung *f*, Hauszeitschrift *f*, Werkzeitschrift *f*	company publication, house journal, house organ, house journal, staff magazine
journal *m* des jeunes *m/pl*	Jugendzeitung *f*	youth paper
journal *m* du matin *m*	Morgenzeitung *f*	morning newspaper
journal *m* du septième jour *m*	Wochenendzeitung *f*	week-end paper
journal *m* du soir *m*	Abendzeitung *f*	evening newspaper
journal *m* d'une concentration *f* de lecteurs *m/pl* dans un grand territoire *m*	Blockzeitung *f*	newspaper with concentration of its readership in a large territory
journal *m* fantôme	Geisterzeitung *f*, Schwindelzeitung *f*	bogus publication
journal *m* financier	Börsenzeitung *f*, Finanzblatt *n*	financial paper
journal *m* gauchiste	linkseingestellte Zeitung *f*	leftist paper
journal *m* hebdomadaire	Wochenzeitung *f*	weekly newspaper
journal *m* illustré	Bildzeitung *f*	illustrated paper
journal *m* indépendant avec une rédaction *f* complète	journalistische Einheit *f*	independent newspaper with a complete editorial staff, journalistic unit
journal *m* intérimaire	Notzeitung *f*	temporary paper
journal *m* intime	Tagebuch *n*	diary
journal *m* le plus lu	meistgelesene Zeitung *f*	most read paper
journal *m* local	Heimatzeitung *f*, Ortszeitung *f*	local paper
journal *m* lumineux	Wanderschriftnachrichten *f/pl*	illuminated newsband, news by electric sign
journal *m* luxueux	Luxusblatt *n*	luxury paper, slick magazine
journal *m* médiocre	minderwertiges Blatt *n*, Schundblatt *n*	trashy paper
journal *m* monopolisateur	Monopolzeitung *f*	monopolistic journal
journal *m* mural	Wandzeitung *f*	wall newspaper
journal *m* officiel	amtliche Zeitung *f*	gazette
journal *m* parlé	Nachrichtensendung *f*, Rundfunknachrichten *f/pl*, Tagesnachrichten *f/pl* im Rundfunk *m*	broadcast news, news bulletin, newscast, topical talk
journal *m* populaire	populäre Zeitung *f*	popular newspaper
journal *m* pornographique	pornografisches Blatt *n*	smut sheet
journal *m* pour concierges *f/pl*	Räuberpistole *f*	penny dreadful
journal *m* pour la clientèle *f*	Kundenzeitschrift *f*	customer magazine, sales *pl* bulletin, shopping news
journal *m* pour l'élite *f*	Qualitätszeitung *f*	high-class paper, prestige paper, quality paper
journal *m* prédaté	vordatierte Zeitung *f*	antedated paper, bulldog edition *am*, early-bird issue *am*, pre-dated paper
journal *m* professionnel	Fachzeitung	business publication, technical publication, trade journal
journal *m* publicitaire	Anzeigenblatt *n*	admag, advertisement magazine, advertiser, free sheet, shopper

journal *m* **sans publicité** *f*	Zeitung *f* ohne Anzeigen *f/pl*	adless newspaper
journal *m* **scandaleux**	Skandalblatt *n*	smut sheet
journal *m* **scolaire**	Schülerzeitung *f*	school journal
journal *m* **se distinguant seulement d'un autre par le titre** *m*	Kopfblatt *n*	reprint with change of title only
journal *m* **sérieux qu'on cite**	oft zitiertes Blatt *n*	newspaper of record
journal *m* **sonore**	Zeitschrift *f* in Schallplattenform *f*	paper in form of records *pl*
journal *m* **sportif**	Sportzeitschrift *f*	sport magazine
journal *m* **télévisé**	Tagesnachrichten *f/pl* im Fernsehen *n*, Tagesschau *f*	television news, television news show
journal *m* **très répandu**	Zeitung *f*, weitverbreitete	widely read newspaper
journal *m* **trompeur**	Geisterzeitung *f*, Schwindelzeitung *f*	bogus publication
journaleux *m*	Skribifax *m*	ink-slinger
journalisme *m*	Journalismus *m*, Pressewesen *n*, Publizistik *f*, Zeitungswesen *n*	journalism, press
journaliste *m*	Journalist *m*	journalist, newspaper man
journaliste *m* **indépendant**	freier Journalist *m*	free lance reporter
journaliste *m* **payé à la ligne** *f*	Journalist *m* mit Zeilenhonorar *n*	space man
journaliste *f* **spécialisée en reportages** *m/pl* **larmoyants**	Heulsuse *f*	sob-sister
journaliste *m* **universel**	Universaljournalist *m*	universal journalist
jugement *m*	Beurteilung *f*	valuation
jugement *m* **de valeur** *f*	Werturteil *n*	value judgment
jumelage *m*	Zusammenschluß *m*	amalgamation, combination
jusqu'à nouvel ordre *m*	bis auf Widerruf *m*	till forbid, until cancelled order
juste prix *m*	angemessener Preis *m*	adequate price
justificatif *m*	Beleg *m*, Durchführungsbestätigung *f*, Zahlungsbeleg *m*	voucher
justificatif *m* **complet**	komplette Belegnummer *f*	complete voucher copy
justificatif *m* **d'annonce** *f*	Anzeigenbeleg *m*	voucher copy
justification *f*	Druckeinstellung *f/typog*, Justierung *f*, Satzbreite *f*, Zeilenlänge *f*	adjustment, justification, length of line, measure
justification *f* **de la colonne** *f*	Spaltenbreite *f*, Zeilenbreite *f*	column measure, column width, length, measure, width of column
justifier	ausschließen (typog), justieren, Zeile *f*, ausschließen	to adjust, to align, to justify, word space
justifier à droite	nach rechts ausschließen	to move to the right
justifier à la gauche	nach links ausschließen	to move to the left
juxtaposition *f* **désordonnée d'annonces** *f/pl*	Anzeigenplantage *f*	cocktail of ads *pl*

K

kiosque *m*	Kiosk *m*	kiosk *brit*, news stand *am*
kiosque *m* **à journaux** *m/pl*	Zeitungskiosk *m*, Zeitungsstand *m*	kiosk *brit*, newsstall, newsstand *am*

L

label *m* de qualité *f*	Gütezeichen *n*	certification mark, quality label, seal of approval
labeur *m*	Schwerarbeit *f*	hard work
lacune *f* dans la publicité *f*	Werbepause *f*	hiatus
lacune *f* dans le marché *m*	Marktlücke *f*	loop-hole in the market, marketing-gap
lacune *f* d'été *m*	Sommerloch *n*	hiatus, seasonal summer decline
lacune *f* d'information *f*	Informationslücke *f*	information gap
laisser en blanc	aussparen *typog*, blank schlagen, blind schlagen	to clear away, to leave blank
laize *f*	Rollenbreite *f*	reel width
laminage *m*	Laminierung *f*	laminating
laminer	laminieren	to laminate
lampe *f* survoltée	Flutlicht *n*	floodlight
lancement *m*	Lanzierung *f*	launching
lancement *m* d'un ballon *m* d'essai *m*	Versuchsballon *m* steigen lassen	kite-flying
lancer	einführen, lanzieren	to introduce, to launch
langage *m* courant	Umgangssprache *f*	colloquial speech
langage *m* technique	Fachsprache *f*	technical language
langue *f* de la publicité *f*	Werbesprache *f*	advertising language
langue *f* littéraire	Schriftsprache *f*	written language
lanterne *f* magique	Laterna *f* magica	living screen
lapsus *m* calami	Schreibfehler *m*	clerical mistake, slip of the pen
lapsus *m* linguae	Sprechfehler *m*	lapse of the tongue
laque *f*	Lack *m*	lacquer, varnish
laque *f* zapon	Zaponlack *m*	Japan enamel, zapon varnish
laquer	lackieren	to lacquer, to varnish
large	breit	expanded, wide
largeur *f*	Breite *f*	width
largeur *f* abregée de la composition *f*	verkürzte Satzbreite *f*	run-around
largeur *f* de la colonne *f*	Spaltenbreite *f*	column measure, column width
largeur *f* de la composition *f*	Satzbreite *f*	measure
largeur *f* de page *f*	Blattbreite *f*	page width
largeur *f* minimum *m*	Mindestbreite *f*	minimum width
lavage *m* de cerveau *f*, lavage *m* de crâne *m*	Gehirnwäsche *f*	brain washing
lavage *m* de machine *f*	Maschinenreinigung *f*	machine washing
le même nom *m* pour des produits *m/pl* différents	gleicher Markenname *m* für verschiedene Produkte *m/pl*	brand-umbrella
lèche-vitrines *m*	Schaufensterbummel *m*	window shopping
lecteur *m*	Leser *m*	reader
lecteur *m* accidental, lecteur *m* aléatoire	Zufallsleser *m*	pass-along reader
lecteur *m* averti	urteilsfähiger Leser *m*	discriminating reader
lecteur *m* de journaux *m/pl*	Zeitungsleser *m*	newspaper reader
lecteur *m* des cartes *f/pl* perforées	Lochkartenleser *m*	card reader
lecteur *m* d'une maison *f* d'édition *f*	Lektor *m*	copy editor
lecteur *m* exclusif	Exklusivleser *m*	exclusive reader
lecteur *m* occasionnel	Gelegenheitsleser *m*	casual reader, occasional reader

lecteurs *m/pl*	Leserschaft *f*	audience, readers *pl*, readership
lecteurs *m/pl* réguliers	regelmäßige Leser *m/pl*	regular readers *pl*
lecture *f*	Lektüre *f*	reading
lecture *f* mécanique	maschinelles Lesen *n*	character recognition
lecture *f* récréative	leichte Lektüre *f*	light reading
lecture *f* sonore	Wiedergabe *f* einer Tonaufnahme *f*	play back
légalisation *f*	Beglaubigung *f*	authentication
légaliser	beglaubigen	to authenticate
légende *f*	Bildunterschrift *f*, Legende *f*, Unterschriftszeile *f*	base line, caption, legend, outline
légende *f* de cliché *m*	Klischeeunterschrift *f*	cut-liner
législation *f* de la publicité *f*	Werbegesetzgebung *f*	advertising legislation
leitmotiv *m*	Leitmotiv *n*	leitmotif
à l'endroit *m*	seitenrichtig	right reading
à l'envers *m*	seitenverkehrt	reversed left to right
letters *f/pl* majuscules	Majuskeln *f/pl*	capital letters *pl*
lettre *f*	Buchstabe *m*, Letter *f*, Type *f*	character, face, letter, type
lettre *f* à la rédaction *f*	Leserzuschrift *f*	letter to the editor
lettre *f* à queue *f*	Zierbuchstabe *m*	ornamental letter, swash letter
lettre *f* aérienne	Flugpostbrief *m*	airmail letter
lettre *f* bas de casse *f*	Kleinbuchstabe *m*, Minuskel *f*	lower case letter, minuscule, small letter
lettre *f* bloquée	Blockade *f*, Fliegenkopf *m/typog*	black, turned letter
lettre *f* circulaire	Rundschreiben *n*	circular letter
lettre *f* crénée	gestürzter Buchstabe *m*	kerned letter
lettre *f* de change *m*	Wechsel *m*	bill
lettre *f* de confirmation *f*	Bestätigungsschreiben *n*	letter of confirmation
lettre *f* de propagande *f*	Werbebrief *m*	advertising letter, sales *pl* letter
lettre *f* de rappel *m*	Mahnbrief *m*	demand-note
lettre *f* de remerciement *m*	Dankschreiben *n*	letter of thanks *pl*
lettre *f* de retrait *m*	Nachfaßbrief *m*	follow-up letter
lettre *f* de vente *f*	Werbebrief *m*	advertising letter, sales *pl* letter
lettre *f* débordante	überhängender Buchstabe *m*	kerned letter
lettre *f* d'envoi *m*	Begleitbrief *m*	covering letter
lettre *f* dont l'adresse *f* est défectueuse	Brief *m* mit fehlerhafter Anschrift *f*	blind letter
lettre *f* d'or *m*	Goldbuchstabe *m*	gilt-letter
lettre *f* en relief *m*	Reliefbuchstabe *m*	relief letter
lettre *f* illustrée	Bilderbrief *m*	illustrated letter
lettre *f* lumineuse	Leuchtbuchstabe *m*	illuminated letter
lettre *f* majuscule	Majuskel *f*	cap
lettre *f* manquante	fehlender Buchstabe *m*	dropped-out letter
lettre *f* minuscule	Minuskel *f*	small letter
lettre *m* moulée	Blockbuchstabe *m*	block capital, block letter
lettre *f* ornée	Zierbuchstabe *m*	ornamental letter, swash letter
lettre *f* publicitaire	Werbebrief *m*, Werbeschreiben *n*	advertising letter, sales *pl* letter
lettre *f* recommandée	eingeschriebener Brief *m*	registered letter
lettre *f* reproduite	vervielfältigter Brief *m*	process letter
lettre *f* schématique	Schemabrief *m*	schematic letter
lettre *f* télégraphique	Brieftelegramm *n*	letter telegram
lettre *f*-réponse *f*	Antwortschreiben *n*	written reply
lettres *f/pl*	Schrifttum *n*	literature
lettres *f/pl* bas-de-casse *f*	gemeine Buchstaben *m/pl*	lower case letters *pl*
lettres *f/pl* bâtardes	Bastardschrift *f*	bastard face, bastard type
lettres *f/pl* capitales	Großbuchstaben *m/pl*	capital letters *pl*, caps *pl*, large print, upper case letters *pl*

lettres f/pl couchées	Schrägschrift f, schrägliegende Buchstaben m/pl	slant letters pl, slanting letters pl
lettres f/pl débordantes	Oberlängen f/pl	ascenders pl
lettres f/pl écrasées	beschädigte Buchstaben m/pl, lädierte Buchstaben m/pl	battered letters pl, broken letters pl
lettres f/pl supérieures	hochgerückte Buchstaben m/pl	superior letters pl
lettreur m	Schriftenmaler m, Schriftzeichner m	lettering artist, lettering man
lettrine f	Initiale f	initial letter
lettriste m	Buchstabenzeichner m, Schriftzeichner m	letter designer, lettering man
leurre m	Köder m	bait, loss leader, lure
levage	Spieß m/typog	rising space, work-up am
lexicographe m	Wörterbuchverfasser m	lexicographer
lexique m	Lexikon n	encyclopaedia, lexicon
lézarde f	Straße f (Satz m), weißer Streifen m im Satz m	channel, river, river of white
liaison f	Zusammenhang m	association, connexion
liant m	Bindemittel n	binder
libelle f	Schmähschrift f	lampoon
liberté f de la pensée f	Gedankenfreiheit f	freedom of thought
liberté f de la presse f	Pressefreiheit f	freedom of the press
liberté f de parole f	Redefreiheit f	freedom of speech
liberté f d'opinion f	Meinungsfreiheit f	freedom of opinion
libraire m	Buchhändler m	bookseller
libre service m	Selbstbedienung f, Supermarkt m	self-service, supermarket
libretto m	Textbuch n	libretto
licence f	Lizenz f	franchise, license
lié au lieu m d'implantation f	standortgebunden	bound to the location
lier	ausbinden	to tie up
lieu m commun	Gemeinplatz m	commonplace, platitude
lieu m d'affichage m	Anschlagort m	place of posting
lieu m de publication f	Erscheinungsort m, Verlagsort m	place of publication, town of publication
lieu m de publicité f	Streuort m	place of advertising
lieu m d'essai m	Testort m	test-town
lieu m d'exécution f	Erfüllungsort m	place of fulfilment
lieu m d'impression f	Druckort m	place of printing
ligature f	Ligatur f	double letter, ligature
lignage m	Anzeigenraum m, Zeilenzahl f	advertising space, amount of space, lineage, number of lines pl
lignage m d'une annonce f	Anzeigengröße f, Gesamtinhalt m einer Anzeige f	advertisement lineage, lineage of an advertisement, space size
lignage m maximum	Höchstgröße f	maximum lineage
lignage f minimum m	Mindestgröße f	minimum lineage
ligne f	Linie f, Zeile f	line, rule typog
ligne f avec le nom m de l'auteur m	Zeile f mit dem Namen m des Autors m	by-line
ligne f bloc	Setzmaschinenzeile f	type bar
ligne f boiteuse	Hurenkind n (typog)	bastard type, widow
ligne f courte	Ausgangszeile f, Kurzzeile f	break-line, broken line, last line, short line, widow
ligne f de blanc	Blindzeile f	blank line, white line
ligne f de division f	Trennlinie f	cut-off-rule, dividing rule
ligne f de fond m	Schlußaussage f	base line

ligne f de la trame f	Rasterlinie f	screen line
ligne f de lettre f	Schriftlinie f	alignment, body line
ligne f de pied m	Fußzeile f	bottom line, foot rule
ligne f de pointillés m/pl	punktierte Linie f, Punktlinie f	dotted line, dotted rule
ligne f d'identification f	Erkennungszeile f	galley line
ligne f duplexée	Auszeichnungszeile f	display line
ligne f en gras	fette Linie f	fat line
ligne f épointée	stumpffeine Linie f	blunt rule
ligne f intervertie	verstellte Zeile f	transposed line
ligne f isolée	Witwe f/typog	widow
ligne f millimètre m	Millimeterzeile f	millimetre line
ligne f pleine	volle Zeile f, voller Spaltensatz m	full line, full measure
ligne f principale	Hauptzeile f, Schlagzeile f	catch line, headline, head line, punch line, shoulder note
ligne f repère	Schlagzeile f	catch line, headline, punch line, shoulder note
ligne f téléphonique	Telefonleitung f	telephone circuit
ligne f transposée	verhobene Zeile f	misplaced line
ligne f tremblée	Wellenlinie f	wavy line, wavy rule
ligne-bloc f	Maschinenzeile f	slug
lignes f/pl croisées	Kreuzlinienschraffur f	cross hatch
lignes f/pl d'une manchette f	Überschriftszeilen f/pl	banks pl
lignomètre m	Zeilenmesser m	line measure, type line scale, type-gauge
limitation f	Beschränkung f	limitation, restriction
limitations f/pl de la publicité f	Werbebeschränkungen f/pl	advertising limitations pl, advertising restrictions pl
limité	begrenzt	limited
limite f minimum	Rentabilitätsschwelle f	break-even point
linéaire	linear	linear
lingot m	Schließsteg m, Steg m/typog	furniture
lingot m de plomb m	Bleisteg m	lead furniture
lingot m évidé	Hohlsteg m	furniture
linguistique	sprachwissenschaftlich	linguistic
linotype f	Linotype-Setzmaschine f, Zeilenguß-Setzmaschine f	linotype
linotypiste m	Linotypesetzer m	linotype operator
liquidation f	Abrechnung f	settlement, statement
liquidation f générale	Totalausverkauf m	clearing of goods pl
liquider	ausverkaufen	to sell off
lire les épreuves f/pl	Abzüge m/pl lesen	to hold copies pl
lire qch. à qn.	vorlesen	to read out
lire sur le plomb m	auf dem Blei n lesen	to read in the metal
lisibilité f	Lesbarkeit f	legibility
liste f	Aufstellung f, Liste f, Verzeichnis n	catalogue brit, inventory, list
liste f aide-mémoire m	Kontrolliste f, Checkliste f	check list, guide-sheet
liste f d'adresses f/pl	Adressenliste f, Versandliste f	list of addresses pl, mailing index, mailing list
liste f de contrôle m	Checkliste f, Kontrolliste f, Prüfliste f	check list, guide sheet
liste f de localités f/pl	Ortsverzeichnis n	gazetteer
liste f de prix	Preisliste f	price list, rate card, rates pl, schedule of prices pl

liste *f* d'emplacements *m/pl*	Standortverzeichnis *n*, Stellenverzeichnis *n*	listing, site list
liste *f* des fournisseurs *m/pl*	Bezugsquellenverzeichnis *n*	directory of suppliers *pl*, list of suppliers *pl*
litho *f*	Lithografie *f*	litho, lithography
lithographe *m*	Lithograf *m*	lithographer
lithographie *f*	Lithografie *f*, Steindruck *m*	litho, lithographic print, lithography
lithographie *f* en couleurs *f/pl*	Farbenlithografie *f*	colour lithography
littérature *f*	Schrifttum *n*	literature
littérature *f* d'anticipation *f*	Zukunftsroman *m*	science-fiction
littérature *f* de bas étage *m*	Schundliteratur *f*	rubbishy literature
littérature *f* divertissante	Unterhaltungsliteratur *f*	fiction
littérature *f* larmoyante	sentimentale Literatur *f*	sob-stuff, squish
littérature *f* publicitaire	Werbeliteratur *f*	advertising literature
littérature *f* spécialisée	Fachliteratur *f*, Sachbuchliteratur *f*	nonfiction, specialised literature
livraison *f*	Lieferung *f*, Zustellung *f*	delivery
livraison *f* à domicile *m*	Lieferung *f* frei Haus *n*	free delivery, house delivery
livraison *f* renvoyée	Rücklieferung *f*	sales *pl* return
livre *m*	Buch *n*	book
livre *m* à feuilles *f/pl* mobiles	Loseblattbuch *n*	loose-leaf book
livre *m* à onglets *m/pl*	Buch *n* mit alphabetischem Register *n*	thumb-indexed book
livre *m* à succès *m*	Erfolgsbuch *n*, meistgekauftes Buch *n*	bestseller
livre *m* bien présenté	extra ausgestattetes Buch *n*	enriched book
livre *m* blanc	Weißbuch *n*	white paper
livre *m* broché	broschiertes Buch *n*, geheftetes Buch *n*	paperback, sewn book
livre *m* broché par boucles *f/pl*	Ringbuch *n*	coil-stitched book
livre *m* d'adresses *f/pl*	Adreßbuch *n*	address book, directory
livre *m* de commerce *m*	Geschäftsbuch *n*	ledger
livre *m* de poche *f*	Taschenbuch *n*	paper book, pocket book
livre *m* d'échantillons *m/pl*	Musterbuch *n*	sample book
livre *m* d'écoulement *m* facile	leichtverkäufliches Buch *n*, schnellverkäufliches Buch *n*	quick seller
livre *m* d'images *f/pl* sur toile *f*	unzerreißbares Bilderbuch *n*	rag-book
livre *m* durable	langlebiges Buch *n*	long seller, steady seller
livre *m* professionnel	Fachbuch *n*	handbook, text-book, trade book
livre *m* relié	fest gebundenes Buch *n*	hardcover
livre *m* technique	Fachbuch *n*	handbook, text-book, trade book
livre-cadeau *m*	Geschenkband *m*	presentation copy
livret *m*	Büchelchen *n*, Textbuch *n*	booklet, libretto
localisation *f*	Lokalisierung *f*	localization
location *f*	Vermietung *f*	leasing, letting
location *f* de films *m/pl*	Filmverleih *m*	film distributors *pl*, film lending institute
locomotive *f*	Zugnummer *f*	puller
locution *f*	Redensart *f*	phrase
logotype *m*	Firmenschriftzug *m*, Logotype *f*, Markenzeichen *n*, Namenszug *m*	device, logotype, name slug, trade mark
loi *f* de presse *f*	Presserecht *n*	press law
loi *f* publicitaire	Werbegesetz *n*	advertising law

loi *f* sur la presse *f*	Pressegesetz *n*	press law
long métrage *m*	abendfüllender Film *m*	full-length film
à long terme *m*	langfristig	long-term
à longue échéance *f*	langfristig	long-term
de longue haleine *f*	langatmig	long-winded
longues *f/pl* du haut *m*	Oberlängen *f/pl*	ascenders *pl*
longueur *f*	Länge *f*	length
longueur *f* de ligne *f*	Zeilenlänge *f*	length of line
longueur *f* de visibilité *f*	Sichtweite *f*	length of visibility
longueur *f* d'onde *f*	Wellenlänge *f*	wave-length
lotissement *m* publicitaire	Anweisung *f* von Werbekosten *pl*, Werbekostenanweisung *f*, Zuteilung *f*	advertising allocation, allotment
loueurs *m/pl* d'adresses *f/pl*	Adressenverlag *m*	address broker, supplier of addresses *pl*
loup *m*	Schnitzer *m*, Versprecher *m*	fluff
loyer *m*	Pachtabgabe *f*	rent
lucratif	gewinnbringend	profitable
lumière *f* d'ambiance *f*, lumière *f* d'arrosage *m*	Flutlicht *n*	floodlight

M

machinateur *m*	Drahtzieher *m*	machinator, wire-puller
machine *f* à affranchir	Frankiermaschine *f*	franking machine
machine *f* à composer	Setzmaschine *f*	composing machine, typesetting machine
machine *f* à écrire	Schreibmaschine *f*	typewriter
machine *f* à écrire automatique	automatische Schreibmaschine *f*, Schreibautomat *m*	automatic typewriter
machine *f* à fondre	Gießmaschine *f*	casting machine
machine *f* à graver	Ätzmaschine *f*, Graviermaschine *f*, Klischeeätzmaschine *f*	engraving machine, etching machine
machine *f* à imprimer	Druckmaschine *f*	letter press, printing press
machine *f* à imprimer à bobines *f/pl*	Rollendruckmaschine *f*	web printing press
machine *f* à numéroter	Numeriermaschine *f*	numbering machine
machine *f* à retiration *f*	Schön-und-Widerdruck-Maschine *f*	perfecting press
machine *f* de la mise *f* en pages *f/pl*	Umbruchgerät *n*	make-up terminal
machine *f* linotype	Linotypemaschine *f*	linotype machine
machines *f/pl* rotatives	Rotationspresse *f*	rotary press
maculature *f*	Makulatur *f*	misprint, spoil, waste paper
maculatures *f/pl*	Einschießbogen *m*	slip sheets *pl*
macule *f*	Fleck *m*	blur, speck
maculer	durchschlagen *typog*	to come through, to strike through, to transpierce
macules *f/pl*	Zwischenblätter *n/pl*	interleaves *pl*
magasin *m*	Laden *m*	retail store, shop
magasin *m* discount *m*	Discountladen *m*	discount shop, discounter
magasin *m* specialisé	Spezialgeschäft *n*	specialty store
magasinage *m* de cliché *m*	Klischeeaufbewahrung *f*	block preservation, block storage
magasins *m/pl* de modes *f/pl*	Modezeitschriften *f/pl*	fashion magazines *pl*

magasins *m/pl* pour ménagères *f/pl*	Hausfrauenzeitschriften *f/pl*	housewives' magazines *pl*
magazine *m*	Magazin *n*, Publikumszeitschrift *f*, Zeitschrift *f*	consumer publication, magazine, periodical, review
magazine *m* de télévision *f*	Programmzeitschrift *f*	television magazine
magazine *f* d'information *f*	Nachrichtenmagazin *n*	news magazine
magazines *m/pl* chics	elegante Zeitschriften *f/pl*	glossy monthlies *pl*
magie *f* noire	schwarze Kunst *f*	black art
magnat *m* de la presse *f*	Pressemagnat *m*	press tycoon
magnétophone *m*	Magnetofon *n*	magnetophone
magnétoscope *m*	Gerät *n* für Filme *m/pl* in Kassettenform *f*, Gerät *n* zur Aufzeichnung *f* von Fernsehsendungen *f/pl*, Tonbandgerät *n*	video recorder, video-tape recorder
maigre	mager	lean, light, thin
main *f*	Buch *n* (25 Bogen *m/pl* Papier *n*), Hand *f* (Hinweiszeichen *n*), Papierlage *f*	index mark, quire, quire (25 sheet)
main *f* de passe *f*	überzählige Exemplare *n/pl*, Überdruck *m* (Überschuß *m*)	overquire, surplus
maintenir, à	es bleibe stehen *typog*, stehen lassen!	stet!
maison *f*	Firma *f*	firm
maison *f* de distribution *f* de films *m/pl*	Filmverleih *m*	film distributors *pl*, film lending institute
maison *f* de vente *f* par correspondance *f*	Versandhaus *n*	mail order house
maison *f* d'édition *f*	Verlag *m*	publishing company, publishing house
maison *f* d'expédition *f*	Versandhaus *n*	mail order house
maison *f* d'héliogravure *f*	Tiefdruckanstalt *f*	photogravure plant
majoration *f*	Zuschlag *m*	additional charge, extra charge
majoration *f* de prix *m*	Mehrpreis *m*, Preisaufschlag *m*, Preisheraufsetzung *f*	additional price, extra charge, surcharge, upward adjustment of prices *pl*
majoration *f* de tarif *m*	Aufschlag *m*	rate increase
majoration *f* pour emplacement *m* de rigueur *f*	Plazierungsaufschlag *m*	surcharge for special position
majuscule *f* imitée	Blockbuchstabe *m*	block capital, block letter
majuscules *f/pl*	Großbuchstaben *m/pl*, Versalien *f/pl*	capital letters *pl*, caps *pl*, large print, upper case letters *pl*
manchette *f*	Kopf *m* (Überschrift *f*), Schlagzeile *f*, Zeitungskopf *m*	catch line, headline, head, heading, mast head, newspaper heading, punch line, shoulder note, top
manchette *f* à droite du titre *m*	Anzeige *f* neben Zeitungskopf *m*, oberer Eckplatz *m* der Titelseite *f*	box on the right of the masthead, ear-pieces *pl*, ears *pl*
manchette *f* sensationnelle	alarmierende Überschrift *f*	scare headline
manchette *f* verbale	aussagekräftige Überschrift *f*	action
mandant *m*	Auftraggeber *m*	client, commissioned by, customer
mandat *m* bancaire	Bankscheck *m*	bank cheque *brit*, check *am*
mandataire *m*	Auftragnehmer *m*	supplier
maniaque *m* de la T.V. *f*	Fernsehsüchtiger *m*	television addict

manier la plume *f*	die Feder *f* führen	to wield a pen
manière *f* de considérer	Betrachtungsweise *f*	slant
manière *f* de s'exprimer	Ausdrucksweise *f*	diction, phraseology, style
manière *f* de travailler	Arbeitsweise *f*	method of operation
manière *f* noire	Schabemanier *f*	mezzotint technique, scratchboard drawing
manifestation *f*	Veranstaltung *f*	performance
manifestation *f* publicitaire	Werbeveranstaltung *f*	publicity event
manipulation *f* de nouvelles *f/pl*, manipulation *f* des informations *f/pl*	Manipulation *f* von Nachrichten *f/pl*, Nachrichtenmanipulation *f*	news management
manipuler	manipulieren	to manipulate
mannequin *m*	Fotomodell *n*, Mannequin *m*, Modell *n*, Vorführdame *f*, Werbedame *f*	demonstrator, mannequin, model, pattern, photographer's model
mannequin *m* mâle, mannequin *m* masculin	männliches Fotomodell *n*, Vorführmann *m*	dressman
manque *f* de netteté *f*	Unschärfe *f*	lack of sharpness
manque *f* de place *f*	Raummangel *m*	pressure of space
manquer de copie *f*	auf Manuskript *n* warten	to wait copy
manques *m/pl*	Mängel *m/pl*	deficiencies *pl*
manuel *m*	Handbuch *n*, Leitfaden *m*	guide, handbook, manual, vademecum
manuel *m* de vente *f*	Verkaufshandbuch *n*	sales *pl* book, sales *pl* manual
manuel *m* pour des représentants *m/pl*	Vertreterhandbuch *n*	sales *pl* manual
manuscrit *m*	Manuskript *n*	copy, manuscript, MS
manutention *f*	Geschäftsführung *f*, Handhabung *f*	handling, management
maquette *f*	Ansichtsskizze *f*, Aufbauskizze *f*, Aufmachungsmuster *n*, Aufriß *m*, Blindband *m*, Entwurf *m*, Handmuster *n*, Ideenskizze *f*, Klebespiegel *m*, Layout *n*, Skizze *f*, Rohentwurf *m*	creative work, design, draft, dummy, layout, make-up, outline, page-plan, rough, rough outline, sketch, tentative work, tracing, visual, visualizing
maquette *f* de la partie *f* publicitaire	Anzeigenspiegel *m*	advertisement make-up, advertisement type area, advertising page plan
maquette *f* définitive	Reinlayout *n*	finished layout
maquette *f* détaillée	detailliertes Layout *n*	comprehensive
maquette *f* d'imprimerie *f*	Blindmuster *n*	dummy
maquette *f* d'une affiche *f*	Plakatentwurf *m*	dummy of a poster, poster design, poster sketch
maquette *f* d'une revue *f*	Blindmuster *n* von Zeitschriften *f/pl*	dummy magazine
maquette *f* très poussée	fertiger Entwurf *m*	comprehensive
maquette *f* typographique	Satzskizze *f*	type layout
maquettiste *m*	Entwerfer *m*, Gestalter *m*, Umbruchredakteur *m*	creative artist, designer, draughtsman, lay out man, make-up editor, visualizer
maquillage *m*	Retusche *f*	retouching
marbre *m*	Druckfundament *n*, Fundament *n* (Schließplatte *f*), Stein *m*	bed, stone

marbre *m* de mise *f* en pages *f/pl*	Umbruchtisch *m*	making up table
marbre *m* de serrage *m*	Schließplatte *f*	imposing stone
marbre *m* porte-forme *m*	Schriftfundament *n*	form bed
marchand *m*	Händler *m*	dealer
marchand *m* ambulant	fliegender Händler *m*	hawker, itinerant salesman
marchand *m* de journaux *m/pl*	Zeitungsverkäufer *m*	newsdealer *am*, newsvendor
marchand *m* forain	fliegender Händler *m*	hawker, itinerant salesman
marchander	aushandeln	to bargain, to negotiate
marchandise *f*	Ware *f*	commodity, goods *pl*
marchandise *f* d'appel *m*	Anreizartikel *m*	loss leader
marchandise *f* rare	Mangelware *f*	shortage goods *pl*
marchandises *f/pl* à transporter par l'acheteur *m*	Abholwaren *f/pl*	cash-and-carry-wares *pl*
marchandises *f/pl* empaquetées	abgepackte Waren *f/pl*	packaged goods *pl*
marché *m*	Absatzgebiet *n*, Markt *m*	market, outlet, sales *pl* area, trading area
marché *m* commun	gemeinsamer Markt *m*	common market
Marché *m* Commun Européen	Europäische Wirtschaftsgemeinschaft *f* (EWG)	European Common Market
marché *m* d'acheteurs *m/pl*	Käufermarkt *m*	buyer's market
marché *m* de consommation *f*	Verbrauchermarkt *m*	consumer market
marché *m* de vendeurs *m/pl*	Verkäufermarkt *m*	seller's market
marche *f* des affaires *f/pl*	Geschäftsgang *m*	trend of business
marché *m* d'essai *m*	Testmarkt *m*	test market
marché *m* du travail *m*	Stellenmarkt *m*	labour market
marché *m* encombré	gesättigter Markt *m*	glutted market
marché *m* étranger *m*	Auslandsmarkt *m*	foreign market
marché *m* gris	grauer Markt *m*	grey market
marché *m* inondé	überschwemmter Markt *m*	glutted market
marché *m* intérieur	Inlandsmarkt *m*	domestic market
marché *m* mondial	Weltmarkt *m*	world market
marché *m* principal	Hauptabsatzgebiet *m*	main market
marché-test *m*	Testmarkt *m*	test market
marge *f*	Anlage *typog*, Rand *m*, Seitenrand *m*, unbedruckter Rand *m*	edge, lays *pl*, margin
marge *f* commerciale	Handelsspanne *f*	trade margin
marge *f* de pied *m*	Fuß *m*, unterer Blattrand *m*	foot, tail
marge *f* de tête *f*	Kopfsteg *m*	head margin, head stick, top margin
marge *f* extérieure	äußerer Papierrand *m*, Außensteg *m*, weißer Rand *m*	fore-edge, fore-edge margin, outside margin
marge *f* intérieure	Bundsteg *m*, Bund *m/typog*, Innenrand *m*	back, back margin, gutter-stick, inner margin
marge *f* supérieure	Kopfsteg *m*	head margin, head stick, top margin
margeur *m*	Anlegeapparat *m*	feeder, margin stop
margeur *m* automatique	Selbstanleger *m*	automatic feeder
margeur *m* de feuilles *f/pl*	Bogenanleger *m*	sheet-feeder
marketing *m*	Marketing *n*, Marktfähigmachung *f*, Marktplanung *f*	marketing
marketing *m* mix *m*	Marketingmix *n*, Marktplan *m*	marketing mix
maroquin *m*	Maroquin *n*	marocco leather

marque *f*	Marke *f*, Zeichen *n*	brand, make, mark, sign
marque *f* de bataille *f*	Kampfmarke *f*	fighting brand
marque *f* de contrôle *m*	Prüfzeichen *n*	test mark
marque *f* de distributeur *m*	Eigenmarke *f*, Handelsmarke *f*, Hausmarke *f*	house brand, own brand, private brand
marque *f* de fabricant *m*	Fabrikmarke *f*, Herstellermarke *f*	manufacturer's brand, producer's brand, trade-mark
marque *f* de fabrique *f*	Warenzeichen *n*	brand, make, trade mark
marque *f* de firme *f*	Firmenzeichen *n*	trade-mark
marque *f* de garantie *f*	Gütezeichen *n*	certification mark, quality label, seal of approval
marque *f* de produit *m*	Produktmarke *f*	brand of a product
marque *f* de standing *m*	Statussymbol *n*	status symbol
marque *f* de tête *f*	Spitzenmarke *f*	brand leader
marque *f* d'éditeur *m*	Verlagssignet *n*	publisher's colophon, publisher's imprint
marque *f* déposée	eingetragenes Warenzeichen *n*, Schutzmarke *f*	registered trade mark, trade-mark
marque *f* d'imprimeur *m*	Druckerzeichen *n*	printer's mark
marque *f* d'origine *f*	Herkunftszeichen *n*	mark of origin
marque *f* du correcteur *m*	Korrekturzeichen *f*	correction mark, proofreader's mark
marque *f* du distributeur *m*	Händlermarke *f*	dealer's brand
marque *f* d'une espace *f* haute	Spieß *m*/*typog*	rising space, work-up *am*
marque *f* figurative	Bildzeichen *n*	symbol
marque *f* graphique	Signet *n*	book mark, colophon
marque *f* symbolique	Bildmarke *f*	symbol
marque *f* typographique, marque *f* verbale	Wortmarke *f*	trade name
marquer les pages *f*/*pl*	paginieren	to number pages *pl*, to page, to paginate
marques *f*/*pl* de compétition *f*	Konkurrenzmarken *f*/*pl*	competing brands *pl*
marqueur *m*	Filzschreiber *m*	felt pen
masquage *m*	Sichtbehinderung *f*, verdeckt stehende Anschlagstellen *f*/*pl*	impediment of visibility, sites *pl* hidden from view
masque *m*	Auflegemaske *f*, Decker *m*	mask, overlay
masquer	abdecken, ausdecken	to block out, to cover, to mask out
masse *f* des consommateurs *m*/*pl*	Verbraucherschaft *f*	usership
masse *f* des lecteurs *m*/*pl*	Leserschaft *f*	audience, readers *pl*, readership
massicot *m*	Papierschneidemaschine *f*	paper cutter
massicot *m* trilatéral à une seule lame *f*	Dreischneider *m*	three side trimmer
massif couloir *m* (métro *m*)	Reihenanschlag *m* in den Gängen *m*/*pl* für einen einzigen Werbungtreibenden *m* (Untergrundbahn)	series *pl* posting in the passage ways *pl* for one advertiser only (Metro)
massif quai *m* (métro *m*)	Reihenanschlag *m* auf den Metro-Bahnsteigen *m*/*pl* für einen einzigen Werbungtreibenden *m*	series *pl* posting on the métro platforms *pl* for one advertiser only
mass-média *m*	Massenmedium *n*	mass medium

mastic *m*	Fisch (typog) *m*, Zwiebelfisch *m*/typog	pi *am*, pie, wrong fount, wrong letter
mât *m* publicitaire	Mastenwerbung *f*, Werbemast *m*	advertising mast, sign mast advertising
mater	mattieren	to frost glass
matériaux *m*/*pl*	Werkstoff *m*	raw material
matériaux *m*/*pl* de composition *f*	Satzmaterial *n*	composing material
matériel *m*	Unterlagen *f*/*pl*	material
matériel *m* d'émission *f*	Sendeunterlagen *f*/*pl*	broadcasting material
matériel *m* de publicité *f*	Werbematerial *n*	advertising aids *pl*, advertising material
matériel *m* d'étalage *m*	Schaufenster-Werbemittel *n*/*pl*	window display material
matériel *m* d'étalage *m* de comptoir *m*	Thekenaufsteller *m*,	counter display, piece,
matériel *m* de vitrine *f*	Ausstellungsmaterial *n* stummer Verkäufer *m*	material for exhibitions *pl* counter dispenser, counter display container, dummy salesman
matériel *m* d'exposition *f*	Ausstellungsmaterial *n*	material for exhibitions *pl*
matériel *m* d'impression *f*	Druckunterlage *f*	printing material
matériel *m* photographique	Fotounterlage *f*	photographic record
matière *f*	Sachgebiet *n*	subject
matière *f* artificielle	Kunststoffe *m*/*pl*	plastics *pl*, synthetic material
matière *f* restée sur le marbre *m*	liegengebliebener Satz *m*	crowded out matter
matière *f* synthétique	Kunststoffe *m*/*pl*	plastics *pl*, synthetic material
matir	mattieren	to frost glass
matrice *f*	Mater *f*, Matrize *f*	flong, mat *am*, matrix, mould, stencil
mauvais goût *m*	Geschmacklosigkeit *f*	bad taste
mauvais usage *m*	Mißbrauch *m*	misuse
mauvaise réputation *f*	schlechter Ruf *m*	bad will
mauvaises nouvelles *f*/*pl*	schlechte Nachrichten *f*/*pl*	black tidings *pl*, ill news
maximum *m* des ventes *f*/*pl*	Verkaufsspitze *f*	sales *pl* peak
médaille *f*	Medaille *f*	medal
médaillon *m*	Hintergrundbericht *m*	close-up
média *m*	Medium *n*	medium
média *m* de base *f*	Hauptwerbemittel *n*	basic medium
média *m* imprimé	Insertionsmedium *n*	printed medium
média *m* principal	Hauptwerbemittel *n*	basic medium
media-planneur *m*	Mediaplaner *m*	media planner
médias *m*/*pl* additionnels	zusätzliche Werbemittel *n*/*pl*	collateral media *pl*
médias *m*/*pl* appuyants	unterstützende Medien *n*/*pl*	supporting media *pl*
médias *m*/*pl* classiques	klassische Medien *n*/*pl*	basic media *pl*, classic media *pl*
médias *m*/*pl* de la publicité *f* dans les moyens *m*/*pl* de transport *m*	Medien *n*/*pl* der Werbung *f* im Verkehr *m*	traffic media
médias *m*/*pl* de presse *f*	Pressemedien *n*/*pl*	press media
médias *m*/*pl* obligatoires	obligatorische Werbeträger *m*/*pl*	obligatory media *pl*
médias *m*/*pl* répandus dans tout le pays *m*	national verbreitete Medien *n*/*pl*	national media *pl*
médias *m*/*pl* sonnants	Tonmedien *n*/*pl*	sound media *pl*
médias *m*/*pl* visuels	visuelle Kommunikation *f*	visual communication
médisance *f*	üble Nachrede *f*	back-biting
méfaits *m*/*pl* de la publicité *f*	Reklameauswüchse *m*/*pl*	misdoings *pl* of advertising

mélange m des encres f/pl	Farbmischung f	ink mixing
mélodie f d'identification f	Erkennungsmelodie f	signature, theme song
membre m d'un cercle m d'édition f	angeschlossene Zeitung f	member of a group of publishers pl
membre m d'une chaîne f volontaire	Kettenladen m	chain store
mémoire m, memorandum m	Denkschrift f	memorandum, record
mémoire f à disques m/pl	Plattenspeicher m	disc memory, disc storage
mémoire f aidée	Erinnerungshilfe f	aided recall
mémoire f spontanée	spontane Erinnerung f	pure recall, spontaneous remembrance
mensuel	monatlich	monthly
mentalité f	Geisteshaltung f	mentality
mentalité f orientée vers la campagne f	kampagnegerechtes Denken n	campaign thinking
mention f	Erwähnung f	mention, quotation
mention m du producteur m	Herstellervermerk m	imprinting
menu m	Speisekarte f	menu card
menus m/pl propos	leichte Plauderei f, Partygespräch n	chatly article, small talk
message m	Botschaft f	message
message m additionnel à la fin f d'un message m publicitaire	abschließender Kaufappell m	rider
message m chiffré	Geheimbotschaft f	cipher message
message m de base f	Grundaussage f, Hauptaussage f	basic message, creative copy
message m publicitaire	Werbeaussage f, Werbebotschaft f, Werbeeinschaltung f, Werbespot m	advertising message, broadcast announcement, commercial, spot, spot announcement
message m publicitaire impayé	unbezahlte Werbebotschaft f	plug
messager m	Bote m	messenger
messagerie f	Pressevertrieb m	distribution of publications pl, newspaper wholesaling
mesures f/pl publicitaires	Werbemaßnahmen f/pl	advertising measures pl
mesures f/pl typographiques (voir appendice)	Punktsystem n (siehe Anhang)	point system (see appendix), typographical units pl of measurement (see appendix)
métal m à caractères m/pl	Letternmetall n, Schriftmetall n	type metal
métamorphose f	Verwandlung f	metamorphosis
métaphore f	bildlicher Ausdruck m	metaphor
métaphorique	metaphorisch	metaphorical
météo f	Wetterbericht m	weather-forecast, weather-report
méthode f colle f et ciseaux m/pl	Schere f-und-Kleister m-Arbeit f	scissors pl-and-paste work
méthode f de distribution f	Absatzmethoden f/pl, Verkaufsmethode f, Vertriebsmethode f	distribution method, marketing techniques pl, selling method
mèthodes f/pl publicitaires	Werbemethoden f/pl	publicity methods pl
méthodes f/pl scientifiques	wissenschaftliche Methoden f/pl	scientific methods pl
méthodologie f publicitaire	Werbemethodik f	advertising methodology
métier m	Gewerbe n	craft, trade

métier *m* publicitaire	Anzeigengeschäft *n*, Werbewirtschaft *f*	advertising business
métrage *m*	Filmlänge *f*, Format *n* der Anschlagstellen *f/pl*, Meterzahl *f*, Werbefilmlänge *f*	footage, length of the advertising film, metric volume
metteur *m* en pages *f/pl*	Metteur *m*	clicker, form-man, lay-out man, make-up hand, maker-up
metteur *m* en scène *f*	Aufnahmeleiter *m*, Filmregisseur *m*	director, film director, film producer
mettre à jour *m*	auf den neuesten Stand *m* bringen	to update
mettre en casse *f*	ablegen (Satz) *m*	to diss (composition), to kill (composition)
mettre en code *m*	kodieren	to code
mettre en crochets *m/pl*	einklammern	to bracket, to put in parentheses *pl*
mettre en demeurre *m*	mahnen	to admonish, to remind
mettre en évidence *f*	hervorheben	to accentuate, to emphasize, to feature, to highlight
mettre en images *f/pl*	verfilmen	to film, to screen
mettre en manchette *f*	in großer Aufmachung *f* bringen	to make a splash
mettre en ordre *m* alphabétique	alphabetisieren	to place in alphabetical order
mettre en page *f*	zurichten	to back-up, to make ready
mettre en pages *f/pl*	umbrechen	to break the line, to make up
mettre en parenthèses *f/pl*	einklammern	to bracket, to put in parentheses *pl*
mettre en relief *m*	hervorheben, unterstreichen	to accentuate, to emphasize, to feature, to highlight, to underline
mettre en renfoncement *m*	einziehen (Zeile)	to indent
mettre en tableau *m*	tabellieren	to tabulate
mettre en train *m*	zurichten	to back-up, to make ready
mettre en vedette *f*	hervorheben	to accentuate, to emphasize, to feature, to highlight
mettre sous enveloppe *f*	einkuvertieren	to put in an envelope
mettre sous presse *f*	in Druck *m* geben	to send to press
mettre un texte *m* en évidence *f*	Auszeichnen *n* eines Textes *m*	to accentuate, to display text matter
mettre un titre *m* en gros caractères *m/pl*	Überschrift *f* in großen Buchstaben *m/pl* setzen	to screamline
mettre une inscription *f* sur	beschriften	to letter
mettre une nouvelle *f* en manchette *f*	Nachricht *f* groß aufmachen	to feature a piece of news
mévente *f*	Absatzflaute *f*	period of dull sales *pl*
mezzoteinte	Schabemanier *f*	mezzotint technique, scratchboard drawing
mi-carton *m*	Halbkarton *m*	thin board
micro *m* secret	verstecktes Mikrophon *n*	bug
microfilm *m*	Mikrofilm *m*	microfilm
microphone *m*	Mikrofon *n*	mike
microsillon *m*	Langspielplatte *f*	microgroove
miette *f* de la semaine *f*	literarischer Leckerbissen *m*	tit-bit
mi-gras	halbfett	half-bold, medium, semi-bold
milieu *m* de page *f*	Mitte *f* der Seite *f*, Seitenmitte *f*	centre of page
millimètre-colonne *f*	Millimeterpreis *m*	column-millimetre
mince	mager	lean, light, thin
miniature *f*	Miniatur *f*	miniature

minimiser	herunterspielen, verniedlichen	to make light, to play down, to soft-pedal
minuscule f	Kleinbuchstabe m	lower case letter, minuscule, small letter
minute f	Konzept n, Pausdruck m	blue print, draft, rough copy
miscellanées f/pl	Vermischtes n	miscellanies pl, miscellaneous items pl
mise à l'impression f	Drucklegung f	going to press, printing
mise f au concours m	Preisausschreiben n	competition, prize contest
mise f au frigo m	auf Eis n legen	to put into cold-storage
mise f au pas m	Gleichschaltung f	bringing into line, equalization
mise f de hauteur f sous cliché m	Klischeeunterlage f	underlay
mise f en avant	Sonderplacierung f	special position
mise f en demeurre f	Mahnung f	reminder
mise f en forme f	Formulierung f	formulation
mise en marche f	Druckbeginn m	start of printing
mise f en musique f	Vertonung f	musical setting, scoring
mise f en page f	Umbruch m, Zusammenstellung f der Seiten f/pl	imposition, make up, page make-up
mise f en page f équilibrée	ausgewogene Aufmachung f	balanced make up
mise f en page f surchargée	überladene Aufmachung f	crowded make up
mise f en pages f/pl des annonces f/pl	Anzeigenumbruch m	advertisement make-up
mise f en place f	Belegung f	booking, placing
mise f en train m	Zurichtung f	make-ready
mise f en œuvre f	Bewerkstelligung f, Einsatz m	implementation, implementing
mise f en valeur f	absatzpolitische Maßnahmen f/pl, Hervorhebung f, Merchandising n	emphasizing, merchandizing
mise sous enveloppes f/pl	Kuvertierung f	putting in an envelope
mise sous presse f	Drucklegung f	going to press, printing
mi-ton	Halbton m	half-tone
mixage m	Tonmischung f	mixing of sounds pl
mobile m	Mobile n	dangler, mobile
mobilophone m	tragbares Funksprechgerät n	walkie-talkie
moche	stümperhaft	buckeye
mode m de comportement m	Verhaltensweise f	habit
mode m de paiement m	Zahlungsweise f	mode of payment
mode m de parution f	Erscheinungsweise f	frequency of publication, publishing intervals pl
mode m de travail m	Arbeitsvorgang m	operating process
mode m d'emploi m	Gebrauchsanweisung f	directions pl for use, instruction booklet
mode m d'expression f	Ausdrucksform f	form of expression
mode m d'impression f	Druckart f, Druckverfahren n	kind of printing process, printing method, printing process
modèle m	Modell n, Satzvorlage f, Schema n, Vorbild n, Vorlage f	copy, layout, mannequin, model, pattern, prototype, schedule, schema
modèle m d'un photographe m	Fotomodell n	photographer's model
modèle m d'utilité f	Gebrauchsmuster n	industrial design
modernisation f	Modernisierung f	modernisation
moderniser	modernisieren	to streamline
modification f	Abwandlung f, Änderung f	amendment, variation

modification f de format m	Formatänderung f	change of measure, change of size, rescale, scaling
modification f de titre m	Titeländerung f	alteration of title
modification f du prix m	Preisänderung f	price alteration, price changes pl, price variance
modifier	abändern	to modify
moine m	Mönchsbogen m	friar
moins m	Minuszeichen n	em-rule
moirage m	Schnürlmoiré n	moiré effect
moiré m	Moiré n	moiré
mois m	Monat m	month
mois m/pl creux de l'été m	Saure-Gurken-Zeit f	dead season, gooseberry season, silly season
mondanités f/pl	Gesellschaftsklatsch m	social gossip, society item, society news
monde m de la presse f	Zeitungsleute pl	newspapermen pl
monde m des spectacles m/pl	Vergnügungsindustrie f	show business
monde m du théâtre m	Theaterwelt f	entertainment world
mondovision f	Satellitenfernsehen n	television by satellites pl
moniteur m	Monitor m	monitor
monochrome	einfarbig	monochrome, single-coloured
monographie f	Monographie f	monograph
monopole m	Monopol n	market monopoly
monopole m publicitaire	Anzeigenmonopol n	advertising monopoly
monotype f	Typenguß-Setzmaschine f	monotype
montage m	Montage f	assembling, mounting, paste up
montage m photographique	Fotomontage f	photo montage, photocomposition, stripping
montant m	Betrag m	amount
montant m d'annonces f/pl	Anzeigenerlöse m/pl	advertisement proceeds pl
montant m de la facture f	Rechnungsbetrag m	invoice amount
monté sur plomb m	Bleifuß m, auf	mounted on metal
montée f des prix m/pl	Preisanstieg m	price advance
monter	aufziehen (Foto) , montieren	to mount
montrer	vorführen, vorzeigen	to demonstrate, to present, to show
morasse f	Bürstenabzug m, letzte Korrektur f, Maschinenabzug m	brush proof, final proof, flat proof, galley proof, press proof, press revise, stone proof
mordre	ätzen	to bite, to engrave, to etch
mors m	Rückenrand m	back edge
morsure f	Ätztiefe f	bite
morsure f de grand creux m	Tiefätzung f	deep-etching
mortalité f des journaux m/pl	Zeitungssterben n	mortality of journals pl
morte-saison f	Saure-Gurken-Zeit f, stille Saison f, tote Saison f	dead season, gooseberry season, off season, silly season, slack period
mot m	Wort n	word
mot m à la mode f	Modewort n	vogue-word
mot m à trait m d'union f	Kuppelwort n	hyphenated word
mot m clé f	Stichwort n	catch word, cue
mot m de code m	Kodewort n	code word
mot m désuet	veraltetes Wort n	obsolete word
mot m d'ordre m	Kennwort n, Parole f	code word, parole
mot m du jour m	Modewort n	vogue-word
mot m étranger	Fremdwort n	foreign word

mot m **forgé**	erfundenes Wort n, Phantasiewort n	coined word
mot m **repère**	Schlagwort n	catch word, slogan
mot m **souche**	Stichwort n	catch word, cue
mot m **téléscopé**	zusammengesetztes Kunstwort n	blend
mot m **vedette** f	Stichwort n	catch word, cue
mot-clé m	Schlüsselwort n	code-word, key-word
motif m	Beweggrund m, Motiv n	motive
motif m **d'achat** m	Kaufanlaß m	buying motive
motif m **de publicité** f	Werbeanlaß m	cause for advertising
motif m **publicitaire**	Bildmotiv n, Werbemotiv n	advertising motif, publicity motif
motivation f	Motivierung f, Verhaltensgrund m	motivation
motivation f **d'achat** m	Kaufmotive n/pl	buying motives pl, reasons pl for buying
motiver	motivieren	to motivate
motrice f	Triebwagen m (Motorwagen m)	tram-car
mots m/pl **d'appel** m	Spitzmarke f	heading
mouchard m	Geheimmikrophon n	bug
mouchoir m **en papier** m **rafraîchissant**	Erfrischungstuch n	refreshment towel
moulage m	Abguß m	casting
moule m	Gießform f	mould
mouler	matern	to mould
mousseline f	Heftgaze f	stitching gauze
mouvement m	Bewegung f	motion, movement
mouvement m **des yeux** m/pl **sur une page** f **d'annonces** f/pl	Blickverlauf m auf einer Anzeigenseite f	ad-page traffic
mouvement m **pour la protection** f **des consommateurs** m/pl	Verbraucherschutzbewegung f	consumerism
moyen m **de communication** f	Kommunikationsmittel n	communication medium, means pl of communication
moyen m **de publicité** f	Werbemittel n	advertising medium
moyen m **d'expression** f	Ausdrucksmittel n	means pl of expression
moyen m **d'information** f	Informationsmedium n	medium of information
de **moyen format** m	mittleres Format n	medium-size
moyen m **mnémotechnique**	Gedächtnishilfe f	memory aid, recall aid
moyenne	Durchschnitt m	average
moyens m/pl **de réalisation** f	Gestaltungsmittel m/pl	art work
moyens m/pl **de transport** m	Verkehrsmittel n	transport systems pl
moyens m/pl **pour aider à la revente** f **par le détaillant** m	Maßnahmen f/pl zur Steigerung f des Absatzes m beim Einzelhandel m	merchandizing
moyens m/pl **publicitaires synthétiques**	Werbemittel n/pl aus Kunststoff	plastic media pl
ms	Manuskript n	copy, manuscript, MS
multicolore	mehrfarbig	multicoloured, polychromatic
multicopie f	Vervielfältigung f	duplication, multiplication
multicopier	vervielfältigen	to duplicate, to mimeograph
multigraphe m	Vervielfältigungsapparat m	duplicator, hectograph
multilithe m	Rotaprintverfahren n	multilith, rotaprint process
multiplication f	Vervielfältigung f	duplication, multiplication
multiplicité f	Vielfältigkeit f	multiplicity
multiplier	vervielfältigen	to duplicate, to mimeograph
mur m **du son** m	Schallmauer f	sound barrier

musée *m* de l'affiche *f*	Plakatmuseum *n*	poster museum
muselement *m* de la presse *f*	Presseknebelung *f*	gagging of the press, muzzling of the press, stifling of the press
musique *f* enregistrée	Schallplattenmusik *f*, Tonkonserve *f*	canned music
mutation *f*	Auswechselung *f*	change
mutation *f* d'emplacements *m/pl*	Ersatzplakatierung *f*	change of posters *pl*
mystification *f*	Täuschung *f*	feint, fraud, shenanigan *am*

N

naissance *f*	Entstehung *f*	origination
nature *f* morte	Stilleben *n*	still life
ne pas publier jusqu'à nouvel avis, à	vor Veröffentlichung *f* Weisung *f* abwarten	to withhold until further notice
nécrologe *m*	Nachruf *m*	obituary notice
négatif *m*	Negativ *n*	negative
négociant *m*	Händler *m*	dealer
négociateur *m*	Unterhändler *m*, Vermittler *m*	intermediary, negotiator
négociation *f*	Verhandlung *f*	negotiation
négocier	aushandeln	to bargain, to negotiate
nègre *m*	im Auftrag *m* und unter dem Namen *m* eines anderen schreibender Autor *m*	ghost writer
néologisme *m*	Wortneubildung *f*	neologism
néophyte *m*	Neuling *m*	beginner, newcomer, tyro
net	scharf	sharp
net d'un texte *m*	Klartext *m*	fair copy, hard copy
netteté *f*	Schärfe *f*	sharpness
netteté *f* des contours *m/pl*	Konturzeichnung *f*	definition of contours *pl*
neutre	überparteilich	neutral, non-partisan
niche *f*	Aussparung *f*	recess
niveau *m*	Niveau *n*	level
nivellement *m*	Nivellierung *f*	levelling
noir au blanc	Konterdruck *m*	counter-proof, reversed impression
nom *m* de guerre *f*	Deckname *m*, Pseudonym *n*	code-word, pen-name, pseudonym
nom *m* de la marque *f*	Markenname *m*	brand name, trade name
nom *m* de plume *f*	Pseudonym *n*, Schriftstellername *m*	pen-name, pseudonym
nom *m* de produit *m*	Produktname *m*	name of a product
nom *m* inventé	Phantasiemarkenname *m*	coined brand name, fancy name
nombre *m*	Zahl *f*	figure, number
nombre *f* de lignes *f/pl*	Zeilenzahl *f*	lineage, number of lines *pl*
nombre *m* de mots *m/pl*	Wortzahl *f*	number of words *pl*
nombre *m* de page *f*	Nummer *f* der Seite *f*	folio
nombre *m* des abonnés *m/pl*	Abonnentenzahl *f*	number of subscribers *pl*
nombre *m* des colonnes *f/pl*	Spaltenanzahl *f*	number of columns *pl*
nombre *m* des lecteurs *m/pl*	Leserzahl *f*	readership figure
nombre *m* des pages *f/pl*	Umfang *m*	size
nombre *m* des personnes *f/pl* touchées par un support *m*	Teilnehmerzahl	audience turnover
nombre *m* des pièces *f/pl*	Stückzahl *f*	number of pieces *pl*
nombre *m* des sièges *m/pl*	Sitzplatzanzahl *f*	seating capacity
nombre *m* impair	ungerade Zahl *f*	odd number
nombre *m* optimal	Bestzahl *f*	optimum number

nombre *m* pair	gerade Zahl *f*	even number
nomenclature *f*	Wortregister *n*	terms *pl* index
non officiellement	inoffiziell	off-stage
non plié	ungefalzt	non-folded
non rogné	unbeschnitten	untrimmed
non transparent	undurchsichtig	opaque
non-conformiste *m*	Außenseiter *m*	outsider
non-exécution *f* d'une commande *f*	Nichtausführung *f* eines Auftrages *m*	non-performance of an order
non-paru	nicht erschienen	non-appeared
normalisé	übersichtlich	clearly arranged, standardized
normes *f/pl*	Richtlinien *f/pl*	guide-lines *pl*, instructions *pl*
note *f*	Anmerkung *f*	note
note *f* au bas *m* de la page *f*, note *f* courante	Fußnote *f*	footnote
note *f* de crédit *m*	Gutschrift *f*	credit note
note *f* de critique *f*	Waschzettel *m*	dope, hand-out, press-release, publisher's blurb, publisher's note, slip
note *f* de pied *m*	Fußnote *f*	footnote
note *f* féminine	weibliche Note *f*	female touch
note *f* marginale	Randbemerkung *f*	marginal note
note *f* sur les étapes *f/pl* de déroulement *m*	Arbeitsablaufblatt *n*	job memorandum, work order
noter un ordre *m*	Auftrag *m* buchen	to book an order
notes *f/pl* marginales	Marginalien *f/pl*	marginal notes *pl*, side-notes *pl*
notice *f*	Impressum *n*	colophon, imprint
notion *f*	Begriff *m*	notion
notoriété *f*	Ansehen *n*, Ruf *m*	reputation
nouveau venu	Neuling *m*	beginner, newcomer, tyro
nouveauté *f* publicitaire	Werbeartikel *m*, Werbeneuheit *f*	advertising novelty
nouvel alinéa *m* !	neuer Absatz *m*!	run out!
nouvel ordre *m*	Nachbestellung *f*	repeat order
nouvelle *f*	Kurzgeschichte *f*, Meldung *f*, Nachricht *f*, Novelle *f*, Zeitungsnotiz *f*	information, news, news item, news report, press item, press notice, short story
nouvelle *f* à la tatare *m*	Tatarennachricht *f*	false news
nouvelle *f* à sensation *f*	Sensationsmeldung *f*	scoop
nouvelle *f* d'horreur *f*	Schreckensnachricht *f*	creepy news
nouvelle édition *f*	Neuauflage *f*	new edition, reprint
nouvelle *f* lancée	Zweckmeldung *f*	tendentious information
nouvelle peinture *f*	Neubemalung *f*	repaints *pl*
nouvelle rédaction *f*	Neufassung *f*	new formulation, remaking
nouvelle *f* sensationnelle	Nachricht *f* auf der Titelseite *f*	front-page news
nouvelle *f* supprimée	unterdrückte Nachricht *f*	blacked out news
nouvelles *f/pl* à la main *f*	Gesellschaftsklatsch *m*, Klatschspalte *f*	social gossip, society item, society news
nouvelles *f/pl* authentiques	amtliche Nachrichten *f/pl*	official news
nouvelles *f/pl* brèves	Kurznachrichten *f/pl*	news in brief
nouvelles *f/pl* câblées	gekabelte Nachrichten *f/pl*	overhead
nouvelles *f/pl* de l'étranger *m*	Auslandsnachrichten *f/pl*	foreign news
nouvelles *f/pl* de presse *f*	Pressenachrichten *f/pl*	press news
nouvelles *f/pl* du pays *m*	Inlandsnachrichten *f/pl*	home news
nouvelles *f/pl* fragmentaires	bruchstückhafte Nachrichten *f/pl*	piecemail information
nouvelles *f/pl* fraîches	neueste Nachrichten *f/pl*	latest intelligence, spot-news
nouvelles *f/pl* sportives	Sportnachrichten *f/pl*, Sportseite *f*	sporting news, sporting page, sportsmen's page

nouvelles *f/pl* **toutes chaudes**	brandneue Nachrichten *f/pl*	news hot from the press
noyau *m* **de lecteurs** *m/pl*	Leserstamm *m*	stock of regular readers *pl*
nuance *f*	Abstufung *f,* Farbschattierung *f,* Farbton *m*	hue, shade, shading, tint
nuance *f* **d'opinion** *f*	feiner Meinungsunterschied *m*	shade of opinion
numéro *m*	Ausgabe *f* (Nummer)	copy, edition, issue, number
numéro *m* **à succès** *m*	zugkräftige Werbung *f*	attractive advertising, audience builder
numéro-clé *f*	Chiffre *f*	box number, key number
numéro *m* **codique**	Schlüsselzahl *f*	key
numéro *m* **de classement** *m*	Standortnummer *f*	press-mark
numéro *m* **de code** *m*	Chiffre *f,* Kennziffer *f*	box number, key number
numéro *m* **de la commande** *f*	Auftragsnummer *f*	order number
numéro *m* **de la page** *f*	Seitennummer *f,* Seitenziffer *f*	folio, page number
numéro *m* **de propagande** *f*	Werbeexemplar *n,* Werbenummer *f*	complimentary copy, publicity copy
numéro *m* **de téléphone** *m*	Telefonnummer *f*	telephone number
numéro *m* **d'essai** *m*	Probenummer *f*	specimen copy
numéro *m* **du secteur** *m* **postal**	Postleitzahl *f*	number of postal district
numéro *m* **inaugural**	Einführungsnummer *f*	introductory number
numéro *m* **justificatif**	Belegexemplar *n*	advertisers' copy, checking copy, voucher copy
numéro *m* **séparé**	Einzelnummer *f*	single copy
numéro *m* **spécial**	Sondernummer *f*	special issue, special number
numéro *m* **spécimen** *m*	Ansichtsexemplar *f*	sample copy, specimen copy
numéros *m/pl* **couplés**	Doppelnummer *f*	combined issues *pl*
numérotage *m,* **numérotation** *f*	Numerierung *f*	numbering, pagination
numéroter	numerieren	to number

O

objectif *m* **marketing** *m*	Verkaufsziel *n*	sales *pl* objective
objectifs *m/pl* **publicitaires**	Werbeziele *n/pl*	advertising objectives *pl*
objectivité *f*	Objektivität *f*	objectivity
objet *m* **publicitaire**	Werbeobjekt *n*	advertising object
objet-réclame *f*	Wertreklame *f*	free gift advertising
observation *f*	Beobachtung *f*	observation
observation *f* **du marché** *m*	Marktbeobachtung *f*	market observation
observations *f/pl*	Bemerkungen *f/pl*	observations *pl*
obsolescence *f*	Veralten *n*	obsolescence
obtention *f* **des informations** *f/pl*	Nachrichtenbeschaffung *f*	collection of information
occasion *f*	Gelegenheitskauf *m*	bargain
occasion *f* **de faire de la publicité** *f*	Werbegelegenheit *f*	advertising facilities *pl*
occasion *f* **de voir**	Sichtmöglichkeit *f*	opportunity to see
occulter	verdunkeln	to black out
octavo *m*	Oktavformat *n*	octave
œuvre *f* **de pionnier** *m*	Pionierleistung	pioneering achievement
Office *m* **de Justification** *f* **des Tirages** *m/pl*	Auflagenüberwachungsstelle *f*	Audit Bureau of Circulations *pl*
office *m* **de presse** *f*	Presseamt *n,* Pressestelle *f*	press office, public relations *pl* office, publicity department
office *m* **de publicité** *f*	Werbestelle *f*	official publicity bureau
officieux	halbamtlich, offiziös	officious, semi-official
offre *f*	Offerte *f*	estimate, offer
offre *f* **au prix** *m* **coûtant**	Angebot *n* zum Selbstkostenpreis *m*	selfliquidation offer

offre f clandestine	verborgenes Angebot n, verstecktes Angebot n	blind offer, buried offer, hidden offer, subordinate offer
offre f concurrentielle	Konkurrenzangebot n	rival supply
offre f de faveur f	Sonderangebot n, Vorzugsangebot n	deal, premium, premium offer, special offer
offre f de prix m	Preisangebot n	quotation
offre f d'emploi m	Stellenangebot n	situation vacant
offre f	Angebot n	offer
offre f ferme	Festangebot n	firm offer
offre f gratuite	Gratisangebot n	free deal
offre f réclame f (sur emballage m)	Prämie f bei Verpackungsteileinsendung f	box-top offer am
offre f sans engagement m	freibleibendes Angebot n	offer without obligation
offre f spéciale	Sonderangebot n	deal, premium, special offer
offres f/pl d'emploi m	Personalanzeigen f/pl	vacancies pl
offrir	anbieten	to offer
offset lithographie f	Offsetdruck m	offset printing
oléographie f	Öldruck m	oleography
ombré	schattiert	shaded
omettre	weglassen	to omit
on dit	Gerücht n	rumour
on indique	verlautet, wie	as reported
on ne parle que de cela	Stadtgespräch n	talk of the town
onglet m	Facette f, Gehrung f, zweiseitiger Ersatzkarton m	bevel, single-leaf cancel
opacité f	Undurchsichtigkeit f	opacity
opaque	undurchsichtig	opaque
opérateur m	Kameramann m, Maschinensetzer m	camera man, machine-compositor, operator
opérateur m amateur m	Radioamateur m	ham
opération f	Arbeitsgang m	process of work, working operation
opération f publicitaire	Werbeaktion f	advertising activity
opérations f/pl publicitaires	Werbetransaktionen f/pl	advertising transactions pl
opinion f	Einstellung f, Meinung f	attitude, behaviour, mental set, opinion
opinion f publique	öffentliche Meinung f	public opinion
opportuniste m	Gesinnungslump m, Konjunkturritter m	opportunist, time-server
optimisme m de commande f	Schönfärberei f	eyewash
or m en feuilles f/pl	Blattgold n	gold leaf
orage m des cerveaux m/pl	Ideenfindung f durch Gruppendiskussion f	brainstorming
orateur m	Redner m	speaker
orchestration f des différents supports m/pl	Mediastrategie f	media strategy
ordinateur m	Computer m, Datenrechner m	computer
ordonnateur m d'art m	Artdirektor m	art buyer, art director
ordre m	Auftrag m, Bestellung f, Reihenfolge f	commission, order
ordre m annuel	Jahresauftrag m	annual order
ordre m collectif	Sammelauftrag m	collective order, omnibus order
ordre m d'affichage m	Plakatierungsauftrag m	billposting order
ordre m d'annonces f/pl	Insertionsauftrag m	insertion order, space order
ordre de préséance f	Rangordnung f	hierarchy, order of precedence
ordre m des mots m/pl	Wortstellung f	word order
ordre m d'essai m	Probeauftrag m	sample order, trial order

ordre *m* d'impression *f* des couleurs *f/pl*	Farbreihenfolge *f*	sequence of colours *pl*
ordre *m* d'insertion *f*	Insertionsauftrag *m*	insertion order, space order
ordre *m* ferme	Festauftrag *m*	definite order, firm order, standing order
ordre *m* occasionnel	Gelegenheitsauftrag *m*	casual order
ordre *m* par exprès *m*	Eilauftrag *m*	express order, rush job
ordre *m* permanent	Dauerauftrag *m*, laufender Auftrag *m*	continuous order, permanent order, standing order
ordre *m* provisoire	provisorischer Abschluß *m*	provisional booking
ordre *m* sans engagement *m*	freibleibender Auftrag *m*	order without obligation
ordre *m* valable jusqu'à révocation *f*	Auftrag *m* auf Widerruf *m*	open order, until cancelled order
ordres *m/pl* à conservation *f* déterminée	Festaufträge *m/pl* auf bestimmte Zeit *f*	fixed period orders *pl*
organe *m*	Organ *n*	medium, publication
organe *m* affermé	Pachtorgan *n*	tied paper
organe *m* de combat *m*	Kampforgan *n*	combat organ
organe *m* de publicité *f*	Werbeträger *m*	advertising medium, advertising vehicle, means *pl* of advertising
organe *m* d'opinion *f*	Meinungsblatt *n*	opinion paper
organe *m* officiel	amtliches Organ *n*	official organ
organigramme *m*	Organisationsschema *n*	organization set-up
organisateur *m*	Veranstalter *m*	organizer
organisation *f*	Organisation *f*	organization
organisation *f* de vente *f*	Verkaufsorganisation *f*	sales *pl* organisation, selling organisation
organiser	organisieren	to organize
organisme *m* professionnel	Berufsverband *m*	professional organization
orientation *f*	Orientierung *f*	orientation
orientation *f* publicitaire	Werbeorientierung *f*	advertising orientation
orienté vers le client *m*	verbraucherorientiert	customer-oriented
oriflamme *f*	Transparent *n*	banner, electric sign, streamer
original *m*	Urtext *m*	original text
original *m* à reproduire	Reproduktionsvorlage *f*	copy for reproduction
origine *f*	Herkunft *f*	origin
ornement *m*	Ornament *m*	ornament
orner	verzieren	to ornament
orthographe *f*	Rechtschreibung *f*	spelling
oukase *m*	Ukas *m*	ukase
outil *m*	Arbeitsgerät *n*	tool
outil *m* de propagande *f*	Werbeinstrument *n*	advertising medium
outrance *f* publicitaire	Werbeübertreibung *f*	puff advertising
outsider *m*	Außenseiter *m*	outsider
ouverture *f*	Auftakt *m*	opening phase
ouverture *f* en fondu *m*	Einblendung *f*	fade-in
ouvrage *m* de référence *f*	Nachschlagewerk *n*	reference book, work of reference
ouvrage *m* de référence *f* sous la forme *f* de livraisons *f/pl* régulières	Nachschlagewerk *n* in Form regelmäßig erscheinender Hefte *n/pl*	part publication
ouvrage *m* d'imagination *f*	Erdichtung *f*	fiction
ouvrage *m* en trois langues *f/pl*	Triglotte *f*	trilingual work
ouvrage *m* spécialisé	Fachbuch *n*	handbook, text-book, trade book
ouvrages *m/pl* artistiques	künstlerische Arbeiten *f/pl*	art work

ouvrier *m* à deux mains *f/pl*	Schweizerdegen *m/typog*	compositor-pressman
ouvrier *m* en conscience *f*	Akzidenzsetzer *m*	advertographer, job compositor
ozalide *m*	Blaupause *f*	blue print, cyanotype, ozalide

P

à la **page** *f*	zeitgemäß	up to date
page *f*	Blatt *n* (Seite *f*) , Bogen *m*, Seite *f*	page, sheet
page *f* **blanche**	leere Seite *f*, Schimmel *m/typog*	blank page, blind print
page *f* **cartonnée**	Kartonseite *f*	board page
page *f* **collective**	Anzeigenkollektiv *n*, Kollektivseite *f*	collective page
page *f* **cornée**	Seite *f* mit Eselsohren *n/pl*	dog-eared page
page *f* **d'annonces** *f/pl*	Anzeigenseite *f*	advertisement page, advertising sheet
page *f* **de couverture** *f*	Umschlagseite *f*	cover page
page *f* **de deux tiers**	Zweidrittelseite *f*	two-thirds page
page *f* **de droite**	rechte Seite *f*	odd page, right-hand page
page *f* **de garde** *f*	Vorsatzblatt *n*	fly bill, fly sheet
page *f* **de gauche**	linke Seite *f*	even page, left-hand page
page *f* **de la femme** *f*	Frauenseite *f*	women's topics *pl*
page *f* **de texte** *m*	Textseite *f*	text page
page *f* **de titre** *m*	Titelseite *f*	front cover, front page, title page
page *f* **départementale**	Bezirksseite *f*	departmental page
page *f* **dernière**	letzte Seite *f*	back page, last page
page *f* **d'opinion** *f*	Meinungsseite *f*	editorial page
page *f* **du faux titre** *m*	Schmutztitelblatt *n*	halftitle page
page *f* **en blanc**	leere Seite *f*, Vakatseite *f*	blank page
page *f* **entière**	ganze Seite *f*	full page
page *f* **impaire**	ungerade Seite *f*	odd page, uneven page
page *f* **intercalaire**	Einschaltseite *f*	inset, interpolated sheet
page *f* **intérieure**	Innenseite *f*	inner page, inside page
page *f* **justificative**	Belegseite *f*	tear sheet
page *f* **littéraire**	Feuilleton *n*	feuilleton
page *f* **modèle** *m*	Probeseite *f*	proof page, specimen page
page *f* **paire**	gerade Seite *f*, Rückseite *f*	even page, even-numbered page, inner form, reverse page
page *f* **recto verso**	Seite *f* mit Vorder- *f* und Rückseite *f*	page work and turn
page *f* **rédactionnelle**	Textseite *f*	text page
page *f* **régionale**	Lokalseite *f*	regional page
page *f* **sans faute** *f*	Jungfer *f/typog*	perfect page
page *f* **spéciale**	Sonderseite *f*	special page
page *f* **spécimen** *m*	Probeseite *f*	proof page, specimen page
page *f* **sportive**	Sportseite *f*	sporting page, sportsmen's page
page *f* **verso**	Rückseite *f*	even-numbered page, inner form, reverse page
page *f* **vierge** *f*	leere Seite *f*	blank page
pages *f/pl* **en regard** *m*	Doppelseite *f*	double page, double spread, opening
pages *f/pl* **jaunes**	Branchentelefonbuch *n*, gelbe Seiten *f/pl*	yellow pages *pl*

pagination *f*	Paginierung *f*, Seitennumerierung *f*	paging, pagination, paging
paginer	paginieren	to number pages *pl*, to page, to paginate
paiement *m*	Bezahlung *f*, Einlösung *f*, Zahlung *f*	payment, redemption
paiement *m* à la commande *f*	Zahlung *f* bei Auftragserteilung *f*	payment with order
paiement *m* à la réception *f* de la facture *f*	Zahlung *f* bei Erhalt *m* der Rechnung *f*	payment on receipt of invoice
paiement *m* comptant	Barzahlung *f*, Lagerverkauf *m*, Verkauf *m* ohne Kredit *m* und Kundendienst *m*	cash-and-carry, spot cash
paiement *m* d'avance *m*	Vorauszahlung *f*	advance payment, prepayment
paiement *m* lors de la réception *f* de la marchandise *f*	Zahlung *f* bei Erhalt *m* der Ware *f*	cash on delivery
paiement *m* par versements *m/pl* fractionnés	Ratenzahlung *f*	part payment
palabre *f*	Hin- und Hergerede *n*	palaver
palette *f*	Palette *f*	palette
palissade *f*	Anschlagfläche *f*	street hoarding
palmarès *m*	Schlagersendung *f*	hit-parade
pamphlet *m*	Pamphlet *m*	lampoon
pan *m* de chemise *f*	Zusatz *m* am Ende eines Artikels *m*	shirt-tail
pancarte *f*	Aufstellplakat *n*, Schaufensterplakat *n*, Werbeaufsteller *m*	counter card, show card, windowcard
panchromatique	lichtempfindlich	panchromatic
panégyrique *m*	Lobrede *f*	eulogy, panegyric
panel *m* des auditeurs *m/pl*	Hörerpanel *n*	listening panel
panel *m* des consommateurs *m/pl*	Verbrauchertestgruppe *f*	consumer panel
panneau *m*	Außenschild *n*, Schild *n*	board, outdoor sign, panel, plate, sign
panneau *m* à l'entrée *f*	Türplakat *n*	front-end space
panneau *m* d'affichage *m*	Anschlagtafel *f*, Anschlagwand *f*, Anschlagzaun *m*, Plakatständer *m*, Plakatwand *f*, Werbeschild *n*	billboard, notice board, poster hoarding, poster panel, sign, stand
panneau *m* d'affichage *m* avec l'addition *f* d'éclairage *m*	Werbefläche *f* mit Beleuchtung *f*	semi-spectacular
panneau *m* d'affichage *m* le long *m* d'une voie *f* ferrée	Streckenplakat *n*	railroad bulletin, roadside hoarding
panneau *m* de fond *m*	Stirnwand *f*	bulkhead
panneau *m* de gare *f*	Bahnhofshallenwerbung *f*	station interior site
panneau *m* de porte *f* d'accès *m*	Türrahmenschild *n*	door panel, poster on door-frames *pl*
panneau *m* de publicité *f*	Reklamefläche *f*, Werbefläche *f*	advertising space, hoarding for posters *pl*
panneau *m* d'entreprise *f*	Firmentafel *f*	name plate
panneau *m* d'escalier *m*	Treppenstufenwerbung *f*	advertising on risers *pl* of staircase, staircase site
panneau *m* longitudinal	Rumpffläche *f*	side panel
panneau *m* métallique	Blechschild *n*	tin plate sign
panneau *m* mural	Wandschild *n*	wall sign
panneau *m* peint	gemalte Anschlagfläche *f*	painted display

panneau *m* **routier**	Hinweisschild *n*, Straßenschild *n*	direction sign, road sign, roadside hoarding
panneau *m* **sur le toit** *m*	Dachschild *n*	banner, roof panel, streamer
panneau *m* **transportable**	auswechselbare Werbefläche *f*, Stellschild *n*	portable panel
panneau-réclame *f*	Plakatzaun *m*, Werbetafel *f*	poster hoarding
panneaux *m/pl* **peints**	gemalte Außenwerbung *f*	painted displays *pl*
panonceau *m*	Aushängeschild *n*, Schild *n*, Werbeschild *n*	billboard, board, panel, plate, sign
panoramarique *f*	Panoramierung *f*	panning
pantographe *m*	Pantograph *m*, Storchschnabel *m*	pantograph
paperasse *f*	Schreiberei *f*	red tape
paperasserie *f*	Papierkrieg *m*	paper-warfare
papeterie *f*	Papierfabrik *f*	paper-mill
papier *m*	Papier *n*	paper
papier *m* **à calquer**	Kohlepapier *n*, Pauspapier *n*	blueprinting paper, carbon paper, tracing paper
papier *m* **à décalque** *f*	Umdruckpapier *n*	transfer paper
papier *m* **à dessin** *m*	Zeichenpapier *n*	drawing paper
papier *m* **à écrire**	Schreibpapier *n*	writing-paper
papier *m* **à imprimer**	Druckpapier *n*	printing paper
papier *m* **à la cuve** *f* **à la machine** *f*	Maschinenbüttenpapier *n*	mould made paper
papier *m* **à la forme** *f*, **papier** *m* **à la main** *f*	handgeschöpftes Büttenpapier *n*	hand made deckle-edged paper
papier *m* **à lettres** *f/pl*	Briefpapier *n*	note-paper
papier *m* **à musique** *f*	Notenpapier *n*	music paper
papier *m* **à prise** *f* **de vue** *f*	fotografisches Papier *n*	photo paper
papier *m* **à report** *m*	Umdruckpapier *n*	transfer paper
papier *m* **amoureux**	saugfähiges Papier *n* (Saugpost *f*)	absorbent paper
papier *m* **anti-macule**	Abschmutzbogen *m*	set-off sheet, tympan-paper
papier *m* **apprêté machine** *f*	maschinenglattes Papier *m*	M. F. (machine finished) paper
papier *m* **au bromure** *m* **d'argent** *m*	Bromsilberpapier *n*	bromide paper
papier *m* **autographique**	autografisches Papier *n*	transfer paper
papier *m* **avec de bois** *m*	holzhaltiges Papier *n*	paper made from wood pulp, wood containing paper
papier *m* **avion** *m*	Luftpostpapier *n*	airmail paper, onionskin
papier *m* **baryté**	Barytpapier *n*	baryta paper
papier beurre *f*	fettdichtes Papier *n*	grease-proof paper
papier *m* **bible**	Bibeldruckpapier *n*, Dünndruckpapier *n*	bible paper, India paper, thin paper
papier *m* **bouffant**	Federleichtpapier *n*	featherweight paper
papier *m* **bulle** *f*	Einwickelpapier *n*, Manilapapier *n*	Kraft paper, manila paper, wrapping paper
papier *m* **buvard**	Löschpapier *n*	blotting-paper
papier *m* **calandré**	geglättetes Papier *n*, Glanzpapier *n*, satiniertes Papier *n*	calendered paper, flint paper, glaced paper, imitation art paper
papier *m* **carbone** *m*	Kohlepapier *n*, Pauspapier *n*	blueprinting paper, carbon paper, tracing paper
papier *m* **charbon** *m*	Pigmentpapier *n*	carbon paper, pigment paper
papier *m* **chiné**	chinesisches Papier *n*	India paper, rice-paper
papier *m* **chromo**	Chromopapier *n*, mattes Kunstdruckpapier *n*	art matt paper *brit*, art matt *am*, chromo paper

papier *m* ciré	Wachspapier *n*	wax paper
papier *m* collé	geleimtes Papier *n*	sized paper
papier *m* commun	Konzeptpapier *n*	scribbling paper
papier *m* continu	endloses Papier *n*	reel paper, web paper
papier *m* coquille *f*	Bankpostpapier *n*	bond paper
papier *m* couché	gestrichenes Papier *n*	coated paper, glazed paper
papier *m* couché de deux pages *f/pl*	zweiseitig gestrichenes Papier *n*	two-sided coated paper
papier *m* couché des deux faces *f/pl*	Kunstdruckpapier *n*	art paper, coated paper, enamelled paper, glossy paper
papier *m* couché mat	mattes Kunstdruckpapier *n*, Papier *n*, mattes	art matt paper *brit*, art matt *am*
papier *m* couverture *f*	Überzugpapier *n*	lining paper
papier *m* crayonneux	Kreidepapier *n*	chalk overlay paper
papier *m* crépon	Kreppapier *n*	crêpe paper, crinkled paper
papier *m* d'argent *m*	Stanniolpapier *n*	tin foil
papier *m* de chancellerie *f*	Kanzleipapier *n*	foolscap paper
papier *m* de chiffons *m/pl*	Hadernpapier *n*	rag paper
papier *m* de Chine *f*	chinesisches Papier *n*, Reispapier *n*	India paper, rice-paper
papier *m* de couleur *f*	buntes Papier *n*, getöntes Papier *n*	colored paper *am*, coloured paper, coloured paper *brit*
papier *m* de couverture *f*	Umschlagpapier *n*	cover paper, cover stock
papier *m* de crêpe *m*	Kreppapier *n*	crêpe paper, crinkled paper
papier *m* de cuve *f*	geschöpftes Papier *n*	hand-made paper
papier *m* de décharge *f*	Abschmutzbogen *m*, Abziehbogen *m*	set-off sheet, tympan-paper, tympan-sheet
papier *m* de décoration *f*	Dekorationspapier *n*	decorating paper, fancy paper
papier *m* de fond *m*	Auskleidepapier *n*, Fondpapier *n*	blanking paper
papier *m* de Hollande *f*	holländisches Papier *n*	hand-made paper
papier *m* de la main *f*	widerstandsfähiges Papier *n*	paper with some substance
papier *m* de rebut *m*	Makulatur *f*	misprint, spoil, waste paper
papier *m* de riz *m*	Reispapier *n*	rice-paper
papier *m* de soie *f*	Seidenpapier *n*	tissue paper
papier *n* de verre *f*	Sandpapier *n*	sandpaper
papier *m* d'édition *f*	Buchdruckpapier *n*	book paper
papier *m* d'emballage *m*	Einschlagpapier *n*, Einwickelpapier *n*, Packpapier *n*	brown paper, Kraft paper, wrapping paper
papier *m* d'emballage *m* à la soude *f*	Natronpackpapier *n*	Kraft paper
papier *m* demi-collé	halbgeleimtes Papier *n*	soft sized paper
papier *m* d'étain *m*	Stanniolpapier *n*	tin foil
papier *m* d'ivoire *m*	Elfenbeinpapier *n*	ivory paper
papier *m* du Japon *m*	Velinpapier *n*	vellum paper, wove paper
papier *m* du tonnerre *m*	aufsehenerregender Artikel *m*	blockbuster
papier *m* d'œuvre *f*	Werkdruckpapier *n*	antique weave paper, book paper
papier *m* édition *f*	antik (Papier)	antique wove
papier *m* émeri	Schmirgelpapier *n*	emery-paper
papier *m* entoilé	Leinenpapier *n*	linen-paper
papier *m* fait de pâte *f* de bois *m*	holzhaltiges Papier *n*	paper made from wood pulp, wood containing paper
papier-film *m*	Filmpapier *n*, Fotopapier *n*	film paper
papier *m* fort	starkes Papier *n*	strong paper

papier *m* fort pour l'impression *f*	bauschiges Papier *n*	bulky paper
papier *m* frictionné	Spaltpapier *n*	cheap paper for wrapping and posters *pl*
papier *m* gaufré	geprägtes Papier *n*	embossed paper
papier *m* glacé	gestrichenes Papier *n*, Glacépapier *m*	coated paper, glazed paper, glossy paper
papier *m* gommé	gummiertes Papier *n*	gummed paper
papier *m* grainé	gekörntes Papier *n*, gemasertes	grained paper
papier *m* granulé	Papier *n*, graniertes Papier *n*, Kornpapier *n*, Maserpapier *n*	
papier *m* gris	Packpapier *n*	brown paper, wrapping paper
papier *m* huilé	Ölpapier *n*	oiled paper
papier *m* imperméable à la graisse *f*	fettdichtes Papier *n*	grease-proof paper
papier *m* imprégné et gaufré	Atlaspapier *n*	satin paper
papier *m* incombustible	feuerfestes Papier *n*	uninflammable paper
papier *m* japon	Japanpapier *n*	India paper, Japan paper
papier *m* journal *m*	Zeitungsdruckpapier *n*, Zeitungspapier *n*	news stock, newsprint paper
papier *m* lissé	Glanzpapier *n*	calendered paper, flint paper, glaced paper
papier *m* mâché	Papiermaché *n*	paper mâché
papier *m* maculé	Makulaturpapier *n*	set-off paper, slip sheets *pl*
papier *m* marbré	Kleisterpapier *n*, marmoriertes Papier *n*	gummed fancy paper, marbled paper
papier *m* mat	mattiertes Papier *n*	dull-finished paper
papier *m* mélangé de fils *m/pl* de soie *f*	Faserpapier *n*	granite paper
papier *m* mince	Dünndruckpapier *n*	bible paper, India paper, thin paper
papier *m* non couché	Naturpapier *n*	uncoated paper
papier *m* ondulé	gewelltes Papier *n*	corrugated paper
papier *m* opaque	nicht durchscheinendes Papier *n*	opaque paper
papier *m* ordinaire	Konzeptpapier *n*	scribbling paper
papier *m* parchemin *m*	Pergamentpapier *n*	thick vellum
papier *m* parchemin *m* imitation *f*, papier *m* parcheminé	fettdichtes Papier *n*	grease-proof paper
papier *m* parfumé	parfümiertes Papier *n*	scented paper
papier *m* peint	buntes Papier *n*	colored paper *am*, coloured paper *brit*
papier-pellicule *f*	Filmpapier *n*, Fotopapier *n*	film paper
papier *m* -pelure *f*	Flugpostpapier *n*, Luftpostpapier *n*	airmail paper, onionskin
papier *m* photographique	Fotopapier *n*	film paper
papier *m* pour affiches *f/pl*	Plakatpapier *n*	poster paper
papier *m* pour cartes *f/pl* géographiques	Landkartenpapier *n*	map paper
papier *m* pour copies *f/pl*	Abzugpapier *n*, Durchschlagpapier *n*, Kopierpapier *n*	copy paper, copying paper, flimsy paper
papier *m* pour héliogravure *f*	Tiefdruckpapier *n*	gravure paper
papier *m* pour illustrations *f/pl*	Illustrationsdruckpapier *n*	supercalendered paper

papier *m* pour impression *f* rotative	Rotationspapier *n*	newsprint paper
papier *m* pour machine *f* à écrire	Schreibmaschinenpapier *n*	typewriter paper
papier *m* pour offset *m*	Offsetpapier *n*	offset paper
papier *m* pour tirage *m* d'épreuves *f/pl*	Andruckpapier *n*	proofing paper
papier *m* quadrillé	kariertes Papier *n*	cross hatched paper
papier *m* quadrillé à millimètre *m*	Millimeterpapier *n*	graph paper
papier *m* réglé	liniiertes Papier *n*	ruled paper
papier *m* roulé	Rollenpapier *n*	reel paper
papier *m* rugueux	Zeitungspapier *n*	news stock, newsprint paper
papier *m* sans pâte *f* de bois *m*	holzfreies Papier *n*	wood-free paper
papier *m* satiné	geglättetes Papier *n*, Glanzpapier *n*, hochsatiniertes Papier *n*, imitiertes Kunstdruckpapier *n*	calendered papier, flint paper, glaced paper, imitation art paper, supercalendered paper
papier *m* sensibilisé	lichtempfindliches Papier *n*	sensitized paper
papier *m* surglacé	Bilderdruckpapier *n*, kalandriertes Papier *n*	art paper, supercalendered paper
papier *m* transparent	durchscheinendes Papier *n*	glassine, translucent paper
papier *m* très calandré pour simili *m*	Autotypiepapier *n*	half-tone paper
papier *m* vélin	Velinpapier *n*	vellum paper, wove paper
papier *m* vergé	geripptes Papier *n*, gestreiftes Papier *n*	laid paper
papier-cache *m*	Abdeckpapier *n*	golden-rod paper, masking paper
papier-cuir *m*	Lederpapier *n*	leather paper
papillon *m*	Aufkleber *m*, Beilagenzettel *m*, Handzettel *m*, Klebezettel *m*, Packungsbeilage *f*, Tektur *f*, Waschzettel *m*	dodger *am*, dope, give-away, gummed label, hand-out, handbill, overlay, package insert, press-release, publisher's blurb, publisher's note, slip, sticker, stuffer, throw-away
papillon *m* des erratas *m/pl*	Korrekturenzettel *m*	errata slip
papillotage *m*	unscharfer Druck *m*, verschwommener Druck *m*	blurred impression, unsharp impression
paquet *m*	Paket *n*, Paket *n* (Satzstück *m*)	parcel, piece of composition
paquet *m* de composition *f*	Satzstück *n*	parcel of type
paquetage *m*	Packung *f*	pack, package
paquetier *m*	Paketsetzer *m*	piece hand
par édition *f*	je Ausgabe *f*	per issue
par ordre *m* alphabétique	alphabetisch	alphabetic
par tête *f*	per Kopf *m*	per capita
parade *f*	Schau *f*	show
parade *f* des succès *m/pl*	Schlagersendung *f*	hit-parade
paragraphe *m*	Absatz *m* (im Text *m*), Absatzzeichen *n*, Abschnitt *m*, Paragraph *m*, Paragraphzeichen *n*	paragraph, section mark
parangonner	Linie *f* halten, Zeile *f* halten	to align, to straighten lines *pl*
paraphe *m*	Namenszeichen *n*, Schriftzug *m*	flourish, initials *pl*, paraph

paraître	erscheinen	to appear, to come out
parc *m* des expositions *f/pl*	Messegelände *n*	fair site
parcheminé *m*	Pergament *n*	parchment
parcourir	durchlesen, überfliegen	to run through, to skim
parenthèses *f/pl*	Parenthesen *f/pl*, runde Klammern *f/pl*	brackets *pl*, fingernails *pl*, parenthesis *pl*, toenails *pl*
parisienne (voir appendice)	Perlschrift *f* (siehe Anhang)	pearl (see appendix)
parler métier *m*	fachsimpeln	to talk shop
parodie *f*	Parodie *f*	parody
paroles *f/pl* vides	leeres Geschwätz *n*	bunkum, hokum
parrain *m*	Förderer *m*	sponsor
part *f* de marché *m*	Marktanteil *m*	market share
partage *m* de commission *f*	Provisionsteilung *f*	commission splitting
partager	aufteilen	to split
parti *m* pris	Voreingenommenheit *f*	bias, prejudice
partial	parteiisch	partial
partie *f* commerciale	Handelsteil *m*	commercial section
partie *f* composante	Bestandteil *m*	component, constituent
partie *f* de son *m* d'une émission *f* télévisée	Tonteil *m* einer Fernseh- sendung *f*	audio
partie *f* d'images *f/pl* d'une émission *f* télévisée	Bildteil *m* einer Fernsehsendung *f*	video
partie *f* finale couronnée de succès *m*, partie *f* finale efficace d'un film *m*	werbewirksamer Filmschlußteil *m*, wirksamer Filmschluß *m*	pay off
partie *f* picturale	Bildteil *m*	pictorial part
partie *f* publicitaire	Anzeigenteil *m*, Inseratenteil *m*	advertisement columns *pl*, advertising section
pas d'alinéa *m* !	kein Absatz *m* !	run-in !
passage *m*	Druckgang *m*, Passus *m*	passage, run
passage *m* souterrain	Unterführung *f*	underground passage
passant *m*	Passant *m*	passer-by
passation *f* d'un ordre *m*	Auftragserteilung *f*	placing of orders *pl*
passe *f*	Zuschuß *m* (Überschuß *m*)	overs *pl*
passer	verblassen	to fade
passer les cahiers *m/pl* en presse *f*	bündeln	to bunch, to bundle
passer sous silence *m*	unter den Tisch *m* fallen lassen	to ignore, to let drop
passer une commande *f*	Auftrag *m* vergeben	to place an order
passe-temps *m* favori	Liebhaberei *f*	hobby
pastel *m*	Pastell *n*	pastel
pastichage *m*	Abklatsch *m*	copy, poor imitation
pâté *m*	gequirlter Satz *m*, Zwiebelfisch *m/typog*	broken matter, pi *am*, pie, wrong fount, wrong letter
pâte *f* de papier *m*	Papiermasse *f*	pulp, stuff
patron *m*	Muster *n*, Schnittmuster *n*	pattern, sample
patronnage *m*	Subvention *f* von Sendungen *f/pl*	sponsorship
pavé *m* de texte *m*	Textblock *m*	bold type, section of copy
pavillon *m* de publicité *f*	Werbepavillon *m*	advertising pavilion
payer les droits *m/pl* d'entrée *f*	verzollen	to clear through customs *pl*
paysage *m* des médias *m/pl*	Medienlandschaft *f*	media scenery
peindre	bemalen	to paint in
peint à la main *f*	handgemalt	hand painted

peintre *m* en lettres *f/pl*	Schildermaler *m*	sign writer
peinture *f*	Anstrich *m*, Malerei *f*	paint, painting
peinture *f* à l'eau *f*	Wasserfarbzeichnung *f*	water-colour drawing
peinture *f* à l'huile *f*	Ölbild *n*	oil painting
peinture *f* murale	Mauerbemalung *f*, Wandbemalung *f*	painted wall, painting on walls *pl*
pêle-mêle *m*	Verschiedenes *n*	miscellaneous column
pelliculage *m*	Hochglanzkaschierung *f*	high gloss lamination
pellicule *f*	Folie *f*	foil
pellicule *f* brillante	Glanzfolie *f*	glossy foil
pellicule *f* galvanoplastique en cuivre *m*	Kupferhaut *f*	electro-shell, galvanic shell
pellicule *f* tramée	Rasterfolie *f*	screen foil
pelliculer	einkopieren	to copy in, to superimpose
peluché	fusselnd	fluffy
peluches *f/pl*	Fussel *m*	fuzz
pelure *f* d'oignon *m*	Dünndruckpapier *n*	bible paper, India paper, thin paper
pendentif *m*	Hängeplakat *n*, Hängeschild *n*	hanger-card, hanging
pénétration *f*	Durchdringung *f*, Wirkungskraft *f*	penetration
pénétration *f* de la presse *f*	Zeitungsdichte *f*	press density
pénétration *f* de la télévision *f*	Fernsehdichte *f*	television density
pénétrer	durchschlagen *typog*	to come through, to strike through, to transpierce
pensée *f* bien tournée	gut formulierter Gedanke *m*	well-phrased opinion
perceptibilité *f*	Erkennbarkeit *f*	perceptibility
percer	perforieren	to perforate
perfection *f*	Vollkommenheit *f*	perfection
perfectionner	vervollkommnen	to perfect
perforation *f*	Ausschnitt *m* (Stanze *f*), Perforation *f*	cut out, perforation, piercing, trimming
perforer	perforieren	to perforate
périmé	veraltet	antiquated, out-of-date
période *f*	Zeitabschnitt *m*	period
période *f* comptable	Abrechnungszeitraum *m*	accounting period
période *f* creuse	Flaute *f*	dullness, flatness
période *f* creuse pour la publicité *f*	Anzeigenflaute *f*	flatness in advertising business
période *f* de conservation *f*	Aushangzeit *f*	period of display
période *f* de démarrage *m*	Anlaufzeit *f*	start time
période *f* de diffusion *f*	Streuperiode *f*, Streuzeitpunkt *m*	advertising period, dispersion period, time of the dispersion of the advertising media
période *f* de garantie *f*	Garantiefrist *f*	guarantee period
période *f* de la diffusion *f* des moyens *m/pl* publicitaires	Streuzeitpunkt *m*	dispersion period, time of the dispersion of the advertising media
période *f* de suspension *f*	Sperrfrist *f*	hold for release, waiting period
période *f* de vogue *f*	Hochkonjunktur *f*	boom
période *f* maximum	Höchstanschlagzeit *f*	period maximum
période *f* publicitaire	Werbeperiode *f*	advertising period
période *f* transitoire	Auslaufzeit *f*, Übergangszeit *f*	stop time, transition period
périodicité *f*	Erscheinungsweise *f*, Periodizität *f*	frequency of publication, periodicity, publishing intervals *pl*
périodicité *f* d'achat *m*	Einkaufshäufigkeit *f*	purchase rhythm

périodique *m*	Zeitschrift *f*	magazine, periodical, review
périodique *m* de culture *f*	kulturelle Zeitschrift *f*	cultural magazine, periodical of culture
périodique *m* de luxe *m*	Luxusblatt *n*	luxury paper, slick magazine
périodique *m* d'une circulation *f* contrôlée et qualifiée	CC-Zeitschrift *f,* Kennzifferzeitschrift *f*	ciphered business journal, qualified and controlled circulation paper
périodique *m* gratuit	Gratisblatt *n*	free publication, giveaway
périodique *m* illustré	Illustrierte *f*	illustrated paper, pictorial, picture paper, review
périodique *m* sans publicité *f* commerciale	Nichtanzeigenträger *m*	periodical without ads *pl*
périodique *m* technique	Fachzeitung	business publication, technical publication, trade journal
périodiques *m/pl*	Periodika *n/pl*	periodicals *pl*
périphrase *f*	Umschreibung *f*	periphrasis
permettre la publication *f*	zum Druck *m* freigeben	to release
permission *f*	Bewilligung *f*	permit
permission *f* d'imprimer	Druckerlaubnis *f,* Druckgenehmigung *f,* Imprimatur *n*	imprimatur, o. k. to print, permission to print, ready for press
persiflage *m*	Verspottung *f*	mocking
personnage *m* dans une marque *f* de fabrique *f*	Figur *f* in einem Warenzeichen *n*	trade character
personnage *m* publicitaire, personnage *m*-type *m*	Reklamefigur *f,* Werbefigur *f*	advertising character, advertising figure, average person
personnalisation *f*	Personalisierung *f*	personifying
personnalités *f/pl*	persönliche Bemerkungen *f/pl*	personal remarks *pl*
personnel *m* du service *m* extérieur	Außendienstmitarbeiter *m/pl*	field force, field staff
personnel *m* pour services *m/pl* d'acceuil *m*	Hostessendienst *m*	hostess service
perspective *f*	Ausblick *m*	vista
pèse-papier *m*	Quadrantenwaage *f*	basic weight scales *pl*
pétard *m*	aufsehenerregende Nachricht *f*	sensational piece of news
petit écran *m*	Fernsehen *n,* Fernsehschirm *m*	telecast, television (TV), TV-screen, video
petit prospectus *m*	Kleinprospekt *m*	leaflet
petit roman *m* bon marché	Romanheft *f*	journal of fiction, penny novellette
petit tirage *m*	kleine Auflage *f*	short run
petite annonce *f*	Gelegenheitsanzeige *f,* Wortanzeige *f*	classified advertisement, composite advertisement
petite bourgeoisie *f*	Kleinbürgertum *n*	petty-bourgeoisie
petite brochure *f*	Kleinprospekt *m*	leaflet
petite interligne *f*	Stückdurchschuß *m*	short lead
petite presse *f* offset	Kleinoffsetpresse *f*	small offset press
petite vitrine *f* murale	Schaukasten *m*	showcase
petites annonces *f/pl*	kleine Anzeigen *f/pl,* Kleinanzeigen *f/pl,* rubrizierte Anzeigen *f/pl*	classified advertisements *pl,* composite advertisements *pl,* small ads *pl,* smalls *pl brit*

petites caps *f/pl*	Kapitälchen *n*	small caps *pl*
petit-fonds *m*	Innenspalte *f*	gutter
petits caractères *m/pl*	kleiner Druck *m*	small print
phase *f* de travail *m*	Arbeitsgang *m*	process of work, working operation
philactère *f*	Sprechblase *f*	balloon caption, bubble, speech balloon
phonéticien *m* publicitaire	Werbephonetiker *m*	advertising phonetician
phonotèque *f*	Tonbandarchiv *n*	record library
photo *f* aérienne	Luftaufnahme *f*, Luftbild *n*	aerial photograph
photo *f* de plateau *m*	Standfoto *n*	action still, cinema still, movie film clip
photo *f* de presse *f*	Pressefoto *n*	press photo
photo *f* de scène *f*	Standfoto *n*	action still, cinema still, movie film clip
photo *f* d'intérieur *m*	Innenaufnahme *f*	indoor photo
photo *f* en couleurs *f/pl*	Farbaufnahme *f*, Farbfoto *n*	colour photograph, colour photography
photo *f* en dégradé	verlaufendes Bild *n*	vignette
photo *f* en plein air *m*	Außenaufnahme *f*	outdoor photo
photo *f* en tons *m/pl* clairs	Foto *n* in hellen Tönen *m/pl*	high key
photo *f* en tons *m/pl* obscurs	Foto *n* in dunklen Tönen *m/pl*	low key
photo *f* flou	unscharfes Foto *n*	high key
photo *f* publicitaire	Werbebild *n*, Werbefoto *n*	commercial photo
photochimie *f*	chemische Lichteinwirkung *f*	photochemistry
photochromie *f*	farbiger Steindruck *m*, Farbfotografie *f*, Fotochrom *n*	colour photography, photochrome
photocompeuse *f*	Filmsetzgerät *n*, Fotosetzmaschine *f*, Lichtsetzmaschine *f*	filmsetting machine, photocomposer, photocomposing machine, phototype setter, video-setter
photocomposeuse *f* électronique	elektronische Fotosetzmaschine *f*	electronic phototypesetting machine
photocomposition *f*	Lichtsatz *m*	film setting, photo lettering, photo typesetting, photo(graphic) composition
photocopie *f*	Ablichtung *f*, Fotokopie *f*	blueprint, photo print, photostatic copy
photogénique	bildwirksam, fotogen	photogenic
photographe *m*	Fotograf *m*	photographer
photographe *m* de presse *f*	Bildreporter *m*, Pressefotograf *m*	camera-man, press photographer
photographie *f*	fotografische Aufnahme *f*, Foto *n*, Fotografie *f*, Lichtbild *n*	photograph, photography, shot, taking of photographs *pl*
photographie *f* de mode *f*	Modefotografie *f*	fashion photography
photographie *f* instantanée	Momentaufnahme *f*	candid picture, snapshot
photographie *f* prise de près	Nahaufnahme *f*	close-up
photographier	aufnehmen (Foto), fotografieren	to photograph, to shoot
photograveur *m*	Chemigraf *m*, Klischeeätzer *m*, Klischeur *m*	blockmaker, engraver, process engraver
photogravure *f*	Chemigrafie *f*, Fotogravur *f*, Klischeeherstellung *f*	photo-engraving, photogravure
photojournalisme *m*	Bildjournalismus *m*, Fotojournalismus *m*	photo journalism, pictorial journalism
photolithographie *f*	Fotolithografie *f*	photo-lithography
photomécanique	fotomechanisch	photomechanical

photomontage *m*	Fotomontage *f*	photo montage, photocomposition, stripping
phototélégramme *m*	Bildtelegramm *n*	telephotograph
photothèque *f*	Fotothek *f*, Lichtbildsammlung *f*	photographic library
phototitreuse *f*	Lichtsetzmaschine *f*	filmsetting machine, phototypesetter, videosetter
phototypie *f*	Fotodruck *m*, Fotosatz *m*, Kollotypie *f*, Lichtdruck *m*, Lichtsatz *m*	collotype, film setting, photo lettering, photo typesetting, photo(graphic) composition
photo-typographie *f*	Autotypiereproduktion *f*, fotomechanischer Druck *m*	block – process, photo-typography
phrase *f* choc *m*	Schlagwort *n*, Schlagzeile *f*, Slogan *m*	catch line, headline, catch word, punch line, shoulder note, slogan
phrase *f* d'accrochage *m*	Werbespruch *m*	advertising slogan, catch line, catch phrase
phrase *f* finale	abschließende Frage *f*	rider
phrase *f* rebattue	abgedroschene Redensart *f*	hackneyed phrase, stock phrase
phraséologie *f*	Ausdrucksweise *f*	diction, phraseology, style
phrases *f/pl* lacrymogènes	tränenreiche Phrasen *f/pl*	hokum
phraseur *m*	Phrasendrescher *m*	phrase-monger
pica (voir appendice)	Pica *f* (siehe Anhang)	pica (see appendix)
pick-up *m*	Tonabnehmer *m*	pickup
pictogramme *m*	Piktogramm *n*	pictograph
pièce *f*	Schriftstück *n*	document, piece of writing
pièce *f* à sensation *f*	Reißer *m*	thriller
pièce *f* à thèse *f*	Problemstück *n*	problem play
pièce *f* courte	Kurzszene *f*, Sketch *m*	blackout
pièce de cabaret *m* artistique	Minisketch *m*	black out
pièce *f* de résistance *f* d'une annonce *f*	Kernstück *m* einer Anzeige *f*	bold type
pièce *f* de théâtre *m*	Theaterstück *n*	play
pièce *f* d'exposition *f*	Exponat *n*, Schaustück *n*	show-piece
pièce *f* larmoyante	Rührstück *n*	sob-stuff
pièce *f* préliminaire	Titelbogen *m*	prelim, title-sheet
pièce *f* radiophonique	Hörspiel *n*	radio drama
pièce *f* spécimen *m*	Ausstellungsstück *n*	exhibits *pl*, show-piece
pied *m* de bois *m*	Holzfuß *m*	wood base, wood mount
pied *m* de cliché *m*	Klischeefuß *m*	block base, block mount
pied *m* de page *f*	am Fuß *m* einer Seite *f*	bottom of page, foot of page
pied *m* photographique	Stativ *n*	camera stand, mounting
pierre *f* à broyer	Farbstein *m*	inking stone
pige *f*, pige *m*	Belegkontrolle *f*, Journalistenhonorar *n*	fee for journalists *pl*, voucher audit, watching of order filling
pige *f* de la concurrence *f*	Konkurrenzbeobachtung *f*	watching of competitive advertising
pigeur *m*	Rechnungskontrolleur *m*	checker
pigiste *m*	freier Journalist *m*, unabhängiger Journalist *m*	free lance journalist, free lance reporter
pignon *m* publicitaire	Giebelwerbung *f*	gable publicity, wall publicity
piller	abschreiben	to pilfer
pinceau *m* à lettres *f/pl*	Schriftpinsel *m*	lettering brush

pionnier *m* **de la consommation** *f*	Konsumpionier *m*	innovator, taste-maker
pionnier *m* **publicitaire**	Werbepionier *m*	pioneer in advertising
piquage *m* **dans le pli** *m* **au fil** *m* **de fer** *m*	Drahtheftung *f*	saddle stitching
piquer travers	Einsteckheftung *f*	stabbing
piqûre *f*	Heftung *f*	stitching
piqûre à cheval *m*	Rückstichbroschur *f*	pamphlet stitching
piqûre *f* **à plat**	seitliche Heftung *f*	side stabbed
piqûre *f* **au bloc** *m*	Blockheftung *f*	block stitching
piste *f* **sonore**	Tonspur *f* eines Films *m*	sound track
pisteur *m*	Kundenwerber *m*	tout
pistolet *m* **à peinture** *f*	Spritzpistole *f*	airbrush
placard *m*	Affiche *f*, Druckfahne *f*, Fahne *f*/typog *f*, Plakat *n*	bill, placard, poster, proof, slip, sticker *am*
placard *m* **dont l'emplacement** *m* **peut varier**	versetzbares Plakat *n*	floating piece
placatif	plakativ	poster-like
place *f* **d'affichage** *m*	Anschlagstelle *f*	billboard, site
place *f* **vacante**	Vakanz *f*	vacancy
placement *m*	Plazierung *f*	placing, position
placement *m* **de faveur** *f*	Vorzugsplazierung *f*	full position *am*, preferred position, special position
placer	unterbringen	to place
placer au centre *m* **de la ligne** *f*	auf Mitte *f* stellen	to place in centre of line
placer plus bas	tiefer stellen	to move down
placer plus haut	höher stellen	to move up
plagiaire *m*	Plagiator *m*	copycat, plagiarist
plagiat *m*	Nachahmung *f*, Plagiat *n*	counterfeit, crib, imitation, plagiarism
plagier	plagiieren	to plagiarize
plan *m*	Plan *m*	plan, schedule
plan *m* **comptable**	Kontenrahmen *m*	payment plan
plan *m* **d'archives** *f/pl*	Archivbild *n*	stock-shot
plan *m* **de campagne** *f* **plan** *m* **de diffusion** *f*	Mediaplanung *f*, Streuplan *m*, Streuplanung *f*, Werbeplan *m*	account planning, advertising programme *brit*, advertising program *am*, advertising schedule, campaign plan, media planning, media schedule, scheduling, space schedule, spread-over
plan *m* **de marketing** *m*	Marketingplan *m*	marketing plan
plan *m* **de publicité** *f*	Werbeplan *m*	advertising programme *brit*, advertising program *am*, advertising schedule, campaign plan
plan *m* **de termes** *m/pl*	Datenplan *m*, Datenschema *n*, Erscheinungsplan *m*	advertising schedule, date schedule, date schedule, insertion schedule, schedule of insertions *pl*, time schedule
plan *m* **de vente** *f*	Absatzplan *m*, Verkaufsplan *m*	distribution plan, selling plan
plan *m* **des délais** *m/pl*	Terminplan *m*	aging schedule, date plan, time schedule

plan *m* des supports *m/pl*	Streuplanung *f*	account planning, media planning
plan *m* média *m*	Mediaplan *m*	media plan
plan *m* publicitaire	Werbeplan *m*	advertising programme *brit*, advertising program *am*, advertising schedule, campaign plan
plan *m* serré	Großaufnahme *f*	close-up, full screen
planche *f*	Ballenbrett *n*, Druckstock *m*	baling board, block *brit*, cut, engraving, plate
planche *f* à contours *m/pl*	Konturplatte *f*	key plate
planche *f* à dessiner	Reißbrett *n*	drawing board
planche *f* de fond *m*	Tonplatte *f*	background plate, ground-tint plate, tint block
planche *f* typographique	Klischee *n*	block *brit*, cliché, cut, plate
planification *f*	Planung *f*	plan, planning
planning *m* publicitaire	Werbeplanung *f*	account planning, advertising planning
plan-paquet *m*	Packungsbild *n* im Film *m*	pack-shot
plaque *f*	Platte *f*, Schild *n*, Stehbild *n*	board, panel, plate, sheet, sign, slab, slide
plaque *f* bi-métal	Bimetallplatte *f*	bimetal plate
plaque *f* de contreplaqué *m*	Sperrholzplatte *f*	plywood plate
plaque *f* de plastique *f*	Plastikplatte *f*	plastic sheet
plaque *f* de zinc *m*	Zinkplatte *f*	zinc plate
plaque *f* d'impression *f*	Druckplatte *f*	engraving plate, printing plate
plaque *f* emaillée	Emailleschild *n*	enamel plate, enamel sign
plaque *f* peinte	bemaltes Schild *n*	painted plate
plaque *f* publicitaire	Werbeschild *n*	billboard, sign
plaque-adresse *f*	Adremaplatte *f*	addressograph plate
plaquette *f*	Broschüre *f*, Plakette *f*	booklet, brochure, folder, pamphlet, plaquette
plastification *f*	Glanzfolienkaschierung *f*	lamination
plastifié sur le dos *m*	gegenkaschiert	laminated on the back
plastique	plastisch	plastic
plat *m*	Film *m* (für Offset *m*)	flat, offset transparency
plate-forme *f*	Plattform *f*	platform
plate-forme *f* média *m*	Mediaplattform *f*	media platform
plein *m*, plein	Anstrich *m* (Buchstabe *m*), kompreß	close-set, solid set, up-stroke
plein pouvoir *m*	Vollmacht *f*	fullness of power
plénitude *f* d'information *f*	Informationsfülle *f*	abundance of information
pléonasme *m*	Pleonasmus *m*	pleonasm
pli *m*	Bruch (Falz) *m*, Falte *f*	crimp, fold
pli *m* accordéon *m*	Leporellofalzung *f*	accordion folding, concertina folding, fanfold form
pli *m* en portefeuille *m*	ausschlagbare Seite *f*, Wickelfalz *m*	gatefold, parallel folding
pli *m* en zig-zag	Leporellofalzung *f*	accordion folding, concertina folding, fanfold form
pliage *m*	Falzung *f*	folding, grooving
pliage *m* croisé	Kreuzbruchfalzung *f*	French fold, right angle folding
pliage *m* en zig-zag	Handharmonikafalzung *f*	concertina folding
plié	gefalzt	folded
plier	falzen	to fold
plis *m/pl* accordéon *m*	Harmonikafalzung *f*, Zickzackfaltung *f*	concertina folding

plisser	falten, Falten f/pl werfen	to crease, to fold
plomb m	Blei n	lead
plume f	Schreibfeder f	pen
plume f à dessiner	Zeichenfeder f	drawing pen
plumitif m	Federfuchser m	pendriver
plusieurs emballages m/pl d'un produit m	mehrere Packungen f/pl eines Produktes n	banded packs pl
plusieurs pièces f/pl dans un même emballage m	Mehrstückpackung f	combipack, multipack, multiple unit item
plusieurs points m/pl qui indiquent l'omission f d'un mot m	Punkte m/pl, die die Auslassung f eines Wortes n anzeigen	leaders pl
plusieurs unités f/pl de vente f dans un même emballage m	Verbundpackung f	combipack
pochette f	Versandtasche f	American envelope
pochette f à anse f	Tragetasche f aus Papier n	paper bag, paper carrier
pochette f d'allumette f	Streichholzbriefchen n	book of matches pl
pochette f de disque m	Schallplattenhülle f	record cover, record sleeve
pochoir m	Schablone f	cut out, jig, pattern, stencil
poids m	Quadratmetergewicht n des Papiers n	paper weight (by grams pl per square meter)
poids m d'un média m	Mediengewicht f	media weight
poids m maximum	Höchstgewicht n	maximum weight
poinçon m	Patrize f, Prägestempel m	counter-die, punch, stamping die
point m	Punkt m	dot, full stop, point
point (voir appendice!)	Achtelpetit f (siehe Anhang!)	12-to-pica (see appendix!)
point m central, point m chaud	Brennpunkt m des Verkaufs m	focal point, focus of sale, hot spot
point m chaud	umsatzstarke Stelle f	focus
point m d'achat m	Kaufort m	point of purchase
point m d'arrêt m	Straßenbahnhaltestelle f	tram stop
point m de saturation f	Sättigungspunkt m	saturation point
point m de trame f	Rasterpunkt m	halftone dot
point m de vente f	Verkaufsort m, Verkaufsplatz m	point of purchase, point of sale
point m de vue f	Gesichtspunkt m, Standpunkt m	aspect, point of view, standpoint
point m de vue f des lecteurs m/pl	freie Aussprache f, Leserforum n	open forum
point m d'exclamation f	Ausrufezeichen n	exclamation mark, exclamation point am
point m d'interrogation f	Fragezeichen n	interrogation point am, question mark
point m final	Schlußpunkt m	full stop, period
point m mort	Gewinnschwelle f	break-even point
point m typographique	typografischer Punkt m	typographic point
pointage m	Belegungsliste f	marked list
pointage m des emplacements m/pl disponibles	Liste f des verfügbaren Anschlagraums m	available sites pl list
pointe f	Pointe f, Radiernadel f	chisel, gag, point
pointes f/pl de vente f	Spitzenverkaufszahlen f/pl	peak sales pl
point-virgule m	Semikolon n, Strichpunkt m	semicolon
polémique f	Meinungsstreit m, Polemik f	controversy, polemics pl
polémique f de presse f	Pressepolemik f	paper war, press controversy
polir au buffle m	schwabbeln	to buff
politicien m	Politikaster m	armchair politician

politique *m*	Politiker *m*	politician
politique *f* de communication *f*	Kommunikationspolitik *f*	communication policy
politique *f* de marketing *m*	Marketingpolitik *f*	marketing policy
politique *f* de vente *f*	Verkaufspolitik *f*	sales *pl* policy
politique *f* des prix *m/pl*	Preispolitik *f*	price policy
politique *f* publicitaire	Werbepolitik *f*	advertising policy
politique *f* rédactionnelle	redaktionelle Tendenz *f*	editorial policy
politisation *f*	Politisierung *f*	politization
polychrome	mehrfarbig	multicoloured, polychromatic
polychromie *f*	Buntdruck *m*, Farbdruck *m*	chromotype, colour printing
polycopie *f*	Vervielfältigung *f*	duplication, multiplication
polycopier	vervielfältigen	to duplicate, to mimeograph
polycopiste *m*	Hektograph *m*	hectograph
polyglotte	mehrsprachig	polyglot
polygraphe *m*	Lügendetektor *m*	polygraph
poncif	abgegriffen	trite
ponctuation *f*	Interpunktion *f*, Zeichensetzung *f*	punctuation
ponctuer	interpunktieren	to put in the stops *pl*
pondérer	gewichten	to weight
popularité *f*	Volkstümlichkeit *f*	popularity
pornographie *f*	Schmutzliteratur *f*	pornography
port *m*	Porto *n*	postage
portage *m*	Zustellung *f* durch Träger *m/pl*	delivery by porters *pl*
portant atteinte *f* aux bonnes mœrs *f/pl*	sittenwidrig	immoral
portatif *m*	Fernsehrequisit *n*, Ständer *m*	bracket, poster site, prop
porte *f* à porte *f*	Haus *n* zu Haus *n*, von, Hauszustellung *f*	door delivery, door-to door
porte-affiches *m*	Schwarzes Brett *n*	advertisement board, notice board
porte-bagages *m/pl*	Gepäckhalter *m*	luggage-rack
porte-copie *m*	Manuskripthalter *m*	copy-holder
portée *f*	Tragweite *f*	bearing
portefeuille *m* de commandes *f/pl*	Auftragsbestand *m*	stock of orders *pl*
porte-journaux *m*	Zeitungsspanner *m*	newspaper-holder
porte-pages *f/pl*	Portepagen *pl*	bearers *pl*
porte-parole *m*	Pressesprecher *m*, Wortführer *m*	speaker, spokesman
porteur *m*	Austräger *m*	delivery man
porteur *m* de journaux *m/pl*	Zeitungsträger *m*	carrier of newspapers *pl*, delivery man
porteur *m* d'une licence *f*	Lizenzträger *m*	licensee
portrait *m*	Konterfei *n*, Personenbildnis *n*	portrait
portrait *m* biographique	biografische Skizze *f*	profile
portrait-charge *f*	Zerrbild *n*	caricature
pose *f* libre	Wildanschlag *m*	fly posting, sniping
poser une affiche *f*	anschlagen	to place bills *pl*, to post bills *pl*, to stick bills *pl*
position *f*	Standort *m*	location
position *f* isolée	alleinstehend (Anzeige *f*)	island position, solus position *brit*
possibilité *f* de la communication *f*	Kommunikationsmöglichkeit *f*	possibility of communication
possibilités *f/pl* de publicité *f*	Werbemöglichkeiten *f/pl*	advertising facilities *pl*, advertising horizons *pl*, possibilities *pl* of advertising

postcalculation *f*	Nachkalkulation *f*	cost-effect calculation, final costing
poste *f* de brouillage *m*	Störsender *m*	blooper, jamming station
poste *m* de radio *f*	Radioapparat *m*, Rundfunkempfangsgerät *n*	wireless set
poste *m* de radio *f* portatif	tragbares Funksprechgerät *n*	walkie-talkie
poste *m* de vente *f*	Verkaufsstelle *f*	sales *pl* office, selling point
poste *m* de vente *f* d'affiches *f/pl*	Plakatladen *m*	poster-shop
poste *m* émetteur *m*	Rundfunkanstalt *f*	broadcasting station
poste *f* fédérale	Bundespost *f*	federal post
postenquête *f*	Nachprüfung *f*	post-testing
postsonorisation *f*	Rückspiel *n*	play back
post-synchronisation *f*	Nachsynchronisierung *f*	post synchronization
pot-de-vin *m*	Schmiergeld *n*	bribe, tip
poteau *m* d'arrêt *m*	Haltestellensäule *f*	bus stop pillar
potentiel	potentiell	potential
potin *m* mondain	Gesellschaftsklatsch *m*	social gossip, society item, society news
pouce *m* (hauteur 27 mm)	Inch *n* (Anzeigengrundmaß)	inch (14 agate lines *pl*)
pour-cent *m*	Prozent *n*	percentage
pourcentage *m*	Prozentsatz *m*	percentage
poussée *f*	neuer Schwung *m*	push
pouvoir *m* d'achat *m*	Kaufkraft *f*	buying power, purchasing power, spending power
pouvoir *m* de choc *m*	Widerhall *m*	impact, response
praticien *m* de la publicité *f*	Werbepraktiker *m*	practitioner in advertising
pratique *f* publicitaire	Werbepraxis *f*	advertising practise
préambule *f*	Einleitung *f*	introduction, preamble
précurseur *m*	Vorläufer *m*	forerunner
prédiction *f*	Vorhersage *f*	forecast
pré-encollage *m*	Vorleimen *n* eines Plakates *n*	preposting
préenquête *f*	Vortest *m*, Voruntersuchung *f*	pilot study, pretest, pretesting
préface *f*	Vorwort *n*	preface
préférence *f* d'une marque *f*	Markenbevorzugung *f*	brand preference
pré-impression *f*	Vordruck *m*/*typog*	preprinting
préjugé *m*	Vorurteil *n*	bias, prejudice
premier folio *m*	Schöndruck *m*	first impression, first run, prime, printing one face, sheetwise
premier jet *m*	roher Umriß *m*, Rohentwurf *m*	dummy, layout, rough outline, visual
premier jour *m* de vente *f*	Erstverkaufstag *m*	first selling day
premier lecteur *m*	Erstleser *m*	primary reader
première correction *f*	Hauskorrektur *f*	first proof, reader's proof
première de couverture *f*	1. Umschlagseite *f*	front cover
première édition *f*	erste Ausgabe *f*, Erstausgabe *f*, Morgenausgabe *f*, vordatierte Zeitung *f*	antedated paper, bulldog edition *am*, early morning edition, early-bird issue *am*, first edition, pre-dated paper
première édition *f* du matin *m*	Postausgabe *f*	mail edition
première épreuve *f*	Rohabzug *m*	first proof, flat proof, foundry proof, rough proof
de première main *f*	aus erster Hand *f*	from first source

première page *f*	bedruckte Vorderseite *f*, erste Seite, Titelseite *f*, Vorderseite *f*	face, first page, front page, front cover, front page, front page, outer form, title page
premières épreuves *f/pl* **d'un film** *m*	Schnellkopie *f* (Film)	rushes *pl*
pré-mise *f* **en train** *m*	Vorzurichtung *f*	pre-makeready
préparateur *m*	Arbeitsplaner *m*	programmer
préparatifs *m/pl* **publicitaires**	Werbevorbereitung *f*	advertising preparations *pl*
préparation *f* **de la copie** *f*	Manuskriptbearbeitung *f*	copy styling
prescription *f*	Vorschrift *f*	prescription
présentateur *m*	Präsentator *m*	introducer, presenter
présentateur *m* **de disques** *m/pl*	Schallplatten-Ansager *m*	disc-jockey
présentateur *m* **du journal** *m* **parlé**	Nachrichtensprecher *m*	newscaster, newsreader
présentation *f*	Aufmachung *f*, Auslage *f*, Ausstattung *f*, Darbietung *f*, Präsentation *f*, Vorführung *f*	demonstration, display, make up, presentation, projection, show
présentation *f* **appétissante**	appetitanregende Aufmachung *f*	appetizing appeal
présentation *f* **condensée**	gedrängte Darstellung *f*	digest, pemmican style
présentation *f* **de la marchandise** *f*	Warendarbietung *f*	merchandizing
présentation *f* **de l'annonce** *f*	Anzeigengestaltung *f*	creative copy and artwork
présentation *f* **de l'intérieur** *m*	Darstellung *f* des Inneren *n*	ghost view
présentation *f* **de masse** *f*	Warenanhäufung *f*	mass-display
présentation *f* **de placards** *m/pl*	Plakataushang *m*	display of posters *pl*
présentation *f* **d'un scénario** *m* **sous forme** *f* **d'une suite** *f* **de dessins** *m/pl*	Entwurfsskizze *f* eines Werbefilms *m*	storyboard
présentation *f* **d'un stand** *m*	Standgestaltung *f*	stand design, stand dressing
présentation *f* **formelle**	Darstellungsform *f*	form of presentation
présentatrice *f*	Ansagerin *f*	female announcer
présenter	aufmachen, vorzeigen	to dress, to make up, to present, to show
présentoir *m*	Ständer *m*	bracket, poster site, prop
présentoir *m* **de sol** *m*	Ausstellungsständer *m*	floor-stand
presse *f*	Presse *f*, Zeitungswesen *n*	journalism, press
presse *f* **à bras** *m*	Handpresse *f*	hand-press
presse *f* **à copier**	Kopiergerät *n*	contact printing machine, photostat
presse *f* **à cylindre** *m*	Schnellpresse *f*	cylinder machine, flat-bed press
presse *f* **à double impression** *f*	Schön-und-Widerdruck-Maschine *f*	perfecting press
presse *f* **à empreindre**	Prägepresse *f*	blocking press
presse *f* **à épreuves** *f/pl*	Abziehpresse *f*	proof press
presse *f* **à genouillère** *f*	Kniehebelpresse *f*	toggle press
presse *f* **à grand tirage** *m*	auflagenstarke Presse *f*	press with a large circulation
presse *f* **à imprimer**	Druckpresse *f*	printing press
presse *f* **à photocopier**	Fotokopiergerät *n*	photo copier, photo copying machine, photostat
presse *f* **à platine** *f*	Tellertiegel *m*, Tiegel *m*, Tiegeldruckpresse *f*	platen machine, platen press, platine
presse *f* **à scandale** *m*	Skandalpresse *f*	gutter press
presse *f* **à sensation** *f*	Sensationspresse *f*	muckraker, stunt press, yellow press
presse *f* **clandestine**	Untergrundpresse *f*	underground press

presse f corrompue	käufliche Presse f	corrupt press
presse f cylindrique à marbre m plan	Zylinderflachformmaschine f	flat-bed cylinder press
presse f de bas étage m	Skandalpresse f	gutter press
presse f de gauche	Linkspresse f	leftist press
presse f de l'étranger m	Auslandspresse f	foreign press
presse f de réputation f douteuse	Winkelblatt n	hedge press, local rag
presse f d'information f	Generalanzeigerpresse f, Nachrichtenpresse f	information press, newspaper press
presse f d'opinion f	Gesinnungspresse f, Meinungspresse f	opinion press, press of opinion
presse f du cœur m	Schnulzenzeitung f	sentimental magazine
presse f économique	Wirtschaftspresse f	commercial press
presse f en blanc	Schnellpresse f	cylinder machine, flat-bed press
presse f illégale	illegale Presse f	illegal press
presse f jaune	Sensationspresse f	muckraker, stunt press, yellow press
presse f mondiale	Weltpresse f	world press
presse f nationale	überregionale Presse f	national press
presse f obscène	Schmutzpresse f	gutter press
presse f pour la population f rurale	Kleinstadtzeitung f	grass roots pl press
presse f professionnelle	Berufspresse f, Fachpresse f	professional press, technical press, trade press
presse f provinciale	Provinzpresse f	provincial press
presse f quotidienne	Tagespresse f	daily press
presse f régionale	Regionalpresse f	regional press
presse f rotaprint	Kleinoffsetmaschine f	rotaprint sheet-fed machine
presse f rurale	Agrarpresse f	farm press
presse f stationnaire	Standortpresse f	stationary press
presse f technique	Fachpresse f	technical press, trade press
presse f urbaine	Großstadtpresse f	big city press, metropolitan dailies pl
pression f publicitaire	Werbepression f	advertising pressure
prestation f	Leistung f	performance
prestation f accessoire	Nebenleistung f	accessorial service
prestation f de service m	Dienstleistung f	service
prestige m	Ansehen n	reputation
prêt à être cliché m	klischierfertig	ready for stereotyping
prêt à expédier	versandfertig	ready for shipping
prêt à imprimer	druckreif	good for printing, o.k. am, ready for press
prête-nom m	Strohmann m	man of straw
prétentions f/pl	Behauptungen f/pl	claims pl
pré-test m	Voruntersuchung f, Werbevortest m	pilot study, pre-test, pretesting
prêteur m	Verleiher m	lender
prévention f	Voreingenommenheit f	bias, prejudice
prévision f	Vorausberechnung f	forecast
prévisions f/pl météorologiques	Wettervorhersage f	weather-forecast
prévoir	disponieren	to dispose, to give instructions pl
prière f d'insérer	Waschzettel m	dope, hand-out, press-release, publisher's blurb, publisher's note, slip

prime *f*	Beigabe *f*, Prämie *f*, Werbegeschenk *n*, Werbeprämie *f*, Zugabe *f*	addition, advertising gift, bonus, free gift, premium, specialty
prime *f* attachée à l'emballage *m*	Prämie *f* auf der Verpackung *f*	on-pack premium
prime *f* auto-payante	selbstfinanzierte Prämie *f*	self-liquidating premium
prime *f* d'encouragement *m*	Anreizprämie *f*, Trostpreis *m*	consolation price, incentive
prime *f* stimulante	kaufanreizende Prämie *f*	incentive premium
principe *m*	Grundsatz *m*	principle
principe *m* d'impression *f*	Druckprinzip *n*	printing process
principes *m/pl* de vente *f*	Verkaufsrichtlinien *f/pl*	principles *pl* of selling
principes *m/pl* publicitaires	Werbegrundsätze *m/pl*	advertising principles *pl*
prise *f* de son *m*	Tonbandaufnahme *f*	electrical transcription, tape recording
prise *f* de son *m* photographique	Lichttonverfahren *n*	photographic sound-recording
prise *f* de vue *f*	Aufnahme *f* (Film), fotografische Aufnahme *f*, Filmaufnahme *f*	shooting of a film, shot, take, taking of photographs *pl*
prise *f* de vue *f* directe	Direktübertragung *f*, Live-Sendung *f*	live broadcast
prise *f* de vue *f* documentaire	Dokumentaraufnahme *f*	documentary photograph
prise *f* de vue *f* en couleurs *f/pl*	Farbaufnahme *f*	colour photograph
prise *f* de vue *f* en masse *f*	Massenaufnahme *f*	crowd shot
prise *f* de vue *f* noir blanc	Schwarzweißaufnahme *f*	black and white reproduction
prise *f* de vue *f* paysage	Landschaftsaufnahme *f*	landscape photo
prise *f* tourne-disque *f*	Tonabnahme *f*	prise pick-up
prix *m*	Preis *m*	price, rate
prix *m* à la livraison *f*	Lieferpreis *m*	delivery price
prix *m* à la production *f*	Erzeugerpreis *m*	producer's price
prix *m* affiché	angekündigter Preis *m*	posted price
prix *m* approuvé	gebilligter Preis *m*, genehmigter Preis *m*	approved price
prix *m* au catalogue *m*	Katalogpreis *m*	list price
prix *m* au tarif *m*	Listenpreis *m*	listprice, scale rate
prix *m* aux milles lecteurs *m/pl*	Tausenderpreis *m*	cost-per-thousand
prix *m* brut	Bruttopreis *m*	gross price
prix *m* courant *m*, prix *m* courant	Preisliste *f*, Tagespreis *m*, Tarif *m*	current price, price list, rate card, rates *pl*, schedule of prices *pl*
prix *m* coûtant	Selbstkosten *pl*	prime cost, selling costs *pl*
prix *m* d'abonnement *m*	Abonnementspreis *m*, Bezugspreis *m*	advertised price, subscription rate, subscription rates *pl*
prix *m* d'achat *m*	Kaufpreis *m*	cost price, purchase-money
prix *m* d'affichage *m* par jour *m* et affiche *f*	Bogentagpreis *m*	posting price per day and poster
prix *m* de barème *m*	Listenpreis *m*	listprice, scale rate
prix *m* de base *f*	Grundpreis *m*	basic rate, flat rate, open-time rate *am*, standard rate
prix *m* de base *f* augmenté	erhöhter Grundpreis *m*	raised standard rate
prix *m* de couplage *m*	Kombinationspreis *m*	combination rate, combined rate
prix *m* de détail *m*	Einzelhandelspreis *m*	retail price
prix *m* de direction *f*	Richtpreis *m*	basic price
prix *m* de fabrication *f*	Herstellungskosten *pl*	manufacturing costs *pl*, production costs *pl*
prix *m* de fantaisie *f*	Mondpreis *m*	fancy price, misleading pricing
prix *m* de lancement *m*	Einführungspreis *m*	early bird price
prix *m* de l'encart *m*	Beilagenpreis *m*	cost of the insert

prix *m* de magasin *m*	Ladenverkaufspreis *m*	shop price
prix *m* de monopole *m*	Monopolpreis *m*	monopoly price
prix *m* de réclame *f*	Werbepreis *m*	knock down price
prix *m* de revient	Selbstkosten *pl*	prime cost, selling costs *pl*
prix *m* de saison *f*	Saisonrabatt *m*	period price
prix *m* de souscription *f*	Subskriptionspreis *m*	subscription price
prix *m* de vente *f*	Verkaufspreis *m*	selling price
prix *m* de vente *f* au numéro *m*	Heftpreis *m*	single copy price
prix *m* de vente *f* barré	durchstrichener Verkaufspreis *m*	crossed out selling price
prix *m* d'insertion *f*	Einschaltpreis *m*	insertion rate
prix *m* double	doppelter Preis *m*	double rate
prix *m* du silence *m*	Schweigegeld *n*	hush money
prix *m* d'une ligne *f*	Zeilenpreis *m*	cost per line, price per line
prix *m* d'une page *f* entière	Seitenpreis *m*	page rate
prix *m* échelonné	gestaffelter Preis *m*	differential price, graduated price
prix *m* excessif	überhöhter Preis *m*	excessive charge
prix *m* fixe	Anzeigenfestpreis *m*, Festpreis *m*, gebundener Preis *m*, Preistreue *f*	controlled price, firm price, fixed selling price, flat rate, one-price, rigid price, standing price
prix *m* forfaitaire	Pauschalpreis *m*	blanket rate, flat rate, lump sum price
prix *m* global	Inklusivpreis *m*	price including
prix *m* imbattable	Tiefstpreis *m*	rock-bottom price
prix *m* imposé	Festpreis *m*, gebundener Preis *m*, Preisbindung *f* der zweiten Hand *f*	controlled price, firm price, fixed selling price, one-price, resale price maintenance, standing price
prix *m* maximum	Höchstpreis *m*	ceiling price
prix *m* minimum	Mindestpreis *m*, niedrigst kalkulierter Preis *m*, Tiefstpreis *m*	bargain level, minimum rate, rock-bottom price
prix *m* modique	niedriger Preis *m*	thrift price
prix *m* moyen	Durchschnittspreis *m*	average price
prix *m* net	Nettopreis *m*	net price, net rate
prix *m* optimum	Optimalpreis *m*	optimum price
prix *m* psychologique	psychologisch richtiger Preis *m*	psychological price
prix *m* réclame	Reklamepreis *m*	cut-rate price
prix *m* recommandé	empfohlener Preis *m*	standard price, suggested price
prix *m* réduit	reduzierter Preis *m*	short price
prix *m* soutenu	Stützpreis *m*	pegged price
prix *m* spécial	Sonderpreis *m*, Spezialpreis *m*, Vorzugspreis *m*	cut price, special rate
prix *m* unitaire	Stückpreis *m*	unit price
prix *m* usuraire	Wucherpreis *m*	exorbitant price
prix *m* vente *f* au détail *m*	Kleinverkaufspreis *m*	retail price
prix-réclame *f*	Sonderpreis *m*, Spezialpreis *m*	cut price, special rate
problème *m* publicitaire	Werbeproblem *n*	advertising problem
procédé *m*	Vorgehen *n*	procedure
procédé *m* argenture par pulvérisation *f*	Silberspritzverfahren *n*	silver spray technique
procédé *m* de copie *f* offset	Offsetkopierverfahren *n*	offset printing-down process
procédé *m* de fabrication *f*	Herstellungsverfahren *n*	manufacturing process
procédé *m* de gravure *f*, procédé *m* de morsure *f*	Ätzverfahren *n*	engraving process, etching process

procédé *m* d'impression *f*	Druckverfahren *n*	printing method, printing process
procédé *m* flexichrome	Handkolorierung *f*	flexichrome process
procédés *m/pl* photomécaniques	Reproduktionstechnik *f*	reproduction technique
procédure *f*	Arbeitsablauf *m*	procedure
processus *m* de concentration *f*	Konzentrationsprozeß *m*	economic concentration
processus *m* de production *f*	Produktionstechnik *f*	production techniques *pl*
procès-verbal *m*	Niederschrift *f*	record, writing down
proclamer	feierlich verkünden	to herald
producteur *m*	Hersteller *m*, Produzent *m*	producer
producteur *m* de films *m/pl*	Filmproduzent *m*	film producer
producteur *m* de films *m/pl* publicitaires	Werbefilmproduzent *m*	producer of advertising films *pl*
production *f*	Erzeugung *f*, Herstellung *f*	production
production *f* des moyens *m/pl* de publicité *f*	Werbemittelherstellung *f*	media *pl* production
produit *m*	Erzeugnis *n*, Produkt *m*	product
produit *m* à la mode *f*	modisches Produkt *n*	fancy article
produit *m* d'appel *m*	Lockartikel *m*	bait, catch-penny article, loss leader, lure
produit *m* de grande consommation *f*	Massenprodukt *n*	mass product
produit *m* de marque *f* déposée	Markenartikel *m*	branded goods *pl*, specialty goods *pl*
produit *m* de mauvaise qualité *f*	minderwertiges Produkt *n*	inferior product, lemon
produit *m* de qualité *f*	Qualitätserzeugnis *n*	quality product
produit *m* imitatif	nachgeahmtes Produkt *n*	imitative product
produit *m* plastique	Plastikerzeugnis *n*	plastic product
produits *m/pl* finis	Fertigprodukte *n/pl*	convenience goods *pl*
professions *f/pl* de la publicité *f*	Werbeberufe *m/pl*	advertising professions *pl*
profit *m*	Gewinn *m*, Nutzen *m*	gain, profit
profitable	gewinnbringend	profitable
programmateur *m*	Programmierer *m*	programmer
programmation *f*	Programmgestaltung *f*	programming
programme *m*	Planung *f*, Programm *n*	plan, planning, program *am*, programme *brit*
programme *m* adjacent, programme *m* d'accompagnement *m*	Beiprogramm *n*	adjacency, supplementary film
programme *m* de la publicité *f*	Werbeprogramm *n*	advertising program *am*, advertising programme *brit*
programme *m* de la radio *f*	Sendeplan *m*	guide sheet
programme *m* de photocomposition *f*	Lichtsatzprogramm *n*	photocomposition programme
programme *m* de radio *f*	Hörfolge *f*	feature programme
programme *m* des travaux *m/pl*	Arbeitsprogramm *n*	programme of work
programme *m* encadrant les émissions *f/pl* publicitaires	Rahmenprogramm *n*	programme framing the commercials *pl*
programme *m* patronné	Patronatssendung *f*, Sponsor-Sendung *f*	sponsored broadcast, sponsored programme, sponsored broadcast, sponsored programme
programme *m* récréatif	Unterhaltungsprogramm *n*	recreational programme
programme *m* télévisé	Fernsehprogramm *n*	television program
programmer	programmieren	to program
progressiste	fortschrittlich	advanced, go-ahead, progressive

projecteur *m*	Projektor *m*	projector
projecteur-diascope *m*	Diabildwerfer *m*	slide projector
projection *f*	Vorführung *f*	demonstration, projection, show
projection *f* dans des localités *f* avec lumière *f* de jour *m*	Hellraumprojektor *m*	film projector usuable in daylight-rooms *pl*
projection *f* de film *m*	Filmvorführung *f*	film projection
projection *f* en salle *f*	Filmwiedergabe *f*	film reproduction
projet *m*	Entwurf *m*, Konzept *n*, Schmierskizze *f*	design, draft, layout, outline, rough, rough copy, sketch, tentative work
projet *m* d'affiche *f*	Plakatentwurf *m*	dummy of a poster, poster design, poster sketch
projet *m* de budget *m*	Etatplan *m*	allocation draft
projet *m* de texte *m*	Textentwurf *m*	draft
projet *m* définitif	Reinzeichnung *f*	final art work, finished drawing
projet *m* gratuit	unverbindlicher Vorschlag *m*	speculative work
promotion *f*	Förderung *f*	promotion
promotion *f* de vente *f*	Absatzförderung *f*, Absatzsteigerung *f*, Verkaufsförderung *f*, Vertriebsförderung *f*	sales *pl* promotion
promotion *f* jumelée	Koppelungsverkauf *m*	banded offer, combination sale
prôner	anpreisen	to plug
pronostic *m*	Prognose *f*	prognosis
propagande *f*	Propaganda *f*, Werbetätigkeit *f*, Werbung *f*	advertising, advertising activity, propaganda, publicity
propagande *f* de bouche *f* à oreille *f*	Mundpropaganda *f*	advertising by word of mouth
propagande *f* électorale	Wahlpropaganda *f*	election propaganda
propagande *f* par stand *m*	Ladenwerbung *f*	shop advertising
propagandiste *m*	Propagandist *m*, Werber *m*	builder-upper, propagandist
propagation *f*	Verbreitung *f*	circulation, coverage, diffusion, dissimination, distribution
propager	propagieren, verbreiten	to disseminate, to propagandize, to propagate
propos *m*	Äußerung *f*	utterance
proposer	vorschlagen	to propose, to suggest
proposition *f*	Exposé *n*, Vorschlag *m*	proposal, proposition, statement
proposition *f* publicitaire	Werbevorschlag *m*	advertising proposal
propositions *f/pl* commerciales	Verkaufsargumentation *f*	purchase proposition
propre annonce *f*	Eigenanzeige *f*	one's own advertisement
propre publicité *f*	Eigenwerbung *f*	house advertising
propriétaire *m*	Verpächter *m*	landlord
propriétaire *m* d'emplacement *m*	Flächengesteller *m*	owner of site
propriété *f* intellectuelle	geistiges Eigentum *n*	intellectual property
prospect *m*	eventueller Kunde *m*, Interessent *m*, möglicher, voraussichtlicher Kunde *m*	prospect
prospecter	hereinholen	to canvass
prospecteur *m* d'emplacements *m/pl*	Abpächter *m*	site getter

prospection _f_	Aufträge _m/pl_ hereinholen, Streuung _f_	canvassing, coverage, diffusion, dispersion, spread
prospection _f_ perdue	Streuverlust _m_	waste dispersion
prospection _f_ publicitaire	Werbestreuung _f_	advertising dispersion
prospectus _m_	Broschüre _f,_ Handzettel _m,_ Prospekt _m_	booklet, brochure, dodger _am,_ folder, give-away, handbill, pamphlet, prospectus, throw-away
prospectus _m_ de voyage _m_	Reiseführer _m_	travel guide
prospectus _m_ distribué en arrasoir _m_	Streuprospekt _m_	throwaway leaflet
prospectus _m_ publicitaire	Werbeblatt _n_	advertising handbill
prote _m_	Faktor _m/typog m_	overseer of composing room
protection _f_ des consommateurs _m/pl_	Verbraucherschutz _m_	consumer protection
protection _f_ des marques _f/pl_	Markenschutz _m,_ Warenzeichenschutz _m_	protection of trademarks _pl,_ trade mark protection
protection _f_ des modèles _m/pl_ et dessins _m/pl_	Gebrauchsmusterschutz _m_	protection of registered design
protection _f_ des prix _m/pl_	Preisschutz _m_	price protection
protège-livre _m_	Schutzumschlag _m_	dust-cover, jacket
prototype _m_	Vorbild _n_	prototype
proverbe _m_	Sprichwort _n_	proverb
provision _f_	Kommission _f_	commission
provisoire	provisorisch	provisional
provocation _f_ à l'achat _m_	Kaufbeeinflussung _f_	inducement to buy
pseudonyme _m_	Deckname _m,_ Pseudonym _n_	code-word, pen-name, pseudonym
psychologie _f_ de la publicité _f_	Werbepsychologie _f_	advertising psychology
publiable	geeignet zur Veröffentlichung _f_	publishable
public, public _m_	öffentlich, Publikum _n_	audience, public
public _m_ des cinémas _m/pl_	Kinopublikum _n_	movie audience
publication _f_	Druckschrift _f_ (Veröffentlichung _f_), Erscheinen _n,_ Organ _n,_ Publikation _f,_ Verlagserscheinung _f_	appearance, medium, printing work, publication
publication _f_ anniversaire, publication _f_ de jubilé _m_	Jubiläumsschrift _f_	anniversary publication, jubilee publication
publication _f_ gratuite	Gratisblatt _n_	free publication, giveaway
publication _f_ médicale	medizinische Zeitschrift _f_	medical journal
publication _f_ occasionnelle	Gelegenheitspublikation _f_	occasional publication
publiciste _m_	Publizist _m,_ Schriftsteller _m_	author, journalist, publicist, writer
publicitaire _m,_ publicitaire	Anzeigenfachmann _m,_ Reklamechef _m,_ werblich, Werbefachmann _m_	adman, advertising, advertising expert, advertising man, build-upper
publicité _f_	Öffentlichkeit _f,_ Publizität _f,_ Werbewesen _n,_ Werbung _f_	advertising, publicity
publicité _f_ à l'écran _m_	Filmwerbung _f_	cinema advertising, moving picture advertising, screen advertising
publicité _f_ à l'étranger _m_	Auslandswerbung _f_	foreign advertising
publicité _f_ à plusieurs voies _f/pl_	mehrgleisige Werbung _f_	split run advertising
publicité _f_ acoustique	akustische Werbung _f_	acoustic advertising

publicité f additionnelle	Zusatzwerbung f	accessory advertising
publicité f aérienne	Himmelsschrift f, Luftschriftwerbung f, Luftwerbung f	aerial advertising, air advertising, sky line advertising, sky typing, sky writing, skyline advertising
publicité f agressive	aggressive Werbung f, herabsetzende Werbung f	competitive copy am, disparaging copy, hard approach, knocking copy brit
publicité f anticyclique	antizyklische Werbung f	anticyclic advertising
publicité f argumentée	Aufklärungswerbung f, begründende Werbung f	product publicity, reason-why advertising
publicité f artistique	Gebrauchsgrafik f, künstlerische Werbung f	advertising art, applied art, artistic advertising, commercial art
publicité f attractive	zugkräftige Werbung f	attractive advertising, audience builder
publicité f attrape-regard m	Blickfangwerbung f	eye-catching advertising
publicité f attrayante	ansprechende Werbung f	appealing advertising
publicité f au format m	seitenteilige Anzeige f	fractional-page advertisement
publicité f au moyen m de coupons m/pl	Kuponwerbung f	coupon advertising
publicité f au point m d'achat m	Werbung f am Kaufort m	point-of-purchase advertising
publicité f au superlatif m	Superlativwerbung f	advertising in superlatives pl
publicité f audio-visuelle	audiovisuelle Werbung f	audio-visual advertising
publicité f auprès des consommateurs m/pl	Konsumentenwerbung f	consumer advertising
publicité f auprès le grand public m	Publikumswerbung f	advertising for the general public
publicité f autorisée	zulässige Werbung f	admissible advertising
publicité f auxiliaire	Ergänzungswerbung f, unterstützende Werbung f, zusätzliche Werbung f	accessory advertising, auxiliary advertising, supplementary advertising
publicité f avec des bandes f/pl dessinées	Bildserienwerbung f	band advertising, strip advertising
publicité f avec primes f/pl	Zugabewerbung f	gift advertising
publicité f balnéaire	Bäderanzeige f	travel advertisement
publicité f bien organisée	gut aufgezogene Werbung f	well-organized advertising
publicité f camouflée	Schleichwerbung f	camouflaged advertising, clandestine advertising, masked advertising, subliminal advertising
publicité f cinématographique	Filmwerbung f, Lichtspieltheaterwerbung f	advertising in cinemas pl, cinema advertising, moving picture advertising, screen advertising
publicité f clandestine	Schleichwerbung f	camouflaged advertising, clandestine advertising, masked advertising, subliminal advertising
publicité f codée	Kennzifferwerbung f	keyed advertising
publicité f collective	Gemeinschaftswerbung f	collective advertising, cooperative advertising brit, group advertising, joint advertising

publicité f collective horizontale	Horizontalwerbung f	horizontal co-operative advertising
publicité f collective verticale	Vertikalwerbung f	vertical co-operative advertising
publicité f combinée	kombinierte Werbung f	co-op advertising
publicité f commerciale	Wirtschaftswerbung f	business advertising
publicité f communale	Gemeindewerbung f	community advertising
publicité f commune	Verbundwerbung f, Werbung f, gemeinsame	co-operative advertising, co-up advertising, tie-up advertising
publicité f concentrée	Schwerpunktwerbung f	zone plan
publicité f concurrente	Konkurrenzwerbung f	competitive advertising
publicité f consommateurs m/pl	Verbraucherwerbung f	consumer advertising
publicité f coordonnée	aufeinander abgestimmte Werbung f, koordinierte Werbung f	coordinated advertising
publicité f courante	gegenwärtig laufende Werbekampagne f	current advertising
publicité f coûteuse	kostspielige Werbung f	expensive advertising
publicité f cyclique	zyklische Werbung f	cyclic advertising
publicité f d'amorçage m	Vorwerbung f	advance publicity
publicité f dans des médias m/pl imprimés	Werbung f in gedruckten Medien n/pl	print advertising
publicité f dans le ciel m	Werbung f auf dem Dach n	sky sign
publicité f dans les aéroports m/pl	Flughafenwerbung f	airport advertising
publicité f dans les cercles m/pl de lecture f	Lesezirkelwerbung f	advertising in circulating magazines pl, advertising in reading circles pl
publicité f dans les cinémas m/pl	Kinowerbung f	cinema advertising, film advertising
publicité f dans les ferry-boats m/pl	Fährschiffwerbung f	ferry-boat advertising
publicité f dans les gares f/pl	Bahnhofswerbung f	railway station advertising
publicité f dans les revues f/pl	Zeitschriftenwerbung f	magazine advertising
publicité f dans les stades m/pl	Bandenwerbung f, Sportplatzwerbung f	advertising in sport fields pl
publicité f dans les taxis m/pl	Taxiwerbung f	taxicab advertising
publicité f dans les terminus m/pl	Stationswerbung f	terminal display
publicité f dans ou sur un autobus m	Autobuswerbung f, Omnibuswerbung f	bus advertising
publicité f dans un tirage m partagé	Teilbelegung f	split run advertising
publicité f d'association f	Anknüpfungswerbung f, kombinierte Werbeaktion f	tie-in advertising, tie-up advertising
publicité f de bouche f à bouche f	mündliche Werbung f	advertising by word of mouth
publicité f de complément m	begleitende Werbung f, zusätzliche Werbung f	accessory advertising, auxiliary advertising, supplementary advertising
publicité f de foire f	Messewerbung f	exhibition advertising
publicité f de grand style m	großzügige Werbung f	large-scale advertising
publicité f de la mode f	Modewerbung f	fashion advertising
publicité f de lancement m	Einführungswerbung f	introductory advertising,

publicité *f* **de maintien** *m*	Erhaltungswerbung *f*	maintenance advertising
publicité *f* **de marque** *f*	Markenartikelwerbung *f*	brand advertising
publicité *f* **de notoriété** *f*	institutionelle Werbung *f*, Prestigewerbung *f*	corporate advertising, goodwill advertising, institutional advertising, prestige advertising
publicité *f* **de pionnier** *m*	Initialwerbung *f*	pioneering advertising
publicité *f* **de porte** *f* **en porte** *f*	Haushaltswerbung *f*	house-to-house advertising
publicité *f* **de prestige** *m*	Goodwillwerbung *f*, institutionelle Werbung *f*, Prestigewerbung *f*, Repräsentationswerbung *f*	corporate advertising, goodwill advertising, institutional advertising, prestige advertising
publicité *f* **de prestige** *m* **pour une société** *f*	Firmenwerbung *f*	institutional advertising
publicité *f* **de rappel** *m*	Erinnerungswerbung *f*	remembrance advertising
publicité *f* **de relance** *f*	Nachfaßwerbung *f*	follow-up advertising
publicité *f* **de soutien** *m*	Ergänzungswerbung *f*, zusätzliche Werbung *f*	accessory advertising, auxiliary advertising, supplementary advertising
publicité *f* **de souvenir** *m*	Erinnerungswerbung *f*	remembrance advertising
publicité *f* **de tourisme** *m*	Fremdenverkehrswerbung *f*	holiday resorts *pl* advertising, tourism advertising, tourist publicity
publicité *f* **de vente** *f* **par correspondance** *f*	Versandhauswerbung *f*	mail order advertising
publicité *f* **de villégiature** *f*	Fremdenverkehrswerbung *f*	holiday resorts *pl* advertising, tourism advertising, tourist publicity
publicité *f* **déceptive**	betrügerische Werbung *f*	deceptive advertising
publicité *f* **déguisée**	Schleichwerbung *f*	camouflaged advertising, clandestine advertising, masked advertising, subliminal advertising
publicité *f* **déloyale**	irreführende Werbung *f*, unehrenhafte Werbung *f*, unlautere Werbung *f*	deceptive advertising, dishonest advertising, false advertising, misleading advertising
publicité *f* **déplacée**	falsch angesetzte Werbung *f*	misplaced advertising
publicité *f* **des biens** *m/pl* **de consommation** *f*	Konsumwerbung *f*	consumer goods *pl* advertising
publicité *f* **des boissons** *f/pl*	Getränkewerbung *f*	beverage advertising
publicité *f* **des détaillants** *m/pl*		retail advertising
publicité *f* **des établissements** *m/pl* **de détail** *m*	Einzelhandelswerbung *f*	retail advertising
publicité *f* **des producteurs** *m/pl*	Herstellerwerbung *f*	producer advertising
publicité *f* **d'exportation** *f*	Exportwerbung *f*	export advertising
publicité *f* **d'information** *f*	Einführungswerbung *f*	introductory advertising
publicité *f* **d'intérieur** *m*	Innenwerbung *f*	indoor advertising
publicité *f* **d'introduction** *f*	Einführungswerbung *f*	introductory advertising
publicité *f* **directe**	Direktwerbung *f*	direct advertising
publicité *f* **directe par la poste** *f*	Direktwerbung *f* durch die Post *f*	direct mail advertising, mailing shot

publicité *f* **directe par voie** *f* **postale**	Postwurfsendungen *f/pl*	boxholder addressing, bulk posting, mail distribution, mailing piece, post office mailing
publicité *f* **discriminatoire** **publicité** *f* **discriminatrice**	herabsetzende Werbung *f*, Komparativwerbung *f*, vergleichende Werbung *f*	comparative advertising, competitive copy *am*, disparaging copy, knocking copy *brit*
publicité *f* **d'opportunité** *f*	Gelegenheitswerbung *f*	opportunity advertising
publicité *f* **du domaine** *m* **des loisirs** *m/pl*	Freizeitbereichswerbung *f*	leisure time publicity
publicité *f* **éclairée**	angestrahlte Werbefläche *f*	floodlight advertisement
publicité *f* **éducative**	belehrende Werbung *f*, erzieherische Werbung *f*	educational advertising
publicité *f* **efficace**	wirksame Werbung *f*	effective advertising
publicité *f* **électronique**	elektronische Werbung *f*	electronical advertising
publicité *f* **émotive**	gefühlsbetonte Werbung *f*	emotional advertising
publicité *f* **emphatique**	hochtönende Werbung *f*	high-pressure advertising
publicité *f* **en commun**	Kollektivwerbung *f*	collective advertising, cooperative advertising *brit*, group advertising, joint advertising
publicité *f* **en couleurs** *f/pl*	Farbanzeige *f*	colour advertisement
publicité *f* **en douceur** *f*	leise Werbung *f*	soft approach
publicité *f* **en étapes** *f/pl*	Stufenwerbeplan *m*	cream-plan
publicité *f* **en faveur** *f* **des produits** *m/pl* **pharmaceutiques**	Pharmawerbung *f*	advertising for drugs *pl*
publicité *f* **en langue** *f* **étrangère**	fremdsprachliche Werbung *f*	advertising in foreign language
publicité *f* **en vitrine** *f*	Schaufensterwerbung *f*	shop window advertising
publicité *f* **enchaînée**	eingeblendete Werbung *f*	tie-in advertising
publicité *f* **envahissante**	anmaßende Werbung *f*	insolent advertising
publicité *f* **éthique**	ethische Werbung *f*	ethical advertising
publicité *f* **extérieure**	Außenwerbung *f*	outdoor advertising
publicité *f* **fallacieuse**	irreführende Werbung *f*	deceptive advertising, false advertising, misleading advertising
publicité *f* **financière**	Finanzwerbung *f*	financial advertising
publicité *f* **générale**	Publikumspropaganda *f*	general publicity
publicité *f* **groupée**	Kollektivwerbung *f*, Verbundwerbung *f*	co-up advertising, collective advertising, group advertising, tie-up advertising
publicité *f* **holographique**	holografische Werbung *f*	holographic advertising
publicité *f* **humoristique**	scherzhafte Werbung *f*	jesting advertising
publicité *f* **illicite**	unerlaubte Werbung *f*	illicit advertising
publicité *f* **illustrée**	Bildwerbung *f*	pictorial advertising
publicité *f* **impeccable**	einwandfreie Werbung *f*	clean advertising
publicité *f* **impériale**	Prestigewerbung *f*	good-will advertising, institutional advertising, prestige advertising
publicité *f* **inadéquate**	unzulängliche Werbung *f*	inadequate advertising

publicité f incitant à l'action f directe	Kaufwerbung f	direct-action advertising
publicité f indécente	anstößige Werbung f	indecent advertising
publicité f indirecte	indirekte Werbung f	indirect advertising
publicité f individuelle	Alleinwerbung f, Einzelwerbung f, Individualwerbung f	individual advertising, isolated advertising
publicité f industrielle	Industriewerbung f	industrial advertising
publicité f informative	informierende Werbung f	informatory advertising, product advertising
publicité f insidieuse	unterschwellige Werbung f	subliminal advertising
publicité f institutionnelle	firmenbetonte Werbung f, institutionelle Werbung f	corporate advertising, goodwill advertising, institutional advertising
publicité f instructive	informierende Werbung f	informatory advertising, product advertising
publicité f intensive	Intensivwerbung f	intensive advertising
publicité f interdite	unzulässige Werbung f	forbidden advertising
publicité f irréprochable	einwandfreie Werbung f	clean advertising
publicité f isolée	Alleinwerbung f	individual advertising, isolated advertising
publicité f locale	Lokalwerbung f, Ortsanzeigen f/pl	local advertising
publicité f lumineuse	Leuchtwerbung f, Lichtwerbung f	animation, electric sign advertising, illuminated advertising
publicité f lumineuse animée	bewegliche Lichtwerbung f	animated electric sign advertising, electric spectaculars pl/am, spectacular
publicité f mécanique	mechanische Werbung f	mechanical advertising
publicité f mensongère	betrügerische Werbung f, irreführende Werbung f, lügnerische Werbung f	deceptive advertising, false advertising, lying advertising, misleading advertising
publicité f mobile	bewegliche Werbung f	mechanical advertising
publicité f moderne	fortschrittliche Werbung f	progressive advertising
publicité f moyens m/pl de transport m	Verkehrsmittelwerbung f	advertising in transport systems pl, transit advertising, transport advertising brit, transportation advertising am, vehicular advertising
publicité f murale	Giebelwerbung f, Mauerwerbung f	gable publicity, wall advertising, wall publicity
publicité f musicale	Werbemusik f	music in advertising
publicité f nationale	überregionale Werbung f	nation-wide advertising
publicité f non classifiée	allgemeine Anzeigen f/pl	display advertisements pl
publicité f non-sélective	ungezielte Werbung f	non-selective advertising
publicité f obsessionnelle	zudringliche Werbung f	obtrusive advertising
publicité f occulte	Schleichwerbung f	camouflaged advertising, clandestine advertising, masked advertising, subliminal advertising
publicité f orale	Flüsterpropaganda f, Schallplattenwerbung f	record advertising, whispering campaign
publicité f originale	ungewöhnliche Werbung f	original advertising

publicité f par affiches f/pl	Anschlagwerbung f, Bogenanschlag m, Plakatanschlagwerbung f	bill posting, poster advertising, sheetage
publicité f par avion m	Flugzeugwerbung f	aeroplane advertising
publicité f par ballons m/pl	Ballonwerbung f	balloon advertising
publicité f par ballons m/pl captifs	Fesselballonwerbung f	advertising by captive balloons pl
publicité f par cerf-volant m	Reklamedrachen m	advertising kite
publicité f par chemin m de fer m	Eisenbahnwerbung f	railway advertising
publicité f par chocs m/pl	Stoßwerbung f	impact advertising
publicité f par diapositif m	Diapositivwerbung f	slide advertising
publicité f par dirigeable m	Luftballonwerbung f	dirigible advertising
publicité f par encarts m/pl dans les livres m/pl en location f	Leihbuchwerbung f	advertising by inserts pl in books pl of a lending library
publicité f par étalage m	Schaufensterwerbung f	shop window advertising
publicité f par film m	Filmwerbung f	cinema advertising, moving picture advertising, screen advertising
publicité f par haut-parleur m	Lautsprecherwerbung f	loudspeaker advertising
publicité f par insetting	Insettinganzeige f	advertisement by insetting, spectacolor advertisement
publicité f par la presse f	Zeitungswerbung f	press advertising
publicité f par l'objet m	Warenprobenverteilung f	free gift advertising, novelty advertising
publicité f par poste f	Postwerbung f	postal advertising
publicité f par primes f/pl	Zugabewerbung f	gift advertising
publicité f par tube m néon	Neonlichtwerbung f	neon tubing
publicité f parlante	mündliche Werbung f, Mund-zu-Mund-Werbung f	advertising by word of mouth, word-of-mouth-advertising
publicite f payée	bezahlte Werbung f	paid advertising
publicité f permanente	Dauerwerbung f	permanent publicity
publicité f personnalisée	personalisierte Werbung f	personalised sales pl technique
publicité f persuasive	überzeugende Werbung f	persuasive advertising
publicité f pleine d'élan m	schwungvolle Werbung f	dynamic advertising
publicité f pour des biens m/pl d'investissement m	Investitionsgüterwerbung f	industrial advertising
publicité f pour le distributeur m	Händlerwerbung f	trade advertising
publicité f pour les voyages m/pl d'avion m	Flugreisewerbung f	airline advertising
publicité f préventive	Präventivwerbung f	preventive advertising
publicité f primaire	Primärwerbung f	primary-demand advertising
publicité f produits m/pl	Aufklärungswerbung f, Produktwerbung f	line advertising, product advertising, product publicity, reason-why advertising
publicité f pseudo-scientifique	scheinwissenschaftliche Werbung f	pseudoscientific advertising
publicité f raccrocheuse	anreißerische Werbung f, marktschreierische Werbung f	ballyhoo am, noisy advertising, puffing publicity
publicité f radiodiffusée	Radiowerbung f	broadcast advertising

publicité *f* radiophonique	Funkwerbung *f*, Hörfunkwerbung *f*, Rundfunkwerbung *f*, Werbefunk *m*	broadcast advertising, commercial broadcasting, commercial radio, radio advertising
publicité *f* radiophonique dans une boutique *f*	Rundfunksendung *f* im Laden *m*	storecasting
publicité *f* rationnelle	vernünftige Werbung *f*	rational advertising
publicité *f* rédactionnelle gratuite	redaktionelle Werbung *f*	editorial publicity, free puff, write-up *am*
publicité *f* relative à l'enfant *m*	Werbung *f*, kindbezogene	kid appeal advertising
publicité *f* relative au produit *m*	Werbung *f*, produktbezogene	product advertising
publicité *f* rentable	einträgliche Werbung *f*	lucrative advertising
publicité *f* répétée	ständig wiederholte Streuung *f*	rotation
publicité *f* retardataire	Nachzügler-Werbesendung *f*	hitchhike
publicité *f* roulante	rollende Werbung *f*	rolling advertising
publicité *f* routière	Straßenwerbung *f*, Streckenwerbung *f*	roadside advertising
publicité *f* saisonnière	Saisonwerbung *f*	seasonal advertising
publicité *f* scientifique	wissenschaftliche Werbung *f*	scientific advertising
publicité *f* se découpant sur le ciel *m*	Werbesilhouette *f*	sky sign
publicité *f* sélective	gezielte Werbung *f*, selektive Werbung *f*, ausgewählte Werbung *f*	selective advertising
publicité *f* sonore	Tonwerbung *f*	sound advertising
publicité *f* sous chiffre *m*	Kennzifferwerbung *f*, Werbung *f* mit Kennziffern *f/pl*	keyed advertising
publicité *f* spécialisée	Fachwerbung *f*	professional advertising
publicité *f* spectacles *m/pl*	Werbung *f* der Vergnügungsbranche *f*	entertainment advertising
publicité *f* subliminale	unterschwellige Werbung *f*	subliminal advertising
publicité *f* substantielle	starke Werbung *f*, umfangreiche Werbung *f*	substantial advertising
publicité *f* subversive	Schleichwerbung *f*	camouflaged advertising, clandestine advertising, masked advertising, subliminal advertising
publicité *f* suggestive	Suggestivwerbung *f*	suggestive advertising
publicité *f* sur billets *m/pl*	Fahrscheinwerbung *f*	ticket advertising
publicité *f* sur des billets *m/pl* de loterie *f*	Losbriefwerbung *f*	advertising on lottery ticket letters *pl*
publicité *f* sur des mâts *m/pl* d'éclairage *m*	Kandelaberwerbung *f*	lamp post advertising
publicité *f* sur des plans *m/pl* de ville *f*	Stadtplanwerbung *f*	advertising on town maps *pl*
publicité *f* sur enveloppes *f/pl* commerciales	Briefumschlagwerbung *f*	advertising on envelopes *pl*
publicité *f* sur enveloppes *f/pl* de paye *m*	Lohntütenwerbung *f*, Lohnbeutelwerbung *f*	pay envelopes advertising
publicité *f* sur façades *f/pl*	Fassadenbeschriftung *f*	advertising on façades *pl*
publicité *f* sur feuillets *m/pl* d'allumettes *f/pl*	Zündholzwerbung *f*	matchbox advertising
publicité *f* sur le lieu *m* de vente *f*	Werbung *f* am Verkaufspunkt *m*	advertising on the point of sale
publicité *f* sur l'emballage *m*	Werbung *f* auf Packungen *f/pl*	package advertising

publicité f sur les soucoupes f/pl de la bière f	Bierdeckelwerbung f	advertising on beer mats pl
publicité f sur les toits m/pl	Dachwerbung f	roof advertisement
publicité f sur l'extérieur m de voitures f/pl	Außenwerbung f an Verkehrsmitteln n/pl	parade poster, travelling display
publicité f sur ou dans véhicules f/pl de transport m	Werbung f in Fahrzeugen n/pl	vehicular advertising
publicité f sur papier m buvard	Löschblattreklame f	blotter advertising
publicité f sur potelets m/pl	Mastenwerbung f	sign mast advertising
publicité f sur trottoir m	Pflasterwerbung f	pavement advertising
publicité f sur wagons m/pl de marchandises f/pl	Güterwagenwerbung f	advertising on goods-trains pl
publicité f systématique	zielbewußte Werbung f	systematic advertising
publicité f tapageuse	marktschreierische Werbung f, Werberummel m	ballyhoo am, hoopla, noisy advertising, puffing publicity
publicité f taquine	Neckwerbung f	teaser advertising
publicité f télévisée	Fernsehwerbung f	commercial television, television advertising
publicité f test m	Versuchswerbung f	advertising test
publicité f tram m	Straßenbahnwerbung f	street car advertising, tramway advertising
publicité f trompeuse	täuschende Werbung f, trügerische Werbung f	false advertising, misleading advertising
publicité f verbale	Mund-zu-Mund-Werbung f	word-of-mouth-advertising
publicité f vigoureuse	nachdrückliche Werbung f	vigorous advertising
publicité f volumineuse		substantial advertising
publicité-métro m	U-Bahn-Werbung f	subway advertising am, underground railway advertising brit
publicité-presse f	Anzeigenwerbung f, Pressewerbung f	press advertising
publier	herausgeben, publizieren, veröffentlichen	to bring out, to issue, to publish
publier un article m simultanément dans plusieurs journaux m/pl	Artikel m gleichzeitig in mehreren Zeitungen f/pl veröffentlichen	to syndicate
publi-information f	PR-Anzeige f	public relations pl report
publiphobie f	Werbefeindlichkeit f	antipathy to advertising
publipostage m	werbliche Postaussendung f	mailing
publi-reportage m	PR-Anzeige f	public relations pl report
puissance f d'expression f	Aussagekraft f	force of expression
puissance f maxima	Spitzenleistung f	top work
puissance f publicitaire	Werbekraft f	pulling power, selling power
pylône m publicitaire	Werbepylon m, Werbeturm m	advertising pylon, advertising tower
pyrogravure f	Brandmalerei f	poker-work

Q

quadrangle m	Viereck n	rectangle
quadrangulaire	viereckig	squared-off
quadrichromie f	Farbätzung f, Vierfarbendruck m	colour process etching, four-colour block, four-colour process
qualité f	Qualität f	quality
qualité f de l'impression f	Druckausfall m	quality of prints pl
qualité f de peu de valeur f	minderwertige Qualität f	cheap quality
qualité f esthétique	ästhetische Qualität f	aesthetic quality
qualité f typographique	Schriftqualität f	quality of type

quart *m* de page *f*	Viertelseite *f*	quarter page
querelleur *m*	Querulant *m*	grumbler
question *f*	Frage *f*	query, question
question *f* suggestive	Suggestivfrage *f*	leading question, suggestive question
question *f* tendancieuse	Suggestivfrage *f*	leading question, suggestive question
questionnaire *m*	Fragebogen *m*	question form, questionnaire
questions *f/pl* d'actualité *f*	Tagesfragen *f/pl*	topics *pl* of the day
qui ne prend pas position *f*	zurückhaltend	non-committal
quinconce *f*	Schachbrettform *f*	in sqares *pl*
quiproquo *m*	Mißverständnis *n*	misunderstanding
quota *m*	Quote *f*	quota
quota *m* de vente *f*	Verkaufsquote *f*	sales *pl* quota
quote-part *f*	Marktanteil *m*	market share
quotidien, quotidien *m*	täglich, Tageszeitung *f*	daily, daily newspaper
quotidien *m* du septième jour *m*	Sonntagsausgabe *f*	Sunday edition
quotidien *m* régional	regionale Tageszeitung *f*	regional daily
quotidiens *m/pl* métropolitains	Großstadtpresse *f*	big city press, metropolitan dailies *pl*

R

rabais *m*	Nachlaß *m*, Preisermäßigung *f*, Rabatt *m*, Rückvergütung *f*	discount, price abatement, rebate, reduction, refund
rabais *m* additionnel	Extrarabatt *m*, Zusatzrabatt *m*	additional account, additional discount
rabais *m* au client *m*	Kundenrabatt *m*	discount for customers *pl*
rabais *m* aux éditeurs *m/pl*	Verlegerrabatt *m*	publisher's discount
rabais *m* commun	Anzeigenrabatt *m* bei Belegung *f* mehrerer Blätter *n/pl* eines Verlages *m*	clubbing offer
rabais *m* de couplage *m*	Kombinationsrabatt *m*	clubbing offer, combined edition discount
rabais *m* de fidélité *f*	Treuerabatt *m*	patronage discount
rabais *m* de lancement *m*	Einführungsrabatt *m*	discount of introduction
rabais *m* de quantité *f*	Mengenrabatt *m*	bulk rate *brit*, frequency discount, quantity discount, space discount, volume discount
rabais *m* de série *f*	Serienrabatt *m*	frequency discount
rabais *m* maximum	Höchstrabatt *m*	maximum rebate
rabais *m* pour les commerçants *m/pl*	Händlerrabatt *m*	dealer rebate
rabais *m* rétroactif	Nachrabatt *m*	retroactive discount
rabat *m*	Klappe *f*, Umschlagklappe *f*	flap
raccourcir	kürzen, verkürzen	to boil down, to compress, to curtail, to shorten
raclette *f*, racleur *m*	Rakel *f*	blade, squeegee
racolage *m*	Kundenfang *m*	crimping, touting
racoleur *m*	Anreißer *m*	tout
radio *f*	Rundfunk *m*	aircast, broadcasting, radio, wireless
radiocommunication *f*	Funkübertragung *f*, Nachrichtenübermittlung *f*	news transmitting, radio communication
radiodiffuser	senden (Radio)	to broadcast, to transmit
radiodiffusion *f*	Rundfunksendung *f*	broadcast, radio casting *am*

radiodiffusion *f* **par fil** *m*	Drahtfunk *m*	broadcasting by wire
radiodiffusion *f* **sonore**	Hörfunk *m*	broadcasting
radio-reportage *m*	Rundfunkbericht *m*	broadcast account
raillerie *f*	Stichelei *f*, witzige Bemerkung *f*	quip, squib
rainage *m*	Falzung *f*	folding, grooving
rainer	nuten	to groove
rainure *f*	Falz *m*	fold, joint
raison *f* **d'achat** *m*	Kaufanlaß *m*	buying motive
ralentisseur *m*	Zeitlupe *f*	slow-motion method
rame *f*	Ries *n*	ream
rang *m*	Setzregal *n*	case stand
rapetisser	verkleinern	to minimise, to reduce
rapiéçage *m*	Flickwerk *n*	patchwork
rappel *m*	Rabattrückbelastung *f*, Rückbelastung *f*	short rate, short rates *pl*
rapport *m*	Bericht *m*, Zeitungsbericht *m*	report
rapport *m* **annuel**	Jahresbericht *m*	annual report
rapport *m* **d'actualité** *f*	Feature *n*, Sachbericht *m*	feature
rapport *m* **de conférence** *f*	Besprechungsbericht *m*	call report
rapport *m* **de contrôle** *m*	Prüfungsbericht *m*	audit report
rapport *m* **de visite** *f*	Besuchsbericht *m*, Vertreterbericht *m*	call report, call slip
rapport *m* **d'exercise** *f*	Jahresbericht *m*	annual report
rapport *m* **d'information** *f* **devant le commencement** *m* **d'une campagne** *f* **publicitaire**	Informationsbericht *m* vor Beginn *f* der Ausarbeitung *f* einer Werbekampagne	start work report
rapport *m* **documentaire**	Dokumentarbericht *m*	background story, feature
rapport *m* **exclusif**	Exklusivbericht *m*	exclusive report
rapport *m* **journalier**	Tagesbericht *m*	daily report
rapport *m* **spécial d'actualité** *f*	besonders gestalteter aktueller Tatsachenbericht *m*	feature
rapport *m* **sur la situation** *f*	Lagebericht *m*	background report
rapport *m* **sur les tirages** *m/pl*	Auflagemeldung *f*	publisher's statement
rapporter	berichten	to report
rapporteur *m*	Berichterstatter *m*	chronicler, correspondent, reporter
rapports *m/pl* **de grandeur** *f*	Größenverhältnis *n*	proportionality
rapports *m/pl* **humains**	menschliche Note *f*	human touch
rapprochement *m* **dans une vue** *f* **de premier plan** *m*	Heranrücken *n* bei Großaufnahme *f* (Film)	zooming
rat *m* **de bibliothèque** *f*	Leseratte *f*	book-hunter, paper worm
ratage *m*	unterdrückte Nachricht *f*	blacked out news
raturer	durchstreichen	to cross out
ravitailleur *m* **des éléments** *m/pl* **d'illustrations** *f/pl*	Bildmaterialbeschaffer *m*	art buyer
rayer	tilgen	to take out
rayon *m*	Abteilung *f*, Regal *n*, Verkaufsständer *m*	department, distribution rack, division, rack, section
rayon *m* **d'action** *f*	Reichweite *f*, Verbreitungsgebiet *n*	circulation area, coverage, covered sector, penetration, range, reach *am*, turnover
rayonnement *m*	Verbreitung *f*	circulation, coverage, diffusion, dissimination, distribution
rayure *f*	Schramme *f*, Streichung *f*	deletion, scar, scratch

réabonnement *m*	Abonnementserneuerung *f*	renewal of subscription
réalisateur *m*	Filmregisseur *m*	film director, film producer
réalisation *f*	Ausführung *f*	execution, realization
réalisation *f* de commandes *f/pl*	Auftragserledigung *f*	carrying out of an order, order filling
réalisation *f* d'un produit *m*	Produktgestaltung *f*	styling
rébus *m*	Bilderrätsel *n*	picture puzzle
rebut *m*	Ausfall *m*	failure rates *pl*, turnout
récapitulation *f*	Zusammenfassung *f*	recapitulation, synopsis
récapituler	zusammenfassen	to accumulate, to cumulate, to recapitulate, to summarize
recensement *m* de la distribution *f*	Absatzzählung *f*, Erfassung *f* der Werbestreuung *f*	census of distribution
récepteur *m*	Empfänger *m*, Rundfunkempfangsgerät *n*	addressee, radio set, recipient, wireless set
récepteur *m* de poche *f*	Taschenradio *n*	pocket-radio
récepteur *m* de télévision *f*	Fernsehapparat *m*, Fernsehempfänger *m*	television receiver, television set
récepteur *m* radio *f*	Radioapparat *m*	wireless set
réception *f* d'annonces *f/pl*	Anzeigenannahme *f*	reception of advertisements *pl*
réception *f* de la presse *f*	Presseempfang *m*	press reception
réception *f* de télévision *f*	Fernsehempfang *m*	television reception
réceptivité *f*	Aufnahmefähigkeit *f*	receptivity
recettes *f/pl*	Einnahmen *f/pl*	receipts *pl*, revenue
recettes *f/pl* publicitaires	Werbeeinnahmen *f/pl*	advertising revenues *pl*
recherche *f*	Nachforschung *f*, Untersuchung *f*	examination, inquiry, research, survey, test
recherche *f* auprès des consommateurs *m/pl*	Verbraucheranalyse *f*, Verbraucherforschung *f*	consumer research
recherche *f* de l'effet *m*, recherche *f* de l'épate *m*	Effekthascherei *f*	claptrap, sensationalism
recherche *f* documentaire	Forschungsarbeit *f*	desk research
recherche *f* du marché *m*	Marktforschung *f*	field investigation, market analysis, market research
recherche *f* économique	Wirtschaftsforschung *f*	commercial research
recherche *f* par lettre *f*	briefliche Befragung *f*	mail research, mail survey, mail research, mail survey
recherche *f* sociale	Sozialforschung *f*	social research
recherches *f/pl*	Forschung *f*	research
recherches *f/pl* relatives à la publicité *f*	Werbeforschung *f*	advertising research
recherches *f/pl* relatives à l'audience *f*	Höreranalyse *f*	audience measurement, listenership research
recherches *f/pl* relatives aux téléspectateurs *m/pl*	Fernsehforschung *f*	television audience research
récit *m*	Pressebericht *m*	press report, write-up *am*
récit *m* d'un témoin *m* oculaire	Augenzeugenbericht *m*	eyewitness account
réclamation *f*	Beanstandung *f*, Mängelrüge *f*, Reklamation *f*	complaint
réclame *f*	Werbung *f*	advertising, publicity
réclame *f* monstre *m*	Riesenreklame *f*	gigantic publicity
récolte *f* des informations *f/pl*	Beschaffung *f* von Informationen *f/pl*	gathering of information
recommandation *f*	Empfehlung *f*	recommendation

recomposer	umsetzen *typog*	to reset
recomposition *f*	Neusatz *m*	re-setting
reconnaissance *f*	Anerkennung *f*	recognition
reconnaître	anerkennen	to recognise
reconnu	anerkannt	accredited, recognised
recouvrement *m*	Überlappung *f*	overlapping
recouvrement *m* des frais *m/pl*	Unkostendeckung *f*	recovery of expenses *pl*
recouvrir	abdecken, überlappen	to block out, to cover, to mask out, to overlap
récrire	neu schreiben, umarbeiten	to reshape, to rewrite
rectangle *m*	Rechteck *n*, Viereck *n*	rectangle, rightangle
rectangulaire	rechteckig	rectangular
rectificatif *m*, rectification *f*	Berichtigung *f*	corrigendum, rectification
rectifier les approches *f/pl*	ausgleichen (Zeile)	to space evenly
recto	rechte Seite *f*	odd page, right-hand page
reçu	Lieferschein *m*	delivery note, receipt
recueil *m* de citations *f/pl*	Zitatensammlung *f*	commonplace-book
recueil *m* de locutions *f/pl*	Sammlung *f* von Redewendungen *f/pl*	phrase-book
recueil *m* en un volume *m*	Sammelband *m*	collected volume, miscellany
recueillement *m* de faits *m/pl*	Faktensammlung *f*	fact-gathering
récupération *f*	Wiedererlangung *f*	recovery
rédacteur *m*	Schriftleiter *m*, Redakteur *m*	editor
rédacteur *m* adjoint	stellvertretender Redakteur *m*	sub-editor
rédacteur *m* au desk *m* rédacteur *m* aux informations *f/pl*	Nachrichtenredakteur *m*	desk editor, news editor
rédacteur *m* de la rubrique *f* culturelle	Kulturredakteur *m*	cultural editor
rédacteur *m* de la rubrique *f* économique	Wirtschaftsredakteur *m*	economic editor
rédacteur *m* de nuit *f*	Nachtredakteur *m*	night editor
rédacteur *m* des illustrations *f/pl*	Bildredakteur *m*	pictures *pl* editor
rédacteur *m* des sports *m/pl*	Sportredakteur *m*	sports *pl* editor
rédacteur *m* du feuilleton *m*	Feuilletonredakteur *m*	literary editor
rédacteur *m* en chef *m*	Chefredakteur *m*, Hauptschriftleiter *m*	editor-in-chief
rédacteur *m* en chef *m* adjoint	stellvertretender Chefredakteur *m*	associate editor
rédacteur *m* gérant	geschäftsführender Redakteur *m*, Redaktionsdirektor *m*	managing editor
rédacteur *m* local	Lokalredakteur *m*	city editor, local editor
rédacteur *m* parlementaire	Parlamentsjournalist *m*	lobby journalist
rédacteur *m* politique	politischer Redakteur *m*	political editor
rédacteur *m* publicitaire	Texter *m*, Werbetexter *m*	copy-writer, script-writer
rédacteur *m* responsable	verantwortlicher Redakteur *m*	responsible editor
rédacteur-concepteur *m*	Texter *m*	copy-writer, script-writer
rédaction *f*	Abfassung *f*, redaktionelle Bearbeitung *f*, Schriftleitung *f*	composition, editorial department, editorial staff, editorialising
rédaction *f* complète	Vollredaktion *f*	complete editorial staff
rédaction *f* d'annonces *f/pl*	Werbetextabfassung *f*	advertising copywriting
rédaction *f*	Redaktion *f*	editorial board, editorial office, editorial staff
redevance *f*	Autorentantieme *f*, Umsatzhonorar *n*	royalties *pl*

rédiger	redigieren	to edit
rédiger à nouveau	umschreiben (neu fassen)	rewriting
rédiger des textes *m/pl*	texten	to copy-write
réduction *f*	Nachlaß *m*, Verkleinerung *f*	discount, rebate, reduction
réduction *f* de faveur *f*	Sonderrabatt *m*	extra discount, special discount
réduction *f* de prix *m*	Preisherabsetzung *f*	mark down, shrinking of prices *pl*
réduction *f* de prix *m* signalé sur le conditionnement *m* ou l'étiquette *f*	Reduzierung *f* des Preises *m* gegenüber dem auf Packung *f* oder Etikett *f* angegebenen	off-label deal
réduction *f* de rabais *m*	Rabattreduzierung *f*	discount reduction
réduction *f* d'un mandat *m*	Auftragskürzung *f*	reduction of an order
réduction *f* du nombre *m* d'affiches *f/pl* commandées	Kürzung *f* der Stellenzahl *f*	reduction of the number of the ordered sites *pl*
réduction *f* du prix *m* de vente *f*	Verkaufspreisermäßigung *f*	deal
réduire	verkleinern	to minimise, to reduce
réduire au silence *m*	zum Schweigen *n* bringen	to silence
réduire au strict minimum *m*	in großen Zügen *m/pl* darstellen	to skeletonize
réduire en proportion *f*	proportional verkleinern	to scale down
refaçon *m* d'un film *m*	Wiederverfilmung *f*	remake
refaçonner	neu verfilmen	to remake
réfection *f*	Neufassung *f*	new formulation, remaking
référence *f* de composition *f*	Satzmuster *n*	composition pattern
référence *f* de source *f*	Quellenangabe *f*	credit
réflecteur *m*	Reflektor *m*	reflector
refondre	umschmelzen	to recast
refrain *m* radiophonique	musikalische Werbung *f*	jingle
refus *m*	Ablehnung *f*, Verweigerung *f*	refusal, rejection
refus *m* de commande *f*	Auftragsablehnung *f*	refusal of an order
refus *m* d'un manuscrit *m*	Ablehnung *f* eines Manuskripts *n*	spike
regard *m* en coulisses *f/pl*	Blick *m* hinter die Kulissen *f/pl*	inside story
régie *f* d'affichage *m*	Plakatpachtung *f*	site leasing
régie *f* d'annonces *f/pl*	Anzeigenregie *f*	advertising management, sole advertising representative
régie *f* de publicité *f*	Anzeigenverwaltung *f*	advertisement administration
région *f*	Gebiet *n*	geographical sector
région *f* d'émission *f* radiophonique	Sendebereich *m*	listening area
région *f* de vente *f*	Verkaufsbezirk *m*	sales *pl* territory
région *f* du représentant *m*	Vertreterbezirk *m*	agent's territory
régisseur *m*	Anzeigenpächter *m*, Werbeflächenpächter *m*, Werbepächter *m*	advertising franchise operator, advertising operator
registre *m*	Register *n*	index, register
registre *m* avec onglets *m/pl* -guides *m/pl*	Daumenregister *n*	thumb-index
registre *m* défectueux	fehlerhaftes Register *n*	out-of-register
registre *m* de l'office *m* de la propriété *f* industrielle	Warenzeichenrolle *f*	trademark's register
registre *m* par matières *f/pl*	Sachregister *n*	subject index, table of contents *pl*

réglage *m*	Werbeeinblendung *f*	chain break, spot announcement
règle *f*	Lineal *n*	ruler
règle *f* à calculer	Rechenschieber *m*	slide rule
règle *f* à dessiner	Reißschiene *f*	drawing rule
règle *f* de conduite *f*	Richtschnur *f*	guidance, rule of conduct
règle *f* graduée	Maßstab *m*	scale, yardstick
règlement *m*	Bezahlung *f*	payment
règlement *m* comptant	Barzahlung *f*	spot cash
réglementation *f*	Regelung *f*	regulation
réglementation *f* de la publicité *f*	Werberegelung *f*	regulation of advertising
réglementation *f* de la terminologie *f*	Sprachregelung *f*	regulation of terminology
réglementations *f/pl* publicitaires	Werbebestimmungen *f/pl*	advertising regulations *pl*
règles *f/pl* de travail *m*	Arbeitsgrundsätze *m/pl*	rules *pl* of work
réglette *f*	Reglette *f*	clump, lead, line-space, reglet
réglette *f* numerotée	Nummernreglette *f*	galley-slug
réglure *f*	Querlinie *f*	cross rule
régression *f* des tirages *m/pl*	Auflagenrückgang *m*	decline in circulation
regroupement *m*	Zusammenschluß *m*	amalgamation, combination
régulateur *m* de marges *f/pl*	Anlegeapparat *m*	feeder, margin stop
réhabilitation *f*	Ehrenrettung *f*	white wash
réimpression *f*	Nachdruck *m/typog,* Neudruck *m,* Wiederabdruck *m*	new edition, new impression, reprint
réimpression *f* fac-similée	Faksimiledruck *m*	facsimile reprint
ré-insertion *f*	Ersatzanzeige *f,* Wiederholungsanzeige *f*	make-good, repeat ad, replacement ad, rerun, run-it-again
réitération *f*	ständige Wiederholung *f*	reiteration
rejet *m*	Ablehnung *f*	rejection
rejeu *m*	Rückspiel *n*	play back
relance *f*	Nachfaßbrief *m*	follow-up letter
relatif à	betreffend	reference, referring to
relation *f*	Beziehung *f*	relation
relations *f/pl* des lecteurs *m/pl* avec leur journal *m*	Leserblattbindung *f*	connexion of readers *pl* with their paper, reader-magazine-relationship
relations *f/pl* extérieures	Öffentlichkeitsarbeit *f,* Vertrauenswerbung *f*	public relations *pl*, publicity
relations *f/pl* humaines	zwischenmenschliche Beziehungen *f/pl*	human relations *pl*
relations *f/pl* internes	innerbetriebliche Beziehungen *f/pl*	intraflow
relations *f/pl* publiques	Meinungspflege *f,* Öffentlichkeitsarbeit *f,* public relations *f/pl,* Vertrauenswerbung *f,* Zielpublizistik *f*	public relations *pl*, publicity
relative à la pratique *f*	praxisbezogen	related to practise
relayer	übertragen	to get across, to relay
relevé *m*	Aufstellung *f*	list
relier par collage *m*	lumbecken	perfect-bind by employing the Lumbeck method, to lumbeck

relieur *m*	Buchbinder *m*	bookbinder
reliure *f*	Bucheinband *m*, Einband *m*	binding, cover
reliure *f* cartonnée	Pappband *m*	stiff paper binding
reliure *f* en demi-cuir *m*	Halblederband *m*	half binding
reliure *f* en matière *f* plastique	Plastikheftung *f*	plastic binding
reliure *f* peau *f* pleine	Lederband *m*	leather binding
reliure *f* spirale	Spiralheftung *f*	spiral stitching
remanier	neu schreiben, neu umbrechen, umarbeiten, überarbeiten	to overrun, to overrun lines *pl*, to reshape, to retouch, to revise, to rewrite
remanier un texte *m*	Text *m* umarbeiten	to rewrite a text
remboursement *m*	Rückvergütung *f*	rebate, refund
remboursement *m* des frais *m/pl*	Spesenvergütung *f*	expense account
remettre une annonce *f*	Inserat *n* aufgeben	to order an advertisement
remise *f*	Preisermäßigung *f*, Rabatt *m*	discount, price abatement, rebate
remise *f* à titre *m* de confrère *m*	Kollegenrabatt *m*	discount granted to colleagues *pl*
remise *f* de copie *f*	Redaktionsschluß *m*	closing date, closing down, copy deadline, forms *pl* close
remise *f* de quantité *f*	Mengenrabatt *m*	bulk rate *brit*, frequency discount, quantity discount, space discount, volume discount
remise *f* des ordres *m/pl*	Rücktrittsrecht *n*	cancellation right
remise *f* spéciale	Sonderrabatt *m*	extra discount, special discount
remonter une nouvelle *f*	eine Nachricht *f* hochspielen	to play up an information, to puff up an information
remorque *f*	Anhänger *m* (Beiwagen *m*)	trailer
remorque *f* du tramway *m*	Straßenbahnanhänger *m*	tram trailer
remplacement *m*	Erneuerung *f*	renewal
remplissage *m*	Füller *m*	cushion, fill-up, filler, quadder
rémunération *f*	Vergütung *f*	bonus, fee
rémunération *f* à la ligne *f*	Zeilenhonorar *n*	penny-a-line payment, space fee *am*
rendement *m*	Leistung *f*	performance
rendement *m* publicitaire	Werbeerfolg *m*, Werbeleistung *f*	advertising performance, advertising result
rendez-vous *m*	Treffpunkt *m*	meeting-place
rendre	wiedergeben	to render, to reproduce
rendus *pl*	Remittenden *f/pl*	overrun, remainders *pl*, returns *pl*
renfoncement *m*	Einzug *m/typog m*, Zeileneinzug *m*	indent, indention
renfoncer	einrücken (einziehen)	to indent
renforcer	verstärken	to intensify
renouvellement *m*	Erneuerung *f*	renewal
renouvellement *m* de l'affiche *f*	Plakatauswechslung *f*	change of the bill
renouvellement *m* d'un ordre *m*	Auftragserneuerung *f*	repeating of an order
renseignements *m/pl*	Informationen *f/pl*	inquiries *pl*
renseignements *m/pl* privés	Nachricht *f* aus erster Hand *f*	inside information
renseignements *m/pl* techniques	technische Daten *m/pl*	mechanical data *pl*
rentabilité *f*	Wirtschaftlichkeit *f*	profitability
rentrer	einrücken (einziehen)	to indent
renversé	kopfstehend	inverted
renverser	umkehren	to reverse, to turn round

renvoi *m* à l'expéditeur *m*	Rücksendung *f*	return consignment
renvoi *m* de marge *f*	Auslassungszeichen *n*	caret mark
répandre	verbreiten	to disseminate
répartition *f*	Aufschlüsselung *f*, Aufteilung *f*	breakdown, classification
répartition *f* des charges *f/pl,* répartition *f* des coûts *m/pl*	Kostenverteilung *f*	account distribution, allocation
répartition *f* des tirages *m/pl*	Auflagenverteilung	circulation breakdown
répartition *f* du budget *m*	Streuplan *m,* Etatverteilung *f*	budget distribution, media schedule, space schedule, spread-over
repatiner	umredigieren	to revise
repère *m*	Passer *m*	register
repérer	einpassen	to register
répertoire *m*	Sachregister *n*	subject index, table of contents *pl*
répertoire *m* de fournisseurs *m/pl*	Bezugsquellenverzeichnis *n*	directory of suppliers *pl*, list of suppliers *pl*
répertoire *m* des annonceurs *m/pl*	Inserentenverzeichnis *n*	list of advertisers *pl*
répertoire *m* encoché	Griffregister *n*	thumb-index
répétition *f*	Wiederholung *f*	duplication, repetition
répétition *f* d'une série *f* d'annonces *f/pl*	Wiederholung *f* einer Anzeigenserie *f*	rotation
repiquage *m*	Aufdruck *m*, Impressum *n*, Mehrdruck *m*, Pflichteindruck *m*	colophon, imprint, overprint
repiquage *m* d'un nom *m* commercial sur l'enveloppe *f*	Firmeneindruck *m* auf Briefumschlag *m*	corner card
repiquer sur	eindrucken	to print on
réplique *f*	Gegenantwort *f*	replication
répondant *m*	Befragter *m*	interviewee, respondent
réponse *f*	Werbeantwort *f*	reply mail, return
réponse *f* payée	Rückporto *n*	return postage
réponse *f* télégraphique	telegrafische Antwort *f*	reply by wire
report *m*	Umdruck *m*	transfer
report *m* documentaire	Bildbericht *m*	documentary report
report *m* du trou *m* de serrure *f*	Schlüssellochbericht *m*	keyhole report
report *m* expressif	Stimmungsbericht *m*	background story
reportage *m*	Pressebericht *m*, Reportage *f*	feature article, press report, report, reporting, running commentary, write-up *am*
reportage *m* de séance *f*	Sitzungsbericht *m*	report of a meeting
reportage *m* en extérieur	Außenbericht *m*	outside broadcast
reportage *m* filmé	Filmbericht *m*	screen record
reportage *m* parlé	Hörbericht *m*	radio report
reportage *m* photographique	Fotoreportage *f*	photographic report, picture story
reportage *m* publicitaire	feuilletonistische Anzeige *f*	advertisement in feuilleton style, advertisement in short story style, advertisement in feuilleton style, advertisement in short story style
reportage *m* sensationnel	Knüller *m*	scoop

reporter	nichtgebrachte Anzeige f, verschieben	hold over, to defer, to postpone, to shift
reporter m	Reporter m	newshawk, newshound, reporter
reporter m à la tâche f	Reporter m für besondere Aufgaben f/pl	assignment-man
reporter m itinérant	reisender Berichterstatter m	roving reporter
reporter-dessinateur m	Pressezeichner m	cartoonist
reporter-photographe m	Bildreporter m	camera-man, press photographer
reporteur m	Umdruckapparat m	offset repro machine
reporteur m d'images f/pl	Bildberichterstatter m	reporter-cameraman
repoussage m	gezeichnete Schrift f, Prägung f, Schriftzeichnen n	embossing, hand lettering
repousser	prägen	to emboss, to stamp
représentant m	Repräsentant m, Vertreter m	agent, representative
représentant m de commerce m	Handelsvertreter m	sales pl representative
représentant m de radiodiffusion f publicitaire	Werbefunkvertreter m	station rep
représentant m d'une agence f de publicité f	Agenturvertreter m	agency representative
représentant m publicitaire	Anzeigenvertreter m	advertisement representative, advertising sales pl executive
représentation f	Darstellung f, Vertretung f	representation
représentation f graphique	grafische Darstellung f	chart, graphic, graphic chart, graphical representation
représenter	darstellen, vertreten	to represent
réprimande f	Hering m (Tadel m)	reprimand, reproof
reprise f	Wiederaufführung f	reprise
reproduction f	Reproduktion f, Wiedergabe f	copy print, reproduction
reproduction f électro-mécanique	elektromechanische Reproduktion f	electromechanical reproduction
reproduction f panchromatique	panchromatische Reproduktion f	panchromatic reproduction
reproduction f souhaitée	Nachdruck m erbeten	please copy
reproduire	vervielfältigen	to duplicate, to mimeograph
reprolithographe m	Reprolithograf m	reprolithographer
réputation f	Ansehen n, Ruf m	reputation
réseau m	Raster m, Sendernetz n, Stellennetz n, Werbeflächengruppe f	Ben Day, holding of outdoor advertising sites pl, network, poster showing, screen
réseau m de vente f	Verkaufsapparat m	sales pl organisation
réseau m d'émetteurs m/pl	Rundfunknetz n	web
réseau m télégraphique	Fernschreibnetz n	telegraphic network
réseau m téléphonique	Fernsprechnetz n	telephone network
réservation f	Reservierung f	booking, reservation
réservation f de temps m d'antenne f	Werbezeitenreservierung f	to clear time
réserve f	Schriftlager n	type stock
réserve f pour la publicité f	Werbereserve f	advertising reserve
réserver	reservieren	to reserve
résiliation f	Annullierung f, Auflösung f	cancellation, dissolution
résiliation f de l'abonnement m	Abonnementskündigung f	subscription stop
résine f synthétique	Kunstharz n	synthetic resin
résistance f à la rupture f	Reißfestigkeit f	tensile strength
résistance f aux intempéries f/pl	Wetterbeständigkeit f	weather resistance
résistance f de l'acheteur m	Kaufhemmung f	buyer's resistance

résistant aux acides *m/pl*	säurefest	acid resisting
résonance *f*	Resonanz *f*	echo, empathy
responsabilité *f* pour dommages *m/pl*	Haftung *f* für Schäden *m/pl*	liability for damages *pl*
responsabilité *f* pour insuffisances *f/pl*	Haftung *f* für Mängel *m/pl*	liability for insufficiencies *pl*
responsabilité *f* quant au délai *m*	Terminhaftung *f*	term-liability
responsable des relations *pl* avec le public *m*	PR-Bearbeiter *m*	public relations *pl* officer
resserrer	kompresser setzen	to close up, to set more solid
ressort *m*	Ressort *n*	beat, department
ressort *m* d'activité *f*	Arbeitsgebiet *n*	field of activities *pl*
reste *m* de papier *m*	Abfall *m*	offcut
restriction *f*	Beschränkung *f*	limitation, restriction
restriction *f* à la concurrence *f*	Wettbewerbsbeschränkung *f*	reduction of competition
restrictions *f/pl* dans le temps *m*	zeitliche Beschränkungen *f/pl*	time limitations *pl*
restrictions *f/pl* de la publicité *f*	Werbebeschränkungen *f/pl*	advertising limitations *pl*, advertising restrictions *pl*
restrictions *f/pl* légales	gesetzliche Beschränkungen *f/pl*	legal restrictions *pl*
résultat *m* de la campagne *f* publicitaire	Streuerfolg *m*	advertising result
résultat *m* de la publicité *f*	Werberesultat *n*	results *pl* of advertising
résultat *m* d'enquête *f*	Umfrageergebnis *n*	survey data
résultats *m/pl* des ventes *f/pl*	Verkaufserfolg *m*	sales *pl* impact
résumé *m*	Abriß *m*, Auszug *m*, Inhaltsangabe *f*, Übersicht *f*, Zusammenfassung *f*	excerpt, extract, recapitulation, summary, survey, synopsis
résumé *m* d'instructions *f/pl*	Zusammenfassung *f* von Unterlagen *f/pl*	briefing
résumer	zusammenfassen	to accumulate, to cumulate, to recapitulate, to summarize
retard *m*	Verzögerung *f*, zeitlicher Unterschied *m*	time-lag
retard *m* dans l'exécution *f* des commandes *f/pl*	Auftragsrückstand *m*	back orders *pl*, delay in the execution of orders *pl*
retard *m* de paiement *m*	Zahlungsverzug *m*	delay of payment
retardement *m*	Zeitverzögerung *f*	time lag
retenir	zurückstellen	to withhold
retenir une édition *f*	die Ausgabe *f* verzögern	to hold an edition
retentissement *m*	Widerhall *m*	impact, response
retenue *f* des emplacements *m/pl*	Anzeigendisposition *f*	placing orders *pl* for space
retiration *f*	Widerdruck *m*	backing up, perfecting, second printing, verso printing
retouchage *m*	Retuschierung *f*	retouching
retouche *f*	Nachbesserung *f*, Retusche *f*	retouching, touching-up
retouche *f* à l'outil *m*	Klischeekorrektur *f*	hand tooling
retouche *f* complète	Vollretusche *f*	full retouching
retouche *f* des couleurs *f/pl*	Farbretusche *f*	colour retouching, dye transfer
retouche *f* sur négatif *m*	Negativretusche *f*	negative retouching
retoucher	retuschieren, überarbeiten	to artist, to retouch, to revise
retoucher à l'outil *m*	nacharbeiten mit der Hand *f*	hand tooling
retoucheur *m*	Retuscheur *m*	retoucher
retour *m*	Rücklieferung *f*	sales *pl* return
retour *m* de coupons *m/pl*	Kuponrücklauf *m*	response
retour *m* en arrière	Rückblende *f*	flash-back

retourner	kontern, umkehren	to reverse, to turn round
retournez la lettre f!	Buchstaben m wenden!	invert letter!
retraduire	zurückübersetzen	to retranslate
retrait m	Schrumpfung f	shrinkage
rétrécir	eingehen (stereotyp.), einlaufen (stereotyp.)	to shrink
rétroactif	rückwirkend	retro-active
rétroaction f	Rückkopplung f, Rückwirkung f	feed-back
réunion f	Veranstaltung f, Versammlung f	meeting, performance
réunion f de table f ronde	Konferenz f am runden Tisch m	round-table meeting
réunion f de travail m	Kursus m, Lehrgang m	workshop
réunion f paritaire	Gespräch n am runden Tisch, Gruppendiskussion f, Konferenz f am runden Tisch m	round-table conference, round-table meeting, round-table discussion
révélateur m	Entwickler m	developer
révélation f	Enthüllung f	disclosure
révéler	enthüllen	to dig out
revendeur m	Einzelhändler m, Wiederverkäufer m	dealer, retailer
revendre	weiterverkaufen	to resell
revenu m	Einkommen n, Erträge m/pl	income, revenue
revenus m/pl d'annonces f/pl	Anzeigeneinnahmen f/pl	ad revenues pl
reviser, revoir	durchsehen, verbessern	to revise
revue f	Blatt n (Zeitung f), Magazin n, Publikumszeitschrift f, Zeitschrift f	consumer publication, journal, magazine, paper, periodical, review
revue f à deux sous m/pl	Groschenheft n	pulp magazine
revue f affermée	Pachtblatt n	leased paper, tied paper
revue f de cinéma m	Filmzeitschrift f	film magazine
revue f de concierge f	Groschenheft n	pulp magazine
revue f de la presse f	Presserundschau f	press review
revue f de publicité f	Werbefachzeitschrift f	advertising magazine
revue f d'entreprise	Hauszeitschrift f	company publication, house journal, house organ, staff magazine
revue f destinée à être recueillie	Zeitschrift f mit Sammelcharakter m	partwork
revue f d'intérêt m général	Familienblatt n	family paper, magazine of general interest
revue f féminine	Frauenblatt n, Frauenzeitschrift f	women's pl magazine
revue f hebdomadaire	Wochenzeitschrift f	weekly magazine, weekly paper
revue f juridique	juristische Zeitschrift f	law review
revue f mensuelle	Monatsschrift f	monthly paper
revue f politique	politische Zeitschrift f	political periodical
revue f pour industriels m/pl	Industrieblatt n	industrial magazine, technical magazine
revue f pour les passagers m/pl	Fluglinienzeitschrift f	inflight magazine
revue f professionnelle	Berufszeitschrift f, Fachzeitschrift f	professional magazine
revue f spécialisée	Zielgruppenzeitschrift f	specialised magazine
revue f syndicale	Gewerkschaftszeitung f	trade-union paper
revue f technique	technische Zeitschrift f	technical publication
revue f trimestrielle	Vierteljahreszeitschrift f	quarterly
revue-programme m de la radio f et de la télévision f	Rundfunk- und Fernseh-Programmzeitschrift f	radio and television program paper

rez-de-chausée *m*	unter dem Strich *m*	in the feuilleton
Rheinländer (voir appendice)	Rheinländer *f* (siehe Anhang)	Rheinländer (see appendix)
rideau *m* réclame *f*	Vorhangwerbung *f*	theatre curtain advertising
risque *m* de vente *f*	Verkaufsrisiko *n*	sales *pl* risk
risques *m/pl* de publicité *f*	Werberisiko *n*	risks *pl* of advertising
ristourne *f* pour clients *m/pl* habituels	Treuerabatt *m*	patronage discount
ritournelle *f* publicitaire	musikalische Werbung *f*	jingle
rivalités *f/pl* de clocher *m*	Lokalpatriotismus *m*	local patriotism
rodomontade *f*	Großsprecherei *f*	bragging
rognage *m*	Beschnitt *m*	cutting, trimming
rogne *f*	Anschnitt *m*	bleed
rogner	beschneiden, kürzen	to boil down, to compress, to crop, to curtail, to make cuts *pl*, to prune, to shorten, to slash, to trim
roman *m*	Reißer *m*, Roman *m*	fiction, novel, thriller
roman *m* à clé *f*	Schlüsselroman *m*	key-novel
roman *m* à gros effets *m/pl*, roman *m* à sensation *f*	Kolportageroman *m*, Schauerroman *m*, spannende Handlung *f*	penny dreadful, shocker, thriller
roman *m* à suites *f/pl*	Fortsetzungsroman *m*	novel in continuations *pl*, serial story
roman *m* à thèse *f*	Tendenzroman *m*	tendency novel
roman *m* bon marché *m*	Groschenroman *m*	dime novel
roman *m* policier	Detektivroman *m*, Krimi *m*	detective novel, whodunit
roman *m* sensationnel	Schauerroman *m*	shocker, thriller
roman-feuilleton *m*	Fortsetzungsroman *m*, Zeitungsroman *m*	novel in continuations *pl*, serial story
rond	rund	round
rossignol *m*	Ladenhüter *m*	dead article, dormant stock, shelf warmer
rotair *m*	Deckenhänger *m*, Mobile *n*	dangler, mobile
rotatif *m* offset *m*	Rollenoffsetmaschine *f*	rotary offset press
rotative *f* hélio en couleur *f*	Mehrfarben-Druckpresse *f*	multiple colour press
rotative *f* typographique à bobines *f/pl*	Hochdruckrollenrotation *f*	web-fed letterpress rotary machine
rotogravure *f*	Fototiefdruck *m*, Heliogravüre *f*, Kupfertiefdruck *m*, Rakeltiefdruck *m*, Rotationstiefdruck *m*, Tiefdruck *m/typog*	copper gravure, copper-plate printing, intaglio printing, photogravure, rotogravure *am*
rouleau *m* à encrer	Massewalze *f*	composition roller
rouleau *m* de carton *m*	Papprolle *f*	paperboard roll
rouleau *m* d'écriture *f*	Schriftrolle *f*	scroll
rouleau *m* de pellicule *f*	Filmrolle *f*	film reel, film roll
rouleau *m* de sortie *f* ralentisseur *m*	Auslageapparat *m*	delivery apparatus roll
rouleau *m* encreur	Farbwalze *f*	inking-roller
roulement *m* de publicité *f*	umlaufende Streuung *f*	rotation
rouler	fortdrucken	to run on
routage *m*	Drucksachenversand *m*, Sortierung *f*, Zeitungsversand *m*	mailing, sorting

route *f* carossable	Fahrstraße *f*	roadside
ruban *m* adhésif	Klebeband *n*	adhesive tape
ruban *m* de machine *f*	Farbband *n*	typrewriter ribbon
ruban *m* magnétique	Magnetband *n*	magnetic tape, videotape
ruban *m* perforé	Lochstreifen *m*	paper tape, punched tape
rubriquard *m*	Kolumnist *m*	syndicated columnist
rubrique *f*	Rubrik *f*, Überschrift *f*	caption, head, heading, headline, special section
rubrique *f* des loisirs *m/pl*	Rubrik *f* für Mußestunden *f/pl*	leisure time
rubrique *f* sportive	Sportteil *m*	sports *pl* page
rue *f*	Gießbach *m*	gutter
ruelle *f*	weißer Streifen *m* im Satz *m*	river of white
ruse *f* publicitaire	Reklametrick *m*	bluff, stunt, trick
rut *m*	Laufzeit *f*	propagation time, running time, transit time
rythme *m*	Rhythmus *m*	rhythm
rythme *m* d'achat *m*	Einkaufsrhythmus *m*, Verkaufsrhythmus *m*	purchase rhythm
rythme *m* de la production *f*	Produktionsablauf *m*	tempo of production
rythme *m* de parution *f*	Erscheinungsrhythmus *m*	rhythm of publication

S

s'abonner à	abonnieren, beziehen (abonnieren)	to subscribe
sac *m*	Beutel *m*	bag
sac *m* cabas	Einholetasche *f*	shopping basket
sac *m* en papier *m*	Einkaufstasche *f* (aus Papier *n*)	paper bag
sac *m* publicitaire	Papierbeutel *m* mit Werbeaufdruck	shopping-bag
saillie *f*	Geistesblitz *m*, witziger Einfall *m*	brain-wave, flash, gag, idea
saisie *f* des textes *m/pl*	Texterfassung *f*	text generation
saison *f* principale	Hauptsaison *f*	busy season, peak season
salaire *m* fixe	Fixum *n*	fixed salary
salle *f* de lecture *f*	Lesesaal *m*	reading-room
salle *f* de rédaction *f*	Redaktionssaal *m*	editorial hall
salle *f* des journaux *m/pl*	Zeitungslesesaal *m*	news-room
salle *f* d'exposition *f*	Ausstellungsraum *m*	show-room
salon *m* de l'automobile *f*	Autosalon *m*	motor-show
salon *m* du livre *m*	Buchmesse *f*	bookfair
sans engagement *m*	unverbindlich	without obligation
sans étiquette *f* politique	unpolitisch	non-political
sans frais *m/pl*	kostenlos	free of charge
sans partie *f* sonore	tonlos	cold
sans rabais *m*	ohne Rabatt *m*	transient rate
sans rémunération *f*	unentgeltlich	free of charge
sans renfoncement *m*	ohne Einzug *m*	flush
sans-filiste *m*	Rundfunkteilnehmer *m*	radio listener, wireless enthusiast
satellite *m* de télécommunication *f*	Nachrichtensatellit *m*	telecommunication satellite
satinage *m*	Politur *f*	burnishing
satiné *m*	Glätte *f*	smoothness
satiné des deux côtés *m/pl*	beidseitig satiniert	calendered on both sides *pl*
satiné d'un côté *m*	einseitig gestrichenes Papier *n*	one-side coated paper
satiné mat	matt satiniert	English finished (E.F.)

satire *f*	Satire *f*	satire
satirique *m*	Witzblatt *n*	comic journal, funnies *pl*, funny paper, humorous paper
satisfaction *f* des besoins *m/pl*	Bedarfsdeckung *f*	supply covering all requirements *pl*
saturation *f* publicitaire	werbliche Übersättigung *f*, Werbemüdigkeit *f*	oversaturation with advertising
sauf erreur *f* ou omission *f*	Irrtümer *m/pl* und Auslassungen *f/pl* vorbehalten	errors *pl* and omissions *pl* excepted
savoir faire	gewußt, wie	know how
savoir-faire *m*	praktisches Wissen *n*, technisches Spezialwissen *n*	know-how
sceau *m*	Siegel *n*, Stempel *m*	seal, stamp
scénario *m*	Drehbuch *n*, Filmdrehbuch *n*, Filmmanuskript *n*	film script, scenario, script, shooting script
scénariste *m*	Filmmanuskriptverfasser *m*	script-writer
scène *f* de la vie *f* de tous les jours *m/pl*	Szene *f* aus dem täglichen Leben *n*	life story
scène *f* publicitaire	Werbekurzspiel *n*	advertising sketch
scène *f* rétrospective	Rückblende *f*	flash-back
schéma *m*	bildliche Darstellung *f*, Plan *m*, Satzvorlage *f*, Schema *n*	diagram, layout, pattern, plan, schedule, schema
schéma *m* d'emplacement *m* de lignes *f/pl*	Zeilenfall *m*	typographical arrangement
schématisation *f*	Schematisierung *f*	schematizing
Schwabach *m*	Schwabacher Schrift *f*	Schwabacher type
scie *f* à ruban *m*	Bandsäge *f*	band saw
science *f* de la publicité *f*	Werbewissenschaft *f*	advertising science
science *f* du journalisme *m*	Zeitungswissenschaft *f*	science of journalism
science *f* spéciale	Fachwissen *n*	special knowledge
script *m*	Drehbuch *n*, Filmdrehbuch *n*	film script, scenario, script, shooting script
sculpture *f* sur bois *m*	Xylografie *f*	wood-engraving
se désabonner à	sein Abonnement *n* abbestellen	to withdraw a subscription
se fondre	verlaufen (Farben *f/pl*)	to blend, to run (colour)
se joignant au texte *m*	textanschließend	facing matter, following matter, next to reading matter
se passer	sich zutragen	to happen
se référant à	betreffend	reference, referring to
se renfermer dans le silence *m*	sich in Schweigen *n* hüllen	to be wrapped in silence
se retirer	einlaufen (sterotyp.)	to shrink
se tromper en parlant	sich versprechen	to make a slip of the tongue
séance *f*	Sitzung *f*	meeting, session
séance *f* cinématographique	Filmvorstellung *f*	cinema performance
séance *f* de discussion *f*	Forum *n*	forum
séance *f* d'essai *m*	Probesprechen *n*	audition
séance *f* de travail *m*	Arbeitssitzung *f*	research *pl* plans *pl* board meeting
séchage *m*	Trocknung *f*	drying
second titre *m*	Untertitel *m*	cut-in, drop head, sub-title, subheading
seconde épreuve *f*	Zweitabzug *m*	second proof
seconde forme *f*	Widerdruck *m*	backing up, perfecting, second printing, verso printing
seconde revision *f*	Zweitkorrektur *f*	second revised proof

secours *m* de vente *f*	Verkaufsunterstützung *f*	trade support
secret *m* commercial	Geschäftsgeheimnis *n*	trade secret
secret *m* de la rédaction *f*	Redaktionsgeheimnis *n*	editorial secret
secret *m* des chiffres *m*/*pl*	Chiffregeheimnis *n*	box security
secrétaire *m*	Schreibtisch *m*	desk,
secrétaire *f* de plateau *m*	Filmsekretärin *f*	script-girl
sécrétaire *m* de rédaction *f*	Redaktionssekretär *m*	copy reader, sub-editor
sécrétariat *m* de rédaction *f*	Redaktionssekretariat *n*	desk
sécrétariat *m* de rédaction *f* d'une agence *f* de presse *f*	Sekretariat *n* einer Presseagentur *f*	desk
secteur *m*	Ressort *n*	beat, department
secteur *m* de vente *f*	Einzugsgebiet *n*	sales *pl* area, trading area
secteur *m* économique des services *m*/*pl*	Dienstleistungsgewerbe *n*	service rendering trade
secteur *m* géographique	Gebiet *n*	geographical sector
secteur *m* publicitaire	Werbesektor *m*	advertising sector
sectio *m* aurea	goldener Schnitt *m*	medial section, sectio aurea
section *f*	Abteilung *f*, Sparte *f*	branch, department, division, section, subject
section *f* rédactionnelle	redaktioneller Teil *m*	editorial matter, editorial section
section *f* shopping *m*	Rubrik *f* shopping *n*	case shopping
séducteurs *m*/*pl* clandestins	geheime Verführer *m*/*pl*	hidden persuaders *pl*
segment *m* du marché *m*	Marktsegment *n*	market segment
seizième de page *f*	Sechzehntelseite *f*	sixteenth of page
sélection *f*	Auswahl *f*	assessment, choice, selection
sélection *f* des couleurs *f*/*pl*	Farbauszug *m*	colour selection, colour separation
sélection *f* des médias *m*/*pl*	Mediaauswahl *f*, Mediaselektion *f*	media selection
sélectionner	auswählen	to choose, to select
sélectivité *f*	Trennschärfe *f*	selectivity
selon plan *m*	planmäßig	according to plan
selon possibilité *f*	nach Möglichkeit *f*	according to possibility
semaine *f* de propagande *f*	Werbewoche *f*	propaganda week
semaine *f* publicitaire	Reklamewoche *f*	propaganda week
semantique *f*	Wortbedeutungslehre *f*	semantic
semestriel	halbjährlich	half-yearly, semi-annual, twice yearly
semi-hebdomadaire	halbwöchentlich	half-weekly
semi-mensuel	halbmonatlich	half-monthly
séminaire *m*	Symposium *n*	symposium
semi-officiel	halbamtlich, offiziös	officious, semi-official
sens *m* commun	gesunder Menschenverstand *m*	common sense
sens *m* de fabrication *f*	Laufrichtung *f*	fiber direction *am*, fibre direction *brit*
sens *m* des formes *f*/*pl*	Formgefühl *n*	feeling for form
sens *m* littéral	Wortsinn *m*	meaning of a word
sensationnalisme *m*	Sensationsmache *f*	sensationalism
sensationnel	sensationell	sensationel
sensibilité *f* à la lumière *f*	Lichtempfindlichkeit *f*	sensitiveness to light
séparation *f* des colonnes *f*/*pl*	Spaltenlinie *f*	column line, dividing rule
séparation *f* des couleurs *f*/*pl*	Farbauszug *m*	colour selection, colour separation
séparer	ausreißen	to pull out
sépia *f*	Sepiazeichnung *f*	sepia-drawing
séquence *f*	Bildfolge *f* im Film	sequence
série *f*	Satz *m* (Sortiment *n*)	set

série f d'annonces f/pl	Anzeigenserie f	serial advertisements pl
série f d'articles m/pl	Artikelserie f	series pl of articles pl
série f de bandes f/pl dessinées	Comicserie f	continuity strip
série f de caractères m/pl	Schriftgarnitur f	series pl
série f d'émission f	Sendereihe f	serial
série f d'images m/pl	Bilderreihe f	picture series pl
sérigraphie f	Seidengazedruck m, Siebdruck m	screen printing, silk screen printing
serpent m de la mer f	Seeschlange f/fig	mare's nest
serrage m	Schließzeug n	metal quoin
serré	kompreß	close-set, solid set
serre-livres m/pl	Bücherstützen f/pl	book-ends pl
serrer	Zwischenraum m verkleinern	to close up, to depress space, to lock up a form, to quoin
serrer une forme f	Form f schließen	to close the form, to lock up a form
service m additionnel	zusätzliche Dienstleistung f	accessorial service
service m après minuit m	Dienst m nach Mitternacht f	lobster shift
service m après-vente f	Kundendienst m	service
service m bénévole	kostenloser Kundendienst m	gratuitous service
service m commercial	Verkaufsabteilung f	sales pl department
service m complet	kompletter Kundendienst m	full service
service f comptabilité f	Buchhaltungsabteilung f	accounting department
service m de distribution f	Zustelldienst m	delivery service
service m de documentation f	Dokumentationsabteilung f	record office
service m de la rédaction f	Textabteilung f	copy department
service m de la vente f	Vertriebsabteilung f	marketing department, sales pl department
service m de matrices f/pl	Materndienst m	matrix service
service m de presse f	Gratisexemplar n, Pressedienst m, Presseexemplar n	news agency, presentation copy, press service, press-copy, specimen copy
service m de publicité f	Anzeigendienst m, Werbeabteilung f, Werbedienst m	advertisement department brit, advertising department, advertising service, publicity department
service m de routage m	Versandabteilung f	postal department, shipping department
service m de surveillance f de la production f	Terminabteilung f	traffic department
service m des annonces f/pl	Anzeigenabteilung f	advertising department
service m des commandes f/pl	Auftragsabteilung f	order department
service m des expéditions f/pl	Versandabteilung f	postal department, shipping department
service m des nouvelles f/pl	Nachrichtendienst m	news service
service m d'information f	Informationsdienst m	information service
service m extérieur	Außendienst m	field service, outdoor duty
service m matrice	Maternkorrespondenz f	mat service, ready print
service m médias m/pl	Medienabteilung f, Streuabteilung f	media department
service m photocomposition	Fotosetzerei f	phototypesetting room
service m photographique	Bilderdienst m, fotografische Abteilung f	art department, photographic service
service m publicité f	Anzeigenabteilung f	advertising department
service m spécial	Sonderleistung f	extra performance
services m/pl de composition f	Setzerei f	case room, composing room

services *m/pl* de la remise *f* de félicitation *f*	Glückwunschdienst *m*	congratulation service
services *m/pl* de l'empaquetage *m* des présents *m/pl*	Geschenkpackungsdienst *m*	gift parcel services *pl*, parcel distribution service
session *f*	Sitzung *f*	meeting, session
seuil *m* d'efficacité *f*	Reizschwelle *f*	sensation level, threshold of sensation
seuil *m* de la rentabilité *f*	Gewinnschwelle *f*, Rentabilitätsschwelle *f*	break-even point
seuil *m* de prix *m*	Preisschwelle *f*	price threshold
seule annonce *f*	einzige Anzeige *f* einer Seite *f*	sole advertisement
siccatif *m*	Sikkativ *n*, Trockenmittel *n*	siccative
siège *m*	Sitz *m*	seat
sigle *m*	Gütezeichen *n*, Kürzel *n*, Signet *n*	book mark, certification mark, colophon, grammalogue, quality label, seal of approval
signal *m* de direction *f*	Hinweisschild *n*	direction sign, road sign
signature *f*	Signatur *f*, Unterschrift *f*	signature
signature *f* de feuille *f*	Bogensignatur *f*	sheet signature
signe *m*	Zeichen *n*	mark, sign
signe *m* d'alinéa *m*	Absatzzeichen *n*	section mark
signe *m* de correction *f*	Korrekturzeichen *f*	correction mark, proofreader's mark
signe *m* de ponctuation *f*	Satzzeichen *n*	punctuation mark
signe *m* distinctif	Abzeichen *n*	badge
signe *m* d'omission *f*	Auslassungszeichen *n*	caret mark
signe *m* «et» commercial	„und"-Zeichen *n*	ampersand
signer	unterschreiben	to approve of, to sign
signet *m*	Lesezeichen *n*, Verlagssignet *n*	bookmark, publisher's colophon, publisher's imprint, reading mark
signet *m* de livre *m*	Buchzeichen *n*	bookmark, bookplate
signification *f* secondaire	Nebenbedeutung *f*	connotation
silence *m*	Sendepause *f*	dead air, station break
silence *m* complet	Totschweigen *n*	blackout
silhouette *f*	Scherenschnitt *m*, Silhouette *f*	silhouette
silhouette *f* découpée	Ausstanzstück *n*	cut out, die cut
silhouetter	freistellen	to drop out, to silhouette
similarité *f* de présentation *f*	Familienähnlichkeit *f*	family likeness
simili *m*	Netzätzung *f*	halftone, screen etching
simili *m* au carré *m*	rechteckige Vollautotypie *f*	square half-tone
simili *m* avec blanc pur	tiefgeätzte Autotypie *f*	deep-etched half-tone
simili *m* détouré	freistehende Autotypie *f*	blocked-out half-tone, outline half-tone, silhouette halftone
simili *m* manquant de creux *m*	flachgeätzte Autotypie *f*	shallow half-tone
similigravure *f*	Autotypie *f*, Netzätzung *f*	autotype, half-tone block *brit*, half-tone plate *am*, halftone, process engraving, screen etching
similiste *m*	Autotypieätzer *m*	process engraver
simplifier	vereinfachen	to simplify
simulation *f*	Simulierung *f*	simulation
simuler	Türken *m/pl* bauen	to feign, to make pass false for right, to simulate
simultané	gleichzeitig	concurrent

situation *f* du marché *m*	Marktlage *f*	level of market demand, market condition, marketing background
sixième de page *f*	Sechstelseite *f*	sixth of page
sketch *m* publicitaire	Werbesketch *m*	advertising sketch
slogan *m*	Werbeschlagwort *n*	slogan
slogan *m* publicitaire	Werbemotto *n*, Werbeslogan *m*	advertising device, advertising motto, advertising slogan
société *f*	Gesellschaft *f*	society
société *f* affiliée	Tochtergesellschaft *f*	affiliate, affiliated company
société *f* ayant pour objet *m* les actualités *f/pl*	Wochenschaugesellschaft *f*	newsreel company
société *f* d'affermage *m*	Pachtunternehmen *n*, Werbepächter *m*	advertising operator, leaseholder
socle *m*	Grundgestell *n*	mount
socle *m* de bois *m*	Holzunterlage *f*	wooden base
soirée *f* de ménagères *f/pl*	Hausfrauenabend *m*	housewives' party
solde *m* de printemps *m*	Winterschlußverkauf *m*	winter sale
solder	abrechnen, ausverkaufen	to account, to invoice, to sell off
soldes *m/pl*	Restauflage *f*	remainders *pl*
soldes *m/pl* après inventaire *m*	Inventurausverkauf *m*	stock-taking sales *pl*
soleil *m*	gequirlter Satz *m*	broken matter
solide à la lumière *f*	lichtecht	fast to light
solidité *f*	Haltbarkeit *f*	solidity
sollicitation *f* de suffrages *m/pl*	Stimmenfang *m*	canvassing
solliciteur *m*	Akquisiteur *m*	canvasser
solo *m*	Einmannschau *f*	one man show
sommaire *m*	Inhaltsverzeichnis *n*	index, table of contents *pl*
sommaire *m* des frais *m/pl*	Kostenübersicht *f*	guide of cost
sommaire *m* des nouvelles *f/pl*	Nachrichtenübersicht *f*	news summary
sommation *f*	Mahnung *f*	reminder
somme *f*	Betrag *m*, Summe *f*	amount
somme *f* globale	Pauschalsumme *f*	lump sum
sommer	mahnen	to admonish, to remind
son *m* réverbéré	widerhallender Ton *m*	resounding
sondage *m*	Stichprobe *f*	sample
sondage *m* de l'opinion *f* publique	Demoskopie *f*	Gallup poll, opinion poll, opinion research, public opinion analysis
sondage *m* d'opinion *f*	Meinungsforschung *f*	opinion poll, opinion research, public opinion analysis
sonder	erforschen, erkunden	to investigate
sonorisation *f*	Beschallung *f*, Vertonung *f*	musical setting, providing of sound effects *pl*, scoring
sonoriser	beschallen, vertonen	to provide with sound, to voice-over
sorte *f*	Sorte *f*	brand, sort
sorte *f* de papier *m*	Papiersorte *f*	kind of paper, paper type
sortes *f/pl* de composition *f*	Satzarten *f/pl*	kinds *pl* of composition
sortie *f*	Erscheinen *n*	appearance
sortie *f* des feuilles *f/pl*	Ausleger *m* (Bogenfänger)	sheet-delivery
sortir	erscheinen, herausgeben	to appear, to bring out, to come out, to issue, to publish
sortir de la ligne *f*	umbrechen	to break the line, to make up
souder	löten, schweißen	to solder

souligner	hervorheben, unterstreichen	to accentuate, to emphasize, to feature, to highlight, to underline
soulignure *f*	Unterstreichung *f*	underlining
soumission *f*	Lieferungsangebot *n*	tender
soupoudrer	bestäuben	to bronze
source *f*	Quelle *f*	source
source *f* **d'adresses** *f/pl*	Adressenquelle *f*	address source
source *f* **d'erreurs** *f/pl*	Fehlerquelle *f*	source of error
source *f* **d'information** *f*	Informationsquelle *f*, Nachrichtenquelle *f*	source of information, stock of information
sous bande *f*	unter Kreuzband *n*	by bookpost
sous le texte *m*	textanschließend	facing matter, following matter, next to reading matter
sous presse *f*	Druck *m*, im	in the press
souscopier	unterkopieren	to underprint
souscripteur *m*	Abonnent *m*	subscriber
souscription *f* **à un abonnement** *m*	Zeitungsbestellung *f*	subscription to a journal
souscrire à	unterschreiben	to approve of, to sign
sous-estimation *f*	Unterbewertung *f*, Untertreibung *f*	understatement
sous-exposition *f*	Unterbelichtung *f*	underexposure
sous-graver	unterätzen	to undercut
sous-louer	untervermieten	to sublet
sous-main *m*	Schreibunterlage *f*	desk pad
sous-titre *m*	Untertitel *m*, Zwischentitel *m*	caption, cut-in, drop head, sub-title, subheading
souvenir *m* **aidé**	Gedächtnisstütze *f*	aided recall
souvenir *m* **de moyens** *m/pl* **publicitaires**	Werbemittelerinnerung *f*	advertising media recall
souvenir *m* **laissé**	Erinnerungswert *m*	memory value, remembrance value, reminder value
souvenir *m* **spontané**	spontane Erinnerung *f*	pure recall, spontaneous remembrance
speaker *m*	Ansager *m*, Rundfunksprecher *m*	announcer, broadcaster, compère, emcee, radio announcer, radio communicator *am*
speakerine *f*	Ansagerin *f*, Bildschirmdame *f*	female announcer
spécialiste *m*	Fachmann *m*	expert, specialist
spécialiste *m* **de la publicité** *f*	Werbefachmann *m*	adman, advertising expert, advertising man
spécialiste *m* **de la recherche** *f*	Ermittler *m*	research worker, researcher
spécialiste *m* **produit** *m*	Markenbetreuer *m*, Produktmanager *m*	brand manager, product manager
spécialistes *m/pl* **de publicité** *f*	Werbespezialisten *m/pl*	hot shops *pl*
spécimen *m*	Einzelnummer *f*, Freiexemplar *n*, Muster *n*, Probe *f*	complimentary copy, free copy, pattern, sample, single copy, specimen, specimen copy
spécimen *m* **de caractères** *m/pl*	Schriftmuster *n*	type specimen
spécimen *m* **de texte** *m*	Leseprobe *f*	specimen
spectacles *m/pl*	Unterhaltungen *f/pl*	entertainments *pl*
spectateur *m*	Filmbesucher *m*, Kinobesucher *m*, Zuschauer *m*	film-goer, viewer *m*
spectatrice *f*	Zuschauerin *f*	viewer *f*

sphère *f*	Kugel *f*	bullet, sphere
sphère *f* d'action *f*	Wirkungsbereich *m*	sphere of action
sphère *f* d'affectivité *f*	Gefühlssphäre *f*	emotional atmosphere
sphère *f* d'influence *f*	Einflußgebiet *n*	sphere of influence
sphère *f* d'intérêts *m/pl*	Interessenbereich *m*	interest pattern, sphere of interests *pl*
split-run *m* test *m*	Split-Run-Test *n*	split-run test
spot *m*	Fernsehspot *m*, Werbespot *m*	announcement, broadcast announcement, commercial, spot, spot announcement
spot *m* court	kurzer Werbefilm *m*, Kurzfilm *m*	quickie
spot *m* en forme *f* d'affiche *f*	Fernsehwerbung *f* in Plakatform *f*	billboard commercial
spots *m/pl* dans le voisinage *m* immédiat d'une émission *f* spécifique	Werbespot *pl* in unmittelbarer Nachbarschaft *f* einer besonderen Sendung *f*	adjacencies *pl*
stade *m*	Stadion *n*	stadium
stagiaire *m*	Auszubildender *m*, Volontär *m*	probationer, trainee
stagnation *f* des tirages *m/pl*	Auflagenstillstand *m*	circulation dullness
stagnation *f* des ventes *f/pl*	Absatzstockung *f*	standstill in market
stand *m*	Stand *m*, Zeitungsstand *m*	kiosk *brit*, newsstall, newsstand *am*, stand
stand *m* de foire *f*	Messestand *m*	exhibition stand
stand *m* de la presse *f*	Pressestand *m*	press-box
stand *m* d'exposition *f*	Ausstellungsstand *m*	exhibition stand
standard *m*	Norm *f*	standard
standard *m* de vie *f*	Lebensstandard *m*	economic status, living standard
standardisation *f*	Normung *f*, Standardisierung *f*, Typisierung *f*	standardization
station *f* d'émission *f*	Sendeanstalt *f*	broadcasting station
station *f* de radiodiffusion *f*	Radiostation *f*, Rundfunkstation *f*	broadcasting station
station *f* de télévision *f*	Fernsehanstalt *f*, Fernsehsender *m*	television station
station *f* pirate *m*	Piratensender *m*	pirate station
station *f* privée	Privatsender *m*	private station
stationnement *m*	Standort *m*	location
station-radio *f*	Sender *m*	broadcaster, station
station-radio *f* de l'étranger *m*	Auslandssender *m*	foreign station
statisticien *m*	Statistiker *m*	statistician
statistique *f*	Statistik *f*	statistics *pl*
statistiques *f/pl* de publicité *f*	Werbestatistik *f*	advertising statistics *pl*
stencil *m*	Matrize *f*, Schablone *f*	cut out, jig, matrix, mould, pattern, stencil
sténo *m* de presse *f*	Pressestenograf *m*	press stenographer
sténographe *m*	Stenograf *m*	shorthand writer
sténographe *m* parlementaire	Parlamentsstenograf *m*	parliament reporter
sténographie *f*	Kurzschrift *f*	shorthand
stéréo *m*	Stereo *n*	electro *am*, electro-type, stereo, stereotype
stéréo *m* cintré	Rundstereo *n*	curved stereo
stéréo-nickel *m*	Nickelgalvano *n*	nickel electro, nickel-faced stereo
stéréophonie *f*	räumliches Hören *n*, Raumton *m*	stereophony
stéréotypage *m*	Plattendruck *m*	stereotype
stéréotypeur *m*	Stereotypeur *m*	plate maker, stereotyper
stéréotypie *f*	Stereotypie *f*	stereotyping
stimulation *f*	Reiz *m*	stimulus
stimulation *f* de la demande *f*	Bedarfsweckung *f*	demand stimulation

stipulation *f*	Abrede *f*, Klausel *f*, Vereinbarung *f*	agreement, stipulation
stipuler	ausbedingen, vereinbaren	to agree, to stipulate
stock *m*	Lagerbestand *m*	stock
stock *m* restant	Restbestand *m*	stock remainder
store *m*	Werbeschild *n* am Verdeck *m*	awning
storyboard *m*	Bild-Drehbuch *n*	storyboard
stratégie *f* de distribution *f*	Absatzstrategie *f*	marketing strategy
stratégie *f* de marché *m*	Marktstrategie *f*	marketing strategy
stratégie *f* marketing	Marketingstrategie *f*	marketing strategy
stratégie *f* publicitaire	Werbestrategie *f*	advertising strategy
stringer *m*	freier Lokalberichterstatter *m*	free lance reporter
structure *f* de la distribution *f*	Vertriebsgefüge *n*	structure of distribution
structure *f* démographique	demografische Struktur *f*	audience composition, demographical structure
structure *f* de tarif *m*	Tarifaufbau *m*	rate structure
structure *f* du programme *m*	Programmstruktur *f*	program structure
structure *f* treillis *m*	Leinenstruktur *f* (Papier)	crash finish
studio *m*	Atelier *n*, Filmatelier *n*, Filmstudio *n*	film studio, studio, workshop
studio *m* de prises *f/pl* de vue *f*	Tonfilmatelier *n*	sound film studio
studio *m* de publicité *f*	Werbeatelier *n*	commercial studio
studio *m* de télévision *f*	Fernsehstudio *n*	television studio
studio *m* publicitaire	Werbestudio *n*	advertising studio
style *m*	Schreibart *f*, Stil *m*	style
style *m* à l'emporte-pièce *m*	kraftvoller Stil *m*	style with punch in it
style *m* ampoulé	schwülstiger Stil *m*	gobbledygook
style *m* de journal *m*	Zeitungsdeutsch *n*	journalese
style *m* de marque *f*	Markenstil *m*	style of marks *pl*
style *m* d'entreprise *f*	Hausstil *m*	house style
style *m* de publicité *f*	Werbestil *m*	graphic design
style *m* énergique	kerniger Stil *m*, Schmiß *m*	punch, vigorous style
style *m* lapidaire	Dreizeilenfall *m*	centred style
style *m* négligé	vernachlässigter Stil *m*	slipshod style
style *m* pince-sans-rire	empfindungsloser Stil *m*	deadpan style
style *m* sans fioritures *f/pl*	klare Ausdrucksweise *f*	plain style
style *m* simple	einfacher Stil *m*	plain style
style *m* télégraphique	Telegrammstil *m*	telegraphic style
styliste *m*	Formgestalter *m*	designer, stylist
styliste *m* de marchandise *f*	Warengestalter *m*	merchandizer
stylo *m*	Füllfederhalter *m*	fountain-pen
stylo *m* à bille *f*	Kugelschreiber *m*	ball-point
subdivision *f*	Unterteilung *f*	subdivision
substantiel	inhaltsreich	full of matter
subventionnement *m*	Subventionierung *f*	subsidizing
succès *m*	Erfolg *m*, Schlager *m*	hit, success, winner
succès *m* de vente *f*	Verkaufsschlager *m*	bestseller
successif	aufeinanderfolgend	successive
succession *f* de publicité *f* par répétition *f* permanente avec un rythme *m* invariable	Werbeserie *f* in ständiger Wiederholung *f* mit gleichem Rhythmus *m*	rotation
succursale *f*	Filialbetrieb *m*, Zweigstelle *f*	branch, integrated store
suggérer	vorschlagen	to propose, to suggest
suggestion *f*	Vorschlag *m*	proposition
suggestion *f* grégaire	Massensuggestion *f*	mass suggestion
suite *f*	Farbandruck *m*, Fortsetzung *f*, Reihenfolge *f*	colour proof, continuation, order, progressive proof

suite f des idées f/pl	Gedankengang m	train of thought
suivant l'ordre m	auftragsgemäß	as per instructions pl
suivre, à	Fortsetzung f folgt, wird fortgesetzt	more to come, to be continued
sujet m	Gegenstand m, Grundthema n	story, subject
sujet m de l'affiche f	Plakatmotiv n	subject of the poster
sujet m publicitaire	Werbethema n	advertising theme
superchérie f littéraire	literarischer Betrug m	fabricated account
supermarché m	Selbstbedienungsladen m, Supermarkt m	supermarket
supplément m	Anhang m, Aufschlag m, Beilage f, Zeitungsbeilage f	annex, appendix, enclosure, extra charge, insert, inset, rate increase, supplement
supplément m balnéaire	Bäderbeilage f	health resort supplement
supplément m d'affiches f/pl pour le remplacement m	Plakatersatzreserve f	renewals pl
supplément m d'annonces f/pl	Anzeigenbeilage f	advertisement supplement
supplément m de mode f	Modebeilage f	fashion supplement
supplément m de prix m	Preisaufschlag m	extra charge, surcharge
supplément m de prix m pour la couleur f	Farbzuschlag m	colour additional charge, colour surcharge
supplément m dominical	Sonntagsbeilage f	Sunday supplement
supplément m feuilleton	Unterhaltungsbeilage f	recreational supplement
supplément m illustré	Bilderbeilage f	pictorial supplement
supplément m littéraire	Literaturbeilage f	literary supplement
supplément m pour la jeunesse f	Jugendbeilage f	youth supplement
supplément m pour les dames f/pl	Frauenbeilage f	ladies' pl supplement
supplément m pour polychromie f	Mehrfarbenzuschlag m	surcharge for multi-color
supplément m pour T.V.	Fernsehbeilage f	TV supplement
supplément m publicitaire encartage m	Werbebeilage f	advertising supplement
supplément m rurale	Landwirtschaftsbeilage f	farmer's supplement
supplément m spécial	Sonderbeilage f	special supplement
supplément m touristique	Reisebeilage f	travel supplement
supplémentaire	zusätzlich	supplementary
support m	Schaufensterständer m, Ständer m, Stütze f	bracket, poster site, prop, support
support m de publicité f	Medium n	medium
support m publicitaire	Werbeträger m, Werbeunterstützung f	advertising medium, advertising support, advertising vehicle, means pl of advertising
suppression f	Streichung f	deletion
suppression f d'un mandat m	Auftragsstreichung f	cancelling of an order
supprimer l'espace m	ohne Zwischenraum m setzen	to close up
sur appel m	auf Abruf m	at our convenience, on call
sur demande f	auf Anfrage f	on request
sur deux colonnes f/pl	Doppelspalte f, zweispaltig	double column, half measure, in double columns pl
sur quatre colonnes f/pl	vierspaltig	four columns pl
sur trois col f de largeur f	dreispaltig	for a 3-column
sur une col f	einspaltig	one column wide, single-column
surcharge f	Satzerschwernis f	difficult matter
surcommission f	Superprovision f	supercommission
surexposition f	Überbelichtung f	overexposure, solarization
surface f	Fläche f	area, surface
surface f d'affichage m	Reklamefläche f, Werbefläche f	advertising space, hoarding for posters pl

surface f de justification f	Satzspiegel m	printing space, type area, type page
surface f de la page f	Größe f einer Seite f, Seitenformat n	page size, size of page
surface f d'impression f	Druckfläche f, Satzspiegel m	printing space, printing surface, type area, type page
surface f du papier m	Papieroberfläche f	surface of paper
surface f mate	matte Oberfläche f	mat surface
surface f utile	Satzspiegel m	printing space, type area, type page
surfaces f/pl peintes	bemalte Flächen f/pl	painted surfaces pl
surglacé	hochsatiniert, scharf satiniert	high-glazing, super-calendered
surimpression f	Aufdruck m, Mehrdruck m, überkopieren, Überdruck m (Aufdruck)	imprint, overprint, overprinting, surprint
surimprimer	überdrucken	to overprint
surjeu m	Rückspiel n	play back
surmontoir m	Flaschenkapsel f	crowner
surmouler	abformen	to duplicate
surplus m	Überschuß m	surplus
surplus m de commandes f/pl	Auftragsüberhänge m/pl	surplus of orders pl
surremise f	Superprovision f	supercommission
surtaxe f	Zuschlag m	additional charge, extra charge
surtaxe m spécial	Sonderzuschlag m	special additional charge
surveillance f	Überwachung f	supervision
surveillance f de presse f	Pressebeobachtung f	watching of the press
surveillant m de la production f	Terminüberwacher m	accelerator, traffic manager
surveiller	überwachen	to watch-dog
surveilleur m du déroulement m de la production f	Überwacher m des Produktionsablaufs m	dispatcher
suscription f publicitaire	Werbeaufschrift f	advertising label
symétrie f	Symmetrie f	symmetry
synchronisation f	Synchronisation f	dubbing, synchronization, voice-over
synthétique	künstlich	artificial
syntonisation f	Abstimmung f	tuning
système m boule f de neige f	Schneeballsystem n	cumulative returns, snowball system
système m de photocomposition f	Lichtsatzsystem n	photocomposing system
système m en points m/pl	Punktsystem n (siehe Anhang)	point system (see appendix)
système m intégré des textes m/pl composés	integriertes Satzsystem n	integrated composition system, integrated typesetting system
système m publicitaire	Werbesystem n	advertising system

T

table f à dessin m	Zeichentisch m	drawing table
table f de montage m	Montagetisch m	illuminated line-up table, stripping desk, stripping table
table f des matières f/pl	Inhaltsverzeichnis n	index, table of contents pl
table f des sources f/pl	Quellenverzeichnis n	list of references pl
table f lumineuse	Montagetisch m	illuminated line-up table, stripping desk, stripping table

table *f* **nominale**	Namensliste *f*	index of names *pl*
table *f* **ronde**	Gespräch *n* am runden Tisch, Gruppendiskussion *f*	round-table conference
tableau *m*	Tabelle *f*	chart, tabulation
tableau *m* **noir**	Schwarzes Brett *n*	advertisement board, notice board
tableautage *m*	Tabellensatz *m*	tabular matter, tabulator matter
tabloïd *m*	Kleinformatzeitung *f*	tabloid
tabulateur *m*	Tabulator *m*	tabulator
tabulation *f*	Tabelle *f*	chart, tabulation
tabuler	tabellieren	to tabulate
tache *f*	Fleck *m*	blur, speck
tâche *f* **assignée**	Aufgabengebiet *n*	assignment, field, scope
tachistoscope *m*	Tachistoskop *n*	tachistoscope
tacticien *m*	Politikaster *m*	armchair politician
tactique *f* **publicitaire**	Werbetaktik *f*	advertising tactics *pl*
taillader	beschneiden, zusammenstreichen	to compress, to contract, to crop, to make cuts *pl*, to prune, to shorten, to slash, to trim
taille *f* **dure**	Stahlstich *m*	steel engraving
taille-douce *f*	Kupferdruck *m*	copper-plate printing
tailler	beschneiden	to crop, to make cuts *pl*, to prune, to slash, to trim
talus *m*	Facette *f*	bevel
talus *m* **de pied** *m*	Fleisch *n* eines Buchstabens *m*	beard, bevelled feet *pl*, blank space, burr
tamiser	sieben	to sift
tampon *m*	Stempel *m*	stamp
tampon *m* **encreur**	Farbkissen *n*	inkpad
tamponner	stempeln	to stamp
tam-tam *m*	marktschreierische Werbung *f*, Werberummel *m*	ballyhoo *am*, hoopla, noisy advertising, puffing publicity
tantième *f*	Gewinnanteil *m*	quota of profits *pl*
tape-à-l'œil *m*	Blickfang *m*, Kitsch *m*	approach, catch phrase, eye appeal, eye catcher, hook, shoddy, sob-stuff, stopper, trash
tapis *m* **roulant**	Transportband *n*	transport tape
tapis *m* **vert**	grüner Tisch *m*	green table
taquoir *m*	Klopfholz *n*	planer
tarabiscoté	gekünstelt	over-elaborate
tarif *m*	Preisliste *f*, Tarif *m*	price list, rate card, rates *pl*, schedule of prices *pl*
tarif *m* **combiné**	kombinierter Anzeigenpreis *m*, kombinierter Tarif *m*	combination rate, combined rate
tarif *m* **couplé**	gekoppelter Tarif *m*	coupled rate
tarif *m* **d'annonces** *f/pl*	Anzeigenpreisliste *f*, Anzeigentarif *m*	advertisement rate card, advertisement rate schedule, advertising charges *pl*, advertising rates *pl*, space rates *pl*
tarif *m* **d'annonces** *f/pl* **valide actuellement**	z.Zt. gültige Anzeigenpreisliste *f*	temporary rate sheet

tarif *m* d'antenne *f*	Sendegebühren *f/pl*, Senderpreis *m*, Tarif *m* für Werbesendungen *f/pl*	commercial rate cards *pl*, radio and television rates *pl*, time charge
tarif *m* de base *f*	Anzeigengrundpreis *m*, Einzelpreis *m*	basic rate, flat rate, one-time rate, open rate
tarif *m* de faveur *f*	Vorzugstarif *m*	preferential tariff
tarif *m* dégressif	Anzeigenpreis *m* entsprechend der tatsächlich abgenommenen Menge *f*	earned rate
tarif *m* de la publicité *f* moyens *m/pl* de transport *m*	Tarif *m* für Verkehrsmittelwerbung *f*	card rates *pl*
tarif *m* de la publicité *f* radiophonique	Tarif *m* für Werbesendungen *f/pl*	time charge
tarif *m* de publicité *f*	Anzeigentarif *m*	advertisement rate schedule, advertising charges *pl*, advertising rates *pl*, space rates *pl*
tarif *m* d'insertion *f*	Anzeigentarif *m*	advertisement rate schedule, advertising charges *pl*, advertising rates *pl*, space rates *pl*
tarif *m* fixe	Einzelpreis *m*, Grundpreis *m*	basic rate, flat rate *brit*, open rate, open-time rate *am*, standard rate
tarif *m* local	Lokaltarif *m*	local rate
tarif *m* minimal	Minimaltarif *m*	minimum tariff
tarif *m* mobile	gestaffelter Preis *m*	differential price, graduated price
tarif *m* par mot *m*	Wortgebühr *f*	charge per word
tarif *m* réajusté	ermäßigter Preis *m*	reduced rate, short rate
tarif *m* réduit	ermässigter Tarif *m*	short rate
tarifs *m/pl* de publicité *f*	Anzeigenpreise *m/pl*	adrates *pl*, advertising charges *pl*, costs *f* of advertisement
tasseau *m* du marbre *m*	Schmitzleiste *f*	bed bearer
taux *m*	Preis *m*	price, rate
taux *m* de commission *f*	Provisionssatz *m*	rate of commission
taux *m* de pénétration *f*	Reichweite *f*	coverage, penetration, range, reach *am*, turnover
taxe *f*	Steuer *f*	tax
taxe *f* pour annonce *f* chiffrée	Chiffregebühr *f*	box fee
taxe *f* sur la valeur *f* ajoutée (T.V.A.)	Mehrwertsteuer *f*	added value tax
taxer	schätzen	to rate
team *m* rédactionnel	Redaktionsgemeinschaft *f*	joint editorial board
technicien de publicité *f*	Werbefachmann *m*	adman, advertising expert, advertising man
technique *f* de clicher	Klischeetechnik *f*	block making techniques *pl*
technique *f* de fabrication *f*	Herstellungstechnik *f*	technique of production
technique *f* de la vente *f* par téléphone *m*	Telefonverkaufskunst *f*	phonemanship
technique *f* de projection *f*	Projektionstechnik *f*	projection technique
technique *f* d'imprimerie *f*	Drucktechnik *f*	printing techniques *pl*
technique *f* du journal *m*	Zeitungstechnik *f*	newspaper technique
technique *f* galvanoplastique	Galvanotechnik *f*	galvanotechnics *pl*
technique *f* photographique	Aufnahmetechnik *f*	photographic technique
technique *f* publicitaire	Werbetechnik *f*	advertising technique

technique f typographique	Satztechnik f	typographical technique
technique-offset m à cylindres m/pl	Rollenoffset n	offset rotary printing
techniques f/pl marchandes	absatzpolitische Maßnahmen f/pl, Absatzvorbereitung f durch Vertriebsplannung f, Einzelhändlerunterstützung f, Merchandising n	merchandizing
teinte f, teinté, teinte f	Farbton m, getönt, Kolorit n	coloured, colouring, hue, shade, tint, tinted
teintes f/pl grises	Grautöne m/pl	grey tints pl
tel	Originalgröße f	as is, same size
télécomposeuse f	Fernsetzmaschine f	teletypesetting machine
télécomposition f	Fernsatz m	teletypesetting
télédiffusion f	Drahtfunk m	broadcasting by wire
télégénique	telegen	telegenic
télégramme m	Telegramm n	cable, telegram
télégramme m de presse f	Pressetelegramm n	press telegram
télégraphie f sans fil m	drahtlose Telegrafie f	wireless telegraphy
télégraphier	drahten, telegrafieren	to telegraph, to wire
télégraphique	telegrafisch	by telegram, telegraphic
télégraphiste m	Telegrafist m	telegraphist
téléimprimeur m	Fernschreiber m	teleprinter, teletyper, ticker
téléobjectif m	Teleobjektiv n	telephoto lens, telephotography
télépathie f	Gedankenübertragung f	telepathy
téléphone m	Telefon n	telephone
téléphone m arabe	Latrinenparolen f/pl	grape-vine
téléphone m intérieur	Haustelefon n	house telephone, interphone
téléphone m rouge	heißer Draht m	hot line
téléphoner	telefonieren	to telephone
téléphonique	telefonisch	telephonic
téléphoniste m	Telefonist m	telephonist
téléphotographie f	Bildfunk m, Bildtelegrafie f, Fernfotografie f, Telefoto n, Teleobjektiv n	photo-telegraphy, telephoto lens, telephotography, wireless picture transmission, wirephoto
téléreportage m	Fernsehreportage f	outside broadcast
téléscripteur m	Fernschreiber m, Hellschreiber m	teleprinter, teletyper, ticker
télésiège m	Sesselbahn f	chair-lift
téléspectateur m	Fernsehzuschauer m	television viewer
télétexte m interactif	Bildschirmtext m	viewdata
télétype m	Fernschreiber m, Hellschreiber m	teleprinter, teletyper, ticker
télétypesetter m	automatische Setzmaschine f, Teletypesetter m	teletypesetter
téléviseur m	Fernsehapparat m	television set
téléviseur m portatif	tragbares Fernsehgerät n	walkie-lookie
télévision f	Fernsehen n	telecast, television (TV), video
télévision f à cassettes f/pl	Kassettenfernsehen n	audiovision, commercial
télévision f commerciale	Werbefernsehen n	television advertising
télévision f couleur f	Farbfernsehen n	colour television
télévision f privée	privates Werbefernsehen n	independent television
télévision f via câble m	Kabelfernsehen n	community antenna television, television via cable
télévision f via satellites m/pl	Satellitenfernsehen n	television by satellites pl
telex m	Fernschreibanschluß m	telex

témoignage *m*	Zeugnis *n*	certificate
témoin *m* auriculaire	Ohrenzeuge *m*	ear-witness
temps *m* d'antenne *f*	Sendezeit *f*	air time, broadcasting time
temps *m* d'antenne *f* disponible	Werbezeiten *f/pl* in Rundfunk *m* und Fernsehen *n*	availabilities *pl* in radio and television
temps *m* d'attente *f*	Wartezeit *f*	waiting time
temps *m* de lecture *f*	Lesedauer *f*	reading duration
temps *m* de pose *f*	Belichtungszeit *f*	exposure
temps *m* d'observation *f*	Betrachtungszeit *f*	looking time, stopping power
temps *m* mort	Sendepause *f*	dead air, station break
tendance *f*	Tendenz *f*	bias, tendency, trend
tendance *f* d'opinion *f*	Meinungstrend *m*	trend of opinion
tendance *f* du marché *m*	Markttendenz *f*	trend
tendance *f* stylistique	Stilrichtung *f*	tendency of style
tendances *f/pl* de fusion *f*	Fusionsbestrebungen *f/pl*	merger movement
teneur *f*	Tenor *m*, Wortlaut *m*	purport, tenor, wording
tenir la manchette *f*	Schlagzeilen *f/pl* machen	to crash the headlines *pl*
tenir secret	geheimhalten	to keep secret
terme *m* d'émission *f*	Ausstrahlungstermin *m*	play date
terme *m* de paiement *m*	Zahlungsfrist *f*	date of payment, term of payment, time of payment
terme *m* de règlement *m*	Zahlungsziel *n*	open terms *pl*
terme *m* de rigueur *f*	äusserster Termin *m*	deadline
terme *m* technique	Fachausdruck *m*, Fachwort *n*, Spezialausdruck *m*	technical term, trade expression, trade word
terminal *m* de composition *f*	Umbruchterminal *n*	graphic terminal, page-proof terminal
terminer l'impression *f*	ausdrucken	to work off
terminologie *f*	Terminologie *f*	terminology
terminologie *f* publicitaire	Werbeterminologie *f*	advertising terminology
terrain *m* de football *m*	Fußballplatz *m*	football ground
terrain *m* de l'exposition *f*	Ausstellungsgelände *n*	exhibition grounds *pl*
terrain *m* de sport *m*	Sportgelände *n*	playing-field
territoire *m*	Gebiet *n*	geographical sector
territoire *m* de vente *f*	Absatzbereich *m*	sales *pl* area, trading area
territoire-test *m*	Testgebiet *n*	test area
test *m*	Test *m*	test
test *m* à l'aveugle	Blindtest *m*, Vergleich *m* anonymer Produkte *n/pl*	blind test
test *m* après parution *f*	Nachtest *m*	post-test
test *m* comparatif	Paarvergleich *m*	duo test, paired comparison
test *m* d'annonce *f*	Anzeigentest *m*	copy test, folder test, impact-test
test *m* d'association *f*	Assoziationstest *m*	association test
test *m* d'axe *m*	Prüfung *f* des Publikumsverhaltens *n*	attitude study, concept-test
test *m* de consommation *f*	Verbrauchertest *m*	consumer test
test *m* de demandes *f/pl*	Anfragentest *m*	inquiry test
test *m* d'efficacité *f*	Wirkungstest *m*	efficiency test
test *m* de lancement *m*	Testkampagne *f*	launching test, test campaign
test *m* d'emballage *m*	Packungstest *m*	packaging test
test *m* de mémorisation *f*	Erinnerungstest *m*	recall test, recognition test
test *m* de produit *m*	Produkttest *m*	product testing
test *m* de produit *m* anonyme	anonymer Produkttest *m*	blind product test
test *m* de reliure *f*	Untersuchung *f* der Anzeigenwirkung *f*	folder test
test *m* de souvenir *m* aidé	Gedächtnisprüfung *f*	recall test
test *m* de souvenir *m* spontané	Erinnerungstest *m*	recall test, recognition test

test *m* d'opinion *f*	Meinungstest *m*	opinion test
test *m* d'une émission *f* radiophonique	Test *m* einer Rundfunksendung *f*	audition
test *m* du texte *m*	Copytest *m*	copytest
test *m* monadique	Geschmackstest *m*	solo test
test *m* préalable	Anzeigenvortest *m*, Vortest *m*	pre-test
test *m* sans visibilité *f* du produit *m*	Anzeigenerinnerungstest *m*	blind product test
test *m* ultérieur	Nachtest *m*	post-test
testage *m* des messages *m/pl* publicitaires	Textprüfung *f*	copy testing
tête *f* de colonne *f*	Kopf *m* der Spalte *f*	top of column
tête *f* de note *f*	Notenkopf *m*	notehead
tête *f* de page *f*	Kopf *m* der Seite *f*	head of page, top of page
tête *f* de tableau *m*	Tabellenkopf *m*	box head
tête *f* imprimante	Kugelkopf *m*	golf-ball typing head
têtes *f/pl* de clou *m*	abgenutzte Schrift *f*	worn-out type
texte *m*	Text *m*	copy, matter, text
texte *m* déjà employé	alter Text *m*	dead copy
texte *m* de l'annonce *f*	Anzeigentext *m*	copy, text
texte *m* délayé	weitschweifiger Text *m*	padded text
texte *m* de liaison *f*	verbindender Text *m*	tie-in
texte *m* différent	wechselnder Text *m*	different text
texte *m* du rabat *m*	Klappentext *m*	advertising text
texte *m* enchaîné	Texteinblendung *f* in Film *m*	faded in text
texte *m* intégral	vollständiger Text *m*	full text
texte *m* même	gleichbleibender Text *m*	same text
texte *m* mis en boîte *f*	vorbereiteter Text *m*	canned copy
texte *m* mutilé	verstümmelter Text *m*	mutilated text
texte *m* original	Originaltext *m*	original copy, verbatim report
texte *m* plein	Fließsatz *m*	solid matter, undisplay
texte *m* principal	Haupttext *m*, Hauptwerbetext *m*, Nachrichtenkörper *m*	body, creative copy
texte *m* publicitaire	Werbetext *m*	advertising text, copy
texte *m* publicitaire extraordinaire	außergewöhnlicher Werbetext *m*	creative copy
texte *m* rédactionnel	redaktioneller Teil *m*	editorial matter, editorial section
texte *m* revu	verbesserter Text *m*	revised text
texte *m* sérieux	seriöser Zeitungstext *m*	pig iron
textuellement	wörtlich	verbatim
théâtre *m* ambulant	Wanderbühne *f*	travelling theatre
thème *m*	Thema *n* einer Anzeige *f*	story, theme
théorie *f* de la communication *f*	Kommunikationstheorie *f*	theory of communication
théorie *f* de la publicité *f*	Werbetheorie *f*	theory of advertising
thermomètre *m* publicitaire	Werbethermometer *n*	advertising thermometer
thermosouder	aufschweißen	to weld on
thésaurus *m*	Wortschatz *m*	thesaurus, vocabulary
tierce *f*	letzte Korrektur *f*	final proof, press revise
tierce épreuve *f*	Maschinenrevision *f*	press revise
tiers *m* de page *f*	Drittelseite *f*	one-third-page
tilde *f*	Tilde *f*	tilde
timbrage *m*	Stempeldruck *m*	seal printing
timbre *m*	Etikett *n*, Stempel *m*	label, stamp, sticker

timbre *m* adhésif *m*	Aufkleber *m*	gummed label, sticker slip
timbre *m* de rabais *m*, timbre *m* d'épargne *f*	Rabattmarke *f*	discount ticket, saving stamp, trading stamp
timbre *m* en relief *m*	Siegelmarke *f*	paper seal
timbre *m* pré-oblitéré	Freistempelung *f*	pre-franked stamp
timbre *m* réclame *f*	Reklamemarke *f*	advertising seal, poster stamp
timbre-poste *m*	Briefmarke *f*	postage stamp
timbre-primes *f/pl*	Rabattmarke *f*	discount ticket, saving stamp, trading stamp
timbrer	stempeln	to stamp
tintamarre *m* de propagande *f*	Propagandagetöse *n*	hullabaloo
tintement *m*	musikalische Werbung *f*	jingle
tirage *m*	Auflage *f*, Reindruck *m*	circulation, clean print, press run
tirage *m* (impression *f*)	Auflagendruck *m*, Druckauflage *f*	circulation run, print figure, print run
tirage *m* à la suite *f*	Druck *m* einer bestimmten Anzahl *f* von Exemplaren *n/pl*	printing of a certain number of copies *pl*
tirage *m* à part *f*	Separatdruck *m*	off-print, separate copies *pl*, special impression
tirage *m* brut	Bruttoauflage *f*	gross circulation
tirage *m* contrôlé	beglaubigte Auflage *f*	audited circulation
tirage *m* d'un journal *m*	Zeitungsauflage *f*	circulation of a newspaper
tirage *m* global	Gesamtauflage *f*	total circulation, total print run
tirage *m* minimum *m*	Mindestauflage *f*	minimum circulation
tirage *m* minimum garanti	garantierte Mindestauflage *f*	guaranted minimum circulation
tirage *m* moyen	durchschnittliche Auflage *f*	average circulation
tirage *m* national	Inlandsauflage *f*	home circulation, national print run
tirage *m* net	Nettoauflage *f*	net circulation
tirage *m* partagé	Anzeigensplit *m*, Inseratvarianten *f/pl* in derselben Ausgabe *f*	split run
tirage *m* partagé entre des partenaires *m/pl*	Auflagensplit *m* unter Partnern *m/pl*	partner split
tirage *m* partiel	Teilauflage *f*	partial circulation
tirage *m* payé	bezahlte Auflage *f*	paid circulation
tirage *m* report *m*	Offsetdruck *m*	offset printing
tirage *m* spécial	Sonderdruck *m*	off-print, separate copies *pl*, special impression
tirage *m* supplémentaire	Auflageerweiterung *f*, erhöhte Auflage *f*	run-on
tirage *m* total	Gesamtauflage *f*	total circulation, total print run
tirage *m* urbain	Stadtauflage *f*	city zone
tiré à part *f*	Fortdruck *m*	production run, running-on
tire-ligne *m*	Reißfeder *f*	drawing pen
tire-l'œil *m*	Blickfang *m*	approach, catch phrase, eye appeal, eye catcher, hook, stopper
tirer	abziehen (Druck), drucken	to impress, to print, to proof, to pull
tirer des épreuves *f/pl*	andrucken	to pull a proof
tiret *m*	Gedankenstrich *m*	dash, em-rule
tiret *m* de séparation *f*	Trennungsstrich *m*	dash
tireur *m* à la ligne *f*	Zeilenschinder *m*	penny-a-liner

tireur *m* des épreuves *f/pl*	Abzieher *m*	proofer
tiroir *m*	Schubfach *n*	pigeon-hole
tissu *m* de mensonges *m/pl*	Lügengewebe *n*	web of lies *pl*
titrage *m*	Betitelung *f*	entitling
titre *m*	Kopf *m* (Überschrift *f*), Titel *m*, Verlagserscheinung *f*	caption, head, heading, headline, heading, headline, printing work, publication, title
titre *m* aligné à gauche	nicht eingezogener Titel *m*	flush head
titre *m* au dos *m* d'un livre *m*	Rückentitel *m*	spine lettering
titre *m* courant	Kolumnenleiste *f*, Kolumnentitel *m*	column heading, running head, running title
titre *m* criard	knallige Überschrift *f*	catchline, scare headline, very striking headline
titre *m* de chapitre *m*	Abteilungstitel *m*, Kapitelüberschrift *f*	section title
titre *m* de colonne *f*	Kolumnentitel *m*	column heading, running head, running title
titre *m* de paragraphe *m*	Spaltenüberschrift *f*	column heading
titre *m* de première page *f* en gros caractères *m/pl*	Titel *m* der ersten Seite *f*	flag
titre *m* de rubrique *f*	Rubriktitel *m*	column title, contents *pl* heading
titre *m* d'un journal *m*	Zeitungstitel *m*	title of a newspaper
titre *m* encadré	eingerahmter Titel *m*	box head
titre *m* en caractères *m/pl* d'affiches *f/pl*	Balkenüberschrift *f*	banner-headline
titre *m* en gras	fetter Titel *m*	fat head
titre *m* en marche *f* d'escalier *m*	stufenförmige Überschrift *f*	step head
titre *m* en ras de marge *f*	vorspringender Titel *m*	shoulder head
titre *m* en vedette *f*	Schlagzeile *f*	catch line, headline, punch line, shoulder note
titre *m* en vedette *f* sans citant le produit *m*	Schlagzeile *f* ohne Produktnennung *f*	blind headline
titre *m* flamboyant	auffallende Titelseite *f*	flag
titre *m* intérieure	Innentitel *m*	half title
titre *m* provisoire	Arbeitstitel *m*	provisional title
titre *m* sans information *f*	Überschrift *f* ohne Information *f*	blind headline
titre *m* sensationnel	senstionelle Überschrift *f*	screamer
titre *m* sur toute la longueur *f*	Titel *m* über Blattbreite *f*	streamer
titre-courant *m*	durchgehender Titel *m*	running head
titre-planche *f*	Titelbild *n*	frontispiece
titulaire *m* du courrier *m* du cœur *m*	Redakteur *m* der Seufzerspalte *f*	love-lorn editor
titulateur *m*	Überschriftenverfasser *m*	caption writer
toile *f*	Leinen *n*, Leinwand *f*	canvas, cloth, linen, screen
toile *f* peinte	bemalte Leinwand *f*	painted cloth
toile-ballon *f*	Ballonleinen *n*	balloon linen
tôle *f* métallique	Blechplatte *f*	metal sheet
ton *m* de couleur *f*	Farbton *m*	hue, shade, tint
ton *m* émouvant	menschliche Note *f*	human touch
tonalité *f*	Tonbeschaffenheit *f*, Tonwert *m*	tonal value, tonality
totalité *f* des emplacements *m/pl* extérieurs d'un autobus *m*	Rundumbeschriftung *f*	solus bus site
touche *f*	Taste *f*	key
toucher	erreichen	to reach

touches *f/pl*	Daumenregister *n*	thumb-index
toupiller	ausfräsen	to cut out, to rout out
tour *m* d'horizon *m*	Überblick *m*	survey
tour *m* d'inspection *f*	Kontrollfahrt *f*	tour of inspection
tour *f* publicitaire	Werbeturm *m*	advertising pylon, advertising tower
tournage *m*	Filmaufnahme *f*	shooting of a film
tourne *f*	Überlauf *m*	jump
tourne-disques *m*	Plattenspieler *m*	record player, recorder
tournée *f* de propagande *f*	Werbefahrt *f*	publicity tour
tournée *f* publicitaire	Werbetournee *f*	advertising tour
tourner à nouveau	Neuaufnahme *f*	retake
tourner la page *f*	Blatt *n* wenden	to turn over the page
tourner un film *m*	filmen	to film, to shoot a film
tournure *f* de phrase *f*	Redewendung *f*	phrase, turn of a sentence
tous droits *m/pl* réservés	alle Rechte *n/pl* vorbehalten	all rights *pl* reserved
tous les six mois *m/pl*	halbjährlich	half-yearly, semi-annual, twice yearly
tout neuf	brandneu	brand-new
toutes les éditions *f/pl*	Gesamtausgabe *f*	all the issues *pl*
trac *m* devant le micro *m*	Mikrofonfieber *n*	mike fever
trace *f* de son *m* d'un film *m*	Tonspur *f* eines Films *m*	sound track
trace *f* d'un film *m*	Bild- oder Tonspur *f* eines Films *m*	track
tract *m*	Flugblatt *n*, Flugschrift *f*, Flugzettel *m*, Prospekt *m*	booklet, chap-book, folder, handbill, leaflet, pamphlet, prospectus, throw-away, tract
traducteur *m*	Übersetzer *m*	translator
traduction *f*	Übersetzung *f*	translation
traduction *f* libre	Übersetzung *f*, freie	loose translation
traduire	übersetzen	to translate
traffic *m* de paiement *m*	Zahlungsverkehr *m*	clearing system
train *m* d'exposition *f*	Ausstellungszug *m*	exhibition train
train *m* urgent	Schnellschuß *m*	hot shot, priority job, rush job
trait *m*	Hauptmerkmal *n* (einer Anzeige *f*) , Schriftzug *m*, Strich *m*	dash, feature, flourish, paraph, stroke
trait *m* anglais	Schabemanier *f*	mezzotint technique, scratchboard drawing
trait *m* d'union *f*	Bindestrich *m*	hyphen
traité *m*	Abhandlung *f*	treatise
traite *f*	Wechsel *m*, Tratte *f*	bill
traitement *m* des nouvelles *f/pl*	Nachrichtenverarbeitung *f*	processing of the news
traitement *m* simultané	Simultanverarbeitung *f*	multi processing, simultaneous operation
tramage *m*	Aufrasterung *f*	Ben Day process, screening
trame *f*	Raster *m*	Ben Day, screen
trame *f* à grain *m*	Kornraster *m*	granulated screen
trame *f* à lignes *f/pl* croisées	Kreuzlinienraster *m*	cross-line screen
trame *f* à points *m/pl*	Punktraster *m*	dot screen
trame *f* collée	aufgelegter Raster *m*	sticked screen
trame *f* de copie *f*	Kopierraster *m*	copying screen
trame *f* de simili *m*	Autotypieraster *m*	halftone screen
trame *f* fine	Feinraster *m*	fine screen
trame *f* fine, à	feingerastert	with fine screen
trame *f* imprimée	Rasterpapier *n*	printed shading tint

trame *f* journal *m*	Zeitungsraster *m*	newsprint screen
trame *f* mécanique	Rasterpapier *n*	printed shading tint
tramway *m*	Straßenbahn *f*	tramway
tranche *f* de publicité *f*	Werbeblock *m*	block of advertisements *pl*
tranche *f* d'or *m*	Goldschnitt *m*	gilt edge
tranches *f/pl* horaires	Werbezeitenblöcke *m/pl*	periods *pl* of commercial emissions *pl*
transcription *f* phonétique	Lautschrift *f*	phonetic transcription
transeurdonnées *f/pl*	Datensender *m*	data transmission
transfert *m* de couleur *f*	Farbdiaabzug *m*	dye transfer
transfiguration *f*	Umgestaltung *f*	transfiguration, transformation
transformation *f*	Umwandlung *f*, Weiterverarbeitung *f*	change, converting
transformation *f* de structure *f*	Strukturwandel *m*	transformation of structure
transistor *m*	Transistor *m*	transistor
transition *f* courte	kurzer Übergang *m*	flash
transition *f* musicale	Klangbrücke *f*, musikalische Überleitung *f*	bridge, sequel
transmettre	übertragen, weiterleiten	to get across, to relay, to transmit
transmission *f*	Übermittlung *f*, Übertragung *f*, Weitergabe *f*	forwarding, passing on, transmission, transmittal
transmission *f* à la presse *f*	Freigabe *f*	handout, release
transmission *f* des informations *f/pl*	Nachrichtensendung *f*, Nachrichtenübermittlung *f*	broadcast news, news bulletin, news transmitting, newscast, radio communication
transmission *f* phototélégraphique	Bildübertragung *f*	photo-telegraphy
transmission *f* radiophonique	Rundfunkübertragung *f*	outside broadcast
transmission *f* radiophonique de sport *m*	Sportübertragung *f*	broadcasting sports *pl*
transmission *f* télévisuelle	Fernsehübertragung *f*	telecast, television transmission *brit*
transparaître	durchscheinen	to show through, to transpierce
transparence *f* de la couleur *f*	Durchsichtigkeitsgrad *m*	ink density
transparént, transparent *m*	durchsichtig, Transparent *n*	banner, electric sign, streamer, transparent
transparent *m* rayé	Linienblatt *n*	guideline
transparent *m* sur les glaces *f/pl*	Seitenscheibenplakat *n*	side window transfer, window sticker
transpercer	durchbohren, durchscheinen, durchschlagen *typog*	to come through, to pierce, to show through, to strike through, to transpierce
transposer	auswechseln, umstellen *typog*	to transpose
travail *m* à la pièce *f*	Akzidenzdruck *m*	job printing, jobbing work
travail *m* artistique	Bildgestaltung *f*, Künstlerarbeit *f*	art work
travail *m* de publicité *f*	Werbearbeit *f*	publicity work
travail *m* de relieur *m*	Buchbinderarbeit *f*	binding
travail *m* de ville *f*	Akzidenzdruck *m*	job printing, jobbing work
travail *m* d'organisation *f*	Stabsarbeit *f*	staffwork
travail *m* en équipe *f*	Gemeinschaftsarbeit *f*, Gruppenarbeit *f*	cooperative work, team-work
travail *m* sédentaire au journal *m*	sitzende Redaktionsarbeit *f*	desk work
travail *m* sur le terrain *m*	Feldarbeit *f*	field-work

travaux *m/pl* d'écritures *f/pl*	Schreibarbeiten *f/pl*	written work
travaux *m/pl* de ville *f*	Akzidenzen *f/pl*	jobbing work
travaux *m/pl* d'impression *f*	Druckarbeiten *f/pl*	printing works *pl*
travaux *m/pl* exceptionnels	Sonderleistung *f*	extra performance
travaux *m/pl* préliminaires, travaux *m/pl* préparatoires	Vorarbeiten *f/pl*	preliminary work
travelling *m*	Kamerawagen *m*	dolly
traverser	durchschlagen *typog*	to come through, to strike through, to transpierce
tréma *m*	Trema *n*, Trennpunkte *m/pl*	diaeresis
tremper	einweichen	to soak
trépied *m*	Stativ *n*	camera stand, mounting
trésor *m* de mots *m/pl*	Wortschatz *m*	thesaurus, vocabulary
tri *m*	Aussortierung *f*	sorting out
tribunal *m*	Gerichtsstand *m*	competent court
tribunal *m* arbitral	Schiedsgericht *n*	court of arbitration
tribune *f* de la presse *f*	Pressetribüne *f*	press gallery
tribune *f* libre	freie Aussprache *f*	open forum
trichromie *f*	Dreifarbenätzung *f*, Dreifarbendruck *m*	three-colour etching, three-colour printing, trichromatic process work
trier	ausmerzen	to expurgate, to sort
tri-hebdo	dreimal wöchentlich	thrice weekly
trimensuel	dreimal monatlich	thrice monthly
trimestriel	alle drei Monate *m/pl*, vierteljährlich	every three months *pl*, quarterly
tringle *f* à journaux *m/pl*	Zeitungshalter *m*	newspaper-holder
tripatouiller	zurechtstutzen	to doctor
triturer	zusammenstreichen	to compress, to contract, to shorten, to slash
troc *m*	Gegengeschäft *n*	barter
trois dimensions *f/pl*, à	dreidimensional	three-dimensional
troisième de couverture *f*	3. Umschlagseite *f*	inside back cover
trolley-bus *m*	Oberleitungsomnibus *m*	trolleybus
tromper	irreführen	to mislead
tronquer	verstümmeln	to garble
trottoir *m*	Gehweg *m*	footpath
trouvaille *f*	Fundgrube *f*	godsend, lucky find
truc *m*	ausgefallene Idee *f*, Dreh *m*, sensationelle Werbung *f*, Trick *m*	gimmick, stunt advertising
trucage *m*	Trickbild *n*	trick picture
tube *m* fluorescent	Leuchtstoffröhre *f*	fluorescent lamp, luminescent lamp
tuyau *m*	Tip *m*, Wink *m*	hint, tip, wrinkle
tuyau *m* exact	sicherer Tip *m*	straight tip
tuyaux *m/pl* confidentiels	vertrauliche Winke *m/pl*	inside dopes *pl*
type *m*	Letter *f*	letter, type
type *m* à toutes fins *f/pl*	Allzweckschrift *f*	all-purpose type face
type *m* de publicité *f*	Werbeart *f*	kind of advertising, type of advertising
type *m* gras	fette Schrift *f*	bold-face type, full faced type, heavy type
type-journal *m*	Zeitungstyp *m*	type of newspaper
types *m/pl* des médias *m/pl*	Mediaarten *f/pl*, Streuarten *f/pl*	types *pl* of media

typographe *m*	Schriftsetzer *m*, Setzer *m*, Typograf *m*	compositor, lettering man, operator, typesetter, typographer
typographie *f*	Buchdruck *m*, Typografie *f*	letter press printing, letterpress, typography
typologie *f*	Einteilung *f* nach Typen *f/pl*	typology
typomètre *m*	Typometer *m*, Zeilenmesser *m*	line measure, type gauge, type line scale, typometer
typon *m*	Film *m* (für Offset *m*)	flat, offset transparency
typo-relief *m*	Thermodruck *m*	thermography

U

unicolore	einfarbig	monochrome, single-coloured
uniformité *f*	Gleichförmigkeit *f*, Uniformität *f*	uniformity
unité *f* journalistique	journalistische Einheit *f*	independent newspaper with a complete editorial staff, journalistic unit
usager *m* de médias *m/pl*	Medianutzer *m*	media user
usages *m/pl* publicitaires	Werbebräuche *m/pl*, Werbeusancen *f/pl*	advertising practices *pl*
utilisation *f*	Verwendung *f*, Verwertung *f*	utilization
utiliser	abwickeln	to wind up
utilité *f*	Nutzen *m*	gain, profit
utopie *f* scientifique-technique	naturwissenschaftlich-technische Utopie *f*	science-fiction

V

vade-mecum *m*	Handbuch *n*	guide, handbook, manual, vademecum
vague *f* de popularité *f*	Woge *f* der Volksgunst *f*	band wagon
valeur *f* affective	Gefühlsansprache *f*	human appeal
valeur *f* commerciale	Firmenwert *m*, Geschäftswert *m*	good will
valeur *f* comme signal *m*	Signalwert *m*	signal-value
valeur *f* d'attention *f*	Aufmerksamkeitswert *m*	attention value
valeur *f* de couleur *f*	Farbwert *m*	value of colour
valeur *f* de mémorisation *f*	Erinnerungswert *m*	memory value, remembrance value, reminder value
valeur *f* de nouvelle *f*	Neuigkeitswert *m*	news value
valeur *f* de rappel *m*	Erinnerungswert *m*	memory value, remembrance value, reminder value
valeur *f* de surprise *f*	Überraschungswert *m*	surprisal value
valeur *f* d'information *f*	Informationswert *m*, Neuigkeitswert *m*	information value, news value
valeur *f* d'usage *m*	Nutzungswert *m*	value in use
valeur *f* indicative	Informationswert *m*	information value, news value
valeur *f* publicitaire	Werbewert *m*	advertising value
valide	gültig	valid
validité *f*	Gültigkeit *f*	validity
vantard *m*	Schaumschläger *m*	windbag
varia	besonders gestalteter aktueller Tatsachenbericht *m*	feature

variante *f*	Abwandlung *f*, Spielart *f*, Variante *f*	variant, variation
variation *f* de la conjoncture *f*	Konjunkturschwankung *f*	market vacillation
variation *f* saisonnière	Saisonschwankung *f*	seasonal fluctuation
variétés *f/pl*	Unterhaltungen *f/pl*	entertainments *pl*
vedette *f*	Filmgröße *f*	star
vedette *f* de l'écran *m*	Filmstar *m*	leading lady, star
véhicule *m* de communication *f*	Kommunikationsmittel *n*, Werbeträger *m*	advertising medium, advertising vehicle, communication medium, means *pl* of advertising, means *pl* of communication
vendable	marktgerecht, verkäuflich	marketable, saleable, vendible
vendeur *m*	Verkäufer *m*	salesman
vendeur *m* ambulant de journaux *m/pl*	ambulanter Zeitungsverkäufer *m*	news-butcher
vendeur *m* de journaux *m/pl*	Zeitungshändler *m*, Zeitungsjunge *m*, Zeitungsverkäufer *m*	news boy, newsdealer *am*, newsvendor, paper-boy
vendeur *m* d'espace *m*	Anzeigenakquisiteur *m*, Verlagsvertreter *m*	advertisement canvasser, advertising solicitor *am*, publisher's representative, space salesman
vendeur *m* muet	stummer Verkäufer *m*	counter display container, counter dispenser, dummy salesman
vendeuse *f*	Verkäuferin *f*	sales *pl* girl
vendre	absetzen (Verkauf), veräußern, vertreiben	to distribute, to sell
vendre la mèche *f*	eine Sache *f* ausplaudern	to blab out a secret
vente *f*	Verkauf *m*, Vertrieb *m*	distribution, sale
vente *f* à crédit *m*	Ratenverkauf *m*	hire-purchase
vente *f* ambulante	Straßenhandel *m*	boy sales *pl*, street sales *pl*
vente *f* à meilleur marché *m*	Schleuderverkauf *m*	dumping, underselling
vente *f* à tempérament *m*	Abzahlungsverkauf *m*, Ratengeschäft *n*	instalment sale, tally business
vente *f* à tout prix *m*	Verkaufen *n* um jeden Preis *m*	hard selling
vente *f* au kiosque *m*, vente *f* au numéro *m*	Einzelverkauf *m* (Zeitungen)	news stand sales *pl*, sale per copy
vente *f* à vil prix *m* ·	Schleuderverkauf *m*	dumping, underselling
vente *f* d'adresses *f/pl*	Adressenverkauf *m*	letter shop
vente *f* d'articles *m/pl* dans des machines *f/pl* distributrices automatiques	Verkauf *m* durch Automaten *m/pl*	automatic selling, vending
vente *f* de fin *f* de saison *f*	Saisonschlußverkauf *m*	seasonal closing-out sale
vente *f* de porte *f* en porte *f*	Direktverkauf *m*	house-to-house selling
vente *f* de soldes *m/pl*	Ausverkauf *m*	clearance sale, selling off
vente *f* de soldes *m/pl* d'été *m*	Sommerschlußverkauf *m*	summer sales *pl*
vente *f* directe	Beziehungskauf *m*, Direktabsatz *m*	direct selling, industrial selling
vente *f* exclusive	Alleinverkauf *m*	exclusive distribution, sole sale
vente *f* liée	Koppelungsverkauf *m*	banded offer, combination sale
vente *f* massive	Massenabsatz *m*	mass selling
vente *f* par correspondance *f*	Versandhandel *m*	mail order trade
vente *f* par téléphone *m*	Telefonwerbung *f*	bell-sell
vente *f* réclame	Reklameverkauf *m*, Werbeverkauf *m*	bargain sale

ventes f/pl avec primes f/pl	Zugabewesen n	giftgiving
ventes f/pl publiques	Versteigerungen f/pl	auctions pl
ventes f/pl réelles certifiées	beglaubigte Auflage f	audited circulation
ventilation f	Aufgliederung f,	breakdown, classification
	Aufschlüsselung f	
verbiage m	Wortschwall m	redundancy, torrent of
		words pl
verbosité f	Wortaufwand m	verbosity
vergeure f du papier m	Formstreifen m im Papier n	wire-mark
vérification f	Kontrolle f, Streuprüfung f	check, check-up, checking
vérification f de l'audience f	Prüfung f der Plakatbeachtung f	poster audience survey
d'affichage m		
vérification f des comptes m/pl	Rechnungsprüfung f	audit
vérification f des stocks m/pl	Bestandsüberprüfung f	shop audit
vérifier	prüfen	to check, to check up, to
		examine
vérifier la facture f	Rechnung f prüfen	to check the invoice, to verify
		the invoice
vernir	lackieren	to lacquer, to varnish
vernis m	Firnis m, Lack m	lacquer, varnish
vernissage m	Besichtigung f vor der	varnishing, varnishing – day
	Eröffnung f, Lackierung f	
vernissage m d'impression f	Drucklackierung f	varnished overprinting
vers m publicitaire	Werbevers m	advertising verse
versement m	Zahlung f	payment
version f	Lesart f	reading, version
version f abrégée	gekürzte Fassung f	cut version
veuve f	Witwe f/typog	widow
victime m de la publicité f	Opfer n der Werbung f	admass
vidéo m	Fernsehen n	telecast, television (TV) , video
vidéophone m	Fernsehtelefon n	videophone
vieille matière f	Altzeug n	old metal
vieille rengaine f	abgedroschenes Zeug n	threadbare story
vieilli	veraltet	antiquated, out-of-date
vient de paraître	neu herausgekommen, soeben	just out, just published
	erschienen	
vieux clichés m/pl	alte Klischees n/pl	dead plates pl
vieux papiers m/pl	Altpapier n	waste paper
vignette f	Namenszug m, Randverzierung f,	book mark, cartouche,
	Signet n, Vignette f	colophon, logotype, mask,
		name slug, ornament,
		vignette
vignette f collante	Klebemarke f	adhesive stamp
vil prix m	Schleuderpreis m	cut rate, cut-throat price, give-
		away price
violon m d'Ingres	Liebhaberei f	hobby
virgule f	Komma n	comma
visa m	Sichtvermerk m	signature
visibilité f	Sichtbarkeit f	approach, visibility
visibilité f étendue	weite Sichtbarkeit f	long approach site
visionner	veranschaulichen	to vizualize
visite f à domicile m	Hausbesuch m	domiciliary visit
visite f des clients m/pl	Kundenbesuch m	business call, calling on
		customers pl

visite f des curiosités f/pl	Besichtigung f	sightseeing
visite f répétée	Wiederholungsbesuch m	call-back
visualiser	gestalten	to shape, to visualize
vitesse f de lecture f	Lesegeschwindigkeit f	reading rate
vitrine f	Auslage f, Schaufenster n, Vitrine f	display, display case, display faces pl, display window, shop window, show window
vitrine f publicitaire	Werbevitrine f	advertising showcase
vitrinette f	Schaukasten m	showcase
vitrophanie f	Fensterklebeplakat n	window sticker, window streamer
vocabulaire m	Sprachschatz m, Wortschatz m	thesaurus, vocabulary
voie f de distribution f	Absatzkanal m, Absatzweg m	channel of distribution, sales pl channel
voie f de prospection f	Streuweg m	channel of dispersion
voiture f d'exposition f	Ausstellungswagen m	exhibition van
voiture f équitée pour la projection f de films m/pl	Filmwagen m	film car
voiture f motrice	Straßenbahntriebwagen m	bloomer am, traction car brit
voiture f spéciale pour la projection f de films m/pl sonores	Tonbildschau f	film-sound transmission car, sound film strip, sound slide film
volet m	Schiebeblende f, Verschluß m, Wischblende f	shutter, wipe
volume m d'annonces f/pl	Anzeigenumfang m	advertisement volume
volume m de la composition f	Satzumfang m	volume of composition
volume m de la publicité f	Streumenge f, Werbevolumen n	advertising volume
volume m publicitaire	Abnahmemenge f, Abschlußmenge f, Anzeigenvolumen n, Werbeanteil m	advertising volume, size of the order, volume of advertising
voussure f	Deckenschild n	ceiling panel
voyage m organisé	Pauschalreise f	package tour
voyageur m de commerce m	Handelsreisender m, Reisender m	commercial traveller, travelling salesman
vue f à vol m d'oiseau m	Vogelperspektive f	bird's eye view
vue f d'ensemble	Überblick m	survey
vue f de premier plan m	Großaufnahme f	close-up, full screen
vulgarisation f	Popularisierung f	popularization

W

western m	Wildwestfilm m	western

X

xérographie f	Trockenkopierverfahren n, Xerografie f	xerography
xographie f	Xografie f	xography
xylographe m	Xylograf m	wood-engraver
xylographie f	Xylografie f	wood-engraving

Y

y compris	inbegriffen	included

Z

zinc m	Zink n	zinc
zincographe m	Chemigraf m	blockmaker, process engraver
zincographie f	Chemigrafie f, Zinkätzung f, Zinkdruck m, Zinkklischee n	photo-engraving, zinc block, zinc etching, zinc block, zinc etching, zincography
zone f **de chalandise** f	Verkaufsbrennpunkt m	focal point of sales pl
zone f **de diffusion** f	Streufeld n, Verbreitungsgebiet n	advertising zone, circulation area, covered sector
zone f **de résidence** f	Ortsgrößenklasse f	town size group

Anhang · Appendix · Appendice
Punktsystem · Point system
Mesures typographiques

Plakatformate · Sizes of posters
Formats d'affiche

Deutsch	English	Français
1. Doppelkrone (engl.) 30 × 20 Zoll = 76 × 51 cm	double-crown (G. B.) 30 × 20 inches = 76 × 51 cm	format double couronne (G. B.) 30 × 20 pouces = 76 × 51 cm
2. Colombier (franz.)	colombier (France) 60 × 80 cm	format colombier 60 × 80 cm
3. 1/1 Bogen (deutsch) 59,4 × 84,1 cm	Bogen (Germany) 59,4 × 84,1 cm	format Bogen (Allemagne) 59,4 × 84,1 cm
4. Einheitsformat (Schweiz) 95 × 128 cm (Holland: 83 × 118)	"Einheits"-size (Switzerland) 95 × 128 cm (Holland: 83 × 118)	format unique (Suisse) 95 × 128 cm (Hollande: 83 × 118)

Punktsystem (Didot)

Punkte	Name (deutsch)	mm	Désignation française
1	Achtelpetit	0,376	1 point
2	Viertelpetit (Non plus ultra)	0,752	2 points
2 1/2	Microscopique	0,940	
3	Viertelcicero (Brillant)	1,128	3 points
4	Halbpetit (Diamant)	1,504	4 points
5	Perl	1,880	5 points (parisienne)
6	Nonpareille	2,256	6 points
6 1/2	Insertio	2,444	
7	Kolonel (Mignon)	2,632	7 points
8	Petit	3,008	8 points
9	Borgis	3,384	9 points
10	Korpus (Garmond)	3,761	10 points
11	Rheinländer	4,137	
12	Cicero	4,513	12 points (Cicéro)
14	Mittel	5,265	14 points
16	Tertia	6,017	16 points
18	1 1/2 Cicero	6,769	
20	Text	7,521	20 points

Punktsystem (Pica)

Points	Englische Namen	Amerikanische Namen	Didot-Punkte	mm
1	12-to-pica	1 point	0,935	0,351
2	6-to-pica	2 Points	1,869	0,703
3	Minikin	Excelsior	2,803	1,054
3 1/2	Brilliant	Brilliant	3,270	1,229
4	Gem	Ruby	3,738	1,405
4 1/2	Diamond	Diamond	4,205	1,581
5	Pearl	Pearl	4,672	1,757
5 1/2	Ruby	Agate	5,140	1,933
6	Nonpareil	Nonpareil	5,607	2,109
6 1/2	Emerald	Emerald	6,074	2,284
7	Minion	Minion	6,541	2,460
8	Brevier	Brevier	7,476	2,812
9	Bourgeois	Bourgeois	8,410	3,163
10	Long Primer	Long Primer	9,345	3,515
11	Small Pica	Small Pica	10,279	3,866
12	Pica	Pica	11,214	4,217
14	English	English	13,083	4,921
16	2-line Brevier	Columbian	14,952	5,624
18	Great Primer	Great Primer	16,821	6,327
20	2-line Long Primer	Paragon	18,690	7,029